Lecture Notes in Computer Science 634

Edited by G. Goos and J. Hartmanis

Advisory Board: W. Brauer D. Gries J. Stoer

D0993625

Lecture Notes in Computer Science   634

Edited by G. Goos and J. Hartmanis

Advisory Board: W. Brauer D. Gries J. Stoer

L. Bougé   M. Cosnard
Y. Robert   D. Trystram (Eds.)

Parallel Processing: CONPAR 92 – VAPP V

Second Joint International Conference
on Vector and Parallel Processing
Lyon, France, September 1-4, 1992
Proceedings

Springer-Verlag

Berlin Heidelberg New York
London Paris Tokyo
Hong Kong Barcelona
Budapest

Series Editors

Gerhard Goos
Universität Karlsruhe
Postfach 69 80
Vincenz-Priessnitz-Straße 1
W-7500 Karlsruhe, FRG

Juris Hartmanis
Department of Computer Science
Cornell University
5149 Upson Hall
Ithaca, NY 14853, USA

Volume Editors

Luc Bougé
Michel Cosnard
Yves Robert
Laboratoire de l'Informatique du Parallélisme IMAG - CNRS
Ecole Normale Supérieure de Lyon
46 Allée d'Italie, F-69364 Lyon Cedex 7, France

Denis Trystram
Laboratoire de Modélisation et de Calcul IMAG - CNRS
46 Avenue Félix Viallet, F-38041 Grenoble Cedex, France

CR Subject Classification (1991): C.1, F.2, B.3, J.0, C.4, D.1, D.4, E.1, G.1 I.4

ISBN 3-540-55895-0 Springer-Verlag Berlin Heidelberg New York
ISBN 0-387-55895-0 Springer-Verlag New York Berlin Heidelberg

© Springer-Verlag Berlin Heidelberg 1992
Printed in Germany

Typesetting: Camera ready by author/editor
Printing and binding: Druckhaus Beltz, Hemsbach/Bergstr.
45/3140-543210 - Printed on acid-free paper

Preface

The past decade has seen the emergence of two highly successful series of CONPAR and VAPP conferences on the subject of parallel processing. The Vector and Parallel Processors in Computational Science meetings were held in Chester (VAPP I, 1981), Oxford (VAPP II, 1984) and Liverpool (VAPP III, 1987). The International Conference on Parallel Processing took place in Nürnberg (CONPAR 81), Aachen (CONPAR 86), and Manchester (CONPAR 88). Thereafter the two series joined and the CONPAR 90 - VAPP IV conference was organised in Zürich.

The next event in the series CONPAR 92 - VAPP V will be organised in 1992 at the Ecole Normale Supérieure de Lyon (FRANCE) from September 1, 1992 to September 4, 1992.

The format of the joint meeting will follow the pattern set by its predecessors. It is intended to review hardware and architecture developments together with languages and software tools for supporting parallel processing and to highlight advances in models, algorithms and applications software on vector and parallel architectures.

More than 230 papers written by authors from 35 countries have been submitted for consideration to CONPAR 92 - VAPP V. Among these papers, the program committee has selected 36 full papers, 58 short papers and several posters. Four invited presentations, four tutorials and various exhibitions will complete the conference. We are pleased to thank the program committee members and the 600 referees (each paper has been evaluated by four referees), for their excellent job in building the scientific content of the conference.

Welcome to the Ecole Normale Supérieure de Lyon during four days of dense and creative scientific activities.

Many thanks to our sponsors:

LIP, IMAG, ENSLyon, C^3, CNRS, DEC, Archipel, AFCET, INRIA, BCS-PPSG, GI-PARS, IEEE, ACM, SI-PARS,

and to Valérie Roger and Jocelyne Richerd, responsible for the secretariat of the conference.

June 1992   Luc Bougé, Michel Cosnard, Yves Robert, Denis Trystram

Committees

Organising Committee

Michel Cosnard	LIP-IMAG - ENS Lyon
Luc Bougé	LIP-IMAG - ENS Lyon
Yves Robert	LIP-IMAG - ENS Lyon
Denis Trystram	LMC-IMAG - Grenoble

Standing Committee

P.C.P. Bhatt	Inst. of Techn. Delhi (India)
K. Boyanov	Acad. Bonchev Sofia (Bulgaria)
H. Burkhart	Univ. Basel (Switzerland)
M. Cosnard	ENS Lyon (France)
L.M. Delves	Univ. of Liverpool (UK)
C. Jesshope	Univ. of Surrey (UK)
H. Jordan	Univ. Colorado (USA)
O. Lange	TU Hamburg-Harburg (FRG)
N. Mirenkov	Acad. of Sciences (USSR)
Y. Muraoka	Waseda Univ. Tokyo (Japan)
W. Händler	Univ. Erlangen-Nürnberg (FRG)
I. Plander	Academy Bratislava (CSFR)
K.D. Reinartz	Univ. Erlangen-Nürnberg (FRG)
E.H. Rothauser	IBM Rüschlikon (Switzerland)
A. Viegas de Vasconcelos	Brussels (Belgium)
R. Wait	Liverpool (UK)

Program Committee

M. Cosnard, Chairman	(ENS Lyon - France)
J.M. Adamo	(ENS Lyon - France)
H. Aiso	(Keio Univ. - Japan)
S. Akl	(Kingston - Canada)
M. Amamiya	(Fukuoka - Japan)
F. Andre	(IRISA, Rennes - France)
M. Annaratone	(Zürich - Switzerland)
A. Apostolico	(Italy and Purdue Univ. - USA)
R.G. Babb II	(Bearverton - USA)
J.C. Bermond	(Valbonne - France)
D. Bini	(Pisa - Italy)
A. Bode	(TU. München - FRG)
L. Bouge	(ENS Lyon - France)
P.C.P. Bhatt	(IIT Delhi - India)
V.P. Bhatkar	(CDAC Pune - India)
R.P. Brent	(Canberra - Australia)
H. Burkhart	(Basel - Switzerland)

F. Dehne	(Ottawa - Canada)
J.M. Delosme	(New Haven - USA)
E. Deprettere	(Delft - Netherlands)
J. Dongarra	(Knoxville - USA)
I. Duff	(UK and Toulouse - France)
P. Feautrier	(Paris - France)
C. Fraboul	(Toulouse - France)
D. Gannon	(Bloomington - USA)
J.L. Gaudiot	(Los Angeles - USA)
A. Gerasoulis	(Rutgers Univ. - USA)
W. Giloi	(TU Berlin - FRG)
G. Hains	(Montréal - Canada)
R.N. Ibbett	(Edinburgh - UK)
H. Imai	(Tokyo - Japan)
C. Jesshope	(Surrey - UK)
H. Jordan	(Colorado - USA)
O. Lange	(TU Hamburg-Harburg - FRG)
M. Langston	(Tenessee - USA)
N.N. Mirenkov	(Acad. of Sciences - USSR)
H. Mühlenbein	(St. Augustin I - FRG)
Y. Muroaka	(Tokyo - Japan)
P. Navaux	(Porto Allegre - Brasil)
D.A. Padua	(Illinois - USA)
D. Parkinson	(Queen Mary College - UK)
B. Philippe	(IRISA Rennes - France)
R.H. Perrott	(Belfast - UK)
G.R. Perrin	(Besancon - France)
B. Plateau	(Grenoble - France)
R. Puigjaner	(Baleares - Spain)
P. Quinton	(Rennes - France)
V. Ramachandran	(Austin - USA)
K.D. Reinartz	(Erlangen-Nürnberg - FRG)
G. Reijns	(Delft - Netherlands)
Y. Robert	(ENS Lyon - France)
D. Roose	(Leuven - Belgium)
W. Rytter	(Warszawa - Poland)
S. Sedukhin	(Novosibirsk - USSR)
B. Sendov	(Sofia - Bulgaria)
S.W. Song	(Soa Paulo - Brasil)
O. Sykora	(Bratislava - CSFR)
M. Tchuente	(Yaoundé - Cameroun)
E.E. Tyrtyshnikov	(Moscow - USSR)
D. Trystram	(Grenoble - France)
M. Valero	(Barcelona - Spain)
M. Vanneschi	(Pisa - Italy)
M. Vajtersic	(Bratislava - CSFR)
P. Vitanyi	(CWI Amsterdam - The Netherlands)
U. Vishkin	(Maryland - USA, Tel Aviv - Israel)
R. Wait	(Liverpool - UK)
H.P. Zima	(Wien - Austria)

Contents

11. Data Parallelism

12. Parallel Algorithms

13. Image Processing

Tolerating Faults in Synchronization Networks

Sandeep N. Bhatt[*]   Fan R. K. Chung [†]

F. Thomson Leighton[‡]   Arnold L. Rosenberg[§]

Abstract. A *synchronization network* (*SN*) consists of processing elements (PEs) at the leaves of a complete binary tree, with routing switches at interior nodes. We study the problem of rendering an SN tolerant to PE failures, by adding queues to its edges. We obtain the following results. In the *worst-case*, an N-PE SN whose edges have queues of capacity $O(\log \log N)$ can tolerate the failure of a positive fraction of its PEs, no matter how the failed PEs are distributed; furthermore, this capacity requirement cannot be lowered by more than a small constant factor. In the *expected-case*, with probability exceeding $1 - N^{-\Omega(1)}$, an N-PE SN whose edges have queues of capacity $O(\log \log \log N)$ can tolerate the failure of a positive fraction of its PEs; we do not know if this capacity requirement can be lowered. We also present an algorithm which, given an SN with queues of capacity C, *salvages* a maximum number of fault-free PEs; the running time is a low-degree polynomial in N even when C is as large as $\log(N/\log N)$.

1 Introduction

A synchronization network (*SN*) consists of processing elements (PEs) that communicate through a complete binary tree interconnection network. The leaves of the tree hold the PEs of the SN (whence N is typically a power of 2); the nonleaf nodes route messages and perform simple combining, broadcast, and accumulation. An SN can be a useful *auxiliary network* when adjoined to a processor network having a richer topology (say, a mesh or hypercube). A variety of computations [4] yield to the simple, fast combining within trees; these are exploited in [3] and [10], where SNs are adjoined to data-processing machines for speedy searching, selection, and combining; most recently, in [5] and [6], SNs have been adjoined to MIMD hypercubes.

[*]Dept. Computer Science, Yale University, New Haven, CT 06520 USA.

[†]Bell Communications Research, 435 South St., Morristown, NJ 07960 USA.

[‡]Dept. of Mathematics and Lab. for Computer Science, MIT, Cambridge, MA 02139 USA.

[§]Dept. of Computer Science, University of Massachusetts, Amherst, MA 01003 USA.

This study is motivated by the vulnerability of aggressive VLSI designs to fabrication defects which almost certainly disable some fraction of the PEs. (Wires and communication nodes, being considerably smaller than PEs, are commensurately less vulnerable to both defects and faults [11].) This has led researchers to seek strategies for retaining a large proportion of the computational power of a processor network even after it has been crippled by PE failures; studies have focused on the hypercube [7], the de Bruijn graph and the butterfly [2], the mesh [12], [9], and the tree [1]. This paper considers the problem of rendering an SN tolerant to PE failures. Although this problem is nominally subsumed by the study of fault tolerance in trees [1], the special structure and mode of use of SNs opens avenues to fault tolerance that are significantly — in fact, exponentially — more efficient than analogous techniques for general tree machines. We achieve the desired tolerance to faults by adding small-capacity queues to the edges of the SN. The quality of our solution is gauged in terms of the capacities of the queues.

Our study considers three possible demands on the design of a fault-tolerant N-PE SN $\mathcal{N}$, delimited by the following scenarios. In the *worst-case* scenario (Section 2), we insist that the fault-tolerant version of $\mathcal{N}$ be able to survive the failure of a positive fraction α of its PEs, no matter how the failures are distributed. We show that if the edges of $\mathcal{N}$ are equipped with queues of capacity[1] $\log^{(2)} N + c(\alpha)$, where $c(\alpha)$ is a constant depending only on the fraction α, then $\mathcal{N}$ can tolerate the failure of any αN of its PEs (Theorem 2.1). Moreover, we show that, this queue-capacity is necessary, to within a small constant factor; i.e., there is a set of αN PEs whose failure render an N-PE SN inoperative unless the edge-queues have capacity $\Omega(\log^{(2)} N)$ (Theorem 2.2).

In the *expected-case* scenario (Section 3), we insist that a set of up to αN PE failures be tolerated *with very high probability*, where the probability is determined by considering the relative frequencies of various failure patterns — assuming processors fail independently with fixed probability. We show that, with probability exceeding $1 - N^{-\Omega(1)}$, the SN, equipped with queues of capacity $O(\log^{(3)} N)$, can tolerate the failure of a positive fraction $\alpha < .7$ of its PEs (Theorem 3.1). It remains an inviting challenge to determine whether or not a smaller queue-capacity suffices.

In the *salvaging* scenario (Section 4), we are given a version of the SN already equipped with queues of some given capacity C. Our task is to determine how to configure $\mathcal{N}$ for a given pattern of failed PEs, in a way that salvages a maximum number of fault-free PEs. The salvage algorithm we present works in an amount of time that grows with the queue-capacity C, but is a low-degree polynomial in N even when C is as large as $\log(N/\log N)$ (Theorem 4.1).

Our results derive from a new notion of graph embedding which is presented in Subsection 1.1. Our lower bounds are among the first based solely on the congestion of embeddings.

---

[1] All logarithms are to the base 2. The iterated logarithm $\log^{(k)}$ is defined by: $\log^{(1)} N = \log N$; $\log^{(k+1)} N = \log\log^{(k)} N$.

Before turning to the formal development, it is worth asking whether or not the added queues degrade computation on the SN enough to negate the benefits of the SN. We believe that the answer is generally no; we justify this belief in terms of one specific application. In [5], [6], SNs are used as a mechanism for synchronizing a MIMD array of microprocessors. It is claimed there that an appropriately designed SN will accumulate and distribute the messages that lead to synchronization in time roughly commensurate with a single instruction cycle of the underlying processor network. In contrast, synchronization using network interconnections takes time proportional to the diameter of the network, with possibly nontrivial delay at each PE. Hence, even if our queues slow the operation of an SN down from a single instruction cycle-time to roughly $\log^{(2)} N$ such cycle-times, the network with the adjoined SN will still synchronize much faster than will the underlying network by itself. Moreover, one could probably design a way to bypass the queues unless they are needed.

1.1 The Formal Setting

Terminology. We label each node of the *height-n complete binary tree* T_n with a distinct binary word of length at most n, so that each node x is adjacent to its successors $x0$ and $x1$. For each $\ell \in \{0, 1, \ldots, n\}$, the 2^ℓ words/nodes of length ℓ form *level* $n - \ell$ of T_n. The unique node at level n is the *root* of T_n, and the 2^n nodes at level 0 are the *leaves* of T_n. We say that node x is a *(proper) ancestor* of node y, or, equivalently, that node y is a *(proper) descendant* of node x, iff the string x is a (proper) prefix of the string y. For each node x of T_n, the *subtree of T_n rooted at x* is the induced subgraph of T_n on the nodes $\{xy : 0 \le |y| \le n - |x|\}$. Finally, a *forest* is a nonempty set of complete binary trees.

Red-Green Graph Embeddings. Let us be given a complete binary tree $\mathcal{H}_n$ (the host tree) whose 2^n leaves have each been colored either red or green. Say that the fraction $0 < G \le 1$ leaves have been colored green. The tree T_n represents the ideal SN we want to implement. Its green leaves represent functional PEs, and its red leaves represent faulty PEs. Let us further be given a complete binary tree $\mathcal{G}_k$ (the guest tree), where $k \le \log G 2^n$. T_k represents the actual SN we want to "salvage" from the fault-laden SN T_n.

A *red-green embedding* (*RG-embedding*, for short) $\langle \mathbf{a}, \mathbf{r} \rangle$ of $\mathcal{G}_k$ in $\mathcal{H}_n$ has two components: (i) an assignment $\mathbf{a}$ of the nodes of $\mathcal{G}_k$ to nodes of $\mathcal{H}_n$ that maps each leaf of $\mathcal{G}_k$ to a unique *green* leaf of $\mathcal{H}_n$, and such that each ancestor x of a node y in $\mathcal{G}_k$ is mapped to an ancestor $\mathbf{a}(x)$ of node $\mathbf{a}(y)$ in $\mathcal{H}_n$[2], and (ii) a routing function $\mathbf{r}$ that assigns to each edge (x, y) of $\mathcal{G}_k$ a path in $\mathcal{H}_n$ that connects nodes $\mathbf{a}(x)$ and $\mathbf{a}(y)$.

---

[2]We term this latter property of RG-embeddings *progressiveness.*As in the ideal SN, messages follow an up-then-down path in a "progressively" salvaged SN.

By extension, an RG-embedding of a *forest* of trees in $\mathcal{H}_n$ is a set of RG-embeddings of the trees in the forest, whose leaf assignments are node disjoint. This node disjointness guarantees that if any subset of the trees in the forest are grown and combined into a single tree, an RG-embedding of that single tree can use the leaf assignments of the forest.

Costs of an Embedding. An RG-embedding $\langle \mathbf{a}, \mathbf{r} \rangle$ of $\mathcal{G}_k$ in $\mathcal{H}_n$ has two costs. The first is the *harvest* of the embedding, which equals the ratio $2^{k-n}/G$ of the number of leaves of $\mathcal{G}_k$ to the number of green leaves of $\mathcal{H}_n$. The second is *congestion*, which equals the maximum, over all edges (x, y) of $\mathcal{H}_n$, of the number of routing paths that cross edge (x, y)[3].

Within this formal setting, the specific problems we study are stated below.

CONGESTION-HARVEST TRADEOFF PROBLEMS. *Determine, as a function of the size parameter n of $\mathcal{H}_n$, the fraction $0 < G \leq 1$ of green leaves, and the desired harvest fraction[4] $0 < H \leq 1/2$, the smallest congestion $C = C(n, G, H)$ for which there is a congestion-C RG-embedding of $\mathcal{G}_{\lfloor \log HG2^n \rfloor}$ in $\mathcal{H}_n$:*
(a) for the worst-case *pattern of red and green leaves in $\mathcal{H}_n$;*
(b) in the expected case, *i.e., with probability $\geq 1 - 2^{-\Omega(n)}$, when leaves of $\mathcal{H}_n$ are colored red and green independently with probability p.*

HARVEST-MAXIMIZATION PROBLEM. *Given an integer $C \leq n$, find the largest k for which there is an RG-embedding of $\mathcal{G}_k$ in $\mathcal{H}_n$ with congestion $\leq C$.*

2 Optimizing Worst-Case Congestion

This section derives upper and lower bounds on the minimum congestion $C_{\min}$ that we must suffer in order to harvest a fraction H of the green leaves in the worst case. As we will see, the bounds are tight to within constant factors.

2.1 An Upper Bound

We formulate and analyze a "greedy" RG-embedding algorithm, in order to obtain an upper bound on the quantity $C_{\min}$. The algorithm proceeds level-by-level, bottom-up from level 0 to level n in $\mathcal{H}_n$. As each node x is encountered, the algorithm assigns node x a label $\lambda(x)$ which is the length-$(n+1)$ binary representation of a nonnegative integer. For such a label $\lambda(x) = \lambda_n(x)\lambda_{n-1}(x)\cdots\lambda_0(x)$, where

---

[3]The *dilation* measure [8] is not relevant here because of the assumed speed of the ideal SN relative to the speed of each individual PE [5].

[4]We cannot aim at harvests exceeding 1/2, because the number of harvested leaves must be a power of 2, but G could be such that the largest power of 2 not exceeding $G2^n$ may be close to $G2^{n-1}$.

- $I(\lambda(x)) = \sum_{i=0}^{n} \lambda_i(x)2^i$, i.e., the integer value of the binary string $\lambda(x)$;

- $S(\lambda(x)) = \{i | \lambda_i(x) \neq 0\}$, i.e., the set of nonzero bit-positions in label $\lambda(x)$;

- $W(\lambda(x)) = |S(\lambda(x))|$, i.e., the *weight*, or, number of nonzero bit-positions in label $\lambda(x)$.

The intended interpretation of the labels is that if node x of $\mathcal{H}_n$ receives label $\lambda(x)$, then there is an RG-embedding of the forest $\{\mathcal{T}_k : k \in S(\lambda(x))\}$ in the subtree of $\mathcal{H}_n$ rooted at x. This interpretation and the progressiveness of RG-embeddings imply that $\lambda_k(x) = 0$ for all $k > \text{level}(x)$.

The Labelling/Embedding Procedure. Let C be the maximum congestion allowed in any RG-embedding. We exploit the fact that all labels have length $n + 1$ by specifying each label $\lambda(x)$ implicitly, via the integer $I(\lambda(x))$.

Algorithm Worst-Case:

Step 0. {Label nodes on level 0 of $\mathcal{H}_n$}
$$\text{Assign each leaf } x \text{ a label } I(\lambda(x)) = \begin{cases} 1 & \text{if } x \text{ is green} \\ 0 & \text{if } x \text{ is red} \end{cases}$$

Step $\ell > 0$. {Label nodes on level ℓ of $\mathcal{H}_n$}

    Substep $\ell.a$ {Assign the string label}
        Assign each level-ℓ node x a label $I(\lambda(x)) = I(\lambda(x0)) + I(\lambda(x1))$

    Substep $\ell.b$ {Combine small embedded trees}
        if there was a chain of carries from bit-positions $k-i, k-i+1, \ldots k-1$
        of $\lambda(x0)$ and $\lambda(x1)$ into bit-position k of $\lambda(x)$
        then embed the roots of copies of $\mathcal{T}_{k-i+1}, \ldots, \mathcal{T}_k$ in node x, **and**
        route edges from those roots to the roots of two copies each of $\mathcal{T}_{k-i}, \ldots, \mathcal{T}_{k-1}$
        that are embedded in proper descendants of x

    Substep $\ell.c$ {Honor the congestion bound C}
        for $k = 0$ **to** $\lceil \log I(\lambda(x)) - C \rceil$
        if $W(\lambda(x)) > C$ **then** $\lambda_k(x) \leftarrow 0$

Theorem 2.1 *Let the 2^n leaves of $\mathcal{H}_n$ be colored red and green, in any way, with $G2^n$ green leaves for some $0 < G \leq 1$. For any rational $0 < H \leq 1/2$, Algorithm* **Worst-Case** *finds an RG-embedding of $\mathcal{G}_{\lfloor \log HG2^n \rfloor}$ in $\mathcal{T}_n$, with congestion $C \leq \log n - \log((1 - H)G) + 1$.*

Proof. It is clear that, for each node x of $\mathcal{H}_n$, Algorithm **Worst-Case** RG-embeds $\mathcal{G}_{\lfloor \log I(\lambda(x)) \rfloor}$ in the subtree of $\mathcal{H}_n$ rooted at node x; hence, overall, the Algorithm RG-embeds the tree $\mathcal{G}_{\lfloor \log I(\lambda(r)) \rfloor}$ in $\mathcal{H}_n$, where r is the root of $\mathcal{H}_n$.

We need only verify that the salvaged tree is big enough when C is as big as the bound in the statement of the Theorem.

Note first that Algorithm **Worst-Case** never requires us to abandon any green leaves as we work up from level 0 through level $C - 1$ of $\mathcal{H}_n$, because the high-order bit of $I(\lambda(x))$ can be no greater than the level of x in $\mathcal{H}_n$. To see what happens above this level, focus on a specific node x at level $\ell \geq C$ of $\mathcal{H}_n$. The congestion bound may require us, in Substep $\ell.c$ of the Algorithm, to abandon one bit in each position $k \leq \ell - C$ of $\lambda(x)$. This is equivalent to abandoning one green-leafed copy of each tree $\mathcal{G}_k$ with $k \leq \ell - C$; however, at most one tree of each size is abandoned, because any two trees of the same size would have been coalesced (by embedding a new root) at this step, if not earlier. It follows that, when the Algorithm processes node x, it abandons no more than $\sum_{i=0}^{\ell-C} 2^i < 2^{\ell-C+1}$ green leaves; hence, at the entire level ℓ, strictly fewer than $2^{\ell-C+1} 2^{n-\ell} = 2^{n-C+1}$ previously unabandoned green leaves are abandoned. Thus, the entire salvage procedure abandons fewer than $(n + 1 - C)2^{n-C+1}$ green leaves due to congestion. Since there are $G2^n$ green leaves in all, we see that more than $(G - (n + 1 - C)2^{1-C})2^n$ green leaves are *not* abandoned due to congestion. Now, at the end of the Algorithm, we may have to abandon almost half of these unabandoned green leaves — because the green leaves we finally use in the RG-embedding must be a power of 2 in number. The Algorithm will have succeeded in salvaging the desired fraction of green leaves as long as the number of salvaged green leaves, which is no fewer than $2^{\lfloor \log(G - (n+1-C)2^{1-C})2^n \rfloor}$, is at least as large $2^{\lfloor \log HG2^n \rfloor}$, the number of green leaves we want to salvage.

Simple estimates show that, if we allow our RG-embedding to have congestion $C = \log n - \log((1 - H)G) + 1$, then we shall have accomplished this task. $\square$

2.2 A Lower Bound

Theorem 2.2 *Let G and H be rationals with $0 < G < 1$ and $0 < H \leq 1/2$. For each n, there exists a coloring of the leaves of $\mathcal{H}_n$ with the colors red and green, with the fraction $G2^n$ leaves colored green, such that every RG-embedding of some $\mathcal{G}_m$ in $\mathcal{H}_n$, where $2^m \geq HG2^n$, has congestion $C > (const) \log n$.*

Proof. Let us be given an algorithm, call it Algorithm **A**, that solves our Congestion-Harvest Tradeoff Problem in the worst-case scenario, while incurring minimal congestion. By Section 2.1, we know that the congestion incurred by Algorithm **A** for *any* coloring of the leaves of $\mathcal{H}_n$, in particular for the advertised malicious coloring, is $C \leq (const) \log n$.

The coloring of $\mathcal{H}_n$ that we claim defies efficient salvage is described as follows (L is a parameter we fix later, and n is a multiple of L): for each level $\ell = 0, L, 2L, \ldots, n$, proceed left to right along the level-ℓ nodes of $\mathcal{T}_n$, coloring red all of the leaves in the subtree rooted at every 2^L-th node encountered. All other leaves are colored red.

This coloring can be viewed as turning $\mathcal{H}_n$ into a complete $(2^L - 1)$-ary tree, all of whose leaves are colored green, providing that we look only at levels whose level-numbers are divisible by L. Therefore, our RG-embedding problem now assumes some of the flavor of the problem of efficiently embedding a complete binary tree into a complete $(2^L - 1)$-ary tree that is only slightly larger (by roughly the factor $1/H$). The results in [8] about a similar problem lead us to expect the large congestion that we now show must occur.

Our coloring of $\mathcal{H}_n$ has left the tree with $(2^L - 1)^{n/L}$ green leaves. The worst-case scenario of our Congestion-Harvest Tradeoff Problem assumes that the number of green leaves in $\mathcal{H}_n$ is a positive fraction $G > 0$ of the total number of leaves, namely, 2^n. Elementary estimates show that this assumption implies that $L \geq \log n - \log^{(2)} n - c(G)$ for some constant $c(G) > 0$ depending only on G. In analyzing our putative Algorithm **A**, we may, therefore, assume that we are dealing with RG-embeddings whose congestions satisfy $C < \frac{1}{3}L$ (or else, we have nothing to prove).[5]

For each $\ell \in \{0, 1, \ldots, n/L\}$, let $M(\ell)$ denote the number of leaves in the largest green-leafed tree that can be RG-embedded at a level-ℓL node of $\mathcal{H}_n$, according to Algorithm **A**. Even if there were no bound on congestion, the similarity of the colored version of $\mathcal{H}_n$ and a complete $(2^L - 1)$-ary tree would guarantee that $M(\ell + 1) \leq (2^L - 1)M(\ell)$ for $0 \leq \ell < n/L$.

In order to appreciate the effect of the bound C on congestion, note that, if the embedding of Algorithm **A** has congestion $\leq C$, then each number $M(\ell)$ must be representable as the sum of no more than C powers of 2; in other words, the binary representation of $M(\ell)$ can have weight no greater than C.[6] It follows in particular that $M(1) \leq 2^L - 2^{L-C}$. Starting from this upper bound on $M(1)$, we derive a sequence of upper bounds on the other numbers $M(\ell)$. It is clerically convenient to number the bit-positions in the shortest binary representation of $M(\ell)$ from left to right, i.e., high order to low order. Moreover, we need only restrict attention to bit-positions $1, 2, \ldots, L$, as will become clear in the course of the argument.

Focus on a specific $\ell \in \{0, 1, \ldots, n/L - 1\}$ and on its associated $M(\ell)$. Note the effect of proceeding from $M(\ell)$ to $M(\ell + 1)$, $M(\ell + 2)$, and so on. When we multiply $M(\ell)$ by $2^L - 1$ (thereby going up L levels in $\mathcal{H}_n$), the multiplication affects only the rightmost 1 in bit-positions $1, 2, \ldots, L$; say this rightmost 1 appears in bit-position k. The effect of the multiplication, in the presence of our bound C on the congestion of the RG-embedding, is as follows. Our assumption that the rightmost 1 appears in bit-position k means that the high-order L bit-positions end with a string $100 \cdots 0$, of length $\min(C - k + 1, L - k) + 1$. The multiplication has the effect of replacing this string with the like-length string

---

[5] Our assumption that $C < \frac{1}{3}L$ simplifies the clerical details of the upcoming argument.

[6] This is true because we focus on *progressive* RG-embeddings. If we allowed arbitrary RG-embeddings, then $M(\ell)$ would be the *algebraic* sum — i.e., the sum/difference — of at most C powers of 2. The added generality of arbitrary RG-embeddings would influence only constant factors in our bounds.

$011\cdots1$. Note that the resulting bit-string satisfies two conditions: (a) it has weight no greater than C, and (b) its rightmost 1 appears in bit-position $\leq L$.

If we continue the process of multiplying by $2^L - 1$ and "pruning" to maintain the bound on congestion, we find that, every so often — we shall estimate how often — a 1 that originated in a bit-positions $k \in \{1, 2, \ldots, C\}$ in the binary representation of $M(1)$, together with every 1 that is "spawned" by it in subsequent multiplications and "prunings," ceases to exist. When such an *annihilation* occurs, we have lost at least the fraction 2^{-k+1} of the green leaves we could conceivably have been salvaging at that point.

The basis for our lower bound on C resides in our ability to bound how many multiplications and "prunings" have to take place before a 1 that began in bit-position k is annihilated. Since each such annihilation loses us a significant fraction of the green leaves, we wish to maximize the stretches of time between annihilations — by having $M(1)$ assume its maximum possible value, namely, $M(1) = 2^L - 2^{L-C}$, and by "pruning" as few leaves as possible after each multiplication. A corollary of this strategy is that we always strive to have the bit-string in positions $1, 2, \ldots, L$ of our expression for the values $M(\ell)$ have maximum possible weight, namely C.

Let us focus on a 1 that originated in bit-position $k \leq C$ in $M(1)$. Once this 1 begins to "move" in the multiply-then-"prune" game — which occurs when it becomes the rightmost 1 in the surviving representation — and until this 1 is annihilated, the configuration of bit-positions $1, 2, \ldots, L$ has the form $11 \cdots 10x$, where (a) bit-positions $1, 2, \ldots, k-1$ contain the string $11 \cdots 1$, (b) bit-position k contains a 0, and (c) bit-positions $k+1, k+2, \ldots, L-1$ contain a bit-string x of weight at most $C - k + 1$.

Since the numerical value of the bit-string x in bit-positions $k + 1, k + 2, \ldots, L - 1$ decreases monotonically during the multiply-then-"prune" game, it follows that, once it starts to move, the 1 that began in bit-position k is annihilated after no more than $\sum_{i=0}^{C-k+1} \binom{L-k}{i} < 2\binom{L-k}{C-k+1}$ steps. Therefore, the *total* time it takes to annihilate the 1 that originated in bit-position k, from the very start of the multiply-then-"prune" game — which is the time required to annihilate every 1 that originated in bit-positions $k, k+1, \ldots C$, is bounded above by

$$T(k) < 2\sum_{i=k}^{C} \binom{L-i}{C-i+1} \leq 2\binom{L-k+1}{C-k+1} < 2\left(\frac{e(L-k+1)}{C-k+1}\right)^{C-k+1}.$$

Now, if we play the multiply-then-"prune" game long enough that we annihilate a 1 in some bit-position $k \leq h =_{\text{def}} -\lfloor \log(1 - H) \rfloor$, then we shall have lost more than the fraction $1 - H$ of the green leaves; hence, we shall have failed in our assigned task of salvaging at least the fraction H of these leaves. Therefore, the depth n of the SN $\mathcal{H}_n$ had better be small enough to preclude our playing the game for this many steps. In other words, we must have

$$\frac{n}{L} \leq (const) \left(\frac{e(L - h + 1)}{C - h + 1} \right)^{C - h + 1}.$$

This inequality implies $C \geq (const)L = \Omega(\log n)$. □

3 Optimizing Expected Congestion

This section derives bounds on the congestion one must incur in order to survive "random" faults. We adopt the model that predominates in the literature by assuming that the PEs of our SNs fail independently, with probability 1/2.[7] It remains an inviting challenge to determine whether or not the upper bound can be lowered.

3.1 An Algorithm with Good Expected Behavior

We show that a modified version of Algorithm **Worst-Case** of Section 2 incurs congestion that is only *triply* logarithmic in the size of the salvaged SN, with extremely high probability, providing that we lower our demands a bit. Specifically, we reduce our demand that we salvage the fraction H of the surviving PEs of our SN to the demand that we salvage only the fraction $0.3H$ of these PEs.

Theorem 3.1 *Let the leaves of $\mathcal{H}_n$ be colored red and green, independently, with probability 1/2. For any rational $0 < H \leq 1/2$, with probability $\geq 1 - 2^{-\Omega(n)}$, a modification of Algorithm **Worst-Case** will find an RG-embedding having congestion $C \leq \log^{(2)} n - \log 0.3(1 - H) + 1$ of some $\mathcal{G}_m$ in $\mathcal{H}_n$, where $m \geq n - \lceil \log 10n \rceil + \lfloor \log 2.5n \rfloor$.*

The major insight leading to the desired modification of Algorithm **Worst-Case** resides in the following combinatorial fact.

Lemma 3.1 *Let each leaf of $\mathcal{H}_n$ be colored red or green, independently, with probability 1/2. Fix any partition of the leaves of $\mathcal{H}_n$ into blocks of size $10n$. Then, with probability $\geq 1 - 2^{-\Omega(n)}$, each block contains at least $2.5n$ green leaves.*

Proof. Focus first on a single block of $10n$ leaves.

$$Pr(< 2.5n \text{ green leaves}) = Pr(> 7.5n \text{ red leaves})$$

$$= 2^{-10n} \sum_{k=7.5n+1}^{10n} (\text{number of ways to choose } k \text{ red leaves})$$

---

[7] Changing the probability 1/2 to any fixed p merely changes the constants in our results.

This last sum is easily transformed to

$$\sum_{k=0}^{2.5n-1} \binom{10n}{k} 2^{-10n} \leq 2 \binom{10n}{2.5n} 2^{-10n} \leq 2 \left(\frac{10e}{2.5}\right)^{2.5n} 2^{-10n} \leq 2 \left(\frac{\epsilon}{2}\right)^{n}$$

for some $\epsilon < 1$. It follows that

$$Pr(\geq 2.5n \text{ green leaves}) \geq \left(1 - 2 \left(\frac{\epsilon}{2}\right)^{n}\right)^{2^{n}/10n} \geq \exp(-c_1 \epsilon^{n}/n) \geq 1 - \frac{1}{n2^{c_2 n}}$$

for some constants $c_1, c_2 > 0$. $\square$

Proof of Theorem 3.1. Lemma 3.1 tells us that when we look at the labels assigned by our greedy algorithm to nodes at or above level $\lceil \log 10n \rceil$ of a randomly colored instance of $\mathcal{H}_n$, then, with very high probability, we find every node having a label $\lambda(x)$ for which $I(\lambda(x)) \geq 2.5n$. Let $m = n - \lceil \log 10n \rceil + \lfloor \log 2.5n \rfloor$. If we now abandon all but exactly $2^{\lfloor \log 2.5n \rfloor}$ of the salvaged green leaves at each of these nodes, we can "assemble" a salvaged copy of the 2^m-leaf SN $\mathcal{G}_m$ without incurring any further congestion. $\square$

4   Optimizing Worst-Case Harvest

Algorithm **Worst-Case** of Section 2.1 is guaranteed to be efficient, both in running time — it operates in time $O(2^n)$, which is linear in the size of $\mathcal{H}_n$ — and in harvest — it salvages the fraction H of the green leaf-PEs. But, it is easy to find examples where a nongreedy strategy allows one to salvage a much larger fraction of the green leaves. In particular, when the green leaves are spread out sparsely, any greedy approach abandons many more green leaves than it has to. One finds an analogous deficiency in a "lazy" salvage strategy — one that coalesces small-order trees as late as possible, rather than as early as possible; lazy strategies abandon too many green leaves when the leaves are packed densely, in clumps. It might be of practical interest, therefore, to find a computationally efficient algorithm that salvages optimally many green leaves, while honoring a prespecified limit, C, on congestion. This section presents such an algorithm.

4.1   The Algorithm

Overview. Our salvage algorithm proceeds up $\mathcal{H}_n$, from level 0 to level n, labeling each node x at level ℓ with a *set* $\Lambda(x)$ of length-$(\ell+1)$ integer vectors. Each vector in $\Lambda(x)$ will indicate one possible salvage decision available to x; in particular, for each vector $\langle \nu_0, \nu_1, \ldots, \nu_\ell \rangle$:

- there is an RG-embedding in the subtree of $\mathcal{T}_n$ rooted at x of a green-leafed forest $\mathcal{F}$ containing ν_k disjoint copies of $\mathcal{T}_k$, for $0 \leq k \leq \ell$;

- $\sum_{k=0}^{\ell} \nu_k \leq C$, so that the bound on congestion is always honored.

When we get to the root of $\mathcal{H}_n$ (where $\ell = n$), we select the largest level k for which some vector in the set that labels the root has $\nu_k > 0$. Our harvest, then, is a green-leafed copy of $\mathcal{G}_k$.

The Labelling/Embedding Procedure. We associate each level-ℓ node x of $\mathcal{H}_n$ with a trie (i.e., a digital search tree) of height $\ell + 1$. This trie will store the label-set $\Lambda(x)$ in the obvious way. We now present the details of Algorithm **Optimal-Harvest**.

Algorithm Optimal-Harvest:

Step 0. {Label nodes on level 0 of $\mathcal{H}_n$}

Assign each leaf x a label $\Lambda(x) = \begin{cases} \{\langle 1 \rangle\} & \text{if } x \text{ is green} \\ \{\langle 0 \rangle\} & \text{if } x \text{ is red} \end{cases}$

Step $\ell > 0$. {Label nodes on level ℓ of $\mathcal{T}_n$}

Substep $\ell.a$ {Assemble the vectors }
Assign each level-ℓ node x a label as follows.
for each pair of length-ℓ vectors $\xi \in \Lambda(x0)$ and $\eta \in \Lambda(x1)$, place the length-$(\ell + 1)$ vector ζ in $\Lambda(x)$, where

$$\zeta_k = \begin{cases} 0 & \text{if } k = \ell \\ \xi_k + \eta_k & \text{if } k \neq \ell \end{cases}$$

Substep $\ell.b$ {Combine small embedded trees}
for each vector ζ of $\Lambda(x)$, **for all** $0 \leq k < \ell$, **if** component ζ_k of ζ is the sum of a nonzero ξ_k (for some $\xi \in \Lambda(x0)$) and a nonzero η_k (for some $\eta \in \Lambda(x1)$), **then** add to $\Lambda(x)$ a vector ζ' that agrees with ζ except in positions $k, k + 1$; specifically:

$$\zeta_i' = \begin{cases} \zeta_{i+1} + 1 & \text{if } i = k + 1 \\ \zeta_i - 2 & \text{if } i = k \\ \zeta_i & \text{otherwise} \end{cases}$$

and embed the root of a copy of $\mathcal{G}_{k+1}$ in x, routing edges from that root to the roots of two copies of $\mathcal{G}_k$ that are embedded in proper descendants of x

Substep $\ell.c$ {Honor the congestion bound C}
for each vector $\xi \in \Lambda(x)$
if $\sum_{k=0}^{\ell} \xi_k > C$ **then** replace ξ in $\Lambda(x)$ by all possible vectors ξ' such that $\xi_k' \leq \xi_k$ for all $0 \leq k \leq \ell$, and such that $\sum_{k=0}^{\ell} \xi_k' \leq C$.

In the full version of the paper we establish the following theorem. The proof is omitted here for lack of space.

Theorem 4.1 *Let the leaves of $\mathcal{H}_n$ be colored red and green, in any way, and let $1 < C \leq n$. Algorithm* **Optimal-Harvest** *finds, in time $O(n^{3C+2}2^n)$, an RG-embedding of some $\mathcal{G}_m$ in $\mathcal{H}_n$, having congestion $\leq C$ and having optimal harvest among embeddings with congestion C.*

Note that for $C = \frac{1}{3}\left(\frac{n}{\log n} - 2\right)$, the time is quadratic in the size of $\mathcal{H}_n$.

ACKNOWLEDGMENTS: The authors thank Don Coppersmith for helpful suggestions. The research of S. N. Bhatt was supported in part by NSF Grant CCR-88-07426, by NSF/DARPA Grant CCR-89-08285, and by Air Force Grant AFOSR-89-0382; the research of F. T. Leighton was supported in part by Air Force Contract OSR-86-0076, DARPA Contract N00014-80-C-0622, Army Contract DAAL-03-86-K-0171, and NSF Presidential Young Investigator Award with matching funds from ATT and IBM; the research of A. L. Rosenberg was supported in part by NSF Grants CCR-88-12567 and CCR-90-13184. A portion of this research was done while S. N. Bhatt, F. T. Leighton, and A. L. Rosenberg were visiting Bell Communications Research.

References

[1] A. Agrawal (1990): Fault-tolerant computing on trees. Typescript, Brown Univ.

[2] F.S. Annexstein (1989): Fault tolerance in hypercube-derivative networks. *1st ACM Symp. on Parallel Algorithms and Architectures*, 179-188.

[3] J.L. Bentley and H.T. Kung (1979): A tree machine for searching problems. *Intl. Conf. on Parallel Processing*, 257-266.

[4] S. Browning (1980): *The Tree Machine: A Highly Concurrent Computing Environment.* Ph.D. Thesis, CalTech.

[5] R.D. Chamberlain (1990): Multiprocessor synchronization network: design description. Tech. Rpt. WUCCRC-90-12, Washington Univ.

[6] R.D. Chamberlain (1991): Matrix multiplication on a hypercube architecture augmented with a synchronization network. Typescript, Washington Univ.

[7] J. Hastad, F.T. Leighton, M. Newman (1989): Fast computation using faulty hypercubes. *21st ACM Symp. on Theory of Computing*, 251-263.

[8] J.-W. Hong, K. Mehlhorn, A.L. Rosenberg (1983): Cost tradeoffs in graph embeddings. *J. ACM 30*, 709-728.

[9] C. Kaklamanis, A.R. Karlin, F.T. Leighton, V. Milenkovic, P. Raghavan, S. Rao, C. Thomborson, A. Tsantilas (1990): Asymptotically tight bounds for computing with faulty arrays of processors. *31st IEEE Symp. on Foundations of Computer Science*, 285-296.

[10] C.E. Leiserson (1979): Systolic priority queues. *1979 CalTech Conf. on VLSI.*

[11] C. Mead and L. Conway (1980): *Introduction to VLSI Systems.* Addison-Wesley.

[12] P. Raghavan (1989): Robust algorithms for packet routing in a mesh. *1st ACM Symp. on Parallel Algorithms and Architectures*, 344-350.

On Incomplete Hypercubes

Pavel Tvrdík

Department of Computers, Czech Technical University,
Karlovo nám. 13, 121 35 Praha, Czechoslovakia
e-mail: tvrdik@cs.felk.cvut.cs

Abstract. New approach to the fragmentation problem of hypercube multiprocessors with dynamic allocation of subcubes is proposed. It is based on constructing Hamiltonian circuits of incomplete hypercubes. The main result is a constructive proof that an n-cube from which up to $n-2$ vertex-disjoint subcubes are removed so that it remains connected is a Hamiltonian graph and its Hamiltonian circuit can be constructed. If the communication subsystem can use a circuit as an efficient broadcasting and communication graph, then the operating system can use this algorithm for allocating nodes of a fragmented hypercube to a user task when there is no subcube large enough to accommodate the task and in the same time the total number of free nodes is sufficient – instead of forcing the user to wait for releasing allocated subcubes or forcing the system to move the running tasks to other parts of the hypercube.

1 Introduction

An *incomplete hypercube* is a graph which arises from a hypercube by removing some edges or by removing some vertices together with all the edges which are incident with them. Here we will deal with incomplete hypercubes from which several subcubes have been removed. The state of a hypercube multiprocessor with dynamic allocation and releasing of subcubes can be modelled using this kind of incompleteness.

Several simple algorithms have been proposed so far for solving the subcube allocation problem in the hypercube multiprocessors (for example, Gray or binary code strategies [1], free-list strategy [4], MSS strategy [3]). They are based on analysis of a global array of allocation bits [1] or of dynamic lists of free subcubes [3, 4]. The performance of these methods is usually poor under realistic conditions of dynamic allocation and releasing of subcubes due to the fragmentation of the incomplete hypercube. Task migration has been proposed to solve the fragmentation problem recently [2], but it suffers a considerable run-time overhead.

Here another approach to the fragmentation problem based on more effective use of incomplete hypercubes by constructing their Hamiltonian circuits is suggested. Incomplete hypercubes lose the advantage of complete hypercubes – their homogenous structure. Nevertheless we can use the same inductive technique as for the complete hypercube based on decomposing the hypercube into two halves. The simplest question we can ask is whether or under which conditions a Hamiltonian circuit/path of an incomplete hypercube can be constructed.

These questions are addressed in this paper. Several new results on constructing Hamiltonian circuits of incomplete hypercubes are presented. The main
result is a constructive proof that an n-cube from which up to $n-2$ vertex-
disjoint subcubes are removed so that it remains connected is a Hamiltonian
graph and its Hamiltonian circuit can be constructed.

If the communication subsystem can use a circuit as an efficient broadcasting
and communication graph, then the operating system can use this algorithm for
allocating nodes of a fragmented hypercube to a user task when there is no
subcube large enough to accommodate the task but in the same time the total
number of free nodes is sufficient. The user does not have to wait until some
of allocated subcubes are released and the system is not forced to relocate the
running tasks.

2 Basic Definitions

The set of integers $\{1,..,n\}$ is denoted $\mathcal{N}$. The set of vertices and the set of
edges of a simple undirected graph G are denoted $V(G)$ and $E(G)$, respectively.
Two subgraphs H_1 and H_2 of G are *vertex-disjoint* if $V(H_1) \cap V(H_2) = \emptyset$.

An edge joining two vertices u and v is denoted $\langle u, v \rangle$. A path with vertices
$u_0, u_1, .., u_k$ and edges $\langle u_i, u_{i+1} \rangle$, $0 \le i \le k-1$, is denoted $\mathrm{p}\langle u_0, u_1, .., u_k \rangle$.
The circuit $\mathrm{p}\langle u_0, u_1, .., u_k \rangle \cup \langle u_k, u_0 \rangle$ is denoted $\mathrm{c}\langle u_0, u_1, .., u_k \rangle$. A Hamiltonian
path of a graph G and with terminal vertices u and v is denoted $\mathrm{hp}\langle u, v : G \rangle$. A
Hamiltonian circuit of a graph G is denoted $\mathrm{hc}\langle G \rangle$.

An *n-dimensional binary hypercube* (or an *n-cube* only), Q_n, is a graph with
2^n vertices labelled by integers $0, 1, .., 2^n - 1$ represented as n-bit binary strings
(called *addresses*) and with edges joining two vertices whenever their addresses
differ in a single bit. We will usually identify the vertices of the hypercube with
their addresses. Hence $u = 010110$ says that the address of vertex u is 010110.
The jth bit of the address of vertex u, called j^{th} *coordinate* of the vertex u, is
denoted $u[j]$.

The dimension of a hypercube Q is denoted $\dim(Q)$. The Hamming distance
between two vertices $u, v \in V(Q_n)$ is denoted $\varrho(u, v)$. The Hamming distance
between subgraphs H_1 and H_2 of Q_n, $\varrho^*(H_1, H_2)$, is defined as:

$$\varrho^*(H_1, H_2) = \min\{\varrho(u, v) \mid u \in V(H_1), v \in \hat{V}(H_2)\}.$$

The set of all coordinates $j \in \mathcal{N}$ in which the addresses of two vertices $u, v \in$
$V(Q_n)$ differ is denoted $\delta(u, v)$. The set of all coordinates $j \in \mathcal{N}$ in which the
addresses of all vertices from $\mathcal{V} \subset V(Q_n)$ do not differ is denoted $\varepsilon(\mathcal{V})$.

Two edges $E_1 = \langle u_1, v_1 \rangle$ and $E_2 = \langle u_2, v_2 \rangle$ of Q_n are said to be *parallel* if
$\delta(u_1, v_1) = \delta(u_2, v_2)$ (or *parallel at the distance* k if $\varrho^*(E_1, E_2) = k$, $1 \le k \le$
$n-1$). Two parallel edges E_1 and E_2 at the distance 1 are denoted $E_1 \square E_2$.

For each $j \in \mathcal{N}$, Q_n can be decomposed along the dimension j into two
$(n-1)$-dimensional subcubes Q^{0j} and Q^{1j} such that

$$\forall u \in V(Q^{0j}); u[j] = 0 \bigwedge \forall u \in V(Q^{1j}); u[j] = 1.$$

A decomposition along the dimension j is written $Q_n = Q^{0j}\|_j Q^{1j}$. For every subgraph H^0 of Q^{0j} there exists its *image* H^1 in Q^{1j}, written $H^1 = \text{img}_j(H^0)$ (and vice versa).

3 Subcubes

Subcubes of the hypercube are denoted by uppercase letters S or R. It follows from the recursive definition $Q_n = Q_i \times Q_{n-i}$, $1 \leq i \leq n-1$, that each k-dimensional subcube of Q_n can be considered a vertex of an $(n-k)$-cube. Each subcube of Q_n can be uniquely specified by an n-bit string of symbols of the set $\Sigma = \{0, 1, *\}$, called the *address* of the subcube. Equally as for vertices, we will identify subcubes with their addresses. Hence $S = 01*10*$ says that the subcube S has the address $01*10*$. $S[j]$ denotes the jth coordinate in the address of S. The set $\mathcal{N} - \varepsilon(V(S))$ is called the *directions* of S, dir(S). Obviously $|\text{dir}(S)| = \dim(S)$ (= the number of symbols $*$ in the address of the subcube S) and $|\varepsilon(V(S))| + \dim(S) = n$.

The notions introduced for vertices of the hypercube can be generalized to the subcubes. The set of all coordinates $j \in \mathcal{N}$ in which subcubes S_1 and S_2 of Q_n differ is denoted $\delta^*(S_1, S_2)$:

$$\delta^*(S_1, S_2) = \{j \in \mathcal{N} \mid \{S_1[j], S_2[j]\} = \{0, 1\}\}.$$

It is clear that $\forall S_1, S_2 \subset Q_n; \varrho^*(S_1, S_2) = |\delta^*(S_1, S_2)|$ and two subcubes S_1 and S_2 of Q_n are vertex-disjoint iff $\delta^*(S_1, S_2) \neq \emptyset$. Two subcubes S_1 and S_2 are said to be *complementary* if $\dim(S_1) = \dim(S_2)$ and there exists $j \in \mathcal{N}$ such that $\delta^*(S_1, S_2) = \{j\}$ and $S_2 = \text{img}_j(S_1)$.

If $\delta^*(S_1, S_2) = \emptyset$, then the graph $S_1 \cap S_2$ is again a subcube of Q_n and its address and dimension uniquely follows from the addresses of S_1 and S_2. To show this, it is useful to define the set Σ to be a poset.

Definition 1. The set $\Sigma = \{0, 1, *\}$ is a poset $\begin{smallmatrix} 0 & & 1 \\ & \diagdown * \diagup & \end{smallmatrix}$ where the symbol $*$ is its bottom element. The partial ordering is denoted by $\sqsubseteq$. The join of two elements a, b of Σ is denoted by $a \sqcup b$ and the meet of two elements a, b of Σ is denoted by $a \sqcap b$.

The following statements are easy to prove.

Proposition 2. *Given two subcubes* $S^a = a_1 \ldots a_n$ *and* $S^b = b_1 \ldots b_n$ *of* Q_n *such that* $\delta^*(S^a, S^b) = \emptyset$, *then* $S^b \cap S^a = c_1 \ldots c_n$ *where* $c_i = b_i \sqcup a_i$.

Proposition 3. *Given two subcubes* $S^a = a_1 \ldots a_n$ *and* $S^b = b_1 \ldots b_n$ *of* Q_n, *then* $S^b \subset S^a$ *iff* $\forall j \in \mathcal{N}; a_j \sqsubseteq b_j$.

Given $V \subset V(Q_n)$, the *subcube of Q_n induced by the set V* is defined to be the least subcube $S \subseteq Q_n$ such that $V \subseteq V(S)$. Two vertices $u, v \in V(Q_n)$ with $\varrho(u, v) = k \leq n$ induce a k-dimensional subcube of Q_n. Two parallel edges at the distance k induce a $(k+1)$-dimensional subcube of Q_n.

Proposition 4. *Given* $V = \{v_1, \ldots, v_m\} \subset V(Q_n)$, *then the address of the sub-cube induced by* V *is* $s_1 \ldots s_n$, *where* $s_j = \sqcap\{v_i[j], i \in \{1, \ldots, m\}\}$, $j \in \mathcal{N}$.

4 Incomplete Hypercubes

As mentioned above, we consider only incomplete hypercubes that result from removing vertex-disjoint subcubes and edges incident with them from the hypercube. This operation of removing a subgraph is called v-difference here (in contrast to the standard difference of two graphs).

Definition 5. The *v-difference* of two graphs G_1 and G_2, $G_1 \ominus G_2$, is defined to be a subgraph of G_1 induced by the vertex set $V(G_1) - V(G_2)$.

Incomplete hypercubes are irregular graphs. They lose the homogenous structure of the complete hypercubes. The general graph-theoretical properties of incomplete hypercubes are poorly understood and there is very little work on that. Nevertheless we can use the same inductive technique as for the complete hypercube, based on decomposing the hypercube into two halves. The simplest question we can ask is whether or under which conditions a Hamiltonian circuit/path of an incomplete hypercube can be constructed.

We will first present several results on constructing Hamiltonian circuits in incomplete hypercubes made by removing up to three subcubes from the hypercube. See [5] for complete proofs of the following four lemmas.

A hypercube with one vertex removed is obviously not Hamiltonian since the circuits in the hypercube have always even length, but its Hamiltonian path between two given vertices exists under certain conditions.

Lemma 6. Let $n \geq 2$ and let u, v, x be three distinct vertices of Q_n. Then there exists a Hamiltonian path $\mathrm{hp}\langle u, v : Q_n \ominus (\{x\}, \emptyset)\rangle$ iff $\varrho(u, x)$ is odd and $\varrho(v, x)$ is odd.

The simplest case of an incomplete hypercube is $Q_n \ominus S$ where $S \subset Q_n$ is a subcube with $1 \leq \dim(S) \leq n - 1$.

Lemma 7. Let $S \subset Q_n$ be an m-dimensional subcube of Q_n such that $1 \leq m < n$. Let $u, v \in V(Q_n \ominus S)$ be two vertices such that $\varrho(u, v)$ is odd. Then there exists a Hamiltonian path $\mathrm{hp}\langle u, v : Q_n \ominus S\rangle$ except the case when $n = 3$, $\varrho(u, v) = 1$, and S is an edge parallel with $\langle u, v \rangle$ at the distance 2.

More incomplete hypercubes can be modelled by removing two subcubes. If one of them is a vertex and the other is at least 1-cube, the incomplete hypercube is not Hamiltonian. If both subcubes are at least 1-cubes, the incomplete hypercube is Hamiltonian.

Lemma 8. Let $n \geq 4$ and let $S_1, S_2 \subset Q_n$ be two vertex-disjoint subcubes of Q_n such that $\dim(S_1) \geq 1$, $\dim(S_2) \geq 1$, and the graph $Q_n \ominus S_1 \ominus S_2$ is connected. Then there exists a Hamiltonian circuit of $Q_n \ominus S_1 \ominus S_2$.

A similar result is for a hypercube with 3 subcubes removed.

Lemma 9. Let $n \geq 5$ and let $S_1, S_2, S_3 \subset Q_n$ be three vertex-disjoint subcubes such that $\dim(S_i) \geq 1$ for $i = 1, 2, 3$, and the graph $Q_n \ominus \cup_{i=1}^{3} S_i$ is connected. Then there exists a Hamiltonian circuit of $Q_n \ominus \cup_{i=1}^{3} S_i$.

5   Main Result

The main result of this paper is stated by the following theorem which was inspired by Lemmas 8 and 9.

Theorem 10. *Let $n \geq 3$ and let $p \geq 0$ and $q \geq 0$ be two integers such that $p + q \leq n - 2$. Let $\mathcal{S} = \{S_1, S_2, .., S_p\}$ be a set of mutually vertex-disjoint subcubes of Q_n such that $\forall i \in \{1, .., p\}; \dim(S_i) \geq 1$ and $G_s = Q_n \ominus \cup_{i=1}^{p} S_i$ is connected. Let $\mathcal{E} = \{E_1, E_2, .., E_q\}$ be a set of mutually vertex-disjoint edges of G_s such that $G_{se} = G_s \ominus \cup_{i=1}^{q} E_i$ is connected. Then there exists a Hamiltonian circuit $C = \mathrm{hc}\langle G_s \rangle$ such that $E_i \in E(C) \; \forall i \in \{1, .., q\}$.*

Proof. The test of connectedness of the graph $G_s = Q_n \ominus \cup_{i=1}^{p} S_i$ is based on finding a set of vertex-disjoint subcubes $\{R_1, .., R_t\}$ such that $G_s = \cup_{i=1}^{t} R_i$ and then on standard partitioning $\cup_{i=1}^{t} R_i$ into connected components. Similarly for $G_{se} = G_s \ominus \cup_{i=1}^{q} E_i$. See [6] for details.

Denote $r = p + q$. Without loss of generality, we may assume that there is no pair of complementary subcubes in $\mathcal{S}$ (since two complementary k-dimensional subcubes form one $(k + 1)$-dimensional subcube) and that $\forall i \in \{1, .., p\}; \dim(S_i) \leq n - 2$ (since $\dim(S_i) = n - 1$ transfers the problem into an $(n - 1)$-subcube of Q_n). Since G_{se} is connected, it follows that at most 2 subcubes can have dimension $n - 2$.

The case $n = 3$ is trivial since $p = 1$ and $q = 0$ or $p = 0$ and $q = 1$. The case $n = 4$ is also simple, there are several nonisomorphic cases and all of them have the required solution. Assume that $n \geq 5$ and that the theorem holds for all $n' < n$ and for all $p' + q' \leq n' - 2$. Let for each $j \in \mathcal{N}$ denote

$$\mathcal{AS}(j) = \{S_i[j] \mid i \in \{1, .., p\}\},$$
$$\mathcal{AE}(j) = \{E_i[j] \mid i \in \{1, .., q\}\},$$
$$\mathcal{PS}_0(j) = \{i \in \{1, .., p\} \mid S_i[j] = 0\},$$
$$\mathcal{PS}_1(j) = \{i \in \{1, .., p\} \mid S_i[j] = 1\},$$
$$\mathcal{PS}_*(j) = \{i \in \{1, .., p\} \mid S_i[j] = *\},$$
$$\mathcal{PE}_0(j) = \{i \in \{1, .., q\} \mid E_i[j] = 0\},$$
$$\mathcal{PE}_1(j) = \{i \in \{1, .., q\} \mid E_i[j] = 1\},$$
$$\mathcal{PE}_*(j) = \{i \in \{1, .., q\} \mid E_i[j] = *\}.$$

Recall that Q^{0j} and Q^{1j} denote the $(n - 1)$-dimensional subcubes of Q_n in the decomposition of Q_n along the dimension j. Let S_i^{0j} and S_i^{1j}, $i \in \mathcal{PS}_*(j)$, denote two subcubes into which S_i is decomposed in the decomposition $Q_n = Q^{0j} \|_j Q^{1j}$. Similarly E_i, $i \in \mathcal{PE}_*(j)$, is split into two vertices E_i^{0j} and E_i^{1j}.

Let

$$G_s^{0j} = Q^{0j} \ominus \bigcup_{i \in \mathcal{PS}_0(j)} S_i \ominus \bigcup_{i \in \mathcal{PS}_*(j)} S_i^{0j},$$

$$G_{se}^{0j} = G_s^{0j} \ominus \bigcup_{i \in \mathcal{PE}_0(j)} E_i \ominus \bigcup_{i \in \mathcal{PE}_*(j)} E_i^{0j},$$

$$G_s^{1j} = Q^{1j} \ominus \bigcup_{i \in \mathcal{PS}_1(j)} S_i \ominus \bigcup_{i \in \mathcal{PS}_*(j)} S_i^{1j},$$

$$G_{se}^{1j} = G_s^{1j} \ominus \bigcup_{i \in \mathcal{PE}_1(j)} E_i \ominus \bigcup_{i \in \mathcal{PE}_*(j)} E_i^{1j}.$$

The induction by decomposing the graph G_{se} along the dimension j can be applied only if G_{se}^{0j} and G_{se}^{1j} are themselves connected. Since G_{se} is connected, it follows that

$$\forall j \in \mathcal{N} \; \exists \langle y_0, z_0 \rangle \in E(G_{se}^{0j}); \; \text{img}_j(\langle y_0, z_0 \rangle) \in E(G_{se}^{1j}).$$

Since the subcubes S_i and the edges E_i are mutually vertex-disjoint, it follows that

$$\forall i_1, i_2 \in \{1, .., p\}, i_1 \neq i_2, \exists j \in \mathcal{N}; \{S_{i_1}[j], S_{i_2}[j]\} = \{0, 1\},$$
$$\forall i_1, i_2 \in \{1, .., q\}, i_1 \neq i_2, \exists j \in \mathcal{N}; \{E_{i_1}[j], E_{i_2}[j]\} = \{0, 1\},$$
$$\forall i_1 \in \{1, .., p\} \, \forall i_2 \in \{1, .., q\} \, \exists j \in \mathcal{N}; \{S_{i_1}[j], E_{i_2}[j]\} = \{0, 1\}.$$

The algorithm proceeds by analyzing individual mutually disjoint conditions that cover all possible cases of decomposing Q_n into two subcubes.

1. $\exists j \in \mathcal{N}; G_{se}^{0j}$ and G_{se}^{1j} are connected $\wedge \; \mathcal{AS}(j) \cup \mathcal{AE}(j) = \{0, 1\} \wedge 2 \leq |\mathcal{PS}_0(j)| + |\mathcal{PE}_0(j)| \leq n - 4$. This condition implies $n \geq 6$ and $\mathcal{PS}_*(j) = \mathcal{PE}_*(j) = \emptyset$. Then a decomposition of Q_n into Q^{0j} and Q^{1j} can be applied. Let $\langle y_0, z_0 \rangle \in E(G_{se}^{0j})$ such that its image $\langle y_1, z_1 \rangle$ in Q^{1j} belongs to G_{se}^{1j}. Let $C_0 = \text{hc}\langle G_s^{0j} \rangle$ such that $\forall i \in \mathcal{PE}_0(j); E_i \in E(C_0)$ and $\langle y_0, z_0 \rangle \in E(C_0)$ (by induction). Let $C_1 = \text{hc}\langle G_s^{1j} \rangle$ such that $\forall i \in \mathcal{PE}_1(j); E_i \in E(C_1)$ and $\langle y_1, z_1 \rangle \in E(C_1)$ (by induction). Then the graph

$$C = (C_0 - \langle y_0, z_0 \rangle) \cup (C_1 - \langle y_1, z_1 \rangle) \cup \langle y_0, y_1 \rangle \cup \langle z_0, z_1 \rangle$$

is the required Hamiltonian circuit of G_{se}.

2. $\exists j \in \mathcal{N}; G_{se}^{0j}$ and G_{se}^{1j} are connected $\wedge \; \mathcal{AS}(j) \cup \mathcal{AE}(j) = \{0, 1\} \wedge |\mathcal{PS}_0(j)| + |\mathcal{PE}_0(j)| = 1$. (The condition when $|\mathcal{PS}_0(j)| + |\mathcal{PE}_0(j)| = n - 3$ has a symmetric solution to this case.) Let us again apply a decomposition of Q_n into Q^{0j} and Q^{1j}. Let $C_1 = \text{hc}\langle G_s^{1j} \rangle$ such that $\forall i \in \mathcal{PE}_1(j); E_i \in E(C_1)$ (by induction). Since $\forall i \in \mathcal{N}; \dim(S_i) \leq n - 2$, it follows that G_{se}^{1j} contains at least one 2-dimensional subcube. A simple analysis reveals that there always exists an edge $\langle y_1, z_1 \rangle \in E(C_1 \cap \text{img}_j(G_{se}^{0j}))$ such that $\forall i \in \mathcal{PE}_1(j); \langle y_1, z_1 \rangle \neq E_i$. Hence we can take its image $\langle y_0, z_0 \rangle \in E(G_{se}^{0j})$, apply the induction for constructing $C_0 = \text{hc}\langle G_s^{0j} \rangle$ such that $\langle y_0, z_0 \rangle \in E(C_0)$, and interconnect again C_0 and C_1 into $C = \text{hc}\langle G_s \rangle$.

3. $\forall j \in \mathcal{N}; (G_{se}^{0j}$ and G_{se}^{1j} are connected $\wedge \; \{0, 1\} \subset \mathcal{AS}(j) \cup \mathcal{AE}(j)) \Rightarrow * \in \mathcal{AS}(j) \cup \mathcal{AE}(j)$. Whenever there exists a decomposition of Q_n into Q^{0j} and Q^{1j} for some $j \in \mathcal{N}$ such that G_{se}^{0j} and G_{se}^{1j} are connected graphs and both Q^{0j} and Q^{1j} contain at least one subcube from $\mathcal{S}$ or one edge from $\mathcal{E}$, then at least one subcube $S_i \in \mathcal{S}$ or edge $E_i \in \mathcal{E}$ is cut into two halves.

3.1. $\exists j \in \mathcal{N}; G_{se}^{0j}$ and G_{se}^{1j} are connected $\wedge \; \{0, 1\} \subset \mathcal{AS}(j) \cup \mathcal{AE}(j) \wedge * \in \mathcal{AE}(j) \wedge * \notin \mathcal{AS}(j)$. If there are more such j, then choose j such that the set $\mathcal{PE}_*(j)$ is minimal. Let $m = |\mathcal{PE}_*(j)|$. Clearly $1 \leq m \leq q$. Assume without loss of generality that $\mathcal{PE}_*(j) = \{1, 2, .., m\}$. The edges $E_1, .., E_m$ are parallel with each other. For each E_i, $i \in \{1,..,m\}$, we have to find an edge E_i' such that $E_i \square E_i'$. If $\exists k \in \{1,..,m\} - \{i\}$ such that $E_i \square E_k$, then put $E_i' = E_k$ and remove E_k from further considerations. For the other edges E_i, there always exists an edge $E_i' \in E(G_{se})$ such that $E_i \square E_i'$. This is because $r \leq n-2$ and for each E_i, $i \in \{1,..,m\}$, there exist $n-1$ edges in Q_n, parallel with E_i at the distance 1. Therefore at least one of them is vertex-disjoint with $p - 1 \leq n-3$ subcubes, members of $(\mathcal{S} \cup \mathcal{E}) - \{E_i\}$. Let m' be the number of these newly constructed squares induced by E_i and E_i'. Clearly $1 \leq m' \leq m$. Let $F_1^0,..,F_{m'}^0$ $(F_1^1,..,F_{m'}^1)$ denote the edges of these squares belonging to Q^{0j} (Q^{1j}), respectively. Let $C_0 = \text{hc}\langle G_s^{0j} \ominus \cup_{i=1}^{m'-1} F_i^0 \rangle$ such that $\forall i \in \mathcal{PE}_0(j); E_i \in E(C_0)$ and $F_{m'}^0 \in E(C_0)$ (by induction). Let $C_1 = \text{hc}\langle G_s^{1j} \rangle$ such that $\forall i \in \mathcal{PE}_1(j); E_i \in E(C_1)$ and $\forall i \in \{1,..,m'\}; F_i^1 \in E(C_1)$ (by induction). Denote by C_1' the circuit $((C_1 \rightleftharpoons F_1^0) \rightleftharpoons \cdots \rightleftharpoons F_{m'-1}^0)$ where the notation $G \rightleftharpoons F_i^0$ is an abbreviation for $(G - F_i^1) \cup E_i \cup E_i' \cup F_i^0$. Then $(C_0 - F_{m'}^0) \cup (C_1' - F_{m'}^1) \cup E_{m'} \cup E_{m'}'$ is the required Hamiltonian circuit $\text{hc}\langle G_{se} \rangle$.

3.2. $\exists j \in \mathcal{N}; G_{se}^{0j}$ and G_{se}^{1j} are connected $\wedge \{0,1\} \subset \mathcal{AS}(j) \cup \mathcal{AE}(j) \wedge * \in \mathcal{AE}(j) \wedge * \in \mathcal{AS}(j) \forall i \in \mathcal{PS}_*(j); \dim(S_i) \geq 2$. We can obviously apply the same inductive construction as in the case 3.1.

3.3. $\exists j \in \mathcal{N}; G_{se}^{0j}$ and G_{se}^{1j} are connected $\wedge \{0,1\} \subset \mathcal{AS}(j) \cup \mathcal{AE}(j) \wedge * \notin \mathcal{AE}(j) \wedge * \in \mathcal{AS}(j) \wedge \forall i \in \mathcal{PS}_*(j); \dim(S_i) \geq 2$.

3.3.1. $|\mathcal{PS}_*(j)| = r - 2$. Recall that $r = p + q$. In any decomposition satisfying the condition 3.3, $r - 2$ subcubes are cut into 2 halves. Clearly $q = 0$. Each coordinate $j \in \mathcal{N}$ such that $\{0,1\} \subset \mathcal{AS}(j)$ can distinguish just 2 subcubes since the coordinate j of the remaining $r - 2$ subcubes equals to $*$. The number of coordinates we need is therefore $r(r-1)/2$. Clearly $r(r-1)/2 \leq n$. It implies $n \leq 6$ and $r = n - 2$ or $n \geq 7$ and $r \leq n - 3$.

3.3.1.1. $n \geq 7 \wedge r \leq n-3$. Each of the subcubes Q^{0j} and Q^{1j} contains $r - 1 \leq n - 4$ subcubes $S_i \in \mathcal{S}$ (and their halves) and/or edges $E_i \in \mathcal{E}$, therefore we can apply the same inductive construction as in the case 1 of this proof.

3.3.1.2. $n = 6 \wedge r = 4$. It is easy to see that in this case there always exist an edge F^0 in G_s^{0j} and an edge F^1 in G_s^{1j} such that $F^0 = \text{img}_j(F^1)$ and F^0 has to belong to any Hamiltonian circuit of G_s^{0j} since each of its two vertices has exactly one neighbour in $G_s^{0j} \ominus F^0$ and similarly for F^1. Hence we can construct $\text{hc}\langle G_s^{0j} \rangle$ and $\text{hc}\langle G_s^{1j} \rangle$ inductively and interconnect them through F^0 and F^1.

3.3.1.3. $n = 5 \wedge r = 3$. The construction is analogous to that in the previous case.

3.3.2. $|\mathcal{PS}_*(j)| \leq r - 3$. Then at least 3 subcubes S_i or edges E_i are not cut by the decomposition of Q_n along dimension j and we can apply the same inductive construction as in the cases 1 or 2.

3.4. $\forall j \in \mathcal{N}; (G_{se}^{0j}$ and G_{se}^{1j} are connected $\wedge \{0,1\} \subset \mathcal{AS}(j) \cup \mathcal{AE}(j)) \Rightarrow \exists i \in \{1,..,p\}; S_i[j] = * \wedge \dim(S_i) = 1$. Any decomposition of Q_n such that G_{se}^{0j} and G_{se}^{1j} are connected and at least one subcube $S_i \in \mathcal{S}$ or one edge $E_i \in \mathcal{E}$

belongs to Q^{0j} and Q^{1j}, respectively, cuts at least one 1-dimensional subcube S_i into 2 halves.

3.4.1. $q = 0$. Then $r = p$.

3.4.1.1. $p = 3$. Since at least one of subcubes S_1, S_2, S_3 is an edge and G_{se} is connected, it follows that $\forall j \in \mathcal{N}; G_s^{0j}$ and G_s^{1j} are connected. Since there is no $j \in \mathcal{N}$ such that $\{S_i[j] \mid i \in \{1,2,3\}\} = \{0,1\}$, it follows that S_1, S_2, and S_3 are three vertex-disjoint edges of three distinct directions inducing a 3-cube, in Q_n, $n \geq 5$. Put $S_1 = \langle u^0, u^1 \rangle$. Since $n \geq 5$, there exists a 3-cube, say R_3, in $Q_n \ominus S_2 \ominus S_3$ such that $\langle u^0, u^1 \rangle \in E(R_3)$. Let $\langle v^0, v^1 \rangle$, $\langle w^0, w^1 \rangle$, and $\langle x^0, x^1 \rangle$ be the other three edges of R_3, parallel with $\langle u^0, u^1 \rangle$ such that $c\langle u^0, v^0, w^0, x^0 \rangle$ is a square in Q_n. Let j be the direction of $\langle u^0, u^1 \rangle$ and let $Q_n = Q^{0j} \|_j Q^{1j}$. Assume without loss of generality that $S_2 \in E(Q^{0j})$, $S_3 \in E(Q^{1j})$, and $c\langle u^0, v^0, w^0, x^0 \rangle \subset Q^{0j}$.

3.4.1.1.1. $n = 5$. The induction cannot be directly applied, but it is easy to see that there exist $C_0 = \text{hc}\langle Q^{0j} \ominus S_2 \ominus \langle u^0, v^0 \rangle \rangle$ such that $\langle w^0, x^0 \rangle \in E(C_0)$ and $C_1 = \text{hc}\langle Q^{1j} \ominus S_3 \ominus \langle u^1, v^1 \rangle \rangle$ such that $\langle w^1, x^1 \rangle \in E(C_1)$. Then the required Hamiltonian circuit is

$$(C_0 - \langle w^0, x^0 \rangle) \cup (C_1 - \langle w^1, x^1 \rangle) \cup \langle x^0, x^1 \rangle \cup \text{p}\langle w^0, v^0, v^1, w^1 \rangle.$$

3.4.1.1.2. $n \geq 6$. The same circuits C_0 and C_1 as in the preceding case can be constructed by induction.

3.4.1.2. $p = 4$.

3.4.1.2.1. $n = 6$. There are two cases. All the subcubes $S_1, \ldots, S_4$ are edges inducing a 4-cube in Q_n or three of them are edges inducing a 3-cube, say R_3, and the fourth subcube is at least 2-dimensional and intersects R_3. In both cases there exist a decomposition of Q_n into Q^{0j} and Q^{1j} such that each subcube Q^{0j} and Q^{1j} contains at least one subcube S_i. Assume without loss of generality that S_1, S_2, S_3 are edges, $\dim(S_4) \geq 1$, $\text{dir}(S_1) = \{j\}$, $S_2 \subset Q^{0j}$, and $S_3, S_4 \subset Q^{1j}$. Put again $S_1 = \langle u^0, u^1 \rangle$ and let $R_3 \subset Q_n \ominus \cup_{i=2}^4 S_i$ be a 3-cube containing $\langle u^0, u^1 \rangle$. Let $\langle v^0, v^1 \rangle$, $\langle w^0, w^1 \rangle$, and $\langle x^0, x^1 \rangle$ be the other three edges of R_3, parallel with $\langle u^0, u^1 \rangle$ such that $c\langle u^0, v^0, w^0, x^0 \rangle$ is a square in Q_n. Let $C_0 = \text{hc}\langle Q^{0j} \ominus S_2 \ominus \langle u^0, v^0 \rangle \rangle$ such that $\langle w^0, x^0 \rangle \in E(C_0)$ (by induction). The induction in Q^{1j} cannot be directly applied, but similarly to the case 3.4.1.2 there exists $C_1 = \text{hc}\langle Q^{1j} \ominus S_3 \ominus S_4 \ominus \langle u^1, v^1 \rangle \rangle$ such that $\langle w^1, x^1 \rangle \in E(C_1)$. Then the required Hamiltonian circuit is again

$$(C_0 - \langle w^0, x^0 \rangle) \cup (C_1 - \langle w^1, x^1 \rangle) \cup \langle x^0, x^1 \rangle \cup \text{p}\langle w^0, v^0, v^1, w^1 \rangle.$$

3.4.1.2.2. $n \geq 7$. The same circuits C_0 and C_1 as in the preceding case can be constructed by induction.

3.4.1.3. $p \geq 5$. Let d be the number of directions $j \in \mathcal{N}$ such that in a decomposition of Q_n into Q^{0j} and Q^{1j} at least one member of S belongs to Q^{0j} and at least one belongs to Q^{1j}. Assume without loss of generality that the set of such directions is $\mathcal{D} = \{1, \ldots, d\}$. Clearly d is also the dimension of the least subcube of Q_n that has a nonempty intersection with each $S_i \in \mathcal{S}$. Denote this subcube by R_d. Then $\mathrm{dir}(R_d) = \mathcal{D}$. Recall that by our assumption

$$\forall j \in \mathcal{D} \, \exists i \in \{1, .., p\}; \dim(S_i) = 1 \wedge \mathrm{dir}(S_i) = \{j\}.$$

Let for all $j \in \mathcal{D}$ denote

$$\mathcal{SO}(j) = \{S_i \in \mathcal{S} \mid \dim(S_i) = 1 \wedge \mathrm{dir}(S_i) = \{j\} \wedge S_i \in E(R_d)\}$$

and $h(j) = |\mathcal{SO}(j)|$. We now derive the lower and upper bounds on the size of d with respect to the number of subcubes p. Clearly $d \leq p$. If $d = p$, then the subcubes $S_1, .., S_p$ are edges of mutually distinct directions inducing a p-cube and $\forall j \in \mathcal{D}; h(j) = 1$. If $d = p - 1$, then either $\exists j' \in \mathcal{D}; h(j') = 2$ and $\forall j \in \mathcal{D} - \{j'\}; h(j) = 1$ or $\exists i \in \{1, .., p\}; \dim(S_i) \geq 2$ and $R_d \cap S_i \neq \emptyset$. Generally, if $d < p$, then there exist a permutation π on $\{1, .., p\}$ and d edges $S_{\pi(1)}, .., S_{\pi(d)}$ such that $\cup_{i=1}^{d} \mathrm{dir}(S_{\pi(i)}) = \mathcal{D}$ (hence inducing R_d). The remaining $p - d$ subcubes (i.e. members of $\mathcal{S} - \{S_{\pi(1)}, .., S_{\pi(d)}\}$) are either edges of $R_d \ominus \cup_{i=1}^{d} S_{\pi(i)}$ or at least 2-cubes intersecting R_d in at least one vertex. The subcube R_d has 2^d edges and $2d + (2^d - d)$ is the maximum number of subcubes that can intersect or belong to R_d. Therefore $p \leq 2^d - d$ and this implies

$$d \geq \left\lceil \log_2(p + \lceil \log_2 p \rceil) \right\rceil.$$

Since $p \geq 5$, it follows that $d \geq 3$. Let $\alpha = \min_{j \in \mathcal{D}} \{h(j)\}$ and let $l \in \mathcal{D}$ such that $h(l) = \alpha$. Let $\beta = |\mathcal{PS}_*(l)| - \alpha$ (i.e. the number of the subcubes whose dimension is at least 2 and that are cut in a decomposition of Q_n into Q^{0_l} and Q^{1_l}). Clearly $\beta \geq 0$. Assume without loss of generality that $\mathcal{PS}_*(l) = \{1, .., \alpha + \beta\}$, $\mathcal{SO}(l) = \{S_1, .., S_\alpha\}$, and $S_i = \langle u_i^0, u_i^1 \rangle \, \forall i \in \{1, .., \alpha\}$. Let Q^{0_l} and Q^{1_l} be a decomposition of Q_n along dimension l such that $u_i^0 \in V(Q^{0_l})$ and $u_i^1 \in V(Q^{1_l}) \forall i \in \{1, .., \alpha\}$. Since $\forall j \in \mathcal{D}; h(j) \geq \alpha$, it follows that $p \geq \alpha d + \beta$ and $n \geq \alpha d + \beta + 2$. Since $Q_n = R_d \times Q_{n-d}$ and $n - d \geq 2$, it follows that there always exist mutually vertex-disjoint 3-cubes $\widetilde{R}_1, .., \widetilde{R}_\alpha$ such that

$$\forall k \in \{1, .., \alpha\}; \quad \widetilde{R}_k \subset (Q_n \ominus \bigcup_{i=1}^{k-1} S_i \ominus \bigcup_{i=k+1}^{p} S_i) \bigwedge \langle u_i^0, u_i^1 \rangle \in E(\widetilde{R}_k).$$

Let $\widetilde{R}_k^0$ and $\widetilde{R}_k^1$ denote the 2-dimensional subcubes of $\widetilde{R}_k$ such that $\widetilde{R}_k^0 \subset Q^{0_l}$ and $\widetilde{R}_k^1 \subset Q^{1_l}$. Let $v_k^0, w_k^0, x_k^0 \in V(\widetilde{R}_k^0)$ such that $c\langle u_k^0, v_k^0, w_k^0, x_k^0 \rangle = \widetilde{R}_k^0$ and similarly for $v_k^1, w_k^1, x_k^1 \in V(\widetilde{R}_k^1)$. Let m_0 and m_1 denote the number of subcubes from $\{S_{\alpha+\beta+1}, .., S_p\}$ in Q^{0_l} and Q^{1_l}, respectively. Then clearly $m_0 + m_1 + \alpha + \beta = p \leq n - 2$. Assume without loss of generality that $S_i \subset Q^{0_l}$ for $\alpha + \beta + 1 \leq i \leq \alpha + \beta + m_0$ and $S_i \subset Q^{1_l}$ for $\alpha + \beta + m_0 < i \leq p$.

3.4.1.3.1. $m_0 = 1$. Let

$$C_1 = \mathrm{hc}\langle Q^{1_l} \ominus \bigcup_{i=1}^{\alpha} \widetilde{R}_i^1 \ominus \bigcup_{i=\alpha+1}^{\alpha+\beta} S_i^1 \ominus \bigcup_{i=\alpha+\beta+2}^{p} S_i \rangle$$

(by induction). Let $\langle y_1, z_1 \rangle \in E(C_1)$ such that $\langle y_0, z_0 \rangle = \text{img}_l(\langle y_1, z_1 \rangle)$ is vertex-disjoint with $S_{\alpha+\beta+1}$. Let

$$C_0 = \text{hc}\langle Q^{0\iota} \ominus \bigcup_{i=1}^{\alpha} \langle u_i^0, v_i^0 \rangle \ominus \bigcup_{i=\alpha+1}^{\alpha+\beta} S_i^0 \ominus S_{\alpha+\beta+1}\rangle$$

such that $\langle w_i^0, x_i^0 \rangle \in E(C_0)$ $\forall i \in \{1, .., \alpha\}$ and $\langle y_0, z_0 \rangle \in E(C_0)$ (by induction). Then

$$C = (C_0 - \bigcup_{i=1}^{\alpha} \langle w_i^0, x_i^0 \rangle - \langle y_0, z_0 \rangle) \bigcup (C_1 - \langle y_1, z_1 \rangle) \bigcup$$

$$\bigcup_{i=1}^{\alpha} p\langle w_i^0, v_i^0, v_i^1, w_i^1, x_i^1, x_i^0 \rangle \bigcup \langle y_0, y_1 \rangle \bigcup \langle z_0, z_1 \rangle$$

is the required Hamiltonian circuit.

3.4.1.3.2. $m_0 > 1 \wedge m_1 > 1 \wedge m_0 \leq \alpha$. Let

$$C_0 = \text{hc}\langle Q^{0\iota} \ominus \langle u_1^0, v_1^0 \rangle \ominus \bigcup_{i=2}^{\alpha} \tilde{R}_i^0 \ominus \bigcup_{i=\alpha+1}^{\alpha+\beta} S_i^0 \ominus \bigcup_{i=\alpha+\beta+1}^{\alpha+\beta+m_0} S_i \rangle$$

such that $\langle w_1^0, x_1^0 \rangle \in E(C_0)$ (by induction). Let

$$C_1 = \text{hc}\langle Q^{1\iota} \ominus \bigcup_{i=1}^{m_0-1} \langle u_i^1, v_i^1 \rangle \ominus \bigcup_{i=m_0}^{\alpha} \tilde{R}_i^1 \ominus \bigcup_{i=\alpha+1}^{\alpha+\beta} S_i^1 \ominus \bigcup_{i=\alpha+\beta+m_0+1}^{p} S_i \rangle$$

such that $\langle w_i^1, x_i^1 \rangle \in E(C_1)$ $\forall i \in \{1, .., m_0 - 1\}$ (by induction). Then

$$C = (C_0 - \langle w_1^0, x_1^0 \rangle) \bigcup (C_1 - \bigcup_{i=1}^{m_0-1} \langle w_i^1, x_i^1 \rangle) \bigcup p\langle w_1^0, v_1^0, v_1^1, w_1^1 \rangle \bigcup \langle x_1^0, x_1^1 \rangle \bigcup$$

$$\bigcup_{i=2}^{m_0-1} p\langle w_i^1, v_i^1, v_i^0, w_i^0, x_i^0, x_i^1 \rangle$$

is the required Hamiltonian circuit.

3.4.1.3.3. $m_0 > \alpha > 1$. Let

$$C_0 = \text{hc}\langle Q^{0\iota} \ominus \langle u_1^0, v_1^0 \rangle \ominus \bigcup_{i=2}^{\alpha} \tilde{R}_i^0 \ominus \bigcup_{i=\alpha+1}^{\alpha+\beta} S_i^0 \ominus \bigcup_{i=\alpha+\beta+1}^{\alpha+\beta+m_0} S_i \rangle$$

such that $\langle w_1^0, x_1^0 \rangle \in E(C_0)$ (by induction). Let

$$C_1 = \text{hc}\langle Q^{1\iota} \ominus \bigcup_{i=1}^{\alpha} \langle u_i^1, v_i^1 \rangle \ominus \bigcup_{i=\alpha+1}^{\alpha+\beta} S_i^1 \ominus \bigcup_{i=\alpha+\beta+m_0+1}^{p} S_i \rangle$$

such that $\langle w_i^1, x_i^1 \rangle \in E(C_1)$ $\forall i \in \{1, .., \alpha\}$ (by induction). Then

$$C = (C_0 - \langle w_1^0, x_1^0 \rangle) \bigcup (C_1 - \bigcup_{i=1}^{\alpha} \langle w_i^1, x_i^1 \rangle) \bigcup \mathrm{p}\langle w_1^0, v_1^0, v_1^1, w_1^1 \rangle \bigcup \langle x_1^0, x_1^1 \rangle \bigcup$$

$$\bigcup_{i=2}^{\alpha} \mathrm{p}\langle w_i^1, v_i^1, v_i^0, w_i^0, x_i^0, x_i^1 \rangle$$

is the required Hamiltonian circuit.

3.4.2. $q > 0$. We can proceed using the same inductive constructions as in the case 3.4.1 and select $l \in \mathcal{N}$ for decomposition of Q_n without considering the edges E_i. If $\mathcal{PE}_*(l) = \emptyset$, the construction remains the same. If $\mathcal{PE}_*(l) \neq \emptyset$, the construction is simplified using the same technique as in the cases 3.1. and 3.2.

This completes the proof since all possible cases have been solved. $\square$

Theorem 10 has two important corollaries.

Corollary 11. *Let* $n \geq 3$ *and* $1 \leq p \leq n - 2$ *be two integers. Let* $S_1, S_2, .., S_p$ *be mutually vertex-disjoint subcubes of* Q_n *such that* $\forall i \in \{1, .., p\}; \dim(S_i) \geq 1$ *and* $Q_n \ominus \cup_{i=1}^{p} S_i$ *is connected. Then the graph* $Q_n \ominus \cup_{i=1}^{p} S_i$ *is Hamiltonian.*

Corollary 12. *Let* $n \geq 3$ *and* $1 \leq q \leq n - 2$ *be two integers. Let* $E_1, E_2, .., E_q$ *be mutually vertex-disjoint edges of* Q_n. *Then there exists a Hamiltonian circuit* $C = \mathrm{hc}\langle Q_n \rangle$ *such that* $E_i \in E(C)$ $\forall i \in \{1, .., q\}$.

6 Conclusions and Future Work

Theorem 10 is the best result we can get if no further conditions or constraints on the size of subcubes S_i or on the placements of subcubes S_i and edges E_i are given. It is easy to find cases for $p + q = n - 1$ such that there exists no Hamiltonian circuit under conditions of Theorem 10. On the other hand, a Hamiltonian circuit exists under certain conditions even if much more than $n - 2$ subcubes are removed. It is an open problem to determine under which conditions a Hamiltonian circuit of more fragmented hypercubes can be constructed. Also the problem how to embed more complicated graphs (e.g. trees) into incomplete hypercubes is to be solved.

References

1. M.-S. Chen and K. G. Shin. Processor allocation in an n-cube multiprocessor using Gray codes. *IEEE Trans. on Computers*, C-36(12):1396–1407, Dec. 1987.
2. M.-S. Chen and K. G. Shin. Subcube allocation and task migration in hypercube multiprocessors. *IEEE Trans. on Computers*, C-39(9):1146–1155, Sept. 1990.
3. S. Dutt and J. P. Hayes. Subcube allocation in hypercube computers. *IEEE Trans. on Computers*, C-40(3):341–352, Mar. 1991.

4. J. Kim, C. R. Das, and W. Lin. A top-down processor allocation scheme for hypercube computers. *IEEE Trans. on Parallel and Distr. Systems*, 2(1):20–30, Jan. 1991.
5. P. Tvrdik. *Spanning subgraphs of hypercubes*. PhD dissertation, Czech Technical University, Prague, 1991.
6. P. Tvrdik. On Incomplete Hypercubes. Research Report DC-92-06, Department of Computers, Czech Technical University, Prague, June 1992.

This article was processed using the LaTeX macro package with LLNCS style

Reducing Network Hardware Quantity by Employing Multi-Processor Cluster Structure in Distributed Memory Parallel Processors

Naoki Hamanaka, Junji Nakagoshi, Teruo Tanaka

Central Research Lab., Hitachi, Ltd.
Kokubunji, Tokyo 185, Japan

Abstract. This paper describes a cluster structure to reduce the amount of network hardware in distributed memory parallel processors. The expected reduction in the data transfer rate as the number of nodes is reduced is avoided by raising the transfer rate of each path. Calculations for typical application programs show that clustering can reduce the hardware quantity by 40% provided that inner-cluster parallel processing efficiency is sufficiently high.

1 Introduction

Recently, the need for detailed numerical simulations has been creating greater demands for high performance computers. Massively parallel processors provide the only hope of fulfilling these demands by using a few thousand nodes, each including high-speed microprocessors, and a network to transfer data between these nodes.

Network architecture is very important in achieving massively parallel processors. The main task in this area is to develop a network with higher data transfer performance and less hardware. Many networks have been proposed, such as our hyper-crossbar network[1].

Another way to reduce network hardware quantity is to use a multi-processor cluster structure. The number of nodes connected by the network can be reduced by clustering a few processors with shared memory. This approach will soon be feasible because a VLSI chip will include several processors[2]. This technique can reduce the quantity of network hardware to about 1/n if each node includes n processors. However, the data transfer rate of the whole network will also be reduced to 1/n because the n processors share one path. To avoid such a decrease in parallel processing performance, the data transfer rate of each path should be increased by increasing the width of the transfer path. Although this increases the hardware quantity, an overall reduction of up to 40% is possible.

This paper discusses the reduction of the network hardware using multi-processor cluster structure by considering characteristics of application programs and intra-cluster parallel processing efficiency.

2 Hardware Quantity of Hyper-Crossbar Networks

2.1 Hyper-Crossbar Network

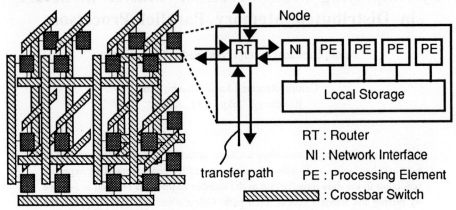

Figure 1. Parallel Processor using Hyper-Crossbar Network.

Figure 1 shows the structure of a parallel processor using a hyper-crossbar network. Nodes are placed three-dimensionally and each includes several processing elements (PEs) and the shared local storage. Crossbar switches are placed in parallel with each dimension to connect nodes. Each node also includes a network interface for controlling data transfer, and a router for connecting the network interface and crossbar switches connected to the node. Each router can route data from a crossbar switch to other crossbar switches to enable data transfer between nodes which are not directly connected by a crossbar switch. Therefore, each router is a small crossbar switch.

Using this network, the mean number of crossbar switches needed to transfer data between source and destination nodes is smaller than in other networks. When every node sends data in the same direction (the typical case in SPMD programming, which is a commonly used style), all data can be transferred completely in parallel.

The above example is a three-dimensional hyper-crossbar network, but other dimensional hyper-crossbar networks are also possible.

2.2 Hardware Quantity

The hardware quantity of a crossbar switch and its router (which is considered to be part of the network) is estimated from the number of crosspoints, which is given by the product of the number of input ports and output ports of each crossbar switch. The number of crosspoints is proportional to the hardware quantity of the crossbar switch minus its control circuit.

Hardware quantity Q of a hyper-crossbar switch is estimated by

$$Q = MW\left((K+1)^2 + \sum_{j=1}^{K} M_j\right) \geq MW\left((K+1)^2 + K\sqrt[K]{\prod_{j=1}^{K} M_j}\right) = MW\left((K+1)^2 + KM^{\frac{1}{k}}\right) \cdots (1)$$

where M is the number of nodes, K is the number of dimensions, Mj is the number of nodes in the j-th dimension, and W is the width of the transfer path in the network. This formula uses the fact that an arithmetical mean is greater than or equal to a geometrical mean. Thus the minimum hardware quantity of the network with M nodes and K dimensions is given when all the Mj's are the same.

The value of K that minimizes Eq. (1) is obtained as a function K=K(M) by solving Eq. (2) numerically.

$$\partial Q/\partial K = MW(2(K+1)+M^{1/K}(1 - (\log M/K))) = 0 \cdots (2)$$

The theoretical minimum hardware quantity for a hyper-crossbar network with M nodes is obtained by assigning K(M) to Eq.(1). Figure 2 shows the result when W=1. This shows that Q can be described approximately by

$$Q = ZWM^{1.2} \cdots (3)$$

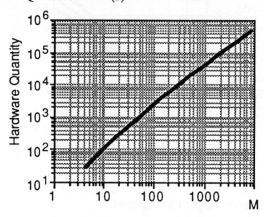

Figure 2. Minimum Hardware Quantity of Hyper-Crossbar Network with M Nodes.

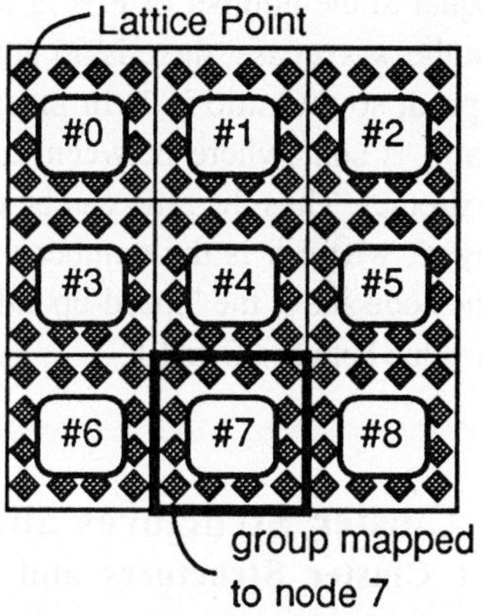

Figure 3. Mapping Example of Two Dimensional Space.

3 Models for the Network Hardware Quantity Estimation
3.1 Model of Application Programs

In this section, typical application programs are modeled. Numerical simulations, which are very important applications for parallel processing, are considered.

In most cases numerical simulations are concerned with continuous systems described by partial differential equations. To solve these equations numerically, continuous spaces are represented by finite lattice points. A value at a lattice point can be determined by values at adjacent lattice points.

Before parallel processing, lattice points should be mapped to nodes. Figure 3 shows an ideal example for two dimensions. Only values of lattice points facing the edge of each group should be transferred since some of their neighboring lattice points are mapped to neighboring groups. Programs can be parallelized into SPMD manner, so data can be transferred through the network without conflict.

When n represents the number of lattice points in a group, the amount of transferred data is proportional to n^p where p is the "transfer index". For the two-dimensional case, $n^p=n^{1/2}$ while the calculation time is proportional to n. For three-dimensional spaces; $n^p=n^{2/3}$. Here, p should be less than 1. The granularity of parallel processing strongly depends on n and p.

3.2 Model of Intra Cluster Parallel Processing Efficiency

In this section, the speed-up ratio in shared-storage parallel processing is modeled. We assume that it can be modeled by figure 4.

When parallel processing in a node is performed ideally, the speed-up ratio is equal to the number of PEs in the node. In the worst case, there is no increase in speed, so the ratio is 1. In practice, the ratio is somewhere between these two extremes. Thus the ratio can be modeled by x^s, where x is the number of PEs in the node and s, the "speed-up index", has a value between 0 and 1.

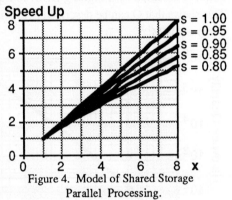

Figure 4. Model of Shared Storage Parallel Processing.

4 Cluster Structures and Network Hardware Quantity
4.1 Cluster Structures and Transfer Path Throughput

A cluster structure reduces the number of nodes, but it decreases the total throughput of the network. Hence, the parallel processing performance decreases. To avoid a decrease in performance, the throughput of the network should be increased. This section discusses the degree of this increase.

The time required to calculate data for all lattice points in a node in one iteration cycle, Tn, and the time required to transfer all data to be transferred in a node in the same cycle, Tt, are estimated by Eq.s (4) and (5), where N represents the total number of PEs, x is the number of PEs in a node and M (= N/x) is the number of nodes in a parallel processor. D represents the number of whole lattice points. A and B are constants. V(x) represents the throughput for each transfer path in the network, and p and s are the transfer index and speed-up index, as before.

$$Tn(x) = A \left(\frac{D}{M}\right) \left(\frac{1}{x^s}\right) = A\left(\frac{D}{N}\right) x^{1-s} \dots (4)$$

$$Tt(x) = \frac{B\left(\frac{D}{M}\right)^p}{V(x)} = B\left(\frac{D}{N}\right)^p \frac{x^p}{V(x)} \dots (5)$$

The execution time should not change even if a cluster structure is employed.

$Tn(1) + Tt(1) = Tn(x) + Tt(x) \cdots (6)$

From Eq.s (4), (5) and (6), we obtain the increase in transfer throughput as

$$\frac{V(x)}{V(1)} = \frac{x^P}{1 - G(x^{1-s} - 1)} \cdots (7)$$

where $G = V(1) \frac{A}{B} (\frac{D}{N})^{1-P} = \frac{Tn(1)}{Tt(1)}$

G represents the granularity. By increasing D/N, we can reduce the data transfer overhead. However, each node has limited memory capacity, so D/N cannot be made so large. The range for G is believed to be 1 to 5 [3].

When the index s is close to 1, $V(x)/V(1)$ becomes x^P, so the transfer throughput is not affected by G. However, when s is not close to 1, the value of $G(x^{1-s} - 1)$ in Eq. (7) is not negligible. As it approaches 1, the value of Eq. (7) approaches infinity. This corresponds to the case when $Tt(x)$ in Eq. (6) is very close to 0 because $Tn(x)$ becomes very close to $Tn(1)+Tt(1)$. When G is greater, the increase of $V(x)/V(1)$ is more sensitive to s.

4.2 Cluster Structures and Network Hardware Quantity

Clustering requires an increase in transfer throughput. This section discusses the relationship between this increase and network hardware quantity.

There are two ways to increase transfer throughput. One is to increase the clock frequency of the network. The other is to increase the width of the transfer path. To determine the effect of clustering, we should increase the transfer throughput by increasing the path width, so that the comparisons are based on the same technology.

In case of hyper-crossbar networks, the hardware quantity can be estimated from

$$Q(x) = ZW(x) (N / x)^{1.2} \cdots (8)$$

which is derived from Eq. (3). In Eq. (8), $W(x)$ represents the width of the transfer path as a function of x. Therefore the ratio of network hardware quantity with clustering and without clustering is given by

$$\frac{Q(x)}{Q(1)} = \frac{ZW(x)(N/x)^{1.2}}{ZW(1)N^{1.2}} = \frac{W(x)}{W(1)x^{1.2}} = \frac{V(x)}{V(1)x^{1.2}} = \frac{1}{x^{1.2-p}} \cdot \frac{1}{1 - G(x^{1-s} - 1)} \cdots (9)$$

where $W(x)$ is proportional to $V(x)$.

When the speed-up index s is very close to 1, Eq. (9) becomes approximately $1/x^{1.2-p}$. Because the transfer index p is less than 1, network hardware quantity can be reduced. When s is not close to 1, the value of Eq. (9) approaches infinity as x increases. When the granularity G is greater, Eq. (9) approaches infinity at low values of x.

Figure 5 shows the ratio of network hardware quantity. Network hardware quantity can be reduced when G=1. When G=5, network hardware quantity can be reduced only if the index s is greater than 0.95.

In this example, the network was a hyper-crossbar network whose exponent of hardware quantity is 1.2 and greater than p. The result is applicable to other networks if its exponent of hardware quantity is greater than p. This condition is a general characteristic of interconnection networks.

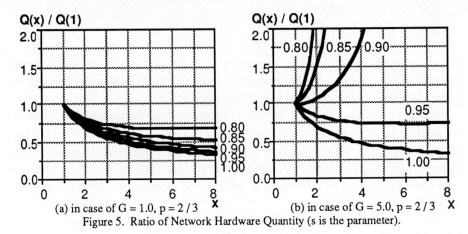

(a) in case of G = 1.0, p = 2 / 3   (b) in case of G = 5.0, p = 2 / 3

Figure 5. Ratio of Network Hardware Quantity (s is the parameter).

Therefore it is concluded that employing the cluster structure reduces network hardware quantity if intra cluster parallel processing efficiency is kept high. Also, the amount of network hardware reduction is greater if its index of hardware quantity and intra-cluster parallel processing efficiency are higher, and the granularity G is lower.

5 Conclusion

The hardware quantity in hyper-crossbar networks can be reduced by clustering. Typical numerical simulations show that clustering can reduce the hardware by more than 40% provided that intra-cluster parallel processing efficiency is sufficiently high.

As the efficiency becomes higher, network hardware quantity becomes smaller. Thus the key technology for clustering is shared-storage parallel processing.

References

[1] Tanaka, T., Hamanaka, N. and Muramatsu, A., "The MIMD Type Parallel Processing Architecture based on Tagged Data Transfer", *Proceedings of the Parallel Processing Symposium*, 1989 (in Japanese).

[2] Hanawa, M., Nishimukai, T., Nishii, O., Suzuki, M., Yano, K., Hiraki, M., Shukuri, S. and Nishida, T., "On-Chip Multiple Superscalar Processors with Secondary Cache Memories", *Proceedings 1991 IEEE International Conference on Computer Design: VLSI in Computers & Processors*, 1991.

[3] Hamanaka, N., Tanaka, T. and Muramatsu, A., "Performance Evaluation of a Numerical Calculation Oriented Macro Dataflow Computer", *Dataflow Workshop*, 1987 (in Japanese).

Connection Machine Results for Pyramid Embedding Algorithms *

Sotirios G. Ziavras

Department of Electrical and Computer Engineering
New Jersey Institute of Technology
Newark, New Jersey 07102, U.S.A.

Abstract

A comparative analysis for four algorithms that embed pyramids into hypercubes is presented in this paper. Relevant results for a Connection Machine system CM-2 with 16,384 processors are included.

1 Introduction

The most important reason for the undisputable success of the hypercube network has been its capability of efficiently emulating a wide variety of important topologies [6]. The N-dimensional *hypercube* H_N is composed of 2^N nodes. If unique N-bit binary addresses are assigned to the nodes of the hypercube, then an edge connects two nodes if and only if their binary addresses differ by a single bit. The *pyramid* structure is composed of successive layers of mesh-connected arrays, where the size of the arrays decreases with the increase of the level number (the base is level 0). Each node, except for nodes at level 0, is directly connected to four children located at the immediately lower level. In the rest of this paper, P_n denotes the pyramid with $2^n \times 2^n$ nodes in its base that comprises $n + 1$ levels.

Section 2 discusses briefly four algorithms that embed pyramids into hypercubes. A comparative analysis that involves all four algorithms is then carried out in Section 3 with results obtained on the Connection Machine. Finally, Section 4 presents conclusions.

2 Pyramid Embedding Algorithms

2.1 Embedding Algorithm I

The first embedding algorithm [1], Algorithm I herein, embeds the P_n pyramid into the H_{2n} hypercube. A one-to-one mapping of nodes from the base of the pyramid onto PEs of the hypercube is accomplished as follows. The n-bit reflected Gray code is used to encode separately the rows and columns in the base. The

---

*This work was supported by the National Science Foundation under Grant CCR-9109084.

RGC	000	001	011	010	110	111	101	100
000	0,1,2,3	0	0	0,1	0,1	0	0	0,1,2
001	0	0	0	0	0	0	0	0
011	0	0	0	0	0	0	0	0
010	0,1	0	0	0,1	0,1	0	0	0,1
110	0,1	0	0	0,1	0,1	0	0	0,1
111	0	0	0	0	0	0	0	0
101	0	0	0	0	0	0	0	0
100	0,1,2	0	0	0,1	0,1	0	0	0,1,2

Figure 1: Mapping the P_3 pyramid onto the H_6 hypercube with Algorithm I. RGC: 3-bit Reflected Gray Code.

binary addresses of the corresponding PEs in the hypercube are found by either interleaving or concatenating the bits of the encoded row and column numbers. PEs having the lower k bits of their encoded row and column numbers equal to 0 will simulate nodes from level k of the pyramid. Fig. 1 shows the mapping of the P_3 pyramid onto the H_6 hypercube; the numbers within the squares represent level numbers. The maximum dilation of this mapping is equal to two. For Algorithm I, the hypercube can not simulate multiple levels of the pyramid simultaneously.

2.2 Embedding Algorithm II

Similarly to Algorithm I, the second embedding algorithm [5], Algorithm II herein, maps the P_n pyramid onto the H_{2n} hypercube. In contrast to Algorithm I, Algorithm II allows multiple levels, excluding the leaf level, to be active at a time. The mapping of nodes from levels 0 and 1 is similar to the mapping produced by Algorithm I. For each set of four PEs representing sibling nodes at level 1 of the pyramid which have a common parent at level 2, the PE chosen to serve as the parent is neighbor to one of the PEs representing the children and all parent PEs for level 2 form mirror images in squares outlined by their children. This procedure is repeated until the apex of the pyramid is reached. Fig. 2 shows an example embedding. The maximum dilation is three.

2.3 Embedding Algorithms III and IV

Two algorithms suggested by Lai and White [2] for embedding a pyramid into a hypercube map distinct nodes of the pyramid onto distinct PEs of the hypercube. They require an H_{2n+1} hypercube for the mapping of the P_n pyramid. Both algorithms are recursive and rather complicated. Their maximum dilation is three and two respectively.

RGC	000	001	011	010	110	111	101	100
000	0,1	0,2	0,3	0,1	0,1	0	0,2	0,1
001	0	0	0	0	0	0	0	0
011	0	0	0	0	0	0	0	0
010	0,1	0	0	0,1	0,1	0	0	0,1
110	0,1	0	0	0,1	0,1	0	0	0,1
111	0	0	0	0	0	0	0	0
101	0	0	0	0	0	0	0	0
100	0,1	0,2	0	0,1	0,1	0	0,2	0,1

Figure 2: Mapping the P_3 pyramid onto the H_6 hypercube with Algorithm II.

3   Comparative Analysis

Results obtained from runs of image processing algorithms on a Connection Machine system CM-2 consisting of 16K PEs are presented here. This system operates in the SIMD mode of computation and the word length of its PEs is one bit. The hypercube is the dominant topology in the system. More specifically, a 10-dimensional hypercube is the backbone (router) of the communication network. Each vertex of this hypercube contains a router node (communication processor) to which sixteen PEs are attached. The communications hardware is capable of combining multiple messages going to the same destination by applying some arithmetic or logical combining operation.

We must emphasize that the results on CM-2 are not always indicative of the performance of pure hypercube systems because of two reasons. Firstly, the routers become the bottlenecks for communication intensive operations because any single router node is shared by sixteen PEs. To alleviate this problem, the results presented in this paper use one PE per router node. Secondly, for algorithms where many-to-one communication operations are followed by the application of associative (reduction) operations on the received data, the Connection Machine routers implement the reduction "on the fly," thus reducing the amount of traffic going to distant PEs as well as the amount of operations performed at the destination.

3.1   Convolution

The convolution algorithm convolves a $k \times k$ window of weighting coefficients with a $2^n \times 2^n$ image matrix. Assuming the assignment of a single pixel to each node in the base of the pyramid, the smallest integer γ is found for which $2^\gamma \geq k$. Then the base is partitioned into square blocks of size $2^\gamma \times 2^\gamma$. Each such partition contains the leaves of a subpyramid whose apex is at level γ. The weighting coefficients are then loaded into the upper leftmost part of each partition. In the Connection Machine, the coefficients are loaded using k^2 broadcasting operations with appropriate sets of PEs selected each time. This part is not included in the total execution time of the presented results. The rest of the PEs in each partition receive a zero as the weighting coefficient. The PEs then multiply the weighting coefficient with their pixel value and send the result to their parent. Parents at level 1 add the values they receive from their children and send the result to their parent. This process continues until the apex of each subpyramid is reached. Each apex at level γ adds the values it receives from its children and sends the result, through the necessary intermediate PEs at lower levels, to the leaf PE in the upper leftmost corner of its partition. Each window in the base that contains the weighting coefficients is then shifted to the right once, multiplications are performed as above, the results are shifted to the left once, and the values are sent to the parents at level 1. The bottom-up and top-down processes described earlier are then applied, with the result now stored in the PE with offset (0,1) in the partition. These steps are repeated $2^{2\gamma}$ times, which is equal to the total number of PEs in each partition.

Results are presented in Table 1 for windows with k from 2 to 8. All times are in msec. The results indicate that there are not any significant differences among the timings of the four embedding algorithms. Therefore, Algorithms I and II are more appropriate than Algorithms III and IV due to their requirement for systems of lower cost. The same table also shows the total time for lateral data transfers at level 0. The relatively small value of the dilation does not have a critical influence due to CM-2's "on the fly" implementation of reduction operations. Algorithms III and IV produce "irregular" embeddings that may increase the overhead resulting from the control structure of application algorithms. This overhead is reduced by generating pointers to parents, children and lateral neighbors during initialization.

Table 2 presents results for the convolution problem when pipelining is implemented. Only communication operations have been pipelined here due to the SIMD mode of computation. The algorithm proceeds in two processing phases. More specifically, in the first phase the algorithm finds all required products between weighting coefficients and pixel values. The results are shifted and stored into the memory of the appropriate PEs in the corresponding partitions. The second phase of the algorithm implements pipelining with bottom-up and top-down communication operations. *Phase 1* in Table 2 denotes the time taken by the first phase. Pipelining can not be implemented with Algorithm II when the window size is smaller than 5×5 because the base of the pyramid can not be simulated simultaneously with other levels.

3.2 Segmentation

The image segmentation technique follows an iterative approach to segmentation and property estimation [7]. An overlapped linked pyramid structure defines a parent-child relationship between nodes in adjacent layers, but, unlike other pyramids, this relationship is not fixed and may be redefined in each iteration. Each node, except for nodes in the base, has a 4×4 subarray of candidate child nodes at the immediately lower level (i.e., 50% overlapping in each of the four directions).

Each iteration links the node to a single one of the four candidate parent nodes.

Our implementation on the Connection Machine uses 8-bit gray level values. Table 3 shows the results for this segmentation algorithm. A total of three images were presented as input to the algorithm. Algorithms I and II assume six levels while Algorithms III and IV assume five levels. Since the time taken by concurrent multilevel processing is only a very small portion of the total execution time, all mapping algorithms yield similar performance.

4 Conclusions

While Algorithms I and II require target systems with approximately half the cost of those required by Algorithms III and IV, Algorithm I is not capable of simulating multiple levels of the pyramid simultaneously. Since a wide variety of pyramid algorithms can take advantage of concurrent multilevel computations, this restriction is a major drawback of Algorithm I. In contrast, Algorithm II does not impose this restriction. For concurrent multilevel computations, this algorithm achieves very good performance, at half the cost, when compared to Algorithms III and IV. Therefore, Algorithm II is a compromise between the pair of Algorithms III and IV and Algorithm I with respect to cost and performance.

Acknowledgment: The author gratefully acknowledges the permission granted to him by Dr. L.S. Davis, Director of UMIACS, for CM-2 access. The computer programming by M.A. Siddiqui is also appreciated.

References

[1] Stout, Q.F., "Hypercubes and Pyramids," *in Pyramidal Systems for Computer Vision*, Cantoni and S. Levialdi (Eds.), Spring-Verlag, Berlin, Heidelberg, Germany (1986), pp. 74-89.

[2] Lai, T.-H. and White, W.,"Mapping Pyramid Algorithms into Hypercubes," *Journal Parallel Distributed Computing*, Vol. 9 (1990), pp. 42-54.

[3] Ziavras, S.G., "Techniques for Mapping Deterministic Algorithms onto Multi-Level Systems," *in Proc. Intern. Conf. Parallel Processing*, Vol. I, Chicago, IL (Aug. 1990), pp. 226-233.

[4] Ziavras, S.G., "Efficient Mapping Algorithms for a Class of Hierarchical Systems," *IEEE Trans. Parallel Distributed Systems*, Accepted for Publication.

[5] Patel, S.C. and Ziavras, S.G., "Comparative Analysis of Techniques that Map Hierarchical Structures into Hypercubes," *in Proc. Parallel Distributed Computing Systems Conf.*, Washington, D.C. (Oct. 1991), pp. 295-299.

[6] Ziavras, S.G., "On the Problem of Expanding Hypercube-Based Systems," *Journal Parallel Distributed Computing*, Accepted for Publication.

[7] Burt, P.J., Hong, T.-H., and Rosenfeld, A., "Segmentation and Estimation of Image Region Properties Through Cooperative Hierarchical Computation," *IEEE Trans. Systems Man Cybernetics*, Vol. 11, No. 12 (Dec. 1981), pp. 802-809.

	Lateral	Total	$k \times k$
Alg. I	3.36	17.61	
Alg. II	3.36	17.82	2×2
Alg. III	5.21	20.24	
Alg. IV	4.82	21.90	
Alg. I	12.78	109.81	
Alg. II	12.53	105.89	3×3
Alg. III	18.55	116.51	
Alg. IV	18.01	107.86	
Alg. I	46.69	577.16	
Alg. II	45.96	547.88	5×5
Alg. III	69.38	593.91	
Alg. IV	67.64	547.67	
Alg. I	46.28	554.14	
Alg. II	46.82	550.76	7×7
Alg. III	70.01	599.93	
Alg. IV	67.66	551.07	
Alg. I	49.21	543.16	
Alg. II	45.83	544.38	8×8
Alg. III	69.26	584.81	
Alg. IV	67.33	541.15	

Table 1: Convolution.

	Phase 1	Total	$k \times k$
Alg. II			2×2
Alg. III	9.36	24.41	
Alg. IV	9.77	24.36	
Alg. II			3×3
Alg. III	32.17	83.68	
Alg. IV	31.83	79.56	
Alg. II	93.26	482.10	5×5
Alg. III	119.11	322.20	
Alg. IV	118.11	307.69	
Alg. II	93.28	500.56	7×7
Alg. III	119.12	329.36	
Alg. IV	118.09	308.11	
Alg. II	93.27	481.65	8×8
Alg. III	119.12	320.83	
Alg. IV	118.08	307.60	

Table 2: Convolution with pipelining.

	Image	Total	Iterations
Alg. I		246.69	
Alg. II	1	255.78	5
Alg. III		212.76	
Alg. IV		212.05	
Alg. I		352.78	
Alg. II	2	351.65	8
Alg. III		310.77	
Alg. IV		322.56	
Alg. I		349.93	
Alg. II	3	351.02	8
Alg. III		311.19	
Alg. IV		322.65	

Table 3: Segmentation.

Interconnection Networks Based on Block Designs

Volker Hatz[*]

Abstract. We discuss a method constructing efficient multiprocessor networks based on combinatorial designs. The principal goal is to reduce the network diameter while keeping the number of processor ports small. With a smart multiplexing technique and the use of a class of bipartite graphs we are able to construct e.g. a 1210 processor machine with 4 ports/processor and diameter 2.

Summary

The efficiency of parallel algorithms often depends on the topology of the underlying network. One goal for hardware designers is to provide networks, which have a small maximum distance and produce minimal overhead for routing (cf. [6]). This would relieve programmers of the problem to place communicating processes on neighbouring processors.

Here, an algebraic method to construct such networks is presented.

1 Introduction

This section gives only a brief overview of the ideas used in the remainder of the paper. For more details we refer to [2] treating this subject more fundamentally.

A *block design* is an incidence structure $\mathbf{D} = (V, B, I)$ consisting of $v = |V|$ points and $b = |B|$ blocks; $I \subseteq V \times B$. Blocks are k-subsets of the point set V. In this paper we will consider only regular 2-designs; i.e. designs with constant point degree r and constant block degree k, where each unordered pair of distinct points occurs in exactly λ blocks, λ is called *index*. Counting arguments show that the equations $vr = bk$ and $k(k-1) = \lambda(v-1)$ hold. Another important relation is Fisher's inequality: $b \geq v$. It implies that $r \geq k$. A simple example of a block design with $V = \mathbf{Z}_7$ and $B \subseteq \binom{V}{3}$ is shown in figure 1. The left picture shows the usual representation of this well known design, while the picture on the right side shows the representation of this design as a *bipartite graph*. All designs can be interpreted as a bipartite graph $G = (V_1 \cup V_2, E)$ by identifying $V_1 = V$ and $V_2 = B$.

Another basic building block of the class of networks to be considered is an ASIC, called the *rotor*, which is a restricted implementation of a crossbar switch with remarkable properties. The rotor device realizes all edges of the complete graph K_n within a minimal number of timesteps by *1-factorizing* it. A 1-factor is a maximal regular subgraph with degree 1. If the sum of disjoint 1-factors results in the original graph, this is called a 1-factorization. A 1-factorization for complete graphs K_n, with

---

[*] This work was done at the Institute for Algorithms und Cognitive Systems, University of Karlsruhe.

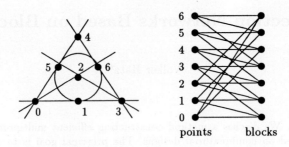

Fig. 1. Simple example of a block design

$n \in 2\mathbb{N}$, is given by the following definition of the edge set for 1-factors F_i (i: vertex i, ∞ is also a vertex):

$$E_{F_i} := \{\{i, \infty\}\} \cup \left\{\{(i-j) \bmod n - 1, (i+j) \bmod n - 1\} \mid j = 1, \ldots, \frac{n}{2} - 1\right\}.$$

By that, we can switch cyclically between $n - 1$ given permutations. An example for the 1-factorization of K_4 is given in table 1.

Table 1. 1-factorization of K_4 ($3 \hat{=} \infty$)

timestep	1-factor	edge 1	edge 2
0	F_0	0,3	1,2
1	F_1	1,3	0,2
2	F_2	2,3	0,1

We have designed an ASIC in CMOS technology which implements a rotor. Compared to crossbar switches the rotor needs less area and almost no control logic (cf. [3]).

2 Design Machines

The theory presented in section 1 is now used to construct a new class of networks: *design machines*. The authors of [1] and [5] have already proposed block designs as interconnection networks for parallel computers. We extend these basic ideas here: busses are replaced by rotors and routing algorithms are presented.

For technical reasons a major goal in network construction is to keep the number of processor ports low. Bermond et al. [1] solved this problem by using busses within block designs. Points were identified with processors, blocks with busses. For larger networks the authors used the *dual design*. Within the dual design points and blocks are interchanged, such that now processors are identified with blocks and busses with points. By Fisher's inequality it follows that the number of processor ports k is now less than the number of processors r attached to one bus. This is highly desirable because the cost for processor ports are high.

However, it has to be remarked that on the other hand the busses would have a high load and thus would not be an efficient means of connecting processors anymore. A better connection strategy was the complete graph in form of a *crossbar switch*. In general, these switches are extremely area consuming and have a considerable overhead in control logic. Therefore, they are not implemented for higher node numbers. Here the superiority of the rotor device comes into play. It needs one port per processor, has minimal control logic and it implements the complete graph.

The new class of networks, which we want to introduce here, is called *design machines*. A main building block of these machines is the rotor.

Definition 1. A *design machine* is a tuple

$$(P, R, H, T_0, \ldots, T_{r-2})$$

such, that $\mathbf{D} = (B, P, I^T)$ is a block design, with $I = \cup_{t=0}^{r-2} T_t$. P is the set of processors, R the set of rotors. $H \subset Aut(\mathbf{D})$ denotes an automorphism group acting on the machine. This is useful to determine embedded groups, and thus naturally embedded networks. T_i is called a *topology instance*. Each T_i represents the topology of a design machine at timestep i.

$DM(n, k)$ is an abbreviation to denote a machine with n processors and k ports.

The next definition helps to describe properties of design machines.

Definition 2. A *slot* is a time interval $[t, t + 1)$ during which a packet can be sent. The *spatial diameter* denotes the well known graph theoretic diameter of a network, whereas the *time&spatial diameter* of a network denotes the maximum of the minimum number of slots that have to be waited until any processor has delivered a packet to any other processor. To determine the spatial diameter of a multiplexed network, we consider the multiplexers as complete graphs.

In [4] we give an algorithm for network construction, which is based on a construction method for block designs. This method is called the development of difference families; a difference family is a set of blocks with certain properties, such that the elementwise operation of a group on the blocks gives rise to a block design. For the general construction it is necessary, that the point degree r is an even number, because only then the complete graph is 1-factorable. By that not all difference families are suitable as a basis for design machines.

Several routing algorithms for design machines are given in [4]. In the following section we consider a small example of a design machine.

2.1 Example: $DM(13, 4)$

In this example we consider a $DM(13, 4) = (\mathbb{Z}_{13}, \mathbb{Z}_{13}, \mathrm{PGL}(3, 3), T_0, T_1, T_2)$, the design machine over the projective plane $PG_{2,3}$. The structure of the topology instances T_0, T_1 and T_2 is developed in the remainder of this section.

For each $PG_{2,q}$ there exists a difference family $D_f = \{B_0\}$ such that the development of the block set $\{B_0, B_0+1, \ldots, B_0+v-1\}$ results in a design **D** isomorphic to $PG_{2,q}$. $D_f = \{\{0,1,3,9\}\}$ is a difference family which can be used to construct a design isomorphic to $PG_{2,3}$. By using the difference family D_f and the operation of the cyclic group C_v on D_f, we obtain the design shown in table 2. Furthermore, table 1 shows how the ports of a rotor are connected in different timesteps according to the 1-factors (port numbers are identified with vertex numbers). The position of the rotors determine the current topology of the network.

Table 2. Structure of $DM(13,4)$

processor	is connected to rotors				processor	is connected to rotors			
0	0	1	3	9	7	7	8	10	3
1	1	2	4	10	8	8	9	11	4
2	2	3	5	11	9	9	10	12	5
3	3	4	6	12	10	10	11	0	6
4	4	5	7	0	11	11	12	1	7
5	5	6	8	1	12	12	0	2	8
6	6	7	9	2					

Using both tables we derive that in timestep 1 processor 0 is connected with processor 4 via rotor 0. That is because in timestep 1 any rotor connects its ports 0 and 3. Furthermore rotor 0 appears in processor 0 in position 0 and in processor 4 in position 3. By the same argument processors 10 and 12 are connected via rotor 0 at the same time. Carrying on we obtain a complete description of the topology instance T_0. T_1 and T_2 can be obtained in the same way. The wiring of $DM(13,4)$ is shown in figure 2.

$$P_0 \; P_1 \; P_2 \; P_3 \; P_4 \; P_5 \; P_6 \; P_7 \; P_8 \; P_9 \; P_{10} \, P_{11} \, P_{12}$$

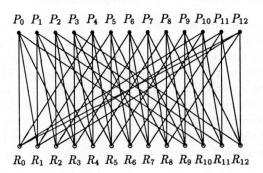

$$R_0 \; R_1 \; R_2 \; R_3 \; R_4 \; R_5 \; R_6 \; R_7 \; R_8 \; R_9 \; R_{10} R_{11} R_{12}$$

Fig. 2. Example of a 13 processor design machine network

$DM(13,4)$ is ideally suited for a class of processors called *Transputers*. Other networks which are ideally suited for Transputers are (e. g.) a machine $DM(111,4)$ with 3 base blocks {0,1,3,24}, {2,12,20,32}, {4,8,30,36}, 111 processors with 4 ports, 37 rotors of size 12 and a machine $DM(1210,4)$ with 10 base blocks constructed over $PG(4,3)$, 1210 processors with 4 ports, 121 rotors of size 40.

Table 3. Some parameters of design machines (dm.: diameter)

type	#proc.	#ports	time&spatial dm.	spatial dm.	#wires
$DM(13,4)$	13	4	2	1	52
torus 4×4	16	4	4	4	32
hypercube 2^4	16	4	4	4	32
$DM(111,4)$	111	4	6	2	444
hypercube 2^7	128	7	7	7	448
hypercube 2^{10}	1024	10	10	10	5120
$DM(1210,4)$	1210	4	39	2	4840

3 Simulation Results

We have completed a simulation toolbox which allows a discrete simulation of interconnection networks. This tool allows to change several parameters and displays a graphical animation of the network traffic for different communication tasks. We are well aware of the deficiencies of our approach since we assume a synchronous machine with uniform packet sizes. On the other hand it is not practical to compare machines without any assumptions of this kind.

Table 4 lists the results for a simulation in which for 100 steps each processor injected a message with 50% probability. The table lists the number of steps needed to deliver a message, the column "fast design machines" shows simulations which assume the presence of a rotor that turns fast enough to provide a virtual complete graph. Here the assumption is, that each processor can only read and write one packet per full turn of the rotor.

Table 4 lists average values since the permutations (destinations) were chosen randomly. A simple routing algorithm was used for all machines (grid: first column then row, hypercube: XOR-mask from left to right). Three of the design machines quoted here have maximum spatial distance 1, i. e. these are machines constructed over $PG_{2,q}$. $DM(111,4)$ has maximum spatial distance 2. The simulations reveal a very interesting property of design machines: store-and-forward chains have almost vanished, since the maximum spatial distance is kept low.

4 Implementation

Finally we want to point out some implementation issues. A small design machine is currently being set up, using transputers as processors. Here synchronization has

Table 4. Simulation results for random-traffic with 50% probability

	grid	hypercube	design machine	fast design machines
13/16 proc.	108.0	105.4	116.6	101.0
31/32/36 proc.	110.2	106.8	119.2	101.2
57/64 proc.	111.0	107.0	114.8	103.6
111/121/128 proc.	117.6	107.0	139.6	103.6

to be done in a locally bounded area and thus is no problem. In larger systems synchronization of the whole system could be done by an optically distributed clock.

The communication speed of the most common Transputer, the T800, is given by 20 MBit/s. Considering the standard Transputer protocol, the speed drops to 1.74 MByte/s. The implementation of our rotor switch is passive and copes well with 20 MHz. Thus it is fast enough to cooperate with Transputers. The "turning" speed is no problem at all, since the ASIC can be clocked with at least 25 MHz. This clocking frequency also determines the length of a slot. Since the rotor is a passive transmitting device, the packet size can be adjusted by changing the clocking frequency. We have not yet done an analysis of optimal slot lengths.

5 Conclusion and Perspective

In summary we have achieved mathematically well described parallel computer interconnection networks.

In comparison to the survey papers of Bermond et al. [1] and Colbourn, van Oorschot [5] we have reported on busless systems, construction methods and routing algorithms. Implementations of the proposed networks are feasible and the simulation results are encouraging.

References

1. J. C. Bermond, J. Bond, M. Paoli, C. Peyrat, "Graphs and Interconnection Networks: Diameter and Vulnerability", in Proceedings of the Ninth British Combinatorial Conference, 1983, pp.1-30
2. T. Beth, D. Jungnickel, H. Lenz, "Design Theory", B.I.-Wissenschaftsverlag, 1985
3. T. Beth, V. Hatz, "A Restricted Crossbar Implementation and its Applications", ACM Computer Architecture News, Vol. 19, December 1991
4. T. Beth, V. Hatz, "Design Machines: Algebraically Well Described Interconnection Networks", to appear in Journal on Designs, Codes and Cryptography
5. C. J. Colbourn, P. C. van Oorschot, "Applications of Combinatorial Designs in Computer Science", ACM Computing Surveys, Vol.21, No.2, June 1989
6. C. Wu, T. Feng, "Tutorial: Interconnection Networks for Parallel and Distributed Processing", Computer Society Press, 1984

Partitioning and mapping communication graphs on a modular reconfigurable parallel architecture

V. DAVID, Ch. FRABOUL, JY. ROUSSELOT, P.SIRON

ONERA-CERT
Département d'Etudes et de Recherches en Informatique
BP 4025 31055 TOULOUSE CEDEX
Email: fraboul@tls-cs.cert.fr

Abstract. A reconfigurable parallel architecture whose interconnection topology can be dynamically modified in order to match the communication characteristics of a given algorithm provides flexibility for efficient execution of various applications. But, due to communication links switching devices design constraints, connecting a large number of processors on a dynamically programmable interconnection structure, leads to the design of a modular interconnection structure. The validation of such a modular reconfigurable interconnection network is based on the demonstration of its ability to support any application coded as communicating sequential processes. This demonstration leads to the mapping problem of any partitionable communicating processes graph on the defined architecture, taking into account communication constraints of the modular and reconfigurable interconnection network.

This paper presents results obtained in the context of a research project named MODULOR which objectives were the design and the realization of a massively parallel reconfigurable computer, as well as of the software tools needed for developing applications that efficiently use reconfiguration potentialities of the architecture.

1 Modular reconfigurable parallel architecture context

Main problems encountered in the design of a reconfigurable processor network architecture are due to the programmable interconnection topology needed for the connection of a large number of processors [2, 3, 7, 8]. The connection of all the communication links of all the processors on a single crossbar switch is often impossible. A larger interconnection network can be obtained by cascading smaller switching elements, but as the number of elementary crossbar switches increases, it becomes costly and difficult to realize and to program, moreover communication time between processors is directly linked to the number of stages needed to build this interconnection network.

Main characteristic of MODULOR architecture is to benefit, as far as possible, from communications locality in order to take into account switching elements size constraints and to minimize communication times as well as interconnection network's complexity. A module allows the connection of a limited number of processors on a first level of communication network, but a second level of interconnection switches is needed for the design of a multimodule architecture [2, 3].

A module is based on the connection of a number N of processors compatible with available crossbar switches characteristics. A first assumption consists in the decomposition of the intra-module interconnection structure into L parts (where L is the number of available communication links per processor). All the links having the same serial number are connected to the same crossbar switch: with this assumption the complexity of each switching element can be divided by the number L of links of each processor.

The multimodule architecture needs another communication level between modules. A second assumption deals with the way of connecting communication links of the M modules to the intermodule interconnection structure. Only S ports are reserved on each crossbar switch of a module for communication between modules. It means that each module has L*S external links connected to the second level of crossbar switches.

Main characteristics of the logical structure of MODULOR architecture are described on Fig.1.

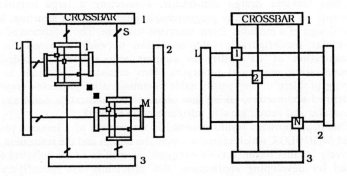

Fig.1 MODULOR multimodule architecture's logical structure

2 Partitioning and mapping a parallel application

The development of parallel applications on such a processor network architecture, generaly uses explicit expression of parallelism handled by message based communicating processes model [6]. A reconfigurable parallel application can be seen by the programmer as a set of algorithmic phases [1, 4]. A phase can be described as processes communicating and synchronizing through messages sent on communication channels. Each process corresponds to an algorithmic entity that can be executed on a processor (a second level of parallelism can be expressed within such an algorithmic entity for exploitation of quasi-parallelism on a processor). A communication graph, where nodes represent processes and edges represent communication channels linking two processes, can be associated to each phase.

In the context of a reconfigurable processor network, mapping such communication graphs only deals with the determination of needed communication links and of corresponding switches settings. But reconfigurable parallel architecture's modularity and interconnection structures characteristics introduce new constraints. In fact, module and intermodule interconnection networks have been designed according their capabilities to map any parallel application coded as communicating processes.

The modularity constraint leads to the study of partitioning heuristics needed to decompose a communication graph into loosely interconnected subgraphs. An application graph is said to be partitionable when the obtained decomposition into subgraphs is compatible with architectural parameters: the number of partitions must be less or equal to the number M of modules, the number of processes per partition must be less or equal to the number N of processors available on each module and the number of external links per partition which must be less or equal to L*S.

Mapping mechanisms are used to allocate any partitionable communication graph on the modular architecture: each subgraph must be allocated to a module of the architecture. The studied mechanisms consist in the determination of module and intermodule communication networks configurations. Formal proofs of mapping potentialities of the proposed architecture that have been settled, directly derive from module and intermodule interconnection structures characteristics.

These partitioning and mapping problems are illustrated on Fig.2.

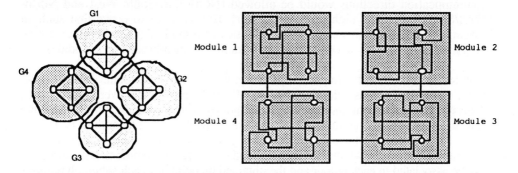

Fig.2 Partitioning of a graph G into 4 subgraphs G1, G2, G3, G4 and mapping on a M=4, N=4, L=4, S=1 multimodule architecture

We developped a polynomial method for splitting a graph into weakly interconnected subgraphs. The algorithm belongs to the class of heuristic algorithms, and is based on the definition of a new affinity function.

Let $G=(X,U)$ be a non oriented graph and $P=(X_1, ...,X_n)$, a partition of G. We will call $A(X_i)$, affinity of X_i, the sum of vertices affinities of X_i with vertices of $X_{j \neq i}$, and $A(P)$, maximal affinity of P, the maximum over i of $A(X_i)$. G is said partitionable for the multimodule Modulor architecture M, N, L, S, iff it exists a partition P of G in at most M parts with at most N vertices with $A(P) \leq L*S$.

Details, results and complexity analysis can be found in [2].

In order to simplify the description of the mapping problem, we will assume in this paper that the communication graph has a number of nodes which is less or equal to the number of available processors, and that the number of edges per node (processes connectivity degree) is less or equal to the number of available links on each processor. If this assumption cannot be verified, a contraction of the graph (equivalent to partitioning problen) must be achieved before mapping and communication links multiplexing facilities must be provided.

3 Mapping a communication graph on a monomodule architecture

Mapping a communicating processes graph on a module of the reconfigurable architecture seems quite easy. All the processors are identical, so we only have to determine which links must be established in order to program the communication links switches. But the module interconnection structure must warrant that all graphs verifying the above assumption can be implemented.

Mapping tentatives of very simple communication graphs show obvious limitations of a module's interconnection scheme as it has been shortly presented above. In fact, an additional assumption is needed: the communication switches of a module must be coupled two by two. As an example, if an Out link of a processor is connected to the North crossbar switch, the corresponding In link has to be connected to the South crossbar switch. In the case of a four links processor, it means that only North/South and East/West links can be established. If the number of links increases, additional communication directions would be allowed (North-East/South-West and North-West/South-East for a eight links processor). But we have to prove that such an assumption doesn't limit mapping potentialities of a module (i.e. a communication graph verifying the size an connectivity constraints can be allocated on a module).

The demonstration of this important property, which validates module's architecture, relies on original graphs colouring methods. It can be proved that every graph which degree is L and verifying the previous assumptions (size and connectivity constaints) can be coloured with C colours (C=L/2) so that each node has at the utmost two edges of the same colour. Such a colouring scheme generates C partial subgraphs which are the reunion of two by two disjoined chains and cycles [2]. A communication direction can be associated to each colour and the obtained mapping for each subgraph requires at the utmost two edges per direction. In conclusion one can verify the absence of edges different from North/South (South/North), East/West (West/East).

Another demonstration of this property has been proposed in the context of a architecture composed of four links processors connected on two crossbar switches [8]. This demonstration is based on the search of Eulerian cycles in a regular 4-valent graph allowing the decomposition of this graph into two regular 2-valent subgraphs.

4 Mapping a communication graph on the multimodule architecture

Mapping a communication graph on the multimodule architecture, leads to more complex problems. If we suppose that the initial graph can be partitioned into loosely interconnected subgraphs, the problem is then to allocate the obtained subgraphs on the modules of the architecture. Communication constraints of module and intermodule networks have to be verified. Mapping of a communication graph on the multimodule architecture assumes that this graph is partitionable.(i.e. its decomposition into subgraphs is compatible with multimodule architecture's parameters). The intermodule interconnection structure must be organised in order to guarantee that any partionable graph can be allocated on the multimodule architecture.

The first approach taken for building the intermodule interconnection network has been to consider a module as a L*S links processor and to connect all the links having the same serial number on the same external crossbar switch. Thus L*S external switches connecting M input links to M outputs links are needed to interconnect M modules.

In this case the multimodule architecture presents the same communication constraints as each module architecture. Thus the colouring mechanisms used for allocating a graph on a module can be generalized. As a colour is associated to each communication direction, an edge will have the same colour when crossing source module network, intermodule network and destination module network.

Unfortunately, simple partitionable graphs counter-examples that cannot be coloured and thus allocated on this multimodule architecture can be shown. In fact one can warrant the allocation of a partitioned graph only if the connectivity degree of each partition is less or equal to 2*S (instead of L*S). It means that in worst cases, all the external links are mapped on the same communication direction.

Thus a second way of connecting the external links of a module has been studied. This design is based on another colouring of partitionable communication graphs: the colouring of intermodule links (communications between partitions) is realized only after colouring edges of each partition's subgraph [2].

An important step of this colouring phase is based on the demonstration that each subgraph of a partitionable graph can admit what we call a S-balanced colouring. It means that the number of external link (which is less or equal L*S) that have the same colour (same communication direction) is less or equal 2*S. This property guarantees the potential utilization of all the external links of a module.

The intermodule colouring mechanism is based on the association of C (number of colours C=L/2) virtual nodes to each module. The 2*S (maximum) corresponding external links are asssociated to each virtual node. A virtual graph composed of C*M nodes which connectivity degree is 2*S is thus obtained and coloured. Each module has S external colours supporting each 2*C external links. An external colour characterizes the external crossbar switch which has to be used.

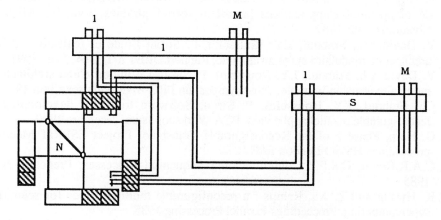

Fig.3 Intermodule communication structure

The intermodule communication structure deriving from this colouring mechanism is described Fig.3. The way of connecting the external links of a module is different from the previous one: each external switch supports all the external links having the same serial number for each communication direction of module's networks. The intermodule interconnection structure is composed of 2*S external switches allowing the connection of M*L/2 input links towards M*L/2 output links.

Conclusion

The studied partitioning and mapping mechanisms have been integrated in a reconfigurable parallel application development software which includes: a graphical editor which allows the description of an application as a set of communicating processes graphs, the software tools dealing with partitioning and mapping of processes graphs on the architecture, and a code generator software allowing the execution of an application on the realized prototype [2, 4].

The validated multimodule architecture has been prototyped. The realized prototype is composed of 4 modules including each 20 INMOS T800 Transputer connected through 4 INMOS C004 switching elements driven by 2 INMOS T414 Transputers. Two types of boards have been designed. A first one inplements each module's interconnection structure. A second one is used for the implementation of intermodule interconnection structure [2, 3].

MODULOR project has been mainly funded by DRET (Direction des Recherches, Etudes et Techniques). Other supports are MRT PRC/ANM (Architectures Nouvelles de Machines), Région Midi-Pyrénées, CEE PCA (Parallel Computing Action).

References

1. F. Boniol, Ch. Fraboul, J.Y. Rousselot, P. Siron, MODULOR: chaîne de développement d'applications parallèles reconfigurables. Journées AFCET, Chamonix, mai 1989
2. V. David, Ch. Fraboul, J.Y. Rousselot, P. Siron, Etude et réalisation d'une architecture modulaire et reconfigurable, Rapport DRET n°1/3364, Mars 1991
3. V. David, Ch. Fraboul, J.Y. Rousselot, P. Siron, Definition d'une architecture modulaire et reconfigurable, 3ème symposium PRC ANM Palaiseau Juin 1991
4. Ch. Fraboul, J.Y. Rousselot, P. Siron, Software tools for developping a reconfigurable parallel application, PCA Workshop Ispra, décembre 1990
5. G. Harp, Phase 2 of the Reconfigurable Transputer Project ESPRIT Meeting proceedings HMSO London 1987.
6. C.A.R.Hoare, C.S.P. : Communicating Sequential Processes, Prentice Hall 1985
7. K. Hwang and Z. Xu, Remps : a reconfigurable multiprocessor for scientific supercomputing, Proceedings Parallel Processing 1985.
8. E.K. Lloyd, D.A. Nicole, Switching Networks for Transputer Links, Proc. of the 8th OCCAM Users Group, Technical Meeting, mars 1988

Generalized Shuffle–Exchange Networks
A Brief Summary

Hans Munthe-Kaas

Dept. of Informatics, University of Bergen, N-5020 Bergen Norway

Abstract. A class of generalized Shuffle-Exchange (SE) graphs is introduced. As permutation networks these have the same functionality as the classical SE net (and contains it as a special case), but some of them possess recursive structures lacking in the classical SE net. This allow them to be constructed from identical or a small number of different building blocks and make them very attractive from a hardware–design point of view. For an extensive account of these graphs and their mathematical properties the reader is referred to [11].

Index Terms interconnection networks, permutation networks, perfect shuffle, shuffle-exchange networks, parallel computers, SIMD computers

1 Introduction

In massively parallel SIMD computers, or data parallel computers, the most common form of interprocessor communication is permutations of the data set, i.e. each (virtual) processor sends out one data item and receive one. A natural efficiency measure for SIMD interconnection networks is therefore the number of *routing steps*, i.e. the number of parallel steps needed to do an arbitrary permutation[1]. The optimal routing problem is discused in a series of papers [6, 9, 10, 12, 13, 21].

We define the *cost* of a network as the product of the routing steps and the number of wires in the network, thus the cost is a price/performance measure. It is relatively easy to show that the cost of any interconnection network must satisfy $c(n) = \Omega(n \cdot \log(n))$, where n is the number of nodes in the network. Figures for some networks are summarized in Table (1). The *Shuffle Exchange* (SE) network [19] is among the few networks with optimal cost complexity. Despite of this, the SE network has not been extensively used in hardware design. The reason for this is probably that the SE network is rather complicated to draw in a nice regular fashion; the graph lacks the recursive structure found in e.g. the Boolean cube and other popular networks. Layouts for the SE network has been studied for VLSI design [7], but due to the lack of recursiveness, the layouts are very complicated.

---

[1] We consider here only static permutations, i.e. permutations that are known in advance, or that are to be performed many times, so that the cost of computing the optimal routing can be neglected. This is relevant for many algorithms and for e.g. measuring the ability of a given network to emulate arbitrary networks.

Network	No. of Routing Steps	No. of Wires	Cost
Complete graph	1	$\Theta(n^2)$	$\Theta(n^2)$
Boolean Cube	$\Theta(\log(n))$	$\Theta(n\log(n))$	$\Theta(n\log^2(n))$
Butterfly	$\Theta(\log(n))$	$\Theta(n\log(n))$	$\Theta(n\log^2(n)$
2–D Mesh	$\Theta(\sqrt{n}))$	$\Theta(n)$	$\Theta(n\sqrt{n})$
Ring	$\Theta(n)$	$\Theta(n)$	$\Theta(n^2)$
Cube Connected Cycles	$\Theta(\log(n))$	$\Theta(n)$	$\Theta(n\log(n))$
(Generalized) SE	$\Theta(\log(n))$	$\Theta(n)$	$\Theta(n\log(n))$

Table 1. Cost complexity for various interconnection networks

2 Definition of Generalized SE Networks

Our basis for searching for generalized versions of the SE net is the following question: *What is the most general form of a network with the same 'permuting functionality' as the (classical) SE net?* In [11] this question is stated in a suitable formal form and it is shown that it is fulfilled if and only if the graph consists of 2^n nodes identified with n-bit binary numbers $g = (g_{n-1}, g_{n-2}, \ldots, g_1, g_0)$; $g_i \in \{0,1\}$, and there exists two permutations of the nodes; $E(g)$ and $S(g)$, such that

$$E(g) = (g_{n-1}, g_{n-2}, \ldots, g_1, \overline{g_0}) \tag{1}$$

and

$$S(g) = (g_{n-2}, g_{n-3}, \ldots, g_0, f(g)) \tag{2}$$

where f is a boolean function satisfying

$$f(g) = f((g_{n-1}, g_{n-2}, \ldots, g_0)) = h((g_{n-2}, g_{n-3}, \ldots, g_0)) \oplus g_{n-1} , \tag{3}$$

for some boolean function h.

Note: A map of the form given in (2) is called a *shift register*, and with the additional property in (3) it is called a *non-singular* (or invertible) shift register. A thorough account for the mathematical properties of shift registers is found in [4].

Definition 1. A *Generalized Shuffle Exchange network*, GSE(n, f), is a graph consisting of $N = 2^n$ nodes $\mathcal{G}$, with edges (g, Eg) and (g, Sg) for all $g \in \mathcal{G}$, where E is defined in (1) and S is a non-singular shift register defined in (2)–(3).

If $f(g) = g_{n-1}$ we get the classical SE net. Given a routing algorithm for the classical SE net, it is easy to derive a routing for any GSE networks, thus all algorithms suited for the classical SE net are trivially moved to any GSE nets. This will in practice also include all algorithms suited for e.g. Boolean Cubes and Butterfly networks (see e.g. [8] for details).

In [11] the connection between GSE graphs and the socalled *de Bruijn graph* [2, 14] is elaborated upon. Via this connection it is prooved that for each n there are exactly $\frac{1}{2}(2^{2^{n-1}} + 2^{2^{n-2}})$ different (i.e. non-isomorphic) GSE(n, f) graphs!

Of special importance for computer hardware dezign is the study of *homomorphisms* of graphs. Homomorphisms of a graph $\mathcal{G}$ onto a graph $\mathcal{H}$ are surjective mappings $\phi : \mathcal{G} \to \mathcal{H}$ such that s.t. $(\phi(g), \phi(g'))$ is an edge of $\mathcal{H}$ if and only if (g, g') is an edge of $\mathcal{G}$. Homomorphisms allow the graph $\mathcal{G}$ to be folded to a simpler form, by collecting nodes into 'supernodes' identified with the nodes of $\mathcal{H}$. In this representation the graph $\mathcal{G}$ has a global structure resembling the graph $\mathcal{H}$, see Figs.(2) and (3). It is shown in [11] that for any graph GSE(m, h) and any $n > m$ there exist a $GSE(n, f)$ and a homomorphism $\phi : GSE(n, f) \to$ GSE(m, h). GSE(n, f) is called a *lifting* of GSE(m, h), and resembles a process where the number of nodes in the network is increased without changing the global structure. It is furthermore shown that for each n there exist two unique graphs GSE(n, f_n) that can be recursively folded n times, each time halving the size. These graphs, shown in Fig.(1) are called the *maximally foldable GSE graphs* and represents the most regular GSE graphs.

3 Linear GSE networks

Whereas the previous section showed that there are a tremendous number of different GSE graphs for each n, we will in this section restrict our attention to a much smaller class of networks, which can be studied in terms of linear recursion theory.

A *linear homogenous* boolean function is a function

$$f((g_{n-1}, \ldots, g_0)) = \sum_{i=0}^{n-1} c_i \cdot g_{n-1-i} \ ,$$

where additions and multiplications are modulo 2. A linear inhomogenous boolean function is defined as

$$\bar{f}(g) = f(g) \oplus 1 \ ,$$

where f is homogenous. A *linear* shift register is a shift register where f is linear (homogenous or inhomogenous), and we define a *linear GSE network* similarly. The mathematical theory for linear shift registers is rich, and a lot is known about their structure (see [4, 17]). The dynamics of a linear shift register is most easily studied by introducing the *characteristic polynomial*[2] defined for a homogenous f as:

$$r(x) = \sum_{i=0}^{n} c_i \cdot x^i \ , \tag{4}$$

where $c_n = 1$. For the results in this paper, we do not need to define the characteristic polynomial for the inhomogenous case, and we will use a bar over the characteristic polynomial to indicate that it corresponds to an inhomogenous recursion. The networks are henceforth written in terms of the characteristic

---

[2] All polynomials are over the binary Galois field $GF[2]$, which means that e.g. $(1 + x) \cdot (1 + x) = 1 + x^2$, since the coefficients are reduced modulo 2.

polynomial as $GSE(r(x))$ or $GSE(\overline{r(x)})$. The maximally foldable GSE graphs, Fig.(1), are given as $GSE((1+x)^n)$ and $GSE(\overline{(1+x)^n})$. Of these the latter family is the nicest; it can be shown that its shuffle orbits are all of equal length $p = 2^{\lfloor \log_2(n) \rfloor + 1}$.

The most important result about linear GSE networks is that the study of homomorphisms can be translated into the study of factorizations of polynomials over $GF[2]$. *There exists a homomorphism* $\phi : GSE(r(x)) \rightarrow GSE(s(x))$ *if and only if* $r(x) = s(x) \cdot t(x)$ *for some polynomial* $t(x)$. Thus the graph $GSE(s(x) \cdot t(x))$ can be folded into a graph with global structure $GSE(s(x))$.

The local structure within each supernode depends on $t(x)$. In general it is possible to arrange the nodes locally such that the local structure in a supernode resembles either the shuffles in $GSE(t(x))$ or in $GSE(\overline{t(x)})$, thus the network can be buildt by two different building blocks. In the case where $t(x)$ and $s(x)$ are relative prime polynomials it is even possible to arrange the nodes such that *every* supernode has the internal structure of $GSE(t(x))$, i.e. the network is buildt from a single building block. These results are summarized in Theorems (2) and (3).

Theorem 2. *Let* $r(x) = s(x) \cdot t(x)$ *where* $\gcd(s(x), t(x)) = 1$. *Then every node* $g_r \in GSE(r(x))$ *can be uniquely identified with a pair of nodes*

$$g_r = (g_s, g_t) \text{ where } g_s \in GSE(s(x)) \text{ and } g_t \in GSE(t(x)),$$

such that shuffle and exchange act according to:

$$E_r(g_r) = (E_s(g_s), E_t(g_t)) \text{ and } S_r(g_r) = (S_s(g_s), S_t(g_t)) \ .$$

In other words: $GSE(r(x))$ is the direct product of $GSE(s(x))$ and $GSE(t(x))$.

Theorem 3. *Let* $r(x) = s(x) \cdot t(x)$. *Then every node* $g_r \in GSE(r(x))$ *can be uniquely identified with a pair of nodes* $g_r = (g_s, g_t)$ *where* $g_s \in GSE(s(x))$ *and* $g_t \in GSE(t(x))$, *such that shuffle and exchange act according to:*

$$E_r(g_r) = (g_s, E_t(g_t)) \tag{5}$$

and

$$S_r(g_r) = \begin{cases} (S_s(g_s), S_t(g_t)) & \text{if leftmost bit in } g_t = 0 \\ (S_{\overline{s}}(g_s), S_t(g_t)) & \text{else} \end{cases} \tag{6}$$

4   Concluding Remarks

A major purpose of this work has been to show that SE-type networks are very attractive from a hardware design point of view, and to tie the bonds between parallel computing and the shift register art.

The theory summarized in this paper has several interesting applications that has not been addressed. One is in derivation of routing and mapping algorithms for SE networks. An other is in construction of optimal layouts (in terms of area usage) for VLSI design of SE graphs. Still another is in partitioning SE networks. It is known that the SE graph cannot be partitioned in smaller SE graphs [18]. Theorems (2) and (3) do, however, show that the generalized graphs can be made partitionalble by adding a small number of additional edges. These issues will be addressed in forthcomming papers.

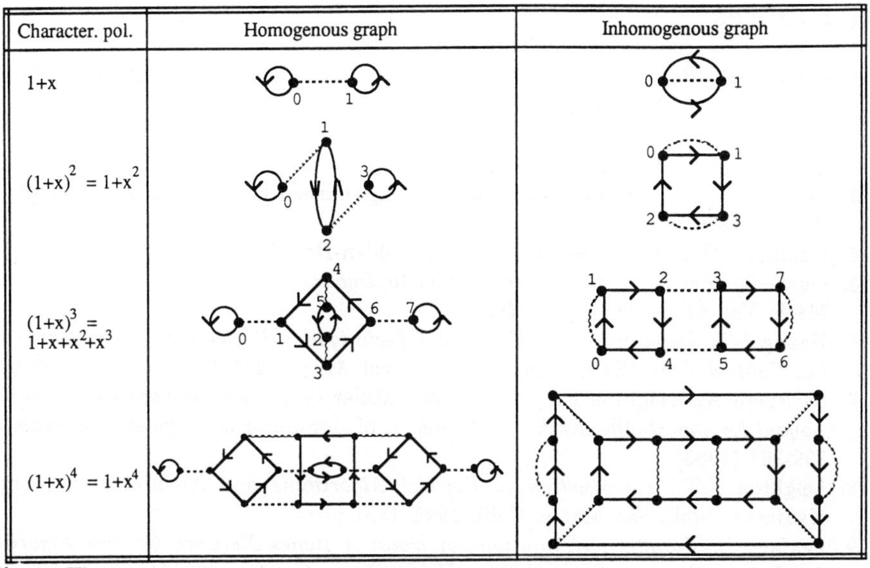

Character. pol.	Homogenous graph	Inhomogenous graph
$1+x$		
$(1+x)^2 = 1+x^2$		
$(1+x)^3 = 1+x+x^2+x^3$		
$(1+x)^4 = 1+x^4$		

Fig. 1. The two families of maximally fodable GSE graphs.

$\overline{1+x+x^2}$ $\overline{1+x^2}$ $\overline{(1+x+x^2)(1+x^2)}$ Building block:

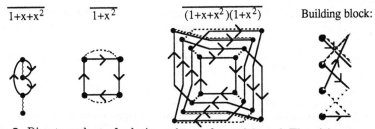

Fig. 2. Direct product of relative prime polynomials, ref. Thm.(3).

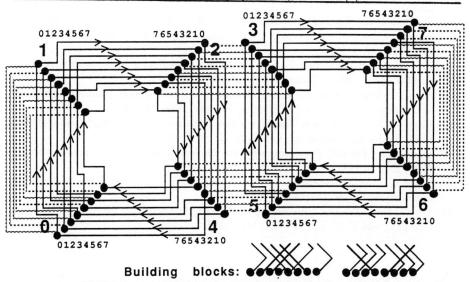

Building blocks:

Fig. 3. $GSE(\overline{(1+x)^6})$, where $\overline{(1+x)^6} = \overline{(1+x)^3 \cdot (1+x)^3}$, ref. Thm.(4).

References

1. Beneš V.E, *Mathematical Theory of Connecting Networks and Telephone Traffic*, New York: Academic Press 1965.
2. Bermond J-C., Peyrat C.: *The deBruijn and Kautz Networks: A Competiton for the Hypercube?*, in Proc. of Hypercube and Distributed Computers, 1989, pp. 279-291.
3. Fredricksen H.: *Lechtures on Recursion*, unpublished lechture notes, University of Bergen, 1970.
4. Golomb S.W.: *Shift Register Sequences*, Holden-Day, San Francisco 1967 (224 pp.).
5. Guckenheimer J.: *A Brief Introduction to Dynamical Systems*, Lectures in Appl. Math. Vol. 17, pp.187-253, 1979.
6. Huang S-T, Tripathi S.K.: *Self–Routing Technique in Perfect-Shuffle Networks Using Control Tags*, IEEE Trans. Comput., vol. 37, pp. 251-256, no. 2 Feb. 1988.
7. Kleitman A., Leighton F.T., Lepley M., Miller G.L.: *An Asymptotically Optimal Layout for the Shuffle–Exchange Graph*, J. of Computer and Systems Sciences 26, 339-361 (1983).
8. Leighton F.T.: *Introduction to Parallel Algorithms and Architectures*, Morgan Kaufman Publ., San Mateo, Calif. 1992. (831 pp).
9. Lenfant J.: *Parallel Permutations of Data: A Benes Network Control Algorithm for Frequently Used Permutations*, IEEE Trans. Comput., vol. C-27,pp. 637-647, no. 7 July 1978.
10. Munthe-Kaas H.: *Practical Parallel Permutation Procedures*, to appear.
11. Munthe-Kaas H.: *Generalized Shuffle Exchange Networks*, Dept. of Informatics, Univ. of Bergen, Rep. no. 61, June 1992, ISSN 0333-3590.
12. Nassimi D., Sahni S.: *A Self-Routing Benes Network and Parallel Permutation Algorithms*, IEEE Trans. Comput., vol. C-30,pp. 332-340, no. 5 May 1981.
13. Parker S.D.: *Notes on Shuffle/Exchange-Type Switching Networks*, IEEE Trans. Comput., vol. C-29,pp. 213-222, no. 3 March 1980.
14. Pradhan D.K., Samtham M.R.: The deBruijn multiprocessor network: A versatile parallel processing and sorting network for VLSI, IEEE trans. on comput. 38 (1989).
15. Pradhan D.K., Kodandapani K.L: *A uniform Representation of Single and Multistage Interconnection Networks Used in SIMD Machines*, IEEE trans. on Comp., vol. C-29, no. 9, 1980.
16. Preparata F.P., Vuillemin J.: *The Cube-Connected Cycles: A versatile network for parallel computation*, Comm. ACM vol. 24 no. 5, 1981.
17. Selmer E.S.:*Linear Rercurrence Relations over Finite Fields*, (mimeograph) Dept. of Mathematics University of Bergen, Norway, 1966, (212 pp.).
18. Siegel H.J.: *The Theory Underlying the Partitioning of Permutation Networks*, IEEE Trans. on Computers, vol. C-29, No. 9, 1980.
19. Stone H.S.: *Parallel Processing with the Perfect Shuffle*, IEEE trans. on comput. C-20, 2, (Feb 1971).
20. Ward M.: *The Arithmetical Theory of Linear Recurring Series* Trans. Amer. Math. Soc. 33 (1931), pp. 153-165.
21. Wu C., Feng T.: *The Universality of the Shuffle-Exchange Network*, IEEE Trans. Comput., vol. C-30, pp. 324-331, May 1981.

This article was processed using the LaTeX macro package with LLNCS style

Execution Replay: a Mechanism for Integrating a Visualization Tool with a Symbolic Debugger [1]

Eric Leu, André Schiper

Ecole Polytechnique Fédérale de Lausanne
Département d'Informatique
CH-1015 Lausanne, Switzerland
leu@lsesun2.epfl.ch

Abstract

Graphical representations of a program execution (also called visualization) have been shown to be useful to understand the behavior of parallel programs. Visualization of an execution is generally done off-line, using an adequate trace generated during execution. However, during the debugging phase, such representations may turn out to be insufficient: use of a symbolic debugger may also be required. The goal of this paper is to show that execution replay is the basic component that must be used to integrate a symbolic debugger with a visualization tool. Such an integration allows a simultaneous use of both tools during an execution, leading to an ideal observation of the execution: low level observation thanks to the debugger, and high level observation thanks to the visualization. This new approach has been implemented for parallel programs running on an iPSC/2.

1 Introduction

Writing efficient parallel programs is a much more complex task than writing sequential programs. Due to this complexity, understanding the behavior or the performance of a parallel program is often difficult. It is however imperative to know exactly what is going on during a program execution in order to detect unsuspected program behaviors and to localize performance bottlenecks and errors. This is generally done in two different ways:

- The first solution consists in setting breakpoints and analysing the process states using a symbolic debugger, as for sequential programming. However, due to the inherent non-determinism of parallel programs, cyclic debugging is often meaningless, which makes symbolic debugging of little use. The notion of execution replay has been suggested to circumvent this problem [2, 8, 10]. The basic idea of execution replay consists of first collecting a judicious trace during an *initial execution* I of a program P. Using this trace, a new execution R of the same program (called a *replay*) is then guided to a deterministic execution equivalent to I. During such a deterministic replay, use of a symbolic debugger becomes meaningful.

- The second solution consists in graphically representing a program execution (also called

---

1 Project funded by the "Fonds national suisse" under contract number 20-28938.90.

visualization). This approach has been shown to be very useful to understand the behavior of parallel programs [1, 9, 12, 13, 14]. Visualization is generally done after the execution of the program, usually on a graphical workstation, using an adequate trace generated during execution (visualization is done *off-line*). In order to limit the amount of information to record, only some very specific events are traced. The objective of visualization is to give the user high level views of an execution.

High level visualization is attractive, but may turn out to be insufficient. While visualizing an execution, and in order to analyse a particular program state, the user may want to access the content of some variables. To get such information from the visualization would require to trace all state changes of each process, which is unrealistic. The goal of the paper is to show that there is another way to combine visualization and access to low level information. The idea is to use execution replay as a basic component on which both a symbolic debugger and a visualization tool are integrated, allowing an ideal observation of the execution: low level observation thanks to the debugger, and high level observation thanks to the visualization. The key concepts are the following:

- as execution replay is deterministic, visualization can be done *on-line* during replay;
- during a deterministic replay, use of a symbolic debugger becomes meaningful;
- if the replay and the visualization are correctly synchronized, simultaneous use of both tools is possible, allowing at any time during visualization to switch between the high level information displayed by the visualizer and the low level information accessible through the debugger.

The technique will be developed in the paper for distributed memory architectures, i.e. communication between processes based on message passing.

The rest of the paper is organized in the following way. In section 2, we start by presenting an example of integration of a visualization tool with a symbolic debugger. To understand how such an integration can be achieved, execution replay has first to be formally defined. This is done in section 3. In section 4, we show how visualization may be done during the replay of a program. Finally, synchronization of both the visualization and the replay are discussed in sections 5 and 6.

2 Example of integration of a visualization tool with a symbolic debugger

Consider a distributed memory architecture. Figure 1 gives an example of integration of a visualization tool with a symbolic debugger that has been implemented on an iPSC/2. The bottom leftmost window is the window of the iPSC/2's symbolic debugger DECON. The other six windows are displayed by the visualization tool ParaGraph [3]. ParaGraph displays information about how and when processes interact during the execution, and shows when processes are idle or busy; it also gives information about the messages exchanged by the processes (type, size, sender, destination process), the message queues on each site, and the degree of parallelism at each instant. Finally, at the end of the animation, general statistics about the execution are computed: average of parallelism, total number of messages, average length of the messages, and so on.

Integration of ParaGraph and DECON means that any of the views displayed by ParaGraph or any information given by DECON can be used simultaneously at any time. More precisely, when a particular configuration is observed in a ParaGraph window, e.g. a process behaves in an unexpected way, the execution (i.e. the replay) may be stopped. Switching to the debugger allows then to obtain any information about the internal state of any process of the application.

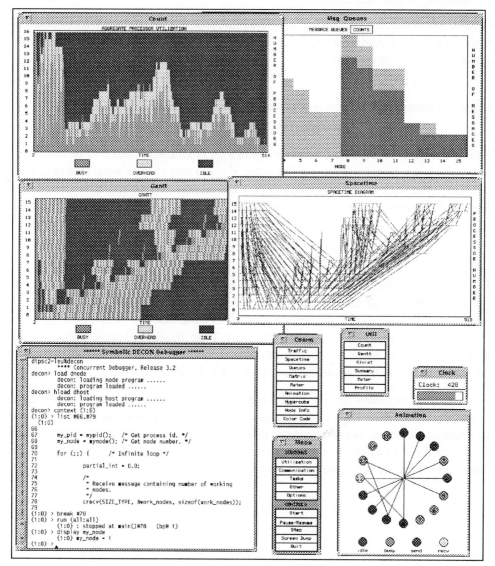

Fig. 1 ParaRex user interface, including both visualization windows and a symbolic debugger window (the graphical windows are produced using the visualization tool ParaGraph [3]).

3 Execution replay

Execution replay is the key component on which both symbolic debugging and visualization will be based. The goal of this section is to present the basic principle of execution replay. In order to formally define this notion and then to model on-line visualization and define synchronization between the visualization and the replay, a program execution model is first introduced in § 3.1. The notion of replay will then be formally defined in § 3.2.

3.1 Modeling a program execution

Consider an execution X of a parallel program P. Suppose that the program P is composed of N processes. The execution of each process p_i may be represented as a sequence of events, called local history of the process:

$$h_i^X = e_{i,0}^X , e_{i,1}^X , e_{i,2}^X , \dots$$

where $e_{i,k}^X$ represents the kth event of process p_i. The set of all events is noted:

$$E^X = \{ e_{i,k}^X \mid 1 \leq i \leq N, 1 \leq k \leq |h_i^X| \}$$

Each event $e_{i,k}^X \in E^X$ represents the execution of a set of statements, and may be considered as a function $\Phi_{i,j}^X$ bringing process p_i from state $s_{i,j-1}^X$ to state $s_{i,j}^X$ (the initial state of process p_i is defined as $s_{i,0}^X$). As we only consider message passing communication, we introduce a relation R between events which is similar to Lamport's *happened-before* relation [6]: $R(e_{i,j}, e_{k,l})$ iff (1) $e_{i,j}$ and $e_{k,l}$ are two events in the same process, $e_{k,l}$ immediately follows $e_{i,j}$ ($e_{k,l} = e_{i,j+1}$), or (2) $e_{i,j}$ is the sending of a message by one process and $e_{k,l}$ is the receipt of the same message by another process.[2][3]

Furthermore, in order to introduce time into our model, we associate with each event $e_{i,k}$ its (local) *start time* ($ts_{i,k}$) and its (local) *finish time* ($tf_{i,k}$). The execution time of event $e_{i,k}$, noted $\Delta t(e_{i,k})$, is equal to the difference between its finish time and its start time: $\Delta t(e_{i,k}) = tf_{i,k} - ts_{i,k}$. For the purpose of modeling, we define T^X as the set of all event timestamps: the timestamp $t_{i,k}^X$ of an event $e_{i,k}^X$ corresponds (arbitrarily) to the local start time of event $e_{i,k}^X$. An execution X may then be modeled as a tuple $< E^X, T^X, R^X >$.

Since parallel programs are inherently non-deterministic, two executions of the same program with the same input data can lead to different behaviors (due to unpredictable communication delays, non-deterministic constructs, etc.). As a consequence, each parallel program P may be considered as a generator of executions: $Gen_P = \{ < E^{Xi}, T^{Xi}, R^{Xi} > , 1 \leq i \}$. We can now formally define the equivalence of two executions:

---

2 We do not consider the transitive closure of the relation!
3 R will be noted R^X when refering to an execution X.

Definition 1

Given an initial state S, two executions X1 and X2 of the same program P are equivalent iff $E^{X1} = E^{X2}$ and $R^{X1} = R^{X2}$.[4] [5]

Proposition 2

If two executions X1 and X2 of a given program P are equivalent, each process of P behaves identically in both executions, i.e. each process executes the same instructions on the same data.

The proof of proposition 2 is out of the scope of this paper. Proposition 2 gives an intuitive interpretation of the equivalence of two executions.

Finally, consider a logical vector time vt, where $vt[i]$ is an event number of process p_i: vt represents a cut of an execution. Each value of vt does however not represent an accessible cut, i.e. a cut that can be reached by an execution [4]. We thus restrict vt to vt_e such that $\forall i,j$, $not\ R(e_{i,\ vte\ [i]\ +1},\ e_{j,\ vte\ [j]})$. The state of an execution X may then be defined as follows:

Definition 3

At a logical time vt_e during execution X, the state $S^X (vt_e)$ of program P is defined as the state of all processes p_i $(1 \le i \le N)$ and all communication channels after execution of events $e_{i,\ vte\ [i]}$.

3.2 Notion of replay

As already mentioned, parallel programs are inherently non-deterministic, i.e. each new execution of the same program with the same input data may behave differently. As a consequence, cyclic debugging, which consists in rerunning the program a certain number of times (each new execution and corresponding breakpoints bringing the programmer closer to the locations of the bugs), becomes meaningless, which makes symbolic debugging of little use. To circumvent this problem, a technique called *execution replay* has been suggested [2, 8, 10]. The basic idea of execution replay is to provide the user with a set of equivalent executions.

Consider an execution X. If X is not monitored by specific hardware (which is the case we consider), no information about the ordering of events of X can be obtained. Instead of X, another execution called execution I ("I" stands for *Initial execution*) has to be considered, during which some information about the ordering of events are recorded in a trace file. This information is then used to force subsequent executions of the same program (called *replays*) to be equivalent to I. Replays are thus deterministic, and full use of a symbolic debugger is then possible. Let us briefly formalize the key concepts of execution replay.

---

4 For this statement to hold, interactions with the external environment must be modeled as a message passing communication with an "*external*" virtual process.

5 T does not appear in this definition!

Consider an execution I and a replay R. Execution I includes some specific events to record the information about the order of events. The execution R (replay) must also include some other events to drive the replay (i.e. to force I and R to be equivalent). We therefore introduce the following notations (see Fig. 2):

- $G^I \subset E^I$ is the set of extra events which generate the replay trace during execution I ("G" stands for Generation). These events will be noted $g^I_{i,k}$, event $g^I_{i,k}$ following immediately event $e^I_{i,k}$. Note that an extra event $g^I_{i,k}$ does not modify the state $s^I_{i,k}$ (the state of process p_i immediately after occurrence of event $e^I_{i,k}$);

- $E^I_G \subset E^I$ is the set of all events $e^I_{i,k}$ after which trace information is recorded (by executing event $g^I_{i,k}$).

Using the trace produced during the initial execution I, the goal of an execution replay technique is to guarantee a replay R equivalent to I: $< E^R - C^R, R^R > = < E^I - G^I, R^I >$, where $C^R \subset E^R$ is the set of extra events $c^R_{i,k}$ executed during execution R to drive the replay (shown in Fig. 2). As for events $g^I_{i,k}$, events $c^R_{i,k}$ are assumed not to modify the state $s^R_{i,k}$ of process p_i.

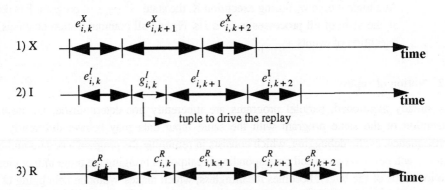

Fig. 2 Representation of process p_i's execution X, I, and R (X = any execution; I = initial execution with trace generation for the replay; R = replay).

Execution replay is really useful if the execution I is equivalent to an execution X without any trace recording. To achieve this goal, the overhead of trace recording in I, i.e. the time spent to generate the replay trace, has to be kept as low as possible. This overhead is given by:

$$\text{Trace recording overhead} = \max_i \left(\sum_k \Delta t (g^I_{i,k}) \right) \tag{1}$$

where $\Delta t (g^I_{i,k})$ is the time spent to generate the replay tuple associated to $e^I_{i,k} \in E^I_G$. In our implementation on an iPSC/2, the overhead is about 1.5% [10]. In this implementation, E^I_G corresponds to the set of all message sendings and receptions, and the size of a trace item is only four bytes long!

4 Visualizing a program execution

Before showing how visualization can be done during an execution replay of the program, it is necessary to model program visualization.

4.1 Modeling program visualization

Visualization consists in graphical representation of specific states $S^X(vt)$. In order to achieve this, one commonly adopted solution is to record during execution specific information in a trace, which is then used *off-line* to graphically represent partial information about states $S^X(vt)$. If we consider ParaGraph for example (see section 2), information collected at run-time only relates to communication, and is generated when messages are sent or received. The trace can be recorded by a hardware monitor, or more generally by a software monitor. In the rest of the paper, we will assume a software monitor. As for execution replay, trace recording is thus considered to be done by adding trace generating events to the execution. Using the formalism introduced in section 3.1, consider an execution $V = < E^V, T^V, R^V >$ ("V" stands for visualization). We define $G^V \subset E^V$ the set of extra events which generate the visualization trace. Events belonging to G^V will be noted $g_{i,k}^V$ (same notation as for events of G^I, see section 3.2): event $g_{i,k}^V$ records a trace item immediately after event $e_{i,k}^V$ ($g_{i,k}^V$ does not modify the state $s_{i,k}^V$).

In full generality, we can consider that each trace event generates a tuple consisting in a timestamp and some specific data: event $g_{i,k}^V$ generates $(d_{i,k}, t_{i,k})$, where $t_{i,k}$ represents the local timestamp of $g_{i,k}^V$ and $d_{i,k}$ some data. Using the tuples $(d_{i,k}, t_{i,k})$, a visualization of the program can be obtained. Consider a logical vector time vt_d, such that for each process p_i, $e_{i,vtd[i]}$ is the event having generated the most recent displayed tuple $(d_{i,k}, t_{i,k})$. The visualized program state at time vt_d is thus an approximation of the program state $S^V(vt_d)$.

Now let us analyze the principal limitations of the visualization. First, consider the time $\Delta t(g_{i,k}^V)$ needed to generate a tuple $(d_{i,k}, t_{i,k})$, where $g_{i,k}^V \in G^V$. The overhead due to the generation of the visualization tuples is thus proportional to the amount of information that is recorded. If too much information is recorded, the visualized execution V may completely differ from an execution X without any trace generation.

Another limitation comes from the *off-line* visualization. As mentioned in section 1, the user can be interested in the value of a particular variable or in the state of a particular process during the visualization. To get such information from the visualization would imply all state changes of each process to be traced, which would precisely lead to an execution with an enormous overhead. The solution to this problem is to run visualization *on-line* during a replay of the program: all information about the program states can then be obtained through a debugger.

4.2 Visualization during the replay

Visualization during the replay is an attractive solution. Two problems still have to be discussed and solved: the generation of the visualization tuples, and the timing component of the tuples.

4.2.1 Generation of the visualization tuples

The first question concerns the generation of the visualization tuples: when do they have to be generated? Suppose the visualization tuples are generated during an initial execution I of the program. This has no meaning for the following reason. Using a symbolic debugger during the visualization may be helpful only if the program state is synchronized with the visualization state (see section 5 for a formal definition). If the visualization tuples are not generated during the replay, it would be difficult to know at what instants the recorded tuples should be displayed. Thus visualization tuples have to be generated during replay and sent directly to the visualization tool.

Consider an initial execution I and a replay RV with an on-line generation of the visualization tuples ("RV" represents replay with visualization). We introduce the following notations (see Fig. 3):

- E_G^{RV}, where $E_G^{RV} \subset E^{RV}$, is the set of events $e_{i,k}^{RV}$ after which visualization tuples will be generated (by events $g_{i,k}^{RV}$);

- G^{RV}, where $G^{RV} \subset E^{RV}$, is the set of extra events $g_{i,k}^{RV}$ generating the visualization tuples during replay RV: $g_{i,k}^{RV}$ generates information related to the occurrence of $e_{i,k}^{RV}$.

As a replay behaves deterministically, the generation of the visualization tuples will *not modify* the replay. Executions I and RV are equivalent: $<E^{RV}\text{-}C^{RV}\text{-}G^{RV}, R^{RV}> = <E^I\text{-}G^I, R^I>$, where $C^{RV} \subset E^{RV}$ is the set of extra events $c_{i,k}^R$ executed to drive replay RV.

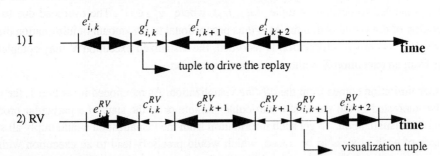

Fig. 3 Representation of process p_i's execution I and RV (I = initial execution with trace generation for the replay; RV = replay with trace generation for the visualization).

4.2.2 "Timing" component of the visualization tuples

As mentioned in section 4.1, a visualization tuple $(d_{i,k}, t_{i,k})$ consists of a data component $d_{i,k}$ and a timestamp $t_{i,k}$. If the tuple $(d_{i,k}, t_{i,k})$ is generated during replay, the only problem open is the generation of the timestamp $t_{i,k}$. Suppose first that the replay time is used, i.e., each tuple $(d_{i,k}, t_{i,k})$ is such that $t_{i,k} = t_{i,k}^{RV}$ (timestamp of $g_{i,k}^{RV}$). Due to the control of the replay and the generation of the visualization tuples, the timing information displayed by the visualization would be distorted. Ideally for $t_{i,k}$ we would like to get the timestamp of event $e_{i,k}^{I}$ of the initial execution I. We suggest the following solution:

1) Each replay tuple generated by event $g_{i,k}^{I}$ (occurring after $e_{i,k}^{I} \in E_{G}^{I}$, see Fig. 3) is completed by a timestamp $t_{i,k}^{I}$ (timestamp of event $g_{i,k}^{I}$). During replay, this timestamp $t_{i,k}^{I}$ will be associated to event $e_{i,k}^{RV} \in E_{G}^{I}$. As a consequence, all visualization tuples $(d_{i,k}, t_{i,k})$ associated to these events (belonging to $E_{G}^{RV} \cap E_{G}^{I}$) will have a nearly exact (and replay independent) timestamp: timestamp of $g_{i,k}^{I}$ is the best approximation of $e_{i,k}^{I}$'s timestamp.

2) For all visualization tuples $(d_{i,k}, t_{i,k})$ associated to events $e_{i,k}^{RV}$ such that $e_{i,k}^{RV} \notin E_{G}^{I}$ (not followed by the generation of a replay tuple during initial execution I), the timestamp $t_{i,k}$ is computed using the timestamp of the latest event $e_{i,j}^{RV}$ belonging to $E_{G}^{RV} \cap E_{G}^{I}$ that precedes $e_{i,k}^{RV}$ (timestamp of $e_{i,j}^{RV}$ is known, see 1):

$$t_{i,k} = t_{i,j}^{I} + t_{i,k}^{RV} - t_{i,j}^{RV} - \sum_{l=j}^{k} \Delta t(c_{i,l}^{RV}) - \sum_{l=j}^{k} \Delta t(g_{i,l}^{RV}) \qquad (2)$$

where $\sum_{l=j}^{k} \Delta t(c_{i,l}^{RV})$ and $\sum_{l=j}^{k} \Delta t(g_{i,l}^{RV})$ are respectively the time spent to control the replay and the time spent to generate the visualization tuples between events $e_{i,j}^{RV}$ and $e_{i,k}^{RV}$.

It may be somewhat difficult to compute the timestamp $t_{i,k}$ given by expression (2). Evaluation of $t_{i,k}$ can however be simplified:

- if only blocking receive primitives are used, component $\sum_{l=j}^{k} \Delta t(c_{i,l}^{RV})$ disappears;
- one reasonable assumption is to consider that the time spent to generate a visualization tuple (i.e. $\Delta t(g_{i,l}^{RV})$) is proportional to the size of the tuple.

Note that expression (2) is meaningful only if the local time of the processes does not progress when a process is blocked on a breakpoint (if this is not the case, $t_{i,k}^{RV} - t_{i,j}^{RV}$ would increase and $t_{i,k}$ could become greater than the next timestamp given by 1).

In the case of the visualization tool ParaGraph [3] considered in our implementation, timestamped visualization tuples are only generated for message sendings and receptions, i.e. only for events associated to the generation of replay tuples. Thus we only had to consider solution 1.

5 Synchronizing the replay with the visualization

Generation of the visualization tuples during replay is not yet enough to enable simultaneous use of the visualization tool and the symbolic debugger. Synchronization of the visualization and the replay is required. Due to the time necessary to display the tuples (communication delay and visualization bottleneck), the delay between the generation of a tuple and its display may be significant. As a consequence, the replay can be *ahead of* the visualization, which makes analysis of the visualized program state with the symbolic debugger not very useful. It should be possible for the user watching the visualization to stop the replay when a particular configuration is observed. The replay should then be in a state compatible with the visualization. Synchronizing the replay with the visualization consists in guaranteeing that at any time all generated visualization tuples $(d_{i,k}, t_{i,k})$ are displayed.

In order to express formally the synchronization, consider the logical vector time vt_d (§ 4.1). At any instant, $e_{i,vtd[i]}$ is the event having generated the most recent displayed tuple. Let's define $succ(vt_d)$ such that for each process p_i, $e_{i,succ(vtd)[i]}$ is the first event after $e_{i,vtd[i]}$ that belongs to E_G^{RV} (i.e. that generates a visualization tuple).

> **Definition 4**
>
> $S^X(vt_e)$ and $S^X(vt_d)$ are *compatible* iff $vt_d \leq vt_e < succ(vt_d)$.

In other words, both states $S^X(vt_e)$ and $S^X(vt_d)$ are compatible if there is no event $e_{i,k}^{RV} \in E_G^{RV}$ such that $vt_e[i] \geq k$ (has occurred during the execution) and $vt_d[i] < k$ (not yet displayed). This leads to the following definition of the synchronization:

> **Definition 5**
>
> The visualization and the replay are *synchronized* iff, at each instant, $S^X(vt_e)$ and $S^X(vt_d)$ are compatible.

Such a synchronization is realized in the following way. Consider the occurrence of an event $g_{i,k}^{RV} \in G^{RV}$ during replay, which generates the visualization tuple $(d_{i,k}, t_{i,k})$. The execution of p_i is suspended just after the emission of the tuple, until an acknowledgement is received from the visualizer. Moreover, the replay of both $e_{i,k}^{RV}$ and $g_{i,k}^{RV}$ together with the reception of the acknowledgement have to be implemented as *atomic actions*, i.e. it should not be possible to set a breakpoint between $e_{i,k}^{RV}$ and $g_{i,k}^{RV}$.[6] Otherwise, $e_{i,k}^{RV}$ could have occurred without the corresponding information from $g_{i,k}^{RV}$ being displayed.

Finally, consider two visualization tuples $(d_{i,k}, t_{i,k})$ and $(d_{j,l}, t_{j,l})$ with $i \neq j$, such that $R(e_{i,k}, e_{j,l})$. Then $(d_{i,k}, t_{i,k})$ should be displayed before $(d_{j,l}, t_{j,l})$, which is equivalent to implementing causal ordering for tuple deliveries on the visualization process (see [5, 11]). With the implementation described above, causal ordering is automatically guaranteed by the

---

6 In the case of an event associated to a message sending or a message reception, a possible solution consists in implementing the generation of the tuple and the reception of the ack in the system library routine (it is generally not possible to step into such a routine with a symbolic debugger).

acknowledgement of the tuples by the visualizer, except for those associated to the sending and the reception of a message. Causal ordering of such tuples can however easily be ensured by the visualizer in an ad-hoc way.

6 Internal synchronization

Synchronization between the replay and the visualization does not ensure that processes progress uniformly. Stopping a process p_i at a breakpoint will not necessarily prevent another process p_j from executing if p_i and p_j do not interact (directly or indirectly). Consider the logical time vt_d of the visualization. Assume that $vt_d[i] = k$ and $vt_d[j] = l$, i.e. $(d_{i,k}, t_{i,k})$ and $(d_{j,l}, t_{j,l})$ are the last displayed tuples generated respectively by p_i and p_j. Stopping process p_i could imply $t_{j,l} \gg t_{i,k}$, which can be considered as undesirable. We define *internal* synchronization (as opposed to the *external* synchronization of the previous section) as follows:

Definition 6

The processes of a program P are *internally synchronized* iff, at each instant and for all processes p_i, p_j, $|t_{i, vtd[i]} - t_{j, vtd[j]}| \le \Delta$, where Δ is an arbitrary constant.

Internal synchronization can be implemented by forcing during replay each process p_i to send periodically (every $\Delta/2$ time interval) an empty but timestamped tuple to the visualization tool. Such tuples have to be acknowledged as normal visualization tuples. However, the acknowledgement will only be sent by the visualizer to a process p_i if, for all other processes p_j, $(t_{i, vtd[i]} - t_{j, vtd[j]}) \le \Delta/2$.

7 Conclusion

Developing efficient parallel software on MIMD machines is a difficult task. Due to the new complexity involved by parallel programming, graphical representations of the program execution have been shown to be useful but not sufficient. Use of a symbolic debugger during visualization of the execution is an attractive solution. We have shown in this paper that execution replay enables to combine a visualization tool giving a high level view of the execution, with a symbolic debugger giving a low level view. Such an integration, allowing the user to switch at any time between both views, turns out to be an extremely powerful paradigm for analysing and understanding the execution of parallel programs. Successive replays will in particular always lead to the same graphical animation of the program execution. Moreover, the timing information given by the visualization will not change from one replay to another.

Once visualization has been integrated with execution replay, many other extensions could be considered. One extension could be to implement particular replays. One example is P-causal replay, a replay ensuring that each breakpoint in a given process P is a causal breakpoint [4]. A P-causal replay can be considered as another kind of internal synchronization. Execution replay, which enables to get rid of the non-determinism of parallel programs, can thus be considered as a basic component on which various debugging tools should be built.

References

[1] T. Bemmerl, O. Hansen, T. Ludwig, "PATOP for Performance Tuning of Parallel Programs", Proc. of CONPAR 90 - VAPP IV conference, Zurich, Switzerland, Sept. 1990.

[2] R. Curtis, L. Wittie, "BugNet: A Debugging System for Parallel Programming Environments", Proc. 3rd Int. Conf. on Distributed Computing Systems, Hollywood, FL, Oct. 1982.

[3] M. Heath, J. Etheridge, "Visualizing the Performance of Parallel Programs", IEEE Software, Sept. 1991.

[4] J. Fowler, W. Zwaenepoel, "Causal Distributed Breakpoints", Proc. 10th IEEE Int. Conf. on Distributed Computing Systems, Paris, May 90.

[5] P, Kearns, B. Koodalattupuram, "Immediate Ordered Service in Distributed Systems", Proc. 9th Symp. on Distributed Computer Systems, IEEE Computer Society, 1989.

[6] L. Lamport, "Time, Clocks and the Ordering of Events in a Distributed System", Communication of the ACM 21 (7), 1978.

[7] L. Lamport, "How to Make a Multiprocessor Computer that Correctly Executes Multiprocess Programs", IEEE Trans. on Computers C-28(9), Sept. 1979.

[8] T. Leblanc, J. Mellor-Crummey, "Debugging Parallel Programs with Instant Replay", IEEE Transactions on Computers C-36(4), April 1987.

[9] T. Leblanc, J. Mellor-Crummey, R. Fowler, "Analysing Parallel Program Executions Using Multiple Views", Journal of Parallel and Distributed Computing 9, 1990.

[10] E. Leu, A. Schiper, A. Zramdini, "Efficient Execution Replay Technique on Distributed Memory Architectures", Proc. of the 2nd European Distributed Memory Computing Conference, LNCS 487, Springer-Verlag, Munich, April 1991.

[11] M. Raynal, A. Schiper, S. Toueg, "The causal Ordering Abstract and a Simple Way to Implement it", Information Processing Letters 39, Sept. 1991.

[12] L. Ni, K. Tai, eds, "Special Issue on Software Tools for Parallel Programming and Visualization", Journal of Parallel and Distributed Computing, Vol. 9 No 2, June 1990.

[13] D. Socha, M. Bailey, D. Notkin, "Voyeur: Graphical Views of Parallel Programs, Special Issue of SIGPLAN Notices, Vol. 24 No 1, Jan. 1989.

[14] J. M. Stone, "A Graphical Representation of Concurrent Processes", Special Issue of SIGPLAN Notices, Vol. 24 No 1, Jan. 1989.

The Software-Monitor DELTA-T and Its Use for Performance Measurements of Some Farming Variants on the Multi-Transputer System DAMP

Andreas Bauch, Thomas Kosch, Erik Maehle and Wolfgang Obelöer

Universität-GH-Paderborn, Fachgebiet Datentechnik
Warburgerstr. 100, W-4790 Paderborn, Germany

Abstract. Monitoring tools will play an important role in future programming environments for parallel computers. In this paper the software-monitor DELTA-T and its use are presented. The DAMP multi-transputer system is chosen as a target system. To show the use of DELTA-T for interactive 'performance debugging' a farm with a hypothetical load is selected. It is shown that the diameter of the topology is important for execution time. In addition to this suitable modifications and the achieved speedups are presented.

1 Introduction

Transputers [INM88b] have proven to be very flexible and powerful components for building highly parallel MIMD systems. There exist already several commercially available machines (e.g. Parsytec Supercluster [FLM92], Meiko Computing Surface [Mei91]) which have been used successfully for a wide spectrum of applications. However, the programming of these parallel computers is rather complicated, cumbersome and still far away from the comfort achieved today for sequential machines.

One aspect in this context is the difficulty for the programmer to find out why his parallel program does not show the expected performance (which is a usual situation at least for the first implementation). What is required are tools for getting detailed insights into the program behaviour, e.g. the load of the various processors, the communication durations, the execution time of individual processes etc. Here, performance monitors [DHK92, Bem90] are adequate tools which will play an important role in future parallel programming environments.

There exist three basic approaches: hardware, software and hybrid monitors. Hardware monitors [TFC90] require probes to be connected with (or integrated into) suitable places in the system (e.g. processor busses, links) which makes them rather costly for large parallel systems with hundreds or thousands of nodes. The same is essentially true for hybrid monitors [DHK92] where the measurement data is generated by small software routines, however collecting, storing and evaluation of the measurement traces still is carried out by an external monitoring device. Software monitors [MaO92] on the other hand are completely implemented in software and thus are easily scalable to arbitrarily high processor numbers. Their main problem is that they can influence the execution of their target programs considerably making the measurement results questionable (*monitor intrusion*). Furthermore it is highly desirable that the application program does not have to be modified for monitoring purposes (*user-transparent monitoring*).

In this paper we will introduce the software monitor DELTA-T (Debugging and Evaluation of the Load of Transputer Applications and Topologies) which has been developed at our institute, especially with the goal of small monitor intrusion and high user transparency in mind. DELTA-T can be executed on each (multi-) transputer system under OCCAM2/TDS [INM88a] or Inmos TOOLSET with OCCAM2 or Parallel C [INM90]. The monitoring system itself has already been described in [MaO91] and [MaO92]. Here we will focus on the application of DELTA-T to typical performance measuring problems. As target system DAMP (Dynamical Adaptable Multi-Processor), a dynamically reconfigurable multi-transputer system also developed by our group [BBM91], was chosen. The sample applications are variants of farming, a very popular parallel program class on transputers.

2 Software Monitor DELTA-T

2.1 Basic Structure

One important characteristic of software monitors is whether the evaluation of measurements is carried out online or offline. For *online* evaluation the measurement data has to be transferred to an external device (usually host workstation) where visualization of the results takes place. This requires either a separate communication network for monitoring (which is not available on standard transputer systems) or it generates an additional load on the application communication net. As communication usually is a very critical issue for parallel programs this latter approach can falsify measurements considerably. Another problem is that the time scale which monitoring is bound to is that of the application program, i.e. at least very short and very long programs are difficult to monitor.

The alternative is storing only measurement traces *online* (in the local node memories) and evaluating them *offline* after program termination on the host system. Clearly, additional monitoring communication is now avoided at the prize of additional memory space for trace buffers. This also restricts the duration of a measurement or respectively its granularity. The offline evaluation allows to set the time scale as required. So, the user can e.g. start with a quick animation of his program and then interactively dive more deeply into critical parts (detailed analysis of computation and communication times etc.).

As small monitor intrusion and interactive 'performance debugging' were two of our main design goals, we decided to implement offline evaluation for DELTA-T. The resulting basic structure is shown in fig. 1. Local monitoring processes running concurrently to the application processes store the measurement traces in the local node memories. After program termination these distributed local traces are merged to a common global one on the disk of the host workstation. Interactive evaluation tools then interprete this traces on different levels (system, node or process level).

For this evaluation it is important to gain a global system view from the distributed subtraces. This is achieved by global time-stamping of all measurement data. So, the evaluation tools can reconstruct the ordering of events and can calculate computation and communication times, processor loads etc. The implementation of this global system time is dependent on the target system. On the DAMP machine we have implemented a special timer on each module with a global starting mechanism and a common global clock [MaO91]. If no such support is available, a scheme for a global software synchronization has been developed [MaO91]. At the beginning and at the end of the parallel program execution a synchronization message is sent through the whole system passing each node in a given order and setting a time-stamp with the actual local time. Because of the synchronous communication of transputers a global time point can easily be derived from these local time-stamps in the offline evaluation phase. During runtime of the program time-stamps are solely based on local timers. After the termination of the parallel program these local times are interpolated between the start and stop synchronization points to reconstruct the global system time. Practical experiments on the Parsytec Supercluster have shown that this scheme allows reasonable accuracy (in the millisecond range) for execution times at least up to some tens of minutes.

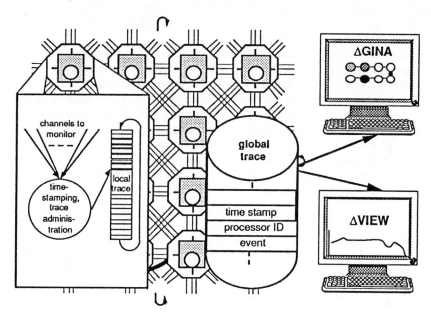

Fig. 1. Basic structure of DELTA-T

2.2 User-Transparent Instrumentation

The following monitoring levels can be distinguished: system, node, process, procedure, statement or hardware level. The most appropriate approach for parallel programs is a hierarchical monitoring concept which allows to switch interactively between several levels. In DELTA-T the first three levels mentioned above are covered by user-transparent instrumentation, the fourth and fifth ones are only supported by manually inserted measurement points in the source code. However, our experience so far indicates that the system, node and process level (including communications) are sufficient for typical practical transputer programs.

In transputers process management as well as interprocess communication are already supported by hardware/firmware (scheduler, autonomous DMA-links etc.). So, at least in OCCAM there is no operating system kernel which could be instrumented for monitoring (the situation is different for TOOLSET/C, because process and communication management is there implemented by library routines which can be instrumented).

In order to achieve user-transparent instrumentation in DELTA-T, so-called spy processes are inserted into the transputer's process queue (see [BoK90] for a similar approach for mono-transputer systems). Depending on the monitoring level there exists a node spy (which is also used for system level monitoring) or a process spy. The node spy is a special process which is inserted in the low priority active process queue on each node before the application starts (fig. 2a). As the hardware scheduler time-slices all active processes according to a simple round-robin strategy, the node spy is executed once each scheduling round and then appends itself again always *at the end* of the process queue. Thus it can record the start/stop events of busy/idle periods on the node level by inspecting whether the queue is empty or not. Remember that all measured events are time-stamped. Therefore, during the evaluation, node or system busy/idle times as well as the mean number of parallel active nodes over time (parallelization profile) can be derived.

For measurements at the process level a spy process is always inserted at the *second place* into the process queue (fig. 2b). Consequently, after the first process has finished its time-slice the spy is executing and after setting its measurement points it inserts itself again at the second place of the queue. Then after execution of the second process the spy gets the processor again etc., i.e. the process spy is running at each process switching. In addition to the events monitored by the node spy it can record busy-times of individual processes and start/stop of communications on the external links (and with some restrictions also on the internal channels), i.e. this spy recognizes each event which causes a process switch (e.g. starting a computation and a communication on an external DMA-link in parallel).

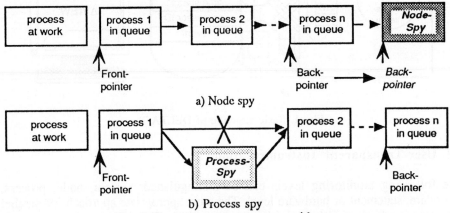

a) Node spy

b) Process spy

Fig. 2. Transputer process queue with spy

Experience shows that the typical intrusion of the node spy is in the range of 1% (execution time of the spy about 20 μs for each scheduling round) that of the process spy is about 5% (execution time 50 μs for each time slice, which is about 2 ms for typical processes) additional execution time. Note that this is achievable because process switching is extremely fast on transputers (microseconds range) and because the spies are hand-coded in assembler. For TOOLSET/C programs the node spy can be used as described. The process spy however has problems to identify the individual processes because process switching occurs usually within library routines. So in this case we are instrumenting the appropriate library calls instead (of course also transparent to the user).

2.3 Evaluation of Measurement Traces

After the execution of an instrumented parallel program the local events in the node trace buffers (which carry globally valid time-stamps eventually interpolated from local ones if there is no common hardware clock) are collected and sorted according to their time-stamps to a global trace on the host. This global trace, consisting of the global times, the events, and the node identities is then scanned and evaluated by two tools ΔGina and ΔView (implemented under SunView and X-Windows respectively on Sun workstations).

ΔGina animates the load of either the nodes (node spy) or the processes and the link communications (process spy) on a user-defineable graphical representation of the system topology (fig. 6). Either gray-scale, colors, pie-charts or numerical values can be chosen to visualize loads. Of course the animation proceeds in a movie-like fashion at a user-selectable speed. So the user can get a very good first impression of the load characteristics of his program and is already able to locate possible performance troublespots.

A more detailed quantitative analysis can be carried out with ΔView which is based on PATOP from the Technical University of Munich [BHL90, BHO92]. This tool currently supports:
- system, node or process level busy time diagrams or histograms (fig. 7a, 7c, 8)
- parallelization profiles (fig. 7b, 8)
- Gantt-charts of process and communication activities (fig. 7d).

As multiple windows can be opened, the user can easily select the suitable information and time-scale for his problem (e.g. process and communication Gantt-charts for two neighboring nodes). Examples of the use of these tools will be discussed in more detail in chapter 4.

3 Multi-Transputer System DAMP

The target system for our investigations of different farming variants is the multi-transputer system DAMP, which is in operation with 64 nodes at our institute. Here, only a brief overview of the DAMP architecture is given, more details can be found in [BBM91].

DAMP is a dynamically reconfigurable system with a distributed switching network. Basic building block is a single type of DAMP-module (fig. 3) which consists of
- a PMU (Processor/Memory Unit) with a transputer T800 plus 8 MByte of RAM
- a local 32x32 crossbar switch (C004) plus control unit for *application communication*
- 8 link adaptors LA (parallel/serial converters with transputer link protocol) providing an additional lower-bandwidth connection to up to 8 neighbors for *system communication*.

From the 32 links of the crossbar switch 4 are connected to the transputer links, 24 (in bundles of 3) to 8 neighboring nodes and 3 are reserved for (optional) I/O purposes. This allows to switch the own transputer links either to one of the 8 neighbors or to I/O as well as connecting incoming links directly to outgoing ones. The latter is used for non-neighbor communications (circuit switching).

In principle DAMP modules can be combined to any physical topology with a node degree up to eight. We have currently chosen an octagonal torus, mainly because of easy physical implementation, simple routing algorithms and satisfactory reconfiguration properties (at least for smaller numbers of nodes). On the other hand simulation studies have shown that for larger systems other topologies, especially DeBruijn graphs, are superior [Bra92]. Fig. 3 shows as an example a 4x4 torus with a binary tree as application topology (bold lines) plus one spare. Note that the connection from PMU21 to PMU42 is switched via the local crossbar of PMU32.

The control of the crossbar switch is done locally by the PMU itself. Once a path is built up, it can be used like a direct link connection (only with a small additional delay caused by the switching gates). More details on the distributed network control and fault tolerance concept can be found in [BBM91] and [BaM91].

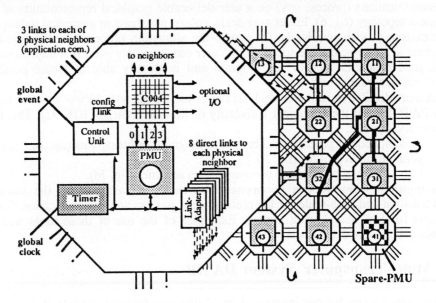

Fig. 3. DAMP module and octagonal DAMP torus

DAMP supports quasi-static as well as dynamic reconfiguration. For quasi-static configurations the switches are set by a configurer *before* the parallel application starts and remain unchanged until its end. The only exception are node or link failures in fault-tolerant configurations (e.g. switching in spares [BaM91]). In dynamic mode communication paths can be established and released at any time according to the requirements of the parallel program. As the support software for dynamic mode and fault tolerance is not yet completely finished, the following practical investigations refer to quasi-static mode only.

4 Example Application: Farming

In the following part the measurements of a farm are described. The farming example is chosen, because its structure is simple and all important facilities of the DELTA-T tool can be shown.

Multiprocessor programs often have large variations of task execution times. Additionally, there is usually little information about execution times. Therefore it is difficult to achieve load-balancing. The farming concept is a simple and easy to implement solution to such problems provided the tasks are independent. There is one master (farmer) and a number of workers. The farmer generates application tasks for the workers and collects the results from them. Each worker waits until it gets a task, then it processes its task and finally sends the result back to the farmer.

It is important to keep the load of the worker at a high level. Therefore the distribution of new tasks and the collecting of results have to be very fast. Shortest computation times can be expected when the farmer directly communicates with each worker, but for this case a fully connected multiprocessor system would be required.

4.1 Implementation of the Example Farm

For our target system DAMP we have quasi-static topologies of maximum node degree 4 and 64 processors (in this case 1 farmer and 63 workers). Here the simplest topology for the farm is a line. Each worker needs to have only a node degree of two, but the diameter increases linearly with the number of workers.

For a uniform analysis of different load characteristics the following assumptions were made. Applications run only at low priority. High priority processes will be used for system services (e.g. fault tolerance, monitoring) only. The farmer (fig. 4a) can be configured to use four different distribution functions (constant, uniform, normal or Erlang) to determine the load for computation and communication (synthetic computation load is realized by a replicated execution of a trigonometric function, communication load is represented by the length of transmitted data). A hypothetical load was chosen, because a wide range of load characteristics can be examined easily. In order to prevent the farmer's activity from influencing the measurement results in the farm itself it is only responsible for generating tasks and collecting application results. For that reason it does not compute any application tasks itself. Furthermore the same farmer is used for all measurements and load characteristics. Only a limited number of tasks (depending on the maximum number of tasks that can be held in the farm) are sent into the farm.

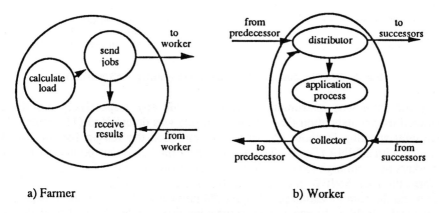

a) Farmer   b) Worker

Fig. 4. Structure of farmer and worker

Our worker (fig. 4b) is split up into three processes (distributor, application process, collector). The distributor waits for a task from its predecessor. A received task is accepted if the application process is not computing a task. Otherwise the task is sent to the successor. The application process executes the task. To gather the results they are received from the application process or from the successor by a collector process and sent to the predecessor. In addition the collector informs the distributor about executed tasks so that it can give a new task to the application process. With this farm (implemented in the Inmos TOOLSET/C) the first measurements were carried out.

4.2 Measurements

Before the evaluation with DELTA-T started, a set of parameters (computation load, communication load, distribution) was determined. First a few program runs with different distribution functions but with same mean values were passed. The appearing effects proved to be independent from the choice of distribution functions for the considered communication and computation loads. Therefore the *uniform* distribution was selected for the following measurements. Now the speedup was measured for different ratios of computation to communication load. Fig. 5 shows a collection of speedup curves. The diagram elucidates that the speedup falls rapidly if the mean communication load is beyond 500 Bytes for all considered computation loads. For this reason a communication load of 500 Bytes (mean value) and a computation load of 1 sec (mean value) were chosen, because these parameters offer the possibility of a significant performance improvement. To get an acceptable execution time the total number of tasks was limited to 5000.

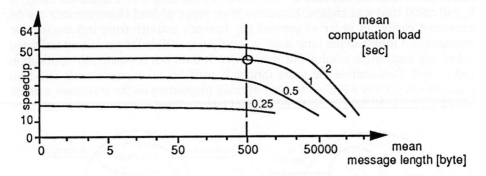

Fig. 5. Speedup curves for the farm line (farmer + 63 worker)

Now the farm was instrumented with the node spy respectively monitoring libraries. First the execution time of the farm line was determined (112.4 sec). The suboptimal speedup is about 45. In a first approach the reason for this can be examined with ΔGINA (fig. 6). The animation of the behaviour points out that not all workers run with high load, i.e. there is a poor load balancing. For a closer look at the farm the tool ΔVIEW was chosen. The system load (fig. 7a) of about 70.25 percent and the parallelization profile (fig. 7b) prove our first assumption. A possible reason for this lack of efficiency may be the administration overhead. This is the load of the farmer node and the overhead of the workers' distributor and collector (fig. 7c). Focussing on the farmer's load yields that during computation it does not exceed a margin of two percent. The maximum of administration overhead appears at the first worker and is less than one percent. Therefore the administration overhead cannot be the bottleneck of the farm.

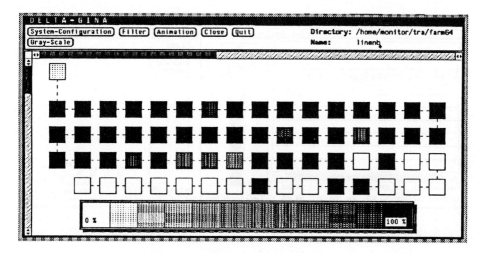

Fig. 6. Animation of a farm line

Now only the distribution of the application tasks remains to be a possible reason for the speedup losses. The Gantt-chart in fig. 7d shows the timing correlation of application processes at two consecutive workers (40, 41). Worker 40 receives a task. After this worker 41 starts. Worker 40 stops *after* worker 41, but gets the next task immediately. Strictly this task cannot have been destined for this worker because the other worker is already waiting for a longer time. (Remember that the farmer only sends a new task into a (saturated) farm if it gets a completed task back.) Consequently, the load cannot be balanced uniformly because workers closer to the farmer in the line catch tasks that are not destined for them.

This effect is grounded in the long communication distance of the line. In order to shorten this distance the workers were organized as a binary tree whose diameter only increases logarithmically with the number of workers. Now every worker has two successors. For every successors there is a counter which registers the number of tasks that are in each branch. Tasks to pass are sent to the branch with the lower count.

The farm tree was measured with the same load and instrumentation as the line. The execution now speeds up to 89.9 sec. The system load grows correspondingly (fig. 8) but the speedup is not optimal yet. The load balance is clearly improved (higher degree of parallelization, fig. 8). But even now the distribution and collection of tasks takes too much time. In order to get a better utilization of each worker a task buffer was implemented into the distributor. This has the effect that the possible number of tasks in the farm increases and the computation gets faster for both (line and tree). Now another question must be answered. What is better: one or multiple buffers? The tree was chosen as an example for this examination. Looking at the execution time or the load the tree with one buffer (fig. 9a) seems to be superior. The length of the fill-up and run-idle phase which is larger for multiple buffers is responsible for this. The degree of parallelization (fig. 9b) however, presents the tree with multiple buffers (5) as the better solution. So, if the fill-up and run-idle time can be neglected in comparison to the total execution time, multiple buffers are preferable for farming on transputer systems. The line is speeding up as well (97.3 sec with 1 buffer, 91.4 sec with 5 buffers).

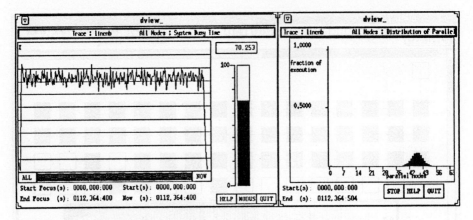

a) System load as a function of time

b) Parallelization profile

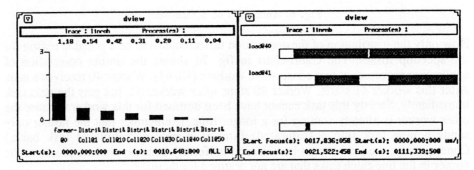

c) Administration overhead
(farmer at node level,
workers at process level)

d) Gantt chart of application processes
of worker 40 and 41

Fig. 7. ΔVIEW evaluation of the farm line

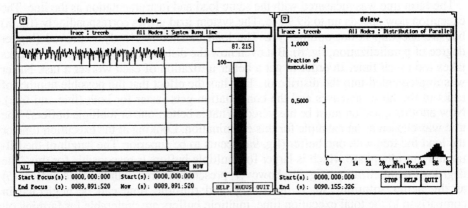

Fig. 8. Load and parallelization profile of the farm tree

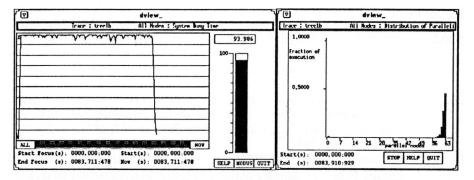

a) Load and parallelization profile with 1 buffer

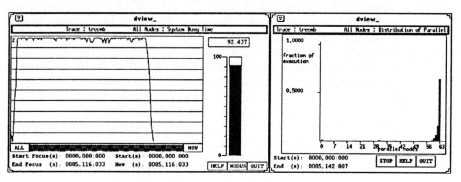

b) Load and parallelization profile with 5 buffers

Fig. 9. Farm tree with buffering

5 Concluding Remarks

In this paper we have described how the software-monitor DELTA-T can be used for 'performance debugging'. This tool offers a global system view (by global time-stamping) and user-transparent instrumentation. Although a detailed analysis of computation and communication times (system, node and process level) is possible the monitor intrusion is very small. The multi-transputer system DAMP with 64 processing nodes acted as the target system (used in quasi-static mode).

A farm with a hypothetical load served as an example for examinations of suboptimal speedup and a lack of performance. During these examinations the software-monitor DELTA-T proved to be a precious help for tuning the speedup of applications. So, the speedup of a farm line could be increased from 45 to 55. If the only possibility is to implement a farm line on the target system, buffering improves the speedup to the level of a farm tree without a buffer. All these improvements could be achieved with a monitoring overhead of about 1%.

Our further work will concentrate on a debugging tool. This tool shall be a debugger combined with a performance monitor. The next generation of transputers, the T9000, has already been announced [INM91]. From our first studies we are very confident that DELTA-T can be ported to large T9000-based multi-processor systems as well.

References

[BaM91]   Bauch, A.; Maehle, E.: Self-Diagnosis, Reconfiguration and Recovery in the Dynamical Reconfigurable Multiprocessor System DAMP. Proc. Fault-Tolerant Computing Systems, Nürnberg 1991, Informatik Fachberichte 283, 18 - 29, Springer-Verlag, Berlin 1991

[BBM91]   Bauch, A.; Braam, R.; Maehle, E.: DAMP - A Dynamic Reconfigurable Multiprocessor System With a Distributed Switching Network. Proc. EDMCC2, Lecture Notes in Computer Science 487, 495-504, Springer-Verlag, Berlin 1991

[Bem90]   Bemmerl, T.: The TOPSYS Architecture.Proc. CONPAR 90-VAPP IV, Lecture Notes in Computer Science 457, 732-743, Springer-Verlag, Berlin 1990

[BHL90]   Bemmerl, T.; Hansen, O.; Ludwig, T.: PATOP for Performance Tuning of Parallel Programs. Proc. CONPAR 90-VAPP IV, Lecture Notes in Computer Science 457, 840-851, Springer-Verlag, Berlin 1990

[BHO92]   Bemmerl, T.; Hansen, O.; Obelöer, W.; Willeke, H.: Adapting the Portable Performance Measurement Tool PATOP to the Multi-Transputer Monitoring System DELTA-T, To appear: Proc. Working Conference on Programming Environments for Parallel Computing, Edinburgh 1992

[BoK90]   Boillat, J. E.; Kropf, P. G.: A Fast Distributed Mapping Algorithm. Proc. CONPAR 90-VAPP IV, Lecture Notes in Computer Science 457, 405-416, Springer-Verlag, Berlin 1990

[Bra92]   Braam, R.: Ein dynamisch rekonfigurierbares Multiprozessorsystem mit einem verteilten Verbindungsnetzwerk, Dissertation, Universität-GH Paderborn 1992

[DHK92]   Dauphin, P.; Hofmann, R.; Klar, R. et al.: ZM4/SIMPLE: a General Approach to Performance-Measurement and -Evaluation of Distributed Systems. To appear: Advances in Distributed Computing: Concepts and Design. IEEE Computer Society Press, 1992.

[FLM92]   Funke, R.; Lüling, R.; Monien, B. et al.: An Optimized Reconfigurable Architecture for Transputer Networks. Proc. 25th Hawaii Int. Conf. on System Sciences (HICSS), vol. 1, 237-245, 1992

[INM88a] Inmos Transputer Development System, Prentice Hall, New York 1988

[INM88b] Transputer Reference Manual. Prentice Hall, New York 1988

[INM90]   Inmos Toolset Manual. SGS-THOMSON Microelectronics Group, First Edition 1990

[INM91]   The T9000 Transputer Products Overview Manual. SGS-THOMSON Microelectronics Group, 1991.

[MaO91]   Maehle, E.; Obelöer, W.: Monitoring-Werkzeuge zur Leistungsmessung in Multi-Transputersystemen. Proc. 2. Int. Fachmesse und Kongreß für RISC/Transputer-Architekturen und Anwendungen, 609-619, VDE-Verlag, Berlin 1991

[MaO92]   Maehle, E.; Obelöer, W.: DELTA-T: A User-Transparent Software-Monitoring Tool for Multi-Transputer Systems. To appear: Proc. EUROMICRO 92, Paris, Sept. 15-17, 1992

[Mei91]   Meiko Computing Surface Overview. Meiko 1991

[TFC90]   Tsai, J. P.; Fang, K.-Y.; Chen, H.-Y.: A Noninvasive Architecture to Monitor Real-Time Distributed Systems. IEEE Computer, vol. 23, no. 3, 11-23, 1990

Visualization of Message Passing Parallel Programs [*]

Thomas Bemmerl[1] and Peter Braun[2]

[1] Intel Corporation, European Supercomputer Development Center (ESDC)
Dornacher Str. 1, W-8016 Feldkirchen bei München
Tel.: +49-89-90992-166, Fax.: +49-89-9039142
e-mail: thomas@esdc.intel.com

[2] Technische Universität München,Institut für Informatik
Lehrstuhl für Rechnertechnik und Rechnerorganisation
Arcisstr. 21, W-8000 München 2, FRG
Tel.: +49-89-2105-2386, Fax.: +49-89-2800-529
e-mail: braunp@informatik.tu-muenchen.de

Abstract. Parallel programming is orders of magnitudes more complex than writing sequential programs. This is particularly true for programming distributed memory multiprocessor architectures based on message passing programming models. Understanding the synchronization and communication behavior of parallel programs is one of the most critical issues in programming distributed memory multiprocessors. The paper describes methods and tools for visualization and animation of the dynamic execution of parallel programs. Based on an evaluation and classification of existing visualization environments, the visualization and animation tool VISTOP (VISualization TOol for Parallel Systems) is presented as part of the integrated tool environment TOPSYS (TOols for Parallel SYStems) for programming distributed memory multiprocessors. VISTOP supports the interactive on-line visualization of message passing programs based on various views, in particular, a process graph based concurrency view for detecting synchronization and communication bugs.

1 Motivation

The operation of parallel programs is often very complex and difficult to understand. Graphical representation can aid human comprehension of complex phenomena with large quantities of data. This is due to the fact that the human visual system is more suited to process information in form of graphical images than in the form of textual images. Apart from understanding the sequential parts of the parallel program, new degrees of freedom lead to additional bugs. In particular, the interaction between processes with respect to synchronization and communication raises new problems. Inadequate synchronization and communication very often results in deadlocks and races. In addition to these correctness bugs, performance issues are extremely critical in parallel programs. A wrong way of using synchronization and communication primitives may lead to performance bottlenecks. But the most complex problem to solve when writing parallel programs is the scalability problem [8]. Programs running on massively parallel architectures consist of hundreds and thousands of interacting processes. This massive amount of processes or information in general has to be handled by the programmer.

---

[*] Funded by the German Science Foundation, Contract: SFB 0342

Graphical visualization techniques are one favorable way of dealing with all the problems stated above. Program visualization systems can be used for many purposes, including, understanding the dynamic behavior of parallel programs for educational purposes, debugging for correctness, performance monitoring and analysis (performance debugging), and visualization of scientific data.

2 Related Work and Basic Problems

In general the purpose of program visualization systems is to gain insight into the dynamic behavior of programs. Myers [17] has proposed to classify program visualization systems by whether they animate code or data, and whether they generate static or dynamic displays. Further criteria for visualization systems can be whether they are active or passive and whether the contents of the displays show the current state or a complete history of events [7].

We choose a different way of classifying visualization systems for parallel programs. Approaches to build visualization and animation systems to support debugging and understanding of parallel programs can be divided into three different categories: *data* oriented visualization systems, *program or system* oriented visualization systems, and *problem* oriented visualization systems. Each approach has its specific strengths and can help a programmer to examine different aspects or bugs in parallel programs. Some systems provide several components which belong to different categories of our classification.

2.1 Data Oriented Visualization Systems

Data oriented visualization refers to the animation of the data calculated by an algorithm. This type of visualization can often be found in scientific computing areas such as simulation, aerospace applications, and fluid dynamics which are required in fields like geology, meteorology, chemistry, and physics. Very advanced techniques are used in these areas to produce animated displays. Although these systems can help the programmer to detect erroneous behavior of a program, the main purpose of this kind of animation systems is to visualize the results of a computation. Thus we do not consider this class of visualization systems in this paper.

However one approach presented in literature should be mentioned for reasons of completeness. Roman and Cox [19] have developed a visualization methodology for parallel programs which is based on correctness proofs. They propose to visualize properties which are used in correctness proofs as data patterns. For example, invariants of an algorithm could be visualized as a stable pattern, progress in an algorithm could be displayed as an evolving pattern. They argue that this approach is especially promising for systems with a large number of processing elements, where the traditional visualization techniques could not be used.

2.2 Program or System Oriented Visualization Environments

These systems emphasize the monitoring of the execution of a parallel program. A parallel program can be observed at different levels of abstraction, for example at the level of the source code, at the level of the underlying operating system, at the level of the process graph or the level of the parallel programming model. Even auralization can effectively enhance one's insight into complex interactions of concurrent applications [10].

In program oriented systems visualization is based on the source code, while in system oriented visualizers the properties of the underlying hardware (number of CPUs, topology of the communication network) or the objects of the operating system (processes) are most important. This group contains textual based tools like PECAN which animates the program code by highlighting the appropriate part as the code is executed [18]. PROVIDE extends the properties of a conventional debugger by the use of graphical displays for continuous process states [16]. Some of the tools use the process graph instead of the source code as a basis for visualization [1]. This is especially appropriate if the same process graph is part of the specification of the parallel program. In Belvedere, the message activity of a parallel program is displayed via the edges of the process graph [12].

However all systems mentioned only support a static process model which is only sufficient for regular types of applications and not general purpose. Most visualization systems for parallel programs focus primarily on performance monitoring rather than on algorithm animation. Examples for system oriented visualization systems are ParVis [14], Traceview [15] and ParaGraph [11]. These are general-purpose trace-visualization tools which can display trace data in different graphical forms. In ParaGraph, the user can select the appropriate visualization method from about 25 different diagrams, which include Gantt charts, Kiviat diagrams, communication traffic diagrams, and space-time diagrams. They display time dependent process activities of the program to be monitored.

2.3 Problem Visualization Systems (Algorithm Animation)

The basic idea in an algorithm animation system is to represent a program's data, actions and semantics in form of graphical views. Adequate abstractions can help to increase the understanding of algorithms. A classical example for an algorithm animation system is the BALSA system and its descendant BALSA-II [7]. Although it has been developed for sequential algorithms, many of its ideas are also useful for animation systems for parallel programs. In the BALSA system, multiple graphical displays of an algorithm in action can be specified by so called "annotations" in the source code of the algorithm. The programmer creates the animation for an algorithm and the end-users execute the animated program. The animation system itself is domain independent. The strength of BALSA is its flexibility which makes it possible to create the best suited abstractions and graphical representations for a given algorithm.

An example of an algorithm animation system which is adapted to parallel programs, is the TANGO algorithm animation system [20]. An animation is composed of basic graphical objects that can change their state (location, size, color) throughout an animation and operations that drive the animation. TANGO uses the "path-transition" animation paradigm to produce smooth color animations for an algorithm. Paths specify the magnitude of modification in image attributes between successive frames. A transition uses path parameters to change the state of an image. Another system is the AFIT Algorithm Animation Research Facility (AAARF). It is a program visualization system for the Intel iPSC/2 hypercube system, which displays animated data in real-time [21].

The drawback with problem-oriented approaches to support debugging is that displays cannot be generated automatically. This problem is widely recognized. So most of the systems provide basic graphical objects which can easily be adapted to a new algorithm like in Voyeur [2]. PARADISE [13] is meant as a meta tool to create visualizers. It aims to make the creation of visualization tools a reasonable task for the non-graphics expert and even for the experienced user.

However in all these systems, the algorithms to be animated should be correct, which makes it difficult to use such systems as a general purpose debugging aid, as you never can tell if a bug is in your application or in the animation itself. The main application area for systems like BALSA is computer-aided instruction.

3 Visualization within the TOPSYS Tool Environment

The major intention of the TOPSYS (TOols for Parallel SYStems) project [3] is to simplify the usage and programming of parallel systems for widening the range of applications for these types of machines. In TOPSYS the visualization system is not an isolated tool for a specific purpose, but it is part of an integrated environment.

TOPSYS is based on a message passing process model implemented with the parallel programming library MMK (Multiprocessor Multitasking Kernel) [6]. MMK supports an object based style of programming and provides three predefined types of objects: tasks, mailboxes, and semaphores. A parallel program consists of multiple interacting instances of objects. Tasks communicate (synchronously or asynchronously) via mailboxes and can be synchronized via semaphores. All MMK objects reside in a global object name space and can be addressed regardless of their processor location and the underlying hardware configuration. MMK objects can be created and destroyed dynamically and thus offer great flexibility for different types of applications. The implementation of the tasks is performed in a sequential programming language (e.g. C or FORTRAN).

3.1 Common Design Concepts of the TOPSYS Environment

A detailed description of the TOPSYS tool environment can be found in [3, 4]. We will therefore only describe the major design concepts of TOPSYS needed for the understanding of the visualization tool in the following section. The implementation of TOPSYS is based on an integrated hierarchical tool model with the following features:

- Implementation of all tools on top of a common distributed monitoring system which uses different instrumentation techniques (software, hardware, hybrid monitoring) with identical functionality.
- All tools are interactive tools which run in parallel to the application being monitored. This enables the user to control the execution run and decide which

information is required during execution. This is the major advantage compared to trace based, off-line systems.

- All tools share a graphical and menu-driven user interface with the same look and feel, i.e. with the same philosophy of usage based on the X Window system.
- All tools can be used in an integrated way on the same program. For example, it is possible to specify a breakpoint in your program with the debugger and start visualization exactly in the routine where a deadlock is assumed.

4   The Visualization Tool VISTOP

The visualization tool VISTOP (VISualization TOol for Parallel systems) animates message passing programs developed with the parallel programming library MMK. VISTOP visualizes the structure of an application in terms of the basic MMK object types task, mailbox and semaphore, which represents the abstraction level of the programmer using the MMK programming model. The visualization approach of VISTOP is program and system oriented as described in section 2.2.

Currently VISTOP supports three different views of the underlying application, the concurrency (communication, synchronization) view, the object creation view, and the system view. They can be displayed together or separately, which can be selected by a control panel. The different views are synchronized and always show a consistent picture of the state of the objects of the application.

For visualization of a distributed application, VISTOP gathers run-time information whenever an interesting event occurs (e.g. communication or creation of a task). Then a snapshot of the state of the objects under supervision is taken and stored in an internal data structure, the "animation queue". The sequence of snapshots that arises from the execution of a program is animated in such a way that transitions between successive snapshots are smooth and continuous, thus giving the user an idea of how one state changes to another. During the animation, each MMK object is represented by a small window containing information about the current state of this object. You can replay the snapshots of an application back and forth, stepping through it manually or automatically.

4.1   The Concurrency View

In order to get insight into the dynamic behavior of a parallel program, it is crucial to understand the communication and synchronization events that occur while an application is executing. In addition to the communications or synchronizations, the corresponding protocol, i.e. whether blocking or non-blocking communication or synchronization library calls are used by the application program, is visualized.

The communication and synchronization events collected by VISTOP at a conceptual level are: a task sending (receiving) a message to a mailbox and a task requesting (releasing) units from a semaphore. However not every communication or synchronization can be executed instantaneously. A target mailbox might be completely filled or a critical section guarded by a semaphore is blocked. In addition, errors or timeouts can occur during communication. All these task states are displayed in VISTOP.

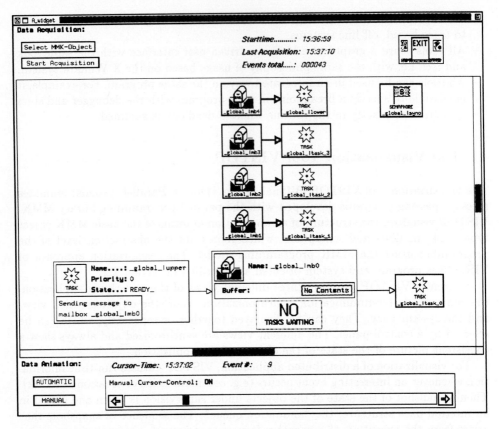

Fig. 1. *VISTOP Concurrency View. A snapshot of a replicated worker program. Task task_1 is just receiving a message while task_1 to task_3 are waiting to receive for a message.*

Visualization Metaphor in the Concurrency View. All interesting MMK objects of an application are displayed in the data display area of the Concurrency window and represented by little icons showing the class and the name of an object. The metaphor used for the animation in the Concurrency view (see. fig. 1) is the following: If a task communicates with a mailbox or a semaphore or if a task has to wait at a mailbox or semaphore, the corresponding task window inserts itself into a queue of tasks waiting at the communication object. For this purpose the task moves from its current location to the last position in the queue. Queues are visualized as chains of arrows between objects. Thin arrows characterize communication while thick arrows indicate that a task really has to wait until its communication request can be satisfied. The direction of an arrow shows the direction of the requested data transfer. When a task has finished its communication, it leaves the queue and the window is moved back to its old position. The associated arrows are deleted.

All windows representing MMK objects can be moved individually by the user. This feature can be used to rearrange the MMK objects to reflect the communication structure of the application. Arrows are rearranged automatically.

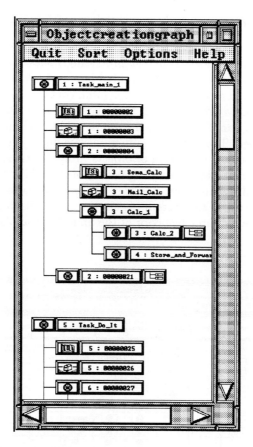

Fig. 2. *VISTOP Object Creation View. This screen dump shows the 2 static tasks Task_main_1 and Task_Do_It and their descendants.*

4.2 The Object Creation View

This view displays the dynamic object creation chain of the MMK objects. This is interesting in very dynamic applications like database systems or tree search algorithms. The MMK objects are represented in form of a graph consisting of at least one tree. An example for an object tree can be seen in figure 2. Each of the tasks that are declared statically form the root of a separate tree. The father entry shows the task that created the child object dynamically. By selecting a node of the graph, additional information about the object is displayed (state of the object, module where the object was created, ...).

When a new object is created, this is animated in the object creation view as follows. First, the position of the object in the tree is determined. All objects below this position move down one line. A "turtle" appears below the task which creates the new task and draws a line from the father to the new object. Now the turtle grows and finally the icon for the new object appears. The animation of the deletion of an object is animated in an analogous way to the creation.

4.3 The System View

This visualization component shows the distribution of the objects of an application onto different processing nodes. Different processing nodes may be located on different machines, when a program is distributed in a network of UNIX workstations. The display is organized as a matrix. Each column contains all objects of one node. An object may be displayed as an icon that shows its type, its name or its object identifier. By selecting an object with the mouse additional information about the object can be obtained. The VISTOP system view is displayed in figure 3.

This view can visualize migration of objects in applications which perform migration with the automatic load balancing facility of the MMK. When MMK objects are created or deleted dynamically, this view shows the location of the objects and their overall distribution in the system. Again the events displayed in this view are animated to show the dynamic behavior of the underlying application.

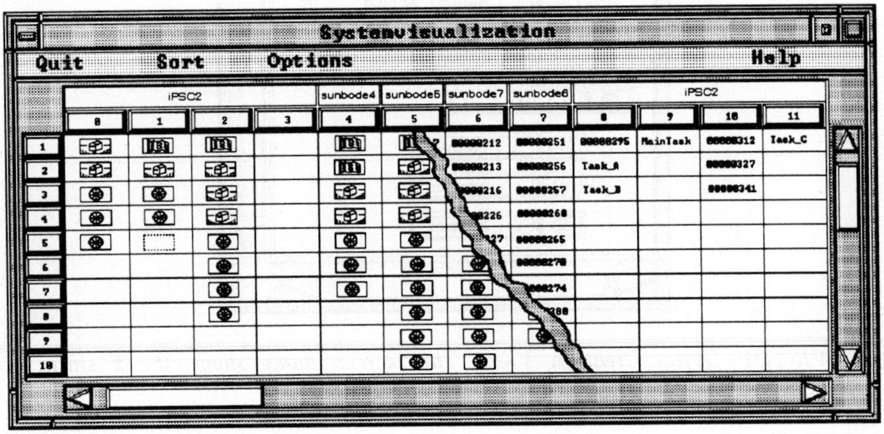

Fig. 3. *VISTOP System View*

4.4 Abstraction in VISTOP

One of the greatest problems for visualization systems of parallel programs is scalability. With the advent of massively parallel systems consisting of many processing nodes, the amount of information provided by a visualization system must be adaptable to the needs of the user of the system in order to be effective.

Selection of Objects. One mechanism in VISTOP to increase scalability is selection of "interesting" objects. When using a visualization system to support debugging and performance monitoring, a user is usually interested in very specific objects and phases during the execution of an application. The user can select the MMK objects which he is interested in via lists. Only those objects are displayed in the animation window. The selection of the appropriate MMK objects for each phase of a computation can be performed any time during the animation. This feature makes it more feasible to visualize an application running on a massively parallel architecture.

Initially each MMK object appears as an icon showing the type of the object and the name of the object thus requiring a minimal amount of space on the screen. However the objects can also be deiconified when the user wants to get extra information, like the number of messages in a mailbox or the scheduling state of a task. In addition, the animation area of each view is much larger than the physical space on the screen. The user can select the appropriate section of the animation area with scroll-bars.

Selection of interesting phases. Parallel programs usually run for a long time because most often the extra effort to build a parallel application is only justified for time consuming problems. Often a user only wants to visualize a key scene of his program. In the TOPSYS environment this can be performed by using VISTOP together with our parallel debugging system DETOP (DEbugging TOol for Parallel Systems). The user starts the program under control of DETOP and specifies a breakpoint at the entry of the routine he wants to visualize. When the breakpoint is reached he starts the visualization tool and examines the interesting part of the application.

While being very helpful to increase the scalability of VISTOP, the mechanisms available in VISTOP to visualize massively parallel applications are not yet sufficient. Further research is going in this direction. For example, it is planned to allow composite objects in VISTOP. The user can combine basic objects (i.e. tasks, mailboxes and semaphores) and compose objects to new objects. Visualization can be performed at any level. The user can switch between different levels by zooming. In the long run, such object hierarchies appropriate for visualization might already be created during the design process for a parallel application.

5 Selected Design Concepts of VISTOP

VISTOP follows a general design concept which is similar to most visualization systems. There is a data acquisition layer which gathers runtime information on a parallel application, a model layer which stores the data of subsequent snapshots and the presentation layer which visualizes the information of the model layer. Figure 4 shows the basic architecture of VISTOP. The model of the concurrent application is contained in a central data structure called "animation queue". It is filled by the data acquisition process. The visualization process reads the data from the animation queue. All action is controlled by the user.

The advantage of having two independent parts for acquisition and animation is obvious: one part can easily be replaced by a different implementation without affecting the other.

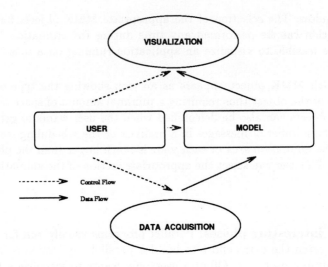

Fig. 4. *General design architecture of VISTOP*

5.1 Data Acquisition in VISTOP

As already mentioned, all tools of the TOPSYS environment are based on a common distributed monitoring system. The monitors which are located on the computation nodes of the target system can be implemented either in software or in hardware. The TOPSYS hierarchical tool model offers a tool interface, the HLTL (High Level Language Tool Layer) interface, which enables to control the execution of a parallel application and to collect runtime data on the execution of the parallel program. There are, for example, commands to start an application, to specify breakpoints, to specify traces and to inspect and modify the state of the objects of the application [5].

In VISTOP the HLTL interface of TOPSYS was used in two different ways to implement two different data acquisition techniques. One version of the visualization tool is based on iterative global breakpoints and state inspection, whereas the second version uses traces for gathering runtime information. All instrumentation is performed automatically at the level of the object code.

5.2 Visualization using Breakpoints

The key idea with this method is to stop an application, whenever an interesting event occurs, by the monitoring system. Then the state of all interesting objects is inspected, stored in the animation queue, and the application is continued.

The major advantage of this data acquisition method is that the state of the application running on a parallel machine is exactly the same that is shown by the visualization system, i.e. on-line. When the user needs additional information of the application (for example values of variables), he can get the information with the debugger. The user may even modify a variable to fix a problem and continue the visualization.

The first version of VISTOP used this method for data acquisition. The drawback of this approach was the heavy intrusion of the data acquisition process into the application to be visualized.

5.3 Visualization using Traces

The use of event traces for visualization and performance analysis systems is much more common in visualization systems described in literature than the method mentioned previously. Traces can be generated very easily either by source code instrumentation or by using an instrumented communication library, like the PICL library [9]. In most systems, data acquisition and visualization is completely independent. When the program is running, the trace data is stored in a file. The analysis of the program execution is performed after the program has finished, i.e. off-line. The user can not modify the execution of the program or get additional information which is not contained in the trace data. Also, the scalability of such an approach is a problem due to the huge amount of data which has to be collected and transferred.

In our current version of VISTOP we try to combine the advantages of an online visualization with those of data acquisition by traces. This is possible because our visualization system is integrated in a tool environment. The monitoring system collects traces of the events required for the visualization. These are visualized in parallel to the program to be analyzed. The user can start the visualization tool any time he wants during the execution of his program and he can suspend the execution, when he needs additional information.

Thus the amount of information collected can be kept to a minimum and intrusion through the monitoring system and data transfer is much less than in the version of VISTOP that used breakpoints for data acquisition. The data acquisition is about 100 times faster than in the previous method.

6   Conclusion and Future Plans

VISTOP as integral part of the TOPSYS tool environment is distributed since two years on a non-commercial basis. Implementations are available for the iPSC/2 and iPSC/860 multiprocessor systems as well as for networks of SUN SPARCstations. Approximately 30 installations are currently in use at 15 different institutions. Most users of VISTOP so far have used the tool for getting an overview on the dynamic behavior and a deeper understanding of their parallel program. Based on a questionnaire among all the current TOPSYS users, the following topics to be worked on have been identified:

Graphical visualization techniques have to be integrated into VISTOP to deal with massively parallel systems incorporating hundreds or thousands of processors (objects). One solution to this problem is zooming and hierarchies of MMK objects.

Application oriented visualization based on primitives offered by VISTOP. Integration of new visualization views better suited for abstractions used within the application program, e.g. visualization of transactions in parallel databases.

Improving the portability and adaptability of VISTOP with respect to different programming models. This means eliminating the restrictions for applications based on message passing programming models.

References

1. M. Aspnäs, R. J. R. Back, and T. Langbåcka. Millipede - A Programming Environment Providing Visual Support for Parallel Programming. In *Proc. of the European Workshops on Parallel Computing*, March 1992.

2. M. L. Bailey, D. Socha, and D. Notkin. Debugging Parallel Programs using Graphical Views. In *Proc. of the Int'l Conf. on Parallel Processing*, pages 46–49, August 1990.

3. T. Bemmerl. The TOPSYS Architecture. In H. Burkhart, editor, *Proc. of CONPAR90 VAPP IV*, volume 457 of *LNCS*, pages 732–743, Zürich, Schweiz, 1990.

4. T. Bemmerl and A. Bode. An Integrated Environment for Programming Distributed Memory Multiprocessors. In A. Bode, editor, *Distributed Memory Computing - 2nd Europ. Conf., EDMCC2*, volume 487 of *LNCS*, pages 130–142, München, April 1991.

5. T. Bemmerl, A. Bode, P. Braun, O. Hansen, T. Treml, and R. Wismüller. The Design and Implementation of TOPSYS. SFB-Bericht 342/16/91 A, Institut für Informatik, Technische Universität München, Juli 1991.

6. T. Bemmerl and T. Ludwig. MMK - A Distributed Operating System Kernel with Integrated Dynamic Loadbalancing. In H. Burkhart, editor, *Proceedings of CONPAR90 VAPP IV*, volume 457 of *LNCS*, pages 744–755, Zürich, Schweiz, 1990. Springer-Verlag.

7. M. H. Brown. Perspectives on Algorithm Animation. In E. Soloway, D. Frye, and S. B. Sheppard, editors, *Human Factors in Computing Systems*, Washington, May 1988.

8. D. A. Reed et al. Scalable Performance Environments for Parallel Systems. In *Proc. of the Sixth Distributed Memory Computing Conference*, pages 562–569, Portland,Or, April 28 - May 1 1991. IEEE.

9. G. A. Geist et al. PICL: A Portable Instrumented Communication Library. Tech. Report. ORNL/TM-11130, Oak Ridge Nat'l Lab., Oak Ridge, Tenn., 1990.

10. Joan M. Francioni, Larry Albright, and Jay Alan Jackson. Debugging Parallel Programs Using Sound. In *Proceedings of the ACM/ONR Workshop on Parallel and Distributed Debugging*, pages 60–68, Santa Cruz, CA, May 1991. ACM/ONR.

11. M. T. Heath and J. A. Etheridge. Visualizing the Performance of Parallel Programs. *IEEE Software*, 8(9):29–39, September 1991.

12. A. A. Hough and J. E. Cuny. Belvedere: Prototype of a Pattern-Oriented Debugger for Highly Parallel Computations. In Sartaj K. Sahni, editor, *Proc. of the International Conference on Parallel Processing*, pages 735–738, August 1987.

13. J. A. Kohl and T. L. Casavant. Use of PARADISE: A Meta-Tool for Visualizing Parallel Systems. In *Proc. of the 5th Int'l Par. Proc. Symp.*, pages 561–567, 1991.

14. L. B. Linden. Parallel Program Visualization Using ParVis. In *Performance instrumentation and visualization*, pages 157 – 187, 1990.

15. A. D. Malony, D. H. Hammerslag, and D. J. Jablonsky. Traceview: A Trace Visualization Tool. *IEEE Software*, 8(9):19–28, September 1991.

16. T. G. Moher. PROVIDE: A Process Visualization and Debugging Environment. *IEEE Transactions on Software Engineering*, 14(6):849–857, June 1988.

17. B. A. Myers. Visual Programming, Programming by Example, and Program Visualization: A Taxonomy. In *Proc. ACM SIGCHI '86*, pages 59–66. ACM, April 1986.

18. S. P. Reiss. PECAN: Program Development Systems that Support Multiple Views. *IEEE TSE*, 11(3):276–285, 1985.

19. G.-C. Roman and K. C. Cox. A Declarative Approach to Visualizing Concurrent Computations. *IEEE Computer*, 38(10):25 – 36, 10 1989.

20. J. T. Stasko. Tango: A Framework and System for Algorithm Animation. *IEEE Computer*, 11(9):27–39, September 1990.

21. E. T. Williams and G. B. Lamont. A Real-Time Parallel Algorithm System. In *Proc. of the 6th Distr. Memory Comp. Conf.*, pages 551–561, Portland, April 28-May 1 1991.

Parallel Physical Optimization Algorithms for Data Mapping

Nashat Mansour
Syracuse Ctr. for Computational Sc.
and
Beirut University College, Lebanon

Geoffrey C. Fox
Northeast Parallel Architectures Ctr.
Syracuse University
Syracuse, NY, U.S.A. 13244

Abstract. Parallel algorithms, based on simulated annealing, neural networks and genetic algorithms, for mapping irregular data to multicomputers are presented and compared. The three algorithms deviate from the sequential versions in order to achieve acceptable speed-ups. The parallel annealing and neural algorithms include communication schemes adapted to the properties of the mapping problem and of the algorithms themselves. These schemes are found useful for providing both good solutions and reasonable execution times. The parallel genetic algorithm is based on a model of natural evolution. The three algorithms preserve the high quality solutions and the non-bias properties of their sequential counterparts. Further, the comparison results show their suitability for different requirements of mapping time and quality.

1 Introduction

Given an algorithm, ALGO, for solving a problem with an underlying data set, DATA, with P objects, the data mapping problem refers to mapping disjoint subsets of DATA to N nodes of a multicomputer such that the parallel execution time of ALGO is minimized. A mapping solution can be represented by a vector, MAP[], with length P; an element n at index p indicates that data object p is mapped to node n. The minimization of execution time of data-parallel programs requires equal distribution of the computation load associated with the data objects and the minimization and balancing of internode communication. Note that minimizing execution time is equivalent to maximizing concurrent efficiency.

The mapping problem is NP-complete, and several heuristics have been proposed for sub-optimal solutions [1,2,3,5,14,15]. These heuristic are fast; but, they usually favor certain problem configurations. Another class of methods consists of physical optimization (PO) methods, which employ techniques from natural sciences; they include simulated annealing [9], neural networks [8] and genetic algorithms [7]. These three paradigms have been applied to data mapping [5,6,10] and their performances have been evaluated. The operation of the PO algorithms is guided by an objective function, OF, that is related to the parallel execution time of ALGO. The PO algorithms yield high quality solutions and have more general applicability than previous heuristics [11]. But, they are slower and, hence, their parallelization is necessary for realistic applications.

In this paper, we briefly present parallel PO algorithms for mapping irregular data to hypercube nodes. This work constitutes a part of an automatic parallelization effort, the

Fortran D programming system [4]. The algorithms are implemented on N_H-node nCUBE/2, and their performances are compared for test cases with different features. A clearer presentation is found in [12].

2 Parallel Simulated Annealing Algorithm

Simulated annealing (SA) starts with some mapping configuration at a high temperature, and the goal is to find a configuration that corresponds to minimum OF. The configuration is cooled down according to a schedule. In sequential SA [11], a number of successive perturbations, N_{attmax}, to the configuration are attempted at each temperature, for thermal equilibrium to be reached. A perturbation, or a move, is accomplished by a random change to an element in MAP[]. Moves are accepted if the change, ΔOF, is negative; otherwise, they are accepted according to a temperature-dependent probability. ΔOF depends on the number of objects mapped to the nodes, denoted by NSUM[n] for node n, and on the change in communication cost [12].

```
while ( T(i) > Tfreeze and NOT converged ) do
    while (not equilibrium) do
        Local SA step;
        Update #attempted and #accepted moves at ω_mvs;
        Communicate boundary info at ω_bdy;
        Update NSUM[] at ω_NS (global sums);
    end_while
    T(i) = k * T(i-1);
end_while (end 1 pass)
```

Fig. 1. PSA node algorithm for data mapping.

A parallel SA (PSA) algorithm is given in Figure 1. It is based on executing sequential SA concurrently and loosely-synchronously in N_H nodes of the nCUBE, where the nodes contain disjoint segments of MAP[], and the associated data subsets. Clearly, PSA is not faithful to the sequential SA because moves can occur concurrently and not successively. Hence, the local nCUBE node view of ΔOF is not always correct. That is, PSA involves inconsistencies related to NSUM[] and the use of outdated nonlocal information. To prevent these inconsistencies from accumulating and degrading the mapping solution, corrections are performed in two ways: a global sum operation to unify NSUM[] in all nodes, and inter-node communication of boundary information. Obviously, it would be disastrous for PSA's speed-up to make these corrections at a high frequency, and low-frequency corrections lead to degeneration. However, as temperature decreases the number of accepted moves decreases and, thus, the likelihood of inconsistencies also decreases; at low temperatures PSA approaches SA. This observation points to a remedy, which is the use of an adaptive correction scheme. In this scheme, the frequency of global summation of the numbers of attempts and accepts, ω_{mvs}, can be annealed, and the frequencies of updating NSUM[], ω_{NS}, and of boundary communication, ω_{bdy}, can be made adaptive to the number of accepted moves. Empirically derived values are: ω_{mvs} is decreased from one every two attempts, at initial temperature, to a few times every N_{attmax}, at freezing temperature, ω_{NS} equals one every few accepted moves, and ω_{bdy} equals one every several accepted moves.

3 Parallel Neural Network Algorithm

The sequential bold neural network (BNN) [6,11] associates a spin $s(e,i)$ with each data object, e, where i corresponds to the i-th bit in a hypercube node label. BNN consists of log_2N iterations and aims for finding quick minima for the energy function, OF. In each iteration, the current subsets of objects are bisected and mapped to subcubes. Such bisection is accomplished in a number of sweeps over the entire problem until convergence. A bisection iteration starts with random spin values, in the -1 to 1 range, and randomly updates these values. The update formula [6] for $s(e,i)$ depends on spin coupling, with neighboring spins, and the sum of spin values, SSUM[], in the spin domain to which $s(e,i)$ belongs. A spin domain, Φ_k, corresponds to a subset of data objects mapped to a subcube, k. At convergence, the spin direction, 1 (up) or -1 (down), determines the new domain (subcube) for a spin (data object).

```
for i = 0 to ( log₂N -1) do
    After 1st bisection: reallocate_spins() and determine my_subcube;
    repeat
        for all spins 0 to P-1
            Global_add(SSUM[] in my_subcube) at ω_ss;
            Communicate_boundary(spin values) at ω_bdy;
            Pick a spin, e, randomly and update s(e,i);
    until (convergence)
    Set bit i in the neurons (0 or 1);
end-for
```

Fig. 2. PNN node algorithm for data mapping.

A parallel NN (PNN) algorithm is shown in Figure 2. It takes a similar approach to that of PSA. It is based on executing BNN loosely-synchronously on N_H disjoint subsets of spins and the associated data objects. Thus, PNN also deviates from the sequential operation of BNN. Similarly to PSA, this involves inconsistencies related to SSUM[] values and the use of outdated values of nonlocal coupled spins. In PNN, we also use a communication scheme which makes use of the properties of NN and the mapping problem. When spin domains are formed, in each bisection iteration, the number of spins changing value/direction decreases as more sweeps are performed. Also, the number of boundary spins coupled to nonlocal peers is only a fraction of the number of local spins. Further, some magnitude of inconsistency can be tolerated as long as it does not accumulate and grow. These observations suggest a communication scheme whereby ω_{ss}, the frequency of global summation to update SSUM[], and ω_{bdy} are attenuated with the number of sweeps. Empirically derived frequencies are: ω_{bdy} equals several (e.g. 10) times for sweep 0 to #SWP1, and then gradually decreases to once per sweep, and ω_{ss} starts with one every few (e.g. 5) spin updates in a sweep until #SWP1, and then decreases to once per sweep. #SWP1 depends on the problem topology and is typically equal to $\sqrt{P}$. To further decrease the cost of updating SSUM[], spins are reallocated to nodes after each bisection pass so that summation will subsequently be needed within smaller subcubes instead of the entire cube. That is, spins are reallocated so that boundaries of spin domains coincide with node boundaries.

4 Parallel Genetic Algorithm

A sequential Genetic Algorithm (GA) starts with a population of possible solutions (individuals), MAP[], and evolves over a number of generations [10]. In each generation, individuals are assigned reproduction trials according to their fitnesses, the reciprocal of OF, and pairs of mates are randomly selected from the reproduction trials list. Then, crossover and mutation are applied to the survivors.

The parallel GA (PGA), described here, is based on Wright's shifting balance theory of natural evolution [16], and is a deviation from the classic GA [7]. In this PGA, the population is divided into disjoint subpopulations, called demes, to which reproduction is restricted. Distributed populations represent better simulation of nature and provide a natural way for preserving genetic diversity and, thus, for circumventing the problem of premature convergence. The demes are allocated to the nCUBE nodes and evolve in three phases. The first and second phases are for random genetic drift and local intrademe selection. In the third phase, interdeme selection takes place; demes with higher fitness expand in size and shift the genetic structure of adjacent demes. The first two phases are simulated by executing a sequential GA, confined to local demes, for D generations. The third phase is accomplished by a one-way migration of the M best individuals from the fitter demes to the less fit neighboring demes. This phase involves communication between physically adjacent nodes in the nCUBE. An outline of PGA is given in Figure 3. The parameters D and M depend on the deme size and the required convergence rate [12]. Clearly, PGA is highly efficient since communication cost is quite small relative to the local computation time. Further, PGA evolves fit solutions in a smaller number of generations than sequential GA [12].

> **repeat**
>   **for** (D drift generations) **do** Perform Sequential GA **endfor**
>   **if** (this is highest peak in neighborhood) **then** Send copies of M migrants;
>   **else** Receive M migrants from fittest neighbor and replace M weakest;
> **until** convergence

Fig. 3. PGA node algorithm for data mapping.

5 Comparison of the PO Algorithms

In this section, comparative experimental results are presented. The data sets used are: FEMW is a 545-point unstructured tetrahedral finite-element discretization of an aircraft wing, GRIDP is a 551-point 2-D grid-based discretization of a broken plate having a large variation in the spatial density of its points, and FEM2 is a 198-point interesting 3-D structure. The test cases are: Test1 is mapping FEMW to N=16, Test2 is FEMW to N=8, Test3 is GRIDP to N=16, and Test4 is FEM2 to N=16. The four test cases provide different geometries, granularities, and graph connectivities.

Figures 4-7 show the solution qualities, i.e. efficiency, and execution times for N_H=N. Results of two faster bisection methods are also included as quality indicators. These are recursive coordinate bisection (RCB) and recursive spectral bisection (RSB) [14]. It is clear from the figures that the PO algorithms produce good sub-optimal solutions; PGA and PSA outperform the bisection methods; PNN outperforms RCB and seems comparable to RSB. The inconsistencies allowed in PSA and PNN do not lead to degeneration, since they are corrected frequently enough by the communication schemes. Comparing the PO algorithms, PGA consistently produces the best solutions followed by PSA and then PNN. Since the solutions of the parallel PO algorithms are consistent with those of their sequential counterparts, our earlier conclusion [11] that this class of algorithms do not exhibit a bias towards particular problem topologies can be reasserted. The execution times of the PO algorithms show that PGA is the slowest and PNN is the fastest.

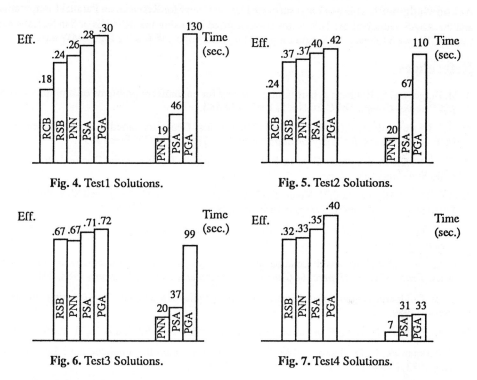

Fig. 4. Test1 Solutions.

Fig. 5. Test2 Solutions.

Fig. 6. Test3 Solutions.

Fig. 7. Test4 Solutions.

There is a significant difference in the memory space requirements between the algorithms. In PGA, information is needed in every node about the whole problem, whereas in PSA and PNN only the local subproblem is considered. This restrains PGA's scalability. One way to alleviate this restriction is to add a preprocessing graph contraction step [11]. PSA and PNN are scalable. Further, the three parallel algorithms are fairly robust with respect to design parameters. However, they are somewhat less robust than their sequential counterparts due to their additional parameters.

6 Conclusions and Further Research

The mapping solutions produced by the three parallel PO algorithms have been found to be good sub-optimal solutions. The shifting balance theory adopted in PGA has provided a suitable model for evolving fit structures. The adaptive communication schemes in PSA and PNN and the spin reallocation in PNN have been found adequate for preserving good solution qualities while limiting the communication overhead.

The three parallel algorithms exhibit diverse properties which make them suitable for different applications. PGA produces the best results, followed by PSA and then PNN. However, PNN is the fastest and PGA the slowest. The test cases considered are rather small. Nevertheless, we are confident that the results, reported in this paper, extend to larger problems. Further work is underway to verify this conjecture [13].

Acknowledgment. This work was supported by the Center for Research on Parallel Computation and the ASAS agency of the U.S. army. It was carried out using the nCUBEs at Sandia Labs and Caltech. We wish to thank H. Simon for providing RSB code and J. Saltz for FEMW data.

References

1. M. Berger and S. Bokhari: A partitioning strategy for nonuniform problems on multiprocessors. *IEEE Trans. Comp.*, Vol C-36,No. 5, 1987, 570-580.

2. N.P. Chrisochoides, E.N. Houstis, and C.E. Houstis: Geometry based mapping strategies for PDE computations. *Int. Conf. on Supercomputing*, 115-127, ACM Press 1991.

3. F. Ercal: *Heuristic approaches to task allocation for parallel computing*. Doctoral Dissertation, Ohio State University, 1988.

4. G. C. Fox, S. Hiranandani, K. Kennedy, C. Koelbel, U. Kremer, C. Tseng, and M-Y. Wu: Fortran D language specification. Syracuse University, NPAC, *SCCS-42*, 1990.

5. G. C. Fox, M. Johnson, G. Lyzenga, S. Otto, J. Salmon, and D. Walker: *Solving problems on concurrent processors*. Prentice Hall 1988.

6. G. C. Fox and W. Furmanski: Load balancing loosely synchronous problems with a neural network. *Proc 3rd Conf. Hypercube Concurrent Computers, and Applications*, 1988, 241-278.

7. D. E. Goldberg: *Genetic algorithms in search, optimization and machine learning*. Addison-Wesley 1989.

8. J. Hopfield and D. Tank: Computing with neural circuits: a model. *Science* 233, 1986, 625-639.

9. S. Kirkpatrick, C. D. Gelatt, and M. P. Vecchi: Optimization by simulated annealing. *Science* 220, 1983, 671-680.

10. N. Mansour and G. C. Fox: A hybrid genetic algorithm for task allocation. *Int. Conf. Genetic Algorithms*, July 1991, 466-473.

11. N. Mansour and G. C. Fox: Allocating data to multicomputer nodes by physical optimization algorithms. To appear in *Concurrency Practice and Experience*.

12. N. Mansour and G.C. Fox: Parallel physical optimization algorithms for allocating data to multicomputer nodes. Syracuse University, NPAC, *SCCS-305*, 1992.

13. N. Mansour and G.C. Fox: For efficient mapping of large problems. In preparation.

14. H. Simon: Partitioning of unstructured mesh problems for parallel processing. *Proc. Conf. Parallel Methods on Large Scale Structural Analysis and Physics Applications*, Permagon 1991.

15. R. D. Williams: Performance of dynamic load balancing algorithms for unstructured mesh calculations. *Concurrency Practice and Experience*, 3(5), Oct. 1991, 457-481.

16. S. Wright: *Evolution and the genetics of populations*. Vol. 3, Univ. of Chicago Press 1977.

Profiling on a Massively Parallel Computer

Jonathan D. Becher
Kent L. Beck

MasPar Computer Corporation
749 North Mary Avenue
Sunnyvale, CA 94086
becher@maspar.com

Abstract. Profiling is critical on massively parallel architectures because the combination of a novel architecture and parallel high-level languages changes the rules of optimal program design. The MasPar profiler provides routine and statement level profiling, interactive browsing, and typeset hardcopy integrated into an existing graphical debugger. This integration allows entire programs or program fragments to be profiled without having to recompile.

1 The Problem

On high performance vector and parallel computers, programmers can significantly improve the execution time of their programs by carefully designing and implementing key algorithms. Profiling is the process of assigning costs to program units (i.e. subroutines and source statements) to identify code that will most benefit from optimization. Although this process is not new [1], the MasPar profiler is the first to be integrated into a graphical debugger and programming environment.

On a massively parallel computer such as the MasPar MP-1, understanding the profile of a program is critical to the successful use of the machine. First, as with any new architecture, the MP-1 changes the rules of effective program design. For example, transferring a floating point number to a neighboring processor is only one-fifth the cost of a floating point multiply, so that algorithms that minimize communication at the expense of computation are not necessarily making optimal use of machine resources. Second, parallel high-level languages provide terse constructs to manipulate large data sets by manipulating a complex instruction stream. In the MasPar languages, a single addition statement may add one or thousands of values, making it difficult to predict the cost of an operation. Finally, the profiler can rapidly identify the computation intensive portions of scalar code, significantly reducing the effort to port existing code to the MP-1. Experience has shown that a few areas of a program cost disproportionately more than others; typically 90% of the parallelization effort is spent on 10% of the code.

2 The Environment

The MP-1 is a distributed memory massively parallel SIMD computer, ranging in size from 1024 to 16,384 processors [2]. Each processing element (PE) is a custom load/store 4-bit processor with 160 bytes of registers and up to 64 KBytes of memory. The PEs are connected by a high-speed two-dimensional toroidal mesh with eight-way nearest neighbor communication (X-Net) and by a circuit-switched hierarchical crossbar that allows arbitrary communications between PEs (router). The PEs are controlled by an array control unit (ACU) that executes scalar instructions, broadcasts instructions to the PE array, and communicates with an attached front end workstation. The ACU and PE array are collectively termed the data parallel unit or DPU.

The MP-1 is programmed in either MPL [3], a parallel extension to C, or MPF, an implementation of Fortran 90 [4]. In MPF, parallel operations are expressed with the Fortran 90 array extensions which treat entire arrays as unitary objects rather than requiring them to be iterated through one element at a time. MPF generates code for both the front end and the DPU, effectively hiding the details of the architecture from the programmer. MPL contains a new type qualifier, `plural`, that allocates a variable on each PE, and communication keywords, `xnet` and `router`, that allow communication between PEs. In contrast to MPF, MPL generates code solely for the DPU and relies on remote procedure calls to the scalar C or Fortran on the front end workstation for operating system or networking tasks.

The MasPar Programming Environment™ (MPPE) is an integrated set of graphical tools that helps in understanding the behavior of massively parallel programs [5]. Using MPPE, the user can control the execution of a program, display the values of variables in a graphical or tabular format, and examine the state of the program or the machine. MPPE contains tools that are specifically designed to support the large data sets used in programming a massively parallel computer but that work equally well on scalar code. A typical debugging session for an MPF program is shown in Figure 1.

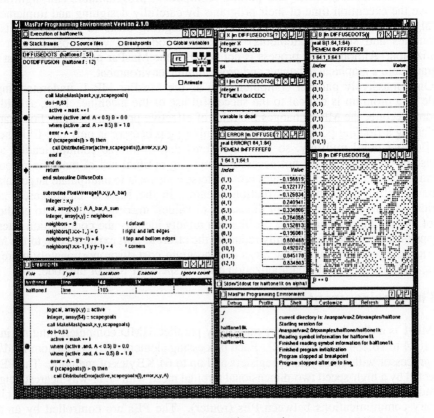

Fig. 1. A debugging session

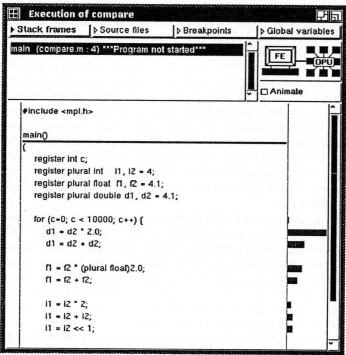

Fig. 2. Profiles integrated into source code

3 The Profiler

Unlike traditional profiling tools, the MPPE profiler is integrated into the debugging environment and does not require recompilation of the user program. In fact, the profiler is a superset of the debugger and uses the same graphical display with an additional bar that displays the relative per-statement costs as histograms (see Figure 2). This integration eliminates the need to master a new tool and allows a program to be profiled and debugged at the same time.

Because the profiler and debugger are integrated, the programmer can use the usual execution control commands (e.g. breakpoints, step, go to line) to collect profile information. Profiles are updated every time the program stops, not just at program termination, allowing the user to sample subsets of the code. Thus, the user is not required to execute the entire program if he is only interested in the profile of a small portion of the code, dramatically increasing productivity. The traditional "whole program" style of profiling is accomplished by running the program from beginning to end. The profiles of multiple runs are accumulated, improving statistics and sharpening performance estimates.

The profile bar displays the relative statement weights as histograms; wider histograms represent statements that take longer to execute. This graphic representation allows quick intuitions into the profile of a program. To determine the actual percentages or absolute number of samples, the user can press the left mouse button to bring up a magnified view. Magnification is a common thread in MPPE: It is used to inspect variables, to zoom in on subsections of arrays, and to provide on-line help.

Four menu options are available from within the profile bar: *view statements, view routines, clear,* and *print*. The view routines and view statements options open new windows indexed onto a sorted list of routine and statement profiles (see Figure 3). The top portion of the window is a table listing routine name, file, number of samples, and percentage of total time; selecting a row displays the associated source code. These windows allow the user to rapidly identify the most costly routines and statements, focusing attention on the areas most likely to benefit from optimization. The clear option resets the accumulated profile information so that individual program subsegments can be profiled without data from previous code. For example, to profile only one subroutine in a program, the user could select *go to routine, clear* the profile information, and *go to line* immediately after the subroutine call. The print option creates a Postscript™ [6] file containing the source code merged with the graphical and tabular profile information. Our output format is an extension to the literate programming work of Marcus and Backer [7].

The profiler is implemented with the help of a device driver that uses the UNIX™ system clock to sample the program counters on the front end and the ACU 256 times a second. While the program is executing, MPPE maps the program counters to source lines so that it can rapidly display the information when the program stops. Because the MP-1 is a SIMD architecture and there is only one instruction stream controlling thousands of PEs, the profiler is spared the job of collecting and synchronizing thousands of program counters. In addition, the asynchronous collection scheme means that profiling has a negligible impact on the runtime of a program (less than 3%). A serendipitous result is that MPPE is always profiling a program, even if the user did not originally request it. If during the debugging session, the user is curious about the profile of the program, a single mouse click will expose the information (see the thin vertical bar in Figure 1 which "hides" the profile bar).

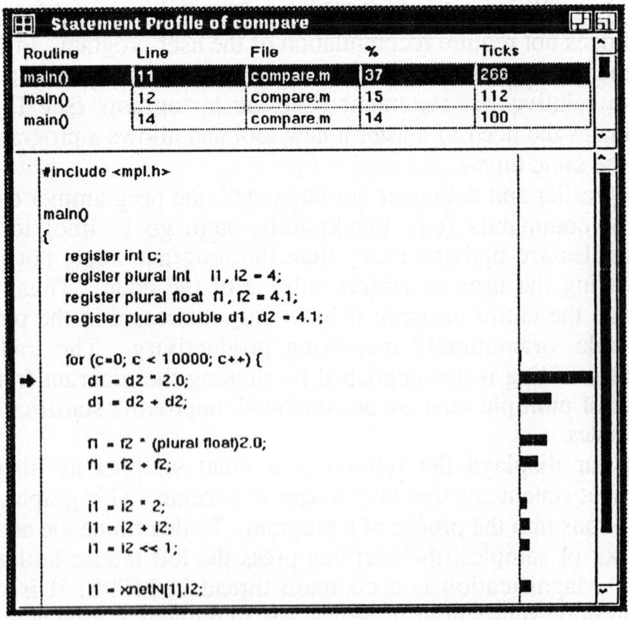

Fig. 3. Sorted statement profiles

4 Case Studies

As previously mentioned, the profiler is invaluable in learning the performance characteristics of the MP-1. Figures 2 and 3 display the profile of a program designed to compare various floating point and integer operations on the PEs. Looking at the relative sizes of the statement profile histograms, we can deduce that a double precision multiply is more than twice as expensive as a double precision addition. The addition, in turn, is about the same cost as a single precision multiply but one and a half times as expensive as a single precision add. These visual intuitions are verified by the statement profile window which lists the actual percentages for each source line. Similar inferences can be made for integer operations.

The profiler is also effective in comparing alternative solutions to a problem. As an example, consider the case in which every PE wishes to send data to the PE four steps away from it. We can imagine that the PEs are arranged in a single strand; those PEs in the bottom right corner "wrap around" and send their data to the PEs in the upper left. This problem can be implemented straightforwardly using the router construct in MPL. Since every PE knows its own linear index (iproc), the destination PE is iproc+4; wrap around is handled transparently by the hardware. The following MPL statement sends the contents of the src variable to the PE a distance four away and stores the result in the dest variable:

```
router[iproc+4].dest = src;
```

Although this code is simple, it can be implemented more efficiently using the xnet construct. The following code achieves the same effect as the router version:

```
xnetE[4].dest = src;
if (ixproc < 4)
    xnetS[1].dest = dest;
```

The first step shifts the data along the horizontal axis four PEs to the east. As with the router, data that falls off the right edge wraps around to the left. The second step shifts the first four columns one PE to the south, completing the data transfer. The statement profile in Figure 4 shows that the xnet solution is approximately seven times more efficient than the router solution.

Although no profiler can solve performance problems, these two examples show how the MPPE profiler can educate the programmer by focussing attention on the areas of the program most likely to yield improvements. It is this knowledge that is key to the successful use of the MP-1.

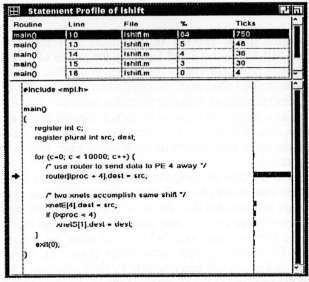

Fig. 4. Statement profile comparison of xnet and router

5 Conclusions

The goal of the profiler was to provide a convenient and intuitive tool that helps programmers to develop highly-tuned applications. By integrating the profiler into an existing graphical debugger, we were able to achieve this goal and provide novel functionality in interactive and on-demand profiling, with minimal additional cognitive load. Customer experience has verified these results and shown that the profiler is an indispensable tool in successfully programming the MasPar computer.

References

[1] "grof: A Call Graph Execution Profiler", S.L. Graham, P.B. Kessler, and M.K. McKusick, *Proceedings of the SIGPLAN '82 Symposium on Compiler Construction*, SIGPLAN Notices, Vol. 17, No. 6, pp. 120-126, June 1982.
[2] "The MasPar MP-1 Architecture", Tom Blank, *Proceedings of the IEEE Compcom*, IEEE, February 1990.
[3] "MPL: A Data Parallel C", Jonathan D. Becher and Kenneth M. Hansen, *MasPar Computer Corporation Technical Report*, TR001.1091, November 1991.
[4] "Software to Support Massively Parallel Computing on the MP-1", Peter Christy, *Proceedings of the IEEE Compcom*, IEEE, February 1990.
[5] *The MasPar Programming Environment Reference Manual*, MasPar Computer Corporation, 1990.
[6] *Postscript Language Reference Manual*, Adobe Systems Inc., Addison-Wesley, 1988.
[7] *Human Factors and Typography for More Readable Programs*, Aaron Marcus and Ronald Backer, Addison-Wesley, 1990.

A Multiprocessor Multiwindow Visualization Subsystem

R. D. Hersch, B. Tonelli, B. Krummenacher

Peripheral Systems Laboratory
Swiss Federal Institute of Technology (EPFL)
CH-1015 Lausanne, Switzerland

Abstract. Multiprocessor systems are available at moderate costs, but they generally lack high-speed multiwindow colour image visualization capabilities. A multiprocessor multiwindow parallel visualization subsystem is presented which can he hooked onto parallel processor arrays or high-speed network interfaces (FDDI, ATM broadband). Thanks to its well-balanced triple transputer architecture, the multi-window display subsystem is capable of simultaneously transferring, clipping and displaying 24bit/pixel colour images at a rate of 18 Mbytes/s. Under optimal conditions it is able to receive, clip and display six full-screen 1024×1024 or twenty-four 512×512 full-colour images/s. Such a display subsystem is one order of magnitude faster than X-window systems running on standard workstations. It satisfies the need for browsing through image data bases and for fast visualization of uncompressed image sequences (scientific data produced by supercomputers, photogrammetry, civil engineering, biology, medicine, etc..).

Keywords: multiprocessor window display, colour image visualization, high-speed browsing

1 Introduction

Thanks to their special-purpose display pipeline, current state of the art workstations are able to display synthesized colour images in real-time. However they prove moderately fast and very expensive for executing general purpose 2-d image processing and visualization tasks which are common when visualizing existing images, such as aerial photographs or medical images [2].

In the near future, high-capacity image servers will be available for storing large quantities of pixel image data [9]. These servers will be accessible through high-speed local area networks or through the future broadband ISDN public network. Browsing at high speed through random sequences of images will become as common as today's fast visualization of text by high-performance editors. Such browsing capabilities will probably be integrated into multimedia interactive environments. Furthermore, simulation programs running on supercomputers will generate image sequences for animated interactive user-driven visualization.

Previous approaches based on the use of multiprocessor arrays for visualization tasks were limited to high-speed graphic image synthesis [1], [4], [6], [8]. In these systems, parallelism and pipelining are combined in order to optimize the graphic visualization pipeline (projection, hidden-surface removal, illumination, segmentation, scan-conversion, clipping). Presently, transputer-driven graphic displays are single processor window servers running X-Windows [11]. To our knowledge, there are no high-speed multiprocessor-multiwindow colour displays optimized for fast display of randomly selected full-colour raster images.

2 General architecture

In order to offer high-speed image visualization which can be interfaced with various devices, such as processor arrays, high-speed local area networks (FDDI) and broadband communication networks, a multiprocessor transputer-based display subsystem was designed for fast interactive multi-window visualization of full-colour 24 bit/pixel images.

This display subsystem consists of one separate processing unit for each of the basic Red, Green and Blue colours (figure 1). Each processing unit consists of a T800 transputer [3] with 4 Mbytes RAM and 2 Mbytes video-ram. The video-ram supports two frame buffers, each of which has a size of 1024 × 1024 pixels. The processor also incorporates 4 serial links each of which offers an effective communication bandwidth of 1.5 Mbytes/s.

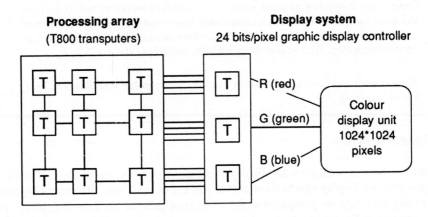

Fig. 1. Visualization subsystem hooked onto a high-performance parallel processing array

The display subsystem incorporates a window manager responsible for the dialog with the application, for filtering input events and for creating and maintaining the window hierarchy. Window server processes running on the R, G and B processors are responsible for the data exchange between the application and the display (figure 2). They receive clipped colour image data in parallel from application processes which they display in the target window. In the case of an event which changes the current state of window overlays, the window manager process updates the information record of each window while specifying its visible rectangular parts and sends messages to the concerned application processes, asking them to regenerate their visible window image parts.

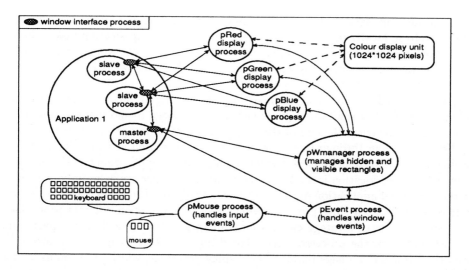

Fig. 2. Multiprocessing window management

3 Multiprocessor-multiwindow display subsystem

Previous research [7] has shown that overlapping window systems offer the greatest flexibility. A multi-window system was therefore designed incorporating window overlapping capabilities; it is fully integrated into the transputer-based multiprocessing environment. The window system supports window sharing and updating operations by application tasks running on several processors. As on most window systems, it also supports scroll bars in the horizontal and vertical directions.

The window system comprises a *window management process* responsible for the dialog with application processes and for the creation and maintenance of data structures reflecting the current state of the the window hierarchy. The *window manager* communicates with the *red, green* and *blue display processes* running in parallel on their respective processors. On request, the display processes create a window frame of the required colour. Once the window has been created, the display processes are ready to receive display data in parallel from application processes.

Input events (mouse, keyboard) are received, transformed into higher order events and directed to their destination by the *event management* process. For example, if in selection mode, the cursor is displaced at a window frame edge, the *event manager* transmits the appropriate high-level event (window move, window resize or window close) to the *window manager*.

Once a window has been created, red, green and blue *display processes* running in parallel are ready to receive display data from application processes. In order to avoid congestion and application deadlocks, application processes are required to ask each of the three colour display processes if they are ready to receive image data of a given size. After an acknowledgement has been issued by each display process, red, green and blue image components are simultaneously sent to the display processes running in parallel on different processors.

Two different window refresh strategies exist [7]. One can either keep window content refresh locally in the display device [10] or ask the application task to be responsible for refreshing the window content upon request by the window manager [5]. Assigning the task of refreshing window content to the window system requires storing the full virtual image contents associated with each window. In the case of many overlapping windows, it would mean storing and managing huge amounts of image information. Such a solution requires either a very large memory space (hundreds of Mbytes) or restricts the size of the largest displayable image. In order to be able to display and pan through large size images like those used in photogrammetry or medicine, we prefer to delegate window refreshing to the application tasks. Whenever a window size or location is modified, the window manager sends an update request to the concerned application master processes. Application masters transmit the update requests to their slave processes which may be running on different processors. This window refresh strategy enables large images to be segmented into parts and be distributed on the processor array. For displaying large images, slave processes send their respective image parts to the display processes, which are responsible for clipping and display.

4 Performances of a T800 transputer based display

Global display subsystem performance depends on communication bandwidth, on the extent to which communication and display are executed in parallel and on the performance of application and display processors during clipping and display operations.

Communication bandwidth is mainly limited by the bandwidth of the transputer serial communication links. But, since link controllers work by direct memory access (DMA), 4 transputer links can simultaneously transfer information into the memory without requiring processor power. Communication and processing can therefore overlap.

The clipping time necessary for displaying an image within a window depends on the complexity of overlapped window parts. It is proportional to the number of rectangles lying within the boundary of a manhattan polygon representing the visible image part. Clipping time was measured to be 100 microseconds for a non-overlapped window and 300 microseconds for a partially covered window, resulting in a polygonal uncovered image part composed of 7 rectangles. Compared to image display time (10 to 100ms, depending on image size), clipping time is negligible.

Pure display time includes clipping time and the time needed to transfer clipped rectangular image parts from the reception buffer into the corresponding parts of the image frame buffer. Measured maximal image display bandwidth by one T800 transputer is 9.5 Mbytes/s. This relatively high speed is obtained thanks to the *move pixel bloc* instruction available in the transputer instruction set.

Figure 3 shows comparative display performances of the three processor T800-based display sub-system, of standard X-window systems running on Sparc 4 and IBM RISC 6000 workstations and of the high-performance Silicon Graphics SG 220 VGX optimized graphic workstation. The tests on the Silicon Graphics were carried out with the GL graphic library using its high-performance buses, its clipping units and its interleaved multibank frame buffer memories.

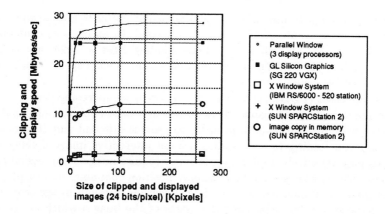

Fig. 3. Comparison of display performances (without communication)

Under X-Windows, Sun Sparcstation 2 or IBM R6000 workstations show display performances which are 10 to 15 times poorer than those of the three processor display. Without X-Windows, a Sun Sparcstation 2 is able to copy a full-colour image from one memory location to another at a speed of 12 Mbytes/s, which is less than half the pure display rate of the parallel display subsystem.

The pure display performance of the high-end Silicon Graphics workstation comes close to the performance of our three processor display subsystem. If we take into account the limited communication bandwidth of the three processor display subsystem (18 Mbytes/s), the Silicon Graphics workstation provides 50% more performance. But, due to its high-performance buses, its interleaved frame-buffer memory banks and its specialized display and clipping hardware, it is one order of magnitude more complex and expensive than the three processor display subsystem.

Global performance tests including parallel communication, clipping and simultaneous display in multiple windows show that the single frame-buffer display subsystem is capable of displaying 24 bit/pixel image data at a rate of 18 Mbytes/s. Communication is running in complete overlap with clipping and display. The display subsystem is extremely well balanced: at full speed, maximal communication bandwidth per single processor is 6.3 Mbytes/s. When displaying the received image parts, each display processor must access the main memory (read and write accesses) at a rate of 12.6 Mbytes/s. The resulting total memory bandwidth of 19 Mbytes/s per processor is close to the maximum available bandwidth for a 32 bit wide memory bank having a cycle time of 200ns.

5 Conclusions

The display subsystem is driven by 3 transputers and offers the external processor array a 18 Mbytes/s communication bandwidth through its 12 communication links. Display resolution is 1024 × 1024 pixels at 24 bit/pixel. Since transputers allow simultaneous communication and processing, previously received colour images are clipped and displayed, while new images are being received. Extensive performance tests show that in single frame-buffer mode, the display is able to receive and visualize colour image data at a rate of 18 Mbytes per second. In an optimal configuration, one can either display six full screen single-window 1024 × 1024 or twenty-four multiwindow 512 × 512 24bit/pixel images per second. Such a speed is sufficient for real-time interactive visualization of image sequences issued by a processor array, by fast network accesses (FDDI, ATM broadband) or by a supercomputer.

The proposed high-speed display device offers new data visualization capabilities. The different windows can be used in order to provide different simultaneous views of the same data, leading to a multidimensional interactive image display device. Since the display is entirely digital and does not require image compression and decompression, display size, scale factor, display position (panning) and display speed can be controlled and modified at any time. Browsing through image sequences at any desired speed and focussing on those parts of the images which are of special interest will prove to be particularly useful for the display of three-dimensional data (scientific images, scanning tomography).

The proposed multiprocessor multiwindow display subsystem is one order of magnitude faster than standard workstation-based multiwindow visualization systems. It satisfies the need for fast image visualization in various disciplines like photogrammetry, civil engineering, biology, and medicine.

References

1. K. Akeley, T. Jermoluk: High-Performance Polygon Rendering. Computer Graphics. Vol. **22**, No. 4 (August 1988) pp 239–246
2. B. Chardonnens, R.D. Hersch, O. Kölbl: Transputer based distributed cartographic image processing. Joint Conference on Vector and Parallel Processing Proceedings VAPP IV. CONPAR 90 (H. Burkhart, Ed.). LNCS 457. Springer Verlag (1990) 336–346
3. M. Homewood et al.: The IMS T800 Transputer. IEEE Micro. Vol. **7**, No. 5 (October 1987) 10–26
4. H. Fuchs, et al.: Pixel.Planes 5: A Heterogeneous Multiprocessor Graphics System Unsing Processor-Enhanced Memories. Computer Graphics. Vol. **23**, No. 3, July 1989, 79–88
5. O. Jones: Introduction to the X-Window System. Prentice-Hall (1989)
6. D. Kirk, D. Voorhies: The Rendering Architecture of the DN10000VS. Computer Graphics. Vol. **24**, No. 4 (August 1990) 299–307
7. B.A. Myers: Window Interfaces: A Taxonomy of Window Manager User Interfaces. IEEE Computer Graphics and Applications. Vol. **8**, No. 3 (September 1988) 65–84
8. J.D. Nicoud, P. Schweizer: Multitransputer Graphics Subsystem. Microprocessors and Microsystems. Vol. **13**, No. 2 (March 1989) 88–96
9. D.A. Patterson, G. Gibson, R.H. Katz: A case for Redundant Arrays of Inexpensive Disks (RAID). Proc. ACM SIGMOD Conf. on Management of Data (1988) 109–116
10. R. Pike: Graphics in Overlapping Bitmap Layers. ACM Trans. on Graphics. Vol. **2**, No. 2 (1983) 135–160
11. R.W. Scheifler, J. Gettys: The X-Window System. ACM Transactions on Graphics. Vol. **5**, No. 2. 79–109

This article was processed using the LaTeX macro package with LLNCS style

Data Race Detection Based on Execution Replay for Parallel Applications

Anton Beranek

Dept. of Computer Science. University of Kaiserslautern

D-W 6750 Kaiserslautern, Germany, email: beranek@informatik.uni-kl.de

Abstract. We describe an integrated approach to support debugging of nondeterministic concurrent programs. Our tool provides reproducible program behavior and incorporates mechanisms to identify synchronization bugs commonly termed data races or access anomalies. Both features are based on partially ordered event logs captured at run time. Our mechanism identifies a race condition that is guaranteed to be unaffected by other races in the considered execution. Data collection and analysis for race detection has no impact on the original computation since it is done in replay mode. The race detection and execution replay mechanisms are integrated in the MOSKITO operating system.

1 The MOSKITO System

This paper describes our approach to support debugging of parallel and distributed applications running on the MOSKITO kernel [1]. Such concurrent programs are difficult to debug because of their nondeterministic nature. For sequential programs an observed error symptom is analyzed by reexecution using a breakpoint debugger. This *cyclic debugging* requires that the program behavior is repeated in successive executions. It is crucial that cyclic debugging becomes applicable to nondeterministic parallel programs.

Similar to systems like Mach [2] or Chorus [3], our model is based on teams of tightly coupled processes executing in a common virtual address space with unrestricted direct access to all team data. Address spaces are protected against each other. Processes of different teams can only interact by various forms of message passing. Process synchronization is based on a team semaphore. The MOSKITO kernel supports preemptive process scheduling and real parallelism within teams. Therefore, it is impossible to base replay on a deterministic, co-routine like scheduling order as found for example in Amoeba [4] or some thread libraries under UNIX.

Section 2 sketches the replay recording and control system. The run time traces allow an equivalent reexecution of faulty programs under the presumption that the team's processes are properly synchronized, i.e. that they do not exhibit *data races* [5,6]. Section 3 describes a tool that automatically identifies data races. It is based on the replay tool.

2 The Replay System

For cyclic debugging an equivalent, reproducible computation that reproduces the same faulty state is necessary. This requires that every process repeats its computation and that the external environment behaves identically. The actual order of concurrent events is only relevant if it affects the computation.

Each process will repeat its computation and produce the same results if:

1.) It starts its computation with the same set of initial data and receives the same input.

2.) Every read instruction obtains the same value from the referenced memory location as in the original execution.

Team input is controlled by capturing hints that allow to reconstruct the return values of kernel calls or the values themselves. Messages as a special case of team input are reconstructed by relating the send events to the corresponding receive events. Refer to [7,8] for a discussion of the aspects of message passing.

In the original execution of the program we collect traces to capture non determinism. In our approach, the tracing subsystem records a set of sequentially ordered event logs for every team of the system to be replayed. All events are derived from kernel calls which also reflect the user's synchronization measures. The processes write their events to the appropriate logs of their team during the calls. We utilize already existing synchronization within the kernel for writing in order to minimize the logging overhead.

A version based approach like Instant Replay [9] is not suitable for our model. With such an approach, a version counter is required for every global data object at run time. As MOSKITO doesn't distinguish shared from private memory within a team and each process can directly access any memory location, we would have to monitor every access.

The replay control system consists of teams that globally coordinate the execution of target teams based on their logs and message flow. All teams are restarted from their initial states or an intermediate global checkpoint. When a process traps into the kernel, it contacts its supervisor. It is allowed to proceed if its actual event is next in the logs. Otherwise it is delayed until all preceding events are replayed.

Equivalent reexecution requires to control interference of concurrently executable accesses of different processes to common data. Synchronization programmed by the user often has subtle errors. For a tool to debug erroneous programs we cannot rely on correct user synchronization. However, we assume that the user *intended* to implement an access policy that enforces the Concurrent Reader, Exclusive Writer (CREW) property which is also required in [9,10]. We believe that this does not impose a serious restriction to application programmers. The replay system guarantees equivalent execution under the presumption of proper CREW synchronization. If this is not the case we consider this to be a synchronization bug. Such programs contain *data race conditions* [5,6]. In the presence of data races the replay may fail to reproduce the error but the logs provide enough information for the automatic race detection tool to locate and replay the race.

3 Data Races

A data race condition or access anomaly occurs if concurrent processes have data conflicts. Such a conflict exists if processes access the same memory location and at least one access is a write operation. A conflict is a data race if the accesses are not synchronized[11]. Our tool applies a dynamic race detection scheme based on the replay facility to detect the variables, processes and statements involved in races.

Replay of an execution that contains data races leads to one of the following situations:
- The replay attempt succeeds in spite of the race and reproduces the observed error.
- At least one team tries to execute a kernel call that does not match the recorded log.
- The events from the log are repeated but the system reaches a different final state.

In the first case the user may not notice the existence of a race unless he explicitly invokes a race check. Otherwise the system will indicate the existence of a race to the user.

Our scheme reports unaffected races first. This is important because they occurred without influence of earlier races. An erroneous program state resulting *after* a race can cause other artificial races to be reported that could not result from any correct state.

The basic idea of the race detection scheme is straightforward. It identifies potentially concurrent execution history intervals of processes between logged replay events and checks their data accesses. We sketch the idea first under the simplifying assumption that all events were totally ordered in a single log for each team.

The execution histories of all processes are divided in consecutive intervals bounded by their logged events. From the log we know which intervals overlapped in the original run. A race condition exists if a memory location is referenced during execution of overlapping intervals of different processes and is written at least once. Only instructions in overlapping intervals can participate in a race.

The algorithm determines the read and write sets of variables accessed in an interval. We define the *current team event* (CTE) as the next event in the log to be replayed. The *last process event* LPE(P_i) is the latest already replayed event of process P_i. The *current interval* CI(P_i) is the interval bounded by LPE(P_i)and the next event recorded for P_i after LPE (P_i). The current read/ write sets CRS(P_i) and CWS(P_i) are the read/write sets of CI(P_i).

At least one race condition between current intervals of two processes P_1 and P_2 exists iff: $CRS(P_1) \cap CWS(P_2) \neq \emptyset \vee CWS(P_1) \cap CRS(P_2) \neq \emptyset \vee CWS(P_1) \cap CWS(P_2) \neq \emptyset$. The addresses involved in races are given by the union of the access set intersections.

Initially, the team is recreated or restarted from a checkpoint state. The processes execute their first CIs and record the CRS and CWS. The process that executed CTE is always selected for continuation. A race check is performed that compares its CRW and CWS to those of the other current intervals. If no race is detected, the selected process executes up to its next event generating the new CRS and CWS. This is repeated until the team log ends or a race is detected.

Imagine a vertical line representing CTE sweeping over the time line diagram in figure 1. All activities of an interval crossed by the line may be concurrent to CTE and to all oth-

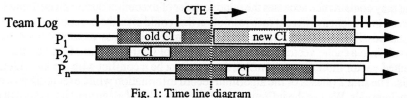

Fig. 1: Time line diagram

er crossed intervals. We always select the CI with the smallest upper bound for comparison and continuation, so all intervals concurrent to CI have already been reexecuted.

If a race is found, the participating processes are replayed and interrupted immediately before they reference a race variable thus presenting a first race state.

We use the protection facilities of the memory management unit (MMU) to record the accessed addresses of an execution interval during the replay. For efficiency reasons the race detection algorithm operates in three replay phases. First, we approximate the access sets by the referenced pages. Intervals with conflict-free page sets cannot participate in races. In a second replay we check accesses to conflicting pages reported in phase 1 in detail. No race exists if different locations are referenced within a page. Identification of page access sets is efficiently supported by the *used* and *dirty* bits set by the MMU. In the second replay we force a page fault exception when the suspected pages are referenced which provides the required address and reference type for the access bit vector. Note that this overhead is not critical since this is performed in replay mode. Additional validation during a third phase presents an unaffected, actual race state. This addresses the problem of inaccurate race reports. It suppresses race artifacts and follow-up race errors.

In fact, the replay system maintains multiple logs per team so ordering of events is only partial. This requires a more complex mechanism to determine potential concurrency between process intervals. Sequential execution within a process together with the sequential recording within the same logs provide a *partially* defined relation 'happened before' (<) on events of different processes similar to [12]. This implies that we may not be able to decide whether an interval precedes another of a different process. Consequently we have to compare the access sets of all intervals that *may have overlapped* to identify a possible race.

We provide a labelling scheme to test concurrency of interval bounds efficiently. Similar representations of the 'happened before' relation are referred to as logical clocks or virtual time stamps [13, 14]. For any two events A, B and their time stamps T(A), T(B) the condition $A < B \Leftrightarrow T(A) < T(B)$ holds. Unordered events have incomparable time stamps.

Time stamps are vectors of size n if n logs are used for each team. We attach a current time stamp to every log and to every process in the replayed team. The logs initially hold $(0,...,0)$, the processes initially have the time stamp of their creation event. On every replayed event, the new time stamp for this event, its log L and the executing process P are formed by the maxima of T_P and T_L in every component. Then the component for the log that stored the event is incremented by 1. This clock scheme takes advantage of the fixed number of logs to build the dependency vector which is beneficial if the number of logs is small (3 in our implementation) compared to the number of processes. It is independent of the number of processes which is important because process creation and termination can be highly dynamic in our system.

Since we use 3 phases the first phase also provides a deterministic schedule that is used to guarantee the same access sequences and execution during the following phases. Execution of concurrent intervals cleared in phase 1 may proceed in parallel. For intervals that may contain race accesses the relative order of execution during phase 1 must be preserved to prevent a different race resolution that could alter the execution.

It is possible to reduce comparison costs by merging access vectors of overlapping intervals into a cache vector containing the union of their accesses. If the comparison to a cached vector indicates no conflict, there cannot be a conflict with the individual intervals. The first 2 phases of the algorithm record information while executing process history intervals. We use the infimum of the lower bounds of all current intervals as a criterion to limit the amount of this information. If the upper bound of an interval is smaller than the infimum, its information can be discarded.

Different resolutions of a race may change the control flow of processes but only one resolution can be traced in a single execution. Access conflicts reported after the first conflicts have been identified may indicate access pairs that in fact cannot occur in arbitrary order, thus giving false race reports. If the algorithm (arbitrarily) schedules interval A before interval B of figure 2a, two races on the variables X and Y would be reported. However, the race on X is impossible. This apparent conflict depends on one particular resolution of the race on Y. The write to X cannot precede the read in interval A in any execution. However, the race on Y is possible.

Some detected races will only occur after a particular resolution of other race events. These races may be artifacts caused by a wrong order of accesses in another race that vanish once this race is fixed. Consider figure 2b. Race R_1 is an artifact if proper synchronization of R2 would prevent the write of R_1 to be executed concurrently with the read. It is mandatory to avoid reporting infeasible races. Also, the system should present those races first, that may affect others and are not artifacts so the user can concentrate on the independent bugs. This is the purpose of the third phase of the algorithm.

A race that was found first can nevertheless be an artifact of another race that would have appeared first under a different schedule. Under schedule A, B, C in figure 2b the race R1 is reported first while R2 is detected first under schedule B, C, A. Therefore, access analysis continues after the first detected conflict in order to identify unaffected race accesses in remaining concurrent intervals. After phase 2 one or more apparent races have been detected. We use the page protection mechanism to replay the processes up to an apparent race event or until they are blocked because of the logged execution order.

If some processes have reached matching conflicting accesses to the same address, these races are feasible. They are first, authentic races in the sense, that they are unaffected of other races possible under the traced kernel event order and the shared data dependences given by the schedule generated by phase 1. By construction as above a valid, deterministically repeatable execution prefix exists that is race free and leads to the displayed races. They can be analyzed and fixed using the replay mechanism and team debugger. Also, all unblocked processes may have reached a reported race access but no matching pair can be found. This occurs if all accesses are to different addresses or the accesses to the same address are all reading (see figure 2c.).

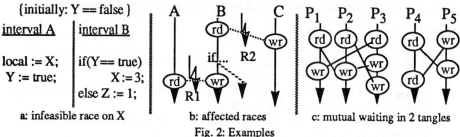

| {initially: Y == false } | | a: infeasible race on X | b: affected races | c: mutual waiting in 2 tangles |

Fig. 2: Examples

In this case not all apparent race conditions detected in phase 2 can occur in the same execution. In order to construct one feasible race, another race, that may also be feasible in another execution, must be resolved in one particular way. In [6,15,16] such races are termed *tangled races*. A different access order in a reexecution can cause a read access to yield a different value which may alter the processes execution so that the race event that we tried to reach will not be reexecuted. Also, a changed computation can generate references to other pages that were not checked and thus constitute an undetected race. However, in the case of a false race as in figure 2a only breaking the false race (that is not yet known to be the false one) will produce the feasible one. We provide a resolution scheme that ensures the same data dependences as during the first phases.

When constructing a first race state in the case of tangled races we exploit our knowledge about the access order under the schedule of phase 1 to achieve deterministic process behavior. We define two attributes on a reexecuted race access that can efficiently be deduced from the known scheduling sequence and the reported apparent races.

A replayed write access to an address X is *safe*, if no concurrent interval that was scheduled earlier accesses X. A read access to X is *safe*, if no concurrent interval that was scheduled earlier is recorded to write X. Other accesses are termed *critical*.

When the detection process blocks, we select a safe current access that must be passed in order to generate the race partner of another current access. This does not alter the observed computation of processes because it guarantees that all read accesses yield the correct version of a shared variable. The algorithm terminates reporting a feasible race. A correctness argument is given in [8]. In case of multiple safe accesses the choice is arbitrary. By breaking a race, we choose one of two execution prefixes that are feasible under the logged kernel event trace. We can parallelize the validation process by replicating the team and breaking different races in each replica. This provides deterministically repeatable executions leading to different race states. The user can switch between them and can derive the correct synchronization by analysis of the consequences of each order.

In the course of debugging a particular race the tool generates a hint whenever a broken race event is encountered. So the user may check whether the access was correct and properly synchronized.

4 Conclusions

We have presented an integrated approach of replay debugging and automatic data race detection for systems based on the team model. Execution replay is always successful if the user provided access synchronization is correct. Otherwise data races exist. Our dynamic race detection scheme utilizes replay to automatically identify such races and provides deterministic replay for them. In case of multiple races in the execution the tool presents those races first that occurred without influence of other race events. For tangled races multiple possible races are presented together with hints that identify potential race accesses that had to be resolved to generate the replayed execution prefix.

References

1. J. Nehmer,T. Gauweiler: Design Rationale for the MOSKITO kernel. ZRI report 13/89, Univ. of Kaiserslautern (1989)
2. M.J. Accetta *et al.*: Mach: A New Kernel Foundation for UNIX Development. Proc. of Summer Usenix, 93-112 (1986)
3. H. Zimmermann *et al.*: Basic concepts for the support of distributed systems: the CHORUS approach. Proc. of the 2nd ICDCS, (1981)
4. I.J.P. Elshoff: A Distributed Debugger for Amoeba. SIGPLAN Notices 24(1)1988
5. D.P. Helmbold, C.E. McDowell: Computing reachable states of parallel programs. Proc. ACM/ ONR Workshop on Parallel and Distributed Debugging, 1991
6. R. Netzer, B. Miller: Improving the accuracy of data race detection. Proc. 3rd Symp. on Principles &Practice of Parallel Programming (1991)
7. A. Beranek: Execution Replay and Data Race Detection for the Debugging of MOSKITO Applications. In: W.Joosen, E. Milgrom (eds.):Parallel Computing: From Theory to Sound Practice,IOS Press, pp 80-91, (1992)
8. A. Beranek: Execution Replay and Race Detection for Debugging MOSKITO Applications. ZRI report, Univ. of Kaiserslautern, (1992)
9. T.J. LeBlanc, J.M. Mellor-Crummey: Debugging Parallel Programs with Instant Replay. IEEE Trans. Comput. C-36, 4, (1987)
10. R.H. Carver, K.C. Tai: Reproducible Testing of Concurrent Programs Based on Shared Variables. Proc. 6th. ICDCS, pp. 428-433, (1986)
11. A. Dinning, E. Schonberg: Detecting Access Anomalies in Programs with Critical Sections. ACM/ONR Workshop on Parallel and Distributed Debugging, (1991)
12. L. Lamport: Time, Clocks and the Ordering of Events in a Distributed System. Communications of the ACM 21(7) (1978)
13. F. Mattern: Virtual Time and Global States of Distributed Systems. Parallel and Distributed Algorithms, pp. 215-226, (1989)
14. C.J. Fidge: Partial orders for parallel debugging. SIGPLAN Notices 24(1),1988
15. J.D. Choi, S.L.Min: Race Frontier: Reproducing Data Races in Parallel-Program Debugging. Proc. 3rd Symp. on Princ. & Practice of Parallel Programming, (1991)
16. R. Netzer, B. Miller: Detecting Data Races in Parallel Program Executions. Proc. 3rd Workshop Prog. Lang. and Compilers for Parallel Computing (1990)

The C_NET Programming Environment: An Overview

J-M. Adamo, C. Bonello, L. Trejo

Laboratoire LIP-IMAG - Ecole Normale Supérieure de Lyon
46, allée d'italie - 69364 LYON cédex 07 FRANCE

Abstract. The paper presents an overview of C_NET, a programming environment that has been specially designed to allow for the development of phase-reconfigurable programs on the SuperNode multiprocessor. The design decisions concerning dynamic-reconfiguration handling are discussed with regard to the architectural constraints of the machine. The software architecture is carefully described.

1   Introduction

C_NET is a programming environment for SuperNode which has been designed so as to take advantage of the dynamic reconfiguration facility available within the machine and to allow for the development of variable-topology programs. This paper provides a brief presentation of C_NET and is organised as follows. In the first section the SuperNode architecture is briefly presented (section 2), next, the features of a computing model that appropriately implements dynamic reconfiguration are discussed in relation with the capabilities of the hardware (section 3). The discussion leads to the conclusion that opting for a phase computing model would be the best choice. In section 4, the C_NET programming environment is described according to the user point of view. The last section describes the C_NET routing facility.

2   SuperNode Architecture

SuperNode is a transputer-based reconfigurable MIMD multiprocessor which can be constituted from 16 to 1024 transputers. The software interface presented in this paper has been developed for a 32-worker SuperNode, but could be extended to larger machines. Each worker-node is a T800 transputer. The nodes communicate with one another across a programmable switch. They can also communicate with a controller down a bus denoted as the control bus. Larger machines can be constructed by recursively combining basic ones.

The switch can be set up dynamically by the controller. The set up time of one bidirectional link is around 3µs, which provides a set up time of about 200µs for the whole switch. The workers are connected with the controller down a second communication medium denoted as the control bus. In the C_NET programming environment the control bus has essentially been used to carry the synchronisation signals of the phase handling machine. Assessing the control bus performances revealed that one cannot expect very fast worker-synchronisation (about 300μs).

3 Handling Dynamic Reconfiguration: A Computation Model

SuperNode provides basic hardware facilities that allow variable-topology algorithms to be implemented on the machine. The development of such algorithms requires a computation model to be devised so that the capabilities of the hardware would be exploited in the most efficient way. Two models are possible in relation with the degree of freedom left to the workers with regard to emitting connection-setting requests (CSR). They are discussed below.

3.1 Asynchronous Model

As the controller is the only place where the switch can be set up and as the control bus is the only channel on which requests can be passed from worker to controller, the CSRs are necessarily processed sequentially. Due to the low speed of the control bus, the connection-setting times can vary from around 100μs when the request is issued while the control bus is free to around 1.5ms when it is fully loaded. Therefore, not only the average-cost of an individual CSR appears to be extremely high but also the connection setting time turns out to be highly non-deterministic as it depends heavily on the load of the control bus.

The switch is flexible enough [6] to allow any less-than-four degree graph to be implemented onto the switch. Unfortunately the resulting connection network is only re-arrangeable. Of course, performing dynamic re-arrangement is possible at the expense of executing some appropriate algorithm at any CSR reception which would make dynamic reconfiguration highly unprofitable. At this stage, it appears quite clearly that the asynchronous computation model does not provide an adequate solution.

3.2 Synchronous Model

The model we are going to propose is a bulk-synchronous one. In such a model, the programs consist of a pair $<P,R>$ where P is a sequence of phases: $P = p^0, p^1 ..., p^n$ and R is a sequence of reconfiguration functions: $R = r^1, r^2, ... r^n$. Each p^i in P is a tuple of software components $p^i = <s^i_0 ,..., s^i_{m(i)}>$ (m(i) stands for the number of workers involved in phase i) together with a one-to-one mapping from the components to the processors. Any software component s^i_k appears to be organised as a sequential triple: $s^i_k = <c1^i_k, cc^i_k, c2^i_k>$. $c1^i_k$ and $c2^i_k$ stand for programs that perform computations but are not allowed to perform interprocessor communications (one or both of these parts might be empty), cc^i_k stands for a program that can perform both computations and communications down the interprocessor channels. The execution of phases and reconfiguration functions is synchronised according to the two following rules:

let us take (p^i, p^{i+1}) a pair of consecutive phases and let r_{i+1} be the $(i+1)^{th}$ reconfiguration function:

(1) the termination point of cc^i_k is synchronised with the starting point of r_{i+1}, $0 \leq k \leq m(i)$,

(2) the starting point of cc_k^{i+1} is synchronised with the termination point of r_{i+1}, $0 \leq k \leq m(i)$.

Note that we do not need for the sequences P and R to be known statically. Indeed, the selection of the pair (p^{i+1}, r^{i+1}) can be decided in the ith stage from the final state computed by p^i. The software component subdivision resulted from our observation that, most often, computation and communication can be sequentialised so that a large part of reconfiguration times can be overlaped with computation times.

Other phase models have recently been proposed by people interested in parallel algorithm complexity. Some try to derive more realistic models of parallel computation from PRAMs [4]; others are looking for something that could be used as a universal model for parallel computation [7]. The phase model presented in this section is based on similar ideas with the difference that in this model each phase is assumed to be executed on the graph that fits, in the best possible way, the needs of the performed data movements. The idea of using and underlying reconfigurable synchronous model is not new. A similar idea can be found in [5].

4 Implementing the Computation Model: the User Point of View

The software interface provides the user with a set of appropriate algorithmic languages that allow the development of phase-reconfigurable programs. The software interface is rooted in a kernel language which, for portability reasons, has been chosen to be C++. The first one (PPL language: Phase Programming Language) is devoted to the description of phase-reconfigurable programs. The second (GCL: Graph-Construction Language) is devoted to the construction of graphs the phases are executed on. The third one (CPL: Component Programming Language) allows for coding the software components that are executed within the phases of the program. Each extension borrows from C++ the data and control structures and contains an additional set of specialised instructions.

4.1 Coding Phase Programs: the PPL Language

PPL [2] is devoted to phase-machine programming. The set of additional instructions essentially provides a means for phase and phase sequence description. Here is the syntax of a phase definition (it will be completed later on along with the router description):

> **upon** topology-function (parameters)
> > **mapping** mapping-function (parameters)
> > { declaration of interprocessor-channels
> > > declaration and placement of software components
> > }

topology-function is the name of a GCL function that defines the graph on which the phase is to be executed. *mapping-function* performs the placement of the graph upon the set of processors by mapping each vertex of the former on a processor of the latter. The code into brackets allows for the declaration and placement of the software components and interprocessor channels onto the nodes and links of the processor graph. Of course, as no routing facility is assumed so far, interprocessor channels are expected to link only pairs of software components that are executed on connected processors.

4.2 Symbolic Definition of Topologies: the GCL Language

Any phase declaration requires the definition of topology on which the phase is to be executed. Symbolic construction of topologies are performed by GCL functions. GCL is a C++ based language extended with the following programming primitives:
• **node** (*number-list*): defines a node and assign a number to it. In general, this number will be subsequently replaced by the number of the processor it is mapped onto (mapping declaration).
• **connect** (*number1, number2*): defines a connection between a pair of previously defined nodes identified by *number1* and *number2*.
• **disconnect** (*number1, number2*): removes every connection existing between two given nodes. It allows for partial graph construction. It can be very useful for defining irregular topologies from regular ones by simply removing certain edges.
• **remove** (*number-list*): removes one or more nodes and all the pending edges. It allows for sub-graph construction.

4.3 Coding the Software Components

A phase definition requires a set of software components to be assigned to the processors involved. The C_NET programming environment has been built upon the Logical Systems C package which provides a set of basic pieces of software: a C compiler, a library of functions (usual C functions, OCCAM-like functions and transputer-instruction-like functions) and a network loader.

The software components can directely be coded within the Logical Systems C package. They can also be coded using the CPL language we have developed. The CPL language has been designed so as to support both the object oriented and communicating processes styles of programming. Such a goal could have been achieved by extending simply C++ with a library of functions specially designed to support the CSP-OCCAM concurrent programming style. However there are major drawbacks in such an approach, in particular, the concurrent programming facilities are superficially introduced into the host programming language so that checking their static semantics is made quite impossible. So, we decided to take the opposite approach and undertook to merge communicating sequential processes as closely as possible within C++ [1].

A special function: *release()* is available in the C_NET system library which allows for overlapping switch reconfiguration with worker computation. The release function should be executed in a software component as soon as it is known that the component no longer needs to perform interprocessor communication. Executing the *release()* function on a worker incurs a signal to be sent to the control bus. Upon reception of a *release* signal from the workers, the controller starts reconfiguring the switch according to the needs of the next phase and then broadcasts a *switch-ready* signal to the workers involved in the next phase as soon as the switch reconfiguration is completed. In the mean time, each worker can complete executing the current phase and can start the next one. A worker attempting to perform an interprocessor communication while the *switch-ready* signal has not yet been received is descheduled. The worker is resumed upon reception of this signal.

5 Extending the C_NET Programming Environment with a Routing Functionality

The idea of a phase-reconfigurable program developed so far aims at avoiding routing as much as possible. This idea clearly conflicts with that of programs with routed messages which constitutes an opposite alternative. Nevertheless, we decided to extend C_NET with a routing facility so as to allow both styles of programming within the programming environment. Furthermore, things have been designed and implemented in such a way that a mixed style of programming is also possible.

Interprocessor communication is performed in the software components either by directly accessing the physical links (level 0) or by using virtual channels (level 1). At level 0, the programs directly read/write on the physical links. At level 1, the processes in the software components can communicate across virtual interprocessor communication channels (VICC). The VICCs can only connect software components loaded on pairs of connected processors. There can be an unlimited number of VICCs between a pair of components. Several VICCs can share one or a pool of several physical links. At level 1 routing must explicitly be performed by the programmer. Extending C_NET with a router allows for achieving a further level of virtualisation (level 2). At this level the VICC are allowed to connect any pair of software components regardless of the way they are placed on the nodes of the physical network. Routing is performed automatically by a router joined to the software components.

The C_NET routing system consists of a parametrised router together with a library of predefined routing data that currently contains data related to the definition of usual topologies: ring, grid, torus, ...

The syntax of the **upon** construct (see section 4.1) has to be completed in order to allow for declaration of routing data.

```
upon topology-function (parameters)
   mapping mapping-function (parameters)
   routing routing_function (parameters),
             virtual_link_nb_function (parameters),
          constructor (parameters), destructor (parameters)
   {  declaration of interprocessor-channels
      declaration and placement of software components
   }
```

routing_function is a function of the routing library or has to be written by the user.*virtual_link_nb_function* returns the number of virtual links that have to be assigned to the physical ones in order to generate a virtual routing graph. It is used to generate buffers that are associated to the physical links. The next two functions are a pair of *constructor* and *destructor* functions intended to perform creation, initialisation and destruction tasks in relation with the need of *routing_function*.

6 Conclusion

The first example on which the programming environment was experimented is the conjugate-gradient (CG) algorithm. The results we have got from experimenting with this algorithm are encouraging. Phase-reconfigurable implementtation of CG was developed and compared with a fixed topology implementation (4x8 torus) [8]. What we have got is consistent with what we were expecting. For small dimensions of the A matrix (up to 64 rows) the reconfiguration time is too high for overlaping it with computation time. As a consequence, the fixed-topology algorithm runs only (very) slightly faster. For larger dimensions of the A matrix the phase-reconfigurable algorithm provides better compared performances. For example, for a 1024x1024 A matrix, the latter runs 5% faster. At first sight, the profit appears not to be sufficiently substantial to be really interesting. Let us note however that the 5% profit results from executing most data movements in logarithmic-time. Now, as we are experimenting on a very small machine (32 nodes) such a profit could not reasonably be expected to be larger. High profits could undoubtedly be achieved on larger machines (say 256, 512 or 1024 nodes). This has been proved by simple extrapolation from what we have got on our 32-nodes machine. We have recently developed a computation model to perform such an extrapolation. In the best situation (1024 processors formated as a 8x128 matrix and a 1024x1024 A-matrix) the predicted speed up rate yield by the model is around 6. Report on this work has been published in [8].

References

1. J-M. Adamo, Extending C++ with Communicating Sequential Processes, Proc. of the Transputing Conf., Santa Clara April 1991, IOS Press.

2. J-M. Adamo, C. Bonello, The PPL language: Reference Manual, LIP research report n° 91-23.

3. J-M. Adamo, N. Alhafez, Un routeur paramètrable pour l'environnement de programmation C_NET, soumis à la letter du transputer.

4. R. Cole, O. Zajicek, The APRAM: Incorporing Asynchrony into the PRAM Model, ACM Symp. on Parallel Algorithm and Architectures (SPAA), 1989.

5. L. Snyder, Introduction to the Proper Parallel Programming Environment, Proc. of the 1983 Int. Conf. on Parallel Processing.

6. D. A. Nicole, Esprit project 1085: Reconfigurable Transputer Processor Architecture, Dept. of Electronics and Computer Science, Univ. of Southampton, Sept. 1988.

7. L. G. Valiant, General Purpose Parallel Architectures, Research Report TR0789, Harvard.

8. J-M. Adamo, L. Trejo, Experimenting Upon the Conjugate Gradient Algorithm within the C-NET Programming Environment, LIP research report n° 92-18.

P++, a C++ Virtual Shared Grids Based Programming Environment for Architecture-Independent Development of Structured Grid Applications

Max Lemke[1] and Daniel Quinlan[2]

[1] Mathematisches Institut der Universität Düsseldorf, Universitätsstraße 1, D-W-4000 Düsseldorf 1; lemke@numerik.uni-duesseldorf.de

[2] Computational Mathematics Group, University of Colorado, Campus Box 170, P.O. Box 173364, Denver, USA-CO 80217-3364; dquinlan@copper.denver.colorado.edu

Abstract. P++ is an innovative parallel array class library for structured grid applications on distributed memory multiprocessor architectures. It is implemented in standard C++ using a serial array class library and a portable communications library. P++ allows for software development in the preferred serial environment and such software to be efficiently run, unchanged, on parallel architectures. The added degree of freedom presented by parallel processing is exploited by use of an optimization module within the array class interface. P++ is based on the combination of the SPMD (Single Program Multiple Datastream) programming model with the VSG (Virtual Shared Grids) principle of data parallelism. Besides different grid partitioning strategies, two communication update principles are provided and automatically selected at runtime: Overlap Update for nearest neighbor grid element access and VSG Update for general grid (array) computations. As opposed to general Virtual Shared Memory implementations, VSG allows for obtaining similar parallel performance as for codes based on the traditionally used explicit Message Passing programming model.

1 Introduction

P++ is an innovative, robust, architecture-independent array class library that simplifies the development of efficient, parallel programs for large scale scientific applications. The target machines are current and evolving massively parallel distributed memory multiprocessor systems (e.g. Intel iPSC/860 and PARAGON, Connection Machine 5, Cray MPP, IBM RS 6000 networks) with different types of node architectures (scalar, vector, or superscalar). Through the use of portable communications and tools libraries (e.g. EXPRESS^{TM} [3]), the requirements of shared memory computers are also addressed. The P++ parallel array class library is implemented in

---

[1] Research supported by the German Federal Ministry of Research and Technology (BMFT) under PARANUSS, Grant ITR 900689; part of the author's dissertation.

[2] Research supported by the National Aeronautics and Space Administration (NASA), part of the author's dissertation.

[3] EXPRESS is a trademark of ParaSoft Corp.

standard C++ using the serial M++^{TM} [4] array class library, with absolutely no modification of the compiler. P++ allows for software development in the preferred serial environment, and such software to be efficiently run, unchanged, in all target environments.

The P++ application class is restricted to structured grid-oriented problems, which form a primary problem class currently represented in scientific supercomputing. This class is represented by dimensionally independent blockstructured grids (1D - 4D) with rectangular or logically rectangular blocks including domain decomposition and adaptive mesh refinement applications, which have motivated this work [1]. The M++ array interface, whose functionality is similar to the array features of FORTRAN 90, is particularly well suited to express the operation and grid structure of these algorithms to the compiler and to the P++ environment at runtime.

The major features of the P++ array class library as a programming environment for structured grid applications are: object oriented indexing of the array objects simplifies development of serial codes by removing error prone explicit indexing common to *for* or *do* loops; algorithm and code development takes place in a serial environment; serial source codes are recompilable to run in parallel without modification; codes are portable between different architectures; vectorization, parallelization and data partitioning are hidden from the user, except for optimization switches; P++ application codes exhibit communication as efficiently as FORTRAN codes with explicit Message Passing; single node performance approximates that of FORTRAN. Thus, P++ makes programming distributed architectures as simple as programming serial architectures without loss of parallel efficiency.

We would like to thank all the people who discussed the P++ development, in particular S. McCormick, K. Witsch, L. Dye, D. Clarkson, D. Balsara, D. Edelsohn, C. Kesselmann, I. Angus, J. Peery, and A. Robinson.

2 Parallelism in P++

P++ is based on the Single Program Multiple Datastream (SPMD) programming model, which consists of executing one single program source on all nodes of the parallel system. Its combination with the Virtual Shared Grids (VSG) model of data parallelism (a restriction of Virtual Shared Memory to structured grids, where communication is controlled at runtime) is essential for the simplified representation of the parallel program using the serial program.

Besides data parallelism, functional parallelism is essential for obtaining high performance. To date only natural functional parallelism, which results from the execution of operations and expressions with different distributed grid variables on different processors, is available within P++. Two different principles for providing very efficient additional functional parallelism through asynchronous scheduling are currently under investigation: Parallel blocks or a *forall*-like functionality at compile time ([1] and CC++ at Caltech); and deferred expression evaluation (across multiple expressions) with runtime dependency analysis.

---

[4] M++ is a trademark of Dyad Software Corp.

2.1 Data Partitioning

Currently *Default Partitioning* of the grid data within P++ consists of even partitioning of each grid variable across all nodes, based on 1D partitioning of the last array dimension [3]. In addition, *Associated Partitioning*, provides for consistently aligned partitionings of grid variables (same size, coarser, or finer) with others (e.g. for multigrid algorithms, Fig.3); *User Defined Partitioning*, which is based on a user filled mapping structure; and *Application Based Partitioning*, which allows for the introduction of user specified load balancing algorithms to handle the partitioning of one of more specified grid variables [2], are available as user supported choices that can override the default. In combination with VSG this allows partitioning to be a parameter of optimization.

2.2 Data Parallelism Based on Virtual Shared Grids (VSG)

The VSG concept gives the appearance of Virtual Shared Memory restricted to array/grid variables. The M++ array syntax provides the means for the user to express the algorithm's data and operation structure to the compiler and runtime system. Computations are based on global indexing. Communication patterns are derived at runtime, and the appropriate send and receive messages of grid portions are automatically generated by P++ selecting the most efficient communication models for each operation: Overlap Update for computations on closely aligned grid portions or VSG Update for general operations between nonaligned grids. The ability of P++ to optimally schedule communication, for each array expression, guarantees that the same minimum amount of data is communicated in the same minimum number of messages as in codes based on the traditional explicit Message Passing programming model. This is a big advantage over the more general Virtual Shared Memory model, where the operating system triggers communication without having information about the algorithm's use of data. In this case, either full memory pages are communicated for each data item of basic type (float, int, ...) in the hope that the succeeding non-local data item is located on the same page as the preceding item, or expensive element by element communication is done.

VSG Update: In the implementation of the general VSG concept, within the VSG Update communication model, we restrict the classical *Owner Computes* rule to binary subexpressions and define the owner arbitrarily to be the left operand. This simple rule handles the communication required in the parallel environment; specifically, the designated owner of the left operand receives all parts of the distributed array necessary to perform the given binary operation. Thus the temporary result and the left operand are partitioned similarly (Fig. 1).

Overlap Update: As an optimization for a broad range of iterative methods we have implemented nearest neighbor access to array elements through the widely used technique of grid partitioning with overlap (currently restricted to width one, see [3]). In this way, the most common type of nearest neighbor grid accesses can be handled by complicated expressions, and the communication limited to one overlap update in the "=" operator (overloaded) for grids. To minimize communication, the necessity of updating the overlapping boundaries is detected at runtime, based on how the overlap has been modified.

```
1.  T = B + C
    P1: T11 = B11 + C1
        receive C21 from P2
        T12 = B12 + C21
    P2: T2 = B2 + C22
        send C21 to P1
    P3: idle
2.  A = T
    P1: send T1 to P3
    P2: send T2 to P3
    P3: receive T1 from P1
        receive T2 from P2
        A = T
```

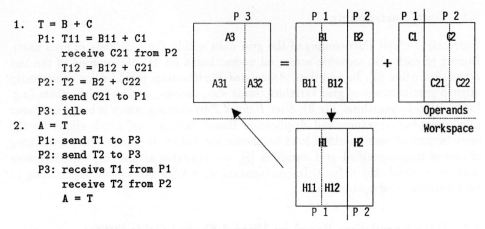

Fig. 1. VSG Update based on Owner Computes: A = B + C on 3 processors

Grids are constructed in a distributed fashion across the processors of the parallel system. All information, required for evaluating expressions, is available from the array syntax and a partitioning table, which stores partitioning information and processor mappings. The number of entries in the table is greatly reduced by grouping associated grids and providing for storage of only the required data on a processor by processor basis. This is necessary due to the large sizes that these tables can be on massively parallel systems. All necessary global information is locally available on each processor with no communication required, again a significant advantage of P++ compared to other developments.

In addition to the above two basic communication models the principle of Deferred Expression Evaluation is under investigation in collaboration with Sandia National Laboratories. Besides other more complicated reasons for its use, this evaluation rule allows for significant expression optimization w.r.t. communication and intermediate array storage minimization. In a vector environment like the Cray Y-MP for example, the given operations that form the array expression are collapsed to form aggregate operators (optionally implemented in FORTRAN), so that the expression can fully exploit the vector hardware (e.g. through chaining and optimal vector register use).

3 Object Oriented Design and User Interface of P++

The basic structure of P++ consists of multiple interconnected classes. The overall structure and the interconnections are illustrated in Fig. 2. The P++ user interface consists of a combination of the M++ array language interface and a set of functions for parallel optimization, the Optimization Manager. Standard C++ I/O functions are overloaded by P++ parallel I/O-Manager functions. The P++ user interface provides for switching between M++ in the serial environment to P++ in the serial or parallel environment.

The Optimization Manager allows for overriding defaults for user control of partitioning, communication, array to processor mappings, communication models of

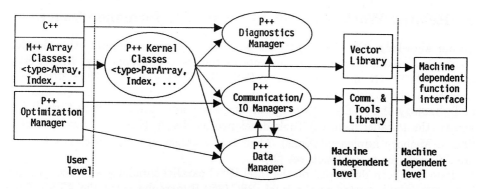

Fig. 2. The object oriented design of the P++ environment.

VSG, parallel I/O system, scheduling, etc. Optimizations of this kind only have significance in a parallel environment. The Optimization Manager is the only means by which the user can affect the parallel behavior of the code. It provides a consistent means of tailoring the parallel execution and performance.

4   P++ Support for Structured Grids — an Example

Although P++ is dimensionally independent, its applications support is demonstrated using a 1D multigrid algorithm on a rectangular domain. The usual way to implement multigrid algorithms on a distributed memory system is to use grid partitioning with overlap [3]. The computational domain (grid) is divided into subgrids which are assigned to processors. The subgrids of the fine grids and the associated ones of the coarse grid are assigned to the same processor. The nearest neighbor computations of each multigrid component can be performed on a subset of the interior points of the local partition in parallel, using the overlap area on partition boundaries. Because details of the algorithm on a small number of points per processor are problematic, agglomeration is one of the strategies that can be used to consolidate the distributed application to a smaller number of processors. Figure 3 shows the automatically selected runtime support of P++ for the interpreted communication patterns of the solver and for the agglomeration strategy. VSG reduces the details of their implementation to defining the fine and coarse grid partitioning.

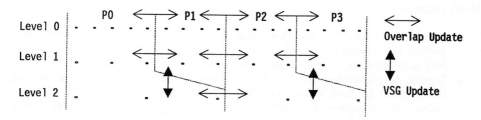

Fig. 3. Standard multigrid partitioning with coarse level agglomeration

5 Related Work, Current State and Performance Issues

To our knowledge the P++ approach is unique. There are several other developments that contain distinct components of the P++ concepts (e.g. High Performance FORTRAN and other parallel FORTRAN dialects, the CC++ declarative concurrent object oriented programming notation developed at California Institute of Technology, the PARAGON programming environment developed at Cornell University, the Parallel Runtime Tools developed at NASA/ICASE or several Virtual Shared Memory implementations). Their major target application classes however are different (for more details see [2]).

P++ has been developed on the Intel iPSC parallel simulator and, recently, has been successfully ported to the Intel iPSC/860 Hypercube using the AT&T C++ Cfront compiler and the Intel NX-2 communications library. It contains all major concepts described above. At some points its functionality is still restricted to the needs within our own set of test problems (e.g. a 3D multigrid code).

Besides a proof of the feasibility of the approach, first results with respect to parallel efficiency have been obtained: Comparisons for P++ and FORTRAN with Message Passing based test codes, respectively, have shown that the number of messages and the amount of communicated data is roughly the same. Thus, besides a negligible overhead, similar efficiency is achieved. With respect to single node performance, optimization has not been finished yet and therefore no comparable results are available. However, our experiences with C++ array language class libraries on workstations and on the Cray Y-MP (in collaboration with Sandia National Laboratories: about 90% of the FORTRAN vector performance is achieved) are very promising. Therefore, altogether, we expect the parallel performance for P++ based codes to be similar to that obtained for optimized FORTRAN codes with explicit Message Passing.

Currently, P++ is used to support the parallelism of a second class library which we have developed to support adaptive mesh refinement (AMR++). This class library abstracts issues of local refinement and, when run with P++, abstracts issues of parallelism. The flexibility of the P++ support for this complex application is demonstrated in [2]. In addition, a version of the P++ Communication Manager based on EXPRESS is under development. For the future it is planned to further develop and optimize P++ for several architectures. Functional parallelism is one of the major aspects that will be tackled.

References

1. Lemke, M.; Quinlan, D.: Fast adaptive composite grid methods on distributed parallel architectures; Proceedings of the Fifth Copper Mountain Conference on Multigrid Methods, Communications in Applied Numerical Methods, Wiley, 1992.
2. Lemke, M.; Quinlan, D.: P++, a C++ Virtual Shared Grids Based Programming Environment for Architecture-Independent Development of Structured Grid Applications; Arbeitspapiere der GMD, No. 611, 20 pages, Gesellschaft für Mathematik und Datenverarbeitung, St. Augustin, Germany (West), February 1992.
3. Lemke, M.; Schüller, A.; Solchenbach, K.; Trottenberg, U.: Parallel processing on distributed memory multiprocessors; Proceedings, GI-20. Annual meeting 1990, Informatik Fachberichte Nr. 257, Springer, 1990.

Detection of concurrency-related errors in Joyce

D. K. Arvind and J. Knight

Computer Science Department,
Edinburgh University,
Mayfield Road, Edinburgh EH9 3JZ,
SCOTLAND

Abstract. EXTENDED PMD is a methodology for detecting communication- and concurrency-related errors in CSP-based languages. A static analysis of the source program is used to build a model which is augmented with dynamic information from a dedicated hardware monitor. These information allow a post-mortem analysis of the program with automatic detection of errors. EXTENDED PMD has been applied to Joyce[1], a semantic variant of CSP based on a subset of common Pascal.

1 Introduction

EXTENDED PMD is a methodology for detecting errors in concurrent software which have dynamic process creation and flexible communication. It uses static analysis of the source code to build a model of the program which is dynamically enhanced with run-time information generated by a dedicated hardware monitor. A *thread* is defined as a unit of scheduling whose lifetime corresponds to the execution of a sequential piece of code. Threads communicate synchronously via *channels*. In Joyce, the status of a thread becomes active on creation, blocked while waiting for communication, suspended while waiting for child threads to terminate, and finally reverts to the invalid state on termination. These changes in the states of threads are recorded by the hardware monitor in a trace file. This trace is complete to allow faithful reconstruction of the execution of the program.

The program graph is a two-dimensional representation of the Joyce program. The nodes of the graph correspond to program constructs. For example, an IF-THEN-ELSE construct is represented as a COND (conditional) node with two child SELEC (selection) nodes. The latter could themselves be parents of sub-graphs which represent the two alternative execution paths. This is treated in greater detail in Section 2.1.

In Joyce, the concurrent processes called *agents* have the same syntax and scoping restrictions as procedures in Pascal. When an agent is called, a process is created which executes the body of the agent. The caller of the agent continues executing and is not suspended as in the case of Occam2. The scoping rules for variables are considerably simpler than in the case of Pascal. There are no global variables except for agent names and type declarations, and variables declared within an agent can only be used within the body of that agent. All shared data, including channels, must therefore be passed via agent parameters. This restricted variable scoping implies that passing a channel to an agent signals its wish to use that channel.

The notion of a Region of Channel Usage (RCU) is introduced for efficient examination of the program graph. An RCU for a channel is the set of threads which have access rights to that channel. This is explained in greater detail in Section 2.3.

2 Extended PMD

2.1 Program Graph

The program graph reflects the structure of the program, records thread information (like identifiers, current positions, and status), and records channel information. Figure 1 illustrates the program graph for a Joyce program. This contains examples of each type of graph node. A horizontal arrow denotes a parent-child relationship; for instance, a LOOP node is the parent of the sub-graph representing the body of the loop. Siblings are connected by a vertical arrow. The concurrency-related constructs in Joyce include agents (the basic unit of concurrency), channel port variable (pointers to channel entities), channel creation, channel input/output, and channel polling statements. These are represented in Fig. 1. Sequential program constructs which are not choice points, such as variable assignment, have no corresponding graph nodes.

2.2 Trace Events

There are two kinds of events – *essential* and *optional*. Essential events are changes in the states of threads which are potential sources of errors. The optional events help map the source of errors as represented in the program graph to line numbers in the program. The complete set of trace events for Joyce is shown in Fig. 2.

The logging of events by the hardware monitor is initiated by the operating system. The essential events correspond to statements which naturally require the operating system to perform specific functions such as thread creation. The overhead in logging such events is therefore small (approx. 3-4 machine instructions). In order to signal the optional events the compiler introduces code to issue explicit requests to the operating system. The overhead here is relatively expensive compared to the class of essential events (approx. 100 machine instructions).

When an agent is called in the program, two sets of information need to be monitored – the identifier of the newly created thread (and its parent), and the parameter information associated with the agent call. The send and receive events are signalled whenever an agent executes a communication statement. This only implies that an agent is ready to communicate; the communication actually executes when two matching agents become ready. The polling event gives the number and identifiers of channels which are involved in a polling loop. The direction fields indicate whether the communication is an input or an output. Thread termination is signalled when a thread terminates normally. Abnormal termination (for example, by an attempted division by zero) produces the halt event.

The optional event, loop exit, signals the completion of an iterative loop. The selection event indicates the choice taken when alternative execution paths are available, for example, in the case statement of a polling loop.

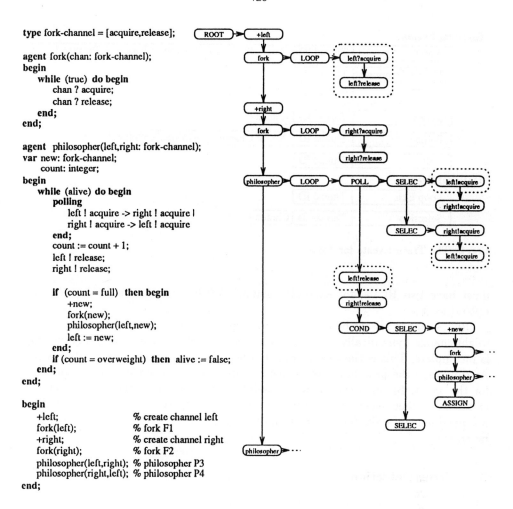

```
type fork-channel = [acquire,release];

agent fork(chan: fork-channel);
begin
    while (true) do begin
        chan ? acquire;
        chan ? release;
    end;
end;

agent philosopher(left,right: fork-channel);
var new: fork-channel;
    count: integer;
begin
    while (alive) do begin
        polling
            left ! acquire -> right ! acquire |
            right ! acquire -> left ! acquire
        end;
        count := count + 1;
        left ! release;
        right ! release;

        if (count = full) then begin
            +new;
            fork(new);
            philosopher(left,new);
            left := new;
        end;
        if (count = overweight) then alive := false;
    end;
end;

begin
    +left;                      % create channel left
    fork(left);                 % fork F1
    +right;                     % create channel right
    fork(right);                % fork F2
    philosopher(left,right);    % philosopher P3
    philosopher(right,left);    % philosopher P4
end;
```

Fig. 1. The Program Graph of the Evolving Philosophers.

2.3 Region of Channel Usage

The RCU of a channel defines the set of threads which may communicate via the channel. This is determined by examining the program graph. In Fig. 1, the RCU of channel *left* is the set of threads in which the channel is used (these are highlighted in the figure). Joyce allows the definition of complex types for channels, *i.e.* the alphabet of symbols which the channel may convey. If two agents wish to communicate they must agree on the object type. Channels therefore have an RCU corresponding to each alphabet of symbols. In Fig. 1, the channels are defined to communicate only *acquire* and *release* tokens. As these tokens define separate alphabets the channels

Essential Events

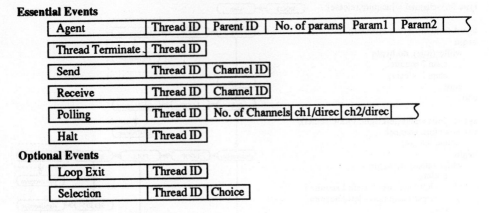

Fig. 2. The Trace Events for Joyce

must have two RCUs, for example, channel *left* has the RCUs *left(acquire)* and *left(release)*.

RCUs cannot always be determined at compile-time because the program graph might change dynamically. Also, RCUs cannot be determined if the program graph is incomplete. This is the case in Fig. 1, when the first agent to be created is *fork*. At this stage the program graph consists only of the root node and the sub-graph for the agent. In this example it is possible to predict, from the source code, the creation of other agents and hence the corresponding RCU. In cases where this is not possible, one waits for the creation of the RCU or for evidence that it will never be created.

2.4 Error Detection

EXTENDED PMD automatically detects two kinds of concurrency-related errors – *deadlock* and *infinite-waiting*. The former is characterized by a cyclic dependency amongst a number of communicating processes, *i.e.* all processes in the deadlocked set solely depend on some other process in the set. This is detected by examining the thread status after each communication event and searching for cycles in the dependency graph.

Infinite-waiting occurs when a communication statement has no potential corre-spondent. On the arrival of a communication event the RCU is searched for such a correspondent. The channel creation and channel assignment statements make this problem non-trivial because channels can be arbitrarily copied and even over-written. A record is maintained noting which agents have access to each channel. Simple data-flow analysis can be used with this record to determine whether an agent is within a given RCU. For example, the IF statement within the agent *philosopher* contains an assignment to a new channel. Clearly the original value of the variable is lost implying that the philosopher agent is no longer in the RCU for the original channel. Instead, the agent is added to the RCU for the newly created channel.

The program in Fig. 1 is a Joyce implementation of the Evolving Philosophers problem[2]. This is an adaptation of Dijkstra's original Dining Philosophers problem in which the activities of five philosophers sitting at a table are followed. Between each philosopher is a fork and at the centre of the table is a bowl of spaghetti. Each philosopher is either thinking, hungry or eating. When hungry he attempts to pick up his neighbouring forks. If either of these are held by his neighbours then he must wait. Once he has both forks he may begin eating and continues to do so until satisfied. He then relinquishes both forks and resumes thinking. The adaptation to the Evolving Philosophers allows the number of philosophers to change dynamically through births and deaths.

Although the forks are resources, in the given implementation they are active agents which repeatedly receive requests for acquisition and return of the fork. The fork agent will only receive an acquisition request if it has the fork. Return is always immediately granted as only one philosopher may have the fork at any time.

To minimize the amount of unnecessary detail we begin with only two philosophers and two forks. The first event in any program is the creation of the root thread. This is followed here by the creation of a fork agent (F1) which immediately enters its while loop and executes a receive on channel *left*. Notice that the channel type is parenthesised in the event.

[agent, root thread, no parent, no params]	% root thread
[agent, thread 1, parent root, 1 param, left]	% fork F1
[receive, thread 1, left(acquire)]	% F1 offers *left*

At this point the error-detection mechanism tries to determine whether the communication event has a correspondent. This is not possible because the agents which use the channel, and therefore form the RCU, have not yet been created. Heuristics can be used to infer this information from the program code but are not considered here. The creation of the other three agents (fork F2, and philosophers P3 and P4) then follow.

In the previous communication F1 offers its fork. Here P3 issues the corresponding communication to acquire it. This corresponds to the first selection in the polling loop. Notice that no polling event is signalled because the communication is not blocked; it immediately executes.

| [send, thread 3, left(acquire)] | % P3 acquires *left* |
| [receive, thread 1, left(release)] | % F1 wants *left* |

P4 now attempts to acquire either of the forks by entering its polling loop. P3 having acquired fork *left* also attempts to acquire *right*. This results in contention; both philosophers attempt to communicate with F2 but only one succeeds (chosen non-deterministically). Here we allow P3 to succeed.

[poll, thread 4, 2 chans, right(!), left(!)]	% P4 wants either
[send, thread 3, right(acquire)]	% P3 requests *right*
[receive, thread 2, right(acquire)]	% F2 releases *right* to P3

Finally, having acquired both forks, P3 eats and releases them (eating does not cause traceable events).

P3 now reaches the conditional (IF) choice point in the program. For demonstration we allow him to take the first selection resulting in the birth of a new philosopher

(P6). A new fork agent is also created which communicates via the channel *new*. Note that this channel identifier is unknown until it is included in some event – here it is included as a parameter in the agent event.

[selection, thread 3, select 1]	% P3 gives birth
[agent, thread 5, parent 3, 1 param, left]	% fork C5
[agent, thread 6, parent 3, 2 param, left, new]	% philosopher P6

After skipping intermediate events we now assume that each philosopher has acquired the fork to his immediate right (*i.e.* P3 acquired *right*, P4 acquired *left*, and P6 acquired *new*). The following events result in deadlock as each philosopher attempts to gain his other fork.

[receive, thread 5, new(acquire)]	% C5 offers *new*
[send, thread 6, new(acquire)]	% P6 acquires it
[poll, thread 3, 2 chans, new(!), right(!)]	% P3 wants either
[receive, thread 2, acquire(right)]	% F2 offers *right*
[selection, thread 3, select 2]	% P3 acquires *right*
[send, thread 3, right(acquire)]	
[receive, thread 1, left(acquire)]	% F1 offers *left*

A cycle in the dependency graph is discovered which involves all six agents. For example, thread 1 is blocked waiting to receive on channel *left*. The only threads capable of matching with this are P4 and P6 (from the RCU of *left*). Thread 1 is thus dependent on 4 and 6. The other threads have similar dependencies and so deadlock is flagged.

3   Conclusion

A methodology has been described for detecting concurrency-related errors in CSP-based languages. The use of static analysis and hardware monitoring minimises any intrusion. The notion of RCU allows efficient detection of these errors. The suitability of EXTENDED PMD for Joyce has been demonstrated.

References

1. Hansen, P (1989), "The Joyce Language Report", In *Software – Practice and Experience*, Vol.19(6), June 1989.
2. Kramer J., Magee J., "The Evolving Philosophers Problem: Dynamic Change Management", In *IEEE Transactions on Software Engineering*, Vol.16(11), November 1990.
3. Arvind, D. K. and Yokotsuka, D., "Debugging concurrent programs using static analysis and run-time hardware monitoring", In Proc. *IEEE Symp. on Parallel and Distributed Processing*, Dallas TX, USA, Dec. 1-5, 1991.

Analysis of an Efficient Distributed
Algorithm for Mutual Exclusion
(Average-Case Analysis of Path Reversal)

Christian LAVAULT
INSA/IRISA (CNRS URA 227)
20 Avenue des Buttes de Coësmes 35043 Rennes Cedex, France.
Email : lavault@irisa.fr

Abstract

The algorithm designed in [12, 15] was the very first distributed algorithm to solve the mutual exclusion problem in complete networks by using a dynamic logical tree structure as its basic distributed data structure, *viz.* a *path reversal transformation* in rooted *n*-node trees ; besides, it was also the first one to achieve a logarithmic average-case message complexity. The present paper proposes a direct and general approach to compute the *moments of the cost of path reversal*. It basically uses one-one correspondences between combinatorial structures and the associated probability generating functions : the expected cost of path reversal is thus proved to be exactly H_{n-1}. Moreover, time and message complexity of the algorithm as well as randomized bounds on its worst-case message complexity in arbitrary networks are also given. The average-case analysis of path reversal and the analysis of this distributed algorithm for mutual exclusion are thus fully completed in the paper. The general techniques used should also prove available and fruitful when adapted to the most efficient recent tree-based distributed algorithms for mutual exclusion which require powerful tools, particularly for average-case analyses.

1 Introduction

A distributed system consists of a collection of geographically dispersed autonomous sites, which are connected by a communication network. The sites — or processes — have no shared memory and can only communicate with one another by means of messages.

In the *mutual exclusion problem*, concurrent access to a shared resource, called the *critical section* (*CS*), must be synchronized such that at any time, only one process can access the (*CS*). Mutual exclusion is crucial for the design of distributed systems. Many problems involving replicated data, atomic commitment, synchronization, and others require that a resource be allocated to a single process at a time. Solutions to this problem often entail high communication costs and are vulnerable to site and communication failures.

Several distributed algorithms exist to implement mutual exclusion [1, 3, 9, 10, 13, 14, 15], etc., they usually are designed for complete or general networks and the most recent ones are often fault tolerant. But, whatever the algorithm, it is either a permission-based, or a token-based algorithm, and thus, it uses appropriate data structures. Lamport's token-based algorithm [9] maintains a waiting queue at each site and the message complexity of the algorithm is $3(n-1)$, where n is the number of sites. Several algorithms were presented later, which reduce the number of messages to $\Theta(n)$ with a smaller constant factor [3, 14]. Maekawa's permission-based algorithm [10] imposes a logical structure on the network and only requires $c\sqrt{n}$ messages to be exchanged (where c is a constant which varies between 3 and 5).

The token-based algorithm $\mathcal{A}$ (see [12, 15]), which is analysed in the present paper, is the first mutual exclusion algorithm for complete networks which achieves a logarithmic average message complexity ; besides, it is the very first one to use a *tree-based* structure, namely a path reversal, as its basic distributed data structure. More recently, various mutual exclusion algorithms (*e.g.* [1, 13], etc.) have been designed which use either the same data structure, or some very close tree-based data structures. They usually also provide efficient (possibly fault tolerant) solutions to the mutual exclusion problem.

The general model used in [12, 15] to design algorithms $\mathcal{A}$ assumes the underlying communication links and the processes to be reliable. Message propagation delay is finite but impredictable and the messages are not assumed to obey the FIFO rule. A process entering the (*CS*) releases it within a finite delay. Moreover, the communication network is *complete*. To ensure a fair mutual exclusion, each node in the network maintains two pointers, *Last* and *Next*, at any time. *Last* indicates the node to which requests for (*CS*) access should be forwarded ; *Next* points to the node to which access permission must be forwarded after the current node has executed its own (*CS*). As described below, the dynamic updating of these two pointers involves two distributed data structures : a waiting queue, and a *dynamic* logical rooted tree structure which is nothing but a path reversal. Algorithm $\mathcal{A}$ is thus very efficient in terms of average-case message complexity, *viz.* $H_{n-1} = \ln n + O(1)$[1].

Let us recall now how the two data structures at hand are actually involved in the algorithm, which is fully designed in [12, 15]. Algorithm $\mathcal{A}$ uses the notion of *token*. A node can enter its (*CS*) only if it has the token. However, unlike the concept of a token circulating continuously in the system, the token is sent from one node to another if and only if a request is made for it. The token (also called *privilege message*) consists of a queue of processes which are requesting the (*CS*). The token circulates strictly according to the order in which the requests have been made.

The first data structure used in $\mathcal{A}$ is a *waiting queue* which is updated by each node after executing its own (*CS*). The waiting queue of requesting processes is maintained at the node containing the token and is transferred along with the token whenever the token is transferred. The requesting nodes receive the token strictly according to the order in the queue. Each node knows its next node in the waiting queue only if the *Next* exists. The head is the node which owns the token and the tail is the last node which requested the (*CS*). Thus, a path is constructed in such a way that each request message is transmitted to the tail. Then, either the tail is in the (*CS*) and it let the requesting node enter it, or the tail waits for the token, in which case the requesting node is appended to the tail.

The second data structure involved in algorithm $\mathcal{A}$ gives the path to go to the tail : it is a logical rooted ordered tree. A node which requests the (*CS*) sends its message to its *Last*, and, from *Last* to *Last*, the request is transmitted to the tail of the waiting queue. In such a structure, every node knows only its *Last*. Moreover, if the requesting node is not the last, the logical tree structure is transformed : the requesting node is the new *Last* and the nodes which are located between the requesting node and the last will gain the new last as *Last*. This is typically a logical transformation of *path reversal*, which is performed at a node x of an ordered n-node tree T_n consisting of a root with $n-1$ children. These transformations $\varphi(T_n)$ are performed to keep a dynamic decentralized path towards the tail of the waiting queue.

In [7], Ginat, Sleator and Tarjan derived a tight upper bound of $\lg n$ for the cost of path reversal in using the notion of *amortized cost* of a path reversal. Actually, by means of combinatorial and algebraic methods on the Dycklanguage (namely by encoding oriented ordered trees T_n with Dyckwords), the average number of messages used by algorithm $\mathcal{A}$ was obtained in [12]. By contrast, the present paper uses direct and general derivation methods involving one-to-one correspondences between combinatorial structures such as priority queues, binary tournament trees and permutations. Moreover, a full analysis of algorithm $\mathcal{A}$ is completed in this paper from the computation of the first and second moments of the cost of path reversal ; *viz.* we derive the expected and worst-case message complexity of $\mathcal{A}$ as well as its average and worst-case waiting time. Note that the average-case analysis of other efficient mutual exclusion tree-based algorithms (*e.g.* [1, 13], among others) may easily be adapted from the present one, since the data structures involved in such algorithms are quite close to those of algorithm $\mathcal{A}$. The analysis of the average waiting time using simple birth-and-death process methods and asymptotics, it could thus also apply easily to the waiting time analysis of the above-mentioned algorithms. In this sense, the analyses proposed in this paper are quite general indeed.

The paper is organized as follows. In Section 2, we define the path reversal transformation performed in a tree T_n and give a constructive proof of the one-one correspondence between priority queues and the combinatorial structure of trees T_n. In Section 3, probability generating functions are computed which yield the exact expected cost of path reversal : H_{n-1}, and the second moment of the cost. Section 4 is devoted to the computation of the waiting time and the expected waiting time of algorithm $\mathcal{A}$. In Section 5, more extended complexity results are given, *viz.* randomized bounds on the worst-case message complexity of the algorithm in *arbitrary* networks. In the Appendix, we propose a second proof technique which directly yields the exact expected cost of path reversal by solving a straight and simple recurrent equation.

2   One-one Correspondences between Combinatorial Structures

We first define a path reversal transformation in T_n and its *cost* (see [7]). Then we point out some one-to-one correspondences between combinatorial objects and structures which are relevant to the problem of computing the average cost of path reversal. Such one-to-one tools are used in Section 3 to compute this

---

[1]Throughout the paper, lg denotes the base two logarithm and ln the natural logarithm.
$H_n = \sum_{i=1}^{n} 1/i$ denotes the n-th harmonic number with the asymptotic value :
$H_n = \ln n + \gamma + 1/2n + O(n^{-2})$ (where γ is Euler's constant : $\gamma = 0.577\ldots$).

expected cost and its variance by means of corresponding probability generating functions.

2.1 Path Reversal

Let T_n be a rooted n-node tree, or an ordered tree with n nodes — according to either [7], or [8, page 306]. A *path reversal* at a node x in T_n is performed by traversing the path from x to the tree root r and making x the parent — or pointer *Last* — of each node on the path other than x. Thus x becomes the new tree root. The *cost* of the reversal is the number of edges on the path reversed. Path reversal is a variant of the standard path compression algorithm for maintaining disjoint sets under union.

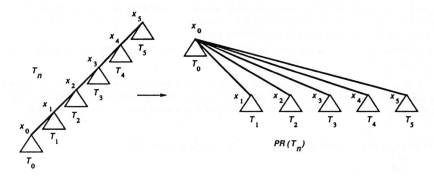

Figure 1: Path reversal φ_{x_0}. The T_i's denote (left/right) subtrees of T_n.

The average cost of a path reversal performed on an initial ordered n-node tree T_n which consists of a root with $n-1$ descendants (or *children*, as in [7]) is the expected number of edges on the paths reversed in T_n (see Figure 1). In words, it is the *expected height of such reversed trees* $\varphi(T_n)$, provided that we let the height of a tree root be 1 : *viz.* the *height* of a node x in T_n is thus defined as being the number of nodes on the path from the node x to the root r of T_n.

It turns out that the average number of messages used in $\mathcal{A}$ is actually the expected cost of a path reversal performed on such initial ordered n-node trees T_n which consist of a root with $n-1$ children. This is indeed the average number of changes of the variable *Last* which builds the dynamic data structure of path reversal used in algorithm $\mathcal{A}$.

2.2 Priority queues, Tournament Trees and Permutations

Whenever two combinatorial structures are counted by the same number, there exist one-one mappings between the two structures. Explicit one-to-one correspondences between combinatorial representations provide coding and decoding algorithms between the stuctures. We now need the following definitions of some combinatorial structures which are closely connected with path reversal and involved in the computation of its cost.

Definitions and Notations 2.1

(i) Let $[n]$ be the set $\{1, 2, \ldots, n\}$. A *permutation* is a *one-one mapping* $\sigma : [n] \to [n]$; we write $\sigma \in S_n$, where S_n is the symmetric group over $[n]$.

(ii) A *binary tournament tree* of size n is a binary n-node tree whose internal nodes are labeled with consecutive integers of $[n]$, in such a way that the root is labeled 1, and all labels are decreasing (*bottom-up*) along each branch. Let $\mathcal{T}_n$ denote the set of all binary tournament trees of size n. $\mathcal{T}_n$ also denotes the set of tournament representations of all permutations $\sigma \in S_n$, considered as elements of $[n]^n$, since the correspondence $\tau : S_n \to \mathcal{T}_n$ is one-one (see [16] for a detailed proof). Note that this one-to-one mapping implies that $|\mathcal{T}_n| = n!$

(iii) A *priority queue* of size n is a set Q_n of keys ; each key $K \in Q_n$ has an associated priority $p(K)$ which is an arbitrary integer. To avoid cumbersome notations, we identify Q_n with the set of priorities of its keys. Strictly speaking, this is a set with repetitions since priorities need not be all distincts. However, it is convenient to ignore this technicality and assume *distinct priorities*. The simplest representation of a priority queue of size n is then a sequence $s = (p_1, p_2, \ldots, p_n)$ of the priorities of Q_n, kept in their order of arrival. Assume the $n!$ possible orders of arrival of the p_i's to be equally likely, a priority queue Q_n (*i.e.* a sequence s of p_i's) is defined as random *iff* it is associated to a random order of the p_i's. There is a one-to-one correspondence between the set T_n of all the n-node binary tournament trees and the set of all the priority queues Q_n of size n. To each one sequence of priorities $s = (p_1, \ldots, p_n) \in Q_n$, we associate a binary tournament tree $\gamma(s) = T \in T_n$ by the following rules : let $\mathrm{m} = \min(s)$, we then write $s = \ell\,\mathrm{m}\,r$; the binary tree $T \in T_n$ possesses m as root, $\gamma(\ell)$ as left subtree and $\gamma(r)$ as right subtree. The rules are applied repeatedly to all the left and right subsequences of s, and from the root of T to the leaves of T ; by convention, we let $\gamma(\emptyset) = \Lambda$ (where Λ denotes the empty binary tree). The correspondence γ is obviously one-one (see [6] for a fully detailed constructive proof).

We shall thus use binary tournaments T_n to represent the permutations of S_n as well as the priority queues Q_n of size n.

(iv) If $T \in T_n$ is a binary tournament, its *right branch* $RB(T)$ is the increasing sequence of priorities found on the path starting at the root of T and repeatedly going to the right subtree. The *bottom* of $RB(T)$ is the node having no right son. The *left branch* $LB(T)$ of T is defined in a symmetrical manner.

2.3   The one-one Correspondence between Q_n and T_n

We now give a constuctive proof of a *one-to-one correspondence* mapping the given combinatorial structure of ordered trees T_n (as defined in the Introduction) onto the priority queues Q_n.

Theorem 2.1 *There is a one-to-one correspondence between the priority queues of size n, Q_n, and the ordered n-node trees T_n which consist of a root with $n-1$ children.*

Proof   There are many representations of priority queues Q_n ; let us consider the n-node *binary heap* structure, which is very simple and perfectly suitable for the constructive proof.

- First, a *binary heap* of size n is an *essentially complete binary tree*. A binary tree is *essentially complete* if each of its internal nodes possesses exactly two children, with the possible exception of a unique *special* node situated on level $(h-1)$ (where h denotes the height of the heap), which may possess only a left child and no right child. Moreover, all the leaves are either on level h, or else they are on levels h and $(h-1)$, and no leaf is found on level $(h-1)$ to the left of an internal node at the same level. The unique special node, if it exists, is to the right of all the other level $(h-1)$ internal nodes in the subtree.
  Besides, each tree node in a binary heap contains one item, with the items arranged in heap order (*i.e.* the priority queue ordering) : the key of the item in the parent node is strictly smaller than the key of the item in any descendant's node. Thus the root is located at position 1 and contains an item of minimum key. If we number the nodes of such a essentially complete binary tree from 1 to n in heap order and identify nodes with numbers, the parent of the node located at position x is located at $\lfloor x/2 \rfloor$. Similarly, The left son of node x is located at $2x$ and its right son at $\min\{2x+1, n\}$. We can thus represent each node by an integer and the entire binary heap by a map from $[n]$ onto the items : the binary heap with n nodes fits well into locations $1, \ldots, n$. This forces a breadth-first, left-to-right filling of the binary tree, *i.e.* a heap or priority queue ordering.

- Next, it is well-known that any ordered tree with n nodes may easily be transformed into a binary tree by the *natural correspondence* between ordered trees and binary trees. The corresponding binary tree is obtained by linking together the brothering nodes of the given ordered tree and removing vertical links except from a father to its first (left) son.
  Conversely, it is easy to see that any binary tree may be represented as an ordered tree by reversing the process. The correspondence is thus one-one (see [8, Vol. 1, page 333]).

Note that the construction of a binary heap of size n can be carried out in a linear time, and more precisely in $\Theta(n)$ sift-up operations.

Now, to each one sequence of priorities $s = (p_1, \ldots, p_n) \in Q_n$, we may associate a unique n-node tree $\alpha(s) = T_n$ in the natural breadth-first, left-to-right order ; by convention, we also let $\alpha(\emptyset) = \Lambda$. In such a representation, $T_n = \alpha(s)$ is then an ordered n-node tree the ordering of which is the priority queue (or heap) order, and it is thus built as an essentially complete binary heap of size n. The correspondence α naturally represents the priority queues Q_n of size n as ordered trees T_n with n nodes.

Conversely, to any ordered tree T_n with n nodes, we may associate a binary tree with heap ordered nodes, that is an essentially complete binary heap. Hence, there exists a correspondence β mapping any given ordered n-node tree T_n onto a unique sequence of priorities $s = \beta(T_n) \in Q_n$; by convention we again let $\beta(\Lambda) = \emptyset$. The correspondence is one-one, and it is easily seen that mappings α and β are respective inverses. $\quad\square$

Let binary tournament trees represent each one of the above structures. Any operation can thus be performed as if dealing with ordered trees T_n, whereas binary tournament trees or permutations are really manipulated. More precisely, since we know that $T_n \longleftrightarrow Q_n \longleftrightarrow T_n \longleftrightarrow S_n$, the cost of path reversal performed on initial n-node trees T_n which consist of a root with $n-1$ children is *transported* from the T_n's onto the tournament trees $T \in T_n$ and onto the permutations $\sigma \in S_n$. In the following definitions (see Section 3.1 below), we therefore let $\varphi(\sigma) \in S_n$ denote the "reversed" permutation which corresponds to the reversed tree T_n.

3 Expected Cost of Path Reversal, Average Message Complexity of $\mathcal{A}$

It is fully detailed in the Introduction how the two data structures at hand are actually involved in algorithm $\mathcal{A}$ and the design of the algorithm takes place in [12, 15].

3.1 The Analysis

From this point the *first moment of the cost of path reversal*, $\varphi : T_n \to T_n$, can be derived. However, if we also desire to know the moments of the cost, we do need the probability generating function of the probabilities $p_{n,k}$, defined as follows.

Let $h(T_n)$ denote the height of T_n, *i.e.* the number of nodes on the path from the deepest node in T_n to the root of T_n, and let $T \in T_{n-1}$.

$$p_{n,k} = \Pr\{cost\ of\ path\ reversal\ for\ T_n\ is\ k\} = \Pr\{h(\varphi(T)) = k\}$$

is the probability that the tournament tree $\varphi(T)$ is of height k. We also have

$$p_{n,k} = \Pr\{k\ changes\ occur\ in\ the\ variable\ Last\ of\ algorithm\ \mathcal{A}\}.$$

More precisely, let a **swap** be any interchanged pair of adjacent prime cycles (see [8, Vol. 3, pages 28-30]) in a permutation σ of $[n-1]$ to obtain the "reversed" permutation $\varphi_x(\sigma)$ corresponding to the path reversal performed at a node $x \in T_n$, that is any interchange which occurs in the relative order of the elements of $\varphi_x(\sigma)$ from the one of σ's elements, and let N be the number of these swaps occurring from $\sigma \in S_{n-1}$ to $\varphi_x(\sigma)$, then,

$$p_{n,k} = \frac{1}{(n-1)!} [\ number\ of\ \sigma \in S_{n-1}\ for\ which\ N = k\ ],$$

since the cost of a path reversal at the root of an ordered tree such as T_n is zero.

Lemma 3.1 *Let* $P_n(z) = \sum_{k \geq 0} p_{n,k} z^k$ *be the probability generating function of the* $p_{n,k}$ *'s. We have the following identity :*

$$P_n(z) = \prod_{j=1}^{n-1} \frac{z + j - 1}{j}.$$

Proof We have $p_{1,0} = 1$ and $p_{1,k} = 0$ for all $k > 0$.

A fundamental point in this derivation is that we are averaging not over all tournament trees $T \in \mathcal{T}_{n-1}$, but *over all possible orders* of the elements of S_{n-1}. Thus, every permutation of $(n-1)$ elements with k swaps corresponds to $(n-2)$ permutations of $(n-2)$ elements with k swaps and one permutation of $(n-2)$ elements with $(k-1)$ swaps. This leads directly to the recurrence

$$(n-1)! \, p_{n,k} = (n-2)(n-2)! \, p_{n-1,k} + (n-2)! \, p_{n-1,k-1},$$

or

$$p_{n,k} = \left(1 - \frac{1}{n-1}\right) p_{n-1,k} + \left(\frac{1}{n-1}\right) p_{n-1,k-1}. \tag{1}$$

Consider any permutation $\sigma = \langle \sigma_1 \ldots \sigma_{n-1} \rangle$ of $[n-1]$. Formula (1) can also be derived directly with the argument that the probability of N being equal to k is the simultaneous occurrence of $\sigma_i = j$ $(1 \le i, j \le n-1)$ and N being equal to $k-1$ for the remaining elements of σ, *plus* the simultaneous occurrence of $\sigma_i \ne j$ $(1 \le i, j \le n-1)$ and N being equal to k for the remaining elements of σ. Therefore,

$$\begin{aligned} p_{n,k} &= \Pr\{\sigma_i = j\} \times p_{n-1,k-1} + \Pr\{\sigma_i \ne j\} \times p_{n-1,k} \\ &= [1/(n-1)] \, p_{n-1,k-1} + [1 - 1/(n-1)] \, p_{n-1,k}. \end{aligned}$$

Using now the probability generating function $P_n(z) = \sum_{k \ge 0} p_{n,k} z^k$, we get after multiplying (1) by z^k and summing,

$$(n-1) P_n(z) = z P_{n-1}(z) + (n-2) P_{n-1}(z),$$

which yields

$$\begin{aligned} P_n(z) &= \frac{z+n-2}{n-1} P_{n-1}(z) \\ P_1(z) &= z. \end{aligned} \tag{2}$$

The latter recurrence (2) telescopes immediately to

$$P_n(z) = \prod_{j=1}^{n-1} \frac{z+j-1}{j}.$$

□

Remark The property proved by Trehel that the average number of messages required by $\mathcal{A}$ is exactly the number of nodes at height 2 in the reversed ordered trees $\varphi(T_n)$ (see [12]) is hidden in the definition of the $p_{n,k}$'s. As a matter of fact, the number of permutations of $[n]$ which contains exactly 2 prime cycles is $\begin{bmatrix} n \\ 2 \end{bmatrix} = (n-1)! \, H_{n-1}$ (see [8]), whence the result.

Theorem 3.1 *The expected cost of path reversal and the average message complexity of algorithm $\mathcal{A}$ is* $E[C_n] = \overline{C_n} = H_{n-1}$, *with variance* $\text{var}(C_n) = H_{n-1} - H_{n-1}^{(2)}$. *Asymptotically, for large n,*

$$\overline{C_n} = \ln n + \gamma + O(n^{-1}) \text{ and } \text{var}(C_n) = \ln n + \gamma - \pi^2/6 + O(n^{-1}).$$

Proof By Lemma 3.1, the probability generating function $P_n(z)$ may be regarded as the product of a number of very simple probability generating functions ($P.G.F.$s), namely, for $1 \le j \le n-1$,

$$P_n(z) = \prod_{1 \le j \le n-1} \Pi_j(z), \text{ with } \Pi_j(z) = \frac{j-1}{j} + \frac{z}{j}.$$

Therefore, we need only compute moments for the $P.G.F.$ $\Pi_j(z)$, and then sum for $j = 1$ to $n-1$. This is a classical property of $P.G.F.$s that one may transform products to sums.

Now, $\Pi'_j(1) = 1/j$ and $\Pi''_j(1) = 0$, hence

$$E[C_n] = \overline{C_n} = P'_n(1) = \sum_{j=1}^{n-1} \Pi'_j(1) = H_{n-1}.$$

Moreover, the variance of C_n is

$$var(C_n) = P''_n(1) + P'_n(1) - P'^2_n(1),$$

and thus,

$$var(C_n) = \sum_{j=1}^{n-1} \frac{1}{j} - \sum_{j=1}^{n-1} \frac{1}{j^2} = H_{n-1} - H^{(2)}_{n-1}.$$

Since $H^{(2)}_{n-1} = \pi^2/6 - 1/n + O(n^{-2})$ as $n \to +\infty$, and by the asymptotic expansion of H_n, the asymptotic values of $\overline{C_n}$ and of $var(C_n)$ are easily obtained. Recall that Euler's constant is $\gamma = 0.57721...$, thus $\gamma - \pi^2/6 = -1.6772...$

Hence, $\overline{C_n} = 0.693...\lg n + O(1)$, and $var(C_n) = 0.693...\lg n + O(1)$. □

Note also that, by a generalization of the central limit theorem to sums of independent but nonidentical random variables, it follows that

$$\frac{C_n - \overline{C_n}}{(\ln n - 1.06772...)^{1/2}}$$

converges to the normal distribution, as $n \to +\infty$.

Proposition 3.1 *The worst-case message complexity of algorithm $\mathcal{A}$ is $O(n)$.*

Proof Let Δ be the *maximum* communication delay time in the network and let Σ be the *minimum* delay time for a process to enter, proceed and release the critical section. Set $q = \lceil \Delta/\Sigma \rceil$, the number of messages used in $\mathcal{A}$ is at most $(n-1) + (n-1)q = (n-1)(q+1) = O(n)$. □

Remarks

- The one-to-one correspondence between ordered trees with $(n+1)$ nodes and the words of lenght $2n$ in the Dycklanguage with one type of bracket is used in [12] to compute the average message complexity of $\mathcal{A}$. Several properties and results connecting the depth of a Dyckword and the height of the ordered n-node trees can be derived from the one-to-one correspondences between combinatorial structures involved in the proof of Theorem 2.1.

- In the first variant of algorithm $\mathcal{A}$ (see [15]) which is analysed here, a node never stores more than one request of some other node and hence it only requires $O(\lg n)$ bits to store the variables, and the message size is also $O(\lg n)$ bits. This is not true of the second variant of algorithm $\mathcal{A}$ (designed in [11]). Though the constant factor within the order of magnitude of the average number of messages is claimed to be slightly improved (from 1 downto 0.4), the token now consists of a queue of processes requesting the critical section. Since at most $n-1$ processes belong to the requesting queue, the size of the token is $O(n \lg n)$. Therefore, whereas the average message complexity is slightly improved (up to a constant factor), the message size increases from $O(\lg n)$ bits to $O(n \lg n)$ bits. The bit complexity is thus much larger in the second variant [11] of $\mathcal{A}$. Moreover, the state information stored at each node is also $O(n \lg n)$ bits in the second variant, which again is much larger than in the first variant of $\mathcal{A}$.

4   Waiting Time and Average Waiting Time of Algorithm $\mathcal{A}$

Algorithm $\mathcal{A}$ is designed with the notion of *token*. Recall that a node can enter its critical section only if it has the token. However, unlike the concept of a token circulating continuously in the system, it is sent from one node to another if and only if a request is made for it. The token thus circulates strictly according to the order in which the requests have been made. The queue is updated by each node after executing its own critical section. The queue of requesting processes is maintained at the node containing the token and is transferred along with the token whenever the token is transferred. The requesting nodes receive the token strictly according to the order in the queue.

In order to simplify the analysis, the following is assumed :

- When a node is not in the critical section or is not already in the waiting queue, it generates a request for the token at Poisson rate λ, *i.e. the arrival process is a Poisson process.*

- Each node spends a constant time (σ time units) in the critical section, *i.e. the rate of service is $\mu = 1/\sigma$.* Suppose we would not assume a constant time spent by each process in the critical section. σ could then be regarded as the maximum time spent in the critical section, since any node executes its critical section within a finite time.

- The time for any message to travel from one node to any other node in the complete network is *constant* and is equal to δ (communication delay). Since the message delay is finite, we assume here that every message originated at any node is delivered to its destination in a *bounded* amount of time : in words, the network is assumed to be *synchronous*

At any instant of time, a node has to be in one of the following two states :

1. *Critical state.*
   The node is waiting in the queue for the token or is executing its critical section. In this state, it cannot generate any request for the token, and thus the rate of generation of request for entering the critical section by this node is zero.

2. *Noncritical state.*
   The node is not waiting for the token and is not executing the critical section. In this state, this node generates a request for the token at Poisson rate λ.

4.1 Waiting Time of Algorithm $\mathcal{A}$

Let $\mathcal{S}_k$ denote the system state when exactly k nodes are in the waiting queue, including the one in the critical section, and let P_k denote the probability that the system is in state $\mathcal{S}_k$, $0 \leq k \leq n$. In this state, only the remaining $n - k$ nodes can generate a request. Thus, the net rate of request generation in such a situation is $(n - k)\lambda$. Now the service rate is constant at μ as long as k is positive, *i.e.* as long as at least one node is there to execute its critical section and the service rate is 0 when $k = 0$. The probability that during the time period $(t, t + h)$ more than one change of state occur at any node is $o(h)$. By using a simple birth-and-death process (see Feller, [4]), the following theorem is obtained :

Theorem 4.1 *When there are k ($k > 0$) nodes in the queue, the waiting time of a node for the token is $w_k = (k - 1)(\sigma + \delta) + \sigma/2$, where σ denotes the time to execute the critical section and δ the communication delay.*
The worst-case waiting time is $w_{worst} \leq (n - 1)(\sigma + \delta) + \sigma/2 = O(n)$.
The exact expected waiting time of the algorithm is

$$\overline{w} = (\sigma + \delta)(\overline{n} - nP_n) - (\delta + \sigma/2)(1 - P_0 - P_n) + 2\delta P_0,$$

where $\overline{n}$ denotes the average number of nodes in the queue and the critical section.

Proof Following equations hold,

$$P_0(t + h) = P_0(t)(1 - n\lambda h) + P_1(t)[1 - (n - 1)\lambda h](\mu h) + o(h)$$

$$\frac{1}{h}(P_0(t + h) - P_0(t)) = -n\lambda P_0(t) + \mu P_1(t) - (n - 1)\lambda \mu h P_1(t). \tag{3}$$

Under steady state equilibrium, $P_0'(t) = 0$ and hence,

$$\mu P_1(t) - n\lambda P_0(t) = 0, \text{ and } P_1(t) = n(\lambda/\mu)P_0(t). \tag{4}$$

Similarly, for any k such that $1 \leq k \leq n$, one can write :

$$
\begin{aligned}
P_k(t+h) = \ & P_k(t)\left[1-(n-k)\lambda h\right](1-\mu h) + \\
& P_{k-1}(t)\left[(n-k+1)\lambda h\right](1-\mu h) + \\
& P_{k+1}(t)\left[1-(n-k-1)\lambda h\right](\mu h) + o(h),
\end{aligned}
$$

and

$$
\frac{1}{h}\left(P_k(t+h)-P_k(t)\right) = -(n-k)\lambda P_k(t) + (n-k+1)\lambda P_{k-1}(t) + \mu P_{k+1}(t) - \mu P_k(t).
$$

Classically, set $\rho = \lambda/\mu$. Proceeding similarly, since under steady state equilibrium $P'_k(t) = 0$:

$$
P_{k+1}(t) = \left[1+(n-k)\rho\right]P_k(t) - (n-k+1)\rho, \tag{5}
$$

and, for any k $(1 \leq k \leq n)$,

$$
P_k(t) = \frac{n!}{(n-k)!}\,\rho^k P_0(t) = n^{\underline{k}}\rho^k P_0(t). \tag{6}
$$

For notational brevity, let P_k denote $P_k(t)$. By Eq. (6), we can now compute the average number of nodes in the queue and the critical section as

$$
\bar{n} = \sum_{k=0}^{n} k P_k = P_0 \sum_{k=0}^{n} k n^{\underline{k}}\rho^k.
$$

Since the system will always be in one of the $(n+1)$ states $S_0, \ldots, S_n$, $\sum_k P_k = 1$. Now using expressions of P_k in terms of P_0 yields

$$
\sum_{k=0}^{n} P_k = P_0 \sum_{k=0}^{n} n^{\underline{k}}\rho^k = 1.
$$

Thus,

$$
P_0 = \left(\sum_{k=0}^{n} n^{\underline{k}}\rho^k\right)^{-1} \quad \text{and} \quad P_i = \frac{n^{\underline{i}}\rho^i}{\left(\sum_{k=0}^{n} n^{\underline{k}}\rho^k\right)}. \tag{7}
$$

Let there be k nodes in the system, when a node i generates a request. Then $(k-1)$ nodes execute their critical section, and one node executes the remaining part of its critical section before i gets the token. Thus, when there are k $(k > 0)$ nodes in the queue, the waiting time of a node for the token is

$$
\begin{aligned}
w_k = (k-1)[\ & time\ to\ execute\ the\ critical\ section\ +\ communication\ delay\ + \\
& average\ remaining\ execution\ time\,],\ or
\end{aligned}
$$

$$
w_k = (k-1)(\sigma+\delta) + \sigma/2 \tag{8}
$$

(where σ denotes the time to execute the critical section and δ the communication delay).

When there are zero node in the queue, the waiting time is $w_0 = 2\delta = total\ communication\ delay\ of\ one\ request\ and\ one\ token\ message$. Hence the expected waiting time is

$$
\begin{aligned}
E[w] = \bar{w} &= \sum_{k=0}^{n-1} w_k P_k = 2\delta P_0 + \sum_{k=1}^{n-1}\left\{(k-1)(\sigma+\delta) + \frac{\sigma}{2}\right\}P_k, \\
&= (\sigma+\delta)\sum_{k=1}^{n-1} k P_k - (\sigma+\delta)\sum_{k=1}^{n-1} P_k + \sigma/2\sum_{k=1}^{n-1} P_k + 2\delta P_0,
\end{aligned}
$$

and

$$
\bar{w} = (\sigma+\delta)(\bar{n}-n P_n) - (\delta+\sigma/2)(1-P_0-P_n) + 2\delta P_0. \tag{9}
$$

By Eq. (9), we know the exact value of the expected waiting time of a node for the token in algorithm $\mathcal{A}$. Moreover, by Eq. (8), the worst-case waiting time is $w_{worst} \leq (n-1)(\sigma+\delta) + \sigma/2 = O(n)$. □

4.2 Average Waiting Time of Algorithm $\mathcal{A}$

The above computation of $\overline{w}$ yields the asymptotic form of an upper bound on the average waiting time $\overline{w}$ of $\mathcal{A}$.

Theorem 4.2 *If $\rho < 1$, the average waiting time of a node for the token in $\mathcal{A}$ is asymptotically (as $n \to +\infty$),*

$$\overline{w} \leq (\sigma + \delta) \left[n(1 - 2e^{-1/\rho}) \right] - (\delta + \sigma/2)(1 - e^{-1/\rho}) + O\left((\sigma/2 + 3\delta)e^{-1/\rho} \frac{\rho^{-n}}{n!} \right).$$

Proof Assume $\rho = \lambda/\mu < 1$. In Eq. (9) we can bound $\overline{w}$ from above when n is large as follows :

First, $1 - P_0 - P_n = 1 - P_0 - n!\rho^n P_0$, where $P_0 = \left(\sum_{i=0}^{n} n^i \rho^i \right)^{-1}$.

Since $\rho < 1$,

$$P_0 \leq \left(n!\rho^n e^{1/\rho} \right)^{-1},$$

and, for large n,

$$1 - P_0 - P_n \leq 1 - \frac{1 + n!\rho^n}{n!\rho^n e^{1/\rho}} \leq 1 - \frac{1}{n!\rho^n e^{1/\rho}} - e^{-1/\rho}. \tag{10}$$

Next,

$$P_n = n!\rho^n P_0 \geq \frac{n!\rho^n}{n!\rho^n e^{1/\rho}} = e^{-1/\rho},$$

and

$$\overline{n} - nP_n = P_0 \sum_{i=1}^{n} in^i \rho^i - nP_n.$$

Now,

$$
\begin{aligned}
P_0 \sum_{i=1}^{n} in^i \rho^i &= \frac{\sum_{j=1}^{n}(n-j)\rho^{-j}/j!}{\sum_{j=0}^{n}\rho^{-j}/j!} \\
&= n - \frac{n}{\sum_{j=0}^{n}\rho^{-j}/j!} - \frac{\sum_{j=1}^{n} j\rho^{-j}/j!}{\sum_{j=0}^{n}\rho^{-j}/j!} \\
&\leq n - \frac{n}{e^{1/\rho}} - \frac{1}{n!\rho e^{1/\rho}}.
\end{aligned}
$$

Therefore,

$$\overline{n} - nP_n \leq n - ne^{-1/\rho} - \rho^{-1}e^{-1/\rho}/n! - ne^{-1/\rho} \leq n(1 - 2e^{-1/\rho}) - \rho^{-1}e^{-1/\rho}/n! \tag{11}$$

Thus, by equations (9), (10) and (11), we have

$$\overline{w} \leq (\sigma + \delta) \left[n\left(1 - 2e^{-1/\rho}\right) - \frac{1}{n!\rho e^{1/\rho}} \right]$$

$$- (\delta + \sigma/2) \left[1 - \frac{1}{n!\rho^n e^{1/\rho}} - e^{-1/\rho} \right] + 2\delta \left(\sum_{i=0}^{n} n^i \rho^i \right)^{-1},$$

which yields the desired upper bound for $\rho < 1$, when n is large :

$$\overline{w} \leq (\sigma + \delta) \left[n(1 - 2e^{-1/\rho}) \right] - (\delta + \sigma/2)(1 - e^{-1/\rho}) + O\left((\sigma/2 + 3\delta)\, e^{-1/\rho} \frac{\rho^{-n}}{n!} \right).$$

$\square$

Corollary 4.1 *If $\rho < 1$, and irrespective of the values of σ and δ, the worst-case waiting time of a node for the token in $\mathcal{A}$ is $O(n)$ when n is large.*

5   Randomized Bounds for the Message Complexity of $\mathcal{A}$ in Arbitrary Networks

The network considered now is general. The exact cost of a path reversal in a rooted tree T_n is therefore much more difficult to compute. The message complexity of the variant $\mathcal{A}'$ of algorithm $\mathcal{A}$ for arbitrary networks is of course modified likewise.

Let $G = (V, E)$ denote the underlying graph of an arbitrary network, and let $d(x, y)$ the distance between two given vertices x and y of V. The diameter of the graph G is defined as

$$D = \max_{x,y \in V} d(x, y).$$

Lemma 5.1 *Let $|V| = n$ be the number of nodes in G. The number of messages M_n used in the algorithm $\mathcal{A}'$ for arbitrary networks of size n is such that $0 \leq M_n \leq 2D$.*

Proof Each request for critical section is at least satisfied by sending zero messages (whenever the request is made by the root), up to at most $2D$ messages, whenever the whole network must be traversed by the request message. □

In order to bound D, we make use of some results of Béla Bollobás about random graphs [2] which yield the following summary results :

Summary Results

1. Consider *very sparse* networks, *e.g.* for which the underlying graph G is just hardly connected. For *almost every* such network, the worst-case message complexity of the algorithm is $\Theta(\frac{\lg n}{\lg \lg n})$.

2. For *almost every* sparse networks (*e.g.* such that $M = O(n/2)$), the worst-case message complexity of the algorithm is $\Theta(\lg n)$.

3. For *almost every* r-regular network, the worst-case message complexity of the algorithm is $O(\lg n)$.

6   Conclusions and Open Problems

The waiting time of algorithm $\mathcal{A}$ is of course highly dependent on the values of many system parameters such as the service time σ and the communication delay δ. Yet, the performance of $\mathcal{A}$, analysed in terms of average and worst-case complexity measures — time and message complexity —, is *quite comparable* with the best existing distributed algorithms for mutual exclusion (*e.g.* [1, 13]). However, algorithm $\mathcal{A}$ is only designed for complete networks and is *a priori* not fault tolerant, although a fault tolerant version of $\mathcal{A}$ could easily be worked out. The use of direct one-one correspondences between combinatorial structures and associated probability generating functions proves here a powerful tool to derive the expected and the second moment of the cost of path reversal ; such combinatorial and analytic methods are more and more required to complete the average-case analyses of distributed algorithms and data structures [5]. From such a point of view, the full analysis of algorithm $\mathcal{A}$ completed herein is quite general. Nevertheless, the simulation results obtained in the experimental tests performed in [15] also show a very good agreement with the average-case complexity value computed in the present paper.

Let $\mathcal{C}$ be the class of distributed tree-based algorithms for mutual exclusion, em e.g. [1, 13]. There still remain open questions about $\mathcal{A}$. In particular, is the algorithm $\mathcal{A}$ average-case optimal in the class $\mathcal{C}$? By the tight upper bound derived in [7], we know that the amortized cost of path reversal is $O(\lg n)$. It is therefore likely that the average complexity of $\mathcal{A}$ is $\Theta(\lg n)$, and whence that algorithm $\mathcal{A}$ is average-case optimal in its class $\mathcal{C}$. The same argument can be derived from the fact that the average height of n-node binary search trees is $\Theta(\lg n)$ [5].

References

[1] AGRAWAL D., A. EL ABBADI, An Efficient and Fault Tolerant Solution for Distributed Mutual Exclusion, *ACM Transaction on Computer Systems, Vol. 9, No 1, 1-20*, February 1991.

[2] BOLLOBÁS B., The Evolution of Sparse Graphs, *Graph Theory and Combinatorics, 35-57*, Academic Press 1984.

[3] CARVALHO O.S.F., G. ROUCAIROL, On Mutual Exclusion in Computer Networks, *Comm. of the ACM, Vol. 26, No 2, 145-147*, February 1983.

[4] FELLER W., *An Introduction to Probability Theory and its Applications*, 3rd Edition, Vol. I, Wiley, 1968.

[5] FLAJOLET P., J. S. VITTER, Average-Case Analysis of Algorithms and Data Structures, *Res. Rep. INRIA No 718*, August 1987.

[6] FRANÇON J., G. VIENNOT, J. VUILLEMIN, Description and analysis of an Efficient Priority Queue Representation, *Proceedings of the 19th Symposium on Foundations of Computer Science, 1-7*, Ann Arbor, October 1978.

[7] GINAT D., D. D. SLEATOR, R. E. TARJAN, A Tight Amortized Bound for Path Reversal, *Information Processing Letters Vol. 31, 3-5*, March 1989.

[8] KNUTH D. E., *The Art of Computer Programming*, Vol. 1 & 3, 2nd ed., Addison-Wesley, Reading, MA, 1973.

[9] LAMPORT L., Time, Clocks and the Ordering of Events in a Distributed System, *Comm. of the ACM, Vol. 21, No 7, 558-565*, July 1978.

[10] MAEKAWA M., A $\sqrt{N}$ Algorithm for Mutual Exclusion in Decentralized Systems, *ACM Trans. on Computer Systems, Vol. 3, No 2, 145-159*, May 1985.

[11] NAÏMI M., M. TREHEL, An Improvement of the log n Distributed Algorithm for the Mutual Exclusion, *Proceedings of the 7th International Conference On Distributed Computing Systems, 371-375*, Berlin, September 1987.

[12] NAÏMI M., M. TREHEL, A. ARNOLD, A log n Distributed Mutual Exclusion Algorithm Based on the Path Reversal, *Res. Rep., R. R. du Laboratoire d'Informatique de Besançon*, April 1988.

[13] RAYMOND K., A Tree-Based Algorithm for Distributed Mutual Exclusion, *ACM Trans. on Computer Systems, Vol. 7, No 1, 61-77*, February 1987.

[14] RICART G., A.K. AGRAWALA, An Optimal Algorithm for Mutual Exclusion in Computer Networks, *Comm. of the ACM, Vol. 24, No 1, 9-17*, January 1981.

[15] TREHEL M., M. NAÏMI, A Distributed Algorithm for Mutual Exclusion Based on Data Structures and Fault Tolerance, *Proceedings of the 6th Annual International Phoenix Conference on Computers and Communications, 35-39*, Scottsdale, February 1987.

[16] VUILLEMIN J., A Unifying Look at Data Structures, *Communications of the ACM, Vol. 23, No 4, 229-239*, April 1980.

Invariance Properties in Distributed Systems

Jörg Schepers *

Institut für Informatik, Universität Kiel, W-2300 Kiel

Abstract

We propose a constructive approach for the specification of distributed systems that allows for a detailed analysis of essential invariance properties like liveness or determinism. A meta-language is defined for the specification of interaction-schemes among processes, each assuring some specific invariance properties. An operational Petri-net semantics, defined for these constructs, allows for an algebraical analysis of invariance properties. The results may be reflected to the process-system and help to identify design errors in the communication and synchronization structure of a distributed system.

1 Introduction

The most important requirements for modern computer systems can be summarized in two terms: efficiency and security. The first one can easily be benchmarked and expressed in units of (relative) execution times. Talking about security, however, is much harder but nevertheless just as important.

For sequential programming paradigms proof systems exist which allow for proving a program to be semantical correct w.r.t. some specification. However, due to their complexity and tediousness they have never been of practical significance. In the last years, new programming paradigms have been developed, especially for the specification of distributed process-systems. Programming languages of this kind, like ADA, OCCAM, CHILL or MODULA-2, support constructs for process creation, communication and synchronization. The semantics of these languages, however, cannot be defined proceeding the old way [Bar86]. Questions for security and correctness get a new dimension in the context of concurrency. Terms like 'determinism', 'liveness', 'deadlocks', 'concurrency' or 'synchronization distance' become important if we reason about properties of distributed systems. All these terms denote invariance properties which can be formalized in various theoretical calculi [Mil89, Ol86]. However, the behavior of concurrently working processes is already very hard to understand for programmers which have learned to think operationally and sequentially. This is the point where they need support, but not in a way where pages of wild-looking, complex formulas of first-order predicate logic have to be used in order to prove a simple while-loop to be correct, but in a comprehensible and pragmatical manner.

In this paper we propose a constructive approach for the specification of distributed systems that also supports a detailed analysis of essential invariance properties like liveness or determinism. For that purpose, we introduce a meta-language for the specification of interaction-schemes among distributed processes. This language may be seen as a level of abstraction at which only events between processes may be specified. Local computations are not in the scope of this level. They may be specified in some imperative or declarative programming language. The meta-language may be implemented as additional part of this underlying language and provided in form of library routines or it may be realized as part of the runtime system that controls the execution of processes.

The basic idea of the meta-language is to support a set of well-defined interaction schemes among processes. These comprise communication interfaces, synchronization concepts and handling of resource conflicts [Broy84]. It is an essential precondition for a detailed and meaningful analysis to restrict the kind of interaction among processes to some well-defined schemes. An unrestricted communication scheme, for example by using shared global variables, results in a mostly

---

*The author is now with Siemens AG / ZFE ST SN 24, Otto-Hahn-Ring 6, W - 8000 München 83, e-mail: js@zfe.siemens.de

unpredictable program behavior. An obvious rule in this context is the following: the more restrictive the communication patterns, the more detailed analyses become feasible.

Following this idea, the meta-language provides several constructs, each assuring some specific invariance properties that are essential for an overall stable system behavior. The more restrictive constructs are used for a system specification, the more invariance properties can be derived statically by an analysis of the communication structure.

Different communication and synchronization schemes are investigated in the next chapter. The rest of the paper is then structured as follows: In chapter 3 we introduce the constructs of the meta-language and define a simple Petri-net semantics for them. Chapter 4 shows how the behavior of a distributed process system can be analyzed by means of techniques known from Petri-net theory. The results are then reflected to the original process-system. The last chapter outlines a realization of the proposed concept and summarizes the experiences that have been made with this system.

2 Interaction Schemes

Basically, two basic mechanisms for process interaction can be identified: communication and synchronization. Some approaches, like ADA or OCCAM, make no distinction between them and allow only for synchronous process communication. In this paper, however, we propose asynchronous communication in combination with flexible synchronization constructs. By this way, we can define adequate operators at the specification level with a well-defined semantics, such that formal analyses and reasoning about their properties become feasible.

Process interaction becomes necessary, if processes want to communicate, synchronize or communication-conflicts have to be solved. Accordingly, we propose the following basic interaction schemes:

Process communication should be feasible via asynchronous communication channels, realized as streams. Streams provide an unidirectional communication link between exactly two processes. Conceptually, there are no synchronization effects, neither to the sender nor to the receiver process. Access conflicts are also excluded, due to an unique sender and receiver.

Process synchronization between two or more processes can be achieved either implicitly by stream capacities or by explicit synchronization interfaces. In the first case, processes become synchronized if a stream capacity is exceeded. Synchronization interfaces allow for process activation not before all input data are available.

Conflict situations between processes may be of different nature. They may occur internally or at the communication level. Internal conflicts occur if a process has to decide whether to send a message or not. This decision is unvisible at the communication level and results externally in non-deterministic process-behavior. External conflicts are defined between two or more processes. They occur if a message should be forwarded to one out of several processes or messages from several processes have to be merged into one stream. This corresponds to forward- and backward-conflicts known from Petri-net theory. They can be solved either non-deterministically or under control of some control-message.

All kind of conflicts result in non-deterministic behavior and, hence, drastically increase the complexity of analyses, because all alternatives of conflict resolution have to be taken into consideration. By this way, invariance properties often get lost and mostly analysis requires exponential-time algorithms which can not be applied to real complex systems. Also, from a pragmatical point of view, conflicts make it more difficult to imagine all possible situations that may occur in complex systems. Non-deterministic effects often cause irreproducible system behavior, that makes systems more unsave. Hence, conflicts should be avoided as far as possible in the design of distributed systems.

Fortunately, in many cases conflicts have no far-reaching effects. Pairs of forward/backward conflicts often compensate each other, such that overall invariance properties can be ensured. Examples for these constellations are realized as process constructs of the meta-language and introduced in the next chapter.

3 The Meta-Language

The objectives of the meta-language are twofold. On the one hand, process constructs which preserve essential invariance properties in distributed systems should be defined. This is a constructive approach for establishing invariance properties in advance, for example, by minimizing conflicts between processes during process specification. On the other hand, the meta-language should provide a formal semantics that allows for constructive analyses of invariance properties.

In order to achieve the first aim the classification of process-interaction schemes, introduced in the previous chapter, constitutes the basis from which concrete process-constructs are built. The second objective can be fulfilled by using Petri-nets for the definition of an operational semantics of the interaction schemes among processes. Petri-nets provide suitable formalisms and techniques for the definition and analysis of invariance properties [Mur89, Rei86]. In contrast to interleaving semantics, wherein concurrency is defined by non-deterministic sequences of events, these terms are strongly separated and defined consistently in the Petri-net model.

We define the external communication behavior of each process construct of the meta-language by means of a simple Petri-net. This net reflects the invariance properties of a specific interaction scheme. A complete definition of the external and internal behavior would require more complex high-level Petri-nets like PrT-nets [Gen79] or Coloured Petri-nets [Jen86]. However, these net classes provide only complex algebraic analysis techniques for invariance properties, because all internal computations of processes have to be considered [Jen81]. For our purpose simple Petrinets are sufficient and reflect exactly those properties we are interested in.

3.1 Petri-nets

We start with some definitions of basic terms from net theory. For more detailed informations concerning Petri-nets we refer to many articles and books published in this area. An overview can be got from [Gen80, Mur89, Rei86].

In Petri-net theory two classes of invariance properties are distinguished: structural invariances and invariances w.r.t. markings. Structural invariances can directly be derived from the netstructure, i.e. without considering an actual marking. Important invariances of this class are S- and T-invariants as well as reproduction-vectors. They are defined as follows:

Definition 3.1 Let $N = (S, T, F, K, W, M)$ be a Petri-net with S a set of places, T a set of transitions, F a flow-relation, K a capacity function for places, W a weight-function on edges and M an initial marking. Let $I : S \times T \rightarrow \mathbb{Z}$ be the incidence matrix induced by F.

- A vector $\Sigma = (\sigma_1, \ldots, \sigma_k) \in \mathbb{Z}^{|S|}$ is a *S-invariant*, if $I^t * \Sigma = 0$ and $\gcd(\sigma_1, \ldots, \sigma_k) = 1$.
- A vector $\Theta = (\theta_1, \ldots, \theta_l) \in \mathbb{Z}^{|T|}$ is a *T-invariant*, if $I * \Theta = 0$ and $\gcd(\theta_1, \ldots, \theta_l) = 1$.
- A T-invariant Θ is called a *reproduction-vector* if $\forall \theta_i \in \{\theta_1, \ldots, \theta_l\} : \quad \theta_i \geq 0$ 3.1 ∎

The existence of S- and T-invariants is a necessary but no sufficient precondition for an overall stable behavior of the net. If T- or S-invariants do not exist, markings are irreproducible or the total number of tokens in the net is unbounded or decreases on the whole.

Structural invariants can be computed easily by solving systems of linear equations. Other important properties, like concurrency, determinism or liveness can only be proved under consideration of all reachable markings. We informally define some of these net-properties.

Definition 3.2 Let N be a Petri-net and M the actual marking of N.

- Activated transitions t_1 and t_2 of N are *in conflict* with each other under M if the firing of one transition would deactivate the other.

- Activated transitions t_1 and t_2 of N are in a *concurrency relation* under M if they are not in conflict with each other.

- N is *live* under M if under all reachable markings from M there exists at least one activated transition. If no transition in a net is activated we call this state of the net a *deadlock situation*.

- N is *persistent* if conflict situations are excluded under all markings reachable from M.

- N is *deterministic* if for all reachable markings from M there exists at least one marking that is reachable from all of them. **3.2 ▪**

All these invariance properties can be defined in a more formal way (see [Mur89, Rei86]). However, these formalisms are beyond the scope of this paper.

It should be noted, that all invariance properties for a complete net, as defined in 3.2, depend on the set of reachable markings. Hence, the complexity for proving those invariance properties is, in general, exponential-time. However, specific subclasses of nets restrict the net-structure in a way, such that certain properties can be proved by efficient algorithms. Two of these subclasses are free-choice and synchronization nets [Rei86]. In synchronization-nets places are connected to exactly one predecessor and successor transition. Conflicts are excluded by this restriction. Free-choice nets allow conflicts, however, places with more than one predecessor or successor transition must be restricted to be the only place in the postset or preset of this transition.

3.2 Process Constructs

Accordingly to the basic interaction schemes of processes, as classified in section 2, we will now define the process constructs of the meta-language. However, we will only define the external operational behavior of the process constructs exactly. Concrete implementations of those constructs depend on the underlying programming language. An example for a concrete realization of the proposed process types as well as an exact formal definition may be found in [Sch90]. An overview of this implementation will be given in section 5.

Process communication is performed via streams that are realized as uni-directional, asynchronous communication channels between exactly two processes. Their operational behavior is modeled by a single place in a Petri-net. This implies that the sequence and types of messages are ignored at this level of abstraction. An optional capacity limit of a stream determines the synchronization distance between sender and receiver process.

Processes may be specified at several levels of abstraction. At the lowest level a program of the underlying programming language specifies the computations performed by a single process. Each process has an unique communication interface that determines the input and output streams. Additionally, it synchronizes the communications performed by the process. A process starts its computations if all input values are available, consumes a fixed number of messages from each input stream and produces a fixed number of output messages that are sent to the output streams after the computation has been terminated.

This regular input/output behavior guarantees an essential invariance property of single processes. The number of messages consumed and produced by each process activation can be determined statically. This behavior exactly corresponds to the behavior of transitions in Petri-nets, so that a single transition suffices to model the external behavior of a simple process.

This technique can also be applied at the process level of the meta-language. A subsystem of processes and streams can be abstracted to a new hierarchical process simply by defining a common communication interface for several processes. At a higher level of abstraction the subsystem behaves like a simple process, however, internally it is recursively built up from other processes and streams. Advantages of this hierarchical process concept, that also allows for a specification of recursive process structures, are a modular system design and a lower complexity of analyses which can be performed at each level of abstraction, separately. This abstraction scheme corresponds to a syntactical refinement of transitions in Petri-nets. Semantic checks for the equivalence of internal and external behavior can be performed during system analysis (see 4.1).

The process concept proposed so far is still too restrictive for the specification of real and complex distributed systems. The interaction schemes of section 2 recommend at least two more basic constructs in order to handle conflict situations among processes.

Forward conflicts can be realized by split-operators, which distribute an incoming message to one of their output streams. The output stream can be determined either randomly or under control of a control-message. The abstract behavior of both types of split-operators can be modeled by the Petri-net[1] shown in fig. 1. This net clearly points out the conflict situation that may occur if an incoming message resides on the input place. Split-operators handling more than one input stream can be defined in the same way.

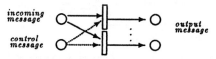

Figure 1: Behavior of the split-operator(s)

As the counterpart to split-operators we define merge-operators, which select (may be under control of some control message) one input stream and forward a message from this stream to the output stream. This behavior can be modeled by the Petri-net[1] shown in fig. 2. Due to the net-structure, backward conflicts may occur if the common output place has a finite capacity.

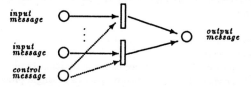

Figure 2: Behavior of the merge-operator(s)

Single uses of merge- and split-operators have a detrimental property; they disturb structural invariance properties of a net and cause an overall non-deterministic behavior. However, if they are used pairwise they partially compensate each other. Two basic programming constructs can be recognized, if we combine a split-operator with a merge-operator and vice versa.

If we combine deterministic split- and merge-operators we will get an alternate-construct with the following external behavior. A control message selects one out of a fixed number of alternative processes. These processes may operate concurrently, but their output messages will be reordered under control of their activation sequence by a deterministic merge-operator. The restriction that all alternative processes must have identical communication interfaces ensures an important external invariance property. With each activation the alternate construct will consume one input message and produce one output message. The net in fig. 3 models this internal behavior. The

---

[1] The exact behavior can only be defined using edge attributes as, for example, in PrT-nets.

external behavior of the whole process construct is the same as that of a simple process and one transition suffices to model this behavior in the operational net semantics.

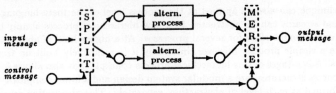

Figure 3: Combination of split and merge to alternate

A similar effect arises if we combine a non-deterministic merge- and a split-operator. The result is a process construct that is usually known as a resource-manager or monitor. The merge-operator non-deterministically generates a sequence of asynchronous requests for an enclosed critical process. The results of this process are then distributed to corresponding output channels under control of an internal control message. The invariance property of this process is an external behavior that guarantees a response for each request. By this way, blocking of a critical region is excluded, conceptually. The internal behavior of this process-type is shown in fig. 4a; for a structural analysis, however, the synchronization-net of fig. 4b models exactly the invariance property of this process type.

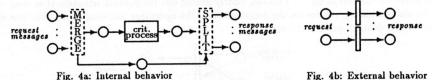

Fig. 4a: Internal behavior   Fig. 4b: External behavior

Figure 4: Critical region enclosed in merge- and split-operators

Several types of external conflicts can be specified by the process constructs described above. Internal conflicts, however, have also to be taken into consideration at the level of process interaction. Externally, they manifest themselves in the following way: Either a process may optionally generate output messages, depending on some internal decision, or it may consume or produce a varying number of messages with each activation. Both forms cause the loss of an important invariance property of simple processes. Their input/output behavior can no longer be defined by a single transition in a Petri-net.

Optional messages can be realized by explicit NULL-messages, which are sent to a special kind of streams, where these messages will be deleted. The external behavior of those filter-streams is defined by the net shown in fig. 5. By that, we can exactly identify places where optional messages may occur and, hence, preserve the invariance properties of single processes.

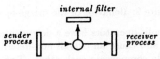

Figure 5: A filter-stream between two processes

Varying numbers of input/output messages can be realized by special process types. We define so-called loop-processes for generators as well as for collectors. Generators consume their input message and produce, depending on some internal computations, a varying number of output messages. Processes of this type may, for example, get a matrix and break it down to single elements, each being sent in a separate output message. Collectors act contrary to this scheme. They consume a varying number of input messages until some internal condition is fulfilled and an output message is sent. The behavior of these process types is defined by the nets from fig. 6. The internal conflicts, causing the external behavior, can be found in the internal control structure of these process types.

Fig.6a: Generator process   Fig.6b: Collector process

Figure 6: Loop - processes

4 Invariance Analyses

The operational semantics of the process constructs proposed in the previous section is defined in a modular fashion by means of simple Petri-nets. These nets can be composed in accordance with the communication structure of a process system. The communication and synchronization behavior of the system is then completely modeled by these Petri-nets. Hence, the results of invariance analyses performed on the Petri-net may be transferred to the process system, directly. If we additionally take into consideration the external invariance properties of specific process constructs, these nets can even be simplified. We abstract from the internal behavior and perform analyses at each level of abstraction, separately. This decreases the complexity of analysis and makes the dependencies among processes more clear.

Essential invariance properties of Petri-nets have been defined in section 3.1. Some of them are easy to prove, but all concerning liveness or deadlock behavior require exponential-time analyses, in general. However, if we cannot verify liveness conditions we often are able to falsify them more easily. This is a method to provide pragmatical useful hints for programmers and help to identify logical errors in the design of the communication and synchronization structure of a distributed system.

4.1 Structural Analyses

Structural invariants, as defined in 3.1, are easy to compute and their non-existence is an obvious indication of instable system behavior. The following lemmas show the pragmatical relevance of these invariants.

Lemma 4.1 Let N be a Petri-net and M an actual marking of N. If M can be reproduced by some firing-sequence of transitions of N, then a reproduction-vector Θ of N exists.   **4.1 ∎**

Proof: The proof is an obvious conclusion from the definition of reproduction-vectors (see [Rei86]).

Pragmatically, this lemma allows to check for cyclic system behavior in a strong sense. If no reproduction-vector exists, then the corresponding process system can never reach the same state twice. In many cases this indicates an incorrect system design. The computation of S-invariants allows for similar conclusions.

Lemma 4.2 Let N be a Petri-net, $\Sigma = (\sigma_1, \ldots, \sigma_{|S|})$ a S-invariant of N, M an actual marking of N and M' any marking reachable from M. The following equality holds:

$$\sum_{s \in S} M(s) \cdot \sigma_s = \sum_{s \in S} M'(s) \cdot \sigma_s$$

4.2 ∎

Proof: This is also a direct conclusion from the definition of S-invariants (see [Rei86]).

The non-existence of S-invariants indicates an overall decreasing or increasing number of tokens in a net. For a process-system this means either more messages are sent than processed or the system deadlocks due to the absence of messages.

Yet another property of pragmatical relevance can be proved by S-invariances. In net theory the capacity of places can be infinite. From the pragmatical point of view this could never be realized and it indicates an unstable system behavior if one channel is filled up with an infinite number of messages. The following lemma helps to find an upper capacity limit for each place in a net, that would never be exceeded.

Lemma 4.3 Let N be a Petri-net with an initial marking M. If a S-invariant $\Sigma = (\sigma_1, \ldots, \sigma_{|S|})$ of N with $\sigma_i > 0 \quad \forall i \in \{1 \ldots |S|\}$ exists, then for each place s_i of N an upper capacity-bound k_i can be found such that for all markings M' reachable from M $M'(s_i) < k_i, \quad \forall i \in \{1 \ldots |S|\}$ holds. **4.3** ∎

Proof: See also [Rei86].

Our approach, that allows for a syntactical abstraction of subsystems to new hierarchical processes, causes still another pragmatical problem. A common communication interface for several (internal) processes requires a special behavior of these processes, which become synchronized by each other by the interface. For example, the simplified process system shown in fig. 7 would cause an external synchronization error, because it can not provide one output message for each input message as required by its external communication interface.[2]

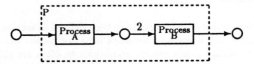

Figure 7: Internal structure of a hierarchical process

However, those internal defects of hierarchical processes can easily be identified if we compute reproduction-vectors for a net, wherein the output tokens of the net are fed back to the input places. This scheme is shown in fig. 8.

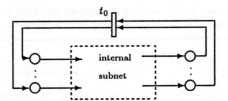

Figure 8: Feed-back network for hierarchical processes

If we compute the reproduction-vectors for those feed-back nets, the following lemmas hold.

Lemma 4.4 Let N_P be a feed-back net for a hierarchical process P. If no reproduction-vector Θ for N_P exists, such that $\theta_{t_0} = 1$ then the internal structure of P can not be synchronized as required by the external communication interface of P. **4.4** ∎

Proof: The lemma is a direct conclusion of lemma 4.1.

However, even if such a reproduction-vector exists, synchronization errors caused by the internal structure of P can not be excluded, in general. They have always to be checked dynamically under consideration of actual input data. The following lemma, however, helps to identify critical processes that may cause synchronization errors at runtime.

Lemma 4.5 Let N_P be a feed-back net for a hierarchical process P. If there exists a transition t_i of N, such that $\theta_{t_i} = 0$ for all reproduction-vectors Θ of N_P, then a firing of t_i disturbs the reproducibility of a marking of N_P. **4.5** ∎

---

[2]Due to its internal structure, process B needs two messages for an activation.

Proof: Also a direct conclusion of lemma 4.1.

Lemma 4.5 helps to identify those processes which disturb an internal invariance property of hierarchical processes if they become activated. Such kind of behavior may be caused by internal conflicts that are resolved non-deterministically. From the pragmatical point of view, determinism is an important invariance property. Unfortunately, it can seldom be proved statically. Only if the communication structure of a distributed system can be completely modeled by a synchronization net and if all processes behave deterministically, an overall deterministic behavior is guaranteed. This means that, if non-deterministic merge- and split-operators or monitor-processes are used, determinism generally gets lost. In particular, this becomes important with respect to deadlocks that may occur in distributed systems. The occurrence of deadlocks in combination with non-determinism often results in irreproducible deadlock-situations which make systems extremely unreliable. Deadlock behavior, however, belongs to the class of invariance properties that have to be analyzed under consideration of actual markings. Those properties are investigated in the next section.

4.2 Liveness Analyses

Decidability of liveness in general Petri-nets is equivalent to the reachability problem of a given marking [Ha74]. Both problems could be proven to be decidable but also to be NP-hard [Sac76, Pet77]. Polynomial algorithms exist only for a special class of Petri-nets, e.g. free-choice nets [Esp89].

Liveness analysis is based on the identification of substructures in a Petri-net, fulfilling certain invariance properties. Especially sets of places which never lose a marking or never become marked are of interest in this context. We define these sets as follows:

Definition 4.6 Let $N = (S, T, F, K, W, M)$ be a Petri-net. Let denote $\bullet s$ the preset of $s \in S$, i.e. $\bullet s = \{t \in T \mid (t, s) \in F\}$ and for $S' \subseteq S$ define $\bullet S' = \bigcup_{s \in S'} \bullet s$. The postsets $s\bullet$ and $S'\bullet$ are defined accordingly.

- A subset $S' \subseteq S$ is a *deadlock* of N if $\bullet S' \subseteq S'\bullet$.
- A subset $S' \subseteq S$ is a *trap* of N if $S'\bullet \subseteq \bullet S'$. **4.6 ∎**

We obviously see that an unmarked deadlock never will become marked, because no transition of its preset can be activated. On the other hand, marked traps will never become unmarked, because all transitions consuming tokens from the trap will also produce tokens for it. In particular, deadlocks comprising marked traps will never become unmarked. This is an essential precondition for liveness and known as Commoner's Property [Ha76].

Theorem 4.7 A free-choice net is live iff it fulfills Commoner's Property. **4.7 ∎**

Proof: The proof is based on the construction of deadlocks and can be found in [Rei86].

Commoner's Property can be proved for bounded free-choice nets by the solution of a linear optimization problem [Esp89]. Hence, liveness of bounded free-choice nets is provable in polynomial time. For synchronization-nets an even more simple result is available.

Lemma 4.8 A synchronization-net is live iff each cycle of the net is being marked. **4.8 ∎**

Proof: The proof directly results from Commoner's Property and the matter of fact, that in synchronization-nets each deadlock is a trap and each cycle is a deadlock.

The lemma can be used to prove liveness of synchronization-nets only by removing all marked places from the net and then verifying the absence of cycles, which is an easy problem known from graph-theory.

The operational external behavior of the process constructs introduced in section 3 is completely defined by means of free-choice nets, as long as no weighted edges are used. Hence, with theorem 4.7 and lemma 4.8 we have suitable results to validate the communication and synchronization structure of distributed systems.

If the operational behavior of a process system can not be modeled by means of free-choice nets we have to look for other criteria of liveness, which can be checked efficiently. Weighted edges in Petri-nets are one reason due to which free-choice nets can not be used and serious problems with respect to liveness analysis are caused. Commoner's Property is not significant in those nets, but we can also identify invariant subnets in order to check important preconditions for liveness.

The main difference between nets with and without weighted edges becomes clear if we investigate the behavior of cycles. If all edges of a cycle are equally weighted a cycle without branches is always live. However, if the edges of a cycle have different weights some additional requirements must be fulfilled in order to prove liveness.

Definition 4.9
Let $N = (S, T, F, K, W, M)$ be a Petri-net and $C = \{(s_1, t_1), (t_1, s_2), \ldots, (s_n, t_n), (t_n, s_1)\} \subseteq F$ a cycle in N. If for all places and transitions of $C \mid \bullet t_i \mid = \mid t_i \bullet \mid = \mid \bullet s_i \mid = \mid s_i \bullet \mid = 1$ holds, we say the cycle is *pure*. For each $t_i \in T$ of C we define a

transition-ratio: $\quad \xi_i = \frac{W(t_i, s_{(i \bmod n)+1})}{W(s_i, t_i)} \quad$ and a *cycle-ratio:* $\quad \Xi = \prod_{i=1}^{n} \xi_i.$

Cycles are called *consuming* if $\Xi < 1$, *producing* if $\Xi > 1$, and *preserving* if $\Xi = 1$. **4.9 ■**

The overall behavior of cycles can be checked by means of the following lemmas.

Lemma 4.10 Consuming pure cycles are not live. **4.10 ■**

Proof: This obvious result could be shown by solving a linear optimization problem for maximal firing sequences (see [Ka66]).

Lemma 4.11 The total number of tokens in producing cycles will grow infinitely. **4.11 ■**

Proof: Similar to lemma 4.10 (see also [Ka66]).

Lemma 4.12 For preserving cycles a positive S-invariant $\Sigma > 0$ can be found. **4.12 ■**

Proof: Let I_c be the incidence-matrix of a cycle C. S-invariants can be computed by

$$I_c^t \cdot \Sigma \;=\; 0$$
$$\Rightarrow \quad \sigma_i \;=\; \xi_i \cdot \sigma_{(i \bmod n)+1} \quad \forall i \in \{1, \ldots, n\}.$$

Mutual substitution of these equations yields

$$\sigma_i = \sigma_i \cdot \prod_{j=1}^{n} \xi_j = \Xi \cdot \sigma_i$$
$$\Rightarrow \quad \Xi = 1 \quad \vee \quad \sigma_i = 0.$$

From the lemma $\Xi = 1$ holds. Hence, a solution can be found by

$$\sigma_1' \;=\; 1 \quad \wedge \quad \sigma_i' \;=\; \prod_{j=i}^{n} \xi_j \quad \forall i \in \{2, \ldots, n\}$$

The S-invariant Σ is then defined by the smallest integer solution $k \cdot (\sigma_1', \ldots, \sigma_n')$ with $k \in \mathbb{N}$. □

We can now use these lemmas to check for some preconditions for liveness in Petri-nets. The results are summerized in the following theorem:

Theorem 4.13 Let N be a Petri-net and C a cycle in N. N is not live if one of the following conditions hold:

   i. C is consuming and for all places s_i of $C \mid \bullet s_i \mid = 1$ holds.

   ii. C is producing and for all places s_i of $C \mid s_i \bullet \mid = 1 \quad \wedge \quad K(s_i) < \infty$ holds.

   iii. C is preserving and condition ii. holds and at least one s_j of C exists with $\mid \bullet s_j \mid > 1$ and s_j is not covered by any S-invariant of N.   **4.13** ∎

Proof: The proofs follow directly from lemmas 4.10 - 4.12.

The computations of cycle-ratios can be performed in polynominal time. A polynomial algorithm for checking initial markings to be sufficient for at least one cyclic run is described in [Sch90].

The formal methods proposed in this section can be used to check for a stable system behavior, statically. They can not be used to prove liveness, which in general is an undecidable problem, but they may be used to validate some necessary preconditions for a deadlock-free and deterministic behavior. All of them can be applied efficiently at several levels of abstraction. The results may directly be mapped to the corresponding processes and give informations about their specific runtime-behavior. More details and further results, e.g. on path and capacity analyses, may be found in [Pan90, Sch90].

5   The GRAPH-system

The proposed concept has been realized in the GRAPH-system, an interactive tool for specification, analysis and execution of distributed processes [Sch90]. In GRAPH a purely functional programming language has been combined with a process-concept, similar to that introduced in section 3. GRAPH provides an interactive user-interface for specification, analysis and execution. Process systems are externally represented as graphs which are variants of Petri-nets. Statical analyses of the communication structure may be performed at each level of abstraction. Several debugging facilities allow for a visualization of the communication behavior and for a stepwise execution under interactive control.

Manifold experiences have been made with the GRAPH-system. Process-specification follows a constructive approach and design errors are detected at an early stage of the design process by means of statical analyses. The graphical representation clearly points out the mutual dependencies among processes and gives an impression of the dynamical behavior. The interactive execution of process systems, that can be visualized at the graphical specification level, is also an extremely helpful tool for debugging and validating the runtime behavior of distributed systems. Due to the modular process concept a distribution on several processors at runtime and a concurrent execution of processes has also been realized without conceptual problems. The streams specified in a process systems can directly be mapped to the communication channels of a multiprocessor machine. From the pragmatical point of view, however, the modular and sometimes restrictive process concept might become a critical factor concerning the acceptance of such an approach. Our experiences show that too much restrictions at the early stages of system design would meet with disapproval. It seems to be better recommended to allow also for some destructive process constructs, w.r.t. invariance properties, and clearly stress their destructive nature during a formal system analysis. A combination of both seems to be most suitable - restrictive processes whenever possible, destructive constructs whenever strictly necessary.

6   Conclusion

The proposed process concept is a constructive approach in order to preserve essential invariance properties in distributed systems. By means of some simple restrictions concerning the communication behavior of processes, a lot of invariance properties can be proved statically only by investigating the communication and synchronization structure of distributed systems. An operational Petri-net semantics forms a sound basis for efficient algebraical invariance analyses. Hence, essential design errors can be avoided at an early stage of system development.

This concept is applicable to a wide range of programming paradigms. Special process types can be defined for each language and realized either by new language constructs, library functions or predefined modules. Similar constructs can be defined if timing constraints have also to be considered as, for example, in real-time applications. Enhanced Petri-net models (timed nets) can be used for this purpose and process constructs have to be defined accordingly.

References

[Bak79]   Baker, H.G.; *Rabin's proof of the undecidability of the reachability set inclusion problem of vector addition systems* ; Computation Structures Group Memo 1979; Project MAC; M.I.T. July 1973

[Bar86]   Barringer, H. ; *A survey of verification techniques for parallel programs* ; LNCS 191, Springer 1986

[Bro84]   Brookes, S.D.; Hoare, C.A.R.; Roscoe, A.W. ; *A theory of communicating sequential processes* ; Jour. of the ACM, 1984, Vol. 31, pp. 560-599

[Broy84] Broy, M.; Bauer, F.L.; *A systematic approach to language constructs for concurrent programs*; Science of Computer Programming, 4, 1984, pp. 103-139 North Holland

[Esp89]   Esparza, J.; Silva, M. ; *A polynomial-time algorithm to decide liveness of bounded free-choice nets*; Internal Report, June 1989

[Gen79]   Genrich, H.J.; Lautenbach, K. ; *The analysis of distributed systems by means of Predicate/Transition nets*; in *Semantics on concurrent computation* LNCS 70; Springer 1979

[Gen80]   Genrich, H.J.; Lautenbach, K.; Thiagarajan, P.S.; *Elements of general net theory*; in *Net theory and applications* (ed. W. Bauer), pp. 21-164 ; LNCS 84; Springer 1980

[Ha74]   Hack, M. ; *The recursive equivalence of the reachability problem and the liveness problem for Petri nets and vector addition systems* ; Proc. 15th Ann. Symp. Switching and Automata, IEEE, 1974

[Ha76]   Hack, M.; *Decidability questions for petri nets*; MIT Technical Report 161, June 1976

[Jen81]   Jensen, K. ; *How to find invariants for coloured Petri nets*; LNCS 118, Springer, 1981, pp. 327-338

[Jen86]   Jensen, K. ; *Coloured Petri-nets* ; Advances in Petri Nets, Part I, LNCS 254, Springer 1986

[Ka66]   Karp, R.M.; Miller, R.E. ; *Properties of a model for parallel computations: Determinacy, Termination, Queueing*; SIAM, Vol. 14, No. 6, 1966, pp. 1390-1411

[La78]   Landweber, L; Robertson, E. ; *Properties of conflict-free and persistent Petri-nets*; Journal of the ACM, Vol. 25, Nr. 3, 1978, pp. 352-364

[Mil89]   Milner, R.; *A Calculus of Communicating Systems*; LNCS 92, Springer 1980

[Mur89]   Murata, T. ; *Petri nets: properties, analysis and applications* ; Proc. of the IEEE, Vol. 77, No.4, 1989

[Ol86]   Olderog, E.R.; *Process theory: semantics, specification and verification*; LNCS 224, pp. 442-509, Springer, 1986

[Pan90]   Pantke, S. ; *Semantische Analyse von* GRAPH *Prozeßsystemen* ; Master Thesis, Univ. of Kiel, 1990

[Pet77]   Peterson, J.L. ; *Petri Nets* ; ACM Computing Surveys, 1977, Vol. 9, No. 3

[Rei86]   Reisig, W.; *Petrinetze*; Springer 1986

[Sac76]   Sacerdote, G. ; Tenney, R.L.; *The decidability of the reachability problem for vector addition systems* ; 1976

[Sch90]   Schepers, J.; GRAPH - Eine auf Petri-Netzen basierende Entwicklungsumgebung für verteilte Systeme; PhD Thesis, University of Kiel, 1990

Synchronization of Parallel Processes in Distributed Systems*

Mikhail Makhaniok[1] and Reinhard Männer[23]

[1] Institute of Engineering Cybernetics, Academy of Sciences of Belarus, Surganov Str. 6, SU–220000 Minsk, Republic Belarus

[2] Lehrstuhl für Informatik V, Universität Mannheim, A5, W-6800 Mannheim, Germany

[3] Interdisziplinäres Zentrum für Wissenschaftliches Rechnen, Universität Heidelberg, Im Neuenheimer Feld 368, W-6900 Heidelberg, Germany

Abstract. In this paper a solution is given for the problem to determine the duration of a parallel asynchronous multi–step process in a homogeneous system of combinational logic. In such a system the problem arises if the processors have different speeds and input data. If so each processor "knows" its own data and the type of the process but in general has no information about the speed of the other processors and their input data.

1 Introduction

In parallel asynchronous systems often the problem arises how to determine the moment when a parallel process will be finished, i.e., when all signals in the system will have settled. An excellent example is the synchronization problem in arbitration systems for multiprocessor buses, i.e., Futurebus+ [1]. The same problem exists, e.g., in a hardware accelerator for speeding up the median search operation [2].

To analyze this synchronization problem we introduce the following notions. We consider a parallel process $\mathcal{P}$ which is carried out by a system $Z = \{P_j, j = 1, \ldots, N\}$ of processors. $\mathcal{P}$ is a multi–step process and every processor is assembled of a number m of processing elements, one per step. The processors are implemented as combinatorial logic so that no synchronization is required between their processing elements. A step is started automatically when the output computed in the previous one is available. Every step consists of two parts, a distributed operation which is executed in parallel by the corresponding processing elements, and a global operation following it (Fig.1). The duration $T(\mathcal{P}, Z)$ of $\mathcal{P}$ is the sum of the execution times of all steps. We define $d_{i,j} = 1$, if P_j takes longest to complete its part of the i-th distributed operation, $d_{i,j} = 0$ else, so that $\sum_{j \in Z} d_{i,j} = 1$. Then the execution time of a single step $i \in \{1, \ldots, m\}$ is the sum of the time τ_i required to execute the i-th global operation plus the time $b_i \sum_{j=1}^{N} (T(j)) d_{i,j}$ to execute the i-th distributed operation. Here $T(j)$ can be considered as a "time unit" which is inversely proportional to the speed of the j-th processor, and b_i is a measure for the complexity of the i-th distributed operation.

---

* This work has been supported by the Deutsche Forschungsgemeinschaft (DFG) under grants 436–WER–113–1–0 (438 113/117/0) and Ma 1150/8-1

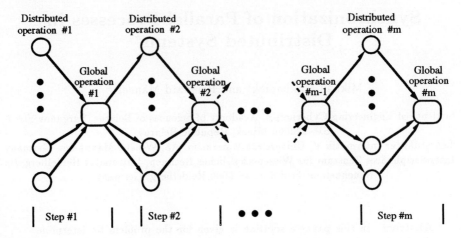

Fig. 1. A distributed multi–step process.

Thus the duration of $\mathcal{P}$ is

$$T(\mathcal{P}, Z) = \sum_{j \in Z} c_j T(j) + \sum_{i=1}^{m} \tau_i \ , \tag{1}$$

where $c_j = \sum_{i=1}^{m} b_i d_{i,j}$ is the number of the individual time units introduced by the j-th processor.

Two cases are distinguished. In the first case the processors have no information about the time units of the others so that the following relation is assumed

$$0 < T(j) < \infty \ . \tag{2}$$

In the second case they can exploit the fact that their speed is bounded, i.e., that

$$T_L \leq T(j) \leq T_H \ . \tag{3}$$

The synchronization in such a system is done as follows [3]. After all processors have been notified of the beginning of the process $\mathcal{P}$ they assert "one" signals onto a wired OR logic line S. During execution each processor P_j waits for a certain time $t(j, \mathcal{P})$ before it removes its "one" from the line S. When S changes to the "zero" state all processors recognize the end of the process. Therefore the total waiting time $t(\mathcal{P})$ for the system is

$$t(\mathcal{P}) = \max_{j \in Z} t(j, \mathcal{P}) \ . \tag{4}$$

It is obvious that $\mathcal{P}$ will be finished correctly if this total waiting time is not less than the duration of the process. This means that the condition

$$t(\mathcal{P}) \geq T(\mathcal{P}, Z) \tag{5}$$

must be true for all possible combinations of $T(j)$ satisfying either (2) or (3).

2   Problem of Investigation

In a parallel asynchronous system each processor P_{j^*}, $j^* \in Z$, knows the type of the process, i.e., all the coefficients c_j, all global operation times τ_i, and its own individual delay $T(j^*)$. However it generally has no information about the delays $T(j)$, $j \in \{Z \backslash j^*\}$ of other processors. Then the following problem arises according to relations (2) and (3). For every processor P_{j^*} the time $t(j^*, \mathcal{P})$ has to be calculated so that condition (5) is fulfilled. It is impossible for any P_{j^*} to determine its own value $t(j^*, \mathcal{P})$ appropriately by its own. Therefore all processors have to co–operate in order to synchronize the parallel process, that is to find the moment when $\mathcal{P}$ will be finished. Following [4] and [5] we formulate below the task of minimizing the total waiting time. We fix the type of the process and introduce the parameter

$$n_j = \frac{t(j, \mathcal{P}) - \sum\limits_{i=1}^{m} \tau_i}{T(j)}, \quad j \in Z , \tag{6}$$

which does not depend on time.

Then, using (1), (4)–(6), we can guarantee that the process will always be finished correctly if at least one relation of the system

$$\begin{cases} n_{j^*} \cdot T(j^*) \geq \sum\limits_{j \in Z} c_j T(j), \\ j^* = 1, \ldots, N \end{cases} \tag{7}$$

is fulfilled for either (2) or (3). To solve the problem one has now to determine the coefficients n_j. However it is not easy in general to calculate any coefficient n_{j^*} using system (7), because n_{j^*} depends on the unknown values $T(j)$, $j \in \{Z \backslash j^*\}$. To eliminate them and to simplify (7) we use the two theorems stated below.

Theorem 1 *At least one relation of the system (7) is fulfilled for arbitrary values* $T(j)$, $0 < T(j) < \infty$, $j = 1, \ldots, N$, *if and only if*

$$\sum_{j \in Z} \frac{c_j}{n_j} \leq 1 . \tag{8}$$

Proof see in [4].

Theorem 2 *At least one relation of the system (7) is fulfilled for arbitrary values* $T(j)$, $T_L \leq T(j) \leq T_H$, $j = 1, \ldots, N$, *if*

$$\sum_{j' \in Z'} \frac{c_{j'}}{n_{j'}} + \frac{T_H}{n_l T_L} \sum_{j'' \in Z''} c_{j''} \leq 1 , \tag{9}$$

where $Z' \bigcup Z'' = Z$, $Z' \bigcap Z'' = \emptyset$, $l, j' \in Z'$, $j'' \in Z''$, $n_l T_L \geq n_{j''} T_H$.

Proof. Let us suppose the contrary. Then

$$n_j T(j) < \sum_{j' \in Z'} c_{j'} T(j') + \sum_{j'' \in Z''} c_{j''} T(j'') \tag{10}$$

for all $j \in Z$. This implies

$$\frac{c_{j'}T(j')}{n_{j'}T(j')} > \frac{c_{j'}T(j')}{\sum\limits_{j'\in Z'} c_{j'}T(j') + \sum\limits_{j''\in Z''} c_{j''}T(l)\frac{T_H}{T_L}}, \quad j' \in Z', \tag{11}$$

$$\frac{c_{j''}T(l)\frac{T_H}{T_L}}{n_l T(l)} > \frac{c_{j''}T(l)\frac{T_H}{T_L}}{\sum\limits_{j'\in Z'} c_{j'}T(j') + \sum\limits_{j''\in Z''} c_{j''}T(l)\frac{T_H}{T_L}}, \quad j'' \in Z''. \tag{12}$$

If we take sum of (11) over $j' \in Z'$ and (12) over $j'' \in Z''$ and add the results we obtain the following contradiction to the assumption (10).

$$\sum\limits_{j'\in Z'} \frac{c_{j'}}{n_{j'}} + \sum\limits_{j''\in Z''} \frac{c_{j''}T_H}{n_l T_L} > \frac{\sum\limits_{j'\in Z'} c_{j'}T(j') + \sum\limits_{j''\in Z''} c_{j''}T(l)\frac{T_H}{T_L}}{\sum\limits_{j'\in Z'} c_{j'}T(j') + \sum\limits_{j''\in Z''} c_{j''}T(l)\frac{T_H}{T_L}} .$$

$\square$

Now we formulate the optimization task for a system that executes the process many times. The function $F(\mathcal{P})$ to be optimized is proportional to the average number of time units in the process. In accordance with the definitions (4) and (6) it can be written as $F(\mathcal{P}) = \sum_{j'\in Z'} a_j n_j$, where a_j are constants which depend on the type and frequency of the process. If all $T(j)$ satisfy condition (2) then a_{j*} is equal to the probability that P_{j*} participates in $\mathcal{P}$. Let p_k, $k = \{1, \ldots, N\}$, be the probability that a group of k processors participate in $\mathcal{P}$. If the coefficients n_j are ordered as $n_1 \geq, \ldots, \geq n_N$, then

$$a_j = \sum_{d=1}^{N-j+1} p_d \frac{C_{N-j}^{d-1}}{C_N^d}, \quad j \in Z, \text{ where } \sum_{d=1}^{N} p_d = 1 .$$

3 Solution of the Optimization Task

To speed up the process one has to minimize $F(\mathcal{P})$ under either condition (8) or (9) and to determine the values n_j, $j \in Z$. For that we will use the two following theorems.

Theorem 3 *If the condition* $\sum\limits_{j\in Z} \frac{c_j}{n_j} = 1$ *holds true then* $\min F = (\sum\limits_{j\in Z} \sqrt{c_j a_j})^2$.

Proof. We use polar coordinates in N-dimensional space $(\sqrt{a_1 n_1}, \ldots, \sqrt{a_N n_N})$. Then from the system

$$\begin{cases} a_1 n_1 = F(\varphi) \prod\limits_{l=1}^{N-1} \sin^2 \varphi_l, \\ a_d n_d = F(\varphi) \cos^2 \varphi_{d-1} \prod\limits_{l=d}^{N-1} \sin^2 \varphi_l, \text{ where } d = 2, \ldots, N-1, \\ a_N n_N = F(\varphi) \cos^2 \varphi_{N-1} \end{cases} \tag{13}$$

one can represent the minimizing function as

$$F(\varphi) = \frac{c_1 a_1}{\prod\limits_{l=1}^{N-1} \sin^2 \varphi_l} + \sum_{d=2}^{N-1} \frac{c_d a_d}{\cos^2 \varphi_{d-1} \prod\limits_{l=d}^{N-1} \sin^2 \varphi_l} + \frac{c_N a_N}{\cos^2 \varphi_{N-1}} .$$

According to the definition of the extremum we have

$$\frac{\partial F(\varphi)}{\partial \varphi_l} = 0, \text{ where } l = 1, \ldots, N-1. \tag{14}$$

Let us consider $l = 1$. From (13) and (14) follow

$$\frac{n_1}{n_2} \cdot \frac{a_1}{a_2} = \frac{\sin^2 \varphi_1}{\cos^2 \varphi_1} \quad \text{and} \quad \frac{c_1 a_1}{\sin^4 \varphi_1} = \frac{c_2 a_2}{\cos^4 \varphi_1} . \tag{15}$$

Eliminating the parameter φ_1 we get $\frac{n_1}{n_2} = \sqrt{\frac{c_1 a_2}{c_2 a_1}}$. In an analog way we obtain $n_j = n_k \sqrt{\frac{c_k a_j}{c_j a_k}}$ for any j and $k \in Z$. Now using condition (8) for all $j = 1, \ldots, N$, we find

$$n_k = \sqrt{\frac{c_k}{a_k}} \left(\sum_{j=1}^{N} \sqrt{c_j a_j} \right).$$

Taking the sum of $a_k n_k$ over all $k \in Z$ yields $\min F = \left(\sum\limits_{j=1}^{N} \sqrt{c_j a_j} \right)^2$. $\qquad \square$

Applying this result to the investigated problem we obtain its solution

$$t(j^*, \mathcal{P}) = T(j^*) \sqrt{\frac{c_j^*}{a_j^*}} \left(\sum_{j=1}^{N} \sqrt{c_j a_j} \right) \text{ for any } j^* \in Z.$$

From the proved theorem follows

Theorem 4 *If the condition* $\sum\limits_{j' \in Z'} \frac{c_{j'}}{n_{j'}} + \frac{T_H}{n_l T_L} \sum\limits_{j'' \in Z''} c_{j''} = 1$, $l \in Z'$, *holds true then*

$$\min F = \left(\sqrt{a_l \left(c_l + \frac{T_H}{T_L} \sum\limits_{j'' \in Z''} c_{j''} \right)} + \sum\limits_{j' \in \{Z' \setminus l\}} \sqrt{c_{j'} a_{j'}} \right)^2 .$$

4 Application

Consider the two following examples.

Example 1. Let three processors participate in a process with $T(\mathcal{P}, Z) = 16T(1) + T(2) + T(3)$, and let $T(j)$ satisfy relation (2). Then according to [3] and [5] one solution is $n_1 + n_2 + n_3 = 54$. If we use theorem 3 then $n_1 + n_2 + n_3 = 36$, and the process can be speeded up by a factor of 1.5.

Example 2. Let us consider three processors with priorities 101, 010, 001; and an arbitration procedure [4] where condition (2) applies. If all processors or the first two participate in the arbitration then the system will execute a process of duration $T(1, Z) = 2T(1) + T(2)$. However, an arbitration between the last two processors requires $T(2, Z) = T(2) + T(3)$. So there are two different processes. Even in this case we find from (13)

$$\frac{2}{\sin^2 \varphi_1 \sin^2 \varphi_2} + \frac{1}{\cos^2 \varphi_1 \sin^2 \varphi_2} = F(\varphi)$$

and

$$\frac{1}{\cos^2 \varphi_1 \sin^2 \varphi_2} + \frac{1}{\cos^2 \varphi_2} = F(\varphi) \ .$$

Then $\cos^2 \varphi_2 = \frac{2}{2+\sin^2 \varphi_1}$, and from $\frac{\partial F(\varphi_1, \varphi_2(\varphi_1))}{\partial \varphi_1} = 0$ we have $n_1 = \frac{2}{\sqrt{3}}(1 + \sqrt{3})$, $n_2 = (1 + \sqrt{3})$, $n_3 = \frac{1}{\sqrt{3}}(1 + \sqrt{3})$.

5 Conclusion

The suggested synchronization method can be used to enhance the performance of distributed asynchronous processes. It gives the possibilities 1) to compute the optimal processors' synchronization delays, 2) to speed up the process without any changes to the processing elements and to the algorithm of the process, 3) to determine the duration of the process for a given system, 4) to find the subprocesses which contribute most to the global waiting time, and 5) to minimize the duration of the process by choosing an appropriate hardware configuration.

References

1. Borrill P.L.: Futurebus+: A Tutorial. VMEbus Applications **4** (1990) 25–34
2. Makhaniok M., Cherniavsky V., Marte C., Männer R.: Data Representation for Median Search Operation. Proc. 6th Int'l Symp. on Comp. & Inform. Sci., Antalya, Turkey **2** (1991) 1011–1017
3. Taub D.M.: Improved Control Acquisition Time for the IEEE 896 Futurebus. IEEE Micro **7** (1987) 52–62
4. Makhaniok M., Cherniavsky V., Männer R., Stucky O.: Reduced Bus Acquisition Time in Distributed Arbitration Systems. Electron. Lett. **25** (1989) 1593–1594
5. Makhaniok M., Cherniavsky V., Männer R., Stucky O.: Massively Parallel Realization of Logical Operations in Distributed Parallel Systems. Proc. Joint Int'l Conf. on Vector and Parallel Processing, Lecture Notes in Comp. Sci. **457**, Springer, Heidelberg (1990) 796–805

This article was processed using the LaTeX macro package with LLNCS style

Statistical Probabilistic Clock Synchronization Algorithm.

Pierre MOUKELI

Laboratoire LIP-IMAG, Ecole Normale Supérieure de Lyon
46, allée d'Italie, 69364 LYON cedex 07 FRANCE

Abstract. Cristian proposed a probabilistic algorithm for clock synchronization. This algorithm however is not adapted to the changing system load, and it needs the knowledge of communication delay distribution. In this paper, we presents an algorithm similar to that of Cristian, which supports system load changes. This algorithm is based on the statistic of the communication delays.

1. Introduction.

A global time reference is useful for many distributed system applications. In the absence of a global hardware time, clock synchronization algorithms are the only mean to build a global time reference on the parallel machines. To do so, Cristian [3] proposed a probabilistic clock synchronization algorithm. The principle of the algorithm is that a processor makes several attempts to read the clock of another processor until the communication round trip delay is close to a given minimum value. Which means that the processor minimizes the error it makes when estimating the current time of the clock it is reading. However, this algorithm is not adapted to the changing system load and it supposes the knowledge of the distribution of communication delays.

In this paper we present a new version of the probabilistic algorithm using the statistics of communication delays to estimate the communication mean delay and standard deviation. From these two values we derive a lower bound of the probability to synchronize clocks, and we dynamically estimate the synchronization interval according to the system load and the desired precision. That is the interval of the round trip delays that can be accepted by a given node to estimate the clock time of another node. An implementation of our algorithm was made on a 32-node SuperNode of the LIP laboratory for the C_NET Debugging System CDS [5] [7]. Section 2 presents the notions of clock theory used in this paper, and states the problem of clock synchronization solved in this paper. Section 3 presents our solution to this problem : the statistical probabilistic algorithm. Section 4 presents implementation.

2. Presentation.

2.1. Basic notions about clocks.

Before presenting the clock synchronization problem, we introduce the notation and the notions used in this paper. Lower case letters refer to real time, and uppercase letters refer to clock time. We make the assumption that each processor P is associated with a hardware clock C_p. We make no distinction between clock and processor. For good clocks, the drift rate ρ is a constant on the order of 10^{-6}, such that :

- $C(t) = (1 + \rho)t.$ (R1)

In the Taylor series expansion of $1/(1 + \rho)$, the second-order terms can be ignored. So,

- $1/(1 + \rho) \approx 1 - \rho$, and $1/(1 -)) \approx 1 + \rho.$ (R2)

We call δ, the maximum deviation of two clocks; and R, the length of the time interval between two resynchronization points. If ϵ is the difference between the minimum and the maximum communication delay, from [1] we know that for N processors :

- $$\epsilon(1 - \frac{1}{N}) \leq \delta min. \tag{R3}$$

2.2. Some clock properties.

We call a good clock any clock verifing the following properties; C is a set of clocks; **T** is a synchronization interval [2] (we make no assumption about faulty clocks) :
• Any clock in C is a continuous function of the real time:
$$\forall C \in C, \forall t \in \Re, \forall d > 0 : C(t) \leq C(t + d). \tag{P1}$$
But generally clocks are discrete functions, so we have :
$$\forall C \in C, \exists g \geq 0, \forall t \in \Re, \forall d \geq g : C(t) \leq C(t + d). \tag{P'1}$$
• The difference between two good clocks is bounded :
$$\exists \delta \in \Re^+, \forall C_i, C_j \in C^2, \forall t \in T : |C_i(t) - C_j(t)| \leq \delta. \tag{P2}$$
• The drift from real time is bounded, and the clock is within an envelop of real time :
$$\exists \rho \in \Re, \forall C \in C, \forall t1, t2 \in T^2, t1 \leq t2 :$$
$$(1- \rho)(t2 - t1) \leq C(t2) - C(t1) \leq (1+ \rho)(t2 - t1). \tag{P3}$$
• A clock C is a good clock during the real-time interval $[t_1, t_2]$ if it is a monotonic, differentiable function on $[T_1, T_2]$, where $C(t_1) = T_1$ and $C(t_2) = T_2$:
$$\exists \rho \in \Re, \forall C \in C, \forall t \in [t_1, t_2] : \left| \frac{dC(t)}{dt} - 1 \right| < \rho. \tag{P4}$$
• The communication delay Δ is small enough so that the clocks can be synchronized at the end of the period R using K messages : $\quad R - K\Delta \leq \dfrac{(1 + \rho)\delta}{2\rho}. \tag{P5}$

2.3. Problem statement.

The clock synchronization problem is formally stated in [2] [4]. We just present an informal description of the solution in [4]; we then show the limitations with that solution. In order to achieve clock synchronization, Cristian [4] presented an original scheme : the probabilistic synchronization algorithm, in which the worst-case skews to synchronize clocks can be made as small as desired. The main idea can be sketched as follow. Each processor P makes several attempts to read the other clocks. At each attempt, the processor P sends a message to the processor Q requesting its clock time. When Q receives that request, it replies by sending a message to P, saying that "Time is T". Whenever P receives that reply, it estimates the round trip delay Δ using its own clock. If Δ is close to the estimated minimum round trip delay, so is the reading error; then P uses T and Δ to estimate the current time of clock Q : P has reached the rapport with Q. Otherwise, P ignores Δ and after a certain amount of time, it makes a new attempt to read Q's clock. By retrying often enough, P can read the other clocks to any given precision with probability as close to one as desired. The upper bound of the interval of acceptable (i.e. close to min) round trip delays is determined according to the desired precision and the supposed known distribution of the round trip delay. Cristian proved that, if T is the time at Q's clock when Q received the request from P; Δ is the half round trip delay experienced by P; min is the estimated minimum half round trip delay; and ρ is the maximum drift rate; then the value displayed by Q's clock when P receives the message "Time is T" is in the interval (called the clock reading interval) :
- $\quad I = [T + (1 + \rho)\Delta min, \ T + 2(1 + 2\rho)\Delta - (1 + \rho)\Delta min]. \tag{R4}$

Cristian [4] used this scheme to derive an algorithm to achieve clock synchronization. There are two main limitations with that algorithm. First, this algorithm badly behaves when the system load increases. Indeed, in such cases, the round trip increases, and so is the number of the attempts to reach the rapport. This can lead to a situation where the synchronization cannot be achieved by that algorithm. Second, the need to know the distribution of communication delay. Unfortunately, in most cases the system load behaves unpredictably and so is the communication delay.

3. Statistical probabilistic algorithm.

To overcome the changing load problem we suggest to estimate dynamically the interval of acceptable round trip delays. One way to do so is to choose the mean of the round trip delay as the center of that interval. Its length must be fixed according to the desired precision. It is shown in [1] (see R5) that it is the reading error (i.e. variation of the round trip) that imposes a bound to the synchronization accuracy. So there is no special need to choose the minimum round trip as the reference unit to compute the current time of the clock being read. This minimum is a constant; any modification of the upper bound of the acceptable round trip delays -as proposed in [4] to deal with the system load- will alter the clock synchronization accuracy. And more generally, the use of constants leads to the lack of flexibility in clock synchronization algorithms. The mean of the round trip delays can be estimated with the average of these delays. By doing so, we also overcome the problem of the round trip delay distribution because the statistics of these delays give a lower bound of the probability to reach the rapport. We are now going to state more formally our solution.

3.1. Attempting to read a remote clock using the mean of the round trip.

To read a remote clock, we adopt the strategy sketched in §2.2 as in [4]. Let P be the requesting processor, Q the replier, T the time carried by Q's reply, Δ the half round trip delay experienced by P, and $\overline{\Delta}$ the round trip mean delay computed by P.

Theorem. If the clock of processors P and Q are correct, and if there exists $\varepsilon \geq 0$ such that $|\Delta - \overline{\Delta}| \leq \varepsilon$, then , the current value $C_Q(t)$ of Q's clock when P receives the "Time is T" message is in the interval: $C_Q(t) \in [T + (1 - 2\rho)(\overline{\Delta} - 2\varepsilon), T + 2(1 + 2\rho)\Delta - (\overline{\Delta} - 2\varepsilon)]$.

Proof. Let P and Q be as defined above. Let $2d \geq 0$ be the real time of the round trip delay between the sending of the request and the receiving of the reply at node P. Let $2\overline{d} \geq 0$ be the real time of the round trip mean delay. Let $\overline{d} + \alpha$ and $\overline{d} + \beta$ be the real time delay experienced by the request and the reply messages, respectively :

$$2d = 2\overline{d} + \alpha + \beta; \tag{1}$$

There exists $\partial \geq 0$, such that : $\partial \geq |d - \overline{d}|;\ 2\partial \geq |\alpha|$ and $2\partial \geq |\beta|$. (2)

$$(1, 2) \Rightarrow 2d - 2\overline{d} + 2\partial \geq \beta. \tag{3}$$

Since P and Q are good clocks : (H)

$$(P3) \Rightarrow C_Q(t) \in [T + (1 - \rho)(\overline{d} + \beta), T + (1 + \rho)(\overline{d} + \beta)]. \tag{4}$$

$$(2, 3, 4) \Rightarrow C_Q(t) \in [T + (1 - \rho)(\overline{d} - 2\partial), T + (1 + \rho)(\overline{d} + 2d - 2\overline{d} + 2\partial). \tag{5}$$

$$(5) \Rightarrow \quad C_Q(t) \in [T + (1 - \rho)(\overline{d} - 2\partial), T + (1 + \rho)(2d - (\overline{d} - 2\partial))]. \tag{6}$$

Since the clock used by processor P to measure $d, \overline{d}$ and ∂ can drift at a rate at most ρ from real time, it follows from (P3) that :

$$(1 - \rho)\Delta \leq d \leq (1 + \rho)\Delta; \quad (1 - \rho)\overline{\Delta} \leq \overline{d} \leq (1 + \rho)\overline{\Delta}; \quad \exists \, \varepsilon \geq 0 : \partial \leq (1 + \rho)\gamma. \tag{7}$$

$$(H), (7) \Rightarrow \quad (1 - \rho)|\Delta - \overline{\Delta}| \leq |d - \overline{d}| \leq (1 + \rho)|\Delta - \overline{\Delta}| \tag{8}$$

$$(R2), (2), (8) \Rightarrow \quad |\Delta - \overline{\Delta}| \leq (1 + 2\rho)\gamma. \tag{9}$$

$$(R2), (6, 7) \Rightarrow C_Q(t) \in [T + (1 - 2\rho)\overline{\Delta} - 2\gamma, T + 2(1 + 2\rho)(\Delta + \gamma) - \overline{\Delta}]. \tag{10}$$

Let $\varepsilon \geq 0$ be : $\varepsilon = (1 + 2\rho)\,\gamma.$ By replacing γ in formulae (9-10) we have :

$$(R2), (9) \Rightarrow \quad |\Delta - \overline{\Delta}| \leq \varepsilon. \tag{11}$$

$$(R2), (10) \Rightarrow C_Q(t) \in [T + (1 - 2\rho)(\overline{\Delta} - 2\varepsilon), T + 2(1 + 2\rho)\Delta - (\overline{\Delta} - 2\varepsilon)]. \tag{12}$$

Cqfd.

This theorem means that if the round trip delay experienced by P to read Q's clock is within a given distance ε from the mean round trip delay, then P can determine an interval which contains Q's clock. The constant ε is the maximum tolerable deviation of the reading error from the mean $\overline{\Delta}$. As argued in [4], the interval (12) is the smallest interval that P can determine in terms of $T, \Delta, \overline{\Delta}$ and ε. Since P does not know where Q's clock is in the interval (12), P minimizes the error it can make in estimating $C_Q(t)$ by choosing the middle of that interval as the estimator C_Q^P of $C_Q(t)$:

$$C_Q^P (T, \Delta, \varepsilon) = T + (1 + 2\rho)\Delta - \rho(\overline{\Delta} - 2\varepsilon). \tag{13}$$

With that estimation, the maximum error P can make in reading Q's clock is the half of the length of the interval (12) : $\quad e = (1 + 2\rho)\Delta - (1 - \rho)(\overline{\Delta} - 2\varepsilon). \tag{14}$

This means that, if Q is a master processor and P a slave, by setting its clock to $C_Q^P (T, \Delta, \varepsilon)$, P is at most at a distance of e from Q. Therefore, e is the minimum synchronization accuracy between P and Q's clocks.

3.2. Estimation of the round trip mean delay.

An efficient and unbiased estimator of the round trip mean delay is the average of the round trip delays experienced by P at every attempt to read Q's clock. At the n_{th} attempt, if $2\Delta_n$ is the round trip delay experienced by P, the average $2\overline{\Delta_n}$ of the round

trip delay is : $\quad \overline{\Delta} \approx \overline{\Delta_n} = \frac{1}{n}\sum_{j=0}^{n}\Delta_j = \frac{n-1}{n}\overline{\Delta_{n-1}} + \frac{1}{n}\Delta_n. \tag{15}$

At every attempt to read Q's clock, P measures the round trip delay $2\Delta_n$ and computes its contribution to the average. From (15) we can see that if $\Delta_n \geq \overline{\Delta_n}$, then $\overline{\Delta}$ increase; otherwise, $\overline{\Delta}$ decrease. With the formulae (13) and (15), P adapts the synchronization to the changes of the systems load which is partially responsible of the above variation of $\overline{\Delta}$. The standard deviation σ of the round trip delay can be estimated with one of the following expressions (efficient and biased estimator, unbiased and not efficient estimator) :

- $$\sigma^2 \approx S^2 = \frac{1}{n}\sum_{j=0}^{n}(\Delta_j - \overline{\Delta})^2; \text{ or } \sigma^2 \approx \hat{S}^2 = \frac{1}{n-1}\sum_{j=0}^{n}(\Delta_j - \overline{\Delta})^2. \quad (16), (17)$$

3.3. A lower bound of the probability to reach the rapport.

The constant ε in (11) is fixed according to the desired minimum accuracy, for example using (R3). A good knowledge of the distribution of Δ leads to a better choice of ε. However this distribution is unknown in most cases. Therefore, we have to estimate it, provided a fixed value of ε. If σ is the standard deviation of the round trip delay, the

Chebychev's theorem yields that :
$$\text{Proba}(|\Delta_n - \overline{\Delta}| \geq \varepsilon) \leq \frac{\sigma^2}{\varepsilon^2} = 1 - p. \quad (18)$$

Then the probability to have $|\Delta - \overline{\Delta}| \leq \varepsilon$ is : $p = 1 - (\sigma^2/\varepsilon^2)$. It is the lower bound of the probability to reach the rapport. This means that, provided a maximum acceptable reading error ε and the statistic of the round trip delay, P can estimate the probability to reach the rapport at the next attempt. The larger ε is, the closer of 1 is the probability to reach the rapport.

3.4. The average number of attempts to reach the rapport.

Since each attempt to reach the rapport needs two messages (request and reply), if p is the probability to reach the rapport, Bernoulli law yields that the average number of messages to achieve synchronization is : $\tilde{n} = 2(1 - p)$. (19)

If the distribution of the round trip delay is unknown, then the lower bound p given by (16) can be used as an estimator of p.

4. Experimental studies.

We implemented our algorithm on the SuperNode and integrated to the C_NET Debugging System [7]. With $\varepsilon = 1 \mu$ (see table), the observed probability to reach rapport was 0,996 with a maximum synchronization error : e = 3 μs (see 14). We reached rapports with one attempt. Meanwhile, with Cristian's algorithm (also implemented) the probability was 0,004 with the same error; and we did not reach the rapport. With $\varepsilon = 2 \mu$s, the probability to reach rapport with our algorithm was 0,999 with a maximum synchronization error of 6 μs. We reached rapports with one attempt. Cristian's algorithm behaved like our one with the same error. For values $\varepsilon > 2 \mu$s, we observed no change in the two algorithm behaviours, apart from the increasing of the error e. The computed lower bound p (18) was not far from the observed probability. It would have been a good estimator of that probability. For normal-like distributions of round trip delays, our algorithm is certainly better than Cristian one; which is the case in our environment.

Reading error ε	Max error e	Cristian scheme	Statistical scheme	Lower bound p
1 μs	3 μs	0,004	0,9956	0,985
2 μs	6 μs	0,999	0,999	0,996

Probability to reach rapport.

Conclusion.

We have presented a new version of the probabilistic algorithm for clock synchronization. This algorithm is based on the use of the statistics of round trip delays. This algorithm is better than Cristian one, if the distribution of these delay is normal-like. Following Chebychev's theorem, we have also derived a lower bound of the probability to reach rapport. This probability can be used to estimate the number of attempts to reach the rapport if the distribution of round trip delay is unknown.

The programmer can make some hypothesis on the distribution of round trip delays and use the statistic of these delays at run time to test these hypothesis. For example, if these delays follow the normal distribution, then : $Z = ((\Delta - \overline{\Delta})/\sigma)$ is bound to follow the normal distribution; which means that : $\overline{Z} = 0$, $\sigma_Z = 1$ (standard deviation of Z), and $Proba(|Z - \overline{Z}| \leq 1,96) \approx 0,95$. The χ^2 test is also very useful. The advantage of such tests is to find a better bound of the probability p in (19) and a better length ε of the interval of acceptable round trip delays.

The improvement made by Alari and Ciuffoletti [6] to Cristian algorithm can also apply to our one. Some of the algorithms currently proposed in the literature for clock synchronization can be improved by a better knowledge of the communication delay. Statistics can be of a good help in that process.

Acknowledgements. Special thanks to J.M. Adamo who encouraged me to produce this paper, and to Christophe Bonello and Luis Trejo, my colleagues in the LSP team and the C_NET project.

References.

[1] Lundelius Jennifer, Lynch Nancy
An Upper and Lower Bound for Clock Synchronization
Information and Control, Vol. 62, N° 2-3, 1984, PP. 190-204
[2] Lamport L., Miller-Smith P.M.
Synchronizing Clocks in Presence of Faults
Journal of the Association for Computing Machinery
Vol. 32, N° 1, January 1985, PP. 52-78
[3] Dolev D., Halpern J.Y., Strong R.
On the Possibility and Impossibility of Achieving Clock Synchronization
Journal of Computer and System Sciences, N° 32, 1986, PP. 230-250.
[4] Cristian Flaviu
Probabilistic Clock Synchronization
Distributed Computing, N° 3, 1989, PP. 146-158
[5] Adamo J.M., Alhafez N., Bonello C., Bonneville J., Moukeli P., Trejo L.
Developing A High Level Programming Environment for SuperNode,
Proc. of Transputer Applications 91, Aug. 28-30, Glasgow, IOS Press.
[6] Alari G., Ciuffoletti Augusto.
Improving the Probabilistic Clock Synchronization Algorithm
Università degli Studi di Pisa -Dipartimento di Informatica
Corso Italia n. 40, 56100 Pisa -Italy
[7] Moukeli Pierre
Designing CDS: the C_NET Debugging System.
Supercomputer Debugging workshop'91
Albuquerque New Mexico (Proceedings to be published)

A SIMD Architecture for Medical Imaging

Wieslaw L. Nowinski

Institute of Systems Science, National University of Singapore
Heng Mui Keng Terrace, Kent Ridge, Singapore 0511

Abstract. This paper addresses parallel processing in 3D medical imaging. A SIMD architecture common for image reconstruction, image processing, and volume visualization is proposed. The ray casting algorithm for volume visualization along with some of its improvements is described. The image-space parallelization of ray casting is given. The parallelization ensures an even load balancing among processors and conflict free memory access without the need of replicating the entire volume data set. This parallelization covers distribution of the volume data set among global memory modules, distribution of the image among local memories, processors - global memory modules mapping, generation and scheduling of image parts, and processor program.

1 Introduction

The major role for 2D medical imaging is diagnosis. Diagnosis, however, is only part of patient care, and it is followed by treatment. In clinical management decisions, computer-assisted surgery, radiation therapy, complex fractures or abnormalities, and many others, 3D medical imaging is required. In 3D medical imaging, the volume data set is formed from multiple 2D slices. In order to generate and visualize volume data, the following sequence of steps has to be performed: *measurement data collection*, *measurement data processing*, *image reconstruction*, *image processing*, and *volume visualization*, see Fig. 1.

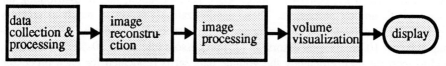

Fig. 1. The sequence of steps in 3D medical imaging

Measurement data may be collected by various medical imaging modalities, such as CT, MRI, PET, SPECT, ultrasound, confocal microscopy. The ways of processing measurement data depend on the imaging modality used. Images are reconstructed from measurement data. For image reconstruction two main groups of methods are used: *transform methods* and *series expansion methods* [8,15]. The most popular image reconstruction method in medical applications is the *convolution method* [8]. To preprocess data and to enhance images, 2D and 3D image processing is required [7,21]. Volume visualization is the most computationally expensive step. Moreover to effectively visualize volume data, it is important to be able to image it from different viewpoints. In general, the techniques for displaying volume data can be classified as follows: *surface-based* techniques, *binary voxel* techniques, and *semi-transparent volume rendering* techniques [14]. The main advantages of volume rendering over other visualization techniques are its superior image quality and ability to generate images without explicitly defining surfaces. On the other hand, however, volume rendering is computationally intensive.

Rendering the volumetric data set involves sampling it and mapping each sampled value to a color and opacity. Then, the contribution from each sample is composited into the image. There are two main approaches to volume rendering: *ray casting* [13,23] and *cell-by-cell projection* [23,24]. Volume images are very large 3D matrices. For example, a volumetric data set consisting of 512^3 samples demands 128MB memory, provided that the data values are bytes. Since all voxels participate in the generation of an image, rendering time grows linearly with the size of the volumetric data set. Therefore to speed up medical imaging and, especially, volume rendering, specialized architectures and parallel processing are required.

For parallel image reconstruction, SIMD [6,16], MIMD [10,11,18], and PRAM [19] architectures have been proposed. The SIMD architectures [6,16] are for the convolution method.

For image processing, a SIMD architecture is considered to be the most suitable [3]. Several architectures for image processing have been reviewed, e.g., in [4,22].

To speed up rendering, several specialized architectures have been developed. A survey and comparison of some of them have been presented in [9]. Moreover, several general-purpose systems, such as Pixel Machine, Silicon Graphics 4D, Pixel-Planes 5, Apollo DN10000VS, or Stellar Graphics Supercomputer GS2000, provide some support for volume visualization.

It should be noted that in subsequent steps of medical imaging, various architectures are used. However, it is more efficiently to use one common architecture specific to image reconstruction, image processing, and especially volume rendering. In this paper we show that a SIMD architecture [16] designed originally for the parallel convolution method can be adapted to volume rendering.

Several approaches have been proposed to parallelize ray casting. The approaches presented in [2,12,25] consist in image-space parallelization, i.e., in distributing the image pixels among processors. These parallelizations, however, result in memory contention and uneven load balancing among processors. For example, in [2] the speedup is below 10 on 100 processors. In [25] processors idle about 30-50% of the time, and to increase their efficiency the volume data set is replicated for each processor. These drawbacks may be avoided by exploiting object-space parallelism inherent in ray casting [20].

In this paper we show that in image-space parallel ray casting it is possible to ensure an even load balancing among processors and to avoid memory contention without the need of replicating the volume data set.

The goals of the paper are threefold:

- Use of the same SIMD architecture for image reconstruction, image processing, and volume visualization.

- Ensure a conflict free memory access for image-space parallel ray casting without the need of replicating the entire volume data set.

- Ensure an even load balancing among processors for image-space parallel ray casting and achieve a high efficiency of their utilization.

The rest of the paper is organized as follows. The SIMD architecture used originally for the parallel convolution method is reviewed in Section 2. The standard ray casting algorithm along with some of its improvements is presented in Section 3. Parallel ray casting using the SIMD architecture is discussed in Section 4. Conclusions are drawn in Section 5.

2 SIMD Architecture

In [16] a SIMD architecture for the parallel convolution method of image reconstruction was designed, see Fig. 2.

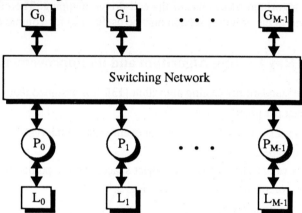

Fig. 2. SIMD architecture

It contains M processors P_i, $i = 0...M$-1. The i-th processor is provided with a local memory L_i. Moreover, the processors have access to a global memory. The global memory is a parallel memory and consists of M memory modules G_i, $i = 0...M$-1. The processors access the global memory modules via a switching network. An image is reconstructed in M steps. In the k-th step, the switching network links the i-th processor with the $((i+k)$ mod $M)$-th memory module, where "mod" denotes the modulo function. This method of linking is suitable to parallelize backprojection used in the convolution method [17]. Thus, the processors - global memory mapping is the following

$$P_i \rightarrow G_{(i+k)\,\mathrm{mod}M}, \qquad i = 0...M-1, \quad k = 0...K-1 \qquad (1)$$

with $K = M$. This way a conflict free memory access is achieved.

There are two spaces in image reconstruction: *image space* and *projection space*. In [18] two types of mapping of the projection space into the image space have been distinguished:

- *pixel-driven mapping* (i.e., for a given pixel all rays influencing it are determined);

- *ray-driven mapping* (i.e., for a given ray all pixels affected by it are determined).

In [19] it has been shown that the type of mapping has a vital influence on memory utilization. Namely for the pixel-driven mapping, a measurement data has to be stored in the global memory, whereas an image is distributed among local memories. Conversely for the ray-driven mapping where an image should be kept in the global memory, while a measurement data is distributed among local memories.

There exist some similarities between image reconstruction and volume rendering. In volume rendering there are also two spaces: *image space* and *object space*. Image reconstruction consists in a suitable mapping of the projection space into the image space. Similarly volume rendering which maps the object space into the image space. Moreover, two types of mapping of the object space into the image space may be distinguished:

- *pixel-driven mapping* (i.e., for a given pixel all cells influencing it are determined);
- *cell-driven mapping* (i.e., for a given cell all pixels affected by it are determined).

Note that the ray casting algorithm exploits pixel-driven mapping, while the cell-to-cell projection algorithm makes use of the cell-driven mapping. Therefore, the architecture presented in the previous section may be useful also for volume rendering.

3 Standard Ray Casting Algorithm and its Improvements

Let us recall the standard ray casting algorithm [13]. It is assumed that:

- one ray is cast per pixel
- volume data set is sampled along a ray at evenly spaced intervals
- all rays are parallel.

For each pixel a ray is cast through the object space, and the points of intersection of the ray with the volume are calculated - see Fig. 3.

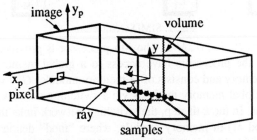

Fig. 3. Geometrical interpretation of ray casting

Samples are drawn at equally spaced intervals along the ray between the points of intersection. Sample points along the ray do not lie, in general, directly on voxels. Therefore, the scalar data value at a desired sample point is calculated using trilinear interpolation from the eight voxels surrounding the sample point. These voxels form a *cell*. A color and opacity for a specific data value are obtained using transform functions (lookup tables). The opacities and colors are then composited with each other on depth-sorted order yielding a color of the pixel.

Trilinear interpolation may be performed in several ways. For example, in [1] it uses 24 multiplications. In [23] a trilinear interpolation equation demands 12 multiplications; in addition to determine coefficients of the equation, a linear system of 8 equations has to be solved. In this paper we use approach presented in [20] which requires 7 multiplications only. The approach consists in decompositing of trilinear interpolation into three steps: 4 linear interpolations along the x axis, 2 linear interpolations along the y axis, and 1 linear interpolation along the z axis. Then for given points a, b linear interpolation of a function f() in the point c is done as follows

$$f(c) = (f(b) - f(a)) h - f(a), \tag{2}$$

where $h = (c - a) / (b - a)$.

Suppose e_x, e_y, e_z denote the size of the cell in x, y, z direction, respectively. Assume that $c_x = 1/e_x$, $c_y = 1/e_y$, $c_z = 1/e_z$. For each sample (x,y,z) the following values are calculated

$$x_0 = xc_x, \qquad y_0 = yc_y, \qquad z_0 = zc_z. \tag{3}$$

Then h_x, h_y, h_z which determine interpolation geometry and indices i_x, i_y, i_z identifying a cell which contains the sample are calculated as follows

$$\begin{cases} i_x = \text{int}(x_0) \\ h_x = \text{fract}(x_0) \end{cases}, \qquad \begin{cases} i_y = \text{int}(y_0) \\ h_y = \text{fract}(y_0) \end{cases}, \qquad \begin{cases} i_z = \text{int}(z_0) \\ h_z = \text{fract}(z_0) \end{cases}. \tag{4}$$

The functions int() and fract() return the argument's integer and fractional part, respectively.

In general, there are two orders of compositing: *front-to-back* and *back-to-front*. For a front-to-back order compositing is done as follows [24]

$$a_{out} = a_{in} + (1 - a_{in}) a, \tag{5}$$
$$c_{out} = c_{in} + (1 - a_{in}) ac, \tag{6}$$

where a, c are opacity and color of a sample, and indices in, out denote values as a ray approaches and leaves the sample, respectively. A front-to-back order, as opposed to a back-to-front one, allows to adaptively terminate ray casting [13]. We reformulate Eqs. (5), (6) in the following way

$$a_1 = (1 - a_{in}) a, \tag{7}$$
$$a_{out} = a_{in} + a_1 \tag{8}$$

and

$$c_{out} = c_{in} + a_1 c. \tag{9}$$

Then compositing (7), (8), (9) uses only 4 multiplications instead of 7 multiplications required in standard compositing (5), (6) (i.e., 1 multiplication for opacity compositing and 2 multiplications for compositing each of the R, G, B colors). In addition, interpolation formulae (2) as well as compositing formula (7), (8), (9) may be expressed by means of the same function

$$p = p(x_1, x_2, x_3, x_4) = (x_1 - x_2) x_3 + x_4. \tag{10}$$

This approach facilitates the design for a processor (see Chapter 4).

4 Ray Casting on the SIMD Architecture

Parallel ray casting demands the volume data set to be kept in the global memory and the image to be distributed among local memories. Then the conflict free memory access condition is satisfied by using Eq. (1). This demands adequate distributions of the volume data set among the global memory modules and the image among the local memories. Recall that mapping (1) requires the global memory to be accessed in K steps. For image reconstruction $K = M$, i.e., the number of steps equals the number of processors. For ray casting K depends on orientation of the volume.

The time of processing of a pixel is proportional to the number of samples drawn along a ray which is cast from the pixel. As one ray cast per pixel and evenly spaced sampling are assumed, the time of processing of any part of the image is proportional to the amount of volume which projected orthogonally onto the image plane gives the considered part of the image. Therefore to ensure an even load balancing, each processor should process the same amount of volume. Let us assume that dimensions of each volume part are the same. Then the even load balancing condition is equivalent to the requirement that each processor processes an image part of the same size and shape. Note that the even load balancing condition has to be satisfied within a given step.

Parallel ray casting is done in K steps. These steps are performed one after another. For each step opacity and color compositing is done for samples along a segment of ray lying in a volume part being processed. The complete opacity and color are obtained using superposition provided that the order of processed volume parts ensures the ray continuity. This way in each step the volume data set may be divided into three subregions: *being accessed (visible)* composed of the volume parts under processing, *previously accessed (transparent)* composed of the volume parts which were processed in the previous steps, and *not accessible (opaque)*. Let $A_{i,k}$ denote the image part processed by the P_i processor in the k-th step. The image-space parallel ray casting algorithm may be formulated as follows

> **procedure** ParallelRayCasting(K,M)
> **begin**
>   **for** $k = 0$ **to** $K - 1$ **do**
>   **for** $i = 0$ **to** $M - 1$ **do in parallel**
>   process the image part $A_{i,k}$
> **end**

Consider the distribution of the volume data set among the global memory modules. Let us divide the volume data set by parallel, equidistant planes into M equal slabs S_i, $i = 0...M-1$. Assume that the slabs are distributed among M global memory modules in such a way that the i-th slab is stored in the i-th global memory module M_i, see Fig. 4. To ensure a cell continuity within a module, the planes have to pass exactly through voxels, and the scalar data values on the planes have to be stored in both neighbouring modules.

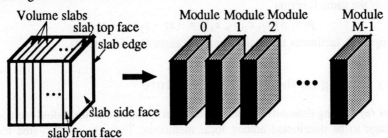

Fig. 4. Distribution of the volume data set among the global memory modules

Consider the most simple case when the volume is rotated about the x axis (the planes dividing the volume are parallel to the $\{y,z\}$ plane). Then the i-th image part is an orthogonal projection of the front and top faces of the i-th slab onto the image plane. In this case a volume part is an entire slab, and the i-th processor accesses only the i-th global memory module. Thus, the processors - global memory modules mapping

$$P_i \rightarrow M_i, \qquad i = 0 \ldots M - 1 \tag{11}$$

matches mapping (1) for $K = 1$.

Suppose the volume is rotated about the y axis. Then orthogonal projections of the slab front faces onto the image plane do not cover the entire region of image. In general in any step, the region of image may be divided into three subregions: *processed, under processing,* and *not processed yet.* Moreover, the contents of more than one slab may contribute to a pixel. A geometrical interpretation of this case for $M = 4$ is given in Fig. 5.

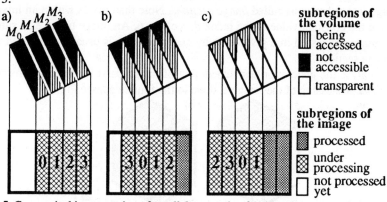

Fig. 5. Geometrical interpretation of parallel ray casting for the volume rotated about the y axis; volume and image for: a) step 0, b) step 1, c) step 2. The numbers denote the indices of processors

The image is generated in three steps, and a slab contains three volume parts. Let $V_{i,k}$ denote the volume part processed by the P_i processor in the k-th step. In the Step 0, the region of image is divided into two subregions: *under processing* and *not processed yet,* see Fig. 5a. The *under processing* region contains 4 (in general M) equal image parts. An image part is an orthogonal projection of the front face of a slab onto the image plane. In the Step 1, all pixels in the image part $A_{3,0}$ are already processed and P_3 starts to process a new image part $A_{3,1}$ lying in the previous step in the *not processed yet* subregion, see Fig. 5b. In the Step 2, the pixels in $A_{2,1}$ are already processed and P_2 starts to process a new image part $A_{2,2}$ lying in the previous step in the *not processed yet* subregion, see Fig. 5c. This way the whole region of image is processed with an even load balancing among processors and without memory contention.

For these steps, the processors - global memory modules mapping is the following

$$P_i \rightarrow M_{(i+k)\bmod 4}, \qquad i = 0, 1, 2, 3, \qquad k = 0, 1, 2. \tag{12}$$

Relationship (12) for any M reads as

$$P_i \rightarrow M_{(i+k)\bmod M}, \qquad i = 0 \ldots M - 1, \qquad k = 0 \ldots K - 1 \tag{13}$$

and it matches Eq. (1).

Consider the most general case when the volume may be rotated about the x, y, and

z axes (a geometrical interpretation of this case for $M = 4$ is presented in Fig. 6).

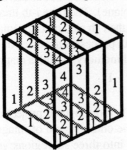

Fig. 6. Projections of the slab edges onto the image plane. For each image section the number of global memory modules to be accessed is given

In general, the contents of more than one slab contribute to a pixel. Let the *memory depth index d* determine the number of global memory modules to be accessed in order to process a pixel. Projections of the slab edges onto the image plane divide the region of image into subregions called *image sections*. Note than pixels within an image section have the constant value of the index d, see Fig. 6. An image part, i.e., a subregion of the image processed in a given step by one processor, is usually composed of several image sections.

Let us analyse the generation and scheduling of image parts for the case presented in Fig. 6. The processing of the image is done in the four steps, see Fig. 7.

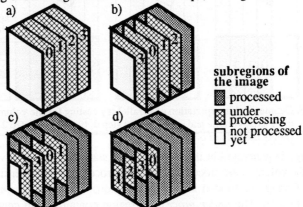

subregions of the image
- ▨ processed
- ▨ under processing
- ☐ not processed yet

Fig. 7. Generation and scheduling of image parts for:
a) step 0, b) step 1, c) step 2, d) step 3

Step 0: The region of image is divided into two subregions: *under processing* and *not processed yet*, see Fig. 7a. The *under processing* region contains 4 (in general M) equal image parts. An image part is an orthogonal projection of the top and front faces of a slab onto the image plane.

Step 1: From the image parts determined in the previous step, image sections with $d = 1$ are subtracted, see Fig. 7b. Since $A_{3,0}$ is already processed (as its $d = 1$), P_3 starts to process a new image part lying in the previous step in the *not processed yet* subregion.

Step 2: Image parts are generated as follows: $A_{i,2} = A_{i,1} -$ (image sections with $d = 2$), $i = 0, 1$; $A_{3,2} = A_{3,1} -$ (image sections with $d = 1$). Since $A_{2,1}$ is already processed, P_2 starts to process a new image part lying in the previous step in the *not processed yet* subregion, see Fig. 7c.

Step 3: $A_{0,3} = A_{0,2} -$ (image sections with $d = 3$); $A_{3,3} = A_{3,2} -$ (image sections with $d = 2$); $A_{2,3} = A_{2,2} -$ (image sections with $d = 1$). As $A_{1,2}$ is already processed, P_1 starts to process a new image part lying in the previous step in the *not processed yet* subregion, see Fig. 7d.

Let us generalize the above considerations. Assume that l_x, l_y, l_z denote the size of the volume in x, y, z direction, respectively. Suppose the vertices of the volume at the initial (unrotated) position are denoted by G_j, $j = 0...7$, and their coordinates are $G_0(-l_x/2, -l_y/2, l_z/2)$, $G_1(-l_x/2, l_y/2, l_z/2)$, $G_2(l_x/2, l_y/2, l_z/2)$, $G_3(l_x/2, -l_y/2, l_z/2)$, $G_4(-l_x/2, -l_y/2, -l_z/2)$, $G_5(-l_x/2, l_y/2, -l_z/2)$, $G_6(l_x/2, l_y/2, -l_z/2)$, $G_7(l_x/2, -l_y/2, -l_z/2)$. Let α, β, γ be the angles of rotation of the volume about the x, y, z axes, respectively. The coordinates of the vertices of the rotated volume H_j, $j = 0...7$, may easily be calculated by multiplying the coordinates of the vertices at the initial position by the rotation matrix R

$$H_j = R \, G_j, \qquad j = 0...7. \tag{14}$$

The rotation matrix R is composed of three matrices R_α, R_β, R_γ describing rotations about the x, y, z axes, respectively [5]. Projections of the rotated vertices onto the image plane determine points W_j, $j = 0...6$, as follows (see Fig. 8):

- W_1 - projection of the nearest vertex (i.e., with the highest value of z coordinate);
- $\{W_0, W_1, W_4, W_5\}$ - region of projections of the slab front faces;
- $\{W_1, W_2, W_3, W_4\}$ - region of projections of the slab top faces;
- $\{W_6, W_2, W_1, W_0\}$ - projection of the side face of the nearest slab (i.e., the slab S_0).

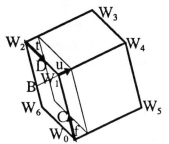

Fig. 8. Projections of the vertices of the rotated volume onto the image plane

The Step 0 may be done provided that the area of the regions $\{W_0, W_1, W_4, W_5\}$ and $\{W_1, W_2, W_3, W_4\}$ is not zero, i.e., provided that in both regions none of three points W_j are collinear; otherwise the way of division of the volume by the parallel planes must be changed. For any M the generation and scheduling of image parts may be done as shown above. In the Step 0 this involves the calculation of projections of the slab top and front faces. In subsequent steps, in order to calculate image parts recursively, the image sections along with their values of the memory depth index have to be calculated.

Below we show another, substantially simplified solution. Let v be a vector by which two subsequent slabs are translated. Its projection onto the image plane is a vector u by which two subsequent image parts are translated

$$u = (W_4 - W_1) / M. \tag{15}$$

Suppose an image part is determined by its corner points. Then W_0, W_1, W_2, and u are sufficient to calculate all image parts in the Step 0

$$A_{0,0} = \{W_0, W_1, W_2, W_2 + u, W_1 + u, W_0 + u\}, \tag{16}$$

$$A_{i,0} = A_{0,0} + iu, \qquad i = 1...M - 1. \tag{17}$$

To generate image parts in subsequent steps, let us introduce two vectors f, t

$$f = C - W_0, \qquad t = D - W_2, \tag{18}$$

where C, D are the points of intersection of the lines $(\{W_0, W_1\}, \{W_0+u, W_6+u\})$ and $(\{W_1, W_2\}, \{W_2+u, W_6+u\})$, respectively (see Fig. 8). Note that the memory depth index increases by 1 along the f vector in the region of projections of the slab front faces. Similarly, the memory depth index increases by 1 along the t vector in the region of projections of the slab top faces. Define the following areas

$$F_{0,k} = \{W_0, W_0 + kf, W_0 + u + (k-1)f, W_0 + u\}, \qquad k = 1...K - 1,$$
$$T_{0,k} = \{W_2, W_2 + kt, W_2 + u + (k-1)t, W_2 + u\}, \qquad k = 1...K - 1. \tag{19}$$

Then the image parts $A_{0,k}$ are generated as follows

$$A_{0,k} = A_{0,0} - F_{0,k} - T_{0,k}, \qquad k = 1...K - 1. \tag{20}$$

In the k-th step the $((M-k) \bmod M)$-th image part is already processed and a new image part in the *not processed yet* subregion is generated. Note that the image parts $A_{(M-k)\bmod M, k-1}$ and $A_{(M-k)\bmod M, k}$ are translated by the vector $-U$, where $U = uM$. Let

$$\delta_{i,j} = \begin{cases} 1 \text{ for } i \geq j, \\ 0 \text{ otherwise.} \end{cases} \tag{21}$$

Then the values of the index i for which $\delta_{i,(M-k)\bmod M} = 1$ determine the image parts to be translated. The first M image parts (for $K > M$) are translated by the vector $-U$, the next M image parts (for $K > 2M$) by the vector $-2U$, etc. In general, in the k-th step an image part is translated by the vector $-\text{int}((k-1)/M+1)U$. Therefore, the subsequent image parts $A_{i,k}$ are generated in the following way

$$A_{i,k} = A_{0,k} + iu - \delta_{i,(M-k)\bmod M} \text{int}((k-1)/M+1)U,$$
$$i = 1...M - 1, \qquad k = 1...K - 1. \tag{22}$$

The number of steps K may easily be calculated by determining the number of image parts which can be placed in the *not processed yet* subregion for $k = 0$. Let B be the point of intersection of the line $\{W_1, W_4\}$ and polyline $\{W_0, W_6, W_2\}$, see Fig. 8. Then

$$K = \text{ceil}\left(\frac{|B - W_1|}{|u|}\right) + 1, \tag{23}$$

where $|\cdot|$ denotes the length of vector, and the ceil() function returns the lowest integer not less than its argument. Note that the minimum number of steps is achieved when the volume is divided into slabs in such as way that the region $\{W_6, W_2, W_1, W_0\}$ has a smaller or equal area than any of the regions $\{W_0, W_1, W_4, W_5\}$ or $\{W_1, W_2, W_3, W_4\}$.

The reformulation of ray casting presented in Section 3 substantially facilitates the design for the processor. In fact, the processor is a simple multiplier/adder performing the function p() (see Eq. (10)) which describes both interpolation and compositing. In addition, it is able to do the AND operation (to perform the int() and fract() functions). In the k-th step the i-th processor runs the following program

```
procedure ProcessImagePart(i,k)
begin
    for all pixels within A_{i,k} do
        for all samples along a segment of ray which is cast from the pixel do
            identify a cell and calculate interpolation geometry - Eqs. (3), (4)
            perform 7 linear interpolations - Eq. (2)
            composite opacity - Eqs. (7), (8)
            composite color - Eq. (9)
end
```

5 Summary and Conclusions

The paper addresses parallel processing in 3D medical imaging. A SIMD architecture common for image reconstruction, image processing, and volume visualization is proposed. The image-space parallelization of ray casting is given. The parallelization ensures an even load balancing among processors and conflict free memory access without the need of replicating the entire volume data set. For M processors and N^3 volume data set, the speedup of image-space parallel ray casting on the SIMD architecture is $M \in [1,N]$. However, a higher speedup results in a greater number of processors and memory modules, as well as a more complicated switching network. A hybrid image-space/object-space parallel ray casting increases the speedup and reduces the cost. The processor (exploiting object-space parallelism) can then be designed either as a multiple multiplier/adder or an application specific integrated circuit [20].

Acknowledgements

The author wishes to thank the Institute of Systems Science, National University of Singapore for support on this research.

References

1. Buchanan D. L. and Semwal S. K.: *A new front to back composition technique for volume rendering*. In: CG International'90 (eds. Chua T. S. and Kunii T. L.), Springer-Verlag Tokyo 1990, 149-174.
2. Challinger J.: *Parallel volume rendering on a shared-memory multiprocessor*. Technical Report UCSC-CRL-91-23, University of California at Santa Cruz, July 1991, 1-23.
3. Danielsson P-E. and Ericsson T. S.: *LIPP - proposals for the design of an image processor array*. In: Computing Structures for Image Processing. Academic Press (ed. Duff M. J. B.), London 1983, 157-178.
4. Duff M. J. B. (ed.): *Computing Structures for Image Processing*. Academic Press, London 1983.
5. Foley J. D., van Dam A., Feiner S. K. and Hughes J. F.: *Computer Graphics. Principles and Practice*. 2nd ed. Addison-Wesley, Reading, Mass. 1990.
6. Gilbert B. K., Kenue S. K., Robb R. A. et al.: *Rapid execution of fan beam image recon-*

struction algorithms using efficient computational techniques and special-purpose processors. IEEE Trans. Biomed. Eng., BME-**28**, 2, 1981, 89-115.

7. Gonzales R. C. and Wintz P.: *Digital Image Processing.* 2nd ed., Addison-Wesley, Reading, Mass. 1987.

8. Herman G. T.: *Image Reconstruction from Projections. Fundamentals of Computerized Tomography.* Academic Press, New York 1980.

9. Kaufman A.: *Volume rendering architectures.* In: Tutorial on Volume Visualization Algorithms, Visualization90, San Francisco, CA, October 23, 1990, 58-65.

10. Kingswood N., Dagless E. L., Belchamber R. M. et al.: *Image reconstruction using the transputer.* IEE Proceedings, **133**, Pt. E. 3, May 1986, 139-144.

11. Lattard D. and Mazare G.: *Parallel image reconstruction by using a dedicated asynchronous celluar array.* In: Parallel Processing for Computer Vision and Display (eds. Dew P. M., Earnshow R. A., and Heywood T. R.), Addison-Wesley, Wokingham 1989, 479-488.

12. Levoy M.: *Design for a real-time high-quality volume rendering workstation.* Conference Proceedings of the Chapel Hill Workshop on Volume Visualization, Chapel Hill, North Carolina, May 18-19, 1989, 85-92.

13. Levoy M.: *Efficient ray tracing of volume data.* ACM Transactions on Graphics, **9**, 4, July 1990, 245-261.

14. Levoy M.: *A taxonomy of volume visualization algorithms.* In: Tutorial on Volume Visualization Algorithms, Visualization'90, San Francisco, CA, October 23, 1990, 6-12.

15. Nowinski W. L.: *Image reconstruction methods and a tool for their investigation.* Journal of New Generation Computer Systems, **1**, 4, 1988, 327-352.

16. Nowinski W. L.: *Parallel implementation of the convolution method in image reconstruction.* Lecture Notes in Computer Science, **457**, 1990, Proceedings of the Joint International Conference on Vector and Parallel Processing CONPAR90/VAPPIV, 355-364.

17. Nowinski W. L.: *Parallel implementation of backprojection in image reconstruction.* Volume on Special Technical Contributions of the Joint International Conference on Vector and Parallel Processing CONPAR90/VAPPIV, 10-13 September 1990, Zurich, Switzerland, C49-C52.

18. Nowinski W. L.: *Memory access synchronization in series expansion methods of parallel image reconstruction.* In: Real-time Systems with Transputers (ed. Zedan, H.), IOS Press, Amsterdam 1990, 295-304.

19. Nowinski W. L.: *The use of a PRAM architecture for parallel image reconstruction.* In: Parallel Computing Technologies (ed. Mirenkov N. N.), Scientific Publishing, Singapore 1991, 215-222.

20. Nowinski W. L.: *Design for a ray casting integrated circuit.* In: Information Processing92-Proc. 12th World Computer Congress, Madrid, Spain, 7-11 September 1992, Vol. I: Algorithms, Software, Architecture (ed. van Leeuwen J.).

21. Rosenfeld A. and Kak A. C.: *Digital Picture Processing.* 2nd ed., Academic Press, New York 1982.

22. Uhr L.: *Parallel architectures for image processing, computer vision, and pattern perception.* In: Handbook of Pattern Recognition and Image Processing (eds. Young T. Y. and Fu K. S.), Academic Press, Orlando 1986, 437-469.

23. Upson C. and Keeler M.: *V-buffer: visible volume rendering.* Computer Graphics, **22**, 4, August 1988, 59-64.

24. Westover L.: *Interactive volume rendering.* Conference Proceedings of the Chapel Hill Workshop on Volume Visualization, Chapel Hill, North Carolina, May 18-19, 1989, 9-16.

25. Yoo T. S., Neumann U., Fuchs H., Pizer S. M., Cullip T., Rhoades J. and Whitaker R.: *Achieving direct volume visualization with interactive semantic region selection.* Proceedings Visualization'91, October 22-25, 1991, San Diego, CA, 58-65.

Computing The Inner Product on Reconfigurable Buses with Shift Switching

R. Lin

Department of Computer Science
SUNY at Geneseo
Geneseo, NY 14454

S. Olariu*

Department of Computer Science
Old Dominion University
Norfolk, Va 23529

Abstract. *The purpose of this work is to present two novel architectures for inner product computation. The proposed architectures incorporate shift switching into the reconfigurable buses. Given two arrays of N elements, each consisting of m bits, our first architecture achieves a latency of $O((logN + logm)t_a + (logN)t_b)$, using Nm^2 basic shift switches and m^2 adders assuming that broadcasting on a bus takes t_b time and an addition takes t_a time. The second architecture extends the first one by pipelining and achieves a throughput of one inner product per time unit, while keeping the latency unchanged. Replacing large number of adders with simple shift switches, both architectures improve the state of the art by reducing the amount of hardware for the computation.*

1. Introduction

Although single-processor computer performance has grown rapidly in the past, it is becoming increasingly clear that this rate of growth cannot be sustained: the speed of light and the laws of quantum mechanics act as formidable barriers that cannot be breached. In the last decade, it has been realized that a different and more cost-effective way to increase the processing power is to turn to parallel and massively parallel computing devices. Recently, massively parallel machines featuring many thousands of cooperating processors have become a reality. However, interprocessor communication and simultaneous memory accesses typically act as bottlenecks in parallel machines, hampering any increase in computational power from translating into increased performance of the same order of magnitude. To overcome the inefficiency of long distance communication among processors, bus systems have been recently added to a number of parallel machines [4, 9, 10]. If the configuration of such a bus system can be dynamically changed, to suit communication needs, it is referred to as *reconfigurable*.

We propose to enhance the well known reconfigurable bus architecture by the addition of a new feature that we call shift switching. Machines featuring a reconfigurable bus system (REBS) include the bus automaton [10], the reconfigurable mesh [9], and the polymorphic torus [4]. REBS have been studied by researchers and have been used extensively in the field of parallel processing [1, 5-10, 15].

There are two major components in a REBS: a local programmable switch within each processor and a bus network whose global configuration can be dynamically changed by adjusting these local switches. The proposed architectures also feature these two basic components. However, what distinguishes our architectures from existing is that we adopt a new class of switch states which are manipulated by each processor. The motivation for this is provided by the observation that for a reconfigurable

---

This author was supported by National Science Foundation under grant CCR-8909996

architecture to yield efficient algorithms, its network configuration must at all times reflect the properties of data distributed in its local processors. In the existing REBS, locally programmable switches are the only tools used in setting up the appropriate configurations. As it turns out, the local switches within processors do not always provide a sufficiently flexible mechanism to take full advantage of the reconfigurability.

Our idea is to enable switches to rotate connections between lines of a bus. We show that this is a simple and powerful approach to improve the flexibility of a reconfigurable system. It is well known that bit operations of shifting and rotating have been successfully used to help carry out many basic arithmetic operations [13]. Recently, researchers have used the operations performed by groups of processors (not by groups of switches) in the design of efficient REBS algorithms [8, 15]. The architectures demonstrated in this paper introduce innovative designs and uses of switches, thus making it possible to simulate arithmetic operations using shifting on buses. It turns out that a reconfigurable bus system properly equipped with these new switches considerably reduces the cost of executing quite a few fundamental parallel algorithms [6, 7].

To illustrate our ideas we present new architectures specialized to compute the inner product of two arrays of N elements, each consisting of m bits. The first architecture is for non-pipelined computation and achieves a latency (i.e. the computation time for an inner product) of $O(\log N + \log m)$, with Nm^2 shift switches and m^2 adders, each about $(m+\log N)/2$ bits. The second architecture is for pipelined computation. With $2Nm^2$ shift switches, we achieve a throughput (i.e. the inverse time between successive completion of two inner products) of one per time unit.

The inner product processor is implemented with a shift switch network, which consists of m reconfigurable buses, each having N shift switch units, and a tree of m^2 adders. The processor is obtained by incorporating the following ideas into the inner product computation:

(1) the multiplication of two m-bit numbers is expressed as the weighted sum of m m-bit numbers; consequently, the inner product is expressed as the weighted sum of m numbers, each is a sum of N m-bit numbers;

(2) the sum of N m-bit numbers is expressed as the weighted sum of m numbers, each is a sum of N binary numbers (thus, the inner product is expressed as m^2 weighted numbers, each is a sum of N binary numbers);

(3) the sum of N binary numbers is implemented by broadcasting a signal pattern "01" along a 2-line bus of N switches for log N times (the configuration of the lines of such buses is set up prior to each broadcasting);

(4) finally, the inner product is obtained by using m^2 such parallel broadcastings with the outputs weighted and added in a full binary tree of adders; we obtain the inner product from the root of the adder tree, achieving $O(\log N + \log m)$ latency.

(5) by spanning log N time broadcasts in log N buses (of width 2), we construct a pipelined architecture which achieves a throughput of one inner product per time unit.

We also compare our architectures with a Carry-Save-Adder implementation (CSA for short) of an inner product processor proposed by Smith and Torng [11]. Their design requires a latency of $O(\log N + \log m)$, or $2(\log N + \log m)t_{csa}$ (here, t_{csa} is the delay for signal propagation from one carry-save adder to another), and achieves a throughput of one per constant time units with $O(Nm^2)$ adder bits. Instead of adder bits, we use switching elements. Thus, we significantly reduce the number of adder bits to about m/N the number used in the CSA design [11]. As it turns out, our results are particularly attractive in the context of matrix multiplication with small m.

The paper is organized as follows: Section 2 introduces the concept of reconfigurable bus system with shift switching (REBSIS, for short). Section 3 presents a REBSIS application for the summation of a binary array. Sections 4 and 5 introduce a non-pipelined inner product processor, along with an inner product algorithm. Section 6 presents our pipelined inner product scheme. Finally, Section 7 summarizes the results.

2. Shift switches for reconfigurable buses

To make the paper self-contained, we shall review the basic structural features of a reconfigurable bus system. For illustration purposes, consider the case of a reconfigurable mesh and refer to figure 1.(a). A reconfigurable mesh consists of an $N \times N$ VLSI array of processors overlaid with a reconfigurable bus system. Every processor features four ports denoted by N, S, E and W. Local connections between these ports can be established under program control creating a powerful bus system that changes dynamically to accommodate various computational needs. We assume a single instruction stream: in each time unit the same instruction is broadcast to all processors, which execute it and wait for the next instruction. The regular structure of the reconfigurable mesh makes it suitable for VLSI implementation. In accord with other workers [1, 4, 9, 15] we assume that broadcasting along buses takes $t_b = O(1)$ or $O(\log N)$ time. Recent experiments with the YUPPIE system [4] seems to indicate that wherever the number of switches (or processors) involved is less than 10^6, the broadcasting delay is a small constant. For our purposes, a switch (see Figure 1.b) can be seen as an array of m identical switching elements, which are under synchronous control of a processor. Every switching element involves a number of lines of buses. Several different *switch states* can be obtained by instructing a switch to set line contacts in different ways. For simplicity, the switches of a REBS are referred to as simple switches as opposed to shift switches introduced below.

We now propose a new type of switch (see Figure 2), which we call a *shift switch*. A REBS equipped with shift switches is referred to as a *REBSIS*. A shift switch can be constructed from simple switches with changes only in internal wiring which guarantees that shift (or rotation) connections between the incoming and outgoing bus lines can be dynamically constructed.

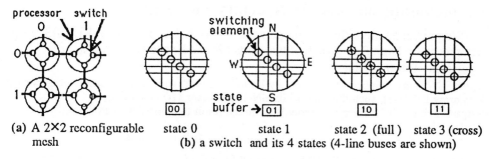

(a) A 2×2 reconfigurable mesh
state 0   state 1   state 2 (full)   state 3 (cross)
(b) a switch and its 4 states (4-line buses are shown)

Fig. 1. Reconfigurable bus system.

In our descriptions of types of shift switches, $S_{m:d}$ stands for a switch featuring m switching elements, with the state changes controlled by d bits. Note that an $S_{m:d}$ has no more than 2^d states. Equipped with an $S_{m:d}$ switch a processor can shift one (or zero) bits of an incoming m-bit signal. For example, for incoming signals: 0010 and 1000 (m=4), the outgoing signals can be 0010 and 1000 (shift 0 bit), or 0100 and 0001 (shift 1 and rotate 1 bit).

In order to simplify the descriptions of shift switch, we assume the following:
(1) Each switch has a d-bit buffer called *state buffer*: if the contents of this buffer is k, then the processor can trigger its switch to state k;
(2) A switch has a special element, called a *rotation element*, to output the *rotation bit* (as it will become apparent in the next section, the rotation bits reflect the status of shifting along the network);
(3) A processor can write into the state-buffer and read the rotation bit .

Figure 2 illustrates an $S_{2:1}$ switch involving two switching elements and 2 states denoted by state 0 (shift 0) and state 1 (shift 1). When a processor sets its switch to state
● 0, the following contacts are established: w (west) and e (east) in every switching element, as well as c (rotate-bit) and g (ground, which provides a 0 signal);
● 1, the following contacts are established: w and i in every switching element, as well as a, b and c in the rotation element (it will soon be clear that c is not the same as but similar to a carry bit of an addition).

It is easy to confirm that in state I_0 (resp. I_1) the passing signal is shifted 0 (resp. 1) lines.

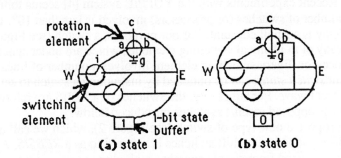

Fig. 2. Shift Switches $S_{2:1}$ and its two tates.

3. Computing the sum of N binary numbers

We present an algorithm to compute the sum of N bits on a linear REBSIS, where each processor has a $S_{m:1}$ switch of two ports (W and E) and two states I_0 or I_1.

Algorithm Binary_Sum
Input: N binary numbers (for simplicity let $m^{(r-1)} \leq N < m^r$, and $m=2^t$ for some integers r and t) in array B[0:N-1], such that, for all $0 \leq i \leq N-1$, processor P(i) holds B(i);
Output: The sum of elements of array B (with the result in register R of P(N-1)).
begin
0.   [Initialization] set R to 0 and set state-buffer(i) to B(i) for $0 \leq i \leq N-1$;

1.   All processors P(i) ($0 \leq i \leq N-1$) do in parallel for k=0 to r -1 (=$\lfloor \log N/\log m \rfloor$) times;

   1.1 P(i) triggers its switch;

1.2 P(0) broadcasts the bit-pattern $\underbrace{000\cdots 1}_{m}$ {1 on line 0, 0 on others} from its W port.

1.3 P(N-1) does the following
    1.3.1 reads bit-pattern received at its E port, encode it to X(k) with t =(log m) bits;
    1.3.2 shifts register R t bits to the right ;
    1.3.3 writes X(k) into the leftmost t bits of register R;
  1.4 P(i) reads the rotation bit, and writes the value into the state-buffer(i);
end

Note for m=2, 1.3.1 should be: reads 1st bit on E port, write it to X(k) (no encodering);

Example 1. Figure 3 shows how the algorithm works for B= (1,1,0,1,1,0,1) and m=2.

We are now in a position to state our first result.

Theorem 1. *On a linear REBSIS of N processors (with bus width m and broadcasting time t_b), the sum of a binary array A(0:N-1) can be computed in O((log N/log m)·t_b) time, using a shift register and no adder.*

Proof. We use algorithm Binary_Sum and

let $C = \sum_{k=0}^{N-1} B(k)$, $m^{(r-1)} \leq N < m^r$ and $m=2^t$; since $C \leq N < m^r$, C can be represented as

$$a(r-1)\cdot m^{(r-1)}+\cdots+a(j)\cdot m^j+\cdots+a(1)\cdot m^1 +a(0) \qquad (A)$$

here the integer a(j) satisfies: $0 \leq a(j) \leq m-1$, for $0 \leq j \leq r-1$ (refer to base m number representation [2]). It is easy to verify by induction that at the end of the k-th iteration, a(k)=X(k). Since step 1.3.2 divides R by 2^t, and step 1.3.3 adds $X(k)\cdot 2^{(r-1)t}$ to R, the value of the expression (A) is obtained in R after log(N+1)/log(m)=r iterations, thus the running time of the algorithm is $r\cdot t_b$ i.e. O((log N/log m)·t_b) . □

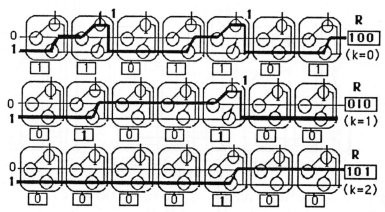

Fig. 3. Summing B= (1,1,0,1,1,0,1). (the end of step 1.3 for k=0,1 and 2 are shown)

4. A non-pipelined architecture

In this section we introduce a non-pipelined inner product architecture which consists of two components: a *switch network*, or a mesh of switches, and an adder tree. Each node of the switch network is referred to as a *switch unit* and consists of a set of switches. Figure 4 features several types of switch units. A switch unit U(m,r,t) contains m·t basic switches (i.e. $S_{2:1}s$). A section of buses can be divided into m partitions, each r buses (of width 2): t sequentially connected basic switches are on the first (in bottom-up order) t (t≤r) buses of each partition, one per bus. When a specific clock cycle comes, all switches turn to new states simultaneously as dictated by the values in the state-buffers. All switches can also be reset to 0 state. For the non-pipelined architecture, all switch units are of the same type, U(m, 1, 1) (Fig. 4(a)), and each rotation bit has a connection to the state-buffer of the same switch, ensuring that the rotation bit can be loaded into the state-buffer in the following clock cycle.

The switch network can be seen as m linear REBSIS, each containing N switch units in a matrix form. A switch unit can receive data from the vertical data input buses in the corresponding column. In this context, each REBSIS is termed a *switch block*.

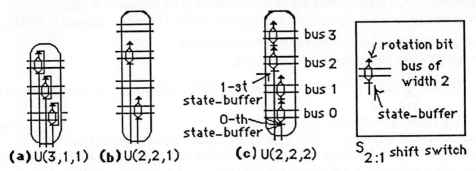

Fig. 4. Shift switch units and their numbering scheme.

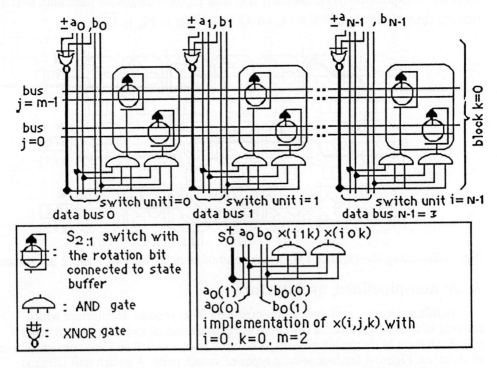

Fig. 5. A Switch block with N=4, m=2, k =0 and its numbering scheme.

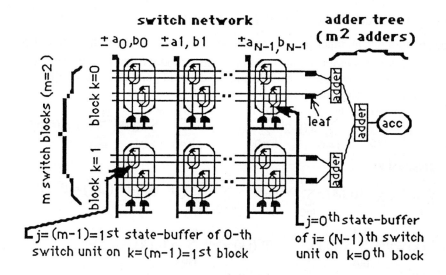

Fig. 6. Inner product processor architecture.

Figures 5 show the architectures and index schemes of a switch block. The overall architecture of the inner product processor is a heterogeneous array connected by the switch network and the adder tree as shown in fig. 6 for N=4 and m=2. The system can broadcast 1's (resp. 0's) to the left entries of all even (resp. odd) lines of the horizontal buses. The right ends of odd lines of all buses constitute the outputs of the network. When input data A and B is fed into the processor from the top of the data buses, the j-th state-buffer (which is on the j-th bus) of the i-th switch unit in the k-th block receives $x(i,j,k)$ or $x'(i,j,k)$ ($0 \leq i \leq N-1$; $0 \leq j,k \leq m-1$) corresponding to the following logic expressions, for two clock cycles (positive and negative) respectively:

$$x(i,j,k) = S_i^+ \cdot a_i(j) \cdot b_i(k), \qquad (0 \leq i \leq N-1); \ (0 \leq j,k \leq m-1)$$

$$\text{or} \quad x'(i,j,k) = S_i^- \cdot a_i(j) \cdot b_i(k), \qquad (0 \leq i \leq N-1); \ (0 \leq j,k \leq m-1) \tag{B}$$

here we assume the binary representation for A(i) (denoted a_i) is $a_i(m)a_i(m-1)..a_i(0)$, for B(i) (denoted b_i) is $b_i(m)b_i(m-1)..b_i(0)$, and $a_i(m)$ and $b_i(m)$ are sign bits, $a_i(k)$ and $b_i(k)$ ($0 \leq k \leq m-1$) are binary digits, also

$$S_i^+ = = \overline{a_i(m) \oplus b_i(m)}, \quad S_i^- = \overline{\overline{a_i(m) \oplus b_i(m)}}$$

$$S_i = S_i^+ - S_i^- = \overline{a_i(m) \oplus b_i(m)} - \overline{\overline{a_i(m) \oplus b_i(m)}} = \begin{cases} 1 & \text{if } a_i(m) = b_i(m) \\ -1 & \text{otherwise} \end{cases} \tag{C}$$

We implement S_i^+ and S_i^- by associating each data bus with a XNOR gate and negating the input array A in the negative cycles, and implement $a_i(j) \cdot b_i(k)$ by associating each switch unit with an AND gate of three inputs (see fig. 5).

The adder tree is a full binary tree with m^2 leaves connected to the outputs of the switch network. Each leaf commits a fixed shift operation with zeros filled, which is simply accomplished in the placement of wires. An internal node of the tree is an adder.

5. A non-pipelined inner-product algorithm

The idea to compute an inner product on the proposed architecture can be described as follows: consider two vectors A and B and their inner product denoted by A·B, with numbers here represented by sign-magnitude and the decimal point of each number being at its right most position (for simplicity). By (B) and (C) we have

$$A \cdot B = \sum_{i=0}^{N-1} s_i \, a_i \, b_i = \sum_{i=0}^{N-1} s_i \sum_{j=0}^{m-1} a_i(j) \cdot 2^j \sum_{k=0}^{m-1} b_i(k) \cdot 2^k = \sum_{k=0}^{m-1} \sum_{j=0}^{m-1} 2^{j+k} \left(\sum_{i=0}^{N-1} s_i \, a_i(j) \, b_i(k) \right)$$

It can be segregated to

$$A \cdot B = \sum_{k=0}^{m-1} \sum_{j=0}^{m-1} 2^{j+k} \left(\sum_{i=0}^{N-1} x(i,j,k) - \sum_{i=0}^{N-1} x'(i,j,k) \right) = \sum_{k=0}^{m-1} \sum_{j=0}^{m-1} \left(IP^+(j,k) - IP^-(j,k) \right) = IP^+ - IP^-,$$

where $IP^+(j,k) = 2^{j+k} \sum_{i=0}^{N-1} x(i,j,k), \qquad IP^-(j,k) = 2^{j+k} \sum_{i=0}^{N-1} x'(i,j,k),$

$$IP^+ = \sum_{k=0}^{m-1} \sum_{j=0}^{m-1} IP^+(j,k), \qquad IP^- = \sum_{k=0}^{m-1} \sum_{j=0}^{m-1} IP^-(j,k)$$

The item $IP^+(j,k)$ $(0 \le j,k \le m-1)$ is evaluated on the j-th bus of the k-th block of the switch network by applying algorithm Binary_Sum. Now Theorem 1 guarantees that it takes $O(\log N / \log m') = O(\log N)$ (note that for our processor m'=2) cycles, which are referred to as positive cycles. The item $IP^-(j,k)$ $(0 \le j,k \le m-1)$ is evaluated on the same bus taking the same amount of clock cycles and is referred to as negative cycles. The result produced on the j-th bus of the k-th block in the t-th cycle needs to be shifted so that it is multiplied by 2^{j+k+t} and the result is referred to as $V(j,k,t)$ (or $V'(j,k,t)$).

Clearly, $IP^+(j,k) = \sum_{t=0}^{\log N - 1} V(j,k,t),$ and $IP^-(j,k) = \sum_{t=0}^{\log N - 1} V'(j,k,t)$

The multiplication of 2^{j+k+t} can be implemented by adding j+k+t zeros at the right end of the registers through the placement of wires. All m^2 results on the registers of right-end of m^2 buses (which are referred to as leaves), as well as the results in the inner nodes of the adder tree, are sent to their parents in each clock cycle. The root of the adder tree accumulates two consecutive sequences, each in logN cycles, (i.e. accumulating positive and negative data respectively), and finally, it results the inner product.

We spell out the details of the algorithm, then evaluate the performance cost.

Algorithm Inner_Prod

Input: A[0..N-1] and B[0..N-1]; the numbers are represented in sign and magnitude, assuming a decimal point is in the rightmost position of each number (for simplicity);

Output: the inner product of A·B from the accumulator of the adder tree.

begin

0. Initialization: reset all switches to I_0 states, and all adder bits to 0;

1. For r=0 to 1 do {the iteration is referred to as positive if r=0, otherwise, as negative}

    1.1. Feed in the i-th data bus with A(i) (r=1), or, -A(i) (r=1) and B(i) $0 \le i \le N-1$;

        {thus the j-th state-buffer of i-th switch unit on k-th block is loaded with a bit

value x(i,j,k) or x'(i,j,k) as shown in (B)}
1.2. For t=0 to (log N)-1 Do {an iteration here is referred to as a cycle}
    1.2.1. trigger all switches to new states;
    1.2.2. send the broadcast signals on the network; {i.e. signal 1 (0) to the left entries of all even (odd) lines of the horizontal buses}
    1.2.3. shift the j-th register (at the end of j-th bus) of k-th block j+k+t bits so that the bit value is multiplied by 2^{j+k+t} for $0 \le j,k \le m-1$; {the result is referred to as $V(j,k,t)$ for r=0, $V'(j,k,t)$ for r=1}
    1.2.4. each adder adds values of two child nodes and the accumulator adds in the value of its child node; {note that all adders (except the accumulator) only deal with numbers of the same sign}
    {note that 1.2.3 and 1.2.4 could also be executed in parallel}
2.   For k=1 to (2·log m) do   {an iteration here is referred to as an additional cycle} each adder adds values of its two child nodes, the accumulator adds the value of its child node and stores the first result after a total of 2·logm+logN cycles, from which the second accumulated result is subtracted in the last cycle.
end.

We now compare the design with that (CSA design) of Smith and Torng [11].

latency: Assume that broadcasting along the whole bus (with N switch elements) takes time t_b, an addition plus a shift operation takes time t_a. Considering algorithm Inner_Prod, step 1.2.2 takes t_b, steps 1.2.4 takes t_a, and each iteration of step 2 takes t_a. Thus, we have the latency: $O(2(\log N)(t_b+t_a)+ 2(\log m)t_a)= O(2(\log N + \log m)t_a + 2(\log N)t_b)$. This is the same as taken by CSA design, which has the value: $O(2(\log N + \log m)t_{csa})$ where t_{csa} is the delay for signal propagation from one carry-save adder to another (see [11]).

hardware: The following table summarizes the hardware requirements for each processor (assume each adder and shift register has an average of (m+logN)/2 bits)

	CSA design	REBSIS design
adder bits	$a_1 =Nm(m+2)+(2m-1)\log N+m(\log m-3)$	$a=m^2(m+\log N)/2$
switching elements		$s= 2Nm^2$
state buffer bits		$b= Nm^2$
rotation elements		$r= Nm^2$
shift register bits		$f= m^2(m+\log N)/2$

Instead of using adder bits, we use switching elements as a major component of the processor with the number of adder bits reduced to m/N as many as used in the CSA design. The precise hardware saving evaluation needs to be determined by further studies and is not provided in this paper. However, in the following we give an evaluation to illustrate the rough hardware reduction (refer to [2]). We assume that one-bit CSA requires about 8 AND/OR gates, a simple switch element is comparable to a single gate, a bit of state buffer requires about 3 gates, a bit of shift register requires 5 gates and a rotation element is comparable to a switching element, thus, the hardware gain denoted as β_1/β_2 can be represented as, $\beta_1/\beta_2 =(8 \cdot a+ s+3 \cdot b+ r + 5 \cdot f) / 8 \cdot a_1 =$
$(8m^2(m+\log N)/2+6Nm^2+5m^2(m+\log N)) / 8(Nm(m+2)+(2m-1)\log N+m(\log m-3))$.
Table 1 shows the values β_1/β_2 for m= 2^2 to 2^5 and N = 2^7 to 2^{13}.

Though the results are approximate, the proposed method does clearly show a promise for the computation, and it is particularly attractive, when (1) fast broadcasting can be well implemented in a VLSI chip, or an optical interconnected network [1, 4] and (2) the value of m is small, thus m/N is small.

To summarize our findings we state the following result.

Theorem 2. *Given two arrays A, B of N elements, each consisting of m bits, the inner product of A·B can be computed in $O((logN + logm)t_a + (logN)t_b)$ time, on a net work consisting of m^2 linear REBSIS of N shift switch units (with bus width m) and a adder tree of m^2 adders , assuming that broadcasting on a bus takes t_b time and an addition takes t_a time .*

Table 1: β_1/β_2 for the REBSIS processors

N	m			
	4	8	16	32
128	0.56	0.70	0.84	0.95
256	0.53	0.65	0.76	0.87
512	0.52	0.63	0.71	0.79
1024	0.51	0.61	0.69	0.75
2048	0.50	0.61	0.68	0.73
4096	0.50	0.60	0.67	0.72
8192	0.50	0.60	0.67	0.71

Table 2: β_1/β_2 for pipelined processors

N	m			
	4	8	16	32
128	0.64	0.80	0.95	1.00
256	0.61	0.75	0.87	0.96
512	0.60	0.73	0.82	0.91
1024	0.59	0.71	0.80	0.87
2048	0.59	0.71	0.79	0.85
4096	0.59	0.70	0.78	0.83
8192	0.58	0.70	0.78	0.83

Note that we restrict ourselves to the use of basic switches (or $S_{2:1}$), in fact, replacing switches of type $S_{2:1}$ by $S_{m:1}$ (m>2) can reduce the running time by a factor of logm (Theorem 1) while increasing by a factor of m the switching elements.

6. A pipelined architecture

An alternative to the non-pipelined architecture is obtained by substituting a pipelined switch network for the above switch network. Figure 7. shows a pipelined architecture for the inner product processor, the left part of which is a switch block for N=4, m=2. The i-th switch unit ($0 \leq i \leq N-1$) is of type U(log N, m, q), where q is determined as follows: let r be the number of rightmost zeros in the binary representation of i+1; now set q=1 if r=0, and set q= (r div 2) + 2, otherwise. It is easy to confirm that the rotation bits of a switch block form m full binary trees. In each clock cycle, for an internal node of each full binary tree formed by the rotation bits, the state-buffer is loaded with the OR value of the rotation bits of its two children, generated in the previous clock cycle. We now compute the inner loop of the Procedure Inner_Prod on the log N levels of the tree in a pipelined fashion. By allowing to feed in a new set of data A and B in the first cycle (referred to as positive cycle), and to feed in -A and B in the second cycle, we construct a pipelined computation on the switch network. To cope with the synchronized operations in the adder tree, we need a shifting mechanism. For this purpose, for all $0 \leq t \leq logN$ and $0 \leq j,k \leq m-1$, we place two identical buffers of (t+1)·2 bits each, in a column at the right end of the (j·logN + t)-th bus of k-th block. In every clock cycle (positive or negative), when a bit value arrives at the left end of each even buffer, all buffer bits, except the top level bits, shift one bit up along the columns.

During the pipelining, in every even cycle a value of $IP^+(j,k)$ corresponding to arrays A and B is concatenated at the j-th top buffer of block k. Then in the next odd cycle $IP^-(j,k)$ is formed. Notice that at the same time the adder tree also works in a pipelined fashion,

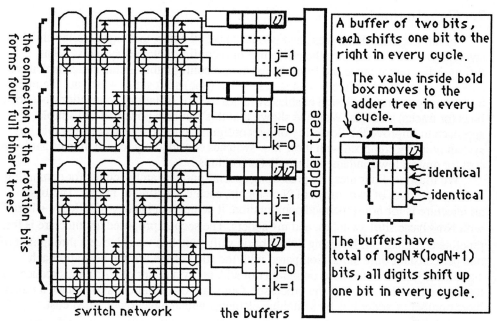

Fig. 7. The architecture of a pipelined inner product processor for N=4, m=2.

so an inner-product can be produced every two cycles. We spell out the detail by following algorithm:

Algorithm Pipe_Inner_Prod

Input: a stream of two array pairs (A and B) of N elements, each consisting of m bits.

Output: the stream of inner products of A.Bs from the accumulator of the adder tree.

Repeat the following

begin {pipelining}

1. Get new arrays A and B;

2. For r=0 to 1 do {an iteration is referred to as positive if r=0, or negative, if r=1}

    2.1. Feed in the i-th data bus with A(i) (r=1), or, -A(i) (r=1) and B(i) 0≤i≤N-1;

    2.2 Do in parallel for (a), (b) and (c) {the time is referred to as a cycle}

    (a) a.1 trigger all switches to new states;

        a.2. send the broadcast signals on the network;

        a.3 move the value in the bold box of top buffers to the adder tree (see fig. 8}

        a.4. shift one bit up for bits in non-top buffers, one bit right for others;

    (b) each adder adds values of its two child nodes;

    (c) the accumulator adds the value of its child, and then for positive cycle, it stores
the result for negative cycle, it subtracts the current result from the first result.

end. {of pipelining}

Table 2 shows the hardware gain β_1/β_2 of a pipelined inner product processor.

We summarize the pipelined inner product computation by

Theorem 3. *The algorithm Pipe_Inner_Prod pipelines the inner product with the latency of $O((\log N + \log m)t_b)$, and throughput of one inner product per time unit, using $2Nm^2$ basic switches and m^2 adders, assuming that an addition takes t_a time and broadcasting on a bus takes t_b time.*

7. Conclusion

In this paper we have presented two instances of a new technique (called shift switching) meant to enhance the efficiency of reconfigurable bus systems. What distinguishes our architecture from the existing reconfigurable architectures is that we adopt a new class of simple switch states, called (line) shift states which are manipulated by each processor. Our design enables switches to shift (rotation) connections between lines (or tracks) of a bus. We have shown that this can be a powerful and simple approach to improve the flexibility of a reconfigurable system. A reconfigurable bus system properly equipped with these new switches considerably reduce time or hardware cost for quite a few fundamental parallel algorithms.

We illustrated our ideas by presenting special-purpose architectures for computing the inner product of two arrays of N elements, each consisting of m bits. The first architecture is for non-pipelined computation: it achieves a latency of $O(logN + logm)$, with Nm^2 basic shift switches, and m^2 adders. The second proposed architecture is for pipeline computation. By using $2Nm^2$ basic shift switches we achieve a throughput of one per constant time units. Compared with the state of the art, the new approach significantly reduces the need on number of adders (by a factor of N/m), thus reduce the total amount of hardware in the processor. Our main contribution is to replace a rather large number of adder bits by switching elements which have lower VLSI cost.

REFERENCES

[1] Y. Ben-Asher, D. Peleg, R. Ramaswam, and A. Schuster, The Power of Reconfiguration, *Journal of Parallel and Distributed Computing*,vol.13 (1991) 139-151.

[2] J. J. F. Cavanaugh, Digital Computer Arithmetic Design and Implementation, New York: McGraw -Hill Book Co. 1984.

[3] H. T. Kung and C. E. Leiserson, Algorithms for VLSI Processor Arrays, *Introduction to VLSI Systems*, C. Mead and L. Conway, Reading MA: Addison-Wesley, 1980.

[4] H. Li and M Maresca, Polymorphic-torus network, *IEEE Trans. Comput.*,38 (9), 1989.

[5] R. Lin, Fast algorithms for the lowest common ancestor problem on a processor array with reconfigurable buses, *Information Processing Letters*, 40, Nov. 1991.

[6] R. Lin , Reconfigurable Buses with Shift Switching - VLSI Radix sort, to appear in *Proc. of International Conference on Parallel Processing*, St. Charles, IL, August 1992.

[7] R. Lin, and S. Olariu, A new method of inner product computation on reconfigurable buses with shift switching, TR 8-92, Dept. of Comp., Sci., Old Dominion Univ. 1992.

[8] R. Lin, S. Olariu, J. Schwing, and J. Zhang, Sorting in $O(1)$ time on an n×n reconfigurable mesh, to appear in *Proc. of 9-th European Workshop on Parallel Computing*, Barcelona, Spain, March 1992.

[9] R. Miller, V. K. Prasanna Kumar, D. Reisis and Q.F. Stout, Mesh with reconfigurable buses, in *Proc. 5th MIT Conference on Advanced Research in VLSI* (1988) 163-1'/8.

[10] J. Rothstein, Bus automata, brains, and mental models, *IEEE Trans. on Systems Man Cybernetics* 18, (1988).

[11] S. P. Smith and H. C. Torng, Design of a Fast Inner Product Processor, in *Proc. IEEE 7th Symposium on Computer Arithmetic*, 1985.

[12] E. E. Swartzlander, Jr., Barry K. Gilbert, and Irving S. Reed, Inner Product Computers, *IEEE Trans. Computers*, C-27, 1, Jan. 1978, pp. 21-31.

[13] E. E. Swartzlander, Jr., *Computer Arithmetic Vol. 1*, (IEEE CSP, CA, 1990).

[14] J. D. Ullman, *Computational Aspect of VLSI*, (Computer Science Press,MD, 1983).

[15] B. F. Wang, G.H. Chen, and F.C. Lin, Constant Time Sorting on a processing array with a reconfigurable bus system, *Information Processing Letters*,vol. 34, no. 4.

A Novel Sorting Array Processor

Stephen P.S. Lam

School of Computing and Mathematical Sciences
Oxford Polytechnic
Headington, Oxford
United Kingdom OX3 0BP

Abstract: Based on a novel array processor architecture, consisting of two tightly-coupled mesh-connected processing cells, a number of highly parallelizable sorting algorithms are realized by match the data flow with the interconnection topology. The sorting algorithms chosen are the odd-even sort, bitonic sort and binary tree sort. Taking the modularity of these algorithms, the array implementation of small sorting modules can be optimised, and nearly optimal sorters can then be constructed for large data sequences by cascading several small sorting modules together. With the novel architecture, vertical connections between cells in adjacent array layers provide additional versatility and expandability, compared with other sorting arrays. Techniques for realizing different sorting algorithms systematically will also been discussed.

1. The Novel Architecture

The novel array processor architecture [1,2], named the TA, comprises two tightly coupled layers of mesh-connected homogeneous sorting cells. The configuration of a 4×4×2 TA with half the number of cells on the top array and the rest on the bottom array is illustrated in Figure 1. Shaded circles are used to distinguish the cells on the bottom array. Each sorting cell is divided into two internal parts, i.e. the computation unit (CP) and the communication unit (CM). The role of CP is determined by the underlying algorithms, for instance it may perform a word compare and exchange operation. The interconnection between neighbouring cells are established through the CM which is set initially to construct a desired data path. Communication between vertically adjacent cells can be achieved via the vertical connections which associate with the same amount of latency as other connections. Data enter and leave the arry through the boundary cells. Data received by a cell are sorted and passed onwards to a neighbouring cell in a single clock cycle. All the sorting cells are operating synchronously. By propagating control words through the CMs, the interconnections between neighbouring cells may be changed in form of wavefronts at run-time. The complexity of each cell is determined by the functionality of the CP and the versatility of the CM. The regularity and locality of the TA are favourable for very large scale (VLSI) or even wafer scale integration, particularly with arrays of fine grain sorting cells.

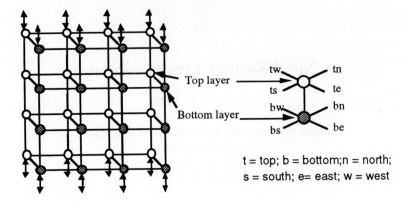

t = top; b = bottom; n = north;
s = south; e= east; w = west

Figure 1: The Novel Array Processor Architecture (TA)

2. Sorting Problems

Sorting [3] a sequence of data elements into a pre-defined order, is one of the most common operations among symbolic processing applications. It is achieved by executing a sequence of simple operations. Sorting problems are also of great theoretical appeal, and their study has generated a significant amount of interesting concepts and mathematics. Besides heavy applications in the organisation of data storage, sorting has also been integrated into many digital signal processing applications. The backbones of many implementation of fast sorting algorithms are efficient communication networks and the applications of parallelization techniques. The array processor realization [4,5] of the parallel sorting algorithms is particularly attractive, as sorting steps are spread over time and space. The integrated sorting arrays are cost-effective and capable of delivering the throughput close to their theoretical lower bounds. To match the data flow, dedicated communication network topologies are developed specifically in association with a large number of sorting cells.

Starting from the simplest sorting algorithm, the sequential bubble sort algorithm which compares each element in a data sequence with all the remaining ones, can easily be reformulated to exploit inherent computational parallelism. The odd-even transposition (OET) algorithm which is a parallel version of the bubble sort algorithm is derived and implemented on linearly connected array processors with $O(n)$ cells, where n is the number of elements to be sorted. As the circuit density continues to increase, the sorting algorithms of this kind with a reasonable number of cells can be integrated on to a single chip. However, the growth of communication between cells and the costs for implementing sophisticated switching networks on silicon urge for more cost-effective network topologies. As the choice of sorting algorithms for a particular application is often determined by the complexity and configuration of sorting cells, dedicated sorters for short data sequences with cascadable features have been risen to high ranks for VLSI implementation.

3. The Cyclic-order OET Bilinear Sorter (COBS)

Sorting one-dimensional data sequences can be accomplished by simply applying the bubble sort algorithm, which has $O(n^2)$ time complexity according to the area-time complexity theory developed by Thompson [7] and Leighton [8]. The OET can be realized on a linearly connected systolic array with $O(n)$ cells and sorts the same sequence in $O(n)$ time steps. Other sorting algorithms based on the fold-over and the zero-time schemes have been reported in [6].

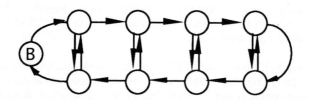

Figure 2(a): The Cyclic-Order OET Bilinear Sorter

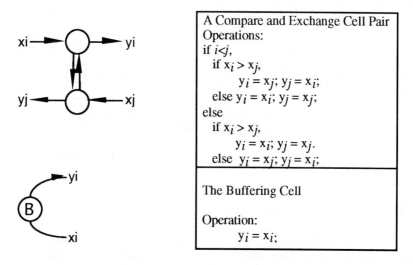

A Compare and Exchange Cell Pair
Operations:
if $i<j$,
 if $x_i > x_j$,
  $y_i = x_j; y_j = x_i$;
 else $y_i = x_i; y_j = x_j$;
else
 if $x_i > x_j$,
  $y_i = x_i; y_j = x_j$.
 else $y_i = x_j; y_j = x_i$;

The Buffering Cell

Operation:
 $y_i = x_i$;

Figure 2(b): The Cell Operations of the COBS

To realize the one-dimensional OET algorithm, a Cyclic-order OET Bilinear Sorter (COBS) is devised by projecting the TA on to the horizontal or vertical direction. The COBS, as shown in Figure 2 (a-b), consists of a bilinear array with (n-1) cells for odd n (n cells for even n) and a buffering unit attached to one end of the array. After elements entering from the left end of the upper array, they propagate round the array from the top cells to the bottom cells via the buffer and end connections in the clockwise direction. After the first few steps, the first entry has reached the opposite end of the array, then the closed loop structure with odd number of cells begins to permutate the data entries and generates all the combination of entry pairs. Simple compare-and-exchange operations are performed simultaneously between vertical adjacent cells. The correctness of the sorted sequence is assured by adding a tag value to each element. The tag values are effectively the indices of the sorted sequence. For instance, to sort a data sequence into an ascending order, each pair of vertical adjacent cells is set in such a way that the bigger element is stored in the top cell and the smaller in the bottom cell, if the tag value of a top cell is bigger than that of the corresponding cell in the bottom array, and vice versa. At the end of each time step, all elements move cyclically. Finally, the sorted data sequence can be collected from either ends of the array after $O(n)$ time steps. In doing so, the overall structure achieves the highest cell utilization compared with other sorting arrays, although the buffering cell is idle, i.e. not computing. The data loading and unloading time is also reduced due to the dynamic movement of data sequence. A sorting array proposed by Megson [9] based on a technique similar to this for bit-level applications achieves only half the cell utilization.

Referring to Figure 3, the COBS is used to sort a tagged data sequence with five elements. The tag number is shown as a subscript attached to each element. The actual sorting step begins at step 3. According to the cell structure described in Figure 2(b), the first exchange occurs at step 4 as the data value 4 with tag number 1 is smaller than the data value 3 with tag number 2. Intermediate data are passed on to the adjacent cells after each sorting step. From step 7 onward, the sorted sequence is then gradually collected from the top rightmost cell of the array. As shown in the Figure 3 that elements are compared in pairs and in parallel.

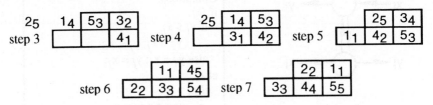

Figure 3: Sorting of 5-Element Data Sequence by the COBS

4. The TA OET Sorter (TOS)

The throughput of the OET algorithm for sorting one-dimensional data sequences can be improved by exploiting computation parallelism in time as well as in space. The incorporation of computation parallelism in spatial domain is achieved by realizing $O(n)\times\lceil n/2\rceil$ compare-and-exchange operations explicitly with $O(n^2)$ cells. The parallel sorting operations are carried out by pipelining a sequence of one dimensional sequences through a mesh-connected array. The sorted data sequences can be collected from the opposite edge of the array at the end of each sorting step.

A TA OET sorter, named the TOS, which basically consists of two $n\times n/2$ mesh arrays with programmable vertical connections, where n is the length of each data sequence. All the interconnections in the array are set before execution. One of the features attributed by the TOS is that the two-layer structure enhances the array flexibility for adapting sorting problems of different sizes by keeping input and output ports on the top and bottom edges of the same side of the TOS and joining the data flow of the two mesh arrays at half way. As the number of cells increases exponentially with the problem sizes, this is the best way for a mesh array to accommodate the expansion without re-constructing the entire array, introducing additional latency by the redundant cells or directing the output data with long connections. With this arrangement, the TOS can be expanded to bigger size by moving the joint between the two array layers further away from their input/output edges.

5. The TA Bitonic Sorter (TBS)

Bitonic merge and the odd-even merge are two powerful sorting techniques used for data sequences with specific ordering. These techniques form the basis of the bitonic sort algorithms proposed by K.E. Batcher [10]. The bitonic sort algorithm can sort a n-element sequence in $O(\log n)$ time steps using an array with $O(n \log n)$ cells. Theoretically, it can be implemented on a linearly connected array with $O(n)$ cells, but there will be heavy traffic between cells. Communication between cells can be achieved either by multiple routing steps or direct connections. The former approach will degrade the throughput and the latter will have devastating effects on VLSI realization. Although the bitonic sorting algorithm is best mapped on to a perfect shuffle network with $n(\log^2 n)$ cells, proposed by Pease and Stone [11], it has also been realized on other network topologies such as linear arrays [12] and mesh arrays [13,14]. Owing to long connections and many cross-over connections involved in the perfect shuffle network, they are undesirable for VLSI implementation. In the following, several small bitonic merge networks with local connections only are developed as basic modules for the construction of larger sorting networks.

A linear array with only local connections and the OET algorithm partially sorts a data sequence in $n + \log(n/2)$ - 1 time steps. Compared with the odd-even merge sort, the latter has poorer performance and requires the two subsequences to be partially sorted. Because of the similarity of the odd-even merge and the bitonic merge algorithms, the embedding of the bitonic merge algorithm is chosen to demonstrate the versatility of the TA.

The networks based on the TA which are developed to perform the Batcher's bitonic sort algorithm on one-dimensional data sequences are named the TA bitonic sorters (TBSs). The TBSs use the same principle as how a perfect shuffle network indexes each element by permuting a binary word corresponding to each element location. In doing so, some of the long connections are avoided as distant elements are placed in neighbouring locations. The locality of interconnections, including unit-distance diagonal connections, renders the small TBSs for VLSI/WSI implementation. As the number of elements n gets bigger than 32, long connections between sorting cells become inevitable and the degree of circuit density may also exceed the circuit capacity of a single dice with respect to current semiconductor technology. Therefore, techniques such as the split merge [4] will have to be employed for $n > 32$.

Figure 4 shows the third stage of the TBS for sorting 8-element data sequences. The horizontal shaded lines correspond to cells for successive sorting steps and the pairs of elements undergoing a comparison-and-exchange (cnx) are indicated by the vertical arrows. The direction of the arrows indicates the locations in which the smaller elements are to be placed. According to the algorithmic flow shown in Figure 4(a), the top four elements correspond to the cells on the first top row in Figure 4(b), and so on, communication between elements at maximum distance of four is required. By splitting elements into two sets which are then entering to the top and bottom boundaries of the TBS on the left, connections of four-unit long are completely avoided. Elements are sorted as they propagate from left to right. In the second sorting step in Figure 4(b), connections of two-unit length are required. To overcome this problem, the middle sorting step is decomposed into three steps with local operations only. As all the cells are operating synchronously, even simple exchange operations will prolong the sorting time. The TBS is modified further by employing diagonal connections of unit length as depicted in Figure 5. As the maximum distance for communication in the first two stage of bitonic sort is two, the same technique used in the third stage applies. The algorithmic flow and the TBS for the first two sorting stages are given in Figure 6(a) and (b). Finally, the three sorting stages are connecting together to form the 8-element TBS, see Figure 7. The TBSs developed can be extended to sort 4, 16, and 32 elements concurrently.

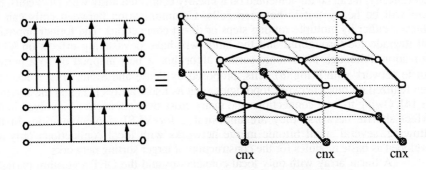

Figure 4: The Third Stage of 8-Element Bitonic Sort
(cnx = compare and exchange and x = exchange only)

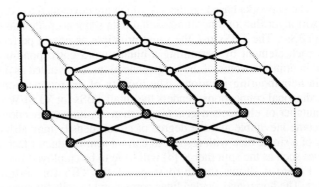

Figure 5: The Third Stage of the Resultant TBS for 8 Elements

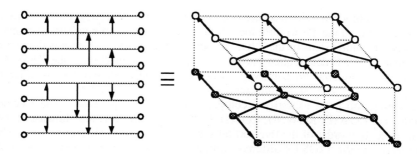

Figure 6: The First Two Stage of the 8-Element TBS

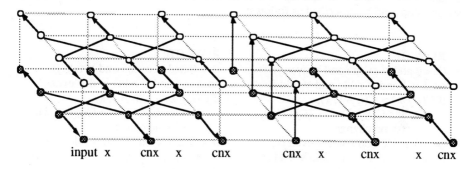

input x   cnx   x   cnx   cnx   x   cnx   x   cnx

Figure 7: The Eight-Element TBS

6. The TA 2-D OET Sorting (T2OS)

Image processing is an area which has great demands for integrated components to perform high speed sorting operations, to be able to implement parallel sorting algorithms for two dimensional data sequences will have significant impacts in this area. Unfortunately, the bitonic sort is not an ideal algorithm for this area of applications because of the complex communication structure. If the network for two-dimensional (2-D) sorting is expanded in the spatial domain as the one-dimensional (1-D) case proposed previously, the number of sorting cells required will increase exponentially with the problem size and the network topology may be expanded to three or more dimensional space. This growth of complexity implies the necessitate of complicated control. An alternative way to sort a 2-D data sequence is to linearize it into a 1-D data sequence and then apply existing sorting algorithms to it. However, the hardware costs or the sorting time may be increased by an order of magnitude. The consequence of this is undesirable and unfavourable for large scale integration on to a chip with limited capacity. Alternatively, a 2-D data sequence can be stored and sorted within a two-dimensional array processor of the same dimensions. Yet, another approach is to break down the data sequence into many small sequences (in rows or columns), to sort each small sequence separately and finally to merge the partially sorted sequences together. In order to develop a sorting network which is favourable for VLSI implementation, the OET algorithm is chosen.

In order to gain maximum cell utilization and efficiency, the OET algorithm is embedded on the TA to form the T2OS. For the sake of comparison with other 2-D sorters, the dimensions of the T2OS are set to $2 \times \sqrt{n} \times (\sqrt{n})/2$, where n is the number of elements in a 2-D data sequence. In this case, the interconnection of the T2OS cells(C) is strictly orthogonal. Each entry of the two dimensional data sequence is stored in C.

The sorting algorithm, which comprises five sorting steps, is executed by activating cell pairs to perform comparison-exchange operations. The five sorting steps, i.e. ROW(I), ROW(II), COL(I), COL(II), and VERT, are shown in Figure 8. The execution order of the five sorting steps is irrelevant to the sorting time. The cell utilization of the T2OS for different sorting steps is summarized in Figure 9. With this particular arrangement, the 2-D sequence is sorted in the snake-like row-major order. If each cell is assigned a coordinate $C(i, j, k)$, where i be the row number, j be the column number and k be the top ($k = 0$) and bottom ($k = 1$) array layers. The five sorting steps can be described as follows:

ROW (I):
($k = 0$ and $\forall$ even i and $\forall$ even j)
or ($k = 1$ and $\forall$ odd i and $\forall$ odd j)
if $C(i, j, k) > C(i, j+1, k)$,
    then $C(i, j, k) \Leftrightarrow C(i, j+1, k)$,
    else no change
($k = 0$ and $\forall$ odd i and $\forall$ even j)
or ($k = 1$ and $\forall$ even i and $\forall$ odd j)
if $C(i, j, k) < C(i, j+1, k)$,
    then $C(i, j, k) \Leftrightarrow C(i, j+1, k)$,
    else no change

ROW (II):
($k = 0$ and $\forall$ even i and $\forall$ odd j)
or ($k = 1$ and $\forall$ odd i and $\forall$ even j)
if $C(i, j, k) > C(i, j+1, k)$,
    then $C(i, j, k) \Leftrightarrow C(i, j+1, k)$,
    else no change
($k = 0$ and $\forall$ odd i and $\forall$ odd j)
or ($k = 1$ and $\forall$ even i and $\forall$ even j)
if $C(i, j, k) < C(i, j+1, k)$,
    then $C(i, j, k) \Leftrightarrow C(i, j+1, k)$,
    else no change

COL (I):
($k = 0$ and $\forall$ even i)
or ($k = 1$ and $\forall$ odd i) and $\forall j$
if $C(i, j, k) > C(i+1, j, k)$,
    then $C(i, j, k) \Leftrightarrow C(i+1, j, k)$,
    else no change

COL (II):
($k = 0$ and $\forall$ odd i)
or ($k = 1$ and $\forall$ even i) and $\forall j$
if $C(i, j, k) > C(i+1, j, k)$,
    then $C(i, j, k) \Leftrightarrow C(i+1, j, k)$,
    else no change

VERT :
$\forall$ even i and $\forall j$
if $C(i, j, 0) > C(i, j, 1)$,
    then $C(i, j, 0) \Leftrightarrow C(i, j, 1)$,
    else no change
$\forall$ odd i and $\forall j$
if $C(i, j, 0) < C(i, j, 1)$,
    then $C(i, j, 0) \Leftrightarrow C(i, j, 1)$,
    else no change

Figure 8: The T2OS Sorting Steps
(continue)

The T2OS accomplishes matrix transposition, where the worst case is to move an element from one corner of the bottom array to the opposite corner on the top layer, in about half of the time taken for conventional mesh arrays.

According to the analytical simulation, the T2OS has approximate ly $O(\sqrt{n} \log^2(n/2)$ time complexity. Compared with the Krammer and Hendrikus's helix array

[15], the T2OS gives slight advantage due to its regularity and locality. With the T2OS, local connections are used between top and bottom arrays instead of long connections used to join cells in opposite edges of helix rings. Compared with a single processor implementing the bubble sort algorithm, the T2OS provides a network with local connections and simple control to sort 2-D data sequences at a moderate speed and its throughput may be improved if a fast parallel sorting algorithm [16] is embedded.

Operation	Count	Utilization
ROW (I)	$n\backslash 2$	$1 - 1/\sqrt{n}$
ROW (II)	$n\backslash 2$	$1 - 1/\sqrt{n}$
COL (I)	$n\backslash 2$	$1 - 2/\sqrt{n}$
COL (II)	$\sqrt{n}(\sqrt{n}-2)/2$	$1 - 2/\sqrt{n}$
VERT	$n\backslash 2$	1

Figure 9: The Cell Utilization and Operation Count of the T2OS

7. Binary Tree

Binary trees are another class of networks which are commonly used in sorting. A simple binary tree network consists of a root node and two leaf nodes. As each leaf node becomes the parent of another two leaf nodes, the number of nodes grows in the powers of two. Binary tree networks may be used to perform searching, sorting, dynamic programming, interpolation and extrapolation. Binary tree networks are particularly suitable for digital computation as each leaf node can be identified by a binary word. Similarly the regularity of binary tree networks allows them to be realized efficiently on silicon wafer. Furthermore, the simplicity of internal structure of each cell encourages wafer-scale integration of medium size networks. Several placement strategies of binary trees have been reported, such as the classical H-tree, fat tree [17], tile-based tree [18], and module-based tree [19]. Important issues of these strategies are to maintain high degree of cell utilization and to keep the connection between two adjacent cells constant.

In a recent article by Latifi and El Amawy [20], binary trees are embedded in three-dimensional rectangular arrays. Their proposed scheme uses a hierarchical strategy, which has also been employed by Youn and Singh [19], to combine the number and type of basic modules in order to construct a tree of arbitrary sizes. Each basic module is a small balanced binary tree embedding in a two-layer mesh array with a spare cell used as a connector to link up with its parent module. The regularity of each module is maintained by restricting all the connections to be orthogonal. To facilitate this, by-pass mechanism is available in each cell. However, the expansion to high dimensionality has ruled out the possibility for large scale integration.

The aims of the development of binary tree networks on the TA is to render VLSI implementation using a systematic approach and to improve the accessibility of the root node without employing long connections. A balanced binary tree is constructed by allocating cells diagonally across the top and bottom arrays to a set of successive leaf nodes and placing other nodes around these cells. With the local connections of the TA including unit-distance diagonal connections between two mesh layers, the maximum length between two adjacent nodes is always 1. The area efficiency can also be maintained at a level close to 100% for small n. According to the estimation of propagation delay suggested by Youn and Singh, the TA with 2^n cells inherits a lower bound of $O(2^{(n-1)/2})$. Data enters and leaves the TA through the edges of the TA.

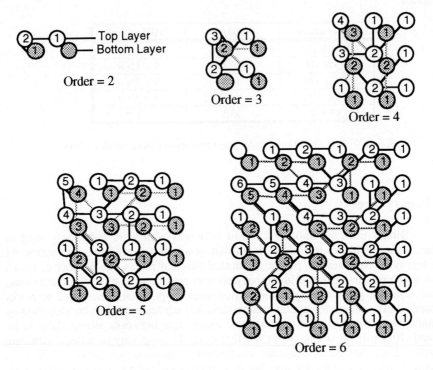

Figure 10: Binary Trees Embedded in TA

According to the systematic approach of cell allocation, balanced binary trees of the order from 2 to 6 are embedded in the TA as shown in Figure 10. In each case, the number of nodes in the top and bottom arrays is roughly equal. The embedding of a binary tree is begun by allocating the root (the biggest label number) to one of the cell at the top left edge of the TA. All the other nodes are placed around the root cell. As the amount of propagation delay introduced by diagonal connections are assumed to be the same as other orthogonal connections, the maximum delay from the root to the lowest nodes is n. For a n-order binary tree with $2^n - 1$ nodes, the minimum number of cells requires to accommodate the tree is $(2n-1) \times n$ and $(2n-2) \times n$ for even and odd n, respectively. Thus, the number of wasted cells is the difference between the number of cells in the TA and the number of cells used to construct the tree. Furthermore, the maximum length between neighbouring nodes is one because no straight through path nor long connections are available.

8. Conclusion

In this paper, sorting networks based on the novel architecture for one- and two-dimensional data have been discussed. In terms of computational efficiency, sorting algorithms based on bitonic merge and odd-even merge are superior to odd-even transposition or bubble sorting algorithms. However, they are relatively more difficult to be realized on locally connected array processors. In some circumstances, the efficiency of the bitonic sorters is overtook by the cost effective of VLSI implementation of other sorting arrays, and hence the odd-even sorters still have their roles to play. Particularly in the areas like image processing high throughput sorting for two dimensional data sequences is of crucial importance, the embedding of connection networks within sorting cells minimizes communication time. The contribution of the TA on different sorting problems is summarized as follow.

Arrays	Algorithms	Number of Cells	Number of Time Steps	Remarks
COBS	OET	$O(n)$	$O(n)$	set-up overlapping
TOS	OET	$O(n^2)$	$O(1)$	expandable
TBS	BIT	$O(n \log^2 n)$	$O(1)$	local connections for small n
T2OS	OET	$O(n)$	$O(\sqrt{n} \log^2 n/2)$	$\approx 100\%$ utilization

The embodiment of the TA has been proven in the realization of various sorting algorithms that the architecture of the TA provides higher efficiency, cell utilization and versatility, compared with conventional mesh arrays. The two mesh-layer structure provides greater connectivity without introducing excessive propagation delay. The vertical connections between the top and bottom arrays allow data to loop round the network dynamically. Larger numbers of boundary cells imply easier input and output interfaces and greater expandability.

References

1   LAM, S.P.S.: **Matrix Vector Multiplication using A $2\frac{1}{2}$-dimensional Systolic Array**, *Electronics Letts.*, vol. 26, no. 18, 1990, pp.1453.
2   LAM, S.P.S.: **A Systolic Implementation of the Jacobi Algorithm**, *Proc. Int. Conf. on Acoustic Speech and Signal Processing*, Toronto, May, 1991.
3   KNUTH, D.E.: **The Art of Computer Programming**, *Addison-Wesley*, Reading, 1973.
4   AKL, S.G.: **Parallel Sorting Algorithms**, *Academic Press*, Orlando, 1985.
5   BITTON, D. et al.: **A Taxonomy of Parallel Sorting**, *Comput. Survey*, vol. 16, no. 3, 1984, pp. 287-318.
6   SHIH, Z.C. and CHEN, G.H.: **Systolic Algorithms to Examine All Pairs of Elements**, *Commu. ACM*, vol. 30, no. 2, 1987, pp. 161-167.
7   THOMPSON, C.D.: **Area-Time Complexity for VLSI**, *Proc. Sym. Theory of Computing*, ACM, N.Y., 1979, pp. 81-88.

8   LEIGHTON, F.T.: **Tight Bounds on the Complexity of Parallel Sorting: Special Issue on Sorting.** *IEEE Trans.*, C-34, 1985, pp. 351-359.

9   MEGSON, G.M.: **Sorting Without Exchanges on a Bit-Serial Systolic Array,** *IEE Proc.*, Pt. G, vol. 137, no. 5, 1990, pp. 345-352.

10   BATCHER, K.E.: **Sorting Networks and Their Applications,** *Proc. Spring Joint Computing Conf. AFIPS,* vol. 32, 1968, pp. 307-314.

11   STONE, H.S.: **Parallel Processing with the Perfect Shuffle,** *IEEE Trans.*, C-20, 1971, pp. 153-161.

12   KUMAR, M. and HIRSCHBERG, D.S.: **An Efficient Implementation of Batcher's Odd-Even Merge Algorithm and Its Application in Parallel Sorting Schemes,** *IEEE Trans.*, C-32, 1983, pp. 254-264.

13   AJTAL, M., KOMLOS, J. and SZEMEREDI, E.: **An O(n log n) Sorting Network,** *Proc. 15 Ann. ACM Sym. Theory of Comput.*, ACM, New York, 1983, pp. 1-9.

14   THOMPSON, C.D. and KUNG, H.T.: **Sorting on a Mesh-Connected Parallel Computer,** *Commu. ACM*, vol. 20, no. 4, 1977, pp. 263-271.

15   KRAMMER, J.G. and HENDRIKUS, A.: **A Fault-Tolerant Two-Dimensional Sorting Network,** *Proc. Conf. Appl. Spec. Array Processors,* edited by S.Y. Kung et al., IEE Comp. Soc., 1990, pp. 317-328.

16   SCHMECK, H.: **A Comparison-Based Instruction Systolic Array,** *Parallel Alg. & Archit.*, M. Cosnard et al. (editors), 1986, pp. 281-292.

17   LEISERSON, C.E.: **Fat-Trees: Universal Networks for Hardware-Efficient Supercomputing,** *IEEE Trans.*, C34, 1985, pp. 892-901.

18   GORDON, D. et al.: **Embedding Tree Structures in VLSI Hexagonal Arrays,** *IEEE Trans.*, C33, 1984, pp.104-107.

19   YOUN, H.Y. and SINGH, A.D: **On Implementing Large Binary Tree Architectures in VLSI and WSI,** *IEEE Trans.*, C38, 1989, pp. 526-537.

20   LATIFI, S. and El-AMAWY, A.: **Efficient Approach to Embed Binary Trees in 3-D Rectangular Arrays,** *IEE Proc.*, vol. 137, Pt. E, no. 2, 1990, pp. 159-163.

The Time-Parallel Solution of Parabolic Partial Differential Equations Using the Frequency-Filtering Method

Graham Horton, Ralf Knirsch and Hermann Vollath

Lehrstuhl für Rechnerstrukturen (IMMD 3), Universität Erlangen-Nürnberg
Martensstr. 3, D-8520 Erlangen

Abstract. We consider the parallel solution of time-dependent partial differential equations. Due to the fact that time is a one-way dimension, traditional methods attack this type of equation by solving the resulting sequence of problems in a sequential manner. Parallel solution methods retain this sequential process, obtaining their parallelism by distributing the problem at each discrete time-step. It has been recently shown that a new approach called *time-parallelism,* which assigns successive time-steps to different processors can also lead to high efficiencies. In this paper we describe such a time-parallel algorithm based on the frequency-filtering scheme of Wittum.

1 Introduction

There exist a variety of publications on the parallel solution of time-dependent partial differential equations. The great majority of this papers deals with parallelism obtained by grid partitioning or domain decomposition strategies, i.e. by splitting up the problem at each discrete time-step. This methods, however, retain the sequential process of the integration in time direction.

A method to parallelize also over the time dimension was suggested by Hackbusch in [3]. This solution procedure based on a multigrid method distributes the problems of *successive* time-steps to *different* processors. Convergence results for this method applied to a simple model problem were presented by Burmeister in [2]. First experimental results of a parallel implementation were presented by Bastian, Burmeister and Horton in [1] for the unsteady heat equation. A time-parallel multigrid solution method for the Navier-Stokes equations was developed by Horton [4]. In [6] Knirsch studied the behaviour of the method when step control mechanisms are applied to the time-parallel algorithm. A similar solution technique for parabolic partial differential equations was presented by Womble in [10].

In this paper we present the experimental results obtained by a time-parallel version of the frequency-filtering scheme of Wittum [9], based on the parallel implementation of Vollath [7] on a Transputer system. The frequency-filtering scheme operates only on one grid level, thus avoiding the necessity of finding coarser grids which may in some cases be inappropriate. The algorithm retains, however, the good convergence properties of the multigrid method.

The system matrix of the frequency-filtering method is of block-tridiagonal form, where the blocks on the main diagonal are itself tridiagonal (sub-) matrices. A parallelization of this method with usual grid partitioning techniques would lead in principle to standard parallel solution methods (e.g. recursive doubling or cyclic reduction). These methods are known to obtain only relatively poor efficiencies. Another parallel ansatz based on a *domain decomposition* approach was presented by Weiler in [8]. Due to the additional arithmetic work needed with this method compared to the sequential algorithm a maximal efficiency of only 50% can be achieved.

In the next section we describe the principle of the time-parallel method and focus on some factors influencing the obtainable speedup. Section 3 gives a short description of the frequency-filtering scheme and the time-parallel version of this solution method. In section 4 we present some results of a parallel implementation on a Transputer system.

2 The Time-Parallel Principle and Influencing Factors

Time-parallel methods can be easily derived from the standard procedure. For the illustration of this principle we consider a parabolic p.d.e. of the form

$$\frac{\partial u}{\partial t} + \mathcal{L}(u) = f(t, x, y), \quad (x, y) \in \Omega \subset R^2, \quad t_0 < t \leq t_{MAX} \tag{1}$$

with an elliptic operator $\mathcal{L}$ and the necessary boundary conditions and starting values at $t = t_0$.

Discretizing this type of equation with standard techniques like finite difference methods in space and the backward Euler formula in time leads to a sequence of problems of the type

$$\frac{1}{\Delta t} u_{k+j} + \mathcal{L}_h u_{k+j} = f_{k+j} + \frac{1}{\Delta t} u_{k+j-1} \quad j = 1, \ldots, m, \tag{2}$$

where $\mathcal{L}_h$ is the discrete analogue of $\mathcal{L}$ and $m\Delta t = t_{MAX} - t_0$. Conventionally, the unknown grid functions $u_{k+1}, u_{k+2}, \ldots$ are calculated in a sequential manner. To obtain a time-parallel method, the equations of several discrete time-steps are considered as a single system. In Fig. 1 the structure of this extended system matrix is shown, obtained by the discretization of a two-dimensional problem on a rectangular grid. Due to the five-point stencil used for the discretization of the space directions the matrix on the main diagonal is of pentadiagonal form. This block system is considered as a whole, whereby each row is assigned one individual processor.

Any standard iterative technique may be used to solve the problem at one discrete time-step. There exist two variants for the treatment of the sub-diagonal with the $-\frac{1}{\Delta t}$-term within the iteration: An explicit use will result in a Block-Jacobi-like procedure whilst an implicit use leads to a Block-Gauß-Seidel-like technique. Note that the communication requirements of the two variants differ strongly in their granularity: For the Block-Gauß-Seidel-like technique a fine-grain granularity can be observed since one communication per grid point is

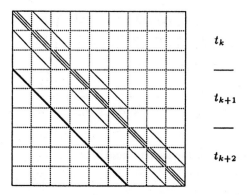

t_k

———

t_{k+1}

———

t_{k+2}

Fig. 1. Extended system matrix of a time-parallel method for 3 time-steps

necessary per iteration. By contrast, only one communication of a large amount of data (i.e. the whole computational grid) is necessary for the Block-Jacobi-like variant (see [6]).

In a time-parallel method each processor performs the same algorithm on the same amount of data, so the algorithmic work per processor is the same as in the traditional time-stepping case. There is, however, a certain number of synchronisations to be done, so the computation time for one iteration will be higher than in the sequential case which will influence the obtainable speedup. In the time-parallel case there are two further factors influencing the overall efficiency of the method: the deterioration of the initial values and the increase of the convergence rate.

When solving time-dependent problems with iterative methods the problem of starting values for the iteration process for a new time-step occurs. Often zero-order extrapolation is performed, i.e the values of the last computed time-step are used. This leads, depending on the solution function, to an increasing starting error with increasing distance from the starting point. In this case, the parallel method will always need more iterations to reduce the error to a given accuracy than the sequential method. This naturally inhibits the obtainable speedup. Methods to improve the starting values are first-order extrapolation or the nested iteration scheme if a time-parallel multigrid method is used. Details of these improvements may be found in [6] and [4].

The second factor influencing the efficiency of the time-parallel method is the convergence rate ρ, defined as the quotient of the norm of the residual r of two successive iterations i and $i + 1$:

$$\rho = \frac{\|r^{(i+1)}\|}{\|r^{(i)}\|} \; . \tag{3}$$

The convergence rate of iterative methods deteriorates, in general, with an increasing number of unknowns. It is therefore to be expected that the convergence

$$A = \begin{pmatrix} A_1^C & A_1^N & O & \cdots & & O \\ A_2^S & A_2^C & A_2^N & \ddots & & \vdots \\ O & \ddots & \ddots & \ddots & & O \\ \vdots & \ddots & \ddots & \ddots & & A_{n-2}^N \\ O & \cdots & O & A_{n-1}^S & A_{n-1}^C \end{pmatrix}$$

Fig. 2. Notation of the entries of the system matrix A

rate will increase with an increasing number of simultaneously computed time-steps. The analytic results for the time-parallel multigrid method of Burmeister in [2] show, however, that its convergence rate is bounded. The convergence behaviour of this method is discussed in [4] and [6] . For the time-parallel version of the frequency-filtering scheme no analytic investigations have been made. In section 4 we will present some numerical results for the time-parallel variant.

3 The Frequency-Filtering Scheme

In order to describe the frequency-filtering method of Wittum [9] we will use the unsteady heat equation

$$\frac{\partial u}{\partial t} - \Delta u = f(t, x, y) \tag{4}$$

on $\Omega = (t_0, t_{MAX}) \times (0,1) \times (0,1)$ as a model problem. Suitable boundary conditions and initial values at $t = t_0$ are provided. The discretization with central differences in space and backward differences in time leads for each grid point $u_{k,i,j}$ to an equation of the following type:

$$\frac{(4 + \frac{h^2}{\Delta t})u_{k,i,j} - u_{k,i-1,j} - u_{k,i,j-1} - u_{k,i+1,j} - u_{k,i,j+1}}{h^2} = f_{k,i,j} + \frac{1}{\Delta t}u_{k-1,i,j}, \tag{5}$$

with $i,j = 1, \ldots, (n-1), k = 1, \ldots, m$. A lexicographic ordering of the $(n-1) \times (n-1)$ equations leads to a block-structured system matrix A as shown in Fig. 2. In the following, the entries of A will be denoted as indicated, where the subscripts C (Center) stands for the entries of the main diagonal and S and N for the southern and northern blocks, respectively. The system of linear equations may then be solved by iterative methods. For this purpose the equation is transformed into a fix point type of the form

$$\mathbf{u}^{(i+1)} = \mathbf{u}^{(i)} - M^{-1}(A\mathbf{u}^{(i)} - \mathbf{f}), \tag{6}$$

where $\mathbf{u}^{(i)}$ denotes the approximation of $\mathbf{u}$ after the i-th iteration. The problem is now to find an appropriate matrix M, often called the *approximated inverse* of

```
PROCEDURE Frequency_Filtering_Scheme(α, n, k)
/* α stretching factor, n grid size, k no. of time-step */
BEGIN
        /* Compute Decompositions of A */
        i = 1;    ν₁⁽ⁱ⁾ = 1;   ν₂⁽ⁱ⁾ = 2;
        WHILE (ν₁⁽ⁱ⁾ < n) DO
                M⁽ⁱ⁾ = Compute_T(ν₁⁽ⁱ⁾, ν₂⁽ⁱ⁾);
                IF ([αν₁⁽ⁱ⁾] > ν₁⁽ⁱ⁾ + 1) THEN    ν₁⁽ⁱ⁺¹⁾ = [αν₁⁽ⁱ⁾];
                                          ELSE  ν₁⁽ⁱ⁺¹⁾ = ν₁⁽ⁱ⁾ + 2;
                        ν₂⁽ⁱ⁺¹⁾ = ν₁⁽ⁱ⁺¹⁾ + 1;    i = i + 1;
        END
        maxit = i − 1;
        /* Iteration process with different decompositions */
        /* M⁽ⁱ⁾ is decomposed in L⁽ⁱ⁾ and U⁽ⁱ⁾ */
        Compute dₖ = fₖ − Auₖ + (1/Δt)uₖ₋₁;
        REPEAT
                FOR i = 1 TO maxit DO
                        Solve L⁽ⁱ⁾vₖ = dₖ;
                        Solve U⁽ⁱ⁾δ = vₖ;
                        Compute uₖ = uₖ + δ;
                        Compute dₖ = fₖ − Auₖ + (1/Δt)uₖ₋₁;
                END
                UNTIL ||d|| < ε;
END.
```

Fig. 3. The frequency-filtering method

A, which minimizes the number of iterations needed to compute an approximation of a specified exactness. Additionally, M should be easily invertible. Wittum uses in [9] the formulation

$$M = (L + T)T^{-1}(U + T) \tag{7}$$

where L and U are lower and upper block-triangular matrices, respectively, and T is a block-diagonal matrix. For the frequency-filtering scheme Wittum constructs the matrix M in the following way. The lower (block) triangular matrix L is obtained by setting all blocks of A except the A_i^S-blocks to zero. The upper (block) triangular matrix U is obtained by setting all blocks of A to zero, except the A_i^N-blocks. For the construction of the tridiagonal blocks T_i of T the recursion

$$
\begin{aligned}
T_1 \mathbf{e}_k &= A_1^C \mathbf{e}_k \\
T_i \mathbf{e}_k &= (A_i^C - A_i^S T_{i-1}^{-1} A_{i-1}^N)\mathbf{e}_k & i = 2, \ldots, n-1, \quad k = 1, 2
\end{aligned}
\tag{8}
$$

```
PROCEDURE Time-parallel Solution of M̄δ = d̄ (k)
/* k number of time-step of processor */
BEGIN
      d_k = f_k - Au_k + (1/Δt)u_{k-1}
      REPEAT
            /* Solve L system line by line */
            FOR i = 1 TO n - 1 DO
                  Receive v_{k-1}[i] from P_{k-1};
                  v_k[i] = Solve_L(d_k[i], v_{k-1}[i]);
                  Send v_k[i] to P_{k+1};
            END;
            δ_k = Solve_U(v_k);
            u_k = u_k + δ_k;
            Receive (u_{k-1}) from P_{k-1};
            Send (u_k) to P_{k+1};
            d_k = f_k - Au_k + (1/Δt)u_{k-1};
      UNTIL ‖d_k‖ < ε;
END.
```

Fig. 4. Time-parallel iteration with semi-sequential smoothing variant

is used. This recursion implies that M is an exact inverse of A in the subspace defined by the vectors e_1 and e_2. Wittum uses for $e_{1,2}$ the *test vectors*

$$e_k = (sin(\nu_k ih\pi))_{i=1,\ldots,(n-1)} \qquad k = 1, 2, \qquad h = \frac{1}{n} \qquad (9)$$

with the so-called *smoothing frequencies* $\nu_{1,2}$. According to the choice of this parameters the properties of the resulting scheme may be influenced. The method will be a *corrector* for $\nu_1 = 1, \nu_2 = 2$, where the test vectors are smooth, which leads to a damping out of low frequencies of the defect. For "bigger" values of $\nu_{1,2}$ higher frequencies of the defect will be damped out and the resulting method will be a *smoother*. It can be seen that for different values of $\nu_{1,2}$ different frequencies in the defect may be *filtered out*.

In [9] Wittum develops an algorithm which simulates the sequence of grids of the multigrid method by performing several iteration steps with different values of $\nu_{1,2}$. The smoothing frequencies $\nu_{1,2}$ for these iterations are determined by the *stretching factor* $\alpha > 1$ and the following definition:

$$\nu_1^{(1)} = 1 \qquad \nu_2^{(1)} = 2$$

$$\nu_1^{(i)} = \begin{cases} [\alpha\nu_1^{(i-1)}] & \text{for} \quad [\alpha\nu_1^{(i-1)}] > \nu_1^{(i-1)} + 2 \\ \nu_1^{(i-1)} + 2 & \text{otherwise} \end{cases} \qquad (10)$$

$$\nu_2^{(i)} = \nu_1^{(i)} + 1 \; .$$

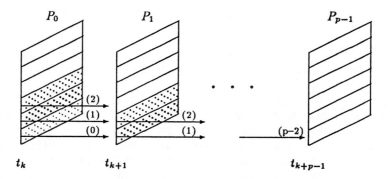

Fig. 5. Illustration of the semi-sequential smoothing variant

The factor α corresponds to the coarsening factor in the multigrid process. The case of standard coarsening would correspond to $\alpha = 2.0$. In Fig. 3 the resulting frequency-filtering scheme is shown. The matrix M is stored as an LU-decomposition, where $L = A^S + T$ and $U = I + T^{-1}A^N$ (see (7)).

To obtain a time-parallel version of the frequency-filtering method the iteration matrices M of several time-steps are combined together. This leads to a block bidiagonal matrix $\overline{M}$ whose block diagonal matrices are the M matrices. The block sub-diagonal of $\overline{M}$ consists of diagonal matrices with the $-\frac{1}{\Delta t}$-term, reflecting the coupling between successive time-steps. For the parallel solution of the resulting system, a $\overline{LU}$-decomposition of $\overline{M}$ is made. The block triangular matrix $\overline{L}$ consists of the matrices $(L + T)$ on the main diagonal and the diagonal matrices with the $-\frac{1}{\Delta t}$-term on the sub-diagonal. The matrices on the main diagonal of $\overline{U}$ is the (block) identity matrix I, which result from $T^{-1}(T + U)$ of (7). The matrices on the upper diagonal are of the form $T^{-1}U$. Note that this product would be a dense matrix. For implementation reasons this product is not stored explicitly but by (just another) LU-factorization of T, which is used to compute multiplications with T^{-1}.

The necessity of a communication between processors working on successive time-steps is limited to the solution of the $\overline{L}$ system, where two smoothing variants may be distinguished. The Block-Gauß-Seidel-like technique, called *semi-sequential smoothing* in [7], is illustrated in Fig. 4. Note that each block of the main diagonal of the $\overline{L}$ system is itself a block-structured L-matrix with the tridiagonal matrices T_i on the main diagonal. As mentioned above, the T_i are stored as LU-decomposition, which implies that intermediate values of a whole line of the computational grid have to be computed before an exchange of data can be performed. The pipeline character of this smoothing scheme can be seen in Figure 5. Regions with the same pattern are computed in parallel and flashes with the same numbers indicate a (possible) parallel communication. We observe that the time to fill the pipeline is longer than in the case of point-wise ILU-decomposition as discussed in [6].

Table 1. Iteration numbers and timings of the time-parallel method

#P	$\lambda = 1$ parallel #It	T[s]	sem.seq. #It	T[s]	$\lambda = 1638$ parallel #It	T[s]	sem.seq. #It	T[s]	$\lambda = 16384$ parallel #It	T[s]	sem.seq. #It	T[s]
1	400	4590	400	4590	1184	12758	1184	12758	1342	14404	1342	14404
2	200	2470	200	2666	593	7027	593	7591	673	7869	673	8510
4	100	1332	100	1506	300	3954	300	4497	345	4447	345	5062
8	67	908	63	975	203	2678	202	3085	188	2481	187	2825
12	62	864	51	811	166	2214	164	2527	139	1859	138	2133
16	61	848	44	717	140	1898	139	2181	113	1536	113	1776

For the second variant of the smoothing procedure the intermediate values v_{k-1} of the preceeding time-step are assumed to be zero. This means that the solution of the L-system in Fig. 4 may be computed without communication. To this Block-Jacobi-like variant we will therefore refer to as *parallel smoothing*. Note, however, that in both variants an exchange of the whole grid is necessary, in order to be able to compute the defect d_k.

4 Experimental Results

The time-parallel variant of the frequency-filtering scheme as decribed in section 3 was implemented on a Transputer system. It was applied to the unsteady heat equation (4) whereby the numerical behaviour of the method for different step-sizes Δt was investigated.

Since the time-parallel variant of the frequency-filtering scheme differs from the original method, a different numerical behaviour of the method than in the conventional time-stepping case is to be expected. This may result in additional iterations to compute the solution compared to the serial case, which will have an impact on the overall efficiency of the parallel method. So the loss in efficiency of the parallel algorithm may be divided in two parts, namely the losses incurred by communications between processors and the losses owing to the additional computational work.

The total efficiency E_{tot} of the time-parallel method may therefore be expressed as the product of the *numeric* efficiency E_{num} and the *parallel* efficiency E_{par} which are defined as follows:

$$E_{par} = \frac{T_{Iter}(1)}{T_{Iter}(p)} \qquad E_{num} = \frac{\#Iter(1)}{p * \#Iter(p)} \qquad E_{tot} = E_{num} * E_{par} \qquad (11)$$

where $T_{Iter}(p)$ represents the computation time for one iteration on p processors, and $\#Iter(p)$ the total number of iterations required by p processors to perform the integration.

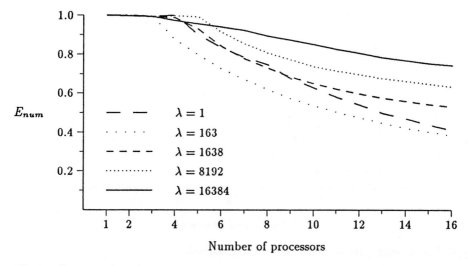

Fig. 6. E_{NUM} with parallel smoothing variant

The numeric efficiency identifies the losses in efficiency due to the increased number of iterations compared to the time-step-by-time-step approach. The parallel efficiency identifies the losses due to communication overhead and synchronization. The classically defined efficiency $E = T(1)/T(p)$ where $T(p)$ represents the total computation time on p processors, was found to be almost equal to E_{tot}. The small difference results from the overhead of the parallel algorithm between iterations.

We tested the behaviour of the two smoothing variants for different values of the parameter λ, which is defined as $\lambda = \frac{\Delta t}{\Delta x^2}$. The measurements were performed on a 128×128 grid where 400 time-steps have been computed. For the convergence criterion ϵ a value of 10^{-7} was stipulated. The right-hand side was choosen to obtain a solution function $u(t, x, y) = t^2 + x^2 + y^2$ and a stretching factor of $\alpha = 2.0$ was used.

In Table 1 iteration numbers and timings of the time-parallel frequency-filtering scheme for different values of λ are presented. For $\lambda = 1$ the method reduces the norm of the residual r to 10^{-14} within one iteration. By one iteration we denote the $\lfloor \log_\alpha n \rfloor$ applications of the matrices M_i constructed with the different frequencies $\nu_1^{(i)}$ and $\nu_2^{(i)}$. In our case this corresponds to 7 smoothing steps on the 128×128 grid. A comparable multigrid solver with an ILU-smoother (two pre- and one post-smoothing step, a coarsest grid of size 4×4 and 6 grid-levels, standard coarsening) needs 5 V-Cycles to achieve the specified accuracy of 10^{-7}. A detailed comparison of the (sequential) frequency-filtering scheme and the multigrid method can be found in [9].

It can be observed that for up to four processors there is no significant increase in the number of iterations compared to the sequential algorithm. The computation times, however, are higher in the semi-sequential smoothing case which is due to the communications involved in the solution of the L-system.

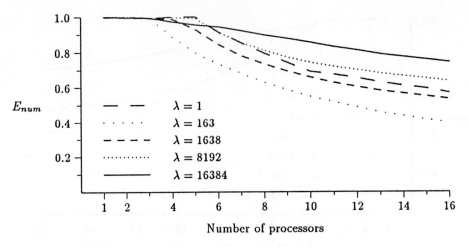

Fig. 7. E_{NUM} with semi-sequential smoothing variant

Figures 6 and 7 show the corresponding numeric efficiency for the parallel and semi-sequential smoothing variants, respectively. It can be seen that the behaviour of the time-parallel method is nearly independent of the smoothing variant. Only for $\lambda = 1$ the semi-sequential smoothing variant achieves a better efficiency. This behaviour of the two smoothing variants differs significantly from the numerical behaviour of the point-wise ILU-scheme described in [6]. Further investigations of the time-parallel frequency-filtering scheme are needed to explain this behaviour.

Besides the numeric behaviour of the time-parallel frequency-filtering algorithm the communication requirements influence the overall efficiency of the method. In Fig. 8 the parallel efficiency E_{par} of the two smoothing schemes is shown for different grid sizes. It can be observed that for both variants E_{par} is independent of the size of the computational grid. The shape of the curves can be explained as follows: For two processors one communication phase is needed for the data exchange. One additional step is needed for three processors. The use of more processors does not increase the number of communication phases since data exchanges are done in parallel. Note that the values of E_{tot} shown in Fig. 8 depend on the architecture of the Transputer system and may vary on different multiprocessor systems.

In Table 2 the total efficiency E_{tot} for both the parallel (*par.*) and the semi-sequential (*sem.*) smoothing variant are presented. Since the numeric efficiency for up to three processors is nearly optimal, the parallel efficiency of the smoothing variants is responsible for the overall efficiency of the time-parallel method. When more than three processors are used the parallel efficiency is a constant factor so that the numerical behaviour is responsible for the values of E_{tot}. Since there is no significant difference in the numerical behaviour of the two variants, the total efficiency depends only on E_{par}, which is better for the parallel smoothing variant.

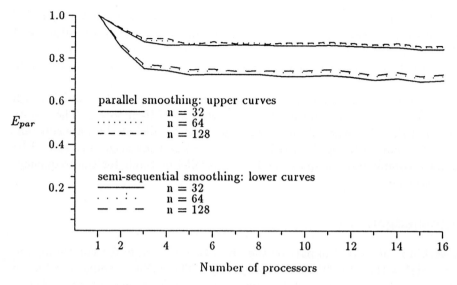

Fig. 8. Comparison of E_{PAR} for the smoothing variants

Table 2. Total efficiency E_{tot} for different values of λ

#P	$\lambda = 1$		$\lambda = 163$		$\lambda = 1638$		$\lambda = 8192$		$\lambda = 16384$	
	par.	*sem.*	*par.*	*sem.*	*par.*	*sem.*	*par.*	*sem.*	*par.*	*sem.*
1	1.00	1.00	1.00	1.00	1.00	1.00	1.00	1.00	1.00	1.00
2	0.94	0.86	0.94	0.86	0.94	0.86	0.94	0.86	0.94	0.86
4	0.89	0.76	0.77	0.67	0.86	0.74	0.89	0.76	0.86	0.74
8	0.65	0.60	0.54	0.46	0.64	0.54	0.71	0.60	0.78	0.67
12	0.47	0.48	0.41	0.36	0.52	0.44	0.60	0.52	0.70	0.60
16	0.35	0.41	0.33	0.29	0.45	0.39	0.54	0.46	0.64	0.54

5 Conclusions and Outlook

In this paper we described the time-parallel ansatz for time-dependent partial differential equations. The principle of time-parallelism was used to construct a time-parallel variant of the frequency-filtering scheme of Wittum [9]. Since the time-parallel scheme differs from the original scheme we used a refined measure for the quality of the method. This enabled us to identify the losses in efficiency due to the numerical behaviour and to the communication costs.

The results obtained by an implementation on a Tranputer system showed that the time-parallel method could achieve good efficiencies. Depending on the value of the parameter λ overall efficiencies between 54% and 78% for the parallel smoothing variant could be achieved. For the semi-sequential smoothing procedure these values were between 46% and 67%. These differences are due to the different communication costs of the variants since the numerical behaviour is almost identical. This differs from the observations made for a time-parallel variant of the point-wise ILU method used as a smoother in a multigrid method as described in [6]. Further research is necessary to explain this behaviour.

Since the principle of time-parallelism makes no assumptions on the solution method in space a combination with space-parallel techniques could be used to increase the degree of parallelism. This has been done by Horton and Knirsch in [5] for the time-parallel multigrid method with an ILU-smoother. The results showed that the efficiencies obtained with the time-parallel method are substantially better than in the grid partitioning case. Similar investigations should be made for a combination of space- and time-parallel methods for the frequency-filtering scheme.

Acknowledgement

This work was supported in part by the "Bundesministerium für Forschung und Technologie" within it's "PARAWAN" project. The authors would also like to thank Gabriel Wittum for helpful discussions on the frequency-filtering scheme.

References

1. P. Bastian, J. Burmeister, and G. Horton. Implementation of a parallel multigrid method for parabolic partial differential equations. In W.Hackbusch, editor, *Proceedings of the 6th GAMM Seminar*, pages 18–27, Braunschweig, 1990. Vieweg.
2. J. Burmeister. Paralleles Lösen diskreter parabolischer Probleme mit Mehrgittertechniken. Master's thesis, Universität Kiel, 1985.
3. W. Hackbusch. Parabolic multi-grid methods. In R. Glowinski and J.-R. Lions, editors, *Computing Methods in Applied Sciences and Engineering, VI*, Amsterdam, 1984. North Holland.
4. G. Horton. *Ein zeitparalleles Lösungsverfahren für die Navier–Stokes Gleichungen.* PhD thesis, Universität Erlangen-Nürnberg, 1991.
5. G. Horton and R. Knirsch. A space- and time-parallel multigrid method for time-dependent partial differential equations. In W. Joosen and E. Milgrom, editors, *Parallel Computing: From Theory to Sound Practice*, Amsterdam, 1992. IOS Press.
6. R. Knirsch. Implementierung eines parallelen Mehrgitterverfahrens zur Lösung instationärer partieller Differentialgleichungen. Master's thesis, Universität Erlangen-Nürnberg, 1990.
7. H. Vollath. Die zeitparallele Lösung von instationären partiellen Differentialgleichungen mit dem Glätter-Korrektor-Verfahren. Technical report, Universität Erlangen-Nürnberg, 1992.
8. W. Weiler. Parallelization of a frequency filtering method by domain decomposition. In W.Hackbusch and G. Wittum, editors, *Proceedings of the 8th GAMM Seminar, in preparation*, Braunschweig, 1992. Vieweg.
9. G. Wittum. Filternde Zerlegungen: Ein Beitrag zur schnellen Lösung großer Gleichungssysteme. Report 90–19, Universität Heidelberg, 1990.
10. D. E. Womble. A time-stepping algorithm for parallel computers. *SIAM Journal on Scientific and Statistical Computing*, 11, No. 5:824–837, 1990.

This article was processed using the LaTeX macro package with LLNCS style

The Combination Technique for Parallel Sparse-Grid-Preconditioning or -Solution of PDE's on Workstation Networks

M. Griebel * and W. Huber ** and U. Rüde *** and T. Störtkuhl *

Institut für Informatik, Technische Universität München
Arcisstrasse 21, D-8000 München 2, Germany
e-mail: griebel/huberw/ruede/stoertku@informatik.tu-muenchen.de

Abstract. In this paper we study the parallel solution of elliptic partial differential equations with the sparse grid combination technique. This new algorithmic concept is based on the independent solution of many problems with reduced size and their linear combination. The resulting algorithm can be used as a solver and within a preconditioner. We will describe the algorithm for two and three-dimensional problems and discuss its parallel implementation on a network of HP720 workstations.

1 Introduction

We present a new parallel method for the solution of elliptic partial differential equations. In this method the solution is obtained by linear combination of discrete solutions on different meshes. A special case is the *combination technique* that needs only $O(h_n^{-1}(\log(h_n^{-1}))^{d-1})$ grid points instead of $O(h_n^{-d})$ for d-dimensional problems, where $h_n = 2^{-n}$ denotes the mesh size. The accuracy of the sparse grid combination solution is of the order $O(h_n^2(\log(h_n^{-1}))^{d-1})$ provided that the solution is sufficiently smooth. This is only slightly worse than $O(h_n^2)$ obtained for the usual full grid solution. In addition to being a solver in its own right, the combination method can be used as a parallel preconditioner for the full grid problem. Then, a basic iterative method is accelerated substantially and shows nearly optimal, i.e. multigrid-like convergence behavior, if the accuracy of the solution is required only up to the truncation error.

The natural coarse grain parallelism of the combination method makes it prefectly suited for MIMD parallel computers and distributed processing on workstation networks. $O((\log(h_n^{-1}))^{d-1})$ problems of the size $O(h_n^{-1})$ must be solved independently and can therefore be computed fully in parallel. Especially for the higher dimensional cases this is a very promising approach. On a computer or a network with $O((\log(h_n^{-1}))^{d-1})$ processors we achieve an overall parallel complexity of only $O(h_n^{-1})$.

* supported by Sonderforschungsbereich SFB 342, TU München,
** supported by Deutsche Forschungsgemeinschaft, AZ Ze 281/3-2,
*** supported by Deutsche Forschungsgemeinschaft, Stipend Ru422/3-1.

For the three-dimensional case, we report the results of numerical experiments on a network of 110 HP720-workstations.

2   The combination method

We consider a partial differential equation

$$Lu = f$$

in the unit cube $\bar{\Omega} = [0,1]^d \subset \mathbb{R}^d$ with a linear, elliptic operator L of second order and appropriate boundary conditions. For reasons of simplicity, first we restrict ourselves to the case $d = 2$ and consider the case $d = 3$ later.

The usual approach is to discretize the problem by a finite element or finite difference method on an equidistant grid $\Omega_{n,n}$ with grid size $h_n = 2^{-n}$ in x- and y-direction and to solve the arising linear system of equations $L_{n,n} u_{n,n} = f_{n,n}$. Then, we get a solution $u_{n,n}$ with error $e_{n,n} = u - u_{n,n} = O(h_n^2)$, if u is sufficiently smooth. Here, we assume that $u_{n,n}$ represents an appropriate interpolant defined by the values of the discrete solutions on grid $\Omega_{n,n}$.

For the solution of the discrete system, one of the most effective techniques is the multigrid method. Roughly speaking, the number of operations is of the order $O(h_n^{-2})$ and is therefore proportional to the number of grid points.

Extending this standard approach, we now study linear combinations of discrete solutions of the problem on different rectangular grids. Let $\Omega_{i,j}$ be the uniform grid on Ω with mesh sizes $h_1 = 2^{-i}$ and $h_2 = 2^{-j}$ in x- and y-direction, respectively.

To this end, we consider the so-called *combination technique*

$$u_{n,n}^c = \sum_{i+j=n+1} u_{i,j} - \sum_{i+j=n} u_{i,j} \tag{1}$$

that has been introduced in [11]. Here, i ranges from 1 to n. This method is illustrated in Fig. 1. Note that our approach can be interpreted as a special case of multivariate extrapolation (see [14]).

Thus, we have to solve n different problems $L_{i,j} u_{i,j} = f_{i,j}$, $i+j = n+1$, each with about 2^n unknowns and $n - 1$ different problems $L_{i,j} u_{i,j} = f_{i,j}$, $i + j = n$, each with about 2^{n-1} unknowns and combine their bilinearly interpolated solutions. This gives a solution defined on the so-called sparse grid $\Omega_{n,n}^s$, see Fig. 2. The sparse grid $\Omega_{n,n}^s$ is a subset of the associated full grid $\Omega_{n,n}$.

3   Properties of the combination method as sparse grid solver

Altogether, the combination method involves $O(h_n^{-1}\log(h_n^{-1}))$ unknowns in contrast to $O(h_n^{-2})$ unknowns for the conventional full grid approach. Additionally,

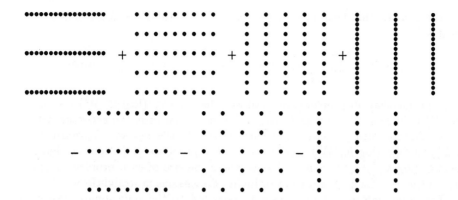

Fig. 1. The linear combination of grids $\Omega_{i,j}$ and solutions $u_{i,j}$ with i+j=n+1 and i+j=n, n=4.

Fig. 2. The sparse grid $\Omega_{4,4}^s$ and the associated full grid $\Omega_{4,4}$.

the combination solution $u_{n,n}^c$ is nearly as accurate as the standard solution $u_{n,n}$. It can be proved (see [11]) that the error satisfies

$$e_{n,n}^c = u - u_{n,n}^c = O(h_n^2 \log(h_n^{-1})),$$

(pointwise and with respect to the L_2- and L_∞-norm). This is only slightly worse than for the associated full grid where the error is of the order $O(h_n^2)$. For the proof we assume that u is sufficiently smooth, so that for $u_{i,j}$ (interpolated from grid $\Omega_{i,j}$ to the domain Ω) an *error splitting* of the form

$$u_{i,j} = u + h_i^2 \omega_1(h_i) + h_j^2 \omega_2(h_j) + h_i^2 h_j^2 \omega_3(h_i, h_j) \tag{2}$$

holds for any fixed point $(x, y) \in \Omega$ with ω_1, ω_2, ω_3 bounded by a constant C. This is a requirement different (and weaker) than what is used for usual Richardson extrapolation. If we insert the error splitting formula (2) into equation (1), we see that the leading error terms cancel. We get the estimation

$$|u - u_{n,n}^c| \leq C \cdot h_n^2 \cdot (1 + 5/4 \log(h_n^{-1})) = O(h_n^2 \log(h_n^{-1})).$$

Related techniques have been studied in [4] where it is shown that the energy-norm of the error is of the order $O(h_n^{-1})$ which is the same as for the full grid approach.

The combination technique can be extended to the three-dimensional case. We get

$$u_{n,n,n}^c = \sum_{i+j+k=n+2} u_{i,j,k} - 2 \cdot \sum_{i+j+k=n+1} u_{i,j,k} + \sum_{i+j+k=n} u_{i,j,k}. \tag{3}$$

This means that all problems in total only have $O(h_n^{-1}(\log(h_n^{-1}))^2)$ instead of $O(h_n^{-3})$ unknowns. Analogous to the two dimensional case, the accuracy deteriorates slightly both pointwise and with respect to the L_2- and L_∞-norm from $O(h_n^2)$ to $O(h_n^2(\log(h_n^{-1}))^2)$. For details of the proof see [11]. Now, we have to solve $O((\log(h_n^{-1})^2)$ different problems where the size of each problem is of the order $O(h_n^{-1})$. The generalization to higher dimensions is straightforward.

The combination technique is not restricted to the unit square. We have successfully treated problems on distorted quadrilaterals, triangles, and more general domains with polygonal boundaries. Additionally, problems with a non-linear operator and PDE-systems like the Stokes' and Navier-Stokes' equations have been solved (see [9]).

To some extent, the combination method even works in the case of non-smooth solutions. Now, h_i^2 and h_j^2 in (2) have to be replaced by h_i^α, h_j^β with appropriate α and β, but, because of the properties of the combination technique, the leading error terms still cancel. However, for problems with severe singularities the appropriate combination of adaptively refined grids is recommended. For further results on the combination method as sparse grid problem solver (see [11], [8], and [14]).

We remark that all the different discrete problems whose solutions have to be combined are totally independent of each other and can be solved fully in parallel. This will be exploited in the parallelization in section 5.

4 The combination method as preconditioner for the full grid problem

So far, we have used the combination method to produce an approximation to the solution on the sparse grid $\Omega_{n,n}^s$. Additionally, the combination method can be used as a *preconditioner* for the problem $L_{n,n}u_{n,n} = f_{n,n}$ on the full grid $\Omega_{n,n}$. Let $P_{i,j}^{n,n} : \Omega_{i,j} \to \Omega_{n,n}$ be the standard bilinear interpolation operator (multigrid-prolongation), and let $R_{n,n}^{i,j} : \Omega_{n,n} \to \Omega_{i,j}$ be a local averaging operator. This is the adjoint operator of $P_{i,j}^{n,n}$ (weighted restriction). Furthermore, let ω denote an appropriate damping factor (e.g. $\omega \in (0.2, 1.0)$). Then, we solve the preconditioned system

$$B_{n,n}^{-1} L_{n,n} u_{n,n} = B_{n,n}^{-1} f_{n,n},$$

where

$$B_{n,n}^{-1} = \sum_{i+j=n+1} P_{i,j}^{n,n} L_{i,j}^{-1} R_{n,n}^{i,j} - \sum_{i+j=n} P_{i,j}^{n,n} L_{i,j}^{-1} R_{n,n}^{i,j} + \omega \cdot (diag(L_{n,n}))^{-1}, \tag{4}$$

by some iterative algorithm, for example the defect correction process or the conjugate gradient method. There, in each iteration step the residual $r_{n,n} = f_{n,n} - L_{n,n}u_{n,n}^{it}$ has to be computed. Here, $u_{n,n}^{it}$ denotes the actual iterate on $\Omega_{n,n}$ before the it-th iteration step. Then, this residual has to be multiplied with $B_{n,n}^{-1}$. Practically, this is done by the combination method with the right hand sides $f_{i,j} = R_{n,n}^{i,j} r_{n,n}$ for the problems on the grids $\Omega_{i,j}$, $i+j = n+1$ and $i+j = n$. In the three-dimensional case an analogous preconditioner can be derived from (3). Note that without a term like $(diag(L_{n,n}))^{-1}$, the preconditioner (4) would be of deficient rank. Then, it can be interpreted as a certain additive MG-coarse grid correction involving multiple coarse grids with multivariate discretizations.

Thus, the combination method is not only useful to produce an approximation of the solution on the sparse grid, but it can also be applied as a preconditioner for the full grid problem to speed up a basic iterative solver. Then, a nearly optimal convergence behavior similar to the FMG-approach can be obtained. The work on the full grid problem necessary to reduce the error to the size of the truncation error is practically independent of h_n. See [10] for a discussion of the convergence acceleration properties of the combination method preconditioner and related techniques.

It is no longer necessary to solve each problem arising in the combination method exactly, if the combination method is only used within a preconditioner. Without significant loss of the error reduction properties of the overall algorithm an appropriate inexact solver can be substituted instead. Here, it is mostly sufficient to use only just a few multigrid V-cycles.

The combination preconditioner can be interpreted as a certain multilevel additive Schwarz algorithm [5]. From this point of view, our combination preconditioner can be seen as a special Schwarz method with maximal overlap but multivariate discretizations. In this sense it is also related to the asynchronous fast adaptive composite grid method [12] and domain decomposition type algorithms (see [13] and the references cited therein). Though these methods are devised as parallel solvers on adapted nonuniform meshes, they share their parallelization properties with the combination technique.

In general, there exist many efficient preconditioners for the (conjugate gradient) solution of the full grid problem. However, while typically the parallelization of the basic iterative method is easy, the parallelization of the preconditioning step may be very difficult. Certain types of preconditioners like, for example, the ILU-approach are not efficiently parallelizable or need modifications of the numerical algorithm that might result in slower convergence rates.

Other types of preconditioners like the hierarchical basis preconditioner of Yserentant [16] or the preconditioner of Bramble, Pasciak, and Xu [3], or even classical multigrid are well parallelizable but do not possess the natural inherent coarse grain parallelism of the combination method.

In contrast to these techniques, the parallelism in the combination technique is more explicit. Similar to the domain decomposition approach, the combination method possesses a natural and simple coarse grain parallelization potential, because all the subproblems are independent. For the combination technique the various parallelization techniques mentioned above can be exploited *additionally* within the subproblem solvers. The parallelism typical for the combination technique becomes particularly attractive for higher-dimensional problems, when $O((\log(h_n^{-1}))^{d-1})$ problems can be solved completely independently in each preconditioning (or solution) step.

5 Parallelization aspects of the combination method

For the combination technique in two dimensions, n different problems each with about 2^n unknowns and $n-1$ problems each with about 2^{n-1} unknowns can be solved *fully in parallel*. In the three-dimensional case, $n \cdot (n+1)/2$ problems with about 2^n unknowns, $(n-1) \cdot n/2$ problems with about 2^{n-1} unknowns, and $(n-2) \cdot (n-1)/2$ problems with about 2^{n-2} unknowns can be solved fully in parallel. The situation for more than three dimensions is analogous. This parallelization potential of the combination method can be gained already on a relatively course grain level.

Additionally, the subproblem solver (e.g. multigrid) can be parallelized. This, however, requires a comparatively fine grain parallelization. In addition to the natural coarse grain parallelism this can only be exploited on massively parallel systems with thousands of processors. Alternatively, the subproblems are ideal for vectorization (see [7]).

Note that the problem size is only dependent on the discretization parameter n. Thus, the number of unknowns for a single problem does not grow with the dimension as it is the case for the domain decomposition approach. However, the number of different problems that can be treated in parallel depends on the dimension.

The independence of the subproblems can be realized by a simple parallel computation model. We propose a farm-like master and slave structure for the coarse grain parallelization. The master distributes the subproblems to be solved to its slaves and collects the results when they all have terminated. This simple structure is suitable because usually the communication is very small compared to the work assigned to each processor. In extreme çases with many parallel tasks, we can avoid the bottlenecks in a $1 \leftrightarrow p$ communication by implementing the master-slave structure with additional *sub-masters* each taking responsibility for a certain number of slaves (see Fig. 5). This approach can be applied recursively.

The different sizes of the various problem classes suggest the following simple load balancing strategy. Assume that p processors are available. First, the n problems of size 2^n are distributed among the processors. We denote the work to solve one of these problems by W. In the case of a multigrid solver, we may assume $W = O(2^n)$. Now, the load of two processors differs at most by W. For two dimensions we are left with $n-1$ problems of size $O(2^{n-1})$ each corresponding to a load of $W/2$. As shown in Fig. 3, two of these problems are used to fill the processors having less load than the others. If, after this step, not all tasks have been assigned to processors, the remaining problems are again evenly distributed among the processors. In the three-dimensional case this algorithm is continued in the canonical way with the problems of size $O(2^{n-2})$.

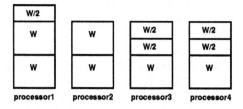

Fig. 3. A simple load balancing strategy, 2D case, $P=4$.

Following this simple strategy, we achieve that the load of two different processors differs at most by $W/2$ for the 2D case and $W/4$ for the 3D case, provided that the number of problems is sufficiently large with respect to the number of processors. In the three-dimensional case, the largest efficiency with the highest speed up for a given n is obtained by using

$$P = \text{int} \left[\frac{n(n+1)}{2} + \frac{(n-1)n}{4} + \frac{(n-2)(n-1)}{8} \right] \tag{5}$$

processors. Note at last that this strategy can be improved somewhat if we exploit the fact that for example the problems on grids $\Omega_{i,j,k}$, $i+j+k = n$ do not possess exactly the same number of unknowns and, therefore, do not require the same work to be solved.

The general coarse grain parallelization concept introduced above cannot only be used for the combination method but also for a broad range of extrapolation and domain decomposition techniques. It is realized with a shell type approach as shown in Fig. 4. The goal of this concept is to separate the numerical problem from the description of its parallelization, as proposed in [6].

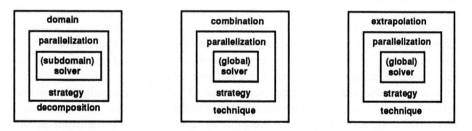

Fig. 4. Shell concept for parallelization of different solution approaches.

Each subproblem is independent of the others. Thus, it is not necessary that the process implementing the solution of a particular subproblem has any information about the other subproblems. This supports a clean modularization that is often neglected in current parallel programming practice. The parallelization strategy is implemented in an outer module. Of course, this is now dependent on the combination technique and would be somewhat different for other problems, like more general extrapolation or domain decomposition methods.

As a benefit from this modularization we get easy extensibility and portability. For example, the subproblem solvers can be exchanged without modification of the combination or the parallelization strategy. Similarly, the load balancing part can be modified without affecting the subproblem solvers. The current codes have already been ported to different MIMD-machines, where all modules have been programmed in C (see [9]). For our workstation version, the single subproblem solvers remain to be implemented in C. The master program, however, is partly implemented as a shell script initiating the distribution of the problems and collecting their results.

This concept has to be altered somewhat if the combination technique is used as a preconditioner for the associated full grid. In this case the full solution must be assembled and its residual must be calculated. To implement this efficiently, a sophisticated re-organization of the data is required, because a parallelization of the residual calculation requires a different parallelization concept.

6 Experiments on a network of high performance workstations

In this section we turn to the results of our numerical experiments. We consider the simple three-dimensional model problem

$$\Delta u = 0 \quad \text{in } \Omega = (0,1) \times (0,1) \times (0,1) \tag{6}$$

with the exact solution

$$u = \sin(\pi x) \cdot \sin(\pi y) \cdot \sinh(\sqrt{2}\pi z)/\sinh(\sqrt{2}\pi)$$

and Dirichlet boundary conditions on $\partial \bar{\Omega}$. As we are interested in the parallelization properties of our method, we neglect the possibilities of using only an inexact solver for the different subproblems arising in the combination method. Furthermore, we focus on the parallelization properties of the combination method itself (as a sparse grid problem solver or as a preconditioner) and not on its interaction with fine grid iterations necessary for a full grid solver.

For the solution of the subproblems we use 10 V-cycles of a multigrid method with one step of lexical Gauss-Seidel pre-smoothing and one post-smoothing. Thus, the computational cost of the parallel tasks is of the same order as the cost of the communication of each solution to the master task. This may become a bottleneck, if really the fully assembled solution is required (see the discussion in section 5). In this sense, the simple Laplace problem is a quite hard test example for the parallel performance of our algorithm. Experiments with more complicated PDE's and PDE-systems like the Stokes' equations gave analogous results. Note that our code uses full 27-point stencils that are derived from the assembly of tri-linear quadrilateral finite elements. Furthermore, the stencil is assembled explicitly at each grid point, simulating the solution of a more general, second order elliptic operator with variable coefficients.

Now we turn to the implementation of the combination method on a network of 110 HP720 workstations. The workstations are organized in 10 clusters. Each cluster consists of a disc-server and 10 discless clients, each with 16MByte main memory (see Fig. 5).

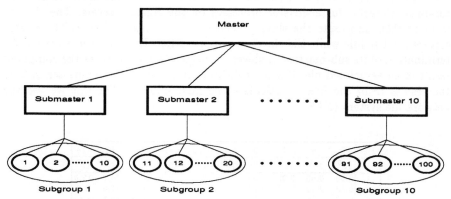

Fig. 5. Workstation network configuration.

It is noteworthy that the total memory capacity of this system is more than 1.6 GByte and thus larger than most machines presently considered as supercomputers. The HP720 workstation is based on HP's Precision RISC-architecture. This architecture achieves a peak-rate of 50 MFlop per second (see [2]), so that the peak rate of the network would be 5.5 GFlop per second.

Similar to vector architectures the peak rate is rarely obtained in practice. Even on a single workstation the peak performance can only be obtained, when floating point operands are stored in registers. The registers can be considered as the top level of a multi-level memory hierarchy, consisting of registers, cache (256 KByte), main memory, and, finally, virtual memory. If data must be transferred from slower to faster memory in the hierarchy, the performance may drop dramatically. Experiments indicate that for practical applications a careful and sophisticated optimization is required to obtain at least about 50% of the single processor peak rate. For a detailed discussion see [2]. Our present code, that has not been specially optimized yet, runs at more than 5 MFlop per second on a single processor.

Of course, the application of the network as a parallel supercomputing system is additionally handicapped by several more constraints. The ethernet connection is very slow compared to the processing speed of a single workstation. Furthermore, it is not possible to use the workstations as a dedicated system. Even at night hours when no regular users are present, it is practically impossible to control the effect of background processes on the elapsed time and performance. This is further complicated by the lack of tools supporting the evaluation of distributed applications in the network. Therefore, our results are based on an idealized measurement system. For each of the parallel tasks we compute the sum of the user and system time and neglect idle times caused by virtual memory effects, disc-IO and background processes. The maximum of these times plus the execution time of the master process are used as the overall time.

The communication demands of our application are so simple that a quite naive implementation already gives quite satisfactory results. A shell script is used to start the execution of the slave processes. This is done in two levels. The top-master starts cluster-master processes on the cluster servers. The cluster-masters then distribute the slave processes on the cluster-clients. The cluster servers are left idle while the slaves are in operation. Each master waits for the termination of its sub-masters or slaves, respectively, which stores the computed result in an associated file. When all slaves have terminated, the master collects the results from the files to calculate the final solution. For this we use the network file system (NFS).

$P \backslash n$	5	6	7	8	9	10	11	12	13	14
$\times$	10^0	10^0	10^1	10^1	10^1	10^2	10^2	10^2	10^2	10^3
1	2.03	6.85	2.09	6.09	16.8	4.48	11.7	29.3	79.2	19.5
3	0.73	2.45	0.74	2.24	6.08	1.66	4.37	10.9	27.0	6.6
6	0.42	1.2	0.4	1.16	3.19	0.87	2.24	5.73	14.1	3.45
12	0.25	0.7	0.22	0.62	1.67	0.47	1.16	2.95	7.07	1.76
25	0.18	0.34	0.1	0.32	0.84	0.22	0.59	1.44	3.44	0.89
50	0.20	0.38	0.08	0.19	0.48	0.12	0.33	0.76	1.93	0.49
100	0.24	0.25	0.08	0.16	0.35	0.08	0.17	0.41	0.99	0.24

Table 1. Times (in sec.) for combination algorithm on $\Omega_{n,n}^s$ on network with P HP720-workstations as slaves.

$P \backslash n$	5	6	7	8	9	10	11	12	13	14
$\times$	10^7	10^7	10^7	10^7	10^7	10^7	10^7	10^7	10^7	10^7
1	0.53	0.54	0.56	0.57	0.57	0.57	0.57	0.57	0.52	0.51
3	1.47	1.52	1.58	1.55	1.58	1.55	1.52	1.54	1.53	1.51
6	2.57	3.10	2.94	2.98	3.01	2.97	2.97	2.92	2.93	2.90
12	4.30	5.31	5.40	5.60	5.76	5.46	5.73	5.68	5.84	5.67
25	5.98	10.9	11.7	10.9	11.4	11.5	11.1	11.7	12.0	11.2
50	5.38	9.79	15.6	18.2	19.9	22.1	20.1	22.1	21.4	20.5
100	4.48	14.9	15.4	21.2	27.5	34.3	38.6	40.1	41.6	42.3

Table 2. Flop per second for combination algorithm on $\Omega_{n,n}^s$ on network with P HP720-workstations as slaves.

With this implementation we measured the times that are shown in Table 1. Table 2 shows the performance. With 100 slave processors we achieved a rate of approximately 400 MFlop per second. On a CRAY YMP with 4 processors, a comparable algorithm (see [8]) ran wat about the same speed. Fig. 6 shows the resulting speed up and efficiency for varying problem sizes and processor numbers. There, an efficiency of more than 70 percent can be seen for a sufficient large value of n.

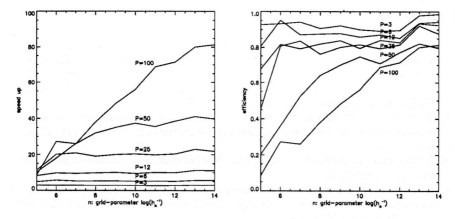

Fig. 6. Speed up and efficiency of the network measured with respect to P slave-workstations.

7 Concluding remarks

In this paper we discussed the distributed and parallel solution of partial differential equations by combination type algorithms on a workstation network. Our experiments indicate an excellent performance potential.

The experiments show that for a certain class of algorithms, including the combination technique, extrapolation, and domain decomposition, a comparatively simple parallel computing model already leads to an efficient parallel implementation.

The concept used to implement the parallel combination technique supports both modularity and portability by providing a strict separation of sequential modules. Their integration in a parallel application is implemented in separate modules.

Further experiments on MIMD-machines (see [9]), however, have shown that the inherent coarse grain parallelism of the combination method is not sufficient to achieve substantially better efficiency rates than our network. A more sophisticated load balancing strategy is necessary to exploit the advantages of massive parallel systems that are equipped with fast communication hardware.

In future research we will carefully optimize the scalar code for the target architectures. Additionally, the software basis will be revised. With parallel development and computing systems like TOPSYS (see [1]) or PVM (see [15]), a software basis becomes available that promises better performance together with improved monitoring and evaluation tools.

For a certain class of practical algorithms with moderate communication requirements we see that a network of workstations can be a quite powerful parallel computing system. We believe that with the development of fast FDDI based communication links a network of workstations will be a real competitor to standard MIMD computers in near future.

References

1. S. BAKER, H.-J. BEIER, T. BEMMERL, A. BODE, H. ERTL, U. GRAF, O. HANSEN, J. HAUNERDINGER, P. HOFSTETTER, R. KNÖDLSEDER, J. KREMENEK, S. LANGENBUCH, R. LINDHOF, T. LUDWIG, P. LUKSCH, R. MILNER, B. RIES, AND T. TREML, *TOPSYS – tools for parallel systems*, SFB Bericht 342/13/91 A, Institut für Informatik, TU München, June 1991.
2. T. BONK AND U. RÜDE, *Performance analysis and optimization of numerically intensive programs*, SFB Bericht, Institut für Informatik, TU München, 1992. in preparation.
3. J. BRAMBLE, J. PASCIAK, AND J. XU, *Parallel multilevel preconditioners*, Math. Comp., 31 (1990), pp. 333–390.
4. H. BUNGARTZ, *Dünne Gitter und deren Anwendung bei der adaptiven Lösung der dreidimensionalen Poisson-Gleichung*, Dissertation, Institut für Informatik, Technische Universität München, 1992.
5. M. DRYJA AND O. WIDLUND, *Multilevel additive methods for elliptic finite element problems*, in Parallel Algorithms for Partial Differential Equations, Proceedings of the Sixth GAMM-Seminar, Kiel, January 19-21, 1990, W. Hackbusch, ed., Braunschweig, 1991, Vieweg-Verlag.
6. R. FÖSSMEIER AND U. RÜDE, *Konzepte und Werkzeuge zur Parallelen Programmierung auf der Unix-Kommando-Ebene*, unix/mail, 2/90 (1990).
7. M. GRIEBEL, *Parallel multigrid methods on sparse grids*, in Proceedings of the Third European Conference on Multigrid Methods, October 1-4, 1990, W. Hackbusch and U. Trottenberg, eds., Basel, 1991, Birkhäuser, pp. 211–221. International Series of Numerical Mathematics, Vol. 98.
8. ——, *The combination technique for the sparse grid solution of PDE's on multiprocessor machines*, SFB Bericht 342/14/91 A, Institut für Informatik, TU München, June 1991.
9. ——, *Sparse grid methods, their parallelisation and their application to CFD*, in Proceedings of parallel CFD92 Conference, New Brunswick N.J., March 1992.
10. ——, *Sparse grid preconditioners*, SFB Bericht, Institut für Informatik, TU München, 1992. in preparation.
11. M. GRIEBEL, M. SCHNEIDER, AND C. ZENGER, *A combination technique for the solution of sparse grid problems*, SFB Bericht 342/19/90, Institut für Informatik, TU München, October 1990. Also in: Proceedings of the International Symposium on Iterative Methods in Linear Algebra, Bruxelles, April 2-4, 1991.
12. S. MCCORMICK, *Multilevel Adaptive Methods for Partial Differential Equations*, SIAM, Philadelphia, 1989.
13. A. QUATERONI, *Domain decomposition and parallel processing for the numerical solution of partial differential equations*, Surv. Math. Ind., 1 (1991), pp. 75–118.
14. U. RÜDE, *Extrapolation and related techniques for solving elliptic equations*, Bericht I-9135, Institut für Informatik der TU München, 1991.
15. V. SUNDERAM, *PVM: a framework for parallel and distributed computing*, tech. report, Emory University, Department of Mathematics and Computer Science, Atlanta, GA 30322, USA, 1991.
16. H. YSERENTANT, *Hierarchical bases*, in Proceedings of the ICIAM 1991, SIAM, 1991.

This article was processed using the LaTeX macro package with LLNCS style

Comparing the DAP, Meiko and Suprenum with a fluid dynamic Benchmark

Michael Schäfer

Lehrstuhl für Strömungsmechanik,
Universität Erlangen-Nürnberg, Cauerstr. 4, D-8520 Erlangen, Germany

Michael M. Gutzmann and Markus Schwehm

Institut für Mathematische Maschinen und Datenverarbeitung VII,
Universität Erlangen-Nürnberg, Martensstr. 3, D-8520 Erlangen, Germany

email: gutzmann@immd7.informatik.uni-erlangen.de

Abstract

An algorithm for the numerical simulation of the fluid flow in a crystal growth process is presented. The algorithm is implemented on three parallel architectures. The performance analysis shows that special care has to be taken for the efficient realization of communication patterns on massively parallel systems.

1 Introduction

The numerical solution of fluid dynamical problems is characterized by very intensive demands on computational power and memory. In our case a 3D fluid flow problem in a Czochralsky crystal growth configuration is given: a silicon crystal is grown from a melt which is heated, while the crystal and the melt are rotated around the main axis in opposite direction, demonstrated by Brown [1]. The numerical simulation of fluid flow in a crystal growth system, as described above, is needed in order to improve the quality of crystals for the manufacturing of highly integrated semiconductor devices. Due to the high complexity of this system, massively parallel computer architectures are recommended to simulate the process.

For such machines the difficulty to reach the required performance lies not only in the arithmetical power of the elementary processors (the best ones today reach 200 MFlops for 64 bit arithmetic), but in connecting 10^3 up to 10^6 or even more of them efficiently. Elementary local and global communication demands can slow down the performance by a factor of ten or more. In large mesh-connected SIMD systems with synchronous communication (no overhead for message passing), the overhead in time usage for some elementary regular communication patterns grows with the square root of the number of processing elements in comparison with the time for arithmetic computation, shown by Strey [10]. Therefore the discussion of suitable interconnection networks for massively parallel supercomputers is very important for the objective to set up a system that is balanced in terms of arithmetical and communicational power, in order to avoid bottlenecks and to use resources efficiently. Different Approaches in performance evaluation of those computers are shown by Erhard [3] and by Gutzmann [5].

The results presented in this paper, which include comparisons of several architectures with different amount and power of processors and various interconnection networks, confirm the importance of efficient communication in very large computer systems.

Since the original 3D problem cannot be computed on any existing machine today, there are many approaches for problem partitioning and for generating test problems. Our investigations are based on a 2D test problem, as described in section 2. The solution algorithm presented in section 3 is implemented on three different types of parallel computers, as described in section 4:

- Distributed Array Processor (AMT, SIMD architecture),
- Transputer System (Meiko, MIMD architecture),
- Suprenum Cluster (Suprenum, MIMD architecture),

On both MIMD architectures there are several different implementations for one test problem. The implementations differ in the degree of parallelism (the total usage of processors solving the problem), and in the grid size of the given problem in order to investigate the efficiency of the architectures under different conditions.

2   The Test Problems

We briefly recall the test problems given in Wheeler [11]. The configuration consists of a vertical cylindrical crucible of radius R_C filled with a melt to a height H and rotating with an angular velocity Ω_C. The melt is bounded above by a coaxial crystal of radius $R_X < R_C$ rotating with angular velocity Ω_C.

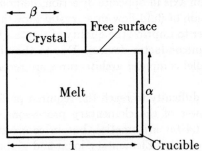

Figure 1: Non-dimensional system configuration.

Figure 1 shows the system configuration. The following assumptions are made:

- The surface of the melt between the crystal and the crucible is assumed to be flat and free of shear stress,

- The crystal is isothermal with temperature T_X,
- the crucible wall is isothermal with temperature T_C,
- the crucible base is a perfect insulator,
- the temperature on the shear stress free surface of the melt behaves linearly from T_X to T_C,
- the melt is an incompressible Newtonian Boussinesq fluid,
- the flow in the melt is axial symmetric.

In the following equations the overbar denotes a dimensional variable. The notations are: (r, z) polar coordinates, t time, u radial velocity, v azimuthal velocity, w axial velocity, p pressure, T temperature, ν kinematic viscosity, g gravitational acceleration and ρ_X density of the melt. The system is non-dimensionalized by:

$$
\begin{aligned}
(\bar{r}, \bar{z}) &= R_C \, (r, z), \\
(\bar{u}, \bar{v}, \bar{w}) &= (\nu/R_C) \, (u, v, w), \\
\bar{p} &= \left(\rho_X \nu^2 / R_C^2\right) p - \rho_X R_C g z, \\
\bar{t} &= \left(R_C^2 / \nu\right) t, \\
\bar{T} &= T_X + (T_C - T_X) \, T.
\end{aligned}
$$

The governing dimensionless equations are

$$
\begin{aligned}
u_t + u u_r + w u_z - v^2/r &= -p_r + \Delta u - u/r^2, \\
v_t + u v_r + w v_z + u v/r &= \Delta v - v/r^2, \\
w_t + u w_r + w w_z &= -p_z + \Delta w + Gr \, T, \\
(ru)_r \, / r + w_z &= 0, \\
T_t + u T_r + w T_z &= \Delta T / Pr,
\end{aligned}
\tag{1}
$$

and the boundary conditions are given by

$$
\begin{aligned}
u = v = w_r = T_r = 0 \quad &\text{for} \quad r = 0, \; 0 \le z \le \alpha, \\
u = w = 0, \; v = Re_C, \; T = 1 \quad &\text{for} \quad r = 1, \; 0 \le z \le \alpha, \\
u = w = T_z = 0, \; v = r Re_C \quad &\text{for} \quad 0 \le r \le 1, \; z = 0, \\
u_z = v_z = w = 0, \; T = (r - \beta)/(1 - \beta) \quad &\text{for} \quad \beta \le r \le 1, \; z = \alpha, \\
u = w = T = 0, \; v = r Re_X \quad &\text{for} \quad 0 \le r \le \beta, \; z = \alpha.
\end{aligned}
\tag{2}
$$

Here a subscript denotes differentiation with respect to the subscript variable and Δ is the axissymmetric Laplace operator in cylindrical coordinates. The occurring non-dimensional parameters are the aspect ratios α, the Reynolds numbers Re_X and the Prandtl and Grashof numbers Pr

$$
\alpha = H/R_C \; \text{and} \; \beta = R_X/R_C,
$$
$$
Re_X = R_C^2 \Omega_X/\nu \; \text{and} \; Re_C = R_C^2 \Omega_C/\nu
$$
$$
Pr = \nu/\kappa \; \text{and} \; Gr = g \hat{\beta} \, (T_C - T_X) \, R_C^3/\nu^2,
$$

where $\hat{\beta}$ is the coefficient of volumetric thermal expansion of the melt.

3 The Solution Algorithm

To approximate (1)-(2) we use finite differences for both space and time discretization. The space discretization is performed on a staggered grid as it was introduced by Harlow-Welch [7]. The staggered arrangement of the unknowns is illustrated in fig. 2. All spatial derivatives are approximated with second order central differences.

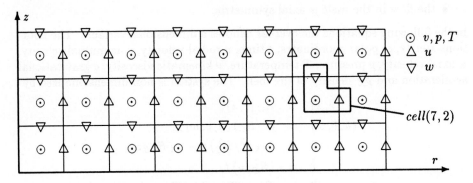

Figure 2: Staggered grid

For time discretization we take the one-step Euler implicit scheme, which is only of first order, but allows for large time steps, since it is unconditionally stable. Starting with some initial values u_h^0, v_h^0, w_h^0, T_h^0 we can successively compute the approximations u_h^{n+1}, v_h^{n+1}, w_h^{n+1}, p_h^{n+1}, T_h^{n+1} to the solution of (1)-(2) at the time levels $t = (n+1)\Delta t$ ($\Delta t > 0, n = 0, 1, \ldots$) from a nonlinear algebraic system of the form

$$\frac{u_h^{n+1} - u_h^n}{\Delta t} + \mathbf{A}_{hu}\left(u_h^{n+1}, v_h^{n+1}, w_h^{n+1}\right) + \mathbf{G}_{hr}p_h^{n+1} = 0,$$

$$\frac{v_h^{n+1} - v_h^n}{\Delta t} + \mathbf{A}_{hv}\left(u_h^{n+1}, v_h^{n+1}, w_h^{n+1}\right) = 0,$$

$$\frac{w_h^{n+1} - w_h^n}{\Delta t} + \mathbf{A}_{hw}\left(u_h^{n+1}, v_h^{n+1}, w_h^{n+1}, T_h^{n+1}\right) + \mathbf{G}_{hz}p_h^{n+1} = 0, \qquad (3)$$

$$\mathbf{L}_{hr}u_h^{n+1} + \mathbf{L}_{hz}w_h^{n+1} = 0,$$

$$\frac{T_h^{n+1} - T_h^n}{\Delta t} + \mathbf{A}_{hT}\left(u_h^{n+1}, w_h^{n+1}, T_h^{n+1}\right) = 0,$$

where $\mathbf{A}_{hu}$, $\mathbf{A}_{hv}$, $\mathbf{A}_{hw}$, $\mathbf{A}_{hT}$, $\mathbf{G}_{hr}$, $\mathbf{G}_{hz}$, $\mathbf{L}_{hr}$ and $\mathbf{L}_{hz}$ are the difference operators corresponding to the space discretization. These operators already include the boundary conditions. The solution of the systems (3) we perform with a pressure correction algorithm that is based on a fractional step method of Chorin [2]. This approach transforms (3) by means of a linearization process and a decoupling of variables into a sequence of linear systems. We only give the algorithm here, details can be found in Schäfer [9]. For each $n = 0, 1, \ldots$ we have to carry out the following steps:

(i) Compute $\tilde{u}_h^{n+1}$ from $\dfrac{\tilde{u}_h^{n+1} - u_h^n}{\Delta t} + \mathbf{A}_{hu}\left(\tilde{u}_h^{n+1}, v_h^n, w_h^n\right) + \mathbf{G}_{hr}p_h^n = 0.$

(ii) Compute $\tilde{w}_h^{n+1}$ from $\dfrac{\tilde{w}_h^{n+1} - w_h^n}{\Delta t} + \mathbf{A}_{hw}\left(\tilde{u}_h^{n+1}, v_h^n, \tilde{w}_h^{n+1}, T_h^n\right) + \mathbf{G}_{hz}p_h^n = 0.$

(iii) Compute $\tilde{p}_h^{n+1}$ from $\mathbf{L}_{hr}\mathbf{G}_{hr}\tilde{p}_h^{n+1} + \mathbf{L}_{hz}\mathbf{G}_{hz}\tilde{p}_h^{n+1} = -\dfrac{\left(\mathbf{L}_{hr}\tilde{u}_h^{n+1} + \mathbf{L}_{hz}\tilde{w}_h^{n+1}\right)}{\Delta t}$

(iv) Compute $u_h^{n+1} = \tilde{u}_h^{n+1} - \Delta t G_{hr}\tilde{p}_h^{n+1}.$

(v) Compute $w_h^{n+1} = \tilde{w}_h^{n+1} - \Delta t G_{hz}\tilde{p}_h^{n+1}.$

(vi) Compute $p_h^{n+1} = p_h^n + \tilde{p}_h^{n+1}.$

(vii) Compute v_h^{n+1} from $\dfrac{v_h^{n+1} - v_h^n}{\Delta t} + \mathbf{A}_{hv}\left(u_h^{n+1}, v_h^{n+1}, w_h^{n+1}\right) = 0.$

(viii) Compute T_h^{n+1} from $\dfrac{T_h^{n+1} - T_h^n}{\Delta t} + \mathbf{A}_{hT}\left(u_h^{n+1}, v_h^{n+1}, w_h^{n+1}, T_h^{n+1}\right) = 0.$

While the correction steps (iv), (v) and (vi) consist in direct computations, each of the steps (i), (ii), (iii), (vii) and (viii) requires the solution of a sparse system of linear equations. For the solution of the systems in (i), (ii), (vii) and (viii), which in general are nonsymmetric, we use the conjugate gradient squared method with two steps of the Jacobi method as a preconditioner (e.g. Schäfer [8]).

The solution of the symmetric positive definite system in (iii) for the pressure correction, which usually takes the major part of the computing time of the algorithm, is computed with an algebraic multigrid method with the damped Jacobi method for smoothing (e.g. Hackbusch [6]).

4 Parallel Architectures

The following parallel architectures are investigated in this paper:

- SIMD: Distributed Array Processor AMT DAP 510,
- MIMD: Meiko Transputer System and Suprenum Vector Multiprocessor

The **AMT DAP** consists of a host connection unit, a master control unit, the processing element and memory array and a fast data channel. The host connection unit provides an interface to the outer world, in our case a SUN workstation, and direct access to the VME bus. The master control unit interprets data parallel code and broadcasts instructions and data to the processing elements. The instructions are executed in parallel synchronously on each processing element (SIMD programming model). The array of the processing elements consists of 1024 1-bit processing elements, arranged in a 32×32 array. Each processing element has 32 k-bit local memory, resulting in a total of 4 M-byte of array memory. The processing elements are interconnected by a mesh nearest neighbor network and additionally a bus system for connecting rows and columns of the array. The fast data channel was not used in this investigation. The DAP was programmed in FORTRAN-Plus, a FORTRAN 77 with data parallel extensions.

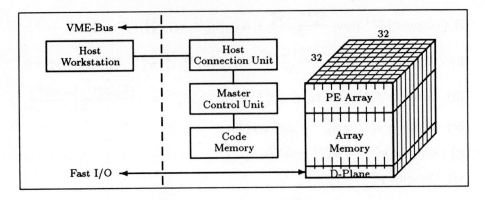

Figure 3: The AMT DAP distributed array processor

The **Meiko** Transputer System is a distributed memory multiprocessor. The system under consideration has 64 nodes, each consisting of one T800 Transputer, which is a RISC processor with arithmetic coprocessor and four communication links. The interconnection network can be set up individually for each application, but remains static during each run. Programming languages are FORTRAN, C and OCCAM; in this investigation, FORTRAN was chosen in order to allow easy porting of the code among the three machines. There are two concepts for the interprocessor communication, which are not integrated into the language: 'channels' and 'transports'. Channels are synchronous accesses to the physical communication links, while transports are symbolic links between processes. Due to the data parallel nature of the application, channels were found to be more efficient. The setup time for communication in the considered system is 22 μs and the transfer rate is 1.4 Mbyte/s per link in each of both directions.

The **Suprenum** vector multiprocessor consists of up to 256 processing nodes. The nodes are grouped in up to 16 clusters, each containing 16 processing nodes, two communication nodes, a disk control node and a diagnostic node. One processing node consists of a M68020 CPU, an arithmetic coprocessor and a vector unit. Interprocessor communication is done via a system of busses. For communication inside a cluster, there exist two cluster-busses, which allow a bandwidth of 160Mbyte/s, but have a long setup time (1ms). Inter-cluster communication is provided by the Suprenum bus which connects up to 16 clusters which are organized like a torus. In Erlangen only one cluster is installed, thus the Suprenum bus is not used. The Suprenum was programmed in Suprenum-FORTRAN, a parallel extension of FORTRAN 77. The language provides instructions for synchronous and asynchronous message-passing between tasks running in parallel.

5   Parallel Implementation

This section describes how the solution algorithm is implemented on the different computer architectures. Although the computations are the same in each implementation, the mapping of the grid nodes on the processing nodes implies communication patterns to be realized on the different interconnection networks. Not only the mapping strategy but also the succession of the communication instructions influences the performance of the implementation.

For the DAP, two programs have to be written: A host program and a data parallel program. The host program loads and stores data and transfers them to the code and array memory of the DAP. Then it gives control to the master control unit, which executes the data parallel code and controls the array of the processing elements. Due to the data parallel nature of the application, the implementation of the solution algorithm is straightforward. A 32×32 grid maps directly to the processing element array. Larger grids are mapped to the array using the 'crinkling' partitioning strategy, i.e. the grid is divided into 32×32 blocks and each block is mapped onto one processing element. This allows for local communication to be realized using the mesh interconnection network and, in case of 'crinkling', some of the local communication can be done inside the local memory of a processing element. For global communication the global bus and the row/column bus system are used.

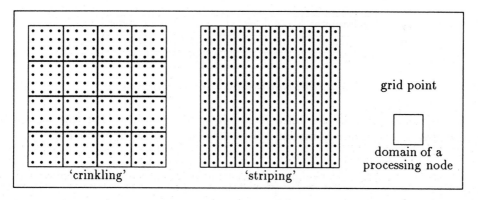

Figure 4: 'Crinkling' versus 'striping'

Both multiprocessor systems have a much lower number of processing nodes than the DAP. Of course one could use a crinkling scheme for the mapping of grid nodes to processor nodes, too. But in comparison with the DAP each communication in the considered message passing systems requires a long set up time (see section 4), and thus it is more efficient to collect all outgoing messages of a processing node and to send all of them in one long message. To optimize this idea, the grid is divided into vertical 'stripes'. Communication in vertical direction is done in the local memory of a processing node, while communication in horizontal direction is done at once in one long message.

The Meiko Transputer System is configured in a row of nodes. Each node is connected to its left and right neighbor. Local communication can be realized in a constant number of steps, while the complexity of global communication grows linearly with the number of processing nodes.

On the Suprenum, the communication between processing nodes has to use the cluster-busses. Local communication has to be done serially via the two busses and therefore, the communication complexity grows linearly with the number of used processing nodes. For global communication a tree-like scheme is implemented, thus communication complexity grows logarithmically with the number of processing nodes.

6 Numerical Results

For our numerical investigations we chose two test cases of the benchmark problem described in section 2. The physical and numerical parameters defining the two test problems are summarized in Table 1. The other parameters are chosen identical for the two problems:

$$\alpha = 1.0, \quad \beta = 0.4, \quad Re_C = 0 \quad \text{and} \quad Pr = 0.05.$$

Problem 1 corresponds to a steady flow, while Problem 2 has a time-dependent solution. The first investigation concerns the performance of the arithmetic and

Parameter	Gr	Re_x	Δt	time steps
Problem 1	10^5	10	0.02	100
Problem 2	10^7	0	0.0001	1000

Table 1: Parameters for the test problems.

the communication of the different computer architectures. For this we ran Problem 1 on the various machines with different numbers of processors.

System	# Proc	Comp. time (s)	local comm.(%)	global comm.(%)
DAP	1024	341	0.8	1.8
Meiko	1	4094	-	-
Meiko	2	2059	0.6	0.1
Meiko	4	1053	2.2	0.2
Meiko	8	512	4.7	0.4
Meiko	16	286	8.8	1.6
Meiko	32	174	15.8	5.4
Suprenum	1	6347	-	-
Suprenum	2	3749	2.5	1.5
Suprenum	4	2095	9.3	5.7
Suprenum	8	1306	14.9	13.3
Suprenum	16	928	23.7	23.4
Sparc 1	1	3414	-	-
Sparc 2	1	1999	-	-

Table 2: Computing times for Problem 1 on different architectures

For these calculations the size of the finest grid was fixed to 64 × 64 and 2 multigrid levels were used. We measured the total computing times as well as the portions of the local and global communication on these total times. The results are summarized in Table 2. For comparison we also included results obtained on a Sparc1 and a Sparc2 workstation.

Concerning the single processor performance one can state that the Sparc processors are superior to the processors in the parallel systems and that one T800 transputer is more powerful than one Suprenum node (factor 1.5). The performance of the DAP approximately corresponds to that of 12 transputers. The performance of the Sparc2 can nearly be reached with 2 transputers.

Comparing the results for the Suprenum and the Meiko Transputer System, one can see that the latter one becomes more and more superior when the number of processors is increased. This is due to the lower communication performance (especially the high setup times) of the Suprenum. Figure 5 shows the deviation of the speedup from the ideal case without communication (dotted lines) for the two systems.

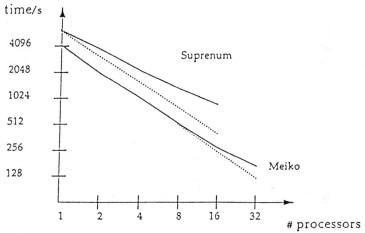

Figure 5: Computing times as a function of the numbers of processors

Simple theoretical considerations suggest that for both MIMD systems the local communication time remains constant with increasing numbers of processors (for 4 and more processors), since in the present implementation (domain decomposition in stripes) the size of the messages to be sent is independent of the number of processors. However, the numerical experiments show that for both systems there is a small increase in the local communication time for increasing processor numbers. This behavior can be explained if one takes a look on the behavior of the involved processes. The sooner a process is ready with his arithmetic work the sooner it enters the communication routine, where it has to wait upon the process to which it should communicate next. This waiting time is part of the local communication time measured. Since the probability of such a behavior increases with the number of processes, the measured local communication time also increases.

Grid size	Meiko 32 processors	Meiko 64 processors	Suprenum 16 processors	DAP 1024 processors
32×32	-	-	6925	-
64×64	1478	-	10438	2858
128×128	4096	5626	22472	-
256×256	14938	12232	68247	-

Table 3: Computing times (sec.) for Problem 2 for different grid sizes

Grid size	CGS		MG	
	Time (sec.)	Percentage (%)	Time (sec.)	Percentage (%)
64×64	310	21.0	1094	74.0
128×128	1307	31.9	2539	61.9
256×256	6989	46.8	7034	47.1

Table 4: Percentage of the CGS and MG method for Problem 2

The global communication time for the Meiko system should theoretically be directly proportional to the number of processors. For the Suprenum with its busses and the tree-like implementation this dependence should be logarithmic. The measured global communication times are in fair agreement with these considerations.

Next we study the dependence of the computing times and on the grid size and the processor number for the computer architectures considered. For this we consider problem 2 with different grid sizes. The number of multigrid levels was chosen such that each processor obtains one column of grid points on the coarsest grid (i.e. $P \times P$ coarse grid for P processors). Table 3 shows the total computing times for the different cases.

The increase in the computing times is lower than 4, if the number of grid points is doubled in each space direction. This is due to the fact that the losses due to the communication overhead becomes smaller, when the number of grid points per processor increases. The influence of the number of grid levels on the efficiency of the algorithm can be seen from the results for the 128×128 grid on the Meiko system with 32 and 64 processors. The time with 64 processors is larger than those with 32 processors. Despite the higher communication requirements with 64 processors, this effect is mainly due to the higher numerical efficiency of the multigrid method with 3 grid levels compared to the 2 grid level case.

In order to compare the behavior of the CGS method and the multigrid method within the solution algorithm the computing times of these parts of the algorithm on the Meiko system with 32 processors are given in Table 4 for different grid sizes. The percentage on the total computing times are also indicated. The portion of the CGS method increases with the number of grid points. This is due to the fact that the convergence rate of the CGS method deteriorate as the grid is refined, while those of the multigrid method are largely independent of the number of grid points.

7 Validation

The validation of the implementation has been done by comparison with results obtained from the flow prediction code FASTEST. This program is used and maintained at the institute of fluid dynamics in Erlangen, for more details refer to Gosman and Peric [4].

8 Conclusion

Three different computer architectures were compared by a fluid dynamic benchmark. One SIMD architecture, the DAP (1024 1 bit processors, synchronous mesh connected network) and two MIMD architectures, the Meiko Transputer System (64 processors, asynchronous direct link connections) and the Suprenum System (16 processors, asynchronous hierarchical bus network).

For orientation: the peak performance of the three systems can be carefully estimated as about 10 MFlops for the DAP, 96 MFlops for the Meiko and 160 MFlops for the Suprenum in vector mode.

The observed fluid dynamic problems are characterized by a data parallelism up to 10^7 points. The relation between arithmetical computation and communication is strongly dependent of the problem and architecture size. The implementation of the problems on the three machines was done in FORTRAN to increase the comparability. The algorithm and the code were not optimized for the different machines.

The results give the best relation between theoretical and measured performance for the DAP. This is independent of any unfairness in comparison which is possible in the area of machine dependent algorithm and code optimization. The results show the existence of an efficiency limit for the Suprenum and the Meiko System even in 'low power' configuration. The efficiency depends on the sizes of the problem and the machine (number of processors). Especially for the Suprenum the benchmark shows a very large gap to the theoretically performance. (It is known that the vectorizing compiler works not well – the difference to a non vectorized code is low).

Our conclusion is that the DAP is more efficient in using hardware resources than the two MIMD architectures in the observed test cases. This can be explained because of the synchronous computing and communication possibilities of the DAP which are well suited for massively data parallel problems. With respect to the total computing time for solving the problem, due to the higher arithmetic performance of the processors, the transputer system clearly is the most powerful.

9 Acknowledgments

The authors thank the Stiftung Volkswagenwerk for the financial support of the work and Dipl.-Inf. M. Hobohm for porting the code to the MIMD machines and for carrying out the numerical experiments in his master thesis.

References

[1] R.A. Brown. Theory of Transport Process in Single Crystal Growth from the Melt. *AICHE Journal*, 34:881–911, 1988.

[2] A.J. Chorin. Numerical solution of the Navier-Stokes equations. *Mathematics of Computation*, 22:745–762, 1968.

[3] W. Erhard, A. Grefe, M. Gutzmann, and D. Pöschl. *Vergleich von Leistungsbewertungsverfahren für unkonventionelle Rechner*, Arbeitsberichte des IMMD (Informatik), Universität Erlangen–Nürnberg, 24(5). 1991.

[4] A.D. Gosman and M. Peric. *User Manual for the FASTEST computer package*. Institute of fluid dynamics LSTM, Erlangen, 1988.

[5] M.M. Gutzmann. Performance Evaluation Of Parallel SIMD-Systems by Interpreting Automatically Transformed Algorithms On Simulated Architectures. In N.N.Mirenkov, editor, *Proceedings of the International Conference Parallel Computing Technologies*, pages 395–406. Computing Center Novosibirsk, USSR, World Scientific, September 1991.

[6] W. Hackbusch. *Multi-Grid Methods and Applications*. Springer, Berlin, 1985.

[7] F.J. Harlow and J.E. Welch. Numerical calculation of time dependent viscous incompressible flow of fluids with free surface. *Physics of Fluids*, 8:2183–2189, 1960.

[8] M. Schäfer. Numerical Simulation of Thermal Convection on SIMD computers. In *Proceedings of the Joint International Conference on Vector and Parallel Processing*, pages 786–795, Berlin, 1990. Springer-Verlag.

[9] M. Schäfer. Parallel Algorithms for the Numerical Simulation of Three-Dimensional Natural Convection. *Applied Numerical Mathematics*, 7:347–365, 1991.

[10] A. Strey. *Ein Vergleich von Verbindungsnetzwerken für große SIMD Parallelrechner*. PhD thesis, Arbeitsberichte des IMMD (Informatik), Universität Erlangen–Nürnberg, 1991.

[11] A. A. Wheeler. Four Test Problems for the Numerical Simulation of Flow in Czochralski Crystal Growth. *Journal of Crystal Growth*, 102:691–695, 1990.

Parallel Detection Algorithm of Radar Signals

Christo A. Kabakchiev, Vera P. Behar

Center of Informatics and Computer Technology
Bulgarian Academy of Science, 1113 Sofia, Bulgaria

Abstract. A parallel structure of an adaptive algorithm for detecting a coherent pulse packet in the Gaussian narrowband noise background is discussed. In synthesis of the considered pulse packet detectors a vector model of input radar signals is assumed. The special attention is paid to different possible levels of paralleling of the signal performance. In order to reduce the processing time a parallel structure of the signal processor realized on the base of matrix systolic processors is also proposed.

1 Introduction

Highly efficient adaptive detectors of moving targets in the background of natural clutter (sea-, ground-, weather-) are the widely known signal processors of the MTD series developed by the Lincoln Laboratory, namely MTD-I, MTD-II, AMTD [4]. One adaptive processor realized the signal performance in the time area is proposed in the paper. It is designed as a multiple channel system for estimating unknown informative signal parameters connected with the coordinates and the velocities of targets [1]. This processor includes an adaptive (self-learning) detector one for each "range-azimuth" channel The target velocity is estimated in only those cases when the target detection is indicated. The structure of detector in each "range-azimuth" channel implies a matched filtration of broadband pulses, filtration of pulse packet and estimation of noise power and futher comparing it to the adaptive threshold. In advance the noise power and width of noise spectrum are estimated on three levels (lower than, equal to and greater than the width of the desired signal spectrum) and stored in a clutter map. Obtained estimates are used in the structure of detectors in the corresponding channel. In other words, these adaptive detectors have in their structure schemes similar to CFAR circuits [6]. After detecting the target a multichannel dopller processing of signals is performed by FFT but only for that "range-azimuth" channel where the target is detected. At first the signal processor performs data from all channels by range for a single channel by azimuth. In practice, this structure of the processor can be realized very difficulty. That's why it is necessary to seek various possibilities for its simplification using parallelism.

2 Adaptive Detection Algorithm

Vectorial models of radar signal and total noise, which are very convenient for application of modern DSP methods [2] will be used to describe the input data. The vector description will result in parallel processing structures. Therefore the input data will be presented as $Y = || \vec{Y}_{2Nn} ||_{KM}$, where K and M are the number of range and azimuth resolution cells respectively. The random process $\vec{Y}_{2Nn}$ is observed at the in-

tion will result in parallel processing structures. There-
fore the input data will be presented as $Y=||\vec{Y}_{2Nn}||$ KM, where
K and M are the number of range and azimuth resolution cells
respectively. The random process $\vec{Y}_{2Nn}$ is observed at the input to the detector in the km -th resolution cell (at the
output of the synchronous rectifier) is a sum of the desired
signal and Gaussian process, i.e.

$$\vec{y}_{2Nn} = \vec{X}_{2Nn} + \vec{N}_{2Nn} \qquad (2.1)$$

where n-is the number of samples in a single pulse, N -is the
number of pulses in a packet. The components $\vec{Y}_{1in}$ and $\vec{Y}_{2in}$
are stored in the processor memory as $(\vec{Y}_{1in}, \vec{Y}_{2in})$. The desired
signal from a point target $\vec{X}_{2Nn}$ is assumed to be as

$$\vec{X}_{2Nn} = \lambda \phi \vec{V} \qquad (2.2)$$

where λ and $\vec{V}$ are non-informative signal parameters. The parameter λ accounts for the average power of the signal from
the target at the detector input. The vector $\vec{V}=(\vec{a}, \varphi)$ accounts
for the random fluctuations of the pulse envelope ($M[a_i]=1$,
$i=1,N$) and the initial phase of the pulses in the packet. The
conversion matrix ϕ accounts for the pulse modulation A_n and
the shape of the directional pattern of the receiving anten-
na l_N, i.e. $\phi = A_n^N l_N I_N$. The total noise $\vec{N}_{2Nn}$ is considered
as an additive sum of
a. White Gaussian noise with a zero mean and dispersion σ_0^2;
b. Narrowband Gaussian noise with a zero mean and great power $\sigma_c^2 >> \sigma_0^2$ in the frequency band ∇f_{cm} .
Hence, the total noise is described as a 2Nn-dimensional narrowband and locally stationary Gaussian process with a zero
mean and covariation matrix

$$R_{2Nn} = M\left\{\vec{y}_{2Nn}\vec{y}^T_{2Nn}\right\} \qquad (2.3)$$

The sample set $\vec{N}_{in}$ is independent and Gaussian distributed
vector with a zero expectation and exponential correlation
matrix K. Therefore, the covariation matrix R_{2Nn} is a diagonal
matrix with a diagonal element K defined as

$K = K_{in}/(2V_s)$, where $V_s = (2\sigma^2)^{-1}, \sigma^2=\sigma_0^2+\sigma_c^2 \qquad (2.4)$

$K = \gamma^{|i-j|}$, where $\gamma = exp\{\nabla f_{cm}/[\nabla f(n-1)]\}, i,j=1,n (2.5)$
The parameter ∇f in (2.5) is the bandwidth of the signal. The
parameter V_s determines the intensity of the total noise and
is an unknown value. The signal-to-noise ratio at the input
of detector is defined as P_c

$$\frac{P_c}{P_m} = V_s \lambda^2 \qquad (2.6)$$

The problem of signal detection with unknown parameters $\lambda_p \vec{V}_p$
in the background of the total noise with unknown intensity
V_{sp} is defined as a statistical problem for testing the hy-
pothesis $\mathcal{H}_0: \{V_s>0; \lambda_p\vec{V}_p=0$ at $p=1\div P\}$ against the following alternatives $\mathcal{H}_p: \{\lambda_p\vec{V}_p\neq 0; V_s>0\}$where p is the number of channels
$(P=K \times M)$. The structure of an adaptive rule for testing the
hypothesis $\mathcal{H}_0$ against the alternatives $\mathcal{H}_p$ is as follows

$$\phi(\vec{y}_{2Nn}) = \begin{cases} 1, \text{if } \max_{p=1..P}\Theta_p(Y_{2Nn})\geq C_{ap} \\ 0, \text{if } \max_{p=1..P}\Theta_p(\vec{y}_{2Nn})<C_{ap} \end{cases} \qquad (2.7)$$

where

$$\Theta_p(\vec{y}_{2Nn}) = \frac{U_p^T B_p^{-1} U_p}{E_y(\vec{y}_{2Nn}^P)} \quad \text{and} \quad E_y(\vec{y}_{2Nn}^P) = \left(\sum_{i=1}^{N} \vec{y}_{in}^T R_{2n}^{-1} \vec{y}_{in}\right)^P \tag{2.8}$$

In practice, it is more convenient the testing rule (2.7) to be presented as:

$$\max_{p=1..P} U_p^T B_p^{-1} U_p \geq E_y(\vec{y}_{2Nn}^P), \text{where} \tag{2.9}$$

where

$$U_p^T(U_1,\ldots,U_N); \quad U_i = \phi_{in}^T R_{2n}^{-1} \vec{y}_{2n} \tag{2.10}$$

$B = Q \, I_N$, where the matrix Q is a diagonal one with Q that are $Q_i = \phi_{in}^T R_{2n}^{-1} \phi_{in}$, where

$$\phi_{in} = \begin{bmatrix} A_n \ell_i & 0 \\ 0 & A_n \ell_i \end{bmatrix}; \quad R_{2n}^{-1} = \begin{bmatrix} K_{1n}^{-1} & 0 \\ 0 & K_{1n}^{-1} \end{bmatrix} \tag{2.11}$$

In the case of the coherent signal $\{V_i = V_j \text{ at } i \neq j\}$ the structure of detection algorithm is presented

$$\left[\sum_{j=1}^{2} \left(\sum_{i=1}^{N} \ell_i A_n^T K_{1n}^{-1} \vec{y}_{in}^{(j)}\right)^2\right]_P \geq C_a^P q^2 \left(\sum_{i=1}^{N} \sum_{j=1}^{2} \vec{y}_{in}^{(j)T} K_{1n}^{-1} \vec{y}_{in}^{(j)}\right)_P$$

where

$$q^2 = \sum_{i=1}^{N} \ell_i^2 A_n^T K_{1n}^{-1} A_n \tag{2.12}$$

According to the expression (2.12) the structure of detection algorithm consists of a stripping filter and a filter matched with a single coherent broadband signal. Therefore, $U_i(\vec{y}_{in})$ can be regarded as a signal at the output of linear filter, i.e. $U_i = W_i^T \vec{y}_{in}$. The filter coefficients, i.e. W_i are defined as

$$W_i = R_{2n}^{-1} \phi_{in} \tag{2.13}$$

As a result of coherent pulse integtation we obtain the following signal:

$$U_0(\vec{y}_{2nN}) = \sum_{i=1}^{N} U_i(\vec{y}_{in}) \tag{2.14}$$

The envelope of the signal U_0 is $\eta = |U_0|^2$. In case of coherent pulse packet detection the structure of detection algorithm is:

$$\max_{k,m} \left[\eta\right]_{k,m} \geq (E_y \cdot C_a q^2)_{k,m} \tag{2.15}$$

This maximum is used to identify the channel number, where some target was detected. All detected targets are accepted to be desired. The statistic E_y in the right-hand side of the expression (2.15) is the structure of a range-azimuth averaging CFAR scheme. It is a joint estimate of noise power, i.e.

$$E_y = \sum_{i=1}^{N} \hat{\sigma}_i^2, \quad \text{where} \quad \hat{\sigma}_i^2 = \vec{y}_{in}^T R_{2n}^{-1} \vec{y}_{in}$$

is the estimate of noise power at the i-th location. The values of C_a corresponding to various false alarm probabilities were obtained in [8,9].

3 Parallel structure of adaptive detector

In a general way the modern parallel computer-system archi-

tectures designed for DSP are described and discussed in [2]
The conclusion is that the systolic compute-system architecture on the base of VLSI are the most pertinent for signal
processing at the operation mode of real time. The maximum
parallelism of signal processing in the area of observation
can be achieved when all (K x M) "range-azimuth" resolution
cells are simultaneously processed by systolic processors.
Each channel is served by his separable signal processor
(group of processors) $SPkm$ (Fig.1).
The necessary number of such processors is N_{Osp} =KM   (3.1)

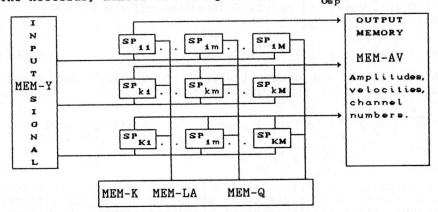

Fig.1 Systolic structure of signal processing
(in the entire area of observation)

In this case the speed of the computing process in each of
channels determines the processing speed for the entire area
of observation. In practice the necessary number of systolic
processors (KM) varies in the range of 15.10^3 to 150.10^3 .As
usual the survey duration of radars($Tsur$),the number of samples in a single pulse (n), the number of pulses in a packet
(N) vary in the range {10 ÷30}[s],{50÷250} and {100÷300} re-
spectivaly.We will consider two manners to speed up the computing process only in the adaptive detector.The substantial
reduction of the processing time Tsp can be achieved by paralleling the computing process. We propose two efficient
systolic architectures of adaptive detector which is very
suitable for signal processing in the "km"-th channel:
for performance with the sliding window by pulses and for
the parallel processing of pulses in a packet (Fig.2). Each
sampled i-th pulse in a packet is sequentialy performed by
systolic processors $SPik$ $(k=1,7)$. The packet of pulses is
performed by systolic processors $SPk(k=1,4)$.All the systolic
processors have a linear matrix of processor elements [2].
Than the necessary number of systolic processors is
$$N1sp = 11   (3.2)$$
In the case when all the pulses in a packet are simultaneously performed using the same systolic structure the numer
of processors is evaluated by $N2sp = 7N + 4$ (3.3)
The systolic matrix of the processors $SPi1$ and $SPi2$ with the
respective processor element is shown in Fig.3. After "2n-1"

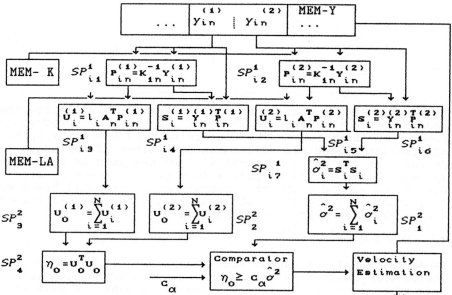

Fig. 2 Parallel flowchart of computing process
in the systolic signal processor SP_{km}

to
MEM-AV

cycles will be obtained the result $\vec{P}_{in}$. The systolic processors $SP_{i3}^1, SP_{i4}^1, SP_{i5}^1, SP_{i6}^1$ consist of only one element (Fig. 4).
After "n" cycles will be the results $S_i^{(1)}, S_i^{(2)}$ and $U_i^{(1)}, U_i^{(2)}$.
The structure of the processors SP_{i7}^1 and SP_4^2 are equal to
that of the processors $(SP_{i3}^1 .. SP_{i6}^1)$. After only 2 cycles
will be formed the results σ_i^2 and η_0. The systolic matrix of
processors SP_1^2, SP_2^2, SP_3^2 is the same, but the result will be
formed after "N" cycles. When the signal processing is realized as a sliding window the processing time is evaluated by

$$T_{1sp}= 3Nn + 2N + 2 \qquad (3.4)$$

The parallel pulse processing in the adaptive detector requires the processing time

$$T_{2sp} = N + 3n + 3 \qquad (3.5)$$

For example, if the adaptive detector in the "km"-th channel
realized as a performance "sliding window" then the signal

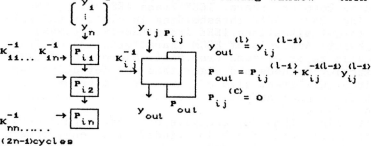

(2n-1)cycles

Fig. 3 Systolic matrix of processor

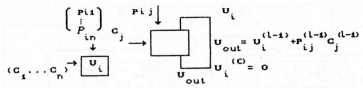

Fig.4 Systolic matrix of processor

processing in the entire area of observation will require according to (3.1) and (3.2) about 10^8 systolic processors (where $Nosp=10^5$, $N=100$, $n=32$). According to (3.3) this number of systolic processors will enhance 70 times if the adaptive detector in the "km"-th channel will be designed as a parallel signal processing of pulses in a packet. However according to (3.4) and (3.5) the computing process will speed up only about 33 times. It is the true that such computer system can be realized only as special VLSI.

4. Conclusion

Vectorial models of signal and total noise are used to describe and design the efficient signal processing in the area of observation in the presence of jamming. A main property of the obtained detection algorithms is that they allow paralleling of the computing process and lead to clear and simple systolic structure of signal processing in the entire area of observation. Two types of systolic structures for DSP, the performance with sliding window by pulses and the paralling processing of pulses in a packet, are proposed in the paper. Their basic characteristics as an amount of the typical processor elements and a processing time are discussed and estimated. It is obvious that such structures are convenient for VLSI realization.

Reference

1. D.Barton: Modern radar analysis,Artech House, 1988
2. S.Kung: VLSI array processors,Prentice-Hall,NJ,1988
3. H.Trees: Detection,estimat. and modulat.theory,JW,1968
4. E.D'Addio,G.Galati Adaptivity and design criteria of a latest-generation MTD processor.IEE Proc.,132,F,(1985)
5. K.Gerlach,G.Andrews:Cascaded detector for multiple high PRF pulse Doppler radars. IEEE Trans,AES-26,5,(1990)
6. H.Rohling: Radar CFAR thresholding in clutter and multiple target situations.IEEE Trans,AES-19,4,(1983)
7. B.Bergkvist: Analysis of ECCM characteristics of frequency agile radar systems.Proc.Milit.Microw. Conf,(1978)
8. C.Kabakchiev:Methods and algorithms for detecting radar signals at different size of parametric a priori information for signal and noice characteristics.DSc dissertation,Sofia,1987
9. V.Behar: Algorithms for analysis of radar signal detectors in conditions of a priori indefinite environment. PhD dissertation,Sofia,1989

Efficient Linear Systolic Array for the Knapsack Problem*

Rumen Andonov [**][1] and Patrice Quinton[2]

[1] Center of Computer Science and Technology, Acad. G. Bonchev st., bl. 25-a,
1113 Sofia, Bulgaria
[2] IRISA, Campus de Beaulieu, 35042 Rennes Cedex, France,
e-mail: quinton@irisa.fr

Abstract. A processor-efficient systolic algorithm for the dynamic programming approach to the knapsack problem is presented in this paper. The algorithm is implemented on a linear systolic array where the number of the cells q, the cell memory storage α and the input/output requirements are design parameters. These are independent of the problem size given by the number of the objects m and the knapsack capacity c. The time complexity of the algorithm is $\Theta(mc/q + m)$ and both the time speedup and the processor efficiency are asymptotically optimal.
A new procedure for the backtracking phase of the algorithm with a time complexity $\Theta(m)$ is also proposed. It is an improvement on the usual strategies used for backtracking which have a time complexity $\Theta(m + c)$.

1 Introduction

Suppose that m types of objects are being considered for inclusion in a knapsack of capacity c. For $i = 1, 2, \ldots, m$, let p_i be the unit value and w_i the unit weight of the i-th type of object. The values w_i, p_i, $i = 1, 2, \ldots, m$, and c are all positive integers. The problem is to find out the maximum total profit without exceeding the capacity constraint, i.e.

$$\max \{\sum_{i=1}^{m} p_i z_i : \sum_{i=1}^{m} w_i z_i \leq c, z_i \geq 0 \text{ integer}, \ i = 1, 2, \ldots, m\}, \tag{1}$$

where z_i is the number of i-th type objects included in the knapsack. This is a classical combinatorial optimization problem with a wide range of application (see Garfinkel and Nemhauser [1], Hu [2], Martello and Toth [3]). If additional constrains $z_i \in \{0, 1\}, i = 1, 2, \ldots, m$ are added to (1), then the restricted problem is called the 0/1 knapsack problem. Problem (1) is well known to be NP-*hard* (see [4], [3]). However it is known that this problem can be solved sequentially in $O(mc)$ time. This time bound is not polynomial in the size of the input since $\log_2 c$ bits are required to encode the input c. Such a time bound is called *pseudo-polynomial* time

---

* This work was partially funded by the French Coordinated Research Program C^3 and by the Esprit BRA project No 3280.
** At the present time at IRISA. Supported by a grant from the MRT.

[4]. Dynamic programming, branch-and-bound and approximate algorithms are the most popular combinatorial optimization techniques for these problems.

With the advent of parallel processors many researchers concentrated their efforts on the development of efficient parallel algorithms for solving the knapsack problem. In this paper we concentrate on one of the most conventional approaches for solving this problem - dynamic programming. This approach is based on the *principle of optimality* of Bellman [5] and usually contains two phases. In the first (forward) phase the maximum value of the objective function is computed, i.e. the value $f_m(c)$ such that $f_m(c) = \max \{\sum_{i=1}^{m} p_i z_i : \sum_{i=1}^{m} w_i z_i \leq c, \ z_i \geq 0 \ \text{integer}, i = 1, 2, \ldots, m\}$. In the second (backtracking) phase the integers $z_i^*, i = 1, 2, \ldots, m$, such that $\sum_{i=1}^{m} p_i z_i^* = f_m(c)$ are found.

In [6] a pipeline architecture containing a linear array of q processors, queue and memory modules is proposed for the knapsack problem by Chen, Chern and Jang. This architecture allows one to achieve an optimal speedup of the algorithm which has a time complexity $\Theta(mc/q + m)$ and an efficiency $E = \Theta(1/(1 + 1/qc))$ which approaches $\Theta(1)$ as c increases.

Our work is related to the design of systolic arrays for dynamic programming problems. The difficulties in this field of research arise from the necessity for the algorithms to meet the requirements of modularity, ease of layout, simplicity of communication and control and scalability. Dynamic programming is a powerful optimization methodology which is worthy of study for its suitability for VLSI systolic implementation. For the 0/1 knapsack problem this approach was considered in the work of Li and Wa [7] and of Lipton and Lopresti [8]. The results obtained are not applicable in the case of the knapsack problem due to a peculiarity in its recurrent formulation. A fixed-size modular linear systolic array (a ring with buffer memory between the last and the first cells) for (1) was proposed for this problem in the paper of Andonov, Aleksandrov and Benaini [9]. It has the drawback that its processor efficiency is small for big values of c.

A new dynamic programming implementation for the knapsack problem is presented in this paper. The architecture is similar to that of [9] - a ring containing a buffer memory and q identical cells, each with a local addressable memory of size α. A new algorithm for the backtracking phase with time complexity $\Theta(m)$ is proposed. It improves on the usual strategies used for backtracking in the knapsack problem (see Hu [2] and Garfinkel and Nemhauser [1]) which have a time complexity $\Theta(m+c)$. Thus this phase of the dynamic programming approach, which is sequential, becomes independent of the parameter c. The problem size memory independence of the algorithm is provided, i.e. the algorithm is designed under the requirement that the cell memory capacity does not depend on the problem size. Hence our algorithm meets all the requirements for VLSI systolic implementation as the algorithm proposed in [9] but substantially improves on its speedup and efficiency. More precisely, the speedup and the efficiency both approach their optimal values respectively $\Theta(q)$ and $\Theta(1)$ as c increases. Therefore we obtain the same speedup and efficiency as in the paper of Chen, Chern and Jang [6]. Note that the algorithm in [6] is not VLSI oriented since it runs exclusively under the assumption that the memory capacity of any processor is at least equal to the knapsack capacity c, i.e. $\alpha \geq c$.

This paper is organized in the following way. Section 2 describes both phases of the dynamic programming approach for problem (1) on a serial machine. Section 3 presents our new algorithm for backtracking and analyses its complexity. In section 4 we discuss our parallel implementation on a linear array containing an unbounded number of cells of storage capacity α. In section 5 the same approach is developed on a ring with a fixed number of cells.

2 Dynamic programming approach for the knapsack problem

In this section we present the dynamic programming approach for the knapsack problem on a serial machine. It consists of two phases - the forward and the backtracking phase.

2.1 Forward phase

Let $f_k(j)$ be the maximum value that can be achieved in (1) from a knapsack of size j, $0 \leq j \leq c$, using only the first k types of objects, $1 \leq k \leq m$. That is

$$f_k(j) = \max \left\{ \sum_{i=1}^{k} p_i z_i : \sum_{i=1}^{k} w_i z_i \leq j, z_i \geq 0 \text{ integer}, i = 1, 2, \ldots, k \right\}. \tag{2}$$

The principle of optimality [5, 1] states that for $\forall k, 1 \leq k \leq m$ and $\forall j, 0 \leq j \leq c$ we have :

$$f_k(j) = \max \left\{ f_{k-1}(j), f_k(j - w_k) + p_k \right\}. \tag{3}$$

The optimal value of (1) $f_m(c)$, can be found in m stages by generating successively the functions $f_1, f_2, \ldots, f_m$ using equation (3) and the initial conditions $f_0(j) = 0$, $f_k(0) = 0$ and $f_k(i) = -\infty$ for $1 \leq k \leq m, 0 \leq j \leq c$ and $i < 0$. By stage k we shall denote the computation of all the values of the function f_k.

Any serial algorithm based on recurrent equation (3) requires $\Theta(mc)$ time to find the optimal value $f_m(c)$. This is the best existing serial algorithm and we shall use its running time to determine the $speedup$ and the $efficiency$ of our parallel algorithm.

The communication required for the execution of equation (3) can be described by means of directed graph, called the $dependence\ graph\ (DG)$. Let N denote the set of natural numbers, i.e. N$=\{0, 1, 2, \ldots\}$. Let $\mathcal{G} = (\mathcal{D}, \mathcal{A})$ be the DG for equation (3), where $\mathcal{D} = \{(j, k) \in \mathbf{N}^2 : 0 \leq j \leq c, 1 \leq k \leq m, \}$ is the set of nodes and $\mathcal{A}$ is the set of directed arcs. Each node $(j, k) \in \mathcal{D}$ of the DG represents an operation performed by the algorithm and the arcs are used to represent data dependencies. For example figure 1 (a) depicts the DG for a knapsack problem, with $m = 3, c = 6, w_1 = 4, w_2 = 3, w_3 = 2$. Each node (j, k) represents one calculation, detailed in figure 1 (b). The peculiarity of this graph is that in any column the dependence vectors depend on the weights $w_i, i = 1, 2, \ldots, m$. Such a dependency is not a $uniform$ dependency. This peculiarity makes the knapsack recurrence equation difficult to transform into a systolic array using the well-known dependence mapping approach (see Quinton and Robert, [10]).

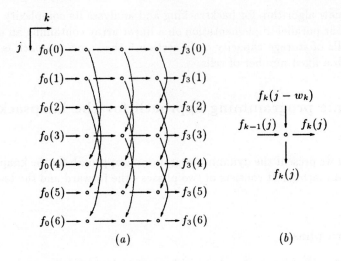

Fig. 1. The dependence graph for the given example

2.2 The classical backtracking algorithm

An approach to find the solution vector $z^* \in \mathbf{N}^m$ such that $\sum_{i=1}^{m} p_i z_i^* = f_m(c)$ is discussed in this section. It is based on the work of Hu [2].

In the course of the forward phase a pointer $u_k(j)$ is associated to any value $f_k(j), (j,k) \in \mathcal{D}$ in such a way that $u_k(j)$ is the index of the last type of object used in $f_k(j)$. In other words if $u_k(j) = r$ this means $z_r \geq 1$, or the r-th object is used in $f_k(j)$ and $z_l = 0$ for all $l > r$. The value $u_k(j)$ is used to keep the history of the first dynamic programming phase.

The boundary conditions for $u_k(j)$ are

$$\forall j : 0 \leq j \leq c : u_1(j) = \begin{cases} 0 \text{ if } f_1(j) = 0 \\ 1 \text{ if } f_1(j) \neq 0. \end{cases}$$

In general we set

$$u_k(j) = \begin{cases} k & \text{if } f_k(j - w_k) + p_k > f_{k-1}(j) \\ u_{k-1}(j) & \text{otherwise.} \end{cases} \tag{4}$$

for $\forall k : 1 < k \leq m$ and $\forall j : 0 \leq j \leq c$.

As shown in [2], definition (4) allows the solution vector $z^* \in \mathbf{N}^m$ of the knapsack problem to be found from the values of the function u_m by the following algorithm:

Hu's backtracking algorithm

$j := c;$
for $k = m$ **downto** 1 **do**
$z_k^* = 0$

> while $u_m(j) = k$ do
> > begin $z_k^* := z_k^* + 1;$
> > > $j := j - w_k$
> > end

This algorithm has time and space complexity $T = \Theta(m + c)$ and $S = \Theta(c + m)$ respectively and it is the best known strategy. Another strategy with time complexity $T = \Theta(m + c)$ and space complexity $S = \Theta(mc)$ is presented by Garfinkel and Nemhauser in [1].

The backtracking phase is sequential and requires at least $\Omega(m)$ operations. In the next section we show how the algorithm above can be modified in order to reach this bound.

3   A modified backtracking algorithm

If we associate a value p_k to any vertical arc $((i, k), (i + w_k, k))$ in column k of the DG for problem (1) then the value $f_n(j)$ for any pair $(j, n) \in \mathcal{D}$ can be regarded as the value of the optimal path $(S_1, S_2, \ldots, S_n)$ from the first stage to the n-th one. We denote by $S_k, k = 1, 2, \ldots, n$, the subpath of the optimal path in column k. The elements of S_k are of the form $((i, k), (i + w_k, k), \ldots, (i + w_k z_k, k)), 0 \le i \le j - w_k z_k,$ where z_k are such that $\sum_{k=1}^{n} p_k z_k = f_n(j)$. Let I_k denote the sequence of the first indices of the elements of the optimal subpath S_k in column k, i.e.

$$I_k = \{i : (i, k) \in S_k\}.$$

Let i_{min}^k denote the minimum index in I_k, i.e.

$$i_{min}^k = \min\{i : i \in I_k\}.$$

By the definition of the function u_k we have

$$u_k(i_{min}^k) < k$$

and

$$\forall i \in I_k : i \ne i_{min}^k \Rightarrow u_k(i) = k.$$

The idea of the modified backtracking algorithm is for any $(j, k) \in \mathcal{D}$ to keep a record of the corresponding value i_{min}^k. In order to generate these values during the forward phase we introduce the function v_k defined as follows:

$$v_k(j) = \begin{cases} v_{k-1}(j) & \text{if } u_k(j) < k \\ j & \text{if } u_k(j) = k \quad \text{and } u_k(j - w_k) < k \\ v_k(j - w_k) & \text{if } u_k(j) = k \quad \text{and } u_k(j - w_k) = k \end{cases} \tag{5}$$

for $\forall k, \forall j : 1 \le k \le m, 0 \le j \le c$ and $v_k(j) = 0$ for $k = 0, 0 \le j \le c$.

When the values of $v_k, k = 1, 2, \ldots, m$, are found, we can easily trace the values z_k that yield $f_k(j)$ for any $j \in I_k$ by the formula

$$z_k = \begin{cases} 0 & \text{if } u_k(j) < k \\ (j - v_k(j))/w_k + 1 & \text{if } u_k(j) = k. \end{cases} \tag{6}$$

In fact (6) determines how many units of object k are used in $f_k(j)$.

Once the value z_k has been computed, the total weight limitation j is reduced to $j_{new} = v_k(j) - w_k$, for which the inequality $u_k(j_{new}) < k$ holds and therefore $u_k(j_{new}) = u_{k-1}(j_{new})$. To find the value z_{k-1} we proceed to check the values $u_{k-1}(j_{new})$ and $v_{k-1}(j_{new})$ in the same way.

The functions $v_k, k = 1, 2, \ldots, m$ are similar to the functions u_k by their properties. For $\forall j : u_k(j) < k$ the function v_k keeps the values of the functions v_{k-1}. This property allows the values $z_k, k = 1, 2, \ldots, m$ to be found from the values of the function u_m and v_m only. The following algorithm is used.

Modified backtracking algorithm

```
j := c;
for k = m downto 1 do
    if u_m(j) < k then z_k* = 0
                else
                   begin z_k* := (j - v_m(j))/w_k + 1;
                         j := v_m(j) - w_k
                   end
```

In this way the values of u_m are used to move back along the k axis of the DG in figure 1. The values of v_m are used to move back along the j axis. Since the computation of z_k^* for any $k, 1 \le k \le m$ requires $\Theta(1)$ operations then we obtain the following property.

Corollary 1. *The modified backtracking algorithm has time and space complexity $T = \Theta(m)$ and $S = \Theta(c + m)$ respectively.*

The computation of the functions $v_k, k = 1, 2, \ldots, m$ can be done simultaneously with the computation of the functions f_k. More details concerning the implementation of the modification proposed are discussed in the next section.

4 Linear systolic arrays

In this section we consider the implementation of the knapsack algorithm in linear arrays composed of q identical cells $C_k, k = 1, 2, \ldots, q$, where $q \ge m$. Each cell C_k has two addressable memories F_k and V_k each of size α, where α is a design parameter. The purpose of F_k and V_k is to save the values of the functions f_k and v_k respectively. We consider successively two cases: $\alpha \ge w_k$ for $\forall k, 1 \le k \le m$, and $\exists k, 1 \le k \le m : w_k > \alpha$. In the first case a straightforward projection of the dependence graph of figure 1 along the j axis provides a systolic array of m cells. This case is described in section 4.1, where we also show how the backward phase can be implemented on the same array. This array is said to be *non modular*, as it cannot accommodate a problem of any size. In the second case it is possible to implement the algorithm on a linear systolic array, by replacing cell C_k of the non modular design by so-called *macro-cells* comprising $\lceil w_k/\alpha \rceil$ cells. Section 4.2 is devoted to this case.

4.1 Non modular systolic array

Forward phase The operation of the systolic array is best explained using the dependence projection method (see [10]) which amounts to scheduling the dependence graph and projecting it along a conveniently chosen direction. A *timing function* is a mapping $t : \mathcal{D} \rightarrow N$, such that if the computation on vertex $v \in \mathcal{D}$ depends on vertex $w \in \mathcal{D}$, then $t(v) > t(w)$. An *allocation function* is a mapping $a : \mathcal{D} \rightarrow [1, q]$, such that $a(v)$ is the number of the processor that executes the calculations attached to vertex $v \in \mathcal{D}$. The mapping a must be chosen in such a way that a processor has no more than one calculation to perform at a given instant. In addition to the previous well known functions, we use the mapping $addr : \mathcal{D} \rightarrow [1, \alpha]$, defined in such a way that $addr(v)$ is the number of the memory location in processor $a(v)$ where data $v \in \mathcal{D}$ is stored.

Obviously, the function $t(j, k) = j + k$ is a timing-function for the dependence graph of figure 1. An allocation function $a(j, k) = k$ corresponds to a projection of the dependence graph along axis j. It yields a linear unidirectional systolic array of m cells. Since for any k, the values $f_k(j), j = 0, 1, \ldots, c$ are computed sequentially and $f_k(j)$ depends on $f_k(j - w_k)$, then the value $f_k(j)$ can be stored in the same memory location in cell C_k as the value $f_k(j - w_k)$. We assume that the memory size α meets $\alpha \geq w_k$, for any $1 \leq k \leq m$. Therefore the address of any data $(j, k) \in \mathcal{D}$ in F_k is $addr(j, k) = 1 + j \bmod w_k$. The total time for the forward phase is

$$t(c, m) = c + m. \tag{7}$$

Backtracking phase The values $u_k(j)$ and $v_k(j)$ are computed and propagated through the considered array simultaneously with the value $f_k(j)$. The computation of the function u_k does not require a supplementary local memory. We show in this section that a memory V_k of size w_k in cell C_k is enough for the computations of the function v_k.

As with the values of the function f_k, the values $v_k(j), j = 0, 1, \ldots, c$ are computed sequentially and $v_k(j)$ depends on $v_k(j - w_k)$, i.e. the value $v_k(j)$ can be stored in the same memory location in V_k as the value $v_k(j - w_k)$. For $j = 0, 1, \ldots, c$ the values of V_k are generated as follows:

$$V_k(j \bmod w_k) = \begin{cases} -1 & \text{if } u_k(j) < k \\ j & \text{if } u_k(j) = k \text{ and } V_k(j \bmod w_k) = -1 \\ V_k(j \bmod w_k) & \text{if } u_k(j) = k \text{ and } V_k(j \bmod w_k) \neq -1 \end{cases} \tag{8}$$

Then the value $v_k(j)$ is defined by

$$v_k(j) = \begin{cases} v_{k-1}(j) & \text{if } f_{k-1}(j) \geq f_k(j - w_k) + p_k \\ V_k(j \bmod w_k) & \text{otherwise} . \end{cases} \tag{9}$$

The values of the functions u_m and v_m leave the last cell C_m and are stored in a supplementary memory of size $2c$. Then the modified backtracking algorithm can' be executed by the host computer.

4.2 Modular systolic array

Let us assume now that the memory size α of the cell is independent of the problem and there exists k, such that $w_k > \alpha$. The idea is to emulate the operation of each elementary cell C_k of the previous linear design by one macro-cell MC_k which is composed of $\lceil w_k/\alpha \rceil$ cells (see figure 2), each one with a memory of size α. The

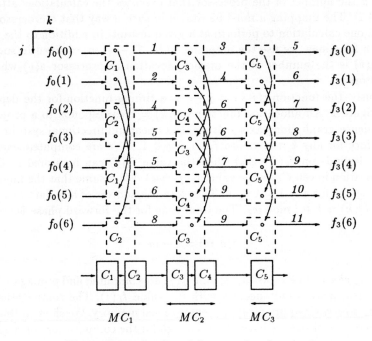

Fig. 2. Example of modular mapping for $\alpha = 2$

mapping of the dependence graph is made as follows. Any computation $f_k(j)$ is performed on macrocell MC_k. The value $\mathrm{addr}(j,k) = 1+j \bmod w_k$ defined in section 4.1 is the address where the value $f_k(j)$ would be stored in MC_k, if α is large enough. Here, the memory w_k is emulated by the memory of the $\lceil w_k/\alpha \rceil$ subcells. To know where $f_k(j)$ is stored in MC_k, we associate with $\mathrm{addr}(j,k)$ a pair $(\mathrm{sc}(j,k), \mathrm{addr}'(j,k))$ which gives respectively the subcell where $f_k(j)$ is stored, and the address in the memory of this subcell. We thus have:

$$\mathrm{sc}(j,k) = \lceil \mathrm{addr}(j,k)/\alpha \rceil$$
$$\mathrm{addr}'(j,k) = \mathrm{addr}(j,k) \bmod \alpha.$$

In this way $f_k(j)$ and $f_k(j - w_k)$ are stored in the same address of the same cell. The calculations executed by a subcell of MC_k are deduced by the following rules. Macro-cell MC_k processes in sequence the calculations associated with nodes (j,k), $0 \leq j \leq c$, of the dependence graph. When a subcell of MC_k receives data which corresponds to $f_{k-1}(j)$, it processes the calculation associated to this value if $f_k(j)$ is stored in its memory, otherwise, it sends this value unchanged to the next subcell. In this way a data $f_{k-1}(j)$ crosses $sc(j,k) - 1$ cells in MC_k without being processed. On the other hand, once computed any value $f_k(j)$ is transmitted forward in the array $\lceil w_k/\alpha \rceil - sc(j,k)$ subcells in order to leave macrocell MC_k. Thus, the new timing-function is given by the following recurrence :

$$t(j,k) = \begin{cases} j + sc(j,k) & \text{if } k = 1 \\ t(j, k-1) + \lceil w_{k-1}/\alpha \rceil - sc(j, k-1) + sc(j,k) & \text{otherwise.} \end{cases} \quad (10)$$

The values of the timing-function for the given example are depicted on the right hand of the corresponding vertices in figure 2.

The operation of one subcell is now described. The value $f_k(j)$ is computed by the subcell $sc(j,k)$ of the macrocell MC_k and is stored in memory location $addr'(j,k)$. All the other cells of the macrocell MC_k merely transmit the value $f_k(j)$. To realize this, we associate a counter $cell(j,k)$ with any data $f_k(j)$. This counter gives the number of elementary cells through which the associated data has to be propagated in order to reach the cell where the value $f_{k+1}(j)$ is computed. According to (10) the counter can be obtained by the formula

$$cell(j,k) = \begin{cases} sc(j, k+1) & \text{if } k = 0 \\ \lceil w_k/\alpha \rceil - sc(j,k) + sc(j, k+1) & \text{otherwise.} \end{cases} \quad (11)$$

From (11) the new allocation function follows easily:

$$a(j,k) = \begin{cases} sc(j,k) & \text{if } k = 1 \\ a(j, k-1) + cell(j, k-1) & \text{otherwise.} \end{cases} \quad (12)$$

During the computations of $f_k(j)$ each cell generates, in addition, the values $v_k(j)$ and $u_k(j)$ needed for the backtracking, as was shown in the previous section. The structure and the program for the forward phase of the cell are depicted in figure 3. To realize this algorithm each subcell of the macrocell MC_k keeps the values p_k, w_k, w_{k+1}, k in registers $p, w, wnext, obj$ respectively. The data input into the left-most cell during the first $c + 1$ instants t, $t = 0, 1, \ldots, c$ are $f_{in} = 0, u_{in} = 0, v_{in} = 0, j_{in} = t$, $cell_{in} = \lceil (1 + t \bmod w_1)/\alpha \rceil$. According to (10) the rightmost cell of the array outputs the value $f_m(c)$ in time $t(c,m) = c + \sum_{i=1}^{m} \lceil w_i/\alpha \rceil$.

From the above discussion we are led to the following result:

Proposition 2. *The algorithm for the modular systolic array requires $c + \sum_{i=1}^{m} \lceil w_i/\alpha \rceil$ time to find $f_m(c)$ on $\sum_{i=1}^{m} \lceil w_i/\alpha \rceil$ processors, each with storage capacity α.*

Corollary 3. *If $\alpha \geq w_i, i = 1, 2, \ldots, m$ then the algorithm presented here requires $c + m$ time to find $f_m(c)$ on m processors.*

5 A Ring

Obviously, the first cell of the linear array from the previous section becomes idle in c time. On the other hand, any data needs $t_{cross} = \sum_{i=1}^{m} \lceil w_i/\alpha \rceil$ time to cross the array and to leave the last cell. Therefore, if $t_{cross} > c$, then the first cell can be

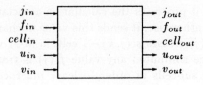

```
repeat
case
    cell_in = 1  → [ {computation}
                     addr  := 1 + j_in mod w;
                     addr' := addr mod α;
                     {compute f_k(j) and store in F}
                     if j_in < w then  F(addr') := f_in
                                 else  F(addr') := max{f_in, F(addr') + p}
                     fi;
                     {compute u_k(j) }
                     if F(addr') ≤ f_in then  u_out := u_in
                                        else  u_out := obj
                     fi;
                     {compute v_k(j) and store in V}
                     if F(addr') ≤ f_in then V(addr') := -1
                                        else
                                            if V(addr') = -1 then V(addr') := j_in
                                            fi
                     fi;
                     if F(addr') ≤ f_in then  v_out := v_in
                                        else  v_out := V(addr')
                     fi;
                     {number of cells to be skipped by f_k(j)}
                     cell_out := ⌈w/α⌉ - ⌈addr/α⌉ + ⌈(1 + j_in mod wnext)/α⌉;
                     j_out := j_in;
                     f_out := F(addr')
                   ]
    cell_in > 1  → [ {transmit}
                     cell_out := cell_in - 1;
                     j_out := j_in;
                     f_out := f_in;
                     u_out := u_in;
                     v_out := v_in
                   ]
end_case
end_repeat
```

Fig. 3. The basic cell and its operation during the forward phase

reused, instead of adding new cells to the array. This idea can be easily extended in the case where we aim to bound the number of the cells used to some fixed number q, where $q \leq \min\{t_{cross}, c\}$. The solution is to add a buffer memory module Q to the array. This memory receives the data from the cell C_q, stores it and sends it to the cell C_1 when this cell becomes idle. The memory Q also saves the vectors u_m and v_m at the end of the forward phase. Therefore a necessary condition for the ring to be able to solve problem (1) is that the size of Q is at least $2m + 4c$. The resulting architecture (see figure 4) is called Ring and is well known from systolic computation [11]. As was shown, the algorithm in the previous section needs t_{cross} cells, each with storage capacity α to solve the knapsack problem. Therefore, the linear array in the ring in figure 4 has to be used $\lceil t_{cross}/q \rceil$ times to solve it. For this purpose, the set

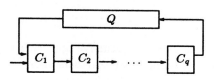

Fig. 4. The Ring

$f_k(j), k = 1, 2, \ldots, m, j = 0, 1, \ldots, c$ is partitioned into $\lceil t_{cross}/q \rceil$ bands and each one of these bands can be executed individually by the linear processor array. Let B_i denote the ith band. The partitioning is performed as follows:

$$f_k(j) \in B_i \Leftrightarrow \lceil a(j, k)/q \rceil = i,$$

where $a(j, k)$ is defined in (12).

Since c values are input in any cell and a data needs q time to pass through C_1 to C_q, then a new set of data (a new band) can be input to the cell C_1 any $\max\{c, q\} = \Theta(c + q)$ time. Obviously, the inequality

$$m\lceil w_{min}/\alpha \rceil \leq t_{cross} \leq m\lceil w_{max}/\alpha \rceil, \tag{13}$$

where $w_{max} = \max_{i=1}^{m}\{w_i\}, w_{min} = \min_{i=1}^{m}\{w_i\}$, is satisfied. Hence, for the running time T_{for} of the parallel forward dynamic programming part we obtain o within a constant factor

$$mw_{min}(c + q)/q\alpha \leq T_{for} \leq mw_{max}(c + q)/q\alpha, . \tag{14}$$

For the total running time T_q we have to add to T_{for} the time needed to load the coefficients $p_i, w_i, i = 1, 2, \ldots, m$ into the cells and the time for the backtracking dynamic programming part, which can be done in additional $\Theta(m)$ time. Therefore, for the total running time T_q from (14) we obtain to within a constant factor

$$mcw_{min}/q\alpha + mw_{min}/\alpha + m \leq T_q \leq mcw_{max}/q\alpha + mw_{max}/\alpha + m.$$

This result confirms once again the observation (see Teng [12] and Andonov and Gruau [13]) that w_{max} and w_{min} are important parameters for the knapsack problem. These influence the running time of the parallel algorithm in contrast to the serial dynamic programming algorithm which depends on m and c only. It is well known that in many practical applications w_{max} is much less than the knapsack capacity c, i.e., $w_{max} \ll c$. A reasonable assumption is that w_{max} and w_{min} do not change as c increases and therefore α/w_{max} and α/w_{min} are constant factors. Hence, we obtain for the total time complexity of our algorithm on the ring

$$T_q = \Theta(mc/q + m). \tag{15}$$

The speedup and the efficiency of the algorithm both approach their optimal values respectively $\Theta(q)$ and $\Theta(1)$ as c increases.

6 Conclusion

Dynamic programming is an effective recursive approach widely used in optimization problems. The results of numerous researchers show that this approach is very suitable for systolic implementation. One interesting exception was the knapsack problem whose dependence graph depends on the weights of the considered objects and lacks the regularity usually required for obtaining a systolic implementation. A method for synthesis of systolic arrays for such class of problems is not yet developed.

In this paper, a previously reported linear systolic array for the knapsack problem is transformed into a more efficient structure. The design parameters (the number of the cells and their memory storage) are problem size independent. To the knowledge of the authors the proposed algorithm is the first processor-efficient VLSI oriented algorithm for the knapsack problem.

Acknowledgements

The authors would like to thank Liam Marnane, Frédéric Raimbault and Nicola Yanev for many helpful discussions. Frédéric Raimbault also wrote a simulation program of the algorithm using the systolic language RELACS.

References

1. R. Garfinkel and G. Nemhauser, *Integer Programming*. John Wiley and Sons, 1972.
2. T. C. Hu, *Combinatorial Algorithms*. Addison-Wesley Publishing Company, 1982.
3. S. Martello and P. Toth, *Knapsack Problems: Algorithms and Computer Implementation*. John Wiley and Sons, 1990.
4. M. Garey and D. Johnson, *Computers and Intractability: a Guide to the Theory of NP-Completeness*. Freeman, San Francisco, 1979.
5. R. Bellman, *Dynamic Programming*. Princeton University Press, Princeton, NJ, 1957.
6. G. Chen, M. Chern, and J. Jang, "Pipeline architectures for dynamic programming algorithms," *Parallel Computing*, vol. 13, pp. 111–117, 1990.
7. G. Li and B. Wa, "Systolic processing for dynamic programming problems," in *Proc. International Conference on Parallel Processing*, pp. 434–441, 1985.
8. R. J. Lipton and D. Lopresti, "Delta transformation to symplify VLSI processor arrays for serial dynamic programming," in *Proc. International Conference on Parallel Processing*, pp. 917–920, 1986.
9. R. Andonov, V. Aleksandrov, and A. Benaini, "A linear systolic array for the knapsack problem," Tech. Rep., Center of Computer Science and Technology, Acad. G. Bonchev st., bl. 25a, Sofia 1113, Bulgaria, 1991.
10. P. Quinton and Y. Robert, *Algorithmes et architectures systoliques*. Masson, 1989. English translation by Prentice Hall, *Systolic Algorithms and Architectures*, Sept. 1991.
11. H. T. Kung, "Why systolic architectures," *Computer*, vol. 15, pp. 37–46, 1982.
12. S. Teng, "Adaptive parallel algorithm for integral knapsack problems," *J. of Parallel and Distributed Computing*, vol. 8, pp. 400–406, 1990.
13. R. Andonov and F. Gruau, "A 2D modular toroidal systolic array for the knapsack problem," in *ASAP'91*,(Barcelona, Spain), September 1991.

This article was processed using the LaTeX macro package with LLNCS style

On the Loading, Recovery and Access of Stationary Data in Systolic Arrays

Jingling Xue

LFCS, Department of Computer Science
University of Edinburgh, Edinburgh EH9 3JZ, UK

Abstract. A space-time mapping that describes a systolic array consists of a scheduling vector that specifies the temporal distribution and an allocation matrix that specifies the spatial distribution. The allocation matrix determines whether a variable is moving or stationary. The space-time mapping provides a complete description of the data flow for moving variables. But it fails to provide any help in handling stationary variables. This paper presents a method for the loading, recovery and access of stationary data in a systolic array. The basic idea is to add new variables, which constitute a specification for the loading, recovery and access of stationary data, to the initial program. This specification leaves open the choice of dependence vectors of the new variables and the scheduling vector. Thus, the search of schemes for handling stationary data reduces to a search of dependence vectors for the new variables and of scheduling vectors.

1 Introduction

We describe a method for the specification of the loading, recovery and access of stationary data in systolic design. We present the method based on input that is in the form of uniform recurrence equations (UREs). We refer to these initial UREs as the *source UREs*. For details about properties of UREs and the mapping of UREs to systolic arrays, see [1] and references therein. We name Φ_V the *the domain of variable V*, the union of all domains of equations with target variable V. Without loss of generality, Φ_V is assumed to be a convex polytope [2]. We name Φ the *index space*, the union of all domains of variables. To simplify presentation, we assume that each variable V is associated with one data dependence vector, denoted ϑ_V.

A space-time mapping, Π, that describes an r-dimensional array from an n-dimensional UREs is a linear transformation from $\mathbf{Z}^n$ to $\mathbf{Z}^{r+1}$:

$$\Pi = \begin{bmatrix} \lambda \\ \sigma \end{bmatrix}$$

$\lambda \in \mathbf{Z}$ is called the *scheduling vector*. Point $I \in \Phi$ is computed at time step λI. $\sigma \in \mathbf{Z}^{r \times n}$ is called the *allocation matrix*. Point $I \in \Phi$ is computed at cell σI. $\mathrm{flow}(V) = \sigma \vartheta_V / \lambda \vartheta_V$ specifies the velocity with which the elements of V travel per step. If $\mathrm{flow}(V) \neq 0$, then variable V is *moving*. The velocity and the distribution of the elements of a moving variable are completely determined by the space-time mapping. If $\mathrm{flow}(V) = 0$, then variable V is *stationary*. A local processor memory is required to store the elements of a stationary variable. A specification for the loading, recovery and access of stationary data needs to be constructed. Since the allocation matrix determines whether a variable is moving or stationary, the method presented here is applied after the allocation matrix has been chosen.

We use the following notations. Let $X \subset \mathbf{Z}^n$ be a convex polytope and $\delta \in \mathbf{Z}^n$. We define $\text{first}(X, \delta) = \{I \mid I \in X \wedge I - \delta \notin X\}$ and $\text{last}(X, \delta) = \{I \mid I \in X \wedge I + \delta \notin X\}$. $\text{in}(X, \delta)$ is the translation of $\text{first}(X, \delta)$ by $-\delta$: $\text{in}(X, \delta) = \{I \mid I + \delta \in \text{first}(X, \delta)\}$. By convention, the input data of V are initialised at $\text{in}(\Phi_V, \vartheta_V)$ and used for the first time at $\text{first}(\Phi_V, \vartheta_V)$. The output data of V are available at $\text{last}(\Phi_V, \vartheta_V)$.

We distinguish three types of equations in the source UREs. An *input equation* is of the form $I \in \text{in}(\Phi_V, \vartheta_V) \twoheadrightarrow V(I) \equiv v_{in_V(I)}$, where in_V is a mapping from $\mathbf{Z}^n$ to $\mathbf{Z}^{i_V}$ $(0 \leqslant i_V \leqslant n)$ and $\{v_{in_V(I)} \mid I \in \text{in}(\Phi_V, \vartheta_V)\}$ contains the input data of V. An *output equation* is of the form $I \in \text{last}(\Phi_V, \vartheta_V) \twoheadrightarrow v_{out_V(I)} \equiv V(I)$, where out_V is a mapping from $\mathbf{Z}^n$ to $\mathbf{Z}^{o_V}$ $(0 \leqslant o_V \leqslant n)$ and $\{v_{out_V(I)} \mid I \in \text{last}(\Phi_V, \vartheta_V)\}$ contains the output data of V. Equations that are neither input nor output equations are called the *computation equations*; each is of the from: $I \in D \twoheadrightarrow V(I) = f(W(I - \vartheta_W), \cdots)$.

For $x, \delta \in \mathbf{Z}^n$, $\text{ray}(x, \delta)$ denotes the set of all points y whose distance to x is a non-negative integral multiple of δ: $\text{ray}(x, \delta) = \{y \mid y = x + m\delta \wedge m \in \mathbf{N}\}$. For $X \subset \mathbf{Z}^n$, we define $\text{rays}(X, \delta) = (\bigcup I : I \in X : \text{ray}(I, \delta))$. For a point K in the domain Φ_V of variable V, we refer to all points of Φ_V contained in $\text{ray}(K, \vartheta_V)$ as a ϑ_V-path. In fact, $\text{first}(\Phi_V, \vartheta_V)$ ($\text{last}(\Phi_V, \vartheta_V)$) is the set of the first (last) points of all ϑ_V-paths. We write $\text{planes}(\Phi, \sigma)$ for the inverse image of the processor space in $\mathbf{Z}^n$ under the space-time mapping: $\text{planes}(\Phi, \sigma) = \{I \mid I \in \mathbf{Z}^n \wedge J \in \Phi \wedge \sigma I = \sigma J\}$; where the *processor space* is the set $\{\sigma I \mid I \in \Phi\}$.

2 The Loading and Recovery of Stationary Data

To specify the loading and recovery of the elements of each stationary variable V, we introduce two variables: *loading variable* L_V for loading the elements of V and *recovery variable* R_V for recovering the elements of V. We must choose dependence vectors ϑ_{L_V} and ϑ_{R_V} such that L_V and R_V are moving.

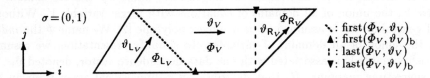

Fig. 1. The construction of loading and recovery variables for stationary variable V ($n = 2$).

The construction of L_V and R_V is symmetrical. Let us consider the loading of the input data first (Fig. 1). The domain Φ_{L_V} of loading variable L_V contains the points that propagate the input data of V during the loading phase:

$$\Phi_{\mathsf{L}_V} = (\text{planes}(\Phi, \sigma) \cap \text{rays}(\text{first}(\Phi_V, \vartheta_V), -\vartheta_{\mathsf{L}_V})) \setminus \text{first}(\Phi_V, \vartheta_V)$$

Since one ϑ_{L_V}-path can load one stationary element only, we must choose dependence vector ϑ_{L_V} such that each ϑ_{L_V}-path contains only one point of $\text{first}(\Phi_V, \vartheta_V)$.

To determine the initialisation of variable L_V with the input data of V, we partition $\text{first}(\Phi_V, \vartheta_V)$ into two subsets: the set $\text{first}(\Phi_V, \vartheta_V)_b$ contains the points that are mapped to border cells and the set $\text{first}(\Phi_V, \vartheta_V) \setminus \text{first}(\Phi_V, \vartheta_V)_b$ contains the points that are mapped to internal cells, where

$$\text{first}(\Phi_V, \vartheta_V)_b = \{I \mid I \in \text{first}(\Phi_V, \vartheta_V) \wedge I - \vartheta_{L_V} \notin \text{planes}(\Phi, \sigma)\}$$

The loading of the input data $V(I - \vartheta_V)$ for $I \in \text{first}(\Phi_V, \vartheta_V)_b$ is unnecessary; $L_V(I - \vartheta_{L_V})$ is initialised with the input value that $V(I - \vartheta_V)$ is initialised with. The initialisation of L_V with the remaining input data is defined as follows. The two sets $\text{in}(\Phi_{L_V}, \vartheta_{L_V})$ and $\text{first}(\Phi_V, \vartheta_V) \setminus \text{first}(\Phi_V, \vartheta_V)_b$ are isomorphic by the bijection:

$$\ell_V : \text{in}(\Phi_{L_V}, \vartheta_{L_V}) \rightarrow \text{first}(\Phi_V, \vartheta_V) \setminus \text{first}(\Phi_V, \vartheta_V)_b, \ \ell_V(I) = J, \text{ where } J \in \text{ray}(I, \vartheta_{L_V})$$

$L_V(I)$ is initialised with the input value that $V(J - \vartheta_V)$ is initialised with. It is then pipelined along ϑ_{L_V} to the corresponding point of $\text{first}(\Phi_V, \vartheta_V)$.

Finally, we initialise variable V with its input data loaded via variable L_V by substituting $L_V(I - \vartheta_{L_V})$ for all arguments $V(I - \vartheta_V)$, for every $I \in \text{first}(\Phi_V, \vartheta_V)$.

Next, we consider the recovery of the output data (Fig. 1). The domain Φ_{R_V} of recovery variable R_V contains the points that propagate the output data of V during the recovery phase:

$$\Phi_{R_V} = (\text{planes}(\Phi, \sigma) \cap \text{rays}(\text{last}(\Phi_V, \vartheta_V), \vartheta_{R_V})) \setminus \text{last}(\Phi_V, \vartheta_V)$$

Since one ϑ_{R_V}-path can recover one stationary element only, we must choose dependence vector ϑ_{R_V} such that each ϑ_{R_V}-path contains only one point of $\text{last}(\Phi_V, \vartheta_V)$.

The recovery of the output data of V is symmetric to the loading of the input data of V. We partition $\text{last}(\Phi_V, \vartheta_V)$ into two subsets: the set $\text{last}(\Phi_V, \vartheta_V)_b$ contains the points that are mapped to border cells and the set $\text{last}(\Phi_V, \vartheta_V) \setminus \text{last}(\Phi_V, \vartheta_V)_b$ contains the points that are mapped to internal cells, where

$$\text{last}(\Phi_V, \vartheta_V)_b = \{I \mid I \in \text{last}(\Phi_V, \vartheta_V) \wedge I + \vartheta_{R_V} \notin \text{planes}(\Phi, \sigma)\}$$

The recovery of the output data $V(I)$ for $I \in \text{last}(\Phi_V, \vartheta_V)_b$ is unnecessary. The recovery of the output data $V(I)$ for $I \in \text{last}(\Phi_V, \vartheta_V) \setminus \text{last}(\Phi_V, \vartheta_V)_b$ is defined as follows. The two sets $\text{last}(\Phi_{R_V}, \vartheta_{R_V})$ and $\text{last}(\Phi_V, \vartheta_V) \setminus \text{last}(\Phi_V, \vartheta_V)_b$ are isomorphic by the bijection:

$$r_V : \text{last}(\Phi_{R_V}, \vartheta_{R_V}) \rightarrow \text{last}(\Phi_V, \vartheta_V) \setminus \text{last}(\Phi_V, \vartheta_V)_b, \ r_V(I) = J, \text{ where } I \in \text{ray}(J, \vartheta_{R_V})$$

To recover stationary variable V, we must initialise R_V with the output data of V. We substitute $R_V(I)$ for all target variables $V(I)$, for every $I \in \text{last}(\Phi_V, \vartheta_V)$. $R_V(I)$ is then pipelined along ϑ_{R_V} to the corresponding point of $\text{last}(\Phi_{R_V}, \vartheta_{R_V})$.

Procedure 1 (Construction of loading variable L_V and recovery variable R_V for stationary variable V of the source UREs given an allocation matrix)

- Delete the input and output equations of variable V.
- The specification of loading variable L_V is as follows:
  - Substitute $L_V(I - \vartheta_{L_V})$ for all arguments $V(I - \vartheta_V)$ of the source UREs, where $I \in \text{first}(\Phi_V, \vartheta_V)$.

- The UREs for loading variable L_V are

$$I \in \text{first}(\varPhi_V, \vartheta_V)_b \rightarrow L_V(I - \vartheta_{L_V}) \equiv v_{inV(I - \vartheta V)}$$
$$I \in \text{in}(\varPhi_{L_V}, \vartheta_{L_V}) \rightarrow L_V(I) \equiv v_{inV(\ell_V(I) - \vartheta V)}$$
$$I \in \varPhi_{L_V} \rightarrow L_V(I) = L_V(I - \vartheta_{L_V})$$

- The specification of recovery variable R_V is as follows:
  - Substitute $R_V(I)$ for all target variables $V(I)$ of the source UREs, where $I \in \text{last}(\varPhi_V, \vartheta_V)$.
  - The UREs for recovery variable R_V are

$$I \in \varPhi_{R_V} \rightarrow R_V(I) = R_V(I - \vartheta_{R_V})$$
$$I \in \text{last}(\varPhi_V, \vartheta_V)_b \rightarrow v_{outV(I)} \equiv R_V(I)$$
$$I \in \text{last}(\varPhi_{R_V}, \vartheta_{R_V}) \rightarrow v_{outV(r_V(I))} \equiv R_V(I) \qquad \square$$

Let us examine the impact of the choice of dependence vectors of loading and recovery variables on the quality of the systolic array. If the domain of a stationary variable V and the domains of their corresponding loading and recovery variables are mutually disjoint (Fig. 1), then each cell is either loading, recovering or computing one element of V at any time step. (If the domains of the loading and recovery variables are disjoint, the two variables can be merged.) Of course, the loading, recovery and computation of V can still be performed concurrently among different cells of the array. To minimise the latency, it is preferable to choose dependence vectors for loading and recovery such that their domains are contained in the index space. However, the choice of these dependence vectors may have to cater for other factors beside the minimisation of latency, e.g., the satisfaction of the requirements on the length and direction of the channels for loading and recovery variables.

3 The Access of Stationary Data

To specify the access of the elements of each stationary variable V, we introduce $n - r - 1$ address variables, $A_V^1, \cdots, A_V^{n-r-1}$. Element $V(I)$ is assigned with location $(A_V^1(I), \cdots, A_V^{n-r-1}(I))$ of the memory at cell σI. Address variables provide the addresses for accessing the stationary data in the local memory of a cell.

If V is stationary, the points of a ϑ_V-path are mapped to the same cell. V is initialised at the first point of the path and then updated at the remaining points. The final output value is available at the last point of the path. It suffices to allocate one memory location for all the points of the path.

We construct address variables $A_V^1, \cdots, A_V^{n-r-1}$ such that all the points in one ϑ_V-path are given the same memory location and different stationary elements that are mapped to the same cell are given different memory locations. The construction of address variable A_V^i is as follows. We choose an n-vector $\pi_{A_V^i}$ and, thus, obtain a sequence of parallel hyperplanes $\text{addr}(\ell_{\min}^{V^i}), \cdots, \text{addr}(\ell_{\max}^{V^i})$ $(\ell_{\min}^{V^i} \leqslant \ell_{\max}^{V^i})$ whose normals are $\pi_{A_V^i}$ and which intersect the domain of stationary variable V. We choose the dependence vector $\vartheta_{A_V^i}$ of address variable A_V^i such that $\vartheta_{A_V^i} \pi_{A_V^i} = 0$ and construct

A_V^i such that $A_V^i(I) = \ell$ ($\ell_{\min}^{V^i} \leqslant \ell \leqslant \ell_{\max}^{V^i}$) for all points I in hyperplane $\mathrm{addr}(\ell)$:

$$I \in \mathrm{addr}(\ell_{\min}^{V^i}) \cap \mathrm{in}(\Phi_V, \vartheta_{A_V^i}) \twoheadrightarrow A_V^i(I) \equiv \ell_{\min}^{V^i}$$

$$\vdots$$

$$I \in \mathrm{addr}(\ell_{\max}^{V^i}) \cap \mathrm{in}(\Phi_V, \vartheta_{A_V^i}) \twoheadrightarrow A_V^i(I) \equiv \ell_{\max}^{V^i}$$

$$I \in \Phi_V \twoheadrightarrow A_V^i(I) = A_V^i(I - \vartheta_{A_V^i})$$

(1)

This implies that the domains of address variable A_V^i and stationary variable V are identical, i.e., that $\Phi_{A_V^i} = \Phi_V$. (The notation σ_i stands for the i-th row vector of σ.) Finally, we must choose $\pi_{A_V^i}$ and $\vartheta_{A_V^i}$ such that

- $\sigma\vartheta_{A_V^i} \neq 0$ (this ensures that A_V^i is a moving variable).
- $\pi_{A_V^i}\vartheta_V = 0$ (this ensures that $A_V^i(I)$ is the same address for all points of a ϑ_V-path).
- $\pi_{A_V^1}, \cdots, \pi_{A_V^{n-r-1}}, \sigma_1, \cdots, \sigma_r$ are linearly independent (this ensures that different elements of stationary variable V that are mapped to the same cell are given different memory locations, because the intersection of $n-1$ mutually non-parallel hyperplanes is one-dimensional).

Procedure 2 (Construction of address variables $A_V^1, \cdots, A_V^{n-r-1}$ for stationary variable V of the source UREs given an allocation matrix)

- The specification of address variables $A_V^1, \cdots, A_V^{n-r-1}$ is given by (1).
- Replace all occurrences of $V(I)$ in the source UREs by $V(A_V^1(I), \cdots, A_V^{n-r-1}(I))$. □

To retain the latency, it is always best to choose the dependence vector of a moving variable as the dependence vector of an address variable.

4 An Example: Square Matrix Product $C = A \times B$

A popular URE specification for the (square) matrix product, say, for sizes of $m \times m$ matrices is given as follows [1, 3]:

$$
\begin{aligned}
0 < i \leqslant m \wedge 0 = j \wedge 0 < k \leqslant m &\twoheadrightarrow A(i,j,k) \equiv a_{i,k} \\
0 < i \leqslant m \wedge 0 < j \leqslant m \wedge 0 < k \leqslant m &\twoheadrightarrow A(i,j,k) = A(i,j-1,k) \\
0 = i \wedge 0 < j \leqslant m \wedge 0 < k \leqslant m &\twoheadrightarrow B(i,j,k) \equiv b_{k,j} \\
0 < i \leqslant m \wedge 0 < j \leqslant m \wedge 0 < k \leqslant m &\twoheadrightarrow B(i,j,k) = B(i-1,j,k) \\
0 < i \leqslant m \wedge 0 < j \leqslant m \wedge 0 = k &\twoheadrightarrow C(i,j,k) = 0 \\
0 < i \leqslant m \wedge 0 < j \leqslant m \wedge 0 < k \leqslant m &\twoheadrightarrow C(i,j,k) = C(i,j,k-1) + A(i,j-1,k)B(i-1,j,k) \\
0 < i \leqslant m \wedge 0 < j \leqslant m \wedge k = m &\twoheadrightarrow c_{i,j} \equiv C(i,j,k)
\end{aligned}
$$

Let us consider the class of one-dimensional arrays described by the allocation matrix (vector) $\sigma = (1, -1, 0)$. Variable C is stationary. First, we consider the loading and recovery of C. We choose $\vartheta_{L_C} = \vartheta_{R_C} = (1, 0, 1)$. Since $\Phi_{L_C} \cap \Phi_{R_C} = \varnothing$, we merge L_C and R_C to one variable denoted P_C. Second, we consider the access of C in local processor memories. There are m $(m-k)$ elements of C mapped to cell 0 $(-k$ or $k)$ $(0 < k < m)$. Only one address variable is needed (since $r = 1$); it is named A_C. We arbitrarily choose $\vartheta_{A_C} = \vartheta_A = (0, 1, 0)$ and $\pi_{A_C} = (1, 0, 0)$. An application of Procs. 1 and 2 rewrites the previous UREs to the following set of equations:

$$0 < i \leqslant m \wedge 0 = j \wedge 0 < k \leqslant m \rightarrow A_C(i,j,k) \equiv i$$
$$0 < i \leqslant m \wedge 0 < j \leqslant m \wedge 0 < k \leqslant m \rightarrow A_C(i,j,k) = A_C(i,j-1,k)$$
$$0 < i \leqslant m \wedge 0 = j \wedge 0 < k \leqslant m \rightarrow A(i,j,k) \equiv a_{i,k}$$
$$0 < i \leqslant m \wedge 0 < j \leqslant m \wedge 0 < k \leqslant m \rightarrow A(i,j,k) = A(i,j-1,k)$$
$$0 = i \wedge 0 < j \leqslant m \wedge 0 < k \leqslant m \rightarrow B(i,j,k) \equiv b_{k,j}$$
$$0 < i \leqslant m \wedge 0 < j \leqslant m \wedge 0 < k \leqslant m \rightarrow B(i,j,k) = B(i-1,j,k)$$
$$i = j - m \wedge k \leqslant i < k + m \wedge 0 < j \leqslant m \wedge k \leqslant 0 \rightarrow P_C(i,j,k) \equiv 0$$
$$i > j - m \wedge k \leqslant i < k + m \wedge 0 < j \leqslant m \wedge k \leqslant 0 \rightarrow P_C(i,j,k) = P_C(i-1,j,k-1)$$
$$i < j + m \wedge k - m < i \leqslant k \wedge 0 < j \leqslant m \wedge k > m \rightarrow P_C(i,j,k) = P_C(i-1,j,k-1)$$
$$0 < i \leqslant m \wedge 0 < j \leqslant m \wedge k = 1 \rightarrow C(A_C(i,j,k)) = P_C(i-1,j,k-1) + A(i,j-1,k)B(i-1,j,k)$$
$$0 < i \leqslant m \wedge 0 < j \leqslant m \wedge 1 < k < m \rightarrow C(A_C(i,j,k)) = C(A_C(i,j,k-1)) + A(i,j-1,k)B(i-1,j,k)$$
$$0 < i \leqslant m \wedge 0 < j \leqslant m \wedge k = m \rightarrow P_C(i,j,k) = C(A_C(i,j,k-1)) + A(i,j-1,k)B(i-1,j,k)$$
$$i = j + m - 1 \wedge k - m < i \leqslant k \wedge 0 < j \leqslant m \wedge k \geqslant m \rightarrow c_{2m-k,j} \equiv P_C(i,j,k)$$

Applying the method in [3], we obtain the following cell program (V^{in} and V^{out} denote the input and output channels for a variable V at a cell, respectively):

$$Z^{\text{out}} = Z^{\text{in}}$$
$$A_C^{\text{out}} = A_C^{\text{in}}$$

$$
\begin{aligned}
&\textbf{if } \varphi \wedge Z^{\text{in}} = z_1 \longrightarrow P_C^{\text{out}} = P_C^{\text{in}} \\
&[\!]\ \varphi \wedge Z^{\text{in}} = z_2 \longrightarrow A^{\text{out}} = A^{\text{in}},\ B^{\text{out}} = B^{\text{in}},\ C^{\text{out}}(A_C^{\text{in}}) = P_C^{\text{in}} + A^{\text{in}} B^{\text{in}} \\
&[\!]\ \varphi \wedge Z^{\text{in}} = z_3 \longrightarrow A^{\text{out}} = A^{\text{in}},\ B^{\text{out}} = B^{\text{in}},\ C^{\text{out}}(A_C^{\text{in}}) = C^{\text{in}}(A_C^{\text{in}}) + A^{\text{in}} B^{\text{in}} \\
&[\!]\ \varphi \wedge Z^{\text{in}} = z_4 \longrightarrow A^{\text{out}} = A^{\text{in}},\ B^{\text{out}} = B^{\text{in}},\ P_C^{\text{out}} = C^{\text{in}}(A_C^{\text{in}}) + A^{\text{in}} B^{\text{in}} \\
&[\!]\ \neg\varphi \qquad\quad \longrightarrow Z^{\text{out}} = Z^{\text{in}},\ A_C^{\text{out}} = A_C^{\text{in}},\ A^{\text{out}} = A^{\text{in}},\ B^{\text{out}} = B^{\text{in}},\ P_C^{\text{out}} = P_C^{\text{in}} \\
&\textbf{fi}
\end{aligned}
$$

Predicate φ is true iff the points being computed are in the index space. The corresponding control variables based on which φ is specified are not shown here.

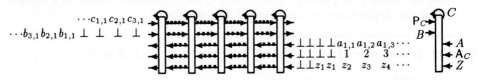

Fig. 2. The one-dimensional array for matrix product ($m = 3$).

Let us choose the scheduling vector $\lambda = (m, m, 1)$. This vector along with the allocation vector $\sigma = (1, -1, 0)$ forms the space-time mapping $\Pi = \begin{bmatrix} m & m & 1 \\ 1 & -1 & 0 \end{bmatrix}$ (Fig. 2).

Acknowledgement

The author is financially supported by UK SERC, Grant no. GR/G55457.

References

1. P. Quinton and V. van Dongen. The mapping of linear recurrence equations on regular arrays. *J. VLSI Signal Processing*, 1(2):95–113, Oct. 1989.
2. A. Schrijver. *Theory of Linear and Integer Programming*. Series in Discrete Mathematics. John Wiley & Sons, 1986.
3. J. Xue. *The Formal Synthesis of Control Signals for Systolic Arrays*. PhD thesis, Department of Computer Science, University of Edinburgh, Apr. 1992.

This article was processed using the LaTeX macro package with LLNCS style

DESIGNING MODULAR LINEAR SYSTOLIC ARRAYS USING DEPENDENCE GRAPH REGULAR PARTITIONS

Jean-Frédéric Myoupo and Anne-Cécile Fabret

L.R.I. URA 410 du CNRS, Bât. 490, Université Paris-Sud
91405 Orsay, France

Abstract: In this paper, we use a variant of the geometric method to derive efficient modular linear systolic algorithms for the transitive closure and shortest path problems. Furthermore, we show that partially-pipelined modular linear systolic algorithms with an output operation, for matrix multiplication, can be as efficient as fully-pipelined ones, and in some cases needs less cells.

1. Introduction

The motivation of this work is to get modular linear systolic algorithms from the existing non modular linear ones in [14, 19] suitable for direct implementation in VLSI. So the starting point of this paper is the non modular linear algorithms in [19]. The result is that we derive a simple mapping technique to design unidirectional modular linear systolic algorithms, for these problems, having bounded I/O requirements. To reach our goal we consider for each problem (of size n) mentioned above the set, denoted $D(n)$, of all its partial computation points in the Space-Time plane. Next we partition $D(n)$ into regular disjoint subsets such that if we can localize the position of one of these subsets in the Space-Time plane, then the localizations of the others are obtained by a simple translation of some vector. The linear algorithms we obtained are efficient and simple. We also show that partially-pipelined linear algorithms for matrix product combined with an output operation can be as efficient as fully-pipelined existing ones and in some cases need less cells. The theorems of this work are proved in [16].

The rest of this paper is organized as follows: In section 2 we present the problems. We use dependence graph regular partitions method to derive modular linear systolic arrays for transitive closure in section 3. In section 4 matrix multiplication is considered. In section 5 we contrast our arrays with the existing ones. The conclusion follows in section 6

2. Statement of the Problems

2.1.The Warshall-Floyd Algorithm

Given the input matrix A, the sequential Warshall-Floyd algorithm to find A^* is well known [see 1 for details]:

$$a_{ij}^{(p+1)} = a_{ij}^{(p)} + a_{ik}^{(p)} \times a_{kj}^{(p)}, \; 1 \leq i, j, k \leq n \qquad (1)$$

This algorithm solves both the transitive closure and the shortest path problems. The difference between the the two problems is the following:

(i). For the transitive closure problem, the input matrix A is the adjacency matrix. The operation + is the Boolean OR operation; the operation * is the Boolean AND operation. The output A* is the transitive closure matrix.

(ii). For the shortest path problem, the input A is the distance matrix. The operation + is the minimum operation; the operation * is the addition operation. The output A^* is the shortest path matrix.

Our goal is to find the solutions of (1) through modular linear systolic arrays. The starting point of this paper is essentially the linear three-pass algorithm for transitive closure in [19] which is derived from the well known Guibas et al. two-dimensional algorithm for transitive closure [4], that is solving (1) reduces to a particular matrix multiplication problem. Our approach is based on the analysis of the set of the partial computation points of (1) in $\mathbb{P}$. Ramakrishnan and Varman [19] exhibit such a non-modular linear three-pass multiplication algorithm to solve the transitive closure problems: They consider the adjacency matrix A and its copy A'. The transitive closure matrix A* is got by a particular matrix multiplication of A by A' in three passes:

$$a^*_{ij} = a^*_{ij} + a_{ik} \times a'_{kj} \qquad (2)$$

For a problem of size n, arising from (2), the set of all its partial computation points, in one pass, will be denoted $D(n)$, it is the dependence graph. A partial computation point arising from (2) in $\mathbb{P}$, in one pass, will be denoted ikj or i.k.j .

Since a calculation arising from (2) must be done in a precise cell and at a precise time, the idea of this paper consists of mapping all these calculations (arising from (2)) in the plane whose axes are the cell's axis and the time axis (Space-Time plane). Hereafter this plane will be denoted $\mathbb{P}$. The data that flows through the linear array (we are designing) is considered as a simple mechanical agent each element of which has a given velocity. Thus each element a_{ij} or b_{ij} when travelling through the array is involved in some calculations which are essential for the computation of solutions of (2). More precisely in $\mathbb{P}$, the trajectory of a token travelling in the array through a channel with a time delay μ between 2 consecutive cells, is a line of slope μ. At some suitable intersections of these lines, the different partial computations of the solutions c_{ij} are performed using (2). Some control signals are also used to avoid undesirable encounters.

This idea was introduced in [2] for matrix product, $C=A*B$ $(c_{ij}=c_{ij}+a_{ik}*b_{kj})$, unfortunately they did not succeed in getting good complexity results. It yields the so called *Parallelogram Method* [25].

3. Linear Systolic Arrays for Transitive Closure and Shortest Path

3.1. Regular Disjoint Partition of $\mathbf{D(n)}$ for the Transitive Closure and Shortest Path

We discuss the way a partial solution arising from (2) is going to be computed during one pass. In order to do this, an analysis of the structure of the equation (2) is necessary. It is important to know from the temporal structure of the computation of a solution of the equation (2) how and when this solution is computed. This may lead us to look for the different temporal steps towards the complete computation of a solution a^*_{ij}. Once these steps are known, we will look for a way of mapping them in $\mathbb{P}$. The conception of the linear algorithm in [19] is hard to follow. It is when trying to understand it that we realize that it derives from a specific partition of the set of the partial computation points arising from the matrix multiplication in one pass: They use two copies of the adjacency matrix A, say A and A'; let a_{ij} denote the $(i, j)^{th}$ entry in A and a'_{ij} denote the same entry in A'; a_{ij} travels in C_a and a'_{ij} travels in $C_{a'}$. Each token travelling in C_a and $C_{a'}$ encounters a delay of 1 and $n+1$ clock cycles respectively between any two consecutive cells. Each cell has a local memory of size n. The three-pass matrix product A×A' in a suitable array then yields the transitive closure matrix A^* of A. Their partition is obtained from the following theorem:

Theorem 3.1 (Ramakrishnan and Varman [19])

(i). There exists a disjoint regular partition of $\mathbf{D(n)}$, in one pass, for the transitive closure or shortest path into n subsets $\mathbf{D_k(n)}$, $1 \leq k \leq n$, in which the size of the local memory of a cell and the delays trough some channels depend on n.
(ii). $\mathbf{D_{k+1}(n)}$ is obtained from $\mathbf{D_k(n)}$ by a translation of the vector $(1, n+1)$.

The Ramakrishnan and Varman partition can be improved in order that only the size of the local memory depends on n: We also use two copies of matrix A, say A and A'. a_{ij} travels in C_a and a'_{ij} travels in $C_{a'}$. Each token travelling in C_a and $C_{a'}$ encounters a delay of 1 and 2 clock cycles respectively between any two consecutive cells. Each cell has a local memory of size n. We get the following partition of $\mathbf{D(n)}$:

Theorem 3.2
(i). There exists a disjoint regular partition of $\mathbf{D(n)}$ for the transitive closure or shortest path into n subsets $\mathbf{D_k(n)}$, $1 \leq k \leq n$, in which only the size of the local memory of a cell depends on n.
(ii). $\mathbf{D_{k+1}(n)}$ is obtained from $\mathbf{D_k(n)}$ by a translation τ_1 of the vector $(0, n+1)$.

3.1.1 Example

For n=3, we have
$\mathbf{D_1}(3)=\{$ 1.1.1, 1.1.2, 1.1.3, 2.1.1, 2.1.2, 2.1.3, 3.1.1, 3.1.2, 3.1.3$\}$; $\mathbf{D_2}(3)=\{$ 1.2.1, 1.2.2, 1.2.3, 2.2.1, 2.2.2, 2.2.3, 3.2.1, 3.2.2, 3.2.3$\}$ and $\mathbf{D_3}(3)=\{$ 1.3.1, 1.3.2, 1.3.3, 2.3.1, 2.3.2, 2.3.3, 3.3.1, 3.3.2, 3.3.3 $\}$.

In the above partition of $D(n)$ each cell has a local memory of size n, that is it depends on the size of the problem. This new partition of $D(n)$ yields the three-pass non-modular linear array for transitive closure in [14]. We recall that our goal is to design modular arrays in which each cell has a local memory of fixed size α. Thus neither this new partition of $D(n)$ is satisfactory. Therefore we have to improve it in order to get what we need.

3.2. Modular linear systolic arrays for transitive closure

From now on, we shall focus only on the transitive closure. The results we obtain can be easily extended to the shortest path. We assume that each cell of the array has a local memory of size α. For $n > \alpha$ and $i = \alpha$, some cells of the array have already used their α storages so that they can no more store any new $a^*{}_{ij}$, $i > \alpha$ (see Fig. 1.b $n=3$ and suppose $\alpha=1$). We keep inserting the coefficients a'_{ij} as in the proof of theorem 3.2. Thus the question is how to insert a_{ij}, $i > \alpha$, so that $a^*{}_{ij}$ should be stored in a cell whose α memory locations are still empty.

3.2.1 Disjoint Partition of $D_k(n)$

All the geometric constructions we are going to carry out now derive essentially from the non-modular case. To illustrate the idea of this paper, let us look at an example for $n=3$ and $\alpha < n$. Each cell of the array can then store only α solutions $a^*{}_{ij}$. Consider $D_1(3)$ of the fig.1b. Each cell of $D_1(3)$ has a local memory of size 3 . The method consists of splitting up $D_1(3)$ into $q(n)+\lceil (r(n)/\alpha) \rceil$ subsets, $n=q(n)k+ r(n)$ (i.e $q(n)$ and $r(n)$ are respectively the quotient and the remainder of the Euclidean division of n by α), such that each cell covered by one of these subsets can store only α elements $a^*{}_{ij}$ and two of them (subsets) have no cell in common:

(i). $n=3$ and $\alpha=1$. Thus $q(n)=3$. Split up $D_1(3)$ of the example 4.1.1 into 3 subsets $D_1{}^1, D_1{}^2$ and $D_1{}^3$. $D_1{}^{\alpha v}$ is a subset of $D_1(3)$ whose elements i1j are such that $(v\text{-}1)p<i\leq pv$, $1\leq v\leq q(n)$.
$D_1{}^1=\{1.1.1,\ 1.1.2,\ 1.1.3\}$, $D_1{}^2=\{2.1.1,\ 2.1.2,\ 2.1.3\}$, $D_1{}^3=\{3.1.1,\ 3.1.2,\ 3.1.3\}$. $D_1 =D_1{}^1 \cup D_1{}^2$ $\cup D_1{}^3$ with $D_1{}^{\alpha v} \cap D_1{}^{\alpha v'} \neq \emptyset$, $v\neq v'$, $1\leq v$, $v'\leq q(n)$, where $\cup$ and $\cap$ are respectively the operations Union and Intersection of sets. $D_k(3)$ is obtained from $D_{k-1}(3)$ by a translation of the vector $(0, 4)$.

(ii). For $n=3$ and $\alpha=2$, thus $q(n)=2$. Split up $D_1(3)$ of the example 4.1.1 into 2 subsets $D_1{}^2$ and $D_1{}^3$: $D_1{}^2=\{1.1.1,\ 1.1.2,\ 1.1.3,\ 2.1.1,\ 2.1.2,\ 2.1.3\}$, $D_1{}^3=\{3.1.1,\ 3.1.2,\ 3.1.3\}$; $D_1(3)=D_1{}^2 \cup D_1{}^3$ and $D_1{}^2 \cap D_1{}^3 \neq \emptyset$. $D_k(3)$ is obtained from $D_{k-1}(3)$ by a translation of the vector $(0, 4)$.

In the general case $n > \alpha$, set $n=\alpha q(n)+r(n)$ and consider $D_1(n)$ of the non modular case. Each cell in $D_1(n)$ must store α elements $a^*{}_{ij}$. Split up this $D_1(n)$ into $q(n)+\lceil (r(n)/\alpha) \rceil$ subsets. These subsets must not have cells in common and the cells covered by each of them (subsets) can store only α solutions $a^*{}_{ij}$.

Definition 1: $D_k{}^{\alpha v}$ is a subset of $D_k(n)$ whose elements i.k.j are such that $\alpha(v\text{-}1)<i\leq \alpha v$. Set $i=kq(i)+r(i)$ where $q(i)$ and $r(i)$ are respectively the quotient and the remainder of the Euclidean division of i by α. Note also that $D_k(n)=D_k{}^{\alpha} \cup D_k{}^{2\alpha} \cup ...\cup D_k{}^{\alpha q(n)+r(n)}$ and $D_k{}^{\alpha v} \cap D_k{}^{\alpha v'} \neq \emptyset$ or $D_1{}^{\alpha v} \cap D_1{}^{\alpha q(n)+r(n)} \neq\emptyset$. $1\leq k\leq n$, $v\neq v'$ and $1\leq v$, $v'\leq q(n)$. Where $\cup$ and $\cap$ are respectively the operations Union and Intersection of sets. $D_k{}^{\alpha q(n)+r(n)}$ is a subset $D_k(n)$ whose elements i.p.j are such that $\alpha q(n)<i\leq \alpha q(n)+r(n)$.

Theorem 3.3

(i). There exists a disjoint regular partition of $D_k(n)$, in one pass, into $q(n)+\lceil (r(n)/\alpha) \rceil$ subsets $D_k{}^{\alpha p}(n)$, $1\leq p\leq q(n)+(1/\alpha)\lceil (r(n)/\alpha) \rceil$, $n=\alpha q(n)+r(n)$, in which no size of the local memory of a cell depends on n.

(ii). $D_k^{\alpha(p+1)}(n)$ *is obtained from* $D_k^{\alpha p}(n)$ *by a translation* τ_2 *of the vector* $(n+\alpha+1, 2n+2\alpha+2)$.

(iii). $D_k(n)$ *is obtained from* $D_{k-1}(n)$ *by a translation* τ_1 *of the vector* $(0, n+1)$.

Proposition 3.1

a)- The number of cells covered by the subset $D_k^{\alpha v}$ is $n+\alpha-1$, $1 \le v \le q(n)$.

b)- The number of cells covered by the subset $D_k^{\alpha q(n)+r(n)}$ $(r \neq 0)$ is $n+r(n)-1$.

Consequently the number of cells in the array is $(n+\alpha-1)q(n)+\lceil(r(n)/\alpha)\rceil(n+r(n)-1)+(\alpha+1)q(n)$.

Remark 1. The channels and controls requirements with characteristics not depending on the size of the problem as well as the operation of a basic cell are described in [16].

4.2.5 The Linear Algorithm

From theorem 3.2, we know how to get $D_1(n)$ in $\mathbb{P}$. Therefore we can determine the times at which the data, the control signals and the addresses, which are involved in the partial computations in $D_1(n)$, are inserted into the array. The matrices A and A' have to be stored between passes. This is done by the host computer which extracts the elements a_{ij} and a'_{ij} at the end of the pass z at precise times and inserts them in the array at the beginning of the pass $z+1$ at precise times, $1 \le z < 3$. The linear array algorithm consists of inserting this data into cell 0 at appropriate clock ticks as described in the following:

1- Begin the first pass at time 0.
2- In every pass z $(1 \le z \le 3)$:
  a)- Insert a_{ij} in C_a at time $(j-1)(n+1)+r(i)+n-2+(q(i)+\lceil(r(i)/\alpha)\rceil-1)(n+\alpha+1)+(z-1)T(n)$, where $i=kq(i)+r(i)$.
  b)- Insert a'_{ij} on $C_{a'}$ at time $(i-1)(n+1)+n-j+(z-1)T(n)$.
  c) Extract a_{ij} from the last cell denoted m_{last} at time $(j-1)(n+1)+r(i)+n-2+(q(i)+\lceil(r(i)/\alpha)\rceil-1)(n+\alpha+1)+m_{last}+(z-1)T(n)$.
  d) Extract a'_{ij} from the last cell denoted m_{last} at time $(i-1)(n+1)+n-j+2m_{last}+(z-1)T(n)$.
Where $m_{last}=(n+\alpha-1)q(n)+\lceil(r(n)/\alpha)\rceil(n+r(n)-1)+2(q(n)+\lceil(r(n)/\alpha)\rceil-1)$ and $T(n)=(n-1)(n+1)+r(n)+(\alpha+3)n+(q(n)+\lceil(r(n/\alpha)\rceil-1)(n+\alpha+1)$.
This completes the description of the algorithm. At the end of the three passes, $a^*_{ij}=1$ if and only if the transitive closure of the matrix A has a 1 in that position. Another weakness of the algorithm in [18] is that one has to wait a pass to be completed before inserting data items for the next pass. In our algorithm, we do not have to wait: All coefficients a_{i1} and a'_{1j} involved in the partial computations in $D_1(n)$ are already extracted when the last coefficient namely a_{nn} (to be inserted in the pass) is inserted. So after inserting a_{nn}, we can insert the data items which are involved in the partial computations of $D_1(n)$ in the next pass.

Proposition 3.2. *(Timing and Task Allocation Functions): The coefficients a_{ik} and a'_{kj} meet in cell $r(i)+j-2+(q(i)+\lceil(r(i)/\alpha)\rceil-1)(n+\alpha+1)$ at time $(k-1)(n+1)+2r(i)+j+n-4+2(q(i)+\lceil(r(i)/\alpha)\rceil-1)(n+\alpha+1)$. Then a^*_{ij} is computed in cell $r(i)+j-2+(q(i)+\lceil(r(i)/\alpha)\rceil-1)(n+\alpha+1)$.*

Theorem 3.4

The transitive closure of an n-square adjacency matrix can be computed in an unidirectional linear array of $n^2/\alpha+O(n)$ cells in time $(3+4/\alpha)n^2+O(n)$.

4. Partially-Pipelined Matrix Multiplication With An Output Operation

This section brings slight modifications of the previous partially-pipelined linear algorithm: Add two new channels C_π, C_c. The tokens travelling in C_π, Cc encounter a delay between two consecutive cells of 1 and $\alpha+1$ clock cycles respectively. π is a boolean control signal travelling in C_π. π is set to 1 and is inserted at the same time with a_{in}, it is set to 0 and is inserted at the same time with a_{ij}, $j \neq n$. Each element of the matrix C is transferred in C_c when it is completely computed. This operation is managed by the signal π. If $\pi=1$ then the element of C which computed is transferred in C_c, otherwise it is not (see [16] for more details).

Theorem 4.1: *The multiplication of two n-square matrices can be computed, including input and output operations, in time $(1+(\alpha+1)/\alpha)n^2+O(n)$ on an array of $n^2/\alpha+O(n)$ cells.*

5. Related Work

Many modular linear systolic array algorithms for transitive closure, shortest path and matrix multiplication have appeared in the literature. In this section, we contrast our results with the previously known ones:

5.1 Transitive Closure

The most popular modular linear arrays for this problems are from Kumar and Tsai [17] and Lee and Kedem[11].
.In the Kumar and Tsai method, each cell has a local memory of size one. Moreover the coefficient a'ij has two channels. Their array is a particular case of ours when $\alpha=1$.

.Lee and Kedem did not give complexity results for their linear algorithm. However, it needs a long preprocessing and moreover it is bidirectional. Therefore it is not fault tolerant.
. The controls relative to the arrays in [15] are unbounded integers depending on the size of the adjacency matrix. Therefore they are somehow non-modular.

5.2 Matrix Multiplication

Many methods to multiply two n-square matrices have proposed among which the so called *Parallelogram method* [1, 25], Kumar and Tsai method[17, 18] and Ramakrishnan and Varman method[20, 21].

. Our design yields almost the same complexity results as the Ramakrishnan and Varman method[20]. However, a selection of an appropriate parameter before inserting the data items in their array is essential.
. The $3n^2-n-1$ time steps required by the " Run Over Technique" in [18] is practically a particular case of our results when $\alpha=1$.. The arrays in [15] need more locations per cell (1.5 times more).

5.2.1 Fully-Pipelined Linear Arrays

Our partially-pipelined linear array with an output operation has the same goal than the fully-pipelined linear arrays: The coefficients of the product of two n-square matrices must be already extracted from the array at the end of the algorithm. Thus we will compare our complexity results with those of the fully-pipelined unidirectional array in [25] which apparently is the previously more efficient one. The comparison is quite difficult since the complexity results of our method depend on α whereas those in [25] depend on X (X is the number of registers in channel C_a). To make this comparison possible we will assume that α and X quantitatively increase in the same order: Therefore our algorithm is as performant, in time, as the one in [25], furthermore it needs few cells. If the previous assumption holds, then X should be at least four times the size of the local memory in each cell in our design. It may have been interesting in [25] to exhibit the controls and to describe their effects.
. In comparison with the arrays in [24], ours are modular and more easy to handle, which is a great advantage. The weakness of the arrays in [21] is that they are bidirectional, therefore non fault tolerant.

6 Conclusion

This paper presents an alternative proposal to the parallelogram and the classical projection (Lee and Kedem) methods. We generalize the work of Prasanna and Tsai [17, 18] by deriving linear systolic arrays in which each cell has a local memory of a constant size α: The array we obtain can solve both transitive closure and matrix multiplication problems. We show that a partially-pipelined linear algorithm, with an output operation, for the matrix multiplication can be as performant, in time, as a fully-pipelined one, and in some cases need less cells. The extension of our design to the shortest path is straightforward.

References

1 A. V. Aho, J. Hopchoft and J. D. Ullman: *The design and analysis of computer algorithms* Addison-Wesley (1974).

2 A. Benaini and M. Tchuente: Matrix product on linear systolic arrays, in *Parallel and Distributed Algorithms*, M. Cosnard and al. eds, North Holland, (1989).

3 A. L. Fischer and H. T. Kung: Synchronizing large VLSI processor arrays. *Proc. Tenth Annual IEEE/ACM Symposium on Computer Architecture*, June 1983, PP. 54-58

4 L. J. Guibas, H. T. Kung and C. D. Thompson : Direct VLSI implementation of combinatorial algorithms; *Proc. Conference on very large Scale Integration: Architecture, Design, Fabrication*; California Institute of Technology (January 1979) pp. 509-525.

5 H.T. Kung: Why systolic architecture. *IEEE Computer*, 15(1) January, 1980, PP. 37-46

6 F. T. Leighton and C.E. Leiserson: Wafer-Scale integration of systolic arrays. *Proc. Twenty-third Symp. Foundations of Computer Science*, November 1982, PP. 297-311.

7 C. H. Huang and C. Langauer: An incremental mechanical development of systolic solutions to the algebraic path problem. *Acta Informatica* 27, (1989), 97-124.

8 S. Y. Kung, P. S. Lewis and S. C. Lo: On optimal mapping algorithms to systolic arrays with application to the transitive closure problem, in *Proc. 1986 IEEE Int. Symp. Circuits Syst.*, PP. 1316-1322.

9 S. Y. Kung and S. C. Lo: A spiral systolic architecture algorithm for transitive closure problems, *Proc. IEEE Int. Conf. Comput. Design*, 1985.

10 S. Y. Kung, S. C. Lo and P. S. Lewis: Optimal systolic design for transitive closure and the shortest path problems; IEEE *Trans. Comput.* C-36, No. 5, 1987, PP. 603-614.

11 P. Lee and Z. Kedem: Synthesizing linear array algorithms from nested for loop algorithms. *IEEE Trans. Comput.*, C-37 (1988), 1578-1598.

12 P. S. Lewis and S. Y. Kung: Dependence graph based design of systolic arrays for the algebraic path problem . *Proc. 12th ann. Asilomar Conf. Signals Syst., Com-put.*, 1986.

13 F. C. Lin and Wu: Systolic arrays for transitive closure algorithms in *Proc. Int. Symp.VLSI Syst. Designs*, Taipei May 1985.

14 J. F. Myoupo : A linear systolic array for transitive closure problems, *Proc. Int. Conf. Parallel Process. (ICPP)*, 1990. Vol. I, PP. 617-618.

15 J. F. Myoupo : A way of deriving linear systolic arrays from a mathematical algorithm description: Case of the Warshall-Floyd Algorithm.*Proc. Int. Conf. Parallel Process. (ICPP)*, 1991. Vol. I, PP. 575-579.

16 J. F. Myoupo and A.C. Fabret: Designing Modular Linear Systolic Arrays Using Dependence Graph Regular Partitions. Rapport Interne, L.R.I., Université Paris-Sud, 1992.

17 V. K. Prasanna Kumar and Y. C. Tsai: Designing linear systolic arrays. *J. parallel distrib. Comput.* 7 (1989), 441-463.

18 S. K. Prasanna Kumar and Y. C. Tsai: On mapping algorithms to linear and fault-tolerant systolic srrays, IEEE *Trans. Comput.* , vol. 38, No. 3 PP. 470-478, 1989.

19 I. V. Ramakrishnan, P. J. Varman : Dynamic programming and transitive closure on linear pipelines; *Proc. Int. Conf. on Parallel Processing, (ICPP)* 1984.

20 I. V. Ramakrishnan and P. J. Varman: An Optimal Family of Matrix multiplication algorithms on linear arrays; *ICPP* (1985), IEEE press, pp.376-383.

21 I. V. Ramakrishnan and P. J. Varman: Synthesis of an optimal family of matrix multiplication algorithms on linear arrays; *IEEE Trans. Computers*, C-35(11), 1986.

22 Y. Robert and D. Trystram: An orthogonal systolic array for the algebraic path problem,*Computing*, 39,PP. 187-199, 1987.

23 G. Rote: A systolic array algorithm for the algebraic path problem; *Computing;* Vol. 34 PP. 192-219, 1985.

24 U. Schwiegelshohn and L. Thiele: Linear systolic arrays for matrix computation. *J. parallel distrib. Comput.* 7 (1989), 28-39.

25 T. Risset: Linear systolic arrays for matrix multiplication: Comparison of existing synthesis methods and new results; Tech. Repport, No. 91-12 LIP, Ecole Normale Supérieure de Lyon, 1991.

26 J. D. Ullman *Computational aspects of VLSI*, Computer Science Press (1984).

27 J. L. A. Van de Snepscheut: A derivation of a distributed implementation of Warshall's algorithm. *Science of Computer Programming* 7 (1986), 55-60.

28 S. W. Warman Jr.: A modification of Warshall's algorithm for the transitive closure of binary relations; *CACM*. Vol. 18 No. 4 PP. 218-220, 1975.

29 S. Warshall: A theorem on boolean matrices; *JACM*, Vol. 9 No.1 PP. 11-12, 1972.

Reducing Symmetric Banded Matrices to Tridiagonal Form – A Comparison of a New Parallel Algorithm with two Serial Algorithms on the iPSC/860*

Bruno Lang

Institut für Angewandte Mathematik, Universität Karlsruhe
Kaiserstrasse 12, W-7500 Karlsruhe 1, Germany

Abstract. We compare three algorithms for reducing symmetric banded matrices to tridiagonal form and evaluate their performance on the Intel iPSC/860 hypercube parallel computer. Two of these algorithms, the routines BANDR and _SBTRD from the EISPACK and LAPACK libraries, resp., are serial algorithms with little potential for coarse grain parallelism. The third one, called SBTH, is a new parallel algorithm. Results on the iPSC/860 hypercube show that this new method may be several times faster than the others, *even when run on a single processor*. In addition, execution on multiple processors yields nearly full speedup.

1 Introduction

Reduction to tridiagonal form is a major step in eigenvalue computations for symmetric matrices. If the matrix is full then usually Householder's or Givens' algorithms are the methods of choice [5, 13]. However, for banded matrices, the case to be considered in the present note, these algorithms are not optimal as they do not fully exploit the band structure. Then each reduction step produces fill-in until eventually the matrix will be full, resulting in $O(n^3)$ time and $O(n^2)$ memory requirements.

A "chasing"-algorithm by H. R. Schwarz [12, 11] avoids this problem by removing *any* fill-in as soon as it occurs. This algorithm is implemented in the routine BANDR of the EISPACK library [4]. The algorithm relies on (fast) Givens rotations to selectively introduce zeroes into the band and to remove intermediate fill-in. The main part of the computations *could* be done with the _AXPY operation of the level 1 BLAS (Basic Linear Algebra Subprograms [10, 3, 2]). However, as the EISPACK library dates back farther than the evolution of the BLAS, the routine BANDR contains no call to the latter.

---

* The numerical experiments were carried out on the 8 node and 128 node iPSC/860 hypercubes of the Advanced Computing Research Facility at Argonne National Laboratory and of Oak Ridge National Laboratory, resp. Many thanks to both institutions. Special thanks to Christian Bischof for initiating my visit at Argonne National Laboratory and to the unknown referee for his valuable comments.

Another version of the same underlying method is due to L. Kaufman [7]; by rearranging the computations she was able to increase the vector lengths, if the bandwidth d is small compared to the matrix dimension n. This algorithm is incorporated into the routines _SBTRD of the recent LAPACK library [1]. Again, rotations are used to transform the matrix, but now in the form of ordinary Givens rotations. This leads to an increased overall floating point operation (*flop*) count of $6n^2d$ versus $4n^2d$ flop of the BANDR version. Another drawback of this method lies in the fact that the bulk of computations is coded in explicit loops since there is no appropriate BLAS routine to cover them.

Both methods make full use of the symmetry in the given matrix and require only the lower (or upper) half of the band to be stored. Thus, $(d+1)n$ memory locations are needed.

The third reduction algorithm SBTH (symmetric banded matrix, reduction to tridiagonal form via Householder transformations) is based – as the name indicates – on Householder transformations. It has some distinct advantages over the above mentioned implementations. First, almost all the computations can be done within the level 2 BLAS; thus, SBTH benefits of a considerably higher *data locality* than the other algorithms, a significant bonus on machines with data caches and with optimized BLAS. On the other hand, the storage requirements of the new algorithm are significantly higher ($2dn$ memory locations). The flop count is roughly the same as for the _SBTRD routines from LAPACK and therefore about 50% higher than that of the EISPACK routine.

As the figures to be presented in Sect. 4 will show, the latter drawback has no major negative impact on the performance of the new algorithm. In fact, if all three algorithms are run on *one* processor of the iPSC/860 hypercube parallel computer, the new method may perform several times better than the other algorithms. In addition, the new algorithm is well suited to parallel execution. Theoretical considerations as well as numerical experiments show that execution of this algorithm on multiple processors will yield nearly full speedup, provided that the matrix is "reasonably large".

The remainder of the note is organized as follows. Section 2 reviews the mathematics of the reduction process and introduces the new serial (block) algorithm. In Sect. 3 we will show how to exploit some of the parallelism inherent in this algorithm. Section 4 contains performance data of experiments on the iPSC/860 hypercube.

2 The reduction process

Throughout the paper, $A = (a_{ij})$ always denotes a symmetric banded matrix of dimension n and (semi-)bandwidth d, i.e. $a_{ij} = 0$ for $|i - j| > d$.

The reduction process consists of applying $n - 2$ orthogonal transformations

$$A^{(\nu+1)} := Q^{(\nu)T} \cdot A^{(\nu)} \cdot Q^{(\nu)}, \qquad \nu = 1, \ldots, n-2, \tag{1}$$

to the matrix $A^{(1)} := A$. The ν-th of these steps eliminates the ν-th column of the band, i.e. the elements $a_{\nu+2,\nu}, \ldots, a_{\nu+d,\nu}$ are made zero. Since all the

$A^{(\nu)}$ are symmetric only their lower triangle will be stored and used during the reduction.

Suppose that for the ν-th step we are able to partition $A^{(\nu)}$ as follows.

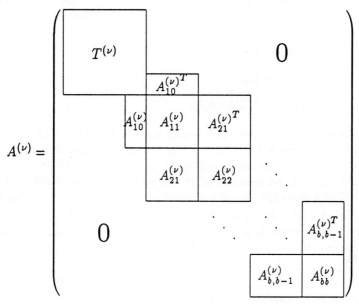

The first $\nu - 1$ columns (and rows) of the band have already been removed; thus, the leading $\nu \times \nu$ submatrix $T^{(\nu)}$ of $A^{(\nu)}$ is tridiagonal. Let $n - \nu = (b-1) \cdot d + r$, $1 \le r \le d$. Then the blocks $A^{(\nu)}_{\beta\beta} \in \mathbb{R}^{d \times d}$ $(1 \le \beta < b)$ and $A^{(\nu)}_{bb} \in \mathbb{R}^{r \times r}$ along the diagonal are symmetric. At the beginning of the algorithm ($\nu = 1$), the subdiagonal blocks $A^{(\nu)}_{\beta+1,\beta} \in \mathbb{R}^{d \times d}$ $(1 \le \beta < b - 1)$ are upper triangular, and $A^{(\nu)}_{b,b-1} \in \mathbb{R}^{r \times d}$ is upper trapezoidal. For $\nu > 1$, however, these subdiagonal blocks will be full. $A^{(\nu)}_{10}$ denotes the first of the remaining columns of the band (except for its first element which is contained in $T^{(\nu)}$).

The corresponding partition of $Q^{(\nu)}$ is

$$
Q^{(\nu)} = \begin{pmatrix}
I_\nu & & & & & 0 \\
& Q^{(\nu)}_1 & & & & \\
& & Q^{(\nu)}_2 & & & \\
& & & \ddots & & \\
0 & & & & & Q^{(\nu)}_b
\end{pmatrix}
$$

with a $\nu \times \nu$ identity matrix I_ν and "suitable" orthogonal blocks $Q_\beta^{(\nu)} \in \mathbb{R}^{d \times d}$ ($1 \le \beta < b$) and $Q_b^{(\nu)} \in \mathbb{R}^{r \times r}$.

Then the transformed matrix $\tilde{A} := Q^{(\nu)^T} \cdot A^{(\nu)} \cdot Q^{(\nu)}$ has a block structure compatible to that of $A^{(\nu)}$. For its blocks we obtain the relations

$$\tilde{A}_{10} = Q_1^{(\nu)^T} \cdot A_{10}^{(\nu)} \quad,$$

$$\tilde{A}_{\beta\beta} = Q_\beta^{(\nu)^T} \cdot A_{\beta\beta}^{(\nu)} \cdot Q_\beta^{(\nu)} \quad (1 \le \beta \le b) \quad,$$

$$\tilde{A}_{\beta+1,\beta} = Q_{\beta+1}^{(\nu)^T} \cdot A_{\beta+1,\beta}^{(\nu)} \cdot Q_\beta^{(\nu)} \quad (1 \le \beta < b) \quad.$$

Remember that, by (1), we also should have $\tilde{A} = A^{(\nu+1)}$. The block decomposition of the matrix $A^{(\nu+1)}$, however, is shifted one column to the right and one row to the bottom as compared to the decomposition of $A^{(\nu)}$ and $\tilde{A}$. This implies that some of the elements of $\tilde{A}$ will no longer be included in the blocks of $A^{(\nu+1)}$. To be more specific, the elements at positions $(2,1), \ldots, (d,1)$ in the first column of each subdiagonal block $\tilde{A}_{\beta+1,\beta}^{(\nu)}$ ($0 \le \beta < b$) will be lost when the block decomposition is shifted. Therefore, we have to make sure that they *already are zero*; this can by enforced by a suitable choice of the transformation matrices $Q_{\beta+1}^{(\nu)}$ (see below).

This leads to the following serial reduction algorithm (for ease of reading, the superscripts (ν) have been dropped):

Algorithm 1 *Serial reduction algorithm*

> **for** $\nu = 1$ **to** $n - 2$
>   *(adopt the block decomposition for step ν)*
>   *determine b and r such that $n - \nu = (b-1) \cdot d + r$ with $1 \le r \le d$*
>   *determine an orthogonal matrix Q_1 such that $\tilde{A}_{10} := Q_1^T \cdot A_{10}$ has the*
>   *form $(*, 0, \ldots, 0)^T$; replace A_{10} by $\tilde{A}_{10}$*
>   **for** $\beta = 1$ **to** b
>   *replace $A_{\beta\beta}$ by $\tilde{A}_{\beta\beta} := Q_\beta^T \cdot A_{\beta\beta} \cdot Q_\beta$*
>   **if** $\beta < b$
>   *determine an orthogonal matrix $Q_{\beta+1}$ such that the first column*
>   *of $\tilde{A}_{\beta+1,\beta} := Q_{\beta+1}^T (A_{\beta+1,\beta} Q_\beta)$ has the form $(*, 0, \ldots, 0)^T$;*
>   *replace $A_{\beta+1,\beta}$ by $\tilde{A}_{\beta+1,\beta}$*

As indicated earlier, the blocks Q_β may be chosen as Householder matrices of size $d \times d$ or – in the case of Q_b – $r \times r$. Q_1 eliminates all but the first elements of A_{10} which is the first of the remaining columns in the band. To determine $Q_{\beta+1}$ ($\beta \ge 1$), one computes the first column of the matrix $A_{\beta+1,\beta} \cdot Q_\beta$ and then choses $Q_{\beta+1}$ to eliminate all but the first elements of this column vector.

Thus, for each value of β, the bulk of computations is comprised in three matrix vector products, a symmetric rank2 update of the block $A_{\beta\beta}$ and a general rank2 update of the block $A_{\beta+1,\beta}$, all of which can be done with level 2 BLAS routines. The remaining $O(d)$ operations are covered by the level 1 BLAS.

It should be noted that – unless tricky programming is used – the band must be moved for each pass through the ν loop. This fact is reflected by the first statement in the loop (*adopt ...*).

3 Exploiting parallelism

While for the BANDR and _SBTRD algorithms it seems to be very difficult to introduce more than a very fine grained parallelism [6], the serial algorithm given in Sect. 2 bears a twofold potential for exploiting parallelism. First, *different* blocks may be transformed simultaneously. In this section we will use a pipelined approach to make use of this medium grained *parallelism between different blocks*. An additional level of parallelism can be obtained by further distributing the work for the transformation of *single* blocks to multiple processors. This – slightly finer grained – *parallelism within the blocks* will not be treated in the present note; details to that topic may be found in [9, 8].

In the sequel, we will always treat the blocks by pairs; to make this explicit we introduce the notation of a *block pair*: $B_\beta := \begin{pmatrix} A_{\beta\beta} \\ A_{\beta+1,\beta} \end{pmatrix} (\beta \geq 0)$.

There are three major steps in changing the serial algorithm into an efficient parallel program which makes best use of the parallelism between different blocks. First, we will make it a *distributed* algorithm. This means that the work is distributed among the processors but that at any given time only one processor is active. Then, a "local view" of the block decomposition introduced in Sect. 2 will be the key for introducing parallelism. Last, we optimize the data layout and the algorithmic flow to improve the performance.

We begin by distributing the block pairs to different processors P_β, $\beta = 0, 1, \ldots$, such that block pair B_β is assigned to processor P_β (cf. the first picture of Fig. 1). The processors are assumed to be linearly connected to form a chain.

To match the data distribution, the work of Alg. 1 must also be distributed among the processors. In each pass through the ν loop, processor P_0 begins by eliminating the first of the remaining columns of the band. Then P_0 sends the transformation matrix $Q_1^{(\nu)}$ to P_1 which transforms its block pair B_1 and thereby generates a new transformation matrix $Q_2^{(\nu)}$. Now P_1 passes this matrix to its successor P_2 which in turn transforms its block pair B_2 and determines $Q_3^{(\nu)}$. Continuing in this way, the activity moves along the chain of processors until all the block pairs are processed. At this moment the block decomposition must be shifted for the next pass through the ν loop. This implies that – except for P_0 – each processor P_β has to send the first column of its transformed block pair to its predecessor $P_{\beta-1}$.

A simple modification of this scheme allows some of the processors to operate simultaneously. The key observation is that the first column of the transformed B_1 is not affected by the ensuing operations in any block pair $B_\beta, \beta > 1$. Therefore, P_1 can send this column back to P_0 as soon as the transformation of B_1 is completed; there is no need to wait until *all* the computations corresponding to $Q^{(\nu)}$ are done. This enables P_0 to *locally* shift its block pair B_0 and to eliminate the $(\nu + 1)$-st column of the band, while P_2 is still transforming its block pair according to $Q_2^{(\nu)}$. The same argument also applies to the other processors P_β. As soon as they receive a column from their successor $P_{\beta+1}$ they locally shift their own block pair and apply the next transformation to it.

Figure 1 gives a sketch of the "start up" of the resulting parallel Alg. 2. To let the complete tridiagonal matrix T assemble in P_0 the ν loop ends with $n - 1$ instead of $n - 2$, as it did in Alg. 1. The additional last pass requires no computation. Of course, we do not send the Householder matrices as such but only the associated Householder vectors.

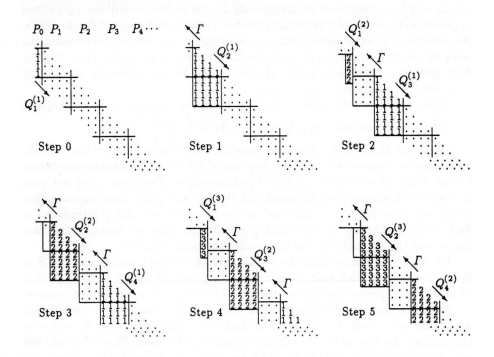

Fig. 1. Computational activity and communication during the "start up" of Alg. 2. The lines indicate the block boundaries; the first picture also includes the distribution of the block pairs to the processors. The matrix elements depicted by digits are modified in the corresponding time step; the digit ν in B_β indicates that this block pair is transformed according to $Q_{\cdots}^{(\nu)}$, i.e., that the transformation is a consequence of the elimination of the ν-th column of the band. The $\bullet$ elements are not touched. Γ stands for the transport of the first column of a block pair, $Q_{\beta+1}^{(\nu)}$ for the newly determined transformation matrix. Communication always takes place at the *end* of the time step, after the computations.

Algorithm 2 *Parallel reduction algorithm, raw version (two different programs for processor 0 and for the remaining processors, resp.).*

P_0 :   for $\nu = 1$ to $n-1$
                determine Q_1 and replace A_{10} by $\tilde{A}_{10}$
                send (Q_1) to P_1
                receive (B_0) from P_1

P_β $(\beta \geq 1)$: for $\nu = 1$ to $n-1$
                if B_β is not empty
                    receive (Q_β) from $P_{\beta-1}$
                    replace $A_{\beta\beta}$ by $\tilde{A}_{\beta\beta}$
                    if $A_{\beta+1,\beta}$ is not empty
                        determine $Q_{\beta+1}$ and replace $A_{\beta+1,\beta}$ by $\tilde{A}_{\beta+1,\beta}$
                    send (first column of B_β) to $P_{\beta-1}$
                    shift B_β to the right/bottom by one column/row
                    if $B_{\beta+1}$ is not empty
                        send $(Q_{\beta+1})$ to $P_{\beta+1}$
                        receive (last column of B_β) from $P_{\beta+1}$

As the transformations according to $Q^{(1)}$ progress along the band, more and more processors become active (cf. Fig. 1), until the end of the band is reached. Later on, as the remaining band becomes shorter, an increasing number of processors falls back to inactivity because their block pairs are "empty". It is not hard to see [9] that on the average, of the $p^* = \lceil (n-1)/d \rceil + 1$ processors which shared the band at the start of the algorithm, only one half will hold a non-empty block pair. Therefore, one half of the available computational power is lost by load imbalance.

In addition, only one half of the processors with non-empty block pairs can work at any given time, as may be observed from Fig. 1. The other processors are idle because they are waiting for transformation matrices from their left neighbors and for columns from their right neighbors. Thus, the attainable speedup is reduced by another factor of 2.

Fortunately there are methods to circumvent much of this loss in efficiency if we are willing to use less than the p^* processors which were assumed for Alg. 2. By halving the number of processors (and slightly changing the data distribution) we can completely eliminate the "idle waiting" time mentioned above, and further reduction of the number of processors (to $n/(10d)$, say) almost eliminates the load imbalance resulting from empty block pairs. The details of these optimizations may be found in [9, 8].

4   Experiments on the iPSC/860 hypercube

The numerical experiments were performed on the 8 node and 128 node iPSC/860 hypercube parallel computers at Argonne National Laboratory and at Oak Ridge National Laboratory, resp.

All programs are written in standard Fortran77, the calls to the BLAS were directed to the optimized assembly-coded BLAS of Kuck and Associates. All computations were done in double precision and do *not* include accumulation of the transformation matrix.

The EISPACK routine BANDR is available via netlib. As the LAPACK library was not yet public at the time of the experiments, we had to use the final test version of the library; thus, the DSBTRD (double precision version of _SBTRD) results are only preliminary. In our SBTH algorithm we exploited only the parallelism between different blocks.

The flop counts are exact for the SBTH algorithm with Householder transformations. We use the *same* flop count for the algorithms BANDR and DSBTRD although they actually have different operation counts: BANDR needs about $4n^2d$ flop, DSBTRD and SBTH require roughly $6n^2d$ flop. Thus, the Mflops performance of the EISPACK routine is overestimated by about 50%.

By adopting this "biased" flop count we are able to compare the *execution time* of the library algorithms BANDR and DSBTRD with the new algorithm SBTH (run on one processor), as well as with each other. For example, if the indicated Mflops rate of BANDR is twice that of SBTH then SBTH needs twice as long to complete. This information seems to be more relevant for practical use than mere Mflops throughput.

From the Mflops/processor figures for parallel execution of the algorithm SBTH one can easily obtain two other figures often reported in the literature: the overall performance (just multiply by the number of processors in use) and the speedup (divide the overall parallel performance by the performance on one processor).

Figure 2 summarizes the measurements for matrices of (semi-)bandwidth $d = 5$ and varying matrix dimension n. The curves indicate that the EISPACK routine is about two times faster than the LAPACK counterpart and three times faster than our algorithm, run on a single processor. But, if the latter is run on multiple processors, and if each processor holds a "sufficient" number of columns (about 100) we obtain nearly full speedup. Thus, the parallel algorithm will be superior if it is run on four processors or more.

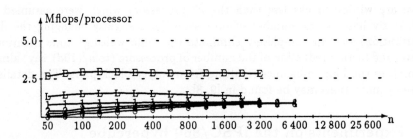

Fig. 2. Performance of the reduction algorithms for (semi-)bandwidth $d = 5$. The "E" and "L" curves correspond to the algorithms of the EISPACK and LAPACK library, resp., which are run on one processor. The curves "1", "2", "4" and "8" (from top to bottom) correspond to the parallel algorithm run on the respective number of processors.

For $d = 10$ the situation has slightly changed, as may be seen in Fig. 3. Now, the parallel algorithm has caught up with the LAPACK routine even if it is run on a single processor.

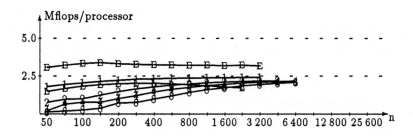

Fig. 3. Performance of the reduction algorithms for (semi-)bandwidth $d = 10$.

It is noteworthy that the *absolute time* for reducing a matrix with semibandwidth 10 with the new algorithm is *less* than for a matrix of the same order with semibandwidth 5, although nearly twice as many operations are needed.

This is due to the varying performance of the underlying BLAS. For very small blocks ($d = 5$) the overhead for calling a subroutine more than outweighs the gain from assembly coding within the BLAS, and therefore a Fortran program with all arithmetic coded in loops would be about twice as fast as the BLAS-based code we used for our timings. With increasing semibandwidth, however, there are *fewer* calls to the BLAS, and the blocks are bigger. Thus, for $d = 10$ our program is competitive with its loop-based counterpart.

For $d = 20$ – and all values of n – the situation has turned completely in favour of the new algorithm (see Fig. 4). It now achieves about 5 Mflops on one processor while the EISPACK and LAPACK routines are well below.

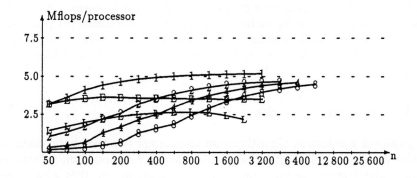

Fig. 4. Performance of the reduction algorithms for (semi-)bandwidth $d = 20$.

Again, the absolute time for reducing a matrix of semibandwidth 20 is less than for a matrix of same order and $d = 10$. This still is an effect of increasing BLAS performance: Doubling the blocksize from 5 to 10 more than doubles the Mflops performance of the BLAS, and it does again for $d = 10/d = 20$.

With increasing semibandwidth the performance of the new algorithm further increases (Figures 5 and 6) and reaches nearly 15 Mflops on one processor for $d = 113$ (the biggest bandwidth in our experiments) which is about four times the highest performance we were able to obtain from the EISPACK and LAPACK routines.

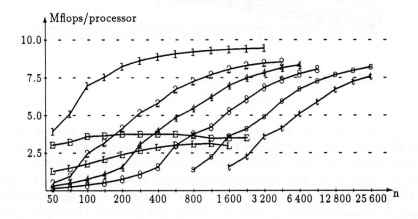

Fig. 5. Performance of the reduction algorithms for (semi-)bandwidth $d = 40$. The curves "s" and "t" correspond to the parallel algorithm run on 16 and 32 processors, resp.

Finally we wish to emphasize that the parallel algorithm *scales* well if the problem size is increased with the number of processors. To this end, we draw the data for (semi-)bandwidth $d = 80$ in a slightly different way: in Fig. 7, we plot the performance against the number of columns *per processor* instead of the matrix dimension n. The figure indicates that the performance per processor is almost independent of the number of processors as long as we keep the number of columns per processor constant. In fact, the curves for 4, 8, 16 and 32 processors nearly coincide.

5 Concluding remarks

We presented a reduction algorithm with an inherent two-level parallelism. The parallelism between different blocks can be efficiently exploited on a distributed memory architecture, as the numerical experiments on the iPSC/860 demonstrate. The performance scales well with the number of processors if the number of columns per processor is kept sufficiently large.

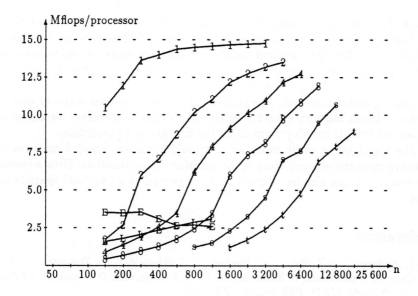

Fig. 6. Performance of the reduction algorithms for (semi-)bandwidth $d = 113$.

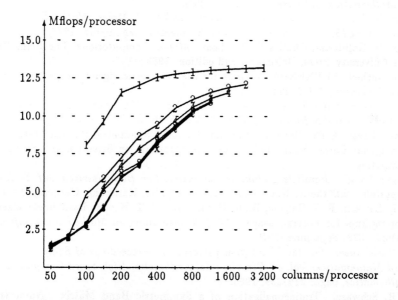

Fig. 7. Performance of the algorithm SBTH for (semi-)bandwidth $d = 80$ as a function of the number of columns per processor. The "x" indicates a single run on 64 processors.

On the iPSC/860 it does not pay to utilize the additional parallelism within the blocks, unless the bandwith is rather large [8]. The reasons for this are twofold. First, the finer grained parallelism requires more communication and more organizational overhead, and second, the BLAS are performing much worse since they are called with smaller submatrices.

The algorithm, however, is equally well suited to shared memory and distributed/shared memory hybrid architectures. On such machines we expect significant additional speedup from using the fine grained parallelism.

The algorithm is easily modified to handle hermitian banded matrices and to incorporate the accumulation of the transformation matrices. Future research will reveal if it can also be adapted to more general (e.g., skyline) sparsity patterns.

References

1. E. Anderson, Z. Bai, C. Bischof, J. Demmel, J. Dongarra, J. Du Croz, A. Greenbaum, S. Hammarling, A. McKenney, and D. Sorensen. *LAPACK User's guide*. SIAM, Philadelphia, PA, 1992.
2. Jack Dongarra, Jeremy Du Croz, Iain Duff, and Sven Hammarling. A set of Level 3 Basic Linear Algebra Subprograms. *ACM Transactions on Mathematical Software*, 16(1):1–17, 1990.
3. Jack J. Dongarra, Jeremy Du Croz, Sven Hammarling, and Richard J. Hanson. An extended set of Fortran basic linear algebra subprograms. *ACM Transactions on Mathematical Software*, 14(1):1–17, 1988.
4. B. S. Garbow, J. M. Boyle, J. J. Dongarra, and C. B. Moler. *Matrix Eigensystem Routines—EISPACK Guide Extension*. Springer-Verlag, Berlin, 1977.
5. Gene H. Golub and Charles F. Van Loan. *Matrix Computations*. The Johns Hopkins University Press, Baltimore, 2nd edition, 1989.
6. Inge Gutheil. SUPRENUM software for the symmetric eigenvalue problem. *Parallel Computing*, 7:419–424, 1988.
7. L. Kaufman. Banded Eigenvalue Solvers on Vector Machines. *ACM Transactions on Mathematical Software*, 10(1):73–86, March 1984.
8. Bruno Lang. A Parallel Algorithm for Reducing Symmetric Banded Matrices to Tridiagonal Form. Submitted to the SIAM Journal on Scientific and Statistical Computing.
9. Bruno Lang. *Parallele Reduktion symmetrischer Bandmatrizen auf Tridiagonalgestalt*. PhD thesis, Universität Karlsruhe (TH), Karlsruhe, Germany, 1991.
10. C. L. Lawson, R. J. Hanson, R. J. Kincaid, and F. T. Krogh. Basic linear algebra subprograms for Fortran usage. *ACM Transactions on Mathematical Software*, 5(3):308–323, September 1979.
11. H. Rutishauser. On Jacobi rotation patterns. In *Proceedings of Symposia in Applied Mathematics, Vol. 15 Experimental Arithmetic, High Speed Computing and Mathematics*, pages 219–239, 1963.
12. H. R. Schwarz. Tridiagonalization of a Symmetric Band Matrix. *Numerische Mathematik*, 12:231–241, 1968.
13. James H. Wilkinson. *The Algebraic Eigenvalue Problem*. Clarendon Press, Oxford, 1965.

This article was processed using the LaTeX macro package with LLNCS style

An Implementation of the BLAS on the i860 : A *RISC* Approach to Software for RISC Devices

Bob Wilkinson[1] and Lawrence S. Mulholland[2]

[1] C.M.S.R., University Of Liverpool ***
[2] Department of Mathematics, University Of Keele †

Abstract. The Liverpool Single-transputer library [10] was ported to the i860 as part of the Esprit Genesis project, P2702. There are approximately 250 routines in this library, including the BLAS (which are a well-known set of subroutines providing functions commonly used in numerical computing, see [8],[3], [2],[1]) and a set of vector routines, known as the FLO routines [9], which define operations on up to as many as five vectors. The transputer version of the library was written almost totally in assembler with individual routines coded separately.

This strategy is expensive to implement on new processors, especially highly structured ones such as the i860. The software was, therefore, implemented with a similar philosophy to that of the hardware designers in designing the hardware. It was coded in a modular form to utilise a few carefully optimised core routines.

The results were encouraging : the number of assembler routines was significantly reduced and large speed-ups were obtained over Fortran.

Keywords: BLAS, RISC, Fortran, hierarchical memory, linear algebra

1 Introduction

There have been profound changes in the design of recent microprocessor hardware. Formerly, the aim was to provide as many functions as possible in hardware (the *CISC* approach). Following analysis of the usage of these devices, it was soon apparent that the processors were executing approximately ten per cent of their instruction set ninety per cent of the time. Those instructions which were used most of the time were the simpler instructions in the instruction set (e.g. adding integers). To better use the silicon, hardware designers decided only to provide these ten per cent of frequently used instructions in hardware, and build up the other instructions from combinations of these (the *RISC* approach).

The level 1 BLAS [8] define operations on one or two vectors e.g. vector scaling by a constant, dot product of two vectors. The level 2 BLAS [3] define operations on a matrix and one or two vectors e.g. matrix-vector product. The level 3 BLAS [2] define operations between matrices. e.g. matrix-matrix product. Our software has a similar hierarchical usage pattern to the instruction set of the CISC processors.

*** Thanks to Cliff Addison and Mike Delves of CMSR for help and comments on this paper. Partial funding for this work was provided by Esprit Genesis project, P2702.
† This work was carried out while the author was at N.A. Software, Liverpool

Those routines which operate on only one or two vectors are more useful than those which operate on four or five. Most of the vector operations involving three, four or five vectors, have common sub-components which operate on one or two vectors [9]. As a consequence of this, and the need to provide a number of variants of each routine, a decision was taken to write the more useful routines in assembler. The more complicated vector routines and the level 2 BLAS were coded as Fortran shells with calls to these assembler routines. The level 2 BLAS generally use a matrix to update a vector. This *re-used* vector is assumed to be cached, and the matrix is assumed to be in external memory. During the T800 implementation the level 3 BLAS were written as Fortran shells to call level 1 and level 2 BLAS. This approach provides quite good performance on the i860, however, better performance was obtained by writing them using calls to an assembler matrix-matrix multiplication primitive, utilising *blocking* ([4],[7]).

In the final version, the library is defined by only 11 assembler source code files. There are also 24 files of *sed* commands, which are used to map one of these *base* source routines on to a *derived* routine. e.g. the vector add routine, _vadd, is a derivative of the vector multiply routine, _vmul.

2   Hardware Considerations

The i860 microprocessor is a very-high performance RISC device, with a peak rate of 80 megaflops ([6]). The architecture includes a number of distinct functional units on the chip, including an integer processor and a floating-point unit. The clock on the i860 works at 40MHz. There are 32 32-bit floating point registers on the chip, which can also be used as 16 64-bit registers. The microprocessor uses wide data paths to be able to sustain high-performance. The register-cache data bus is 128 bits wide; the external data bus is 64 bits wide. The register-cache bus can transfer data on each clock cycle, whereas the external data bus can return data on alternate clock cycles. Thus, the internal bandwidth is a factor of four higher than the external bandwidth. The i860 multiplexes the external address and data buses (some processors provide separate external buses for instructions and data accesses).

The i860 has an 8K data cache and a 4K instruction cache. The instruction cache is used to store the most recently used instructions. The data cache is used to store that data which has been loaded most recently using the ld or fld instructions. i.e. not using the pfld instruction which *does not* disturb the cache. The data cache is arranged in two banks with a 32-byte line size, and it uses *write-back* caching.

Since the i860 comprises a number of discrete functional units, there is a certain amount of implicit parallelism. There are instructions for the floating-point unit which use the floating-point adder and multiplier concurrently (known as *dual-operation* mode) which chain the output of the multiplier to one of the inputs of the adder. In *dual-operation* mode two operations are performed per cycle in single-precision (giving rise to a maximum megaflop rate of 80), and two operations are performed on alternate cycles in double-precision. It is also possible to program the i860 in a manner (known as *dual-instruction* mode) in which alternate integer and floating-point instructions in the source code are executed simultaneously. *Dual-operation* instructions can be used in *dual-instruction* mode, too. An algorithm must map well on to the architecture to realise the full potential of the machine.

All of the functional units on the i860 use *pipelining*. The integer unit uses a four-stage pipeline (fetch, decode, execute and write). In general, load instructions work with a five-stage pipeline, however, the instruction which explicitly loads from external memory, `pfld`, uses a three-stage pipeline explicitly (which gives rise to six cycles in total). The floating-point adder has a three stage pipeline, and the multiplier has three stages in single precision, and two stages in double precision.

Pipelined and non-pipelined instructions are provided for the floating-point units. In non-pipelined mode the adder returns a result in three clock cycles. In pipelined mode the adder returns a result each clock cycle. In non-pipelined mode the multiplier returns a result in three cycles in single-precision, and four cycles in double-precision. In pipelined mode the multiplier returns a result each cycle in single-precision, and on alternate cycles in double-precision.

This implementation of the BLAS involved using the integer and floating-point processors, and the data cache. In general, the routines used the integer unit to test the input parameters, and to branch to code blocks. It was then used for loop control and loading data for the floating-point registers; either from the data cache, or from external memory. It was also used for manipulating the sign bits of data. The appropriate floating-point units were used for the routines; wherever possible *dual-operation* mode was employed. In all cases involving floating-point operations *dual-instruction* mode was used.

3 Software Considerations

3.1 Vector Routines : Level 1 BLAS and FLO Routines

Reducing the Amount of Source Code in the Library. Where possible the source code was written to solve generic problems. For example, the code to add a scalar to a vector is very similar to that which subtracts a vector from a scalar. The mapping between the *generic* source code and any *specific* piece of source code was kept inside a small file, which contains a list of editor commands. When the *specific* source code was created, it was compiled to object code, and placed in the library. The *specific* source code may be discarded. This way of organising the source code involves having less code to maintain. Any general changes across the small set of software can be made by modifying the *generic* case, and re-*making* (and retesting) the new object codes. The *generic* source code has mnemonic labels placed inside it to facilitate the production of new object codes.

Provision of Special Cases. It was *essential* to write separate code blocks for small problems (when the data is in the cache), and for larger problems (when some of the data is not in the cache). This was because code which uses the cache can load data at about four times the rate possible if the data were coming from external memory (640 MBytes/s vs. 160 MBytes/s).

Only when vectors are small can they be found in the cache. A vector of length greater than the cache-size will *never* be (totally) in the cache. It must be assumed that small objects are available in the cache, and that as much work as possible is performed on a *cache-full* of memory.

This leads to the following: under a certain problem size the data is assumed to be cached, and above this some of the data is assumed to be in main memory. The *cachesize* parameter is defined in an `include` file for the routines. Consideration of these aspects of cache use in a hierarchical memory system is important. The performance of the processor will never get anywhere near its theoretical peak value without a high rate of data throughput.

The *stride* of the vectors being manipulated needed to be considered, too. In the case of `real` numbers, the general (i.e. non-unit stride) case only permits the use of the instruction which loads four bytes at a time. However, by recognising the special cases of unit-strided problems, it is possible to increase the cache-register bandwidth by a factor of four by using the instruction which loads sixteen contiguous bytes of data per cycle.

The performance gains obtainable by using the above prior knowledge outweigh the coding costs. Notice that the general case is not the most common (the routines are usually called with unit-strided vectors). The decision paths taken by the _**axpy** routines are as documented in Fig. 1.

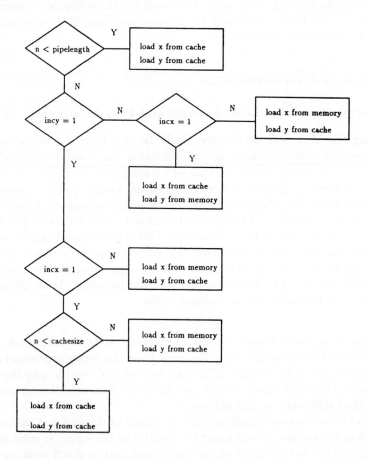

Fig. 1. Flow chart implemented for _axpy

A further implication is that non-unit strided vectors (e.g. rows of Fortran matrices) should not be assumed to be cached, since the objects of which they are a part will probably be too large for the cache (which can hold 8Kbytes). If they are small enough to fit in the cache the penalties associated with reading from main memory rather than the cache will necessarily be small in absolute terms - it is a small problem.

Subroutines to handle specific forms of data access were written for the real cases of the _dot and _axpy routines. The single-precision routines are named :

- sdotcc, sdotmc
- saxpycc, saxpymc, saxpycm

The routines whose names end in the letters cc take both the x and y vectors from the cache. The routines whose names end in the letters mc take the x vector from the main memory, and the y vector from the cache. Saxpycm takes the x vector from the cache, and the y vector from the main memory.

It was found experimentally that the inclusion of these specific versions of _axpy and _dot results in an improvement in performance in the level 2 BLAS by a factor of between 2 and 3.

Strip Mining. If a problem re-uses a large vector which will not fit into the data cache, many cache misses will be encountered, leading to performance degradation. This phenomenon is known as *cache thrashing*. In such cases, it is better to divide the problem into smaller sub-problems (a technique known as *strip-mining*). Those vector routines in the library which have not been explicitly coded in assembler have been written in Fortran and stripmined calling the underlying assembler routines.

It is clear that many of the points raised here will be applicable to other devices (especially those which use a cache and registers, and have a set of floating point unit instructions distinct from the set of integer unit instructions). It should be possible to follow the same approach as outlined here, in order to implement the BLAS routines on other *superscalar* processors, such as the T-9000 or the IBM RS-6000.

3.2 Matrix-Vector Routines : Level 2 BLAS

Introduction. The level 2 and level 3 BLAS were originally defined because it proved impossible on advanced vector architectures to achieve high performance solely based on assembler-coded level 1 BLAS.

The assembler routines used take advantage of the hierarchical memory structure and so have performances which depend on the size of the cache of memory. In writing subroutines which call assembler routines, strategies were adopted that led to algorithms which took account of the cache-size and split the problem into a series of cache-manageable blocks. The results show that if this is carefully done, and if a suitably extended set of optimised level 1 routines are available, then the level 2 codes (and hence the level 3 codes) can be efficiently implemented in pure Fortran77. In addition, the results show that implementations of the level 3 BLAS are best designed by adopting more than one strategy to accommodate the various problem shapes that arise.

Strip Mining. For matrix-vector operations the idea of stripmining reduces to the slicing of a target vector into a set of subvectors of length less than cache-size. Each subvector is then the subject of a sequence of _axpy or _dot operations. To illustrate the technique, consider the case of **strmv** which performs the level 2 operation $x \leftarrow Ax$ where A is lower(say)-triangular. Fig. 2 shows how the stripmining transforms the operation into a set of sub-operations.

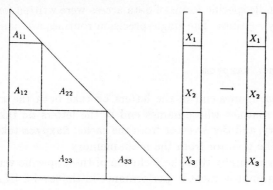

Fig. 2. 3-block partitioning in stripmined **strmv**

In general, if the vector x is sliced into r blocks then the algorithm breaks down into the following loop of subproblems:

$$
\begin{aligned}
&\text{DO } 10 \ k = r, 1, -1 \\
&\qquad x_k \leftarrow A_{k,k} x_k \\
&\qquad \text{IF(} k.\text{NE}.1 \text{) } x_k \leftarrow x_k + A_{k-1,k} \begin{bmatrix} x_1 \\ \vdots \\ x_{k-1} \end{bmatrix}
\end{aligned}
$$

10 CONTINUE

Every one of the level 2 BLAS can be similarly broken down into a loop of subproblems, and each subproblem is equivalent to a level 2 BLAS operation applied to a vector of limited length.

Calling Level 1 BLAS Assembler Codes. The new versions of the level 2 BLAS use the following level 1 codes: _scal, _axpy, _dot, _copy,[8] and the FLO routine _vclr [9]. The performance of the _axpy and _dot assembler codes, which replace the innermost loops of all the level 2 BLAS, is critical to their performance. From an analysis of the performance of _axpy and _dot it is clear that the greatest improvements in performance will come when the cached vector is of unit stride and the lengths of the vectors used in level 1 calls are a proportion of, but not exceeding, the cache-size of the machine used. Thus a good speed-up factor for _gemv (the general matrix-vector multiplication routine) would be expected when the y vector is of unit stride and has dimension close to cache-size. On the other hand, in routines for banded matrices, the vector lengths are at most the bandwidth when _axpy or _dot forms of operations are performed; this means that for small bandwidths, the likely speed-up in performance will be relatively moderate.

On the face of it, _gemv should not seem worthy of special consideration, however, its very generality allows for a case where the simplest vectorising philosophy will lead to very poor performance results. The case in point is where the matrix multiplier has few rows but many columns (*i.e.* M small, N large). In this case, the usual course of applying a sequence of _axpy operations will be inefficient because the vectors will be of length M. However, if the rows of the matrix were accessed by a constant (non-unit) stride then a sequence of _dot operations can be applied with vector lengths of N; for small values of M this approach is likely to achieve performances superior to those of the _axpy approach. To illustrate this point, Fig. 3 shows the respective timings of the unit-stride _axpy and M-stride _dot methods, for various values of M (N kept constant at 1000), as applied in sgemv. From Fig. 3 it can be seen that the

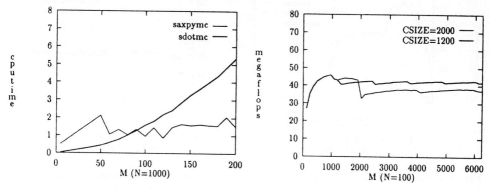

Fig. 3. A graph of cputime v M for 100 iterations of unit-strided sgemv

Fig. 4. A graph of megaflops v M for 10 iterations of unit-strided sgemv

sdotmc method outperforms the saxpymc method for all values of M less than 75. This cut-off mark of $M = 75$ has been found, by experimentation, to be invariant under $N \geq 100$. As a result of experiments, the dotmc approach has been included in the code for the _gemv subroutines and is invoked whenever the leading dimension of the matrix is less than the (experimentally determined) constant CUT. The included piece of code, invoked when $lda < CUT$, has also been stripmined to take account of the case $N > cache\text{-}size$.

Cache Size Assumptions. In the various codes the paramete $CSIZE$ (the block-size, or assumed cache-size) is set at a vector length appropriate to the data-type, assuming that the actual cache-size is 8Kb. This assumption may seem to reduce the portability of the routines, since their implementation may take place on architectures containing larger (or smaller) caches, but, the actual performances remain close to optimal over a wide range of assumed cache-sizes. That is, there may be no need to alter the settings of $CSIZE$ in many instances, provided $CSIZE$ is smaller than the maximum physical cache-size. Meaningful results on the effect of stripmining can be obtained by employing versions of _gemv on matrices with a large number of rows and a fixed small number of columns. Fig. 4 plots the performance of **sgemv** against number of rows of the matrix for two different block sizes.

It can be seen that a block-size which is approximately two-thirds of the actual cache-size provides for a better overall performance than a block-size close to the cache-size. Fig. 4 also shows that stripmining allows a level of performance, close to the maximum, to be maintained for problem sizes many times greater than the cache-size. It seems clear from these graphs, at least for the _gemv routines, that it is better to stripmine using a block-size which is some proportion of the actual cache-size rather than attempt to fill the cache with a block of the target vector. The reason for this is that the performance of the level 1 assembler routines tails off as the vector length comes close to cache-size, as shown in Fig. 5.

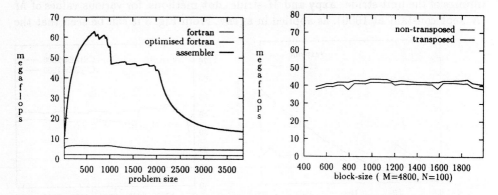

Fig. 5. Performance characterisation of 1000 **Fig. 6.** A graph of megaflops v block-size for iterations of unit-strided **saxpy**   10 iterations of unit-strided sgemv

In order to determine the optimal block-size in the case of _gemv Fig. 6 plots the performances of **sgemv** against various block-sizes, with M fixed at 4800 and N fixed at 100. This figure shows that there is a wide range of block-sizes which would provide a satisfactory level of performance although the optimal performance level is achieved as a plateau in one region: for block-sizes between 984 and 1128. A satisfactory strategy, in the case of the _gemv routines, is to choose a block-size which is approximately one-half of the actual cache-size. These results were measured on a Meiko MK086 board. A peak rate of 62 MegaFlops was obtained in preliminary timings on the new MK096 board.

3.3 Blocked Level 3 BLAS

High performances may be achieved by the level 3 BLAS (see [2]) by writing them in terms of the stripmined level 2 BLAS. Although this technique is convenient, it is not ideal with respect to maximising the number of operations on cache-resident data. The cache would be more efficiently used in this instance by storing there a rectangular block of one matrix and a contiguous piece of another at any one time. This strategy is referred to in the literature as blocking (see for example [4],[7]).

The most efficient blocking algorithms will be those which break down the operations into a set of dot-products operating on cache-resident data. This is because `dot` routines are intrinsically faster than `axpy` routines; the difference in performance is particularly marked for small vector lengths.

The core of the blocking algorithms for the level 3 BLAS are either written to call level 1 assembler routines, or to call the assembler matrix multiply routines. The former approach has the disadvantage that each level 1 operation will operate over small vector lengths (and thus limiting the performance) due to the smallness of the cache; the latter approach, on the other hand, performs a set of back-to-back level 1 operations without the overhead of successive 'CALL' statements.

4 Results

General Comments. $N_{\frac{1}{2}}$ and r_∞ are as defined in [5]. All timings were recorded on a Meiko MK086 board. All Fortran routines were compiled using Green Hills i860 compiler, `if77860`. No compiler flags were explicitly set : the default options were used. The processor clock speed is 40 MHz, and the attached DRAM memory is 3-cycle. Normalised data is used for the timings.

In practice, it has been observed that the speed of some of the vector routines (involving double-precision arithmetic and dual-operation mode) is much less than would be expected. This may be a manifestation of the speed of the attached memory, or else there may be a bug in the hardware that was used to time the routines, or perhaps, it is a software problem. The performance of the routines appears to be better on newer hardware, such as the Meiko MK096 board.

The Tables 1, 2 and 3 contain results for benchmarks. These are artificial (especially Table 1) in that they perform more than one iteration of the problem with the same data set. This is, however, necessary since one iteration does not take sufficient time to be measured accurately. Table 4 compares the megaflop rates of some higher level routines, with and without, using the BLAS library.

4.1 Level 1 BLAS Results

Table 1. Performance Table for 50 Iterations of Unit-Strided Real Level 1 BLAS

generic routine	Single Precision r_{max}	$n_{r_{max}}$	Double Precision r_{max}	$n_{r_{max}}$	generic routine	Single Precision r_{max}	$n_{r_{max}}$	Double Precision r_{max}	$n_{r_{max}}$
_dot	56.3	432	18.4	776	_rot	39.2	936	26.3	264
_dotcc	57.3	440	18.0	288	_rotm	39.6	448	26.0	216
_dotmc	47.1	1176	18.5	768	_copy	189.6	1032	187.5	480
_axpy	55.2	672	17.7	624	_swap	431.1	552	424.9	272
_axpycc	55.2	672	16.5	264	_nrm2	51.7	1656	19.2	3192
_axpymc	45.7	1344	17.8	648	_asum	7.3	792	5.7	456
_axpycm	16.7	1152	8.3	840	_scal	34.9	1160	17.5	560
					i_amax	9.1	1912	8.4	824

Comments. Megaflop rates are given for those routines which perform arithmetic, and bandwidths (in MBytes per second) are given for `_copy` and `_swap`.

No $n_{\frac{1}{2}}$ figures have been given for the vector routines since the hierarchical memory structure gives performance which varies non-linearly with problem size - see Fig. 5. The figures $n_{r_{max}}$ are the problem size at which the highest performance figures, r_{max}, are obtained.

Table 1 was compiled by running each program over a number of problem sizes, and choosing that which gave the largest assembler megaflop or bandwidth rate for fifty iterations. The Fig. 5 runs **saxpy** over a thousand iterations. There is a discrepancy in the peak rate between **saxpy** over fifty and a thousand iterations. This is due to the fact that the first iteration will take longer than any subsequent iterations, because on the first iteration the data must be brought in to the cache from external memory. In general, cached data should be re-used wherever possible.

The results are quite encouraging, however, much better results are obtained from calling the routines with unit-strided vectors.

4.2 Level 2 BLAS Results

Table 2. Performance Table for Real Level 2 BLAS

generic routine	Single Precision		Double Precision		generic routine	Single Precision		Double Precision	
	r_∞	$n_{\frac{1}{2}}$	r_∞	$n_{\frac{1}{2}}$		r_∞	$n_{\frac{1}{2}}$	r_∞	$n_{\frac{1}{2}}$
_gemv	45.0	93	21.9	50	_trsv	35.0	244	17.4	122
_gbmv	22.8	80	18.7	65	_tbsv	32.5	129	20.0	87
_symv	34.3	204	17.0	90	_tpsv	27.0	197	20.0	142
_sbmv	33.0	101	17.5	46	_ger	16.5	59	8.3	24
_spmv	24.2	131	18.3	89	_syr	14.5	97	7.7	35
_trmv	30.9	221	18.3	107	_spr	9.7	54	6.2	23
_tbmv	28.8	121	18.5	63	_syr2	14.4	99	7.7	36
_tpmv	23.3	157	19.9	117	_spr2	9.6	53	6.2	23

Comments. All results in Table 2 are for square, non-transposed matrices and for unit-stride vectors. If matrices are triangular then they are non-unit upper triangular. The results for lower-triangular matrices will be the same as those for the upper-triangular matrices above; but there is a variation, in general, between non-transposed and transposed forms of the level 2 operations. In theory it would be expected that the triangular and symmetric routines would have values of $n_{\frac{1}{2}}$ approximately double the values for the general matrix equivalents; this is verified by Table 2.

The results of the higher-level BLAS are limited by the memory capacity (4Mb) of the machine on which the subroutines were timed. The limitation arises from the storage of large square matrices, and, in particular, means that it is not possible to provide meaningful data on the effect of stripmining, for vector lengths greater than $CSIZE$, on all level 2 BLAS excepting _gemv and _ger. In some cases it also means that the maximum possible performance can only be estimated by the maximum performance obtained, even when it is clear that performance levels are still rising as the memory capacity of the machine is reached.

4.3 Level 3 BLAS Results

Table 3. Performance Table for Real Level 3 BLAS

Parameters			Generic	Single Precision		Double Precision	
transa	transb	side	routine	r_∞	$n_{\frac{1}{2}}$	r_∞	$n_{\frac{1}{2}}$
'n'	'n'	-	_gemm	43.2(41.2)	20 (87)	19.3(21.6)	16(52)
't'	't'	-	_gemm	29.6(40.5)	16 (69)	16.7(17.0)	16(41)
-	-	'r'	_symm	33.8(21.5)	19(118)	17.1(13.3)	17(66)
't'	-	-	_syr2k	35.8(12.1)	42 (88)	15.6(7.0)	41(35)
't'	-	-	_syrk	40.3(12.6)	45(88)	17.4(7.1)	48(32)
'n'	-	'r'	_trmm	31.1(15.4)	106(57)	16.0(14.5)	58(70)
'n'	-	'l'	_trsm	30.6(30.8)	113(114)	15.8(15.1)	61(91)

Comments. Table 3 summarises the performance results of the real level 3 BLAS. All matrices are square, uplo is set at 'u' and diag is set at 'n'. The r_∞ figures, given in megaflops, are estimated by the peak rate of performance obtained. The figures in parenthesis give the corresponding performance of the level 3 BLAS which are written in terms of the level 2 BLAS. All level 3 BLAS have been written in blocked form, with a switch which decides whether to call a matrix-multiply routine or perform a sequence of calls to a dot routine. Currently the switch is set so that the matrix-multiply routine is called provided both dimensions of the matrix-block, resident in the cache, are divisible by 8 (as required by the matrix-multiply routine).

These preliminary performance results indicate that, for square problems, the blocked versions of _trsm and _trmm have similar rates of performance to the versions which call level 2 BLAS, the blocked _gemm routines perform better for some settings of transa and transb and worse for others, the blocked _symm routines perform better (especially for small and moderate problem sizes), and the blocked rank-update routines _syrk and _syr2k perform much better than the versions calling level 2 BLAS.

Some preliminary timings on the blocked level 3 BLAS applied to non-square problems have also been performed. These timings indicate that the versions calling level 2 BLAS are superior when the number of columns of the target matrix is very small, whereas the blocked versions are superior when the number of rows of the target matrix is small. The peak performances are not greatly altered, however, the $n_{\frac{1}{2}}$ figures are generally lower for the blocked versions, implying that these versions should be used for small problem sizes.

Given these preliminary results, it would seem that the best overall approach to providing a set of robust high-performance implementations of the level 3 BLAS is to incorporate both the 'level 2' and the blocked versions into a hybrid set. This hybrid set would include some internal parameters (kept to a practicable number) that would determine the choice of version to be used given the passed parameter list.

Clearly there is much further work to be done in the design of suitable implementations, for cache-based architectures, of the level 3 BLAS and higher-level routines;

such implementations are likely to employ similar strategies to those used in this paper.

4.4 Higher Level Linear Algebra Routine Results

Table 4. Performance Table for Higher Level Linear Algebra Routines

Routine	With Fortran BLAS	With Assembler BLAS	speedup
Eq01	3.3	24.9	7.5
Invpd	6.7	29.0	4.3

Comments. This table gives megaflop rates for a random sample of routines in the Liverpool Higher Level Single Processor Library (see [9]), using fortran or assembler BLAS. Eq01 solves an $n \times n$ system of linear equations, $Ax=b$. Invpd calculates the inverse of a symmetric positive definite matrix. Both problems are computed in single precision, and the matrices are of size 600 square.

References

1. D.S. Dodson, R.G. Grimes, and Lewis J.G. Sparse extensions to the fortran basic linear algebra subprograms. *ETA-TR-63*, aug 1987.
2. J.J. Dongarra, J. Du Croz, I. Duff, and S. Hammarling. A set of level 3 basic linear algebra subprograms. *ANL-MCS-TM 88 (Revision 1)*, 1988.
3. J.J. Dongarra, J. Du Croz, S. Hammarling, and J. Hanson, R. An extended set of fortran basic linear algebra subprograms. *ACM Trans. Math. Softw.*, 14(1):1–18, mar 1988.
4. J.J. Dongarra, P. Mayes, and G. Radicati di Brozolo. The ibm risc system/6000 and linear algebra operations. Technical report, LApack Report Ref. No. 28, dec 1990.
5. R.W. Hockney and C.R. Jesshope. *Parallel Computers*. Adam Hilger, second edition, 1988.
6. Intel. *i860 Microprocessor Reference Manual*. Intel, 1990.
7. M.S. Lam, E.E. Rothberg, and M.E. Wolf. The cache performance and optimisations of blocked algorithms. In *Fourth Intern Conf. on Architectural Support for Programming Languages and Operating Systems (ASPLOS IV)*, Palo Alto, California, 1991.
8. C.L. Lawson, R.J. Hanson, D.R. Kincaid, and F.T. Krogh. Basic linear algebra subprograms for fortran usage. *ACM Trans. Math. Softw.*, 5(3):308–323, sep 1979.
9. N.A. Software Limited. *Liverpool Single-Processor Assembler Library Manual*. N.A. Software Limited, Merseyside Innovation Centre, 131 Mount Pleasant, Liverpool, L3 5TF, July 1991.
10. D.C.B. Watson, R. Wilkinson, P.G.N. Howard, and C.J. Willis. Machine code implementations of basic vector subroutines for the t800. In L. Freeman and C. Phillips, editors, *Applications of Transputers 2*, pages 541–546. IOS Press, Amsterdam, 1990.

This article was processed using the LaTeX macro package with LLNCS style

Partitioning and Mapping for Parallel Nested Dissection on Distributed Memory Architectures

Pierre Charrier[1] and Jean Roman[2]

[1] CeReMaB, Université Bordeaux I, 33405 Talence Cedex, France
[2] LaBRI, ENSERB et Université Bordeaux I, 33405 Talence Cedex, France

Abstract. In this paper, we consider the parallel implementation of a block Cholesky factorization based on a nested dissection ordering for unstructured problems. We focus on loosely coupled networks of many processors with local memory and message passing mechanism. More precisely, we study a parallel block solver associated with refined partitions from the separator partition; the aim is to find the partition corresponding to *the correct granularity* leading to a high quality mapping (in terms of load balancing for the processors, of average length for the routing paths, and of average edge contention on the network). Then, we propose a refinement algorithm leading to this good granularity, and we provide some numerical measurements using the mapping tool included in the ADAM environment.

1 Introduction

This paper deals with the study of a parallel implementation of a block Cholesky factorization algorithm for large sparse matrices.

The target architecture is a loosely coupled network of many processors with local memory and message passing mechanism. We focus on a programming framework in which the user expresses its algorithms as a set of communicating processes which pass messages [1, 2]; the structure of the interprocess communication graph is without any topological restriction, but is supposed to be fixed during the whole parallel execution. The main interest of such a programming method is to be independent from the network topology, and to allow a better portability when changing the structure of this interconnection network. In such a framework, the programming environment must provide a general tool that performs in advance the computation of the static mapping of processes on the processors (each processor supports multiprogramming), and the computation of all communication paths used by processes assigned to non-neighbouring processors in the network [3, 4]; for this mapping step, it is important to compute precisely and in advance the computation cost of each process and the communication cost of each channel.

In this context, the most crucial issues in parallel performance are the adjustment of the granularity of processes, the control of the communication overhead and the achievement of a good load balancing for the processors.

Indeed, excessive fine-grained algorithms don't perform well on MIMD distributed memory machines. The potential gain from parallelism is overwhelmed by substantial overheads associated with coordinating a huge number of processes each performing not enough computation; in particular, a large number of exchanges of short messages is heavily time-consuming, on most current communication systems, because message initiation takes relatively long time with respect to message delivery. Moreover, the quality of the many-to-one embedding of the communication graph on the graph describing the (loosely coupled) network of processors becomes worse if the communication graph is too much dense; the control of the communication overhead requires to minimize the length of the routing paths and the global edge contention on the network (the sharing of a communication link by two or more paths) [5, 6].

At the opposite, a granularity that is too large doesn't take enough advantage of parallelism; it can lead to load-balance problems and, at the worst, to work starvation. From a theoretical point of view, little can be said about correct granularity, apart from the fact that a *crossover point* exists beyond which an application is too fined-grained to perform well.

In this paper, we consider a column block Cholesky factorization based on partitions of the unknowns of the system. We achieve a distributed implementation by assigning one process to each element of the partition; in this context, *the choice of a good granularity consists in the choice of a good partition.*

The useful mathematical tools for the analysis of these implementations are the classical graph model associated with Gaussian elimination [7], and the concept of quotient graph by a partition of vertices [8].

In [9, 10], the authors studied such a parallel implementation in the particular case of a nested dissection ordering with the separator partition induced [11, 12] for families of graphs satisfying general separator theorems. This partition is logically structured as a tree, and leads to a loosely coupled implementation which takes advantage of the parallelism induced by sparsity; the main results achieved are that the density of the communication graph is uniformly bounded, and that this graph can be constructed from data in linear time. Unfortunately, the granularity is too large, and the amount of computation is not well balanced between processes (most of the parallelism is obtained between the processes associated with the smaller separators which are the leaves of the separator tree, when most of the computation is performed by those associated with the few larger separators which are nearest the root); then, a high quality mapping is hard to achieve.

The aim of this paper is to study a parallel implementation of our block factorization scheme with a finer granularity obtained by refining the separator partition; compared with the previous implementation, we exploit a second level of parallelism in the computations inside the dense blocks. Our algorithmic framework is closely related to the supernodal algorithmics [13, 14, 15, 16]. The main objective is here to study the effect of the decreasing of the granularity on the quality of the mapping; indeed, refining the separator partition improves the load balancing but, at the same time, makes more difficult the embedding step owing to the increasing of the density of the communication graph. To deal with the granularity issue for our problem, we propose a general implementation with a granularity *knob*, and we adjust it by a preprocessing algorithm.

The paper is organized as follows. Section 2 introduces the parallel block factorization scheme used, and provides the structure of the weighted communication graph. In section 3, we make an asymptotic study of the density of the communication graph with respect to the decreasing of the granularity (cf. theorems 7 and 8). Lastly, section 4 presents an algorithm to adjust the correct granularity. Then, some measurements illustrating the improvement of the quality of the mapping are provided; these measurements are performed using the mapping tool proposed in the ADAM environment [17]. Because of the restriction on the number of pages, we omitted the most technical proofs; for details see [18].

2 Parallel block factorization scheme

We consider the factorization $M = LDL^T$ of a large, sparse, symmetric positive definite, irreducible $n \times n$ matrix M. Let $G = (V, E)$ be the n-vertex undirected graph associated with M, and let G^* be the elimination graph [7].

2.1 Definitions and notations

First, let us recall some fundamental definitions (see for instance [8, 19, 7, 11]).

Definition 1. A subset C of vertices is a separator of the graph $G = (V, E)$ if the vertices of G can be partitioned into three sets A, B, C such that no vertex in A is adjacent to any vertex in B.

A balanced separator tree partition is a partition of the vertices of G into a tree of separators as follows. The root of the tree is a separator C for G; the two subtrees (with common ancestor C) are balanced separator tree partitions of the two subgraghs of G induced by the subsets A and B obtained by separation.

A nested dissection ordering based on a balanced separator tree partition with root C, is an ordering that assigns the highest numbers to the vertices of C (in any order), and numbers each subtree in a nested dissection ordering (recursively) with consecutive numbers.

We consider a nested dissection ordering associated with a separator partition $\mathcal{C} = \{C_i\}_{i=1,N}$. The ordering of the N separators in the separator tree is a postordering; it corresponds to the elimination ordering of the n vertices of G. Then, we introduce refined partitions from the separator partition.

Definition 2. $\Pi = \{\Gamma_k\}_{k=1,P}$ is a partition of V refined from $\mathcal{C}$ iff: $\forall i \in [1, N]$, C_i is the union of the subsets Γ_k for $k \in [a_i, b_i]$, with $[1, P] = \bigcup_{i=1,N} [a_i, b_i]$.

Among all possible refined partitions Π, the coarsest partition is $\mathcal{C}$, and the finest one is V itself. Lastly, we will use the quotient graph concept.

Definition 3. The quotient graph of $G = (V, E)$ with respect to partition Π is the graph $Q(G, \Pi) = (\Pi, \mathcal{E})$ with $(\Gamma_i, \Gamma_j) \in \mathcal{E}$ if and only if there exists $x \in \Gamma_i$ and $y \in \Gamma_j$ such that $(x, y) \in E$.

2.2 Block data structure and sequential factorization algorithm

We consider a refined partition $\Pi = \{\Gamma_k\}_{k=1,P}$ of the unknowns of the system (or of the vertices of the graph) given by $\Gamma_k = \{x_j,\ p_k \leq j \leq d_k\}$ with $p_1 = 1$, $p_{k+1} = d_k + 1$ for $1 \leq k \leq P - 1$, $d_P = n$.

We associate with this partition a data structure composed of P column blocks for the factored matrices L and D (the matrix D is stored instead of the diagonal of L). The column block k, corresponding to the unknowns belonging to Γ_k, is composed of the following blocks:

one diagonal block $M_{k,k} = (M_{ij})$ with $p_k \leq j \leq i \leq d_k$,

s_k *off-diagonal blocks* $M_{(p),k} = (M_{ij})$ with $\alpha_{k,p} \leq i \leq \beta_{k,p}$ and $p_k \leq j \leq d_k$. $\alpha_{k,p}$ and $\beta_{k,p}$ are defined such that for all $i \in [\alpha_{k,p}, \beta_{k,p}]$, there exists j, $p_k \leq j \leq d_k$ with $L_{ij} \neq 0$, and $\Gamma_{n(k,p)}$ is defined as the element of Π such that $p_{n(k,p)} \leq \alpha_{k,p} \leq \beta_{k,p} \leq d_{n(k,p)}$.

Lastly, we note $M_{(q),(p)} = (M_{ij})$ with $\alpha_{k,q} \leq i \leq \beta_{k,q}$, $\alpha_{k,p} \leq j \leq \beta_{k,p}$.

The off-diagonal blocks in this structure are connected to the existence of edges in $Q(G^*, \Pi)$; then, the structure of column blocks is captured by the quotient of the elimination tree by the partition Π (*block elimination tree*). The final values of the coefficients of the blocks of L and D are computed by a column oriented algorithm; the initial non zero values of the coefficients are those of M.

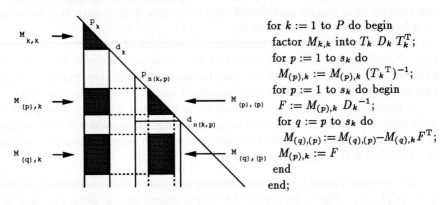

```
for k := 1 to P do begin
    factor M_{k,k} into T_k D_k T_k^T;
    for p := 1 to s_k do
        M_{(p),k} := M_{(p),k} (T_k^T)^{-1};
    for p := 1 to s_k do begin
        F := M_{(p),k} D_k^{-1};
        for q := p to s_k do
            M_{(q),(p)} := M_{(q),(p)} - M_{(q),k} F^T;
        M_{(p),k} := F
    end
end;
```

Fig. 1. Block structure and factorization algorithm

2.3 Construction of the block data structure

The block data structure for the factored matrices L and D can be constructed using a block symbolic factorization algorithm as proposed in [19]; the correctness of this algorithm is based on the equality $Q(G, \Pi)^* = Q(G^*, \Pi)$, and its time and space complexities grow as the total number of off-diagonal blocks.

Theorem 4 [18] gives sufficient conditions on partitions Π in terms of elimination forest [20, 21, 22] that insure this commutation property.

Theorem 4. *Let us assume on partition Π the property (ΓP): For all j, $1 \leq j \leq P$, the elimination forest of the diagonal block associated with Γ_j in L is a tree. Then, $Q(G, \Pi)^* = Q(G^*, \Pi)$.*

Let us assume on partition $\mathcal{C}$ the property (CP): For every i, $1 \leq i \leq N$, the elimination forest of the diagonal block associated with C_i in L is a simple chain. Then, every refined partition Π of the partition $\mathcal{C}$ verifies (ΓP).

First, let us notice that for the finest partition of the family, i.e. for V itself, the property (ΓP) is, of course, always satisfied. In the opposite case, for the separator partition $\mathcal{C}$, which is the coarsest partition of the family, property (ΓP) means that each separator C_i belongs to only one connected component of the subgraph it separates; this is exactly the sufficient condition given in [19] for the commutation property $Q(G, \mathcal{C})^* = Q(G^*, \mathcal{C})$. Such a condition on the separator construction is quite natural.

In fact, we want the stronger condition (CP) on partition $\mathcal{C}$ that insures the condition (ΓP) for *every* refined partition Π. In [18] we study how to obtain this property for some classical separation algorithms by choosing a judicious internal ordering for the separators. In all the following, *we will assume that the condition (CP) is satisfied*; in particular, this property will be used in section 4 in order to define a practical implementation of the refinement procedure.

2.4 Parallel block factorization scheme

Now, we consider a distributed implementation of the block factorization algorithm in the programming framework described in the introduction. First, we must define the processes and the communication graph; next, we associate a computation cost with each process and a communication cost with each channel.

- We associate a process with each element of the partition Π. The local data of the kth process is the kth column block of the data structure for L. We will use the following notations with $1 \leq k \leq P$:
$$I(k) = \{i > k \ / \ \exists p, 1 \leq p \leq s_k \text{ with } n(k, p) = i\},$$
$$J(k) = \{j < k \ / \ \exists p, 1 \leq p \leq s_j \text{ with } n(j, p) = k\}.$$
$I(k)$ is the set of column blocks i of L modified during the factorization by the column block k; in the same way, $J(k)$ is the set of column blocks j of L which modify the column block k.

Then, the process k sequentially performs the three following steps:

a step of receipts: the process k receives blocks from all processes j of $J(k)$; after receipt, it alters the concerned local data. The corresponding instruction in the sequential algorithm is formally $M_{(y),(x)} := M_{(y),(x)} -$ "block received". We note that all these alterations (only substractions) can be performed in any order; so, we will take advantage of this property of nondeterminism in the programming [2].

a step of local computation: as soon as all the receipts have been performed, a local computation is done: the factorization of $M_{k,k}$ into $T_k\, D_k\, T_k^{\mathrm{T}}$, and then the modification of the s_k off-diagonal blocks $M_{(p),k} := M_{(p),k}\,(T_k^{\mathrm{T}})^{-1}$.

a step of emissions: the process k computes blocks locally and sends them to the processes i (considered in increasing order) of $I(k)$; for each such process i and for all p such that $n(k,p) = i$, this step consists in the computation and in the emission of the lower triangular block $M_{(p),k}\, F^{\mathrm{T}}$, and of the rectangular blocks $M_{(q),k}\, F^{\mathrm{T}}$ for $q > p$. Here, we note that the process k does not need to wait for a process i of $I(k)$ to be ready to accept its message; so, communication between processes can be performed using asynchronous message passing [2].

We can characterize the communication graph of this parallel algorithm as $Q(G^*, \Pi)$, the quotient graph of G^* by the partition Π.

Example 1. We consider a 7×7 finite element grid graph with a nested dissection ordering; the block data structure for the factored matrix associated with a separator partition containing 31 elements is depicted below. For $k = 7$, we have $J(k) = \{1, 2, 3, 4, 5, 6\}$ and $I(k) = \{15, 31\}$.

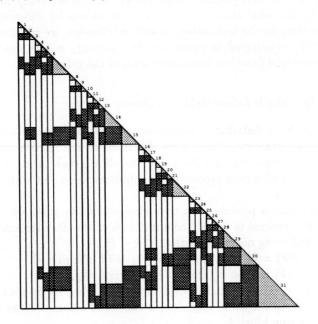

Fig. 2.

• We define the cost of a process as the sum of the numbers of operations required to perform each step. Moreover, we define the cost of each edge as the total number of data transmitted on the corresponding channel. Lemma 2.1 in [18] gives the values of these costs *as a function of the sizes of the blocks in the data structure.*

Remark. From the block data structure computed by the block symbolic factorization, we can construct straightforwardly the communication graph, and we can *exactly* compute the cost of each vertex and of each edge. Then, these costs are used as input data for the mapping tool.

For our example, the weighted communication graph is depicted below (we give the cost for each edge, and for each process we indicate its number followed by its cost). We can notice that the separator partition leads to *badly distributed costs* on this graph; the granularity is clearly too coarse.

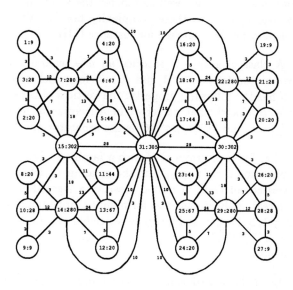

Fig. 3.

To conclude this section, we give the relationship between the partitioning method presented in this paper and the supernodal structure [13, 14, 15, 16].

Indeed, the sets Γ_k of partitions Π are closely related to the concept of supernodes; in particular, for finite element grid graphs $p \times p$ with $p = 2^q - 1$, the Γ_k are exactly supernodes and the separators are exactly the fundamental supernodes associated with the nested dissection ordering. For general graphs, it may happen that some of the blocks defined above are not completely dense; in fact, supernodal partition is, in this case, a *strictly refined* partition of C.

However, when (CP) is satisfied, the partition C is characterized by the following property: no column in a separator can be totally computed until after the whole computation of all columns belonging to all descendant separators in the separator tree; moreover, the separators are the *maximal sets* verifying this property. So, the partition C is the coarsest partition which captures the whole *parallelism induced by sparsity*.

3   Study of the weighted communication graph

In section 2, we have introduced the communication graph associated with a parallel block solver for Cholesky factorization; this solver is defined on partitions refined from an initial partition of separators.

In this section, we quantify the concepts of separation and of refinement in an asymptotic way; the aim is to achieve complexity bounds for the density of the communication graph in order to estimate the influence of the topological structure of this communication graph on the quality of the mapping. Moreover, these asymptotic definitions are well suited for the solution of the *divide and conquer recurrences* leading to these complexity bounds. First, we recall the definition of a separator theorem (see for instance [11]).

Definition 5. A class of graphs S satisfies an $n^\sigma-$ separator theorem, $1/2 \leq \sigma < 1$, if there are constants $\alpha < 1$ and $\beta > 0$ for which any n-vertex graph $G = (V, E)$ in S has the following property: the vertices of G can be partitioned into three sets A, B, C such that no vertex in A is adjacent to any vertex in B, $|A| \leq \alpha n$, $|B| \leq \alpha n$, and $|C| \leq \beta n^\sigma$. C is the separator of G.

We assume that for each graph G of such a family S, there exists a balanced separator tree partition $C = \{C_i\}_{i=1,N}$ in the meaning of definition 1; moreover, we order the vertices of G by a nested dissection algorithm. Separator theorems relevant to real applications exist for planar graphs (and 2D finite element graphs) with $\sigma = 1/2$ [11, 23], and for some restricted classes of 3D finite element graphs with $\sigma = 2/3$ [24]. Now, we quantify the refinement of the separators by the following definition.

Definition 6. Let θ be a real constant satisfying $0 \leq \theta \leq 1$. We say that $\Pi = \{\Gamma_k\}_{k=1,P}$ is a partition of V $\theta-$ refined from C iff for all refined subset Γ of a separator C, $|\Gamma|$ is a $\Theta(|C|^\theta)$ (uniformly with respect to S).

Remark. The partitions C and V correspond respectively to $\theta = 1$ and to $\theta = 0$.

The edges of the communication graph are connected to the existence of off-diagonal blocks in the block data structure for the factored matrix L. So, in order to study the properties of this graph, we first give at theorem 7 [18] complexity bounds for the total number of these off-diagonal blocks as a function of σ and θ. To achieve these bounds, we restrict our study to the family S_δ which is composed of the graphs of S with *maximum vertex degree δ*.

Theorem 7. *Let $G = (V, E)$ be a n-vertex graph belonging to S_δ ordered by a nested dissection algorithm, and let $\Pi = \{\Gamma_k\}_{k=1,P}$ be a partition of V $\theta-$ refined from C. If $\omega = \sigma(1-\theta/2)$ then the number of off-diagonal blocks grows as*

- $\mathcal{O}(P)$ *for $\omega < 1/2$,*
- $\mathcal{O}(P \log(P))$ *for $\omega = 1/2$,*
- $\mathcal{O}(P^{2\omega})$ *for $\omega > 1/2$.*

Then, we can state the main result of this section.

Theorem 8. *For $\theta > \theta_c = 2 - 1/\sigma$, there exists a sequential algorithm, whose time and space complexities grow linearly with P, that computes the communication graph and performs the allocation of local data to the processes. Moreover, this communication graph has uniformly bounded density, that is to say we have a loosely coupled parallel implementation.*

Proof. For given values of σ and δ, $1/2 \leq \sigma < 1$, $\delta > 0$, and using theorem 7, we deduce that for $\theta_c < \theta \leq 1$, the number of off-diagonal blocks grows as $\mathcal{O}(P)$.

Now, the communication graph can be deduced straightforwardly from the block data structure (cf. paragraph 2.3), and the number of edges of this graph is bounded by the number of off-diagonal blocks. This ends the proof. □

Remark. For instance, for planar graphs and for graphs arising in 2D finite elements problems [11, 23] $\sigma = 1/2$, and therefore $\theta_c = 0$; this means that partitions with a uniformly bounded size of blocks do not lead to communication graphs with uniformly bounded density. For cube graphs and and for some restricted classes of 3D finite element graphs [24], $\sigma = 2/3$ and therefore $\theta_c = 1/2$; for cube graphs, separators are planar grids and the size of blocks in such separators must be greater than the size of a row of the grid (at least asymptotically) in order to keep a communication graph with uniformly bounded density.

4 Influence of the granularity on the mapping

In the introduction, we claimed that a practical way to deal with the granularity issue is to build applications in which the granularity can be tuned. For the parallel Cholesky solver described in section 2, the granularity is not fixed; in fact, it depends on the partition which must be considered as an adjustable parameter of the algorithm.

The load balancing obtained by the mapping step will be all the better as the computation costs of the processes are already well distributed on the communication graph. Let us recall that the communication graph associated with the separator partition leads to a too coarse granularity, and doesn't satisfy this property (cf. figure 3). The theoretical asymptotic analysis of section 3 proves that a fine-grained algorithm obtained by refining too much the separator partition can lead to an implementation which is no longer loosely coupled.

So, we proceed in two steps: first, we use a preprocessing algorithm whose aim is to adjust the granularity, and secondly we perform the mapping of this graph; in this last step, we take account of the hardware characteristics of the target architecture.

In this section, we describe our refinement algorithm, and we give some practical results illustrating its efficiency on the quality of the mapping.

4.1 Refinement algorithm

We propose an iterative algorithm that gradually refines the partition until the achievement of a well balanced communication graph; the correctness of this algorithm is based on the property (CP) satisfied by the partition C (cf. theorem 4). We use the following notations with $1 \leq k \leq P$: $c(k)$ is the computation cost of the process k, c_{mean} is the average cost, Δ is the maximum difference with respect to the mean, and lastly $\delta_{process}$ is the relative difference with respect to the mean in the sense of the L^1 norm. For a given partition Π, the Block Symbolic Factorization (named BSF) computes the communication graph and provides these quantities.

begin
iteration:=0; compute the separator partition and perform the BSF on $\Pi = C$;
repeat
  iteration:=iteration+1;
  for $k := 1$ to P do (⋆ *computation of a finer partition* ⋆)
    if $c(k) - c_{mean} > \alpha * \Delta$ then refine the set Γ_k
    of the current partition into $\min(\lceil c(k)/c_{mean} \rceil, |\Gamma_k|)$ subsets;
  perform the BSF on the new partition Π
until $| \delta_{process}^{iteration-1} - \delta_{process}^{iteration} | \leq \varepsilon$
end.

    Here, $0 < \alpha < 1$ is a parameter which controls, at each iteration, the size of the choosen processes to be refined; ε controls the convergence.

4.2 Mapping results and conclusion

Now, we study the influence of this refinement algorithm on the quality of the mapping according to the following criteria: the *load balancing* of the processors, the average length of the *routing paths* and the average *link contention* of the network. The mapping software used (included in the ADAM environment [17]) is based on an improved version of Bokhari's algorithm [3], and the choosen architecture is a hypercube with 128 nodes.

    We consider a 47×47 grid graph ($n = 2209$ vertices). The vertices are numbered using George 's nested dissection method [7], which is based on the $n^{1/2}-$ separator theorem satisfied by this class of graphs. Moreover, we will use this ordering algorithm with a variable threshold s of separation; all subgrids with p vertices and $p \leq s$ will not be separated, and so we use a more general ordering scheme consisting of a more or less incomplete nested dissection.

    From a separator partition, and for each iteration of our refinement algorithm, we compute a mapping. The table 1 provides some measurements about these experiments. P is the number of processes, NE is the number of edges in the communication graph and D is its density ($D = NE/P$), $\delta_{process}$ and $\delta_{mapping}$ are the relative differences with respect to the mean (in the sense of the L^1 norm) for the costs of the processes and the loads of the processors; lastly, RL is the average length of the routing paths and LC is the average link contention (average number of communication paths per physical link).

5. S. H. Bokhari. Communication overhead on the INTEL iPSC-860 hypercube. Interim Report 10, ICASE, May 1990.

6. S. H. Bokhari. Complete exchange on the INTEL iPSC-860. Technical Report 91-4, ICASE, January 1991.

7. J. A. George and J. W. H. Liu. *Computer solution of large sparse positive definite systems.* Prentice Hall, 1981.

8. P. Charrier and J. Roman. Etude de la séparation et de l'élimination sur une famille de graphes quotients déduite d'une méthode de dissections emboîtée. *RAIRO Informatique théorique et Application*, 22(2):245–265, 1988.

9. P. Charrier and J. Roman. Study of the parallelism induced by a nested dissection method and of its implementation on a message passing multiprocessor computer. Rapport interne I-8722, Université Bordeaux 1, July 1987.

10. P. Charrier and J. Roman. Parallel implementation of block cholesky method in the programming environment of the distributed memory multiprocessor CHEOPS. In *Proceedings of the fifth International Symposium on Numerical Methods in Engineering, Vol. 2.* Springer-Verlag, 1989.

11. J. R. Gilbert and R. E. Tarjan. The analysis of a nested dissection algorithm. *Numerische Mathematik*, 50:377–404, 1987.

12. J. Roman. Calcul de complexité relatifs à une méthode de dissection emboîtée. *Numerische Mathematik*, 47:175–190, 1985.

13. C. Ashcraft and R. Grimes. The influence of relaxed supernode partitions on the multifrontal method. *ACM Trans. on Math. Software*, 15:291–309, 1989.

14. C. Ashcraft, R. Grimes, J. Lewis, B. Peyton, and H. Simon. Progress in sparse matrix methods for large linear systems on vector supercomputers. *Intern. J. Supercomp. Appl.*, 1(4):10–29, 1987.

15. J. W. H. Liu, E. Ng, and B. W. Peyton. On finding supernodes for sparse matrix computation. Technical report ORNL/TM-11563, Oak Ridge National Laboratory, 1990.

16. E. Ng. Supernodal symbolic Cholesky factorization on a local-memory multiprocessor. Technical report ORNL/TM-11836, Oak Ridge National Laboratory, 1991.

17. P. Charrier, S. Chaumette, M.C. Counilh, J. Roman, and B. Vauquelin. A programming environment for distributed memory computers - application to scientific computing. In *Proceedings of the 13th world congress on computation and applied mathematics - IMACS'91, Vol. 3*, 1991.

18. P. Charrier and J. Roman. Partitioning and mapping for parallel nested dissection on distributed memory architectures. Rapport interne I-9212, Université Bordeaux 1, March 1992.

19. P. Charrier and J. Roman. Algorithmique et calculs de complexité pour un solveur de type dissections emboîtée. *Numerische Mathematik*, 55:463–476, 1989.

20. J. W. H. Liu. The role of elimination trees in sparse factorization. *Siam J. Matrix Anal. Appl.*, 11:134–172, 1990.

21. R. Schreiber. A new implementation of sparse Gaussian elimination. *ACM Trans. Math. Software*, 8:256–276, 1982.

22. E. Zmijewski and J. R. Gilbert. A parallel algorithm for sparse symbolic Cholesky factorization on a multiprocessor. *Parallel Computing*, 7:199–210, 1988.

23. R. J. Lipton and R. E. Tarjan. A separator theorem for planar graphs. *Siam J. Appl. Math.*, 36:177–189, 1979.

24. G. L. Miller and W. Thurston. Separators in two and three dimensions. In *Proceedings of the 22th Annual Symposium on Theory of Computing.* ACM, 1990.

iteration	0	1	2	3	4	0	1	2	3
P	511	695	745	865	959	255	340	404	419
NE	1830	10802	14357	20657	26180	870	3255	5347	6385
D	3.58	15.54	19.27	23.88	27.30	3.41	9.57	13.23	15.24
$\delta_{process}$	1.28	0.85	0.79	0.72	0.65	0.84	0.44	0.31	0.30
$\delta_{mapping}$	0.84	0.21	0.08	0.01	0.005	0.63	0.11	0.01	0.01
RL	1.54	2.49	2.53	2.56	2.54	2.06	2.53	2.57	2.59
LC	6.30	60.00	81.16	118.04	148.31	4.00	18.38	30.68	36.86

Table 1.

The choosen value of α is 0.4. We perform two tests for the values of the separation threshold $s = 4$ and $s = 10$; the five leftmost columns correspond to five iterations for the first test, and the four rightmost columns correspond to four iterations for the second one.

The first thing to note is the significant improvement of $\delta_{process}$ and $\delta_{mapping}$ which stabilize in very few iterations; moreover, we achieve a very good load balancing in only two or three iterations.

On the other hand, the link contention of the network strongly increases as the number of edges and the density of the communication graph. The average routing length significantly increases at the first iteration, and then has only a slow variation; after the first iteration, 85% of the routing paths have a length between 1 and 4.

About the influence of the parameter s, we can notice that the initial partition for $s = 4$ leads to a communication graph with more vertices and more edges; moreover, the balancing for the computation costs is worse (cf. $\delta_{process}$) than for $s = 10$. However, the refinement algorithm provides a good and nearly equivalent load balancing (cf. $\delta_{mapping}$) for the two tests.

These results show that it is important to refine the initial separator partition, and that the partition corresponding to a correct granularity can be achieved after only a few iterations (two or three for these examples); indeed after this crossover point, the potential gain from a better load balancing will be overwhelmed by a substantial overhead due to the link contention. Lastly, this foreseeable small number of iterations leads to a poor time-consuming refinement algorithm.

References

1. H. E. Bal, J. G. Steiner, and A. S. Tanembaum. Programming languages for distributed computing systems. *ACM Computing Surveys*, 21(3):261–322, 1989.
2. M. C. Counilh and J. Roman. Expression for massively parallel algorithms - description and illustrative example. *Parallel Computing*, 16:239–251, 1990.
3. F. André and J. L. Pazat. Le placement de tâches sur des architectures parallèles. *TSI*, 7(4):385–401, 1988.
4. T. Muntean and E. G. Talbi. Méthodes de placement statique des processus sur architectures parallèles. *TSI*, 10:355–374, 1991.

On the Accuracy of Solving Triangular Systems in Parallel–III

Nai-kuan Tsao

Department of Computer Science, Wayne State University
Detroit, MI 48202, U.S.A.

Abstract. In this paper we present a component-wise error analysis of two different algorithms - one sequential and the other parallel - for solving triangular systems. The results show that each of the computed components of the solution vector using the parallel algorithm is an extended sum of slightly perturbed exact terms whose relative error bounds are comparable to those generated by the usual sequential algorithm. Hence in a backward sense the parallel algorithms are equivalent to the usual sequential algorithm.

1 Introduction

Given error-free L, b and it is desired to find x such that

$$(1.1) \qquad Lx = b, \quad L = \begin{bmatrix} 1 & & & \\ -l_{21} & 1 & & \\ \vdots & \ddots & \ddots & \\ -l_{n1} & \cdots & -l_{n,n-1} & 1 \end{bmatrix}, \quad b = \begin{bmatrix} b_1 \\ b_2 \\ \vdots \\ b_n \end{bmatrix}, \quad x = \begin{bmatrix} x_1 \\ x_2 \\ \vdots \\ x_n \end{bmatrix}.$$

The exact solution to (1.1) can be expressed as

$$(1.2) \qquad x = M_{n-1} \ldots M_1 b, \quad M_i = I + l_i e_i^T, \quad l_i = [0(1:i), l_{i+1,i}, \ldots, l_{ni}]^T$$

where the expression $r(j : k)$ is used to denote a sub-vector of identical components r placed in the the j-th through k-th positions of the larger vector. Now in (1.2) the order of matrix-matrix or matrix -vector multiplications is not specified. Using right to left order of matrix-vector multiplications, we have the usual sequential algorithm as given below:

Algorithm 1.
$b^{(0)} = b$
for $i = 1$ to $n - 1$ do
$\quad b^{(i)} = fl(M_i b^{(i-1)})$
$x = b^{(n-1)}$

where $fl(.)$ denotes the actually computed results of the arguments.

On the other hand for $n = 2^\nu$ one can also devise a divide-and-conquer type of execution for (1.2) as follows:

Algorithm 2.
for $i = 1$ to $n - 1$ do
$\quad M_i^{(0)} = M_i$
$b^{(0)} = b$
for $j = 0$ to $\nu - 1$ do
$\quad$ for $k = n/2^{j+1} - 1$ downto 1 do
$\quad\quad M_k^{(j+1)} = fl(M_{2k+1}^{(j)} M_{2k}^{(j)})$
$\quad\quad b^{(j+1)} = fl(M_1^{(j)} b^{(j)})$
$x = b^{(\nu)}$

Mathematically Algorithm 1 is equivalent to Algorithm 2 if exact computations were possible. In actual computation Wilkinson [1] has shown that if $\bar{x}$ is the computed solution vector due to Algorithm 1, then

$$(L + \delta L_s)\bar{x} = b, \quad \|\delta L_s\| \le nu\|L\|$$

where $\|.\|$ stands for the ∞-norm, u is the machine unit roundoff, while in [2] Sameh and Brent have also shown that if $\bar{x}$ is the solution vector due to Algorithm 2, then

$$(L + \delta L_p)\bar{x} = b, \quad \|\delta L_p\| \le \alpha(n) u \kappa^2(L)\|L\|$$

where $\alpha(n) = O(n^2 \log n)$, and $\kappa(L)$ is the condition number of L.

Thus it appears that Algorithm 2 is much worse-off than Algorithm 1 because of the larger upper bound of the perturbation matrix. However, in [3,4] Tsao has shown that Algorithm 1 and 2 are really 'equivalent' using either the component-wise first order error bounds for the computed solution vector or their associated error complexity measures. Both approaches are forward error analysis in their nature.

In this paper we give an alternative backward error model to show that Algorithms 1 and 2 are indeed 'equivalent': that the computed component x_i of the solution vector x using either algorithm can be expressed as an extended sum of perturbed products of original data represented as the determinant of a lower Hessenberg matrix, confirming further the conclusions given in [3,4]. Section 2 gives some preliminary results. Section 3 contains the major results. Some concluding remarks are given in Section 4.

2 Some Preliminary Results

Given (1.1) let us define a normalized lower Hessenberg matrix

$$(2.1) \quad H = [h_{ij}] = \begin{bmatrix} b_1 & -1 & & & \\ b_2 & l_{21} & -1 & & \\ b_3 & l_{31} & l_{32} & \ddots & \\ \vdots & \vdots & \vdots & \ddots & -1 \\ b_n & l_{n1} & l_{n2} & \cdots & l_{n,n-1} \end{bmatrix}, \quad 1 \le i \le n, \; 0 \le j \le n - 1.$$

Let $H_{c_1,\ldots,c_j}^{r_1,\ldots,r_k}$ or $H[r_1,\ldots,r_k; c_1,\ldots,c_j]$ be used to denote the submatrix formed by the common elements of rows $r_1,\ldots,r_k$ and columns $c_1,\ldots,c_j$. For $k = j$ then

$H_{c_1,\ldots,c_j}^{r_1,\ldots,r_k}$ or $H[r_1,\ldots,r_k;c_1,\ldots,c_j]$ is again a normalized lower Hessenberg matrix and its determinant is denoted by $D_{c_1,\ldots,c_j}^{r_1,\ldots,r_k}$. For simplicity contiguous rows or columns are denoted by

$$r_s : r_t = r_s, r_s + 1, \ldots, r_t - 1, r_t, \quad \text{or } c_s : c_t = c_s, c_s + 1, \ldots, c_t - 1, c_t.$$

In case $r_s > r_t$ or $c_s > c_t$, then they are vacuous. Thus $H_{s:t}^{i:j}$ or $H[i:j;s:t]$ is the submatrix formed by rows i to j and columns s to t inclusive. For $i = s + 1$ and $j = t + 1$ then $H^{i:j} = H_{i-1:j-1}^{i:j}$ and its determinant simplified to $D^{i:j}$. For a given vector c, we will use $c[s : t]$ to denote the sub-vector formed by the s-th through t-th components inclusive. In general the various determinants of the matrix H satisfy the following lemma[5]:

Lemma 2.1 For $1 \le i \le s \le t \le n$, then

$$D^{i:t} = U(i,s)(H_{i-1:s}^{s+1:t})^T V(s,t)$$

where

$$U(i,s) = [\,1 \quad D^{i:i} \quad D^{i:i+1} \quad \ldots \quad D^{i:s}\,],$$
$$V(s,t) = [\,D^{s+2:t} \quad D^{s+3:t} \quad \ldots \quad D^{t:t} \quad 1\,]^T.$$

Now take column j $(s + 1 \le j \le t)$ of the matrix $(H_{i-1:s}^{s+1:t})^T$, then it is the last row of the matrix $H_{i-1:s}^{i:s,j}$, which is also a normalized lower Hessenberg matrix. Thus $D_{i-1:s}^{i:s,j}$ can easily be expressed as a sum of two products by expanding its last column. Applying the above idea repeatedly to the computation of $U(i,s)(H_{i-1:s}^{s+1:t})^T$ gives us the following lemma:

Lemma 2.2 For $1 \le i \le s \le t \le n$, then

$$D_{i-1:s}^{i:s,j} = D_{i-1:s-1}^{i:s-1,j} + D_s^j D^{i:s}, \quad s + 1 \le j \le t$$

and

$$D^{i:t} = W(i,s,t)V(s,t), \quad W(i,s,t) = [\,D_{i-1:s}^{i:s,s+1} \quad D_{i-1:s}^{i:s,s+2} \quad \ldots \quad D_{i-1:s}^{i:s,t}\,].$$

Lemma 2.2 is the foundation of Algorithms 1 and 2 as we shall see next.

To relate the intermediate results of Algorithm 1 with the various determinants of the matrix H, we have the following theorem:

Theorem 1 If exact computations were possible, then the computed $b^{(i)}$ due to Algorithm 1 are such that for $0 \le i \le n - 1$,

$$b^{(i)} = [\,D^{1:1} \quad D^{1:2} \quad \ldots \quad D^{1:i} \quad D_{0:i}^{1:i,i+1} \quad D_{0:i}^{1:i,i+2} \quad \ldots \quad D_{0:i}^{1:i,n}\,]^T.$$

Proof We prove by induction on i. For $i = 0$ the theorem is trivial as $b^{(0)} = [\,D_0^1 \quad D_0^2 \quad \ldots \quad D_0^n\,]^T$ which is true. Assume the theorem is true for $i \le j$. For $i = j + 1$, then we have, from Algorithm 1, that

$$b^{(j+1)} = M_{j+1}b^{(j)} = (I + l_{j+1}e_{j+1}^T)b^{(j)}$$
$$= b^{(j)} + b^{(j)}[j + 1 : j + 1]\,[\,0(1 : j + 1) \quad D_{j+1}^{j+2} \quad \ldots \quad D_{j+1}^n\,]^T.$$

By construction

$$b^{(j+1)}[1:j+1] = b^{(j)}[1:j+1] = [D^{1:1} \quad D^{1:2} \quad \cdots \quad D^{1:j+1}]^T.$$

By using Lemma 2.2 we also obtain

$$b^{(j+1)}[k:k] = b^{(j)}[k:k] + D^{1:j+1}D_{j+1}^k$$
$$= D_{0:j}^{1:j,k} + D^{1:j+1}D_{j+1}^k = D_{0:j+1}^{1:j+1,k}, \quad j+2 \le k \le n.$$

Therefore $b^{(j+1)}$ is correct. This completes the proof. **Q.E.D.**

The structures of the various intermediate results of Algorithm 2 are given by the following lemmas[2]:

Lemma 2.3 The general $M_m^{(j)}$ can be partitioned as

$$M_m^{(j)} = \begin{bmatrix} I_{p_m^{(j)}} & & \\ & L_m^{(j)} & \\ & R_m^{(j)} & I_{q_m^{(j)}} \end{bmatrix}, \quad 1 \le m \le n/2^j - 1, \quad 0 \le j \le \nu$$

where $p_m^{(j)} = m2^j - 1$, $q_m^{(j)} + 2^j + p_m^{(j)} = n$, $L_m^{(j)}$ and $R_m^{(j)}$ are 2^j by 2^j unit-diagonal lower triangular and $q_m^{(j)}$ by 2^j matrix, respectively, and $I_{p_m^{(j)}}$ and $I_{q_m^{(j)}}$ are identity matrices of appropriate dimensions.

Lemma 2.4 To compute $M_k^{(j+1)}$ and $b^{(j+1)}$, the given $M_{2k+1}^{(j)}$ and $M_1^{(j)}$ are partitioned as in Lemma 2.3, and $M_{2k}^{(j)}$ is partitioned as in Lemma 2.3 with $R_{2k}^{(j)}$ further partitioned as $R_{2k}^{(j)} = [U_{2k}^{(j)} \quad V_{2k}^{(j)}]$ where $U_{2k}^{(j)}$ and $V_{2k}^{(j)}$ are general 2^j by 2^j and $q_{2k}^{(j)} - 2^j$ by 2^j matrices, respectively. Then

$$M_k^{(j+1)} = \begin{bmatrix} I_{p_k^{(j+1)}} & & \\ & L_{2k}^{(j)} & \\ & X & L_{2k+1}^{(j)} \\ & Y & R_{2k+1}^{(j)} & I_{q_{2k+1}^{(j)}} \end{bmatrix}$$

where

$$X = fl(L_{2k+1}^{(j)}U_{2k}^{(j)}), \quad Y = fl(R_{2k+1}^{(j)}U_{2k}^{(j)} + V_{2k}^{(j)}),$$

and

$$b^{(j+1)} = \begin{bmatrix} b^{(j+1)}[1:2^j-1] \\ b^{(j+1)}[2^j:2^{j+1}-1] \\ b^{(j+1)}[2^{j+1}:n] \end{bmatrix}$$

where

$$b^{(j+1)}[1:2^j-1] = b^{(j)}[1:2^j-1], \quad b^{(j+1)}[2^j:2^{j+1}-1] = fl(L_1^{(j)}b^{(j)}[2^j:2^{j+1}-1]),$$

$$b^{(j+1)}[2^{j+1}:n] = fl(R_1^{(j)}b^{(j)}[2^j:2^{j+1}-1] + b^{(j)}[2^{j+1}:n]).$$

We have the following theorem:

Theorem 2 If exact computations were possible, then

$$L_m^{(i)} = [l_{st}^{(i)}], \quad 1 \leq m \leq n/2^i - 1, \quad 0 \leq i \leq \nu, \quad 1 \leq s,t \leq 2^i$$

where

$$l_{st}^{(i)} = \begin{cases} 0 & \text{if } s < t, \\ 1 & \text{if } s = t, \\ D_{p_m^{(i)}+t:p_m^{(i)}+s-1}^{p_m^{(i)}+t+1:p_m^{(i)}+s} & \text{if } s > t \end{cases}$$

and

$$R_m^{(i)} = [r_{st}^{(i)}], \quad 1 \leq m \leq n/2^i - 1, \quad 0 \leq i \leq \nu, \quad 1 \leq s \leq q_m^{(i)}, \quad 1 \leq t \leq 2^i$$

where

$$r_{st}^{(i)} = D_{p_m^{(i)}+t:p_m^{(i)}+2^i}^{p_m^{(i)}+t+1:p_m^{(i)}+2^i,p_m^{(i)}+2^i+s}$$

and

$$b^{(i)} = \begin{bmatrix} D^{1:1} & D^{1:2} & \cdots & D^{1:2^i-1} & D_{0:2^i-1}^{1:2^i-1,2^i} & D_{0:2^i-1}^{1:2^i-1,2^i+1} & \cdots & D_{0:2^i-1}^{1:2^i-1,n} \end{bmatrix}^T.$$

Proof We prove by induction on i. For $i = 0$ the theorem is true as

$$p_m^{(0)} = m - 1, \quad q_m^{(0)} = n - m, \quad L_m^{(0)} = I_1, \quad r_{s1} = D_{m:m}^{m+1:m,m+s} = D_m^{m+s},$$

for $1 \leq s \leq n - m$, and $b^{(0)} = \begin{bmatrix} D_0^1 & D_0^2 & \cdots & D_0^n \end{bmatrix}^T = b$ as desired. Assume the theorem is true for $i \leq j$. For $i = j + 1$, then we have, by Lemma 2.4, that

$$M_k^{(j+1)} = \begin{bmatrix} I_{p_k^{(j+1)}} & & & \\ & L_{2k}^{(j)} & & \\ & X & L_{2k+1}^{(j)} & \\ & Y & R_{2k+1}^{(j)} & I_{q_{2k+1}^{(j)}} \end{bmatrix}, \quad \begin{array}{l} X = L_{2k+1}^{(j)}U_{2k}^{(j)}, \\ Y = R_{2k+1}^{(j)}U_{2k}^{(j)} + V_{2k}^{(j)}. \end{array}$$

Consider the computation of X first. By the induction assumption, the (s,t)-th component of X is given as

$$x_{st} = L_{2k+1}^{(j)}[s;1:2^j]U_{2k}^{(j)}[1:2^j;t]$$

$$= \begin{bmatrix} D^{p_{2k+1}^{(j)}+2:p_{2k+1}^{(j)}+s} & D^{p_{2k+1}^{(j)}+3:p_{2k+1}^{(j)}+s} & \cdots & D^{p_{2k+1}^{(j)}+s:p_{2k+1}^{(j)}+s} & 1 \end{bmatrix} Z$$

where

$$Z = \begin{bmatrix} D_{p_{2k}^{(j)}+t:p_{2k}^{(j)}+2^j}^{p_{2k}^{(j)}+t+1:p_{2k}^{(j)}+2^j,p_{2k}^{(j)}+2^j+1} \\ D_{p_{2k}^{(j)}+t:p_{2k}^{(j)}+2^j}^{p_{2k}^{(j)}+t+1:p_{2k}^{(j)}+2^j,p_{2k}^{(j)}+2^j+2} \\ \vdots \\ D_{p_{2k}^{(j)}+t:p_{2k}^{(j)}+2^j}^{p_{2k}^{(j)}+t+1:p_{2k}^{(j)}+2^j,p_{2k}^{(j)}+2^j+s} \end{bmatrix}.$$

By Lemma 2.2, we have

$$x_{st} = D^{p_{2k}^{(j)}+t+1:p_{2k+1}^{(j)}+s} = D^{p_k^{(j+1)}+t+1:p_k^{(j+1)}+2^j+s} = l_{2^j+s,t}^{(j+1)}, \quad 1 \le s, t \le 2^j.$$

Thus $X = L_k^{(j+1)}[2^j + 1 : 2^{j+1}; 1 : 2^j]$ and it is easy to show that

$$L_{2k}^{(j)} = L_k^{(j+1)}[1 : 2^j; 1 : 2^j], \quad L_{2k+1}^{(j)} = L_k^{(j+1)}[2^j + 1 : 2^{j+1}; 2^j + 1 : 2^{j+1}].$$

Therefore we have shown that

$$\begin{bmatrix} L_{2k}^{(j)} & \\ X & L_{2k+1}^{(j)} \end{bmatrix} = L_k^{(j+1)}$$

as desired. Similarly, one can also show that $\begin{bmatrix} Y & R_{2k+1}^{(j)} \end{bmatrix} = R_k^{(j+1)}$ and that $b^{(j+1)}$ has the correct components as prescribed in the theorem. This completes our proof. **Q.E.D.**

From Theorems 1 and 2 we see that the exactly computed final b vectors due to Algorithms 1 and 2 are identical. Furthermore, all intermediate and final results are determinants of normalized lower Hessenberg matrices of various sizes. Now the determinant of a normalized Hessenberg matrix can also be expressed as an extended sum of products of the various coefficients of the matrix. In fact the total number of such products depends only on the dimension of the matrix. It is easily shown that there are 2^{i-1} terms of such products in the determinant of an i by i normalized lower Hessenberg matrix. Thus mathematically Algorithm 1 is equivalent to Algorithm 2 as they both give us the required determinants for the solution vector x. The main difference between these two algorithms lies in the different ways the required determinants are evaluated: it is sequential in Algorithm 1, and parallel in Algorithm 2.

3 Main Results

In actual computation using a normalized floating-point system with a τ-digit base β mantissa, the following equations can be assumed [5] to facilitate the error analysis of general arithmetic expressions using only $+, -,$ or $*$ operations:

$$(3.1) \qquad fl(x \# y) = (x \# y)\Delta, \quad \# \in \{+, -, *\}$$

where

$$1 - u \le |\Delta| \le 1 + u, \quad u \le \begin{cases} \beta^{1-\tau}/2 & \text{for rounded operations} \\ \beta^{1-\tau} & \text{for chopped operations} \end{cases}$$

and x and y are given machine floating-point numbers and $fl(.)$ is used to denote the computed floating-point result of the given argument. We shall call Δ the unit Δ-factor. For convenience, the same set of notations are used to represent the various computed determinants.

Consider Algorithm 1 first. From Algorithm 1 and Theorem 1 we see that the essential computation needed to obtain $b^{(j+1)}$ from $b^{(j)}$ is

$$D_{0:j+1}^{1:j+1,k} = fl(D_{0:j}^{1:j,k} + D^{1:j+1}D_{j+1}^k), \quad j + 2 \le k \le n.$$

By (3.1) we have

$$D_{0:j+1}^{1:j+1,k} = D_{0:j}^{1:j,k}\Delta_1 + D^{1:j+1}D_{j+1}^k\Delta_1\Delta_2 = \det \begin{bmatrix} D_{0:j}^{1:j+1} & -1 \\ D_{0:j}^{1:j,k}\Delta_1 & D_{j+1}^k\Delta_1\Delta_2 \end{bmatrix}.$$

Since normally we do not know the exact value of any specific Δ , we shall use the generic Δ^r to represent the product of r possibly different Δ-factors. Using this notation, we then have

$$D_{0:j+1}^{1:j+1,k} = \det \begin{bmatrix} D_{0:j}^{1:j+1} & -1 \\ D_{0:j}^{1:j,k}\Delta & D_{j+1}^k\Delta^2 \end{bmatrix}.$$

Expanding $D_{0:j}^{1:j+1}$ and $D_{0:j}^{1:j,k}$ by similar recurrences, we obtain

$$D_{0:j+1}^{1:j+1,k} = \det \begin{bmatrix} \det \begin{bmatrix} D^{1:j} & -1 \\ D_{0:j-1}^{1:j-1,j+1}\Delta & D_j^{j+1}\Delta^2 \end{bmatrix} & -1 \\ \det \begin{bmatrix} D^{1:j} & -1 \\ D_{0:j-1}^{1:j-1,k}\Delta & D_j^k\Delta^2 \end{bmatrix}\Delta & D_{j+1}^k\Delta^2 \end{bmatrix}$$

$$= \det \begin{bmatrix} D^{1:j} & -1 & \\ D_{0:j-1}^{1:j-1,j+1}\Delta & D_j^{j+1}\Delta^2 & -1 \\ D_{0:j-1}^{1:j-1,k}\Delta^2 & D_j^k\Delta^3 & D_{j+1}^k\Delta^2 \end{bmatrix}.$$

Note the above expression is obtained by multiplying the $\Delta-$factor associated with $D_{0:j}^{1:j,k}\Delta$ to the last row of $D_{0:j}^{1:j,k}$. Repeated expansions of the first column using similar recurrences eventually gives us the following theorem:

Theorem 3 The computed $D^{1:i}$ due to Algorithm 1 is such that for $1 \leq i \leq n$,

$$D^{1:i} = \det \hat{H}, \quad \hat{H} = \begin{bmatrix} D_0^1 & -1 & & & \\ D_0^2\Delta & D_1^2\Delta^2 & -1 & & \\ \vdots & \vdots & \ddots & \ddots & \\ D_0^{i-1}\Delta^{i-2} & D_1^{i-1}\Delta^{i-1} & \cdots & D_{i-2}^{i-1}\Delta^2 & -1 \\ D_0^i\Delta^{i-1} & D_1^i\Delta^i & \cdots & D_{i-2}^i\Delta^3 & D_{i-1}^i\Delta^2 \end{bmatrix},$$

and the coefficients of $\hat{H}$ are given as

$$\hat{h}_{ij} = \begin{cases} D_j^i\Delta^{i-j+1} & \text{for } i \geq j > 0, \\ D_0^i\Delta^{i-1} & \text{for } j = 0, \\ -1 & \text{for } j = i+1, \\ 0 & \text{otherwise.} \end{cases}$$

From Theorem 3 we see that each computed x_i or $D^{1:i}$ is actually the determinant of a perturbed neighboring system. Furthermore, the neighboring system for x_i is a sub-system of that of x_j for $i < j$. By expanding the right hand side determinant, we see also that each computed x_i or $D^{1:i}$ is the sum of 2^{i-1} products of perturbed original data. Thus, if $D^{1:i}|_{exact} = \sum_{j=1}^{2^{i-1}} D^{1:i}(j)$, then $D^{1:i} = \sum_{j=1}^{2^{i-1}} D^{1:i}(j)\Delta^{\sigma_j}$ by expanding the right hand side determinant. Furthermore, it is easy to show that

$$\frac{|D^{1:i}(j)\Delta^{\sigma_j} - D^{1:i}(j)|}{|D^{1:i}(j)|} \leq |\Delta^{2(i-1)}-1| \leq 2(i-1)u+O(u^2), \quad 1 \leq j \leq 2^{i-1}, \quad 1 \leq i \leq n.$$

Thus term-wise the relative error is bounded by $2(i-1)u + O(u^2)$ which is not bad at all.

For Algorithm 2 the strict equality in Theorem 3 is no longer possible. This can be illustrated by the computation of x_4. Assuming the inner product is evaluated from right to left, then the computed x_4 is given as

$$(3.2) \quad x_4 = fl(D^{1:2}D^{3:4} + D_{0,1}^{1,3}D_3^4 + D_{0,1}^{1,4}) = D^{1:2}D^{3:4}\Delta^2 + D_{0,1}^{1,3}D_3^4\Delta^3 + D_{0,1}^{1,4}\Delta^2.$$

Now the computed intermediate results in the above expression can certainly be modeled by

$$D^{1:2} = \det \begin{bmatrix} D_0^1 & -1 \\ D_0^2\delta & D_1^2\delta^2 \end{bmatrix}, \quad D^{3:4} = \det \begin{bmatrix} D_2^3 & -1 \\ D_2^4\delta & D_3^4\delta^2 \end{bmatrix},$$

$$D_{0,1}^{1,3} = \det \begin{bmatrix} D_0^1 & -1 \\ D_0^3\delta & D_1^3\delta^2 \end{bmatrix}, \quad D_{0,1}^{1,4} = \det \begin{bmatrix} D_0^1 & -1 \\ D_0^4\delta & D_1^4\delta^2 \end{bmatrix},$$

where δ is used instead of Δ to distinguish the two different stages of computation. The above expressions can not be combined in (3.2) to give a neat expression such as the one obtained from Theorem 3 for $n = 4$. This is because, for example, the δ^2 factor associated with D_3^4 in $D^{3:4}$ is in general different from the Δ^3 factor associated with the $D_{0,1}^{1,3}D_3^4$ term in (3.2). And it is necessary to allocate some part of Δ^3 to D_3^4 in order to construct the over all model. However, the computed x_4 using Algorithm 2 is still the extended sum of 2^3 perturbed products of the original data. Furthermore, if we do not deem it important to distinguish between δ and Δ, and the various Δ factors are carefully allocated to the various intermediate determinants, then the computed x_4 using Algorithm 2 can still be expressed compactly as the determinant of a certain Hessenberg matrix. For this example x_4 can be rewritten as

$$x_4 = D^{1:2}(D^{3:4}\delta_r^2) + (D_{0,1}^{1,3}\delta_r)(D_3^4\delta_c^2) + (D_{0,1}^{1,4}\delta_c^2)$$

where the subscript c or r is used to indicate that the associated δ factor should be multiplied to the first column or the last row, respectively, of the determinant model inside the same pair of parentheses. Now x_4 can be expressed compactly as

$$x_4 = \det \begin{bmatrix} D_0^1 & -1 & & \\ D_0^2\delta & D_1^2\delta^2 & -1 & \\ D_0^3\delta^2 & D_1^3\delta^3 & D_2^3\delta^2 & -1 \\ D_0^4\delta^3 & D_1^4\delta^4 & D_2^4\delta^3 & D_3^4\delta^2 \end{bmatrix}.$$

In other words, any one of the 2^3 perturbed products of the original data which constitute x_4 can be obtained by identifying one of the 2^3 products obtained by expanding the right hand side determinant. Furthermore, the $\delta-$factor associated with a specific coefficient can assume different perturbations if the specific coefficient is involved in the computation of more than one intermediate determinant. For example, the δ^2 associated with D_3^4 above represents two possibly different perturbations—one in the calculation of $D^{3:4}$ as δ^2 and the other in the final inner product evaluation as $\delta_c^2 = \Delta^2$ in (3.2) to give x_4. In general we have the following theorem:

Theorem 4 If in Lemma 2.2 the $D^{i:t}$ is evaluated as

$$D^{i:t} = fl(W(i,s,t)V(s,t)), \quad 1 \leq i \leq s \leq t \leq n,$$

where $W(i,s,t)$ and $V(s,t)$ are defined in Lemmas 2.1 and 2.2 and the summations in the inner product are executed from right to left, then the computed $D^{i:t}$ is a sum of 2^{t-i} products of perturbed original data compactly represented by

$$D^{i:t} = \det \bar{H}, \quad \bar{H} = \begin{bmatrix} D_{i-1}^i & -1 & & & \\ D_{i-1}^{i+1}\delta & D_i^{i+1}\delta^2 & -1 & & \\ \vdots & \vdots & \ddots & \ddots & \\ D_{i-1}^{t-1}\delta^{t-i-1} & D_i^{t-1}\delta^{t-i} & \cdots & D_{t-2}^{t-1}\delta^2 & -1 \\ D_{i-1}^t\delta^{t-i} & D_i^t\delta^{t-i+1} & \cdots & D_{t-2}^t\delta^3 & D_{t-1}^t\delta^2 \end{bmatrix}$$

and

$$\bar{h}_{jk} = \begin{cases} D_k^j \delta^{j-k+1} \text{ for } j > k, \ i+1 \leq j \leq t, \ i \leq k \leq t-1, \\ D_{i-1}^j \delta^{j-i-1} \text{ for } k = i-1, \ i \leq j \leq t, \\ -1 \text{ for } i \leq j = k \leq t-1, \\ 0 \text{ otherwise.} \end{cases}$$

where the generic δ^k associated with each coefficient is the product of k possibly different $\delta-$factors representing different perturbations if the specific coefficient is involved in the computation of more than one intermediate determinant.

Proof We prove by induction on $t - i + 1$, the number of rows or columns of the particular determinant. For $t - i + 1 = 1$ or $t = i$, then the theorem is true as $D^{i:i} = D_{i-1}^i$ and there is only one product in the sum. Assume the theorem is true for $t - i + 1 \leq r$. Now for $t - i + 1 = r + 1$, we have

$$D^{i:t} = fl(W(i,s,t)V(s,t)), \quad 1 \leq i \leq s \leq t \leq n.$$

Since the inner product summations are evaluated from right to left, the repeated applications of (3.1) (with Δ replaced by δ) to the above inner product gives us

$$D^{i:t} = D_{i-1:s}^{i:s,s+1}D^{s+2:t}\delta^2 + D_{i-1:s}^{i:s,s+2}D^{s+3:t}\delta^3 + \ldots + D_{i-1:s}^{i:s,t-1}D^{t:t}\delta^{t-s} + D_{i-1:s}^{i:s,t}\delta^{t-s-1}.$$

It is easily seen that the number of products in the above expression is given as

$$2^{s-i+1}2^{t-s-2} + 2^{s-i+1}2^{t-s-3} + \ldots + 2^{s-i+1}2^0 + 2^{s-i+1} = 2^{t-i}.$$

We now allocate the various δ−factors as follows:

$$D^{i:t} = D_{i-1:s}^{i:s,s+1}(D^{s+2:t}\delta_c^2) + (D_{i-1:s}^{i:s,s+2}\delta_r)(D^{s+3:t}\delta_c^2) + \ldots +$$
$$(D_{i-1:s}^{i:s,t-1}\delta_r^{t-s-2})(D^{t:t}\delta_c^2) + (D_{i-1:s}^{i:s,t}\delta_r^{t-s-1})$$

where the subscripts c and r are interpreted as before. Now $D_{i-1:s}^{i:s,s+1}$ is the principal sub-determinant of dimension $s - i + 2$ of $D^{i:t}$. By our induction assumption it is already in our desired form. For $D^{s+2:t}\delta_c^2$ the resultant first column is given as $[\, D_{s+1}^{s+2}\delta^2 \quad D_{s+1}^{s+3}\delta^3 \quad \ldots \quad D_{s+1}^t \delta^{t-s} \,]^T$ which is precisely in the desired form for the nontrivial parts of the $(s + 1)$st column of $D^{i:t}$. Similarly, the first $s - i + 2$ elements of the rows $s + 2, \ldots, t - 1, t$ of $D^{i:t}$ are formed correctly as the last rows of $D_{i-1:s}^{i:s,s+2}\delta_r, \ldots, D_{i-1:s}^{i:s,t-1}\delta_r^{t-s-2}, D_{i-1:s}^{i:s,t}\delta_r^{t-s-1}$, respectively. And the nontrivial elements of the columns $s + 2, \ldots, t - 1$ are formed by the first columns of $D^{s+3:t}\delta_c^2, \ldots, D^{t:t}\delta_c^2$, respectively. This completes our proof. **Q.E.D.**

By Theorems 3 and 4 we conclude that Algorithms 1 and 2 are indeed equivalent — that the computed x_i using either algorithm is a sum of 2^{i-1} perturbed terms and term-wise the relative error of the perturbation is bounded by $2(i-1)u+O(u^2)$.

4 Concluding Remarks

To illustrate our points, we re-examine one 4 by 4 system used in [2]. The given system is

$$\begin{bmatrix} 1 & & & \\ 1.07 & 1 & & \\ 1.02 & 1.10 & 1 & \\ \alpha_1 & \alpha_2 & \beta & 1 \end{bmatrix} \begin{bmatrix} x_1 \\ x_2 \\ x_3 \\ x_4 \end{bmatrix} = \begin{bmatrix} 1 \\ 2.07 \\ 3.12 \\ \gamma \end{bmatrix}$$

where

$$\alpha_1 = 0.993(10^{14}), \quad \alpha_2 = -(\alpha_1 + 4), \quad \beta = -0.34(10^{-3}), \quad \gamma = -4.00017.$$

The condition number of the coefficient matrix is about $O(10^{28})$. The exact solution is

$$x_1 = x_2 = x_3 = 1, \quad x_4 = 0.17(10^{-3}).$$

For simplicity we shall use a normalized floating-point system with a 17-digit base 10 mantissa using rounded operations. Using either Algorithm 1 or Algorithm 2, the first three components of the solution vector are obtained exactly. For x_4's, they are different. Using Algorithm 1, we obtain

$$x_4 = fl(\gamma - \alpha_1 - \alpha_2 - \beta) = (\gamma - \alpha_1)\Delta_1 - \alpha_2 - \beta = -\beta, \quad (\gamma - \alpha_1)\Delta_1 = \alpha_2$$

and x_4 is such that

$$x_4 = \det \begin{bmatrix} 1 & -1 & & \\ 2.07 & -1.07 & -1 & \\ 3.12 & -1.02 & -1.10 & -1 \\ \gamma\Delta_1 & -\alpha_1\Delta_1 & -\alpha_2 & -\beta \end{bmatrix}.$$

Using Algorithm 2, we first obtain

$$
M_1^{(1)} = \begin{bmatrix} 1 & & & \\ & 1 & & \\ & -1.1 & 1 & \\ & w & -\beta & 1 \end{bmatrix}, \quad b^{(1)} = \begin{bmatrix} 1 \\ 1 \\ 2.1 \\ v \end{bmatrix}
$$

where

$$
w = fl(1.1\beta - \alpha_2) = (1.1\beta - \alpha_2)\Delta_2, \quad v = fl(\gamma - \alpha_1) = (\gamma - \alpha_1)\Delta_1 = \alpha_2.
$$

Then we have

$$
\begin{aligned}
x_4 &= fl(w - 2.1\beta + v) = (w - 2.1\beta)\Delta_3 + v = 10^{-3}, \\
(w - 2.1\beta)\Delta_3 &= -0.99300000000003999(10^{14}).
\end{aligned}
$$

The computed x_4 now satisfies the equation

$$
x_4 = \det \begin{bmatrix} 1 & -1 & & \\ 2.07\Delta_3 & -1.07\Delta_3 & -1 & \\ 3.12\Delta_3 & -1.02\Delta_3 & -1.10\Delta_2 & -1 \\ \gamma\Delta_1 & -\alpha_1\Delta_1 & -\alpha_2\Delta_2 & -\beta \end{bmatrix}.
$$

Thus the computed x_4's are equal to the exact determinants of some perturbed systems. This is most satisfactory. Although x_4 obtained by Algorithm 1 is not too accurate with a relative error of 1, it is much closer to the exact solution than that obtained by using Algorithm 2. The reason is simple: there is only one roundoff error incurred in computing x_4 using Algorithm 1 and there are three such occurrences in computing w, v and finally x_4 using Algorithm 2. The error is large because of the unfortunate cumulative effect of the individual errors.

On the other hand, if the fourth equation of our example is changed and we have

$$
\begin{bmatrix} 1 & & & \\ 1.07 & 1 & & \\ 1.02 & 1.10 & 1 & \\ \beta & \alpha_1 & \alpha_2 & 1 \end{bmatrix} \begin{bmatrix} x_1 \\ x_2 \\ x_3 \\ x_4 \end{bmatrix} = \begin{bmatrix} 1 \\ 2.07 \\ 3.12 \\ \gamma \end{bmatrix},
$$

then again we obtain exact solutions for the first three components of the solution vector using either algorithm. For x_4, we obtain, by using Algorithm 1,

$$
x_4 = fl(\gamma - \beta - \alpha_1 - \alpha_2) = fl(-3.99983 - \alpha_1 - \alpha_2) = fl(\alpha_2 - \alpha_2) = 0.
$$

By using Algorithm 2, we have

$$
M_1^{(1)} = \begin{bmatrix} 1 & & & \\ & 1 & & \\ & -1.1 & 1 & \\ & w & -\alpha_2 & 1 \end{bmatrix}, \quad b^{(1)} = \begin{bmatrix} 1 \\ 1 \\ 2.1 \\ v \end{bmatrix}
$$

where $v = fl(\gamma - \beta) = -3.99983$,

$$w = fl(1.1\alpha_2 - \alpha_1) = fl(-0.1092300000000044(10^{15}) - \alpha_1)$$
$$= -0.2085300000000044(10^{15}),$$

and so

$$x_4 = fl(w - 2.1\alpha_2 + v)$$
$$= fl(w + 0.2085300000000084(10^{15}) + v) = fl(4 + v) = 0.00017$$

which is exact! Again the reason is simple: there is still one roundoff error incurred in computing x_4 using Algorithm 1, this time in the opposite direction, yet there is none incurred in computing w, v and finally x_4 using Algorithm 2.

We conclude that our error models given in Theorems 3 and 4 are realistic and Algorithms 1 and 2 are equivalent.

References

[1] J. H. Wilkinson, Rounding Errors in Algebraic Processes, Prentice-Hall, Englewood Cliffs, N.J., 1963.
[2] A. H. Sameh and R. P. Brent, Solving triangular systems on a parallel computer, SIAM J. Numer. Anal., 14(1977), pp. 1101-1113.
[3] N. K. Tsao, On the accuracy of solving triangular systems in parallel, Applied Numerical Mathematics, 7(1991), 207-215.
[4] N. K. Tsao, On the accuracy of solving triangular systems in parallel - II, Applied Numerical Mathematics, 9(1992), 73-89.
[5] Don Heller, A determinant theorem with applications to parallel algorithms, SIAM J. Numer. Anal., 11(1974), 559-568.
[6] N. K. Tsao, Error complexity analysis of algorithms for matrix multiplication and matrix chain product, IEEE Trans. on Computers, C30(1981), 758-771.

Linear Algebra Calculations on the BBN TC2000

Patrick R. Amestoy[1], Michel J. Daydé[2,4], Iain S. Duff[1,3], and Pierre Morère[2]

[1] CERFACS, 42 av. G. Coriolis, 31057 Toulouse Cedex, France
[2] ENSEEIHT-IRIT, 2 rue Camichel, 31071 Toulouse CEDEX, France
also [3] Rutherford Appleton Laboratory, OXON OX11 0QX, England.
also [4] visiting scientist in the Parallel Algorithms Group at CERFACS

Abstract. The BBN TC2000 is a distributed-memory multiprocessor with up to 512 RISC processor nodes. The originality of the BBN TC2000 comes from its interconnection network (Butterfly switch) and from its globally addressable memory. We evaluate, in this paper, the impact of the memory hierarchy of the TC2000 on the design of algorithms for linear algebra. On shared memory multiprocessor computers, block algorithms have been introduced for efficiency. We study here the potential and the limitations of such approaches on the BBN TC2000.
We describe the implementation of Level 3 BLAS and examine the performance of some of the LAPACK routines. We also study the factorization of sparse matrices based on a multifrontal approach. The ideas introduced for the parallelization of full linear algebra codes are applied to the sparse case. We discuss and illustrate the limitations of this approach in sparse multifrontal factorization. We show that the speed-ups obtained on the class of methods presented here are comparable to those obtained on more classical shared memory computers.

1   Introduction

We discuss in this paper an efficient implementation of linear algebra kernels on the BBN TC2000 computer.

The BBN TC2000 is a MIMD multiprocessor based on the Motorola 88100 RISC processor. The TC2000 has from 4 to 512 processor nodes. Each processor node of the configuration includes from 4 to 16 Mbytes of memory, one 88100 processor, and two 88200 cache management units. The size of each cache is 16Kbytes, one is dedicated to data, the other to instructions. The peak performance of the 88100 is 20 MFlops using single precision, and 10 MFlops using double precision. The nodes communicate through a high performance switch (the butterfly switch). It provides transparent access by each processor to all locations in memory, whether local to a processor or remote on another processor. Each node has a switch interface, the memory of the individual nodes forms a pool of shared memory which is accessible by all the processor nodes. Thus this architecture is hybrid in the sense that it exhibits features of both shared and distributed memory architectures. Therefore, efficient code design for this type of computer retains aspects of both programming paradigms : communication and synchronization are effected through the shared memory, but the cost of accessing local data (physically on the same node as the processor) versus remote data makes data locality crucial. We use the BBN Fortran programming language that includes extensions such as the parallel do construct and extensions for distributing the data.

In this paper, we consider the implementation of full and sparse linear algebra kernels. We evaluate the impact of the memory hierarchy of the TC2000 on the design of algorithms. We have developed a parallel version of the Level 3 BLAS kernels (see [6]). The Level 3 BLAS kernels are expressed in terms of matrix-matrix operations and operations involving triangular blocks (see [5]). This blocking technique provides a natural way for parallelizing the kernels and allows efficient exploitation of the memory hierarchy on the BBN TC2000. In the case of full linear algebra, we examine the performance of some of the LAPACK codes using a preliminary version of real and double precision Level 3 BLAS that we have developed. In sparse linear algebra, we study **LU** factorization based on a multifrontal approach (see [7] and [8]). The multifrontal algorithm uses an *elimination tree* which reflects the parallelism arising from the sparsity. The parallelism from the elimination tree is combined with a node-level parallelism that exploits ideas used in full linear algebra.

We first recall, in Section 2, the main memory features of the BBN TC2000. We describe in Section 3 the parallel implementation of the BLAS routines. In Section 4, we show that with an efficient design of the BLAS routines a large part of the parallelism involved in full linear algebra methods can be captured. Performance analysis of classical LAPACK routines (**LU** and Cholesky factorizations) is used to illustrate the discussion. The same ideas are applied in Section 5 to sparse matrix factorization.

2   Memory organization on the BBN TC2000

The memory hierarchy consists of the remote memory, the local memory, the local cache of the 88100, and the internal registers of the 88100. The crucial aspects of this memory organization are the cost of accessing remote versus local memory, and the use of the caching mechanism. This is illustrated in Table 2.1 where we study the influence of the data locality on the average memory access time.

Data can be logically declared as *private* or *shared*. Data that are declared shared are allocated to the physical memory of a single node. Therefore, memory contentions will occur when a shared array is frequently accessed by all the processors. To overcome this problem, there exist extensions to the Fortran language which enable the user to distribute the elements of shared arrays over all the nodes. This can be done by declaring an array as *shared scattered*, in which case the columns of the array are distributed over the nodes. Unfortunately this way of storing arrays is not fully Fortran compatible since the entries in a column are not stored in contiguous memory locations within the global memory. We prefer to use another extension *shared interleaved arrays* since, in this case, the array is distributed over all the nodes of the machine by pieces of size the length of the cache lines (16 bytes, or four reals or two double precision words). In other words, the local node memories can be seen as banks of a classical shared memory computer.

	Number of processors							
	1	2	4	8	12	16	20	24
private	0.35							
shared data								
uncached	0.56	1.26	2.22	5.40	8.74	12.04	15.41	18.50
cached (writethru)	0.36	0.57	0.82	1.99	3.25	4.46	5.72	6.90
cached (copyback)	0.36	0.57	0.83	1.99	3.22	4.42	5.73	6.88
interleaved data								
uncached	2.00	2.01	2.01	2.05	2.10	2.17	2.25	2.33
cached (writethru)	0.80	0.80	0.81	0.81	0.83	0.84	0.86	0.88
cached (copyback)	0.80	0.81	0.81	0.81	0.82	0.84	0.86	0.89

Table 2.1 : Average time in microseconds for reading one element
of a 1,000,000 single precision real array.

Three cache policies can be used by the programmer: *uncached*, *writethru*, and *copyback*. With a writethru strategy, data modified in the cache are updated immediately in the memory. In this way, the main memory is always up-to-date. Using copyback, modified cache lines are updated in memory only when they have to be removed from the cache (for example when flushing a cache line). Therefore, the memory is not always up-to-date. Private data are always cached using copyback. There is no hardware or software policy for maintaining the cache coherency. Shared data are by default non-cachable, but the programmer can override the default cache policies and manage the cache coherency. Fortran extensions are then designed to specify the caching mechanism and to force flushing of the caches. Note that the copyback policy is generally the more efficient since it causes the less amount of traffic between the caches and the memory.

To illustrate the influence of the data locality on the access time, we report in Table 2.1 the access times for reading a single precision real (32-bit) array of size 1,000,000. We examine the most classical combinations of types: private, shared (local or remote), or shared interleaved and cache strategies: uncached, writethru or copyback. Timings in Table 2.1 show that the data locality and the cache strategy are key issues that must be taken into account to reach good performance.

The TC2000 is a virtual memory system and memory paging is crucial when dealing with large amounts of data. As soon as the amount of data exceeds the capacity of the node memory, swapping occurs and causes great overheads. Memory paging has an important effect on data storage. If the amount of local data (either private or local shared data) exceeds the capacity of one node, it is preferable to declare it as interleaved. The amount of physical memory allocated for storing interleaved memory pages can be specified explicitly. Therefore, interleaved memory can be set up in such a way that a high amount of memory pages can be physically stored in the memory nodes, thus avoiding swapping with disk.

3 Level-3 BLAS on the BBN-TC2000

This work is a logical continuation of previous studies on the implementation of Level 3 BLAS on a Transputer network (see [2]) and our studies on the design of a blocked parallel version of Level 3 BLAS for various shared memory vector multiprocessors (see [4], and [5]). A first version of this BLAS package was distributed in September 1991. This package is available without payment and will be sent to anyone interested.

We have developed two versions of the Level 3 BLAS : one serial and one parallel. In our parallel version, the assumption is that the arrays involved in the calculations are shared. We advise the user to interleave shared data (see Table 2.1). In the serial version, we have not made any assumptions, but it is clear that it is preferable to use these kernels on private data.

We have used the blocked version of Level 3 BLAS, which we developed (see [4]), as a platform both for the serial and the parallel versions of Level 3 BLAS for the TC2000. Our implementation combines the use of blocking and loop-unrolling techniques. It is based on the use of the matrix-matrix multiplication kernel GEMM. The calculations within the Level 3 BLAS are partitioned across submatrices so that they can be expressed as sequences of operations involving matrix-matrix multiplications and operations involving triangular matrices. The size of the submatrices is controlled by a parameter that depends on the characteristics of the target machine. Here the main parameter to be considered is the size of the local cache.

Under simple assumptions, the Level 3 BLAS we have developed manage the cache coherency. We have inserted cache flushes and invalidates in the codes so that arrays can always be cached using a writethru strategy. In order to use copyback, the arrays must start at the beginning of a cache line (for example they could be declared within a shared, interleaved, copyback COMMON) and their leading dimension should be a multiple of the cache line length. With this quite simple assumption, we guarantee that the processors work on independent cache lines.

We first implement a tuned serial version of the Level 3 BLAS (plus some tuned Level 2 BLAS kernels such as GEMV and TRSV) for single and double precision real matrices. These codes are targeted to be efficient when data are local to the processor in charge of the calculations (but it is not necessary). The calculations are blocked in order to make use of the GEMM kernel. This blocking allows an efficient reuse of data held in the cache. Depending on the kernel and on the precision (single or double) we determine empirically the best value of the blocking parameter (typical values are 32 or 64).

We use tuned Fortran code to perform operations on the submatrices. The loops are unrolled and we try to minimize the number of dependencies within the calculations so that the hardware can pipeline sequences of independent load/stores, floating-point additions and multiplications simultaneously. Another key factor for minimizing traffic on the interconnection network (that is for decreasing the proportion of remote references) is to copy the most frequently referenced shared data into private data storage. This data duplication is one of the main mechanisms used in the design of our parallel BLAS. It can also be beneficial when an uniprocessor code has to deal with a large amount of data that causes memory paging. In this case, we use shared interleaved data instead of local data (either private or shared) and data duplication between shared interleaved and private memory. Nevertheless, copying data between private and shared (remote or interleaved) memory represents a non negligible cost that makes it efficient only for large enough matrices.

The parallel version of Level 3 BLAS uses shared cached or uncached, interleaved or non interleaved matrices. As in the serial version, the calculations are blocked across submatrices. We have seen in [5] that loop level parallelism can be sufficient to parallelize our blocked implementation of the BLAS. We have used the same approach on the BBN using parallel loop extensions. In order to map the calculations on the memory hierarchy efficiently (to avoid remote accesses), the submatrices are first copied to the private memory of each processor (in small working arrays), then the calculations are performed and the results copied back to the shared memory. The blocking parameter is set accordingly depending both on the memory hierarchy as well as the number of processors available. Therefore, depending on the number of processors available and on the size of the matrices involved, the operations are carried on 16-by-16, 32-by-32, or 64-by-64 submatrices.

We present in Table 3.1 a summary of the performance we have obtained with

Kernel	Precision	uniproc.	Number of processors					
			1	2	4	8	16	24
GEMM	single	7.8	6.6	13.4	26.2	52.1	98.8	124.4
	double	2.6	2.5	4.9	9.7	19.2	37.2	47.0
SYMM	single	6.8	6.2	12.4	24.9	49.5	92.3	123.6
	double	2.0	2.5	5.0	9.8	19.3	38.2	51.9
SYRK	single	7.8	4.7	8.6	15.1	30.2	54.7	54.3
	double	1.7	1.7	4.0	7.8	15.7	29.2	29.2
SYR2K	single	7.7	5.0	9.6	18.2	36.5	66.3	66.1
	double	1.6	1.8	4.4	8.6	17.6	33.2	33.3
TRMM	single	7.1	6.0	12.0	23.9	47.6	92.8	114.9
	double	2.5	2.5	5.0	9.9	19.5	38.2	51.6
TRSM	single	7.6	5.3	10.6	21.4	41.6	80.7	103.6
	double	2.6	2.2	4.4	8.7	17.2	33.1	45.3

Table 3.1 Performance in MFlops of parallel Level-3 BLAS using 512-by-512 matrices.

our parallel version of BLAS on 512-by-512 matrices. Note that we only use Fortran programming. The matrices are all shared interleaved copyback. This data storage does not always correspond to the most efficient uniprocessor code. Therefore, we also report the performance of the uniprocessor code (using local shared copyback matrices). The size of the matrices is not big enough for reaching peak performance. However, we have obtained a rate of 150 MFlops using 24 processors for SGEMM on a 1536-by-1536 matrix.

4   Using parallel Level-3 BLAS in full linear algebra

We study, in this section, the parallelization of LAPACK codes corresponding to blocked **LU** factorization (GETRF) and blocked Cholesky factorization. Parallelism is only exploited within the Level 3 BLAS. We use our tuned version of the BLAS. All the matrices are declared as shared, interleaved, copyback.

We show, in Table 4.1, the performance of the right-looking variant of the blocked **LU** factorization. We use the left-looking variant (JKI variant) for the factorization of a block column since it is the most efficient from our experience. Note that this unblocked code only calls Level 1 and Level 2 BLAS. The best uniprocessor version corresponds to the version using shared interleaved copyback data because the amount of memory space required for a 2000-by-2000 matrix exceeds the amount of physical memory on one node. Therefore, using local data (either private or shared copyback), memory paging cannot be avoided. In the same table, we also present the performance of the LAPACK code corresponding to

Fact.	Precision	Number of processors					
		1	2	4	8	16	24
LU	single	5.4	10.1	18.1	31.1	49.1	60.6
	double	2.0	3.7	6.7	11.3	18.8	24.1
Cholesky	single	6.1	11.6	21.4	38.6	67.6	91.3
	double	2.3	4.4	8.3	14.8	25.9	35.9

Table 4.1 Performance in MFlops of right-looking **LU** factorization and J variant of Cholesky factorization using 2000-by-2000 matrices.

the J variant of the blocked Cholesky factorization. The unblocked code used for factorizing one diagonal block is the top-looking variant (J variant) since it is the most efficient.

5 Sparse multifrontal method

5.1 Introduction

We consider, in this section, the direct solution of large sparse sets of linear equations on the BBN TC2000 computer. The algorithm is based on a multifrontal approach ([7] and [8]). In a multifrontal approach, parallelism is exploited by using the sparsity through an elimination tree. Each edge of the elimination tree corresponds to an assembly while each node is associated with an elimination process on a full frontal matrix. For the elimination process, we use a row oriented (frontal matrices are stored by row) adaptation of the KIJ-SAXPY (see for example [4]). At the k-th step of this block form, a block row of the factors is computed and the corresponding transformations, based on Level-3 BLAS kernels, are applied to the remaining reduced matrix. The parallelism from the elimination tree can thus be combined with a node-level parallelism that exploits ideas used in full linear algebra.

We discuss, in this section, different strategies for adapting our shared-memory multifrontal method for the TC2000. Two straightforward implementations of the shared-memory multifrontal code are described in Section 5.2. In Section 5.3, we apply the techniques used for the parallelization of full linear algebra code (see Section 4).

A medium size sparse matrix, *BCCSTK15* from the Harwell-Boeing set (see [9]), will be used to illustrate our discussion. The matrix is of order 3948 with 117816 nonzeros. A minimum degree ordering is used during analysis and the number of floating-point operations involved during the factorization is 443 Million. We use

Computer	nprocs	multifrontal factorization			
		(1)		(2)	
		Mflops	(speedup)	Mflops	(speedup)
Alliant FX/80	8	15	(1.9)	34	(4.3)
IBM 3090J/6VF	6	126	(2.1)	227	(3.8)
CRAY Y-MP	6	529	(2.3)	1119	(4.8)

Table 5.1.1 Performance summary of the multifrontal factorization on matrix BCSSTK15. -in columns (1) we exploit only parallelism from the tree; -in columns (2) we combine the two levels of parallelism.

double precision (64-bit) arithmetic. We recall, in Table 5.1.1, the performance obtained on a range of shared memory multiprocessors (see [1]).

5.2 Shared memory based multifrontal algorithm

In our first two implementations of the code, the BBN TC2000 is used as a classical shared memory multiprocessor computer. The versions of the multifrontal code presented in this section are thus straightforward adaptations of the shared memory multifrontal code [1]. In *version 1* of the code, all data are declared shared. Note that data declared shared are physically allocated (see Section 2) to the memory of the processor declaring them for the first time. As a result, most data are located on the physical memory of the processor activating all the parallel tasks. Therefore, with version 1, we only use a small part of the bandwidth of the interconnecting network. One way to overcome this problem is to uniformly distribute the shared data over the physical memory of the computer. This is done using interleaving (see Section 2). It is independent of the number of processors used during factorization. This leads to *version 2* of the code. In both versions we use uniprocessor tuned versions of the shared BLAS library described earlier. We also use the optimal value for the Alliant FX/80 (see [1]) of the block parameters controlling the second level of parallelism.

We show, in Table 5.2.1, timings obtained for the numerical factorization of our test matrix (BCSSTK15) from the Harwell-Boeing set [9]. We see, in Table 5.2.1, that, on one processor, version 1 is much faster than version 2 where shared data are uniformly distributed over the physical memory of the TC2000. However, we observe that the uniprocessor Megaflop rate of version 1 (1.35 Mflops) is much smaller that what could have been expected from the performance of the tuned uniprocessor Level 3 BLAS (see Section 3). To factorize our test matrix, we need more than twice the size of the shared memory available on one processor. The BBN is a virtual memory computer and page swapping on the disk memory is thus required with version 1 of the code. This explains the relative low uniprocessor performance obtained with version 1.

Nb of procs	1	2	3	4	6	8	16	20	24	26
version 1										
(1)	328	226	217	186	190	191	198	171	166	206
(2)		227	170	151	117	105	103	100	99	95
version 2										
(1)	490	330	261	247	221	218	225	224	215	214
(2)		300	213	179	129	117	102	98	84	83

Table 5.2.1 Performance summary of two straightforward implementations of the multifrontal method (in seconds) on matrix BCSSTK15.
-in rows (1) we exploit only parallelism from the tree;
-in rows (2) we combine the two levels of parallelism.

Moreover, we see in Table 5.2.1 that the difference in performance between the first two versions reduces when we increase the number of processors. With version 2, shared data are distributed over all the processors. We thus decrease the average data access time by increasing the number of processors used during numerical factorization and we obtain better speed-ups with version 2 than with version 1. Furthermore, the comparison with the speedups obtained on shared memory multiprocessors (see Table 5.1.1) shows that, with version 2, a large part of the potential parallelism of the tree is exploited. Although the speedup is relative to a low uniprocessor performance, it shows that the average memory access time to interleaved data is not very sensitive to an increase in the number of processors and in the memory traffic. It thus confirms the timings obtained in Table 2.1 for interleaved data.

We have seen, in this section, that with shared data as in version 1, we only use a small part of both the physical memory and the bandwidth of the computer. This results in small multiprocessor speed-ups and in page swapping problems that will increase with the size of the problem. With version 2, we overcome these problems by interleaving the shared data over the physical memory of all the processors. This leads to a slower uniprocessor code having a good parallel behaviour.

5.3   Private BLAS based multifrontal method

Clearly, the first two straightforward ways of implementing the multifrontal method on the BBN TC2000 do not take into account the main characteristics of the computer sufficiently. The multifrontal numerical factorization is based on an elimination tree where the nodes correspond to assembly and elimination operations. Most of the floating-point operations involved during factorization come from the node elimination step. We can thus apply, to the sparse multifrontal method, the ideas introduced in Section 4 for full linear algebra codes.

In *version 3* of the multifrontal code, shared blocks of data involved in the block KIJ-SAXPY scheme are moved to temporary private working arrays prior to computation. At the end of the computation, performed in private memory, we then update the original shared block of data. To enhance performance, all data are cached with a writethru strategy and interleaving is used to smooth the access time to shared data. Note that, to prevent cache inconsistency problems, cache flush instructions must be inserted in the code.

Furthermore, we can reduce the amount of data transfers between private and shared memory when the elimination process at a node, k say, does not generate additional parallelism. This can be detected during the assembly process of node k and will only depend on the choice of the blocking parameters controlling the second level of parallelism. In this case, the frontal matrix is assembled in a private working array on which we perform all the elimination operations. Note that at the end of the elimination process, we must store in shared memory the **LU** factors and the block of data, the so called *contribution block*, that is needed when assembling the frontal matrix of the father of node k. On the other hand, if a node elimination process generates parallel tasks based on block spawning then we assemble the corresponding frontal matrix in the shared interleaved memory. Data moves are then required during the elimination step to perform BLAS-3 kernels on private data. In this case, to enhance the performance of the kth step of the KJI-SAXPY scheme, we also copy the block row on which elimination operations are performed to a private working array. In this way, all the BLAS-2 based operations of the KJI-SAXPY scheme are performed in the private area. Note that once the current block row has been factored, we need to update the corresponding block in the shared area before starting the parallel updating of the remaining rows in the frontal matrix.

In a non-uniform memory environment, the parallelization of a node process implies overheads of communication over and above those for a sequential node elimination step. We thus need a good control of the second level of parallelism to prevent speed-down due to communication overheads. We have found experimentally that, for a parallel node process, a good compromise is reached with a block size for the KIJ-SAXPY algorithm equal to 10. The number and the granularity of the parallel tasks generated during node-level parallelism is then controlled by user-defined parameters. We show in Table 5.3.1 the timings corresponding to the best values of the block parameters.

Results presented in Table 5.3.1 clearly illustrate the gain coming from the modifications of the code both in terms of speed-up and performance. In row (1) of Table 5.3.1, we have assumed that the private working arrays are large enough to store the largest frontal matrix. In this case, most floating-point operations are performed in private memory. Only the contribution blocks and the **LU** factors need to be stored in the shared interleaved memory. Note that, with Matrix BC-SSTK15, the largest frontal matrix is of order 533. It thus requires 2.2Mbytes

Nb of procs	1	2	3	4	6	8	16	20	24	26
version 3										
(1)	216	145	113	105	94	91	87	84	84	85
(2)		174	124	95	75	63	48	42	39	38

Table 5.3.1 Performance summary in seconds on matrix BCSSTK15.
-in row (1) we exploit only parallelism from the tree;
-in row (2) we combine the two levels of parallelism.

of memory which is less that the private memory of a processor (13Mbytes). We notice that the speed-ups coming from the use of only parallelism from the tree (see row (1) in Table 5.3.1) are comparable to the speed-ups obtained on shared memory computers (see Table 5.1.1).

We also observe, in Table 5.3.1, that, although the second level of parallelism nicely supplements that from the elimination tree, it does not provide all the parallelism that one could expect (see Table 5.1.1). Furthermore, on a small number of processors, the gain coming from the node-level parallelism does not balance the overhead due to data transfer between private and shared memory. Reducing the overhead due to data transfers, creating more parallelism, and controlling the node-level parallelism better are important issues that we need to address to obtain higher and more stable performance.

6 Concluding remarks

The advantage of the shared virtual memory available on the TC2000 is that it provides very convenient means for porting library codes from classical shared memory architectures. We have been able to run a subset of the LAPACK library using both serial and parallel versions of the Level 3 BLAS. We have also successfully applied (see version 1 to 3) the same ideas to the porting of a sparse multifrontal code. Most of the tuning done on the BBN TC2000 was aimed at efficiently mapping the code into the memory hierarchy within one node while avoiding remote memory references.

We have shown that blocking techniques provide a natural way for parallelizing the kernels and allow an efficient exploitation of the memory hierarchy on the BBN TC2000. We have noticed, for example, that our parallel version of matrix-matrix multiplication (GEMM) on 1024-by-1024 matrices achieves 150 MFlops and 55 Mflops on 25 nodes using single precision and double precision arithmetic respectively.

In full linear algebra, we have obtained good performance using simple BLAS-

3 based parallelism. The main limitation of our approach is due to the fact that, with Level 3 BLAS based parallelism, we cannot keep a high number of processors busy. Increasing the size of the matrices factorized would of course increase the percentage of Level 3 BLAS operations. However, it is clear that a parallelization over the kernels (see for example [3]) needs to be implemented to increase the parallelism of the methods and to reduce the amount of data transfers from private to shared interleaved memory. With a BLAS-3 based parallelization of the second level of parallelism (version 3) we reach a maximum speed-up of 5.7 while, with version 4 of the code, we obtain a speed-up of 7.

Much work still needs to be done on the sparse multifrontal method. Experiments on a wider range of test problems must be performed to generalize our conclusions. We also need to study the influence of numerical pivoting on the performance of the code. Further improvements of the sparse multifrontal code will involve a more distributed type of algorithm.

References

[1] P. R. AMESTOY, (1991), *Factorization of large sparse matrices based on a multifrontal approach in a multiprocessor environment*, PhD Thesis TH/PA/91/2, CERFACS, Toulouse.

[2] P. BERGER, M. J. DAYDÉ, AND P. MORÈRE, (1991), *Implementation and Use of Level 3 BLAS kernels on a Transputer T800 Ring Network*, Tech. Rep. TR/PA/91/54, CERFACS, Toulouse, France.

[3] K. DACKLAND, E. ELMROTH, B. KÅGSTRÖM, AND C. VAN LOAN, (1991), *Parallel block matrix factorizations on the shared memory multiprocessor IBM 3090 VF/600*, Tech. Rep. Report UMINF-91.07, University of Umeå, Sweden.

[4] M. J. DAYDÉ AND I. S. DUFF, (1991), *Use of Level 3 BLAS in LU factorization in a multiprocessing environment on three vector multiprocessors, the ALLIANT FX/80, the CRAY-2, and the IBM 3090/VF*, Int. J. of Supercomputer Applics., 5, 92–110.

[5] M. J. DAYDÉ, I. S. DUFF, AND A. PETITET, (1992), *A Parallel Block Implementation of Level 3 BLAS Kernels for MIMD Vector Processors*, Tech. Rep. TR/PA/92/74, CERFACS, Toulouse, France.

[6] J. J. DONGARRA, J. DU CROZ, I. S. DUFF, AND S. HAMMARLING, (1990), *A Set of Level 3 Basic Linear Algebra Subprograms*, ACM Trans. Math. Softw., 16, 1–17.

[7] I. S. DUFF AND J. K. REID, (1983), *The multifrontal solution of indefinite sparse linear systems*, ACM Trans. Math. Softw., 9, 302–325.

[8] I. S. DUFF AND J. K. REID, (1984), *The multifrontal solution of unsymmetric sets of linear systems*, SIAM J. Matrix Anal. and Applics., 5, 633–641.

[9] I. S. DUFF, R. G. GRIMES, AND J. G. LEWIS, (1989), *Sparse matrix test problems*, ACM Trans. Math. Softw., 15, 1–14.

Parallel Homotopy Algorithm For Large Sparse Generalized Eigenvalue Problems: Application to Hydrodynamic Stability Analysis

G. Chen[1], H. B. Keller[2], S. H. Lui[3] and B. Roux[1]

[1] Institut de Mécanique des Fluides
1, rue Honnorat, 13003 Marseille, France

[2] Applied Mathematics 217-50, California Institute of Technology
Pasadena, CA 91125, U.S.A

[3] Dept. of Mathematics, Hong Kong University of Science and Technology
Hong Kong

Abstract. A parallel homotopy algorithm is presented for finding a few selected eigenvalues (for example those with the largest real part) of $Az = \lambda Bz$ with real, large, sparse, and nonsymmetric square matrix A and real, singular, diagonal matrix B. The essence of the homotopy method is that from the eigenpairs of $Dz = \lambda Bz$, we use Euler-Newton continuation to follow the eigenpairs of $A(t)z = \lambda Bz$ with $A(t) \equiv (1-t)D + tA$. Here D is some initial matrix and "time" t is incremented from 0 to 1. This method is, to a large degree, parallel because each eigenpath can be computed independently of the others. The algorithm has been implemented on the Intel hypercube. Experimental results on a 64-node Intel iPSC/860 hypercube are presented. It is shown how the parallel homotopy method may be useful in applications like detecting Hopf bifurcations in hydrodynamic stability analysis.

1 Introduction

We consider the generalized eigenvalue problem

$$Az = \lambda Bz \,, \tag{1}$$

with real, large, sparse, and nonsymmetric square matrix A and real, singular, diagonal matrix B. By a large sparse matrix we mean one that is prohibitively expensive to factorise by either a QR or a LU decomposition needed for the standard eigenvalue problem or by the QZ algorithm [1] for the generalized eigenvalue problem. We must therefore rule out all these traditional algorithms. Such sparse generalized eigenvalue problems are often encountered in linear hydrodynamic stability analysis, in which the matrix A arises from the discretization of the Navier-Stokes equations (by finite difference or finite element methods), and B is usually called "mass matrix" which is singular due to the continuity equation (and possibly to the boundary conditions). Usually, only certain eigenvalues and corresponding eigenvectors are required. These are either the ones closest to some complex number or the ones in some part of the complex plane. Projection methods, like the Lanczos and Arnoldi methods, are popularly used because they avoid factorising the matrix [2, 3].

With advances in parallel processing technology, it is now feasible to achieve high performance in solving truly complex problems. However, in order to use those general purpose computers in a specific application, algorithms that are to a large extent parallel in nature need to be developed. Homotopy algorithm is one of the parallel algorithms for eigenvalue problems. Remarkable numerical results have been obtained by using the homotopy algorithm for the tridiagonal symmetric matrix eigenvalue problem [4, 5]. Very recently, Li, Zeng and Cong [6] developed a homotopy algorithm for real nonsymmetric eigenvalue problems. Its performance is very encouraging. However, if the matrix is large and sparse, this algorithm suffers a serious drawback. In the reduction of the given matrix to a similar matrix in upper Hessenberg form by the Householder transformation, the matrix usually loses its sparsity. Hence the algorithm requires the explicit storage of the entire matrix. This may pose a problem if the matrix is so large that not all its entries can be accommodated within the main memory of the computer.

In this paper, we present a homotopy continuation algorithm for finding a few selected eigenvalues (for example those with the largest real part) and corresponding eigenvectors of Eq.(1). The essence of the homotopy method is that from the eigenpairs of

$$\mathbf{D}\mathbf{z} = \lambda\mathbf{B}\mathbf{z}, \tag{2}$$

we use Euler-Newton continuation to follow the eigenpairs of

$$\mathbf{A}(t)\mathbf{z} = \lambda\mathbf{B}\mathbf{z}, \tag{3}$$

where $\mathbf{A}(t) \equiv (1-t)\mathbf{D} + t\mathbf{A}$. Here $\mathbf{D}$ is some real initial matrix and "time" t is incremented from 0 to 1. At $t = 1$, we have the eigenpairs of Eq. (1). A great advantage of the homotopy method is that it is, to a large degree, parallel because each eigenpath can be computed independently of the others. With a special choice of initial matrix D, the storage requirement is proportional to the number of nonzero elements of the given matrix.

In §2, we describe the homotopy algorithm for computing the eigenpaths including the choice of the initial matrix $\mathbf{D}$, stepsize selection and the method of solution of the linear systems which arise in the Newton iteration. This algorithm was developed in [7]. We have implemented a parallel program on the Intel hypercube, which is a distributed-memory, message-passing, multiprocessor machine. The results of numerical tests obtained on a 64-node Intel iPSC/860 hypercube are presented in §4 and our conclusion follows in §5.

2 Numerical Algorithm

2.1. Following the eigenpaths

Let $H: C^n \times C \times [0, 1] \to C^{n+1}$ be defined by

$$H(z,\lambda,t) = (1 - t)\begin{pmatrix} Dz - \lambda Bz \\ n(z) \end{pmatrix} + t\begin{pmatrix} Az - \lambda Bz \\ n(z) \end{pmatrix}$$

$$= \begin{pmatrix} A(t)z - \lambda Bz \\ n(z) \end{pmatrix} \tag{4}$$

where $A(t) \equiv (1-t)D + tA$, with $0 \le t \le 1$.

Here, D is the initial matrix and $n(z)$ is a normalisation equation. In our implementation of the homotopy algorithm, we use

$$n(z) \equiv \begin{pmatrix} (z^*z - 1)/2 \\ \mathrm{Im}\, z_j \end{pmatrix} = 0 \tag{5}$$

where the superscript $*$ denotes the conjugate transpose of a complex vector, z_j is the Jth component of z and is required to be nonzero (its imaginary part is put to zero). The normalisation (5) is not analytical as complex equations but their real forms are infinitely differentiable. In practice we choose J so that $|\mathrm{Re}\, z_j| \ge |\mathrm{Re}\, z_i|$ for all $i = 1,..., n$.

Let $DH = (H_z, H_\lambda, H_t,)$, where H_z, H_λ, H_t denote the partial derivatives of H with respect to z, λ, and t respectively. When DH has full rank at $(z_0, \lambda_0, t_0) \in H^{-1}(0)$, the local solution set of $H(z, \lambda, t) = 0$ consists of a smooth 1-manifold $(z(s), \lambda(s), t(s))$ passing through (z_0, λ_0, t_0). Such a curve $(z(s), \lambda(s), t(s))$ is called an eigenpath. To follow an eigenpath $\Gamma = (z(s), \lambda(s), t(s))$ through (z_0, λ_0, t_0), we apply the usual Euler-Newton continuation method.

Namely, we first calculate the tangent vector $(\dot{z}, \dot{\lambda}, \dot{t})$ at (z_0, λ_0, t_0) on Γ by solving

$$H_z\dot{z} + H_\lambda\dot{\lambda} + H_t\dot{t} = 0 , \tag{6}$$

with the normalization

$$\| \dot{z} \|^2 + | \dot{\lambda} |^2 + | \dot{t} |^2 = 1, \tag{7}$$

We have used dot to denote derivative with respect to s.

Using the Euler prediction

$$(z_0{}^1, \lambda_0{}^1, t_0{}^1) = (z_0, \lambda_0, t_0) + ds\, (\dot{z}, \dot{\lambda}, \dot{t}) \tag{8}$$

with stepsize ds, we apply Newton's method to $\mathbf{H} = 0$ with initial guess $(z_0{}^1, \lambda_0{}^1, t_0{}^1)$. Newton iteration will converge quadratically to the solution at a later time t_1 provided $t_1 - t_0$ is small enough.

It should be noted that in the Newton's corrections, we employ the pseudo-arclength method due to Keller [8]. That is, we augment $\mathbf{H} = 0$ with the equation

$$\mathrm{Re}\,[\,\dot{z}^* (z - z_0) + \overline{\dot{\lambda}}\,(\lambda - \lambda_0)\,] + \dot{t}\,(t - t_0) - ds = 0, \tag{9}$$

which represents the plane perpendicular to the tangent vector $(\dot{z}, \dot{\lambda}, \dot{t})$ at a distance ds from (z_0, λ_0, t_0). This method is used to follow successfully the eigenpath in the case where (z_0, λ_0, t_0) may be close to a bifurcation point.

In [6, 7], a method is developed to identify the bifurcation point and continuously follow the bifurcation branches. In practice we have two cases to consider (see Fig. 1):

1. Γ is a real eigenpath (Fig. 1a). On the opposite side of this bifurcation point, a complex eigenpath and its complex conjugate emerge. Using the tangent vector $\phi = (\dot{z}, \dot{\lambda}, \dot{t})$ at the bifurcation point, we need only to follow one of the bifurcation branches with the initial tangent vector $i\phi$ or $-i\phi$.

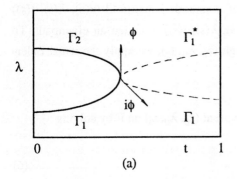 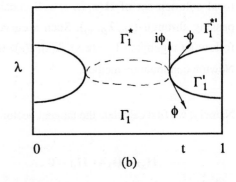

Fig. 1. Transition from (a) real eigenpath to complex eigenpath; (b) complex eigenpath to real eigenpath, at a bifurcation point. Dotted lines denote complex eigenpath.

2. Γ is a complex eigenpath (Fig. 1b). On the opposite side of this bifurcation point, two real eigenpaths emerge. We follow them in real space with the real tangent vectors ϕ and $-\phi$ respectively. Because the problem is being solved in real space, there is no chance of converging back to the complex solution. In our parallel implementation, the processor which became idle at a bifurcation point (in case 1) can be invoked to carry out the computation along one of those directions. This will be described in §3.

2.2 Choice of Initial Matrix D

We first rescale the given n x n matrices A and B so that the largest element of A (in absolute value) equals to one. Using Gerschgorin's theorem, we obtain a number r such that all the eigenvalues of A lie within a circle of radius r in the complex plane. The initial matrix D is chosen as a diagonal matrix whose elements are the diagonal elements of A, possibly perturbed so that

$$| a_{ii} - d_{jj} | > 2r/n^{3/2}, \ i \neq j , \tag{10}$$

where a_{ij} denotes the (i, j) entry of A and d_{jj} denotes the (j, j) diagonal entry of D. More precisely, we define d_{11} to be a_{11}, and for $i > 1$, we take d_{ii} to be $a_{ii} + \delta$, where δ is the smallest number in magnitude which makes d_{ii} satisfy (10) for all $j < i$. With this choice of D, the initial tangents $(\dot{z}, \dot{\lambda}, \dot{t})$ at $t = 0$ are easily computed. There is no theoretical justification for the bound in (10). From numerical experiments on random matrices, the spectrum of D seems to be reasonably distributed with this bound.

2.3 Solution of Nonsymmetric Linear Systems

To compute the tangent vector and each Newton iteration, large, sparse, nonsymmetric linear systems must be solved. Due to memory, operation count, and parallelization considerations, iterative methods are used to solve these linear systems. In our implementation, we employ the conjugate gradients squared (CGS) algorithm [9] which is being widely used to solve large sparse linear systems. This method is simple to implement and has low storage requirements. In order to improve the convergence rate, we use the preconditioning techniques based on the incomplete Gaussian elimination [10].

2.4 Stepsize Control

1. Initial stepsize

Let $(\dot{z}, \dot{\lambda}, \dot{t})$ be the unit tangent with $\dot{t} > 0$ at the initial point $(z_0, \lambda_0, 0) \in H^{-1}(0)$. If $\dot{t} \approx 1$, then the size of $(\dot{z}, \dot{\lambda})$ is relatively small and the eigenpath may be close to a straight line. A larger stepsize ds therefore can be used. In this case, we choose $ds = \dot{t}$. When $\dot{t} \ll 1$, we use $ds = \max\{0.01, |\dot{t}|^5\}$.

2. Increasing and cutting the stepsize

Let (z_0, λ_0, t_0) and (z_1, λ_1, t_1) be two points on the eigenpath with $t_0 < t_1 < 1$, we choose stepsize ds_2 for next point (z_2, λ_2, t_2) as follows:

$$ds_2 = ds_1 \{ \text{Re } (\dot{z}_1^* \dot{z}_0 + \overline{\dot{\lambda}_1} \dot{\lambda}_0) + \dot{t}_1 \dot{t}_0 + 0.5 \}, \tag{11}$$

where ds_1 is the stepsize used to obtain (z_1, λ_1, t_1) from (z_0, λ_0, t_0). The idea is that when the two previous tangents are parallel, then we increase the stepsize by 50%. If the tangents are perpendicular, we decrease the stepsize by a half. We use the above scheme until the time t is close to one; then we solve the problem $H(z, \lambda, 1) = 0$.

Whenever the iteration in the Newton correction step fails to converge after, say, 8 iterations, we cut the stepsize by half and restart the correction step.

3 Parallel Implementation

We have implemented our algorithm on the Intel iPSC/860 which is a MIMD machine consisting of 64 processors in an hypercube connection. Each such processor, also called a node, executes its own program on data in its own memory. The nodes are controlled by another processor, called the host, which loads the programs into the nodes and starts them. Host and nodes communicate by message passing. Communication between nodes are also performed by sending and receiving messages, either synchronously, i.e., the processing stops until a message is sent or received; or asynchronously, where processing and communication overlap.

It is seen, therefore, that an algorithm is well suited on such a machine if it may be set as several independent processes, each working on its own data with a minimum of interprocess communication.

The homotopy method is, to a large degree, parallel in the sense that each eigenpath can be computed independently of the others. If the matrices **A** and **B** are stored in each node, then there is no communication overhead at all other than the trivial broadcast of the location of bifurcation points.

The problem considered, i.e., equation (1), is a special case of the generalized eigenvalue problem. When **B** is a singular diagonal matrix with m zero diagonal elements, the characteristic polynomial det $(A - \lambda B) = 0$ is of degree equal to (n-m), where n is the dimension of **A**. Thus, there is not a complete set of eigenvalues for the problem. The missing eigenvalues may be regarded as "infinite". In the present paper, we intend to find the eigenvalue of (1) with the largest real part.

Computations of several test problems using random matrices **A** and **B** have been carried out. We observe that most of the eigenpaths move in a relatively simple fashion as t progresses. That is, there are no wild oscillations and the eigenpaths, in general, maintain their order where they are ordered according to $Re(\lambda)$. However, we have not been able to derive a mechanism to guarantee that an eigenpath will end up (at t = 1) having an eigenvalue with the largest real part. This is the reason for which several eigenpaths have to be followed. This increases the likelihood that one of them will be the relevant.

In practice, to find an eigenvalue with the largest real part, we reorder the initial matrix **D** so that d_{ii}/b_{ii} is in descending order for $b_{ii} \neq 0$, where d_{ii} and b_{ii} denotes the (i, i) diagonal entry of **D** and **B** respectively. Then we compute k (<<n-m) eigenpairs by following the eigenpaths $(z(s), \lambda(s), t(s))$ which start from the eigenpairs of (2) corresponding to the k largest eigenvalues. Each node (processor) then follows k/p eigenpaths, where p is the number of nodes to be used (for simplicity, we assume that k/p is an integer). For a sample of ten random 640 by 640 matrices **A** and **B**, and for $k \geq 8$, the largest (real part) eigenvalue was found among the first k eigenpaths computed.

Using p nodes, the parallel homotopy algorithm consists of the following steps:

1. Initiating

The non-zero entries of the matrix **A**, and the diagonal elements of the matrix **B** are stored in two one-dimensional arrays, say **RA** and **b** respectively. To locate a special entry of **A**, two address arrays **IR** and **IC** are needed. **IR**(i) gives the address in **RA** of the first non-zero entry in row number i in **A**. **IC**(j) gives the column number (in **A**) of the entry

RA(j). **IR** has dimension n+1, while **RA** and **IC** have dimension nz, where nz is the number of non-zero elements of **A**.

Let us identify the nodes to be used by 0, 1,..., p-1, respectively. Node 0 reads input data from the file in which n, nz, **b**, **RA**, **IR** and **IC** are stored. Then we send these data to all other nodes from node 0. After this point, each node has the necessary data to follow the eigenpaths.

2. Following the eigenpaths

Divide the number of eigenpaths as equally as possible among the p nodes. Each node builds the initial matrix **D** and then follows its own eigenpaths concurrently, with the procedure described in §2.

3. Broadcasting the bifurcation points

The eigenpaths start off from **D** and advance using the Euler-Newton continuation, solving the problem in real space. When it detects that it is going backwards in time, i.e., $\dot{t}$ < 0, then a bifurcation point has been passed. We identify this point first and store the values of (λ, t) at this bifurcation point in an array. We then broadcast these values to all other nodes. When a real eigenpath encounters a bifurcation point (Fig. 1a), it first checks whether the bifurcation point has been visited before. If it has been, then, the node stops following this path. By this way, only one path of a complex conjugate pair of paths is computed. This node is then free to compute one of the two real eigenpaths, say Γ_1' in Fig. 1b.

With the above considerations at the bifurcation points, computation time (and cost) would be reduced.

4 Numerical Experiments

In this section we present numerical results of our implementation of the parallel homotopy algorithm for two examples. All computations were done on the 64-node "Gamma" machine of CCSF at Caltech with double precision.

Our first example is just a test case, constructed as follows:

$$A = \begin{pmatrix} C & -I & & \\ -I & C & & \\ & & & -I \\ & & -I & C \end{pmatrix}, \text{ where } C = \begin{pmatrix} 4 & a & & \\ b & 4 & & \\ & & & a \\ & & b & 4 \end{pmatrix}$$

with $a = -1 + \delta$, $b = -1 - \delta$, $\delta = 0.5$ (asymmetry parameter). We take B to be the unit matrix. The problem therefore becomes a standard eigenvalue problem $Az = \lambda z$. The dimensions of matrices C and A are 32 and 640 respectively. The number of non-zero elements of A is 3096. We computed the 64 eigenpairs corresponding to the 64 largest eigenvalues of the initial matrix D. The performance for this test example is shown in Table 1. The speedup S_p on p nodes is defined as

$$S_p = T_1 / T_p , \tag{12}$$

where T_1 is the execution time using one node, and T_p is the execution time using p nodes. The efficiency, E_p, is the ratio of the speedup and p. For this test example, we obtained an efficiency higher than 86%.

TABLE 1. Performance of the parallel homotopy algorithm, n = 640, nz = 3096.

Number of Nodes p	Execution Time (sec)	Residual $\max_i \| Az_i - \lambda z_i \|_2$	Speedup S_p	Efficiency E_p
1	4736	1.2657×10^{-11}		
4	1331	1.4567×10^{-11}	3.6	0.889
8	671	1.2789×10^{-11}	7.1	0.881
16	338	1.7524×10^{-11}	14.0	0.876
32	170	1.6435×10^{-11}	27.9	0.870
64	86	1.2534×10^{-11}	55.0	0.860

As expected, the largest eigenvalue ($\lambda = 7.7036491$) was found by following the first eigenpath, i.e., the eigenpath with the largest eigenvalue of the initial matrix.

Our second example is concerned with the prediction of the transition from steady to oscillatory surface-tension-driven flows in a liquid bridge [11]. The governing equations of the problem for velocity $U \equiv (u, v, w)$, temperature Θ, and pressure p in the liquid bridge of volume $V = \{ (r, \theta, z) \mid 0 \leq r \leq R, 0 \leq \theta \leq 2\pi, -L \leq z \leq L \}$ are the Navier-Stokes and energy equations:

$$U_t + Re \ (U \cdot \nabla) \cdot U = - \nabla p + \nabla^2 U, \tag{13}$$
$$\nabla \cdot U = 0, \tag{14}$$
$$\Theta_t + Re \ (U \cdot \nabla) \ \Theta = 1/Pr \ \nabla^2 \Theta, \tag{15}$$

with appropriate boundary conditions. Re and Pr denote the Reynolds-Marangoni and the Prandtl numbers, respectively. For a given fluid, molten silicon, for example, we have a Prandtl number of 0.023. The flow behaviour is then characterized by the Reynolds-Marangoni number. At sufficiently low values of Re, the flow is laminar, steady and axisymmetric. When Re exceeds a critical value, the flow undergoes a transition to an oscillatory mode of convection which depends on the boundary conditions. Such transition in fact corresponds to a Hopf bifurcation where a generalized eigenvalue of the discretized Jacobian matrix of the linearized perturbation equations of (13-15) crosses the imaginary axis. We describe briefly here the method used to solve the stationary equations and to compute the eigenvalues of the perturbation equations.

The spatial finite difference discretization of (13-15) yields a system of ordinary differential equations of the form

$$M \frac{\partial x}{\partial t} = f(x, \lambda, \mu), \tag{16}$$

where x is the solution vector (velocities, pressures and temperatures), λ is the bifurcation parameter (Re in the present case), and μ is the vector of the remaining fixed parameters in the problem. For fixed λ, the steady-state solution (which is assumed to be axisymmetric) x_0 of (16) will satisfy the equation

$$f(x_0, \lambda, \mu) = 0, \tag{17}$$

The stability of the steady-state $x_0 (\lambda)$ can be analyzed by taking small perturbations of the form $\zeta(r, z)e^{\sigma t + in\theta}$ and linearizing (16) about x_0, obtaining

$$f_x \zeta = \sigma M \zeta, \tag{18}$$

where n is the azimuthal wave number and f_x is the Jacobian matrix.

As Re is varied, an axisymmetric steady-state solution may lose stability in one of two ways. One or more generalized eigenvalues of (18) may cross the imaginary axis with zero imaginary part. This case corresponds either to a limit point or to a bifurcation to another steady solution. Alternatively the eigenvalue may cross the imaginary axis at a nonzero imaginary value. This corresponds to a Hopf bifurcation to a periodic solution.

At Re = 71739 for n = 0, we solved the axisymmetric steady equations (17) using the Newton-Raphson method. The computation, using the above presented parallel homotopy algorithm, proceeds by following the first 8 eigenpaths on 8 nodes. The resulting eigenvalues with the largest real part among the 8 computed are the complex conjugate pair $\sigma = -41.36 \pm 404\ i$. To locate a nearby Hopf bifurcation, we solved an extended steady-state system of equations proposed in [12] using the steady state solution, the imaginary part of eigenvalue ($\sigma_i = 404$) and the corresponding eigenvectors at that guessed Reynolds-Marangoni number. After 6 iterations, the system converged to a Hopf bifurcation point at a critical Reynolds-Marangoni number of 78000 and an angular frequency $\sigma_i = 446.2$. This result is obtained on a variable (r, z) mesh, 21x41. The dimension of the generalized eigenvalue problem is 2340x2340 with 18885 non-zero elements of the Jacobian matrix.

5 Conclusion

We have presented a homotopy method for solving a real, large, sparse generalized eigenvalue problem. The essence of the method is that all the eigenpairs can be obtained by following the eigenpaths starting from an initial known generalized eigenvalue problem. The algorithm presented here is well suited for parallel computer architectures because of the independence of the eigenpaths to be followed.

By a special choice of the initial matrix and following only several eigenpaths, we determined selected eigenvalues, for example those with the largest real part. Such an approach, which is of interest in linear stability analysis for hydrodynamic problems, has been applied to a concrete problem of finding the Hopf bifurcation point for surface-tension-driven flows in a liquid bridge.

It would be interesting to compare the present algorithm with the widely used Arnoldi algorithm described in [13].

Acknowledgments

Most of the work of the author (G. C) was done during a visit to the Center for Research on Parallel Computation at Caltech with support from "Conseil Régional Provence-Alpes-Côte d'Azur (France)". All the 64-node computations have been performed on the "Gamma" machine of the Caltech Concurrent Supercomputing Facilities.

References

1. C. B. Moler and G. W. Steward: An algorithm for generalized matrix eigenvalue problems, *SIAM J. Numer. Anal.* **10**, 241-256 (1973)

2. W. Kerner: Large-scale complex eigenvalue problems, *J. Compt. Phys.* **85**, 1-85 (1989)

3. Y. Saad: Numerical solution of large nonsymmetric eigenvalue problems, *Computer Physics Comm.* **53**, 71-90 (1989)

4. T. Y. Li and N. H. Rhee: Homotopy algorithm for symmetric eigenvalue problems, *Numer. Math.* **55**, 265-280 (1989)

5. T. Y. Li, H. Zhang and X. H. Sun: Parallel homotopy algorithm for the symmetric tridiagonal eigenvalue problem, *SIAM J. Sci. Stat. Comput.* **12**, 469-487 (1991)

6. T. Y. Li, Z. G. Zeng and L. Cong: Solving eigenvalue problems of real nonsymmetric matrices with real homotopies, *SIAM J. Numer. Anal.*, to appear

7. S. H. Lui: Ph.D Thesis part 2, Parallel homotopy method for the real nonsymmetric eigenvalue problem, California Institute of Technology, Pasadena, 1991

8. H. B. Keller: Numerical solutions of bifurcation and nonlinear eigenvalue problems. In: P.H. Rabinowitz (ed.): *Applications of bifurcation theory*, New York, Academic Press 1977

9. P. Sonneveld: CGS, A fast Lanczos-type solver for nonsymmetric systems, *SIAM J. Sci. Stat. Comput.* **10**, 36-52 (1989)

10. H.P. Langtangen: Conjugate gradient methodes and ILU preconditioning of non-symmetric matrix systems with arbitrary sparsity patterns, *Int. J. Numer. Meth. Fluids* **9**, 213-233 (1989)

11. J-J. Xu and S. H. Davis: Convective thermocapillary instabilities in liquid bridges, *Phys. Fluids* **27**, 1102-1107 (1984)

12. A. D. Jepson: Ph.D Thesis part 2, Numerical Hopf bifurcation, California Institute of Technology, Pasadena, 1981

13. R. Natarajan: An Arnoldi-based iterative scheme for nonsymmetric matrix pencils arising in finite element stability problems, *J. Compt. Phys.* **100**, 128-142 (1992)

Parallel Algorithms for Solving Linear Recurrence Systems

Przemysław Stpiczyński

Numerical Analysis Department, Marie Curie-Skłodowska University

20-031 Lublin, POLAND

Abstract. We present two parallel algorithms for solving linear recurrence systems $R < n, m >$ where m is relatively small, which can be simply implemented on message passing multiprocessors. Theorems concerning their time complexity are also given together with the criterion when each of them should be used. If m is $O(1)$ then the algorithms are effective .

1. Introduction

The final phase of some numerical methods reduces to the solution of a linear recurrence system $R < n, m >$ of order m for n equations. Many parallel algorithms for this problem have been proposed [1-3,5-8,10]. The main result concerning the complexity of the problem is due to Kuck, who showed [7] that it can be solved on p processors in T_p steps, where $T_p < (2 + \log_2 m) \log_2 n - \frac{1}{2}(1 + \log_2 m) \log_2 m$ and $p \leq \frac{1}{2} m(m+1)n + O(m^3)$ if $1 \leq m \leq n/2$, otherwise $p \leq n^3/68 + O(n^2)$.

In this paper we present two new medium grain parallel algorithms for solving $R < n, m >$, which can be simply implemented on message passing multiprocessors [4,9] on condition that the number of available processors is less than n/m. We also state theorems concerning the time complexity of the algorithms, estimate the optimal number of processors to perform each of them and compare their performance.

2. Model of computation

Let us consider the following model of computation. It consists of p processors P_j, $j = 1, .., p$, each with its own memory and no global memory is available. The machine operates in an asynchronous MIMD mode. Communications are by rendez-vous and there is no overlap between communications and computations. Each processor P_j (except P_p) can send data to P_{j+1} using the "**send** *data*" primitive routine. On the other hand, using the "**receive** *data*" primitive routine, the processor P_{j+1} can read data sent by its left neighbour.

To study the complexity of the algorithms, we make the following assumptions:

(a) a time step for an arithmetic operation lasts τ_a and it is constituted by one multiplication plus one addition;

(b) it lasts $m\tau_c$ to transfer m floating point words between two processors.

3. Description of the methods

Let us consider a linear recurrence system $R < n, m >$ of order m for n equations, where $m \leq n - 1$ [3,8]:

$$R < n, m >: \quad x_k = \begin{cases} 0 & \text{if } k \leq 0 \\ f_k + \sum_{j=k-m}^{k-1} a_{kj} x_j & \text{if } 1 \leq k \leq n \end{cases}. \quad (3.1)$$

Computing x_k for $1 \leq k \leq n$ reduces to the solution of the system of linear equations

$$(I - A)\mathbf{x} = \mathbf{f} \qquad (3.2)$$

where $\mathbf{x} = (x_1, .., x_n)^T$, $\mathbf{f} = (f_1, .., f_n)^T$ and $A = (a_{ik})$, $a_{ik} = 0$ for $i \leq k$ or $i - k > m$.

Without loss of generality, let us assume that n is divisible by p and $n/p > m$. Let $q = n/p$. If we assign for $j = 1, .., p$

$$
L_j =
\begin{pmatrix}
1 & & & & & & \\
-a_{r+2,r+1} & 1 & & & & & \\
\vdots & \vdots & \ddots & & & & \\
-a_{r+m+1,r+1} & \cdots & -a_{r+m+1,r+m} & 1 & & & \\
& \ddots & & \ddots & \ddots & & \\
& & -a_{jq,jq-m} & \cdots & -a_{jq,jq-1} & 1
\end{pmatrix}, \qquad (3.3a)
$$

$$\mathbf{x}_j = (x_{(j-1)q+1}, \ldots, x_{jq})^T, \qquad \mathbf{f}_j = (f_{(j-1)q+1}, \ldots, f_{jq})^T \qquad (3.3b)$$

$$
U_j =
\begin{pmatrix}
0 & \cdots & 0 & -a_{r+1,r-m+1} & \cdots & -a_{r+1,r} \\
\vdots & & & \ddots & & \vdots \\
& & & 0 & & -a_{r+m,r} \\
& & & & \ddots & 0 \\
& & & & & \vdots \\
\mathbf{0} & & & \cdots & & 0
\end{pmatrix}, \qquad \text{for } j = 2, .., p, \quad (3.3c)
$$

where $r = (j-1)q$, then the system (3.2) can be written as

$$
\begin{pmatrix}
L_1 & & & \\
U_2 & L_2 & & \\
& \ddots & \ddots & \\
& & U_p & L_p
\end{pmatrix}
\begin{pmatrix}
\mathbf{x}_1 \\ \mathbf{x}_2 \\ \vdots \\ \mathbf{x}_p
\end{pmatrix}
=
\begin{pmatrix}
\mathbf{f}_1 \\ \mathbf{f}_2 \\ \vdots \\ \mathbf{f}_p
\end{pmatrix}. \qquad (3.4)
$$

This yields

$$\mathbf{x}_1 = L_1^{-1}\mathbf{f}_1 \quad \text{and} \quad \mathbf{x}_j = L_j^{-1}\mathbf{f}_j - L_j^{-1}U_j\mathbf{x}_{j-1} \text{ for } j = 2, .., p. \qquad (3.5)$$

Let U_j^k denotes the k-th column of U_j. Thus $U_j\mathbf{x}_{j-1} = \sum_{k=1}^{q} x_{(j-2)q+k}U_j^k$, but $U_j^k = 0$ for $k = 1, .., q - m$, so

$$L_j^{-1}U_j\mathbf{x}_{j-1} = \sum_{k=q-m+1}^{q} x_{(j-2)q+k}L_j^{-1}U_j^k = \sum_{k=0}^{m-1} x_{(j-1)q-k}L_j^{-1}U_j^{q-k}. \qquad (3.6)$$

Finally from (3.5) using (3.3) and (3.6) we have

$$\mathbf{x}_1 = L_1^{-1}\mathbf{f}_1 \quad \text{and} \quad \mathbf{x}_j = \mathbf{z}_j - \sum_{k=0}^{m-1} x_{(j-1)q-k}\mathbf{y}_j^k \text{ for } j = 2, .., p, \qquad (3.7)$$

where $L_j\mathbf{z}_j = \mathbf{f}_j$ and $L_j\mathbf{y}_j^k = U_j^{q-k}$ for $k = 0, .., m - 1$.

To implement the method (3.7) on the parallel machine, let us assume that the system (3.2) is divided into p subsystems due to (3.4) and each P_j holds L_j, U_j and $\mathbf{f}_j$. Under the above conditions we can give the following algorithm.

ALGORITHM 1

Processor P_1:
begin
    solve $L_1\mathbf{x}_1 = \mathbf{f}_1$
    send $(x_{q-m+1}, x_{q-m+2}, .., x_q)$
end

Processor P_j, $j = 2, .., p$:
begin
    solve systems $L_j\mathbf{z}_j = \mathbf{f}_j$, $L_j\mathbf{y}_j^k = U_j^{q-k}$ for $k = 0, .., m-1$
    receive $(x_{(j-1)q-m+1}, x_{(j-1)q-m+2}, .., x_{(j-1)q})$
    compute $(x_{jq-m+1}, x_{jq-m+2}, .., x_{jq})$ /* (3.7) */
    if $j \neq p$ **then send** $(x_{jq-m+1}, x_{jq-m+2}, .., x_{jq})$
    compute $(x_{(j-1)q+1}, .., x_{jq-m})$ /* (3.7) */
end

Let us consider another parallel method for solving (3.4) which sometimes can work faster than the algorithm presented above. Let the k-th unit vector of $\mathbb{R}^q$ be denoted by $\mathbf{e}_k$. Thus for $j = 2, .., p$

$$U_j = -\sum_{k=1}^{m}\sum_{l=k}^{m} \beta_j^{kl} \mathbf{e}_k \mathbf{e}_{q-m+l}^T, \quad \text{where} \quad \beta_j^{kl} = a_{(j-1)q+k,(j-1)q-m+l}.$$

This yields $\mathbf{x}_j = L_j^{-1}\mathbf{f}_j + \sum_{k=1}^{m}\sum_{l=k}^{m} \beta_j^{kl} L_j^{-1}\mathbf{e}_k \mathbf{e}_{q-m+l}^T \mathbf{x}_{j-1}$ for $j = 2, .., p$. Let us assign for $j = 2, .., p$

$$\mathbf{z}_j = L_j^{-1}\mathbf{f}_j , \quad \mathbf{y}_j^k = L_j^{-1}\mathbf{e}_k \text{ and } \alpha_j^k = \sum_{l=k}^{m} \beta_j^{kl} \mathbf{e}_{q-m+l}^T \mathbf{x}_{j-1} \text{ for } k = 1, .., m.$$

$$(3.8)$$

Finally, using (3.8) we can compute the solution of (3.4):

$$\mathbf{x}_1 = L_1^{-1}\mathbf{f}_1 \text{ and } \mathbf{x}_j = \mathbf{z}_j + \sum_{k=1}^{m} \alpha_j^k \mathbf{y}_j^k \text{ for } j = 2, .., p. \qquad (3.9)$$

The parallel algorithm based on (3.9) can be described as follows.

ALGORITHM 2

Processor P_1: the same action as P_1 in Algorithm 1

Processor P_j, $j = 2, .., p$:
begin
    solve systems $L_j\mathbf{z}_j = \mathbf{f}_j$, $L_j\mathbf{y}_j^k = \mathbf{e}_k$ for $k = 1, .., m$
    receive $(x_{(j-1)q-m+1}, x_{(j-1)q-m+2}, .., x_{(j-1)q})$
    compute α_j^k for $k = 1, .., m$
    compute $(x_{jq-m+1}, x_{jq-m+2}, .., x_{jq})$ /* (3.9) */
    if $j \neq p$ **then send** $(x_{jq-m+1}, x_{jq-m+2}, .., x_{jq})$
    compute $(x_{(j-1)q+1}, .., x_{jq-m})$ /* (3.9) */
end

4. Complexity of the algorithms

In this section we present theorems concerning the time complexity of the parallel algorithms for solving (3.2). First, let us prove the following theorem.

Theorem 1. *The system (3.2) can be solved by one processor in time*

$$T_1(n) = m \left(n - \tfrac{m+1}{2}\right) \tau_a. \tag{4.1}$$

Proof: Using a sequential algorithm based on (3.1), we obtain

$$T_1(n) = \sum_{k=1}^{m-1} k\tau_a + m(n-m)\tau_a = m \left(n - \tfrac{m+1}{2}\right) \tau_a \qquad \square$$

Theorem 2. *The time complexity of Algorithm 1 is*

$$T_{p,1}(n) = m \left[mp + (m+2)q - \tfrac{1}{2}(m^2 + 6m + 1)\right] \tau_a + (p-1)m\tau_c \tag{4.2}$$

where p is a number of processors and $q = n/p > m$.

Proof: Let us consider the critical path of the algorithm. First, each processor (except P_1) has to solve $m+1$ systems of linear equations. Due to Theorem 1 it takes $t_1 = m(m+1)\left[q - \tfrac{1}{2}(m+1)\right]\tau_a$. Then each processor P_j (except P_1 and P_p) has to receive m numbers, then to compute m last components of $\mathbf{x}_j$ and to send them to its neighbour. It takes $t_2 = (p-2)(m\tau_c + m^2\tau_a)$. Finally, the processor P_p has to receive m numbers and then to compute x_p. It can be done in time $t_3 = m\tau_c + qm\tau_a$. Summing the quantities t_1, t_2, t_3 we complete the proof. $\square$

To study the complexity of Algorithm 2, let us make the following observations.

Observation 1. *A system of linear equations $L\mathbf{x} = \mathbf{e}_k$, where $q - k > m$ and $L \in \mathbb{R}^{q \times q}$ is like (3.3a) can be solved sequentially in time*

$$t_k(q) = m \left(q - k - \tfrac{m+1}{2}\right) \tau_a. \tag{4.3}$$

Proof: Let $\mathbf{x} = (x_1, x_2, \ldots, x_q)^T$. We have $x_i = 0$ for $i = 1, .., k-1$ and $x_k = 1$. Thus it remains to solve the system $L'\mathbf{x}' = \mathbf{f}'$ where $L \in \mathbb{R}^{(q-k) \times (q-k)}$ and $\mathbf{x}', \mathbf{f}' \in \mathbb{R}^{q-k}$. The matrix L' is like (3.3a), so using (4.1) we complete the proof. $\square$

Observation 2. *A sequence of systems of linear equations $L\mathbf{x} = \mathbf{e}_k$, $k = 1, .., m$ where $L \in \mathbb{R}^{q \times q}$ is like (3.3a) and $q > 2m$ can be solved sequentially in time*

$$t_{1,m}(q) = m^2(q - m - 1)\tau_a. \tag{4.4}$$

Proof: Due to Observation 1

$$t_{1,m}(q) = \sum_{k=1}^{m} t_k(q) = \sum_{k=1}^{m} m(q - k - \tfrac{m+1}{2})\tau_a = m^2(q - m - 1)\tau_a \qquad \square$$

Now we can state the theorem concerning the time complexity of Algorithm 2.

Theorem 3. *The time complexity of Algorithm 2 is*

$$T_{p,2}(n) = m\left[(\tfrac{3}{2}m + \tfrac{1}{2})p + (m+2)q - (m^2 + \tfrac{9}{2}m + \tfrac{1}{2})\right]\tau_a + (p-1)m\tau_c \quad (4.5)$$

where $p < \frac{n}{2m}$ is a number of processors and $q = n/p$.

Proof: As in the proof of Theorem 2, let us study the critical path of the algorithm. First each processor (except P_1) has to solve $m+1$ systems of linear equations. Theorem 1 and Observation 2 imply that

$$t_1 = m(q - \tfrac{1}{2}(m+1))\tau_a + m^2(q - m - 1)\tau_a = m(m+1)[q - (m+\tfrac{1}{2})]\tau_a.$$

Next, each processor P_j (except P_1 and P_p) has to receive m numbers, then to compute coefficients α_j^k for $k = 1,..,m$ and to compute m last components of $\mathbf{x}_j$. Thus

$$t_2 = (p-2)(m\tau_c + \tfrac{1}{2}m(m+1)\tau_a + m^2\tau_a).$$

The processor P_p receives data from P_{p-1} and computes α_p^k for $k = 1,..,m$. Because of each vector $\mathbf{y}_j^k$ for $j = 2,..,p$ and $k = 1,..,m$ has at least $k-1$ zero components, the computing of $\mathbf{x}_j$ takes $(qm - \tfrac{1}{2}m(m-1))\tau_a$. So

$$t_3 = m\tau_c + \tfrac{1}{2}m(m+1)\tau_a + (qm - \tfrac{1}{2}m(m-1))\tau_a = m\tau_c + m(q+1)\tau_a \quad \square$$

5. Comparison of the algorithms

Let us assume that the number of available processors p is less than $\frac{n}{2m}$, what implies that the dimension of subsystems assigned to processors is greater than $2m$. Under this assumption we will compare the performance of the presented parallel algorithms.

Let us compute the difference between the quantities (4.2) and (4.5).

$$T_{p,1}(n) - T_{p,2}(n) = m[\tfrac{1}{2}m(m+1) - \tfrac{1}{2}(p-2)(m+1) - 1]\tau_a$$

Thus $T_{p,1}(n) - T_{p,2}(n) > 0$ for $p < m + \frac{2m}{m+1}$. This yields

Corollary 1. *Algorithm 2 gives better time complexity results when the number of processors is less than $m + \frac{2m}{m+1}$.*

Let us consider the function $f(p) = T_{p,1}(n)$. It achieves its minimum at the point

$$p_1^* = \sqrt{\left(\frac{m+2}{m+\rho}\right)n}, \quad \text{where } \rho = \tau_c/\tau_a. \quad (5.1)$$

Depending on the relation between $f(\lfloor p_1^* \rfloor)$ and $f(\lceil p_1^* \rceil)$, we obtain $\lfloor p_1^* \rfloor$ or $\lceil p_1^* \rceil$ as the optimal number of processors to perform Algorithm 1. Analogously, the function $g(p) = T_{p,2}(n)$ achieves its minimum at the point

$$p_2^* = \sqrt{\left(\frac{2m+4}{3m+2\rho+1}\right)n}. \quad (5.2)$$

Thus, depending on the relation between $g(\lfloor p_2^* \rfloor)$ and $g(\lceil p_2^* \rceil)$, we can estimate the optimal number of processors to perform Algorithm 2. We also get the following corollary.

Corollary 2. *If m is $O(1)$ and the number of processors is optimal then the algorithms work in time $O(\sqrt{n})$.*

Let us define the asymptotic efficiency of a parallel algorithm as

$$e_\infty = \lim_{n \to \infty} T_1(n)/(p^* T_{p^*}(n)) \tag{5.3}$$

where p^* is the optimal number of processors.

From (5.3) using (5.1), (4.2) and (5.2), (4.5) we can compute the asymptotic efficiency of Algorithm 1 and Algorithm 2 respectively. The results yield the final corollary.

Corollary 3. *If m is $O(1)$ then the asymptotic efficiency of the algorithms is $\Theta(1)$ (i.e. the algorithms are effective).*

We have presented two new algorithms for solving linear recurrence systems $R < n, m >$ which can be implemented on message passing multiprocessors. If m is $O(1)$ then the algorithms work in time $O(\sqrt{n})$ what gives worse time complexity in comparison with the algorithms presented in the literature, but they use only $O(\sqrt{n})$ processors, thus their asymptotic efficiency is $\Theta(1)$. Other algorithms which run in time $O(\log n)$ need $O(n)$ proocessors.

References

1. A. Borodin, I. Munro: The computational complexity of algebraic and numerical problems. New York:American Elsevier 1975
2. S.-C. Chen: Speedup of iterative programs in multiprocessing systems. Dissertation. Dept. of Computer Sci., University of Illinois Urbana 1975
3. S.-C. Chen, D.J. Kuck: Time and parallel processor bounds for linear recurrence systems. IEEE Trans. on Computers 24, 701-717 (1975)
4. M. Cosnard, B. Tourancheau, G. Villard: Gaussian elimination on message passing architecture. In E.N. Houstis et al. (eds.): Supercomputing. Lecture Notes in Computer Science 297. Berlin: Springer 1988. pp. 611-628
5. D. Heller: A survey of parallel algorithms in numerical linear algebra. SIAM Review 20, 740-777 (1978)
6. L. Hyafil, H.T. Kung: The complexity of parallel evaluation of linear recurrences. Journal of ACM 24, 513-521 (1977)
7. D.J. Kuck: Structure of Computers and Computations. New York: Wiley 1978
8. J. Modi: Parallel Algorithms and Matrix Computations. Oxford: Oxford University Press 1988
9. Y. Robert, B. Tourancheau, G. Villard: Data allocation strategies for Gauss and Jordan algorithms on a ring of processors. Inf. Proc. Letters 31, 21-29 (1989)
10. A.H. Sameh, R.P. Brent: Solving triangular systems on a parallel computer. SIAM J. Numer. Anal. 14, 1101-1113 (1977)

A New Parallel Factorization $A = DD^t BC$ for Band Symmetric Positive Definite Matrices

Ilan Bar-On and Ophir Munk

Technion - Israel Institute of Technology,
Departement of Computer Science,
Technion City, Haifa 32 000, Israel.

Abstract. We present a new factorization for band symmetric positive definite (s.p.d) matrices which is more useful for parallel computations than the classical Choleskey decomposition method. Let A be a band s.p.d matrix of order n and half bandwidth m and let $p = 2^k$ be the number of processors. We show how to factor A as $A = DD^t BC$ using approximately $4nm^2/p$ parallel operations, which is the maximum number of operations used by any processor. Having this factorization, we improve the time to solve $Ax = b$ by a factor of m using approximately $4nm/p$ parallel operations. There are more applications to our algorithm, such as calculating $\det(A)$, using iterative refinement methods, or computing eigenvalues by the inverse power method. Numerical experiments indicate that our results are as good as LINPACK which is a Fortran machine-independent software for numerical linear algebra.

1 Introduction

The solution of large and band symmetric positive definite linear systems is involved in many mathematical applications. Let n denote the matrix order and m its half bandwidth. In the classical (serial) way in order to solve $Ax = b$ we first factor the s.p.d matrix, A, as $A = LL^t$ (known as the Choleskey decomposition) in $O(nm^2)$ time and then solve the linear system $LL^t x = b$ in two steps: 1. Solve $Ly = b$ 2. Solve $L^t x = y$. Each step takes $O(nm)$ time. Having the factorization at hand (a "preprocessing" stage) enables the solution of $Ax = b$ in $O(nm)$ time. Parallel solutions of the band triangular system $LL^t x = b$ have failed to use $O(nm)$ operations. They require $O(nm^2)$ operations and were shown to be numerically unstable [3]. In this case there is no gain in factoring A as $A = LL^t$. In [1] Bar-On gave a practical and efficient parallel algorithm for solving the linear system $Ax = b$ that runs in $O(nm^2/p)$ time for $p \leq nm/\log n$ processors. His algorithm does not use the traditional Choleskey decomposition. In this paper we go one step further by factoring A as $A = DD^t BC$ using approximately $4nm^2/p$ parallel operations. Having this new factorization, we improve the time for solving $Ax = b$ by a factor of m to approximately $4nm/p$ parallel operations.

2 Parallel Factorization $A = DD^t BC$.

Let A be a band s.p.d matrix of order n and half bandwidth m, and let p be the number of processors. We assume for simplicity that $n = qm$, $p = 2^k$, $q = sp$, where

$$
\begin{pmatrix}
A_1 & U_1^t & & & \\
U_1 & A_2 & U_2^t & & \\
& \ddots & \ddots & \ddots & \\
& & \ddots & \ddots & \ddots \\
& & & U_{q-2} & A_{q-1} & U_{q-1}^t \\
& & & & U_{q-1} & A_q
\end{pmatrix}
\quad
\begin{pmatrix}
0 & U_{r_i} & A_{r_i+1} & U_{r_i+1}^t & & 0 & 0 & 0 \\
\vdots & 0 & U_{r_i+1} & A_{r_i+2} & U_{r_i+2}^t & & \vdots & \vdots \\
\vdots & \vdots & & \ddots & \ddots & & 0 & \vdots \\
0 & 0 & 0 & & U_{r_i+s-1} & A_{r_i+s} & U_{r_i+s}^t & 0
\end{pmatrix}
$$

$$\underbrace{}_{Q_i} \quad \underbrace{}_{M_i} \quad \underbrace{}_{R_i}$$

Fig. 1. Matrix A (on the left) and A_i^0, the ith s-group of A (on the right).

q, s, k are integers. A can be viewed as a tridiagonal block matrix, see Fig. 1. Here, $U_i, A_i \in M(m \times m)$, U_i is upper triangular, A_i is s.p.d. We refer to the $m \times n$ sub-matrix $(\, 0 \ U_{i-1} \ A_i \ U_i^t \ 0 \,)$ as the ith virtual row of A, and to the $n \times m$ sub-matrix $(\, 0 \ U_{i-1} \ A_i \ U_i^t \ 0 \,)^t$ as the ith virtual column of A. An r-group is a sub-matrix of A that contains r consecutive virtual rows of A. A is initially divided into p s-groups, where s-group i contains virtual rows $(i-1)s+1, \ldots, is$ for $i = 1, \ldots, p$. Processor P_i is assigned to s-group i, denoted by A_i^0, see Fig. 1. Here, $M_i \in M(n/p \times n/p)$ is s.p.d., $R_i, Q_i \in M(n/p \times m)$, $r_i = (i-1)s$. M_i, Q_i and R_i correspond to the principal sub-matrix of s-group i, its (i-1)sth virtual column and its (is+1)st virtual column respectively. The factorization is executed in two phases: a **diagonalization** phase, where the DD^t factor is found and an **elimination** phase where the B and C factors are found.

2.1 Diagonalization Phase

In this phase we diagonalize s-group i, $i = 1, \ldots p$, by multiplying it by M_i^{-1}. This is done as follows: P_i, $i = 1, \ldots, p$, finds the $L_i L_i^t$ Cholesky decomposition of M_i (which is s.p.d) and then multiplies Q_i and R_i by $(L_i L_i^t)^{-1}$ by solving $2m$ band linear systems corresponding to the $2m$ columns of Q_i and R_i. As a result we get $\tilde{Q}_i = (L_i L_i^t)^{-1} Q_i$ and $\tilde{R}_i = (L_i L_i^t)^{-1} R_i$. The resulting sub-matrix is shown in Fig. 2. Here, $E_i^0, G_i^0, F_i^0, H_i^0 \in M(m \times m)$. P_i uses $O(nm/p)$ space to store $\tilde{Q}_i$, $\tilde{R}_i$ and L_i, see [2] for more details. We define the D factor by the block diagonal matrix $D = \text{diag}(L_1, \ldots, L_p)$. In [2] we show that the D factor can be calculated and stored in $O(nm^2)$ time using $O(nm)$ space.

2.2 Elimination Phase:

In this phase we use $\log p$ iterations to bring A to a form (denoted by matrix C) which is suitable for parallel computations. Initially there are p s-groups denoted by A_i^0, $i = 1, \ldots, p$. The kth $(1 \le k \le \log p)$ iteration starts with $p/2^k$ $(2^k s)$-groups. We denote by A_i^k, $1 \le i \le p/2^k$, the ith $(2^k s)$-group in the kth iteration. A_i^k is the union of the $(2i\text{-}1)$st and the $2i$th $(2^{k-1} s)$-groups from the previous iteration (i.e. A_{2i-1}^{k-1} and A_{2i}^{k-1}), see Fig. 2.

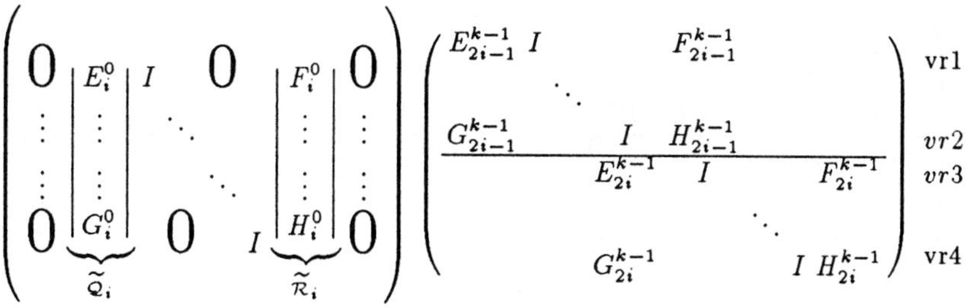

$$\begin{pmatrix} 0 & \begin{matrix} E_i^0 & I \\ \vdots & \vdots \\ 0 & G_i^0 \end{matrix} & \begin{matrix} 0 \\ \ddots \\ 0 \end{matrix} & I & \begin{matrix} F_i^0 \\ \vdots \\ \vdots \\ H_i^0 \end{matrix} & \begin{matrix} 0 \\ \vdots \\ \vdots \\ 0 \end{matrix} \\ & \underbrace{\qquad}_{\widetilde{\mathcal{Q}}_i} & & \underbrace{\qquad}_{\widetilde{\mathcal{R}}_i} & \end{pmatrix} \begin{pmatrix} E_{2i-1}^{k-1} & I & & F_{2i-1}^{k-1} & & \\ & \ddots & & & & \\ G_{2i-1}^{k-1} & & I & H_{2i-1}^{k-1} & & \\ & & E_{2i}^{k-1} & I & & F_{2i}^{k-1} \\ & & & & \ddots & \\ G_{2i}^{k-1} & & & & I & H_{2i}^{k-1} \end{pmatrix} \begin{matrix} vr1 \\ \\ vr2 \\ vr3 \\ \\ vr4 \end{matrix}$$

Fig. 2. s-group i at the end of the diagonalization phase (on the left) and the ith $(2^k s)$-group at the beginning of the kth iteration of the elimination phase (on the right).

We have two objectives: **objective 1** - elimination of E_{2i}^{k-1} and H_{2i-1}^{k-1} in parallel. **objective 2** - elimination of G_{2i}^{k-1} and F_{2i-1}^{k-1} in parallel. The following discussion concerns only A_i^k. Let "$vr1$" and "$vr2$" denote the first and last virtual rows of A_{2i-1}^{k-1}. Let "$vr3$" and "$vr4$" denote the first and last virtual rows of A_{2i}^{k-1}. We denote by P_{vr1}, P_{vr2}, P_{vr3} and P_{vr4} the processors assigned respectively to $vr1$, $vr2$, $vr3$ and $vr4$. Execution of **objective 1**: P_{vr2} sends $vr2$ to P_{vr3} and at the same time P_{vr3} sends $vr3$ to P_{vr2}. Then P_{vr3} subtracts E_{2i}^{k-1} times $vr2$ from $vr3$ (to eliminate E_{2i}^{k-1}) and at the same time P_{vr2} subtracts H_{2i-1}^{k-1} times $vr3$ from $vr2$ (to eliminate H_{2i-1}^{k-1}), see Fig. 3. Execution of **objective 2**: P_{vr3} sends $vr3$ to P_{vr1} and at the same time P_{vr2}

$$A_i^k = \begin{pmatrix} E_{2i-1}^{k-1} & I & & F_{2i-1}^{k-1} & & \\ & \ddots & & & & \\ G_{2i-1}^{k-1} & & I - H_{2i-1}^{k-1}E_{2i}^{k-1} & 0 & & -H_{2i-1}^{k-1}F_{2i}^{k-1} \\ -E_{2i}^{k-1}G_{2i-1}^{k-1} & & 0 & I - E_{2i}^{k-1}H_{2i-} & & F_{2i}^{k-1} \\ & & & & \ddots & \\ G_{2i}^{k-1} & & & & I & H_{2i}^{k-1} \end{pmatrix} \begin{matrix} vr1 \\ \\ vr2 \\ vr3 \\ \\ vr4 \end{matrix}$$

Fig. 3. Elimination phase. After the accomplishment of **objective 1**.

sends $vr2$ to P_{vr4}. Then P_{vr1} subtracts $F_{2i-1}^{k-1}(I - E_{2i}^{k-1}H_{2i-1}^{k-1})^{-1}$ times $vr3$ from $vr1$ (to eliminate F_{2i-1}^{k-1}) and at the same time P_{vr4} subtracts $G_{2i}^{k-1}(I - H_{2i-1}^{k-1}E_{2i}^{k-1})^{-1}$ times $vr2$ from $vr4$ (to eliminate G_{2i}^{k-1}), see Fig. 4. This completes the kth iteration. The next iteration starts with A_i^{k+1} with the same basic structure as A_i^k, and the whole process begins again. Since the number of groups is halved in each iteration (and the number of virtual rows in each group is doubled) – after $\log p$ iterations the elimination phase terminates with one (ps)-group. In [2] we give an example.
Time and space complexity: Let T_p denote the running time of the parallel algorithm with p processors. In [2] we show that our algorithm is efficient with

$$
A_i^k = \begin{pmatrix}
E_i^k & I & & & 0 & & & F_i^k \\
& \ddots & & & & & & \\
G_{2i-1}^{k-1} & & I - H_{2i-1}^{k-1}E_{2i}^{k-1} & & 0 & & & -H_{2i-1}^{k-1}F_{2i}^{k-1} \\
-E_{2i}^{k-1}G_{2i-1}^{k-1} & & 0 & & I - E_{2i}^{k-1}H_{2i-1}^{k-1} & & & F_{2i}^{k-1} \\
& & & & & \ddots & & \\
G_i^k & & 0 & & & & I & H_i^k
\end{pmatrix}
\begin{matrix}
vr1 \\ \\ vr2 \\ vr3 \\ \\ vr4
\end{matrix}
$$

Fig. 4. Elimination phase. At the end of the kth iteration.

$T_p = O(nm^2/p)$ for $p \le q/\log q$, $q = n/m$. We also show that the additional space used to store the main diagonal of C is $2m^2(p-1)$ numbers.

2.3 Description of the B factor

Let B_k, $1 \le k \le \log p$, be the matrix that performs the kth iteration of the elimination phase, then, by defining B as $B \equiv B_1^{-1}B_2^{-1}\cdots B_{\log p}^{-1}$ we get that $A = DD^tBC$. Let $B_{k,i}$ be a matrix of order $\frac{n}{p}2^k$ that performs the kth iteration on A_i^k. Fig 5 show the structure of $B_{k,i}^{-1}$. B_k^{-1} is the direct sum of the square

$$
\underbrace{\begin{pmatrix}
I & & & & 0 \\
& \ddots & & & \\
& & I & -H & \\
& & -E & I & \\
& & & & \ddots \\
0 & & & & I
\end{pmatrix}}_{B_{k,i,1}}
\underbrace{\begin{pmatrix}
I & & & -FZ \\
& \ddots & & \\
& & I & \\
& & & I \\
& & & & \ddots \\
& -GY & & & I
\end{pmatrix}}_{B_{k,i,2}}
\underbrace{\begin{pmatrix}
I & & & FZ \\
& \ddots & & \\
& & \begin{pmatrix} I & -H \\ -E & I \end{pmatrix}^{-1} & \\
& & & \\
& GY & & & I
\end{pmatrix}}_{B_{k,i}^{-1}}
$$

Fig. 5. $B_{k,i,1}$ - the matrix that performs **objective 1**, $B_{k,i,2}$ - the matrix that performs **objective 2** and $B_{k,i}^{-1}$

sub-matrices $B_{k,i}^{-1}$. ¿From the structure of B_k^{-1}, it can be seen that the elements of the product $\prod_{i=1}^{\log p} B_i^{-1}$ fit right into B, with no intermixed operations. This is exemplified and discussed in more details in [2].

Space complexity: In [2] we show that the total space used for the storage of B is $4m^2(p-1)$ numbers and the total space used to store D, B and C is no more than $3nm + 6m^2p \le 6nm$ for $p \le n/(2m)$.

2.4 k-cube implementation

Let $\vec{S}_i$ be a sequence of 2^i numbers defined as follows:

$$\vec{S}_i \stackrel{\text{def}}{=} \begin{cases} \{0,1\} & \text{if } i = 1 \\ \{0[\vec{S}_{i-1}], 1[\overleftarrow{S}_{i-1}]\} & \text{if } i > 1 \end{cases} \tag{1}$$

Here $\overleftarrow{S}_i$ (with left arrow) has $\vec{S}_i$'s numbers in a reversed order. $0[\vec{S}_i]$ (or $1[\vec{S}_i]$) is a sequence obtained by appending bit 0 (or 1) before each number in $\vec{S}_i$. Every number in $\vec{S}_i$ is represented by i bits. For example: $\vec{S}_2 = \{00, 01, 11, 10\}$ and $\vec{S}_3 = \{000, 001, 011, 010, 110, 111, 101, 100\}$.

If we divide $\vec{S}_k$ into any 2^w, $(w \leq k)$, equal sized subsequences, then it is clear that within each subsequence the two extreme and the two middle numbers differ in exactly one bit.

By the k-cube definition a cube's corner, with k bits address, is connected to k other corners whose binary address differ from its own by one bit. We design a new strategy for message passing - in **objective 1** we change the roles of P_{vr2} and P_{vr3} - P_{vr2} calculates what P_{vr3} had to calculate and vice versa (in any case both processors have $vr2$ and $vr3$). Then in **objective 2** P_{vr2} will send $vr3$ to P_{vr1} (doing P_{vr3}'s job) and P_{vr3} will send $vr2$ to P_{vr4} (doing P_{vr2}'s job). Hence, in the kth iteration, data is transferred only between the two middle virtual rows of A_i^k ($P_{vr2} \Leftrightarrow P_{vr3}$) and the two extreme virtual rows of A_{2i-1}^{k-1} and A_{2i}^{k-1} ($P_{vr1} \Leftarrow P_{vr2}$, $P_{vr3} \Rightarrow P_{vr4}$). Let P_i's , $i = 1, \ldots, p$, address be the ith element of $\vec{S}_k$ where $p = 2^k$, then whenever P_i sends data to P_j ($i \neq j$) there is a direct linking between them.

3 Applications for the DD^tBC factorization

3.1 Calculation of det(A)

In [2] we show how to calculate $\det(A)$ in $O(n/p + m^3 + \log p) = O(n/p)$ time.

3.2 Parallel Solution of $Ax = b$

Given A factored as DD^tBC we find the solution x in three steps: 1. Solve $DD^tz = b$. 2. Solve $By = z$. 3. Solve $Cx = y$.

Step 1: Since D is the direct sum of p lower triangular matrices, $D = \text{diag}(L_1, L_2, \ldots, L_p)$, it is clear that step 1 can be solved independently and in parallel by each processor. Processor P_i solves $L_i \tilde{z}_i = b_i$ and then $L_i^t z_i = \tilde{z}_i$ where z_i and b_i denote the corresponding sub-vectors of z and b. Therefore, step 1 takes $O(\frac{n}{p}m)$ time.

Step 2: This step consists of $\log p$ iterations. In the kth iteration, $k = 1, \ldots, \log p$, we solve the system $B_k^{-1} z_{k+1} = z_k$, or $z_{k+1} = B_k z_k$, where $z_1 = z$ and $y = z_{\log p+1}$. We note that B_k is the direct sum of the $p/2^k$ block matrices $B_{k,i}$, $1 \leq i \leq p/2^k$ corresponding to the $p/2^k$ ($s2^k$)-groups in the kth iteration. Therefore, we execute $z_{k+1,i} = B_{k,i,2}B_{k,i,1}z_{k,i}$ where $z_{k,i}$ and $z_{k+1,i}$ denote corresponding sub-vectors of z_k and z_{k+1}. It is clear that we actually perform on $z_{k,i}$ the same row operations that were executed on A_i^k during the elimination phase. More details can be found in [2] where we show that step 2 takes $O(m^2 \log p)$ time.

Step 3: The solutions are found in $\log p$ steps as follows: In step k, $k = \log p - 1, \ldots, 1$, we find in parallel the solutions corresponding to $vr2$ and $vr3$ of each $(2^k s)$-group. Then, in a final step, each processor finds independently and in parallel the solutions corresponding to the remaining $(s - 2)$ virtual rows of its s-group. In [2] we give a pseodo code for this step and show that it takes $O(\frac{n}{p}m + m^2 \log p)$ time. **Conclusion:** The solution of $Ax = b$ is efficient with $T_p = O(nm/p)$ for $p \le q/\log q$, $q = n/m$.

4 Numerical Experiments

In this section we present some numerical results we have obtained from the solution of $Ax = b$. We have generated a random s.p.d matrix A and a random vector x, and produced the solution vector $b = Ax$. We then solved the system using LINPACK and our parallel factorization. The experiments indicate that our results are as good as those of LINPACK, regardless of the number of processors or bandwidth. For more details see [2]. In Table 1 $n = 8192$, $m = 16, 4, 8, 2$, $p = 16, 32, 64, 128$.

estimated condition number	3.54D+06		3.88D+06	
	$m = 16$, $p = 16$	LINPACK	$m = 8$, $p = 32$	LINPACK
maximum absolute error	0.678D-10	0.677D-10	0.108D-09	0.108D-09
average absolute error	0.156D-11	0.167D-11	0.157D-11	0.116D-11
maximum relative error	0.620D-07	0.138D-06	0.398D-08	0.379D-08
average relative error	0.251D-10	0.338D-10	0.109D-10	0.841D-11

estimated condition number	4.26D+06		1.25D+07	
	$m = 4$, $p = 64$	LINPACK	$m = 2$, $p = 128$	LINPACK
maximum absolute error	0.131D-09	0.109D-09	0.315D-09	0.403D-09
average absolute error	0.786D-12	0.857D-12	0.925D-12	0.110D-11
maximum relative error	0.114D-07	0.548D-07	0.752D-08	0.116D-07
average relative error	0.739D-11	0.131D-10	0.585D-11	0.853D-11

Table 1. Comparison of our factorization with LINPACK

References

1. Ilan Bar-On. A practical parallel algorithm for solving band symmetric positive definite systems of linear equations. *ACM Transactions on Mathematical Software*, 13(4):323–332, 1987.
2. Ilan Bar-On and Ophir Munk. A new parallel factorization $A = DD^t BC$ for band symmetric positive definite matrices. Tech. Rep. #721, March 1992.
3. A. H. Sameh and R. P. Brent. Solving triangular systems on parallel computers. *SIAM J. Numer. Anal.*, 14:1101–1113, 1977.

Computation of the Eigenvalues of Real Symmetric Matrices using a Processor Farm

L. C. Waring and M. Clint

Department of Computer Science, The Queen's University of Belfast, BELFAST BT7 1NN, Northern Ireland.

Abstract. A parallel implementation of an algorithm to compute the eigenvalues of a real symmetric matrix using a MIMD machine is described. An array of Transputers configured in a ring topology is used as a processor farm for the computation. The speedup obtained by using P processors asymptotically approaches P when the size of the problem becomes large.

Keywords: Linear algebra, matrix multiplication, orthogonalisation, Transputers, ring topology, processor farm.

1 Introduction

In this paper a parallel algorithm, SPOT, for the computation of the eigenvalues of real symmetric matrices is described. SPOT is a specialisation of an algorithm POT [1], [2] for the computation of both eigenvalues and eigenvectors of real symmetric matrices. Both algorithms are particularly suitable for implementation on an array of transputers using the processor farm approach. SPOT uses only half the storage required by POT and, because the eigenvectors are not computed, is significantly faster.

2 The Special Parallel Orthogonal Transformation (SPOT) Algorithm

SPOT is based on the following recursive equations in which A is the n x n target matrix and Λ is an n x n diagonal matrix whose diagonal elements are the eigenvalues of A. Generate a sequence of similar matrices $\{B_k\}$ according to:

(a) $B_0 = A$ (b) $B_k = U_k^T . B_{k-1} . U_k$, $k >= 1$

where the sequence of orthogonal matrices $\{U_k\}$ is generated according to:

$U_k = gramschmidt\ (\ transform\ (B_{k-1})).$ Then $\lim_{k \to \infty} \{B_k\} = \Lambda.$

Although no proof of convergence is available yet for the algorithm, it appears to converge monotonically. The function *transform* generates from its argument a non-orthogonal transformation matrix whose columns are then orthonormalised using the function *gramschmidt*. A detailed discussion of *transform* is given below. The function *gramschmidt* is implemented using the modified Gram-Schmidt procedure [3]. The recursive equations above give rise to the simple iterative representation given below:

```
repeat
    U := transform (B);
    U := gramschmidt (U);
    B := U^T . B . U
until B is diagonal;
```

The procedure will return Λ in the array B which initially holds A. The algorithm is based on the operations of matrix multiplication, orthogonalisation and transformation.

2.1 Transform

The construction of the transformation matrix resembles in some ways that used in parallel implementations of Jacobi's method [4], [5]. The difference is that a 2 x 2 transformation is defined for each of the $n(n - 1) / 2$ off-diagonal elements of B_k rather than for an appropriately selected subset of approximate size $n / 2$ which allows non-interfering transformations to be applied in parallel. The ij^{th} $(i <> j)$ element of the transformation matrix generated in SPOT is $\tan(\theta_{ij})$, where θ_{ij} is the Jacobi rotational angle corresponding to that position. Each diagonal element of the transformation matrix is unity. Thus, dropping the subscripts for B_k and U_k for convenience:

$$u_{ij} = \frac{2\,b_{ij}}{d_{ji} + sign(d_{ji})\sqrt{d_{ji}^2 + 4 * b_{ij}^2}}, \quad i > j$$

where $d_{ji} = b_{jj} - b_{ii}$, $u_{ii} = 1$ and $u_{ij} = -u_{ji}$, $i < j$

If $b_{jj} - b_{ii} = 0$ then $sign(d_{ji}) = -1$

Clearly the complexity of the transform operation is $O(n^2)$.

2.2 Matrix Multiplication

Each iteration in the description of SPOT given above requires the evaluation of two matrix products to be performed. Each product has complexity $O(n^3)$. Rather than use two separate matrix products a double matrix multiplication is employed as described below. This operation can be implemented very efficiently using a processor farm.

2.3 Gram-Schmidt Orthogonalisation

The Gram-Schmidt orthonormalisation procedure [3] is based on the operations of vector inner product computation, vector addition and the multiplication of vectors by constants. The complexity of the orthonormalisation operation is $O(n^3)$ and an efficient implementation with asymptotic speedup of P on a farm of P processors has been reported in [6].

3 The Execution Environment

Using the ParSys Supernode the algorithm has been implemented on rings of 16 and 32 transputers, as shown in Fig. 1.. The justification for this choice is that the operations to be parallelised, particularly the Gram-Schmidt orthogonalisation, fit naturally onto this configuration.

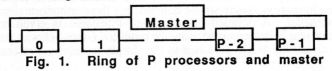

Fig. 1.   Ring of P processors and master

Message sending between the processors is handled by a communications shell [7] which allows bidirectional traffic on the ring. Use of this shell enables messages to be addressed to a numbered processor rather than to a channel.

The program is controlled by a master, or root Transputer, which initiates the sending of message packets to the processors in the farm. These packets contain either data in the form of a set of vectors and/or an instruction to carry out an operation.

The double matrix multiplication and Gram-Schmidt operations are farmed onto the network. An asymptotic speedup of P can be achieved for both operations. The operation transform, which is suitable for parallel implementation is, however, executed sequentially on the master processor since its complexity is only $O(n^2)$.

4. The Implementation

4.1 Double Matrix Multiplication

The double matrix product $M = U^T.B.U$ is evaluated as a single operation. Each processor in the farm has the task of computing, when activated, a column of M. The computation is organised as follows. A copy of the matrix B is initially sent to all processors. The matrix U is available at each processor after the Gram-Schmidt orthonormalisation procedure has been applied (see below). Computation of columns of the double product M is initiated by sending a command message from the master to each processor in the farm. This message consists simply of the index of the column to be computed. On completion of this task the worker returns a message to the master which consists of the column of M, its index and the identification number of the worker processor which has performed the computation. The master overwrites the appropriate column of its copy of B with the column of M which it receives. While there are still columns to be allocated, the master then sends another command signal to the worker. Whenever a command has been transmitted for each of n columns it remains only for the master to collect the final columns of M from the workers. The matrix B is then updated at each of the worker processes.

4.2 Orthonormalisation

Orthonormalisation consists of the generation of a set of n mutually orthogonal and normalised vectors from a set of n independent vectors. In SPOT it is required to orthonormalise the columns of the matrix U.

Suppose that the ith column of U is denoted by u_i. Then the orthonormalisation process may be described as follows:

(0) set i to 0   (1) normalise u_i by dividing it by $\|u_i\|_2$

(2) replace u_k, k = i+1, i+2 ... n by $u_k - (u_i^T * u_k) * u_i$

(3) increment i by 1 and repeat (1) and (2) until i > n-1

The columns of U are distributed over the worker processors as follows. Suppose for convenience that n = mP for some integer m, where P is the number of processors. Assume that the processors are numbered 0 to P-1, then processor 0 is allocated columns 0, P, 2P, . . , (m-1)P of U; processor 1 is allocated columns 1, P+1, 2P+1, . . .,(m-1)P+1 of U, and so on.

The first step of the orthonormalisation procedure consists of processor 0 normalising u_0. When this has been done the normalised vector is transmitted to all of the other workers in the ring. Immediately a worker receives a normalised vector it begins to modify its local vectors according to (2) above. When a vector has been normalised it plays no further part in the computation, except that other vectors are orthogonalised with respect to it. When all of the vectors have been orthogonalised with respect to the normalised vectors the process outlined above is repeated for the modified vector u_1, and continues in a similar fashion until all of the vectors have been normalised. When this point is reached all of the vectors will be mutually orthogonal.

In the implementation used in SPOT the columns of U are not orthonormalised in strictly left to right order. The convergence rate of SPOT is improved if its columns are orthonormalised in an order corresponding to decreasing order of magnitude in the current eigenvalue approximations. These approximations are given by the diagonal elements of B. The orthonormalisation algorithm outlined above may be trivially modified to incorporate this strategy. The farmed orthonormalisation process is described in detail in [6], in which it is also shown that an asymptotic speedup of P is achieved.

5 Realisation in Occam

The parallel algorithm has been expressed in Occam 2 [8]. Details of some of the main components of the implementation are given in the annotated fragments of code below.

5.1 The Master Process

```
sendB ()                    -- the matrix B is sent to all processors
WHILE (NOT converged)       -- main loop
  SEQ
    transform ()
    gramschmidt ()
```

matrixmultiply ()

The $O(n^2)$ operation transform is performed sequentially on the master processor. The other $O(n^3)$ operations are farmed onto the network.

5.2 The Worker Processes

5.2.1 Computation

A worker process repeatedly receives messages from the master process and performs the tasks indicated by the messages: cin6 ? d;n::x

5.2.1.1 Double Matrix Product

The matrix B is initially sent to each processor before the start of the main iterative loop of the master process. Computation of the matrix product $U^T.B.U$ is initiated by sending a message to a worker indicating which of its columns it is to compute. Receipt of a message packet of counted array length 2 indicates that this double matrix product is to be performed.

```
    IF
        n = 2                 -- compute column of U^T.B.U
        SEQ
            j := x[1]         -- column number
            SEQ i = 0 FOR s
                SEQ           -- multiply B on column j of U to get column of B.U
                    z := 0.0 (REAL32)
                    SEQ k = 0 FOR s
                    z := z + (B[i][k] * U[k][j])
                    c[i] := z
            SEQ i = 0 FOR s
                SEQ           -- multiply U^T on column of B.U to get column of U^T.B.U
                    z := 0.0 (REAL32)
                    SEQ k = 0 FOR s
                        z := z + (U[k][i] * c[k])
                    rx[i] := z
```

5.2.1.2 Orthonormalisation

Receipt of a message packet of counted array length 1 indicates that Gram-Schmidt orthonormalisation is to be performed.

The columns of U are ordered, according to decreasing order of magnitude of the diagonal elements of B, and a roughly equal number of them is allocated to each processor. The columns allocated to a processor are normalised in turn and, when each normalisation is completed, the remaining columns assigned to that processor are orthogonalised with respect to it. Each normalised column is then propagated around the ring of processors, each of which orthogonalises its non-orthonormalised columns with respect to it, until it arrives at the processor preceding the one which originally transmitted it. Details of the procedures are given in [6]. When the Gram-Schmidt procedure has been completed the orthonormalised matrix U is stored at each processor. The process is terminated when the eigenvalues are correct to six significant figures, that is, when the ratio of the absolute value of the largest diagonal element of B to the absolute value of the largest off-diagonal element exceeds 10^6. The first worker process in the ring is responsible for accumulating the information on which convergence is decided.

5.2.2 Data Transmission and Storage

A message packet which contains a column of U to be stored has an appropriate tag in element s of the counted array; element s+1 contains the column number. Each processor is supplied with a copy of U. If the receiving processor is not the last processor in the ring then the packet is passed on to the next processor while the column of U is being stored.

```
x[s] = storeU
  SEQ
    PAR
      IF                        -- if not last processor then
        p <> (P - 1)            -- pass on message to next
          SEQ                   -- d = next processor address
            d := route[p]
            cout6 ! d;n::x
        TRUE
          SKIP
      SEQ
        j := x[s + 1]           -- copy data into column of U
        SEQ i = 0 FOR s
          U[i][j] := rx[i]
    SEQ k = 1 FOR s - 1
      SEQ                       -- get remaining columns of U
        cin6 ? d;n::x
        PAR
          IF
            p <> (P - 1)
              SEQ
                d := route[p]
                cout6 ! d;n::x
            TRUE
              SKIP
          SEQ
            j := x[s + 1]
            SEQ i = 0 FOR s
              U[i][j] := rx[i]
```

The columns of B are transmitted and stored similarly.

6. Results

The performances of the parallel algorithm on farms of 16 and 32 processors have been assessed for sets of randomly generated matrices with orders ranging from 32 to 384. Fig. 2. gives the time taken to execute the algorithm for matrix sizes ranging from 32 to 384. The computation was performed in single precision arithmetic. The number of iterations for the sequential and parallel implementations of the algorithm were identical in all cases except for the matrix of size 384 for which the parallel version required one more iteration.

SIZE	ITERATIONS	SEQUENTIAL TIME (sec)	16 PROCESSORS TIME (sec)	SPEEDUP	32 PROCESSORS TIME (sec)	SPEEDUP
32	11	4.61	2.76	2.086	3.18	1.812
64	13	43.00	15.00	3.584	13.86	3.879
96	15	165	42.70	4.831	35.01	5.881
128	16	424	85	6.236	66	8.030
160	19	981	157	7.400	117	9.929
192	20	1781	251	8.426	181	11.685
224	20	2823	359	9.337	252	13.303
256	21	4640	565	10.265	387	14.968
288	21	6600	753	10.956	503	16.401
320	24	10339	1073	11.543	705	17.568
352	25	14324	1488	12.033	955	18.749
384	26 / 27	19332	2015	12.454	1269	19.775

Fig. 2. Comparison of implementations of SPOT

The single Transputer on which the sequential implementations were executed has a clock speed of 25 MHz, while the processors in the network have 20 MHz clocks. This was taken into account when calculating the speedup by multiplication by the appropriate factor.

A graphical representation of the speedups obtained by using the farmed version of the algorithm is shown in Fig. 3..

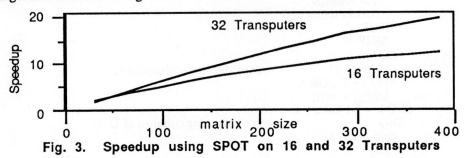

Fig. 3. Speedup using SPOT on 16 and 32 Transputers

The graphs support the remarks made earlier about the predicted asymtotic speedup.

The computation of the $O(n^2)$ operation, transform, on a single processor does not affect the asympotic behaviour of the algorithm. The ring of 16 transputers shows a speedup close to the theoretical maximum for the larger matrices. For the 32 processor implementation the speedup achieved was still increasing when the memory limits of the processors was reached. The order of the largest matrix which could be handled was constrained by the memory capacity available. The memory directly available to each processor was 4 Megabyte. A T800 Transputer is capable of directly addressing 4 Gigabytes of storage. Thus, in principle, matrices of order in excess of 10,000 could be handled if full memory capacity were installed.

7   Conclusions

An efficient method of implementing an eigenvalue algorithm, SPOT, using a MIMD processor farm has been described. The efficiency of the distributed algorithm approaches unity as the size of the matrix becomes large.

8   Acknowledgement

The Occam implementations were developed using the facilities of The Queen's University Parallel Computer Centre.

References

[1] Clint, M., Holt, R., Perrott, R. and Stewart, A. A comparison of two parallel algorithms for the symmetric eigenproblem, Int. Jnl. Comp. Math. 15 (1984) 291 - 302.

[2] Clint, M., Holt, R., Perrott, R. and Stewart, A DAP Fortran subroutine for the eigensolution of real symmetric matrices, Comput. J. 28 (1985) 340 - 342.

[3] Golub, G. and van Loan, C. Matrix Computations, North Oxford Academic (1983).

[4] Modi, J. J. and Pryce, J. D. Efficient implementation of Jacobi's diagonalisation method on the DAP, Num. Math. 46 (1985) 443 - 454.

[5] Weston, J. S. and Clint, M. Two algorithms for the parallel computation of eigenvalues and eigenvectors of large symmetric matrices using the ICL DAP, Parallel Computing 13 (1990) 281 - 288

[6] Waring, L. C. and Clint, M. Improved parallel Gram-Schmidt orthogonalisation on a network of transputers. Applications of Transputers 3, Durrani, T. S., Sandham, W. A. , Soraghan, J. J. and Forbes, S. M. (Editors), (1991) vol 1, 117 - 122.

[7] Waring, L. C. A general purpose communication shell for a network of Transputers, Microprocessing and Microprogramming 29, vol 2 (1989/90) 107 - 119.

[8] The Occam 2 Reference Manual, INMOS Ltd.

Numerical Performance of an Asynchronous Jacobi Iteration

J.M.Bull[1] and T.L.Freeman[2*]

[1] Centre for Novel Computing, Department of Computer Science,
University of Manchester, Manchester, M13 9PL, UK.
[2] Department of Mathematics,
University of Manchester, Manchester, M13 9PL, UK.

Abstract. We examine the effect of removing synchronisation points from a parallel implementation of a simple iterative algorithm—Jacobi's method for linear systems. We find that in some cases the asynchronous version requires *fewer* iterations to converge than its synchronous counterpart. We show that this behaviour can be explained in terms of the presence or absence of oscillations in the sequence of error vectors in the synchronous version, and that removing the synchronisation point can damp the oscillations.

1 Introduction

There are a number of problems in linear and nonlinear numerical algebra where the solution vector $\mathbf{x}^\star$ can be obtained by an iterative method. Such a method generates a sequence of vectors $\mathbf{x}(t), t = 1, 2, 3, \ldots$, so that $\mathbf{x}(t) \to \mathbf{x}^\star$ as $t \to \infty$. Typically $\mathbf{x}(t+1) = \mathbf{f}(\mathbf{x}(t))$, where $\mathbf{f}(\mathbf{x}) = (f_1(\mathbf{x}), f_2(\mathbf{x}), \ldots, f_n(\mathbf{x}))^T$ is the iteration function. They are suitable for implementation on a parallel computer, by assigning subsets of the elements of $\mathbf{x}$ to the different processors. On each iteration a processor updates its elements of $\mathbf{x}(t)$, broadcasts the results to the other processors and in turn receives the other elements of $\mathbf{x}(t)$ from the other processors. However speedup is limited because of the synchronisation point in each iteration (to exchange the latest values of $\mathbf{x}(t)$). What happens if we remove the synchronisation point from the algorithm and allow it to run in an *asynchronous* (or *chaotic*) mode? In general this will affect both the efficiency of the algorithm, and the necessary and sufficient conditions required to ensure convergence. As regards efficiency, we expect there to be a trade-off between a reduced time per iteration (by removing the synchronisation point) and a slower rate of convergence, resulting from the use of older data when computing the next iterate. We examine these issues for a simple iterative method— Jacobi's algorithm for the solution of a system of linear equations. We find that in some cases the convergence rate is *improved* by the switch to the asynchronous implementation. We present results for several linear systems, which are chosen to demonstrate that under some circumstances the removal of the synchronisation point damps oscillatory behaviour in the iteration.

* The second author acknowledges the support of the NATO Collaborative Research Grant 920037.

2   Parallel Jacobi algorithms

The classical Jacobi algorithm (denoted J) for the system of linear equations $Ax = b$ where A is an $n \times n$, non-singular, matrix can be written as:

Choose a starting vector $\mathbf{x}(0)$
for $t = 1, 2, 3, \ldots$,
    for $i = 1, 2, \ldots, n$,

$$x_i(t) = \left(b_i - \sum_{j=1}^{i-1} a_{ij} x_j(t-1) - \sum_{j=i+1}^{n} a_{ij} x_j(t-1) \right) \Big/ a_{ii}$$

    end
    if convergence test is satisfied **then** stop
end

If we let $A = L + D + U$, where L is strictly lower triangular, D is diagonal, and U is strictly upper triangular, then the algorithm can be written as

$$\mathbf{x}(t) = M_J \mathbf{x}(t-1) + D^{-1} \mathbf{b},$$

where $M_J = -D^{-1}(L + U)$ is the *Jacobi iteration matrix*.

A natural parallel version of this algorithm is obtain by assigning sets of the x_i to processors. At each step every processor computes the new values of its set of the x_i. It then broadcasts these to every other processor, then waits until it has received the new values of the x_i from every other processor before proceeding with the next step. Note that within each processor we can implement the algorithm in a Gauss-Seidel fashion by using any new values of the x_i that are available. This algorithm, denoted JLGS (Jacobi with local Gauss-Seidel), usually converges faster than the standard Jacobi algorithm (particularly when p is small) at no extra cost. As described above, it is a synchronous version (which we will denote SJLGS) since, after each processor has broadcast, it blocks until it has received elements of $\mathbf{x}(t)$ from all the other processors. To obtain an asynchronous version of the algorithm (AJLGS), we simply remove this synchronisation point and allow the messages from the other processors to be received at any point in the iteration. Each processor proceeds with the computations, using the most recently received values of the elements of $\mathbf{x}$ when it requires them. Synchronous and asynchronous versions of the standard Jacobi algorithm (SJ and AJ respectively) can of course be derived in exactly the same way.

We mention here the conditions for convergence of the algorithms. For SJ the condition $\rho(M_J) < 1$, where M_J is the Jacobi iteration matrix and $\rho(.)$ denotes the spectral radius of a matrix, is necessary and sufficient (see Section 10.1.2 of [5]). For AJ a sufficient condition is $\rho(|M_J|) < 1$, where $|M_J|$ denotes the matrix whose (i, j) entry is the absolute value of the (i, j) entry of M_J. (see Section 6.2 of [2],[3], [4] and [6]). This condition also seems to be necessary in practise, even though it cannot be demonstrated formally (see Section 6.3.1 of [2], and [3]). The same results also apply to JLGS given a suitable redefinition of the iteration matrix.

3 Results

We now present the results of implementations of SJLGS and AJLGS on the Intel iPSC/2 and iPSC/860 hypercubes at the SERC Daresbury Laboratory. A diagonally dominant matrix A of dimension n was constructed by adding nI_n to a matrix with random entries uniformly distributed on $[0, 1]$. The vector $\mathbf{b}$ was chosen to ensure that the solution vector $\mathbf{x}^\star = A^{-1}\mathbf{b} = (1, 1, \ldots, 1)^T$. The initial vector $\mathbf{x}_0$ was defined by $(x_0)_i = 5i$, $i = 1, \ldots, n$. Single precision (32 bit) arithmetic was used and the iteration was deemed to have converged when $\|\mathbf{x}(t) - \mathbf{x}^\star\|_\infty < 4 \times 10^{-6}$. Each implementation was run on 2, 4, 8 and 16 processors. Table 1 gives the number of iterations and total time required for problems of dimensions $n = 128$ and $n = 512$ on both the iPSC/2 and iPSC/860. Because AJLGS is a chaotic implementation the number of iterations can vary from one run to the next. The figures given here are the median number of iterations from a set of five runs. The most interesting feature

Table 1. Number of iterations and total time required by SJLGS and AJLGS for $n = 128$ and $n = 512$ on the iPSC/2 and iPSC/860

				No. of processors			
				2	4	8	16
iPSC/2	$n = 128$	SJLGS	No. of iterations	17	22	24	26
			Time (ms)	946	694	424	357
		AJLGS	No. of iterations	18	24	26	20
			Time (ms)	945	712	465	316
	$n=512$	SJLGS	No. of iterations	18	23	26	28
			Time (ms)	15585	10094	5935	3521
		AJLGS	No. of iterations	16	19	23	29
			Time (ms)	13146	7959	5012	3464
iPSC/860	$n=128$	SJLGS	No. of iterations	17	22	24	26
			Time (ms)	152.1	120.6	51.2	53.2
		AJLGS	No. of iterations	15	17	19	19
			Time (ms)	142.7	89.0	43.2	44.6
	$n=512$	SJLGS	No. of iterations	18	23	26	28
			Time (ms)	2294.3	1506.2	906.7	582.5
		AJLGS	No. of iterations	18	21	24	25
			Time (ms)	2477.8	1465.0	875.5	526.4

of these results is that the asynchronous version AJLGS often converges in fewer iterations than its synchronous counterpart. This is counterintuitive, since we might expect the asynchronous version, which is likely to be making use of less up-to-date information when computing its iterates, to converge more slowly. We will seek an explanation for this behaviour in the next section. A second observation is that the asynchronous version often requires more time to execute each iteration—in Intel Fortran the overhead incurred in maintaining asynchronous communication can be larger than the synchronisation overhead of synchronous communication.

4   Oscillations of the errors

We suspect that the faster convergence rate of AJLGS is due to damping of oscillations of the iterates generated by the synchronous version of the algorithm about the solution $\mathbf{x}^*$. We note that this damping effect only appears if the time required to pass messages between processors is not much greater than the time required for each processor to perform its part of an iteration. To analyse this effect further we consider the general iteration

$$\mathbf{x}(t+1) = M\mathbf{x}(t) + \mathbf{c}.$$

We will assume that $\rho(M) < 1$, ensuring convergence to a fixed point $\mathbf{x}^*$. If we define the error vector at step t by $\mathbf{e}(t) = \mathbf{x}(t) - \mathbf{x}^*$, then it is easy to show that $\mathbf{e}(t) = M^t\mathbf{e}(0)$. We wish to measure the (degree of) oscillation in the series $\mathbf{e}(0), \mathbf{e}(1), \mathbf{e}(2), \ldots$. A natural measure is provided by the series

$$C(t) = \frac{\mathbf{e}(t)^T\mathbf{e}(t+1)}{\|\mathbf{e}(t)\|_2\|\mathbf{e}(t+1)\|_2} \quad t = 0, 1, 2, \ldots,$$

where we note that $C(t), t = 0, 1, 2, \ldots$, are the cosines of the angles between successive error vectors. We restrict attention to the case when M and $\mathbf{c}$ are real. Let $\lambda_1, \lambda_2, \ldots, \lambda_n$, be the eigenvalues of M, ordered so that $|\lambda_1| \geq |\lambda_2| \geq \ldots \geq |\lambda_n|$, and let $\mathbf{y}_1, \mathbf{y}_2, \ldots, \mathbf{y}_n$, be the corresponding eigenvectors. There are two important cases:

1. λ_1 is real and $|\lambda_1| > |\lambda_2|$.
2. λ_1 is complex, $\lambda_2 = \lambda_1^*$ and $|\lambda_1| > |\lambda_3|$.

Suppose further that $\mathbf{e}(0) \in \text{span}\{\mathbf{y}_1, \mathbf{y}_2, \ldots, \mathbf{y}_n\}$. (If M is diagonalisable then this will be true for any $\mathbf{e}(0)$.) Then

$$\mathbf{e}(0) = \sum_{j=1}^n c_j\mathbf{y}_j \quad \text{and} \quad \mathbf{e}(t) = \sum_{j=1}^n c_j\lambda_j^t\mathbf{y}_j.$$

In case 1., $\mathbf{e}(t) \to c_1\lambda_1^t\mathbf{y}_1$ as $t \to \infty$. This is equivalent to applying a naïve power method to M, and $\mathbf{e}(t)$ converges to a multiple of the eigenvector $\mathbf{y}_1$. Thus $C(t) \to 1$ if $\lambda_1 > 0$ (corresponding to no oscillations in the error terms) and $C(t) \to -1$ if $\lambda_1 < 0$ (corresponding to the strongest possible oscillations in the error terms).

Case 2. is more complicated, but it can be shown that

$$C(t) \to \frac{\cos\phi + B\cos(2\phi t + \beta)}{[1 + D\cos(2\phi t + \delta)]^{1/2}[1 + E\cos(2\phi t + \epsilon)]^{1/2}}$$

where $\phi = \arg(\lambda_1)$ and B, D, E, β, δ and ϵ depend on M and $\mathbf{e}(0)$ but not on t. In this case there is always some degree of oscillation in the error terms.

This analysis applies equally to J and JLGS given suitable definitions of the iteration matrix M. We will restrict our attention to J, however, because we can readily construct systems which display each type of behaviour. We now describe such systems, and present the results of solving them using both synchronous (SJ) and asynchronous (AJ) versions of the standard Jacobi algorithm.

Let J_n be an $n \times n$ matrix with zero diagonal and ones in all off-diagonal positions. We define the following matrices:

$$P_\alpha = \alpha n I_n - J_n, \quad Q_\alpha = \alpha n I_n + J_n, \quad \text{and} \quad R_{\mu,\nu} = nS + J_n,$$

where S is a diagonal matrix with $S_{ii} = \mu$ if i is odd and $S_{ii} = \nu$ if i is even. If $M_J(A)$ denotes the iteration matrix of the Jacobi algorithm applied to the linear system $Ax = b$, then it can be shown that $M_J(P_\alpha)$ has a dominant eigenvalue $\lambda_1(M_J(P_\alpha)) = (1 - 1/n)/\alpha$. Similarly $\lambda_1(M_J(Q_\alpha)) = -(1 - 1/n)/\alpha$. For certain choices of μ and ν, and for even n, $M_J(R_{\mu,\nu})$ has a complex pair of dominant eigenvalues.

In [1] numerical results are given for a linear system derived from the five point finite-difference method for Laplace's equation on a rectangular grid. This system does not fit into any of the above categories as, although $\lambda_1(M_J)$ is real and positive, $\lambda_2(M_J) = -\lambda_1(M_J)$. In this case, $C(t) \rightarrow (c_1^2 - c_2^2)/(c_1^2 + c_2^2)$ as $t \rightarrow \infty$. Since $(c_1^2 - c_2^2)/(c_1^2 + c_2^2)$ can take any value between -1 and 1, the degree of oscillation of the iterates about the solution tends to a constant determined solely by the initial vector $x(0)$.

5 Further results

Table 2 shows the results of solving linear systems with coefficient matrices $P_{1.1}$, $P_{2.0}$, $Q_{1.1}$, $Q_{2.0}$ and $R_{1.0,-10.0}$ for $n = 128$, using SJ and AJ on the Intel iPSC/2. The right hand side vector b is chosen so that the solution $x^* = (1, 1, \ldots, 1)^T$, and the initial vector is chosen so that $C(t) = 1$ for every t for P_α, and $C(t) = -1$ for every t for Q_α. Because these problems are not as well conditioned as those of Section 3 the convergence condition for the iteration is relaxed to $\|e(t)\|_\infty < 6 \times 10^{-5}$.

We observe that for the cases where $C(t) = -1$ ($Q_{1.1}$ and $Q_{2.0}$) and therefore the iterates of SJ are highly oscillatory, the number of iterations required by AJ is consistently less than is required by SJ, and substantially so when the convergence is slow ($Q_{1.1}$). Conversely when $C(t) = 1$ ($P_{1.1}$ and $P_{2.0}$) and there are no oscillations in the iterates of SJ, AJ requires more iterations than SJ. For the linear system $R_{1.0,-10.0}x = b$, AJ sometimes requires fewer iterations than SJ, sometimes more.

This numerical evidence supports our hypothesis that the asynchronous version (AJ) is damping out oscillatory behaviour. Some further experimentation with small matrices confirms that the same effect is also present when the JLGS algorithm is used, although it is less marked. The matrices of Section 3 have $\lambda_1(M_J)$ real and negative, and so we expect that the iterates will oscillate and hence that convergence can be accelerated by using the asynchronous version of algorithm. In many cases this behaviour is observed. The results of [1] show that AJ requires more iterations than SJ for the linear system derived from Laplace's equation. We must assume that in this case either $x(0)$ was such that $C(t)$ tended to a positive constant value, or the communication/computation ratio was high.

6 Conclusions

The results of Section 3 show that an asynchronous version of Jacobi's method sometimes requires fewer iterations to converge than the corresponding synchronous

Table 2. Number of iterations and total time required by AJ and SJ for selected test problems on the iPSC/2.

Problem			No. of processors			
			2	4	8	16
$P_{1.1}\mathbf{x} = \mathbf{b}$	SJ	No. of iterations	158	158	158	158
		Time (ms)	8709	4842	2676	2052
	AJ	No. of iterations	173	199	197	179
		Time (ms)	10302	6509	3936	2910
$P_{2.0}\mathbf{x} = \mathbf{b}$	SJ	No. of iterations	24	24	24	24
		Time (ms)	1323	734	407	311
	AJ	No. of iterations	27	30	29	25
		Time (ms)	1609	983	551	408
$Q_{1.1}\mathbf{x} = \mathbf{b}$	SJ	No. of iterations	156	156	156	156
		Time (ms)	8598	4780	2643	2024
	AJ	No. of iterations	36	46	62	48
		Time (ms)	2143	1504	1176	782
$Q_{2.0}\mathbf{x} = \mathbf{b}$	SJ	No. of iterations	24	24	24	24
		Time (ms)	1323	735	406	310
	AJ	No. of iterations	18	23	20	15
		Time (ms)	1073	751	382	242
$R_{1.0,-10.0}\mathbf{x} = \mathbf{b}$	SJ	No. of iterations	21	21	21	21
		Time (ms)	1157	643	356	271
	AJ	No. of iterations	18	22	19	15
		Time (ms)	1072	719	362	243

version. This is contrary to the expectation that removing synchronisation points will cause older data to be used when computing iterates, and hence delay convergence. We have shown, using carefully designed test problems, that this accelerated convergence occurs when the errors in the synchronised Jacobi algorithm are oscillatory and that the removal of the synchronisation points has a damping effect. However, the details of the mechanism responsible for this are not yet well understood.

References

1. BAUDET, G.M. (1978) Asynchronous iterative methods for multiprocessors *J. Assoc. Comp. Mach.* 25, 226–244.
2. BERTSEKAS, D.P. AND J.N. TSITSIKLIS (1989) *Parallel and Distributed Computation: Numerical Methods.* Prentice Hall, New Jersey.
3. BULL, J.M. (1991) Asynchronous Jacobi iterations on local memory parallel computers. M. Sc. Thesis, University of Manchester, Manchester, UK.
4. CHAZAN, D. AND W. MIRANKER (1969) Chaotic relaxation. *Linear Algebra and its Applications* 2, 199–222.
5. GOLUB, G.H. AND C.F. VAN LOAN (1989) *Matrix Computations (2nd edition)* Johns Hopkins, Baltimore.
6. LI, L. (1989) Convergence of asynchronous iteration with arbitrary splitting form. *Linear Algebra and its Applications* 113, 119–127.

This article was processed using the LaTeX macro package with LLNCS style

Matrix Inversion Algorithm for Linear Array Processor

E. I. Milovanović, I. Ž. Milovanović and M. K. Stojčev*

Faculty of Electronic Engineering, University of Niš
P.O. Box 73, 18000 Niš, Yugoslavia

Abstract. The paper presents parallel algorithm for computing the inversion of a dense matrix based on Gauss–Jordan elimination. The algorithm is proposed for the implementation on the linear array at a processor level which operate in a pipeline fashion. Two types of architectures are considered. One which uses serial data transfer (AP/S) and another which uses parallel data transfer (AP/P) between neighboring processors. The speed up of AP/S and AP/P are $O(n/2)$ and $O(4n/5)$, respectively.

1   Introduction

The problem of inverting a real matrix of order n is one of the central problems in numerical linear algebra. Several VLSI architectures and algorithms have been proposed for performing matrix inversion. A parallel algorithm for matrix inversion based on Givens plane rotations was described by El–Amawy in [2] and El–Amawy and Dharmarajan [3]. The algorithm inverts a dense matrix of order $n \times n$ on systolic array consisting of $n^2 + n$ processing elements (PE), in $5n$ time units, including I/O time. Aleksandrov and Djidjev [1] have described the architecture of a systolic processor for matrix inversion based on Gauss–Jordan method. The systolic processor consists of $n \times n$ PEs. Parallel Gauss–Jordan algorithm suitable for implementation on pyramidal multiprocessor system was analyzed by Geus et all [4]. This paper describes a parallel algorithm for inversion of dense matrices, of order n, based on modified Jordan's method. The described algorithm is implemented on linear array of n processors which operate in a pipeline fashion. Two types of architectures are considered: linear array of processors which uses serial data transfer (AP/S) and linear array which uses parallel data transfer between the neighboring processors (AP/P).

2   Mathematical Background

Let $Q = (q_{ij})$ is a nonsingular matrix of order $n \times n$ with all main minors different from zero. The objective of this paper is to determine an inverse matrix of matrix Q. A recursive procedure based on Jordan's method will be used

---

*This work was supported by the Serbian Sciense Council.

for calculating an inverse matrix. Using this procedure a sequence of matrices $C_k = \left(q_{ij}^{(k)}\right)$, $k = 0, 1, \ldots, n$, is obtained in the following way:

a) $C_0 \equiv Q$.

b) From $C_{k-1} = \left(q_{ij}^{(k-1)}\right)$ matrices L_k and R_k are formed as follows:

$$
L_k = \begin{bmatrix}
1 & \cdots & -\dfrac{q_{1k}^{(k-1)}}{q_{kk}^{(k-1)}} & \cdots & 0 \\
\vdots & & & & \\
0 & \cdots & \dfrac{1}{q_{kk}^{(k-1)}} & \cdots & 0 \\
\vdots & & & & \\
0 & \cdots & -\dfrac{q_{nk}^{(k-1)}}{q_{kk}^{(k-1)}} & \cdots & 1
\end{bmatrix} ,
\tag{1}
$$

$$
R_k = \begin{bmatrix}
q_{11}^{(k-1)} & \cdots & q_{1,k-1}^{(k-1)} & 0 & q_{1,k-1}^{(k-1)} & \cdots & q_{1n}^{(k-1)} \\
\vdots & & & & & & \\
q_{k1}^{(k-1)} & \cdots & q_{k,k-1}^{(k-1)} & 1 & q_{k,k+1}^{(k-1)} & \cdots & q_{kn}^{(k-1)} \\
\vdots & & & & & & \\
q_{n1}^{(k-1)} & \cdots & q_{n,k-1}^{(k-1)} & 0 & q_{n,k+1}^{(k-1)} & \cdots & q_{nn}^{(k-1)}
\end{bmatrix} .
\tag{2}
$$

c) From matrices L_k and R_k, $k = 1, 2, \ldots, n$, the matrix C_k is obtained according to the equality

$$
C_k = L_k R_k , \quad k = 1, \ldots, n .
\tag{3}
$$

Finally, an inverse matrix of matrix Q is equal to C_n, i.e. $C_n = Q^{-1}$.

With a goal to describe parallel procedure clearly, we will rewrite equality (3) in the following form:

$$
C_k = V_k + D_k + Z_k W_k ,
\tag{4}
$$

where matrices V_k and D_k and vectors Z_k and W_k are given as:

$$
V_k = \begin{bmatrix}
0 & \cdots & 0 & -\dfrac{q_{1k}^{(k-1)}}{q_{kk}^{(k-1)}} & 0 & \cdots & 0 \\
\vdots & & & & & & \\
0 & \cdots & 0 & \dfrac{1}{q_{kk}^{(k-1)}} & 0 & \cdots & 0 \\
\vdots & & & & & & \\
0 & \cdots & 0 & -\dfrac{q_{nk}^{(k-1)}}{q_{kk}^{(k-1)}} & 0 & \cdots & 0
\end{bmatrix} ,
\tag{5}
$$

$$D_k = \begin{bmatrix} q_{11}^{(k-1)} & \cdots & q_{1,k-1}^{(k-1)} & 0 & q_{1,k+1}^{(k-1)} & \cdots & q_{1n}^{(k-1)} \\ \vdots & & & & & & \\ q_{k-1,1}^{(k-1)} & \cdots & q_{k-1,k-1}^{(k-1)} & 0 & q_{k-1,k+1}^{(k-1)} & \cdots & q_{k-1,n}^{(k-1)} \\ \vdots & & & & & & \\ 0 & \cdots & 0 & 0 & 0 & \cdots & 0 \\ q_{k+1,1}^{(k-1)} & \cdots & q_{k+1,k-1}^{(k-1)} & 0 & q_{k+1,k+1}^{(k-1)} & \cdots & q_{k+1,n}^{(k-1)} \\ \vdots & & & & & & \\ q_{n1}^{(k-1)} & \cdots & q_{n,k-1}^{(k-1)} & 0 & q_{n,k+1}^{(k-1)} & \cdots & q_{nn}^{(k-1)} \end{bmatrix}, \tag{6}$$

$$Z_k^T = \begin{bmatrix} -q_{1k}^{(k-1)} & \cdots & \dfrac{1}{q_{kk}^{(k-1)}} & \cdots & -\dfrac{q_{nk}^{(k-1)}}{q_{kk}^{(k-1)}} \end{bmatrix} \tag{7}$$

$$W_k = \begin{bmatrix} q_{k1}^{(k-1)} & \cdots & q_{k,k-1}^{(k-1)} & 0 & q_{k,k+1}^{(k-1)} & \cdots & q_{kn}^{(k-1)} \end{bmatrix}. \tag{8}$$

The described mathematical model can be efficiently implemented on linear array of n homogeneous processors. The global scheduling strategy is as follows. The elements of vector Z_k and matrix V_k are calculated in processor P_k. Processor P_k distributes the obtained results to all other processors in the system, which then calculate the column elements of matrix

$$F_k = D_k + Z_k W_k . \tag{9}$$

Namely, processor P_k calculates j–th ($j \neq k$) column of matrix F_k.

If we assume that i–th column of matrix Q is stored in local memory of processor P_i, then in each step processor P_i calculates i–th column of matrix C_k ($k = 1, n$).

In the j–th iteration step each processor performs one of the following group of tasks:

$$T_j^j = \{C_{jj}^{(j)}, \ldots, C_{nj}^{(j)}, C_{1j}^{(j)}, \ldots, C_{j-1,j}^{(j)}\}$$
$$\equiv \left\{ \frac{1}{C_{jj}^{(j-1)}}, -\frac{C_{j+1,j}^{(j-1)}}{C_{jj}^{(j-1)}}, \ldots, -\frac{C_{n,j}^{(j-1)}}{C_{jj}^{(j-1)}}, -\frac{C_{1,j}^{(j-1)}}{C_{jj}^{(j-1)}}, \ldots, -\frac{C_{j-1,j}^{(j-1)}}{C_{jj}^{(j-1)}} \right\},$$
$$j = 1, \ldots, n , \tag{10}$$

or

$$T_i^j = \{C_{ji}^{(j)}, C_{j+1,i}^{(j)}, \ldots, C_{ni}^{(j)}, C_{1i}^{(j)}, \ldots, C_{j-1,i}^{(j)}\}$$
$$\equiv \left\{ \frac{C_{ji}^{(j-1)}}{C_{jj}^{(j-1)}}, C_{j+1,i}^{(j-1)} - \frac{C_{j+1,j}^{(j-1)}}{C_{jj}^{(j-1)}} C_{ji}^{(j-1)}, \ldots, C_{ni}^{(j-1)} - \frac{C_{nj}^{(j-1)}}{C_{jj}^{(j-1)}} C_{ji}^{(j-1)}, \right.$$
$$\left. C_{1i}^{(j-1)} - \frac{C_{1j}^{(j-1)}}{C_{jj}^{(j-1)}} C_{ji}^{(j-1)}, \ldots, C_{j-1,i}^{(j-1)} - \frac{C_{j-1,j}^{(j-1)}}{C_{jj}^{(j-1)}} C_{ji}^{(j-1)}, \right\},$$
$$i, j = 1, n \quad \text{and} \quad i \neq j . \tag{11}$$

Index i in T_i^j represents index of a column which is modified (i.e. the processor which performs the modification), while the iteration step is denoted by j. Element calculation ordering in each processor is explicitly defined by (10) or (11).

3 Hardware Structure of Linear Array Processor

In the text that follows we will describe two types of linear array processors. The first uses serial and the second parallel data transfer between the neighboring processors.

3.1 Array Processor with Serial Data Transfer (AP/S)

The structure of AP/S for matrix inversion is given in Fig.1. AP/S consists of n processors. Each processor has four communication channels. Two of them are used for connection with left and right neighbors, while the two others are used for connection with the host. Communication between processors and processor and host is achieved using message passing technique.

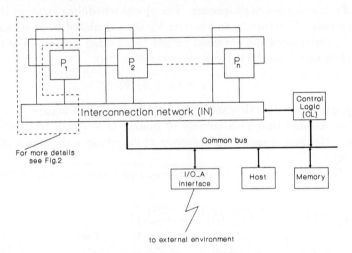

Fig.1. Structure of the system based on the linear array processor with serial interconnection.

3.2 Array Processor with Parallel Data Transfer (AP/P)

The structure of the system for matrix inversion is given in Fig.2. The system is organized in three hierarchical levels. At the highest level is the host. It is connected via global bus with up to 15 processors at the second hierarchical level (denoted as IP in Fig.2). Each processor at this level is connected with up to 15 processors at the third level. The processors at the third level are organized as linear array of processors (denoted as AP/P in Fig.2). The communication between two neighboring processors in AP/P is achieved by common memory module which can be realized as dual–port RAM (DP in Fig.2).

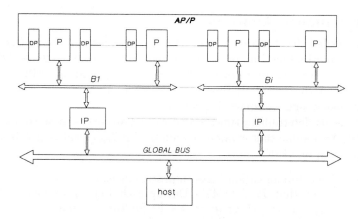

Fig.2. Structure of the system based on linear AP with parallel data transfer.

4 Realization of Matrix Inversion Algorithm

In the text that follows we will describe the realization of the proposed algorithm for matrix inversion. The algorithm starts with P_1 calculating the first element which belongs to the first column of matrix C_1. After that, the result is transferred to processor P_2. Since P_2 has received the result from P_1 it performs two activities. First, it transfers the result obtained from P_1 to P_3, and then calculates the first element which belongs to the second column of C_1. From the processor's point of wiev, CPU's and communication channels activities are performed concurrently. In this way an overlapping of communication and calculation activities is achieved. Element calculation ordering is explicitly defined by (10) or (11). A parallel program sequence, in pseudo code, which corresponds to described mathematical model is as follows:

for $j := 1$ **to** n **do**
 P_j executes: $\;<\; C_{jj} := 1/C_{jj}; \;>$
  for $i := 1$ **to** n **do inparallel**
  P_i executes: $\quad<\quad$ **if** $i = j$ **then**
      for $k := 1$ **to** $n - 1$ **do**
       $r = (k + j - 1) \bmod n + 1;$ $\left.\begin{array}{c} \\ \\ \\ \end{array}\right\} T_j^j$
       $C_{rj} := -C_{rj}/C_{jj}$
      endfor
     else
        $C_{ji} := C_{ji}/C_{jj}$
      for $k := 1$ **to** $n - 1$ **do**
       $r := (k + j - 1) \bmod n + 1$ $\left.\begin{array}{c} \\ \\ \\ \end{array}\right\} T_i^j$
       $C_{ri} := C_{ri} - C_{ji} * C_{rj}$
      endfor
     endif $>$
    endparallel
 endfor

5   Performance Analysis

Time needed to calculate an inverse matrix of a given square matrix of order n by Jordan method on a uniprocessor system is $T_1 = n(2n^2 - 2n + 1)T$, where T is a needed time to perform one floating point operation (FPO). Namely, we assume that the execution time of FPO is dominant over execution time of operations like assign, compare, logical, etc.

Now, let us determine a time needed to find an inverse matrix using AP/S and AP/P. We assume that communication time is T_{com}, and that T is a needed time to perform one FPO.

AP/S: The communication between processors is performed in a serial fashion so we assume that $T_{com} = 4T$. During each step processors perform an operation of type $a := a/b$ or $a := a + bc$ for time T and $2T$, respectively. Since the communication and calculation activities are overlapped the duration of each step is determined by T_{com}. Further, we assume that a time to feed–in and feed–out the array processor is $T_{i/o} = 2nT_{com}$. According to the previous assumptions, the total execution time to find an inverse matrix of a given square matrix of order n is

$$T_{\Sigma S} = T_{i/o} + T_{cal} = 2nT_{com} + (n^2 + 2n - 2)T_{com} = (n^2 + 4n - 2)T_{com} = (n^2 + 4n - 2)4T .$$

The speed up of linear array processor which consist of n processors is

$$SS = \frac{T_1}{T_{\Sigma S}} = \frac{n(2n^2 - 2n + 1)T}{(n^2 + 4n - 2)4T} = O(n/2) .$$

AP/P: In the case of AP/P architecture, the communication between the processors is performed in a parallel fashion, so we assume that $T_{com} = 0.1T$. Having in mind the hierarchical structure of the system, we assume that the time to feed–in and feed–out AP/P in the worst case is $T_{i/o} = 4n^2T_{com}$. The total execution time to find an inverse matrix of a given square matrix of order n is

$$T_{\Sigma P} = T_{i/o} + T_{cal} = 4n^2T_{com} + (n-1)T_{com} + \left(T + (n-1)2T\right)n = nT(2.5n - 0.9) .$$

The speed up of the system is

$$SP = \frac{T_1}{T_{\Sigma P}} = \frac{n(2n^2 - 2n + 1)T}{n(2.5n - 0.9)T} = O(4/5n) .$$

References

1. L.G. Aleksandrov and H.N. Djidjev, Solving systems of linear equations on a systolic processor, *Technical Report*, Center of Informatics And Computer Technology, BAN-Sofia, 1-8 (1989).

2. A. El-Amawy, A Systolic Architecture for Fast Dense Matrix Inversion, *I.E.E.E. Transactions on Computers* **38**, 449-455 (1989).

3. A. El-Amawy and K.R. Dharmarajan, Parallel VLSI algorithm for stable inversion of dense matrices, *IEE Proc.,Pt E.* **136**, 575-580 (1989).

4. L. Geus, W. Henning, M. Vajteri and J. Volkert, Matrix inversion algorithms for a pyramidal multiprocessor system, *Computers and Artificial Intelligence* **7**, 65-79 (1988).

Massively Parallel Preconditioners for the Sparse Conjugate Gradient Method

Serge Petiton[1,2] and Christine Weill-Duflos[1,3]

[1] Site Expérimental en Hyperparallélisme, ETCA, France
[2] Department of Computer Science, Yale University, New Haven, CT
[3] MASI, Université P. et M. Curie, France

Abstract. We study the conjugate gradient method to solve large sparse linear systems with two ways of preconditioning : the polynomial and the ILU preconditionings. A parallel version is evaluated on the Connection Machine 2 (CM-2) with large sparse matrices. Results show that we must find a tradeoff between high performance (in terms of Mflops) and fast convergence. We first conclude that to find efficient methods on massively parallel computers, especially when irregular structures were used, parallelising usual algorithms is not always the most efficient way. Then, we introduce the new massively parallel hybrid polynomial-$ILUTmp(l, \epsilon, d)$ preconditioning for distributed memory machines using a data parallel programming model.

1 Introduction

Solving linear algebra problems is an important issue for massively parallel architectures. Data structures are often matrices and connectivity graphs arising from meshes. The problems usually solved on these architectures often have a very large size. We present in this paper a preconditioned conjugate gradient method to solve large sparse systems with two preconditionings in their parallel versions : a polynomial and a ILU preconditioning. We compare their performance and then we propose some improvement to obtain a good massively parallel preconditioning. Then, we describe the $ILUTmp(l, \epsilon, d)$ preconditioning with some parameters. Thus we propose to associate the high throughput of one with the fast convergence of the other in a hybrid method which includes both of the previous methods.

2 Preconditioned Conjugate Gradient (PCG) Method

2.1 Problem and Method

We are interested in the following problem from linear algebra, solving the system : $Ax = b$, where A is a large sparse symmetric positive definite matrix.
The conjugate gradient method is an interesting method to solve large sparse symmetric positive definite linear systems. In the cases of ill-conditioned problems or very large systems, the convergence can be obtained after a high number of iterations. To improve the usual conjugate gradient method, it is possible to combine it with a preconditioning, see [4]. The goal is to find a matrix M so that the condition number of $M^{-1}A$ is better than that of A and that $Mz = r$ is easy to solve.
We describe below the Generalized Conjugate Gradient of Hestenes and Stiefel (GCGHS) algorithm. We use the preconditioning matrix M.

– First step : choose x_0, then

$$r_0 = M^{-1}(b - Ax_0) \tag{1}$$

$$\rho_0 = (r_0, r_0), v_0 = r_0 \tag{2}$$

– Second step : repeat for $i = 0, 1, \ldots$ until convergence

$$w_i = M^{-1}Av_i \tag{3}$$

$$\alpha_i = \rho_i/(w_i, v_i) \tag{4}$$

$$x_{i+1} = x_i + \alpha_i v_i \tag{5}$$

$$r_{i+1} = r_i - \alpha_i w_i \tag{6}$$

$$\rho_{i+1} = (r_{i+1}, r_{i+1}) \tag{7}$$

$$\beta_i = \rho_{i+1}/\rho_i \tag{8}$$

$$v_{i+1} = r_{i+1} + \beta_i v_i \tag{9}$$

2.2 Preconditionings

We present differents types of preconditionings :

– Incomplete LU (ILU) preconditionings : the family of ILU preconditionings includes many variations. We can define an ILU preconditioning as follows : $M = LU$ with $M_{i,j} = A_{i,j}$ for $A_{i,j} \neq 0$, L is a lower triangular and U an upper triangular with an unit diagonal matrix, and $L_{i,j} = 0$, $U_{i,j} = 0$ if $A_{i,j} = 0$.

– Polynomial preconditionings : the aim is to find a matrice's polynomial represention M^{-1}. The simplest polynomial (there are more efficient polynomials, see [1] and [4]) which approximates A^{-1} is given by the truncated Neuman series : $s(A) = I + R + R^2 + \cdots + R^k$ with $R = I - A$ and $\|R\| < 1$, ($M = s(A)^{-1}$).

On sequential machines, the ILU preconditioning is the more often used and one of the best in terms of the number of iterations.

3 PCG Method for Sparse Matrices on the CM-2

3.1 Data Mapping on the Processors Grid

The data mapping is chosen to optimize communications when computations on vectors and matrices are executed, see [6]. Let N be the matrix size and C be the degree of row equal to the degree of column. Thus we choose the processor grid's size equal to $N \times C$. Let the processors be described in the following way P_{i_g, j_g} with $i_g \in \{0, \ldots, C - 1\}$, $j_g \in \{0, \ldots, N - 1\}$. The mapping of the problem is on a data parallel programming model :

– Scalars are the same on all processors $P_{i_g, j_g} \forall i_g, \forall j_g$.
– Vectors (size N) are mapped on each row of processors so each column of processors, $P_{i_g, j_g} \forall i_g$, contains the same vector component.
– The matrix A is mapped on the processor grid after a column compress : $A_{i,j} \neq 0$ is mapped on the processor P_{i_g, j_g}, with $j = j_g$ and i_g the compress index row. The format of the matrix is described in [2].
– Matrices L and U are mapped according to the A sparse compressed format, L is stored in the lower part of the compressed format and U in the upper.

3.2 Test Matrix Patterns

We use different patterns of matrices to measure performance. The first one is the C-distributed : non-zero diagonals are uniformly distributed with the main diagonal always non-zero. The second pattern is the so called C-diagonal : all the non-zero diagonals are concentrated around the main diagonal. The C-diagonal q-perturbed pattern is obtained from the C-diagonal after a random perturbation of its pattern. The decision to perturbe the pattern follows a probability q. Then each element of a q-perturbed C-diagonal matrix has a probability q to be at a random distance of the main diagonal. More details in [2] and [3].

3.3 Preconditionings on the CM-2

For the polynomial preconditioning, on each iteration of the method, we had to compute $s(A)x$. We choose the option to compute directly $s(A)x$ by a succession of appropriate matrix-vector multiplication instead of computing first $s(A)$ by matrix-matrix multiplication and then $s(A)x$ with one matrix-vector multiplication. The first issue avoids matrix-matrix multiplication which is time consuming and doesn't preserve sparse pattern.

The ILU preconditioning generates the following sparse computations : first the matrix-vector multiplication, then, at each iteration the method solves two sparse triangular systems, the third sparse operation is the ILU factorization of A.

4 Numerical Experiments

We present in this section times corresponding to one iteration of PCG algorithm. For polynomial preconditionings we used the Communication Compiler for general communications. We measured performance for the programs :
- CG : conjugate gradient without preconditioning.
- PPCGk : PCG algorithm with a Neuman polynomial of degree k.
- ILUPCG : preconditioned conjugate gradient with an ILU factorization.
In the following, let be K equal to 1024. Let the vpr be the number of virtual processors under the number of physical processors. Notice that the regular communications generated in the special case of C-diagonal matrices are not take into account to optimize the general communications.

4.1 Results for PPCGk, k=2, 4, 6.

Performance on C-distributed Matrices The first observation, on reading Table 1, shows that the performance increases with N when C is fixed.

When the vpr and C are given, we observe that if the number of processors is doubled (8K to 16K), the performance is also doubled. For example, with $C = 8$, we obtain 16 Mflops with $N = 32K$ on 8K processors ($vpr = 32$) and 32 Mflops when $N = 64K$ on 16K processors ($vpr = 32$). We can reasonably expect to reach, on 64K processors, performance that is 4 times higher than on 16K with the same vpr and C.

Performance on C-diagonal and C-diagonal perturbed matrices Results given in Fig. 1 show that the C-distributed matrices are a worse case for the performance measured because they give lower performance than the perturbed matrices with a probability equal to 1 (i.e. with a completly random pattern).

The reason of these difference in the performance in terms of Mflops between the matrix patterns, comes from general communications. All the other communication

N	C	CG		PPCG2		PPCG4		PPCG6	
		time (ms)	throughput (Mflops)	time (ms)	throughput (Mflops)	time (ms)	throughput (Mflops)	time (ms)	throughput (Mflops)
4K	4	4.2	17	7.4	21	10	23	13	24
64K	4	30	38	70	35	110	34	150	34
128K	4	55	42	130	38	200	38	270	37
2K	8	4.4	12	7.9	16	12	17	15	18
32K	8	28	30	61	33	94	34	130	35
64K	8	53	32	120	34	180	35	250	35

Table 1. *Performance on C-distributed matrices on a 16K CM-2, with the Communication Compiler.*

q	CG		PPCG2		PPCG4		PPCG6	
	time (ms)	throughput (Mflops)	time (ms)	throughput (Mflops)	time (ms)	throughput (Mflops)	time (ms)	throughput (Mflops)
0.0	30	78	52	94	73	104	95	106
0.1	33	70	62	79	89	85	117	86
0.3	38	61	76	64	113	67	150	67
0.5	41	56	86	57	130	59	174	58
0.8	45	52	96	51	146	52	197	51
1.0	46	50	101	49	154	49	208	48

Table 2. *Performance on C-diagonal perturbed with a probability q matrices on a 16K CM-2, $N = 128K$, $C = 4$. We use the Communication Compiler.*

types and operations are the same when N and C are fixed. With the chosen mapping the general communications are dependent on the distance from the coefficient to the main diagonal, see [2] and [6]. In the C-distributed matrices case, there is always a coefficient at the greatest distance from the main diagonal, i.e. $N/2$, and in the C-diagonal case the non-zero coefficients are at most $C/2$ distance from the main diagonal. The C-diagonal perturbed case described the intermediate values when q varies from 0 to 1. The measures (Fig. 1) confirm these affirmations.

We can generally expect with real world problems to obtain better performance. Reasonably on a 64 K CM-2 we can go beyond 200 Mflops when the problem size is large enough.

4.2 Performance for ILUPCG

The performance obtained for ILUPCG, is clearly very poor : 5 to 10 kflops for matrix of size 4K. We do not use the Communication Compiler. But, even if the Communication Compiler was used, the performance would be multiplied by a factor 10 to 20 (see [2]) and it would still be poor performance. We can give some explanations. First, the triangular systems resolution is a recursive operation : to compute a coefficient, we need the previous ones for lower systems or the following ones for upper systems. Very few operations can be executed in parallel. And the sparser the matrix, the lower the parallelism because there are less non-zero coefficients and thus less available processors are running. Thus the sparse triangular systems resolution generates many general communications which take lots of time compared with a computation operation. But these communications are necessary to preserve the generality of the algorithm implementation.

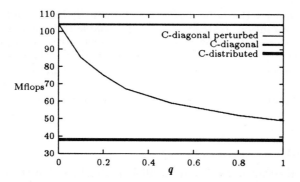

Fig. 1. *Performance of PPCG4 on the 16K CM-2 when* $C = 4$ *and* $N = 128K$.

5 Research of a good Massively Parallel Preconditioning

We observed previously a relationship between the general communications time and the distance of the coefficients to the main diagonal. We propose the following *ILU* factorization for a given matrix $A : ILUmp(d)$ with

$M = LU$ with $M_{i,j} = (LU)_{i,j} = A_{i,j}$ if $A_{i,j} \neq 0$ and $d(A_{i,j}) \leq d$ where $d(A_{i,j})$ represents the distance from $A_{i,j}$ to the main diagonal, and d is a parameter in relation with the architecture; the coefficients at a distance greater than d are replaced by 0 in L and U.

When the d parameter decreases from N (total matrix) to 0 (just the main diagonal), we measured an improvement of general communications performance by about a factor 20% (for $d = 1$) with C-distributed matrices. We must find a tradeoff between communications times and the iteration count to achieve convergence to determine some d optimal value.

Then, we propose a massively parallel *ILU* factorization based on the $ILUT(k, \epsilon)$ proposed by Y. Saad in [5] and on the $ILUmp(d)$ factorization previously described. Then, we define the $ILUTmp(l, \epsilon, d)$ incomplete factorization as follows :

$M = LU$ with $M_{i,j} = A_{i,j}$ if $\|A_{i,j}\| > \epsilon\|row(i)\ of\ A\|$ and $d(A_{i,j}) \leq d$; with less than lC elements per columns of L and U. We describe this algorithm below :

for $i = 1 \ldots N$ do
    $L_{i,i} = A_{i,i} - \sum_{k=1}^{i-1} L_{i,k}U_{k,i}$
    for $j = i + 1 \ldots N$ do
        if $|A_{j,i}| > \epsilon\|row(j)\ of\ A\|$ then
            $L_{j,i} = A_{j,i} - \sum_{k=1}^{i-1} L_{j,k}U_{k,i}$
            if $d(A_{j,i}) \leq d$ then fill-in of L with l coefficients
        else $L_{j,i} = 0$
    end for j
    $U_{i,i} = 1$
    for $j = i + 1 \ldots N$ do
        if $|A_{i,j}| > \epsilon\|row(i)\ of\ A\|$ then
            $U_{i,j} = (A_{i,j} - \sum_{k=1}^{i-1} L_{i,k}U_{k,j})/L_{i,i}$
            if $d(A_{j,i}) \leq d$ then fill-in of U with l coefficients
        else $U_{i,j} = 0$
    end for j
end for i

The major reason for the poor performance of the ILU preconditioning is the triangular system resolution. Instead of solving a sparse triangular system, we can approximate the LU resolution by a polynomial which gives an approximation of $(LU)^{-1}$. Such hybrid preconditionings were studied in [1]. Then, we propose the Polynomial-$ILUTmp(l, \epsilon, d)$ as a massively parallel hybrid preconditioning for the PCG method. Let $Pk - ILUTmp(l, \epsilon, d)$ be this new preconditioning with k the degree of the polynomial. We can also study others polynomials as Chebychev polynomials.

6 Conclusion

We note in experimenting on massively parallel architecture that the major problem when using sparse irregular structures, is the communications between the different processors. Thus, to adapt usual algorithms on these machines, we must reduce and optimize communications cost in comparison with the initial algorithm. One way to efficiently exploit parallelism is to use hybrid methods associating high parallelism degree and numerical efficiency : as we can see the faster is not the most efficient. We used this method to find tradeoffs between these two factors and thus find an expected good massively parallel preconditioning for the conjugate gradient method. Our goal is to study in more detail hybrid preconditionings to define some convergence rate optimum factors. The $Pk - ILUTmp(l, \epsilon, d)$ preconditioning introduced is a tradeoff between high performance (in terms of Mflops) and fast convergence with respect to the results described above. We still have to analyze it with very large sparse matrices from large applications and compare both the performance and the accuracy of this new preconditioning for the conjugate gradient with other preconditionings on massively parallel machines.

Acknowledgements

The authors wish to thank Youcef Saad and Steven Ashby for useful discussions on the subject of this paper. This work has been supported in part by PRC C^3 of the french CNRS.

References

1. S. Ashby. *Polynomial Preconditioning for Conjugate Gradient Methods*. PhD thesis, Department of Computer Science, University of Illinois at Urbana-Champaign, 1304 W. Springfield Avenue Urbana, IL 61801, december 1987.
2. S. Petiton. *Massively Parallel Sparse Matrix Computations*, Tech. Report YALEU/DSC/RR-878, Dept. Computer Science, Yale University, 1992.
3. S. Petiton and C. Weill-Duflos *Very Sparse Preconditioned Conjugate Gradient on Massively Parallel Architectures*. Proceedings of the 13th IMACS World Congress on Computation and Applied Mathematics, Dublin, 1991.
4. Y. Saad. *Practical use of polynomial preconditionings for the conjugate gradient method.* SIAM J. SCI. STAT. COMP., 6(4), October 1985.
5. Y. Saad. *ILUT : a dual thresholdind ILU preconditioning technique.* Tech. Report to appear, Dept Computer Science, University of Minnesota, 1992.
6. J. Saltz, S. Petiton, H. Berryman, and A. Rifkin. *Performance effects of irregular communications patterns on massively parallel multiprocessors.* Journal of Parallel and Distributed Computing, 8 (1991).

A Block Algorithm for Orthogonalization in Elliptic Norms

S. J. Thomas

Département d'informatique et de recherche opérationnelle
Université de Montréal.

Abstract

The need for block formulations of numerical algorithms in order to achieve high performance rates on pipelined vector supercomputers with hierarchical memory systems is discussed. Methods for analysing the performance of standard kernel linear algebra subroutines, such as the BLAS (levels 1, 2 and 3), are reviewed. We extend the L_2 block Gram–Schmidt algorithm of Jalby and Philippe to orthogonalization in *elliptic* norms induced by the inner product $u^T M u$, where $M = B^T B$ is a positive definite matrix. A performance analysis of this block algorithm is presented along with experimental results obtained on the Cray–2 supercomputer.

1. Introduction. A constraint on achieving fast instruction execution rates on the current generation of parallel vector supercomputers is limited memory bandwidth. It is not uncommon for each processor of such a machine to contain multiple floating point vector pipelines capable of operating in parallel and of producing one result per clock cycle. Moreover, arithmetic operations often can be overlapped by 'chaining' compound add/multiply units. In theory, this can result in impressive peak instruction execution rates. However, it is usually difficult to deliver arithmetic operands to the vector pipelines at a sufficient rate. To significantly increase memory transfer rates, current generation vector supercomputers employ a hierarchical memory architecture. Typically a high-speed cache (local memory, vector register files etc.) is placed between the very fast CPU registers and the large slow main memory of a machine with the result that the initial memory access time for a cache memory can be several times faster than for main memory. Sophisticated numerical algorithms exploit a hierarchical memory organization to achieve the highest possible memory transfer rates. Algorithms must not only employ vectorization and concurrency on such machines, but they must also possess a certain amount of data locality. The result is that the designer of numerical algorithms is faced with the additional task of managing the movement of data between different levels in the memory hierarchy. Data locality can be improved by employing 'block' variants of traditional numerical linear algebra algorithms. Typically, this is achieved by formulating an algorithm with respect to BLAS3 matrix–matrix operations such as matrix multiplication. Basic matrix–matrix primitives such as these are now available as standard kernel subroutines for parallel vector supercomputers. The basic linear algebra subroutines (BLAS levels 1, 2, and 3) are part of LAPACK, which is a package of numerical linear algebra codes for high-performance scientific computing [1]. Gallivan *et al* [2], [3] have analysed the performance of such block algorithms on machines containing high–speed cache memories.

The class of machines studied consists of a multiprocessor MIMD parallel machine, with n_p processors. In particular, all processors may access a small fast cache of size CS words and a large, but much slower, global main memory. It is assumed that any processor can read or write to any location in the cache or main memory. To analyse the performance of block algorithms on this type of architecture, the authors of [3] propose that the effects of data locality, concurrency and vectorization can be studied by applying a 'decoupling' strategy. The total computation time T of an algorithm is broken down into two components: the arithmetic time T_a and the data loading time T_l. If it is assumed that the cache is infinitely large, then T_a represents the execution time of an algorithm when there is no memory hierarchy present. Thus, T_a varies according to the degree of vectorization and concurrency that is possible. One can account for the scheduling of arithmetic operations for SIMD execution across several pipelines or MIMD parallelism by letting $T_a = n_a \tau_a$, where n_a is the number of arithmetic operations (flops) and τ_a is the average time to complete a single operation. The data loading component T_l represents the additional time required to load data from the main memory into a cache of size CS. Given n_l the number of data transfers required and τ_l, the average load time, this component can be expressed as $T_l = n_l \tau_l$. Therefore, the total computation time can be given as the sum: $T = n_a \tau_a + n_l \tau_l$. However, it should be noted that the possible overlap of computation with data loading is not excluded by this model, and could result in a reduction of τ_l according to the cache prefetch policy employed. Despite the rather complicated factors which influence the parameters τ_a and τ_l, it is still possible to study the relationship between data locality and performance. The approach taken in [3] is to consider the 'relative' cost of data loading $T_l / T_a = \lambda \mu$, where the authors define a *cache-miss* ratio $\mu = n_l / n_a$ and a *cost* ratio $\lambda = \tau_l / \tau_a$. For machines that implement a specific cache prefetch policy, it is often possible to reduce λ so that the cache–miss ratio has less of an impact on performance. However, for most machines a lower bound on λ can be given and the problem reduces to minimizing the factor μ through algorithm design. If the time components are regarded as parameterized cost functions, then T_a and T_l can be minimized separately to optimize performance. A region in each parameter space is found that is close to the minimum of the cost function.

2. BLAS3 primitives. Since block formulations of algorithms employ BLAS3 primitives, our first task is to determine the performance characteristics of these matrix operations for a general architectural model. Thus, we apply the analysis techniques introduced in [3] to the most basic BLAS3 primitive; $C = C + AB$, where C, A and B are $n_1 \times n_3$, $n_1 \times n_2$, and $n_2 \times n_3$ matrices. If $n_2 = k \ll n_1, n_3$, then this operation is referred to as a rank-k update, but may also represent a dense matrix multiplication when A, B, and C are all large matrices. When $n_2 = 1$, for example, this primitive reduces to the BLAS2 rank–1 update. Both vectorization and concurrency are present in our model architecture, with data movement between two memory levels in the memory hierarchy. To optimize the performance of the above BLAS3 primitive on such a machine, consider a partitioning of the matrices C, A, and B into submatrices of dimension $m_1 \times m_3$, $m_1 \times m_2$ and $m_2 \times m_3$, where $n_1 = k_1 m_1$, $n_2 = k_2 m_2$, and $n_3 = k_3 m_3$. The 'individual' block operations $C_{ij} = C_{ij} + A_{ik} B_{kj}$ can be performed in parallel across n_p processors. Moreover, these operations can be pipelined for SIMD execution via multiple vector pipelines. Optimal block size selection for m_1, m_2 and m_3 can be determined by minimizing T_a, the arithmetic time component, and T_l, the data loading component associated with these operations. Consider the kernel algorithm for one such block operation:

```
do r = 1, m₃
    do t = 1, m₂
        do s = 1, m₁
            c_sr ← c_sr + a_st b_tr
end
```

where we denote matrix elements by variables which are lowercase letters. The outermost loop iterations can be performed in parallel. The two inner loops represent an m_2–adic operation. The latter can be implemented by a *multiply–add* vector instruction, which happens to be the best combination of operations for most vector supercomputers. In particular, fast execution rates for this operation can be achieved on register–to–register machines such as the CRI Cray–2. Values of m_1, m_2 and m_3 that minimize T_a are generally machine dependent. For register–to–register machines, m_1 should be a multiple of the vector register length (64 words for the Cray–2). The value of m_2 should be large enough to achieve a significant fraction of the peak speed of the multiply–add. Finally, m_3 should be a multiple of the number of processors, n_p (four for the Cray–2).

It is assumed, when executing a block matrix–multiply, that the submatrices A_{ik} are loaded from main memory into the cache only once for each execution of the j–loop. Furthermore, we assume that C_{ij} and B_{kj} are repeatedly loaded into the cache. If L denotes the total number of element loads from main memory into the cache, then it follows that: $L = n_1 n_2 + n_1 n_2 n_3 \rho(m_1, m_2)$, where $\rho(m_1, m_2) = m_1^{-1} + m_2^{-1}$. Thus, minimization of the load time is equivalent to minimizing $\rho(m_1, m_2)$ subject to the constraints imposed by a cache of fixed size CS. If it is assumed that a block A_{ik} remains in the cache then $m_1 m_2$ cache memory locations are required. When m_2 exceeds the number of vector registers available for the multiply–add computation, an additional $m_2 p$ cache elements will be needed in order to store columns of B_{kj}. Therefore, minimization of the load time T_l for the BLAS3 primitive is equivalent to the minimization of $\rho(m_1, m_2)$ subject to $m_2(m_1 + p) \leq CS$, $1 \leq m_1 \leq n_1$ and $1 \leq m_2 \leq n_2$, where the value of m_3 is arbitrary. The constraints described above represent a rectangle and a hyperbola in the (m_1, m_2) parameter plane. It is shown in [3] that a solution to this optimization problem lies in one of four different regions (solution regimes) of the bounding rectangle. Since the number of memory element loads into cache is given by $L \equiv n_l$ and since the number of arithmetic operations (flops) required for the BLAS3 primitive is $n_a = 2 n_1 n_2 n_3$, the resulting cache–miss ratio $\mu = n_l / n_a$ is: $\mu = 1/(2m_1) + 1/(2m_2) + 1/(2n_3)$. We recall that T_a is minimized for large positive values of m_1 and m_2, thus insuring efficient use of vector pipelines. Except for cases where the matrix dimensions n_1, n_2 and n_3 are small, the data load time T_l is minimized for the positive values of m_1 and m_2 specified in the abovementioned regimes. Therefore, the decoupling strategy proposed by Gallivan and his co–workers is an effective means of determining optimal blocksize values, since m_1 and m_2 can be chosen to simultaneously minimize T_a and T_l.

3. Orthogonalization in elliptic norms.

Let B be a *known* full–rank matrix of dimension $m \times p$, with $m \geq p$, and let M be the positive definite $p \times p$ matrix defined by $M = B^T B$. For a $p \times 1$ vector u, an *elliptic* norm is induced by the inner product $u^T M u$: $\|u\|_M = \|Bu\|_2 = (u^T B^T B u)^{1/2} = (u^T M u)^{1/2}$. The vector u can be considered as representing, in an oblique coordinate system, the vector whose representation is the $m \times 1$ vector Bu in an orthonormal system. It is for this reason that the matrix B is sometimes referred to as an oblique transformation. Now consider a $p \times n$ matrix S, with $p \geq n$, and suppose that we wish to orthogonalize the columns of S with respect to such an elliptic norm. (The M–orthogonalization of a set of vectors is a basic step in methods for the solution of large symmetric systems of linear equations by iterative techniques and for the generalized eigenvalue problem $Ax = \lambda M x$.) To formulate a modified Gram–Schmidt algorithm in an elliptic norm one can simply take inner products with respect to the matrix M in the traditional L_2 method. However, slightly more efficient variants of this algorithm are given in [6]. For example, if the Cholesky factor B is known instead of M, then an algorithm which avoids matrix–matrix multiplication to form M can be obtained by replacing M with $B^T B$ and separating the individual matrix–vector products.

Algorithm PGSM (Product Gram–Schmidt in the M–norm)

> for $j = 1$ to n do
> > (1) $v_j := B s_j^{(j)}$
> > (2) $\rho_{jj} := \|v_j\|_2$
> > (3) $g_j := s_j^{(j)} \rho_{jj}^{-1}$
> > (4) $q_j := v_j \rho_{jj}^{-1}$
> > (5) $t_j := B^T q_j$
> > for $k = j + 1$ to n do
> > > (6) $\rho_{jk} := t_j^T s_k^{(j)}$
> > > (7) $s_k^{(j+1)} := s_k^{(j)} - \rho_{jk} g_j$
> > end
> end

The complexity of the above algorithm is $4mpn + 2pn^2$. We note that the same basic operations found in the L_2 modified Gram–Schmidt algorithm are employed. In particular, step (6) above is an inner product (sdot) and step (7) is the vector triad (saxpy). However, steps (1) and (5) are BLAS2 matrix–vector products (sgemv) and these two operations account for the additional $4mpn$ flops. To generalize the results of Jalby and Philippe [5] to orthogonalization in elliptic norms, we remark that at step (7) of PGSM,

$$s_k^{(j+1)} = s_k^{(j)} - g_j g_j^T M s_k^{(j)} = (I - g_j g_j^T M) s_k^{(j)},$$

and thus the elementary operators $I - q_j q_j^T$ of the traditional Gram–Schmidt algorithm are simply transformed to $I - g_j g_j^T M$ when an elliptic norm is employed. Now suppose that the original $p \times n$ matrix S is partitioned into d blocks: $S = [S_1, S_2, \ldots, S_d]$, where a block S_j is of size n_j, $n_1 + n_2 + \cdots + n_d = n$. In order to generalize the algorithm to block form, we can define the block–operator:

$$
\begin{aligned}
I - G_j G_j^T M &= (I - g_{n_{j-1}+n_j} g_{n_{j-1}+n_j}^T M) \cdots (I - g_{n_{j-1}+1} g_{n_{j-1}+1}^T M) \\
&= (I - G_j T_j^T)
\end{aligned}
$$

where $T_j = M G_j$. Consequently, elliptic algorithms can be generalized to block form by programming the latter expressions as follows.

Algorithm BGSM (Block Gram–Schmidt in the M–norm)

> for $j = 1$ to d do
> > (1) $(G_j, T_j, R_{jj}) := PGSM(S_j^{(j)})$
> > for $k = j + 1$ to d do
> > > (2) $R_{jk} := T_j^T S_k^{(j)}$
> > > (3) $S_k^{(j+1)} := S_k^{(j)} - G_j R_{jk}$
> > end
> end

4. Performance Analysis of BGSM. Given the matrices $B(m \times p)$ and $S(p \times n)$, where $m \geq p \geq n$, we recall the performance analysis of the L_2 block algorithm BGS given in [3], [5]. It can be shown that, from the standpoint of block operations, Algorithms BGS and BGSM are basically identical. In fact, if we adopt a block partitioning with $n = d\omega$, then we see that Algorithm BGSM employs the matrix primitives:

1. Algorithm PGSM applied to the $p \times \omega$ block $S_j^{(j)}$.

2. A matrix multiplication of the form $C = AB$, A is $\omega \times p$ and B is $p \times (n - j\omega)$. $(R_{jk} = T_j^T S_k^{(j)}, k = j + 1, \ldots, d.)$

3. $C = C - AB$, C is $p \times \omega$, A is $p \times \omega$ and B is $\omega \times (n - j\omega)$. $(S_k^{(j+1)} := S_k^{(j)} - G_j R_{jk}, k = j + 1, \ldots, d.)$

It is possible to derive a load function $L(\omega) \equiv n_l$ for Algorithm BGSM by employing the analysis techniques described in sections 3 and 4. Despite the fact that $L(\omega)$ can be algebraically complex it is still possible to characterize the performance of the block algorithm by approximations to the cache–miss ratio over two separate intervals. An approximation to the cache–miss ratio valid over the interval $1 \leq \omega \leq CS/p$ is $\mu \approx 1/(2\omega) + \eta_1$, where η_1 is proportional to $1/n$. The minimum of this function occurs at $l = CS/p$, when $\mu = p/(2CS)$. For $CS/p \leq \omega \leq n$ it can be shown that the approximation,

$$\mu \approx \frac{1}{2\omega}\left(1 - \frac{\gamma}{n}\right) + \frac{\omega}{2}\left(\frac{1}{n} + \frac{1}{CS}\right) + \eta_2$$

where $\gamma = l^3 + 3l - 3$ and η_2 is proportional to $1/n$ holds. The above function is a hyperbola, which reaches a minimum at $\omega \approx \sqrt{CS}$ and increases thereafter from $\sqrt{CS}$ to n. If $\omega = n$, then $\mu \approx 1/2$ corresponding to the BLAS2 algorithm. Since algorithm BGS and BGSM employ the same operations, except for the additional (sgemv) operations and a normalization, we expect that the above cache–miss ratio approximations should be applicable.

We note, however, that the performance of the algorithm is characterized only partially by these approximate functions. If we assume that $m = p$, then the complexity of Algorithm BGSM is $4m^2n + 2mn^2$. Moreover, when $m \gg n$ the first term dominates. Thus, we propose that the performance of the block algorithm should more closely follow the performance of the (block) matrix–multiplies: $V_j = BS_j$, $T_j = B^T Q_j$, $j = 1, \ldots d$, when $\omega \approx CS/m$. The cache–miss ratio for the these block matrix multiplies is given by: $\mu_{min} = 1/\sqrt{CS} + n_p/(2CS) + 1/(2n_3)$ and when $n \gg \sqrt{CS}$ it follows that $\mu \approx 1/\sqrt{CS}$.

5. Experimental Results. Performance tests were carried out on the National Center for Supercomputer Applications (NCSA) Cray–2 supercomputer at the University of Illinois at Urbana–Champaign. Although the Cray–2 is a four processor vector supercomputer, only one processor was employed in our benchmarks. Each processor has a clock cycle time of 4.1ns, resulting in a theoretical peak rate of 243.9 Mflops for single floating point operations and 487.8 Mflops for compound add/multiply operations. The overall design of the Cray–2 is based upon a register–to–register architecture. Each processor has a $16k$ element, 64–bit word local memory. This local memory replaces the 64 element, 64–bit T (backup scalar) and 64 element, 24–bit Cray X–MP or 32–bit Cray Y–MP B (backup address) registers. There is one port to local memory for each processor, just as there is one port to common memory. The latency to local memory is about 4 clock periods compared to about 20 clock periods for common memory. After this startup time, subsequent vector elements can move at one word per clock period for either memory.

For our tests of the BGS algorithm we employed a 1024×512 randomly generated matrix A. The performance of the algorithm is given in Figure 1, containing plots of Mflops per second versus blocksize ω. The peak speed of the Cray–2 and the Mflops rate of the BLAS2 MGS algorithm are represented by straight lines. In the case of Algorithm BGSM we generated a 1024×1024 matrix B and a 1024×512 matrix S. This results in $4m^2n = 2.15$ Gflops for the matrix multiply component and $2mn^2 = 0.536$ Gflops for the Gram–Schmidt component of the algorithm. Clearly, we expect the former to dominate the computation. Performance results are presented in Figure 1. For comparison purposes we have plotted the performance curve of the associated block matrix multiply in Figure 1. The results indicate that BGSM exhibits the composite behaviour of BGS and the matrix multiply. Finally, we ran a benchmark of the LAPACK block Householder algorithm on a 1024×1024 matrix.

Acknowledgements. The author would like to thank Prof. Ray Zahar for many helpful suggestions which greatly improved the manuscript. Dr. John Larson of the Center for Supercomputing Research and Development (CSRD) of the University of Illinois at Urbana–Champaign generously provided computing time on the NCSA Cray–2. Bill Harrod and Ed Anderson of Cray Research Inc. provided the author with pre–release versions of LAPACK routines and instructions on their use. Finally, it was very kind of Professors W. Jalby and B. Philippe to make their BGS code available on the NCSA Cray–2 and Cray Y–MP for benchmarking.

References

[1] K. GALLIVAN, W. JALBY, and U. MEIER, "The use of BLAS3 in linear algebra on a parallel processor with a hierarchical memory", *SIAM J. Sci. Stat. Comput.*, **8** (1987), pp. 1079–84.

[2] K. GALLIVAN, R. J. PLEMMONS, and A. SAMEH, "Parallel algorithms for dense linear algebra computations", *SIAM Review*, **32** (1990), pp. 54–135.

[3] K. GALLIVAN, W. JALBY, U. MEIER, and A. SAMEH, "The impact of hierarchical memory systems on linear algebra algorithm design", *Intl. J. Supercomputer Appl.*, **2** (1987), pp. 1079–1084.

[4] W. JALBY and U. MEIER, "Optimizing matrix operations on a parallel multiprocessor with a hierarchical memory system", *ICPP Proceedings*, pp. 429–32, 1986.

[5] W. JALBY and B. PHILIPPE, "Stability analysis and improvement of the block Gram–Schmidt algorithm", *SIAM J. Sci. Stat. Comput.*, **6** (1991), pp. 26–50.

[6] S. J. THOMAS and R. V. M. ZAHAR, "Efficient Orthogonalization in the M–norm", *Congressus Numerantium*, vol. 80, 1990.

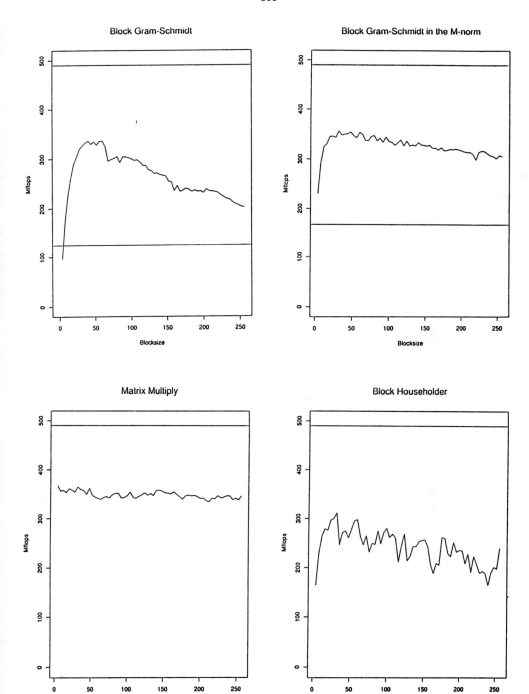

Asynchronous Polycyclic Architecture*

Geraldo Lino de Campos

Escola Politécnica da Universidade de São Paulo

São Paulo 05508, Brazil

e-mail: RTC@BRFAPESP.BITNET

Abstract The Asynchronous Polycyclic Architecture (APA) is a new processor design for numerically intensive applications. APA resembles the VLIW architecture, in that it provides independent control and concurrent operation of low-level functional units within the processor. The main innovations of APA are the provision for multiple threads of control within each processor, the clustering of functional units into groups of functional units that show very weak coupling with each other, decoupled access/execute and eager execution. A supercomputer implementing this architecture is currently being designed, using commercially available parts.

1 Introduction and motivation

Development of the Asynchronous Polycyclic Architecture (APA) concept was spurred by the needs of Project Omicron, an academic research effort. The project's main goal (expected to be achieved sometime in 1994) is to design and build a supercomputer for numerical applications, with a real-world performance in the same range of the then current supercomputers. APA processors are expected to provide better sustained performance in real-world problems than standard vector processors with the same peak capacity.

Since the constraints of a typical University research budget excluded expensive solutions like custom ECL circuits or exotic packaging and cooling, we were forced to develop a novel architecture that is better matched to the needs of real-world computations than the standard vector processor design, but is still realizable by using commercially available components.

We began our design effort with a critical evaluation of existing architectures. Current vector processors are machines architecturally designed in the early seventies. Since then much effort has been put in research in computer architectures, and many important results had been achieved, but had no influence on supercomputer architectures. A basic assumption was that there should be ways to use these results in high-performance machines, if there is no need of compatibility with older architectures.

* This research was partly supported by the CNPQ grant 501971/91-2.

Such an evaluation required a performance yardstick. Given our emphasis on sustained speed in real-world problems, we decided to compare the alternatives by their average performance on some representative benchmark, rather than by their theoretical peak performance under ideal conditions. As pointed out in [8], peak performance adds only to the price of a machine.

Since numerical algorithms typically spend most of their time in the innermost loops, we chose a standard collection of simple loops, the Lawrence Livermore Kernels (LLK) [9] as our benchmark. The performance of many supercomputers in these loops is well known, and the loops are simple enough to be compiled and simulated by hand for all the alternative designs that we had to consider. It is instructive to consider that the real speed observed is a very small fraction of the maximum speed.

This evidence strongly suggests that the traditional vector processor architecture is somewhat ill-adapted to the very tasks for which it was designed. The explanation for this paradox is quite simple: the vector architecture was designed with individual operations in mind, while the real problem is to process entire inner loops, not individual operations. Loops contain recurrences and conditionals, situations that are not considered in the design of vector architectures.

In vector architectures, the main source of inefficiency is the lack or inadequacy of support for operation involving recurrences or conditionals. Following up on the RISC analogy, it seems reasonable to assume that, by breaking up the special instructions of standard vector processors into simpler ones, one would obtain substantially better overall performance from the same amount of hardware. What is needed is an architecture that can offer reasonable performance on general loops, containing recurrences and conditional tests, instead of one that concentrates on optimizing only a few restricted vector forms.

Our proposed Asynchronous Polycyclic Architecture implements this principle by combining the basics of the VLIW architecture [6] with the decoupled access/execute concept [13], and with extensions for loop execution, for conditional execution of instructions, for fetching large amounts of data and for an autonomous operation of groups of functional units, and eager execution for hiding memory latency (in *eager* execution, a instruction is executed as soon as their operands are available and there is a free unit to do the operation, even when it is not sure if the control flow will warrant the need for the instruction; in *lazy* execution an instruction is executed only when reached by the control flow).

Sections 2 and 3 describe the generic APA concept in more detail, and provide arguments in support of these claims. Section 4 briefly outlines an interconnect network specially designed for connecting the above processing units to the memory subsystem. Section 5 describes one specific instance of the architecture, the preliminary design of the Omicron supercomputer. Section 6 offers some concluding remarks

2 Description of the APA

The Asynchronous Polycyclic Architecture resulted from a critical analysis of the characteristics of the VLIW architecture. The detailed evolution leading to the APA can be found in [2]; it will be only summarized here.

A VLIW processor [6] is conceptually characterized by a single thread of execution, a large number of data paths and functional units, with control planned at compile time, instructions providing enough bits to control the action of every functional unit directly and independently in each cycle, operations that require a small and predictable number of cycles to execute, and each operation can be pipelined, i. e., each functional unit can initiate a new operation in each cycle.

On examining the conceptual characterization, it becomes clear that the rationale is to have a large degree of parallelism and a simple, and therefore fast, control cycle. Closer scrutiny of the conditions above shows that they are sufficient for the goal, but most are not necessary, at least in the length stated.

The evolution took place in 4 steps:

First, the access/execute concept [13] was introduced. The motivation was practical considerations on memory access.

The ideal memory subsystem for any supercomputer should have large capacity, very low access times, and very high bandwidth, at a low cost. Real memories must compromise some of these goals. If a large capacity is required, cost and size limitations almost force the usage of relatively slow dynamic memories. Besides, numerically intensive applications require a very high memory bandwidth.

General purpose architectures rely almost invariably on caches to speed up execution, exploiting the locality of memory references. Although this is the case with general computing loads, this assumption can be wildly wrong with numerically intensive programs, since dealing with large arrays is incompatible with any realistically sized cache. This conclusion is reported for quite different machines [1, 5, 12].

The way to go is to have extensive interleaving in the memory; the latency may be high, but as long as it is possible to maintain a large number of outstanding requests, it will be possible to obtain operands at the necessary rate.

It is therefore unfeasible to have a predictable access time for the functional units in charge of memory accesses, due to the static unpredictability of memory bank conflicts. This can be circumvented by considering that the processor remains synchronous in virtual time, stalling if data is not available when expected, but this may have a substantially adverse effect on performance.

The first new APA feature solves the memory access problem by decoupling the process of memory access. Two kinds of functional units are used: the first, called the *address unit*, generates and sends the required addresses to the memory subsystem; the second, called the *data reference unit*, is responsible for reordering data words coming from memory and upon request sending them to the other functional units. This is an asynchronous counterpart to the decoupled access/execution concept introduced by [13].

Address units may operate in two modes: single address and multiple address. In the single address mode, its role is only to receive an address calculated by an arithmetic unit and to send it to the memory subsystem; in the multiple address mode, its role is to autonomously generate the values of a set of arithmetic progressions, until a specified number of elements are generated; this mode is used for reference to (a set of) arrays. Once started, the address unit can proceed asynchronously with the main flow of control: it generates as many addresses as the memory subsystem can accept, waits if the memory subsystem cannot accept new requests, resumes execution when this condition is withdrawn and stops when all addresses have been generated.

As a consequence, the memory subsystem operates at full capacity and the main flow of control is not disturbed by saturation of the memory subsystem. As for hardware, fewer bits are required in the instruction, since the units are controlled by their own instructions, and also fewer ports are required in the central register file, since the address processors can use a local copy of the required registers.

The second step was extending this concept of asynchronous operations to the other functional units, each with its own flow of control.

Experience in programing such a machine shows that it is unduly complicated. Very few situations require this full splitting of the functional units. A hierarchical system is adequate for almost all situations: the functional units can be divided into groups, composed of a certain number of arithmetic units, each capable of forking the operation of address units.

The third step resulted from the fact that experience in programming also shows that the communication between groups is infrequent. An important consequence is that there is no need to share a central register file among groups; each group can use its own, provided it is able to send values to the other groups. This communication is done by a private bus connecting the functional units together.

Three additional features are required for an efficient usage of above characteristics: eager execution, delayed interrupts and a tagged memory system. To keep the functional units busy, values should be calculated as soon as possible, regardless of the possibility of the control flow rendering them unnecessary. A consequence is that abnormal conditions (like division by zero, references to invalid addresses, etc) can arise.

To postpone the resulting interrupts, every word is composed of a tag and a value fields, both in the central register file and in memory. When an operation encounters an error condition, a number associated with this error condition is placed in the tag, and the address of the offending instruction is placed in the value field of the result word. All operations performed with a word containing a non-zero tag will have the original word as its result, thus preserving the error nature and the address of the offending instruction. If both operands have non-zero tags, one is arbitrarily chosen for the result.

Real interrupts occurs only when the word's value is effectively used. A value is effectively used when the computation can not proceed without the use of value. This may be a somewhat elusive concept, and a precise characterization is beyond the scope of this paper. In a simple approach, a value is effectively used when used as a final result, in output operations; in a more restrictive context, when used in an unavoidable operation, as determined by the execution flow graph.

The hardware must have special instructions that generate an interrupt when a value is effectively used. It is up for the compilers do determine when this is the case.

Efficient execution of loops is obtained by use of a variant of polycyclic support; since its basics are described elsewhere [4, 12], it will not be described in detail here. The main difference from the implementation used in the Cydra 5, described in the above references, is that there are no explicit predicates; predicates are implied in the "age" of the iteration. This allows the hardware to support automatic prolog and epilog generation. The hardware also supports predicate-controlled execution of instructions.

The result of these characteristics is a processor with higher performance as compared to an equivalent VLIW, implemented with register files with fewer ports, and with dynamic instruction word size: each group is small, and at any moment only the active ones must fetch instructions. For instance, the machine resulting from the dimensioning studied in the next section uses register files with only two write ports, and instructions of only 80 bits. Figure 1 depicts the evolution from the VLIW to the APA architecture.

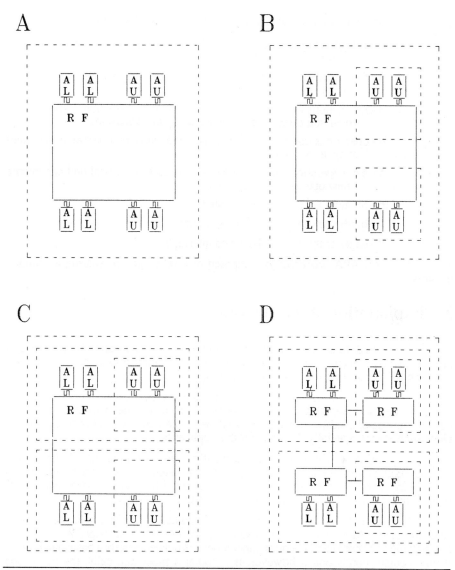

Figure 1 - Evolution from VLIW to APA architecture

In this drawing, dotted lines represent flow of control, AL stands for Arithmetic Logic Unit, and AU for Address unit.

In A, the traditional VLIW architecture. In B, evolution to the access/execute architecture. In C, the introduction of groups. Experimental analysis of programs for this architecture shows that each autonomous set may have its own copy of the register file, as shown in D. Data is exchanged via an internal bus. Other essential features for making this possible are not shown.

In short, the architecture of one APA group is characterized by:

1 - a large number of data paths and functional units, with control planned at compile time;

2 - functional units which are divided into groups; each group has its own register file and its own flow of control;

3 - instructions providing enough bits to control the action of every functional unit directly and independently in each cycle;

4 - operations that require a small and predictable number (in virtual time) of cycles to execute;

5 - each operation can be pipelined, i. e., each functional unit can initiate a new operation in each cycle.

6 - memory accesses are decoupled;

7 - hardware support for loop execution;

8 - eager executions and delayed interrupts.

An APA *processor* is composed of a set of groups sharing a common memory.

3   Exploitation of parallelism

As defined above, a group is a unit of execution. It can be considered as a dual of the pipe in vector machines. In the same way a vector processor can have several pipes, an APA processor may have several groups.

These several groups share a common view of memory, and must be interconnected to a common memory subsystem. Here again, the problem is not one of latency, but one of bandwidth. Section 4 describes a interconnection network, called the *Omicron Network*, specially designed for this application.

With a processor having several groups, fine-grain parallelism is exploited within groups; medium-grain parallelism, if present in loops, is exploited within a processor. Coarse-grain parallelism can be exploited by several processors; in this regard, the APA is not different from other architectures.

Exploitation of the medium-grain parallelism, which is a distinctive characteristic of the APA, is done in blocks contained in innermost loops. We call *inner block* all the code contained inside an inner loop; it is not necessarily a basic block, since it may contain conditionals; however, if it contains procedure calls, the inner loop condition allows only the call of procedures that do not contain loops.

The following considerations are based on simple compiler technology; the use of program transformations and other techniques already developed for vector machines will lead to considerable increase in performance.

Every inner block can be characterized in one of the following categories:

3.1– Blocks without data or control dependencies

These blocks can be divided among a sufficient number of groups to allow the use of all bandwidth to memory and all functional units. This category also includes a few particular cases of easily resolved cases of data dependency, like the sum of products.

As an example, the loop

```
    DO 1 I = 1, N
1   S = S + A(I) * B(I)
```

can be split to

```
    DO 1 I = 1, N, 2           DO 1 I = 2, N, 2
1   S = S + A(I)*B(I)      1   S = S + A(I)*B(I)
```

each executed in a different group, followed by the addition of the values of S.

It should be noted that since each group has its own set of registers, there is no renaming problem with S and I; each value will be kept in a register with the same number, but on a different register file.

3.2– Blocks with control dependencies

Blocks with control dependencies have their performance limited by latency of the instructions that establish conditions and by the branch instructions. This can be improved in two ways. To a limited extent, it can be circumvented by the predicated-controlled execution. A more general solution is to divide the loop among a sufficiently large number of groups, each processing a fraction of the iterations.

3.3– Blocks with data dependencies

It is generally difficult or impossible to parallelize blocks with data dependencies in a straightforward manner. If the data dependency is immediate and the block is short, a technique that might be used is to increase the data dependency length and execute the resulting blocks on several groups. This technique is generally limited to an expansion from a dependency of one to two dependencies of two.

As an example, the following loop

```
     DO 11 K = 2, N
11   X(K) = X(K-1) + Y(K)
```

can be split to

```
                               X(2) = X(1) + Y(1)
     DO 11 K = 3, N, 2         DO 11 K = 4, N, 2
11   X(K)=X(K-2)+Y(K-1)+Y(K)   11  X(K)=X(K-2)+Y(K-1)+Y(K)
```

The net result is that the APA not only allows the "vectorization" of a larger class of loops then the traditional vector architecture, but allows the parallelization of a large class of loops.

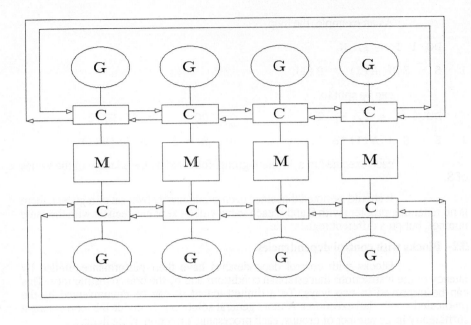

Figure 2 - An 8 x 8 omicron network

G are groups, M are memory modules and C are Omicron switches. Requests from the groups are routed to the memory modules or to the adjoining switches, depending on the address requested.

4   The Omicron Interconnect Network

A detailed description and evaluation results of the omicron interconnect network is beyond the scope of this paper; the following presentation intends to give a few general ideas to clarify the configuration of an APA processor.

To be used in the manner discussed above, independent groups must have a common view of memory. They will be able to operate efficiently only if there is an efficient way to interconnect memory modules (eventually composed of a fairly large number of memory sub-modules) to the groups.

Fortunately, this problem is alleviated by the fact that, due to memory access decoupling, the performance is sensitive to memory bandwidth and not to the access time. This allows the design of a specific interconnect network, called the Omicron network. This network is composed of switches, connected to the groups, to the memory modules and to the adjoining switches. Fig. 2 shows an omicron network, interconnecting 8 groups to 4 dual-ported memory modules.

Each omicron switch is composed of switches that can route a request originated from a group to the adjoining memory module or to neighboring switches, and, in the case of read requests, route back the datum. The innovation is to use a queue in the inputs, to hold requests until there is a free path to the next destination of the request, until the final destination is reached. Although this may add considerably to latency, the obtainable bandwidth is very high, except when the demand rate approaches unity (one request per group per cycle).

The above consideration holds for Omicron networks of up to 8 switches per ring per memory port. Systems with more elements can be constructed by serial connection of switches. An important result is that the first level reduces the request rate to the effective capacity of the switches, and hence subsequent levels do not affect the bandwidth to a significant degree.

5 Dimensioning an APA processor

This section describes one specific instance of the architecture, the preliminary design of Project Omicron supercomputer.

5.1– General aspects

As explained above, reasonably sized data caches are usually useless for processing involving large vectors. Elimination of data caches also avoids cache coherence problems among different groups. Caches are provided for code, however, since the locality of code references is independent of the nature of data accesses. Each group has its own code cache.

To simplify design and implementation, both in hardware and in software, all IO will be implemented by a separate IO processor. A standard RISC server will be used.

The processor will be built with ECL technology, using BIT B3130 floating point processors and Motorola ECLinPS series for logic; the main memory, however, will use standard MOS memories. The target cycle time is 10 ns; this is the value assumed in the foregoing simulations.

A basic word length of 64 bits will be used. This word can also be regarded as two 32 bits words, each with an 8 bit tag, resulting in an 80 bits physical word.

The arithmetic units will be pipelined and capable of integer and floating point operations. The latency of all operations is of 5 cycles, except for divisions and square roots, with 25 and 45 cycles; these last operations are not pipelined.

The structure will be modular, allowing systems with 2, 4, 8 and 16 groups. Each pair of groups will be connected to one memory module. The processor with 16 groups corresponds to the drawing of fig 3.

Simulation studies shown that each memory module should have 32 interleaved sub-modules to allow for two simultaneous reads and two simultaneous writes, limits imposed by technical restrictions on size and density of the backplane.

5.2– Dimensioning the group

The methodology adopted for dimensioning the number of arithmetic units per group and the number of groups was to evaluate the performance when executing the Lawrence Livermore Kernels.

The 24 Lawrence Livermore Kernels [9] were used; kernels 14 and 22 were dropped so as to avoid precision considerations with the functions involved.

The kernels were compiled by hand, with care to use only optimizations that can be expected from a good compiler. The effect of memory conflicts was taken into account. Asymptotic performance means that the inicialization code was neglected; it usually amounts to less the 10 instructions.

In a first stage the study was conducted for architectures with one group, varying from 1 to 16 arithmetic units; table 1 shows the result, with emphasis on the increment of the geometric mean from one to the next configuration.

As can be seen, there are no significant benefits in using more then 2 arithmetic units within a group. This topic is currently receiving much attention, and, with adequate interpretation, the same conclusion has been found in different situations [7, 11, 14], and appears to be a quite general property of programs.

The number of functional units has therefore been fixed as two. There are two couples of address units, one for reads and one for writes; each is composed of one single reference and one multiple reference unit. A branch unit completes the set.

5.3– Dimensioning the number of groups

Table 2 shows the same results for configurations with 2, 4, 8 and 16 groups of 2 arithmetic units. Here, the column increment shows the performance

Table 1 - Performance of one group

Number of arith-metic units	Asymptotic Performance in MFlops					Increment of the geometric mean over previous value (%)
	Minimum	Harmonic mean	Geometric mean	Arith-metic mean	Maximum	
1	16	42	48	49	97	-
2	20	61	84	98	187	75
3	20	63	93	117	276	11
4	20	64	98	127	355	5
5	20	66	104	139	401	6
6	20	67	115	171	528	6
7	20	68	116	174	528	< 1
8	20	68	117	182	673	< 1
...						
16	20	68	117	182	673	< 1*

* relative to 8 arithmetic units

Table 2 - Performance of several groups

| Number of groups | Asymptotic Performance in MFlops | | | | | Increment of the geometric mean over a single group configuration (%) | Increment of the geometric mean over a configuration with the same number of arithmetic units (%) |
	Minimum	Harmonic mean	Geometric mean	Arithmetic mean	Maximum		
2	20	78	123	156	360	46	25
4	20	92	196	296	720	133	67
8	20	102	315	577	1414	275	169
16	20	106	426	937	2880	407	264

increase over a single group with the same number of arithmetic units. As can be seen, the exploitation of fine and medium grain parallelism, allowed by the APA offers an improvement of up to 3.5 times in performance, for configurations with the same hardware resources. What is more important, the improvement increases as the number of arithmetic units increases. Table 2 takes in consideration the reduction in memory bandwidth introduced by the omicron network as the number of groups increase.

As a result, it is worthwhile to use up to 16 arithmetic units in the APA architecture, while only 2 makes sense with a conventional polycyclic architecture. What is more, this can be achieved with register files having the same number of ports and instructions that have the same basic size in both cases.

6   Conclusions

The first conclusion is that there is no reduction in performance when the functional units of a VLIW processor are split into groups with a private register file and autonomous control. On the contrary, this splitting allows the exploitation of medium-grain parallelism, resulting in an increase of performance. This splitting also allows hardware implementations with register files of only two write ports, and the use of dynamical instruction sizing: each group has its own instruction stream, which is used only when required by the available parallelism.

Results of the analysis and simulation of an APA processor are presented, showing a performance increase of 3.5 times in the geometrical mean of the full Lawrence Livermore Kernels over a conventional VLIW machine with polycyclic extensions.

The inclusion of the features needed to asynchronous operation not only increased the performance but resulted in a more easily implementable hardware and in shorter instructions.

A final note is about software. It is generally regarded that the horizontal architectures are inferior to other architectural alternatives on the ground that code is not portable between implementations with different numbers of functional units. This may be true if one takes a strict view about the concept of object code. Nevertheless, if we call object code the result of compilation just prior to final code generation, the horizontal architectures can be code-compatible.

The CONVEX series of machines proves that it is possible to break the compilation process in a series of front-ends for different languages, followed by a generic optimizer and a generic code generator [3]. For a horizontal architecture, we can call object code the output of the optimizer, distribute it under this form, and customize it for a specific machine.

7 Bibliography

1. Abu-Sufah, W and Mahoney, A. D., "Vector Processing on the Alliant FX/8 Processor", Proc. Int'l Conf. Parallel Processing, 559-563, 1986.

2. Campos, G. L., Asynchronous Polycyclic Architecture, Proc. of the 12th Word Computer Congress, vol I- Algorithms, Software, Architecture, Sept 1992.

3. Chastain, M et al., "The Architecture of the CONVEX C240", Proc. of the Fifth Conf. on Multiprocessors and Array Processors, 28-31, March 1989.

4. Dehnert, J. C., Hsu, P. Y. T.., Bratt, J. P., "Overlapped Loop Support in the Cydra 5", 3rd Int. Conf. on Architectural Support for Programming Languages and Operating Systems, 26-38, April 1989

5. Diede, T., et al. "The Titan Graphics Supercomputer Architecture", IEEE Computer 21 (9):13-30, September 1988.

6. Fisher, J. A. "Very Long Instruction Word Architectures and the ELI-512", IEEE Conf. Proc. of the 10th Annual Int. Symp. on Comput. Architecture, 140-150, June 1983.

7. Jouppi, N. P. and Wall, D. W., "Available Instruction-level Parallelism for Superscalar and Superpipelined Machines", 3rd Int. Conference on Architectural Support for Programming Languages and Operating Systems, 272-282, April 1989.

8. Jouppi, N. P., "Architectural and Organizational Tradeoff in the Design of the MultiTitan CPU", IEEE Conf. Proc. of the 16th Annual Int. Symp. on Comput. Architecture, 281-289, May 1989.

9. McMahon, F. H. "The Livermore Fortran Kernels: A Computer Test of the Numerical Performance Range," Lawrence Livermore Nat'l Laboratory Report No. UCRL-53745, Livermore, CA, Dec. 1986.

10. McMahon, F. H. "The Livermore Fortran Kernels Test of the Numerical Performance Range", in "Performance Evaluation of Supercomputers", 143-186, edited by Martin, J. L.., North Holland, 1988.

11. Oyang, Y. et al, "A Cost-Effective Approach to Implement a Long Instruction Word Microprocessor", Computer Architecture News 18(1):59-72, March 1990.

12. Rau, B. R., Yen, D. W. L. and Towle, R. A. "The Cydra 5 Departmental Supercomputer", IEEE Computer 22 (1):12-35, February 1989.

13. Smith, J. E., "Decoupled Access/Execute Architecture Computer Architectures", ACM Trans. Computer Systems, 2(4):298-308, Nov 1984.

14. Smith, M. D., Johnson, M. and Horowitz, M. A. "Limits on Multiple Instruction Issue", 3rd Int. Conference on Architectural Support for Programming Languages and Operating Systems, 290-302, April 1989.

A Comparison of Two Memory Models for High Performance Computers

Peter L. Bird[1]   Nigel P. Topham[2]   Sathiamoorthy Manoharan[2]

bird@ACRI.fr   npt@dcs.ed.ac.uk   sam@dcs.ed.ac.uk

Abstract

High performance scientific computers require high bandwidth memory systems. The size of data sets for large scientific codes implies the need for a memory system which contains independent, interleaved banks. We compare the performance of two different control structures for an interleaved memory: bank buffering and address stream lookahead. We show that a centralized lookahead memory controller provides equivalent memory performance to a bank buffering system while simplifying implementation.

1   Introduction

Advances in device technology have permitted a significant increase in the execution speeds of function units for high performance computers. These increases have aggravated the disparity between the CPU speed and the bandwidth capability of storage sub-systems. Two distinct design techniques have evolved to match the capabilities of the two sub-systems: *caches* and *interleaved memory systems*.

A cache is a small high speed storage buffer close to the CPU. The *size* and *speed* of the cache are inversely related, however, so they are of declining utility for large data sets.

An *interleaved storage organization* partitions the physical address space of the machine into N concurrently accessible *banks*. A bank *conflict* occurs when an address references an already active bank. A bank conflict requires that subsequent storage references to the active bank be delayed until the active reference has completed. This usually delays the entire address stream. The effectiveness of interleaved memories is determined by the *number of banks*, the *bank cycle time*, the *operand referencing pattern* and the capacity for *reordering references*.

Although a high degree of interleave reduces the probability of a bank conflict, it complicates the overall system design since the *fan in* and *fan out* to the banks is increased which may, in turn, increase the overall system clock period.

A faster bank cycle time will reduce the duration of inactivity for a bank, but it might reduce the overall storage capacity of the system since smaller chips would be required and will probably increase both the cost and cooling requirements.

If operand referencing can be spread across all banks of the system, a high degree of concurrent bank usage is possible. In classical interleaved memories this can only occur when the striding value for an array is *coprime* with the interleave factor of the storage system. *Address remapping algorithms* [3] can reduce the impact of bad reference patterns by permuting the address space in more intelligent ways than the simple modulo-hashing which is normally used.

The effective bandwidth of an unbuffered interleaved memory is $O(N^{\frac{1}{2}})$ [2]. Doubling throughput requires a quadrupling of the number of banks. By introducing re-ordering mechanisms the irregularity of memory referencing patterns can be smoothed and better bank utilization achieved, resulting in higher system throughput. This paper compares two schemes for "*out-of-order*" processing of address streams: Lookahead where a small *re-ordering* buffer is used to centrally schedule operand references to the storage system and Bank Queueing where each bank maintains a small buffer for addresses.

---

[1] Advanced Computer Research Institute, 1 Blvd Vivier-Merle, 69443 Lyon, Cedex 03 France.

[2] Computer Science Department, Edinburgh University, J.C.M.B., Mayfield Rd., Edinburgh EH9 3JZ, UK.

In the experiments presented in this paper, we have assumed two hardware structures which optimize machine performance. *Decoupling* [4] is a machine organization which separates operand referencing (i.e. addressing) from arithmetic operations. *Bank remapping* [3] is a technique for transforming striding operand references into a uniform random distribution across the memory banks. While these are important topics, the length of this paper prevents a through treatment of them.

2 Centralized Lookahead Controller

The lookahead controller provid. ; effective bank utilization by examining a 'window' of operands for bank scheduling. A block diagram of the lookahead controller is shown in Figure 1. There are three major components of this system: a *reordering buffer* (ROB), a

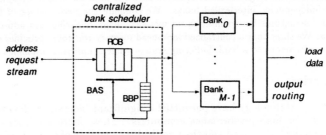

Figure 1: Lookahead Control System

bank active scoreboard (BAS) and a *bank busy pipeline* (BBP). The BAS records currently active banks, and its size is therefore equal to the number of banks in the system. The BBP is a delay line which notes the time when each active bank will become idle. Its length is therefore equal to the *bank cycle time*. The *degree of lookahead* of the system is defined as the length of the ROB minus one. At the beginning of each cycle several concurrent activities occur:

1. Any new addresses from the address generator are appended to the ROB.

2. The bank activity for all of the operands in the ROB are checked using the BAS. The oldest operand in the ROB whose bank is inactive is selected for dispatch.

3. The bank number at the front of the BBP is used to clear the BAS entry for that bank. The bank number for the 'selected' operand (from step 2) is appended to the BBP and the bank number is used to set the BAS.

The BAS and BBP are both simple structures and their implementations are straightforward. The logic to select the next available operand in the ROB is also quite simple. The resequencing of load data can be accomplished with a modulo *sequence counter*; the target cell in the CPU for a load datum can be allocated when the load address is first sent to the memory system.

The centralized controller maintains the entire memory system state at every cycle in its BAS and BBP, thus bank behaviour is entirely deterministic. The scheduling of the *output router* (to determine which bank is to deliver the load datum) can also be provided by the BBP.

A more complete examination of a lookahead controller is presented in [1].

3 Bank Buffering Queues

This storage system architecture uses a collection of FIFO queues at the front of each bank to hold the set of outstanding references to the bank. Consider Figure 2. When a *load* or *store* address is passed to the storage system, a subset of bits in the address is used to select the bank number of the operand. The remainder of the address is appended to the *input queue* (IQ) at the front of the bank and is used to index the datum in the bank. At the start of each memory cycle several concurrent operations take place:

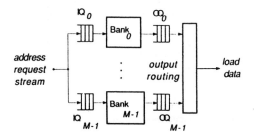

Figure 2: Buffered Bank System

- All *idle* banks with a non-empty IQ initiate the processing of that request.

- If a bank has completed the processing of a *load* request, the loaded datum is appended to the *output queue* (OQ) for the bank. If the OQ is not full, the bank is marked *idle*.

- The set of OQs are examined. The 'earliest' completed *load* reference is moved by the *output routing* logic to CPU.

There are several implementation concerns for this type of architecture. Consider the problem of *queue-to-queue* transfers between the address generator and the IQ. These transfers must take place over a relatively large distance in the machine. Control signals representing the full state of the IQ could take more than one cycle to propagate back to the address generator. Therefore, the depth of the IQ must be sufficient to absorb any objects which are in-transit[1].

The behaviour of the banks themselves when processing their input stream is unpredictable. It is easy to construct an addressing stream whereby two banks will initiate load references on the same cycle, and thus complete the load request at the same time. The output routing structure must maintain all bank states so as to select the appropriate datum to deliver.

4   Experiments

We ran a series of experiments to compare the performance of these two memory organizations over four kernels from the *Livermore Loops*. We generated *scripts* for both the address generation and arithmetic execution instructions of the decoupled system. To mirror the overall decoupled system behaviour, the two script files executed asynchronously. If the resources required for a script were unavailable (such as a queue *empty* for a 'read' operation), the script was frozen until the resource became available. These scripts capture the temporal characteristics of programs without requiring a full functional simulation.

Each simulation trial provided a measure of the arithmetic instruction dispatch rate of the CPU. This measures CPU *efficiency*. This is defined as: $\frac{operations}{cycles}$. The numerator is a count of the number of arithmetic instructions while the denominator is the simulated execution time required to complete the script. The graphs presented below indicate the values for efficiency over a range of memory system configurations. The four kernels chosen for script generation were:

- *Hydro Fragment (loop 1)*: Three vector references[2] with unity strides. The performance demonstrated for this loop was the highest of all the kernels.

- *Banded Linear (loop 5)*: A vector referencing pattern with shifting striding factors.

- *Equation of State (loop 7)*: Ten array references (one store and nine loads), with six of the load references from a window over the same array. This induces bank conflicts.

---

[1] We have not modelled the delay of control signals for buffered banks in our experiments.

[2] There are actually four vectors referenced in the program. One of the vector references is a reused expression. We assume that an optimizing compiler could detect this and remove the duplicate reference.

- *ADI Integration (loop 8)*: Twenty-one, three-dimensional array references displaying *loop-carried* dependencies.

As mentioned in the introduction, the performance of an interleaved memory system depends upon: the *number of banks* and the *bank cycle time*. Let BCT be the *bank cycle time*, and let B be the number of banks in the system. A memory system can be *overbanked* (when $BCT < B$), *critically banked* (when $BCT = B$) or *underbanked* (when $BCT > B$).

Section 4.1 presents a simple comparison of the performance of the two memory architectures. Section 4.2 compares the two schemes when the configuration of the storage system is critically banked. Section 4.3 discusses configurations required to achieve equivalent performance for these loops.

4.1 Simple Comparisons

In this section, we provide comparisons of the performance of the two architectures across the range of kernels we selected for the simulations. Figures 3 and 4 compare the *relative gain* in performance achieved by using lookahead versus bank queueing.

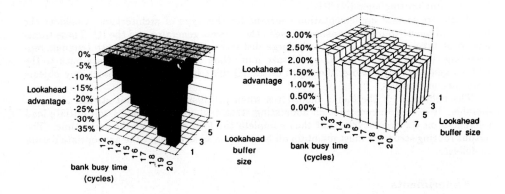

Figure 3: Comparisons using *Hydro-fragment* and *Banded Linear Equations*

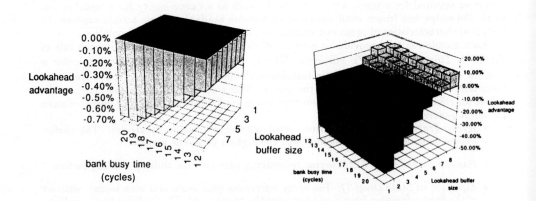

Figure 4: Comparisons using *Equations of State* and *ADI integration*

We fixed the number of banks for this set of simulations at 16. We also fixed the depth of the input queues for the bank queueing scheme to be two elements deep per bank. In all of these figures, one dimension varies the bank cycle time, while the other varies the degree of lookahead. We varied the values of the bank cycle time so as to show systems which were underbanked, overbanked, and critically banked within the same two-dimensional graph. Our principal aim in displaying the data in this format was to expose the design space of the memory system in terms of pairs of pertinent parameters. Often it is possible to see trade-off regions in the design space where one can reduce an expensive parameter without reducing performance.

Consider the Hydro Fragment kernel in figure 3. When the memory system is not underbanked, both schemes display equivalent performance (close to 100% efficiency) for a modest degree of lookahead. The Banded Linear Equations kernel in the same figure shows a modest improvement in performance for lookahead over bank queueing, throughout the design space investigated. Performance for the Equation of State kernel is shown in figure 4. While bank queueing shows better performance over the entire design space we studied, in all cases the performance improvement is less than 1%. Finally, the performance for the ADI integration kernel is also shown figure 4. For all bank cycle times, a modest degree of lookahead (on the order of 5 to 6) shows a performance improvement over bank queueing. In all of these trials, a modest degree of lookahead of the address stream provides a performance which is equivalent to bank queueing with two private buffers per bank.

4.2 "Critical Banking" Comparisons

In this section, compares the performance of bank queueing and lookahead in memory systems which are *critically banked*.

For the trials presented in figure 5, the bank cycle time was varied so that at all times

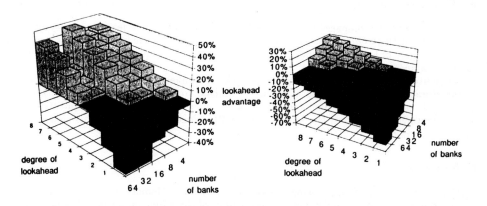

Figure 5: Comparison of schemes at critical banking (Q = 1) and (Q=2)

it was equivalent to the number of banks in the system, thus ensuring a critically banked memory system. Both graphs illustrate the percentage gain in CPU efficiency through the use of lookahead compared with bank queueing, one with a bank buffer size of one, and the other with a size of two. It is interesting to note that for 4 and 8-bank systems with a buffer depth of one, a modest degree of lookahead yields 20–40% higher performance than bank queueing. Even when the input buffer depth is increased to two, a modest degree of lookahead still provides a 20% performance advantage.

4.3 Achieving Equivalent Performance

In both storage architectures, a certain number of cells are devoted to buffering to provide "out-of-order" referencing capability. In this section, we relate the amount of cells required for equivalent system performance. We compare the efficiency of the two architectures for critically banked systems, since these configurations provide the highest degree of stress for reordering schemes.

Table 1 compares the number of cells required for two implementations of bank buffering

Banks	Eff	Lk	Q_1	Eff	Lk	Q_2
4	66.59	1	4	76.88	3	8
8	66.19	3	8	71.79	4	16
16	55.07	3	16	70.04	6	32
32	52.75	5	32	–	–	–
64	27.82	4	64	–	–	–

Table 1: Comparison of Buffer Utilization for Lookahead and Bank Queues

with those required for lookahead to achieve an equivalent degree of performance on a critically banked system running the livermore kernel #8: ADI Integration. The bank buffering schemes have either 1 or 2 cells allocated per bank queue; column 'Q_1' presents a queueing system with 1 cell allocated per bank; 'Q_2' has 2 cells per bank.

The efficiency columns for both sets of trials are low; this is because we have chosen a critically banked system for examination. Recall, for example, that an 8 bank system has a bank cycle time of eight. This constraint places a heavy pressure on the reordering capability of a memory system to achieve any degree of performance. In all cases the lookahead system performed as well as the bank queueing model using only a very small number of lookahead cells.

5   Conclusions

In this paper we have compared two schemes for the control of an *interleaved memory system*: *Lookahead* and *Bank Queueing*. Through a series of simulations, we have demonstrated that a modest degree of lookahead exhibits a performance which is equivalent to, or better than, the performance of bank queueing.

In addition to a straightforward implementation, lookahead permits a centralized control of the storage system. Whereas a lookahead scheme simplifies operand routing, the decentralized operation of the banks in the bank queueing scheme leads to complicated logic for the routing of data from the banks to the CPU, since contention for this shared path cannot be predicted.

References

[1] P. Bird and R. Uhlig "Using Lookahead to Reduce Memory Bank Contention for Decoupled Operand References," *Proceedings of the Supercomputing '91 Conference*, November 1991, pp. 187–196.

[2] T. C. Chen, Parallelism, Pipelining and Computer Efficiency, Computer Design, January 1971, pp.69–74.

[3] B. Rau, "Pseudo-Randomly Interleaved Memory," *Proceedings of the 18th International Symposium on Computer Architecture*, May 1991, pp 74-83.

[4] J. Smith, S. Weiss and N. Pang, "A Simulation Study of Decoupled Architecture Computers", *IEEE Transactions on Computers* C-35(8), August 1986, pp 692–702.

A Decoupled Multicomputer Architecture with Optical Full Interconnection

A.B. Ruighaver

Department of Computer Science, University of Melbourne,
Parkville, Victoria 3052, Australia

Decoupled architectures have been proposed in sequential processing to increase performance when memory access delays are a bottle-neck. Communication delays are expected to be the major bottle-neck in future large-scale parallel computers. Although optical technology is often used to improve the throughput of each connection, such communication systems still have significant data transfer delays. We believe that providing more parallel connections, by increasing the density of topologies, is a more effective approach to reduce the communication bottle-neck.

We are currently evaluating the first prototype of a new decoupled multicomputer architecture supporting static allocation and static scheduling of data processing tasks. The decoupling of communication and computation in this prototype not only supports efficient allocation of data processing resources, but at the same time also allows efficient scheduling of data transfers on the interconnection system to minimize the effect of data transfer delays.

1. Introduction

Although parallel processing has been one of the most important research topics in the last decade, a real breakthrough in the application of large-scale parallelism has been prevented by a communication bottle-neck. The applicability of the few existing multicomputer systems is restricted to applications with a regular structure or to applications with abundant parallelism of medium-to-large granularity.

In a real-time environment, where the requirement of a fast response often leads to a low ratio of problem parallelism versus system parallelism, transfer delays will limit the maximum speed-up. Exploiting more parallelism by reducing the granularity of the parallel tasks will in such a situation just increase the time that each processor has to wait for its data to arrive.

Transfer delays in current large-scale parallel architectures are not only caused by the latency of each connection, but are also the result of a restricted topology. The latest generation of multicomputers is equipped with routing hardware to speed up the transfer of single packets, but the contention in the interconnection system will still prevent the efficient exploitation of small-to-medium granularity parallelism.

Most research in optical communication tries to exploit the enormous throughput of optical links [Acampora88, Dowd91]. Just increasing the throughput of a network, however, does not necessarily reduce the data transfer delays. This is not a problem in Local Area Networks and Metropolitan Area Networks, where large packets of data need to be transferred, but does limit the application of these networks in future parallel architectures.

Because optical interconnections do not have problems with capacitance and inductance, bit rates above 1 Gbit/s are easy to achieve. But even at 1 Gbit/s it will still take at least 32 ns to put 32 bits of data on a single link. Bit-parallel data transfer will be necessary to reduce this delay. More important, however, is the need to reduce routing delay and contention. Routing may become simpler when optical switching technology matures, but optical interconnection systems will have to rely on denser topologies for further reductions in data transfer delays.

In our view, the use of the enormous communication capability of optical links can be exploited most advantageous in communication systems which use the broadcasting property [Fried86] of optics. Broadcasting is less expensive than point-to-point interconnections, because of a reduction in transducers on the transmitting side. A simple example of the implementation of optical broadcasting can be found in optical systems for clock distribution [Clymer86]. Most schemes for distribution of clock signals can be easily extended to broadcast a larger number of signals. In a multicomputer architecture these signals may contain data produced by more than one Processing Element. We call the resulting communication concept *multiple broadcasting* (figure 1).

Initial research on the use of multiple broadcasting for the communication between Processing Elements, together with Frietman at the Technical University Delft, led to a proposal for full interconnection using full bit-parallel optical links [Frietman87]. Our decoupled multicomputer prototype, described in this paper, provides full interconnection using of-the-shelf bit-serial components. We believe, however, that reducing the interconnections per link, while maintaining full interconnection, is not a correct solution for a massive parallel architecture.

Although bit-parallel full interconnection is to be preferred to minimize data transfer delays, only a few applications will be able to take advantage of the abundant throughput provided. For a large-scale system, it is possible to achieve a significant reduction in interconnections and cost, with only a small increase in effective data transfer delays. An extended description of multiple broadcasting topologies providing virtual full interconnection can be found in [Ruighaver90].

In dense topologies there are many parallel routes from one PE to another. When all PE's are trying to transfer data simultaneously, efficient dynamic routing will be impossible. We believe the success of these dense topologies will depend on efficient static scheduling of data transfer to maximize utilization of the communication hardware and to minimize the delay of critical data transfers.

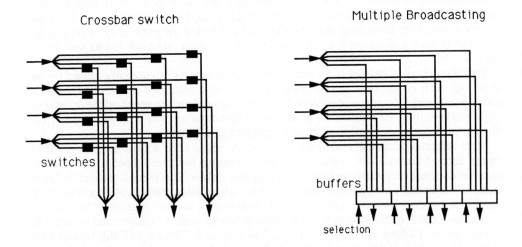

Figure 1:   Comparing multiple broadcasting with a normal optical crossbar switch implementation.

2. A Decoupled Multicomputer Architecture.

Decoupled architectures have been proposed in sequential processing to increase performance when memory access delays are a major bottle-neck [Smith86]. Even with the dense multiple broadcast topologies, made possible by the application of optical technology, communication will still be limiting the speed-up of many applications. Our decoupled multicomputer architecture aims to provide support for separate optimization of data processing and data communication.

A decoupled multicomputer has more in common with a Very Long Instruction Word [Fisher84] architecture than with current message-passing multicomputers. In a VLIW machine, the allocation of parallel data processing tasks to the available functional units is done at compile time, together with the scheduling of these tasks in a single thread of computation. The result is an efficient exploitation of small granularity parallelism, but only on a small scale.

Trying to achieve a similar efficiency in a large-scale multicomputer is not as simple as in the smaller VLIW architecture. Since all functional units in a VLIW computer operate in a lock-step manner, the pattern and timing of the production and consumption of data items is easy to predict. The movement of data on the different data paths can therefore be coded in the same instruction stream that controls the processing of the data in the functional units.

In a large-sale multicomputer it is not feasible to keep the instruction streams in each processing element in lock-step nor is it easy to predict the exact timing of each data transfer. A message-passing multicomputer normally solves this problem by allocation of several independent threads to each processing element. When a thread is waiting for a data transfer it will be suspended and another thread will be executed. Although it is possible to schedule the threads in a predetermined order, the combination of data communication and data processing within each thread makes a static scheduling extremely difficult unless explicitly specified by the programmer.

Dynamic scheduling of threads within a processing element prevents efficient scheduling of data transfer. Most current multicomputer architectures simply transfer messages in the order in which they are produced. Since this order is not known beforehand, extensive identification of each message is required.

Our decoupled multicomputer architecture is based on a semi-dataflow execution model, with objects that consume only data available in their own registers and also store the produced data in their own registers. Both allocation and scheduling of these objects is static, allowing all data processing code in each processing element to be linked in a single thread. Copying of produced data items to other objects is done explicitly. Since the code of the objects is executed in a predetermined order, the production and consumption of data items follows a pattern that is known beforehand. This enables efficient transfer of 32 or 64 bit sized data items, by removing the software overhead of message passing.

Since the PE's are not operating in lock-step we have to allow for slight variations in timing. To prevent unnecessary idle time of the CPU it will be necessary to decouple the transfer system from the CPU with first-in first-out buffers (fifo's). Currently we are evaluating a single small fifo between the CPU and the transmitting side of the network. As long as sufficient parallelism is available, the data transfer code is inserted in the data processing code with the aim to keep at least one data item in the fifo. When the application is compute bound the fifo may become empty and the data transfer system will sometimes be idle. When the application is communication oriented, the fifo will keep the utilization of the network high and the CPU will be idle whenever it tries to put a new data item in a full fifo.

3. The Optoelectronic Multicomputer Architecture.

Our first prototype of a decoupled multicomputer architecture (figure 2) is based on AMD29050 RISC processing elements. The PE's are interconnected with bit-serial broadcasting channels using FDDI optical LAN chips. Each processing element consists of a processor board and a communication board. The AMD29050 is the highest performance member of the 29000 architecture, with a fast Floating Point unit integrated with the CPU.

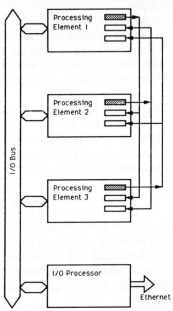

Figure 2:   Multiple broadcasting for a small system with 3 PE's

The interconnection system, shown in figure 3, is working at the FDDI speed of 100 Mbit/s per connection. All PE's in our prototype broadcast at the same time to every other PE, the current network provides full interconnection. A single 32 bit data transfer on this bit-serial interconnection system takes approximately 800 ns. This includes writing of the data to the send buffer, but not the fetching of data from the receive buffer. Less than half of this delay is the actual transfer of bits on the link, the other half is mainly caused by pipeline delay in the FDDI encoders. Obviously, FDDI has not been designed for small data transfers over short distances, and we are currently implementing bit-parallel data links to further reduce the transfer delay.

If we include all overheads in our current implementation of multiple broadcasting, each Processing Element has access to 32 bits of data from all other processing elements every 1200 ns. As our prototype allows for simultaneous data transfer and data processing, this limits the granularity of parallelism on this prototype to tasks with a minimum execution time of 1200 ns per data item produced. As long as the granularity exceeds this minimum there will be no need for the scheduler to minimize communication.

In our programming environment, the responsibility of scheduling the parallel task system on the limited number of available PE's is given to the loader. Since minimization of communication is no longer a basic requirement, the scheduler will be able to achieve near optimal utilization of the processors for most applications using simple heuristic bin-packing algorithms [Bruno86, Ruighaver86].

In 1200 ns our prototype PE, running at 20Mhz, can reduce a vector of six single precision floating point numbers. This is, therefore, the minimal granularity supported for this application. Half of this time is used to transfer the six data elements from the data transfer buffers into the registers of the AMD 29050 [Ruighaver91] and the resulting performance is only 5 MFLOP.

The more data operations are performed per data fetch the better the performance will become. However, to achieve the minimal execution time per task of 1200 ns the granularity of the tasks will also need to be larger. A linear combination of two vectors, each with six single precision numbers and one vector already available in the register file, also has an execution time of approximately 1200 ns. The performance of about 12 MFLOP is more than double the performance of the reduction operation.

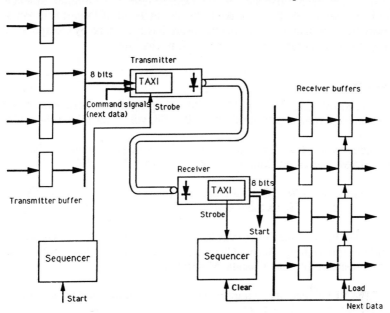

Figure 3:   A single link for pipelined data transfer of 32 bits. Each LED can drive several fibers.

4. Conclusion

A decoupled multicomputer architecture combines static scheduling of data processing tasks with efficient low-latency transfer of small data items of 32 or 64 bits. As our interconnection system supports (virtual) full interconnection, efficient mapping of problem parallelism on the limited system parallelism will no longer be the responsibility of the programmer. As long as sufficient parallel tasks are available with a granularity exceeding the maximal latency of the network, communication overhead will not have to be considered by the (static) load balancing algorithms.

The decoupling of the transfer of operands between PE's and the processing of these operands within a PE is essential to achieve high performance in applications with small granularity parallelism. When the transfer time of the communication system becomes of the same magnitude as the processing time of the computations, the performance will depend on the amount of overlap between the computation and communication.

In our current small prototype we have implemented support for the decoupling of data processing from data transfer with a single fifo between the CPU and the data transmission hardware. It is the responsibility of the system software to schedule the data transfers to keep this fifo partly filled as much as possible.

The performance of our first prototype is promising, it supports efficient exploitation of parallelism at a granularity of 1200 ns. Only the execution of vector reductions is disappointing, owing to the lack of communication bandwith between the receive buffer and the 29050.

5. Acknowledgements.

This project has been financed by the Department of Computer Science of the University of Melbourne and I would like to thank our Head of Department Peter Thorne for his support. The detailed design of the hardware has been done by George Semkiw and the actual implementation has been the work of John Horvath.

6. References.

Acampora A.S., Karol M.J., Hluchyj M.G., "Multihop lightwave networks: A new approach to achieve terabit capabilities", Proc. ICC'88, vol. 1, pp 1478-1484, 1988.

Bruno, J.L. and Downey, P.J., "Probabilistic bounds on the performance of list scheduling", SIAM Journal on Computing, Vol. 15, No.2, May 1986.

Clymer D. C., Goodman J.W., "Optical clock distribution to silicon chips", Optical Engineering, Vol. 25, No. 10, October 1986.

Dowd P.W., "High Performance Interprocessor Communication Through Optical Wavelength Division Multiple Access Channels", Proc. 18th International Symposium on Computer Architecture, Toronto, Canada, May 1991.

Fisher J.A., "The VLIW machine: a multiprocessor for compiling scientific code", IEEE Computer, Vol. 17, No. 7, July 1984.

Fried J.A., "Optical I/O for high speed CMOS systems", Optical Engineering, Vol. 25, No. 10, October 1986.

Frietman E. E. E, Ruighaver A.B., "An Electro-Optic Data Communication System for the Delft Parallel Processor", Computer Architecture News, Vol. 15, No. 4, 1987.

Ruighaver, A.B., "Hierarchical Programming and the DPP84", Ph.D.Thesis, Technical University Delft, December 1986.

Ruighaver, A.B.,"A modular network for dense optical interconnection of Processing Elements", Computer Architecture News, Vol 18, No. 2, June 1990.

Ruighaver, A.B.,"The Melbourne University Optoelectronic Multicomputer Project" Supercomputer, Vol. VIII, No. 6, November 1991, pp. 22-32.

Smith J.E., Weiss S., Pang N.Y., "A Simulation Study of Decoupled Architecture Computers", IEEE Transactions on Computers, Vol. C35, No. 8, August 1986.

Very High Speed Vectorial Processors Using Serial Multiport Memory As Data Memory

A. MZOUGHI, M. LALAM and D. LITAIZE

I. R. I. T. /Université Paul Sabatier, Toulouse, France, e-mail : mzoughi@irit.fr

Abstract. Complex scientific problems involving large volumes of data need a huge computing power. Memory bandwidth remains a key issue in high performance systems. This paper presents an original method of memory organization based on serial multiport memory components which allows simultaneous access to all ports without causing either conflict between them or suspension. The resulting process for information exchange gives a cost effective realization of a data memory for vector processors. The memory bandwidth can be considerably increased in a modular manner, without practical implementation constraints.

Keywords : serial multiport memory, memory bandwidth, realignment network, vector processor.

1 Introduction

Performance improvements in scientific processing may be made in 2 different ways :
- by increasing the number of processors, connected to a common memory, [1, 2] or organized in networks [3]. Nowadays program parallelism in these computers is performed more or less automatically but with different results.
- by using a fast processor specialized in vector calculation [4, 5]. This solution is well adapted to sequential programming [4, 6] since the vectorisation of calculations is carried out automatically in a satisfactory way . Combining these two solutions is, of course, possible, but involves a significant volume of data. The main obstacle when the performance is to be increased becomes the memory-processors network [7]. The existing solution to this problem increases bandwidth to the detriment of complexity, reliability and paradoxically of speed.
A new approach to this problem involves the use of serial multiport memories and an original network. This study presents a vector processor architecture based on serial multiport memory, which is called VEC-SM2 (VEC corresponds to VECtor and SM2 to Serial Multiport Memory).

2 Definition of a Serial Multiport Memory Component

Fig. 1 shows the structure of a Serial Multiport Memory Component (SMMC). It consists of a conventional RAM of word size n, connected in parallel to P shift registers called Memory Shift Registers (MSRs) functioning at a frequency of f MHz.
Example : Considering a RAM cycle time of 80 ns, a shift frequency of 200 MHz, and a MSR size of 72 bits = 64 + 8 bits (parity, Hamming code), then :

VEC-SM2 : This project is supported by the CNRS, the Regional Council of Midi Pyrénées and the French Industry and Research Ministry.

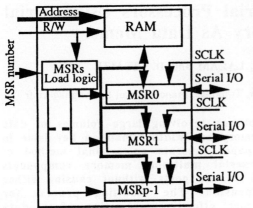

the MSR emptying time(t_f) is :

$t_f = 72 \times 1/(200 \times 10^6) = 360$ ns.

Adding some residual times, we obtain roughly **400 ns**. The RAM can continuously feed **5 MSRs** within the emptying time, using these values.

More generally, if P is defined as the number of MSRs in the SMMC, then the optimal value P is given by :

P = t_f/RAM cycle time.

Fig. 1. Serial Multiport Memory Component

3 Organization of a Serial Multiport Memory

A simple association of SMMCs will give the organization presented in fig. 2.

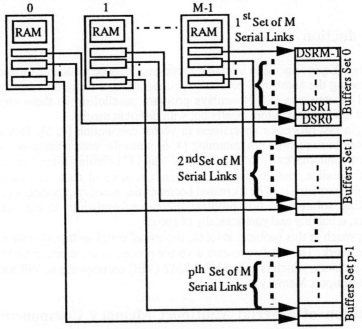

Fig. 2. Organization of a Serial Multiport Memory

A row of MSRs is linked with M (number of SMMCs) Destination Shift registers (DSRs) by M Serial Links (SLs) These M DSRs act as buffers. The memory organization will then have P sets of M SLs and P sets of buffers of M words. We will not discuss these sets of buffers further, but simply note that the memory is thus able to provide P sets of M words at each emptying time interval (t_f) of a MSR. The memory bandwidth obtained is : **Memory Bandwidth = MB = PxM/t_f.**

Example : if we use the same values (§ 2) with M=100 then MB = 1,25 Gigawords/s. We will now discuss the potential benefit of serial multiport memory in comparison with classical memory.

4 Memory Organization of the Cray-2

It is divided into four quadrants [9]. Each quadrant consists of 32 memory banks, each of them divided into 8 memory planes. The vector unit has 8 registers of 64 words, i.e. 512 words of 64 bits. Each quadrant will move 128 words to the vector registers in 128 clock cycles, since the clock cycle is 4.1 ns, 512 ns are needed. The quadrant is organized so that it will be requested every clock cycle and the memory bank every 4 clock cycles. In other words the quadrant functions at a frequency of 250 MHz. The complex interleaving avoids access conflicts to a bank, but the 256 Megawords size requires : 128x8x64 = 65536 components of 256 Kbits. As each memory bank has a data bus of 64 wires, a total number of 64x32x4=8172 wires is needed. This explains the difficulty of scalability in this organization.

5 Comparison of Cray-2 Memory and the SMM

The memory quadrant is synchronous and uses complex interleaving due to the increased number of bus wires, supplying 128 words in 512 ns. Once the first word has been obtained in the first bank, new data is available every 4 clock cycles. Figure 3 illustrates the general timing.

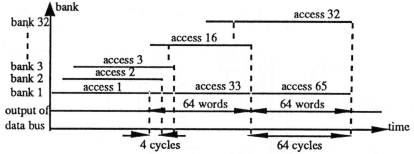

Fig. 3. Chronogram of memory access to one quadrant of Cray-2

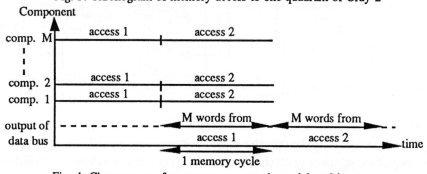

Fig. 4. Chronogram of memory access to the serial multiport memory

Let us now reconsider the memory organization of fig. 2 with a shift frequency of 200 MHz, a memory access time of 80 ns, thus P=5 MSRs. Owing to the much reduced number of wires on the bus, simple interleaving is used. With M=100 SMMCs we obtain 5 sets of buffers of 100 words, and a memory bandwidth of 1,25 Gigawords/s, against 1 Gigaword/s for Cray-2 (fig. 4). The SMMC is considered here from a logical point of view. Its realization, using the same size and components as the Cray-2 memory would necessitate the same number of such components, but with a much simpler interface; a total number of wires MxP=500. We can now compare both organizations in the following table :

Cray-2	Serial Multiport Memory
Complex interleaving	Simple interleaving
Quadrant has a transfer frequency of 250 MHz	MSR has a transfer frequency of 200 MHz
Access is synchronous	Access is synchronous or asynchronous
128 words required 512 ns per quadrant, so 512 words in 512 ns	P*M words in 400 ns, with M=200, P=5 1000 words in 400 ns
Incrementation is complex and limited	Incrementation is easy and large
4 buses of 64 bits	P*M Serial links (1 serial link = 1 bus)
4 parallel quadrants	P groups of pipeline registers (1 group=M)

6 Connection of a Pipeline Operator to a SMM

In the very general case of a classical diadic operation, the pipeline operator of a vector processor has two input feeding pipelines (operands of the operator) and an output pipeline for receiving the results. Let us leave aside the data alignment network for the moment. The architecture proposed in fig. 5, allows the operator to be fed continuously, as each group of DSRs corresponding to a row of MSRs is organized as a set of buffers, and the data is correctly aligned. It shows the interconnection of M SMMCs to a pipeline operator, each SMMC being equipped with 3 MSRs.

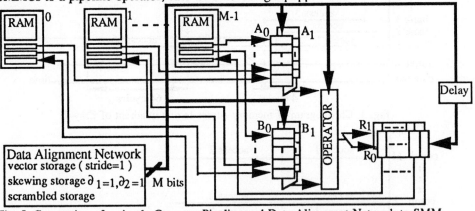

Fig. 5. Connection of a simple Operator Pipeline and Data Alignment Network to SMM

In addition to the operator, it has two sets of buffers (A_0, B_0), (A_1, B_1) working in flip flop mode, allowing the operator to be fed continuously, and one set (R_0, R_1) at the output of the operator to receive the results. They work as follows : $(A_i, B_i) --> R_i$ i mod 2-1. This implies that, while the operands contained in (A_i, B_i) are being processed, (A_{i+1}, B_{i+1}) are fed, and vice versa. The association of a large number of SMMCs allows the number of buses to be increased, yet without having a large number of wires. As a result we can envisage the simultaneous exchange of NxN words. This provides a considerable advantage in calculation and matrix representation. If M is a power of 2, address calculation is simpler and faster than for a prime number of classical memory banks [9]. In order to enlarge access capability to the SMMC, we will attach an address generator/controller to each of them, whose role is to compute the address and control access to the component, which can then be addressed individually, in groups or globally (using the same or different steps). A memory access will give M words simultaneously. These M words are then transferred through the SLs to the corresponding set of buffers in an order which is not necessarily that expected. An original circuit for data realignment has been designed to retreive the original order (fig. 5), which is not a permutation of operands but is deduced from a pre-established order before data is driven to the operator.

6 Data Alignment Network, Originality of Approach

A set of buffers is composed of M serial inputs and one parallel 64 bit output (fig. 6). This approach to data realignment overcomes most of the problems posed by practical implementation of data alignment networks. The solution is very simple since we use serial links. Data is not rearranged during the transfer, but instead processed in an alignment system taking into account operands in the buffer, and imposing the required order (skewing and periodic access [10], scrambled storage [11]). There is no permutation during data transmission. The operand selection for the operator is performed by a shift register, a logical entity easy to implement. The network is modular and easily extensible. Cascading shift registers is simple, and does not require the notion of multiple stages. The system can provide periodic and scrambled permutations. It can be used for different data organizations. Two networks of realignment (one at the input and the second at the output of the operator) are unnecessary. A single network is sufficient. The network shown in fig. 6 is made up of two shift registers SR-A and SR-B of M bits and of a FIFO file organized in words of M bits. The signals $S_0, S_1, \ldots S_{M-1}$ give us the output order of the operands buffer. At a given time only one signal S_i is active (i.e. only one bit at level 1, for example, at the output of the SR-B).

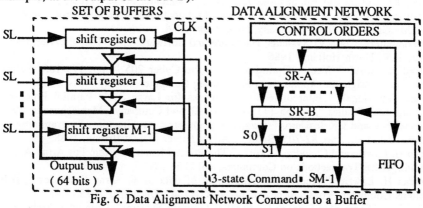

Fig. 6. Data Alignment Network Connected to a Buffer

- The alignment of the operands which have been stored in memory following vector storage (the vector's element of order i is associated to the address i mod M) is done by the SR-B, whose bit "1" at the output is shifted at each clock cycle.

- The alignment of the operands which have been stored in memory following the skewed storage ($\partial_1=1$, $\partial_2=1$, Lawrie's principle [11]) is done through two shift registers SR-A and SR-B, both of them simulating the working of two nested loops.
- The alignment of the operands stored in memory following scrambled storage is realized by the FIFO file. If the speed up of the operator is four times as large as the access to the FIFO, then four FIFO files have to be put in parallel, those files containing consecutive orders which might be arranged horizontally across them. Those orders' orthogonal arrangement known as memory interleave would be used to speed up a single port FIFO system.

7 Conclusion

Serial multiport memories are used in an MIMD architecture project with shared memory [12], whose evaluation was done in our laboratory a prototype of which is already under way. Using the same principles, we plan to use serial multiport memory in a vector processor context. The proposed architecture of VEC-SM2 is representative of two architecture families, those of Cray and Cyber. In fact, VEC-SM2 feeds pipeline operators by registers and thus uses the same philosophy as the Cray, except that in VEC-SM2 the vector registers are managed by hardware and are transparent to the user, feeding being done from memory. In this way we also use the philosophy of Cyber. The large number of simultaneous accesses to the memory, the short memory busy time, and the use of buffers in flip flop mode, guarantee a continuous data flow to the pipeline operator, consequently allowing it to compute at its maximum rate. The transmission speed obtained, in the previous examples, can easily be realized with current technology. Faster speeds can be obtained with more elaborate technology.

References

1. Kenneth E. Batcher ,"Design of a Massively Parallel Processor", pp.104-108, Tutorial Supercomputers design and applications Kai Hwang Computer Society Press, 1984.
2. Burton J. Smith, "Architecture and applications of the Hep Multiprocessor Computer System", pp. 231-238, Tutorial Supercomputers Design and Applications Kai Hwang Computer Society Press, 1984.
3. Tse-Yun Feng, "A Survey of Interconnection Networks", pp. 109-124, Tutorial Supercomputer Design and Applications Kai Hwang Computer Society Press, 1984.
4. Kai Hwang and Fayé A. Briggs, "Computer Architecture and Parallel Processing", pp. 145-320, Mc Graw Hill Book Company, New York, 1984.
5. Supercomputers, Class VI Systems, Hardware and Software, pp. 1-168, Elsevier Science Publishers B.V, North Holland, 1986.
6. Clifford N. Arold, " Vector Optimisation on the Cyber 205 ", pp. 179-185, Tutorial Supercomputer Design and Applications Kai Hwang Computer Society Press, 1984.
7. Howard Jay Siegel, " Interconnection Networks for Large Scale Parallel Processing Theories and case Studies ", pp. 35-173 , D.C. Heath and Company , Massachusetts, 1985.
8. RW Hockney and CR Jesshop, " Parallel Computers : Architecture, Programming and Algorithms ", 2nd ed. , pp. 82-205, Bristol : Adam Hilger , Great Britain, 1988.
9. Duncan H. Lawrie and Chandra R. Vora, " The Prime Memory System For Array Access" pp. 435-442, IEEE Transactions on Computers, vol C-31 , N° 5, may 1982.
10. Duncan H. Lawrie, " Access and Alignment of data in an Array Processor ", IEEE Transactions Computer, Vol C-24 N° 12, pp. 1145-1154 , December 1975.
11. De-lei Lee, "Scrambled Storage for Parallel Memory Systems", Computer Architecture News, Vol. 16, N°2, pp. 232-239, May 1988.
12. D. Litaize, A. Mzoughi, C. Rochange, P. Sainrat, "Towards a Shared-Memory Massively Parallel Multiprocessor", The 19th ISCA ,Vol. 20, N° 2, pp. 70-79, May 1992.

Resource Management on a Packet-based Parallel Graph Reduction Machine

J.A. Keane and K.R. Mayes,

Centre for Novel Computing, Dept. of Computer Science, University of Manchester, U.K.

Abstract. This paper is concerned with resource management on Flagship: a packet-based parallel graph reduction machine specifically designed to support the efficient execution of functional languages. Much of the system software of the machine was implemented *above* the computational model. The major concerns of the system software were the sharing of resources in a way that is compatible with a declarative approach, and to enable the distributed resources of the machine to be used in an efficient manner whilst maintaining consistency of these resources. The paper concentrates on describing how the kernel was structured into a set of resource managers. The resource managers were in turn structured in order to optimise access to distributed resources.

1 Introduction

The Flagship project aimed to produce a complete computing system based on a functional programming style. The machine architecture was a set of processor-store pairs (PEs). Programs were evaluated using graph reduction. Each node of a graph was held in a uniquely-addressed store location as a packet. A packet is physically a collection of contiguous storage locations in a linearly addressable store. The identifier of a packet is the global address where it can be located in this store. Each packet had a header which contains information about the nature of the packet, and a body which held items containing addresses of, i.e. pointers to, packets, so forming the arcs of the graph. The reduction process involved examining the type field of the root packet of a rewrite, and then rewriting the packet and its arguments according to the "rules" associated with that packet type.

Operating systems are inherently *reactive*, i.e. they cannot be characterised simply as a function from their inputs to their outputs. The Flagship approach [3] was to consider it both more natural and more efficient to express the behaviour of such systems using a collection of state variables that are updatable over the course of time, and whose value at any instant represents the state of the computation at that instant. This state had to be isolated from the declarative aspects of the machine, and supported with respect to distribution.

Functional languages, being deterministic, are unable to express the behaviour of reactive systems. However, because the machine supported the efficient execution of functional languages, the pure functional language Hope+ [9], extended with the notion of updatable state, was used as the implementation language for the system software. The occurrence of state introduces problems of consistency with respect to updates. Consistency of state is related to the property of *serialisabiltiy*: i.e. concurrent execution of multiple operations have the same effect as some serial execution. Those actions which can be serialised are termed *atomic* actions.

The purpose of this paper is to show how the Flagship approach to resource management: (1) permitted the sharing of resources in a way that is compatible with the declarative approach and (2) enabled efficient use of resources whilst maintaining consistency. The layout of the paper is as follows: in section 2 the structure of the system software is discussed, section 3 deals with the kernel level, and the structuring of the kernel into resource managers is dealt with in section 4.

2 Structure of the Flagship System Software

This section shows how the system software [7] was supported by the low-level rewrite mechanism. At the primitive level, primitive actions on the computational graph, such as overwriting a node or redirecting an arc, are atomic. At the rewrite level, a single rewrite, which may consist of many component primitive actions, is atomic. The system software is supported by the rewrite level. The lowest part of the system software is the guardian level. Here, atomicity of actions is guaranteed by a *guardian mechanism*. Atomic actions at this level consist of more than one rewrite.

1. Primitive level: Primitive actions such as overwriting a node or redirecting an arc were implemented at this level. Packet representation of graph nodes, primitive packet types, packet states, and firing packets and returning values are provided at the primitive level in the Basic Execution Mechanism (BEM) [10].

2. Rewrite level: This level presents rewrites as atomic actions to the guardian layer. It also supports the concept of the *environment* of a rewrite. The environment provided the contextual information necessary for the execution of a rewrite. One such component of an environment was the Flagship *process*: the unit of scheduling of resources for a computation [7]. That is, a process is the entity to which resources (such as cpu time and store) were allocated; a system software process approximately corresponds to a functional program. The BEM, mentioned above, actually provided more than the machine primitives: (1) it provided facilities for performing several primitive actions, involved in a rewrite, as an atomic action, and (2) it established the environment in which the rewrite occurred.

The MONSTR computational model [2], running on the BEM, imposed constraints on rewrites involving a *stateholder* packet (whose value is updatable). There could only be one stateholder involved in a rewrite, and the rewrite must be executed on the PE where the stateholder was created and permanently resides. Stateholder packets thus have a *locality property* whereby they are never copied and are never exported from their original PE. This property is used in the guardian level to ensure that access to a stateholder is serialised. MONSTR permitted state to be used, in an otherwise declarative computational model, in a clean and controlled way.

3. Guardian level: A *Flagship Abstract Data Type (FADT)* [6] was the unit of abstraction, design and decomposition for the system software. The state of an FADT instance is accessible only via operations defined in the FADT definition. The effects on the state of an FADT instance of these operations are serialised.

The behaviour of the Flagship system software was expressed using a representation of state. State was represented by a *state variable*, which is a stateholder at the rewrite level. However, at the guardian level, this stateholder was embedded in a software structure. This structure containing the stateholder was termed a *guardian* and provided the means whereby FADT instances were implemented at the level of the operating system kernel. The Flagship guardian is similar to the concepts of *guardians* [4] and resource *managers* [1]. The guardian ensured that concurrent actions on the stateholder value each be *atomic and serialised* in their effect. A *guardian mechanism* ensured that an operation application has sole access to the state value for the duration of that application. The guardian mechanism accessed the current state value in the stateholder, allowed the application of an operation to this value, updated the state in the stateholder with the new value and delivered the result of the operation to the caller. This mechanism was supported by features provided by the rewrite level, i.e. the atomic nature of rewrites and the locality property of stateholders.

3 Kernel Level System Software

The Flagship kernel consisted of a set of resource manager subsystems, each responsible for managing a particular resource. The design was such that these resource managers execute in parallel. The state of each subsystem was embedded in structures which are instances of FADTs. Each subsystem itself consisted of instances of particular resource manager FADTs executing in parallel.

The state of an FADT instance may only be accessed by operations (state transition functions) defined for the FADT. Both the state representation and the state transition functions were inaccessible to the caller. The only visible "handles" on an FADT instance were a set of interface functions which had no explicit reference to the state in their signatures. It is these which were accessible to users of the FADT instance. The transformation of a state transition function into an interface function was achieved internally by the guardian mechanism which ensured that access to the FADT instance was serial. Thus an FADT instance in Flagship kernel consisted of a set of interface functions, all of which refer (internally) to the same stateholder.

Each interface function is represented by a triple of items within a packet. Each triple has the form (g, stf, SH), where SH is the stateholder, g represents the guardian mechanism code and stf represents the state transition function code. Thus, for each FADT instance there is a set of interface functions, each referring to the same SH and each stf representing an allowed operation on that FADT. FADT instances communicated by calling each other's operations, and this communication was implemented as a rewrite. The interface function packet, (g, stf, SH), may persist, awaiting the next call. The interface function application, (g, stf, SH, in), is an invocation of an operation of a particular FADT instance with *input* parameters.

FADTS are themselves a system resource. The kernel subsystem responsible for managing the *FADT resource* was the ADT Manager. In particular, ADT manager was responsible for the *dynamic* creation of instances of FADTs. Like other subsystems, ADT Manager consisted of FADT instances. Such *system* FADT instances were created *statically* to solve the problem of creating the initial entities of the system. Initial kernel resources were allocated via a statically-created initial process which served statically-created initial instances of, for example, Store Manager FADTs.

The ADT Manager subsystem provided an operation which created an instance of an FADT. It required, as parameters, the initial state and the state transition functions of the FADT instance to be created. Additionally, the PE where the stateholder of the new FADT instance was to reside was also specified. This operation returned the set of interface functions representing the newly-created FADT instance.

The Flagship system software was written in the functional language Hope$^+$ extended with updatable state. Those parts of the Hope$^+$ program representing the state-based components of the system software were transformed into the stateholders of the machine by means of the creation of FADT instances by the ADT Manager subsystem. This action of ADT Manager was accomplished using routines which directly manipulated the graph reduction primitives at the Primitive Level.

4 Resource Management in the Kernel

The kernel resource managers are structured using the FADT as the unit of design. A *global resource manager* FADT instance is invoked when there is a need to co-ordinate kernel activity across the machine. The stateholder for such a global manager instance is located on a particular PE, and consequently must be accessed on that PE. This represents a bottleneck if many requests are made, as the requests cannot be handled in parallel. Consequently the resource managers were structured so that most activity occurred on a local (per PE) level rather than invoking global activity. This has manifested itself in the presence of *local resource managers* on each PE, each represented by an FADT instance. When a local resource manager is accessed, the particular instance accessed is the instance on the current PE.

1. Store Manager: The proposed Store Manager [8] provides an example of structuring in relation to global/local concerns. There were three classes of FADTs in the design of this subsystem, each of which represented a level – global, process, local – in the subsystem. At any time, the store management subsystem would consist of one instance of a Global store manager, one instance of a Process store manager for each process, and one instance of a Local process store manager for each PE (the neighbourhood) on which each process is running. This structure represents a separation of concerns:

- *global-level concerns*: i.e. of process creation in relation to system-global resource management,
- *process-level concerns*: In that a process may execute on a neighbourhood of PEs, there is a further distinction possible between: (1) management of process-global resources and (2) *processor-level concerns*, such as management of the allocation of resources to the process on each PE in its neighbourhood.

Initiation of activity in the store management subsystem relating to a process occurred via the single instance of Global store manager. However, once the management FADT instances for that process have been set up, the management of store for that process becomes autonomous and can occur in parallel with store management of all other processes. PE-local store management was designed to allow the allocation of store in parallel to the same process on different PEs.

2. SCET Manager: The Static Copying Environment Table (SCET) Manager [5] had two purposes: (1) it exploited locality of reference in functional programs, and (2) it assisted in the PE-local handling of requests to resource managers.

The SCET mechanism enabled locality of reference within functional programs to be exploited on Flagship. Briefly the purpose of this mechanism was to ensure that whenever a copy of a function definition or constant data is held in one of the PEs, it is always located in a well-known place. A *logical* SCET was conceptually a tuple *(Master SCET, set (Local SCET))*, where each master SCET and its associated local SCETs reside on separate PEs. Each Master and Local SCET consist of *(SCET index, SCET entry)* tuples, where the SCET entry is conceptually another tuple *(global address, local address)*. This mechanism essentially provided a local copy of a packet at the *local address*. If no local copy exists then one is made from the *global address* and stored at the *local address* (recall the store is globally addressable). The SCET was an aspect of the environment of a computation.

When an environment for a *new* computation was created on a PE, this PE was designated as the *root* PE for the environment. As part of this creation a Master SCET was associated with the new environment on that PE. The new packets that represent the computation will be loaded on to this PE. As part of this loading process both the *global-address* and *local address* part of all the Master SCET entires were set to the address where their associated packets are located.

As a computation spread across its neighbourhood to a PE where the environment associated with the computation had not yet been established, a similar procedure occurred. The difference was that the *global addresses* was made available in the local SCET associated with the environment but the *local addresses* were all set to the *NULL* value. As the computation proceeded, the BEM and the copying mechanism of the machine ensured that, local copies of SCET entires were made and the *local address* updated appropriately.

As discussed earlier, a rewrite on a PE needed to access the PE-local resource managers. This is also achieved via the SCET mechanism. When a rewrite required access to a particular resource manager interface function, the SCET index associated with the required operation was planted in the requesting rewrite. The rewrite thus used the SCET to access the appropriate local resource manager instance interface function on that PE. A given interface function of a given class of resource manager was addressed via the same index in each Local SCET. However, at that index, each Local SCET contained a reference to the *local* resource manager interface. This interface would be associated with a different FADT instance on different PEs.

The use of the SCET mechanism to support the access of *local* FADT instances by the SCETs extended its original purpose as a copying mechanism. The stateholder which holds the state of an FADT instance *cannot* be copied. Thus each local SCET was assigned the appropriate resource manager interface before access was made to its associated SCET index, so that a local copy always existed and the normal copying was inhibited. This use of the SCET enabled efficient and uniform access to the local resource manager interfaces.

5 Conclusions

Flagship was a graph reduction machine which supported both declarative and state-based computations. The decision that application-level and system software-level computations require state has been reflected in the basic rewrite mechanism of the machine and at all subsequent levels.

The system software was written in Hope+ to utilise the parallelism of the graph reduction machine. The mapping of functional programs representing the system software onto the stateholders of the machine was achieved by the ADT Manager subsystem of the system software, creating FADT instances to serialise access to, and thus maintain the consistency of, the stateholders of the machine.

Factors involved in distributing resource management have been discussed, and the Flagship approach, of maximising the autonomous local processing, has been described. The general structure of the Store Manager subsystem has been described. The SCET Manager subsystem has been dealt with to show how it assisted the PE-local handling of system software requests.

The Flagship project has ended but there remains considerable interest in the use of functional languages extended with state-based ADTs to implement system software on highly parallel machines.

Acknowledgements

The authors wish to thank the people involved in the Flagship project at the University of Manchester and at ICL, West Gorton, especially Steve Leunig, the designer of the system software, and Richard Banach, John Sargeant and Brian Warboys for constructive criticism of earlier drafts of this paper. Flagship was a UK Alvey Project, IKBS 049, this work partly supported by SERC grant GR/E 21070.

References

[1] Arvind & J.D. Brock, Resource Managers in Functional Programming, Journal of Parallel and Distributed Computing 1, pp. 5-21, 1984.

[2] R.Banach & P. Watson, Dealing with State on Flagship: The MONSTR Computational Model, *CONPAR 88*, Cambridge University Press, pp. 595-604, 1989.

[3] R. Banach, J. Sargeant, I. Watson, P. Watson & V. Woods, The Flagship Project, IEE/BCS UK IT 88, Conference Publication, Swansea, pp. 242-245, 1988.

[4] J.B. Dennis, Data Should Not Change: A Model for a Computer System, Laboratory for Computer Science, CGS Memo 209, MIT Cambridge, Mass., 1981.

[5] J.A. Keane, *Aspects of Binding in a Declarative System*, MSc. Thesis, University of Manchester, 1989.

[6] S.R. Leunig, Abstract Data Types in the Flagship System Software, Flagship Document FLAG/DD/303, ICL, 1987.

[7] S.R. Leunig, Design Description of the System Software. Flagship Document FLAG/DD/3SD.016, ICL, with draft changes, August, 1988.

[8] K.R. Mayes, Store manager subsystem, Flagship Document FS/DD/3FS.001, University of Manchester, 1988.

[9] N. Perry, Hope+, Internal Document IC/FPR/LANG/2.5.1/7, Department of Computing, Imperial College, London, 1987.

[10] P. Watson, The Flagship Basic Execution Mechanism, Flagship Document FS/MU/PW/018-87, University of Manchester, 1987.

A Large Context Multithreaded Architecture*

R. Govindarajan and S.S. Nemawarkar
Dept. of Electrical Engineering
McGill University
Montreal, H3A 2A7, CANADA
{govindr,shashank}@pike.ee.mcgill.ca

Abstract

Multithreaded architectures synthesize von Neumann computation model with data-driven evaluation to take advantage of both computation models. In this paper we propose the design and performance evaluation of a Large Context Multithreaded (LCM) architecture. The salient features of the proposed architecture are: (i) a layered approach to synchronization and scheduling of the three levels of program hierarchy, (ii) support for a large resident context to improve locality, and (iii) a novel high-speed buffer organization to ensures 100% data availability. Initial simulation results indicate that the proposed architecture is capable of sustaining very high processor utilization.

1 Introduction

Hybrid von Neumann/dataflow architectures [1, 2, 5, 7] have the potential to satisfy the increasing demands on very high computation speed. In the hybrid computation model, a program is a partially ordered graph of nodes. The nodes, called *threads*, consist of a sequence of instructions which are executed in the conventional von Neumann way. Individual threads, however, are scheduled in a dataflow-like manner, driven by the availability of necessary input operands to the threads. Also, in the hybrid evaluation model, when a long latency operation is encountered in a thread, the processor changes context — starts executing instructions from another thread — in order to keep the processor busy all the time. A suspended thread, suspended due to a long latency operation, becomes enabled for execution only when the request corresponding to the long latency operation is satisfied by the memory system. Thus, the hybrid evaluation model combines the advantages of von Neumann execution with that of data-driven evaluation while carefully avoiding their drawbacks.

Several architectural proposals to exploit locality at thread level have been reported in the literature [1, 2, 5, 7]. (The reader is referred to [4] for a survey on multithreaded architectures.) Unlike the above architectures, with the exception of [3], in our architecture exploiting locality can be extended from a single thread to a collection of threads. Our Large Context Multithreaded architecture (henceforth referred to as the LCM architecture) supports a layered approach to synchronization and scheduling. Also, a novel high-speed buffer organization has been proposed in our architecture that results in zero load stall in the execution pipe.

---

*This work was supported by MICRONET — Network Centres of Excellence, Canada.

The rest of this paper is organized as follows. In the following section, the LCM model is described. We present the details of the LCM architecture in Section 3. The performance results of a single processor LCM architecture are reported in Section 4. Section 5 summarizes and concludes this paper.

2 The LCM Model

The execution model of the LCM architecture is discussed in this section.

2.1 Program Hierarchy

In the LCM model, a program is represented by a collection of code blocks each corresponding to a function/procedure body. A code block is divided into several threads. Threads are extracted from the dataflow graph of a code block using either depth-first or breadth-first partitioning strategy [5]. At the lowest level of program hierarchy is the instruction sequence in a thread. In the LCM model, instructions in a thread are fetched from the program memory and executed as in a von Neumann machine.

2.2 Synchronization and Scheduling

First we consider code blocks. Each invocation of a code block is called an *activation*. Associated with each activation is a set of memory locations required to store the local variables. These memory locations collectively are referred to as the *frame* or the *context* of the activation. Initially an activation is *dormant*. It becomes *enabled* whenever at least one thread in the activation is enabled. The frame corresponding to an enabled activation can be loaded in the high-speed buffer, if enough free space is available in the high-speed buffer. Then the activation or the context is said to be *resident*. The LCM architecture can support multiple resident contexts. A context remains resident as long as there is at least one enabled thread in the activation to be executed. An activation either *terminates* when all threads in the activation have terminated. An activation becomes *suspended* when there is at least one thread in the activation which is not enabled.

A thread becomes *enabled* when it has received the necessary operands on all its input arcs. In the LCM model thread synchronization can be classified as *internal* or *external* depending on whether the thread received all its operands from within the frame or from outside. External synchronization is performed in a special hardware unit called the thread synchronization unit. On the other hand, internal thread synchronization is performed in high-speed buffer locations. An *enabled* thread becomes *ready* when the corresponding context is made resident. A *ready* thread waits for processor *resources*. A *resource* is a set of processor registers, including the program counter and the base address register. When a thread acquires a free *resource*, it is said to be in the *executing* state. A thread in the *executing* state can run to completion without requiring further synchronization.

Instructions from a thread are executed sequentially. However in executing instructions in a pipelined manner, data hazards can occur due to inter-instruction dependency. To solve data hazard, we follow an interleaved execution of thread with some compile-time information to improve the execution efficiency. The details are presented in Section 3.7.

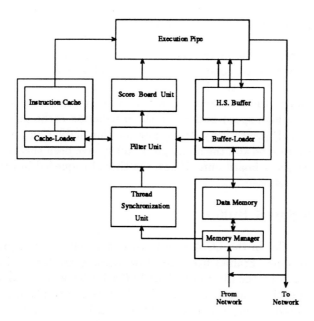

Fig. 1 - A Single Processor LCM Architecture

2.3 High Speed Buffer

A novel implementation idea used in the LCM architecture is to pre-load the necessary frame in the high-speed buffer prior to scheduling the instructions. This, together with dataflow synchronization, ensures that all operands necessary for executing the instructions in an enabled thread are available in the high-speed buffer. In the cache terminology this corresponds to 100% hit ratio.

3 The LCM Architecture

The LCM architecture consists of a number of processing elements connected by an interconnection network. However, in this paper, we will concentrate on the architecture of a single processing element and its performance. The organization of a single processing element is shown in Fig. 1. The various functional units are described below.

3.1 The Memory Unit

The memory unit consists of a simple memory manager and a data memory. The memory manager is responsible for allocating frames dynamically when the new activations are invoked and for deallocating the frame when an activation terminates. It also handles access to data structure memory. In the current implementation only array data structures are supported. Once a frame is allocated for a new activation, tokens belonging to that frame are sent to the thread synchronizing unit.

3.2 The Thread Synchronization Unit

The thread synchronization unit performs external synchronization. It is similar to the explicit token store matching unit of the Monsoon architecture [6]. When all synchronization requirements of a thread have been satisfied, the thread becomes enabled and is then sent to the filter unit.

3.3 The Filter Unit

The filter unit performs the prioritized scheduling of threads. If the incoming thread belongs to an already resident context, then the thread is sent to the score board Unit. Otherwise the filter unit checks whether new contexts can be made resident. If not, the thread is queued in the filter unit. If a new context can be loaded, then the filter unit instructs the the high-speed buffer and the instruction cache unit (to be described in Section 3.5) to load, respectively, the frame for this activation and the code block. When the instruction cache and the high-speed buffer have been successfully loaded, the thread is sent to the score board unit. If not, the thread is queued in the filter unit until a resident context is released.

3.4 The High-Speed Buffer

The high-speed buffer in the LCM architecture is a multi-ported cache-like memory with 1 cycle access time. Frames from the slow memory are loaded in the high-speed buffer when instructed by the filter unit. The buffer loader will always find a free block in the buffer, since such a request is issued by the filter unit only when there is a free block in the high-speed buffer. Unlike conventional caches, the high-speed buffer is not transparent. The start address where the frame is loaded is sent along with the thread. Buffer loader either flushes a frame or writes back the frame into the slow main memory when the corresponding activation has terminated or has suspended[1].

3.5 The Instruction Cache

The instruction cache unit in the LCM architecture is similar to the instruction cache in conventional machines.

3.6 The Score Board Unit

The score board unit receives *ready* threads either from the filter unit (after external thread synchronization) or from the execution pipe (internally synchronized threads). A *ready* thread is sent to the execution pipe if there is a free *resource*. Otherwise it is queued in the score board unit until a *resource* becomes available.

3.7 The Execution Pipe

The execution pipe is a *smooth* pipeline with four stages, namely instruction fetch, decode, execute and result store. The execute stage itself consists of a number of arithmetic pipelines. Instructions in a thread are executed sequentially, fetching the necessary operands from the high-speed buffer. The interleaved execution of threads is supported in the following way in the LCM architecture. With each instruction we associate a stall value, computed at compile-time, which indicates how many stall cycles are required before the next instruction can be fetched. The stall value is stored in the stall register. If the stall register has a value greater than zero, then the next instruction will not be

---

[1] Due to lack of space, the details of how the termination or suspension of an activation is conveyed to the buffer loader are not presented in this paper.

fetched from this thread. Instead, a different *resource* is used and instructions in the corresponding thread will be executed. During each cycle, the stall registers of all *resources* will be decremented by one. Whenever the stall register value becomes zero, the next instruction in that thread is ready for execution.

4 Simulation Results

The performance of a single processor LCM architecture is evaluated using deterministic discrete-event simulation. The behavior of each functional unit was simulated. Constant service time, in number of clock cycles, is assigned to each functional unit. Two scientific benchmark programs — SAXPY (with 512 elements) and matrix multiplication (of two square matrices of order 24) — were run on the simulator.

Table 1. Performance of a Single Processor LCM Architecture

Parameters	SAXPY	Matrix Multiplication
Idle Cycles	93	45
Execution Cycles	10844	143710
Utilization	0.99	1.00

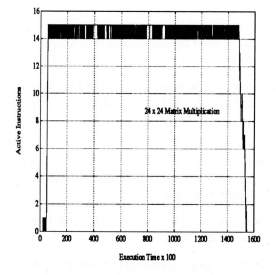

Fig. 2 – Active Instructions in the Execution Pipe

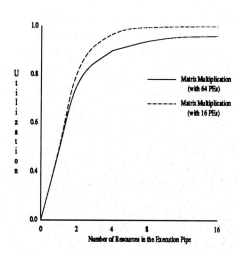

Fig. 3 – Effect of Resources on Utilization

Table.1 summarizes the idle cycles, the execution time, and the utilization of the execution pipe for the two benchmark programs. The architectural configuration used 16 resident contexts and 16 *resources*. The utilization of the pipelined execution unit is defined as the ratio of busy cycles to the total execution time. The simulation results clearly show that the execution pipe was busy almost all the time, resulting in a very high utilization value very close to 1. For instance, in the matrix multiplication program, during the entire execution period, the pipeline was idle for only 50 cycles.

At each time step the number of instructions that are ready for execution (excluding those which are stalling due to data dependency) is measured. Fig. 2 plots this graph. When the architecture uses 16 *resources*, we find that the number of active instructions is close to 15 all the time. This indicates that only a few threads in the *executing* state stall at any time step and there is sufficient number of active threads to do a thread-switch.

Fig. 3 shows the effects of the number of *resources* on the utilization. It can be seen that when the number of *resources* is 6 or more, the utilization is close to 1. The number of *resident* contexts supported by the LCM architecture has a similar effect on the utilization.

5   Conclusions

In this paper the design of a large context multithreaded architecture has been proposed. The salient features of the architecture are (i) its ability to exploit locality in the entire activation of a code block, (ii) the layered approach followed in the synchronization and scheduling of the various levels in program hierarchy, and (iii) the novel high-speed buffer organization which ensures 100% data availability. Initial simulation results of a single processor LCM architecture predict very high processor utilization. We are currently studying the performance of the multiple processor LCM architecture.

References

[1] A. Agarwal, B. H. Lim, D. Kranz, and J. Kubiatowicz. APRIL: A processor architecture for multiprocessing. In *Proceedings of the 17th International Symposium on Computer Architecture*, pages 104–114, 1990.

[2] Robert Alverson et al. The Tera computer system. In *Proceedings of the 1990 International Conference on Supercomputing, June 11–15, 1990, Amsterdam, Netherlands*, pages 1–6, 1990.

[3] David E. Culler, Anurag Sah, Klaus Eric Schauser, Thorsten von Eiken, and John Wawrzynek. Fine-grain parallelism with minimal hardware support: A compiler-controlled threaded abstract machine. In *ASPLOS IV: Architectural Support for Programming Languages and Operating Systems*, pages 164–175, 1991.

[4] J.B. Dennis and G.R. Gao. Evolution of multithreaded architectures. In *Multithreaded Architectures*. Kluwer Academic Publishers, 1992. to appear.

[5] R. A. Iannucci. *Parallel Machines: Parallel Machine Languages*. Kluwer Academic Publishers, Boston, MA, 1990.

[6] G. M. Papadopoulos and D. E. Culler. Monsoon: An explicit token-store architecture. In *Proceedings of the Seventeenth Annual International Symposium of Computer Architecture, Seattle, WA*, pages 82–91, 1990.

[7] Burton J. Smith. Architecture and applications of the HEP multiprocessor computer system. In *SPIE Real-Time Signal Processing IV*, volume 298, pages 241–248, 1981.

On the Practical Efficiency of Randomized Shared Memory

Hermann Hellwagner

Siemens AG · ZFE ST SN 21
P.O.Box 83 09 53, W–8000 Munich 83
E-Mail: hermann@christine.zfe.siemens.de

Abstract. This paper analyzes the efficiency of Randomized Shared Memory (RSM) in terms of constant factors. RSM or memory hashing, that is, pseudo-random distribution of global memory addresses throughout local memories in a distributed-memory parallel system, has been proven to enable an (asymptotically) optimally efficient implementation of scalable and universal shared memory. High memory access latencies are hidden through massive parallelism. Our work examines the practical relevance and feasibility of this potentially significant theoretical result. After an introduction of the background, principles, and desirable properties of RSM and an outline of the approach to determine RSM efficiency, the major results of our simulations are presented. The results show that RSM efficiency is encouragingly high (up to 20% efficiency of idealized shared memory), even in an architecture modelled on the basis of state-of-the-art technology. Performance-limiting factors are identified from the results and architectural features to increase efficiency are proposed, most notably extremely fast process switching and a combining network. Several novel machine designs document the increased interest in RSM and hardware support.

1 Introduction

Parallel MIMD-type computers have traditionally been divided into two classes: shared-memory and distributed-memory systems. Most shared-memory machines to date have been built around a common bus and with physically common memory. Well-known examples are Sequent and Alliant multiprocessors. Due to the use of centralized resources, such systems are confined to relatively small scale, comprising tens of processors at most. In contrast, a distributed-memory architecture allows nodes (processor plus local memory) to be added more readily, without incurring a bottleneck directly. Highly parallel systems such as Intel and NCube hypercube machines and transputer arrays are therefore based on this approach.

In terms of convenience of programming and ease of use, though, shared-memory systems are widely preferred over their distributed-memory counterparts. The development and functionality of systems and support software, such as compilers, debuggers, and load balancing tools, usually benefits from the single global memory provided by the hardware. Application writers often find it more convenient to base their parallel code on the shared-variable programming model, without being concerned with explicit partitioning and mapping of data to individual memories, and exchanging data among nodes via messages.

In the design of massively parallel computers that are destined to meet the need for ever higher computing performance, an attempt is being made to combine the advantages of the two architectures: the superior scalability of distributed-memory hardware, and the convenience of software development provided by a shared-memory image. One of the approaches to achieve this goal is Distributed Shared Memory (DSM), a concept that has attracted substantial research interest in recent years [5, 11]. Most of the DSM schemes proposed and implemented to date employ some form of *caching* and elaborate protocols to ensure coherence of multiple copies of shared data items. Because of possibly expensive coherence maintenance activities and the potential risks of page thrashing and false sharing, the scalability and universal efficiency of such DSM systems is still an open question.

It is therefore worthwhile to investigate an alternative approach to scalable shared memory. Recent work in theoretical computer science showed how to implement *provably scalable* and *universally efficient* DSM [14, 15]. The proposal is based upon global memory *hashing*, that is, pseudo-random distribution of the global address space among the nodes' local memories. High memory access latencies are masked through massive parallelism. It was shown that in these settings shared memory can be emulated optimally (in an asymptotic sense) on a distributed-memory machine, provided that its interconnection network meets certain requirements and that sufficient parallelism for latency hiding is available. In the sequel, the term *Randomized Shared Memory (RSM)* will be used to denote this proposal for shared memory realization.

From a practitioner's point of view, this approach is counter-intuitive in that any locality of reference is destroyed by hashing and, intuitively, one would anticipate very poor performance. Due to its desirable theoretical properties, though, RSM is an interesting and potentially significant proposal. Whether or not RSM is feasible in practice depends on how efficiently it can be implemented in a real system. It is the purpose of this paper, therefore, to determine the practical efficiency of RSM in a state-of-the-art architecture through simulations, to point out architectural features that will increase this efficiency, and, thus, to establish the practical relevance of the theoretical results on RSM.

The remainder of the paper is organized as follows. Section 2 briefly and informally introduces the theoretical background, the principles, and properties of RSM. Section 3 outlines the performance evaluation approach adopted to determine RSM efficiency. In section 4, the major results of our simulations are presented. Section 5 summarizes sources of inefficiencies that can be identified from the performance results, proposes architectural means to overcome them, and gives examples of parallel machine designs that incorporate such features.

2 Randomized Shared Memory

2.1 Background

RSM was introduced in the theoretical literature in the framework of studying emulations of an idealized shared-memory machine, the *Parallel Random Access Machine (PRAM)*, on realistic distributed-memory hardware. The PRAM model essentially consists of a (possibly infinite) number of processors, accessing and communicating via a global memory (possibly of infinite size). The processors operate synchronously; in each step of the computation, every processor can make an access to common memory. Memory accesses are of uniform cost and take unit time; there is no notion of memory locality.

The PRAM model abstracts from any architectural and hardware details and constraints, and allows parallel computation to be studied *per se*. It has therefore extensively been used to develop and study (efficient) parallel algorithms, to devise techniques for parallel algorithm design, and to develop a parallel complexity theory [4, 9].

To make this substantial body of literature and knowledge more relevant and easier to use in the context of practical problems and machines, theoreticians devised ways to emulate the PRAM on (models of) real machines. Exploiting earlier results, such as those of [10], Valiant has made a notable contribution by disclosing a method of optimally emulating (in an asymptotic sense) a PRAM on a distributed-memory and loosely-coupled machine such as the hypercube even [14, 15]. The work presented in this paper draws upon Valiant's results, one key element of which is efficient shared memory emulation through memory randomization.

2.2 Memory Randomization

Fig. 1 illustrates the basic principle of memory randomization. The technique randomly distributes global data and, at run time, global accesses on a *per-word* basis throughout the system's memory modules, i.e., the nodes' local memories. Randomization is applied to global data only. Data that are private to a node can be held in a conventionally addressed portion of the node's local memory.

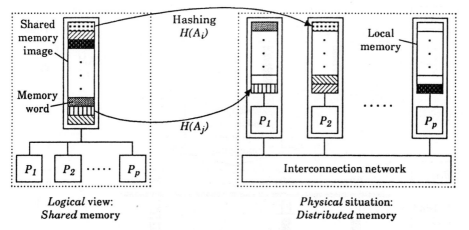

Fig. 1 Randomized Shared Memory

The purpose of hashing is to spread out global addresses and accesses as uniformly as possible across the memory units of the system, avoiding to overload individual units even if the memory accesses are arbitrarily non-uniform. Similarly, memory request/reply traffic in the interconnection network is randomized and the danger of hot spots or systematic blocking, which may severely impair machine performance, is reduced.

It must be noted that fig. 1 gives a simplified picture of memory randomization in depicting a *single* hash function H only. For the theoretical analysis, however, two hashing steps (and functions) are required, *global* and *local* hashing. These functions must satisfy the property to generate a provably (approximately) even distribution of global memory locations throughout the memory units *(universal hashing)*. Their computation involves evaluating a polynomial of degree O (log p) where p is the number of nodes in the system, which would cause substantial hardware and run-time overhead in a real machine. For a more detailed explanation the reader is referred to [6]; the rigorous mathematical treatment is given in [14].

Fortunately, for practical purposes, a *linear* hash function of the type $H(A) = (bA + c)$ mod m, where m is the number of global memory locations, $0 \leq b \leq m-1$, and b and m are relatively prime, was reported to be sufficient [1, 12]. The universality property does no longer hold for these functions, however. Due to the advantages of simple hardware implementation and fast evaluation, a single, linear hash function was assumed for the RSM evaluation reported here.

2.3 Optimal PRAM Emulation and Bulk-Synchronous Parallelism

Valiant's results are potentially highly significant in that they show a method of (asymptotically) *optimal* PRAM emulation on a distributed-memory system. The PRAM is emulated on a so-called *bulk-synchronous parallel (BSP) computer*. Fig. 2 illustrates the basic idea of the emulation of a single PRAM step.

A PRAM algorithm utilizes v virtual processors (VPs). The VPs execute synchronously in PRAM steps, in each step performing operations as given exemplarily for VP$_1$. (For sake of illustration, the steps shown are of coarser grain than those introduced above.) Each PRAM step is emulated by a BSPC *superstep* as follows. The PRAM VPs are mapped to processes on the p physical processors (PPs) of the BSP machine evenly. Thus, every PP executes multiple processes concurrently. The PRAM shared memory is randomized throughout the local memories of the BSPC. Then, with high probability, a global memory request issued by a BSP process will result in a message being sent to the PP hosting the requested data. In that case, the requesting process is descheduled, and another process resumes execution. Thus, frequent process switching is employed to hide the communications latencies involved in memory accesses. At

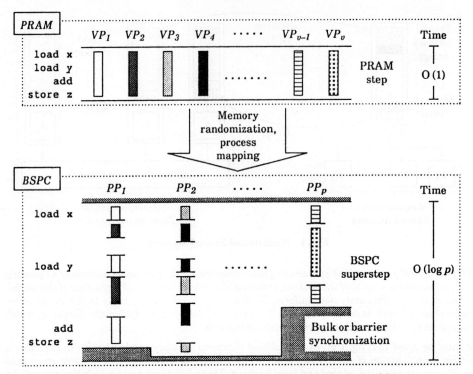

Fig. 2 Optimal PRAM emulation on a bulk-synchronous machine

the end of a superstep, each process explicitly issues a synchronization request, resulting in global synchrony being established eventually, at which point the next superstep may start.

The major prerequisite for efficient execution is a sufficient degree of parallelism (*excess parallelism* or *parallel slackness*) exhibited by an application program. As an example, consider the emulation of an exclusive-read, exclusive-write (EREW) PRAM on a BSP computer. In that case, $\log p$ BSP processes must be available on each PP. (In general, $v \geq p \cdot \log p$ must hold.) It can be shown, then, that on each PP the $\log p$ processes (VPs) are executed (emulated) in $O (\log p)$ time; see fig. 2. Since a PRAM step is assumed to take unit time, this respresents a PRAM emulation of optimal asymptotic efficiency. The detailled analysis as well as results for other PRAM variants can again be found in [14].

The BSP machine's interconnect must provide sufficient network throughput and low (upper-bounded, logarithmic) latency. It has been shown that hypercube and butterfly topologies satisfy this condition. It must be noted that other forms of synchronizations are not prohibited by the bulk-synchronous model [14].

In effect, the analysis shows that any program written in a high-level shared-memory programming model can be emulated on the BSP model and, thus, on a real, distributed-memory system with only a *constant-factor loss of efficiency*.

3 Performance Evaluation Approach

3.1 Evaluation Method—Simulation

In order to be able to judge the practical relevance of RSM, we have aimed at determining the constant factor involved in the PRAM emulation approach described above by extensive *simulations*.

The scope of the simulations encompasses in full detail the global memory access behaviour of the application processes and all resulting activities, such as process scheduling, address translation (hashing), communications, and memory accesses. To comply with the semantics of the BSP execution model, the processes' global synchronization behaviour and resulting activities are modelled and simulated as well. Fig. 3 depicts the basic activities that are simulated on a *per-process basis*.

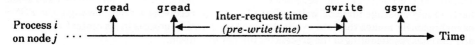

Process i on node j $\cdots$

gread   gread   Inter-request time   gwrite   gsync
(pre-write time)
→ Time

Fig. 3 Activities of application processes considered in RSM simulations

A process makes global memory accesses by issuing gread and gwrite requests and joins the barrier synchronization procedure by issuing gsync. In the intervals denoted as *inter-request (pre-read, pre-write,* and *pre-sync) times* the process is assumed to perform local computations and to access local or private data conventionally. The process is assumed to occupy the CPU without being descheduled or interrupted; the CPU is *active* during these intervals.

On a global memory request, if the requested data item is not found in local memory, and on a global synchronization point, the requesting process is descheduled and another process takes over control, in turn occupying the CPU for an amount of time determined by its next inter-request time. Descheduling does not occur if a requested global data item is available in local memory. Further activities are detailled in the next subsection.

The simulator for RSM performance analysis is an extension of an interconnection network simulator developed at Siemens within the same project. It is briefly described in [7]. The main benefit of building upon an existing network simulator is that all the network properties (such as throughput and latency) and dynamic effects (like contention) are captured in close detail. This is particularly important for the RSM simulations since network behaviour to a high degree determines the efficiency of RSM.

3.2 Architectural Model

The architectural model is based on the new generation of transputer components, the Inmos T9000 processor and C104 routing switch [8], with the extension of a *RSM Server (RSMS)* assumed on each node. The RSMS is a memory management unit that implements the global memory abstraction for the processor. Fig. 4 shows a diagram of the resulting node model.

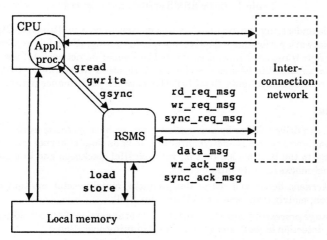

Fig. 4 Node model

As shown in the figure, the RSMS accepts global memory and global synchronization requests from the CPU, and takes over responsibility to satisfy the request. In doing that, it performs address translation (hashing), tests whether the data happen to be local, and either accesses local memory and makes the data available to the CPU, or it initiates process switching and creates and sends a (read or write) request message to the remote node.

On the remote node, the RSMS accepts the request from the network, performs the memory access (a DMA) on behalf of the requester without intercepting the CPU, and creates and sends back a reply message (data or write acknowledge). On receiving a reply message, the RSMS asynchronously makes the data available for the requesting process in its context in memory, and initiates rescheduling of the process for further execution.

In our model, the RSMSs are also responsible for global synchronizations. Since barrier synchronization performance was not a focus of our investigations, only a simple *message-based*, *centralized* scheme was implemented. Clearly, such a scheme is not scalable and needs additional hardware support to be efficient. It was, however, regarded as sufficient for our purposes. A more detailed description of RSMS functionality is given in [6].

The T9000 transputer was regarded as particularly well-suited for these investigations because of its hardware support for process scheduling and communications, making these functions very fast. To make global memory management comparably fast, we modelled the RSMS as a hardware unit similar in performance to the T9000 communications coprocessor. Table 1 gives the basic performance figures assumed for the RSMS. Note that process switching is modelled to take 1 µs only, assuming that the T9000 will be comparable with its predecessors in terms of scheduling performance. Address translation is assumed to involve evaluating a *linear* hash function via special-purpose hardware.

Function	Time [µs]
Address translation and test	0.1
Access of global data in local memory	0.1
Message create and dispatch	0.6
Message receive and analyze	0.4
Process scheduling	1

Table 1   Basic RSMS performance figures

The interconnect underlying the simulations was chosen to be a multi-stage, Clos-type, four-fold replicated network performing adaptive wormhole routing. (Four-fold replication denotes that each of the four transputer links is connected to a separate network.) It was shown in [7] that these networks offer the best cost/performance ratios of the networks that can be built from C104-type routing components. Refer to [7] for network performance figures.

3.3   Workloads

The simulations are driven either by *application traces* or by a *synthetic workload*. The traces capture the global memory access and synchronization behaviour of kernel routines, which are written according to the BSP model; that is, with parallel slackness and in a superstep-wise fashion. The benchmarks fall into three classes:

▸ *Numerical kernels:* dense and sparse dot products, matrix-vector multiplication, matrix multiplication, matrix transpose, and 1D complex FFT;

▸ *Low-level image processing operations* (each in several versions): thresholding, lowpass filtering, edge detection (Sobel), and growing and thinning operations;

▸ *PRAM-specific routines:* parallel prefix (sum) and list ranking.

The programs are coded in occam using the *BSP-occam library* [2], a set of routines that allow global data structures to be declared and accessed (various gread and gwrite routines) and global synchronizations to be performed (gsync). The traces were generated by this BSP machine emulation package running on small T800 transputer arrays (5, 16, or 17 nodes).

The traces contain information as principally depicted in fig. 3. For each process, the sequence of global requests is given in correct temporal order. For global memory accesses, the *global (logical)* addresses are recorded as well. Inter-request times are either read from trace files or generated during simulation runs using a simple synthetic timing model.

The traces are valuable in that RSM performance figures can be obtained on the basis of *realistic* global memory access and synchronization patterns. Their drawback is that they are confined to a fixed, small number of nodes.

In order to be able to address scalability issues and to facilitate systematic investigations of load characteristics and their impact on RSM performance, a synthetic load generator has been added to the simulation tool. It allows for variations in the following parameters: number of nodes (system size), number of processes per node, number of supersteps, number of accesses per superstep and process, size of global address space, and (global) read/write ratio.

The *spatial* distribution of global memory requests is chosen such that the processes do not interfere with each other. Each process is assigned a section of the global address space to which it has exclusive access rights; accesses within a section are randomly distributed. Clearly, this load will yield *best-case* RSM performance figures.

3.4 Evaluation Criteria

For determination of the loss of efficiency in the PRAM emulation, the *elapsed time* (simulated program run time) is split into four parts:

▸ *Average CPU active time and rate (percentage of elapsed time)*
  As explained above, a CPU is *active* when an application process is currently executing. Thus, the average CPU active time is given by the sum of all inter-request times of all processes divided by the number of processors in the system.

▸ *Average CPU waiting time and rate*
  A CPU is *waiting* during global address translation, local access to a global data item, and process (de)scheduling. The main constituent of CPU waiting time is the process switching time ($>90\%$).

▸ *Average CPU memory idle time and rate*
  A CPU is idle when no application process is available to be executed; all processes are inactive. A CPU is *memory idle* when all processes are waiting for their global memory requests to be satisfied.

▸ *Average CPU sync idle time and rate*
  A CPU is *sync idle* when all processes wait for a global synchronization event (the current superstep) to be finished.

The *constant-factor loss of efficiency* C is then defined as

$$C := 1 / (\text{avg. CPU active rate}).$$

In an idealized machine (e.g., a PRAM) with ideal global memory, zero-time process switching and perfectly synchronous operation, the CPUs would be fully active, yielding $C = 1$. $C > 1$ in a real system is caused by the global memory emulation, process switching time, barrier synchronisation latencies, and potentially insufficient degree of excess parallelism. Note that the factor C must be interpreted relative to an *idealized* implementation of a given program, not a different realistic implementation. That is to say that a message-passing version of the program or an implementation on physically shared memory would also have some $C > 1$.

The four constituents of CPU time allow the major sources of inefficiencies to be localized and accessed quantitatively.

4 Results—RSM Efficiency

4.1 Traces

A set of representative programs/traces has been selected for presentation of the major results of our simulation studies. Their basic features are summarized in table 2. Fig. 5 depicts the results for these traces.

Characteristics	Matrix mult. 10	Matrix mult. 15	Matrix mult. 20	Thresh-olding	Low-pass filter	Par. prefix sum	List rank-ing
# nodes # processes/node # supersteps	17 ≤4 4	17 ≤4 4	17 ≤4 4	16 400 2	16 400 4	17 ≤4 448	5 10 22
# global reads # global writes	32000 6400	32000 6400	32000 6400	19184 6400	166704 7056	12230 16230	42000 28701
Avg. pre-read time [µs] Avg. pre-write time [µs] Avg. pre-sync time [µs]	0.2 0.4 0.1	0.3 0.6 0.1	0.4 0.8 0.1	0.05 1 0.05	0.07 0.05 0.44	0.25 0.25 0.1	0.25 0.25 0.1

Table 2 Characterization of sample traces

The matrix multiplication program/trace is representative for the numerical benchmark kernels. Results of three simulation runs using the matrix multiplication trace are shown. As can be seen from table 2, the only difference lies in the inter-request (pre-read and pre-write) times chosen for the simulations. In other words, the versions differ in the frequency (rate) at which global memory accesses are issued. The numbers characterizing the different results largely correspond to the average number of local processor cycles (assuming 25 ns cycles, i.e., a 40 MHz T9000). That is, a global access is issued after every 10, 15, and 20 cycles, respectively, of a process' local activity.

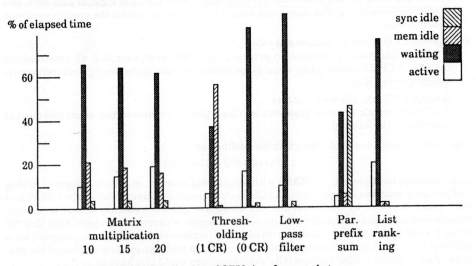

Fig. 5 Distribution of CPU time for sample traces

The CPU efficiency (active rate) for the matrix multiplication simulations varies from about 10% to nearly 20%, which means a constant-factor loss of efficiency C in the range of 5 to 10. This is regarded as encouragingly high, given the high global memory access rates assumed (and probably the anticipation that RSM will perform very poorly). Notice that the CPU efficiency is highly sensitive to the global access rate, increasing almost linearly with decreasing access frequency for these examples. Thus, quite good efficiency can be expected when global requests occur at a coarser grain.

The graphs show a high percentage of CPU waiting time (in excess of 60%), clearly identifying the process switching time to be the major bottleneck in the emulation. CPU memory idle time is up to about 20% for the matrix multiplication results, indicating that the degree of excess parallelism (up to four processes per node) is not sufficient to completely mask global memory access latencies. CPU sync idle times are close to negligible.

The image processing programs/traces are represented by the thresholding and lowpass filtering operations. Two variants of thresholding are shown, one of them with a massively concurrent read (CR) operation. At the beginning of the first superstep, all processes of the application (400 processes on each of the 16 nodes) access a common variable (the threshold value) which leads to massive congestion at the RSMS responsible for the variable and in the interconnection network ('hot spot' behaviour). Since the CR requests are generated at a very high rate and the RSMS can only serially service them, the processors run out of active processes and become idle eventually. This results in CPU memory idle time becoming the dominant factor of this program and efficiency being poor, despite the massive parallelism provided.

The CR is eliminated in the second version of this program by replicating the threshold value and making it accessible concurrently. As a consequence, CPU efficiency becomes acceptable and memory idle time vanishes. Note the very high CPU waiting time, caused by very fine-grain processes (high global access rate) and frequent process switching. This situation is even more pronounced in the lowpass filter result, due to the extremely high access rate (table 2). Again, process scheduling time is heavily limiting performance and efficiency.

Finally, both PRAM-specific operations are shown. The parallel prefix yields an interesting result in which CPU sync idle time is the dominating constituent. This is due to the program being coded in a highly synchronous fashion, with an average of less than one global memory access per process happening between superstep barriers. The result indicates that the message-based barrier synchronization scheme is prone to becoming a bottleneck under unfavourable circumstances. This issue is also addressed below.

The list ranking code is an example of a good BSP program. Memory latencies are almost completely masked by the ten processes per node. A CPU efficiency of 20% is achieved, in spite of high global memory access rates (an average of 10 cycles of local activities only). The efficiency is only limited by context switching time.

4.2 Synthetic load

The synthetic workloads allow us to address scalability aspects and the impact of the degree of excess parallelism on RSM performance. As stated above, the synthetic load does not contain any systematic accesses that would lead to destination address conflicts and performance degradation. Hence, the results shown subsequently exhibit best-case RSM performance in the architectural settings assumed.

Fig. 6 depicts, for various system sizes (number of nodes p), the decrease of simulated program run time with increasing degree of excess parallelism (number of processes per node). In excess of 100000 global memory accesses are simulated, with a read/write ratio of 3 and an average pre-read and pre-write time of 0.2 µs and 1 µs, respectively; this means an average of 400 ns of local activity, before the executing process issues a global memory access.

The curves initially show substantial increase of RSM performance with increasing parallel slackness, due to increasingly effective latency hiding. At $\log p$ processes per node, however, the curves flatten; little further performance can be gained by adding still more processes.

That is, in larger systems, almost exactly log p processes per node suffice to fully hide global memory latencies, which closely corresponds to Valiant's theoretical claim. (Clearly, this holds for the specific architectural model and simulation parameters underlying these experiments. Changing the assumptions would cause a constant-factor increase or decrease of the degree of excess parallelism.)

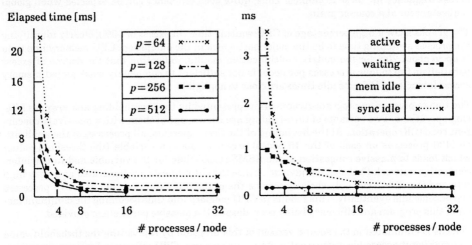

Fig. 6 Simulated program run time for varying degree of parallelism

Fig. 7 Distribution of CPU time for varying number of processes per node ($p = 256$)

Apparently, the results of fig. 6 indicate that there is a source of inefficiency imposing an upper bound on achievable performance. Further note that doubling system size, while leaving the number of processes per node unchanged, does *not* halve elapsed time. In analyzing these effects, we have split up the simulated execution time into its four constituent parts. Fig. 7 displays the result for a system of size $p = 256$ nodes.

For these experiments, overall CPU active time was assumed as constant in terms of absolute time, yielding up to 20% efficiency for 32 processes per node. The decline of CPU memory idle time clearly illustrates the requirement of log p-degree of excess parallelism for latency hiding (in absence of CRs or otherwise systematic destination address conflicts).

Similar to the trace results, the CPU waiting time accounts for up to 60% of elapsed time and again represents the major performance-limiting factor of the global memory emulation. In addition, CPU synchronization idle time is very significant, accounting for about 20% of elapsed time for 32 processes per node, for instance. This is due to the centralized synchronization scheme implemented in the model which clearly is *not* scalable and evolves to a serious source of inefficiency in systems of size $p \geq 128$ nodes. For comparison purposes, a binary tree-style, message-based barrier synchronization scheme was implemented as well. Results indicate better scalability, but still high barrier synchronization latencies (due to synchronization request and acknowledge messages being propagated log p levels up and down the tree), rendering this type of synchronization impractical as well.

Apart from these two factors, process switching time and non-scalable, inefficient global synchronization scheme, no impediments to a scalable and efficient RSM implementation have been found using the synthetic workload, i.e., assuming best-case global access behaviour. For example, the interconnection network, although heavily loaded, could satisfactorily cope with memory request/reply traffic. Thus, this work principally confirmed the desirable theoretical properties and encouraging efficiency of RSM while simultaneously identifying architectural sources of inefficiencies.

5 Conclusions

In the course of optimal PRAM emulation, RSM has been shown to be an attractive approach to implement scalable, universal, and theoretically efficient shared memory. In this paper, we have analyzed the efficiency of RSM in terms of constant factors in order to establish its relevance and feasibility for practical use, i.e., possible implementation in future massively parallel shared-memory computers.

In principle, the practical efficiency of RSM was found to be encouragingly high, in case sufficient parallelism was provided to effectively mask memory access latencies. Up to 20% efficiency of idealized shared memory were attained, assuming a parallel architecture that is principally implementable with today's technology and for global memory access rates that are quite high, but which may be regarded as representative for fine-grained parallel shared-memory programs.

Through simulations, the following were identified to be major architectural bottlenecks, limiting or impairing RSM performance:

▸ *process switching time*, although assumed to be highly efficient (1 μs);

▸ the *interconnection network* in case of concurrent read (or write) accesses to global memory; and

▸ the *message-based, centralized* barrier synchronization mechanism.

Similarly, inefficiencies caused by application programs were found to be: insufficient degree of excess parallelism, concurrent reads (or writes) to global data, extremely high global memory access rate, and overly synchronous algorithms.

To overcome the above bottlenecks and, thus, increase RSM efficiency up to practical levels, the following architectural features are proposed to be incorporated in future scalable shared-memory machines:

▸ *extremely fast (or zero-time) process switching* as implemented by multiple-instruction-stream (multi-threaded) processors;

▸ a *combining network* that is able to on-the-fly combine memory reads (and preferably also writes) concurrently bound for the same locations, and uncombine replies; and

▸ an *efficient and scalable synchronization mechanism*.

It must be noted that a combining network is not only required to support scalable and efficient RSM, but also desirable to implement high-level, powerful memory access primitives like fetch&op or the (multi-)prefix operator [12] which enable scalable parallel algorithms to be written with relative ease. Also, scalable and efficient synchronization can be directly implemented by global memory supported by a combining network, as shown in [1]. Taking these additional benefits into account, the cost of a combining network may well be justified.

There are several novel machine designs incorporating RSM and (part of) the supporting architectural and hardware features, documenting increased interest in the RSM approach and scalable shared memory. The BBN Monarch design [13] is characterized by an ambitious combining network supporting many thousands of processors and RSM with thousands of memory modules. The Tera Computer [3] hides access latencies to RSM by massively multi-threaded processors (up to 128 instruction streams). Finally, the PRAM machine designed at the University of Saarbrücken [1] which is an improvement of the Fluent machine proposal [12], combines memory hashing, multi-threaded processors, a combining network, and the multiprefix memory primitive in a synchronous machine, aiming at providing a PRAM implementation with the theoretical properties achieved as far as possible. Unfortunately, the Monarch and Fluent machines will remain paper designs. It will be interesting to see RSM be implemented in the other machines.

Acknowledgment

Thanks are due to Holm Hofestädt and Axel Klein for helpful discussions, and Erwin Reyzl for advice during simulator development. The work reported in this paper has been carried out within the context of the cooperative project PUMA (Parallel Universal Message-passing Architectures) and has partly been funded under ESPRIT P2701. The support of the project partners in providing the traces is gratefully acknowledged.

References

[1] F. Abolhassan, J. Keller, W. J. Paul, *On the Cost-Effectiveness and Realization of the Theoretical PRAM Model*, Report SFB 124/D4, 09/1991, Univ. Saarbrücken (1991).

[2] J. Allwright, "BSP-Occam: A Parallel Language Based on a Distributed Virtual Shared Memory", submitted to *Software: Practice and Experience* (1992).

[3] R. Alverson, D. Callahan, D. Cummings, B. Koblenz, A. Porterfield, B. Smith, "The Tera Computer System", *ACM SIGARCH Computer Architecture News 18, 3 (Proc. 1990 Int'l. Conf. on Supercomputing)*, pp. 1–6.

[4] A. Gibbons, W. Rytter, *Efficient Parallel Algorithms*, Cambridge University Press, Cambridge (1988).

[5] H. Hellwagner, *A Survey of Virtually Shared Memory Schemes*, SFB Report No. 342/33/90 A, Techn. Univ. Munich (1990).

[6] H. Hellwagner, "Virtually Shared Memory Architectures for Scalable Universal Parallel Computers", in H. Schwärtzel (ed.), *Applied Computer Science and Software (Proc. Int'l. Symp.)*, Springer-Verlag (1991), pp. 91–112.

[7] H. Hofestädt, A. Klein, E. Reyzl, "Performance Benefits from Locally Adaptive Interval Routing in Dynamically Switched Interconnection Networks", in A. Bode (ed.), *Distributed Memory Computing (Proc. EDMCC 2)*, LNCS 487, Springer-Verlag (1991), pp. 193–202.

[8] Inmos Ltd., *The T9000 Transputer Products Overview Manual*, First Edition, 1991.

[9] R. M. Karp, V. Ramachandran, "Parallel Algorithms for Shared-Memory Machines", in J. van Leeuwen (ed.), *Handbook of Theoretical Computer Science*, North-Holland, Amsterdam (1990).

[10] K. Mehlhorn, U. Vishkin, "Randomized and Deterministic Simulations of PRAMs by Parallel Machines with Restricted Granularity of Parallel Memories", *Acta Informatica 21* (1984), pp. 339–374.

[11] B. Nitzberg, V. Lo, "Distributed Shared Memory: A Survey of Issues and Algorithms", *COMPUTER 24, 8* (1991), pp. 52–60.

[12] A. G. Ranade, S. N. Bhatt, S. L. Johnsson, "The Fluent Abstract Machine", in J. Allen, F. T. Leighton (eds.), *Advanced Research in VLSI (Proc. 5th MIT Conf.)*, MIT Press, Cambridge, MA (1988), pp. 71–93.

[13] R. D. Rettberg, W. R. Crowther, P. P. Carvey, R. S. Tomlinson, "The Monarch Parallel Processor Hardware Design", *COMPUTER 23, 4* (1990), pp. 18–30.

[14] L. G. Valiant, "General Purpose Parallel Architectures", in J. van Leeuwen (ed.), *Handbook of Theoretical Computer Science*, North-Holland, Amsterdam (1990).

[15] L. G. Valiant, "A Bridging Model for Parallel Computation", *Comm. ACM 33, 8* (1990), pp. 103–111.

KOAN: a Shared Virtual Memory for the iPSC/2 hypercube

Zakaria Lahjomri and Thierry Priol

IRISA/INRIA, Campus de Beaulieu
35042 Rennes Cedex, FRANCE

Abstract. In this paper, we describe the salient features of an implementation of a shared virtual memory (SVM), named KOAN, running on an iPSC/2 hypercube. A SVM provides to the user an abstraction from an underlying memory architecture. A SVM is a virtual address space that is shared by a number of processes running on different processors of a distributed memory parallel computer. This concept allows the user to program his application without explicit message passing. The performances of our SVM are given as well as some preliminary results on a parallel matrix multiply algorithm.

1 Introduction

Programming distributed memory parallel computers (DMPC) using a Shared Virtual Memory (SVM) seems to be in fashion. However, there is few operating systems available for DMPCs which implements such concept. Most of the implementations of shared virtual memory have been done for networks of workstations, one can cite IVY [8], Gothic [10, 15, 13], Clouds [14], Munin [3], Memnet [5], Mach [17] and Chorus [16]. These implementations concern only high latency networks and do not allow the comparison of the efficiency of different strategies for parallelizing algorithms on DMPCs. SHIVA [9] seems to be the only attempt to implement a SVM on a hypercube multicomputer (Intel iPSC/2). However, it appears that this implementation has been done at the user's level without modifying the iPSC/2 operating system and consequently adds a lot of overhead. Moreover, results on its experimentation with parallel applications have not yet been published. Distributed memory parallel computers with a hypercube or 2D-mesh topology have been commonly used for designing and testing parallel algorithms. Several results on these parallel algorithms have been widely published. Hence, it would be interesting to compare these results with those obtained by using a SVM on the same machine. This paper is a first step in this direction. We present an implementation of a SVM, named KOAN, on an iPSC/2 hypercube that allows us to compare the benefits of using either shared variables or message passing as a communication mechanism between parallel processes. It does not address a new SVM algorithm, such algorithms are now well known.

An outline of the paper is as follow. Section 2 introduces briefly the concept of shared virtual memory. Our implementation of a shared virtual memory on an iPSC/2 hypercube is presented in section 3 whereas section 4 gives some results about the performance of KOAN. Section 5 gives the performance obtained with a matrix multiply algorithm. Finally, in section 6 we give some concluding remarks.

2 Shared virtual Memory

A Shared Virtual Memory (SVM) provides to the user an abstraction from an underlying memory architecture. This concept [8] is somewhat similar to the one which is currently used on classic mainframe computers. However, it differs in the fact that this virtual memory is shared by several processors. It provides a virtual address space that is shared by a number of processes running on different processors of a distributed memory parallel computer. In order to distribute the virtual address space, the SVM is partitioned into pages[1] which are spread among local processor memories according to a mapping function which ensures that each processor has roughly the same number of page. Each local memory is subdivided into two parts. The first one is used for storing the code of processes and their local variables whereas the second part acts as a large software cache for storing pages as shown in figure 1. Since the size of the physical memory on a processor is much less than the size of the SVM, the part of the local memory, which acts as a cache, is managed according to a LRU (Least Recently Used) policy. A memory management unit (MMU) is needed to provide the user with a linear address by translating virtual addresses to physical ones. An algorithm that implements a shared virtual memory has to solve three problems: *cache coherence*, *page ownership* and *page replacement*. The following sections present some existing solutions for solving these problems and those we chose in implementing KOAN.

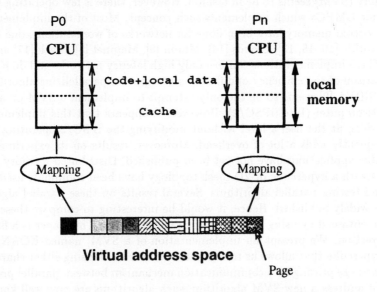

Fig. 1. Mapping a Shared Virtual Memory on DMPC.

---

[1] the granularity afforded by hardware virtual memory

2.1 Cache coherence protocol

Since processors may have to read from or to write to the same page, several processors have a copy of a page in their cache. If one processor modifies its copy, other processors run the risk of reading an old copy. A cache coherence protocol is needed to ensure that the shared address space is kept coherent at all times. A memory is considered *coherent* if the value returned by a read from a location of the shared address space is the value of the latest store to that location [4]. Cache coherence protocol can be divided into two categories. The first one assumes that there is only one copy of a page with write access mode and all other copies are in read-only access mode. The processor that has written most recently into the page is called the *owner* of the page. When a processor needs to write to a page, that is not present in its cache or is present in read-only mode, it sends a message to the owner of the page in order to move it to the requesting processor. Then it invalidates all the copies in the system by sending a message to the relevant processors. This strategy is called the *invalidation* approach. The second category allows several processors to have a copy in write access mode. The processor that does the write has to update all the copies of the page by sending a message to the relevant processors. This technique is called *distributed write* in [1] or *write-back* in [8]. A cache coherence protocol based on this approach is expensive and difficult to implement efficiently on "general- purpose" DMPCs. Every write to a shared page must generate a fault on the writing processor and a small message is sent to update all the copies. Sending small messages is very costly due to the latency of the interconnection network of DMPCs. Consequently, the invalidation technique seems to be the best approach for DMPCs. The faulting management mechanism of a MMU is sufficient to implement this approach efficiently. Moreover, the granularity of an access is the size of a page which is large enough to amortize the latency of the network.

2.2 Page ownership

When a processor needs to access a page, either in write or read access mode, which is not located in its cache, it must ask the owner to send it a copy of the page. This problem is related to the cache coherence protocol described previously. With the invalidation protocol, there is always one owner for a page and the ownership changes according to the page requests coming from other processors. Therefore, the problem is how to locate the current owner of a given page considering that the owner of a page changes. A solution is to update a database that keeps track of the movement of pages in the system. This database can be either *centralized* or *distributed* [8]. In the centralized approach, a processor (called the manager) is in charge of updating the database for every page. When a processor needs a page, it sends a request to the manager which forwards the request to the owner of the page. Consequently, the manager is aware of all the movement of pages in the system. However, it is a bottleneck since one processor (i.e. the manager) receives requests from all other processors. The user's process running on the manager will be interrupted frequently and this approach will also create potential contention into the network. Distributing the database on several processors is a means to avoid these drawbacks. There are two ways to distribute the database:

- *Fixed distributed manager*

  Each processor knows exactly the owner of a subset of pages. The subset is fixed by a mapping function that takes the page number as an argument and returns the processor number of the owner. The function $H(p) = p \bmod N$ is an example of such mapping function, where p is the page number and N is the number of processors in the system.

- *Dynamic distributed manager*

  Each processor has partial knowledge for every page of the virtual address space. Each processor knows a probable owner. This information is updated by the page fault handler or the servers. In the worst case, several processors are needed to determine the "true" owner of a page. K. Li [8] has proved that a page request reaches always the true owner eventually.

Formal analyses of these three approaches for solving the ownership problem can be found in [8]. They show that the best results are obtained with a dynamic distributed manager.

2.3 Page replacement among processors

The problem arises when a processor is the owner of all the pages located in its cache and there is no more space in the cache. If it requests a new page, it has to find space in its cache. It cannot throw away a page from its cache since it owns all the pages. Moreover it cannot save the pages on external high speed storage devices, like disks, since most of DMPCs do not offer such things. Consequently, it has to find a processor which has either a copy of the page or enough space in its cache. If another processor has a copy of the page to be stored, it requires only ownership migration. Otherwise, it requires both page saving and ownership migration. A solution to this problem is proposed in [8] for the dynamic distributed ownership approach. Section 3.4 describe a new one for the fixed distributed ownership approach.

3 Implementing KOAN on an iPSC/2 hypercube

The KOAN SVM is embedded in the operating system of an iPSC/2 hypercube. It allows the use of fast and low-level communication primitives as well as a Memory Management Unit (MMU). It differs from SHIVA described in [9] in that it is an operating system based implementation. It appears that the implementation of SHIVA has been done at the user's level without modifying the iPSC/2 operating system and consequently adds a lot of overhead. We present briefly the architecture of the iPSC/2 and its operating system in section 3.1. Finally, section 3.2 describes our SVM implementation.

3.1 The iPSC/2 hypercube

The iPSC/2 system consists of two main components: the cube and the system resource manager. The cube houses all the nodes which are connected by the hypercube network. Each node consists of one Intel 80386 microprocessor augmented by an 80387 floating point co-processor and 4 Mbytes of local memory. The node is equipped with the Direct Connect Module (DCM) for high speed routing message between nodes. These DCMs allow programmers to view the network as a fully connected graph. Each processor can send a message directly to any other processor. This is very useful for implementing our shared virtual memory because the communication graph is not known in advance.

Software development tools are available on the System Resource Manager (which acts as a host processor), which is connected to node 0 via a special link. The SRM performs compilation, program loading and I/O operations for the cube.

The operating system of the iPSC/2 consists of two parts. The first part runs on the SRM and consists of several UNIX processes. It allows several users to run their programs simultaneously by splitting the cube into sub-cubes. Each is assigned to a user. Several commands have been added to allow the management of sub-cubes or parallel processes. As for the second part, it is a small kernel, called NX/2, which runs on each processor of the cube. It handles memory and process management as well as interprocess communication.

3.2 KOAN design choices

The KOAN SVM implements the fixed distributed manager algorithm as described in [8] with an invalidation protocol for keeping the shared memory coherent at all times. This algorithm offers a suitable comprise between its implementation easiness and its efficiency. It is implemented using a set of handlers and servers. In each processor, two exception handlers are used to trap page faults. A read fault handler manages the page faults which occur when a processor needs to read from a page not located in its cache. If a processor needs to write to a page which is in read-only access mode or not located in its cache, the write fault handler is called. Seven servers are needed to process page requests and page invalidations. The handlers and servers share two data structures:

- A page table, arranged in a two level hierarchy, is used by the MMU for translating virtual addresses to physical ones. It also contains several fields, one of which indicates the access rights associated with a page. This choice is dictated by the MMU included in the 80386.
- A table located in each manager. It has as many entries as pages associated with the manager. For each entry, a field contains the processor numbers that have read copies of the page. Another field store the current owner of the page.

The handlers and servers run concurrently and must be synchronized if several processes, running either on the same processor or on a remote processor, generate multiple page faults on the same page. An implementation requires both system processes as well as semaphores in order to synchronize them. Unfortunately, the NX/2 operating system does not provide such mechanisms. Its kernel is driven by interrupts (system calls, exceptions, external interrupts). The implementation, suggested by K. Li, must be modified to compensate for the missing primitives. The following section outlines the synchronization protocol we designed in order to implement the cache coherence protocol.

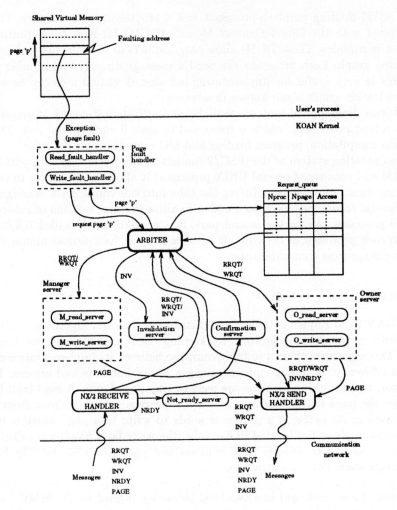

Fig. 2. KOAN synchronization protocol.

Type	Description
RRQT	page request in read mode
WRQT	page request in write mode
INV	invalidation request
NRDY	rejected message
	which contains either RRQT, WRQT or INV
PAGE	a page

Table 1. Message types

3.3 Implementing the cache coherence protocol

Let us outline our synchronization protocol. As shown in figure 2, the KOAN kernel consists of seven servers and two handlers. The servers are installed in the receive interrupt routine of NX/2 where they process all the requests coming from remote processors. The handlers are activated by the MMU when a page fault occurs. The servers and handlers are described in table 2.

Name	Description
Read_fault_handler	Called by the MMU when read page fault occurs
Write_fault_handler	Called by the MMU when write page fault occurs
M_read_server	Processes page requests by the manager (read access)
M_write_server	Processes page request by the manager (write access)
O_read_server	Processes page requests by the owner (read access)
O_write_server	Processes page requests by the owner (write access)
Invalidation_server	Change the access of a page to nil access
Confirmation_server	Processes confirmation messages
Not_ready_server	Resends a request rejected by a remote processor

Table 2. Servers and handlers

In each processor, the KOAN kernel must serialize both the local requests (page faults) and remote requests (pages requests, invalidations) which occur on the same page. This is done by using an *arbiter*. All incoming messages, listed in table 1, are processed by the arbiter which can choose to forward the request to the relevant servers, to store it in a queue called *request_queue*, or to reject the messages by sending it back. Moreover, if a page fault occurs on a page which is currently being processed by the arbiter, handlers must wait until the arbiter has finished processing the page request. Requests stored in the queue are processed when the arbiter has received a confirmation message indicating the completion of the previous page request.

Let us describe how requests are processed by each processor. In each processor, the arbiter manages a table called *busyout[]*. This table has an entry for each page assigned to the processor (manager). Initially, each entry of *busyout[]* is set to false. When the entry p of *busyout[]* is true, it means that this page is currently being processed by one of the manager servers. This entry is set to false when the manager receives a *confirmation* message that tells it the end of the processing of the request.

A request for page p coming from remote processors is first processed by the arbiter. Two cases may happen:

1. If page p is not currently processed by one of the manager servers (*busyout[p]*=false), the arbiter sets *busyout[p]* to true and sends the request to one of the servers regarding to the required access mode.
2. If page p is currently processed by one of the manager servers (*busyout[p]*=true), two cases may happen:
   (a) The manager is in page fault on the same page. If so, the arbiter rejects the request by sending a NRDY message back (the request is holden in

the NRDY message). Indeed, request cannot be stored in the request queue because it is processed when a *confirmation* message is received. Since the manager does not send such message to itself, if the request is stored in the queue it will never be processed when the page fault will end. When a rejected request will be received by the processor which has sent it, the *not_ready_server* running in this processor will resend the request stored in the NRDY message.

(b) Page p is currently processed for another processor q which is distinct from the manager. In that case, the arbiter stores the request in the request queue. When the arbiter will receive a *confirmation* message from processor q for page p, it will get the oldest request on page p from the request queue and will send it to the relevant servers.

Finally, if a page fault on page p occurs in the manager, it is sent to the arbiter. If this latter is currently processing a remote request for page p from a processor q, it stores the request (the page fault) in the request queue. This request will be processed later when the manager will receive a *confirmation* message from processor q.

3.4 A solution to the page replacement problem

In this section, we describe our solution to the page replacement problem. The physical address space of each processor contains different kinds of pages. Pages in *read-write* access mode, which are owned by the processor, belong to a set denoted P_{owner}, pages in *read-only* access mode belong to a set called P_{read}, and unused physical memory pages belong to a set named P_{free}. When a page fault occurs and there is no unused physical memory page available, the KOAN kernel invokes the following page replacement algorithm:

1. If P_{free} is not empty, delete a page p from P_{free} and return p.
2. Else, if P_{read} is not empty, delete a page p from P_{read} with a LRU policy (Least Recently Used) and return p,
3. Else, choose a page p with a LRU policy in the set P_{owner}.

A page chosen for replacement in the set P_{read} or P_{free} can be thrown away, but a page belonging to the set P_{owner} requires an ownership migration which consists of sending it to another processor. The following algorithm is used to find a processor that is able to receive a page in its local memory:

1. The faulting processor sends a request for ownership migration to the manager of the page.
2. When the manager receive this request, it checks if the requesting processor is still the owner of the page. If this is the case, the manager chooses one processor q with the procedure *Find_processor*, sends q to the requesting processor and waits for confirmation. Otherwise the manager sends a message named *resolved* to the requesting processor which means that the problem is solved because the requesting processor has already lost the ownership of the page.

3. If the requesting processor receive the message *resolved*, it can replace the page immediately, otherwise it sends the page to processor q and then replaces the page.

4. The processor q receives the page, notes that it is the new owner of this page and sends a confirmation to the manager.

Let us describe how the manager finds a processor which has enough room in its local memory (procedure *Find_processor*). A local counter *count* is maintained on each processor which represents the number of pages owned by a processor at a given time. *count* is increased when the processor acquires the ownership of a page and is decreased when it relinquishes the page. When the counter *count* reaches a threshold S_1, the processor broadcasts a message named *full_cache* to all managers. When count reach a threshold S_2, the message *have_space* is broadcast. We can easily prove the correctness of this algorithm if the size of the shared memory address space, T, is bounded by:

$$T \leq N * (M_i - K + N - 1) \qquad (1)$$

where M_i is the size of the memory space on processor i, N is the number of processors and K is equal to $(S_1 - S_2)$.

4 Performance

Number of processors	Read page fault		Write page fault	
	best times (ms)	worst times (ms)	best times (ms)	worst times (ms)
2	2.995	3.170	3.110	3.133
4	3.059	3.560	3.144	3.742
8	3.104	3.615	3.274	4.701
16	3.255	3.783	3.355	6.654
32	3.412	3.955	3.447	10.110

Table 3. KOAN page fault times.

We have performed measurements in order to determine the cost of various basic operations for both read and write page faults of the KOAN shared virtual memory. We used the *uclock* timer designed by P. Jacobson et al. [7] which has microsecond resolution. For each type of page fault (read or write), we have tested the best and worst possible situation on different numbers of processors. A page fault that occurs on the manager, which is also the owner, represents the best case for both read and write page faults. The worst case for read page fault occurs when the three entities are distinct processors : the faulting processor, the manager and the owner of the page are as far apart as possible. The worst case for write page fault is similar, but in addition all processors have a copy of the faulting page. The experimental protocol consists of measuring the page fault service once since the timer has microsecond resolution. The best and worst times for both read and write page faults are shown in table 3. They can be compared to the time needed to send a 4096 bytes message (a page) between two neighboring processors: 2.17 *ms*. One can observe that both best times and worst times increase when the number of processors grow up. This is due to the increasing distance between the faulting processors, the manager and the owner of the requested page. The slope is much higher for write page fault, in the worst case, since the manager has to send an invalidation message for each processor. These results are slightly differents from those predicted with SHIVA [9]. It is due to our implementation which is quite different. Moreover, page fault costs for SHIVA have been extrapolated or predicted from timings taken of various primitive operations of the NX/2. These timings depends of the release of NX/2 they used.

5 Application performance

The application we reported was a basic matrix multiply algorithm ($A = B \times C$) programmed in C language. The outer loop is distributed among the available processors. The two input matrices as well as the resulting matrix are stored in the shared virtual memory. Table 4 summarized the results we obtained with different matrix sizes and numbers of processors. Serial times were computed using the local memory for storing the three matrices. For matrix size 128 × 128 and 32 processors, an examination of the post-mortem statistics gathered by the KOAN SVM shows that the average time for solving a read page fault (resp. write page fault) is 6.91 *ms* (resp. 4.72 *ms*). These results are differents from those presented in table 3 since page fault costs depend on the network traffic. Consequently, the significance of page fault costs, measured without page requests traffic, have to be put in perspective.

Matrix size	2 PE	4 PE	8 PE	16 PE	32 PE
96 × 96	1.98	3.84	7.26	0.81	0.51
128 × 128	1.94	3.87	7.54	13.93	1.26
160 × 160	1.99	3.94	7.69	14.24	3.33
192 × 192	1.99	3.97	7.75	14.71	25.73
224 × 224	1.99	3.96	7.79	15.02	27.45
256 × 256	2.00	3.97	7.83	15.21	28.27
512 × 512	2.00	3.98	7.92	15.65	30.47

Table 4. Speedup results

The preliminary results indicate very good speedups except when the matrix size is small (96 × 96 or 128 × 128) and when the number of processors is greater than 16. It is mainly due to the fact that several rows of the resulting matrix are stored in the same page. As the number of processors increases, the probability of having several processors that modify different rows stored in the same page makes greater. Since the cache coherence protocol allows only one writer by serializing the page requests and invalidating the copies, processors wait most of their time for having the page.

Matrix size	2 PE	4 PE	8 PE	16 PE	32 PE
96 × 96	1.98	3.86	7.26	12.00	16.20
128 × 128	1.94	3.87	7.51	13.75	20.71
160 × 160	1.99	3.97	7.69	14.21	24.45
192 × 192	1.99	3.97	7.75	14.68	26.12
224 × 224	1.99	3.96	7.81	15.02	27.46
256 × 256	2.00	3.97	7.83	15.20	28.30
512 × 512	2.00	3.98	7.91	15.61	30.41

Table 5. Speedup with a weak cache coherence protocol.

Since several processors have to write into different locations of a page which is used to store a part of the resulting matrix, we can let them modify concurrently their own copy of a page. Giloi et al. [6] have suggested using two new constructs: *begin_weak* and *end_weak* which delimit a program section in which a weak coherency protocol is used instead of a strong coherency protocol. When a *end_weak* is executed, all the copies of a page which have been modified in the weak block are merged into one page that reflects all the changes. The user has to modify his parallel program in order to add these new constructs in the right places. Such strategy has been implemented in KOAN. Table 5 presents the results obtained with this strategy. For small matrices and a large number of processors, speedups have been improved significantly.

6 Conclusion and future works

The works that are described in this paper represents a first step which consists in implementing and evaluating a shared virtual memory on distributed memory parallel computers. Ongoing efforts are targeted at the comparison of various parallel implementations (data and control parallelism, functional decomposition) on DMPC for a representative set of numerical and non-numerical algorithms. First experiments are described in [2] and [12, 11]. Finally, we are designing a high level software interface to KOAN in order to simplify the use of our shared virtual memory on the iPSC/2 hypercube.

References

1. J.K. Archibald. *The Cache Coherence Problem in Shared-Memory Multiprocessors.* PhD thesis, University of Washington, 1987.
2. D. Badouel, K. Bouatouch, Z. Lahjomri, and T. Priol. *KOAN: a versatile tool for parallelizing realistic rendering algorithms.* Technical Report 1505, INRIA, 1991.
3. John K. Bennett, John B. Carter, and Willy Zwaenepoel. *Munin: Distributed Shared Memory Based on Type-Specific Memory Coherence.* Technical Report Rice COMP TR89-98, Rice University, November 1989.
4. L.M. Censier and P. Feautrier. A new solution to coherence problems in multicache systems. *IEEE Trans. on Computers.*, C-27(12):1112–1118, Dec 1978.

5. G. Delp and D. Farber. *MemNet: An Experiment on High-Speed Memory Mapped Network Interface.* Technical Report 85-11-IR, University of Delaware, 1986.

6. W.K. Giloi, C. Hastedt, F. Schoen, and W. Schroeder-Preikschat. A distributed implementation of shared virtual memory with strong and weak coherence. In Arndt Bode, editor, *Distributed Memory Computing*, pages 23–31, LNCS 487, Springer-Verlag, April 1991.

7. P. Jacobson and E. Tarnvik. *A High Resolution Timer for the Intel iPSC/2 Hypercube.* Technical Report UMINF 91-04, University of Umea, Institute of Information Processing, Department of Computer Science, March 1991.

8. Kai Li. *Shared Virtual Memory on Loosely Coupled Multiprocessors.* PhD thesis, Yale University, September 1986.

9. Kai Li and Richard Schaefer. A hypercube shared virtual memory system. *Proceedings of the 1989 International Conference on Parallel Processing*, 1:125–131, 1989.

10. B. Michel. *GOTHIC Memory Management : a Multiprocessor Shared Single Level Store.* Technical Report 1202, INRIA, March 1990.

11. T. Priol and Z. Lahjomri. Experiments with shared virtual memory and message-passing on ipsc/2 hypercube. In *International Conference on Parallel Processing*, To appear, August 1992.

12. T. Priol and Z. Lahjomri. *Trade-offs Between Shared Virtual Memory and Message-passing on an iPSC/2 Hypercube.* Technical Report 637, IRISA, 1992.

13. I. Puaut, M. Banâtre, and J. P. Routeau. Early experiences with the gothic distributed operating system. In *Proc. of the Symposium on Experiences with Distributed and Multiprocessor Systems (SEDMS II)*, pages 271–282, Atlanta, Georgia, March 1991.

14. Umakishore Ramachandran and M. Yousef A. Khalidi. An implementation of distributed shared memory. *Distributed and Multiprocessor Systems Workshop*, 21–38, 1989.

15. B. Rochat. Implementation of a multi-cache system on a loosely coupled multiprocessor. In *Proc. of 5th Distributed Memory Computing Conference*, pages 676–681, IEEE, Charleston, April 1990.

16. V. Abrossimov and M. Rozier. Generic virtual memory management for operating system kernels. In *12th ACM Symposium on Operating System Principle*, December 1989.

17. M. Young, A. Tevanian, R. Rashid, D. Golub, J. Chew, W. Boloski, D. Black, and R. Baron. The Duality of Memory and Communication in the Implementation of a Multiprocessor Operating System. In *Eleventh ACM Symposium on Operating Systems Principles*, pages 63–76, 1987.

This article was processed using the LaTeX macro package with LLNCS style

A Scalable Distributed Shared Memory

Stephan Murer, Philipp Färber
Institut für Technische Informatik und Kommunikationsnetze, ETH Zürich
ETH-Zentrum, CH-8092 Zürich, Switzerland
E-Mail: murer@tik.ethz.ch, faerber@tik.ethz.ch

Abstract. Parallel computers of the future will require a memory model which offers a global address space to the programmer, while performing equally well under various system configurations. We present a logically shared and physically distributed memory to match both requirements. This paper introduces the memory system used in the ADAM coarse-grain dataflow machine which preserves scalability by tolerating latency and offers programmability through its object-based structure. We show how to support data objects of arbitrary size and different access bandwidth and latency characteristics, and present a possible implementation of this model. The proposed system is evaluated by analysis of the bandwidth and latency characteristics of the three different object classes and by examination of the impact of different network topologies. Finally, we present a number of simulation results which confirm the previous analysis.

1. Introduction

Parallel computers are one possible way to overcome the physical limits that bound the computing power of a single processor. Moreover, parallel computers may yield very high computing power at a good price/performance ratio because no extreme, and therefore expensive, technologies have to be used. Thus, very much effort is invested into design and implementation of parallel computer systems. There are three issues one has to face when designing such systems:

1. The architecture must be scalable. In other words, given enough algorithmic parallelism and within some limits computation speed increases proportionally with the number of processors. Two system requirements follow directly from the scalability issue: First, the system must not include any common resources, like shared memory or shared buses. Second, the network topology must be extendible (cf. Section 5.3. "Network Scalability"). Economically scalability makes sense because the price/performance ratio is better for highly parallel machines with cheap processors than for machines with a few highly optimized processors. Furthermore, in a scalable architecture the same components (hardware and software) can be used for a large family of computers.

2. Any kind of parallelism should be exploitable with good efficiency. In other words, the machine must support *general purpose computation*, leading to the following system requirements: load must be balanced dynamically at runtime, variable granularity of parallelism should be supported efficiently, the hardware structure should not be tailored toward one specific application resulting in suboptimal performance for other problems, and, finally, communication and computation performance must be balanced. The "computer as a universal machine paradigm" is the basis of the economic success of computers and should not be sacrificed with parallel machines. General purpose machines are mass products with advantage of cheap hardware production and high quality software. The success of personal computers is a good example of these effects.

3. Architecture and algorithm should be decoupled to make the machine really *programmable*. The same program, or at least the same source with recompilation

should run on any configuration of the system efficiently. Today, software development is the dominant part of total system cost. Therefore, it is unacceptable that a program must be rewritten on each particular parallel system to achieve good performance. Thus, synchronization must be cheap and the network structure must be hidden from the programmer. Finally, the memory must provide a global address space.

Today, there are mainly three different parallel architectures. Bus-coupled, *shared memory architectures* are programmable and well suited for general purpose computation; however, they are not scalable beyond a few dozen processors. On the other hand, *message passing architectures* are scalable up to hundreds of processors, but the programming is very architecture dependent. *SIMD machines* are scalable to thousands of processors, though their programming model is restricted to one form of parallelism only.

From the above requirements one complication becomes obvious: Where programmability requires a shared memory model for all processors, scalability disallows the use of a physically shared memory. Although this seems to be a contradiction on first sight, close analysis reveals that a logically shared but physically distributed memory can be realized by sacrificing uniform access times. Accesses to remote memories take more time than accesses to local memory. In this paper, a concept for a non-uniform access memory is presented and analyzed.

Non-uniform latency memory architectures have been implemented both in hardware and in software [4, 5, 13]. However, whereas in these works the main focus was on minimizing access latency, our approach is based on dataflow ideas [2] to tolerate rather than minimize access delays. In such a model, bandwidth limitations become a more crucial issue than long delays.

2. Architectural Overview

2.1. Distributed Shared Memory and Latency Tolerance

Scalability means an n-fold increase in performance for a system using n times as many processors. As we postulate a global address space for programmability reasons, total memory traffic can also be expected to increase by a factor of n. In order to obtain the necessary bandwidth, we therefore use a distributed memory system with a number of memory modules proportional to the number of processors.

However, although such a physically distributed memory provides the required access bandwidth, it also introduces large delays for access to data on physically remote modules. In conventional architectures, this problem of high memory latencies leads to a stalling of the processor until the requested data item is returned. This strategy is not acceptable for a scalable multiprocessor, especially when a distributed memory system with potentially high access delays is used. In order to prevent idle wait cycles, a processor should delegate data requests to functional units which resolve memory accesses concurrently, so that program execution can continue. Thus, instead of having to minimize access latency to reduce idle time, such a system is capable of *tolerating* non-uniform memory delays.

In order to supply the independent instructions necessary for continuation of execution, efficient context switching may be required. The following section presents the architecture for a design, in which latency tolerance is achieved by using dataflow synchronization.

2.2. The ADAM Architecture

In the proposed system, all references to non-local memory locations are implemented as split-phase transactions. Encountering a load instruction, the execution unit issues a load request to a special functional unit, the *object manager*. It marks the register where the result is expected as empty by clearing its *present bit*, a special bit associated with each register, and continues execution. In the meantime, the object manager may return the result into the designated register and set the present bit. If the result is needed before the request has returned (present bit still cleared), a context switch occurs to an independently executable part of the program. Figure 1 illustrates the split phase memory transaction.

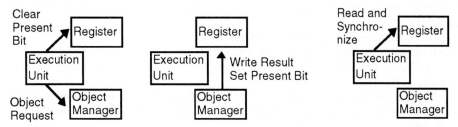

Fig. 1. The three phases of the split-phase memory transaction

This idea of synchronization based on the presence or absence of data is generally known as dataflow. In fact, the described memory system is part of the coarse-grain dataflow machine ADAM (Advanced DAtaflow Machine), which is designed for a medium-scale number (several hundred) of similar processing elements, interconnected via a packet-switched network. Each node consists of an execution unit, several functional units, and a memory module containing local and global data. Figure 2 shows the node structure relevant to the memory system.

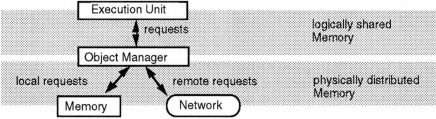

Fig. 2. Structure of one processing node

During execution of a program, a large number of small processes, called codeblocks, is created dynamically and distributed evenly across all processing nodes. Special functional units support load balancing and context management. The context of an executing codeblock basically consists of a program counter and a set of registers, which are used for dataflow synchronization in the manner described above. Context switch time is reduced to a few machine cycles by the use of a large number of register sets. This large synchronization space, called the *frame space*, allows an efficient implementation of dataflow-like codeblock scheduling. A detailed description of the ADAM architecture can be found in [9, 11].

In order to generate the necessary parallelism, programs are written in a functional programming language, such as SISAL [10] or MFL, which was designed as an integral part of the entire ADAM architecture. Through data dependence analysis, a compiler extracts a high degree of parallelism and generates codeblocks of various sizes in order to optimize code granularity.

3. Object-Based Memory

3.1. The Object-Based Memory Interface

All memory modules, together with the object managers, present themselves to the compiler as a global object memory (see fig. 2). Objects are arbitrarily-sized pieces of memory, accessible by a reference and an index into the object. Thus, the reference to a data word consists of two parts: the object reference and an index to specify the desired word within the object. The following list shows the basic operations provided for object manipulation:

- LOAD(obj, idx): reads the contents of the object's indicated field.
- STORE(obj, idx, val): writes a value into the specified object field.
- BLOCKMOVE(obj1, idx1, obj2, idx2, size): allows one to copy entire blocks of memory from one object to another.
- REF(obj): increments the first word (index 0) of an object, which serves as a reference count. Reference counting must be performed explicitly by the application using the object.
- ALLOCATE(class, size): allocates an object of the given class (see next section) with its reference count set to 1. The object manager reserves the requested amount of memory and returns the object reference.
- DEALLOCATE(obj): decrements the object's reference count and frees its allocated memory if the value reaches 0.

This way of defining the memory interface bridges the semantic gap between programming language and machine architecture by supporting the use of structured data objects. Representation of data as structured objects is attractive not only for object-based languages, but also supports many dataflow languages (e.g. I-structures in Id [3]). As will be described in the next section, this scheme also allows to take an object's specific access characteristics into account by assigning them to special classes.

3.2. Three Classes of Objects for Different Access Patterns

A truly programmable system has to free the programmer from the need to specify which data items will be needed where in the program. Especially in a system based on the dataflow paradigm, where processes are scheduled dynamically, compile-time data placement does not make much sense at all. On the other hand, we cannot ignore the fact that the physical location of data in memory has a critical impact on execution time, e.g., a frequently accessed local variable should not reside on the far end of the machine.

In order to support dynamic data placement, the memory system differentiates between three object classes with different typical access characteristics. By matching an object's expected request pattern to one of these classes, access latencies and bandwidth requirements can be optimized.

1. *Local Objects* are stored in a processor's local memory module. They can be accessed quickly by that processor, but cause increasing latencies for requests from more distant processors. Using local objects in sequential program parts yields normal uniprocessor performance. When a local object is shared among many processors, however, it may represent a hot spot .
2. *Distributed Objects* are spread out over all memory modules, so that the index of an object request determines the actual location of the cell. Assuming a system with p processors, the object's first cell is stored on module #0, the second on module #1, and the p+1st cell on module #0 again. The average latency of a distributed object access is fairly high, but p simultaneous requests can theoretically be handled in paral-

lel. Typically, the distributed class is used for large objects which are read and written by many processors in parallel.

3. *Replicated Objects* are stored as individual copies in each memory module. Since they are local to every processor, read access latency is minimal. Write requests are sent to all modules using an efficient broadcast mechanism. Simultaneous writes to replicated objects cause contention and are serialized by the broadcast medium. Therefore, this class should only be written by few processors simultaneously. The replicated class is typically used for special objects like code and constants.

Figure 3 illustrates graphically how the different classes of objects are stored in memory:

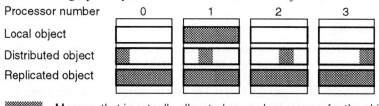

= Memory that is actually allocated on each processor for the object.

Fig. 3. Memory allocation for three different object classes

These three object classes could be extended to match different access patterns more exactly. For example, instead of spreading distributed objects across the entire system, they could be allocated in a locally restricted processor range in order to profit from locality without introducing access bottlenecks. Also, replications of objects might not be needed in every memory module, so that a distributed object consisting of replicated fields would combine the advantages of both classes.

On the other hand, a large number of object classes complicates the implementation of the memory system, which has to perform the different address translations efficiently in hardware. Also, the difficulty for the compiler to automatically choose object classes increases with their number and complexity. Therefore, it is reasonable to restrict the number of classes to the three basic types.

4. Implementation

So far, we have presented the underlying principles of the ADAM memory system, leaving many implementation issues unspecified. Although this results in flexibility in hardware design, it still has to be shown that there exists at least one way to implement these principles. This section discusses some implementation issues which are special to the presented memory system. They have been validated using accurate simulation on the register transfer level and are currently being built into a hardware prototype of the ADAM design.

4.1. Messages

Remote requests are sent across the network as packets, or messages, of variable lengths. The first word of a message specifies the destination in its processor field; following words contain other arguments, such as read or write data or the return address. For example, the remote load and store requests and their replies take format of figure 4.

In the current implementation, all requests (except for BLOCKMOVE operations) refer to only one single memory location. The return address refers to the register location in the frame space which is used for synchronization. The registers are memory mapped, so that they can be addressed in the same format as all memory locations.

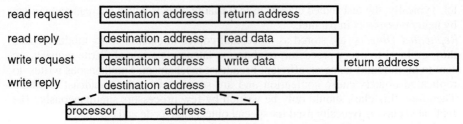

Fig. 4. Format of memory request and reply messages

4.2. Addressing

The object oriented memory is organized as a large heap with efficient object allocation and deallocation, using one of the well-known memory management schemes, such as the Buddy-System [7]. As explained above, object fields are specified by a pair of addresses, the object reference and the index. The object reference is divided into a processor and a base address field. Objects have a minimum size of 4 words, so that the two least significant bits of the object reference can be used to code the object class.

The following figure shows the address fields of an object reference:

Proc	Object Base	Class		Index

Depending on the object class (cf. section 3.2), the object manager has to handle a request in one of three ways. If the class is 'replicated', the request can be satisfied locally by reading the local memory at address [ObjectBase + Index], or by broadcasting the data in the case of a write. If the class is 'local', the requested memory location resides on the specified processor and might require a remote access to the address [ObjectBase + Index] on processor [Proc]. The field of an object of class 'distributed' is located on processor number [Index MOD N] where N is the total number of processors. The requested physical address is [ObjectBase + Index DIV N]. Note that these address calculations have to be carried out at run time, since the number of processors is not known to the compiler. However, if N is a power of 2, the operations DIV and MOD reduce to simple bit field extraction. Table 1 summarizes this address mapping.

class	processor number	physical address
local	**proc**	**OBase + Index**
distributed	**Index** MOD **N**	**OBase + Index** DIV **N**
replicated	(any)	**OBase + Index**

Table 1. Address translation for different object classes

Local objects are allocated and deallocated directly by the object manager of the corresponding processor. Since replicated and distributed objects occur in all memory modules, their allocation is performed by sending a message to a central object manager (e.g., of processor 0) who administrates a separate a dress range designated to common objects. Figure 5 shows the memory map of a four processor system with 16 words of memory each, after allocation of four different objects with common object space growing downward from the top of memory. Note that the allocation of an object does not imply an initialization of all of its fields, so that objects can be allocated and deallocated very quickly. Contention caused by central administration of the common object space will remain low as those classes are usually used for large objects only.

Name	Size	Class	Object Base	alloc. Processor
LA	4	local	0	0
LB	8	local	0	2
R	4	replicated	12	0
D	8	distributed	10	0

Address	Processor 0	Processor 1	Processor 2	Processor 3
0	LA[0]		LB[0]	
1	LA[1]		LB[1]	
2	LA[2]		LB[2]	
3	LA[3]		LB[3]	
4			LB[4]	
5			LB[5]	
6			LB[6]	
7			LB[7]	
8				
9				
10	D[0]	D[1]	D[2]	D[3]
11	D[4]	D[5]	D[6]	D[7]
12	R[0]	R[0]	R[0]	R[0]
13	R[1]	R[1]	R[1]	R[1]
14	R[2]	R[2]	R[2]	R[2]
15	R[3]	R[3]	R[3]	R[3]

Fig. 5. Memory map of an N-processor system

4.3. Broadcasts

The broadcast mechanism necessary for writes to replicated objects has not been specified yet. A separate broadcast bus connecting all object managers provides good latency characteristics and does not load the packet-switched data network, but implementation of a broadcast bus shared by a large number (over 100) of nodes is difficult.

Instead, the existing network can also be used for writes to replicated objects. Compared to a broadcast bus, however, distributing requests over a logical tree significantly increases write latency and consumes network bandwidth, so that block move operations with large packets should be used to reduce routing overhead.

5. Analysis

5.1. Latency Hiding

Although the ADAM architecture is designed to tolerate memory latency by using split-phase operations, large delays may still cause performance degradation. Figure 6 illustrates an example in which two context switches are needed to hide the memory latency T_{lat} for accessing the object A.

Had the request returned before the result was needed ($T_{lat} < T_I$), execution could have proceeded uninterrupted. The scheduling of a sufficient number of interleaving instructions between data request and usage is a common compiler strategy for latency hiding [6, 12]. In most cases, however, there are not enough independent instructions available to 'bridge' the request delay.

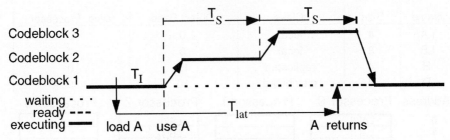

Fig. 6. Tolerating latency by context switching

The general case, therefore, requires one or several context switches in order to supply the processor with useful work. Assuming an average codeblock execution time between context switches T_S, the number of necessary context switches to hide the latency T_{lat} is thus $n_s = (T_{lat} - T_I) / T_S$.

n_s thus indicates the number of independent codeblocks required on each processor, which is determined by the program's parallelism and the code granularity generated by the compiler. Apparently, tolerating large memory latencies requires a higher degree of parallelism.

It is interesting to note that a slow context switch time increases T_S and therefore the tolerable latency, but since this time does not contribute to the computation at all, it should be minimized.

5.2.   Latency and Bandwidth Characteristics of Object Classes

In order to benefit from the assignment of objects to different classes, their expected access patterns should be matched by the latency and bandwidth characteristics of the class. Although the exact characteristics depend on the specific implementation, their general qualities are constant. Table 2 lists those values.

The variables T_{mem}, T_{bus} and T_{hop} refer to the latency of a local memory access, the broadcast bus delay and the time for one packet hop, respectively. The number of hops a request needs to travel varies according to the locality of its object class. Local requests usually refer to adjacent nodes (average distance d_l), whereas distributed object requests on average have to travel across half the network (distance d_d). Also, the number of hops depends on the chosen network topology, which also determines the connectivity c as the number of links connecting each of the p processors.

	Access Latency		Access Bandwidth	
Object Class	local	remote	T_{mem} dominates	T_{hop} dominates
local	T_{mem}	$T_{mem}+d_l\,T_{hop}$	$\dfrac{1}{T_{mem}}$	$\dfrac{c}{T_{hop}}$
distributed	T_{mem}	$T_{mem}+d_d\,T_{hop}$	$\dfrac{p}{T_{mem}}$	$\dfrac{c\,p}{T_{hop}}$
replicated (R)	T_{mem}		$\dfrac{p}{T_{mem}}$	
(W)	T_{bus}		$\dfrac{1}{T_{bus}}$	

Table 2. Latency and bandwidth characteristics for different object classes

Note that the given estimates neglect any delays caused by contention and thus should be interpreted as 'best case' estimates.

In terms of access latencies, the choice of object class does not appear to matter, except that the writing of replicated objects uses the broadcast bus instead of the network. The extra delay dT_{hop} for remote accesses is hidden by the system's latency tolerance.

The bandwidth estimates presented on the right-hand side of the table are much more critical to system performance, since latency can be tolerated dynamically whereas total system bandwidth is limited by the static architecture.

Relating the term of each estimate to the expected demand rate for the object shows which classes to use for which access pattern. Local objects cannot be accessed more than once per memory cycle and therefore represent a bottleneck if simultaneously requested by a large number of processors. Bandwidth of distributed objects scales with the number of processors, which corresponds to the number of potential requesters. Access to replicated objects only scales for read accesses - they reside in every processor's local memory - whereas writes are serialized by the single broadcast bus, thus limiting the number of simultaneous writers to one.

5.3. Network Scalability

During program execution, dynamic load balancing evenly distributes requesting code-blocks, whereas the use of distributed objects leads to a homogenous data distribution. Therefore, the typical network load during program execution on the ADAM architecture approaches a uniform random distribution of messages sent across the network. Assuming such a uniform distribution of requests allows for a simplified analysis of the requirements for the interconnection network.

A program's request rate of r data items per network cycle and processor determines the ratio between network and processing performance required for a balanced system. As a rule of thumb for standard scientific applications, this ratio equals about the execution rate of floating point operations. Since the processing performance in instructions per cycle is usually given by the fastest available uniprocessor architecture, a multiprocessor designer must scale the network performance to this number. Although the presented memory system allows trading off access latency for memory bandwidth, the question of how much bandwidth is actually needed remains.

For a scalable system showing linear speed-up, the request rate r only depends on the program and not on the number of processors p. Since every request has to travel an average distance of n_{hops} across the network, the total network load equals $r \cdot n_{hops} \cdot p$ package-hops per cycle. In a homogenous network, there is a total of $c \cdot p$ links, c being the connectivity or number of links per processor. The network utilization ρ simply is the ratio of used to existing links, yielding

$$\rho = \frac{r \, n_{hops} \, p}{c \, p} = \frac{r \, n_{hops}}{c} \, .$$

As the average number of hops and the connectivity are a function of the chosen network topology, the number of processors needed to reach 100% network utilization is a direct function of the topology and r.

Table 3 shows those terms for four different network topologies. The Ring and Torus networks are closed and every link has independent channels for each direction.

The limit of scalability is reached for a network utilization close to 1, which is not unreasonably high given the random request distribution and assuming modest buffering. In practice, this limit indicates that the achieved speed-up is less than linear, so that the increase in execution cycles due to contention results in a reduced request rate r and ρ remains below 1.

Topology	c	n_{hops}	$\rho = \dfrac{n_{hops}}{r} \dfrac{1}{c}$	$\rho \geq .5$ for	$\rho \geq 1$ for
Ring	2	$\dfrac{p}{4}$	$\dfrac{p}{8}$	$p \leq \dfrac{4}{r}$	$p \leq \dfrac{8}{r}$
Torus	4	$\dfrac{\sqrt{p}}{2}$	$\dfrac{\sqrt{p}}{8}$	$p \leq \left(\dfrac{4}{r}\right)^2$	$p \leq \left(\dfrac{8}{r}\right)^2$
Hypercube	$\log_2 p$	$\dfrac{\log_2 p}{2}$	$\dfrac{1}{2}$	$r \leq 1$	$r \leq 2$
Fully Con.	$p-1$	1	$\dfrac{1}{p-1}$	$r \leq \dfrac{p-1}{2}$	$r \leq p-1$

Table 3. Network characteristics for different topologies

There is a basic difference between the first two and the last two examined topologies concerning their scalability (see last column). While hypercube and fully connected networks are truly scalable, i.e. only limited by the request rate and not by the number of processors, the size of a system using ring or torus topologies is limited. On the other hand, a fully connected network is impossible to realize for a large system, and its potential bandwidth exceeds normal requirements by far. Even the much more modest increase in links per processor for the hypercube network may lead to implementation problems, since this number is usually given by the node hardware. For a more detailed analysis of the trade-offs involved in choosing a network topology, see [1].

The following section will present a confirmation of these estimates by simulation results.

6. Simulation Results

In order to confirm the analysis presented in the last section, we have used a simulator which was written to validate the entire ADAM design. Simulation takes place on the register transfer level, allowing for precise modeling of communication processes inside the machine. The execution unit is non-pipelined and instructions typically take 5 - 10 simulation cycles to complete. Network delay and topology as well as the delay of the broadcast bus can be specified. The simulator runs on an Apple MacIntosh® workstation and on a Parsytec MultiCluster® with 32 processors.

For a simulation load, we chose a 64 by 64 matrix multiplication program, using one codeblock per row for initialization and one codeblock per element to compute the output matrix. Since load and data are dynamically distributed, this program represents the typical memory request pattern which can be expected for most large parallel applications. Execution time is mainly determined by the large number of remote data requests, so that it reflects memory system performance. In the presented graphs, we use efficiency as a performance measure, which is defined as execution speed-up relative to a one processor system divided by the number of processors. An efficiency of 1 means linear speed-up.

6.1. Object class

In order to illustrate the importance of choosing object classes appropriately, the two input matrices have been implemented as local, parallel, and distributed objects. The delay of one package hop was set to 32 simulation cycles using a hypercube network topology.

For comparison, broadcast delays were also set to 32 cycles, although smaller values are more realistic for efficient bus implementations. One processor needs about $30 \cdot 10^6$ simulation cycles to execute 4292 codeblocks. Figure 7 shows the respective efficiency, or processor utilization, for up to 256 processors.

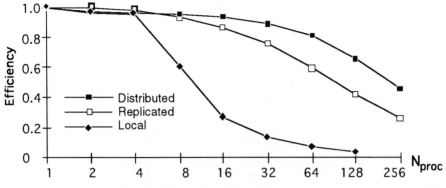

Fig. 7. Efficiency of different object classes

The results clearly show that local objects represent a significant bottleneck limiting scalability to less than 8 processors, whereas access bandwidth to distributed and replicated objects scales with the number of processors. Although a similar number of requests is issued by each processing element in all three cases, the number of destinations for these requests differs significantly. In the version using local objects, where the two input matrices were dynamically allocated on nodes 0 and 1, only these two object managers have to reply to all requests, which leads to heavy contention.

Requests to common objects, on the other hand, avoid hot spots by distributing their destinations evenly. Part of the decrease in efficiency for large numbers of processors is due to the reduction in parallelism per processor. The version using replicated objects achieves linear speed-up during the actual matrix multiplication, but suffers from bandwidth problems during the initialization phase, which is serialized on the broadcast bus. As will be shown in the section 6.3, this effect may have a large impact on total system performance as network latency increases.

6.2. Network Topology

For a comparison between simulation results and the analysis in section 5.3, we will first compute the request rate r for the given program (using distributed objects).

Since the major part of program execution time is used for output element computation, we neglect the initialization phase and the writes to the output matrix. This leaves 4096 codeblocks each loading $2 \cdot 64$ elements for computation of the product sums. Since every load request results in a corresponding reply message, there are $2 \cdot 2 \cdot 64 \cdot 4096$, or about 10^6 requests generated during the $30 \cdot 10^6$ cycles it takes the program to execute on one processor. This number has been confirmed using load counts during simulation. Assuming a package hop delay (network cycle) of 32 processor cycles, the request rate evaluates to

$$r = \frac{10^6 \text{ requests}}{30 \cdot 10^6 \text{ cycles}} \cdot \frac{32 \cdot \text{ cycles}}{\text{netw. cycle}} = 1.07 \text{ requests per network cycle.}$$

Using the formulas presented in the last column of table 3, we can derive a scalability limit of 7 processors for the ring, or 55 processors for the torus topology. These numbers are confirmed by the efficiency plots shown in figure 8. Linear speed-up (efficiency of 1) is achieved up to a certain number of processors, but then decreases rapidly as the network saturates. This agreement confirms the assumption of a uniform request distribution for the given example.

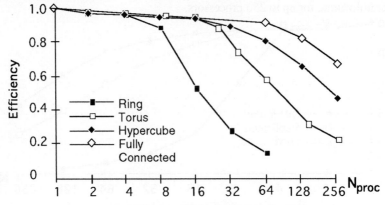

Fig. 8. Efficiency of different network topologies

The efficiency degradation of the examples using scalable topologies is related to a decrease in parallelism per processor as well as load distribution overhead, which increases with the number of processors. The worse performance of the hypercube topology can be explained by the fact that, even though the network has not reached saturation, contention occurs more frequently than in the fully connected network.

6.3. Network Speed

In a latency-tolerant system, network performance is mostly determined by its throughput. Besides changing network topology, as discussed in the last section, an increase in throughput can be achieved by increasing the number of physical wires per link or by speeding up the network clock rate. Both means have the effect of reducing the latency of one packet hop and hence the number of requests per network cycle. The following parallelism profiles show the effect of increasing network latency in a hypercube system of 256 processors executing the matrix multiplication.

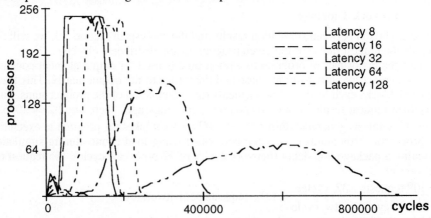

Fig. 9. Parallelism profile for different latencies using distributed objects

Each graph shows the total number of cycles spent on program execution during one machine cycle, thus reflecting the momentary speed-up. After the initialization phase with a speed-up of maximal 32, parallelism increases up to a limit. As load distribution involves the same network latencies, it takes longer to supply all processors with work and to reach maximal speed-up for higher network delays. The area under the different graphs is proportional to the total number of executed instructions and therefore about constant.

The graph shows that for delays of up to 32 processor cycles, the increase in network latency is tolerated well and maximum parallelism is reached during the computation phase. As network delay increases further, more requests are issued in the time needed for a packet hop, so that contention causes more and more processors to spend idle time waiting for requests to return. Maximal speed-up is thus dominated by the network delays instead of the number of processors, so that the system is no longer scalable

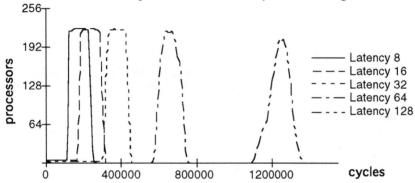

Fig. 10. Parallelism profile for different latencies using replicated objects

Storing the input matrices as replicated objects yields a different picture (Fig. 10).

Here, the actual matrix multiplication is performed in almost constant time, since all reads are local and only writes to the (distributed) output matrix and the load balancing are affected by an increase in network delay. However, the serial broadcasting of the input matrices during the initialization phase disallows latency hiding, and thus takes a number of cycles proportional to the delay time, assuming similar latencies for network and broadcast bus. Comparing total execution time of this example to figure 9 shows that the memory system shows better performance when distributed objects are used for the matrix multiplication. In general, however, the compiler's choice of whether to use replicated instead of distributed objects has to depend on the actual implementation's network and broadcast latencies and on the number of expected read accesses.

7.   Conclusions

We have presented a scalable memory system architecture, which preserves the intuitive view of a shared address space without causing performance degradation in a parallel system using several hundred processors. The ADAM coarse-grain dataflow architecture incorporates the proposed principles by using split-phase memory transactions combined with fast context switching in order to tolerate access latencies.

Through analysis and simulation, we have evaluated the presented concepts and implementation suggestions. Object-based addressing does not only support the programmer by providing a memory structure semantically close to typically used data structures, but it also improves system performance by assigning objects to specific classes according to their access characteristics. The concept of latency tolerance was shown to preserve scalability despite slow memory accesses, as long as the network bandwidth suffices to deliver all requests.

Currently, the ADAM design is being implemented on distributed hardware, so that its scalability can be verified for more complicated programs of bigger sizes.

Acknowledgments

We would like to express our thanks to all the other members of the ADAM project team, especially O. Maquelin for providing the simulator, which we used to obtain the presented results. Our special thanks go to Marty Billingsley for her help in putting the paper into readable English and to Prof. Albert Kündig for providing the research facilities. Part of the ADAM project has been supported by grant no. 2.309-0.86 of the "Schweizerischer Nationalfonds".

References

1. Agarwal, A. "Limits on Interconnection Network Performance," IEEE Trans. on Parallel and Distributed Systems, Vol. 2, Oct 1991, pp 398-412.

2. Arvind and R. A. Ianucci. "Two Fundamental Issues in Multiprocessing," Proceedings of DFVLR - Conference 1987 on Parallel Processing in Science and Engineering, Bonn-Bad Godesberg, D, 6-1987.

3. Arvind, R. S. Nikhil and K. K. Pingali. "I-Structures: Data Structures for Parallel Computing," Workshop on Graph Reduction, Los Alamos, NM, 10-1-1986.

4. Bennett, J.K. et al, "Munin: Distributed Shared Memory Based on Type-specific memory coherence," Proceedings of the Second Symposium on Principles and Practice of Parallel Programming, Seatlle, Wash, Mar. 1990, pp. 168-175

5. BBN. "Inside the BBN TC2000," Cambridge, Mass., Feb. 1990.

6. Gibbons, P.B. and S.S. Muchnik, "Efficient Instruction Scheduling for a Pipelined Processor," SIGPLAN '86 Symp/ on Compiler Construction, ACM, Palo Alto, CA, Jun 1986.

7. Knuth, D. "The Art of Computer Programming," Eddison Weslsy, 1968.

8. Li, K. and R. Schaefer, "A Hypercube Shared Memory System," Proceedings of the 1989 International Conference on Parallel Processing, St. Charles, Ill, Aug. 1989, pp I-125-132.

9. Maquelin, O. "ADAM: a Coarse-Grain Dataflow Architecture that Adresses the Load Balancing and Throttling Problems," Proceedings of CONPAR 90-VAPP IV, Zürich, September 1990, Springer LNCS 457.

10. McGraw, J. et al., "SISAL, Streams and Iterations in a Single Assignment Language," Lawrence Livermore National Laboratory Report 1985.

11. Mitrovic, S. et al. "A Distributed Memory Multiprocessor Based on Dataflow Synchronization," Proceedings of International Phoenix Conference on Computers and Communication, March 1990

12. Murer, S. "A Latency Tolerant Code Generation Algorithm for a Coarse G¹.in Dataflow Machine," Proceedings of CONPAR 90-VAPP IV, Zürich, September 1990, Springer LNCS 457.

13. Pfister et al, "The IBM Research Parallel Processor Prototype (RP3): Introduction and Architecture," Proceedings of the 1985 International Conference on Parallel Processing, St. Charles, Ill, Aug.1985, pp 764-771.

14. Schwehm, M. and A. Strey, "A Comparison of Interconnection Networks for Large SIMD Parallel Computers," Proceedings of the International Conference on Parallel Computing Technologies, Novosibirsk, USSR, Sept. 1991.

Cost prediction for load-balancing: application to Algebraic Computations

J.L. Roch, A. Vermeerbergen and G. Villard

Laboratoire LMC-IMAG, 46 Av. F. Viallet,
F38031 Grenoble Cédex
e.m. *jlroch@imag.fr, vermeer@mistral.imag.fr, gvillard@imag.fr*

Abstract

A major feature of Computer Algebra, and more generally of non-numerical computations, is the dynamical and non-predictable behaviour of the executions. We then understand that statical analysis should imperatively be completed by dynamical analysis in order to reach the best distribution of the tasks among the processors. In this paper, we present a new load-balancing system for parallel architectures with great numbers of processors. Being well suited for Computer Algebra and based on the notion of granularity, it is original in the sense that it takes into account the tasks complexity as a consistent information in order to achieve efficiency.

1 Introduction

Algebraic computations are intrinsically dynamic: in most cases, the effective cost of a computation cannot be predicted. The main reason is that the intermediate coefficients growth is difficult to estimate precisely since it relies on a lot of parameters. Therefore, the taking into account of a small number of these parameters, in order to characterize the inputs (as it is done from a practical point of view), leads to too large and often unrealistic upper bounds on the results. For instance, a matrix multiplication may be efficiently parallelized on 64 processors using a block repartition [9]. If the input data are *well conditioned*, i.e., at the level of the algorithm the basic operations have almost the same cost, this parallelization is efficient. However, in general, the basic operations are not equivalent. For instance, some coefficients may be polynomials with 1000 monomials, while others may be small integers or even zeros. Although it is useful, the static repartition is insufficient.

Consequently, even if the considered problem is highly parallel ($\mathcal{NC}$ class), the static parallelization of a general algebraic algorithm is a difficult issue. Indeed, given a number of processors, a good parallelization consists in equitably distributing the work load, so as to guarantee the best possible processors use. But this work load is related to the inputs and cannot be statically determined. A dynamic load-balancing mechanism is thus necessary to decide how the parallelism has to be exploited (i.e., at which level of granularity it is needed to work, which computations need to be distributed...) in order to decrease the total computation time [1].

In the framework of Computer Algebra, we show how the cost of an algorithm at its current level of granularity (assuming that all the operations have the same cost), is a consistent information which the load-balancer has to take into account in order to achieve efficiency. This fundamental property leads to the specification of a new load-balancer, based on tasks complexity, and dedicated to computer algebra. This approach is different from the ones which do not take into account the cost of tasks to be distributed [1, 6, 10].

Moreover, our target model suffers no limitation: we assume that a large number of processing units are available (more than one thousand). This number imposes two constraints to a load-balancing mechanism:

- it leads to thiner granularities. A new general methodology is thus needed to develop high-level parallel applications. At a given level of granularity, the design should take advantage of previous improvements obtained at lower granularity levels. We show how a load-balancer taking into account tasks granularity can satisfy this condition.
- In order to ensure coherence in the distribution, a global control is needed. Even if the former is centralized, its management must be distributed to avoid bottlenecks. The solution we chose consists in using a classical token-ring strategy [2].

Load-balancing characteristics and specifications given in this paper are dedicated to computer algebra algorithms, but the system is designed for any target architecture (as far as it includes many processors). The described specifications may be implemented on either distributed memory machines, shared memory machines or workstation networks. Two groups of parameters (corresponding to either machine-dependent characteristics or to algorithm-dependent properties) are used to achieve adequation between the load-balancer and the target architecture. An evaluation is in progress on a 128 transputers network [14]. Our target domain of computer algebra are arithmetic, linear algebra [13] and lattice basis reduction.

2 Algebraic Computations Requirements

This section intends to point out the specific characteristics and requirements of Algebraic Computations. These are mainly the dynamic behaviour of the executions and the fact that at a given level of granularity, a static parallelization is both irrelevant and incomplete.

2.1 Parallelization Driven by a High Level Cost

The execution cost of an algebraic algorithm strongly relates to its inputs, which are often very complex to describe. For example, let us consider a generic algorithm for matrix multiplication with coefficients in a commutative ring $\mathcal{R}$. Its cost may only be described by the number of operations performed in $\mathcal{R}$: this cost is thus related to the sole dimension of the input matrices, assuming that basic operations in the ring $\mathcal{R}$ are performed in constant time. However, the effective time spent for two given entry matrices, with coefficients in a given ring, actually corresponds to the number of binary operations performed. For instance, the effective cost of a matrix multiplication may only be due to the product of two coefficients, which cost can be distinguished only at a lower granularity level.

For instance, let $\mathcal{R} = \mathbb{Z}[X]$: the effective cost depends on the dimensions of two matrices, on the number of monomials in each polynomial coefficient, and on the size of the integer coefficients of each monomial. If the multiplication to is the following:

$$
\begin{pmatrix} P & 0 & 0 & \dots & 0 \\ 0 & Q & 0 & \dots & 0 \\ 0 & 0 & 1 & \dots & 0 \\ \vdots & \vdots & \vdots & \ddots & \vdots \\ 0 & 0 & 0 & \dots & 1 \end{pmatrix} \times \begin{pmatrix} P & 0 & 0 & \dots & 0 \\ 0 & Q & 0 & \dots & 0 \\ 0 & 0 & 1 & \dots & 0 \\ \vdots & \vdots & \vdots & \ddots & \vdots \\ 0 & 0 & 0 & \dots & 1 \end{pmatrix} \quad with \quad \begin{cases} P = 1000! X^{10} + 1 \\ Q = \sum_{i=0}^{1000} X^i \end{cases}
$$

then the effective cost will mainly results from the multiplication of large integers, i.e. 1000! × 1000! and the product of large polynomials, i.e. $Q \times Q$.

This is a major remark in computer algebra: it means that, most of the time, the cost of a high level computation cannot be predicted. In the example, the main operations needed to parallelize are the multiplication of integers and the product of polynomials; in these operations, the parallelism involved concerns lower granularity operations. This parallelism, related to the inputs, cannot be found statically in the algorithm, but rather dynamically when this algorithm is to be applied on specific data.

Nevertheless, the cost of an algorithm, evaluated at a given level of granularity, constitutes a significant information. If this cost is high enough, then a parallelization of the algorithm at this level may be worth doing. If it is low, no parallelization should be useful at this level –because of communication overheads– though lower level operations may be efficiently performed in parallel (such as in the above, for example). Let us notice that this cost could be automatically evaluated [8].

2.2 Levels of Parallelization: An Example

Let us consider the following recursive algorithm for matrix product over a ring $\mathcal{R}$:

```
MatrixMultiplication(M ∈ R^{r×n}, N ∈ R^{n×n}) ==
    if (r == 1) return( VectorMatrixProd(M, N) )
    else
        M_H := the r/2 first rows of M ; M_L := the r/2 last rows of M
        R_H := MatrixMultiplication(M_H, N)      (1)
        R_L := MatrixMultiplication(M_L, N)      (2)
    return( MatrixMultiplication(R_H, R_L) )
```

Let $T(r, n)$ be the cost of this computation, assuming that computations in $\mathcal{R}$ are performed in constant time. The cost of the sequential execution for two $n \times n$ matrices is $T_{seq}(n, n) = 2.T_{seq}(\frac{n}{2}, n)$. Computations (1) and (2) may easily be performed in parallel: the first splitting of the recursion involves two processors, and thus the cost of the total parallel execution is: $T_{par}(n, n) = T_{par}(\frac{n}{2}, n) + T_{com}(M_H, M_L, N, R_H, R_L)$. A more precise definition of T_{com} relates to the parallel model:

- On a shared-memory architecture, T_{com} corresponds to the time spent in accessing the shared data (for instance, protected by semaphores). Thus, T_{com} may be assumed to be a machine-dependent constant, but independent on the size of the shared data.
- On a distributed memory architecture, T_{com} corresponds to the time needed for communicating data from one processor to another (point to point communication, between neighbour processors or performed by a router). Thus T_{com} may be assumed to be a linear function in the size of the shared data.

On both models, T_{com} is at most linear in the size of the shared data. As T_{seq} here is a super-linear function and T_{com} is linear, it exists n_0 so that: $n > n_0 \implies T_{par}(n, n) \leq T_{seq}(n, n)$. Parallel execution of sub-multiplications (1) and (2) will be interesting if: $T_{par}(n, n) \leq T_{seq}(n, n)$. if $n < n_0$, a parallel execution of both sub-multiplications will be interesting only if the operations performed in $\mathcal{R}$ (considered as basic operations at the level of the algorithm) can themselves efficiently be performed in parallel. In this case, the benefit brought by parallelism is not due to parallel execution of (1) and (2), but by the inherent parallelism of (1) and (2).

A simple way to exploit parallelism at every granularity level is to perform the operations in $\mathcal{R}$ using similar recursive algorithms. This process is repeated and controlled by the effective cost of the operations at the current granularity level. Thus, it automatically decreases the granularity, exploiting parallelism at each level where gains can be guaranteed.

2.3 Theoretical Overhead

The overhead of this scheduling strategy may be theoretically evaluated if enough processors are available. Let us consider a problem involving n entries, which may be split into p instances of the same problem, each involving $\frac{n}{K}$ entries (the time of the lifting process is assumed to be a constant). Let us denote $T_{//}$ the time of the direct parallelization of this problem, involving $n^{\log_2 p}$ processors. On a shared memory model, the total overhead of the load-balancing will be $\log_k n$ for a parallel execution involving $n^{\log_2 p}$ processors, and the total parallel time will be $T_{//} + \log_k n$. On a distributed memory model, this total execution time will be $T_{//} \log_k n$.

As an example, if we consider Gaussian elimination, the overall cost of our strategy will be $n \log n$ using n^2 processors, which is within a $\log n$ factor of the best known parallelization. Morerover, on the one hand the dynamic strategy avoids useless computations (of zeros, for instance), and on the other hand it is well suited to a direct computation.

3 Load-Balancing : High-Level Specifications

The specific requirements of Algebraic Computations presented above and the related *top-down* approach for the granularity, led to the main choices we have made for the load-balancer. In the following, these high-level specifications are presented both from the user's point of view and from the machine designer's point of view. The user manages the parallelism at its own level of granularity, usually a coarse one. In other words, the user specifies a static mapping of his coarse granularity tasks which is relevant at this level. The inherent parallelism to the arithmetic operations called by the user, although appropriate to a static mapping because of its lower granularity, is then automatically exploited by the load-balancer.

To express the dynamic parallelization, several choices are possible [3, 5, 10]. As far as algebraic computation is concerned, mainly by independent AND parallelism (modular computations, distributed computations) and OR parallelism (probabilistic algorithms, several strategies with no deterministic choice) [11], we have chosen, in order to express parallelism, to use *Fork* (OR-parallelism) primitives and *Fork-Join* (AND-Parallelism) primitives, well suited for an effective computation. In any case, this choice is not restrictive: any primitive allowing *dynamic process creation* and *Rendez-Vous* is convenient. A peculiar choice does not modify the general specification of the presented load-balancer.

In order to stick to the framework of the *remote processes activations*, we have increased the usual *Fork* and *Join* functionalities. In this section, we will use two new functions, *RemThreadFork* and *RemJoin*, which stand for *Fork* and *Join* on possibly distinct processors. They will be described in detail in section 5.

3.1 User Application

The user will manage the parallelism of its application at two levels: he starts by writing a distributed application using the usual rules and parallel language facilities to communicate.

These communications will transit onto the *user network* (see section 4 for a description of the different networks of the load-balancer). At this level, we indeed offer the possibility to completely control the data distribution, the synchronization points and the data exchanges. This corresponds to the highest level of granularity, with a relevant user mapping. Between two data transfers, the user may then exploit a parallelism also inherent to the arithmetic operations he calls, but too difficult to map because of its lower granularity. The example in section 3.2 below shows how to operate in this case, i.e., how to call the load-balancer. Our approach is illustrated in figure 1: the user statically maps its application on its private network, his processes may then call the load-balancer.

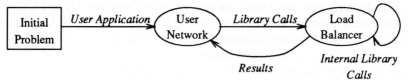

Figure 1 : General behaviour of a user application

3.2   Describing Load-Balancing : the Granularity Threshold

We have seen how the parallel processes are activated. We now show how the cost predictions are taken into account in order to dynamically allow the load-balancer to decrease the granularity and reach the more convenient one. Let us take a typical example. We can write a function which will realize the product of two quantities a and b.

```
mul( *res,a,b )
   case ugdecision( mul,a,b )
   seq :  /* Sequentially on this processor */
      seqmul( &res,a,b )
   par :
      aH = high weights of a ; al = low weights of a
      taskH = DefRemThread( fork,mul,ArithmCost(mul,aH,b),
         CommCost(aH,b), *resH, aH, b ,
         comm.  for resH, comm.  for aH, comm.  for b )
      myfork = DefFork(1)
      /* Computations on high and low weights are done
       in parallel, probably on distinct processors */
      RemThreadFork(myfork,taskH)
      mul( &res,al,b )
      RemJoin( myfork )
      add( &res,resH,resl )
   endcase
```

From the weights of a and b, a prediction will be done during the execution for the cost of the operation. The weight of an operand is a relevant information on it, much cheaper to manipulate than the operand itself, e.g. the binary length for an integer, the dimension for a matrix, the depth for an expression tree. . . This prediction will allow the evaluation of a *user granularity decision* (ugdecision in the example) to seq if it is not worthwhile running the parallel algorithm instead of the sequential one, and to par in the other case. In other words, the prediction may be formulated by using the notion of threshold : on this side of a given *user granularity threshold* (the details are given in section 4), the product –at this level of granularity– will be made sequentially; beyond, part of the work will be taken on by the load-balancer. Let us yet notice that if the function parameters are known, the *user granularity threshold* may be statically computed (unlike the other thresholds involved in the load-balancer (section 4)).

3.3   Parameterizing the Load-Balancer

A general purpose load-balancer will behave differently according to the current application and the current machine: adjusting some basic parameters from some relevant criteria. As it is, the ones that have to be considered, are not known for Computer Algebra applications: our work consists in pointing them out and proving their relevance. In order to do so, the load-balancer must allow the consideration of the largest possible number of situation. A good solution is to parameter the load-balancer as much as possible. This will be done at three main stages, from the user level to the run-time system level:

- the load-balancer must let the user adjust the behaviour of the automatism, being given its own problem and its own knowledges.
- The hardware and software costs of the machine may considerably influence the decision whether to export a given task or not.
- During execution, the arithmetic load of the processors and the communication load of the network have also to influence the exportation decisions.

The decisions related to the first point will obviously belong to the user: he will guide the load-balancer behaviour via its own *user granularity thresholds* previously introduced. Relating to the other two points, the *machine threshold* and the *load threshold* will be detailed in section 4 in order to take into account both hardware and software characteristics of the machine and the loads of the system. These three thresholds are intended to dynamically lead the system to better tasks distributions.

3.4   Control and Communications

We terminate this section on the high-level specifications of the load-balancer with some basic principles. They have been applied in order to distribute a *global control* and to simplify the aspects of the different communications which take place.

Control Unit
Interface
Operative Unit

Figure 2 : Abstract view of the load-balancer.

In an abstract manner, a load-balancer is composed of three main parts. The same division will be used in order to distinguish three main types of communication (in addition to the user communications). The three main parts of an abstract load-balancer are,

- a *Control Unit* taking the mapping decisions,
- an *Operative Unit* receiving orders from the *Control Unit*, appling them and executing the user application.
- a *Control/Operative Interface* linking the *Control Unit* and the *Operative Unit*. Via this interface, the *Control Unit* sends orders and the *Operative Unit* sends the loads measurements.

This division is directly implemented by our load-balancer (section 4). Indeed, we have divided the processes in *controllers* and *workers*, and the communications will transit onto the following inter-processes "parallel networks":

- the *user network* on which transit the messages explicitly communicated by the user,
- the network dedicated to the global control, i.e., to the management of the resources : the *token network*,
- the *mapping network* which plays the role of the interface between the *controllers* and the *workers*,
- the network used by the workers to exchange the data (parameters and results) of the exported tasks : the *inter-workers network*.

The reader will refer to figure 3 for a global view of these different networks. The position of our scheduler in the taxonomy[4] is dynamic, adaptive, heuristic and it has an intermediate position between centralized and distributed control. Note that we do not stick to this terminology, as our scheduler is not *load-balancing* in the sense of[4].

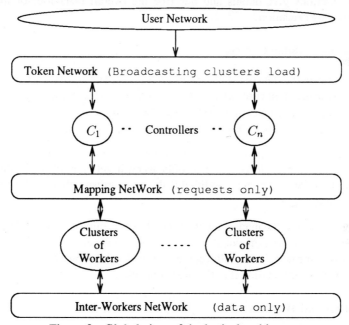

Figure 3 : Global view of the logical architecture

4   Logical Architecture of the Load-Balancer

We may now detail the logical architecture of the load-balancer. The algorithms of the principal tasks which are involved will be given in the next section which will be concerned by the balancer implementation on a distributed architecture. We have *processors* and *processes* which execute on the former.

4.1   Global View

We introduce here a classification of the different processors and processes of the balancer. The processors differ in the processes they execute and the networks they belong to.

Processors. Processors are of two types: the *controllers* and the *workers*. To each controller a cluster of workers is associated, being divided into two groups:

- the *global workers*, also called global resource, are ready to receive the tasks from any other worker.
- the *local workers*, also called *local resources*, which will only receive tasks from the processors of the same cluster or from themselves.

These two latter notions will allow to establish and test the influence of proximity relations between the processors.

Processes. In the same way, we point out three types of process:

- the *resource managers*, managing the arithmetic requests and transmitting the informations concerning the *mapping of the exported tasks*,
- the *arithmetic processes*.

The following sections give details and describe the overall behaviour of the different processes during the execution.

4.2   Distributing a Global Control

As previously noticed, the state of the global resources is kept up-to-date by the circulation of a token between the different controllers. This token encodes the number of global workers ready to be allocated for some extra work: it indicates to the controller to which cluster the workers belong. The following points are always satisfied:

- at a given time, only one processor has the token and can modify it,
- a processor allocates a global resource only when it gets the token; in this case, the only field of the token which is modified is the one corresponding to the cluster of the allocated worker.

Given those assumptions, the management of the global resources is particularly simple: a controller receiving a request of global resource from its cluster waits for the token. Once the operation is performed, it may allocate an available global worker, and consequently modifies the token before sending it to the next controller.

4.3   Controllers and Workers

The controllers : they are dedicated to the management of the resources. In order to do so, they concurrently execute a *global resource manager* and a *local resource manager*. The first manager allocates resources only at each reception of the token, whereas the second one may always allocate some (provided a local worker is available): it itself manages the corresponding informations.

The workers : they execute the exported arithmetic operations. Notice that a worker is not only passive (reception of orders): since the operation it has been asked to execute may involve *remote thread activations*, the worker may become producer –active– and ask for the exportation of its tasks. For the parameters and results exchanges, the global workers use the *inter-workers network* while the local ones communicate within themselves using the intra-cluster *mapping network*.

4.4 Processes and Interconnections

In the present section, we are concerned by more general descriptions about their behaviours.

The global resource managers : on the one hand, the *global resource manager* has to receive the requests from the *local resource manager*, to wait for the token , to modify it for the resource allocation, and finally to answer to the request by communicating with the *mapping process* which is associated to it. The *global resource manager* is thus connected on the *token network* and has two other links: a first one able to receive the requests and a second one able to answer to them. On the other hand, when receiving the token, the manager compares it to its old value, to know if one of the workers of its cluster has been allocated. If yes, it gets in touch with the concerned worker via the mapping processes so that the connection between workers can be established.

The local resource managers : in an analogous way, the *local resource manager* has to receive the request from the local *mapping process*. And, whether there is an available local processor or not, it directly answers to the *mapping process* or relays the request to the *global resource manager*.

The mapping processes : placed on all the processors of the network, their role is to collect the resource requests from the user application and from the exported processes, to relay those requests to the *resource managers*, to get the corresponding answers, and finally to inform the source processor and the one chosen for the exportation of their respective identification (so that they can subsequently exchange their data).

The user or exported processes : these are all the processes which may ask for a resource to export some arithmetic tasks. We have yet seen that the requests are sent to the *mapping processes*. The answers may then be either the identification of a found worker or a negative answer. Once they are virtually connected by their respective *mapping process*, these application processes only communicate via their *inter-workers network* (in order to exchange parameters and results).

4.5 Global Description of Remote Process Activation

We are now ready to give an overall description of a *remote process activation* from the resource request to the reception of the operation result (assuming a free resource is available in the network). After a call to *RemThreadFork* (section 5), the father process (i.e., which has called the activation) will go on executing on the same processor. Concurrently, the requests are sent to the resources-management processes to find other processors for the execution of the sons arithmetic tasks. If those tasks have arithmetic costs which are high enough (depending on the overall load) and if other processors have been found to be unemployed, the corresponding works are exported. Otherwise, the sons will also execute on the original processor. After that, the *RemJoin* synchronization (section 5) simply consists in a transfer of the operation results between the processes concerned. Seven main steps are distinguished.

1. The source process asks for a request to its mapping process, and waits for an answer.
2. The mapping process relays the request to the mapping process of the controller and then to the local resource manager.
3. If a local resource is available the local resource manager sends its answer via the mapping processes, otherwise it relays the request to the global manager.
4. If it is in touch, the global manager waits for the token, takes a decision and sends its answer via the mapping processes.

5. The mapping processes establish the connection between the source process and the chosen destination resource.
6. The source and the destination resource exchange the parameters of the exported operation.
7. The source and the destination resource exchange the result of the exported operation.

In the situation where no free resource is found in the network the global manager simply sends a negative answer to the source process which then itself executes the work which could have been exported.

4.6 Thresholds

We have seen at section 3.2 and 3.3 that to use the notion of *threshold* is a good way to formulate the predictions and the exportation decisions. These decisions are taken at three different levels, to each level corresponds a particular *threshold*.

The granularity threshold : as presented in section 3.2, the user may use a threshold to decide whether to export an operation or not. For instance, after a study of the theoretical cost of his parallelization he may force the system to reach a desired level of granularity, to find the best compromise between arithmetic and communication costs before beginning the exportations. In order to do so, the user will write a *user granularity decision* function, according to the arithmetic operations he uses and the argument types he manipulates. Using constants delivered by the system (as elementary computation, communication or memory management cost) and given an operation and a type, this function will return par or seq indicating whether the work may be parallelized or not.

The machine thresholds : a lot of characteristics of the machine, both hardware and software, must statically influence the behaviour of the load-balancer. We may point out for example:
  – the ratio of the atomic communication cost over the arithmetic one. If it increases, such a ratio will clearly decrease the volume of remote processes.
  – The distances in the network. The *global manager* and the *local manager* must have different thresholds if the *local resources* are reachable at a low cost compared to the *global resources* one.
  – The ratio of the process creation cost over the arithmetic one. The remarks are the same than above.
  – The different arithmetic units capabilities. The availability of some dedicated or powerful arithmetic units must lead to thresholds depending on the types of the free resources.

Those characteristics will be taken into account by using system-defined constants and, as previously, a *machine-granularity-decision* function.

The load thresholds : The decisions and the parameters we have discussed above rely on statically defined data. This will be completed by dynamically assigned parameters to take into account mainly the load of the system. During execution, the load of the networks (the volume of routed data) and the arithmetic load of the processors should clearly influence the balancer behaviour and allow to take the final exportation decisions.

Calibrating the load threshold : Among the three types of threshold mentioned above, both the granularity and the machine ones can be determined in a deterministic way in the general case. The former is a function issued from concerns about algorithms complexity and the later is a set of physical constants that can be determined by a series of preliminary tests. This is not the case of the load threshold in our general context: network load cannot be predicted during the execution. This problem can be tackled by using the temporal locality hypothesis on the network load, that is to say, the network load varies slowly and continuously with time. This method has already been successfully assumed in close contexts. For example, this hypothesis in used in [15] on communication costs and task executions time in a bi-processors to feed exact equations giving the frequency for load-balancer invocations. In our first implementation, we locally estimate an expected communication cost by using routers statistics. This local estimation is expected to be satisfying enough and meets the stability requirement of [7]. However, our model has an intrinsic global state stored in the token.

5 Implementation on a Distributed Architecture

The model we propose for load-balancing is designed for any parallel architecture. For instance, it could be easily implemented on shared memory computers: they are well suited for a global management of resources or to private data exchanges between pairs of processors. In the same way, the distributed memory architectures naturally provide the notion of network and the facilities for the management of many communicating processes. Furthermore, this second model does not lead to any serious limitation concerning the number of processors: this is the reason why (PAC [11, 12] has privileged this alternative) all the implementation part of the paper will rely on a distributed memory model.

5.1 Target Model and Mapping

Our abstract-machine model consists in processes communicating by using a message-passing protocol using `send` and `receive` functions with the appropriate processes identifier (receiver or sender). The processes presented at section 4.4 are gathered together and simultaneously executed on processors. This mapping of the processes on the processors satisfies the two following rules: 1) One *mapping process* is placed on each processor, 2) If a *global (resp. local) resource manager* is placed on a processor, a *local (resp. global) resource manager* is placed on the same processor. These two rules don't lead to any serious limitation, the processes may be combined in many ways and mapped on many topologies. For instance, one may choose to map any number of controllers and workers on a given processor, and may fix any ratio between the numbers of local and global resources, depending on the different costs. The reader will refer to the section 6 for a detailed example of an implementation of the balancer on a 2-dimensional torus topology.

6 Evaluation

The evaluation of the model presented in this paper is currently under progress on a 128-processors computer [14]. Tests will be soon available, concerned with linear algebra problems [13] and lattice basis reduction. For the sake of simplicity the target topology is a 2 dimensioned torus of $P \times Q$ processors which has to be viewed as P horizontal rings and Q vertical rings. One of the P horizontal rings is both the *user network* and the *token network*. Each node of this ring is thus a *controller* and the corresponding vertical ring gives the cluster of his *workers*. Consequently the *mapping processes* may be connected essentially using those vertical rings, and the messages for the *inter-workers network* will be routed using all the torus links except those of the controller ring. Besides its simplicity and its regularity, such a topology allows to easily implement deadlock-free routing algorithms for the three system networks, and the two dimensions offers a lot of different situations for each value of P and Q [13].

7 Conclusion

We have presented a new load-balancing system, well suited to Computer Algebra. An application written with our model of *Remote process activation*, and based at each granularity level on previous developments at lower granularity levels, will automatically execute at its best granularity on any given architecture. This has been made possible simply by considering the tasks complexity as a consistent information, and always by taking into account the machine constants. Besides, this model is general enough in order to to find other applications in other domains.

References

1. G. Bernard, D. Steve, and M. Simatic. Placement et migration de processus dans les systèmes reépartis faiblement couplés. *TSI*, 10 (5):375–392, 1991.
2. D.P. Bertsekas and J.N. Tsitsiklis. *Parallel and distributed computation*. Prentice-Hall, 1989.
3. G. Booch. *Software engineering with Ada*. Benjamin-Cummings Publishing Company, 1983.
4. T. Casavant and J. G. Kuhl. A taxonomy of scheduling in general-purpose distributed computing systems. *IEEE Transactions on Software Engineering*, 14(2):141–154, February 1988.
5. K. Clark and S. Gregory. Parlog: Parallel programming in logic. In J.S. Kowalik, editor, *Parallel Computation and Computers for Artificial Intelligence*, pages 109–130. Kluwer Academic Publishers, 1988.
6. A. Beaumont et al. Flexible Scheduling of OR-Parallelism in Aurora: The Bristol Scheduler. In *PARLE'91*, pages 403–420, Eindhoven, The Netherlands, 1991. Springer-Verlag, LNCS 506.
7. D. Ferrari and S. Zhou. An empirical investigation of load indices for load-balancing applications. In P.J. Courtois and G. Latouche, editors, *PERFORMANCE '87*. Elsevier Science Publishers B.V. (North-Holland), 1988.
8. Ph. Flajolet and J.S. Vitter. Average-case analysis of algorithms and data structures. In J. van Leuwen, editor, *Handbook of Theoretical Computer Science*, pages 431–524. Elsevier, 1990.
9. G. Fox and al. *Solving problems on concurrent processors*. Prentice-Hall, 1988.
10. R.H. Halstead. Parallel computing using multilisp. In J.S. Kowalik, editor, *Parallel Computation and Computers for Artificial Intelligence*, pages 21–49. Kluwer Academic Publishers, 1988.
11. J.L. Roch. The PAC System and its Implementation on Distributed Architectures. In *Computer with Parallel Architectures : T. Node, ed. D. Gassilloud, J.C. Grossetie, Kluwer Ac. Pub.*, 1991.
12. J.L. Roch, F. Siebert, P. Sénéchaud, and G. Villard. Computer Algebra on a MIMD machine. *ISSAC'88, LNCS 358 and in SIGSAM Bulletin, ACM*, 23/11, p.16-32, 1989.
13. F. Siebert and G. Villard. PAC : First experiments on a 128 transputers Meganode. In *International Symposium on Symbolic and Algebraic Computation, Bonn Germany*, 1991.
14. Telmat. TNode Overview. Technical Report Doc-1.02-3.2, Telmat Informatique, 1990.
15. M.C. Wikstrom, J.L. Gustafson, and G.M. Prabhu. A meta-balancer for dynamic load balancers. Technical Report TR91-04, Iowa State University/Ames, Iowa 50011, January 1991.

This article was processed using the LaTeX macro package with LLNCS style

Envelopes in Adaptive Local Queues for MIMD Load Balancing

Konstantin Shteiman   Dror Feitelson[1]

Larry Rudolph   Iaakov Exman

Department of Computer Science
The Hebrew University, 91904 Jerusalem, Israel
E-mail: rudolph@cs.huji.ac.il

Abstract

Envelopes, a run-time mechanism which automatically supports adaptive local queues for MIMD load balancing, are proposed and demonstrated. Envelopes promote generality and language simplicity, while sustaining efficiency.

The local queues, one for each *PE*, contain a get_work task which pulls activities from a global list. In addition, they contain one or more envelopes within which activities are actually performed. These queues are adaptive because each get_work task competes with its own envelopes. The more load the *PE* has, the less additional work it will get. Envelopes are reused for successive activities, thus increasing the granularity. New envelopes are only created to cope with program data and synchronization dependencies, thereby avoiding deadlocks.

Experiments with envelopes performed and efficiency results are reported.

keywords: *envelopes, run-time systems, MIMD, load balancing, granularity, shared memory*

1   Introduction

Dynamic, run time mapping and scheduling of parallel activities to the processors in a multicomputer involves subtle tradeoffs between system overhead, balanced load, and program characteristics. There have been two major approaches. On the one hand, programs can be written to make use of the exact amount of available parallelism; i.e. the parallel machine is exposed and there is only one process per processor (PE); either the programmer or an automatic parallelizer (of some data parallel language) generates such restrictive code (see, e.g., [5]). The other approach gives the programmer freedom to dynamically create as much parallelism as dictated by the problem and the system allocates one process to each parallel activity in the program. A light-weight process mechanism is needed so that the cost of context switching is not prohibitive. We advocate the latter approach and provide support of ultra-light-weight tasks in the run-time system. We contend that efficient support is possible at run time without detailed knowledge about the program.

[1]Current address: IBM T. J. Watson Research Center, P. O. Box 218, Yorktown Heights, NY 10598

This work has been funded in part by the US-Israel BSF Grant No. 88-00045 and the France-Israel BSF Grant No. 3310-2-90

Our goal is to achieve *generality*, with a load-balancing mechanism flexible enough to deal both with fine and coarse-grained activities, without sacrificing *efficiency* by requiring only a minimum of system overhead. We suggest a new mechanism, termed **envelopes**, that adopts to the programs characteristics. Each long-lived, interacting activity, will be allocated to a process that will be managed by the operating system; each short-lived, noninteracting activity will be executed within an existing process. The system will create only as many processes (envelopes) as are really needed.

To make these ideas more concrete and to provide a real implementation, we make use of our locally developed *ParC* language, a superset of the *C* language for parallel programming in a shared memory environment. The main additions to C are two block-oriented parallel constructs: **parblock** and **parfor** both of which indicate that iterations of the loop body or of the constituent blocks can be executed in parallel. Each sub-block or iteration is called an *activity*. The **sync** instruction of *ParC* implements a barrier synchronization among the parallel activities. Each construct can be tagged as light-weight thereby indicating to the compiler that the activities are all independent and can be grouped together at compile time.

In secection 2 we briefly review the basic work distribution mechanism, and then define and discuss envelopes. The implementation and experiments performed are described in section 3. A discussion concludes the paper.

2 Run-Time Task Distribution with Envelopes

It is the job of the scheduler to spread out the activities so they can be executed in parallel on different processors. Here we review the basic mechanism for distributing the activities.

Each time an activity within the user's program reaches a parallel construct, it creates a *spawn descriptor* in the shared memory and then suspends itself (see Fig. 1) The spawn descriptor specifies the number of activities that should be spawned, the code that they should execute, and possibly arguments that should be passed to them. A single global work-pile maintains a set of descriptors.

Each activity is executed within the confines of an *envelope*. An envelope is just a process, however, in order to avoid the overhead of creating and destroying processes, the (envelope) process can be reused to execute many activities (Figure 2). The goal is to have the correct number of envelopes executing.

In addition, local and unique to each PE, is a particular task, referred to as the **get_work** task whose job is to get additional work (activities) from the global workpile of spawn descriptors to be executed by the PE. The **get_work** task on each processor looks at the global workpile and creates a new envelope if it finds activities that have not yet been scheduled. The envelope executes activities in a serial loop, with one activity executed in each iteration. Whenever an activity terminates, the envelope gets a new one.

Only when the there are no more activities does the envelope terminate. Thus if the activities are indeed independent and fine-grained, there is a good chance that one envelope per processor will be needed to execute all the activities.

An envelope is preempted if an activity suspends execution due to its algorithm, or if the envelope executes for longer than a system time quantum. Only if an envelope is preempted, may a new one be created by **get_work**. In effect, the granularity

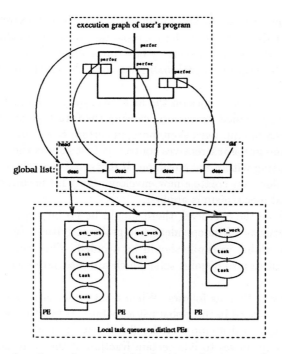

Figure 1: A spawn descriptor is created in the shared memory for each parallel construct. The get_work tasks, which are local to each PE, take descriptors from global workpile. They creat new envelopes representing user's parallel activities and then compete with them for the PE cycles.

```
get_work :  loop forever {
            1. if (global list not empty) create an envelope task
            2. yield processor }


envelope:   while (global list not empty) {
            1. reset timer
            2. execute one activity
            3. if (last in spawn descriptor) report to parent }
            delete the envelope task
```

Figure 2: *High level description of the get_work task and of an envelope. Each processor has one get_work task in its local queue, and it creates additional envelopes as necessary.*

is decreased on-line only when absolutely necessary. In the extreme case, this may degenerate to the naive algorithm where a separate process is created for each activity at the outset. We may create too many envelopes when independent tasks are very long, but then the overhead is still small relative to the total execution time.

Note that the frequency with which the get_work task executes is inversely proportional to the number of envelopes on the local task queue. Thus, it will be scheduled more often on lightly loaded processors, causing them to take more work [4].

Performance can be improved even more, in certain cases. Instead of creating new envelopes each time get_work receives control, it first checks the running time of the last activity executing within the envelope. If it started recently, i.e. not more than a time-quantum, it does not create a new envelope. Only if the running activity started long ago, the usual mechanism is applied.

To further reduce the overhead, there should be no interprocessor interaction involved in the execution of independent fine-grain activities. In particular, possible contention for the global workpile should be avoided. This can be achieved by partitioning the activities into disjoint sets, which are associated with the different processors.

The mechanism is then as follows: When a set of activities should be spawned, a spawn descriptor is placed in the global list as before. When the get_work task on any processor finds a spawn descriptor in the global list, it creates a local *representative* of the descriptor and moves to it a certain fraction of the activities. All local representatives are linked together, creating a local list. Envelopes loop and take activities for execution from the local representatives (and not from the global list of spawn descriptors as before) that avoids redundant locks of the global list.

How to divide the activities between the representatives? Equal division may not be optimal if the activities are not identical. A better approach is to always allocate $1/P$ of the remaining activities. Polychronopoulos and Kuck [3] showed theoretically that independently of the startup time of the P processors that are scheduled under this policy, all processors finish executing a parallel construct within B units of time difference from each other (where B is the execution time of one activity).

3 Measurements on a Testbed

We have implemented envelopes on a MIMD computer, the *Makbilan* research multiprocessor. Makbilan consists of up to 16 processor boards (with Intel 386 processors) in a Multibus-II cage. Memory on remote boards may be accessed through the bus, thus supporting a shared-memory model.

The local kernel on each board is Intel's RMK, which is a real-time kernel designed to use hardware support provided by the 386 and the Multibus II. get_work and envelopes are implemented by RMK tasks.

Each board has a local copy of the run-time library, complete with local data structures. Global data structures in shared memory are used only when activities executing on one board need to influence the execution of other activities on other boards.

The codes we used as examples are given in Table 1 (the code is shorthand that captures the essence of the real code). The statement "delay (1ms)" means that the body of the parallel loop is a function that executes for 1 millisecond. This time interval is much less than the system time-quantum and the parallel activity can be thought as light-weight.

In order to analyze the behavior of envelopes we consider some characteristic program structures.

- *A number of independent parallel activities.* In the basic `get_work` approach a distinct task would be created for each "branch" of the execution graph. With envelopes, all the tasks could be executed by one envelope per *PE*. Thus we economize overhead for task creation and context-switching. There is still overhead for multiple locks of the global queue.

- *Activities depend on one another.* For example they can do barrier synchronization. In this case the envelopes have no effect since a distinct task is to be created for each activity to avoid an infinite wait.

- *Independent groups with internal dependencies.* In this case we have M groups of N activities. In the default version $M * N$ tasks would be created (one for each activity). The envelopes version will involve not many more than $(N + M)$ envelopes (of the order of the number of one group's members!). Since the activity tree is scanned in breadth-first manner, M envelopes will be created first – one for each group; then N envelopes will be created – one for each activity of the leftmost group. When the work is done, the same envelopes will serve the second group etc. Thus the expected improvement is significant.

In the first experiment, 10,000 light-weight activities are spawned. Envelopes are seen to improve performance, but they suffer from contention for the global list. This is solved by using representatives.

The second one is identical, except for using the `lparfor` construct. This construct tells the compiler that the spawned activities are light, and that they should be chunked into P equal chunks, one per processor. Thus the compiler substitutes the user directive to spawn 10,000 activities by a directive to spawn just P activities, and in addition generates code by which these activities each perform $10,000/P$ of the original loop bodies. For the very fine grain activities in the example, this is very efficient; using envelopes doesn't change anything because there is actually only one RMK task on each processor. Note that using the version with representatives in the first experiment leads to the same performance as that of `lparfor` (2.02 ms in both cases). Thus there's no need for this language construct; the run-time system can achieve the same effect automatically.

The third experiment concerns 1000 activities that perform a barrier synchronization, i.e. there are interdependencies among them. In order to do so all of the activities have to be spawned, so the envelopes gain no advantage. In other words, here we are at the other end of the spectrum where the number of the tasks (envelopes) is equal to the number of activities. We have even a small decrease in speed because of additional overhead for locks of the global descriptor list. Using representatives (the third column) improves the situation a little since it avoids the overhead for global locks. However, if there are multiple sets of synchronizing activities, as in the last experiment, envelopes can be reused for different activities.

Due to space limitations, we present only a limited number of experiments. The results of the more detailed experiments, however, almost all fall within the range of the results presented here.

	code	time[s]		
		default	envelopes	representatives
1a	parfor 10000 delay(1 ms);	4.02	3.36	2.02
1b	lparfor 10000 delay(1 ms);	2.02	2.02	2.02
2a	parfor 1,000 sync;	4.95	5.12	5.02
2b	parfor 100 parfor 100 sync;	7.50	2.85	2.50

Table 1: *Experimental results using* envelopes.

4 Discussion

We have proposed and implemented envelopes as a mechanism for run-time load balancing and granularity control on MIMD computers. Envelopes are a transparent instrument to keep simplicity and generality of the parallel programming language. One of the novel aspects of this work is that envelopes deal with dependencies among activities in run-time, and not just independent tasks as most previous work [3, 2]. The experiments performed with typical program structures show that envelopes actually support both coarse and fine-grain activities automatically with high efficiency. In order to minimize overhead, there is no task migration between PE's. We also take advantage of locality, by means of representatives of the descriptors in the global list of work.

References

[1] Y. Ben-Asher, D. G. Feitelson, and L. Rudolph, "*ParC — an extension of C for shared memory parallel processing*". Oct 1990. Manuscript, Dept. Computer Science, The Hebrew University of Jerusalem. Submitted for publication.

[2] E. Mohr, D. A. Kranz, and R. H. Halstead, Jr., "*Lazy task creation: a technique for increasing the granularity of parallel programs*". *IEEE Trans. Parallel & Distributed Syst.* 2(3), pp. 264–280, Jul 1991.

[3] C. D. Polychronopoulos and D. J. Kuck, "*Guided self scheduling: a practical scheduling scheme for parallel supercomputers*". *IEEE Trans. Comput.* C-36(12), pp. 1425–1439, Dec 1987.

[4] L. Rudolph, M. Slivkin-Allalouf, and E. Upfal, "*A simple load balancing scheme for task allocation in parallel machines*". In 3rd *Symp. Parallel Algorithms & Architectures*, pp. 237–245, Jul 1991.

[5] V. Sarkar, *Partitioning and Scheduling Parallel Programs for Multiprocessors*. MIT Press, 1989.

Dynamo – A Portable Tool for Dynamic Load Balancing on Distributed Memory Multicomputers

Erik Tärnvik

Institute of Information Processing, Department of Computing Science,
University of Umeå, S–901 87 Umeå, Sweden, Email: erikt@cs.umu.se

Abstract. Dynamic load balancing is an important technique when developing applications with unpredictable load distribution on distributed memory multicomputers. A tool, *Dynamo*, that can be used to utilize dynamic load balancing is presented. This tool separates the application from the load balancer and thus makes it possible to easily exchange the load balancer of a given application and experiment with different load balancing strategies.

1 Introduction

The distribution of workload is a basic and important aspect to consider when developing programs on parallel computers. The present paper describes a portable tool that can be used to utilize dynamic load balancing on distributed memory multicomputers (*DMM*).

There exists problems where the distribution of workload in a *DMM* can not be predicted. In such cases, the workload should be balanced at run-time. This is known as the *dynamic load balancing* problem. In the general case, the optimal solution to this problem is known to be NP-complete [2]. However, heuristic methods can be used to implement suboptimal dynamic load balancing strategies.

Problem areas known to exhibit computational characteristics that benefit from dynamic load balancing includes searching problems, e.g. branch-and-bound algorithms [6] used to solve different optimization problem, such as combinatorial optimization or global optimization [1], and problems solved by Monte Carlo type algorithms [4], e.g. particle dynamics.

Section 2 discusses the design of the Dynamo tool and the programming interfaces. In Sect. 3 an example application using Dynamo is presented. Finally, in Sect. 4 we draw some conclusions and give an outline of future work.

2 Dynamo

The Dynamo tool relies heavily on the idea that the application should be separated from the load balancing operations. This functionality separation is necessary if the load balancing mechanism is to be handled by a distributed operating system on future parallel systems. Dynamo addresses the following issues:

- The easy exchange of load balancers allows for testing of load balancing strategies on different types of applications without changes to the load balancer.

- A library of load balancers can be built from which the developer can choose and experiment with different load balancers for a given application in order to achieve maximum performance.
- An application can be ported to different target architectures provided that the tool is available on the target environment.
- Dynamo can be ported. In it's present implementation, Dynamo is written in C and built on the PICL (Portable Instrumented Communication Library) communication library of Oak Ridge National Laboratory [3].
- Dynamo provides tracing facilities which supports performance evaluation and debugging tools, e. g. visualization and execution playback using Paragraph [5].

Dynamo is not intended to be responsible for the actual load balancing of application programs. Dynamo provides a framework for the development of load balancers. A prototype of Dynamo has been implemented for the Intel iPSC/2 *DMM* system.

2.1 Tasks

The smallest executable part of a Dynamo program is the *task*. A task is a part of the solution to a problem, and partitioning a large problem into tasks is the programmers responsibility.

A Dynamo task is defined by its *dataset*, which is the data associated with the task. The operations on the datasets are not a part of the task, but must be present on each processor in order to support the execution of a task on all processors. The task dataset in itself might be anything the application decides it to be. The only requirement is that at the time of spawning of a task, the dataset occupies a contiguous portion of memory. If this is not the natural way to store a task dataset, the dataset has to be packed and unpacked by the application before communicating with Dynamo. There are two reasons for this requirement:

1. In order to support datasets occupying non-contiguous memory, a set of location attributes (or some similar scheme) would be necessary.
2. If noncontiguous datasets were supported, they would have to be packed into contiguous memory before communication anyhow, in order to minimize communication overhead.

In addition to its dataset, a task has a number of attributes. The *type* attribute is used to distinguish different task types from each other. The *origin* attribute is automatically assigned by Dynamo when a task is created and identifies the processor on which the task was originally created. The *location* attribute is a pointer to the task's dataset. This is used by the application and the load balancer to access the dataset. The *size* attribute holds the size of the dataset referred to by the location attribute. The combination of location and size gives Dynamo enough knowledge to handle task datasets. The *priority* attribute is an estimate of how important a certain task is to the solution of a problem. Some load balancer use a priority queue, based on this attribute, for task management. For other applications, the notion of priority might not be applicable. *Cost* gives an estimate of the processor resources needed to execute the task. The cost attribute is only relative to the other tasks present in the system. This attribute may be used by some load balancers to improve the balancing of the workload in the system.

2.2 Dynamo Programming

A Dynamo system consists of a number of processors, each having a local memory and the capability to communicate with at least one neighbor. Initially, the problem to solve consists of a number of tasks (see Sect. 2.1) distributed on the processors. Each processor is capable of executing any task in the system, and each task may generate new tasks when executed.

Dynamo consists of two parts, the application interface (DAI) and the balancer interface (DBI). There is also a set of utility functions, mainly concerned with task handling, available in both interfaces. Each interface is independent of the other, meaning that the application can make no assumptions on how the load balancer is performing it's responsibilities, and vice versa.

In a Dynamo application, each node of the parallel system holds a copy of the application code and the load balancer. The load balancer is responsible for the management of the local task queue and makes decisions on task redistributions. The load balancer also handles requests for work both from the local application and from remote processors. The local application code is responsible for notifying the load balancer of new tasks that arise during the execution of the local application.

The DAI is the primary tool in developing load balanced applications using Dynamo. The application can be developed without specific reference to load balancing operations. Table 1 summarizes the functions available to the programmer.

Dynamo features a built-in distributed termination algorithm. The termination function *dai_Terminated* triggers this algorithm by first checking with the load balancer (see Sect. 2.3) if it is ready to terminate. The termination algorithm is a modified version of an algorithm described by Eriksson [1].

2.3 The Load Balancer

The load balancer interface is a collection of functions that supports the load balancer in task queue management and interprocessor communications, both of which are handled by Dynamo (see Table 1).

In addition to tasks, Dynamo provides two datatypes, *requests* and *load*, which support requests for work and the exchange of load information, respectively.

Since the order in which tasks are handled may have a strong influence on the execution profile of a program regardless of load balancing strategy, the decision on how to queue tasks in the local load balancer is determined by the application, not by the load balancer. DYNAMO provides queue types that store tasks in stacks, regular queues, priority queues based on the *priority* and *cost* attributes, and user definable priority queues.

The load balancer is implemented by one function. Program 1 is an example of a simple load balancer which sends every fifth task to a randomly chosen processor.

The load balancer function is called by Dynamo when a task is locally or remotely spawned or requested, and whenever load information arrives. The message parameter (*msg*) indicates the reason for the present call of the balancer.

The *DYN_INIT* message is used when *dai_Init* is called. This call should be used to perform initialization of task queues etc. *DYN_LOCALREQUEST* is used if the local application requests a task. If possible, the load balancer should return

Table 1. Partial summary of application and load balancing programming interfaces

Function	Description
dai_Init(balancer, maxsize, storage)	Initializes Dynamo and specifies which load balancer to use. *Maxsize* is maximum task size, *storage* indicates task storage method.
dai_MakeTask(type, loc, size, priority, cost)	Used to create a task.
dai_KillTask(task, dealloc)	Removes a task from memory.
dai_Request()	Request a task from Dynamo. Returns NULL if the call is unsuccessful.
dai_Spawn(task)	Adds a task for Dynamo to administrate.
dai_Terminated()	Returns a truth value indicating if the system has terminated. This function triggers a distributed termination algorithm, and may be called repeatedly until it returns *TRUE*.
dbi_InitQueue(type)	Creates a queue.
dbi_Add(queue, task)	Adds a task to a queue.
dbi_PopFirst(queue)	Removes a task from a queue and returns it.
dbi_IsEmpty(queue)	Checks if a queue is empty.
dbi_SendTask(task, proc)	Sends a task to processor *proc*.
dbi_MakeLoad(qLen, loadL, loadD)	Creates a load information storage cell.
dbi_KillLoad(load)	Releases the memory used by load.
dbi_SendLoad(load, proc)	Sends load information to *proc*.
dbi_MakeRequest(value)	Creates a request for work.
dbi_KillRequest(request)	Releases memory used by a request.
dbi_SendRequest(request, proc)	Sends a request to another processor.

an appropriate task. If the load balancer is out of tasks, a *NULL* value should be returned to the application. The *DYN_SPAWN* message indicates a local spawning of a task. *DYN_RECEIVED* signals the arrival of a task from another processor. The *DYN_REQUEST* message is generated when a request is received from another processor. If the request is accepted, the load balancer may send one or more tasks to the requesting processor. *DYN_LOAD* indicates the arrival of load information from another processor. The *DYN_TERMINATE* message indicates that the local application is executing the termination procedure and wants to know if the load balancer is ready to terminate. Normally, this will be the case if the load balancer is out of local tasks. The load balancer should return a truth value indicating if this is the case.

3 An Example Application

An example application using Dynamo has been developed. The application uses a branch-and-bound (B&B) algorithm [6] to solve a 0–1 knapsack problem: Given a set $A = \{a_1, a_2, \ldots, a_n\}$ of objects, each having an integer profit p_i and an integer weight w_i, find $x_i \in \{0, 1\}$ so that the sum $\sum_{i=1}^{n} x_i p_i$ is maximized under the constraint $\sum_{i=1}^{n} x_i w_i \leq c$ where c is referred to as the capacity.

This is a well studied NP-complete [2] combinatorial optimization problem were several algorithms, both sequential and parallel, using different approaches have been

```
int SimpleScheduler(msg, pointer)
int msg; char *pointer;
{       static Queue tq; static int send = 1;
        switch (msg) {
        case DYN_INIT:
                tq = dbi_InitQueue(pointer, NULL);
                return 0;
        case DYN_LOCALREQUEST:
                return dbi_PopFirst(tq);
        case DYN_SPAWN:                                             10
                if (!(send++ % 5) && nprocs > 1) {
                        dbi_SendTask(pointer, dbi_RandomNode(me, nprocs));
                        dai_KillTask(pointer, TRUE);
                        return 0;
                } /* Fall through to next case */
        case DYN_RECEIVED:
                dbi_Add(tq, pointer);
                return 0;
        case DYN_TERMINATE:
                return dbi_IsEmpty(tq);                             20
        ...
        }
}
```

Program 1 Portion of a simple load balancer function

published [8, 9]. We have used a parallelized version of an B&B algorithm by Martello and Toth [9]. Table 2 presents results using a customized task storage method and a receiver initiated load balancing strategy [10, 11]. Note that superlinear speedup is not uncommon for this type of algorithm [7]. Larger problems are needed to obtain higher efficiency on large number of processors. Dynamo has been used to experiment with different load balancing strategies. An experimental version of an extension to Paragraph has been used to evaluate the load balancing strategies.

Table 2. 0–1 Knapsack problem on iPSC/2. $n = 300$, $c = 140000$, $\overline{w_i} = 2000$.

Processors	time (s)	Nodes examined	Efficiency (%)
1	22.08	24758	100
2	10.55	29962	105
4	5.26	29891	105
8	3.06	30507	90
16	2.13	33983	65
32	1.67	42571	41
64	1.39	62678	25

4   Conclusions and Future work

A tool for the utilization of dynamic load balancing which separates the load balancing operations from the application has been developed and a prototype has been implemented and tested on a iPSC/2 hypercube system. An example application has been implemented and the results indicate that it is possible to successfully separate the load balancing operations from the application.

There are several possible directions for future research. The implementation of several different applications and load balancers is necessary in order to gain additional experience on the general applicability of the Dynamo tool. One important aspect to investigate is scalability of load balancers.

We also have an interest in extending Dynamo in order to handle problems where data locality is essential if maximum efficiency is to be reached. The possibilities for visualized performance monitoring will be further investigated.

Acknowledgements

The author would like to thank Prof. Bo Kågström and Peter Jacobson for valuable comments on the manuscript. Financial support has been received from the Swedish Board of Technical Development (STU) under contract STU-89-02578P.

References

1. J. Eriksson. Parallel global optimization using interval analysis. Technical Report UMINF-91.17, Inst. of Information Proc., University of Umeå, S-901 87 UMEÅ, 1991.
2. M. R. Garey and D. S. Johnson. *Computers and Intractability: A guide to the theory of NP-Completeness*. Freeman New York, 1979.
3. G. A. Geist, M. T. Heath, B. E. Peyton, and P. H. Worley. *PICL - A Portable Instrumented Communication Library*. Oak Ridge Nat. Lab., Oak Ridge, TN 37831, 1990.
4. R. V. Hanxleden and L. R. Scott. Load balancing on message passing architectures. *Journal of Parallel and Distributed Computing*, 13:312–324, 1991.
5. M. T. Heath and J. A. Etheridge. Visualizing performance of parallel programs. Technical Report ORNL/TM-11813, Oak Ridge Nat. Lab., Oak Ridge, TN, May 1991.
6. J. M. Jansen and F. W. Sijstermans. Parallel branch-and-bound. *Future Generation Computer Systems*, 4:271–279, 1989.
7. T-H. Lai and S. Sahni. Anomalies in parallel branch-and-bound algortithms. *Comm. ACM*, 27:594–602.
8. J. Lin and J. A. Storer. Processor-efficient hypercube algorithms for the knapsack problem. *Journal of Parallel and Distributed Computing*, 11:332–337, 1991.
9. S. Martello and P. Toth. *Knapsack Problems: Algorithms and computer implementations*. John Wiley & Sons, 1990.
10. E. Tärnvik. A parallel branch-and-bound algorithm for the 0–1 knapsack problem. (in preparation), University of Umeå, 1992.
11. Erik Tärnvik. Dynamo – a portable dynamic load balancing tool. Technical report, University of Umeå, 1992.

Semantics and compilation of the data-parallel switch statement

Jean-Luc Levaire *

LIP, ENS Lyon,
46 Allée d'Italie,
F-69364 Lyon Cedex 07, France.
Electronic Mail: jllevair@lip.ens-lyon.fr

Abstract. We study the semantics and the compilation of the data-parallel extension of the C switch statement, as found in the MPL and POMPC data-parallel extensions of C. We first present a small language which embodies the main concepts of the data-parallel programming model, together with its formal operational semantics. We give an implementation of the parallel switch statement in this language. Then, we describe an optimized compilation method used in the POMPC compiler, and give a formal correctness proof for this optimization. The case of the MPL compiler is then discussed.

1 Introduction

Many parallel computers are currently available, such as the Connection Machine, the Maspar MP-1 [1], the Wavetracer Series and the POMP (Petit Ordinateur Massivement Parallèle) machine now under development [7]. These machines correspond to a common execution model, the SIMD (Single Instruction Multiple Data) model, which can be characterized as follows [11]. We consider a set of processors, each managing a private memory. The processors are controlled by a unique external sequencer, which broadcasts the common instruction to be executed. Thus, all processors do the same instruction, but on their own data. An inhibition mechanism, called the *context*, is associated to each processor. A processor context may be either *active* or *idle*. A processor modifies its local memory only if its context is in the *active* state. This facility is essential to implement parallel conditioning branch. Finally, a global bus links the set of processors to the sequencer, and computes the *global or* of the elements of a boolean vector, componentwisely distributed on the processors. This feature enables the sequencer to detect the termination of loops.

Various programming languages for these machines have been proposed, often derived from existing sequential languages. A number of them are extensions of the C language: C* [5] for the Connection Machine, MPL [8] for the Maspar MP-1 , Multi-C [12] for the Wavetracer Series, and POMPC [9] for the POMP machine. All these languages implement the data-parallel programming model. Among them, MPL and POMPC propose a wide range of parallel control structures. They extend the three classical loop statements while, for and do to parallel control structures,

---

* This work has been supported by the French CNRS Coordinated Research Program on Parallelism C^3 and the French Department of Defense DRET contract N° 91/1180.

with their associated statements **break** and **continue**. Both of them also provide a parallel extension of the **switch** statement, called **switchwhere** in POMPC and **switch** in MPL.

In this paper, we study the compilation technique used by the POMPC compiler to implement the **switchwhere** statement. We first give the definition and the semantics of a small data-parallel language called $\mathcal{L}$. It can be seen as an "assembly" language as it is very close to the SIMD execution model. We also define an higher-level "intermediate" language $\mathcal{L}'$, and its compilation into $\mathcal{L}$. We define the **switchwhere** construction in $\mathcal{L}'$, and give the $\mathcal{L}$ program resulting from its compilation. Then, we present the optimized compilation method used in the POMPC compiler. This optimization is made at the level of the $\mathcal{L}$ language, and we formally prove that the primitive $\mathcal{L}$ program and its optimized version are equivalent. This demonstrates the correctness of the implementation of the **switchwhere** construction in the POMPC compiler. In the last part, we extend this study to the implementation of the data-parallel **switch** statement proposed by the MPL compiler.

2 Implementation of data-parallel languages

2.1 A simple data-parallel language and its semantics

Bougé and Garda proposed in [3] a small data-parallel language called $\mathcal{L}$. It has been designed to be as simple as possible, and yet expressive enough to serve as a representative framework for semantic studies. The $\mathcal{L}$ language includes five constructions: assignation, communication, sequencing, iteration and conditioning. A Structured Operational Semantics [10] for $\mathcal{L}$ consists in defining a transition system. For each construction of the language, we give a set of rules or axioms which describe the possible transitions of an idealized SIMD machine. The states $\langle P, \sigma, ct \rangle$ of the transition system, are made of the remaining program P to be executed, the environment σ which binds identifiers X to vectorial values $\sigma(X)$, and a stack ct of contexts. Contexts are boolean vectors which handle the processor activity. A processor is *active* if and only if its corresponding element in the context has the *true* value tt. A stack is useful here to implement nested conditional structures.

In the following, $X, Y \ldots$ denotes parallel variables (also called vectors), and u, $v \ldots$ denotes processor locations. $X|_u$ is the element of X located on the processor whose address is u. All expressions in $\mathcal{L}$ are *local*: the value of an expression on a processor depends only on the values of variables located on this processor. The evaluation of the expression E in the environment σ will be denoted $[\![E]\!](\sigma)$. $\bullet$ is the terminated program and ϵ the empty stack. By convention $Pop(\epsilon) = \epsilon$ and $Top(\epsilon) = Tt$, the true boolean vector. Finally, we define the *active* and the *globalor* predicates as follows

$$active(u) \equiv (Top(ct)|_u = tt)$$
$$globalor(B, \sigma) \equiv \exists u\, ([\![B]\!](\sigma)|_u \wedge active(u))$$

where B is a boolean vectorial expression.

Assignment The instruction $X := E$ stores into variable X the value of the local expression E. An idle processor leaves its local memory unchanged.

$$\langle X := E, \sigma, ct \rangle \longrightarrow \langle \bullet, \sigma', ct \rangle$$

with
> $\sigma'(X)|_u = [\![E]\!](\sigma)|_u$ if $active(u)$;
> $\sigma'(T)|_u = \sigma(T)|_u$ if $T \neq X$ or $\neg\, active(u)$.

Communication On each *active* processor P_u, the instruction **get** X **from** A stores into $X|_u$ the old value of X located on the processor whose adress is $[\![A]\!](\sigma)|_u$.

$$\langle \text{get } X \text{ from } A, \sigma, ct \rangle \longrightarrow \langle \bullet, \sigma', ct \rangle$$

with
> $\sigma'(X)|_u = \sigma(X)|_{\sigma(A)|_u}$ if $active(u)$;
> $\sigma'(T)|_u = \sigma(T)|_u$ if $T \neq X$ or $\neg\, active(u)$.

Sequencing The construction $P; Q$ executes P then Q.

$$\frac{\langle P, \sigma, ct \rangle \longrightarrow \langle P', \sigma', ct' \rangle \quad P' \neq \bullet}{\langle P; Q, \sigma, ct \rangle \longrightarrow \langle P'; Q, \sigma', ct' \rangle} \qquad \frac{\langle P, \sigma, ct \rangle \longrightarrow \langle \bullet, \sigma', ct' \rangle}{\langle P; Q, \sigma, ct \rangle \longrightarrow \langle Q, \sigma', ct' \rangle}$$

Iteration The construction **while** B **do** P **end** iterates program P up to a point where the boolean expression B evaluates to false at each *active* processor. Notice that this construction does not modify the context stack.

$$\frac{globalor(B, \sigma)}{\langle \text{while } B \text{ do } P \text{ end}, \sigma, ct \rangle \longrightarrow \langle P; \text{while } B \text{ do } P \text{ end}, \sigma, ct \rangle}$$

$$\frac{\neg\, globalor(B, \sigma)}{\langle \text{while } B \text{ do } P \text{ end}, \sigma, ct \rangle \longrightarrow \langle \bullet, \sigma, ct \rangle}$$

Conditioning The construction **where** B **do** P **end** inhibits, during the execution of program P, those active processors whose boolean expression B evaluates locally to false. The new activity vector corresponds to the boolean vector $Top(ct) \wedge [\![B]\!](\sigma)$. It is pushed upon the context stack. To keep track of the conditioned blocks, we introduce the new syntactic construction **begin** P **end**.

$$\langle \text{where } B \text{ do } P \text{ end}, \sigma, ct \rangle \longrightarrow \langle \text{begin } P \text{ end}, \sigma, ct' \rangle$$

with $ct' = Push(Top(ct) \wedge [\![B]\!](\sigma), ct)$. The two following rules express that P is executed up to its termination, and, at that time, the former activity is restored by popping the context stack.

$$\frac{\langle P, \sigma, ct \rangle \longrightarrow \langle P', \sigma', ct' \rangle}{\langle \text{begin } P \text{ end}, \sigma, ct \rangle \longrightarrow \langle \text{begin } P' \text{ end}, \sigma', ct' \rangle}$$

$$\langle \text{begin } \bullet \text{ end}, \sigma, ct \rangle \longrightarrow \langle \bullet, \sigma, Pop(ct) \rangle$$

2.2 Handling control transfer instructions: multitype conditioning

We extend in [4] the $\mathcal{L}$ language in order to handle parallel control transfer statements, such as **break** and **continue** in MPL or POMPC. These statements can be considered as jumps to the end of blocks. In the $\mathcal{L}$ language, the **where** construction implements such jumps but in an implicit manner. On entering a **where** block, active processors which do not satisfy the conditional expression directly jump to the end of the block. We generalize this mechanism by introducing an *explicit* "jump to the end of the current block" instruction, called **escape**. On executing it, all active processors become idle up to the termination of the enclosing **where** block. This effect can be easily obtained by anding the top of the stack ct with the negation of the current activity vector.

Nevertheless, this extension is still too poor to express *both* the **break** and the **continue** statements. The first one is a jump to the end of the loop body, the second one is a jump to the end of the current loop. We need to distinguish various types of conditioning blocks, each of them equipped with its own **escape** instruction. Let $\mathcal{L}'$ be the $\mathcal{L}$ language with N conditioning constructions **where**$_i$, $1 \leq i \leq N$, and N respective instructions **escape**$_i$, instead of the original **where** statement. We now consider, in place of a context stack ct, a set (ct_i) of context stacks. Each stack ct_i is associated with the corresponding type of conditioning. It handles the processor activity with respect to this type. Thus, the new activity of processor P_u located at u will be the conjunction of its activities relative to each type. We redefine the *active* predicate as follows

$$active(u) \equiv \bigwedge_i (Top(ct_i)|_u = tt).$$

The semantics of $\mathcal{L}'$ for assignment, communication, sequencing and iteration is the same as for $\mathcal{L}$, substituting (ct_i) for ct. The semantics of multitype conditioning is directly derived from the semantics of conditioning in $\mathcal{L}$. We introduce labeled **begin**$_k$ P **end** constructions to keep track of the conditioned blocks and of their types.

$$\langle \text{where}_k \ B \ \text{do} \ P \ \text{end}, \sigma, (ct_i) \rangle \longrightarrow \langle \text{begin}_k \ P \ \text{end}, \sigma, (ct_i') \rangle$$

with $ct_k' = Push(Top(ct_k) \wedge [\![B]\!](\sigma), ct_k)$ and $ct_i' = ct_i$ for $i \neq k$.
Body P is then normally executed within the block (see the corresponding rule in the semantics of $\mathcal{L}$). On exiting it, stack ct_k is popped.

$$\langle \text{begin}_k \bullet \text{end}, \sigma, (ct_i) \rangle \longrightarrow \langle \bullet, \sigma, (ct_i') \rangle$$

with $ct_k' = Pop(ct_k)$ and $ct_i' = ct_i$ for $i \neq k$.

The **escape**$_k$ instruction masks the top of the stack ct_k with the negation of the current activity. Active processors become thus idle with respect to the enclosing type k block. It has no effect on idle processors.

$$\langle \text{escape}_k, \sigma, (ct_i) \rangle \longrightarrow \langle \bullet, \sigma, (ct_i') \rangle$$

with $ct_k' = Push(\neg(\bigwedge_i Top(ct_i)) \wedge Top(ct_k), Pop(ct_k))$ and $ct_i' = ct_i$ for $i \neq k$.

Notice that escaping out of the scope of a block results in becoming idle up to the end of the program. This corresponds to the data-parallel extension of the **exit** instruction of the C language.

Let us illustrate the multitype conditioning mechanism by expressing some POMPC control structures in $\mathcal{L}'$. The **where**, **whilesomewhere**, **forwhere** and **dowhere** constructions of the POMPC language are the respective parallel extensions of the **if**, **while**, **for** and **do** statements of C. The semantics of the **where** is the same as in $\mathcal{L}$. The semantics of the loops is the following. At *each* iteration, all active processors evaluate the loop condition. The loop terminates if all of them evaluate it to false. Otherwise, active processors such that this condition is false become idle up to the end of the *iteration*. On executing a **continue** statement, the *currently* active processors become idle up to the end of the iteration. On executing a **break** statement, they become idle up to the end of the loop. We express these constructions in $\mathcal{L}'$ with three types of conditioning blocks. Type 1 corresponds to the usual **where** structure. Type 2 and type 3 are respectively used to handle the **continue** and the **break** statements: the effect of **continue** is achieved by the **escape**$_2$ statement, and that of **break** by the **escape**$_3$ one. The expression in $\mathcal{L}'$ of the POMPC control structures is given in Fig. 1.

whilesomewhere (*cond*) {P}	dowhere (*cond*) {P}	forwhere (*start, cond, incr*) {P}
where$_3$ true do while *cond* do where$_1$ *cond* do where$_2$ true do *P* end end end end	where$_3$ true do where$_2$ true do *P* end; while *cond* do where$_1$ *cond* do where$_2$ true do *P* end end end end	*start*; where$_3$ true do while *cond* do where$_1$ *cond* do where$_2$ true do *P* end; *incr* end end end

Fig. 1. Expression of the POMPC parallel control structures in $\mathcal{L}'$.

2.3   Implementing multitype conditioning

Multitype conditioning can be implemented in $\mathcal{L}$ with counters. The idea of the implementation is the following. A (vectorial) stack ct_i can be seen as a set of boolean substacks $ct_i|_u$. The rules of the semantics of $\mathcal{L}'$ imply that an idle processor remains idle at least up to the end of the enclosing block. This actually means that a tt value is never pushed upon a $f\!f$ value in the substacks $ct_i|_u$. As $Top(\epsilon) = Tt$, we can also consider that a stack $ct_i|_u$ has an infinite number of tt at its bottom. Consequently, the only required information concerning a stack $ct_i|_u$ consists in the numbers of $f\!f$ located at its top, that is a single positive number. A vectorial stack ct_i can thus be viewed as a vector Cnt_i of counters.

This allows to define an implementation function ϕ which maps a program P of $\mathcal{L}'$ to a program $\phi(P)$ of $\mathcal{L}$. We consider N *new* variables Cnt_i to be used as counters.

We manage them so that, at each point of the computation of $\phi(P)$, $Cnt_i|_u$ is exactly the number of $f\!fs$ at the top of substack $ct_i|_u$. Hence, the processor located at u is active in P if and only if $\bigwedge_i (Cnt_i|_u = 0)$. Function ϕ is defined in Fig. 2.

$$\phi(X := E) = \text{where } (\textstyle\bigwedge_i Cnt_i = 0) \text{ do } X := E \text{ end}$$

$$\phi(\text{get } X \text{ from } A) = \text{where } (\textstyle\bigwedge_i Cnt_i = 0) \text{ do get } X \text{ from } A \text{ end}$$

$$\phi(P;Q) = \phi(P); \phi(Q)$$

$$\phi(\text{while } B \text{ do } P \text{ end}) = \text{while } ((\textstyle\bigwedge_i Cnt_i = 0) \wedge B) \text{ do } \phi(P) \text{ end}$$

$$\phi(\text{where}_k \ B \text{ do } P \text{ end}) = \text{where } \neg(Cnt_k = 0 \wedge B) \text{ do } Cnt_k := Cnt_k + 1 \text{ end};$$
$$\phi(P);$$
$$\text{where } (Cnt_k > 0) \text{ do } Cnt_k := Cnt_k - 1 \text{ end}$$

$$\phi(\text{escape}_k) = \text{where } (\textstyle\bigwedge_i Cnt_i = 0) \text{ do } Cnt_k := 1 \text{ end}$$

Fig. 2. Implementation of multitype conditioning: the function ϕ.

We refer the interested reader to [4] for a formal correctness proof of this implementation: in a certain sense, P and $\phi(P)$ compute the same function. In this definition, $\phi(P)$ never appears inside a **where** block. This implies that the set $\phi(\mathcal{L}')$ (image of $\mathcal{L}'$ programs by ϕ) is included in the class of $\mathcal{L}$ programs where no nested conditioning appears. The processor activity in such programs can be handled by a single bit per processor, rather than a boolean stack. This demonstrates that high level data-parallel languages can be efficiently implemented by means of counters on machines with a single activity bit.

3 Compiling the data-parallel switch construction

3.1 Expressing the POMPC switchwhere control structure with multitype conditioning

The POMPC **switchwhere** construction is the parallel extension of the **switch** construction of the C language. It supports the **break** statement, and its syntax is the familiar one (see Fig. 3). E denotes a vectorial expression, c_i are *distinct* scalar constants, and P_i are programs. We will assume that E is a local expression. Observe that MPL and POMPC require that no **cases** clauses appear after the **default**. The semantics of this construction can be described as follows. Let Aux be the value of E on entering the **switchwhere** block. An *active* processor P_u will execute program $P_j; P_{j+1}; \ldots; P_n; P_{n+1}$ if there exists j so that $Aux|_u = c_j$. (Observe that such a j is unique since constants c_i are distinct.) Otherwise, that is if $\bigwedge_i (Aux|_u \neq c_i)$, P_u will execute program P_{n+1}. Finally, on executing a **break** statement within a

switchwhere block, each *currently* active processor becomes idle up to the end of the block.

The sequential **switch** statement is usually viewed as a conditional jump. Its data-parallel extension can also be viewed as a jump, with a different jump label for each processor. But in the SIMD execution model, the control flow is unique. Consequently, the **switchwhere** statement is implemented by executing the sequence of programs $P_1; \ldots; P_{n+1}$, and the effect of the jump is achieved by setting the activity of each processor according to its jump label. If processor P_u has to execute $P_j; \ldots; P_{n+1}$, then its context is set to idle during the execution of each P_i for $1 \leq i < j$, and then set to active during the execution of each P_i for $j \leq i \leq n+1$.

Let us express the **switchwhere** statement in terms of where_k structures in $\mathcal{L}'$. We use a new auxiliary variable Aux, not used elsewhere, to hold the value of E at the beginning of the **switchwhere**. A where_1 block is associated to each **case** clause and contains the corresponding program. The block condition expresses that the value of Aux is equal to the current **case** clause constant or to the one of the preceding clauses. Thus, processor P_u is active during the execution of program P_j if and only if $\bigvee_{i \leq j}(Aux|_u = c_i)$. The condition associated to the **default** clause is simply the value true so that every processor active before the **switchwhere** will execute program P_{n+1}. Actually there is no need to associate a where_1 block to this clause. We only keep it in order to simplify the optimization correctness proof. As for the loop structures, we encapsulate this sequence of where_1 blocks with a type 3 conditioning block to handle the **break** statements. The effect of **break** is thus achieved by an escape_3 statement in programs P_i. Finally, the scalar constants c_i are promoted to parallel constants C_i. The program is presented in Fig. 3.

switchwhere $(E)\{$	where_3 (true) do
	$Aux := E;$
case $c_1 : P_1;$	where_1 $(Aux = C_1)$ do P_1 end;
$\vdots$	$\vdots$
case $c_k : P_k;$	where_1 $(Aux = C_1 \vee \ldots \vee Aux = C_k)$ do
	P_k
	end;
$\vdots$	$\vdots$
$default : P_{n+1};$	where_1 (true) do
	P_{n+1}
	end;
$\}$	end

Fig. 3. Expressing the **switchwhere** in $\mathcal{L}'$.

As described in the previous section, function ϕ implements in $\mathcal{L}$ the multitype conditioning of $\mathcal{L}'$ (see Fig. 2). We can thus apply directly this function to this program. The resulting program in $\mathcal{L}$, called *Dir*, is given in Fig. 4, in correspondence with the initial POMPC construction.

Original program	Direct implementation in $\mathcal{L}$ via ϕ: the Dir program	
switchwhere $(E)\{$	where $\neg(Cnt_3 = 0)$ do $Cnt_3 = Cnt_3 + 1$ end; where $(\bigwedge_i Cnt_i = 0)$ do $Aux := E$ end;	$\Big\} Dir_0$
case c_1 :	where $\neg(Cnt_1 = 0 \wedge Aux = C_1)$ do $Cnt_1 := Cnt_1 + 1$ end;	
$P_1;$	$\phi(P_1);$	
$\vdots$	$\vdots$	
$P_k;$	$\phi(P_k);$ where $(Cnt_1 > 0)$ do $Cnt_1 := Cnt_1 - 1$ end;	
case C_{k+1} :	where $\neg(Cnt_1 = 0 \wedge (Aux = C_1 \vee \ldots \vee Aux = C_{k+1}))$ do $\quad Cnt_1 := Cnt_1 + 1$ end;	$\Big\} Dir_k$
$P_{k+1};$	$\phi(P_{k+1});$	
$\vdots$	$\vdots$	
$P_n;$	$\phi(P_n);$ where $(Cnt_1 > 0)$ do $Cnt_1 := Cnt_1 - 1$ end;	
default:	where $\neg(Cnt_1 = 0 \wedge (\text{true}))$ do $\quad Cnt_1 := Cnt_1 + 1$ end;	$\Big\} Dir_n$
P_{n+1}	$\phi(P_{n+1});$ where $(Cnt_1 > 0)$ do $Cnt_1 := Cnt_1 - 1$ end;	
$\}$	where $(Cnt_3 > 0)$ do $Cnt_3 := Cnt_3 - 1$ end;	$\Big\} Dir_{n+1}$

Fig. 4. The Dir program.

3.2 The POMPC compiler optimization

The POMPC compiler implements an optimized compilation of the switchwhere statement. In the Dir program, the condition associated to a where$_1$ block implies that of the next blocks. If a processor becomes active (with respect to conditioning type 1) at the beginning of $\phi(P_i)$, then it will also be active (wrt type 1) at the beginning of $\phi(P_{i+1}), \cdots, \phi(P_{n+1})$. Conversely, if a processor is idle (wrt type 1) at the beginning of $\phi(P_i)$, then it has remained idle (wrt type 1) during $\phi(P_1), \cdots, \phi(P_{i-1})$. Finally, a processor idle (wrt type 1) before the switchwhere remains idle during all the $\phi(P_i)$ executions.

The manipulation of the Cnt_1 counter can thus be described as follows. At the beginning of the switchwhere, Cnt_1 is incremented on every processor. So, currently idle processors have their Cnt_1 value greater or equal than 2. Then, between $\phi(P_i)$ and $\phi(P_{i+1})$ programs, we have three cases for a processor P_u.

▷ $Cnt_1|_u = 1$ and $Aux|_u = c_{i+1}$: Processor P_u satisfies the current clause, but did not satisfy the preceding ones. Moreover it was active (wrt type 1) before the switchwhere statement. It is turned active by setting its $Cnt_1|_u$ value to 0.

▷ $Cnt_1|_u = 1$ and $Aux|_u \neq c_{i+1}$: Processor P_u does satisfy neither the current clause nor the preceding ones. However, it was active before the switchwhere.

$Cnt_1|_u$ is leaved unchanged, and we say that processor P_u is in a *waiting* state.

▷ $Cnt_1|_u = 0$ or $Cnt_1|_u \geq 2$: Processor P_u is respectively active (wrt type 1), or was idle (wrt type 1) before the switchwhere. In both cases, $Cnt_1|_u$ remains unchanged.

Figure 5 presents this mechanism on an example. Before the switchwhere (Fig. 5a), processors P_0 and P_3 are active, whereas P_1 and P_2 are idle. On entering (Fig. 5b), P_0 and P_3 are turned to the waiting state ($Cnt_1 = 1$). At some case (Fig. 5c), P_3 satisfies the test and it is turned active, whereas P_0 remains waiting. At the end of the switchwhere, the initial value of Cnt_1 (Fig. 5a) is restored by decrementing all positive $Cnt|_u$ values. The program in $\mathcal{L}$, called Opt, is presented in Fig. 6.

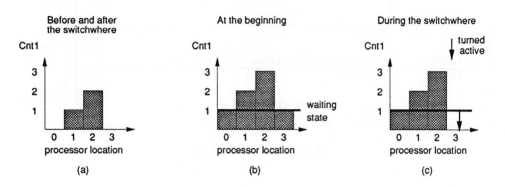

Fig. 5. Manipulation of Cnt_1 in the POMPC compiler.

This implementation presents obvious advantages over the previous one. There is only one manipulation of counter between the $\phi(P_i)$ programs. Moreover the expression of the condition associated to each manipulation is much simpler.

3.3 Correctness of the optimization

Based on the semantics of $\mathcal{L}$, we can express the equivalence of programs. The correctness of the optimization amounts to prove the equivalence of the two programs Dir and Opt. We first give some definitions. A program P *terminates* from initial environment σ and context ct if there exists a finite sequence of transitions $\langle P, \sigma, ct \rangle = S_0 \longrightarrow S_1 \longrightarrow \ldots \longrightarrow S_n = \langle \bullet, \sigma', ct' \rangle$. Observe that this sequence is unique because $\mathcal{L}$ is deterministic. The *result* of such a computation, denoted $[\![P]\!](\sigma, ct)$, is the pair (σ', ct'). If there exists an infinite sequence of transitions $\langle P, \sigma, ct \rangle = S_0 \longrightarrow S_1 \longrightarrow \ldots$, then P diverges and $[\![P]\!](\sigma, ct)$ is denoted $\bot$. We can now define the equivalence $\equiv$ of $\mathcal{L}$ programs as follows. Two programs are equivalent if and only if they yield the same result from any initial state.

Definition 1. Let P, Q be two programs in $\mathcal{L}$. $P \equiv Q$ if and only if for all σ, ct

$$[\![P]\!](\sigma, ct) = [\![Q]\!](\sigma, ct)$$

Theorem 1 expresses the correctness of the optimization.

Original program	POMPC implementation: the Opt program	

switchwhere $(E)\{$	where $\neg(Cnt_3 = 0)$ do $Cnt_3 := Cnt_3 + 1$ end;
	where $(\bigwedge_i Cnt_i = 0)$ do $Aux := E$ end;
	$Cnt_1 := Cnt_1 + 1$;
		$\left.\right\} Opt_0$

case c_1 :	where $(Cnt_1 = 1 \wedge Aux = C_1)$ do $Cnt_1 := Cnt_1 - 1$ end;	
P_1;	$\phi(P_1)$;	
$\vdots$	$\vdots$	
P_k;	$\phi(P_k)$;	$\left.\right\} Opt_k$
case c_{k+1} :	where $(Cnt_1 = 1 \wedge Aux = C_{k+1})$ do $Cnt_1 := Cnt_1 - 1$ end;	
P_{k+1};	$\phi(P_{k+1})$;	
$\vdots$	$\vdots$	
P_n;	$\phi(P_n)$;	$\left.\right\} Opt_n$
default:	where $(Cnt_1 = 1)$ do $Cnt_1 := Cnt_1 - 1$ end;	
P_{n+1}	$\phi(P_{n+1})$;	
$\}$	where $(Cnt_1 > 0)$ do $Cnt_1 := Cnt_1 - 1$ end; where $(Cnt_3 > 0)$ do $Cnt_3 := Cnt_3 - 1$ end;	$\left.\right\} Opt_{n+1}$

Fig. 6. The Opt program.

Theorem 1 $Dir \equiv Opt$

We decompose the two programs respectively into the programs Dir_i $(0 \leq i \leq n+1)$ and Opt_i $(0 \leq i \leq n+1)$ as shown in Fig. 4 and Fig. 6: $Dir = Dir_0; Dir_1; \ldots; Dir_{n+1}$ and $Opt = Opt_0; Opt_1; \ldots; Opt_{n+1}$. The equivalence of programs Dir and Opt is directly deduced from the following lemma.

Lemma 1 For all i, $1 \leq i \leq n+1$, $(Dir_0; Dir_1; \ldots; Dir_i) \equiv (Opt_0; Opt_1; \ldots; Opt_i)$

Proof. The proof of Lemma 1 is done by induction on i. We introduce a predicate $\Pi_i(\sigma)$ which characterizes the Cnt_1 value before executing Dir_i and Opt_i. It keeps track in the induction of the Cnt_1 updates. $\Pi_i(\sigma)$, $1 \leq i \leq n$, is defined as follows: for all location u, if the value of $\sigma(Cnt_1)|_u$ is strictly lower than 2, then it is 0 if and only if there exists $1 \leq j \leq i$ so that the value of $\sigma(Aux)|_u$ is equal to $C_j|_u$.

$$\Pi_i(\sigma) = \forall u \, [(\sigma(Cnt_1)|_u < 2) \Rightarrow ((\sigma(Cnt_1)|_u = 0) \Leftrightarrow (\vee_{j \leq i} \sigma(Aux)|_u = C_j|_u))]$$

Lemma 1 is deduced from the three following propositions.

Proposition 1 Both Dir_0 and Opt_0 terminate. $[\![Dir_0]\!](\sigma, ct) = [\![Opt_0]\!](\sigma, ct) = (\sigma', ct)$ and $\Pi_1(\sigma')$ holds.

Proposition 2 For any $1 \leq i \leq n$, if $\Pi_i(\sigma)$ holds then

▷ either both Dir_i and Opt_i diverge.
▷ or $[\![Dir_i]\!](\sigma, ct) = [\![Opt_i]\!](\sigma, ct) = (\sigma', ct)$ and $\Pi_{i+1}(\sigma')$ holds for $i < n$.

Proposition 3 $Dir_{n+1} \equiv Opt_{n+1}$.

The proof of Prop. 1 is directly derived by studying the value of Cnt_1 after executing Dir_0 and Opt_0. Proposition. 2 holds because the environment after executing the $\phi(P_i)$ program still satisfies the Π_i predicate. This comes from the absence of **escape**$_1$ statement in the compiled POMPC program P_i, since there is no way to escape a **where** block in POMPC. This fact ensures that the following updates of Cnt_1 in Dir_i and Opt_i are equivalent, and also that $\Pi_{i+1}(\sigma')$ holds. Finally, Dir_{n+1} and Opt_{n+1} are the same program, hence their equivalence.

4 Extension to the MPL language and conclusion

We present here a simplified version of the implementation of the MPL data-parallel **switch** statement. Its semantics is the same as that of the POMPC **switchwhere** statement. The MPL compiler implements the parallel control structures by means of a vectorial boolean stack s. s is used to maintain the processor activity during the program execution. At the beginning of conditioning blocks and loops, the current activity vector is pushed upon the stack s. It can thus be restored at the end of blocks by popping s. In case of loops, two extra stack levels are reserved in s to handle respectively the **break** and the **continue** statements. If the component located at u of such a level has the true value, then processor P_u has executed the corresponding statement. These three vectors allow to compute the current activity vector within the loop. At the beginning of a parallel **switch** statement, the current activity vector

switchwhere $(E)\{$	$Aux := E; Break := Ff; Case := Ff;$
	$Oldactive := Active; Active := Ff;$
$\vdots$	$\vdots$
case C_k :	**where** $(Oldactive \wedge Aux = C_k)$ **do**
	$\quad Active := Tt; Case := Tt$
	end
	$Active := Active \oplus Break;$
$P_k;$	**where** $Active$ **do** P_k **end**;
$\vdots$	$\vdots$
default:	**where** $(Oldactive)$ **do**
	$\quad Active := active \vee \neg Case$
	end;
	$Active := Active \oplus Break;$
$P_{n+1};:$	**where** $Active$ **do** P_{n+1} **end**;
$\}$	$Active := Oldactive;$

Fig. 7. MPL implementation of the parallel **switch** statement.

is also pushed upon s. As for loops, a stack level is reserved to handle the **break** statement. An additional level is used to keep track in the **switch** of processors which have satisfied one of the **case** clause. It allows to compute the processor activity in the `default` clause. We present in Fig. 7, according to the code generated by the MPL compiler, a $\mathcal{L}$ program which corresponds to the MPL implementation of the parallel `switch` statement. In this program, the new auxiliary variables *Oldactive*, *Break* and *Case* emulate the corresponding levels of stack s, whereas variable *Active* corresponds to the current activity vector.

In the P_k programs, the effect of the `break` statement is achieved by the instructions $Break := Tt; Active := Ff$. Moreover, at the end of each inner conditionning block of P_k, the statement $Active := Active \oplus Break$ is executed after restoring the activity. Processors which have executed a `break` in the block are thus set idle up to the end of P_k execution.

The compilation technique used in MPL to implement the parallel `switch` statement is similar as the one of the POMPC compiler: the activity updating before the k-th `case` clause only depends on the current activity and on the value of constant C_k. The only difference is the use of a vectorial boolean stack to handle the processor activity, instead of counters.

We formally proved in this paper the correctness of the POMPC compiler optimization. This result completes the proof of the whole compiler as far as usual control structures are concerned. Data-parallel languages also provide specific constructions as the C* and POMPC `everywhere`, called `all` in MPL. A future work will consist in integrating them in the $\mathcal{L}$ language and to study their implementation.

References

1. Blank T. The MasPar MP-1 Architecture. Proc. of the 35th IEEE Computer Society Int. Conf. (Spring Compcon 90), San Fransisco, 1990, pp. 20–24.
2. Bougé L. On the semantics of languages for massively parallel SIMD architectures. Proc. Parallel Arch. and Lang. Europe Conf. (PARLE), Eindhoven, Lect. Notes in Comp. Science 506, Springer Verlag, 1991, pp. 166–183.
3. Bougé L., Garda P. Towards a Semantic Approach to SIMD Architectures and their Languages. Proc. LITP Spring School on Theor. Comp. Science, La Roche Posay, France, 1990, Lect. Notes in Comp. Science 469, Springer Verlag, pp. 142–175.
4. Bougé L., Levaire J-L. Control structures for data-parallel SIMD languages: semantics and implementation. To appear in Fut. Gen. Comp. Sys., Volume 8, Issue 3 and 4, Elsevier Science Publishers, 1992.
5. C* Programming Guide. Thinking Machine Corporation, 1990.
6. Hoogvorst P., Keryell R., Matherat P., Paris N. POMP or how to design a massively parallel machine with small developments. Proc. Parallel Arch. and Lang. Europe Conf. (PARLE), Lect. Notes in Comp. Science 505, Springer Verlag, 1991, pp. 83–100.
7. MasPar Parallel Application Language Reference Manual. MasPar Computer Corporation, 1990.
8. Paris N. Définition de POMPC. Research Report 92-5, LIENS, Ecole Normale Supérieure, Paris, 1992.
9. Plotkin G. An operational semantics for CSP. D. Bjorner (Ed.), IFIP TC-2 Working Conference, Garmish-Partenkirchen, RFA, 1982.
10. Rice M.D., Seidman S.B., Wang P.Y. A formal model for SIMD computation. Frontiers of massively parallel computation, IEEE computer Society Press, 1988.
11. The MultiC programming language. Wavetracer, 1991.

This article was processed using the LaTeX macro package with LLNCS style

K–Project / First Step : to improve Data Manipulations and Representations on Parallel Computers.

by Hassane ESSAFI, Marc PIC, Didier JUVIN.

Commissariat à l'Energie Atomique, C.E.N. Saclay, DTA/DEIN/SLA
91191 Gif-sur-Yvette Cedex.
E-Mail : `hessafi, mpic@chouette.saclay.cea.fr`

Abstract. Large array processing can be done efficiently by a linear processor array. We developed a SIMD line-processor computer and a high-level programmation's environment including a C-like Array Programming Language with Object-Oriented abilities in order to compute physical problems. We based our work on the problem of manipulation, high-level representation and machine-level mapping of data. We try to find hardware and software solutions to provide an easy way to program parallel computer and an efficient use of SIMD parallelism.

1 Introduction.

The need to solve large and complex problems quickly for various application areas has led to build massively parallel machines. Dramatic advances in VLSI and declining cost of processing offer new possibilities to design with low cost parallel computers. Our research project is dedicated to scientific modeling of hydrodynamic flows by cellular automata and more generally to modeling of Partial Differential Equations (P.D.E.) by Lattice Gases [HUMIE87]. So the objects we have to manipulate are tables of several dimensions with big number of elements. It necessitates parallel computing performances [CHASE91] and an efficient manipulation of big tables, both at machine level and at users level : the mapping of data on the processors must permit quick and conflict-free access, and the high-level code must be easy to use for a scientific standard programmer. Thus we developed a SIMD parallel computer and a complete programmation environment oriented both to help programmers to manipulate easily and in a natural way the N-dimensional arrays of data and to improve the efficiency of organization of data in computer memories.

The computer (called SYMPATI 2) is a Line Processor Array. Originally it was designed for image processing [JUVIN88],[ESSAF88]. The performances obtained in this area led us to apply this machine in other domains like hydrodynamics simulation. The environment includes a low-level language (called 4LP), an intermediate set of library (VSIMD language) and a high-level C-like language (called $T{+}{+}$). This paper presents our machine, our environment of programmation and our work to improve the three following points :

- machine-level data-mapping of arrays and consequences on hardware.
- architecture of hardware array of processors to insure the scalability
and facilitate the use.
- high-level representation of data to make easier parallel programmation.

2   Hardware and Software solutions for machine-level data mapping.

A critical point in the design of massively parallel machine is the ability to have an access to data at a rate compatible with the processor's speed. By access we mean fetching the required data in the memory and routing the operands to processing elements through the network. We based our work on interleaved memory system. Maximum speed in two-dimensional arrays processing will be reached only if for a given matrix of data, the desirable subpart called template (e.g. rows, columns, square subarrays) can be fetched in one memory cycle, that means all the data elements comprising the desirable subpart must be stored in different memory banks. All skewing schemes of data organization can only offer free access to limited template [BUDNI71], [LAWRI75], [LEE88]. Three points need to be studied in data-organization : mapping in different memories without conflict, conserving adjacency of data and being easily implemented in hardware. In the algorithms performed for many-dimension tables computation (Image Processing, Numerical Analysis, Lattice Gases, Cellular Automata, P.D.E. Models...) the template is often square, rows, columns. With structures having number of memory banks equal to number of processors, it is not possible to have free access to those three templates. The only skewing schemes which could allow free access to each of these templates have the number of memory bank primer to the number of processing elements. But those type of skewing schemes are difficult to implement on hardware architecture [cf BURROUGHS comp uter]. Fortunately, we note that the operations required on square template can be easily replaced by operations involving only rows or columns template. The inverse is not obvious. So we prefer to define the data organisation function which allows access to in parallel without conflict in rows or columns [SHAPI78], [WIJSH87]. For a two-dimensional array, the data organisation we adopted is the helicoidal scheme $f(i,j) = (i+j)$ modulo M, where M is the number of the Processing Elements of the structure, (i,j) the position of the point P in the array and $f(i,j)$ the running number of the processor where the data will be stored. This architecture provides an high processing speed for certain operations like the matrix transposition. The ability of SYMPATI 2 to transpose a two-dimensional array quickly drives us to use a two-dimensional memory plane to represent a N-dimensional object. More precisely, we decide to use a N-dimensional tree mapping. Furthermore, it is possible to keep a reduce property of adjacency, not simultaneously, but dimension after dimension. This reduced property is sufficient in numerous cases and particularly in a big part of physical problems. We adopt helicoidal trees as atomic objects for data-mapping. We decompose our N-dimensional array following one privileged dimension that we associate with the line of processors in as many sub-arrays as necessary. This organization optimizes the management of the processing elements by the Control Unit.

Hardware architecture : SYMPATI 2.

We have already developed a SIMD architecture in collaboration with IRIT at Toulouse. This architecture called SYMPATI 2 is well suited to image processing and to matrix computations. In order to process two-dimensional matrices, the data in SYMPATI 2 are hardwarely organized in a one-level helicoidal way, making it possible to reach either a row or a column segment without conflict. In the case of two-dimensional array this ability is not only used to exchange data but to really process in 2D the images or the matrices. SYMPATI 2 is composed of two main components, the Command Unit part and the Processing Elements (PEs). The command Unit is responsible for controlling the PEs, the propagation of the process to the entire matrix, even if the number of PEs is smaller than the number of elements in the matrix. It is a hardware virtualization. The Control Unit (CU) is also responsible for controlling the interfaces with the inputs and the outputs and with the host. It is composed by : - a common memory storing the constant elements, the memory of instructions and its module managements. - a scanning part, used to iterate the algorithms defined for one pixel to all the elements of the matrix; the image to be processed may be scanned , according to one out of four possible scanning modes, which are defined from by the segment type (a row or a column segment), the segment displacement type which may be along a line (row or column) or along a band. Furthermore, it makes it possible to perform segments overlapping and forward , or backward matrix scanning. The processing Elements were designed in our laboratory and founded by A.T.&T. in standard cell ASIC integrating 4 Processing Elements in HCMOS 1.2 micron technology (90000). Each P.E. consists of a processing part, and an addressing part: - The processing part includes 16 bit ALU for usual operations (logical, arithmetical and 8*8 bit multiplier) and a scratch pad of registers. But it also comprises specific components, in particular, an interconnection network, allowing the connection between the ALU input, and the required output, and 4 work flags necessary for performing conditional sequences. - The addressing part allowing helicoidal access mode and also indexed access mode. The helicoidal mode is dedicated to two-dimensional processing and to N-dimensional tree (coded in 2D image) processing. The operations performed in Tensors (N-dimensional Trees) computing require to access for each element to its neighbourhood. Due to the large number of Processing Elements the majority of the existing parallel architecture favour access only to centre element, however it is necessary, if we want to have an efficient architecture, to facilitate access, either to the centre element or t o its neighbourhood. Therefore, in each cycle, one can get information from the memory banks or from the registers where it is directly connected and computes the result and store it in its registers or in its memories. The only restriction is that both memory read and write operations are not allowed to be in the same cycle. Another point we elaborate on the hardware configuration is the border effect.

3   High-level Representation of Data : the T++ Environment of Programmation.

The environment of programmation of SYMPATI 2 is composed of three layers. A first layer is the low-level language 4LP. The high-level language is called T++. It is a C-like parallel array language. The intermediate layer is interfacing the high-level design of data-representation produced by T++ and the low-level data-mapping to generate to use 4LP. It is called VSIMD. VSIMD libraries are divided in two parts : computation sub-library and communications sub-library. The communications sub-library routes the data-segment from specific modules to required module. It is specially designed to process non-uniform remapping of data in which it is necessary to calculate a table of index containing for each processor the point with which they have to communicate.

High-level languages have radically improved the quality, costs, reliability and availability of software for sequential architecture of computer. We could hope the same thing for parallel architecture. Hardware progression of parallel computer was faster than progression in parallel software development, and now the need of evolved languages for scientific applications on parallel computers increases strongly. But scientific users need to have simple working environment to develop their programs, and low-level languages are not adapted to their work.

$T++$ is an high-level parallel language that we have made to enhance the capabilities of our machine and to bring to user a high-level interface with parallelism. $T++$ is structured using the two lower level of programmation VSIMD and 4LP.

$T++$ is an Object-Oriented C-like programming language. We choose C++ as prototype for our high-level language in order to allow sequential-C programmers to bring their applications at a low cost. Most scientific applications in the world are developed in FORTRAN today, but advantages of C in various parts of computer science are well-known [MACDO91], and it allows us to strongly structured our data-manipulations and simultaneously to create our own structures of data. C++ Object-Oriented programmation brings interesting features for users and keeps the advantages of C language [KILLI91].

$T++$ is an array-parallel language which means that elementary objects produced and used by $T++$ are N-diemsnional arrays manipulated like scalars [JUDZ91].

The language $T++$ is designed to run on a tandem constituted of a scalar host and of a SIMD grid, but only 4LP is machine-dependant, so $T++$ is a portable language. The implementation of $T++$ uses a C++ library, containing the definition of the objects, and the methods used to treat tensors (N-dimensions arrays). A pre-treatment to process hard points of syntax converts source file in a C++ code. Then the includes and the objects and properties are linked to this code. All are compiled to produce two final codes : one for the scalar host (master of control) and the other for the parallel SIMD structure. The two codes are launched by an exchange controller designed to supervised the two processes.

Nota : Indexed Parallel Operations.

Let us describe a case in which it is necessary to use indexed parallel operations : to compute directly a shrink of a table in which the original table of data loses one point over two and is transformed in a smaller table. The matrix corresponding to the image undergoes the following transformation on each line : On one line, point 0 of Original Image will go in point 0 of Processed Image. Point 2 of O.I. will go in point 1 of P.I. Point 4 of O.I. will go in point 2 of P.I., etc... It can be expressed by the following notation : for all values of i taken in the good set, B(i) = A(2i), where A is a line of the original image and B the processed line. i is a bounded variable, which play no global role in the process, but which is locally necessary. More generally, we can write : B(i) = A(f(i)), for all i, where f() is the non-uniform remapping function. It brings us to mathematical operations like Rotations or Arnold's Transform are not applied on the values taken in memory but on the position in this memory. The transformation is calculated on the coordinates and it requires an exchange of values located in different memories and on different processors. This problem raises two questions : firstly, how to solve by software or by hardware the non-uniform position exchange of data ; secondly, there is a syntax problem to write the exchange property in a formal way. It is necessary to compute the address of the target processor before sending it to the "index address" part of the chip in order to place the good value not only in the good memory bank but also in the good memory place.Thus, it takes a very long time to remap the arrays, the longest path can be as long as the number of processors in SYMPATI, and each step of this algorithm uses eighteen instructions in 4LP. In order to reduce this waste of time we develop hardware solution SYMPATI X to overlap the computing operations with the communication operations. SYMPATI X is composed of two main parts SYMPATI 2 and an autonomous network. Each processor is connected to this network. In irregular exchange each processor sends data to the network which assumes to transfert it to the right processor. At the same time, the processors continue their computation. Performances obtained by this network are under evaluation using VHDL modeling [COLLE92]. The general problem of repositioning data in memory can be written as such : Let A and B be two arrays, and i one vector of coordinates, and f() the remapping function, then, B (i) = A (f(i)). But in this expression i is a bounded variable, just as a convenience to note the problem and to indicate that this operation must be done for all the values of i. Bounded variables are not exactly in the spirit of a standard-C language, but we think it is a necessary harm. It is an open problem but we introduce dumb objects in our language. They are used conventionally to note an operation to do for all the values that could take this variable. Notation is as follows :

$$\text{dumb } i;$$
$$B(i) = A(5*i+3i*i);$$

Others solutions are possible to express this type of instructions, but they always use explicit declaration of the communication processes [M ASPAR], [PARIS92].

4 Conclusion.

The SYMPATI 2 machine, developed in collaboration with IRIT at Toulouse is able to manipulate two-dimensional arrays with a single line of processors and without conflict in the access of data by rows or by columns. It supports virtualization by means of hardware architecture. The hardware of SYMPATI 2 solves also the problem which appear when the number of elements to compute is not a multiple of the number of processors. SYMPATI 2 accepts a purely local declaration of instructions. The access of memory on SYMPATI 2 supports to scan data by rows, by columns, or by bands, what is efficient to transpose a matrix. Those points and particularly the last helps the production of parallel programmation environment.

The use of a matrix-trees representation with the ability to quickly exchange two dimensions allows us to manipulate the N-dimensional tables on a one-dimension grid of processors (as well as on a m-dimensional grid). It is efficient to compute hydrodynamic simulation, lattice gases methods to solve P.D.E., cellular automata, and many other problems. Now, a software solution uses the two-dimensional exchange ability of SYMPATI 2, with computing address exchange, to quickly process N-dimensional grid. But an architecture based on SYMPATI 2, and using only a one-dimensional grid of processors can be conceived to compute the N-dimensional exchange using hardware speed. Such a computer can be equally a solution to the problem of the extension of the numbers of Processing Elements without exponential extension of the connections.

The $T++$ programing language provides a C-like approach of the programmation of parallel computer with object-oriented features. With its structure in three layers it could be port on other parallel computer, as well on hypercubic and pyramidal machines. It allows users to manipulate N-dimensional arrays like scalars, in a simple and natural but formal way. It supports C++ syntax. We port a version of T++ on CM-2.

In the future we plan to install our language on other parallel computers. We will work on problems related to the dumb variables, distance of use, and interpretation of complex syntaxic definitions. We think that the introduction of dumb variables in a C environment can provide a real programmation improvement in future developments. We think also that the problem of data mapping, treated by mixed hardware and software methods, is one key of the efficiency of the parallel computing of tomorrow.

BIBLIOGRAPHY

[BUDNI71] BUDNIK P., KUCK D.J., "the organization and use of parallel memories", IEEE Trans. Comput. C-20(1971), 1566-1569.

[CHASE91] CHASE C.M., CHEUNG A.L., REEVES A.P., SMITH M.R., "Paragon : a parallel programming environment for scientific applications using communications structures", International Conference on Parallel Processing, 1991, II-211.

[COLLE92] COLLETTE T., ESSSAFI H., JUVIN D., KAISER J., "SYMPATI X : A SIMD computer performing the low and intermediate levels of image processing", PARLE, 06/1992.

[ESSAF88] ESSAFI H., "Les processeurs lignes en traitement d'images", Thesis 1988, Université Paul Sabatier, Toulouse.

[HUMIE87] d'HUMIERE D., FRISCH U., HASSLACHER B., LALLEMAND P., POMEAU Y., RIVET J.-P., "Lattice Gas Hydrodynamics in two and three dimensions", Complex Systems 1 (1987), 649-707.

[JUDZ91] JU D.-Z., CHING W.M., "Exploitation of APL data-parallelism on a shared -memory MIMD machine", ACM SIGPLAN Notices, 6/1991, 4, 61-72.

[JUVIN88] JUVIN D., BASILLE J.L., ESSAFI H., LATIL J.Y., "SYMPATI 2, a 1.5 D processor array for image application", Signal Processing IV : Theories and Applications, J.L. Lacoume, A. Chehikian, N.Martin, nad J. Malbos, Elsevier Science Publishers B.V. (North-Holland), 1988.

[KILLI91] KILLIAN M.F., "Object-oriented programming for massively parallel machines", International Conference on Parallel Processing, 1991, II-227.

[LAWRI75] LAWRIE D.H., "Access and alignment of data in an array processor", IEEE Trans. Comput. C-24(1975), 1145-1155.

[LEE88] LEE D., "Scrambled storage for parallel memory systems", Internat. Symp. Comput. Architecture (1988), 232-239.

[MACDO91] MACDONALD Tom, "C for numerical computing", J. of Supercomputing, 5 (1991), 31-48.

[SHAPI78] SHAPIRO H. D., "Theoretical limitations on the effective use of parallel memories", IEEE Trans. Comput. C-27, (1978).

[WIJSH87] WIJSHOFF H.A.G., VAN LEEUWEN J., "On linear skewing schemes and d-ordered vectors", IEEE Trans. Comput., C-36 (1987), 233-239.

F-Code: A Portable Software Platform for Data-Parallel Languages

V.B. Muchnick*and A.V. Shafarenko
Department of Electronic and Electrical Engineering
University of Surrey

Abstract

A unified approach to the implementation of a variety of data-parallel programming languages on a variety of SIMD, multi-SIMD, and SIMD-simulating MIMD hardware platforms is presented. The essence of this approach is the provision of a formally defined high-level intermediate language (f-code) developed to represent the semantics of data-parallel processing in full as well as data management and control primitives inherent in Fortran, Pascal and C.

Since the Program Committee in their ultimate wisdom accepted this text as a *short* paper we will not discuss the importance of portable software platforms (PSP) for the implementation of data-concurrency on a variety of parallel architectures. We shall only define a PSP as a programming language that has:

1. high-level semantics with all sorts of abstractions inherent in high-level languages, such as tuples, pointers, data types, etc;

2. primitive syntax, which makes it easy for the top-level compiler to generate the code from the source program;

3. architecture neutrality, that is the PSP should by all means avoid machine-dependent presumptions as to the number and configuration of processors, the structure of the interconnect etc. No PSP construct must depend of such parameters. Consequently, PSP instructions can only have symbolic form and use only symbolic addressing. An example of PSP for serial processing is given in [DRA 91].

This paper describes a new PSP called f-code (see also [Bolychevsky 92]), developed to support data-parallel, and to some extent process-parallel, languages. It can be targeted from any data-parallel extension of Fortran, C, or Pascal. It can be used to compile occam and Ada as well, again with any reasonable data-parallel extensions or packages. At the moment a compiler targeting f-code from EVAL [Muchnick 92] is available as well as a demonstrator implementation of the PSP. Below we shall briefly outline the main features of f-code

---

*permanent address: IA&E, Novosibirsk 630090 Russia

Concurrency

F-code is a PSP for parallel processing. Primarily it expresses data parallelism through operations on nonscalar objects. This means that, say, adding a matrix to a matrix is not a sequential loop in f-code, but rather an atomic action performed on all matrix elements simultaneously.

The novelty of the f-code approach to data parallelism is that it supports the whole conceivable variety of parallel operations by providing a rank coercion mechanism, which allows one to apply parallel operators to any combination of objects, no matter if they have matching ranks or not. This is done in a regular way and involves just one notion of operand *orientation*. Also, a reasonable default is provided for the case of shape mismatch. Wherever the ranks are same or coerced: f-code supplies a shape coercion rule.

Another sort of concurrency that f-code aims to accurately represent is the concurrency of evaluating the operands to an operation. It may be called *functional* parallelism, since this property is inherent in any functional programming language. For example, the LISP expression

```
(TIMES (DIFFERENCE A B)(ADD C D))
```

can first compute the difference and then the sum, or the other way round. The same may be true, however, with an imperative language, e.g. the Fortran expression

```
(A+B+SIN(X**2))*(G/A*EXP(-R))
```

may evaluate the first bracket first, but it may start with the last one, still the result will not be different (this is not always true since the imperative languages allow the use of side-effecting functions, which is why we prefer to call this concurrency functional: pure functional languages do not allow side effects).

Although functional concurrency is non-parametric, and thus the gain is never as dramatic as one from the use of data concurrency, it is nevertheless important to allow for functional concurrency as an auxiliary mechanism to implement parallelism of data. It can be used for static scheduling of data flow in a multiprocessor, but also an additional source of parallelism to hide the latency of remote memory access in a distributed system.

Whereas data concurrency should be introduced by provision of nonscalar operations, functional parallelism manifests itself in the notion of expression. Typical assembly languages do not have this notion, so functional concurrency is only implicitly present in the assembler program. It is therefore desirable to preserve this concurrency in the PSP notation if the PSP is to support data parallelism. This is the reason that the syntax of f-code is made similar to that of Lisp: the f-program is a tree encoded in the form of list. Each vertex of the tree is a function (f-instruction) invocation with its subtrees executing in parallel for most of the vertex labels (or, f-instructions).

It should be emphasised that the support of functional concurrency in f-code does *not* mean that f-code is a functional language. A functional PSP would not be able to support imperative languages because of the principal divergencies in the two programming paradigms. Naturally f-code has to support actual variables and assignment, so it does not possess referential transparency.

Data

Most of the programming languages introduce a concept of type. Being a PSP f-code suggests a consistent generalisation of those concepts in application to data parallelism. The f-code convention allows f-instructions to be stripped of unwieldy attribute specifications, at the same time providing for inferability of those attributes when the platform is to be compiled. In addition, f-code introduces implicit coercions.

All that helps generating compact f-programs from language compilers and minimises interpretation overheads where the platform is to be interpreted.

Type and sort

F-code types are subdivided into a fixed set of strong "basic" types which form a hierarchy in the sense of compatibility:

$$logical < character < integer < real < complex$$

and structural metatypes, or templates, which are user-defined and "soft" so that any pointer can be dereferenced using any metatype.

Since data-parallel computation normally involves geometric transformations that select and reorder elements of nonscalar objects and since the results of such selections can act as objects in their own right, it is important to provide some sort of address arithmetic. The general mechanism of pointers is softly typed to allow for structures, therefore a nonscalar object can not be represented by a conforming nonscalar aggregate of pointers without discarding its type; even if it could it would not be efficient to dereference this aggregate every time the value is required: array objects are normally stored in memory in some regular way, which implies that the pointer array in question would often be redundant.

In order to solve this problem, every object is ascribed an attribute of *sort*, which can be *value*, *name*, or *target*. A target (which is indeed a target for assignment) is a strongly typed object each element of which refers to a value element whose type is equal to, or senior than, the type of the target (thus the compatibility of basic types is taken into account). Note that the type hierarchy for targets is reversed, because whereas one can raise a value from, say, integer to real or any higher type, an object of real type can be assigned values of integer or any junior type. The f-functions that provide access to variables can yield not only values but targets as well, which can be processed geometrically and still remain strongly typed even after they are mixed up with other targets to form the left-hand side of an assignment. Thus, f-code promotes a greater functional concurrency by allowing expressions on the left-hand side. Other PSPs for data-parallel processing, such as VSA [Jesshope 90] were less neutral architecturally and therefore had to rely upon masked assignment only.

It should be emphasised that the fact that targets refer to values elementwise is an f-code concept. F-code does not assume any specific way the targets are implemented. In particular there is no need to maintain an address table to represent a target if the object the target refers to can be characterised with a simple descriptor.

A target can not be dereferenced since its type is generally incompatible (lower) than the one of the value that would come out as the result, in the sense of type hierarchy of values. There are situations where a target is required not only for assignment, but also for dereferencing (which is the case with read/write variables). In that case a name is used which has a rigid (incoercible) type and which subsumes the functionalities of a value and a target.

The above conventions of sort are part of the f-code paradigm; the important thing is that they constitute a mechanism that makes it redundant to specify access to data objects in each f-instruction. As well as type, the sort attribute is *inferable* in the f-program, the absolute minimum of access specification is therefore required.

Variables and scopes

The main mechanism of memory scheduling in f-code is a stack, since this is the case in many of the top level languages. Also, stack scheduling in a functional type platform (which f-code actually is) is natural: evaluation of a program is effected through recursive function invocation, which uses a stack anyway.

Specifically, f-code supports a lazy function which creates a variable that exists during the lifetime of the function invocation. One of the arguments of this function (executed after the creation of the variable) is the scope of the variable. Access to the stack variable inside the scope is either through its identifier (similar to LISP, f-system maintains a dictionary of the active associations of all identifiers occurring in the f-program) or through a pointer to it.

F-code supports the traditional primitives to control heap memory as well.

Polymorphism and inferability

Generally speaking, the majority of f-instructions are polymorphic. For example, f-function DYADIC with operator ADD does integer addition when the operands are integer and real addition when they are real. It also works when the types of the operands differ from each other, in which case it coerces the data with the lower type. A more dramatical example of polymorphism is f-function COMPOSE which glues two objects. This function admits the operands of all sorts and types and works differently for values, names and targets.

Polymorphism drastically reduces the proliferation of f-functions thus facilitating interpretation of f-code. However, if an f-program is to be compiled, polymorphism may present a problem, since the f-compiler has to know for which type data the f-function should execute (in other words, data attributes have to be inferred). The solution suggested by f-code is to allow polymorphism inside an f-module only. Every identifier can therefore be retraced to the outmost environment where it is explicitly associated with some object. The variables that are essentially external parameters of the module do not have such an environment inside the module. To avoid the polymorphism caused by those parameters, there is a special f-function which coerces a variable to some specified attributes.

Control

The semantics of f-code is purely operational: there is neither predefined program structure nor restrictions whatsoever as to allowed combinations of instructions. Even the scoping of data is determined by lazy evaluation of f-functions, put another way, by the enforced ordering of argument evaluation for a function. The only way not to break the operational semantics and at the same time avoid an explicit instruction address space is to get the flow of data through the function calls that form the f-program to carry some control tokens which cause decision making at control vertices of the program graph.

In effect, the sole reason for control constructs in an imperative language is to determine the order in which assignments are executed. Since the assignment statement regarded as a function has only a side effect, which is changing the value of the left-hand side, f-code defines its main effect as returning some normal completion code. The completion code (or, *token*) is merely an integer scalar value, which may be returned by any "ordinary" f-function, like the one performing an arithmetic operation. To enforce sequential composition of assignments f-code introduces a set of lazy functions which evaluate their arguments in some order. The action such functions perform on the argument values (completion codes) is to test the tokens and decide whether the execution should be continued; these control functions yield completion codes themselves to allow for nesting of control constructs.

It should be noted that this approach to organisation of control assumes only reducible data-flow graphs can be represented by f-code, i.e. such as the language compiler generates from fully structured source programs (see Aho and Ulman [Acho 86]). Although this involves some technical difficulties at the stage of code generation from unstructured languages like Fortran, it does, however, facilitate optimisation techniques on f-code. Another important fact is that the conversion of f-code branches to a linear representation can always be performed at the f-code compilation stage and therefore does not have to be emulated at run-time.

The overall control model is exemplified in Fig 1. In essence, the virtual f-machine operates in two modes, the eager and the lazy one. The lazy mode is usually triggered by an assignment completion. The eager mode is entered every time a new assignment (or stand-alone expression, for example, an IF condition) is to be executed. In a way the eager (functionally parallel) evaluation of expressions is subordinated to the lazy (sequential) execution of the program as it should be. Still, a sequential piece of code can be included in an eager span of the program if necessary (the most obvious example is the C operator ?: that is lazy yet computational, i.e., it returns a result object.) This is achieved

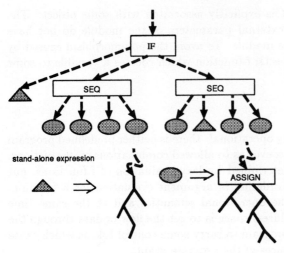

stand-alone expression

Fig 1. Control example in f-code. Solid lines denote eager evaluation with returning object data. Dashed arrows stand for lazy evaluation. The second argument of the last SEQ is a stand-alone expression which computes a token possibly terminating the SEQ.

through a special two-argument lazy f-function which has one token argument, which it fires first and then absorbs, and one object argument that it passes on. Above the invocation locus of this function the evaluation becomes eager.

Implementation

F-code has been implemented on a serial machine[1]. F-code compilers for i860 and transputer networks will be available by the end of 1992.

We acknowledge the financial support from the Royal Society and PARSEQ Ltd.

References

[Acho 86] Aho, A.V., Sethi, R., Ullman, J.D. *Compilers*, Addison-Wesley (Reading MA).

[Bolychevsky 92] Bolychevsky, A.B., Muchnick, V.B., Shafarenko, A.V. *F-code specification*, Internal report, Department of Electronic and Electrical Engineering, University of Surrey.

[DRA 91] *TDF specification*, Defence Research Agency, RSRE Malvern.

[Jesshope 90] Jesshope, C.R. The VSA: an abstract definition and interface for data-parallel program generation. *Computer and Artificial Intelligence*, 9, 441–459.

[Muchnick 92] Muchnick, V.B., Shafarenko, A.V. *The language EVAL and its implementation*, to be published Chapman Hall (London).

---

[1] We owe this implementation to D.Barsky of IA&E

A Parallel Best-first B&B with Synchronization Phases

Marc Gengler and Giovanni Coray

Swiss Federal Institute of Technology Lausanne - EPFL-DI-LITH, CH-1015 Lausanne

Abstract. We present a new parallel best-first Branch and Bound algorithm conceived for machines with distributed memory. Based on the notion of problems having the same lower bound, the algorithm evaluates these problems in parallel, during each phase of its execution. These computationally intensive phases alternate with control phases where synchronization and information exchange between processors takes place. We propose a probabilistic model for predicting the performances of this algorithm and discuss the results obtained on a MIMD multiprocessor for the Asymmetric Non-Euclidean TSP.

1 Introduction

Section (2) analyses the behavior of the B&B algorithm and introduces the notion of *fringes* within a B&B tree. (3) defines the algorithm proposed in this paper whereas (4) presents a probabilistic model which allows us to estimate the size of the fringes. Section (5) describes the Traveling Salesman Problem and the implementation we used on an Intel iPSC/2 hypercube. (6) discusses the results obtained, (7) concludes.

2 Presentation and Analysis of the B&B

2.1 The Sequential B&B

B&B optimization has been formalized in several ways, either by abstract specification [Mit 70, Rin 74, Gen 92] or by analogy with problem solving strategies known in the AI framework which also base on state space enumeration. B&B partially enumerates a set of states in order to find the optimum in this set. It is an algorithm of *combinatorial optimization* mostly applied to *NP-complete* problems [Rou 87, Joh 90]. Hence, the state space is generally very large.

In this paper we only consider the case of minimization. Let S be the set of *solution candidates* and let f be a *cost* function which attributes a value in a totally ordered set R to the elements of the solution space S. $f^* = f_S^* = \text{Min}\{f(x) \mid x \in S\}$ then yields the minimal cost. $S^* = \{x \in S \mid f(x) = f^*\}$ is the set of *optimal solutions*. The B&B computes a subset of S^*.

B&B proceeds by *decomposition* of a problem into several sub-problems, the *branching* scheme β. Problems which cannot be decomposed are evaluated by f. Hence, it is convenient to represent a problem by a tree. At any given moment of its execution, B&B will have developed a part of the tree and has a set of problems, the terminal nodes of this partial tree, also called *open* nodes. β chooses a node among the open nodes, decomposes it into sub-problems which it adds back to the other nodes. Depending on the manner we choose a node, we speak of *depth-first* strategy if at every moment β chooses the open node which is the deepest and leftmost in the tree; of *breadth-first* if β considers the shallowest leftmost sub-problem; of *random* if β makes a priori any selection or of *best-first*, a strategy we will define later.

B&B consistently updates the value of a *best current solution* **BS** which is the optimum of the costs of the terminal nodes evaluated so far. **BS** is initialised to a value $\mathbf{BS}_{init}$ known to be *no* better than f^* or to an arbitrarily bad value. During its execution B&B updates the value of **BS** so that it corresponds at every moment to the best known solution. At the end of the execution of B&B, we have $\mathbf{BS} = f^*$.

The last important notion is that of an *optimistic estimation function*, also called *lower bound*. This function, which we will denote *oe*, under-estimates the cost of a node X: $oe(X) \leq Min\{f(x) \mid x \in X\}$. As soon as the optimistic estimation of an intermediate node X is greater than **BS**, we can decide to ignore this node without risking to *cut off* the optimal terminal node(s). As a fact, we have $f^* \leq \mathbf{BS} \leq oe(X) \leq f_X^*$ and X does not engender the (unique) optimal solution. A branching function β which chooses to always decompose the node having the best optimistic estimation implements the *best-first* strategy. As the state space is generally very large, preventing all exhaustive enumeration, the *cut* condition takes all its importance. It is crucial that

$$\mathbf{BS} \leq oe(X) \tag{1}$$

be verified for a large number of nodes X. In order to increase the probability for a node X to verify (1) we need a value of $oe(X)$ as large as possible, i.e. close the optimal solution in the tree X. Optimizing *oe* only depends on the problem considered. The condition (1) may as well be verified more often if we have a small **BS**, i.e. close to f^*. This supposes that the algorithm has already found a node with nearly optimal cost or that the initial value $\mathbf{BS}_{init}$ is close to f^*.

2.2 Analysis of the B&B

We were interested in the influence of $\mathbf{BS}_{init}$ on the efficiency of the B&B. We explored the B&B tree of a minimization problem with a unique optimal solution using a random strategy and choosing different initial values for $\mathbf{BS}_{init}$. (*Fig.* 1) shows the average behavior of the algorithm and allows several important conclusions.

• First of all, any large value for $\mathbf{BS}_{init}$ does not permit us to significantly reduce the number of nodes explored. This is explained by the fact that B&B will quickly find a better node. Thus, $\mathbf{BS}_{init}$ has to be very close to f^* in order to notably speed up the B&B algorithm.

• Next, we see that, as soon as $\mathbf{BS}_{init} = f^*$, our random B&B explores the same tree all the time. This fact is explained by the following argumentation. As $\mathbf{BS}_{init} = f^*$ is never updated the order in which we explore the tree is of no relevance. The fact that a node is cut off, i.e. (1) being true, does not depend on the moment at which we process this node. More generally, B&B explores exactly - at least if we search all optimal solutions - those nodes X for which we have

$$oe(X) \leq f^* \tag{2}$$

Hence, (2) delimits the sub-tree to explore. Notice that this tree corresponds to the minimal tree which has to be considered in order to certify that $\mathbf{BS}_{init}$ is indeed equal to the optimal value f^*. This tree is illustrated in ($Fig.$ 2).

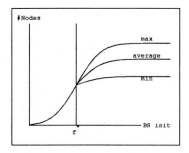

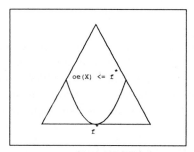

Fig. 1. *This figure gives the minimum, maximum and average number of nodes explored by the random B&B depending on the value of the best initial solution.*

Fig. 2. *This figure illustrates the tree composed of nodes verifying $oe(X) \leq f^*$.*

The tree given in ($Fig.$ 2) is unique only in the case B&B searches all solutions. In the opposite case, there is a family of terminal nodes (X_i) with optimal cost f^*. Each X_i gives birth to a tree A_i like the one of ($Fig.$ 2), trees which as an evidence are not all of the same size. As our strategy of choice is random, B&B may generate any tree of the family (A_i) and thus develop different numbers of nodes. For the ease of our discussion, we will suppose that B&B computes all the solutions and thus needs to develop the union of the trees of the family (A_i).

• The last observation is the behavior of the random B&B when the value $\mathbf{BS}_{init}$ is strictly lower than f^*. The nodes to explore are then determined by the equation $oe(X) \leq \mathbf{BS}_{init} < f^*$ and correspond to the nodes one needs to visit for certifying that a cost as low as $\mathbf{BS}_{init}$ could not be realised ($Fig.$ 3). This tree decreases very quickly in size with $\mathbf{BS}_{init}$ ($Fig.$ 1).

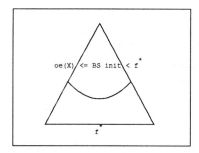

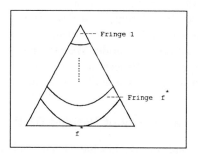

Fig. 3.
This figures illustrates the tree composed of nodes verifying $oe(X) \leq \mathbf{BS}_{init} < f^*$.

Fig. 4. *Fringe Fr_i contains all nodes of tree A_i not belonging to A_{i-1}.*

2.3 The Notion of Fringes

In the common case of a discrete optimistic estimation function oe the values of oe form a finite set (v_i) of numbers in the interval $[0, f^*]$. For each v_j of (v_i) we may construct the tree A_j of nodes X such that $oe(X) \leq v_j$ as well as the set of fringes (Fr_i) composed of the nodes belonging to A_i without belonging to A_{i-1}. The problems of the fringe Fr_j have the optimistic estimation v_j and are sketched in (*Fig.* 4).

(*Fig.* 1) indicates that the trees (A_i) and hence the fringes (Fr_i) increase quickly in size. If the function t_A associates to the index of a tree A_j its average size, then we define the function t_{Fr} which gives the average size of a fringe Fr_j as $t_{Fr}(j) = t_A(j) - t_A(j-1)$. If the number of values the optimistic estimation might take is small, then the function t_A is likely to increase exponentially. And so does t_{Fr}. Thus the processing of one fringe is an important step of computation. This will be the basic hypothesis for the development of the algorithm presented in section (3).

3   The Algorithm

The parallel algorithm presented in this paper is based on the notion of fringes in the B&B tree. Each fringe is explored in parallel by all available processors. Fringes are processed in increasing order of their oe-value. The complete computation of one fringe is terminated by a synchronization phase which allows the processors to exchange the following informations. Has the solution been found within the last fringe? If so, all processors agree to terminate. If not, all the processors determine the next fringe to be processed. Before having a closer look at the parallel algorithm, we analyze its sequential counterpart and give a short survey of parallel B&B algorithms found in the literature for various machine architectures.

3.1   The Sequential Version

This algorithm explores the sequence of fringes taking the nodes one by one. Since all the nodes of one fringe have the same optimistic estimation which is better than the estimation of subsequent fringes, we execute in fact a classical *best-first* B&B.

However, the point of view adopted in this paper for the best-first B&B is remarkably different. Best-first B&B is not defined in terms of the operations to be done on the best node of the list but on the set of all nodes with the same estimation as the best node. We rather express the best-first B&B in the following, more general, way. Process all the nodes with best estimation; if the solution is not found start again for the nodes with the next best estimation.

3.2   A Survey of Parallel B&B

Different approaches have been implemented in the parallelization of best-first B&B [Rou 89]. The main distinction criterion is certainly the existence of one unique open-list, an approach termed *horizontal*, as opposed to multiple private open-lists, called the *vertical* approach.

The horizontal approach has been implemented on shared memory machines as well as on distributed memory machines.

On shared memory machines the parallelization of the best-first B&B is straightforward. All the processors access the open-list, retrieve problems from it and insert newly generated nodes into it. This technique presents the big handicap of having all the processors access one single data structure in *mutual exclusion*.

On distributed memory machines, the implementation of a unique open-list is realised by a *master-slave* scheme. One distinguished processor keeps the open-list, hands out problems to the slave processors and collects from those the nodes to be inserted in the list [Kin 89]. The master quickly becomes a bottleneck.

The vertical approach has only been realised on distributed memory machines. Each processor treats a *part* of the global tree. The processors evolve *independently* from each other, work on their private open-list and exchange informations only in cases they could update their local best solution or in order to avoid an unequal partition of the global work (processors staying idle).

Once again, the efficiency of the parallel algorithm is very disappointing as soon as the number of processors is important or the tree to explore is huge. This degrading of performances is mostly due to a lack of information available locally on each processor. There may be only one processor containing nodes of the minimal tree while the other processors work on problems which are of no interest for determining the solution.

3.3 A Synchronized Parallel B&B

Having presented this algorithm at the beginning of this section, we will now define it in detail. This algorithm shuns the drawbacks of the horizontal approach by not managing any data structure consulted and modified by all the processors. Every processor has its own open-list. We also avoid the disadvantages of the vertical approach. No processor will develop nodes the sequential version could cut off. This parallel algorithm is truly a best-first B&B. These effects are obtained by means of synchronization phases and information exchange inserted between the computation of the different fringes. The correctness of the algorithm is proven in [Gen 92].

The Principles of the "Fringe Enumerating Algorithm" are the following. Between two synchronization phases, all the processors treat problems of the same fringe, every processor treating the problems which are in its local memory. At every synchronization phase all the processors are informed whether the solution has been found during the last computation. If not, the next fringe to be treated is determined by all the processors. Moreover, the processors may statically equilibrate their load for the next fringe. Between two synchronization phases, there is no information exchange concerning B&B, but the processors may do dynamic load balancing.

The Synchronization. A processor which has explored all its nodes in the current fringe or found a solution in the current fringe enters the synchronization phase. In section (5.2) we describe the way synchronization and static load balancing is done in our iPSC/2 implementation.

Starting the Algorithm. When the algorithm is started, one single processor has the root node. As it is not worth parallelizing the processing of the few first fringes, we will englobe those into one phase by means of an *initial optimistic estimation*, OE_{init}. All the problems with an optimistic estimation lower than OE_{init}

are processed during the first phase of computation. It will be reasonable to have all processors cooperating on this increased first phase.

Shared Memory. Although we used the terminology of distributed memory machines, our algorithm may be run on shared memory machines. On such a machine all processors will access private open-lists without any critical section. During the synchronization the local open-lists will be trimmed and redistributed.

Random Behaviors of the B&B. We completely ignored trees for which B&B, searching one solution, may show anomalous behavior and which are responsible for super- or sub-linear speedups in parallel B&B implementations. This behavior is observed for a sequential B&B which makes random choices among problems having the same optimistic estimation. The random behavior is common to both sequential and parallel executions. In the parallel setting of our algorithm, only the processing of the last fringe, i.e. the fringe containing the solution, is influenced. We may find a solution very quickly or on the contrary wait until nearly the last node has been developed. All this is purely a matter of chance. Our algorithm may show the same anomalous behavior as all the other parallel B&B implementations.

4 The Probabilistic Model

The parallel algorithm presented in section (3) is efficient only if nearly all the fringes include a large number of sub-problems which seems to be the case according to (*Fig.* 1). We now introduce a probabilistic model which allows us to estimate the average size of the fringes. This model is used to characterize a broad class of problems for which the algorithm is well adapted. In this sense our model differs from other studies in the literature which try to estimate f^* [Smi 84, Wah 82].

4.1 The Limits of the Model

In order to be able to carry out the calculations, we limit ourselves to regular B&B trees with constant *branching factor* b and constant *maximal depth* p. The model may be extended to all trees for which we are able to determine the number of nodes at any given depth. We suppose that the difference of the optimistic estimations between a father node and a son node is a random variable $d = oe(son) - oe(father)$ having a *mean* ex_d and a *standard deviation* σ_d. We only consider continuous functions in our model and further admit that all over the tree the differences between father and son estimations are independent from each other. This indispensable restriction for all modeling is certainly the hypothesis the most prone to criticism.

4.2 The Calculi in the Model

We need to know the average optimistic estimation of the nodes. With the root estimation assumed to be zero, the estimation of any node X at depth q is the random variable oe_X, sum of q times the random variable d, and can be approximated by a *Gauss* function g_q with mean $q * ex_d$ and standard deviation $\sqrt{q} * \sigma_d$.

$$g_q(x) = \frac{1}{\sqrt{2\,\pi\,q\,\sigma_d}}\; e^{-\frac{(x-q\,ex_d)^2}{2\,q\,\sigma_d^2}} = \mathcal{G}^x(q\,ex_d, \sqrt{q}\,\sigma_d) = \mathcal{G}^x_{ex_d,\sigma_d}(q) \qquad (3)$$

We then normalize the Gauss functions of (3) by weighting them with the relative frequency of the nodes at that depth q, see (4), and define the distribution function D_{ex_d,σ_d} as given by (5).

$$\mathcal{G}^{x,norm}_{ex_d,\sigma_d}(q) = \frac{(b-1)\,b^{q-1}}{b^p - 1}\;\mathcal{G}^x_{ex_d,\sigma_d}(q) \qquad (4)$$

$$D_{ex_d,\sigma_d}(x) = \sum_{i=1}^{p} \mathcal{G}^{x,norm}_{ex_d,\sigma_d}(i) \qquad (5)$$

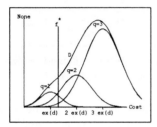

Fig. 5. *Graphical representation of the cost function D and the normalized Gauss functions for different values of the depth q.*

The formulae (6) and (7) then give the average size of a fringe with optimistic estimation x resp. the average size of the tree composed of nodes with an optimistic estimation not exceeding x. One might try to find a more compact and easily manipulable expression than (5). In particular (*Fig. 5*) shows that D is quite close to a Gauss function. Nevertheless, this may only be the case if the Gauss functions are "broad". Hence, we impose the ratio ex_d and σ_d to be included between two constants.

$$t_{Fr}(x) = \frac{b\,(b^p - 1)}{b - 1} D_{ex_d,\sigma_d}(x) \qquad (6)$$

$$t_A(x) = \frac{b\,(b^p - 1)}{b - 1} \int_{-\infty}^{x} D_{ex_d,\sigma_d}(t)\,dt \qquad (7)$$

We numerically compute a Gauss approximation of (5) and determine two values ex and σ such that (8) holds. Alternatively, letting $\sigma_d = \alpha * ex_d$ and $x_n = x/(p * ex_d)$ we obtain $\mathcal{D}_\alpha$ (9) and may determine $ex_{\mathcal{D}}$ and $\sigma_{\mathcal{D}}$ such that (10) holds.

$$D_{ex_d,\sigma_d}(x) \sim \mathcal{G}_{ex,\sigma}(x) \qquad (8)$$

$$\mathcal{D}_\alpha(x_n) = ex_d * D_{ex_d,\sigma_d}(x) \qquad (9)$$

$$\mathcal{D}_\alpha(x_n) \sim \mathcal{G}_{ex_{\mathcal{D}},\sigma_{\mathcal{D}}}(x_n) \qquad (10)$$

$$ln\left(\frac{\mathcal{D}_\alpha(x_n)}{\mathcal{D}_\alpha(ex_{\mathcal{D}})}\right) = -\frac{1}{2\,\sigma_{\mathcal{D}}^2} * t + c \quad \text{if} \quad t = (x_n - ex_{\mathcal{D}})^2 \qquad (11)$$

We may now determine the maximum of $\mathcal{D}_\alpha$ for different maximal depths and different values of α. The results are shown in (*Fig. 6*). For p large enough and α not too large we find, independently of the branching factor b, the maximum for $x_n = ex_{\mathcal{D}} = 0.9174$. The value of standard deviation of $\mathcal{D}_\alpha$ is obtained from (11) and (10) by using a least-squares linear fit on equation (11), see (*Fig. 7*). The value of

σ_D is next determined of the form $\sigma_D \sim p^a * \alpha^b$ by a linear regression. Independently of the branching factor we get $\sigma_D \sim p^{-1/2}$. Thus by (8,10)

$$\mathcal{D}_\alpha(x_n) \sim \mathcal{G}_{ex_D,\sigma_D}(x_n) = \mathcal{G}_{0.9174,f*p^{(-1/2)}}(x_n)$$
$$D_{ex_d,\sigma_d}(x) \sim \mathcal{G}_{ex,\sigma}(x) = \mathcal{G}_{0.9174*p*ex_d,f*\sqrt{p}*\sigma_d}(x) \tag{12}$$

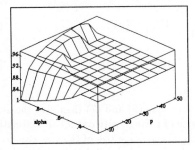
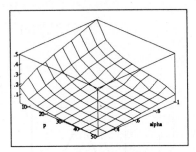

Fig. 6. *Plot of the maximum of $\mathcal{D}_\alpha$ for p from 5 to 50 and α from 1/4 to 1.*

Fig. 7. *Plot of the coefficient σ_D for p from 5 to 50 and α from 1/4 to 1.*

In the previous formula, we cannot give a more precise value to the factor f than the bound $1 \leq f \leq 1.2$. Globally (12) affirms that the computational complexity of a B&B algorithm is mainly given by the size of the few last fringes. Indeed, $ex \sim p*ex_d$ and $\sigma \sim \sqrt{p}*\sigma_d$ which correspond to $g_p(x)$ which gives the distribution of the nodes at the maximal depth p. The approximations are valid if the ratio between the mean and the standard deviation verifies $1/4 \leq \sigma_d/ex_d \leq 1$. In such cases the fringes increase exponentially in size. The same is true for other trees, see [Gen 91].

Under the above conditions, the Fringe Enumerating Algorithm should behave well on the average. For certain problems, we could nevertheless develop trees where the size of the fringes is quite variable or small. For such problems, our algorithm would then need a dynamic mechanism for collapsing small fringes. This decision could be taken during synchronization, all processors agreeing to explore a certain number of small fringes before synchronizing again.

5 The Test Case and the Implementations

5.1 The TSP

The Traveling Salesman Problem, **TSP** for short, consists in searching the cheapest tour through a given number of cities. The problem is described by a matrix indicating the distances between any two towns. Our distances are randomly chosen between 0 and some given maximum distance, the distribution being uniform.

The optimistic estimations are computing according to [Lit 63]. The distance matrix is first reduced, i.e. one subtracts the minimum of each line and each column, the sum of subtracted values giving a lower bound to any tour. A problem is branched into two different sub-problems, one containing an arc $k \rightarrow l$, the other not. The arc $k \rightarrow l$ is chosen according to the following heuristiç: among the arcs $x \rightarrow y$ with distance zero choose $k \rightarrow l$ such that for all p and r the value $cost(k,l) =$

$Min_{p \neq l}(k \rightarrow p) + Min_{r \neq k}(r \rightarrow l)$ is maximum. For the sub-problem which does not take the arc $k \rightarrow l$ we give a infinite distance to that arc, reduce the new matrix and add the newly subtracted values together with $cost(k, l)$ to the old optimistic estimation. For the problem selecting the arc $k \rightarrow l$ we take out the line k and the column l. This yields a smaller problem. Moreover, we compute the longest chain m to n containing $k \rightarrow l$ and forbid the arc $n \rightarrow m$ which would yield to short a tour. Again the matrix obtained is reduced, the newly subtracted values being added to the old optimistic estimation.

5.2 The Parallel Algorithm

Our implementation of the parallel algorithm on an Intel iPSC/2 hypercube is a very simple one. In order to speed up the starting up of the algorithm we decide to uniformly develop the tree to a depth $d + 2$ on 2^d processors. We may thus develop useless nodes. At the end of this initial phase every processor has four nodes.

From this point on we apply the standard Fringe Enumeration Algorithm without collapsing fringes. This may induce very short computation times between two synchronization phases. Some processors could even stay completely idle during one phase. In this case, the processors decide to nevertheless develop one local (maybe useless) problem outside of the current fringe before synchronizing. As soon as a processor finds a solution it broadcasts a *stop* signal.

We finally describe the way the load balancing is done at the beginning of a new fringe. It can be considered "static" since there will be no dynamic load balancing during the computation within one fringe. The implementation of the synchronization heavily uses the hypercube topology. Each processor only exchanges informations with all its direct neighbors beginning with the lowest dimension. Thus all processors communicate on dedicated physical links and there are no contentions.

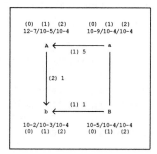

Fig. 8. *Diagram showing the synchronization and load balancing (see text).*

Having finished its work in the current fringe, a processor determines its next local fringe and the number of such nodes (state (0) in *Fig.* 8). Neighbors in the first dimension (A and a, B and b) then exchange these informations and compute the best fringe in that dimension and its size. In (*Fig.* 8) processor A is informed that there is a better next fringe than its local 12. Moreover the processors equilibrate the number of nodes without actually sending them.

The 9 nodes initially held by processor a are distributed between A and a, the processor with a capital letter getting the 9th node. The processors are now in state (1) and start the same protocol for the next dimension which results in state (2). The information exchange is now finished, all processors *globally* know the next fringe and the number of nodes they will get within this fringe. The load is perfectly balanced.

The processors now start to actually send problems to each other so as to equally distribute the total work. From the sequence of memorized states (0) - (1) - (2), every processor may compute the number of problems it has to send or receive in every dimension. (*Fig.* 8) shows the number of problems sent between processors. The total number of 16 nodes will be perfectly distributed on the processors. The synchronization phase is linear in the dimensions, i.e. logarithmic in the processors.

6 Results and Improvements

6.1 The Test Problem

We now present the results obtained for the **TSP** on an Intel iPSC/2 hypercube. In a first version we use the algorithm as described in (5.2). As there are only 4Mbyte of memory on each PE, the size of the **TSP** was chosen as a small 40 towns problem which needs less than 2000 open nodes. Even small sub-problems use the same storage as larger ones leading to a constant time memory management that doesn't handicap the sequential algorithm. The distances between any two towns are chosen by a uniform random generator and vary from 1 to 50. A value of 50 gives us relatively hard problems, either larger or smaller values yield simpler problems.

The results of a typical run with a maximum of 1201 open problems are shown in (*Tab.* 1). The first column gives the execution times in milli-seconds and the speedup obtained. The last column shows the cumulated time of the synchronization steps. It represents the time from the moment a node falls idle in the current fringe until the moment the computation of the next fringe is started. We see that these times are all relatively important. More complete measurements show in column two the average maximum waiting time on any processor from the moment the processor is idle until one of its neighbors is idle. Column three shows the total idle and information exchange times, the difference between column three and four is the time needed for exchanging problems in order to balance the workloads. We easily see that the bad performances come from the idle times of the processors. Thus a simple static load balancing at the beginning of every fringe is not sufficient.

#p	Time and (speedup)	Aver. max wait	Idle & info.	Sync. time
1	60711 (1.00)	0	0	0
2	32229 (1.88)	732	1767	1805
4	19183 (3.16)	1146	3349	3390
8	11215 (5.41)	524	2888	2930
16	7377 (8.23)	366	3000	3036

Table 1. *Execution and synchronization times for one problem instance.*

#p	Time and (speedup)	Aver. max wait	Idle & info.	Sync. time
1	60711 (1.00)	0	0	0
2	33176 (1.83)	248	2129	2249
4	18152 (3.34)	119	2084	2207
8	9701 (6.26)	75	1485	1590
16	6566 (9.25)	66	1467	1550

Table 2. *Execution and synchronization times for one problem instance obtained with the adapted algorithm.*

6.2 Dynamic Behavior of the Workload

Analyzing the **TSP** algorithm of section (5.1), we first notice that the computational complexity for branching a problem is not constant. Moreover, it is possible for son nodes to have the same optimistic estimation as their father. Hence, a fringe may increase while it is explored destroying the good initial load balancing. Thus, we need an additional load balancing scheme within a given fringe.

As dynamic load balancing mechanism is always a complicated procedure we preferred to integrate additional synchronization phases into one given fringe simply by not allowing a processor to treat problems newly created within the current fringe. The processors rather synchronize once more and redistribute those new problems. Introducing this mechanism into the existing code is very easy and needs only a few additional lines.

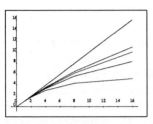

Fig. 9. *Speedups on 1, 2, 4, 8 and 16 PE's for problems of different sizes.*

(*Tab.* 2) shows the performances obtained with this new algorithm applied to the same problem instance as before. The synchronization times are improved and can be considered as being very good given the fact that we now have a large number of synchronizations, typically 50. This shows that the synchronization paradigm coupled with static load balancing performs quite well and is not too time-consuming.

6.3 Statistics

(*Fig.* 9) shows the average speedups obtained on problems of different sizes. We distinguished four classes with maximum open-lists of 0-500, 500-1000, 1000-1500 and 1500-2000 problems and with average sequential execution times of resp. 19.56 ± 13.12, 45.12 ± 17.32, 75.95 ± 30.41 and 106.89 ± 37.19 seconds. The larger the problems the better the speedups, but the speedup is far from optimal for 16 nodes. This can be explained by (*Tab.* 3) which considers the same individual problem as before.

#p	Effic.	Modified efficiency	Ratio of nodes	#nodes develop.
1	1.00	1.00	1.00	1201
2	0.91	0.98	0.96	1252
4	0.84	0.95	0.92	1300
8	0.78	0.94	0.92	1306
16	0.58	0.76	0.76	1578

#p	List 0-500	List 500-1000	List 1000-1500	List 1500-2000
1	324	639	1221	1734
2	168	318	653	911
4	98	172	344	476
8	65	102	186	253
16	51	69	108	142

Table 3. *Comparing the number of nodes developed in sequential and in parallel.*

Table 4. *Comparing the average maximal sizes of the open-lists in sequential and parallel.*

The first column gives the global efficiency, the second one the efficiency when we subtract the synchronization time. This value is roughly the same than the ratio of sequentially and parallelly branched nodes (columns three and four). We conclude that the problems are in fact too small for such large a number of processors. Not all processors will always obtain nodes within the current fringe and will then develop one local (maybe useless) node. Thus, the parallel algorithm does too much work. This explanation is confirmed by the speedups of 4, 7.49, 13.66 and 23.37 we get on larger (40 towns and 5000 open nodes) problems executed on 4, 8, 16 and 32 processors. The speedup is nearly linear except for 32 processors where the problems are again too small.

Finally, let us point out that the static load balancing regularly distributes the sub-problems on all processors allowing larger problems to be solved. (*Tab.* 4) shows the average maximum number of nodes in the open-list of any processor for the problems of (*Fig.* 9).

7 Conclusion

Our analysis of the B&B algorithm led to a tree development strategy by fringes, naturally amenable to parallelization on a MIMD architecture using phases with intermediate synchronization for information exchange and (possibly) load balancing. The tree explored in parallel is exactly the minimal tree considered by the sequential best-first B&B. This is obtained by a judicious choice of the moments at which the processors exchange information. Probabilistic modelization of regular search trees shows the optimality of the parallelization strategy. The implementation of a **TSP** shows the feasibility of our synchronization and load balancing scheme on an iPSC/2. The approach is scalable and behaves well on large numbers of processors from the point of view of speedup as well as from the point of view of memory utilization.

References

[Gen 91] M. Gengler, *A Best-first Parallel B&B with Synchronization Phases on Distributed Memory Machines*, Tech. Rep. 76, Laboratoire d'Informatique Théorique, EPFL-DI, Lausanne (CH), 1991.

[Gen 92] M. Gengler, *Axiomatique du Branch-and-Bound*, Tech. Rep. 77, Laboratoire d'Informatique Théorique, EPFL-DI, Lausanne (CH), 1992.

[Joh 90] D. S. Johnson, *A Catalog of Complexity Classes*, in *Algorithms and Complexity*, Handbook of Theoretical Computer Science, Vol. A, J. Van Leeuwen (ed.), pp. 67-161, Elsevier & MIT Press, Amsterdam (NL) & Cambridge (USA), 1990.

[Kin 89] G. A. P. Kindervater, *Exercises in Parallel Combinatorial Computing*, PhD. Thesis, CWI, Amsterdam (NL), 1989.

[Lit 63] J. D. Little, K. G. Murty, D. W. Sweeney, C. Karel, *An Algorithm for the Traveling Salesman Problem*, Operations Research 11, pp. 972-989, 1963.

[Mit 70] L. G. Mitten, *B&B Methods: General Formulation and Properties*, Operations Research 18, pp. 24-34, 1970.

[Rin 74] A. H. G. Rinnooy Kan, *On Mitten's Axioms for Branch-and-Bound*, Tech. Rep. W/74/45/03, Graduate School of Management, Delft (NL), 1974.

[Rou 87] C. Roucairol, *Du séquentiel au parallèle: La recherche arborescente et son application à la programmation quadratique en variables 0.1*, Thèse d'Etat, Univ. Paris 6, Paris (F), 1987.

[Rou 89] C. Roucairol, *Parallel Branch and Bound Algorithms - an Overview*, in *Parallel and Distributed Algorithms*, M. Cosnard et al. (eds.), Elsevier, Amsterdam (NL), 1989.

[Smi 84] D. R. Smith, *Random Trees and the Analysis of Branch and Bound Procedures*, Journal of the ACM, Vol. 31, *No* 1, pp. 163-188, 1984.

[Wah 82] B. Wah, C. Yu, *Probabilistic Modeling of B&B Algorithms*, in *Proc. COMPSAC*, pp. 647-653, 1982.

This article was processed using the LaTeX macro package with LLNCS style

On Tests of Uniform Tree Circuits

Hongzhong Wu

FB14-Informatik, Universität des Saarlandes
W-6600 Saarbrücken, Germany

Abstract. This paper explores the structure of test complexity classes of uniform tree circuits. We prove that the test complexity of a balanced uniform tree circuit is either $O(1)$ or $\Omega(\lg n)$, the test complexity of balanced uniform tree circuits based on commutative functions can be divided into constant, logarithmic and polynomial classes, and balanced uniform tree circuits based on monotonic functions are all $\Theta(n^r)$ $(r \in (0,1])$ testable.

1   Introduction

The circuit illustrated by Fig. 1 has a tree-like structure. It is regarded as a uniform tree circuit if all its cells $C_1^{(1)}$, $C_1^{(2)}$, ..., $C_{m^2}^{(3)}$ realize the same function. We use the symbol $T^{(n)}$ to denote a balanced uniform tree circuit with n primary inputs. A cell realizing a function f is called f cell. The test complexity of $T^{(n)}$ is defined to be the minimal number of test patterns required to test $T^{(n)}$ completely. It is measured as a function of the number of the primary inputs in $T^{(n)}$.

The key to the test of a VLSI system lies in the test of its combinational logic parts. Many combinational circuits, special for fast computations, consist of tree circuits. To analyze the test complexity of these tree circuits is helpful to the design, optimization and test of a VLSI system.

It has been shown, e.g., in [5], that for an n-input fanout-free tree circuit, the number of single and multiple fault detection tests lies between $2\sqrt{n}$ and $n + 1$. If fanouts are allowed inside a cell, the scene will change. The test complexity of tree circuits for computations over monoids has been deeply studied and surprisingly divided into constant, logarithmic and polynomial classes [2]. It indicates that the test complexity of a tree circuit could jump from one class to another when the definition of its basic cell is modified. It motivates us to analyze the test complexity of a tree circuit and study the possibility of modifying it to change its test complexity from a high class to a low one, for instance from $\Omega(\lg n)$ to $O(1)$ or from $\Omega(n^r)$ $(r \in (0,1])$ to $O(\lg n)$.

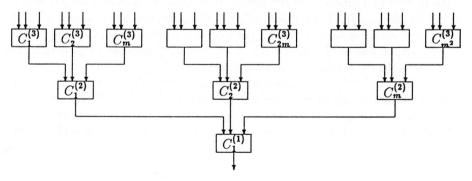

Fig. 1: A uniform tree circuit

The result in [2] is obtained under the assumption that the function implemented by the basic cell has the associative law. This condition is a limitation in practice. For example, the boolean function NAND does not have the associative law. In this paper, we drop this condition and consider a more general problem. Suppose that tree circuits are based on functions having the commutative law instead of the associative law. What is the classification of the test complexity of such kind of tree circuits? This paper answers this question.

In next section we will define the test problem and make some conventions. In the same section we will prove that a balanced uniform tree circuit is either $O(1)$ or $\Omega(\lg n)$ testable. In the third section we will show that the test complexity of balanced uniform tree circuits based on commutative functions can be divided into constant, logarithmic and polynomial classes, namely, $O(1)$, $\Theta(\lg n)$ and $\Omega(n^r)$ $(r \in (0,1])$. The fourth section shows that a balanced uniform tree circuit based on a monotonic function is $\Theta(n^r)$ $(r \in (0,1])$ testable.

2   Uniform Tree Circuits

Let $B = \{0,1\}$ and f be a surjective function from B^m to B. Assume that all cells in the circuit illustrated by Fig. 1 implement the same function f. In other words, all cells in the circuit are identical, and they make up a uniform tree circuit based on f.

To facilitate our discussion, we introduce some terminologies and conventions.

We assign every line and cell in $T^{(n)}$ a unique level. Here levels are arranged in ascending order from the primary output to the primary inputs of $T^{(n)}$. The primary output is assigned level 0. A cell C and all its input lines are in level $k+1$ if the output of the cell C is in level k. A tree circuit is said to be of l-level if it has l levels. Fig. 1 shows a 3-level tree circuit having the cell $C_1^{(1)}$ at the first level, $C_1^{(2)}$, $C_2^{(2)}$, ..., $C_m^{(2)}$ at the second level, and $C_1^{(3)}$, $C_2^{(3)}$, ..., $C_{m^2}^{(3)}$ at the third level.

There are various faults and fault models. In this paper, the *cell functional fault* model will be assumed. This means that a fault in a cell changes the function assigned to the cell. Furthermore, we will hold that there is only one faulty cell in the whole tree circuit that causes a discrepancy between the practical output and the expected one for some inputs.

A $T^{(n)}$ is recognized to be defective if one of its cells is faulty. An f cell is considered to be faulty if for an element $X \in B^m$ applied to it, the corresponding output is $\overline{f(X)}$ instead of the desired $f(X)$. In order to detect this fault, one has to apply X to the faulty cell and sensitize that fault, and then drive a diagnosis signal to the output. When the output line of the faulty cell is not primary, one has to propagate the diagnosis signal to the primary output for observing it.

An element $X \in B^m$ is an assignment to an f cell. Both terms *element* and *assignment* are interchangeable throughout this paper. For $X \in B^m$, we use $H_w(X)$ to denote its *Hamming weight* which is the number of 1 components in X. For $X, Y \in B^m$, we use $H_d(X,Y)$ to denote their *Hamming distance* which is the number of bits in which X and Y differ. We partition B^m into $m+1$ classes in the following way.

$$B_i = \{X \mid X \in B^m, H_w(X) = i\} \quad \text{for } i \in [0,m]$$

B_i denotes the ith class including every X whose Hamming weight is i. The following conventions will be used throughout.

$$(x_1, ..., x_m) \geq (y_1, ..., y_m) \iff \forall i \in [1, m]x_i \geq y_i$$
$$(x_1, ..., x_m) > (y_1, ..., y_m) \iff (x_1, ..., x_m) \geq (y_1, ..., y_m) \wedge \exists i \in [1, m]x_i > y_i$$
$$(x_1, ..., x_m) \leq (y_1, ..., y_m) \iff \forall i \in [1, m]x_i \leq y_i$$
$$(x_1, ..., x_m) < (y_1, ..., y_m) \iff (x_1, ..., x_m) \leq (y_1, ..., y_m) \wedge \exists i \in [1, m]x_i < y_i.$$

Let $\overline{1} = 0$ and $\overline{0} = 1$. We use symbols D and $\overline{D}$ to denote two different *diagnosis signals*. The diagnosis signal D has the value 1 in the normal circuit and 0 in the faulty circuit. Another diagnosis signal $\overline{D}$ has the value 0 in the normal circuit and 1 in the faulty circuit [4].

Assume that $H_d(X, Y) = 1$, $f(Y) = \overline{f(X)}$, and X and Y differ only in their ith component x_i and y_i. We say that the assignment X can propagate a D signal on the ith input if $x_i = 1$, otherwise a $\overline{D}$ signal. The assignment X can deliver a D signal to the output if $f(X) = 1$, otherwise a $\overline{D}$ signal.

Definition 1 : *Assume that $u, v \in \{D, \overline{D}\}$ are two diagnosis signals. We say that v is a successor of u if u can be transformed into v through an f cell.*

Definition 2 : *$X \in B^m$ is logic 1 critical if*
$$\forall Y \in B^m \left\{ Y > X \wedge H_d(X, Y) = 1 \Longrightarrow f(Y) = \overline{f(X)} \right\}.$$
$X \in B^m$ is logic 0 critical if
$$\forall Y \in B^m \left\{ Y < X \wedge H_d(X, Y) = 1 \Longrightarrow f(Y) = \overline{f(X)} \right\}.$$
$X \in B^m$ is full critical if it is logic 1 as well as 0 critical.
We say a function f has C-property(cancellation) if every $X \in B^m$ is full critical.

The C-property generalizes the group-condition in [2]. A full critical assignment X can propagate a diagnosis signal on every input of an f cell and can simultaneously propagate m diagnosis signals altogether.

Definition 3 : *A diagnosis signal $u \in \{D, \overline{D}\}$ on a line has one unit of diagnosis information for the line. Assign X to an f cell. We say that the corresponding diagnosis signal got from the output of the f cell can contain $\frac{i}{m}$ units of diagnosis information for each of the m inputs, provided that with the assignment X one can simultaneously propagate at most i diagnosis signals on the m inputs.*

By using the concept of the *diagnosis information* one can measure the propagatability of the diagnosis signals for an assignment X applied to an f cell.

Lemma 1 $\forall X, Y \in B^m \{H_w(X) = H_w(Y) \Longrightarrow f(X) = f(Y)\}$ if f has C-property.

The proof for this lemma is trivial. $\qquad\square$

It is obvious that if f has C-property, then

$$\forall i \in [0, m) \forall X \in B_i \forall Y \in B_{i+1} \{f(X) = \overline{f(Y)}\}$$
$$\forall X, Y \in \bigcup_{0 \leq 2i \leq m} B_{2i} \{f(X) = f(Y)\}, \quad \forall X, Y \in \bigcup_{1 \leq 2i+1 \leq m} B_{2i+1} \{f(X) = f(Y)\}$$

This states that every assignment $X \in B_i$ applied to an f cell can simultaneously propagate i D as well as $m - i$ $\overline{D}$ signals on the inputs of the cell if f has C-property.

Theorem 1 *If f has C-property, then $T^{(n)}$ is $O(1)$ testable, else $T^{(n)}$ is $\Omega(\lg n)$ testable.*

Proof : We dispose first the *if* part. Assume that f has C-property, Fig. 1 illustrates part of the circuit under consideration, and $C_1^{(1)}$, $C_1^{(2)}$, ..., are all identical cells realizing the same function f. By assigning $X \in B^m$ to $C_i^{(3)}$ one can propagate m diagnosis signals on inputs of $C_i^{(3)}$ simultaneously, since every $X \in B^m$ is full critical. By applying 2^m distinct assignments in B^m to $C_i^{(3)}$ one can propagate 2^{m-1} D signals as well as 2^{m-1} $\overline{D}$ signals on every input of $C_i^{(3)}$. Note that

$$\# \bigcup_{0 \leq 2i \leq m} B_{2i} = \# \bigcup_{1 \leq 2i+1 \leq m} B_{2i+1}.$$

By assigning 2^m distinct assignments to $C_i^{(3)}$ one can deliver 2^{m-1} D signals and 2^{m-1} $\overline{D}$ signals to its output. Furthermore, the 2^m distinct assignments in B^m can test the cell $C_i^{(3)}$ completely.

With the diagnosis signals got from outputs of $C_i^{(3)}$ ($i \in [1, m^2]$) one can construct a complete test set for every cell $C_i^{(2)}$ at the second level. With the diagnosis signals got from outputs of $C_i^{(2)}$ ($i \in [1, m]$) one can form a complete test set for the cell $C_1^{(1)}$. This indicates that for a given $T^{(n)}$ based on f one can always construct 2^m n-bit patterns which completely test every cell in $T^{(n)}$. Thus $T^{(n)}$ is constant testable.

Now turn our hand to proving the *only if* part. Assume that f has not C-property. Then there are $X \in B_i$ and $Y \in B_{i+1}$, so that $f(X) = f(Y)$. It means that either of X and Y applied to an f cell can simultaneously propagate $m - 1$ diagnosis signals at the very most. Let ν denote the minimum number of diagnosis signals got from the primary output of an l-level uniform tree circuit. We can inductively prove that $\nu \geq l$.

For $l = 1$, $T^{(n)}$ is a single cell, and $\nu \geq 1$. Assume that $\nu \geq i$ holds for $l = i$. Suppose that $l = i + 1$. Each of the m inputs of the cell with the primary output is linked directly to the output of an i-level tree circuit, and at least i diagnosis signals on it has to be propagated. On the assumption that there are two distinct assignments $X, Y \in B^m$, so that $H_d(X, Y) = 1$ and $f(X) = f(Y)$, either of X and Y can propagate simultaneously $m - 1$ diagnosis signals at most. Thus $\nu > \frac{m \times i}{m}$. Putting it differently, $\nu \geq i + 1$.

A balanced uniform tree circuit with n primary inputs has at least $\lceil \log_m n \rceil$ levels. It is an immediate conclusion that $T^{(n)}$ is $\Omega(\lg n)$ testable. **Q.E.D.**

There are also other $O(1)$ testable circuit families [3].

Assume that a complete test set of an f cell delivers ν_0 $\overline{D}$ signals and ν_1 D signals to the output. If there is a constant t, so that with t patterns one can propagate ν_0 $\overline{D}$ signals and ν_1 D diagnosis signals assigned to every input of cells at the same level of $T^{(n)}$ to the primary output, then we say that every level of $T^{(n)}$ is constant testable. It is obvious that a balanced uniform tree circuit is $O(\lg n)$ testable if every level is constant testable.

Lemma 2 $T^{(n)}$ *is $\Omega(n^r)$ ($r \in (0, 1]$) testable if there is no full critical element in B^m.*

Proof : Assume that there is no full critical element in B^m. Every assignment applied to an f cell can simultaneously propagate $m - 1$ diagnosis signals at most. Then through a level the number of diagnosis signals on lines will be multiplied by $\frac{m}{m-1}$ at least. It implies that to propagate a diagnosis signal assigned to every primary input we have to deliver at least $(\frac{m}{m-1})^{\log_m n}$ diagnosis signals to the primary output of $T^{(n)}$. Clearly,

$$(\frac{m}{m-1})^{\log_m n} = n^{1-\log_m(m-1)}, \quad 0 < 1 - \log_m(m-1) \leq 1.$$

The lemma follows. $\hspace{6cm}$ **Q.E.D.**

3 Commutative Tree Circuits

We have proved that a $T^{(n)}$ is either $O(1)$ or $\Omega(\lg n)$ testable in the last section. In this section we show that a uniform $T^{(n)}$ based on a commutative function is either $O(\lg n)$ or $\Omega(n^r)$ ($r \in (0,1]$) testable. In other words, the test complexity of balanced uniform tree circuits based on commutative functions can be divided into three classes, namely, $O(1)$, $\Theta(\lg n)$ and $\Omega(n^r)$ ($r \in (0,1]$).

Assume that B^m has full critical elements. We define a function P from the set of full critical elements in B^m to the integer field.

$$P(X) = H_w(X) - mf(X) \tag{1}$$

where X is a full critical element in B^m.

Lemma 3 $T^{(n)}$ is $\Omega(n^r)$ ($r \in (0,1]$) testable if $P(X) < 0$ for every full critical element $X \in B^m$.

Proof : Assume that a nonfull critical assignment can simultaneously propagate k_0 diagnosis signals at most, and a full critical assignment can simultaneously propagate k_1 D signals at the very most, and can only generate a D signal.

Without loss of generality, we assume that $T^{(n)}$ has m^l primary inputs and l is even. Let $k = \max\{k_0, k_1\}$, and $\mu = \frac{2km-k^2}{m^2}$. We prove bellow that a diagnosis signal on the primary output can contain at most $\mu^{\frac{l}{2}}$ units of diagnosis information for every primary input.

For $l = 0$, it is trivial. Assume that for $l = 2i$, a diagnosis signal on the primary output of $T^{(n)}$ can contain at most μ^i units of diagnosis information for every primary input.

Suppose that $l = 2i + 2$, and $T^{(n)}$ is an l-level uniform tree circuit based on f. In $T^{(n)}$ each input of a cell at the second level is linked directly to the output of a $2i$-level balanced uniform tree circuit based on f.

On the assumption that $P(X) < 0$ for every full critical assignment $X \in B^m$, then a $\overline{D}$ signal on the output of an f cell can only be derived from a nonfull critical assignment, and contain only $\frac{k_0}{m}$ units of diagnosis information for every input of the cell. This indicates that a $\overline{D}$ signal on either the primary output or lines in level 1 can contain no more than $\frac{k_0}{m}$ units of diagnosis information for every connected line in level 2.

A D signal on the primary output can be derived from either a full critical assignment or nonfull critical assignment applied to the cell in level 1. For the latter case, such a D signal can contain no more than $\frac{k_0}{m}$ units of diagnosis information for every line in level 1. For the former case, the D signal is derived from a full critical assignment X which can propagate $H_w(X)$ D signals and $m - H_w(X)$ $\overline{D}$ signals simultaneously. Then this D signal can contain no more than $\frac{H_w(X) + \frac{k_0}{m}(m - H_w(X))}{m}$ units of diagnosis information for every connected line in level 2. Clearly,

$$\frac{2km - k^2}{m^2} \geq \max \left\{ \frac{k_0}{m}, \ \frac{H_w(X) + \frac{k_0}{m}(m - H_w(X))}{m} \right\}.$$

It implies that a diagnosis signal on the primary output can contain at most μ units of diagnosis information for every connected input of a cell at the second level, and $\mu \cdot \mu^i$ units of diagnosis information for every primary input at the very most. Then $\mu^{-\frac{l}{2}}$ patterns are necessary to propagate one unit of diagnosis information for every primary input to the primary output. Note that

$$\mu^{-\frac{l}{2}} = \mu^{-\frac{\log_m n}{2}} = n^{1 - 0.5 \log_m (2km - k^2)}.$$

Then we have Lemma 3. **Q.E.D.**

Lemma 4 $T^{(n)}$ is $\Omega(n^r)$ $(r \in (0, 1])$ testable if the unique full critical element X belongs to B_m, and D signal is not a successor of $\overline{D}$.

Proof : Without loss of generality, assume that $T^{(n)}$ is an l-level tree circuit with m^l primary inputs.

On the assumption that D is not a successor of $\overline{D}$, no $\overline{D}$ signal on the primary inputs can be transformed into D signal, and no $\overline{D}$ signal can be propagated with a full critical assignment.

Consider only the propagation of a $\overline{D}$ signal from each of the primary inputs to the primary output. To propagate a $\overline{D}$ signal from each of the m inputs of a cell to its output $\frac{m}{m-1}$ assignments are necessary and $\frac{m}{m-1}$ $\overline{D}$ signals will be delivered to the output line. Assume that $(\frac{m}{m-1})^i$ patterns are necessary to propagate a $\overline{D}$ signal on each of the primary inputs of an i-level balanced uniform tree circuit to its primary output and deliver $(\frac{m}{m-1})^i$ $\overline{D}$ signals to the primary output. Thus we can state that $(\frac{m}{m-1})^{i+1}$ patterns are necessary to propagate a $\overline{D}$ signal from each of the primary inputs of an $i + 1$ levels balanced uniform tree circuit to its primary output and deliver $(\frac{m}{m-1})^{i+1}$ $\overline{D}$ to the primary output. Note that

$$\left(\frac{m}{m-1}\right)^{\log_m n} = n^{1 - \log_m(m-1)}, \quad 1 - \log_m(m - 1) \in (0, 1].$$

The lemma follows. **Q.E.D.**

Lemma 5 $T^{(n)}$ is $\Omega(n^r)$ $(r \in (0, 1])$ testable if $P(X) > 0$ for every full critical element $X \in B^m$.

The proof for this lemma is similar to that for Lemma 3. □

Lemma 6 $T^{(n)}$ is $\Omega(n^r)$ $(r \in (0, 1])$ testable if the unique full critical element X belongs to B_0, and $\overline{D}$ signal is not a successor of D.

The proof for this lemma is similarly to that for Lemma 4. □

Lemma 7 $T^{(n)}$ is $O(\lg n)$ testable if $X \in B_m$ is a full critical element, and D is a successor of $\overline{D}$ signal.

Proof : With a proper assignment one can transform a $\overline{D}$ signal assigned to an input of an f cell into a D. This indicates that with m proper assignments one can separately transform m $\overline{D}$ signals assigned to m inputs of an f cell into m D signals. Furthermore, one can simultaneously propagate m D signals assigned to the m inputs of a cell. It implies that $m + 1$ assignments are enough to propagate a D signal as well as a $\overline{D}$ from every input of cells at the same level to the primary output. Thus every level of $T^{(n)}$ is constant testable, and $T^{(n)}$ is $O(\lg n)$ testable. **Q.E.D.**

Lemma 8 $T^{(n)}$ is $O(\lg n)$ testable if $X \in B_0$ is a full critical element, and $\overline{D}$ is a successor of D signal.

The proof for this lemma is similar to that for Lemma 7. $\qquad\qquad\square$

Lemma 9 $T^{(n)}$ is $O(\lg n)$ testable if there are two full critical elements $X, Y \in B^m$ so that $P(X)P(Y) < 0$.

Proof : For a commutative function f, if $H_w(X) = H_w(Y)$, then $f(X) = f(Y)$, and X and Y have the same propagatability of the diagnosis signal.

Without loss of generality, we assume that $f(X) = 1$, $f(Y) = 0$, $H_w(X) = i$ and $H_w(Y) = j$. Then $P(X) = i - m$, and $P(Y) = j$.

With j assignments in B_i, one can propagate $j \cdot i$ D signals and $j(m - i)$ $\overline{D}$ signals on inputs of an f cell and deliver j D signals to the output. With $m - i$ assignments in B_j, one can propagate $(m - i)j$ D signals and $(m - i)(m - j)$ $\overline{D}$ signals on inputs of an f cell and deliver $(m - i)$ $\overline{D}$ signals to the output. With j assignments in B_i and $m - i$ assignments in B_j, one can simultaneously propagate $m \cdot j$ D signals and $m(m - i)$ $\overline{D}$ signals on m inputs of an f cell.

We can conclude that by applying j assignments in B_i and $m - i$ assignments in B_j to an f cell, one can propagate j D signals and $m - i$ $\overline{D}$ signals on each of the m inputs and deliver j D signals and $m - i$ $\overline{D}$ signals to the output. There is a constant t, and all diagnosis signals derived from testing all cells at the same level in $T^{(n)}$ can be propagated to the primary output with t n-bit patterns. Thus, one can test every level of $T^{(n)}$ through t n-bit patterns. $T^{(n)}$ is $O(\lg n)$ testable. **Q.E.D.**

Theorem 2 $T^{(n)}$ is either $O(\lg n)$ or $\Omega(n^r)$ $(r \in (0, 1])$ testable.

Proof : Given an f function from B^m to B, only following eight cases can happen.
1. There is no full critical element in B^m.
2. $P(X) < 0$ for every full critical element $X \in B^m$.
3. $X \in B_m$ is the unique full critical element, and D is not a successor of $\overline{D}$.
4. $P(X) > 0$ for every full critical element $X \in B^m$.
5. $X \in B_0$ is the unique full critical element, and $\overline{D}$ is not a successor of D.
6. $X \in B_m$ is a full critical element, and D is a successor of $\overline{D}$.
7. $X \in B_0$ is a full critical element, and $\overline{D}$ is a successor of D.
8. There are two full critical elements $X, Y \in B^m$ so that $P(X)P(Y) < 0$.

According to Lemma 2 through 6, $T^{(n)}$ is $\Omega(n^r)$ $(r \in (0, 1])$ testable for the first five cases. For the last three cases, $T^{(n)}$ is $O(\lg n)$ testable based on Lemma 7 through 9. **Q.E.D.**

The following corollary is an immediate consequence of Theorem 1 and 2.

Corollary 1 *The test complexity of balanced uniform tree circuits based on commutative functions can be divided into three classes, namely,* $O(1)$, $\Theta(\lg n)$ *and* $\Omega(n^r)$ $(r \in (0, 1])$.

4 Monotonic Tree Circuits

The test complexity of unate circuits based on AND/OR gates are discussed in detail in [1,7]. The paper [8] shows that balanced uniform tree circuits based on unate functions are all $\Omega(n^r)$ $(r \in (0, 1])$ testable. In this section we study the test complexity of uniform tree circuits based on monotonic functions.

Definition 4 : *A function f is said to be monotonic if*

$$\forall X, Y \in B^m \{X > Y \Longrightarrow f(x) \geq f(y)\} \vee \forall X, Y \in B^m \{X < Y \Longrightarrow f(x) \leq f(y)\}.$$

Assume that $T^{(n)}$ is an l-level uniform tree circuit based on f. Let $\nu_1^{(i)}$ and $\nu_0^{(i)}$ denote the minimum number of D and $\overline{D}$ signals delivered to every input of an f cell in level $l - i$, respectively. A rough relationship among these parameters can be described through the inequality (2).

$$\begin{bmatrix} \nu_1^{(i)} \\ \nu_0^{(i)} \end{bmatrix} \geq \begin{bmatrix} a_{00} & a_{01} \\ a_{10} & a_{11} \end{bmatrix} \begin{bmatrix} \nu_1^{(i-1)} \\ \nu_0^{(i-1)} \end{bmatrix} + \begin{bmatrix} c_1 \\ c_0 \end{bmatrix} \tag{2}$$

The parameters $a_{00}, a_{01}, a_{10}, a_{11}, c_0$ and c_1 are all determined by the definition of function f.

When the equality in (2) is satisfiable, then (2) represents that the number of diagnosis signals delivered to the output of a cell is a linear function of the number of diagnosis signals on inputs of the cell. We call (2) *recurrence formula of the test complexity* of f. The matrix and constant vector in (2) are called *rotation matrix* and *translation vector* of f, respectively.

A monotonic function is monotonic increase if

$$\forall X, Y \in B^m \{X > Y \Longrightarrow f(x) \geq f(y)\}$$

else is monotonic decrease. At first we study the test complexity of uniform tree circuits based on monotonic increase functions.

Theorem 3 $T^{(n)}$ *based on a monotonic increase function is* $\Theta(n^r)$ $(r \in (0, 1])$ *testable.*

Proof: We construct two subsets of B^m.

$$\begin{aligned} \mathcal{E} &= \{X \mid f(X) = 1 \wedge \forall Y \in B^m \{Y < X \Longrightarrow f(Y) < f(X)\}\} \\ \mathcal{N} &= \{X \mid f(X) = 0 \wedge \forall Y \in B^m \{Y > X \Longrightarrow f(Y) > f(X)\}\} \end{aligned}$$

Set $\mathcal{E}$ is an *antichain* in which no element is comparable with others. Set $\mathcal{N}$ is also an antichain.

It is not difficult to see that every element in $\mathcal{E}$ is 0 critical, while every element in $\mathcal{N}$ is 1 critical. A D signal can only be propagated through assignments in $\mathcal{E}$, while a $\overline{D}$ signal can only be propagated through assignments in $\mathcal{N}$. $\mathcal{E}$ and $\mathcal{N}$ have no common element, and we call them D and $\overline{D}$ *critical antichains*, respectively.

For $Y_j = (y_1 \cdots y_i \cdots y_m) \in B^m$ we define $\Pi_i Y_j = y_i$, and $\overline{Y_j} = (\overline{y_1} \cdots \overline{y_i} \cdots \overline{y_m})$. Set $s = \#\mathcal{E}$ and $t = \#\mathcal{N}$. Let

$$\alpha^{-1} = \max\left\{ \min\left\{ \sum_{X_j \in \mathcal{E}} z_j \Pi_i X_j \left(\sum_{1 \le j \le s} z_j \right)^{-1} \middle| i \in [1,m] \right\} \middle| z_j > 0, \ j \in [1,s] \right\}$$

$$\beta^{-1} = \max\left\{ \min\left\{ \sum_{Y_j \in \mathcal{N}} z_j \Pi_i \overline{Y_j} \left(\sum_{1 \le j \le t} z_j \right)^{-1} \middle| i \in [1,m] \right\} \middle| z_j > 0, \ j \in [1,t] \right\}$$

By repeatedly applying an assignment $X_j \in \mathcal{E}$ z_j times to an f cell one can propagate $z_j \Pi_i X_j$ D signals on the ith input of the cell. By applying $\sum_{1 \le j \le s} z_j$ assignments in $\mathcal{E}$ one can propagate $\sum_{X_j \in \mathcal{E}} z_j \Pi_i X_j$ D signals on the ith input of the cell. The formula

$$\min\left\{ \sum_{X_j \in \mathcal{E}} z_j \Pi_i X_j \left(\sum_{1 \le j \le s} z_j \right)^{-1} \middle| i \in [1,m] \right\}$$

define the minimum rate between the minimum number of D signals on an input and the number of assignments used in $\mathcal{E}$. The parameter α^{-1} represents the maximum efficiency of propagating a D signal on an input of the f cell by using an assignment in $\mathcal{E}$. Similarly, β^{-1} represents the maximum efficiency of propagating a $\overline{D}$ signal on an input of the f cell by using an assignment in $\mathcal{N}$.

To propagate a D signal from every input of an f cell one has to use α assignments in $\mathcal{E}$ and deliver α diagnosis signals to the output. Similarly, to propagate a $\overline{D}$ signal from every input of an f cell one has to use β assignments in $\mathcal{N}$ and deliver β $\overline{D}$ signals to the output. It is easy to see that $\alpha, \beta \ge 1$ and $1 < \alpha\beta < m^2$.

An assignment $X \in B^m \setminus \mathcal{E} \cup \mathcal{N}$ can not be used to propagate diagnosis signals at all; for testing a cell completely, every assignment $X \in B^m$ has to be applied to it, however.

Set $c_1 = \sum_{X \in B^m} f(X) - s$ and $c_0 = \sum_{X \in B^m} \overline{f(X)} - t$. Then $c_1 + c_0$ equals the number of elements which are included in neither $\mathcal{E}$ nor $\mathcal{N}$.

In order to propagate $\nu_1^{(i-1)}$ D signals from each of the m inputs of an f cell and to completely test the cell itself, one has to drive $\nu_1^{(i-1)}\alpha + c_1$ D signals to the output. In order to propagate $\nu_0^{(i-1)}$ $\overline{D}$ signals from each of the m inputs and to completely test the cell itself, one has to deliver $\nu_0^{(i-1)}\beta + c_0$ $\overline{D}$ signals to the output.

We can determine that the recurrence formula of the test complexity of f is

$$\begin{bmatrix} \nu_1^{(i)} \\ \nu_0^{(i)} \end{bmatrix} = \begin{bmatrix} \alpha & 0 \\ 0 & \beta \end{bmatrix} \begin{bmatrix} \nu_1^{(i-1)} \\ \nu_0^{(i-1)} \end{bmatrix} + \begin{bmatrix} c_1 \\ c_0 \end{bmatrix}.$$

Assume that $T^{(n)}$ is an l-level tree circuit, and $\nu_0^{(0)} = \nu_1^{(1)} = 1$. Putting it differently, only one D signal and one $\overline{D}$ signal are assigned to every primary inputs. We have thus

$$\begin{bmatrix} \nu_1^{(i)} \\ \nu_0^{(i)} \end{bmatrix} = \begin{bmatrix} \alpha & 0 \\ 0 & \beta \end{bmatrix}^i \begin{bmatrix} \nu_1^{(0)} \\ \nu_0^{(0)} \end{bmatrix} + \sum_{j=0}^{i-1} \begin{bmatrix} \alpha & 0 \\ 0 & \beta \end{bmatrix}^j \begin{bmatrix} c_1 \\ c_0 \end{bmatrix} = \begin{bmatrix} \alpha^i \\ \beta^i \end{bmatrix} + \sum_{j=0}^{i-1} \begin{bmatrix} c_1 \alpha^j \\ c_0 \beta^j \end{bmatrix}$$

$$\nu_1^{(l)} = \begin{cases} \Theta(\alpha^l) & : & \alpha > 1 \\ \Theta(l) & : & \alpha = 1 \wedge c_1 > 0 \\ \Theta(1) & : & \alpha = 1 \wedge c_1 = 0 \end{cases} \quad \nu_0^{(l)} = \begin{cases} \Theta(\beta^l) & : & \beta > 1 \\ \Theta(l) & : & \beta = 1 \wedge c_0 > 0 \\ \Theta(1) & : & \beta = 1 \wedge c_0 = 0 \end{cases}$$

We know that $l \geq \log_m n$. Let $\lambda = \log_m \alpha$ and $\mu = \log_m \beta$. We have

$$\nu_1^{(l)} = \begin{cases} \Theta(n^\lambda) & : & \alpha \geq 1 \\ \Theta(\log_m n) & : & \alpha = 1 \wedge c_1 > 0 \\ \Theta(1) & : & \alpha = 1 \wedge c_1 = 0 \end{cases} \quad \nu_0^{(l)} = \begin{cases} \Theta(n^\mu) & : & \beta \geq 1 \\ \Theta(\log_m n) & : & \beta = 1 \wedge c_0 > 0 \\ \Theta(1) & : & \beta = 1 \wedge c_0 = 0 \end{cases}$$

As mentioned, either α or β is greater than 1 for a monotonic function f. Let $\nu = \nu_1^{(l)} + \nu_0^{(l)}$ and $r = \max\{\lambda, \mu\}$. Then $\nu = \Theta(n^r)$ $(r \in (0,1])$.   Q.E.D.

We suppose further that f is a commutative and monotonic increase function. It is easy to see that there is an $i \in [1, m-1]$ so that

$$\forall X \in \bigcup_{j \leq i} B_j \{f(X) = 0\} \wedge \forall Y \in \bigcup_{j > i} B_j \{f(Y) = 1\}.$$

Then $f(X)$ is a "threshold k" function from B^m to B (see page 110 in [6]).

$$f(x_1, \ldots, x_m) = \begin{cases} 1 & : & \sum_{1 \leq i \leq m} x_i \geq k \\ 0 & : & \text{otherwise} \end{cases}$$

The D and $\overline{D}$ critical antichains are

$$\mathcal{E} = \left\{ (x_1 \cdots x_m) \,\Big|\, \sum x_i = k \right\} \quad \text{and} \quad \mathcal{N} = \left\{ (x_1 \cdots x_m) \,\Big|\, \sum x_i = k-1 \right\}.$$

Every assignment in $\mathcal{E}$ can propagate k D signals simultaneously, while every assignment in $\mathcal{N}$ can propagate $m - k + 1$ $\overline{D}$ simultaneously. The components of the rotation matrix and the translation vector can be determined as follows.

$$\alpha = \frac{m}{k}, \quad \beta = \frac{m}{m-k+1}, \quad c_1 = \sum_{k+1 \leq i \leq m} \binom{m}{i}, \quad c_0 = \sum_{0 \leq i \leq k-2} \binom{m}{i}.$$

Assume that $T^{(n)}$ is an l-level uniform tree circuit based on the "threshold k" function. According to Theorem 3 we can determine that

$$\nu = \nu_1^{(l)} + \nu_0^{(l)} = \Theta(\alpha^{\log_m n}) + \Theta(\beta^{\log_m n}) = \Theta(n^{1-\log_m k}) + \Theta(n^{1-\log_m(m-k+1)}).$$

Take $r = \max\{1 - \log_m k, 1 - \log_m(m - k + 1)\}$. We have thus $\nu = \Theta(n^r)$.

Example 1: Estimate the test complexity of $T^{(n)}$ based on the boolean function $f(x, y) = x \wedge y$. We can determine that the D and $\overline{D}$ critical antichains are $\mathcal{E} = \{(1,1)\}$ and $\mathcal{N} = \{(0,1), (1,0)\}$. The recurrence formula of the test complexity of f is

$$\begin{bmatrix} \nu_1^{(i)} \\ \nu_0^{(i)} \end{bmatrix} = \begin{bmatrix} 1 & 0 \\ 0 & 2 \end{bmatrix} \begin{bmatrix} \nu_1^{(i-1)} \\ \nu_0^{(i-1)} \end{bmatrix} + \begin{bmatrix} 0 \\ 1 \end{bmatrix}.$$

Thus

$$\nu_0^{(l)} = 2^l + c_0 \sum_{0 \leq j \leq l-1} 2^j = 2^{l+1} - 1, \quad \nu_1^{(l)} = 1, \quad \nu = \nu_1^{(l)} + \nu_0^{(l)} = 2n.$$

It has been shown that $T^{(n)}$ based on $f(x,y) = x \wedge y$ can be tested completely with $n+1$ patterns [5]. This conclusion is slightly different from our result since the fault models used here and adopted in [5] are not the same. In [5] only stuck-at-1 and stuck-at-0 faults are considered, i.e., the assignment $(0,0)$ does not need to be assigned to an f cell. Here we assume the cell functional fault model, so that every assignments in B^2 needs to be assigned to an f cell. For instance, we hold that there can exist a fault in an f cell, and only the assignment $(0,0)$ can sensitize it. This implies that $c_0 = 1$. The value of $\nu_0^{(l)}$ is equal to the sum of two terms 2^l and $c_0 \sum_{0 \le j \le l-1} 2^j$. If we set $c_0 = 0$ and omit the second term, then $\nu_0^{(l)} = 2^l$, and $\nu = n+1$. This new result is completely consistent with that got in [5].

In the same way we can determine that $\nu = 2n$ for the case $f(x,y) = x \vee y$.

Based on Theorem 3, $\nu = \nu_1^{(l)} + \nu_0^{(l)}$ can be exactly evaluated, provided f is a monotonic increase function. In case f is not a monotonic increase function, it may be possible to find a monotonic increase function g and to embed f into g. The test complexity of $T^{(n)}$ based on g can be determined. Thus the test complexity of $T^{(n)}$ based on f can be indirectly estimated [8].

Theorem 4 $T^{(n)}$ *based on a monotonic decrease function f is $\Theta(n^r)$ ($r \in (0,1]$) testable.*

Proof : The proof for this theorem is similar to that for Theorem 3 in the most ways. For monotonic decrease function f

$$\forall X, Y \in B^m \{X > Y \Longrightarrow f(X) \le f(Y)\}.$$

We define two subsets of B^m.

$$\mathcal{E} = \{X \mid f(X) = 0 \wedge \forall Y \in B^m \{Y < X \Longrightarrow f(Y) > f(X)\}\}$$
$$\mathcal{N} = \{X \mid f(X) = 1 \wedge \forall Y \in B^m \{Y > X \Longrightarrow f(Y) < f(X)\}\}$$

It is obvious that both sets $\mathcal{E}$ and $\mathcal{N}$ are antichains. All D signals can only be propagated with assignments in $\mathcal{E}$, while all $\overline{D}$ signals can only be propagated with assignments in $\mathcal{N}$.

In the same way used for proving Theorem 3 we define the parameters α, β, c_0 and c_1 and the recurrence formula of the test complexity of f. We have

$$\begin{bmatrix} \nu_1^{(i)} \\ \nu_0^{(i)} \end{bmatrix} = \begin{bmatrix} 0 & \beta \\ \alpha & 0 \end{bmatrix} \begin{bmatrix} \nu_1^{(i-1)} \\ \nu_0^{(i-1)} \end{bmatrix} + \begin{bmatrix} c_0 \\ c_1 \end{bmatrix}$$

for $i \in [1, l]$. Assume that $\nu_0^{(0)} = \nu_1^{(0)} = 1$. We can inductively prove that

$$\nu_0^{(2i)} = \alpha^i \beta^i + c_1 \sum_{j=0}^{i-1} (\alpha\beta)^j + c_0 \alpha \sum_{j=0}^{i-1} (\alpha\beta)^j$$

$$\nu_1^{(2i)} = \alpha^i \beta^i + c_0 \sum_{j=0}^{i-1} (\alpha\beta)^j + c_1 \beta \sum_{j=0}^{i-1} (\alpha\beta)^j$$

$$\nu_0^{(2i+1)} = \alpha^{i+1} \beta^i + c_1 \sum_{j=0}^{i} (\alpha\beta)^j + c_0 \alpha \sum_{j=0}^{i-1} (\alpha\beta)^j$$

$$\nu_1^{(2i+1)} = \alpha^i \beta^{i+1} + c_0 \sum_{j=0}^{i} (\alpha\beta)^j + c_1 \beta \sum_{j=0}^{i-1} (\alpha\beta)^j$$

hold for $2i \in [0, l)$. Assume that $l = 2k$. Then $\nu = \nu_0^{(2k)} + \nu_1^{(2k)} = \Theta((\alpha\beta)^{\frac{l}{2}})$.
We know that $l \geq \log_m n$. Thus

$$\nu = \Theta((\alpha\beta)^{\frac{\log_m n}{2}}) = \Theta(n^{\frac{\log_m \alpha\beta}{2}}).$$

Let $r = \frac{\log_m \alpha\beta}{2}$, then $r \in (0, 1]$, and $\nu = \Theta(n^r)$. **Q.E.D.**

Example 2: Estimate the test complexity of $T^{(n)}$ based on function $f(x, y) = \overline{x \wedge y}$. It is obvious that f is a monotonic decrease function. We can determine that the D and $\overline{D}$ critical antichain and the recurrence formula of the test complexity of f are $\mathcal{E} = \{(1, 1)\}$, $\mathcal{N} = \{(1, 0), (0, 1)\}$, and

$$\begin{bmatrix} \nu_1^{(i)} \\ \nu_0^{(i)} \end{bmatrix} = \begin{bmatrix} 0 & 2 \\ 1 & 0 \end{bmatrix} \begin{bmatrix} \nu_1^{(i-1)} \\ \nu_0^{(i-1)} \end{bmatrix} + \begin{bmatrix} 0 \\ 1 \end{bmatrix}.$$

Here $m = 2$, and $\alpha\beta = 2$. According to Theorem 4, $\nu = \Theta(n^{\frac{\log_2 \alpha\beta}{2}}) = \Theta(n^{\frac{1}{2}})$. $T^{(n)}$ based on f is $\Theta(n^{\frac{1}{2}})$ testable.

Acknowledgement

I am grateful to Prof. G. Hotz for his supervision, and wish to thank Uwe Sparmann for many stimulating discussions and help. The work was supported by DFG, SFB 124, TP B1.

References

1. Akers, S.B.: Universal Test Sets for Logic Networks, IEEE Trans. On Comput. Vol. C-22 No.9 pp.835-839, 1973.

2. Becker, B., U. Sparmann: Computations over Finite Monoids and their Test Complexity, FTCS 19 pp.299-306, 1989.

3. Becker,B., J. Hartmann: Optimal-Time Multipliers and C-Testability, 2nd Annual ACM Symposium on Parallel Algorithms and Architecture pp.146-154, 1990.

4. Breuer, M.A., A.D. Friedman: **Diagnosis & Reliable Design of Digital Systems**, Computer Science Press, INC. 1976.

5. Hayes, J. P.: On Realizations of Boolean Functions Requiring a Minimal or Near-Minimal Number of Tests, IEEE Trans. On Comput. Vol. C-20,No. 12, pp.1506-1513, 1971.

6. Hotz, G.: **Schaltkreistheorie**, Walter de Gruyter · Berlin · New York 1974.

7. Reddy, S.: Complete Test Sets for Logic Functions, IEEE Trans. on Compt. Vol. C-22, No. 11 pp.1016-1020, 1973.

8. Wu, H,: On the Test Complexity of Uniform Tree Circuits, Technical Report 1992. SFB 124, TP B1, Universität, des Saarlandes, Germany.

Improved Parallel Sorting of Presorted Sequences
(Extended Abstract)

Jingsen Chen   and   Christos Levcopoulos

Department of Computer Science, Lund University, Box 118, S-221 00 Lund, Sweden

Abstract. An adaptive parallel sorting algorithm is presented, which is cost optimal with respect to the number of oscillations in a sequence (Osc). More specifically, the algorithm sorts any sequence X of length n in time $O(\log n)$ by using $O(\frac{n}{\log n} \cdot \log \frac{Osc(X)}{n})$ CRCW PRAM processors. This is the first adaptive parallel sorting algorithm that is cost optimal with respect to Osc and, hence, it is also optimal with respect to both the number of inversions (Inv) and the number of runs ($Runs$) in the sequence. Our result improves previous results on adaptive parallel sorting.

1   Introduction

Measuring the order information in partially sorted input sequences, and designing optimal sorting algorithms that adapt optimally to the measures of presortedness has recently received much attention [5, 8, 9, 10, 11, 15, 16, 18]. Intuitively, a measure of presortedness is an integer function on the sequence that presents the distance between the sequence and the sorted sequence in some specific way. An adaptive sorting algorithm is optimal with respect to a given measure if it sorts all sequences in $O(n \log n)$ time in the worst case, but has a linear bound when its input sequences have a high degree of sortedness according to the given measure. Mannila [15] formalized the concept of presortedness and of adaptive sorting algorithms. Several measures of presortedness have been proposed, for example, the number of pairs of elements out of order (Inv), the number of consecutive ascending subsequences of maximum length ($Runs$), the minimum number of elements needed to be removed from X to leave a sorted sequence (Rem), the maximum distance between an element of the sequence and its correct position (Max), and the intensity of oscillations in the sequence (Osc).

Various sequential sorting algorithms that utilize presortedness in the sequence have been developed. However, designing optimal sorting algorithms in parallel models of computation has not been deeply studied. Although there are some known optimal parallel sorting algorithms, for example, AKS sorting network [1] and Cole's parallel merge sort [6], they do not utilize the existing order within the sequence to be sorted. Except for the measures of presortedness Inv, Max, Rem, and $Runs$ [2, 4, 12, 13], no optimal parallel sorting algorithm, which is adaptive to any other measures, is known in any parallel model of computation.

In this paper, we develop an adaptive parallel sorting algorithm that is optimal with respect to Osc. The algorithm sorts any sequence X of length n in $O(\log n)$ time provided $O(\frac{n}{\log n} \cdot \log \frac{Osc(X)}{n})$ processors are available on an arbitrary CRCW PRAM. Such an algorithm is *cost optimal* in the sense that it has a time processor product equal to the sequential lower bound for the problem under consideration. Since *Osc* is a superior measure to *Inv*, *Max*, and *Runs* [14], our parallel algorithm is also optimal with respect to all of them. This algorithm is the first adaptive parallel sorting algorithm that is cost optimal with respect to *Osc*, which improves previous results on adaptive parallel sorting.

2 The Adaptive Parallel Sorting Algorithm

Let $X = \langle x_1, \cdots, x_n \rangle$ be a sequence of n distinct elements drawn from some totally ordered set and $|X|$ be the length of X. We denote the cardinality of a set A by $\|A\|$, and we let $\log x$ mean $\log_2(\max\{2, x\})$. By $X \leq Y$ we mean that $x \leq y$ for any $x \in X$ and $y \in Y$. For $X = \langle x_1, \cdots, x_n \rangle$ and $Y = \langle y_1, \cdots, y_m \rangle$, the concatenation XY of X and Y is the sequence $\langle x_1, \cdots, x_n, y_1, \cdots, y_m \rangle$. For every element x in X, denote $Cross(x)$ by $\{j \mid 1 \leq j < n \text{ and } \min\{x_j, x_{j+1}\} < x < \max\{x_j, x_{j+1}\}\}$. $Osc(X)$ is then defined to be $\sum_{i=1}^{n} \|Cross(x_i)\|$. Osc is a quite powerful measure, as shown in [14] that every Osc-optimal sorting algorithm is also optimal with respect to Inv, $Runs$, and Max. A sequential Osc-optimal sorting algorithm, *Adaptive Heapsort*, has been presented in [14], which sorts any sequence X in $\Theta(|X| \log \frac{Osc(X)}{|X|})$ comparisons. To design our Osc-optimal parallel sorting algorithm, we shall first describe a parallel algorithm that sorts any sequence X with $Osc(X) \geq n \log^{\varepsilon} n$ in time $O(\log n)$ by using CRCW-PRAM $O(\frac{n}{\log n} \cdot \log \frac{Osc(X)}{n})$ processors, where $\varepsilon > 0$ is a constant. In what follows, we always assume that the number of CRCW processors available is $\lceil \frac{n}{\log n} \cdot \log \frac{Osc(X)}{n} \rceil$.

Algorithm 1 *Let $k = \log n$ and $m = \lfloor \frac{n}{\log n} \rfloor$.*

1. *Choose every $(\log n)$-th element to be in a subset X' of X; that is, $X' = \{x_{i \cdot k} \mid 1 \leq i \leq m\}$; Sort X' in parallel into $\{y_1 < y_2 < \cdots < y_m\}$;*
2. *Partition X stably into blocks $X_j = \{x \mid y_{j-1} < x \leq y_j\}$ ($1 \leq j \leq m+1$), where $y_0 \triangleq -\infty$ and $y_{m+1} \triangleq +\infty$.*
3. *Equally distribute the processors to every block, and sort each block in parallel.*

We show in the following that each step of this algorithm can be done $O(\log n)$ time.

(**1**) Step 1 can be done in $O(\log n)$ time since we have $\frac{n}{\log n}$ processors and the number of elements to be sorted is $\frac{n}{\log n}$.

(**2**) To partition X, we shall keep a sequence $Z = \langle z_1, \cdots, z_n \rangle$ of n integers where the i-th element is the block's index which x_i belongs to. By sorting Z stably, we obtain the partition of X. More precisely, Step 2 consists of three substeps:
Step 2.1. Distribute the processors evenly among the elements of X. Each processor takes a block of consecutive elements and calculates their "ranks" in the ordered set $\{y_1 < y_2 < \cdots < y_m\}$. The rank of element x_i will be stored in z_i; i.e., $z_i = j$ if and only if $y_{j-1} < x_i \leq y_j$. This step will stop if some processor has finished its work and all processors have been working in $\Theta(\frac{\log n}{\log \frac{Osc(X)}{n}})$ time.

Step 2.2. Collect stably together all elements whose ranks have not been found in the previous substep and redistribute equally the idle processors among all these elements. Now, each processor takes a new block of elements and performs the rank-finding task as in the previous substep. Step 2.2 (and hence Step 2.1) will be repeated until all ranks have been computed. The outcome of Step 2.2 is the sequence $Z = \langle z_1, \cdots, z_n \rangle$ of integers between 1 and $m + 1$ $(m = \lfloor \frac{n}{\log n} \rfloor)$.

Step 2.3. Assign X_j to be $\langle x_{j_1}, x_{j_2}, \cdots, x_{j_k} \rangle$, where $z_{j_1} = z_{j_2} = \cdots = z_{j_k} = j$ and $j_1 < j_2 < \cdots < j_k$.

All these three substeps can be done in $O(\log n)$ time. In fact:

(2.1) After the first round of the processor distribution, there are $\frac{\log n}{\log \frac{Osc(X)}{n}}$ elements per processor. As assigned above, Step 2.1 will stop in $O(\frac{\log n}{\log \frac{Osc(X)}{n}})$ time.

(2.2) To confirm that Step 2.2 will be repeated at most $O(\log \frac{Osc(X)}{n})$ times, we need the following lemma (the proof appears in the full paper).

Lemma 1. *If we know the rank of x_i, then $\log \|Cover(x_i, x_{i+1})\|$ comparisons are sufficient in the worst case to compute the rank r of x_{i+1} in $\{y_1 < y_2 < \cdots < y_m\}$, where $Cover(x_i, x_{i+1}) = \{x_j \mid 1 \leq j \leq n \text{ and } \min\{x_i, x_{i+1}\} < x_j < \max\{x_i, x_{i+1}\}\}$.*

Notice that the redistribution of the processors costs $O(1)$ time [7] due to the fact that the number of processors available now is at least $n \log \log n$ and we redistribute the processors immediately after some processor has finished its work in Steps 2.1 and 2.2 (i.e., the processors are doing useful work all the time). Since $\sum_{i=1}^{n-1} \log \|Cover(x_i, x_{i+1})\| = O(n \cdot \log \frac{Osc(X)}{n})$ [14], we know that there are at most $O(\log \frac{Osc(X)}{n})$ iterations of Step 2.2, each requiring $\frac{\log n}{\log \frac{Osc(X)}{n}}$ time (for Step 2.1). Therefore, after $O(\log \frac{Osc(X)}{n} \cdot \frac{\log n}{\log \frac{Osc(X)}{n}}) = O(\log n)$ time, we know all the ranks.

(2.3) In Step 2.3, the task we want to perform is to stably sort n integers in range $[1..\lfloor \frac{n}{\log n} \rfloor + 1]$ on CRCW PRAM in $O(\log n)$ time with $\frac{n}{\log n} \cdot \log \frac{Osc(X)}{n}$ processors. Since $Osc(X) \geq n \log^\varepsilon n$, and since the integers to be sorted are of range from 1 to $\lfloor \frac{n}{\log n} \rfloor + 1$, we can use the integer sorting algorithm in [3] to complete Step 2.3.

(3) We shall now prove that Step 3 of sorting all blocks can also be done in $O(\log n)$ time. To this end, we associate each block X_j with a value $Cost(X_j) \triangleq |X_j| \log |X_j|$ and verify our claim by checking the sizes of the blocks.

(3.1) Firstly, all blocks of size smaller than $\log^\sigma n$ $(0 < \sigma < 1)$ can be sorted in at most $O(\log n)$ time. In fact:

(i) Since $Osc(X) \geq n \log^\varepsilon n$, every processor gets $\frac{\log n}{\log \log n}$ elements in all these "smaller" blocks. Running every processor to sort its elements in time $O(\frac{\log n}{\log \log n})$, and redistributing the processors among unfinished blocks, we can spend $\log \log n$ time per element (the redistribution of the processors takes $O(1)$ time [7]). Because every block can be sorted sequentially in $O(\log^\sigma n \cdot \log \log n) = O(\frac{\log n}{\log \log n})$ time, we could have sorted all "smaller" blocks after $O(\log n)$ parallel time.

(ii) If some processor P_k takes more than one smaller blocks, for example, blocks

$X_{i_1}, X_{i_2}, \cdots, X_{i_k}$ such that $\sum_{j=1}^{k} Cost(X_{i_j}) \approx \log n$, then let P_k take $\Theta(\frac{\log n}{\log\log n})$ elements. Similarly, blocks $X_{i_1}, X_{i_2}, \cdots, X_{i_k}$ can be sorted in $O(\log n)$ time.

(3.2) For all blocks of size larger than $\log^\sigma n$, an upper bound of $O(\log n)$ parallel sorting time is still achievable, as will be shown below. Notice that the input sequence of Step 3 is $X' = X_1 X_2 \cdots X_{m+1}$ where every element of X_i is less than every element in X_j whenever $i < j$. Therefore, $Osc(X) \geq Osc(X')$ and running Adaptive Heapsort on X' can be regarded as running simultaneously the algorithm on X_i $(1 \leq i \leq m+1)$.

(i) If the size of a block is at most $\frac{\log n}{\log\log n}$, then, with a procedure similar to that above, we can sort all such blocks in $O(\log n)$ time.

(ii) For all blocks $\{X_i\}$ of size $\{n_i\}$, $\frac{\log n}{\log\log n} < n_i \leq \log^2 n$, since we have now $\Omega(\frac{n}{\log n} \cdot \log \frac{Osc(X)}{n}) = \Omega(\frac{n \cdot \log\log n}{\log n})$ processors, every processor has at most $\frac{\log n}{\log\log n}$ elements. Since the total cost for sorting X' is at most $O(n \cdot \log \frac{Osc(X)}{n})$ and every block X_i can be sorted in $O(n_i \cdot \log\log n)$ time, we afford to assign $\lfloor \frac{Cost(X_i)}{\log n} \rfloor$ processors to each block X_i. With this amount of processors, we can sort all blocks in $O(\log n)$ parallel time by using any $O(\log n)$-time optimal parallel sorting algorithm.

(iii) For any block X_j with $\|X_j\| \geq \log^2 n$ and $Cost(X_j) > \log n$, we will assign $\lfloor \frac{Cost(X_j)}{\log n} \rfloor$ processors to it. With these processors, we can sort X_j in $O(\log n)$ time. Actually, for any block $\mathcal{B}$ with $\|\mathcal{B}\| \geq \log^2 n$, we can prove that $O(Cost(\mathcal{B}))$ is the optimal cost for sorting such a block sequentially. That is, $O(Cost(\mathcal{B}))$ is the sequential time allowed if we want to sort the sequence X optimally and adaptively. To see this, we only need to show that the number of oscillations contributed to $Osc(x)$ by the elements in $\mathcal{B}$ is $\Omega(\|\mathcal{B}\|^2)$. This is because that, in this case, the lower bound for adaptively sorting this block is $\Omega(\|\mathcal{B}\| \cdot \log \frac{Osc(\mathcal{B})}{\|\mathcal{B}\|}) = \Omega(Cost(\mathcal{B}))$, where $Osc(\mathcal{B})$ means the summation of the value of $Cross(\cdot)$ regarding to X over all elements in $\mathcal{B}$. The lemma below confirms our claim (the proof appears in the full paper).

Lemma 2. *For any block $\mathcal{B}$ in Step 3, if $\|\mathcal{B}\| \geq \frac{\log^2 n}{\log\log n}$, then $Osc(\mathcal{B}) \geq \frac{1}{4}(\frac{\|\mathcal{B}\|}{\log n})^2$.*

Therefore, $O(n_i \log \frac{Osc(X_i)}{n_i}) = \Theta(n_i \log n_i) = O(Cost(X_i))$ for any block X_i with size $n_i \geq \log^{2+\sigma} n$. Since $O(\sum_i n_i \log \frac{Osc(X_i)}{n_i}) = O(n \log \frac{Osc(X)}{n})$, we have enough processors to be distributed such that each block X_i has got $\lfloor \frac{Cost(X_i)}{\log n} \rfloor$ processors. We can perform a sorting task on X_i by running any $O(\log n)$-time optimal parallel sorting algorithm on X_i with its associated processors. The total cost for sorting X' is then $O(\sum_i n_i \log \frac{Osc(X_i)}{n_i}) = \Theta(n_i \log n_i) = O(n \log \frac{Osc(X)}{n})$, and we can complete the sorting tasks in $O(\log n)$ parallel time by evenly distributing the processors among unordered elements (i.e., those elements for which we have not found the sorted positions yet) using a redistribution procedure in [7]. In sum, Step 3 takes $O(\log n)$ time and we have that:

Theorem 3. *Given a sequence X of length n, there is an $O(\log n)$-time CRCW PRAM algorithm that sorts X by using $O(\frac{n \log\log n}{\log n} + \frac{n}{\log n} \cdot \log \frac{Osc(X)}{n})$ processors, which is cost optimal provided that $Osc(X) \geq n \log^\varepsilon n$, where $\varepsilon > 0$ is a constant.*

For sorting adaptively any sequence X with $Osc(X) < n \log^\varepsilon n$, we shall employ a slightly different sorting algorithm.

Algorithm 2 *Let* $k = \log\log n$ *and* $m = \lfloor \frac{n}{\log\log n} \rfloor$.

1. *Choose every* $(\log\log n)$-*th element to be in a subset* X' *of* X; *that is,* $X' = \{x_{i\cdot k} \mid 1 \le i \le m\}$; *Sort* X' *in parallel into* $\{y_1 < y_2 < \cdots < y_m\}$ *using Algorithm 1*;
2. *Partition stably* X *into blocks* $\{X_i\}_{1 \le i \le m+1}$ *such that every element* x *in* X_i *satisfies* $y_{i-1} < x \le y_i$ ($y_0 \triangleq -\infty$ *and* $y_{m+1} \triangleq +\infty$).
3. *Equally distribute the processors to every block, and sort each block in parallel.*

Notice that this algorithm uses Algorithm 1 as a subroutine and applies a different strategy from Algorithm 1 to complete its second step. The following step-by-step analysis shows that each step of Algorithm 2 takes time no more than $O(\log n)$.

(1) Note that the number of elements to be sorted is $n' = \frac{n}{\log\log n}$. Since $\frac{n' \log\log n'}{\log n'} + \frac{n'}{\log n'} \cdot \log \frac{Osc(X')}{n'} \le c \cdot \frac{n}{\log n} \le c \cdot \frac{n}{\log n} \cdot \log \frac{Osc(X)}{n}$, we can complete Step 1 in $O(\log n)$ time by Theorem 1, where $c > 0$ is a constant.

(2) Similar to Algorithm 1, let $Z = \langle z_1, \cdots, z_n \rangle$ be the rank sequence of X; i.e., $z_i = j$ if and only if $y_{j-1} < x_i \le y_j$.
(2.1) Distribute the processors evenly among the elements of X. Each processor takes a block of consecutive $\log\log n$ elements and computes their "ranks" in the ordered set $\{y_1 < y_2 < \cdots < y_m\}$ by a binary and exponential search [16]. We shall throw away such a block when searching for some element in the block costs more than $\log(\sqrt{\log n})$ time. Notice that each one of these blocks contributes to the number of oscillations $Osc(X)$ with at least $\sqrt{\log n}$. Therefore, the number of the blocks been thrown away is at most $\frac{n \log^\varepsilon n}{\sqrt{\log n}}$ since $Osc(X) < n \log^\varepsilon n$. The number of elements deleted during this step is thus at most $\frac{n \log^\varepsilon n}{\sqrt{\log n}} \cdot \log\log n \le \frac{n}{\log\log n}$, which can be sorted separately and merged with the sorted sequence output at the end of Step 3. The cost of the rank-finding is at most $O(\log n)$ and its outcome is the sequence $Z = \langle z_1, \cdots, z_n \rangle$ of integers between 1 and $m + 1$ ($m = \lfloor \frac{n}{\log\log n} \rfloor$).
(2.2) Notice that every block Z_j of elements ranging from $(j-1) \cdot \log\log n$ to $j \cdot \log\log n$ ($1 \le j \le \lfloor \frac{n}{\log\log n} \rfloor + 1$) has at most $\sqrt{\log n} \cdot \log\log n \le \frac{\log n}{\log\log n}$ elements. Therefore, we can assign X_j to be $\langle x_{j_1}, x_{j_2}, \cdots, x_{j_k} \rangle$ in $O(\log n)$ time, where $z_{j_1} = z_{j_2} = \cdots = z_{j_k} = j$ and $j_1 < j_2 < \cdots < j_k$.

(3) Step 3 of sorting all blocks can also be done in $O(\log n)$ time:
(3.1) Since for every $\log n$ elements we have $\log \frac{Osc(X)}{n}$ processors, we can sort all blocks of size smaller than $\log^\sigma n$ ($0 < \sigma < 1$) in $O(\log n)$ time. In fact, we first distribute processors evenly among the elements of smaller blocks. Each processor sorts its associated elements by Adaptive Heapsort [14] and we redistribute the idle processors immediately when they finish their works. Notice that each such block can be sorted in $O(\log^\sigma n \cdot \log\log n) = O(\frac{\log n}{\log\log n})$ time sequentially. Since sorting sequentially all these smaller blocks costs $O(n \log \frac{Osc(X)}{n})$, and since all processors

are occupied all the time, all smaller blocks can be sorted in $O(\log n)$ time.

(3.2) For all blocks of size larger than $\log^\sigma n$, we can perform a sorting procedure similar to the Step 3.2 of Algorithm 1 but on all larger blocks. Evenly distributing processors among the elements and doing the same redistributions of the processors as above, we can sort the blocks in due time.

Hence, each step of Algorithm 2 can be done in time $O(\log n)$. For any sequence X to be sorted, we first run Algorithm 2 on X in $O(\log n)$-time. If the output sequence is sorted, then we are done. Otherwise, running Algorithm 1 on X again, we can complete the sorting task in $O(\log n)$-time. In summary:

Theorem 4. *Given a sequence X of length n, there is a cost optimal CRCW PRAM algorithm that sorts X in $O(\log n)$ time by using $O(\frac{n}{\log n} \cdot \log \frac{Osc(X)}{n})$ processors.*

References

1. M. Ajtai, J. Komlós, and E. Szemeredi: Sorting in $c \log n$ parallel steps. *Combinatorica* **3**, 1-19 (1983)
2. T. Altman and B. S. Chlebus: Sorting roughly sorted sequences in parallel. *Information Processing Letters* **33**, 297-300 (1989/90)
3. P. C. P. Bhatt, K. Diks, T. Hagerup, V. C. Prasad, T. Radzik, and S. Saxena: Improved deterministic parallel integer sorting. *Inform. Comput.* **94**, 29-47 (1991)
4. S. Carlsson and J. Chen: An optimal parallel adaptive sorting algorithm. *Information Processing Letters* **39**, 195-200 (1991)
5. J. Chen and S. Carlsson: On partitions and presortedness of sequences. *Proceedings of the Second Annual ACM-SIAM Symposium on Discrete Algorithms*, 62-71 (1991)
6. R. Cole: Parallel merge sort. *SIAM Journal on Computing* **17**, 770-785 (1988)
7. R. Cole and U. Vishkin: Approximate parallel scheduling. Part I: The basic technique with applications to optimal parallel list ranking in logarithmic time. *SIAM Journal on Computing* **17**, 128-142 (1988)
8. C. R. Cook and D. J. Kim: Best sorting algorithm for nearly sorted lists. *Communications of the ACM* **23**, 620-624 (1980)
9. E. W. Dijkstra: Smoothsort, an alternative for sorting in situ. *Science of Computer Programming* **1**, 223-233 (1982)
10. R. G. Dromey: Exploiting partial order with quicksort. *Software-Practice and Experience* **14**, 509-518 (1984)
11. V. Estivill-Castro and D. Wood: A new measure of presortedness. *Information and Computation* **83**, 111-119 (1989)
12. C. Levcopoulos and O. Petersson: A note on adaptive parallel sorting. *Information Processing Letters* **33**, 187-191 (1989)
13. C. Levcopoulos and O. Petersson: An optimal parallel algorithm for sorting presorted files. *Proc. 8th Conf. Found. Soft. Tech. Theore. Comput. Sci.*, 154-160 (1988)
14. C. Levcopoulos and O. Petersson: Heapsort - adapted for presorted files. *Proceedings of the First Workshop on Algorithms and Data Structures*, 499-509 (1989)
15. H. Mannila: Measures of presortedness and optimal sorting algorithms. *IEEE Transactions on Computers* **C-34**, 318-325 (1985)
16. K. Mehlhorn: *Data Structures and Algorithms Vol. 1: Sorting and Searching*. Springer-Verlag, Berlin, Heidelberg, 1984.
17. O. Petersson: Adaptive sorting. Ph. D. Thesis, Lund University, Sweden (1990)
18. S. S. Skiena: Encroaching lists as a measure of presortedness. *BIT* **28**, 775-784 (1988)

This article was processed using the LaTeX macro package with LLNCS style

MIMD Dictionary Machines:
from Theory to Practice*

Thibault Duboux, Afonso Ferreira**, Michel Gastaldo***

Laboratory LIP - IMAG
ENS-Lyon, 69364 Lyon cedex 07, France
e-mail: {duboux,ferreira,gastaldo}@lip.ens-lyon.fr

Abstract. We describe the implementation of a dictionary structure on a distributed memory parallel computer. The dictionary is an important data structure used in applications such as sorting and searching, symbol-table and index-table implementations. Theoretical as well as practical aspects of the development of the application are discussed. Our target machine was a Volvox IS860 with 8 nodes, each composed of one Transputer T800 from INMOS plus an Intel i860. Extensive testing was carried out and the results reported. We also address problems and solutions connected to the programming environment of such a machine.

1 Introduction

The dictionary is an important data structure used in applications such as sorting and searching, symbol-table and index-table implementations [8]. The dictionary task can be loosely defined as the problem of maintaining a set of data elements each of which is composed of a key-record pair (k,r), where k is the search key and r the associated record. It supports a set of instructions on its entries, for instance: Insert(k,r), Delete(k), Find(k), Extract min.

The use of special purpose parallel architectures for implementing dictionary machines has been widely studied in the literature. Some papers report on specialized topologies [1, 2, 5], while others use existing and widely available processor networks [4, 9, 10]. Since those parallel dictionary machines are primarily intended for implementation in VLSI, one of their main characteristics is the complete processor utilization, i.e., there is one data item per processor in the system.

In this paper, we consider the implementation of a dictionary on the Volvox IS860, a MIMD parallel computer from Archipel Co. To our knowledge, this is the first time an experiment with implementation of a dictionary machine on a distributed memory parallel computer is reported. Our goals are to show how a parallel computer can be fully used, time and memory wise, and to describe how such a complex architecture can be programmed to its best with regard to a useful application.

Our paper is organized as follows. First we describe the target parallel computer, and its operating system. Then the implementation details are given, concerning the

---

* Support from DRET and from the PRC C3 of the French CNRS are acknowledged

** On leave from the Institute of Mathematics and Statistics of the University of São Paulo and member of Project 30.01 of the Program BID/USP.

*** Partially supported by a DRET fellowship.

data-structuring techniques used, the algorithms to be programmed, and the global behavior of the parallel dictionary machine. Finally, some results of our experiments are shown, and figures comparing different implementations are analyzed. We close the paper with some concluding remarks and ways for further research.

2 Programming Environment

The Machine. The Volvox IS860 Supercomputing server is a full implementation of the MIMD distributed memory architecture and of the CSP message passing model. It has 8 available nodes, accessed via communication boards laying in a Sun SPARC workstation (the host). The architecture of the Volvox Supercomputing can be extended to 48 nodes, or more in a near future. All the applications described henceforth take into account the extensibility of the machine. Each physical node is composed by a T800 Transputer with 4 reconfigurable communication links, as a Communication Processor, and an *Intel i860* as an Application Processor. A 16MBytes RAM is independently accessed by the two processors via a shared memory optimized mechanism.

Trollius Operating System. Trollius is a programming environment for distributed memory multicomputers [6], mainly used on Transputer based machines. As a programming environment, it encompasses an operating system, a command line interface and library functions. Its goal is to provide basic services needed for communication and process control. User is are free to choose the system layer with the right functionality and overhead. Thus, performance is achieved by supporting several layers of message-passing. Moreover, "virtual circuits" allow a series of messages to bypass the kernel, thus greatly increasing the speed of message passing. Below we give a succinct description of such layers from the closest to the physical structure of the machine to the farthest.

- *Local layer*: used for inter-processes communications on the same node.
- *Physical layer*: offers only neighbor-to-neighbor communications. It uses Transputer primitives of communication on synchronized physical links.
- *Datalink layer*: manages the physical links, by message bufferization and multiplexing, when several processes run on the same processor.
- *Network layer*: adds an implicit "store and forward" routing to the Datalink layer functionalities.
- *Transport layer*: communications are done with the "request-to-send" protocol. It guarantees that messages are transmitted and received. This is very useful during debugging, although it implies worse performances.

3 Implementation

The implementation described below is based on a ring of dictionary machines (DM) connected to the host. Instructions to be executed circulate along this ring. Each DM processes a subset of the instructions, to be defined later, and forward the other instructions to the next DM. Input (output) is supposed to come (go) from (to) users outside the machine, being supported by the host.

Local Data Organization. Each DM should handle a data structure based on balanced trees. Several data structures yield such balancing, but just a few can support exact balancing along with logarithmic time split and concatenate operations. We have chosen to use binary colored trees (BCT) which are the implementation of the 2-3-4 trees [7]. A BCT is a binary search tree, with only one key per inner node. Each node is red or black, depending on the color of the link to its father. The root is black, and its color is never modified. An inner node has always two sons. Two successive nodes cannot be red. The height H of BCT's is such that $\log_2 N \leq H \leq 2 * \log_2 N$. (Therefore, algorithms on BCT's have the same asymptotical time complexity as on 2-3-4 trees).

Local Processing of Instructions. Instructions sent by the host are analysed by the processors on the ring. Once a processor has selectioned a particular instruction to treat, it shall access the local data structure, i.e., its own BCT. We present below the algorithm for BCT's, corresponding to the Insert instruction.

This instruction can be described in three steps:

1 - among the leaves, locate the position in which the element has to be inserted (if the key already exists, Insert fails with a message to the host).

2 - transform the leaf just before the position found, into a red node with two children: one is the former leaf, the other is the element to be inserted.

3 - eliminate successive, eventually created, red nodes in the new tree. This is done by a traversal of the tree from the inserted node to the root; rotations are performed each time two successive red nodes are encountered.

The parallel Dictionary Machine. We now describe the global behavior of the proposed dictionary machine. As seen before, each physical node is a dictionary machine by itself, and they are connected along a ring architecture. Because of the internal organization of the nodes of the Volvox parallel computer, we implemented a client/server protocol. The instructions circulate along the ring, starting at the host. The Transputers must select only those concerned by its *working domain*. Furthermore a Transputer must also forward output messages that arrive from its predecessor in the ring. The binary colored tree storing the elements of the dictionary is managed by the i860, which is used as the actual processing element of the application. The i860 executes the current instruction, modifying the data structure. Eventual output messages are sent by the i860 to its neighbor on the ring, under the control of Trollius.

The working domain of a node is given by a lower and an upper bounds on the key values. Any instruction containing a key into that interval should be treated by that node. The working domains are a partition of the set of possible values for the keys. It is clear that, in order to have a good load balancing of the system, the working domains should be defined in such a way that every node is involved in the processing of roughly the same number of instructions. For instance, if the distribution law of the instruction keys is known beforehand, then such a good partition is easy to obtain. On the other hand, if such a law is unknown or changeable, then a dynamic updating of the working domains becomes primordial to ensure load balancing.

Communications between the two processors of a single node are performed via the shared memory, which stores a circular queue containing the instructions selected by the T800, waiting to be processed by the i860. The head of the queue is controlled by the i860, i.e., every time an instruction is extracted to be executed, the i860 updates the pointer to the head in the shared memory. Similarly, the T800 controls the tail of the same circular queue. Every time an instruction is selected from the instruction flow in the ring, it is inserted into the queue, and the T800 updates the pointer to the tail of the queue. A major difficulty encountered when implementing the circular queue was the sharing of variables between the i860 and the T800. This is due to the use of a cache by the i860.

Another point which is worth mentioning is the importance of a good operating system. On the one hand we need an improved memory management with garbage collection to deal with the large amount of memory allocation and release. On the other hand, the choice of the right layer of message passing is very subtle, trading off performance against control and debugging facilities (see analysis below).

4 Experimental Results

In order to establish a common pattern for comparisons, and to take into account the input/output and system constraints, we have run the same program in different sequential/parallel architectures. The full configuration of the machine is able to treat almost two million instructions in approximately eight minutes. That number of instructions equals the total capacity of our dictionary machine. In order to allow comparisons, a Sun 4/25 Sparc Station with virtual memory processed some half a million elements in about four minutes.

Single Processor Implementations. Three different types of processors have been used to test the dictionary machine in a single processor. Figure 1 compares the times obtained with a Sun 4/25 Sparc Station, a T800 and a i860. We can easily see that the T800 is not efficient with memory management and pointer manipulations. It showed the worst performance: 44 minutes to fill-up the dictionary with 230000 elements. The i860 is definitely more powerful than the Transputer: it needs 530 seconds to perform the same number of insertions.

The two benchmarks given above are useful to compute the speedup of the parallel implementation, since they use the same type of processing elements. However, the performance is worth measuring is the one of the Sparc station, for when no parallel computer is available one should use a powerful sequential machine to develop applications. Sun 4/25 can insert 440000 elements in 210 seconds. This can be explained by the fact that only scalar operations are performed, and that memory management is done by Trollius for both the i860 and the T800.

Single Processor Ring Implementations. Selecting instructions and processing are simultaneously executed on one processor per node instead of using the two available processors on each node. So, rings are composed by only one type of processor. Surprisingly, the results obtained (with the *transport layer* of message passing)

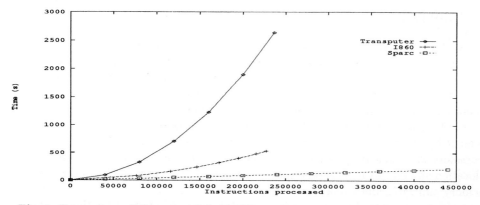

Fig. 1. Comparison of the sequential executions

imply that the ring composed by Transputers is better than the one composed by i860's. This is due to the physical architecture of the machine: a communication from a i860 must be forwarded by the associated Transputer to circulate on a physical link. Moreover, the difference between the two performances is large (by a factor 2) because communicating takes much longer than computing.

Full Machine Implementation. We show in Fig. 2 how important is the choice of the layer of message passing. It also reflects the way the application was actually developed. First we have programmed and debugged it under transport layer. All Trollius tools are available and communications are safe (really synchronized by *rendezvous*). More than an hour was necessary to perform one million insertions. Then, as debugging became less important, we changed message layers, getting closer to a lower level programming. When the program ran perfectly, we changed to physical layer, since Trollius tools were no longer needed and we wanted good performances. We were thus able to insert 1.8 million elements in less than eight minutes.

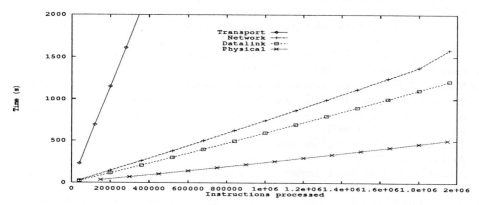

Fig. 2. The different layers of message passing on our implementation

5   Conclusion

Our goal, in this paper, was twofold. Primarily we wanted to report on an application development on a MIMD machine, with all the problems that can appear in such an attempt. Secondly, we showed that parallel computers can be fully used, i.e., that not only megaflops can be achieved by coupling several processors together, but also an efficient utilization of the total memory is possible.

The Volvox machine presents the interesting feature of composing each processing element by two processors. In order to use the computer to its best, we made both processors work concurrently on the dictionary instructions. A great deal of memory allocation and release was necessary, as well as a perfect understanding of the shared memory and cache functionalities.

As far as program development is concerned, we conclude that for this machine one should start programming with high level Trollius communication tools, in order to be able to debug code and, mainly, communications. Then, step by step, the programmer can relax constraints on debugging and get better performances by using lower level tools.

Regarding the application itself, we recall that we supposed in this paper that the distribution law of the instructions was known beforehand. Therefore, each node's working domain was static. We are currently working on a dynamic version of a dictionary machine, where such a law is unknown. As explained in [3], more complex operations on the local data structures are required, and system load balance, through the exchange of dictionary elements, has to be implemented.

References

1. M.J. Atallah and S.R. Kosaraju: A generalized dictionary machine for VLSI. IEEE Trans. on Computers **34** (1985) 151–155
2. K. Cheng and Z. Fan: A generalized Simultaneous Access Dictionary Machine. IEEE Trans. on Computers **40** (1991) 149–158
3. F. Dehne and M. Gastaldo: A note on the load balancing problem for coarse grained hypercube dictionary machines. Parallel Computing (1990)
4. F. Dehne, N. Santoro: An optimal VLSI dictionary machine for hypercube architectures. Parallel and Distributed Algorithms, M. Cosnard (ed.) North Holland (1989) 137–144
5. H.F. Li and D.K. Probst: Optimal VLSI dictionary machines without compress instructions. IEEE Trans. on Computers **39** (1990) 332–340
6. M.Loi et B.Tourancheau: Trollius: un systeme d'exploitation pour ordinateur multi-processeur à mémoire distribuée. Rapport technique LIP 91-02 (1990)
7. K. Melhorm: Data structure and Algorithms I : Sorting and searching. Brauer, Rozenberg, Salomaa (ed.) (1984)
8. T.S.Narayanan: A survey of Dictionary Machines. Technical Report CSD-86-2 Concordia University (1986)
9. A.R. Omondi, J. D. Brock: Implementing a dictionary on hypercube machines. Proc. Int. Conf. on Parallel Processing (1987) 707–709
10. A.M. Schwartz and M.C. Loui: Dictionary machines on cube-class networks. IEEE Trans. on Computers **36** (1987) 100–105

This article was processed using the LaTeX macro package with LLNCS style

Parallel Searching for 3D-Objects

Frank Klingspor, Dietmar Luhofer, Thomas Rottke

FernUniversität

Post Box 940

5800 Hagen 1

Abstract

The major problem in three-dimensional geometric applications such as the computation of arbitrary polyhedra intersections is the great diversity of possible configurations of geometric objects. Thus, even seemingly straight-forward operations often require an enormous number of floating-point computations. This problem can be alleviated by an appropriate preprocessing of the objects involved. For this purpose, we suggest tetrahedronizing geometric objects and organizing the tetrahedra in a *topological B*-Tree*. The topological B*-Tree can function both as an index and as an object data structure and is thus ideally suited for a wide spectrum of geometric applications. Furthermore, it can easily be used to support parallel algorithms. Parallel search algorithms can only be efficient if the data is very evenly distributed among the available parallel resources. For this purpose, we have developed a geometric hashing method extended by a special control mechanism. Using the topological B*-Tree to support preprocessing of geometric objects leads to a significant reduction in the number of required floating-point operations and therefore in execution time.

Keywords:

geometric searching, parallel topological B*-Trees, data distribution, polyhedra intersections, minimal distance

1 Introduction

Non-standard data bases for non-point geometric objects are used, among others, in the fields of process animation, image processing, graphical data processing and computer aided design. Many applications in which geometric objects are stored in a database require not only an index structure which supports geometric queries (e.g., point queries, line queries, polygon queries, volume queries and closest pair or nearest neighbour queries), but also an object data structure which supports geometric operations such as detection or computation of intersections, distance computations, etc. However, selecting geometric objects can be quite expensive. There are essentially two reasons for this:

- A great deal of data is required to describe geometric objects (such as polygons or polyhedra). Therefore, access to secondary memory can become a bottleneck to the system.
- Complicated floating point computations (e.g., polygon or polyhedra intersections) are required in order to decide whether a specific object is to be selected. As a result, the processor can also become a bottleneck.

Fast access to geometric objects can only be achieved by the application of parallel resources (both processor and memory).

We will first introduce our basic data structure the topological B*-Tree and its parallel variant followed by a short excursion into the problem of data distribution of parallel discs. The rest of this paper is dedicated to polyhedra computations, concentrating mainly on the problem of polyhedra intersections. However, in the course of this discussion, it will become clear that the data structure (topological B*-Tree) and algorithmic approach proposed here can basically be used for any geometric operation on complex objects (e.g., polyhedra). Finally, we will close with some brief comments on related topics of further research, in particular the use of parallelism in connection with geometric algorithms using the topological B*-Tree.

2 Related Works

There are numerous proposals for geometric index structures and object data structures, respectively, in the relevant literature. Specifically, for 3d-objects, the most frequently recommended structures are octrees [11], BSP trees [2] and variants of these. The most common index structures are R-trees [3], grid files [8] and hash tables [7]. The structure of an R-tree is dependent on the order in which objects are inserted. This can adversely affect the efficiency of query processing. On the other hand, for certain object configurations, the directory of a grid file can grow more than linearly with data size [10]. Efficient hashing methods usually require advance knowledge of the data distribution in question. However, for most applications, such advance knowledge is not available. Especially for parallel processing of indexes, a structure such as a B*-tree, which is more robust in these respects, would be desirable.

BSP trees have the drawback that too much redundant information is stored, as there are normally multiple references to objects. This results in higher memory requirements than are absolutely necessary. This is not always acceptable, especially if the structure is also to be stored in external memory, as is usually the case. Furthermore, octrees and BSP trees can degenerate in a similar manner to ordinary binary trees.

3 Topological B*-Trees

B*-Trees have proven to be particularly well suited as index data structures for data with scalar keys in data base applications [1]. In particular, because of their well structured nature (balanced, linear ordering, all nodes with the exception of the root at least half full) B*-Trees are independent of data distribution and the order in which objects are inserted. In order to preserve as many as possible of the desirable characteristics of the B*-Tree for representing geometric indexes while at the same time obtaining a data structure that can be used for parallel processing in a transputer network [4] [5], we have expanded the classical B*-Tree to a *topological B*-Tree*[9]. The keys of the topological B*-Tree correspond to axis-aligned subspaces of a universal space. The differences of the topological B*-Tree as compared to the classical B*-Tree are a result of the geometric interpretation of this key (axis-aligned rectangles). The method of always splitting a node relative to the median key value - as in the case of the classical B*-Tree - is not well suited for use with geometric objects. The main problem is that there are configurations of objects such that these objects cannot be disjointly separated by splitting relative to a single key value.

On the other hand, if one permits subregions to overlap the tree becomes susceptible to the insertion order of objects. The solution we have chosen is to define an additional, non-geometric and universally applicable criterion according to which objects are separated in such cases. To this end, we define a key to consist of two parts:
- Domain (the rectangular region in which objects may be located) and
- Range (the rectangular region in which objects are located).

Domain and range both consist of a rectangular subregion parallel to the coordinate axes of the universal space and a volume interval: an object must be located in the subregion determined by the value of its key, and its volume must lie within the volume interval given in the key (see Figure 1). Using this key, objects that cannot be separated according to geometric location are separated according to volume. As a further advantage, objects can be linearly ordered in the tree according to their volume, thereby retaining most of the characteristics of the classical B*-Tree.- While arbitrary (axis-aligned) rectangular regions may be used for the range, it is sufficient to use only regular rectangles, i.e. rectangular regions that come about by repeatedly splitting regions in half. In any case, the range is always a subset of the corresponding domain.

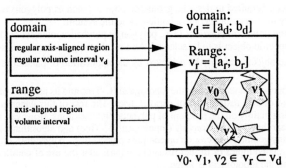

$$v_0. \ v_1, v_2 \in v_r \subset v_d$$

Figure 1: structure of key

An entry of the tree is split according to the following scheme: First, the median line of the domain is determined, and the objects are separated according to whether they intersect the median line or not (*normal split*, see Figure

2, region 1). The latter objects make up a new entry in which all objects lie either to one or the other side of the median line. Should a split of this entry later become necessary, it can therefore simply be split along the median line (*area split*, see Figure 2, region 2a). Parts 3a and 3b show the two new subregions produced by such an area split. Those objects that intersect the median line can be further separated according to their volume (*volume split*, see Figure 2, region 2b). Parts 3c and 3d show the two new subregions that result from a volume split of the subregion IIb. Geometric objects are inserted into the topological B*-Tree according to their bounding box and their volume.

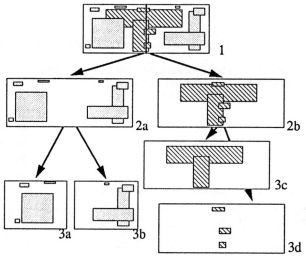

Figure 2: split process

A search query is processed in two steps as follows: First, all objects whose bounding box intersect the search region are selected. The second step, then, consists of deciding whether these objects actually lie within the search region. Note that the intersection of an object with the search region does not necessarily follow from the intersection of its bounding box with that region.

If objects are composed of a large number of atomic sub-objects (e.g., polygons composed of triangles, polyhedra composed of tetrahedra) then these objects themselves can be represented in the form of a topological B*-Tree by storing their atomic components in such a tree.

It turns out in numerous empirical results that the topological B*-Tree provides good average performance and outperforms optimal clustering in volume queries.

4 Parallel topological B*-Trees

There are two ways to use topological B*-Trees for parallel searching:
- One partitions the data (n geometric objects) into disjoint subsets of equal size and constructs a topological B*-Tree for each data subset (array parallelism). Provided all data subsets require approximately the same amount of processing time, the speed-up attained by this sort of partitioning is linear. The degree of partitioning should therefore linearly depend on the expected size (or, in the case of real time applications, on the worst case size) of the response set (set of objects selected by a given query). To this end, one tree is created for every expected element of the response set. If the data is very evenly distributed (i.e., same distribution density in all partitions) one can expect one response per tree and query. Under these conditions, all $O(m)$ responses to a query on $O(m)$ trees are found in expected time of $O(\log n)$. In comparison, the sequential variant of the topological B*-Tree requires $O(\log n)$ time for each object of the response set, resulting in a total of $O(m \log n)$ time for $O(m)$ objects in the worst case. Therefore, parallelism by partitioning is the optimal solution given homogenous distribution density in all partitions.
- Parallelism is achieved by superimposing a pipeline structure on the topological B*-Tree. This type of parallelism only makes sense if continuous search queries are to be expected. Each node of the tree is then assigned its own process which during a given time slice searches all entries of this node in response to at most one query. For the next time slice, the query is passed on to the processes corresponding to descendant nodes

determined by the relevant entries of the previous time slice. In this way, q queries can be processed in $O(q + \log n)$ time. If q is very large with respect to n then an average time of $O(1)$ per query is required.

5 Data Distribution

It is particularly important to have as even a distribution as possible among the various parallel trees or parallel disks. Three ways to achieve this are:
- geometric clustering,
- hashing,
- random assignment of data to a partition.

The results of our research have led us to the conclusion that two factors are of particular importance in choosing a distribution method:
- Data distribution should be as homogenous as possible across partitions.
- The partitions should be of nearly equal size, as even slight differences in size can lead to significant differences in the number of accesses per partition.

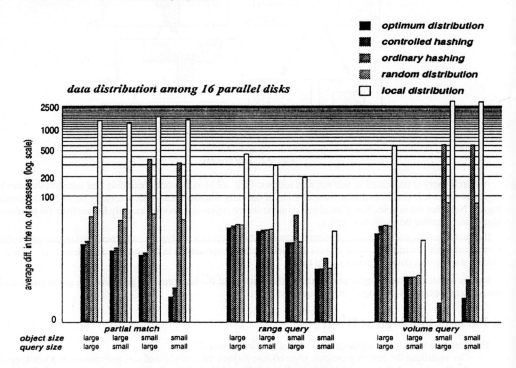

Figure 3: Test results for distribution on parallel disks.

Typical results of our performance tests for queries of types partial match, range query and volume query are summarized in Figure 3. For the sake of simplicity, we have only listed the results for very large and very small objects and queries respectively. The test results for non-extreme (i.e., neither very small nor very large) sizes of objects or queries respectively are monotonically dependant on object and query size.

For our tests, the objects were distributed among 16 parallel disks. We executed 1024 queries of each query type and counted the resulting number of accesses to each disk. The y-axis shows the average differences in the number of accesses as compared to the average number of accesses per partition during a query. The set of objects used consisted of 8192 polygons which were made up of an average of 384 points each.

For large objects, the volume of the bounding box of a polygon reached up to 1/4 of the volume of the universal space. Small objects contained polygons whose bounding box had at most 1/512 of the volume of the universal space. Large query regions covered up to 1/8 of the universal space, small query regions at most 1/128.

Figure 4 contains an analysis of variance for the data shown in Figure 3. It can be seen, that the evenness of the data distribution depends more than 60% on the chosen distribution mechanism. The effects of the object size, query type and query size are negligible. On the other hand, the size of the query answer could be regarded as an error variable, which can not be controlled. The error effect of 10% could be explained in this way. Figure 5 compares the different distribution methods with respect to distribution homogeneity of the partitions and standard deviation of the partition sizes respectively.

It turns out that geometric clustering is not at all suited as a partitioning method: neither are the partitions of nearly equal size nor is data distribution homogenous. It can occur that only one tree is active during a search query. Random partitioning does lead to more or less homogenous data distribution. However, there are still differences in partition size, which can lead to significant differences in required processing time. The same can be said for hashing. To distribute geometric objects, we used an extended hashing method (hashing according to the bounding box and volume of an object) with a control mechanism to ensure that the difference between partition sizes did not exceed a certain value. This method proved to be very nearly optimal.

Analysis of Variance:

Source of Variation	Percentage of Variation	degrees of freedom	Mean Square	F Computed	F Tabled
factor A: query type	1.16%	1	67.55	198.08	3.85
factor B: object size	1.47%	1	82.25	249.99	3.85
factor C: query size	2.00%	1	116.41	341.33	3.85
factor D: cluster type	63.60%	1	3694.90	10834.41	3.85
A x B	1.51%	1	87.49	256.55	3.85
A x C	0.32%	1	18.54	54.37	3.85
A x D	0.60%	1	35.06	102.81	3.85
B x C	6.29%	1	365.57	1071.96	3.85
B x D	5.86%	1	340.37	998.06	3.85
C x D	4.58%	1	266.22	780.62	3.85
error	11.93%	1	0.34		
					significance level: 0.05

Figure 4: analysis of variance for Figure 3

	optimal distribution	controlled hashing	ordinary hashing	random distribution	local distribution
F Computed	203.41	214.01	218.19	240.23	2186.44
F Tabled	261.00	261.00	261.00	261.00	261.00
standard deviation	0.00	0.37	21.96	22.74	648.43

Figure 5: distribution homogeneity and standard deviation of size

6 Conclusions

Using parallel topological B^*-Trees as recommended here, access times for complex geometric objects can be significantly reduced and one can reduce the execution time required for geometric algorithms operating on such objects as well. In summary, the main advantages are:

- The topological B^*-Tree is well suited for parallel processing, i.e., all parallel resources are evenly used.
- Index and object data structures are homogenous, which leads to simpler algorithms.
- Parallel access to external data
- With the help of large, distributed internal memory, a large number of objects can be buffered internally.
- The parallel index can be adapted to different data distributions and query profiles by using an appropriate node size as well as an appropriate degree of partitioning.
- A well structured representation of complex objects leads to a saving of processor time (e.g., for the computation of geometric intersections).
- A substantial speed-up can be attained for sequential algorithms such as polyhedra intersections.
- Topological B^*-Trees were specifically developed to support parallel processing of geometric data. As such, they can easily be used to support parallel geometric algorithms.

References

[1] Bayer, R. and McCreight, E., *Organization and maintenance of large ordered indexes*, Acta Informatica, 1 (1972), pp. 173 - 189.

[2] Fuchs, T., *On visible surface generation by a priori tree structures*, Computer Graphics, 14, pp. 124-133.

[3] Guttman, A., R-trees: *A dynamic data structure for spatial searching*, ACM SIGMOD, 1984, pp. 47 - 57.

[4] Klingspor, F. and Rottke, T., *Realzeitzugriff auf ausgedehnte geometrische Objekte in einem Transputernetz*, Proc. of the TAT '91, Informatik-Fachberichte, Springer, (1991).

[5] Klingspor, F.and Rottke, T., *Realzeitzugriff auf ausgedehnte geometrische Objekte mit parallelen topologischen B^*-Bäumen*, Proc. of the PEARL 91, Informatik-Fachberichte, Springer, (1991).

[6] Klingspor, F., Luhofer, D., Rottke, T., *Intersection and Minimal Distance of 3d-Objects*, Computer Animation, 1992, to appear.

[7] Kriegel, H.P., Seeger, B., *PLOP-Hashing: A Grid File without Directory*, Proc. 4th Int. Conf. on Data Engineering, 1988, pp. 369 - 376.

[8] Nievergelt, J.H. et al., *The grid file: An adaptable, symmetric multikey file structure*, ACM TODS 9, 1984, pp. 38 - 71.

[9] Rottke, T., *Parallele Suchprozesse in der geometrischen Datenverarbeitung*, Technischer Bericht, Fachbereich Informatik, FernUniversität Hagen, to appear.

[10] Rottke, T. et al., *On the Analysis of Grid Structures for Spatial Objects of Non-Zero Size*, Graph-Theoretic Concepts in Computer Science, 1987.

[11] Samet, H., *The Quadtree and Related Hierarchical Data Structures*, ACM Computing Surveys, 1984, pp. 187 - 260.

Parallel Gcd and Lattice Basis Reduction

J.L. Roch and G. Villard *

LMC-IMAG, 46 Av. F. Viallet F38031 Grenoble Cédex.
jlroch, gvillard@imag.fr

Abstract. Gcd and lattice reduction are two major problems in the field of Parallel Algebraic Computations. To know if they are in $\mathcal{NC}$ is still an open question. We point out their correlations and difficulties. Concerning the lattice basis reduction which is of sequential cost $O(n^7)$, we propose a parallelization leading to the time bound $O(n^3 \log^2 n)$ for the reduction of good lattices. Experimentations show that high speed-ups can be obtained.

Throughout the paper we refer to [34], many mathematical points are not detailed in this short presentation concerned with results which have relevance to parallelism.

1 Introduction

The L^3 lattice basis reduction algorithm of A.Lenstra, H.Lenstra and L.Lovász [17] that we intend to parallelize has remarkably wide application areas in the field of Computer Algebra. The most famous one is polynomial factorization since the authors gave in 1982 a polynomial-time solution for $\mathbf{Q}[x]$. Reduction is also used for factorization over algebraic number fields [16, 10] or for factorization of integers [26]. The algorithm is also used to break knapsack public-key cryptosystems [18, 14, 21, 20, 32]. Such a great interest for the L^3 fundamental technique has led authors to improve the original method and reduce its computational cost [8, 29, 27]. But none of these studies seems to be helpful to derive the parallel complexity of basis reduction. However, to decide whether the problem of computing a reduced basis, called $\mathcal{SHORT}$ $\mathcal{VECTORS}$ in [35], has a fast parallel algorithm is still an open question. In particular, $\mathcal{GCD}$ $\mathcal{OF}$ $\mathcal{TWO}$ $\mathcal{INTEGERS}$ is $\mathcal{NC}$-reducible to $\mathcal{SHORT}$ $\mathcal{VECTORS}$. Besides, it is shown in [6] that the L^3-reduction leads to a multidimensional Euclidean algorithm.

The first part of the paper (sec. 2) is a brief survey on gcd. On the one hand $\mathcal{GCD}_{\mathbf{Q}[x]}$ is known to be in $\mathcal{NC}$ [35, 9], on the other hand, to decide whether $\mathcal{GCD}$ $\mathcal{OF}$ $\mathcal{TWO}$ $\mathcal{INTEGERS}$ can be computed fast is still an open question [4, 12]. The second part (section 3) shows the problems encountered while parallelizing the lattice basis reduction. From the sequential algorithm to the implementation on an existing parallel machine, the difficulties are presented, and solutions are proposed.

2 Greatest Common Divisor

We briefly present the main approaches used for the computation of the gcd of two elements in a $E = \mathbf{Z}$ and $E = \mathbf{Q}[x]$. In the following, $M(n)$ denotes the sequential complexity of

---

* This work was supported in part by the *PRC Mathématiques et Informatique* and by the *Groupement C^3* of the french *Centre National de la Recherche Scientifique*.

the multiplication. In the integer case, $M(n)$ is bounded by $O(n \log n \log \log n)$ and in the polynomial case, by $O(n \log n)$.

Sequential algorithms. The properties of an euclidean domain lead to either the *Euclid's algorithm* or the *binary one* [31] which complexities are $O(n^2)$ [3]. Fast algorithms has been derived using the *divide and conquer* technique [15, 13, 19], especially the *Schönage's algorithm* which complexity is $M(n) \log n$ [28].

Direct parallelization : Brent-Kung's algorithm. The algorithm proposed by Brent and Kung [1] uses a systolic array: the number of steps, linear in the length of the operands, is preserved, but each step is parallelized. In the *polynomial case* the complexity is $O(n)$ on a linear array of n processors. Despite of carry propagation the algorithm may be surprisingly suited to the integer case. Nevertheless, for large inputs, the saving of time is disappointing in comparison with the fast sequential Schonhage's algorithm.

Parallel polynomial case. To give better parallel algorithms, two basic ideas may be used: introducing redundancy and describing the function to compute as an algebraic expression, reducible to a problems in $\mathcal{NC}$). Those ideas may be successfully applied to gcd computation in $\mathbf{Q}[x]$, using the theory of subresultants [2]. Polynomial gcd is $\mathcal{NC}$-reducible to the problem of solving linear systems, $\mathcal{DET}_\mathbf{Q}$, and is in $\mathcal{NC}^2$ [35].

Parallel integer GCD : sublinear algorithms. In the integer case, carry propagation makes gcd computation hard to parallelize, and this problem is not known to be either complete for $\mathcal{P}$ or in $\mathcal{NC}$ or $\mathcal{RNC}$. The best known algorithm is $\mathcal{P}$-uniform and is sublinear: its complexity is $O\left(n \log \log n / \log n\right)$ using $O(n^2 \log^2 n)$ processors [11].

3 Lattice Reduction

We begin with some basic definitions and results. For detailed explanations of the sequential algorithm and of its complexity the reader will refer to [17]. We then introduce the problem of size-reduction. The other sections are dedicated to our main result. We firstly present the heuristic on which the parallel algorithm is based and give empirical observations showing that it is a satisfying approach. Next, we derive the algorithm itself and give its complexity from an asymptotical point of view. Finally, using a distributed memory computational model, we show that the algorithm can be efficiently implemented on $O(n^2)$ processors. Empirical results are presented in the last section.

3.1 Basic concepts of lattice reduction

Let $b_1, b_2, \ldots, b_n \in \mathbf{Z}^n$, be n linearly independent vectors. The lattice L in $\mathbf{Z}^n$ generated by the basis $(b_1, b_2, \ldots, b_n)$ is the additive subgroup $\sum_{i=1}^n \mathbf{Z} b_i$. We define the lengh B of the basis to be the largest Euclidean norm $|b_k|$, $|b_i| \leq |b_k| = B$, $1 \leq i \leq n$. L will also denote the $n \times n$ matrix which rows are the vectors b_i. Another basis $L' = b'_1, b'_2, \ldots, b'_n \in \mathbf{Z}^n$ generates the same lattice if and only if for some unimodular matrix U (i.e. $det(U) = \pm 1$), $L' = UL$. To the ordered basis $b_1, b_2, \ldots, b_n$ we associate the Gram-Schmidt orthogonalization $b_1^*, b_2^*, \ldots, b_n^* \in \mathbf{Q}^n$ and the Gram-Schmidt coefficients μ_{ij}:

$$b_i^* = b_i - \sum_{j=1}^{i-1} \mu_{ij} b_j^*, \; and \; \mu_{ij} = \frac{(b_i, b_j^*)}{|b_j^*|^2}, \; \mu_{ii} = 1, \; 1 \leq j < i \leq n. \qquad (1)$$

The L^3 *reduction algorithm* transforms the input basis into a basis consisting in short vectors or equivalently of nearly orthogonal vectors. A basis is called *size-reduced* if $|\mu_{ij}| \leq$

$1/2, 1 \leq j < i \leq n$. A basis which is size-reduced is called L^3-*reduced* if:·

$$|b_i^* + \mu_{i,i-1} b_{i-1}^*|^2 \geq \frac{3}{4} |b_{i-1}^*|^2 \quad for \quad 1 < i \leq n. \tag{2}$$

We know from [17] that if L is a lattice with L^3-reduced basis $b_1, b_2, \ldots, b_n$, then for every nonzero $x \in L$,

$$2^{\frac{n-1}{2}} |x| \geq |b_1|. \tag{3}$$

The first vector of the reduced basis is a relatively short vector in the lattice. A L^3 execution produces a somewhat bubble-sort sequence of the two following transformations:

Swap. Choose i, $1 < i \leq n$, such that (2) is not satisfied and interchange b_{i-1} and b_i. Update the orthogonalization.

Translation. Choose i and j, $1 \leq j < i \leq n$, such that $|\mu_{ij}| > 1/2$ and translate b_i respectively to b_j: if r is the integer nearest to μ_{ij} replace b_i by $b_i - r b_j$.

Complexity of the reduction. It can be shown [17] that $\mathcal{S} = O(n^2 \log_{2/\sqrt{3}} B)$ is an upper bound on the number of swaps that are necessary to reduce a basis. Assuming that the classical arithmetic procedures are employed, the number of arithmetic operations needed for each swap or size-reduction (in order to update the orthogonalization) is at most $O(n^2)$ and the integers on which these operations are performed are of binary length $O(n \log B)$. Consequently the algorithm runs in $O(n^6 \log^3 B)$ binary steps. To use either the original L^3-reduction or one of the improvements previously cited will always preserve the factor $\mathcal{S}$ in the complexity. A main problem from a parallel point of view is thus to reduce this factor (section 3.3). But we have seen that one cannot hope to provide fast algorithms for $\mathcal{SHORT\ VECTORS}$ unless progress is made on computing gcds of integers in parallel.

3.2 Parallel size-reduction

Let $M = \{m_{ij}\} \in \mathbf{Q}^{n \times n}$ a lower triangular matrix with all its diagonal coefficients equal to 1 (M will be the matrix of the Gram-Schmidt coefficients). The problem is to transform the matrix M using unimodular transformations such that it satisfies $|m_{ij}| \leq 1/2, 1 \leq j < i \leq n$. It is shown in [17, 8] that the number of arithmetic operations needed in sequential is $O(n^3)$. Assuming that the numerators and the denominators of the $|m_{ij}|$ are initially bounded by β, the integers on which these operations are performed are of binary length $O(n + \log \beta)$. From a parallel point of view, for every j the μ_{ij}, $2 \leq i \leq n$ can be reduced simultaneously: the parallel size-reduction runs in $O(n)$ steps.

Proposition 1. *Let β be an initial bound on the numerators and the denominators of the $|m_{ij}|$. On $O(n^3 \log \beta \log^2(n \log \beta))$ processors, the parallel size-reduction runs in $O(n \log^2(n \log \beta))$ binary arithmetic steps.*

Proof. The integers on which the operations are performed are shown [34] to be of binary length $O(n \log \beta)$. Noticing that n^2 operations on integers are performed simultaneously, and using that $O(t \log t \log \log t)$ processors are needed to operate on integers of length t, the number of processors is bounded as announced. On such integers the operations are parallelized in $O(\log^2(n \log \beta))$. Noticing that $O(n)$ steps are needed, the proposition is obtained. $\square$

Remark (Coefficient growth). Let us notice that during the parallel size-reduction the integers will have length as large as $O(n \log \beta)$ versus $O(n + \log \beta)$ for the sequential algorithm. This could appear to be a major drawback. Contrary to that, on the one hand, this seems to be necessary in order to decrease the parallel complexity. On the other hand we have proven for particular lattices (see proposition 4 below) that coefficients are not so big.

3.3 Heuristic for parallel reduction

The main difficulty when parallelizing the L^3algorithm is to reduce the factor S which appears in the sequential complexity. The idea we use for our parallel algorithm is that several swaps may probably be done simultaneously at each step of the reduction.

Heuristic 1. *We use P processors, $1 \leq P \leq n$. A basis can be reduced in T phases, each consisting in at most $P/2$ simultaneous swaps among all the possible swaps (b_i, b_{i+1}) for i odd, next $P/2$ simultaneous swaps among all the other possible swaps (b_{i-1}, b_i).*

Let $\sigma(k)$, $1 \leq k \leq T$, be the number of swaps performed at the phase k. We do not yet know how to show, even in particular situations, that $\sigma(k)$ is strictly greater than 1 and/or near to P. This would justify our heuristic and above all, give the complexity of our parallel algorithm. However, we have obtained relevant empirical observations on $\sigma(k)$. Many swaps can always be done in parallel. With test lattices of definitely different types, the average value of $\sigma(k)$ using $n/2$ processors is proportional to n, nearly equal to $2n/3$. That is to say, the heuristic leads to the empirical value $T = O(n \log B)$ in the worst case [34].

3.4 All swaps parallel reduction

Our *all swap parallel reduction* algorithm is based on the previous heuristic, it consists in swapping as much as possible in parallel as long as the basis is not reduced. A basis is reduced in T phases, each phase performing up to n swaps, updating the orthogonalization and size-reducing the basis.

Proposition 2. *On $O(n^4 \log B \log^2(n \log B))$ processors, being given an input basis of dimension n and length B, each phase of the all swaps reduction runs in $O(n\log^2(n\log B))$ binary arithmetic steps. With $T = O(n \log B)$ and $\log B = O(n)$, the complexity of the whole reduction is thus $O(n^3 \log^2 n)$ using $O(n^5 \log^2 n)$ processors.*

Proof. This result may be found in [34]. It essentially relies on modifications of the arguments laid out in [17] so they fit to our parallel framework and on the proposition 1 applied with $\log \beta = O(n \log B)$. □

3.5 On distributed architectures

Our model consists of P processors, each has its own memory and can communicate by a message passing protocol with its neighbours. We assume that $O(l)$ is the binary cost for communicating an integer of length $O(l)$. Using a ring topology, a naive implementation can be based on the parallelization of each swap of pair of vectors and of each translation. The S steps of the sequential reductions are preserved. The algorithm may be viewed as a Gaussian elimination. Applying the numerous results of the litterature on the subject as [25, 5, 22], the data repartition and the arithmetic and communication costs may be discussed.

Distributed all swaps reduction. In order to efficiently use $O(n^2)$ processors, we implement the algorithm based on the heuristic of simultaneous swaps. We use a 2-d torus to benefit both of simultaneous swaps and of the parallelization of each vector operations.

The three matrices which give the vectors b_i and b_i^*, and the coefficients μ_{ij} have to be distributed among the processors. Communications are minimized if one proceed by firstly distributing the columns of the matrices according to the horizontal dimension of the torus. Each of the p_v horizontal rings will thus manage n/p_v rows (vectors of the basis) and perform the associated operations. In particular, p_v translations will be feasible simultaneously. In the same way, we distribute the rows of the matrices according to the vertical dimension.

Consequently, each of the p_h vertical rings will manage n/p_h column operations during the swaps: $p_h/2$ swaps will be done in parallel.

Let us give an overall description of each of the $\mathcal{T}$ phases. Six main successive steps may be distinguished:

1. The processors of the first horizontal ring (labelled $(p_h, 0)$) pairwise exchange the data necessary to the swap decisions: processor $(p_h, 0)$ with $(p_{h+1}, 0)$ then with $(p_{h-1}, 0)$.

2. A *all to all* allows every processor to know all the swaps of the phase.

3. The swaps are performed. Communications on the horizontal rings allow the column operations, afterwards, communications on the vertical rings allow the row operations.

4. The columns of the matrices are vertically duplicated. At the end of this step, every processor (p_h, p_v) of a given vertical ring stores complete columns.

5. The previous duplication allows to perform the translations in parallel using a *broadcast* or a *pipeline strategy* on every horizontal ring.

6. End detection: after a *all to all*, every processor knows if it still remains any swap to perform.

The two major communication costs come from step 4 and step 5 of each phase. It can be shown [34] that $O(np_h l/p_v)$ binary steps are required. The length l of the integers is discussed in proposition 4.

With a good choice of the distribution of the matrices, the computations may be equidistributed. For integers of length l we have $O(n^2 l^2/p_v)$ for the binary arithmetic complexity.

Proposition 3. *Using $O(n^2)$ processors and assuming that the integers involved in the computations are at most of length $O(l)$, each phase of the all swaps parallel reduction needs at most $O(nl^2)$ binary arithmetic steps and $O(nl)$ binary communication steps.*

The assertion can be deduced from a detailed cost study [34] with $p_h = p_v = n$. □

As noticed in section 3.2 for parallel size-reduction, our algorithm involves larger integer than the sequential one. This did not matter in the previous sections since the complexity study was done from an asymptotical point of view. On the contrary, with a limited number of processors, replacing l by $O(n^2 \log B)$ in the proposition 3 leads to prohibitive costs. The solution has been given in [34].

Proposition 4. *Using $O(n^2)$ processors, each phase of the all swaps parallel reduction of a subset lattice needs at most $O(n^3 \log^2 nB)$ binary arithmetic steps and $O(n^2 \log nB)$ binary communication steps. With $\mathcal{T} = O(n \log B)$ the complexity of the whole reduction is $O(n^4 \log^3 nB)$.*

Proof. Most of the lattices used by the applications have a particular structure. Especially, the subset sum lattices [14]. They are used to find $x_i = 0$ or $1, 1 \le i \le n$, such that, given the $n + 1$ integers $a_i, 1 \le i \le n$, and M, we have $x_1 a_1 + \ldots + x_n a_n = M$. Those lattices are given by:

$$L = \begin{bmatrix} 1 \ldots 0 & -a_1 \\ \vdots \ddots \vdots & \vdots \\ 0 \ldots 1 & -a_n \\ 0 \ldots 0 & M \end{bmatrix}. \tag{4}$$

The Gram-Schmidt orthogonalization of L leads to the following relations:

$$B^2 \ge |b_i^*|^2 \ge 1, \ 1 \le i \le n-1, \ and \ B^2 \ge |b_n^*|^2 \ge 1/nB^2. \tag{5}$$

Instead of $|b_i^*|^2 \geq 1/B^{2n}$ in the general case. We have shown in [34] that with such a bound, the proposition 1 can be applied with $\log \beta = O(\log nB)$ in order to give $l = O(n \log nB)$. By replacing this value in proposition 3, we terminate the proof. □

3.6 Performance results

We have implemented the naive parallelization of the sequential reduction, say *algorithm L^3-PR*, and the distributed all swaps reduction, say *algorithm AS-PR*. This work has been done in the frame of the *PAC project* [23, 30]. Our target machine is a *Méganode* [33] based on 128 transputers T800 [7].

Data. The tests presented here are concerned with the subset-sum lattices. The coordinates of the input basis were smaller that 2^{150}. Therefore, the computations on the basis are done modulo integers as large as 2^{150} and, the computations on the orthogonalization are done by exact arithmetic on integers as large as 2^{400}.

Speed-ups As usual let us now discuss the measured speed-ups of the algorithms. Even from an empirical point of view, the case $P \ll n$ is definitely not interesting: there is no difficulty to obtain speed-ups near to P for both algorithms and no conclusion can be made concerning the complexity. In the case $P \approx n$ for a subset sum 36-lattice, the speed-ups of L^3-PR remain lower than 6. Those bad performances are essentially due to the communication cost which tends to predomine as P increases. Consequently, although its implementation is easy, the algorithm L^3-PR presents no interest but for a small number of processors. Contrary to that, *AS-PR* on a similar subset sum 36-lattice leads to a speed-up of 17.4 on a ring of 18 processors.

p_h	1	6	20	30
$p_v = 1$	1	5.3	18.4	23.9
$p_v = 3$	1.6	11.3	43.7	59.6

Table 1 : *AS-PR*, speed-ups for subset sum lattices with $n = 60$.

The most interesting case is $P > n$. Table 1 summarizes the good results obtained with *AS-PR*. It can be seen that on a 90 ($p_h = 30$, $p_v = 3$) processors torus an efficiency of 65% is obtained for $n = 60$, despite of the fact that the infinite precision arithmetic is not appropriate to a low granularity static mapping.

Further studies.

Although progress has to be made before one can hope to provide fast algorithms for *gcd* and *lattice basis reduction*, efficient implementations and high speed-ups can be obtained. We may also noticed that our implementations could suffer from the static mapping of the parallel tasks on the network topology but studies on *dynamic load-balancing* [24] should soon permit to go beyond the limits currently imposed.

References

1. R.P. Brent and H.T. Kung. Systolic VLSI arrays for linear-time gcd computation. In *VLSI'83*. Anceau-Aas Eds, Elsevier Science Publishers, North-Hollland, 1983.

2. G.E. Collins. Subresultants and reduced polynomial remainder sequences. *J. ACM*, 14:128–142, 1967.

3. G.E. Collins. The average running-time of Euclid's algorithm. *SIAM J. Computing*, 3:1–10, 1974.

4. S.A. Cook. The classification of problems which have fast parallel algorithms. In *Int. Conf. Foundations of Computation Theory, Borgholmm 1983, LNCS 158 pp 78-93*, 1983.

5. M. Cosnard, , B. Tourancheau, and G. Villard. Gaussian elimination on message passing architectures. In *Supercomputing, E.N. Houtis et al. eds, LNCS 297*, 1988.

6. J. Hastad, B. Helfrich, J.C. Lagarias, and C.P. Schnorr. Polynomial time algorithms for finding integer relations among real numbers. In *3rd Symposium on Theoretical Aspects of Computer Science, LNCS*, volume 210, pages 105–118, 1986.

7. INMOS. The transputer data book, 1989. Press Ltd, Bath UK.

8. E. Kaltofen. On the complexity of finding short vectors in integer lattices. In *Proc EUROCAL 83 (London) Springer LNCS 162 pp 236-244*, 1983.

9. E. Kaltofen. Processor efficient parallel computation of polynomial greatest common divisors. Technical report, Rensselaer Polytechnic Institute, 1990.

10. R. Kannan, H.W. Lenstra, and L. Lovász. Polynomial factorization and nonrandomness of bits of algebraic and some transcendental numbers, 1984. Carnegie-Mellon University Cs-84.

11. R. Kannan, G. Miller, and L. Rudolph. Sublinear parallel algorithm for computing the greatest common divisor of two integers. *SIAM J. Comput.*, 16 1, 1987.

12. R.M. Karp and V. Ramachandran. Parallel algorithms for shared-memory machines. In J. van Leuwen, editor, *Algorithms and Complexity*, pages 869–932. Elsevier, 1990.

13. D.E. Knuth. The analysis of algorithms. In *Congrès int. Math. Nice*, volume 3, pages 269–274, 1991.

14. J.C. Lagarias and A. Odlyzko. Solving low-density subset sum problems. *Journal of ACM*, 32 1 pp 229-246, 1985.

15. D.H. Lehmer. Euclid's algorithm for large numbers. *AMMM*, 45:227–233, april 1938.

16. A.K. Lenstra. Factoring polynomials over algebraic number fields. In *Proc EUROCAL 83 (London) Springer LNCS 162 pp 245-254*, 1983.

17. A.K. Lenstra, H.W. Lenstra, and L. Lovász. Factoring polynomials with rational coefficients. *Math. Annalen*, 261 pp 513-534, 1982.

18. R.C. Merkle and M.E. Hellman. Hiding information and signatures in trap-door knapsacks. *IEEE Trans. Inf. Theory*, IT 24 pp 525-530, 1978.

19. R.T. Moenck. Fast computation of gcd. In *5 th. ACM Symp. Theory Comp.*, pages 142–151, 1973.

20. V. Niemi. A new trap-door in knapsacks. In *Advances in Cryptology, EUROCRYPT '90, LNCS 473 pp 405-411, Springer-Verlag*, 1991.

21. S.P. Radziszowski and D.L. Kreher. Solving subset sum problems with the LLL algorithm. In *Third SIAM Conference on Discrete Mathematics, Clemson, SC.*, 1986.

22. Y. Robert, B. Tourancheau, and G. Villard. Data allocation Strategies for the Gauss and Jordan Algorithms on a Ring of Processors. *Information Processing Letters*, 31, 1989.

23. J.L. Roch, F. Siebert, P. Sénéchaud, and G. Villard. Computer Algebra on a MIMD machine. *ISSAC'88, LNCS 358 and in SIGSAM Bulletin, ACM*, 23/11, p.16-32, 1989.

24. J.L. Roch, A. Vermeerbergen, and G. Villard. Load-balancing for algebraic computations. In *CONPAR 92, Lyon, France*, LNCS, September 1992.

25. Y. Saad. Gaussian elimination on hypercubes. In *Parallel Algorithms and Architectures, Eds M. Cosnard et al., North-Holland*, 1986.

26. C.P. Schnorr. Factoring integers and computing discrete logarithms via diophantine approximation. In *EUROCRYPT'91, Brighton-U.K., LNCS 547*, pages 281–293, 1991.

27. C.P. Schnorr and M. Euchner. Lattice basis reduction: improved practical algorithms and solving subset sum problems. In *FCT91, Lect. Nt. Comp. Sc.*, 1991.

28. A. Schönhage. Schnelle berechnung von kettenbruchtenwicklungen. *Acta Informatica*, 1:139–144, 1971.

29. A. Schönhage. Factorization of univariate integer polynomials by diophantine approximation and an improved basis reduction algorithm. In *11th ICALP, LNCS 172*, 1984.

30. F. Siebert and G. Villard. PAC : First experiments on a 128 transputers Meganode. In *International Symposium on Symbolic and Algebraic Computation, Bonn Germany*, 1991. ACM Press.

31. J. Stein. Computing gcd without division. *J. Comp. Phys.*, 1:397–405, 1967.

32. J. Stern and P. Toffin. Cryptanalysis of a public-key cryptosystem based on approximations by rational numbers. In *Advances in Cryptology, EUROCRYPT '90, LNCS 473 pp313-317, Springer-Verlag*, 1991.

33. Telmat. TNode Overview. Technical Report Doc-1.02-3.2, Telmat Informatique, 1990.

34. G. Villard. Parallel lattice basis reduction. In *International Symposium on Symbolic and Algebraic Computation, Berbeley California USA*. ACM Press, July 1992.

35. J. von zur Gathen. Parallel algorithms for algebraic problems. *SIAM J. Comput.*, 13 4, pp 802-824, 1984.

Parallel Minimum Spanning Forest Algorithms on the Star and Pancake Interconnection Networks

Selim G. Akl and Ke Qiu

Department of Computing and Info. Science
Queen's University
Kingston, Canada

Abstract. Parallel algorithms are described for computing minimum spanning forests in both sparse and dense weighted graphs. The algorithms are designed to run on the star and pancake interconnection networks. Their time complexities match those of the equivalent hypercube algorithms, thanks mainly to a novel routing scheme. The latter unifies data routing on the star and pancake networks, and makes these networks as powerful as the hypercube when solving a host of problems, and it allows a certain class of algorithms designed for the hypercube to be implemented directly on the star and pancake networks without time loss. These results take added importance when one recalls the many attractive properties that the star and pancake networks possess by comparison with the hypercube, in particular their smaller degree and diameter.

1 Introduction

Let V_n be the set of all $n!$ permutations of symbols 1, 2, ..., n. For any permutation $v \in V_n$, if we denote the ith symbol of v by $v(i)$, then v can be written as $v(1)v(2)\cdots v(n)$. A *star interconnection network* on n symbols, $S_n = (V_n, E_{S_n})$, is an undirected graph with $n!$ nodes, where each node v is connected to $n - 1$ nodes which can be obtained by interchanging the first and i^{th} symbols of v, i.e., $(v(1)v(2)\cdots v(i)v(i + 1)\cdots v(n), v(i)v(2)\cdots v(i - 1)v(1)v(i + 1)\cdots v(n)) \in E_{S_n}$, for $2 \leq i \leq n$. We call these $n - 1$ connections *dimensions*. Thus each vertex is connected to $n - 1$ vertices through dimensions 2, 3, ..., n. S_n is also called an n-star. Fig. 1(a) shows S_4. A *pancake interconnection network* on n symbols, $P_n = (V_n, E_{P_n})$, is an undirected graph with $n!$ nodes, where each node v is connected to $n - 1$ nodes which can be obtained by flipping the first i symbols of v, i.e., $(v(1)v(2)\cdots v(i - 1)v(i)v(i + 1)\cdots v(n), v(i)v(i - 1)\cdots v(2)v(1)v(i + 1)\cdots v(n)) \in E_{P_n}$, for $2 \leq i \leq n$. The dimensions for P_n are defined similarly. P_n is also called an n-pancake. Fig. 1(b) shows P_4. Clearly, $S_n = P_n$, for $n \leq 3$. Since the following discussion and results apply to both networks, we henceforth use X_n to denote either S_n or P_n.

Both the star and pancake are attractive alternatives to the hypercube, a popular network for interconnecting processors in a parallel computer, and compare favorably with it in several aspects [1, 2]. For example, the degree of X_n is $n - 1$, i.e., sublogarithmic in the number of vertices of X_n, while a hypercube with $\Theta(n!)$ vertices has degree $\Theta(\log n!) = \Theta(n \log n)$, i.e., logarithmic in the number of vertices. The same can be said about the diameter of X_n.

Let $X_{n-1}(i)$ be a sub-graph of X_n induced by all the vertices with the same last symbol i, for some $1 \le i \le n$. It can be seen that $S_{n-1}(i)$ is an $(n-1)$-star and $P_{n-1}(i)$ is an $(n-1)$-pancake, both of them defined on symbols $\{1, 2, \cdots, n\} - \{i\}$. Thus, X_n can be decomposed into n X_{n-1}'s: $X_{n-1}(i)$, $1 \le i \le n$ [1, 2]. For example, S_4 in Fig. 1(a) contains four 3-stars, namely $S_3(1)$, $S_3(2)$, $S_3(3)$, and $S_3(4)$, respectively. P_n can also be decomposed similarly.

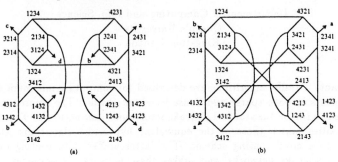

Fig. 1. (a) A 4-Star S_4, (b) A 4-Pancake P_4

Let m_1 and m_2 be two distinct symbols from $\{1, 2, ..., n\}$. We use the notation $m_1 * m_2$ to represent a permutation of $\{1, 2, ..., n\}$ whose first and last symbols are m_1 and m_2, respectively, and $*$ represents any permutation of the $n-2$ symbols in $\{1, 2, ..., n\} - \{m_1, m_2\}$. Similarly, m_1* is a permutation of n symbols whose first symbol is m_1, and $*m_2$ is a permutation of n symbols whose last symbol is m_2.

This paper is organized as follows. Section 2 presents routing algorithms on the star and pancake networks. These routing algorithms are then used in Section 3 to implement two optimal minimum spanning forest algorithms for the hypercube on the star and pancake networks, resulting in optimal algorithms on the latter. Our concluding remarks are offered in Section 4 in which we also compare the power of the hypercube to that of the star and pancake networks.

2 Routing on X_n

Consider the following problem: Given $X_{n-1}(i)$, and $X_{n-1}(j)$, with $i \ne j$, it is required to exchange the contents of the processors in $X_{n-1}(i)$ with the processors in $X_{n-1}(j)$. By exchanging the contents of $X_{n-1}(i)$ with $X_{n-1}(j)$ we mean that the content of each processor in $X_{n-1}(i)$ $(X_{n-1}(j))$ is routed to a processor in $X_{n-1}(j)$ $(X_{n-1}(i))$ such that no two processors in $X_{n-1}(i)$ $(X_{n-1}(j))$ send their contents to the same processor in $X_{n-1}(j)$ $(X_{n-1}(i))$. In other words, the mapping defined by such an exchange is a bijection between $X_{n-1}(i)$ and $X_{n-1}(j)$. We can view this problem as copying the contents of $X_{n-1}(i)$ and $X_{n-1}(j)$ to each other in arbitrary order. This can be accomplished in constant time as shown in Procedure COPY.

Procedure COPY (i, j)

1. **do in parallel for all vertices** $*i$, $*j$
   send content to neighbor along dimension n
2. **do in parallel for all edges** $(i * k, j * k)$, such that $k \ne i, j$,
   exchange contents between $i * k$ and $j * k$.

3. do in parallel for all vertices $i * k, \, j * k, \, k \neq i, j$
send content to neighbor along dimension n. $\Box$

For S_n, it is easy to see from Procedure COPY that vertex $ajbi$ in $S_{n-1}(i)$ corresponds to vertex $aibj$ in $S_{n-1}(j)$, where a and b are permutations of symbols in $\{1, 2, ..., n\} - \{i, j\}$, such that the set of symbols in a is disjoint from the set of symbols in b, and $|a| + |b| = n - 2$, where $|a|$ and $|b|$ are the number of symbols in a and b, respectively. Note that either a or b could be empty, but not both. For P_n, vertex $ajbi$ in $P_{n-1}(i)$ corresponds to vertex $ai\bar{b}j$ in $P_{n-1}(j)$, where $\bar{b} = b_k b_{k-1}...b_1$ if $b = b_1 b_2...b_k$. Therefore, the mapping defined by procedure COPY is a bijection between the vertices of $X_{n-1}(i)$ and $X_{n-1}(j)$.

We now extend the above result as follows. Let I: $i_1, i_2, ..., i_l$ and J: $j_1, j_2, ..., j_l$ be two sequences from $\{1, 2, ..., n\}$ such that no two elements of I are equal, no two elements of J are equal, and $\{i_1, i_2, ..., i_l\} \cap \{j_1, j_2, ..., j_l\} = \emptyset$. It is desired to exchange the contents of $X_{n-1}(i_1), X_{n-1}(i_2), ..., X_{n-1}(i_l)$ with $X_{n-1}(j_1), X_{n-1}(j_2),$ $..., X_{n-1}(j_l)$ such that the contents of $X_{n-1}(i_m)$ are exchanged with $X_{n-1}(j_m)$, for $1 \leq m \leq l$. This task can also be achieved in constant time by procedure GROUP-COPY given below.

Procedure GROUP-COPY (I, J)

1. do in parallel for $1 \leq m \leq l$
COPY (i_m, j_m). $\Box$

It can be shown easily that the given conditions imply that no conflict will occur.

3 Minimum Spanning Forest Algorithms

Let $G = (V, E)$ be a weighted undirected graph and let $|V| = N$ and $|E| = m$. A *minimum spanning forest* (MSF) of G is a spanning forest such that the sum of the weights of its edges is minimum. Two commonly used sequential algorithms for finding a MSF of a given graph are the algorithms of Kruskal and Prim [5]. Kruskal's algorithm has a running time of $O(m \log m)$. If, however, the edges of G are given sorted in non-decreasing order of their weights, then Kruskal's algorithm finds a MSF of the graph in $O(m)$ time [4, 5]. Prim's algorithm has a running time of $O(N^2)$. Our MSF algorithms are modeled on two algorithms for the hypercube [4]. Due to space limitations, we only present one such algorithm on the hypercube and X_n. The reader is referred to [7] for a description of the other algorithm.

3.1 Hypercube MSF Algorithm

This algorithm is based on the idea that when a total order is defined on the edges of G, the edges of an arbitrary subgraph which are not in its MSF cannot be in the final MSF of the entire graph G. Thus the MSF of G is obtained by successive elimination of non-MSF edges. One such a total order $\prec$ on the edges in E can be defined as follows: $e_i \prec e_j \iff (w(e_i) < w(e_j)) \vee ((w(e_i) = w(e_j)) \wedge (i < j))$, where $w(e)$ is the weight associated with edge e. This order $\prec$ will be used for comparing edges in all the algorithms in this paper.

Each processor is initially assigned a maximum of $\lceil m/p \rceil$ edges, where $p = 2^d$ is the number of processors in the hypercube. During the first phase, each processor first sorts its $\lceil m/p \rceil$ edges. If $\lceil m/p \rceil > N$, then each processor finds the MSF for the edges assigned to it using Kruskal's algorithm. Note that the order in which the edges of the MSF are selected produces a list of edges sorted in non-decreasing order of their weights. The second phase consists of d steps of merging. During the jth step, $j = 0, 1, 2, ..., d - 1$, processor A_k receives the list of MSF edges constructed by its neighbor $A_{k+2^{d-j-1}}$, for $0 \leq k < 2^{d-j-1}$. The two lists of sorted edges are then merged in A_k. If the total number of edges of the two lists at A_k is less than N and $j \neq d - 1$, then no further processing is required in A_k. Otherwise, Kruskal's algorithm is applied to the merged list and the edges not in the partial MSF will be discarded. In any case, after these computations, A_k will contain a sorted list of size less than N. The final MSF will be contained in A_0. The time complexity for this algorithm is $O(\frac{m}{p} \log \frac{m}{p} + N + N \log \frac{m}{N})$.

3.2 Star and Pancake MSF Algorithms

Most hypercube algorithms are of the type ASCEND or DESCEND, or some variation thereof [6]. For a hypercube of $p = 2^d$ processors, at the kth step of an algorithm of type DESCEND, a $(d + 1 - k)$-dimensional hypercube is, in effect, divided into two $(d - k)$-dimensional hypercubes, for $k = 1, 2, ..., d$. In some cases, of particular interest in this paper, the algorithms continue to work on only one of the two smaller hypercubes and the same process is continued recursively. The algorithms can then be viewed as applying a *dimension-shrinking* process, each time shrinking a hypercube to one half of its previous size.

The hypercube algorithm for computing the MSF presented in Section 3.1 can be directly implemented on the star and pancake networks using a dimension-shrinking mechanism on X_n described below.

Case 1: n is a power of 2, i.e., $n = 2^k$ for some positive integer k, and dimension-shrinking can be done in the usual way: In the first step, each processor in $X_{n-1}(j)$ communicates with a processor in $X_{n-1}(j + 2^{k-1})$, for $1 \leq j \leq n/2$. This way, n X_{n-1}'s have been reduced to $n/2$ X_{n-1}'s. Then the same process is repeated. After $k = \log n$ steps, X_n has been reduced to $X_{n-1}(1)$.

Case 2: n is not a power of 2, i.e., $n = 2^k + c$, $0 < c < 2^k$. We first reduce n X_{n-1}'s to 2^k X_{n-1}'s by letting the processors in $X_{n-1}(2^k + i)$, $1 \leq i \leq c$, communicate with the processors in $X_{n-1}(i)$. The same dimension-shrinking as in Case 1 is then performed. The total number of steps is therefore $\lceil \log n \rceil$.

In both cases, all the communications are achieved by calling Procedure GROUP-COPY, and the number of steps needed is $\lceil \log n \rceil$. After $\lceil \log n \rceil$ steps, we are down to $X_{n-1}(1)$, which in turn consists of $n - 1$ X_{n-2}'s, and the same procedure is applied. Thus the overall number of steps needed to perform a dimension-shrinking in X_n is equal to $\sum_{i=2}^{n} \lceil \log i \rceil = O(\log n!) = O(\log p)$, where $p = n!$ is the number of processors in X_n.

In the X_n version of the MSF algorithm from 3.1, each processor is initially assigned a maximum of $\lceil \frac{m}{p} \rceil$ edges, and hence the first phase requires $O(\frac{m}{p} \log \frac{m}{p})$ time. During the second phase, there are r steps in which Kruskal's algorithm is not applied because the number of edges in each processor is less than N, where

$r = \sum_{i=q}^{n} \lceil \log i \rceil + s$, $0 \le s < \lceil \log(q-1) \rceil$, for some $2 \le q \le (n+1)$. Thus, $(2^s q(q+1) \cdots (n-1)n) \times \frac{m}{p} < N$. However, after one additional step, we have either $(2^{s+1} q(q+1) \cdots (n-1)n) \times \frac{m}{p} \ge N$, if $s \le \lceil \log(q-1) \rceil - 2$, or $((q-1)q(q+1) \cdots (n-1)n) \times \frac{m}{p} \ge N$, if $s = \lceil \log(q-1) \rceil - 1$. In any case, we always have $(q-1)q \cdots (n-1)n \times \frac{m}{p} \ge N$. For these r steps, the total time required to transmit and merge the lists is on the order of:

$$\{[1 + 2 + 2^2 + \cdots + 2^{\lceil \log n \rceil - 1} + n] +$$
$$[1 + 2 + 2^2 + \cdots + 2^{\lceil \log(n-1) \rceil - 1} + (n-1)]n +$$
$$[1 + 2 + 2^2 + \cdots + 2^{\lceil \log(n-2) \rceil - 1} + (n-2)](n-1)n + \cdots$$
$$[1 + 2 + 2^2 + \cdots + 2^{\lceil \log q \rceil - 1} + q](q+1) \cdots (n-1)n +$$
$$[1 + 2 + 2^2 + \cdots + 2^s]q(q+1) \cdots (n-1)n\} \times (m/p),$$

which is $O(2^s q(q+1) \cdots (n-1)n \times \frac{m}{p}) = O(N)$. For the next $\sum_{i=2}^{n} \lceil \log i \rceil - r$ steps in which Kruskal's algorithm is applied due to the fact that the size of edge list in each processor is larger than N, we have

$$\sum_{i=2}^{n} \lceil \log i \rceil - r \le \sum_{i=2}^{q-1} \lceil \log i \rceil$$
$$= O(\log((q-2)!)).$$

Since $(q-1)q \cdots (n-1)n \times \frac{m}{p} \ge N$, we have

$$\frac{m}{N} \ge \frac{p}{(q-1)q \cdots (n-1)n} = \frac{n!}{(q-1) \cdots n} = (q-2)!$$

This means that the number of steps where Kruskal's algorithm has to be performed on lists longer than N (but less than or equal to $2N$) is $O(\log((q-2)!)) = O(\log \frac{m}{N})$. The first phase of the algorithm takes $O(\frac{m}{p} \log \frac{m}{p})$ time, while the first r steps of the second phase takes $O(N)$ time. The rest of the algorithm takes $O(\log \frac{m}{N})$ steps, each requiring $O(N)$ time to perform Kruskal's algorithm. Thus, the time complexity for the X_n MSF algorithm is

$$T = O(\frac{m}{p} \log \frac{m}{p} + N + N \log \frac{m}{N}). \tag{1}$$

This time matches that of the same algorithm on the hypercube which is somewhat surprising since the star and pancake have sub-logarithmic degree and diameter in the total number of vertices. A further discussion of this issue is offered in Section 4. Since the time required by this algorithm on X_n is the same as that on a hypercube, the following argument from [4] applies here as well. Sequentially, Kruskal's algorithm takes $O(m \log m)$ time, which means that the speedup achieved by the parallel algorithm is $O(m \log m)/T$. This is optimal when $p \le (m \log m)/N(1 + \log(m/N))$ for graphs of any edge density. For dense graphs with $m = \Theta(N^2)$ edges, the algorithm requires $O(N \log N)$ time using $\Theta(N)$ processors, whereas, for sparse graphs with $m = \Theta(N)$ edges, it requires $O(N)$ time with $\Theta(\log N)$ processors.

The second hypercube MSF algorithm can also be implemented on X_n easily with the same time complexity [7]. This algorithm is more efficient for dense graphs. It should be noted that in both algorithms, p must also be chosen so that $p = n!$, for some integer n.

4 Conclusion

We have presented MSF algorithms on the star and pancake networks. The time complexities of these algorithms match those of the equivalent hypercube algorithms, thanks mainly to a novel routing scheme. The latter unifies data routing on the star and pancake networks. Furthermore, it makes these networks as powerful and as efficient as the hypercube when solving a host of problems, as explained below.

Those hypercube algorithms that fall in ASCEND/DESCEND class can be divided further into two sub-classes according to whether or not they preserve the ordering of the processors while ascending or descending, i.e., whether or not a processor ranked k^{th} in one sub-cube has to communicate with a processor also ranked k^{th} in another sub-cube. Examples of algorithms in the first sub-class are Batcher's bitonic merging and sorting algorithms. Algorithms that belong to the second sub-class include broadcasting, prefix sums computation, and load balancing. It is obvious that using Procedure GROUP-COPY, we can implement on the star and pancake networks any algorithm for the hypercube that is in the second sub-class, directly and without time loss. Our MSF algorithms provide further examples of algorithms in the second sub-class, since the shrinking process is independent of the processor rankings as long as one processor in one sub-cube (or X_{n-1}) is able to communicate with another processor (regardless of its rank) in another sub-cube (or X_{n-1}).

In [3], Das et al. describe several parallel graph algorithms on unweighted graphs for hypercube computers. These algorithms are for finding a spanning forest, the connected components, a fundamental cycle set, and the bridges of a graph, as well as for checking whether a graph is bipartite. All of these algorithms fall into the second sub-class mentioned above. Consequently, they can all be implemented directly on the star or the pancake networks without time loss.

References

1. S.B. Akers and B. Krishnamurthy, "A Group Theoretic Model for Symmetric Interconnection Networks," *IEEE Trans. on Compu.*, Vol. c-38, No. 4 (1989) 555-566.
2. S.B. Akers, D. Harel, and B. Krishnamurthy, "The Star Graph: An Attractive Alternative to the *n*-cube," *Proc ICPP*, (1987) 393-400.
3. S.K. Das, N. Deo, and S. Prasad, "Parallel Graph Algorithms for Hypercube Computers," *Parallel Computing*, Vol. 13 (1990) 143-158.
4. S.K. Das, N. Deo, and S. Prasad, "Two Minimum Spanning Forest Algorithms on Fixed-size Hypercube Computers," *Parallel Computing*, Vol. 15 (1990) 179-187.
5. E. Horowitz and S. Sahni, *Fundamentals of Computer Algorithms*, Computer Science Press, Rockville, Maryland, 1978.
6. F.P. Preparata and J. Vuillemin, "The Cube-Connected-Cycle: A Versatile Network for Parallel Computation," *Comm. of the ACM*, Vol. 24, No. 5 (1981) 300-309.
7. S.G. Akl and K. Qiu, Parallel Minimum Spanning Forest Algorithms on the Star and Pancake Interconnection Networks, Technical Report No. 91-323, Dept. of Computing and Info. Sci., Queen's University, Kingston, Canada, 1991.

This article was processed using the LaTeX macro package with LLNCS style

Parallel algorithms for the distance transformation

Hugo Embrechts and Dirk Roose

Katholieke Universiteit Leuven
Dept. Computerwetenschappen
Celestijnenlaan 200A
B-3001 Heverlee, Belgium
Tel ++32 (0) 16-20 10 15
Fax ++32 (0) 16-20 53 08
Hugo.Embrechts@cs.kuleuven.ac.be
Dirk.Roose@cs.kuleuven.ac.be

Abstract. The distance transformation (DT) is a basic operation in image analysis where it is used for object recognition.

We present several approaches for the parallel calculation of the distance transform. They are of the kind "divide-and-conquer" and are similar in this respect to the parallel algorithm we have developed for component labelling. Concrete algorithms and their performance will be discussed for the city block (CB) distance and the Chamfer 3-4 distance that are approximations for the Euclidean Distance.

This paper contains a description of the algorithms, a complexity analysis, a discussion on load imbalance and timings obtained on an iPSC^{T}/2.

Keywords : distance transformation, MIMD machines, divide and conquer, image analysis.

1 Introduction

A DT converts a binary image consisting of foreground and background pixels, into an image where all background pixels have a value equal to the distance to the nearest foreground pixel.

Computing the Euclidean distance from a pixel to a set of foreground pixels is essentially a global operation and therefore needs a complicated and time-consuming algorithm. However, reasonable approximations to the Euclidean distance measure exist that allow algorithms to consider only a small neighbourhood at a time. They approximate a global distance by the sum of local distances, i.e.

distances between adjacent pixels. Two of the in [1, 2] proposed distance measures are the City Block distance and the Chamfer 3-4 distance. They are defined by the masks of figure 1. The DT applied to an image with one foreground pixel centered at the middle of the image is shown in figure 2. The DT is a basic op-

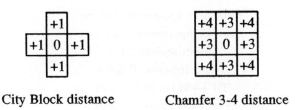

City Block distance   Chamfer 3-4 distance

Fig. 1. These masks show for the indicated distance measures the distance between the central pixel and the adjacent pixels. The distance between two image points a and b is defined as the sum of the distances between adjacent pixels in the path connecting a and b, that minimizes this sum.

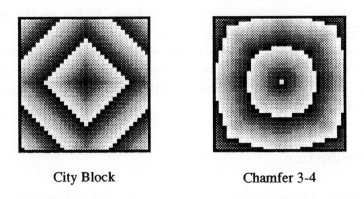

City Block   Chamfer 3-4

Fig. 2. The DT of an image with one foreground pixel centered in the middle of the image for the City Block and Chamfer 3-4 distances. Growing distance is represented by a greytone repeatedly varying from black to white (to accentuate the contours of the DT).

eration in image analysis where it is used for object recognition. It can be used for computing skeletons in a non-iterative way. Further applications are merging and segmentation, clustering and matching [1]. The DT is also an important instrument in path planning.

We present parallel algorithms suited for MIMD-machines. Algorithms for SIMD-machines can be found in e.g. [3].

2 The sequential algorithm

The sequential algorithm is a known algorithm [1] consisting of two passes during which the image is traversed, once from top to bottom and from left to right, and the second time in reverse order. When a pixel is processed, its distance value (infinity if not yet determined) is compared to the distance value of a number of neighbours augmented by their relative distance and is replaced by the smallest resulting value. This causes the distance values to propagate from the object boundaries in the direction of the scan and yields, after the second pass, the correct DT-values.

We describe this in more detail for the CB distance. During the first pass each background pixel takes as value

$$a_{i,j} \leftarrow \min(a_{i,j-1} + 1, a_{i-1,j} + 1). \tag{1}$$

Foreground pixels take value zero. During the second pass the pixel values are replaced by

$$a_{i,j} \leftarrow \min(a_{i,j}, a_{i,j+1} + 1, a_{i+1,j} + 1). \tag{2}$$

The formulae for the Chamfer 3-4 distance are similar.

3 Introduction to the parallel solution

Parallelism is introduced by the 'divide-and-conquer' principle. This means that the image is subdivided into as many subregions as there are processors available ; the operation to be parallelized, in our case the DT, is calculated on each sub-region separately and these local DTs have to be used in one way or another to calculate the global DT on the image. An alternative for the 'divide and conquer' solution is processing the image in a (possibly coarse-grained) systolic fashion [6].

Let LDT (local distance transform) denote the DT applied to a subregion or, where indicated, a union of neighbouring subregions and GDT (global distance transform) the DT applied to the whole image. Then the parallel algorithm consists of the next three steps :

I. On each subregion the LDT is calculated *for the boundary pixels* of that subregion.

II. The GDT values *for the boundary pixels* are calculated out of the LDT values.

III. On each subregion the GDT values for the internal pixels are determined out of the GDT values for the boundary pixels and the local image information. We call this part IDT (internal DT).

Step I and III are actions that can be performed for each subregion independently, whereas step II needs a data exchange between subregions. For step II no internal pixel values are needed, however, as can be seen from figure 3. The first

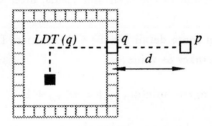

Fig. 3. The distance from p to the foreground pixel in the indicated subregion closest to p is $d + \text{LDT}(q)$.

step could be done by executing the sequential DT algorithm on each subregion and retaining the boundary values. However, in [4] we present a shorter one pass algorithm which scans the image from the borders to the interior and in which each pixel is traversed at most once.

For step II we consider two possible solutions. The first solution is similar to the hierarchical approach we used for component labelling [5]. In this approach the LDT values are determined recursively for the boundary pixels of the union of a number of subregions for which the LDT values are already determined. This is done, until the LDT values for the boundary of the whole image are determined. These are by definition the GDT values. Then the GDT values for the same unions of subregions are calculated, but in reverse order.

The second solution for step II consists of an inter-subregion propagation in successive directions. The feasibility of this approach, however, and the complexity of the resulting algorithm depend on the distance measure used.

For both algorithms we assume the number of subregions horizontally and vertically a power of 2.

The step III of the parallel algorithm is done by executing the sequential algorithm on each subregion starting from the original image data and the GDT values on the boundary pixels obtained in step II.

4 The hierarchical algorithm

Consider a sequence of gradually becoming coarser partitions p_l of the image for $l = 1, 2, \ldots, L$, with the finest partition p_1 being a partition of the image containing as many subregions as there are processors available. Each of the other partitions p_l $(l \neq 1)$ consists of subregions that each are the union of two subregions of p_{l-1}. The coarsest partition p_L contains as only subregion the image itself. See figure 4.

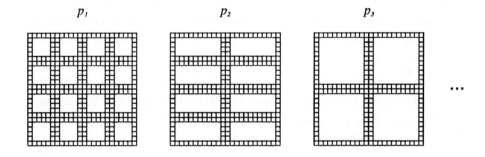

Fig. 4. A hierarchical partition of the image, when a machine with 16 nodes is used. During step II only boundary pixels and associated values are considered.

The *LDT on partition* p_l for $1 \leq l \leq L$ is defined as the result of the DT on each of the subregions of p_l separately. The GDT is, as before, defined as the result of the DT on the whole image.

For $l = 2, 3, \ldots, L$ the LDT on p_l for the border pixels on the subregions of p_l are computed from the LDT on p_{l-1} for the border pixels on the subregions of p_{l-1}. At the end of this bottom up process the LDT on p_L is known for the image border pixels. The latter are the GDT values. From these GDT-values and the previously computed LDT on p_{L-1} the GDT-values on the border pixels of the subregions of p_{L-1} are computed. The following steps of the top down pass are similar.

It is clear that for the CB distance these actions can be done in linear time. In [4] we show that also for the Chamfer 3-4 distance this can be done in linear time.

4.1 Processor task distribution

Each processor is assigned one subregion of which it receives the image data and for which it computes the LDT on the boundary. In order to compute the GDT-values on the boundaries recursively as described above, processors have to cooperate. We discuss two possible task distributions.

Agglomerated computation On a particular recursion level l each subregion of the current partition is processed by one processor. This means that processors become idle on each recursion level. During the bottom up pass each pair of processors that process neighbouring subregions of p_l whose union is a subregion of p_{l+1} exchange the values of the LDT on p_l on the common boundary in order to compute the LDT on p_{l+1}. One of the processors of each pair sends the computed values to the other one and becomes idle, while the other processor continues execution on recursion level $l + 1$. During the top down pass the latter processor activates the former one by sending the GDT-values for the pixels for which it received the values of the LDT on p_{l+1} during the bottom up pass.

This scheme is optimised to eliminate communication during the top down pass. In this case all processors remain active and a processor executes the same code as the processor to which it sends results in the scheme described above.

This approach is similar to the one we used for component labelling [5].

Distributed computation The hierarchical algorithm can be implemented without agglomerating pixel values of a subregion boundary of a higher level partition into one processor. In this approach all processors remain active while executing different jobs, but the formulas need to be computed in several steps. This implementation is described in [4].

5 The directional algorithm

This algorithm is an alternative to the hierarchical algorithm to compute the GDT values on the borders of the subregions out of the LDT values. In this case distances are propagated between border pixels of different subregions in a number of directions. With propagation we mean that, if two pixels differ by more than their relative distance, then the bigger of the two values is replaced by the smaller one augmented by their relative distance. For the CB distance the directional algorithm consists of a vertical and a horizontal 'inter-subregion' propagation. For the Chamfer 3-4 distance also diagonal 'inter-subregion' propagations are necessary.

These inter-subregion propagations of distances do not yield immediately the correct GDT values for all pixels on the borders of the subregions. However, this step provides sufficient information for the third step of the algorithm, i.e. the internal DT (IDT), to compute the correct GDT values for all pixels.

6 Asymptotical complexity

In this section we assume an image of $n \times n$ pixels and p processors.

6.1 Local computations

The computation of the LDT-values of the boundary pixels of a subregion, as well as the IDT can be performed in an amount of time asymptotically proportional to the number of pixels of the image.

6.2 Global computations

The computation of GDT-values out of LDT-values for the border pixels of the subregions consists of computation and communication. The latter can be divided into the initiation and the actual transfer of messages. A summary of the complexity figures derived in this section is shown in table 1.

The hierarchical algorithm

	hierarchical alg.		direct. alg.
	agglom.	distrib.	
City Block			
t_{start_up}	$O(\log p)$	$O(\log^2 p)$	$O(\log p)$
$t_{transfer}$	$O(n)$	$O(\frac{n}{\sqrt{p}})$	$O(\frac{n}{\sqrt{p}})$
t_{comp}	$O(n)$	$O(\frac{n}{\sqrt{p}})$	$O(\frac{n}{\sqrt{p}})$
Chamfer 3-4			
t_{start_up}	$O(\log p)$	$O(\log^2 p)$	$O(\log p)$
$t_{transfer}$	$O(n)$	$O(\frac{n}{\sqrt{p}})$	$O(\frac{n}{\sqrt{p}} \log p)$
t_{comp}	$O(n)$	$O(\frac{n}{\sqrt{p}})$	$O(\frac{n}{\sqrt{p}} \log p)$

Table 1. A summary of the Complexity analysis of the global computations of the presented DT algorithms.

Agglomerated computation Since the number of messages sent on each recursion level is constant and since initiating a message takes constant time, the total start up time is proportional to the number of recursion levels $L = \log_2 p$.

The transfer time is proportional to the amount of data sent. The amount of data sent on recursion level l is proportional to the size of a subregion of p_l being

$$S_l = O(\frac{n}{2^{(L-l)/2}}). \tag{3}$$

Therefore

$$t_{transfer} = O(\sum_{l=1}^{L} \frac{n}{2^{(L-l)/2}}) = O(n). \tag{4}$$

The computational complexity is also $O(n)$ as the data are processed in linear time.

Distributed computation On recursion level l the LDT on p_{l+1} is calculated on the borders of each of its subregions by a group of 2^l processors. The operations to be done on recursion level l can be done in $O(l)$ steps. In each of these steps an amount of data proportional to the boundary length of the subregions of p_l divided by the number of processors 2^l is transferred and processed :

$$O(\frac{n}{\sqrt{p}} \frac{2^{l/2}}{2^l}). \tag{5}$$

The total start up time is therefore

$$t_{start\_up} = O(\sum_{l=1}^{L} l) = O(L^2) = O(\log^2 p) \tag{6}$$

and the total amount of execution and transfer time

$$t_{transfer} = t_{comp} = O(\sum_{l=1}^{L} \frac{n}{\sqrt{p}} \frac{2^{l/2}}{2^l} l) = O(\frac{n}{\sqrt{p}}). \tag{7}$$

The directional algorithm The directional algorithm consists of calculating a number of partial minima that determine the complexity indicated in table 1.

7 Timing and efficiency results

We used as test images two artificial images, one entirely filled with foreground pixels (FULL) and one with one foreground pixel centered in the middle of the image (CENTER) as in figure 2. In [4] we give timings for other images.

7.1 The sequential DT algorithm

Table 2 yields the execution time of the sequential DT algorithm, and consequently the IDT, on one node of the Intel iPSC/2 for the CB distance.

	City Block		Chamfer 3-4	
	the IDT	the LDT	the IDT	the LDT
FULL	428	12	345	22
EMPTY	794	228	1933	359

Table 2. The execution time in milliseconds of the IDT and LDT algorithms on one node of the iPSC/2 for images with 256×256 pixels.

The execution time of the sequential DT algorithm is proportional to the number of pixels of the image. However, the execution time is data dependent and is mainly determined by the ratio r of the number of background pixels to the total number of pixels. Therefore, the execution time of the sequential DT is

$$t^{IDT} = \alpha n^2 (1 + \beta r) \tag{8}$$

with α and β data independent constants. The constants can be derived from table 2. For the CB distance $\beta \approx 1$, for the Chamfer 3-4 $\beta \approx 4$.

7.2   The LDT algorithm

Table 2 yields the execution time of the LDT algorithm on one node of the Intel iPSC/2.

The execution time t^{LDT} as a function of the image size n has two components

$$t^{LDT} = \alpha' n^2 + \beta' n. \tag{9}$$

The first component represents the time spent on traversing background pixels of the image and grows proportional to the number of pixels of the image. The second component represents the time spent on building and using data structures and grows proportional to the image size.

Both α' and β' are data dependent. The α' is large for an image with a considerable amount of background pixels near the image border. The data dependence of β' is less important.

7.3   The computation of the GDT out of the LDT on the border pixels

The execution time of this part of the algorithm is data independent and can be expressed as a function of p and n for each approach [4].

7.4   Efficiency of the parallel algorithm

The parallel efficiency, as a function of the size of the image, is shown in figure 5 for a sample image. From the asymptotical complexity figures of section 6 we learn that for large image sizes the execution time of the global computations is negligible with respect to the the execution time of the IDT and the LDT parts of the algorithm. The ratio of the latter two mainly determines the efficiency. For smaller images the LDT part gets more important with respect to the IDT part because of the linear term in (9). The image size for which the two parts take an equal amount of time is typically 32 pixels for both distance measures. For smaller images also the global computations get more important.

A factor that influences the efficiency too, is the load balance of the algorithm, which is discussed in the next section.

processor configuration : ·············2 × 1 ········ 4 × 2 ‒ ‒ ‒ ‒ 8 × 4
·········2 × 2 ‒ ‒ ‒ ‒ ‒ 4 × 4 ‒ ‒ ‒ 8 × 8

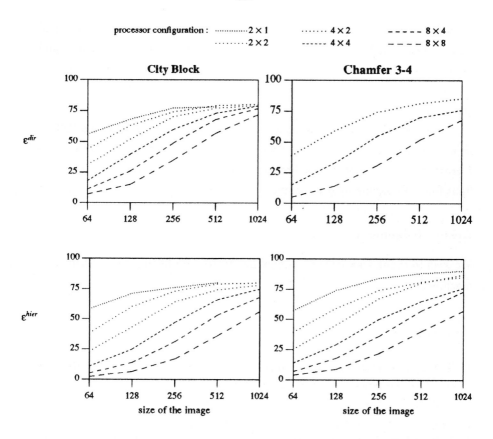

Fig. 5. The parallel efficiency, as a function of the image size, for the image CENTER, when the hierarchical algorithm with agglomerated calculation or the directional algorithm is used.

7.5 Load balance

Load imbalance occurs, when a part of the algorithm takes more time on one processor than on the others and the processors have to wait for one another. A measure for the load imbalance of a part of the algorithm is

$$I = \frac{t^{max} - t^{av}}{t^{av}} \tag{10}$$

with t^{max} and t^{av} the maximal and average execution times of the part of the algorithm under investigation. We can distinguish two sources of load imbalance.

A first source of load imbalance is caused by the data dependence of the LDT part of the algorithm as discussed in section 7.2. This is practically unavoidable, because for most images at least one subregion contains a considerable amount of background pixels and determines the execution time of the LDT part of the algorithm.

A second source of load imbalance is the data dependence of the IDT algorithm. From a statistical point of view we can expect that the load imbalance I grows with the number of subregions. However, in [4] we derive a hard upper limit for the possible load imbalance [5].

Acknowledgements

We wish to thank Oak Ridge National Laboratory for letting us use their iPSC/2 machine.

References

1. G. Borgefors. Distance transformations in arbitrary dimensions. *Computer Vision, Graphics and Image Processing*, 27(3):321–345, 1984.
2. G. Borgefors. Distance transformations in digital images. *Computer Vision, Graphics and Image Processing*, 34(3):344–371, 1986.
3. G. Borgefors, T. Hartmann, and S. L. Tanimoto. Parallel distance transforms on pyramid machines : Therory and implementation. *Signal processing*, 21:61–86, 1990.
4. H. Embrechts and D. Roose. Parallel algorithms for the distance transformation. Technical Report TW151, Katholieke Universiteit Leuven, 1991.
5. H. Embrechts, D. Roose, and P. Wambacq. Component labelling on an MIMD multiprocessor. *Computer Vision, Graphics and Image Processing : Image Understanding*. to appear.
6. S. Miguet. Distance transform on a ring of processors. In M. Cosnard and C. Giraud, editors, *Working Conference on Decentralized Systems*, pages 285–296. North-Holland, 1990.

This article was processed using the LaTeX macro package with LLNCS style

A Multiprocessor System for Displaying Quadric CSG Models

Reinier van Kleij[1] and Frido Kuijper[2]

1. Delft University of Technology, The Netherlands. Email: rein@duticg.tudelft.nl
2. TNO Physics and Electronics Laboratory, The Netherlands. Email: frig5@fel.tno.nl

Abstract. Constructive Solid Geometry (CSG) is a method for defining solid objects as a combination of simple primitives. We present a multiprocessor system for interactive display of CSG models. Several techniques are compared to find an optimum system. Using exact models instead of polygon-approximated models improved the scalability.

1 Introduction

Constructive Solid Geometry (CSG) is a powerful technique for modelling complex mechanical parts. With CSG, simple parametrised objects, called primitives, are positioned in space and dimensioned using geometric transformations. By applying volumetric set operations (union, intersection, difference) the primitives are combined into composite objects to which the set operations can also be applied. The set operations are stored in the nodes of the so-called CSG tree; the primitives are stored in the leafs. The root node represents the composite object.

The CSG scanline algorithm [1] gives reasonable display times on general-purpose workstations, but is too slow for interactive display. We have developed an extendible multiprocessor display system based on the T800 transputer. The system achieves interactive display times for CSG models. We have experimented with methods to distribute the work among the processors. Using an exact representation of the quadrics instead of a polygon-approximated one benefits the scalability.

This paper is structured as follows. Section 2 gives a description of the CSG scanline algorithm for quadrics, which served as our starting point. Section 3 describes the techniques we have investigated. Section 4 discusses the implementation and the results. Section 5 gives some conclusions.

2 A CSG Scanline Algorithm for Quadrics

Atherton [1] has developed an elegant algorithm for displaying polyhedral CSG models, which is based on the standard scanline visible-surface algorithm for polyhedral objects. The scanline algorithm consists of two parts: the preprocessing part and the scan conversion part. In the preprocessing part, the primitives in the CSG model are transformed to image space and the edges are sorted into edge-buckets. An edge-bucket is a linked list of edges that occur for the first time at the scanline the bucket belongs to. The preprocessing needs to be done for all primitives before the scan conversion part can start.

The scan conversion part draws the image in scanline order. Two important data structures are used during scan conversion. The Active Edge List (AEL): the list of all edges intersecting the current scanline, sorted from left to right. Two adjacent edges determine a span. The Active Face List (AFL): the list of all faces that might be visible on the current span. The AEL is updated when the next scanline is to be drawn. A scanline is drawn from left to right, span after span.

The visible face on a span is determined by sorting the faces in the AFL and classifying each face using the CSG tree. The first face, which is classified as on the composite object is the visible face. When there are intersections, the span is subdivided on the intersection and the above procedure is repeated for the two subspans. Bronsvoort [3] gives a number of efficiency improvements. The CSG scanline algorithm is efficient by exploiting coherence between scanlines, between spans and on the spans. In order to display CSG models with quadrics, both the preprocessing part and the scan conversion part of the algorithm need to be adjusted [5]. The use of quadrics results in a small geometric database and reduces the amount of data, that has to be communicated in a multiprocessor environment.

3 Multiprocessing Techniques for Scanline Algorithms

Our goal was to develop a multiprocessor system that displays CSG models within a few seconds. To parallelize the CSG scanline algorithm we used the data decomposition approach. This approach works well, because the data can be divided in chunks with equal workloads. We use a static data scheduling approach, which implies that after a primitive is preprocessed, the results need to be broadcast to all other processors.

3.1 Parallel Preprocessing

For preprocessing we use the processor farm model with a demand-driven task scheduling strategy [6]. Each processor requests the primitives for preprocessing from the host. Since the preprocessing accounts for a small part of the display times, we did not put much effort in optimizing it.

3.2 Parallel Scan Conversion

Parallel scan conversion is achieved by computing different parts of the image in parallel. As the scanline algorithm exploits coherence in the scan conversion part, we tried to preserve it. The screen is subdivided into strips (see Figure 1a). We first look at strips of one scanline. To equally distribute the work among the processors, we have experimented with normal and data pipeline interleaving.

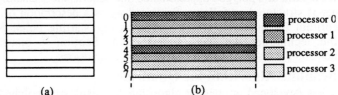

(a)　　　　　　(b)

Fig.1. Strip subdivision of the screen (a) and normal interleaving (b)

Normal interleaving
Each processor processes the same number of scanlines e.g. processor 0 processes scanlines 0, N, 2N, ..., processor 1 processes scanlines 1, N+1, 2N+1, etc., with N is the number of processors (see Figure 1b). This scheme has a drawback: a large number of processors gives a large distance between the scanlines of one processor and the coherence between scanlines is lost.

Data pipeline interleaving
Blonk et al [2] proposed an interleaving method, in which no coherence between scanlines is lost, by using the data pipeline concept. The computations for a scanline are divided into two tasks: the update task, in which the AEL is updated and the draw task, in which the scanline is drawn. Each update task is executed with coherence by using the AEL of the previous scanline, which is received from the previous processor in the pipeline. On finishing the update task, the resulting AEL is sent to the next processor in the pipeline, and a draw task is created and stored in the draw task queue. The draw tasks are read from the draw task queue and executed semi-parallel with the update tasks (see Figure 2a). Since the update tasks are executed

sequentially, efficiency is reduced by a start-up delay and a pipeline delay [2]. Moreover, since the update tasks accounts for 5% of the workload, the speed-up factor is limited by 20 (Amdahl's Law [7]).

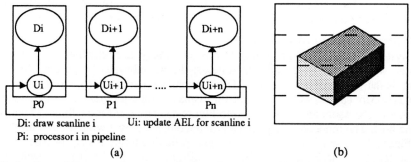

Di: draw scanline i   Ui: update AEL for scanline i
Pi: processor i in pipeline

(a)   (b)

Fig.2 . Control flow mapping onto a pipeline of processors (a) and static, equal strips (b).

To solve the limited scalability of both interleaving techniques, we cluster the processors into groups, which compute strips consisting of more than one scanline. The scanlines in the strip can be distributed among the processors in the group by using normal or data pipeline interleaving. We have experimented with three strip scheduling strategies to distribute the strips among the groups: static, equal strips, dynamic strips with global seeking and dynamic strips with mate seeking.

Static, equal strips
With static, equal strips the screen is divided into N equal strips, with N the number of groups. A disadvantage is the uneven load balance, because images tend to be more complex near the centre of the screen (see Figure 2b).

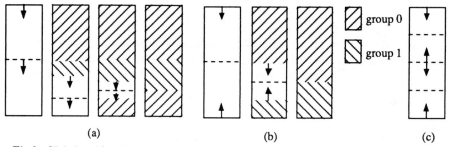

(a)   (b)   (c)

Fig.3. Global seeking (a) and mate seeking (b) with two groups and screen subdivision for mate seeking for 4 groups (c).

Dynamic strips with global seeking
This strategy is based on task stealing [4]. When a group of processors has finished its strip, it sends a request to the other groups to steal work from them; if there is a group that has enough work left, it gives it to the requesting group. In this way the work is distributed evenly among the groups of processors (see Figure 3a). Some overhead is introduced: when a group gets work from another group, the AEL of the first scanline, which might be distant from the last drawn scanline, needs to be computed.

Dynamic strips with mate seeking
To minimize the number of screen subdivisions, we developed the mate seeking technique, in which two neighbouring groups, called mates, start drawing their strip working in opposite direction towards each other. Only when they reach the same

scanline, the groups need to steal work from the other groups (see Figure 3b). So groups of processors can work on adjacent scanlines as long as possible. This is achieved at the cost of some additional communication to check whether two groups have reached the same scanline. Figure 3c gives an example of the initial screen subdivision and the drawing directions in the strips, when there are four groups.

4 Implementation and Results

The system was implemented under Helios on a Parsytec MultiCluster-2 transputer system, which consists of three subsystems: the IO subsystem with a 4 Mb T800, which is the host processor, and a GDS-2 graphics board, the processing subsystem with 32 2 Mb T800's, which are used for display, and a programable link switch to which all processors are connected (see Figure 4). The solid modelling system runs on the host. The renderers are physically interconnected by a wrap-around mesh [7]. In Figure 4 a row of squares depicts a group that compute a strip in parallel. We define the MxN architecture to be the configuration with M groups, each group consisting of N processors, arranged in a MxN wrap-around mesh. Measurements of the display times of the test models (see Figure 10) were done to see, which concepts are most efficient. Also we wanted to find out whether the use of an exact representation of the quadrics did benefit in a multiprocessor environment. All times are given in seconds.

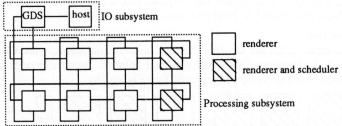

Fig.4. The implemented system and the physical connections for a 2x4 architecture.

Testing the interleaving techniques was done with the Hobin and Bing models. From Figure 5 we see that normal interleaving performs best and we can conclude, that the pipeline delay and the start-up delay are worse than the increased scanline-coherence exploitation.

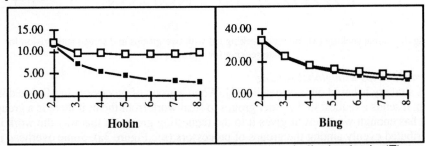

Fig. 5. Scan conversion times with normal (■)and data pipeline interleaving(□).

From Figure 6 we see that global seeking is slightly better than mate seeking, because mate seeking results in more communication than global seeking. So the optimum system uses global seeking and normal interleaving. From Figure 7 we see that the system with 32 processors performs best with an 8x4 architecture. Comparing the results for the 32x1, 1x32 and the 8x4 architecture, we see that clustering processors in groups benefits the system.

	2x2x2	3x3x3	4x4x4	Hobin	Mig	Bing
Static strips	2.26	4.34	7.50	2.07	3.53	7.69
Global seeking	2.06	3.70	6.23	1.72	2.55	4.61
Mate seeking	2.20	3.79	6.61	1.76	2.57	4.52

Fig.6. Display times for the three strip scheduling techniques using a 8x4 architecture

	2x2x2	3x3x3	4x4x4	Hobin	Mig	Bing
32x1	2.40	3.90	6.92	2.04	2.94	5.31
16x2	2.28	3.93	7.10	1.89	2.81	5.04
8x4	2.06	3.70	6.23	1.72	2.55	4.61
4x8	2.20	3.63	6.50	1.77	2.45	4.61
2x16	2.50	3.92	6.66	2.13	2.72	4.40
1x32	2.62	4.01	6.75	2.36	3.03	4.54

Fig. 7. Display times for different dimensions of the optimum system.

To test the scalability of the system, measurements for all models were done with different numbers of processors, ranging from 1 to 32. We define the efficiency as $E_N = T_1/(T_N*N) * 100\%$ where T_1 is the display time on 1 processor and T_N is the display time on N processors. In Figure 8 we see that the efficiency decreases rapidly; this is because of the low performance of the Helios communication for the preprocessing results, the pixel colours and the strip scheduling requests.

	2x2x2	3x3x3	4x4x4	Hobin	Mig	Bing
1	100%	100%	100%	100%	100%	100%
4	88%	89%	91%	78%	83%	92%
8	83%	85%	86%	74%	76%	88%
16	71%	73%	75%	61%	56%	76%
32	50%	57%	58%	40%	36%	55%

Fig.8. Efficiency of the optimum system with increasing number of processors

To get insight in the benefits of using quadrics exactly instead of polygonal models, we have done measurements with a polygonal Bing model. From Figure 9 we see that the efficiency decreases less with quadrics than with polygons with an increasing number of processors.

	1		4		8		16		32	
polygon	68.82	100%	19.91	86%	10.78	80%	7.83	55%	6.01	36%
quadric	79.08	100%	21.50	92%	11.28	88%	6.51	76%	4.48	55%

Fig. 9. Display times and efficiency for the quadric and polygonal Bing model for an increasing number of processors

5 Conclusions

We have developed a multiprocessor display system for quadric CSG models with interactive display times. Due to the expensive communication primitives under Helios, the attempt to exploit coherence as fully as possible was not successful. An analytical model of the implementation might help to predict, whether data pipeline interleaving and mate seeking pay off in other environments. Clustering processors in groups working on strips of more than one scanline turned out to be a good idea. The use of exact representations for quadrics resulted in a better scalable system. Future scanline interleaved graphics architectures based on general-purpose processors should have efficient and scalable communication facilities, supporting both point-to-point communication and broadcasting.

588

Acknowledgements
We would like to thank Wim Bronsvoort, Erik Jansen, Ad Langenkamp and Frits Post
for the stimulating discussions and FEL TNO for using its hardware facilities.

References
1. Atherton PR (1983) A scan-line hidden surface removal procedure for
   constructive solid geometry. *Computer Graphics* **17**(3): 73-82
2. Blonk M, Bronsvoort WF, Bruggeman F, de Vos L (1988) A parallel system for
   CSG hidden-surface elimination. In: *Parallel Processing, Proceedings IFIP WG
   10.3 Working Conference on Parallel Processing*, Cosnard M, Barton MH and
   Vanneschi M (eds), Elsevier Science Publishers, Amterdam, pp 139-151
3. Bronsvoort WF (1990) Direct display algorithms for solid modelling. Ph.D.
   Thesis. *Delft University Press.*
4 Holliman NS (1990), Visualising solid models: An exercise in parallel
   programming. School of Computer Studies and Mechanical Engineering,
   University of Leeds, United Kingdom
5 van Kleij R (1992) Efficient Display of Quadric CSG Models. *Computers in
   Industry* **19**(2):201-211
6. May D, Shepard R (1987) Communicating process computers. *Inmos Technical
   Note 22*, Inmos Ltd, Bristol.
7. Quinn MJ (1987) Designing efficient algorithms for parallel computers. New
   York, McGraw-Hill

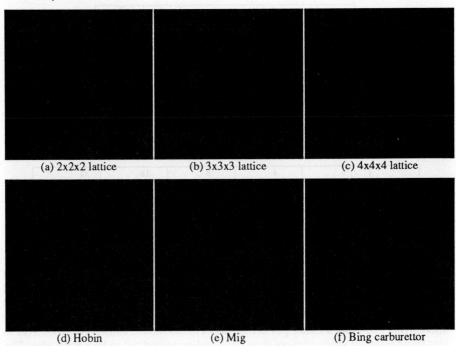

(a) 2x2x2 lattice	(b) 3x3x3 lattice	(c) 4x4x4 lattice
(d) Hobin	(e) Mig	(f) Bing carburettor

Fig. 10. Test models used for measurements (display resolution: 512x512 pixels).

Efficient Image Computations on Reconfigurable Meshes[†]
(Preliminary Version)

Stephan Olariu[‡], James L. Schwing, and
Jingyuan Zhang

Department of Computer Science
Old Dominion University
Norfolk, VA 23529-0162
U.S.A.

ABSTRACT

The reconfigurable mesh combines two attractive features of massively parallel architectures, namely, constant diameter and a dynamically reconfigurable bus system. Being mesh-based, the reconfigurable mesh is eminently suitable for applications in image processing and computer vision. Common wisdom has it that buses are entities created in support of communicational needs of the task at hand. The authors have recently proposed a new way of looking at a reconfigurable bus system. They have shown that buses can be used as computational devices as well as topological descriptors. The purpose of this work is to present additional results of this on-going project. Specifically, we show novel algorithms for image segmentation and labeling, along with a number of algorithms for describing the shape of objects in the image. We discuss using the buses to compute the area, perimeter, and convex hull of every object in the image.

Index Terms: reconfigurable meshes, bus systems, image processing, computer vision, robotics, segmentation, component labeling, area, perimeter, convex hull

1. Introduction

Typical computer and robot vision tasks found today in industrial, medical, and military applications involve digitized images featuring millions of pixels. The enormous amount of data contained in theses images, combined with real-time processing requirements have suggested massively parallel architectures as the only way to achieve the level of performance required for vision tasks.

Among these, the mesh-connected architecture has emerged as one of the most natural choices for solving a large number of computational tasks in image processing, computational geometry, and computer vision. This is due, in part, to its simple interconnection topology and to the fact that many problems feature data that maps easily onto the mesh structure. In addition, meshes are particularly well suited for VLSI implementation. However, due to their large communication diameter, meshes tend to be slow when it comes to handling data transfer operations over long distances. In an attempt to alleviate this problem, mesh-connected machines have been enhanced by the addition of various reconfigurable features. Examples include the *bus automaton* [24], the *reconfigurable mesh* [14], and the *polymorphic torus* [12]. Among these, the reconfigurable mesh has emerged as a very attractive and versatile architecture.

Computer vision tasks are traditionally partitioned into three distinct categories, depending on the

† This work was supported by NASA under grant NCC1-99
‡ Additional support by the National Science Foundation under grant CCR-8909996 is gratefully acknowledged

types of objects they operate on. It is fairly standard to refer to the computational tasks involving two-dimensional arrays of pixels as *low-level* tasks. At the other end of the spectrum, *high-level* vision deals with more refined structures and are closely related to scene analysis. Intermediate level tasks are usually referred to as *mid-level*. Just as low-level vision tasks, they operate on two-dimensional arrays of pixels. Their primary role, however, is to create symbolic representations of the image under investigation.

In the last four years, a number of algorithms for low and mid-level image processing tasks on reconfigurable meshes have been proposed in the literature [7-10,15,21,22]. We shall refer to these algorithms as *traditional* because they all use buses in essentially the same way: to help ferry data around.

Recently, the authors have proposed a new way of looking at a reconfigurable bus system. Specifically, they have observed that up to now, buses and subbuses have been used exclusively to ferry data around. However, it is often the case that several distinct buses are created within a reconfigurable mesh; moreover, examples in image processing show that one cannot rely on processors outside of these buses to carry out meaningful computation. It is then necessary to have the processors on the various buses carry out the computation at hand (e.g. identifying and labeling a connected component). With this in mind the authors have proposed to buses as computational devices or as topological descriptors. They have shown how buses can be used to devise fast algorithms for the Hough transform [19] and for the connected component labeling problem [17]. Both algorithms are either simpler or faster than the best algorithms to date.

The purpose of this paper is to show other non-traditional uses for buses in support of fast image processing and computer vision algorithms. Specifically, with an $N \times N$ binary image stored one pixel per processor in a reconfigurable mesh of the same size, we show that the split and merge segmentation technique can be performed in $O(\log N)$ time. This is then shown to lead to a novel component labeling algorithm running in $O(\log N)$ time.

The remainder of this paper is organized as follows: Section 2 briefly discusses the computational model and introduces terminology about buses, along with a technical result of an independent interest; Section 3 outlines the proposed segmentation algorithm and its applications to component labeling, perimeter, and area computations for all the objects in the given image; Section 4 outlines an algorithm that allows computing the convex hulls of all the objects in the image.

2. Background

The computational model used throughout this work is the *reconfigurable mesh*. An $N \times N$ reconfigurable mesh consists of N^2 identical processors positioned on a square array. The processor located in row i and column j ($1 \leq i, j \leq N$) is referred to as $P(i,j)$. Every processor has 4 ports denoted by N, S, E, and W. In each processor, ports can be dynamically connected to suit computational needs. Our computational model allows at most two connections to be set in each processor. These however must involve a disjoint set of ports.

We assume a SIMD model; all the processing elements have a constant number of registers of $O(\log N)$ bits and a very basic instruction set; a processor can perform in unit time standard arithmetic and boolean operations. By adjusting the local connections within each processor several subuses can be established. At any given time, only one processor can broadcast a value onto a bus.

Throughout this work we shall take the view that buses are dynamic entities that are created, under program control, to fulfill computational needs. Every bus has a *positive* direction and a *negative* direction: corresponding to each direction there exists a first and a last processor on the bus. We assume that every processor that belongs to a bus can determine the positive (resp. negative) direction on the corresponding bus by checking local conditions only.

A bus is best thought of as a doubly-linked list of processors, with every processor on the bus being aware of its immediate neighbors, if any, in the positive and negative direction. When restricted to a given bus, the processors will be assumed to have two ports: one is the positive port, the other being the negative one. The positive (resp. negative) *rank* of a processor on a bus is taken to be one larger than the number of processors preceding the given processor when the bus is traversed in the positive (resp. negative) direction. A bus is said to be *ranked* when every processor on the bus knows its positive and negative rank. Buses that are not ranked are called unranked. The *length* of a bus coincides with the highest rank of a processor on that bus.

Consider an arbitrary unranked bus B of length N. Every processor on the bus is assumed to store an item form a totally ordered universe. We are interested to solve the following problem. In [16,20] the authors have shown that in spite of the fact that the bus is not ranked, the prefix maxima of the items stored by processors on B can be determined efficiently. Specifically they have the following result.

Proposition 2.1. ([16]) The prefix maxima of the items stored by the processors on an unranked bus of length N can be computed in $\Theta(\log N)$ time using the processors on the bus only. $\square$

Quite often, the dynamic setting of connections within a reconfigurable mesh will result in establishing a number of buses, some of them being closed. Such is the case, for example, in image processing applications wherein buses are "wrapped" around connected components in the given image [16,17]. Subsequent computation calls for selecting a name for the component. This is typically done by labeling the component by the identity of its pixel with the least column number. Put differently, it is necessary to elect a *leader* on a closed bus. In [16] it has have shown that this can be done efficiently, by reducing the problem to computing the maximum. Specifically, we have the following result.

Proposition 2.2. Consider an unranked closed bus of N processors, with every processor holding an item from a totally ordered universe. The processor that holds the maximum of these items can be identified in $\Theta(\log N)$ time using the processors on the bus only. $\square$

Similarly, let B a ranked bus of length N, with each processor on the bus holding an item. We want to compute the prefix sums of all these items. By adapting an algorithm of Miller *et al.* we have

Proposition 2.3. ([16]) The prefix sums of the items stored by the processors on a ranked bus of length N can be computed in $O(\log N)$ time by the processors on the bus. $\square$

The problem of ranking a bus dynamically constructed within a given image seems to be a challenging problem. We now describe an $O(\log N \log^* N)$ algorithm to perform this task. Our algorithm is a straightforward adaptation of an elegant result of Cole and Vishkin [3]. They define the $r-ruling$ set problem as follows. Let $G=(V,E)$ be a directed graph such that the in-degree and the out-degree of every vertex is exactly one. For obvious reasons Cole and Vishkin call such a graph a *ring*. A subset U of V is an r-ruling set if (1) no two vertices in U are adjacent and (2) for each vertex v in V there is a directed path from v to some vertex in U whose edge length is at most r. They also prove the following result.

Proposition 2.4. ([3]) A two-ruling set of a ring with N vertices can be obtained in $O(\log^* N)$ time using N processors in the EREW-PRAM. $\square$

As noted by Cole and Vishkin [3] the same algorithm applies to models of computations where only local communications between successive nodes in the ring are allowed. This is precisely the case of an unranked bus. To rank an arbitrary bus B of length N we repeatedly find a 2-ruling set in B and eliminate the nodes in the current ruling set after having added the value they contain to the next remaining element. Clearly, this process terminates in $O(\log N)$ iterations. Consequently we have

Lemma 2.5. An arbitrary unranked bus of length N can be ranked in $O(\log N \log^* N)$ using the processors on the bus only. $\square$

At present it is not known whether this algorithm is best possible. In the remainder of this work we often start out with unranked buses and assumed that they can be ranked in $O(T(N))$ time.

Throughout this paper we assume a binary image I of size $N \times N$ pretiled in a reconfigurable mesh of the same size.[1] We let pixel(i,j) denote the pixel in row i and column j of I, with pixel$(1,1)$ situated in the north-west corner of the image. For the purpose of this paper, the neighbors of pixel(i,j) are pixel$(i,j-1)$, pixel$(i,j+1)$, pixel$(i-1,j)$, and pixel$(i+1,j)$. In this context, two pixels pixel(i,j) and pixel(i',j') are said to be *connected* if there exists a sequence of pixels originating at pixel(i,j) and ending at pixel(i',j'), such that consecutive pixels in the sequence are neighbors. A maximal region of pairwise connected 1-pixels is referred to as a component. Component labeling algorithms known to date are either derived from the ideas in [11] or else are divide-and-conquer based. Our approach is different.

To avoid the need of handling tedious special cases, we further assume that the image does not

---

1 For convenience N is assumed to be a power of 2.

contain any one pixel wide regions or protrusions. As pointed out by Dinstein and Landau [4] this assumption can be accommodated by simple morphological operations. A 1-pixel pixel(i,j) is termed a *boundary* pixel if the 3×3 window centered at pixel(i,j) contains both 0 and 1-pixels. A processor storing a boundary pixel will be termed a *boundary processor*.

3. Image segmentation

Image segmentation is one of the most important computational steps in automated image analysis because it is at this moment that objects of interest are identified and extracted from the image for further processing. The purpose of image segmentation is to partition the image at hand into disjoint regions (or objects) that are meaningful with respect to some application. The partition generated by image segmentation typically features the following properties: (1) every region is homogeneous with respect to some classifier, and (2) adjacent regions are significantly different with respect to the chosen classifier.

Image segmentation has been well studied and numerous image segmentation techniques have been proposed in the literature [1,2,5,6,23,25,26]. An important image segmentation technique is called *region growing*. The basic scheme involves combining pixels with adjacent pixels to form regions. Further, regions are combined with adjacent regions to form larger regions. One of the segmentation techniques often associated with region growing is referred to as *split and merge* [1]. The idea is as follows: once a relevant homogeneity criterion χ has been chosen, the image at hand is tested. If χ is satisfied, then there is nothing else to do. Otherwise, the image is partitioned into four quadrants and χ is tested for each of them in parallel. Quadrants that satisfy the criterion are left alone; those that do not are further subdivided recursively. In the merge stage, adjacent homogeneous regions are combined to form larger and larger regions.

We are restricting our discussion to the segmentation of binary images, the general case of gray-level images will be addressed in a subsequent paper. The split stage is done in the obvious way: any region of all 1's or all 0's is homogeneous and is no longer subdivided. Notice that checking a region for homogeneity is done in O(1) time. Therefore the split stage takes O(log N) time altogether. In addition, every homogeneous region has a boundary bus wrapped around it. Due to the particular shape of these buses, every boundary bus knows its leader defined as the processor on the bus holding the pixel with least row and column number.

The merge stage proceeds to combine adjacent homogeneous regions by in a canonical way: that is we proceed to merge regions in reverse order of the split. It is easy to see that combining adjacent regions is done by merging the individual boundary buses into a new boundary bus wrapped around the resulting region. Using techniques developed in [21], we ensure that the merge phase is carried out in O(1) time. At the end of each step in the merge phase, every newly created boundary bus knows is leader. Therefore we have

Theorem 3.1. The segmentation problem for binary images of size $N{\times}N$ can be solved in O(log N) time on a reconfigurable mesh of size $N{\times}N$. □

It is important to note that our segmentation algorithm has a number of interesting consequences. First, note that for binary images the segmentation problem is identical to the component labeling problem. We have therefore a novel algorithm for the latter task.

Theorem 3.2. The component labeling problem for binary images of size $N{\times}N$ can be solved in O(log N) time on a reconfigurable mesh of size $N{\times}N$. □

As another application, note that for every object in the image obtained at the end of the segmentation algorithm, the length of the corresponding boundary bus is precisely the perimeter of the object. Therefore, to obtain the perimeter we first need to rank every boundary bus and then the perimeter of all the objects in the image can be computed in O(1) time. Thus we have

Theorem 3.3. The perimeter of all the objects in a binary image of size $N{\times}N$ can be solved in O($T(N)$+log N) time on a reconfigurable mesh of size $N{\times}N$, where $T(N)$ is the time needed to rank a bus of length N. □

Note that using the result in Lemma 2.5, we obtain the following corollary of Theorem 3.3.

Corollary 3.4. The perimeter of all the objects in a binary image of size $N{\times}N$ can be solved in O(log N log$^*N$) time on a reconfigurable mesh of size $N{\times}N$. □

Yet another application of the segmentation algorithm is the computation of the area of every object in the image at hand. Again, we rely on the boundary buses. Specifically, we let every processor in the object connects its EW ports. In every row of the mesh, the rightmost processor belonging to some object broadcasts its column number westbound on the horizontal bus in its row. The leftmost processor in that row belonging to the same object as the sender can compute the number of pixels in the object lying in that row. If boundary buses are ranked, then it is a simple problem of computing the sum of all the items held by the boundary processors. By Proposition 2.3 this sum can be computed in $O(\log N)$ time. We thus have

Theorem 3.5. The area of all the objects in a binary image of size $N \times N$ can be solved in $O(T(N) + \log N)$ time on a reconfigurable mesh of size $N \times N$, where $T(N)$ is the time needed to rank a bus of length N. $\square$

As before, note that using the result in Lemma 2.5, we obtain the following corollary of Theorem 3.5.

Corollary 3.6. The area of all the objects in a binary image of size $N \times N$ can be solved in $O(\log N \log^* N)$ time on a reconfigurable mesh of size $N \times N$. $\square$

We note that the results stated in Theorems 3.4 and 3.5 are a factor of $O(\log^* N)$ away from the results obtained by Jenq and Sahni [7] using divide and conquer. However if the boundary buses are ranked, then our results match the corresponding results in [7]. At present it is not known whether boundary buses obtained at the end of our segmentation algorithm can be ranked in $O(\log N)$ time or not.

4. Computing the convex hulls of objects

An important descriptor of an object is the convex hull of its boundary [1,6,23]. The problem that we address in this section is to compute the convex hulls of all the objects in the image at hand. Our idea is novel. We assume that every object in the image space is uniquely identified by its boundary bus. This is not an unreasonable assumption, for these buses are either available as a result of a segmentation operation or else can be created in $O(1)$ time using the method described in [16]. Let B be the boundary bus associated with an object in the image space. Note that establishing a positive and negative direction on this bus is direct and can be computed locally by looking at a 3×3 window. To be more specific, we can impose the counterclockwise direction (with respect to the interior of the object) as positive.

We identify the processors $P(i,j)$ and $P(i',j')$ with smallest and largest column numbers on B. These two processors partition B into an upper subbus and a lower subbus. We only show how to identify the extreme points of the upper subbus. To begin, compute the prefix maxima of column numbers along the upper bus, from $P(i,j)$ to $P(i',j')$ and eliminate processors for which the prefix maximum is greater than their column number. By Proposition 2.1 this can be done in $O(\log N)$ time. The remaining processors form a monotone subbus.

In $O(1)$ time we identify processors on this monotone subbus that contain local minima with respect to row numbers. Processors on the subbus between consecutive local minima become inactive. In at most $O(\log N)$ iterations there is only one minimum left. Clearly, the remaining processors hold pixels belonging to the convex hull. Note that the only processors used in this process are those belonging to B. Note further that the convex hull of every object in the image at hand is computed in parallel. Since, obviously the buses involved are disjoint, no conflict will ever occur. The following result summarizes our findings.

Theorem 4.1. Computing the convex hulls of all the object in a binary image of size $N \times N$ stored one pixel per processor by a reconfigurable mesh of the same size can be solved in $O(\log N)$ time. $\square$

The result in Theorem 4.1 improves by a factor of $O(\log N)$ the running time of the fastest known algorithms to date [15,19]. However, we don't know whether this result is time optimal. We conjecture that it is and pose it as an open problem.

References

1. D. H. Ballard and C. M. Brown, Computer Vision, Prentice-Hall, 1982.
2. W.-E. Blanz, D. Petkovic, and J. L. C. Sanz, Algorithms and Architectures for Machine Vision, in C. H. Chen, ed., *Signal Processing Handbook*, M. Dekker, New York, 1989.
3. R. Cole and U. Vishkin, Deterministic coin tossing with applications to optimal parallel list ranking, *Information and Control*, 70, (1986), 32-53.
4. I. Dinstein and G. M. Landau, Parallel algorithms for contour extraction and coding, *Proc. SPIE Conference on Parallel Architectures for Image Processing*, 1990, 156-161.
5. M. Fairhurst, Computer Vision and Robotic Systems, Prentice-Hall, Englewood Cliffs, NJ, 1988.
6. R. M. Haralick and L. G. Shapiro, Computer and robot vision, Vol. 1, Second Edition, Addison-Wesley, 1992.
7. J.-F. Jenq and S. Sahni, Reconfigurable mesh algorithms for the area and perimeter of image components, *Proc. International Conference of Parallel Processing*, 1991, III, 280-281.
8. J.-F. Jenq and S. Sahni, Reconfigurable mesh algorithms for image shrinking, expanding, clustering, and template matching, *Proceeding of the 5th International Parallel Processing Symposium*, 1991, 208-215.
9. J.-F. Jenq and S. Sahni, Histogramming on the reconfigurable mesh computer, *Proceeding of the 6th International Parallel Processing Symposium*, Beverly Hills, 1992, 258-261.
10. J.-F. Jenq and S. Sahni, Reconfigurable Mesh Algorithms for the Hough Transform, *Proc. International Conference on Parallel Processing*, 1991, III, 34-41.
11. S. Levialdi, On shrinking binary picture patterns, *Comm. of the ACM*, 15, (1972), 7-10.
12. H. Li and M. Maresca, Polymorphic-torus network, *IEEE Transactions on Computers*, vol. C-38, no. 9, (1989) 1345-1351.
13. H. Li and M. Maresca, Polymorphic-torus architecture for computer vision, *IEEE Trans. Pattern Analysis and Machine Intelligence*, vol. 11, no. 3, (1989) 233-243.
14. R. Miller, V. K. Prasanna Kumar, D. Reisis, and Q. F. Stout, Meshes with reconfigurable buses, *Proceedings of the Fifth MIT Conference on Advanced Research in VLSI*, (1988) 163-178.
15. R. Miller, V. K. Prasanna Kumar, D. Reisis, and Q. F. Stout, Image Computations on Reconfigurable VLSI Arrays, *Proc. 1988 IEEE Conf. on Computer Vision and Pattern Recognition*, 925-930.
16. S. Olariu, J. L. Schwing, and J. Zhang, Efficient image processing algorithms for reconfigurable meshes, *Proc. Vision Interface'92*, Vancouver, British Columbia, 1992, to appear.
17. S. Olariu, J. L. Schwing, and J. Zhang, Fast Component Labeling on Reconfigurable Meshes, *Proc. International Conference on Computing and Information*, Toronto, 1992, 121-124.
18. S. Olariu, J. L. Schwing, and J. Zhang, Fast Computer Vision Algorithms on Reconfigurable Meshes, *Image and Vision Computing Journal*, to appear.
19. S. Olariu, J. L. Schwing, and J. Zhang, Computing the Hough Transform on Reconfigurable Meshes, *Proc. of Vision Interface'92*, Vancouver, British Columbia, to appear.
20. S. Olariu, J. L. Schwing, and J. Zhang, Computing on buses, with applications to image processing and computational geometry, Department of Computer Science, Old Dominion University, Norfolk, Virginia, Tech. Report in preparation.
21. S. Olariu, J. L. Schwing, and J. Zhang, Integer Problems on Reconfigurable Meshes, with Applications, *Proceedings of the 29th Annual Allerton Conference on Communications, Control, and Computing*, 821-830, 1991.
22. D. Reisis, An efficient convex hull computation on the reconfigurable mesh, *Proceeding of the 6th International Parallel Processing Symposium*, Beverly Hills, 1992, 142-145.
23. A. Rosenfeld and A. Kak, Digital Picture Processing, Academic Press, vol. 1-2, 1982.
24. J. Rothstein, Bus automata, brains, and mental models, *IEEE Trans. on Systems Man Cybernetics* 18, (1988).
25. D. Vernon, Machine vision, automated visual inspection and robot vision, Prentice-Hall, 1991.
26. M. Willebeek-Lemair and A. P. Reeves, Region growing on a highly parallel mesh-connected SIMD computer, *Proc. Frontiers of massively Parallel Computing*, 1988, 93-100.

A Multiscale parallel thinning algorithm

Jean-Luc Levaire and Stephane Ubeda[†] [*]

LIP, ENS Lyon,
46 Allée d'Italie,
F-69364 Lyon Cedex 07, France.
Electronic Mail: ubeda@lip.ens-lyon.fr
[†]Current Address: EPFL CH-1015 Lausanne, Switzerland.

Abstract. This paper presents a new parallel thinning algorithm. Thinning algorithms based on contour tracing are strongly sequential and irregular, with a complexity of $O(n^2)$. Thinning algorithms using parallel neighboring operations are regular with a complexity of $O(n^3)$.

The parallel thinning approach we propose uses the notion of multi-scaling. This new algorithm keeps the regularity and parallelism of the neighboring operator while achieving a cost of $O(n^2)$. Complexity analysis and comparison with a well-known thinning algorithm using a SIMD machine are presented.

1 Introduction

Thinning is widely used in pattern recognition and particularly when objects can be described in terms of lines or strokes [1]. It reduces an object into a set of lines called the skeleton.

A first method [1, 2] repeatedly traces the contour of objects, computing at each iteration a contour inner to the previous one. A contour point can compute its new location only knowing its neighborhood. An iteration that checks the complete contour involves thus $O(N)$ operations for a $N \times N$ picture. A second method consists in iteratively removing all the contour points of the objects, except those points that belong to the skeleton. Whether a point belongs to the contour or to the skeleton can be checked using a mask-matching method over points and their neighborings. An iteration checks every pixel and involves thus $O(N^2)$ operations for a $N \times N$ picture. The number of iterations of a thinning algorithm is proportional to the maximum thickness of the objects, that is N. The effective complexities of these two thinning approaches are then respectively $O(N^2)$ and $O(N^3)$.

In this paper, we first give some formal definitions about skeletons and present a brief survey of parallel thinning algorithms. We introduce the concept of *pattern*, an object merging pixels in 2×2 squares. We extend standard topological definitions to this object and describe a pattern thinning algorithm based on the latter method, dividing the cost by 8. In a next section, we show that, at some iterations, patterns can also be considered as pixels. The pattern method can thus be applied to this new image. This yields a scale reduction thinning algorithm with a $O(N^2)$ complexity, and its regularity allows to parallelize it easily. This has to be compared with the

---

[*] This work was supported by EEC ESPRIT Basic Research Action 3280 "*NANA*" and the CNRS Coordinated Research Program C^3.

$O(N^3)$ complexity of standard parallel thinning algorithms. An evaluation of the cost of the different algorithms is done in the last section, and experimental results are also presented.

2 Definition of a skeleton

Thinning can be defined as transforming a plane set with a non empty interior into a curve set which has an empty interior. Intuitively this curve set should have the following features.

Condition 1 *Preserve homotopy (connectivity in the 8 directions).*

Condition 2 *Preserve end points.*

The first condition is a basic requirement for all thinning algorithms. The second one has unfortunately no easy formal definition. Usually, an end point is an object pixel with a single neighbor in the object. Using this definition, many noisy branches may occur in the resulting skeleton. All other usual conditions are weaker.

Condition 3 *Be 1-pixel thick.*

Condition 4 *Be minimaly d_8-connected.*

A postprocessing step can force the skeleton to match these non-critical conditions.

Condition 5 *Be isotropic.*

The skeleton must run along the medial axis of the object. The thinning operation has to delete pixels symmetrically to avoid directional bias.

Condition 6 *Have some noise immunity*

The resulting skeleton should depend little on small perturbations in the object's contour.

3 Review of parallel thinning algorithms

There exists many ways to compute the survival condition of a pixel during a thinning process. Some care has to be taken when using thinning operators in parallel mode. Fully parallel thinning operators (i.e. the pixel value at iteration k depends only on the values of its neighboring pixels at iteration $k - 1$) have difficulties in preserving the connectivity of an image [3].

Three methods have been proposed to overcome this problem. The first two methods partially serialize the algorithms by breaking a given iteration into distinct subiterations. A first way is to use distinct thinning operators for each subiteration (this is called *suboperator method*), with some direction bias effect [4]. The second method consists in splitting the picture in distinct subdomains (this is called *subdomain method*). The same operator is used on a single subfield in each subiteration. The picture decomposition is usually a chess-like partitioning [5]. Finally, a third solution consists in extending the mask dimension [6, 7, 8].

4 Pattern Thinning Algorithm

This algorithm is based on subdomain decomposition, and aims to reduce the number of thinning iterations. Our new thinning operator uses a set of 2×2 pixels as target window (i.e. this set is removed or not by the operator). This window is called a *pattern*. A $N \times N$ picture can now be considered as a $\frac{N}{2} \times \frac{N}{2}$ square set of *patterns*. We define *pattern-adjacence* and *thinning window* as follows.

Definition 1. A pattern X is adjacent to a pattern Y if there exists a pixel p in X and a pixel q in Y such that p and q are adjacent.

Definition 2. The pattern thinning window of a pattern P, denoted $PTW(P)$, is the set of patterns which contains P and its 8 neighboring patterns.

The algorithm computes the survival condition of a pattern with respect to the value of its different neighboring patterns. The basic idea of the algorithm is to use a standard thinning operator (Olszewski operator [9]) at the level of patterns instead of pixels. We define a *subpattern* thinning window as follows.

Definition 3. We call subpattern thinning window, denoted $SPTW(P)$, of a pattern window $PTW(P)$ the 9 binary values corresponding to a 3×3 window where

- a 1 is set in the center of $SPTW(P)$ if P is not empty;
- a 1 is set in $SPTW(P)$ if the corresponding pattern in $PTW(P)$ is pattern-adjacent to P;
- a 0 value is set in all other cases;

The survival condition for patterns is no longer the same as the one for pixels, although it is derived from it. We first define a notion of *potentially deletable* patterns, which corresponds to the survival condition of the standard algorithm.

Definition 4. A pattern P is potentially deletable if the removing (i.e. transformation of a 1 value into a 0 value) of the center of $SPTW(P)$ does not affect the Euler number of $SPTW(P)$.

This survival condition is strengthened in order to preserve the connectivity. If a pattern P is potentially deletable, then there exists a path *in the subpattern window* between patterns adjacent to P. We have to check that this path is preserved when removing P, in other words, that all patterns in this path are pairwise adjacent.

Definition 5. Let P be a pattern. Let $(P_0, \ldots, P_k)$ denote the (clockwise) sequence of patterns adjacent to P P is deletable if P is potentially deletable, and the two following conditions hold:

- P is at least adjacent to two patterns (i.e. $k > 1$)
- for all $0 \leq i < k - 1$, there exists a pixel p in P_i which is adjacent to a pixel of P and to a pixel of P_{i+1}, and there exists a pixel q in P_{i+1} which is adjacent to a pixel of P and to a pixel of P_i

Finally, this algorithm decomposes the image in two subdomains A and B as the standard one. The computation of the pattern survival condition can be performed with simple byte logical operations. Ending the algorithm with a standard thinning iteration allows to satisfy condition 3.

5 Parallel Thinning Algorithm Using Scale Reduction

Let us study more precisely the previous algorithm. At the end of a single iteration, we denote Ω the set of patterns different from an *empty* and a *full* block. If $\Omega = \emptyset$, we can then consider that the current picture is a binary $\frac{N}{2} \times \frac{N}{2}$ picture and thus compute its skeleton with the previous method. We divide once again the dimension of the picture, what we call a *reduction*. A *reduction fault* iteration is a thinning iteration where $\Omega \neq \emptyset$. When a reduction fault occurs at some iteration, other reductions may be performed in further iterations (see Fig. 1). Such faults are called *non final* reduction faults.

$$\text{PTW(P)} \qquad \begin{array}{ccc} 1 & 1 & 1 \\ 1 & 1 & 1 \\ 1 & 1 & 0 \end{array} \qquad \text{SPTW(P)}$$

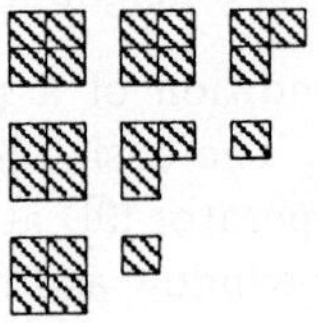

Fig. 1. A non final reduction fault

A *final* reduction fault may occur if there exists a pattern P in Ω, which preserves the connectivity of an object (not deletable with at least two neighbors), or which is extremity of an object (with 0 or 1 neighbor). Such final faults stop the reduction process. However, it is sometimes possible to consider such patterns as *full block* patterns if this does not connect two distinct objects nor creates a hole in the picture. The reduction thinning algorithm iteratively computes a pattern thinning iteration possibly followed by a reduction step.

Algorithm 1 *Reduction Thinning:*

$$I \leftarrow Reduce(I); lr \leftarrow 1$$
repeat
$\qquad DA \leftarrow PatternDeletableSet(A); I \leftarrow I - DA;$
$\qquad DB \leftarrow PatternDeletableSet(B); I \leftarrow I - DB;$
$\qquad OMEGA \leftarrow PartiallyFilledPatternSet(I);$
$\qquad$ **if** $((DA \cup DB) \neq TerminalSet(DA \cup DB)) \wedge (OMEGA = \emptyset)$
$\qquad\qquad I \leftarrow Reduce(I); lr \leftarrow lr + 1$
endif
until $((DA \cup DB) = TerminalSet(DA \cup DB))$

At the end of this algorithm, the output picture is an encoded pattern picture with a scale reduction level of lr (a $\frac{N}{2^{lr}} \times \frac{N}{2^{lr}}$ picture). We have to restore the original size of the picture by performing lr steps of a restoring algorithm. This algorithm consists in the sequential application of a restoring step (pattern to pixel) and a standard thinning iteration. It can be improved by merging the restoring step and the standard thinning step into a single operator step.

6 Analysis and experimental results

6.1 Cost Analysis

We present in Tab. 6.1 the theoretical number of thinning operations performed by each algorithm. This number corresponds to the number of operations performed to thin a picture made of a single $N \times N$ square object. As thinning operations only apply to object pixels, we have evaluated the sum of the number of object pixels at the beginning of each iteration. Notice that, for a square object, a reduction is always performed at each iteration for the scale reduction algorithm.

standard	$N^2 + (N-2)^2 + (N-4)^2 + \ldots + 1$	$\frac{N^3}{6} + O(N^2)$
pattern	$\left(\frac{N}{2}\right)^2 + \left(\frac{N}{2} - 2\right)^2 + \left(\frac{N}{2} - 4\right)^2 + \ldots + 1$	$\frac{N^3}{48} + O(N^2)$
scale	$N^2 + \frac{N^2}{4} + \frac{N^2}{16} + \ldots + 1$	$\frac{4}{3}N^2 + O(N)$

Table 1. Theoretical evaluation of thinning operations

6.2 Experimental results

We have implemented the three algorithms on a SIMD MasPar MP-1 computer composed of 1,024 processors connected with their eight neighbors on a 2D mesh. The results are compared according to 3 criteria: the number of iterations, the number of operator applications and the effective execution time. The two first criteria are standard measures of the efficiency of a thinning algorithm because they are machine-independent and implementation-independent. As we can see on Tab. 6.2, the improvement between the standard thinning algorithm and pattern thinning algorithms is in accordance with the theoretical evaluation.

Image size		64			128			256			512		
Square image	Standard	15	58	0.009s	28	440	0.21s	54	3456	1.07s	136	27106	7.3s
	Pattern	8	20	0.18s	15	74	0.24s	28	504	0.76s	54	3712	4.16s
	Scale	8	20	0.17s	9	23	0.18s	10	39	0.20s	11	103	0.28s
Chinese ideogram	Standard	3	12	0.01s	5	72	0.1s	6	384	0.21s	9	2304	0.82s
	Pattern	2	8	0.16s	3	28	0.18s	5	136	0.29s	6	640	0.81s
	Scale	2	8	0.15s	3	28	0.17s	4	42	0.20s	5	120	0.32s

Table 2. Number of iterations, thinning operations per processor and total time

On the other hand, execution times improvement between the standard algorithm and the pattern algorithms is not as great as we could expect with respect to the number of operations. Remember that the quantity of control code is increased for the pattern and scale thinning algorithms. Figure. 6.2 shows a set of skeletons obtained with the 3 described algorithms on a 128 × 128 Chinese character. It is clear that the improvement of execution times does not induce any loss in the visual quality of the result.

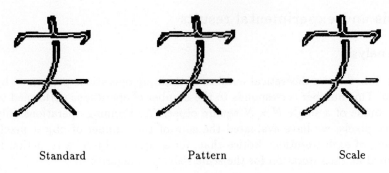

Standard   Pattern   Scale

Fig. 2. Resulting skeletons of the 3 algorithms

7 Conclusion

Pyramidal algorithms as well as pyramidal machines have received a lot of attention. In this paper we present a new pyramidal approach of thinning. Our initial motivation—getting the most out of our SIMD computer—has led to a new efficient algorithm. Our thinning algorithm produces skeletons in accordance with standard thinning criteria but with some specific topological properties (straight lines) and multiresolution aspects. The practical impacts of those properties must be detailed.

Standard parallel thinning operators involve algorithms with a cost in $O(n^3)$. Sequential thinning algorithms based on contour tracing have a cost in $O(n^2)$. The main advantage of our new thinning approach is to propose a parallel thinning operator in a thinning algorithm having a cost in $O(n^2)$.

References

1. T. Pavlidis. A thinning algorithm for discrete binary images. *Computer vision and image processing*, 20:142–157, 1980.
2. C. Arcelli and G. Sanniti di Baja. A thinning algorithm based on prominence detection. *Pattern Recognition*, 13(3):225–235, 1981.
3. C.J. Hilditch. Comparison of thinning algorithms on a parallel processor. *Computer Vision, Graphics and Image Processing*, 1(3):115–132, 1983.
4. C. Arcelli. Pattern thinning by contour tracing. *Comp. Graph. and Image Proc.*, 17:130–144, 1981.
5. Z. Guo and R.W. Hall. Parallel thinning with two-subiteration algorithms. *Comm. ACM*, 32:359–373, 1989.
6. C.M. Holt, A. Stewart, M. Clint, and R.H. Perrott. An improved parallel thinning algorithm. *Comm. ACM*, 30:156–160, 1987.
7. R.T. Chin, H.K. Wan, D.L. Stover, and R.D. Iverson. A one-pass thinning algorithm and its parallel implementation. *Comp. Vision, Graph. and Image Proc.*, 40:30–40, 1987.
8. V. Poty and S. Ubeda. Parallel thinning algorithm using $k \times k$ mask. In *Int. Coll. on Parallel Image Proc.*, 337–352, 1991.
9. J. Olszewski. A flexible thinning algorithm allowing parallel, sequentiel and distributed application. *To appear in ACM Trans. on Mathematical Sofware*.

This article was processed using the LaTeX macro package with LLNCS style

Static Scheduling of Parallel Programs for Message Passing Architectures

Apostolos Gerasoulis and Tao Yang

Department of Computer Science, Rutgers University
New Brunswick, NJ 08903, USA
Email: gerasoulis or tyang@cs.rutgers.edu

Abstract. We discuss the static scheduling and code generation problem for message passing architectures. Using ideas from successful manually written programs for message passing architectures we have developed several new automatic algorithms for scheduling and code generation. These algorithms have been implemented in a preliminary software system named PYRROS. The purpose of this paper is to provide a justification of our approach and choice of algorithms.

1 Introduction

Several new architectures based on the message passing paradigm of computation have been announced recently, e.g. CM-5 from Thinking Machines, INTEL PARAGON and nCUBE-2 . However, programming such architectures is extremely difficult. This is because both data and programs must be partitioned, distributed to the processors and then their execution must be coordinated.

Because of these programming difficulties, many researchers have been investigating the construction of compilers for automatic parallelization and scheduling [7, 9, 11]. Even though automatic parallelization (and vectorization) at the fine grain level has been extremely successful this has not been the case for message passing architectures. As far as we know no compiler exists, that will take a sequential program as input and automatically generate a parallel program for message passing architectures. Furthermore, considering the difficulty of the interprocedural analysis problem to determine data dependence, it is a grand challenge to build a compiler that will automatically parallelize sequential programs with good performance for scalable architectures.

In this paper, we discuss the problem of programming and compiling for message passing architectures. From a theoretical point of view the scheduling and code generation problem is very difficult, NP-complete, but in practice parallel programs are written routinely with excellent performance. Our emphasis has been in developing algorithms which are practical and at the same time perform as well as the "best" hand-written programs.

We have built a prototype named PYRROS [17] to test our ideas and algorithms. Preliminary results are very promising. The current PYRROS prototype has complexity "almost" linear to the size of the task graph in both computational and space complexity and can handle large task graphs. As far as we know this is the first programming tool in the literature that produces scheduled code for *arbitrary* static task graphs on real scalable architectures such as nCUBE-2 and iPSC/860.

PYRROS could be useful in many ways. We mention a few. It can be used as a parallel language for a user to define a parallel program without being involved in low level programming for scheduling and synchronization. It can be used to determine a good partitioning for a given algorithm and architectures via experimentation. Since PYRROS can estimate the numbers of processors for maximum performance at compile time, a scalable architecture could be utilized better in a multi-user environment. Since it automatically generates programs it could be used to program irregular task graphs, an area which suffers from low utilization of parallel architectures e.g. sparse matrix computations in numerical computing and VLSI chip design. Another application is to assist in the development of good scalable computational libraries and kernels, by providing a testbed for comparing a handwritten library program with an automatic generated PYRROS program.

The area of compiling and scheduling for parallel architectures is very active. There are several other systems related to PYRROS. PARAFRASE-2 [11] by Polychronopoulos et. al., is a parallelizing compiler system that performs dependence analysis, program partitioning and dynamic scheduling on shared memory machines. SCHEDULER by Dongarra and Sorensen [2] uses centralized dynamic scheduling which performs well for the shared memory model of computation but is not suitable for message passing architectures. The Kali parallel programming language by Koelbel and Mehrota [9] is currently targeted at DOALL parallelism and can generate parallel codes for the INTEL hypercube. Kali does not address the issues of scheduling and it can be used only for regular task graphs that can be expressed using the DOALL constructs. HYPERTOOL by Wu and Gajski [15] uses the same model of computation and produces codes for the hypercube simulator SIMON. TaskGrapher by El-Rewini and Lewis [4] schedules task graphs but does not generate codes.

In this paper we provide an overview of the algorithms in PYRROS and explain the reasons behind their choice. Details of the algorithms can be found in a series of papers by the authors. We also describe experiments and applications of PYRROS. For example, a new result here is the application of PYRROS on irregular task graphs arising from sparse matrix computation.

2 The PYRROS software tool

The PYRROS tool and its functions are shown in Figure 1. The input to PYRROS is a DAG program and a special task graph language has been developed to define the input. The computational model chosen is the static *macro dataflow* model of computation because such a model performs well for scalable message passing architectures. This model is similar to the classic dataflow model except that nodes in the dataflow graph represent a large segment of program such as subroutines instead of fine grain operations. For this model each task receives the input, performs its execution and immediately sends the data to its successor tasks, e.g. Wu and Gajski [15], Sarkar [13], Kim and Browne [10].

An important part of PYRROS is its scheduling algorithms. PYRROS uses a multistep method to schedule task graphs shown in Figure 1. This approach has been very successful in the literature, e.g. Sarkar [13]. In the first step a task graph is clustered using a scheduling algorithm on unbounded number of processors of a completely connected architecture. In the next steps, the clusters are merged if the number of clusters is larger than the number of processors, and then are mapped onto the physical architecture.

Another important part of PYRROS is the code generation part that utilizes the scheduling result to insert communication primitives, select and devise efficient communication procedures, incorporate a deadlock free communication protocol, and also perform optimizations such as removal of redundant communication primitives. We describe all of these in detail in [17].

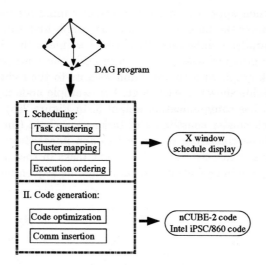

Fig. 1. The system organization of PYRROS prototype.

The current prototype produces non-uniform programs for both regular and irregular task graphs. While Single Program Multiple Data (SPMD) style programming suffers from high overhead for irregular graphs and poor load balancing, it could perform well for uniform task graphs for some applications. We plan to extend PYRROS to incorporate SPMD programming as an option.

3 The PYRROS rationale and approach

In this section we explain in more detail the rationale and approach behind PYRROS. Our goal is the development of a system that produces code which compares well on average with the best hand-written programs. The reasons for the success of hand-written programs for specific applications are:

- The parallelism can be identified accurately at any level of granularity. Currently no automatic parallelization compiler is available to fully identify parallelism at all levels of granularity.
- The data and programs can be distributed so that the parallel architecture is fully utilized.

In order to develop a practical system that produces code which is competitive to the "best" hand-written programs, we analyzed the performance of many hand-written programs. We discovered an underlying theory that provides a justification for such a performance. We then used this theory to develop algorithms whose performance comes close to the "best" hand-written programs. We discus our results in the following sections.

3.1 Clustering and the granularity theory

Clustering. A common approach in parallel programming for message passing architectures is to *cluster* the tasks in the dataflow graph first and then schedule the clusters onto the parallel architecture. By clusters we mean that it is determined at compile time that a group of tasks will be executed in the same processor. In Figure 2(a) we show a task graph with computation weights to the right of each node and communication weights shown in each edge. For example node n_1 has computation 1 and edge (n_1, n_2) has communication weight 3. In Figure 2(b) we show one clustering in which each cluster constitutes of tasks on a chain (linear path). We call such clustering a *linear* clustering as opposed to *non-linear* clustering shown in Figure 2(c) which contains at least two independent tasks in the same cluster. In this example, n_4 and n_5 are independent and they must be sequentialized in execution.

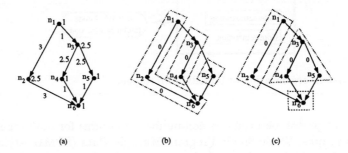

(a) (b) (c)

Fig. 2. (a) A Task Graph (b) A linear clustering (c) A nonlinear clustering

Granularity. What is so special about linear clustering? Linear clustering preserves the parallelism embedded in DAGs while nonlinear clustering does not. Linear clustering is widely used in the literature particularly for coarse grain dataflow graphs, e.g. [12]. In Gerasoulis and Yang [5] we developed the theory that explains the advantages of linear clustering. We introduced a quantification of the *granularity* using a ratio of computation to communication costs taken over all fork and joins subgraphs of a task graph. For example, the granularity of the graph in Figure 2(a) is $g = 1/3$ which is derived as follows: Node n_1 is a fork and its *grain* is $g_1 = 2.5/3$, the ratio of the minimum computation weights of its successors n_2 and n_3, which is 2.5, and the maximum communication cost of the outgoing edges, which is 3. Node n_2 is both a fork and a join and the grain for the join is $1/3$ which is the computation weight of its only predecessor n_1 and the cost of the edge (n_1, n_2), while the grain for the fork is the weight of n_6 over the weight of (n_2, n_6) which is again $1/3$. We finally determine the granularity as the the minimum grain over all nodes of the graph which in our case is $g = 1/3$.

When the granularity is greater than one then the graph is called *coarse grain* otherwise it is called *fine grain*. In [5] we show the following two important theorems:

Theorem 1 *For coarse grain task graphs a linear clustering attains the optimum scheduling.*

Unfortunately determining the optimum linear clustering is NP-complete, but there is a nice performance guarantee property that linear clustering satisfies.

Theorem 2 *For coarse grain task graphs every linear clustering is within a factor of two of the optimum scheduling.*

An Example. To appreciate the importance of these results and their impact in the development of PYRROS let us consider the LINPACK benchmark example for Gauss Jordan (GJ) algorithm.

```
for k = 1 to n
    for j = k + 1 to n + 1
    ┌─────────────────────────────────┐
    │ T_k^j : {   a_{k,j} = a_{k,j}/a_{k,k}    │
    │           for i = 1 : n and  i ≠ k │
    │             a_{i,j} = a_{i,j} − a_{i,k} * a_{k,j} │
    │           end}                    │
    └─────────────────────────────────┘
    end
end
```

Fig. 3. The kji form for the Gauss-Jordan algorithm with interior loop task partitioning.

One of the data partitionings used for message passing architectures for the Gauss-Jordan algorithm is the interior loop partitioning, see Figure 3. Task T_k^j defined in Figure 3 uses column k to modify column j of the matrix A. The coarse grain data dependence graph is given in Figure 4, see [1]. Task T_k^j is a functional task with input data being the columns k and j, and output data the column j. Task T_k^{k+1} is a broadcasting node, sending the same column $k + 1$ to all T_{k+1}^j, $j = k + 2 : n + 1$ tasks. Our data units are the columns of the matrix on which the tasks operate.

Computing the weights. Communication and computation weights are estimated as follows. We can either symbolically compute the time that it takes to execute and communicate the data for each task or perform an average case estimation if this is not possible, see Sarkar [14]. For the example above there are approximately $n\omega$ operations for each task, where ω is the time that it takes for each operation, $a_{i,j} = a_{i,j} - a_{i,k} * a_{k,j}$. For the communication cost we assume the linear model used in most message passing architectures, see Dunigan [3]. Thus it costs $\alpha + n\beta$ time to transfer a vector of size n between two neighbors processors, where α is the start up time and β is the transmission rate. These communication and computation parameters can be found in the literature, [3]. For example, for the nCUBE-2 hypercube we have

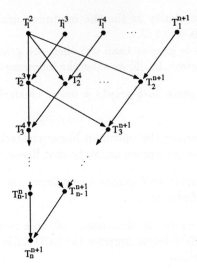

Fig. 4. The Gauss-Jordan DAG. The node computation cost for all nodes is $\tau = n\omega$ and edge communication cost for all edges is $c = \alpha + n\beta$.

used $\omega = 2.38\mu s$, $\alpha = 160\mu s$ and $\beta = 2.4\mu s$ per word transfer for single precision arithmetic.

Natural clustering. For this important GJ example, most of hand-written programs [12] use the locality assumption or owner computes rule, i.e. columns are modified in the processor that have been mapped, to derive the following *natural* clusters:

$$M_{j-1} = \{T_1^j, T_2^j, \ldots, T_k^j, \ldots, T_{j-1}^j\}, \quad j = 2 : n + 1.$$

For each cluster M_{j-1}, column j remains local in that cluster while it is modified by columns $1 : j - 1$. The tasks in M_{j-1} are chains in the task graph in Figure 4, which implies that linear clustering was the result of the locality assumption. We have shown in [5] that this natural linear clustering is also the optimum linear clustering for this graph on machines with clique or hypercube topology as long as the granularity defined by the following ratio

$$g = \frac{n\omega}{\alpha + n\beta}$$

is greater than one. If the granularity is less than one then then natural linear clustering could be a poor choice as it will be seen in the next subsection.

3.2 Importance of automatic scheduling tools

Given a set of parallel tasks with precedence constraint, manually-supplied scheduling may perform well for some cases, but it is difficult and tedious for a user to develop such a schedule. A good automatic scheduling tool can efficiently find near-optimal solutions comparable or superior to user's results.

We demonstrate the importance of automatic scheduling using the following example. For Figure 4, assume the parameters $\alpha = 10$, $\beta = \omega = 1$ and $n = 4$.

For these parameters the computation weight $\tau = 4$, the communication weight $c = \alpha + n\beta = 14$ and the granularity $g = 4/14$ which implies that the task graph is fine grain. As we mentioned above when a program is manually written for a library such as LINPACK, the clustering must be given in advance. Let us assume that the widely used natural linear clustering defined previously is used. This implies that $\{T_1^2\}$, $\{T_1^3, T_2^3\}$, $\{T_1^4, T_2^4, T_3^4\}$ and $\{T_1^5, T_2^5, T_3^5, T_4^5\}$ will constitute separate clusters.

At this point the user, executing the program with natural clustering, cannot determine how many processors to choose so that the parallel time is minimized. If he chooses $p = 4$, since the degree of parallelism of the graph is 4, then the scheduling result on 4 hypercube processors is displayed in Figure 5(a) and the parallel time (PT) will be 58 time units. Each computation weight is 4 and communication weight is 14 but T_2^4 must waits $2 * 14$ time units to receive the data from task T_1^2 since processors P_0 and P_3 are at a distance 2 from each other.

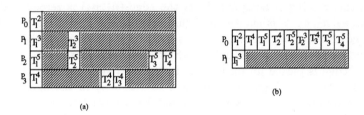

(a)

(b)

Fig. 5. (a) The natural clustering with $PT = 58$. (b) PYRROS result with $PT = 36$.

On the other hand, if clustering is determined automatically using a good algorithm then a better utilization of the architecture and shorter parallel time can be accomplished. In Figure 5(b) we show the scheduling produced automatically by the system. PYRROS using the DSC (dominant sequence clustering) algorithm [16] determines that $p = 2$ processors are sufficient for scheduling this fine grain task graph and the parallel time is reduced to 36 time units. Thus PYRROS is useful in determining the number of processors suitable for executing a task graph. This demonstrates one advantage of an automatic scheduling system over a manually written program.

The reason for this poor performance of the natural linear clustering is that the granularity is less than one for this size of the problem. If we choose the parameters $\alpha = 10$, $\beta = 1$, $\omega = 4$ and $n = 4$ then $g = 8/7$ and the graph becomes coarse grain. The natural clustering results in parallel time 106 which is optimum as it is proven in [5], and PYRROS derives a scheduling with parallel time 120.

To summarize, the granularity and clustering theory raised an interesting question. To succeed in automatic code generation we need to develop an automatic scheduling algorithm that has low complexity to be practical, gives linear clusters when the granularity is greater than one and non-linear when the granularity is less than one.

3.3 PYRROS Algorithms

PYRROS first uses the DSC algorithm to cluster tasks by scheduling tasks on an unbounded number of fully-connected processors. DSC traverses the given graph and performs a sequence of edge zeroing operations. Each step tries to reduce the parallel time using the nonlinear clustering strategy if a task subgraph is fine grain and linear clustering if a task subgraph is coarse grain. This algorithm has been shown to be superior to many other algorithms from the literature [16, 6] in terms of both parallel time and algorithm complexity. The complexity of this algorithm is almost linear to the size of a graph.

Initially every task is its own cluster. For example, Figure 6(a) is the initial clustering. The *dominant sequence* is the longest path in the scheduled graph and is shown with thick arrows. The dominant sequence determines the parallel time which is $PT = 11$ initially. The first edge in DS is zeroed and the parallel time is reduced to $PT = 10$, shown Figure 6(b) along with the new $DS = < n_1, n_3, n_5 >$. A zeroing is accepted as long as the parallel time does not increase from the previous step. Thus this zeroing is accepted. Next the edge (n_1, n_3) is zeroed and the new $DS = < n_1, n_2, n_3, n_5 >$ is shown in Figure 6(c) with $PT = 8$, so this zeroing is also accepted. Notice that an ordering has been imposed between the independent tasks n_2 and n_3 shown by a pseudo-edge. Since the only unexamined edge in DS is (n_3, n_5) this edge is picked up for zeroing in the next step and the parallel time of the clustering shown in Figure 6(d) reduces to $PT = 7$. In the final step (n_1, n_2) is chosen for zeroing, but this zeroing cannot be accepted since the parallel time increases to $PT = 8$.

In the third step shown in Figure 6(c) an ordering algorithm is needed to order the tasks in the non-linear cluster and then the parallel time must be computed to get the new DS. One of the key ideas in the DSC algorithm is that it computes the schedule and parallel time incrementally from one step to the next in $O(\log v)$ time. Thus the total complexity is $O((v + e) \log v)$ time. If the parallel time was not computed incrementally, then the total cost would be greater than $O(v^2)$ which will not be practical for large graphs.

A good clustering algorithm does not completely solve the problem of scheduling in the case that the number of clusters is larger than the number of processors. We further use a load-balance and physical mapping heuristic to map clusters onto p physical processors and use critical path information to order the task execution within each processor.

Using the scheduling results from these algorithms we proposed new code generation algorithms, optimized communication, improved memory utilization, eliminated redundant communication and developed deadlock free communication protocol. The complexity of these algorithms for scheduling and code generation is almost linear to the size of a task graph. More details can be found in [17].

4 Experiments

4.1 The Gauss-Jordan algorithm

This experiment uses the block version BLAS-3 of the GJ algorithm. The number of tasks and edges in the GJ task graph of this example is $v = n^2/2$ and $e = n^2$. A

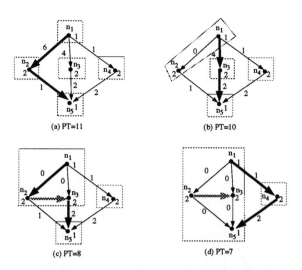

(a) PT=11 (b) PT=10

(c) PT=8 (d) PT=7

Fig. 6. The clustering refinements in DSC. Thick arrows show DSs.

system with $O(v^2)$ complexity will be impractical for this example.

We have also written a parallel program manually that uses natural clustering and wrap mapping along the gray code ring, following the approach by Saad [12] . The sequential time is $1150sec$ for 1000×1000 linear algebraic system in nCUBE-2. In Figure 7, we compare the performance of automatically-generated code by PYRROS with our handwritten manual program. This experiment shows that the performance of the parallel code generated by PYRROS is comparable to that of the hand-written version.

4.2   The sparse irregular task graph computation

One of the advantages of PYRROS is that it can handle irregular task graphs as well as regular ones. We present an example to demonstrate the importance of this feature.

Many problems in scientific computation involve sparse matrices. Generally dense matrix algorithms can be parallelized and vectorized fairly easily and attain good performance for most of the architectures. However if the matrices are sparse, the performance of the dense matrix algorithms is usually poor for most architectures. Thus the parallelization and efficient implementation of sparse matrix computations is one of the grand challenges in parallel processing research.

An example is the area of circuit simulation and testing where the solution of a sets of differential equations are often used. These problems are solved numerically by discretizing in time and space to reduce the problem to a large set of nonlinear equations. The solution is then derived by an iterative method such as Newton-Raphson which iterates over the same dataflow graph since the topology of the iteration matrix remains the same but the data change in each step. The following table shows the number of iterations of an iterative method over the same dataflow graph of several classes of problems taken from Karmarkar [8]. For example for

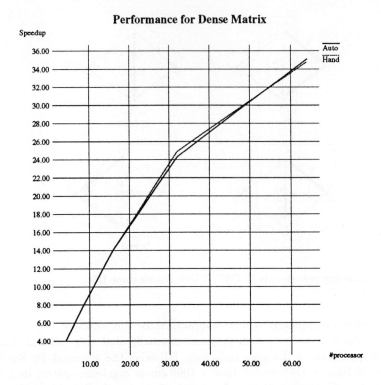

Fig. 7. PYRROS vs. hand-written on nCUBE-2 for dense matrices and $n = 1000$.

Partial Differential Equations it took 12566 iterations for two problems over the same dataflow task graph.

LP Problems	Partial Differential Eqns		Fractional Hypergraph Covering			Control Systems		
Problem number	1	2	1	2	3	1	2	3
Repetition count of dataflow graph	1428	12556	16059	6299	7592	708	1863	7254

The PYRROS algorithms could be very useful for this important class of problems. For the circuit simulation problem the LU decomposition method is used to determine the dataflow graph. Because many of the tasks in the graph perform updating with zeros, a naive approach is to modify the classical algorithms for finding LU so that the zero operations are skipped at run time. Such an approach is very inefficient because of the high overhead in operation skipping and also because of the difficulty in load balancing arithmetic. By traversing the task graph once we can delete all the zero nodes to derive the sparse irregular task graph. This traversal could be costly if it is done only once but this overhead is spread over many iteration and is usually insignificant, especially for symmetric matrices.

There are other methods such as elimination tree algorithms that produce sparse graphs. The PYRROS system is perfect for such problems since it can produce schedules that load balance arithmetic and also generate parallel code.

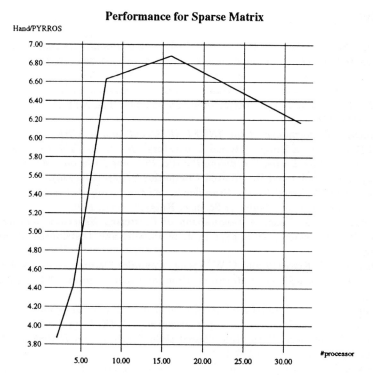

Fig. 8. PYRROS vs. hand-written on nCUBE-2 for sparse matrices with $n = 500$.

We have used PYRROS to schedule sparse LU graphs and compared it with a hand-written program using the natural linear clustering strategy. PYRROS achieved a substantial improvement. Figure 8 gives the result for a matrix size 500. On average PYRROS code is 5 time faster than the hand-written program.

5 Conclusions

The PYRROS experiments have demonstrated that good performance of automatically generated code is feasible provided that task and edge weights are known at compile time. In the future we plan to investigate the performance of PYRROS ideas on a wider range of applications.

Acknowledgments

Partial support has been provided by a Grant No. DMS-8706122 from NSF and the Air Force Office of Scientific Research and the Office of Naval research under grant N00014-90-J-4018. We thank Weining Wang for developing the task graph language parser, Milind Deshpande for the X window schedule displayer, Probal Bhattacharjya for the graph generator of sparse matrix solver, Ye Li for programming the Intel i860 communication routines.

References

1. M. Cosnard, M. Marrakchi, Y. Robert, and D. Trystram, *Parallel Gaussian Elimination on an MIMD Computer*, Parallel Computing, vol. 6, pp. 275-296, 1988.
2. J. J. Dongarra, and D.C. Sorensen, *SCHEDULE: Tools for Developing and Analyzing Parallel Fortran Programs*, in D.B. Gannon, L.H. Jamieson and R.J. Douglass, editors, *The Characteristics of Parallel Algorithms*, pp 363-394. The MIT Press, Cambridge, Massachusetts, 1987.
3. T.H. Dunigan, *Performance of the INTEL iPSC/860 and nCUBE 6400 Hypercube*, ORNL/TM-11790, Oak Ridge National Laboratory, Oak Ridge, TN, Nov. 1991.
4. H.El-Rewini and T.G. Lewis, *Scheduling Parallel Program Tasks onto Arbitrary Target Machines*, J. of Parallel and Distributed Computing 9, 138-153(1990).
5. A. Gerasoulis and T. Yang, *On the Granularity and Clustering of Directed Acyclic Task Graphs*, TR-153, Dept. of Computer Science, Rutgers Univ., 1990.
6. A. Gerasoulis and T. Yang, *A Comparison of Clustering Heuristics for Scheduling DAGs on Multiprocessors*, To appear in J. of Parallel and Distributed Computing, Dec. 1992.
7. S. Hiranandani, K. Kennedy and C.W. Tseng, *Compiler Optimizations for Fortran D on MIMD Distributed-Memory Machines*, Proc. of Supercomputing '91, IEEE, pp86-100.
8. N. Karmarkar, *A New Parallel Architecture for Sparse Matrix Computation Based on Finite Project Geometries*, Proc. of Supercomputing '91, IEEE, pp358-369.
9. C. Koelbel, P. Mehrotra, *Supporting Shared Data Structures on Distributed Memory Architectures*, Ppopp 1990, pp 177-186.
10. S.J. Kim and J.C Browne, *A General Approach to Mapping of Parallel Computation upon Multiprocessor Architectures*, Int'l Conf. on Parallel Processing, vol 3, pp. 1-8, 1988.
11. C. D. Polychronopoulos, M.B. Girkar, M. R.Haghighat, C.L. Lee, B.P. Leung, and D.A. Schouten, *The Structure of Parafrase-2: an Advanced Parallelizing Compiler for C and Fortran*, in D. Gelernter, A. Nicolau and D. Padua (Eds.), *Languages and Compilers for Parallel Computing*, 1990.
12. Y. Saad, *Gaussian Elimination on Hypercubes*, Parallel Algorithms and Architectures, Cosnard, M. et al. Eds., Elsevier Science Publishers, North-Holland, 1986.
13. V. Sarkar, *Partitioning and Scheduling Parallel Programs for Execution on Multiprocessors*, The MIT Press, 1989.
14. V. Sarkar, *Determining Average Program Execution Times and their Variance*, SIG-PLAN 1989, pp298-312.
15. Min-You Wu and D. Gajski, *A Programming Aid for Hypercube Architectures*, The Journal of Supercomputing, vol. 2, pp. 349-372, 1988.
16. T. Yang and A. Gerasoulis, *A Fast Scheduling Algorithm for DAGs on an Unbounded Number of Processors*, Proc. of Supercomputing '91, IEEE, pp 633-642, Nov. 1991.
17. T. Yang and A. Gerasoulis, *PYRROS: Static Task Scheduling and Code Generation for Message-Passing Multiprocessors*, Proc. of 6th ACM International Conference on Supercomputing, Washington D.C., July, 1992.

This article was processed using the LaTeX macro package with LLNCS style

A Polynomial Time Method for Optimal Software Pipelining

Vincent H. Van Dongen
Centre de recherche informatique de Montréal
Montréal, CANADA H3T 1P1

Guang R. Gao and Qi Ning
McGill University, School of Computer Science
Montréal, CANADA H3A 2A7

Abstract

Software pipelining is one of the most important loop scheduling methods used by parallelizing compilers. It determines a static parallel schedule – a periodic pattern – to overlap instructions of a loop body from different iterations. The main contributions of this paper are the following: First, we propose to express the fine-grain loop scheduling problem (in particular, software pipelining) on the basis of the mathematical formulation of *r-periodic scheduling*. This formulation overcomes some of the problems encountered by existing software pipelining methods. Second, we demonstrate the feasibility of the proposed method by presenting a polynomial time algorithm to find an *optimal schedule* in this r-periodic form that maximizes the computation rate (in fact, we show that this schedule maximizes the computation rate theoretically possible).

1   Introduction

The efficient exploitation of fine-grain parallelism in loops has been a major challenge in the design of optimizing compilers for high-performance computer architectures. Fine-grain loop scheduling involves the detection of parallelism from a partially ordered set of operations of the loop body which are to be performed repetitively over a sequence of iterations. With loop-carried dependencies, the dependency relation between operations in the loop is a digraph with cycles, thus presenting a specific challenge to the effectiveness of classical scheduling theory.

Recently, *software pipelining* has been proposed for fine-grain loop scheduling. This method derives a static parallel schedule – a periodic pattern – that overlaps instructions of a loop body from different iterations. Software pipelining has been proposed for high-performance pipelined processor architectures, as well as super-scalar and VLIW architectures [1, 2, 3, 5, 6, 11, 13, 15, 17].

To motivate our work, we briefly discuss two existing approaches for software pipelining. In the first approach [2, 3, 8], a compiler emulates the execution of the loop under a certain operational model, until a periodic pattern is "discovered" which often consists of instructions from a number of consecutive iterations. In the technique proposed in [2], the instructions are scheduled as early as possible by a *greedy* machine model with the constraint of having *bounded gaps* between the computations. This technique is called *OPTimal loop parallelization (OPT)* (a particular case of *Perfect Pipelining*). In [8], the loop is modeled by a timed Petri net executed under the "earliest firing rule". There are two problems with this approach: (1) for loops with multiple *critical cycles*, no polynomial time bound is known to occur for such a periodic pattern; (2) the patterns may be exponential in size under the earliest firing rule [14].

The second approach generates a fixed scheduling pattern for one iteration, and repeats it for all iterations with a specific initiation time interval. For an idealized unbounded parallel processor system, an interesting solution is presented in [19]. The problem is formulated as a linear algebraic problem. By doing so, a polynomial time algorithm in $O(n^4)$ is derived. In [11], the author gives a mathematical (linear programming) formulation of the scheduling problem, and tries to minimize the initiation interval between the successive iterations.

However, the requirement that only regular schedules (such that all iterations are scheduled in the same manner) are considered may exclude some optimal solutions. This was demonstrated in [10], and an improvement was suggested in which the loops may first be subjected to an *unrolling* transformation.

In this paper, we propose a different alternative, based on an elegent and powerful scheduling technique for Karp-Miller computation graphs [16]. Using this technique, the schedule is of the form

$$t(i,v) = \lfloor \frac{T \cdot i + A[v]}{r} \rfloor,$$

where the parameters T, r and $A[v]$ are integers, and $t(i,v)$ is the starting time of the ith occurrence of the vth statement of the loop body. (Throughout this paper, $\lfloor \frac{a}{b} \rfloor$ denotes the floor of $\frac{a}{b}$, i.e. the largest integer less or equal to $\frac{a}{b}$, while $\lceil \frac{a}{b} \rceil$ is the ceil of $\frac{a}{b}$, i.e. the smallest integer larger or equal to $\frac{a}{b}$.) In this form, the schedule is periodic with periodicity r, period T and offset time $A[v]$. Surprisingly, this mathematical form of schedule and its exact analytical solution didn't receive a great deal of attention from previous work in the area of software pipelining.

There are several reasons which motivated us in adopting this formulation to fine-grain loop scheduling. Intuitively these reasons are: (1) The formulation does not have the restriction that the schedule must follow an earliest firing rule. In fact, the values computed for the offsets in general will be different from those derived from the methods of [2, 3, 8]. (2) The formulation also does not have the restriction that the schedule of each individual iteration must be the same. In fact, the schedule of two consecutive iterations may not be the same, but will repeat every r iterations; hence called *r-periodic*. (3) As a result, the formulation provides a uniform analytical framework to express the time-optimal loop scheduling problem. That is, we have a single mathematical formulation which considers both software pipelining and loop unrolling.

The main contribution of this paper is the following. We propose to express the fine-grain loop scheduling problem (in particular, software pipelining) on the basis of the mathematical formulation of r-periodic scheduling. It overcomes some of the problems encountered by existing software pipelining methods as described above. We demonstrate the feasibility of the proposed method by presenting a polynomial time algorithm to find the *optimal schedule* in this r-periodic form that maximizes the computation rate.

This paper is a short version of [18]. It is organized as follows. In section 2, we present two examples of loops scheduled with the proposed model. In section 3, we present our program model; i.e., the type of loops to which our scheduling technique applies. We also review the notion of dependence graph as a basis for later sections. Then, in section 4, the main results of this paper are presented. Section 5 presents our conclusions and ideas for future work.

2 Motivating examples

We hereafter consider two examples of loop scheduling. The first one is very simple. Its schedule of optimal computation rate is 1-periodic. In that case, the loop is easily rewritten in terms of its *prelude* (sometimes called *prologue*), *pattern* and *postlude* (sometimes called *epilogue*). The second example illustrates the case when the optimal schedule is 3-periodic.

Example 2.1 Consider the following simple example.

$$
\begin{aligned}
&\textbf{for } i = 0 \text{ to } N - 1 \quad \textbf{do} \\
&\qquad a[i] = a[i-1] + R[i]; \\
&\qquad b[i] = a[i] + c[i-1]; \\
&\qquad c[i] = b[i] + b[i-1]; \\
&\qquad \textbf{od}
\end{aligned}
\tag{1}
$$

The dependence graph of this loop is shown in figure 2(a). (For those who are not familiar with the concept of dependence graph, see the next section.) If all instructions take one unit of time, the schedule of maximal computation rate is

$$ t(i, v) = 2 \cdot i + A[v], $$

with $A[a] = 0$, $A[b] = 1$, $A[c] = 2$ (where $A[a]$, $A[b]$ and $A[c]$ denote the values of $A[v]$ for the instructions computing $a[i]$, $b[i]$ and $c[i]$ respectively). The computation rate is $1/2$; every two units of time, a new iteration begins. The resulting schedule of the first three iterations is shown in figure 1. All iterations are clearly scheduled the same manner. We call this type of schedule *regular* or *1-periodic*.

time	i=0	i=1	i=2
0	a		
1	b		
2	c	a	
3		b	
4		c	a
5			b
6			c

Figure 1: For the loop (1), the optimal schedule is 1-periodic.

Clearly, the instructions executed from time $t = 2$ to $t = 3$ form a *pattern* for the loop. In other words, the loop can be rewritten in terms of this *pattern*, a *prelude* (instructions before the pattern) and a *postlude* (instructions after the pattern). The loop (1) is rewritten:

```
%prelude
a[0] = a[−1] + R[0];
%pattern
  for i = 0 to N − 2   do
                b[i] = a[i] + c[i − 1];
                a[i + 1] = a[i] + R[i + 1]||
                c[i] = b[i] + b[i − 1];
                od
%postlude
b[N − 1] = a[N − 1] + c[N − 2];
c[N − 1] = b[N − 1] + b[N − 2];
```

Note that in the *pattern*, the two instructions $a[i + 1]$ and $c[i]$ are executed in parallel; this is here simply noted with the delimiter "$||$". Note also that in this case, the number of instructions in the pattern is equal to n, the number of instructions in the original loop.

□

Example 2.2 Consider the following example whose dependence graph is shown in figure 2(b).

$$
\textbf{for } i = 0 \text{ to } N - 1 \quad \textbf{do}
$$

$$
\begin{aligned}
a[i] &= h[i - 1] + R[i]; \\
b[i] &= a[i] + a[i - 1]; \\
c[i] &= b[i] + b[i - 1]; \\
d[i] &= c[i] + c[i - 1]; \\
e[i] &= d[i - 1] + d[i - 2]; \\
f[i] &= e[i - 1] + e[i - 2]; \\
g[i] &= f[i] + X[i]; \\
h[i] &= g[i] + Y[i]; \\
i[i] &= d[i] + j[i - 1]; \\
j[i] &= i[i] + Z[i]; \\
\end{aligned}
\tag{2}
$$

$$
\textbf{od}
$$

Assume that all instructions are unit-delays. The optimal schedule is then given by

$$
t(i, v) = \lfloor \frac{8 \cdot i + A[v]}{3} \rfloor,
$$

with $A[f] = 0$, $A[a] = 1$, $A[g] = 3$, $A[b] = 4$, $A[e] = 5$, $A[h] = 6$, $A[c] = 7$, $A[d] = 10$, $A[i] = 13$, and $A[j] = 16$. The resulting schedule of the first five iterations is shown in figure 3. Clearly, the first three iterations are scheduled differently, but the fourth iteration is scheduled as the first one, etc. We call such a schedule *3-periodic*.

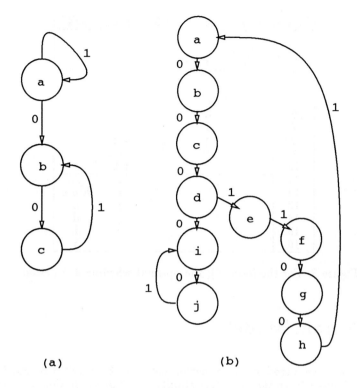

Figure 2: Dependence graphs: (a) for the loop (1) and (b) for the loop (2).

The *pattern* of the loop includes the instructions executed from time $t = 3$ to time $t = 10$ included. Its size is $3n$, where n is the number of instructions in the original loop. Also, the pattern is a loop of the form:

for $i = 0$ **to** $(N - 1)$ **div** 3 **step** 3 **do begin**

The postlude will also be a bit more complicated than in the 1-periodic case because it will depend on the value of N mod 3.

The scheduling method proposed in this paper enables the user to automatically find this schedule of optimal computation rate. Other methods are restricted to 1-periodic schedules [11]. Using that model in this example would result in a computation rate of 1/3 instead of 3/8, which is 12.5% slower. (The largest rate gives the the fastest timing.) In [10], it is shown that x-periodic schedules can be found by unrolling the loop x times and by applying a 1-periodic schedule on the unrolled loop. This is therefore an alternative to the one-step analytical procedure presented hereafter.

In this paper, we have also extended our procedure to find the optimal schedule of a given periodicity. This will enable the user to find efficiently for example this 1-periodic schedule of rate 1/3 whose resulting pattern and postlude are simpler.

□

time	i=0	i=1	i=2	i=3	i=4
0	a f				
1	b g e				
2	c h	f			
3	d	g a			
4	i	h b e			
5	j	c	a f		
6		d	b g		
7		i	c e h		
8		j	d	a f	
9			i	b g e	
10			j	c h	f
11				d	g a
12				i	h b e
13				j	c
14					d
15					i
16					j

Figure 3: For the loop (2), the optimal schedule is 3-periodic.

3   Program Model

In this section, we introduce the program model to be handled by our transformation techniques. We take the opportunity to recall the notion of dependence graph and its connected components.

Our program model consists of a class of *loops* which define a number of arrays (vectors). To simplify the model, we allow loops of the following form:

$$
\begin{aligned}
&\textbf{for } i = 0 \textbf{ to } N-1 \quad \textbf{do} \\
&\qquad S_0; \\
&\qquad S_1; \\
&\qquad ... \\
&\qquad S_{n-1}; \\
&\textbf{od}
\end{aligned}
$$

which has the following features:

- The loop has a unit step size.
- Each of the n statements in the loop body, S_v ($0 \leq v \leq n-1$), is an assigment statement defining an array (vector). All the statements in the body are of the form:

$$a[i] = f(b[i-d], ...) \tag{3}$$

where

- a and b are two vectors of N entries computed by two statements in the loop
- $a[i]$ is the ith component of a
- $b[i - d]$ is some component of b
- d is a constant integer
- f is some elementary function whose arguments are either external inputs or are of the form $b[i - v]$

In (3), the constant d is called a *dependence distance*. When $d = 0$, we call it *intra-body dependence* else it is a *loop-carried dependence*.

The basic model provides a framework to capture a reasonably wide class of loops important in scientific computation. First, the majority of time in such programs is spent in innermost loops. The main data structures computed in such loops are *arrays* and a significant fraction of their index expressions are in the form allowed by our model. For example, statements of the form

$$a'[i - u] = f(b[i - d], ...)$$

can be temporally transformed into (3) by simple renaming of $a'[i - u]$ into $a[i]$; the input arguments of the form $a'[i - d']$ must then be transformed accordingly into $a[i + u - d']$. The kernel of the body are statements defining arrays. If an assignment to a scalar variable appear in the loop body, it can be temporally transformed into an array by *scalar expansion* — a technique frequently used in vectorization/parallelization. Also, if the index range of the loop is different from $[0, N - 1]$, and/or if the step of the loop is different from one, the loop can be first normalized. as explained in [20].

Some statements of the loop can be conditional. This particular case requires a particular attention, as explained in [18].

Let us now recall the definition of *dependence graph*. The dependence graph contains as many node as there are statements in the loop body. Each of its n nodes represents in fact a particular statement. Each node v is labeled $E[v]$ which represents the time it takes to execute S_v. When all statements are unit-delays, $E[v] = 1$. The arcs between the nodes represent dependences between the associated statements. There is an arc going from node u to node v if S_v has for input argument the output variable of S_u. Now, if there are several dependences from node u to node v, only the one of minimal dependence distance is of importance (the others can be safely eliminated); the arc will be noted with that value $d[u][v]$.

It is important to observe that the number of arcs of the dependence graph, which will be noted m, is in $\mathcal{O}(n)$. Indeed, for each node, the number of incoming arcs is less than the number of arguments of the corresponding statement. Each statement being *elementary*, the number of arguments is a constant independent on n. Thus, m is in $\mathcal{O}(n)$.

4 Periodic schedules

One approach for scheduling a given loop is by looking at a partial execution history of the loop, say the first i iterations [2]. A *greedy schedule* is obtained when the statements of those i iterations are scheduled as soon as they are ready for execution. Scheduling a large enough portion of a loop's execution history in this way reveals some repetitive behavior, which can be used to obtain a good schedule [2, 8].

A drawback with the greedy schedule is that gaps of increasing length can appear between the statements. In [2], a scheduling method is presented that keeps the gaps of constant minimal size without affecting the optimality of the final code. Yet, the pattern cannot be kept of polynomial size.

On the other hand, some people suggested the use of *regular* schedules [11, 4, 19]. In that case, all iterations are scheduled in the same manner and the pattern is equal to the size of the original loop body. However, these schedules can not always achieve the maximal computation rate as demonstrated by the second example of section 2. In [10], a solution has been proposed that a loop be first unrolled x times before the application of Lam's scheduling method [11]. It was demonstrated that this combined method may achieve the maximal computation rate with a properly chosen x.

In this paper, we are interested in a uniform analytical framework to express the time-optimal loop scheduling problem for software pipelining, without requiring an extra unrolling phase. We are interested in x-periodic schedules, since they can always achieve the maximal computation rate and we present an efficient analytical method for computing them. We suggest to use schedules of the form

$$t(i, v) = \lfloor \frac{T \cdot i + A[v]}{r} \rfloor, \tag{4}$$

where $t(i, v)$ represents the starting time of the ith instance of statement S_v. The parameters of such a schedule are the following.

- T is an integer called the *period* (or *initiation interval*) of the schedule.

- r is a non-negative integer called the *periodicity*; T and r are relatively prime.

- $A[v]$ ($v \in [0, n-1]$) is a positive integer called the *offset* for statement S_v.

This class of schedules has shown to be very useful. In [16], its was proven that these schedules can always achieve the optimal computation rate for Karp-Miller computation graphs. We therefore apply this technique to loop scheduling.

Given a schedule of the form (4), its *computation rate* is r/T. Indeed, every T time units, a new set of r iterations starts executing. Note that in the particular case when $T = 0$, the computation rate is infinite. In loop scheduling, this simply means that the loop can be executed as a *forall*, all instances in parallel.

Our problem is to find the schedule of the form (4) that maximizes r/T while satisfying all the data dependence constraints. For all dependence $d[u][v]$ of the dependence graph, the schedule must satisfy

$$t(i, v) - t(i - d[u][v], u) \geq E[u], \tag{5}$$

where $E[u]$ represents the execution time of node u. With a schedule of the form (4), this constraint (5) is equivalent to

$$\lfloor \frac{T \cdot i + A[v]}{r} \rfloor - \lfloor \frac{T \cdot (i - d[u][v]) + A[u]}{r} \rfloor \geq E[u]. \tag{6}$$

If a schedule satisfies the data dependence constraints, we say that it is *valid*. To find a valid schedule of the form (4), we first consider as in [16] the use of the rational schedule

$$t^*(i, v) = \frac{T \cdot i + A[v]}{r}.$$

We will call $t^*(i, v)$ the approximant of $t(i, v) = \lfloor t^*(i, v) \rfloor$.

As proven in [18],

- If $t^*(i, v)$ is valid then $\lfloor t^*(i, v) \rfloor$ is valid.

- The computation rate of $t^*(i, v)$ is equal to the one of $\lfloor t^*(i, v) \rfloor$.

Based on these two properties, the strategy to compute a schedule of the form (4) is to find its approximant first. The approximant is subject to the constraint

$$t^*(i, v) \geq E[u] + t^*(i - d[u][v], u)$$

for all $d[u][v]$. This constraint is equivalent to

$$T \cdot d[u][v] + A[v] - A[u] \geq r \cdot E[u]. \tag{7}$$

In [16], it is shown that the maximal value of r/T that satisfy these constraints for all $d[u][v]$ of the dependence graph is a particular application of the well-known *Minimum Cost-to-Time Ratio Cycle (MCTRC)* problem. Let us recall this problem here.

Consider any simple cycle c of the dependence graph. To this cycle corresponds a particular value of the ratio

$$\frac{\sum_c E[u]}{\sum_c d[u][v]},$$

where $\sum_c E[u]$ is the sum of the operator delays along that cycle and $\sum_c d[u][v]$ is the sum of the dependence vectors. Clearly, because of (7) and because it is a cycle, the value of T/r must satisfy the constraint:

$$\frac{T}{r} \geq \frac{\sum_c E[u]}{\sum_c d[u][v]}. \tag{8}$$

This constraint must be satisfied for all simple cycle of the dependence graph. In other words, the problem is to find the simple cycle c of minimum ratio

$$\frac{\sum_c d[u][v]}{\sum_c E[u]}. \tag{9}$$

This is a particular application of the *Minimum Cost-to-Time Ratio Cycle (MC-TRC)* problem where the cost is given by the dependence values $d[u][v]$'s and the operator delays by the values of $E[u]$'s.

Let us briefly recall the complexity for solving that problem. A full description of the algorithm can be found in [12]. But basically, the idea is to use a binary search to find the appropriate value of T/r. By doing so, $\mathcal{O}(\lg n)$ particular shortest path problems are to be solved. (It is shown hereafter that the test of a particular value of T/r is achieved by solving a particular shortest path problem.) As explained in [12], the shortest path problem is solved in $\mathcal{O}(mn)$ when using Bellman-Ford algorithm. Because m is here in $\mathcal{O}(n)$, the complexity is in $\mathcal{O}(n^2)$. This complexity is further improved when using the recent Gabow-Tarjan's algorithm [7] which is in $\mathcal{O}(\sqrt{n}\, n \lg n)$ in our case. Thus the overall complexity is clearly polynomial. It is in $\mathcal{O}(n^2 \lg n)$ when using Bellman-Ford algorithm and in $\mathcal{O}(\sqrt{n}\, n \lg^2 n)$ when using Gabow-Tarjan algorithm.

In [16], it is proven that the minimum value of (9) computed on all simple cycles of the dependence graph gives the maximal computation rate that can ever be achieved by any schedule. This result is directly applicable here.

Note that once the value of T/r is known, the values of $A[v]$'s can be easily computed. Indeed, these values must obey the constraints (7) which can be rewritten

$$A[u] - A[v] \leq T \cdot d[u][v] - r \cdot E[u]. \tag{10}$$

As explained in [12], this problem is a particular shortest path problem. As explained here above, it can be solved in $\mathcal{O}(n^2)$ with Bellman-Ford algorithm and in $\mathcal{O}(\sqrt{n}\, n \lg n)$ with Gabow-Tarjan algorithm.

Theorem 1 *The schedule of the form (4) that achieves the maximal computation rate can be computed in polynomial time.*

Proof   See the above discussion. ∎

5   Conclusions

We share the points of view put forward by [9]: Loop unrolling and software pipelining are among the most important methods proposed for fine-grain loop scheduling, and the suitability of the two techniques and their relation remain to be "the most significant open research area in pipelined processor design"[9].

In this paper, we present a uniform analytical framework to express the time-optimal loop scheduling problem. That is, we have a single mathematical formulation which considers both software pipelining and loop unrolling. The paper is a short version of [18] in which:

- We establish polynomial bounds for the optimal schedule, i.e. bounds on its period, its periodicity, the pattern size, and the computation rate.

- We show that the optimal schedule of a given periodicity can be found by solving an additional shortest path problem.

- We show that the optimal schedule of a given computation rate can be found by solving a particular shortest path problem.

- We illustrate what can be done in the presence of conditionals.

- We show how the connected components of the dependence graph can be used to accelerate the computation of the schedule.

- An example of a forall loop is given and treated with the general scheduling technique of this paper.

Yet, there are important aspects this paper has not addressed. One question is the handling of resource constraints in the mathematical framework proposed in this paper. At this moment, we can only suggest to apply list-scheduling on the pattern of the optimal schedule. Another question is how to extend the proposed method to multidimensional loops. Finally, an implementation of this method in a real life compiler will also be an interesting task by itself. We are currently exploring these problems.

Acknowledgments

We wish to express our gratitude to P. Wong and M. Latendresse for their fruitful remarks.

References

[1] A. Aiken. Compaction-based parallelization. (PhD thesis), Technical Report 88–922, Cornell University, 1988.

[2] A. Aiken and A. Nicolau. Optimal loop parallelization. In *Proceedings of the 1988 ACM SIGPLAN Conference on Programming Languages Design and Implementation*, June 1988.

[3] A. Aiken and A. Nicolau. A realistic resource-constrained software pipelining algorithm. In *Proceedings of the Third Workshop on Programming Languages and Compilers for Parallel Computing*, Irvine, CA, August 1990.

[4] Ron Cytron. Doacross: Beyond vectorization for multiprocessors. *Proceedings of the 1986 International Conference on Parallel Processing*, pages 836–844, August 1986.

[5] K. Ebcioğlu. A compilation technique for software pipelining of loops with conditional jumps. In *Proceedings of the 20th Annual Workshop on Microprogramming*, December 1987.

[6] K. Ebcioğlu and A. Nicolau. A global resource-constrained parallelization technique. In *Proceedings of the ACM SIGARCH International Conference on Supercomputing*, June 1989.

[7] H. Gabow and R. Tarjan. Faster scaling algorithms for network problems. *SIAM J. Computing*, October 1989.

[8] G. R. Gao, Y. B. Wong, and Qi Ning. A Petri-Net model for fine-grain loop scheduling. In *Proceedings of the '91 ACM-SIGPLAN Conference on Programming Language Design and Implementation*, pages 204–218, Toronto, Canada, June 1991.

[9] J. L. Hennessy and D. A. Patterson. *Computer Architecture: A Quantitative Approach*. Morgan Kaufmann Publishers, Inc., 1990.

[10] R. B. Jones and H. A. Allan. Software pipelining: A comparison and improvement. In *Proceedings of the 23th Annual Workshop on Microprogramming and Microarchitecture*, pages 46–56, Orlando, Florida, November 1990.

[11] Monica Lam. Software pipelining: An effective scheduling technique for VLIW machines. In *Proceedings of the 1988 ACM SIGPLAN Conference on Programming Languages Design and Implementation*, pages 318–328, Atlanta, GA, June 1988.

[12] Eugene Lawler. *Combinatorial Optimization: Networks and Matroids*. Saunders College Publishing, 1976.

[13] A. Nicolau, K. Pingali, and A. Aiken. Fine-grain compilation for pipelined machines. Technical Report TR-88-934, Department of Computer Science, Cornell University, Ithaca, NY, 1988.

[14] Pierre Peladeau. On the length of the cyclic frustrum in a sdsp-pn. Technical Report ACAPS Technical Note 31, McGill University, Montreal, 1991.

[15] B. R. Rau and C. D. Glaeser. Some scheduling techniques and an easily schedulable horizontal architecture for high performance scientific computing. In *Proceedings of the 14th Annual Workshop on Microprogramming*, pages 183–198, 1981.

[16] Raymond Reiter. Scheduling parallel computations. *Journal of the ACM*, 15(4):590–599, 1968.

[17] R. F. Touzeau. A FORTRAN compiler for the FPS-164 scientific computer. In *Proceedings of the ACM SIGPLAN '84 Symposium on Compiler Construction*, pages 48–57, June 1984.

[18] V. Van Dongen and G. Gao. A polynomial time method for optimal software pipelining. Technical Report ACAPS Tech. Memo 37, McGill University, School of Computer Science, 1992.

[19] A Zaky and P. Sadayappan. Optimal static scheduling of sequential loops on multiprocessors. In *Proceedings of the 1989 Internat. Conf. on Parallel Processing*, volume 3, pages 130–137, 1989.

[20] Hans Zima and Barbara Chapman. *Supercompilers for Parallel and Vector Computers*. ACM Press, New York, 1990.

Scheduling Loops on Parallel Processors: A Simple Algorithm with Close to Optimum Performance

Franco Gasperoni[1] and Uwe Schwiegelshohn[2]

[1] gasperon@cs.nyu.edu
CIMS-NYU, 251 Mercer Street, New York, NY 10012
[2] uwe@watson.ibm.com
IBM Research Center, P.O. Box 218, Yorktown Heights, NY 10598

Abstract. This paper addresses the NP-hard problem of scheduling a cyclic set of interdependent operations, representing a program loop, when a finite number of identical processors are available. We give a simple and efficient algorithm producing close to optimum results. As a side result our algorithm guarantees optimality when the number of processors is infinite.

1 Introduction

With advances in hardware technology most of today's high performance microprocessors and computers offer some degree of parallelism. To take advantage of this concurrency a common approach has been to employ parallelizing compilers which automatically extract the parallelism present in sequential programs. Most of the concurrency present in these applications is expressed in the form of loops and considerable efforts have been devoted to loop parallelization ([6, 7, 8, 9] to name a few). Because this problem is NP-hard when the target machine has finite resources (see section 2), loop parallelization algorithms have assumed infinitely many processors or have validated performance results only by means of benchmarking. Our goal is to provide a simple and efficient loop parallelization algorithm with close to optimum performance when the number of available processors is finite.

In our machine model time is viewed as a discrete rather than continuous entity. A time instant is called a "cycle" or "execution cycle". The machine itself consists of p identical processors. There is no preemption: once started, an operation has to be executed without interruption. Two type of processors will be considered: pipelined and unpipelined. In the pipelined case p new operations can be *initiated* every cycle even though the operations initiated in the previous cycle may not have completed yet. In the unpipelined case a new operation can be initiated on a given processor only if the operation previously *executing* on that processor has completed. Note that if all operations take one cycle to execute the two machine models are equivalent.

A program loop is modeled as a doubly weighted directed graph $G = (O, E, \delta, d)$, called dependence graph, where the vertex set O is the set of operations to execute, δ is a mapping from O in the positive integers giving the duration of each operation, E is the edge set of G and d a mapping from E into the non-negative integers. E and d specify operation dependences. More specifically an edge $e = (op, op') \in E$ with weight $d(e)$ states that for every iteration $i \geq d(e)$ of the loop, operation op' depends on the outcome of operation op in iteration $i - d(e)$ and cannot be initiated until its completion. The only restriction imposed on the edge weight function d is that every cycle in G contain at least one edge with positive weight. An example of a program loop and the corresponding dependence graph is given in figure 1.

Let $\mathbb{N}$ denote the set of non-negative integers and let $|S|$ denote the cardinality

```
FOR i IN 0..n LOOP
    a[i] := a[i]+d[i-2];  -- op₁
    b[i] := a[i]/e[i-2];  -- op₂
    c[i] := a[i]*e[i-2];  -- op₃
    d[i] := c[i]+b[i-1];  -- op₄
    e[i] := e[i]+b[i]  ;  -- op₅
END LOOP;
```

(a)

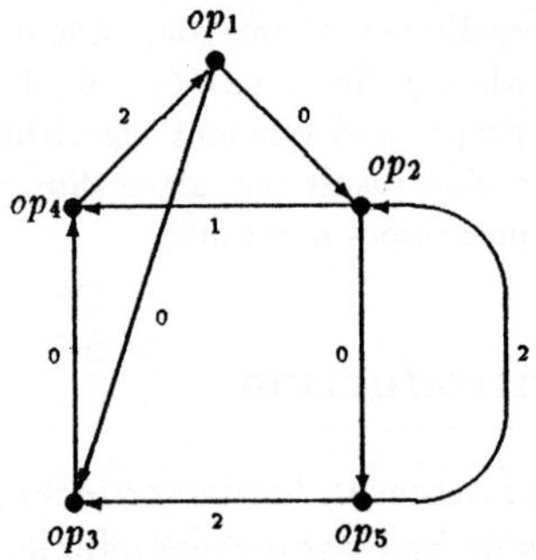

(b)

Fig. 1. (a) Some loop. (b) The dependence graph G for the loop in (a). Each edge e is labeled by its $d(e)$ value. Operation durations are 1 cycle except for op_2, $\delta(op_2) = 2$.

of a set S. Given a loop under the form of a dependence graph $G = (O, E, \delta, d)$ and a p processors machine, the LOOP PARALLELIZATION PROBLEM consists in:

Constructing a schedule σ, that is a mapping from $O \times \mathbb{N}$ into $\mathbb{N}$ (where $\sigma(op, i)$ denotes the execution cycle in which the instance of operation op in iteration i is initiated) such that the following constraints are met:

Resource constraint: In the case of pipelined processors no more than p operations are *initiated* in the same cycle:

$$\forall t \in \mathbb{N} \quad |\{(op, i) \,:\, \sigma(op, i) = t\}| \leq p$$

In the case of unpipelined processors no more than p operations are *executing* in the same cycle:

$$\forall t \in \mathbb{N} \quad |\{(op, i) \,:\, \sigma(op, i) \leq t < \sigma(op, i) + \delta(op)\}| \leq p$$

Dependence constraint: the schedule σ respects loop dependences, that is:

$$\forall e = (op, op') \in E \quad \forall i \in \mathbb{N} \quad \sigma(op, i) + \delta(op) \leq \sigma(op', i + d(e))$$

Cyclicity constraint: σ must be expressible in the form of a loop, that is there exists a non negative integer λ, called the initiation interval of σ, such that:

$$\forall op \in O \quad \forall i \in \mathbb{N} \quad \sigma(op, i) = \sigma(op, 0) + \lambda \cdot i$$

Because the input loop is supposed to execute many iterations we will focus on the asymptotic behavior of σ. The initiation interval λ is therefore a natural performance estimator of σ ($1/\lambda$ measures σ's throughput). Note that if the target machine has an infinite number of processors and the dependence graph of the input loop is acyclic, λ can be null. This type of schedule has infinite throughput.

Let $n = |O|$ denote the number of operations, m the number of edges in the input dependence graph, $\delta_{max} = \max_{op \in O} \delta(op)$ and p the number of processors. Our algorithm is simple, runs in $Order(n\,m\,\log(n\,\delta_{max}))$ time and yields a schedule whose initiation interval λ_∞ is optimum when infinitely many processors are available ($p = \infty$). When $p < \infty$ let λ_{opt} denote the optimum initiation interval and let λ denote the initiation interval generated by our algorithm. Then for pipelined processors we guarantee that

$$\lambda - \lambda_{opt} \leq \left(1 - \frac{1}{p \cdot \delta_{max}}\right) \cdot \lambda_\infty \quad \text{and} \quad \frac{\lambda}{\lambda_{opt}} \leq 2 - \frac{1}{p \cdot \delta_{max}}$$

whereas and for unpipelined processors we guarantee:

$$\lambda - \lambda_{opt} \leq \left(1 - \frac{1}{p}\right) \cdot (\lambda_\infty + \delta_{max} - 1) \quad \text{and} \quad \frac{\lambda}{\lambda_{opt}} \leq 2 - \frac{1}{p} + \frac{p-1}{p} \cdot \frac{\delta_{max} - 1}{\lambda_{opt}}$$

Previous work in loop parallelization by Iwano & Yeh [6] assumes $p = \infty$. Their relatively complex algorithm yields an optimum schedule whose running time is $Order(n\,m\,\log(n\,\delta_{max}\,d_{max}))$, where $d_{max} = \max_{e \in E} d(e)$. Zaky & Sadayappan [9] have employed an algebraic approach to solve the same problem. Their polynomial time algorithm, however, has greater running time complexity than the combinatorial technique of Iwano & Yeh. The result of Iwano & Yeh and Zaky & Sadayappan can be adapted to machines with $p < \infty$ processors only if $\delta_{max} = 1$. In this case the performance of the generated schedule is at most a factor $2 - 1/p$ from the optimum. The work of Munshi & Simons [8] assumes $\delta_{max} = 1$ and infinitely many processors. Their machine model, however, differs from ours in that operations of a same loop iteration are required to execute on a same processor. This restriction makes the loop parallelization problem NP-hard even in the absence of resource constraints. Munshi & Simons give a simple linear time algorithm yielding a schedule whose performance is at most 3 times the optimum. They also give polynomial time algorithms for optimally solving some special cases.

2   The Loop Parallelization Algorithm

In its general form the problem studied in this paper is NP-hard. This can be easily seen by reducing the acyclic scheduling problem (called precedence constrained scheduling problem in [4]), to the loop parallelization problem. Informally the acyclic scheduling problem is the acyclic version of the loop parallelization problem. An instance of the acyclic scheduling problem consists of a directed *acyclic* graph $G' = (O, E)$, a duration function δ, a number p of processors and a deadline D. Again the vertex set O represents a set of operations and the acyclic edge set E embodies the dependences between these operations. Each operation op requires $\delta(op)$ cycles to complete. The goal is to decide whether there exists a schedule σ_a, that is a mapping from O into the non-negative integers, such that the processor and dependence constraints are satisfied and the length of schedule σ_a, $\max_{op}(\sigma_a(op) + \delta(op))$ is less then the deadline D. In its full generality the acyclic scheduling problem is NP-hard [4].

To reduce the acyclic scheduling problem to the loop parallelization problem we create a loop (and the corresponding dependence graph) where each iteration has the same operations and dependences as those indicated by the acyclic graph G'. In addition for all $i \geq 1$, all the operations in iteration i are set to depend on all the operations of iteration $i - 1$. The duration function δ is unchanged. Suppose we could build in polynomial time an optimum schedule for the previously constructed loop and the number of processors p. Let λ_{opt} denote the initiation interval of such loop schedule. Then by comparing the deadline D with λ_{opt}, which is nothing but the completion time of the last operation scheduled in the zero-th iteration, it would be possible to decide, in polynomial time, whether the given instance of the acyclic scheduling problem has a solution or not.

As previously mentioned the acyclic scheduling problem is, in its full generality, NP-hard. However when $p = 2$ and operations take a single cycle to execute, a polynomial time algorithm for the acyclic scheduling problem was presented by Coffman & Graham [2]. It is open whether for unit time operation durations and any fixed $p \geq 3$ the acyclic scheduling problem can be solved in polynomial time [4]. However if operations are allowed to last 1 and 2 cycles and the processors are unpipelined, the acyclic scheduling problem is NP-complete even for $p = 2$.

The algorithm of Coffman & Graham builds on the *list scheduling* framework [1]. List scheduling algorithms work as follows. Operations are ordered in a priority list. At any given instant where a processor is available an operation is initiated by selecting the first operation in the priority list all of whose predecessors in the dependence graph have finished executing. For an unpipelined p processor machine any list scheduling algorithm guarantees a schedule length at most $(2 - 1/p)$ times the optimum [1]. If the processors are pipelined this bound can easily be shown to be $(2 - 1/(p \cdot \delta_{max}))$ (see next section). If operations have arbitrary durations these optimality bounds are the best known so far.

As the reduction at the beginning of this section shows, every polynomial time approximation algorithm for the loop parallelization problem can be used to approximate optimality for the acyclic scheduling problem. Thus the goal of our algorithm is to generate a loop schedule whose worst case performance is as close as possible to $(2 - 1/(p \cdot \delta_{max}))$ times the optimum in the pipelined case and $(2 - 1/p)$ in the unpipelined case.

The overall idea of the algorithm is to decouple the processor constraint from the cyclic dependence constraints. In a first step we relax the restriction on the number of processors to pinpoint critical operation dependences and determine the optimum initiation interval λ_∞ for $p = \infty$. The value λ_∞ plays a critical role when re-introducing processor constraints. In fact we use this best possible initiation interval to break dependence cycles and generate an acyclic dependence graph. Effectively we have transformed the loop parallelization problem into an acyclic scheduling problem. By employing a simple list scheduling algorithm on the acyclic dependence graph we finally derive the core of our loop schedule.

2.1 Optimal Loop Parallelization for Infinite Processor Machines

The idea of the algorithm in the $p = \infty$ case is to start operations as early as possible, in a controlled fashion. The critical cycle of the input dependence graph determines the optimum initiation interval λ_∞ from which the earliest starting time of any operation is easily computed.

Input: A dependence graph $G = (O, E, \delta, d)$.
Output: A loop schedule σ_∞ which meets the cyclicity and dependence constraints stated in the introduction and is optimum when infinitely many pipelined or unpipelined processors are available.
Algorithm:

1. Associate to each edge $e = (op, op') \in E$ the length $t(e) = \delta(op) - \rho \cdot d(e)$, where ρ is some parameter. Add a vertex s to G and the edges (s, op) for each $op \in O$. Set the length of these edges to 0. Find λ_∞, the smallest non-negative integer value of ρ such that G has no positive length cycle. If G is acyclic then $\lambda_\infty = 0$. Otherwise as every cycle of G contains at least one edge e such that $d(e) \geq 1$, λ_∞ is in the interval $[0, n \, \delta_{max}]$ and can be computed in $Order(n \, m \, \log(n \, \delta_{max}))$ time by employing the Bellman-Ford single source longest paths algorithm [3] in conjunction with a binary search on the interval $[0, n \, \delta_{max}]$. If we take the newly introduced vertex s as the source in the Bellman-Ford algorithm, the above procedure also yields the length of the longest path from s to any operation op when λ_∞ is substituted to ρ. Let $t(s, op)$ denote such longest path.

2. For all $op \in O$ and $i \in \mathbb{N}$:

$$\sigma_\infty(op, i) = t(s, op) + \lambda_\infty \cdot i$$

Figure 2 illustrates the above algorithm on the loop of figure 1. Note that if we allowed time to be continuous rather then discrete, i.e. a real instead of an integer, we can obtain a schedule with better throughput than the schedule of figure 2, namely $\lambda_\infty = 3/2$ rather then $\lambda_\infty = 2$. Alternatively if we keep time discrete but allow "loop unrolling" we can still guarantee a throughput of two iterations every 3 cycles, which corresponds to $\lambda_\infty = 3/2$. For a formal treatment of these two extensions please refer to [5].

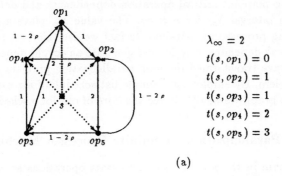

$$\lambda_\infty = 2$$
$$t(s, op_1) = 0$$
$$t(s, op_2) = 1$$
$$t(s, op_3) = 1$$
$$t(s, op_4) = 2$$
$$t(s, op_5) = 3$$

(a)

time	iter. 0	iter. 1	$\cdots$
0	op_1		
1	op_2	op_3	
2	op_4	op_1	
3	op_5	op_2	op_3
4		op_4	
5		op_5	

(b)

time	iter. 0	iter. 1	$\cdots$
0	op_1		
1	op_2	op_3	
2	$\times$	op_4	op_1
3	op_5	op_2	op_3
4		$\times$	op_4
5		op_5	

(c)

Fig. 2. (a) The transformed graph. Dotted edges have length 0. (b) Schedule for the pipelined case. (c) Schedule for the unpipelined case.

Theorem 1. *Given a dependence graph $G = (O, E, \delta, d)$ the previous algorithm generates a schedule meeting the dependence and cyclicity constraints stated in the introduction. Furthermore the schedule is optimum when infinitely many pipelined or unpipelined processors are available.*

Proof. The schedule generated by the previous algorithm clearly meets the cyclicity constraint. To show that dependence constraints are also satisfied consider an edge $e = (op, op') \in E$. We would like to show that

$$\forall i \in \mathbb{N} \quad \sigma_\infty(op, i) + \delta(op) \leq \sigma_\infty(op', i + d(e))$$

By virtue of the longest path inequalities one can write

$$t(s, op) + \delta(op) - \lambda_\infty \cdot d(e) \leq t(s, op')$$

and therefore

$$\sigma_\infty(op, i) + \delta(op) = t(s, op) + \lambda_\infty \cdot i + \delta(op) \leq$$

$$\leq t(s, op') + \lambda_\infty \cdot (i + d(e)) = \sigma_\infty(op', i + d(e))$$

Thus it remains to show that σ_∞ is optimum. If G is acyclic then $\lambda_\infty = 0$ and σ_∞ is clearly optimum. If G contains a cycle and σ_∞ is not optimum there must exist a cyclic schedule σ_0 which meets G's dependence constraints and has an initiation interval $\lambda_0 \in \mathbb{N}$ such that $\lambda_0 < \lambda_\infty$. Let C be an arbitrary cycle in G, $\delta(C)$ the sum of the durations of the operations traversed by C and $d(C)$ the sum of the dependence distances of the edges comprising C. Let op be any operation in C, then

$$\sigma_0(op, 0) + \delta(C) \leq \sigma_0(op, d(C)) = \sigma_0(op, 0) + \lambda_0 \cdot d(C)$$

Thus for every cycle C in G we have $\delta(C) - \lambda_0 \cdot d(C) \leq 0$ which contradicts the fact that λ_∞ is the smallest integer to verify this inequality.

2.2 The Parallelization Algorithm for Finite Processor Machines

Given a dependence graph G, the algorithm for the finite processor case converts G into an acyclic dependence graph G' and invokes a list scheduling algorithm on G' to construct the core of the loop schedule. The dependence graph G' is obtained by deleting certain critical edges from G. The difficult part when cutting edges is to shorten dependence paths as much as possible while making sure that dependence constraints will not be violated when constructing a list schedule from G'. The schedule generated in the infinite processors case will be the base for the edge deletion procedure.

Input: A dependence graph $G = (O, E, \delta, d)$ and a number of processors p.
Output: A cyclic schedule σ meeting the processor and dependence constraints as well as the performance bounds stated in the introduction.
Algorithm:

1. Do step 1 of the loop parallelization algorithm for infinite processor machines, that is compute λ_∞ and $t(s, op)$ for each $op \in O$.
2. Let $e = (op, op')$ be an edge of G and let $\pi(op) = t(s, op) \bmod \lambda_\infty$ if $\lambda_\infty > 0$ and $\pi(op) = 0$ if $\lambda_\infty = 0$. Then we delete e from G if and only if

   $$\pi(op') < \pi(op) + \delta(op)$$

   Note that if $\lambda_\infty \leq 1$ all edges get deleted. The resulting graph G' is acyclic (see lemma 2). This step takes $Order(m)$ time.
3. For the purpose of pipelined processors we define $\Delta(op)$ for each $op \in O$ to be $\Delta(op) = \min(\delta(op), \lambda_\infty - \pi(op))$. Note that if $\Delta(op) < \delta(op)$ we must have $\lambda_\infty < \pi(op) + \delta(op)$ which implies that every edge (op, op') in G has been deleted since $\pi(op') \leq \lambda_\infty$.
4. Consider the acyclic scheduling instance whose dependence graph is G'. Operation durations are given by the function δ if the processors are unpipelined and by the function Δ if the processors are pipelined. Use any list scheduling algorithm to generate a schedule σ_a that can be executed

on a p pipelined/unpipelined processors machine and meets G' dependences. In addition for pipelined processors we require that no operation op is scheduled before cycle $\pi(op)$. This step takes $Order(m + n \log n)$ time.

5. Let $\mu(op) = \lfloor t(s, op)/\lambda_\infty \rceil$ if $\lambda_\infty \geq 1$ and $\mu(op) = t(s, op)$ if $\lambda_\infty = 0$. Let λ be the length of σ_a, that is $\lambda = \max_{op}(\sigma_a(op) + \Delta(op))$ for pipelined processors and $\lambda = \max_{op}(\sigma_a(op) + \delta(op))$ for unpipelined processors. Then for all $op \in O$ and $i \in \mathbb{N}$:

$$\sigma(op, i) = \sigma_a(op) + \mu(op) \cdot \lambda + i \cdot \lambda$$

Figure 3 illustrates the above algorithm on the loop of figure 1.

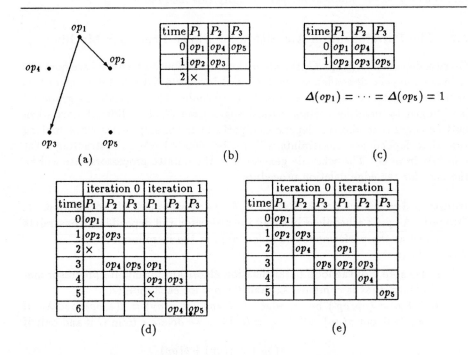

Fig. 3. (a) The graph G'. (b) The schedule σ_a when 3 unpipelined processors P_1, P_2 and P_3 are available. (c) The schedule σ_a for the pipelined case. (d) The overall schedule for the unpipelined case. (e) The overall schedule for the pipelined case.

Note that in point 5 of the algorithm we could have used $\mu(op) = t(s, op)$ for all values of λ_∞. This modification has the advantage of simplyfing the proof that dependences are preserved in σ (theorem 3), but has the disadvantage of delaying roughly by a factor of λ_∞ cycles the materialization of the steady state. In other words if $\mu(op) = t(s, op)$ the last operation of the 0-th iteration initiates in cycle

$\max_{op}(\sigma_a(op) + \lambda \cdot t(s, op))$ whereas for the value of μ used in the algorithm it initiates in cycle $\max_{op}(\sigma_a(op) + \lambda \cdot \lfloor t(s, op)/\lambda_\infty \rfloor)$.

The first step in proving the correctness of the algorithm is to show that schedule σ_a can be constructed, that is the graph G' obtained in step 2 of the algorithm is acyclic.

Lemma 2. *The graph G' obtained in step 2 of the previous algorithm is acyclic. Furthermore let the duration of a path $P = (op_1, op_2), (op_2, op_3), \cdots, (op_{c-1}, op_c)$ of G' be defined as:*

$$\delta(P) = \sum_{i=1}^{c} \delta(op_i) \quad \text{for unpipelined processors}$$

$$\Delta(P) = \pi(op_1) + \sum_{i=1}^{c} \Delta(op_i) \quad \text{for pipelined processors}$$

Then for all paths P of G'

$$\delta(P) \le \lambda_\infty + \delta_{max} - 1 \quad \text{and} \quad \Delta(P) \le \lambda_\infty$$

Proof. Let C be a cycle in G comprising edges $(op_1, op_2), \ldots, (op_c, op_1)$. Suppose that no edge was deleted from C. Then

$$\forall 1 \le i \le c \quad \pi(op_i) + \delta(op_i) \le \pi(op_{1+i \bmod c})$$

Thus $\pi(op_1) + \delta(op_1) \le \pi(op_1)$, a contradiction.

For the second part of the lemma let $P = (op_1, op_2), (op_2, op_3), \cdots, (op_{c-1}, op_c)$ be a path of G'. Because of the edge deletion condition we must have

$$\forall 1 \le i < c \quad \pi(op_i) + \delta(op_i) \le \pi(op_{i+1})$$

therefore by adding these $c - 1$ inequalities together we obtain:

$$\pi(op_c) \ge \pi(op_1) + \sum_{i=1}^{c-1} \delta(op_i)$$

Thus for unpipelined processors $\delta(P) \le \pi(op_c) + \delta(op_c) \le \lambda_\infty - 1 + \delta_{max}$. For pipelined processors given the remark of step 3 of the algorithm and the fact that for $1 \le i < c$, op_i has an outgoing edge in G' we have $\delta(op_i) = \Delta(op_i)$. Furthermore since $\lambda_\infty - \pi(op_c) \ge \Delta(op_c)$ we easily obtain

$$\lambda_\infty \ge \pi(op_1) + \sum_{i=1}^{c} \Delta(op_i)$$

Theorem 3. *Given a dependence graph $G = (O, E, \delta, d)$ and p pipelined or unpipelined processors, the previous algorithm generates a schedule meeting the resource, dependence and cyclicity constraints stated in the introduction.*

Proof. Regardless of processor type the schedule σ generated by the algorithm clearly satisfies the cyclicity constraint.

Because the schedule σ is obtained by infinitely repeating the pattern given by the acyclic schedule σ_a and because the value of λ is chosen so that no two consecutive repetitions of σ_a overlap, σ meets processor constraints if and only if σ_a does, which is guaranteed by step 4 of the algorithm.

It remains to show that σ meets the dependence constraints. This is true if and only if

$$\forall e = (op, op') \in E \quad \forall i \in \mathbb{N} \quad \sigma(op, i) + \delta(op) \leq \sigma(op', i + d(e))$$

Because of the definition of σ the previous inequality can be rewritten as

$$\sigma_a(op) + \delta(op) + \lambda \cdot \mu(op) \leq \sigma_a(op') + \lambda \cdot (d(e) + \mu(op'))$$

the proof that the above inequality holds relies on the longest paths inequality

$$t(s, op) + (\delta(op) - \lambda_\infty \cdot d(e)) \leq t(s, op')$$

There are two cases to consider depending on whether edge $e = (op, op')$ has been deleted by the algorithm in step 2. If e has not been deleted then $\lambda_\infty > 0$, $\Delta(op) = \delta(op)$ and both pipelined and unpipelined cases can be treated equally. Namely in both cases $\sigma_a(op) + \delta(op) \leq \sigma_a(op')$. Furthermore by dividing the longest path inequality by λ_∞ and taking the floor one obtains $\mu(op) \leq d(e) + \mu(op')$ and consequently by combining the two previous inequalities one can see that the dependence constraint is respected in σ when edge $e = (op, op')$ has not been deleted.

If on the contrary edge e has been deleted in step 2 then it must be that $\pi(op') < \pi(op) + \delta(op)$. Let us first assume tha $\lambda_\infty > 0$. Then $t(s, op) = \pi(op) + \mu(op) \cdot \lambda_\infty$. Thus by rewriting the longest path inequality as:

$$\pi(op) + \delta(op) + \mu(op) \cdot \lambda_\infty - d(e) \cdot \lambda_\infty \leq \pi(op') + \mu(op') \cdot \lambda_\infty$$

one derives $0 < \mu(op') + d(e) - \mu(op)$. If $\Delta(op) = \delta(op)$ then regardless of the processors type one can write

$$\sigma_a(op) + \delta(op) - \sigma_a(op') \leq \lambda \leq \lambda \cdot (\mu(op') + d(e) - \mu(op))$$

and thus the dependence constraint is met. It remains to consider the case when processors are pipelined and $\Delta(op) < \delta(op)$. Again from the longest path inequality we derive

$$\pi(op) + \Delta(op) + \delta(op) - \Delta(op) + (\mu(op) - d(e)) \cdot \lambda_\infty \leq \pi(op') + \mu(op') \cdot \lambda_\infty$$

Because of the definition of Δ we have $\pi(op) + \Delta(op) = \lambda_\infty$ thus

$$\lambda_\infty \leq \pi(op') - (\delta(op) - \Delta(op)) + \lambda_\infty \cdot (\mu(op') + d(e) - \mu(op))$$

because $\pi(op') - (\delta(op) - \Delta(op)) < \lambda_\infty$ it must be that $0 < \mu(op') + d(e) - \mu(op)$ and therefore for all $\lambda \geq \lambda_\infty$ we have

$$\lambda \leq \pi(op') - (\delta(op) - \Delta(op)) + \lambda \cdot (\mu(op') + d(e) - \mu(op))$$

because $\sigma_a(op') \geq \pi(op')$ we obtain

$$\sigma_a(op) + \Delta(op) \leq \sigma_a(op') - (\delta(op) - \Delta(op)) + \lambda \cdot (\mu(op') + d(e) - \mu(op))$$

By simple algebraic manipulation we arrive to

$$\sigma_a(op) + \delta(op) - \sigma_a(op') \leq \lambda \cdot (\mu(op') + d(e) - \mu(op))$$

Thus provided $\lambda_\infty > 0$ the dependence constraint embodied by edge $e = (op, op')$ is met in all cases.

To show that the theorem equally applies to the case $\lambda_\infty = 0$ it suffices to show that $0 < \mu(op') + d(e) - \mu(op)$. The proof then proceeds as in the case $\lambda_\infty > 0$ for both type of processors. To show that the above inequality holds one needs to remark that when $\lambda_\infty = 0$ the longest path inequality becomes $0 < \delta(op) \leq \mu(op') - \mu(op)$ and therefore $0 < \mu(op') + d(e) - \mu(op)$.

Theorem 4. *Let G be a dependence graph, λ the initiation interval of the schedule generated by our algorithm when p processors are available, λ_{opt} the best possible initiation interval and λ_∞ the optimum performance when infinitely many processors are available. Then for pipelined processors*

$$\lambda - \lambda_{opt} \leq \left(1 - \frac{1}{p \cdot \delta_{max}}\right) \cdot \lambda_\infty \quad and \quad \frac{\lambda}{\lambda_{opt}} \leq 2 - \frac{1}{p \cdot \delta_{max}}$$

and for unpipelined processors

$$\lambda - \lambda_{opt} \leq \left(1 - \frac{1}{p}\right) \cdot (\lambda_\infty + \delta_{max} - 1) \quad and \quad \frac{\lambda}{\lambda_{opt}} \leq 2 - \frac{1}{p} + \frac{p-1}{p} \cdot \frac{\delta_{max} - 1}{\lambda_{opt}}$$

Proof. Let us first consider the simpler case of unpipelined processors. Clearly λ_{opt} is bounded by the duration of operations in O and the number of available processors p: $\sum_{op \in O} \delta(op) \leq p \cdot \lambda_{opt}$. Let ϕ denote the overall time in σ_a when no more than $p-1$ processors are busy. Because σ_a is generated by a list scheduling algorithm there must exist a dependence path P in G' such that $\phi \leq \delta(P)$. Thus by employing the previous inequality and the result of lemma 2 we obtain

$$p \cdot \lambda \leq \sum_{op \in O} \delta(op) + (p-1) \cdot \phi \leq p \cdot \lambda_{opt} + (p-1) \cdot (\lambda_\infty + (\delta_{max} - 1))$$

which implies the stated results since clearly $\lambda_\infty \leq \lambda_{opt}$.

The case of pipelined processors is similar. Let $H_1, H_2, \cdots, H_p$ respectively denote the overall number of cycles in the acyclic schedule σ_a in which no operation is initiated on processors $1, 2, \cdots, p$. Let P be the path in G' with greatest $\Delta(P)$. Because σ_a is generated using a list scheduling algorithm at least one operation is initiated every δ_{max} cycles, thus

$$\sum_{i=1}^{p} H_i \leq p \cdot \Delta(P) - \frac{\Delta(P)}{\delta_{max}} \leq p \cdot \lambda_\infty - \frac{\lambda_\infty}{\delta_{max}}$$

Since $|O| \leq p \cdot \lambda_{opt}$ we derive

$$p \cdot \lambda = |O| + \sum_{i=1}^{p} H_i \leq p \cdot \lambda_{opt} + p \cdot \lambda_\infty - \frac{\lambda_\infty}{\delta_{max}}$$

which yields the desired results since $\lambda_\infty \leq \lambda_{opt}$.

3 Conclusion

In this paper we have presented a simple and efficient loop parallelization algorithm. The algorithm guarantees optimality when the number of processors is infinite and a worst case performance of roughly twice the optimum when only finitely many processors are available.

The algorithm described in this paper can easily be extended to accomodate non integer operation durations and initiation intervals. It can also be extended to allow for a more general definition of cyclicity (for both extensions see [5]).

Acknowledgments. We wish to thank the anonymous referees for their comments which have improved the clarity and correctness of the paper.

References

1. E. G. COFFMAN, *Computer and Job-shop Scheduling Theory*, John Wiley and Sons, New York, New York, 1976.
2. E. G. COFFMAN AND R. L. GRAHAM, *Optimal scheduling for two processor systems*, Acta Informatica, 1 (1972), pp. 200–213.
3. T. H. CORMEN, C. E. LEISERSON, AND R. L. RIVEST, *Introduction to Algorithms*, MIT Press and Mc Graw Hill, 1990.
4. M. R. GAREY AND D. S. JOHNSON, *Computers and Intractability - A Guide to the Theory of NP-Completeness*, Freeman, New York, New York, 1979.
5. F. GASPERONI AND U. SCHWIEGELSHOHN, *Efficient algorithms for cyclic scheduling*, IBM technical report RC 17068, August 1992.
6. K. IWANO AND S. YEH, *An efficient algorithm for optimal loop parallelization*, in International Symposium on Algorithms, Springer-Verlag, Aug. 1990, pp. 201–210. Lecture Notes in Computer Science 450.
7. M. LAM, *Software pipelining: An effective scheduling technique for VLIW machines*, Proceedings of the SIGPLAN'88 Conference on Programming Language Design and Implementation, June 1988, pp. 318–328.
8. A. MUNSHI AND B. SIMONS, *Scheduling loops on processors: algorithms and complexity*, SIAM Journal of Computing, 19 (1990), pp. 728–741.
9. A. ZAKY AND P. SADAYAPPAN, *Optimal static scheduling of sequential loops on multiprocessors*, in International Conference on Parallel Processing, IEEE, Aug. 1989, pp. III–(130–137).

This article was processed using the LaTeX macro package with LLNCS style

Automatic Parallelization of Grid-based Applications for the iPSC/860

Edward J. Kushner

Intel Supercomputer Systems Division,
15201 NW Greenbrier Pkwy, Beaverton, OR 97006
kushner@ssd.intel.com

Abstract

The need to invest considerable time and effort to modify programs written in FORTRAN 77 so that they run in parallel has impacted the use of MIMD computers like the iPSC/860. The difficulty associated with very large codes has provided motivation for a number of research efforts to develop tools that reduce the parallelization effort. Very recently, these efforts have progressed to the point where semi-automatic parallelization is possible for a very important class of problems, the so called grid-based applications.

Three examples of such tools are FORGE 90, Pfortran and Fortran Linda. This paper describes success in using these tools to parallelize 3 grid-based applications. All three tools were used on a numerical weather prediction benchmark. In addition FORGE 90 was applied to two other programs from the NAS collection of parallel benchmarks. All 3 programs are of the order of a few thousand lines of FORTRAN 77 code and were converted to run in parallel using FORGE 90 in a day or two. Parallelization by hand took 2 - 3 week while the use of Pfortran and Fortran Linda each required about a week. Comparison of performance results for the various methods indicates that FORGE 90 achieves about 50 to 65% of the performance of the hand-coded version while Pfortran and Linda achieves 75 to 90% of the same performance.

1 Introduction

The need to invest considerable time and effort to modify application codes written in FORTRAN 77 so that they run in parallel has impacted the use of distributed-memory message-passing computers. For SIMD systems the approach is usually to rewrite the application in FORTRAN 90 and then invoke the automatic message-passing facility of these machines. For MIMD systems like the iPSC/860, the approach is to modify the code in a few areas by the insertion of message-passing routines that allow for parallel execution. In many instances the strategy for parallelization is fairly obvious and the problem is correct and timely implementation. A class of problems with these characteristics are grid-based applications where typically the finite difference method is used to discretize some physical phenomena over a 2D or 3D region of space.

The need to convert these applications to run in parallel with a minimum of effort has provided motivation for a number of research efforts. One approach is the on-going effort to specify and to develop compilers to support FORTRAN D, a version of FORTRAN 90 enhanced with data decomposition specifications [1]. The goal of the FORTRAN D project is to develop compilers that automatically insert message-passing routines given an application-specific decomposition provided by the user. The decomposition is specified by inserting directives into the source code. An emerging standard with the functionality of FORTRAN D is High Performance Fortran[2].

A related approach is to develop preprocessors or translators that take a code for which a decomposition has been provided and output code in FORTRAN 77 that contains all necessary message-passing routines. Hypertasking [3], Pfortran [4] and Fortran Linda[5] are three of several examples.

A third approach is represented by FORGE 90 [6]. Here the approach is to use a sophisticated parallelization tool that does not require the insertion of directives into the source code. Typically the only modifications that are needed are those to optimize performance.

The purpose of this paper is to describe success that has been achieved using FORGE 90, Pfortran and Linda to parallelize three different grid-based applications All three programs are of the order of a few thousand lines of Fortran. As of this writing (June '92) results had been obtained for all three tools on one program. For the other two programs results have been obtained for FORGE 90 only.

2   FORGE 90

FORGE 90 is an interactive programming environment that modifies large scientific and engineering programs so that they run in parallel on distributed memory computers. It is under development by Applied Parallel Research and has been built around the FORGE data base analyzer [7]. Since it is an extension of FORGE, it uses the capability of the tool to analyze and understand very large programs. In particular, it has access to information regarding global control and data flow, can track global use of variables and can understand data dependencies among separate parts of program units.

It is important to point out that FORGE 90 is not a fully automated solution to the parallelization problem as the user must be mindful of a domain decomposition that is reasonable for the application.

The user interface is implemented as a windowing system on a workstation that is menu-driven using either the keyboard or the mouse. A work session begins with the selection of the PARALLELIZE FOR DISTRIBUTED MEMORY option within FORGE. The user then has the option of specifying a domain decomposition first and then distributing each loop that contains references to decomposed arrays or distributing loop iterations first and then specifying a domain decomposition that matches the loop distribution. The former can be used with relatively simple applications where one decomposition is sufficient while the latter is used with more complex applications that require additional decompositions. The APPSP program described below is an example of an application with multiple decompositions.

Arrays are decomposed by specification of the following three items.

Block or cyclic

Dimension to be distributed

Fully dimensioned or shrunk allocation of data

The first two items indicate that as of this writing, the tool does not allow either decompositions that are both block and cyclic or multidimensional decompositions. In the case of the third item, fully dimensioned allocation means that each processor needs sufficient memory to store all arrays prior to decomposition. Shrunk arrays means that each processor needs space only for that portion of decomposed arrays for which it is responsible. Use of shrunk arrays creates a parallel version that is more efficient in the use of memory but usually is less efficient in execution time.

The result of a work session with FORGE 90 is the creation of a directory structure and associated files that contain information regarding the parallelization. The user then invokes a postprocessor to use this data base to construct a parallel version of the original source code. The output of the postprocessor is then compiled and linked with a run time library to give an executable file.

3 Pfortran

Pfortran was developed at the University of Houston and has been used extensively to parallelize applications in molecular dynamics[8]. It extends the FORTRAN77 language to allow the user to directly address data that is resident in the memory of another processor. This is done either through the use of the @ operator or by using special reduction functions. As an example of the @ operator, the following piece of code indicates that the array x on processor i is to have the same value as the array y on processor 0.

x@i = y@0

The Pfortran translator takes code written in this way and outputs FORTRAN77 code with message-passing calls automatically inserted. Unlike FORGE 90, it makes no attempt to automatically distribute the data among the processors. Thus the user of Pfortran must implement a data decomposition just as if the parallelization is to be done manually. The tool is then used to generate message-passing routines automatically.

4 Fortran Linda

Linda is a commercial product of Scientific Computing Associates. It has been used for some time to implement the manager-worker parallel programming model. Recently, a Fortran version has become available and this version has been used to implement domain decompositions that are typical of grid-based applications. From the perspective of this paper, its use is very similar to that of Pfortran. That is, after the user has implemented a data decomposition, the tool inserts message-passing routines automatically. The piece of code in the previous section would be implemented in the following way with Fortran Linda

```
if (mynode.eq.0) out("some_string",int,y)
```

```
if(mynode.eq.i) in("some_string",int,x)
```

An advantage in using Linda is that the it runs on a wide variety of computer from shared-memory parallel systems to collections of widely-distributed workstations. Pfortran, on the other hand, is only intended for distributed-memory, message-passing systems. Thus, a code written in Linda is portable over a wider variety of parallel computers.

5 NWP Benchmark

The Numerical Weather Prediction benchmark is one component of the Parallel Benchmark Suite specified by the Forecast System Laboratory of the National Oceanic and Atmospheric Administration of the US Government[9]. The benchmark implements the shallow-water equation and is representative of the computational issues that arise in atmospheric models[10]. The program is written in 3200 lines of FORTRAN 77 divided into 13 subroutines. In addition to extensive calculations associated with 3-dimensional arrays, the program requires periodic output of data to a disk file.

Parallelization by hand using a decomposition of the third dimension required modifications to 17 DO loops. About two weeks were necessary. A similar effort using FORGE 90 was done in one day with most of the time spent optimizing performance over initial results. The time that was required using Pfortran and Linda was about a week for each. The explanation for less time for code conversion when FORGE 90 was used is that the data decomposition had to be done by hand for both Pfortran and Linda. A comparison of performance results and memory requirements among the four methods can be found in Table 1 and Table 2. Some minor modifications were needed before the results in the tables were realized for FORGE 90.They include

1) Removal of all references to decomposed arrays in I/O statements through the use of temporary buffers

2) Interchange of the order of nested DO loops so that the distributed index is the outermost

Table 1: Performance Results For NWP Benchmark - 50x50x51 Problem Time in Seconds (Speedup)

Parallelization	1 Node	4 Nodes	8 Nodes
Manual	4320	1658 (2.6)	1163 (3.7)
FORGE 90 Full Arrays	4452	2196 (2.0)	1668 (2.6)
FORGE 90 Shrunk Arrays	4632	2460 (1.8)	1776 (2.4)
Pfortran	4320	1886 (2.3)	1238 (3.5)
Fortran Linda	4320	1982 (2.2)	1454 (3.0)

Speedup computed from results for 1 node with manual parallelization

Table 2: Memory Required per Node For NWP Benchmark (Mbytes)

Parallelization	1 Node	4 Nodes	8 Nodes
Manual	24.0	8.3	5.8
FORGE 90 Full Arrays	24.0	24.0	24.0
FORGE 90 Shrunk Arrays	24.0*	13.5*	12.0*
Pfortran	24.0	8.7	6.2
Fortran Linda	24.0	8.3	5.8

* Estimated due to dynamic memory allocation

3) Addition of an outer loop that is executed one time in order to optimize the inter-processor communication that FORGE 90 generates. This was done for 8 of the 17 loops that were parallelized

In the case of Pfortran and Linda, many more changes were necessary to implement a decomposition of the third dimension.

6 The MGRID Benchmark from the NAS Suite of Parallel Benchmarks

The Numerical Aerodynamics Simulation (NAS) Program at the NASA Ames Research Center has developed a collection of benchmarks that characterize the computational requirements associated with aerodynamic simulations [11]. One of these is a simplified 3D application that requires 4 iterations of a V-cycle multigrid algorithm. The program consists of 850 lines of Fortran in 14 routines. A characteristic of the benchmark that did not appear in the NWP benchmark was the use of "work" arrays for each of the 4 large arrays of the program. Each work array in turn contained sufficient space to accommodate all 4 grids that are required for the 4 iterations of the V-cycle.

Parallelization by hand was done by Jim Patterson of Boeing Computer Services and required about 3 weeks to generate an initial version that ran reasonably well in parallel with a 2-dimensional decomposition of the data. Since FORGE 90 was not able to generate a 2D decomposition as of this writing, automatic parallelization was based on a simplifier 1D decomposition in the third dimension. About a day was required to do this using fully dimensioned arrays with another day required for an implementation based on shrunk arrays. Most of the time was spent in the determination that a simple DO loop had to be added to the program to partition the work arrays into parts associated with each cycle of the algorithm.

Performance results with manual and automatic parallelization can be found in Table 3. The availability of only 8 nodes with sufficient memory explains the lack of results for 16 nodes when FORGE 90 was run with fully dimensioned arrays. A comparison between the two methods is less than ideal as the hand-coded version is based on a 2D decomposition while FORGE 90 was limited to 1D. Thus some narrowing of the gap, especially when the number of nodes is large, can be expected when the tool becomes capable of multi-dimensional decompositions.

7 The APPSP Benchmark

The APPSP benchmark is another component of the NAS suite of parallel benchmarks. It is a simplified version of an actual fluid flow code that lacks the complexity of the real program but retains all the essential computational structure. The benchmark solves the Navier-Stokes equation using an implicit solution algorithm. The resulting system of linear equations is solved using the diagonal form of the approximate factorization algorithm[12].

The program is written in 3600 lines of FORTRAN 77 code divided among 25 subroutines. A characteristic of the benchmark that did not exist for the other two applications was recursion in all three directions when updating array values. This fact necessitated the use of more than

Table 3: Performance Results in Seconds (Speedup) For MGRID Benchmark (128x128x128 Grid)

Parallelization	1 Node	8 Nodes	16 Nodes
Manual	190.8	25.2 (7.6)	13.2 (14.5)
FORGE 90 Full Arrays	191.3	37.8 (5.0)	
FORGE 90 Shrunk Arrays	215.8	54.9 (3.8)	34.3 (5.6)

Table 4: Performance Results For APPSP Benchmark - Time in Seconds and Speedup for 1 Iteration on 32x32x32 Grid

Parallelization	1 Node	16 Nodes	32 Nodes
Manual	12.9		.66 (19.7)
FORGE 90 Full Arrays	13.2	1.78 (7.2)	1.38 (9.3)
FORGE 90 Shrunk Arrays	13.0	1.69 (7.6)	1.34 (9.7)

one decomposition in order to avoid sequential execution of some of the 34 parallelizable loops in the program.The transition between the two decompositions was done using a distributed matrix transpose for both manual and automatic parallelization. In the case of FORGE 90, the transpose operation is built into the tool and is not visible to the user.

A comparison of performance results with manual and automatic parallelization can be found in Table 4. In both instances, the decomposition was in the third dimension for 27 loops and in the second dimension for the 7 loops with recursion in the third dimension. About two weeks were required for manual parallelization while somewhat less than a day were needed using FORGE 90. Results for manual parallelization were obtained using an initial implementation written by Jim Patterson of Boeing Computer Services that required that the number of nodes be equal to the size of the problem. Hence results for the table were obtained only when 32 nodes were used.

The results for FORGE 90 were generated after two minor changes were made. They were

(1) Removal of a WRITE statement associated with an error exit from one of the loops.

(2) Replacement an * in a DIMENSION statement with a parameter that represented the actual value.

8 Concluding Remarks

It is now feasible to use software tools to parallelize grid-based application for distributed-memory message-passing computers. Unlike vectorizers or shared-memory parallel compilers, these tools are not fully automatic at this time. For all three tools, the user must understand the application well enough to have a reasonable domain decomposition in mind. Implementation of this domain decomposition is automatic with FORGE 90, but must be done manually for Pfortran and Linda. All three tools then automatically insert message-passing routines.

The data for the NWP benchmark indicate that FORGE 90 gives 50 to 65% of the performance of a parallelization done by hand. The performance for the other tools is significantly better (75 - 90%). Superior performance by Pfortran and Fortran Linda is to be expected as both these tools require more effort. Work is now under way with the other two benchmarks to determine if the relative performance of these tools can be generalized.

The availability of semi-automatic parallelization tools gives the user a number of choices for parallelizing grid-based applications. At one end is FORGE 90 which can be used to get an application up and running in parallel very quickly. Better performance results can be obtained with more effort using Pfortran or Linda. If additional performance is needed, a number of optimizations can be done within the context of a manual parallelization.

References

1. Fox, G. et al. "FORTRAN D Language Specification", Syracuse Center for Computational Science SCCS-42c, April 1991.

2. Loveman, D. and Steele G. "High Performance FORTRAN Draft Proposal", presented at the Rice University HPF Forum, March, 1992.

3. Baber M. "Hypertasking Support for Dynamically Redistributed and Resized Arrays on the iPSC", The Sixth Distributed Memory Computing Conference Proceedings, April 1991, pp. 59 - 66.

4. Scott, R., Clark, T. and Bagheri, B. "Pfortran: a parallel dialect of Fortran",University of Houston Research Report UH/MD-131, March 1992

5. "Original Linda",Scientific Computing Associates publication 1990.

6. MIMDizer User's Guide, Pacific-Sierra Research Corporation, July 1991.

7. FORGE User' Guide, Pacific-Sierra Research Corporation, July 1991

8. Clark, T., McCammon, J. A. and Scott, R. "Parallel Molecular Dynamics",University of Houston Research Report UH/MD - 101, Nov. 1991.

9. FSL Parallel Benchmark Suite, National Oceanic and Atmospheric Administration, Boulder Colorado, Nov. 1991.

10. Hoffman, G. R., Swarztrauber, P. and Sweet, R., "Aspects of Using Multiprocessors for Meteorological Modelling", Springer-Verlag, New York, 1988.

11. Bailey, D. et al. "The NAS Parallel Benchmarks",NASA Ames Research Center, Report RNR-91-002, Jan.1991.

12. Weeratunga, S. et al. "The Application Benchmarks", Chapter 3 from The NAS Parallel Benchmarks, Jan 1991, p.35.

Semantic Analysis for Parallelizing C

Pierre David

Laboratoire MASI - Institut Blaise Pascal
Laboratoire LPTL
Université Pierre et Marie Curie
75252 Paris Cedex 05 - France
email : pda@masi.ibp.fr

Abstract. Automatic parallelization of C language programs is a difficult task due, for example, to side effects within expressions and access to memory via pointers. We describe a method based on semantic analysis of the language, in order to detect parallelism in complex programs using pointer arithmetic. We define semantic domains which respect the type system of the language, and use them to synthesize effect of the program through functional objects called transformations.

Keywords: automatic parallelization, compilation, pointers, side effects, C language, types.

1 Introduction

In the past few years, a considerable amount of work has been done in the field of automatic parallelization [13]. However, most of these efforts have been applied to the Fortran language, which is undoubtedly the most widely used language in science and engineering. In comparison, very little time has been devoted to more recent imperative languages such as Pascal, C or Ada.

C offers some interesting facilities, even in the area of intensive computing [11]. Among its strong features, C is widely used and taught, it is stable (there is a norm), it simplifies portability problems, it is efficient, it is adapted to many problems from numeric simulations to graphic manipulations (domains where a large demand exists for parallel computing).

Some efforts have been made to specify some parallelized versions of C ([9] for example). In this paper, however, we focus on the problems one must face in order to automatically detect parallelism in C programs. The most important ones are:

- side effects in expressions (including assignment) hinder further analysis,
- some operators (&& for example) are sequential,
- numerous data types and sizes of manipulated objects,
- the for loop, on which all parallelizers rely, does not have the same semantics as the Fortran DO loop,
- using small functions is considered good programming style,
- operator & allows variable modification in a subtle way, making obsolete all methods to build the dependence graph used for Fortran,
- pointer arithmetics makes determination of modified variables much more complex, and the presence of cast operator, union types and parameter passing allow type system violation.

Some attempts have been made to solve some of these problems. These works fall into two categories:

1. works done on pointer and dynamically allocated data structures. Many of them are not applied to a particular language ([5, 8] among others), but rare are those directly applied to C [4]. In these works, major problems we cited, such as pointer arithmetic or side-effects in expressions, are not addressed.
2. works dedicated to the C language and some of the problems we mentioned.
A compiler for a multi-processor and vector machine is described in [1]. The pragmatic approach, in a industry context, is to use the AT&T compiler as the front-end of a parallelizer. For loops are converted to while loops, side effects are removed from expressions and procedure inlining is described. However, authors do not detail their work.
The Parafrase-2 parallelizer [10] includes a pre-processor and a post-processor for the C language. However, they are not sufficient to do a good job on C. Authors admit that dependence analysis in the presence of pointers is not implemented.

As we can see, very few satisfying solutions have been given to our problem. We cannot afford to address all problems at the same time. So, our goal is to be able to parallelize significant programs (using arrays, pointers and pointer arithmetic, complex expressions). This paper describes the first step in this direction: semantic analysis of assignments, conditionals and sequences (no loops). Due to space requirements, this is just an outline. More detailed discussion is in [6] or [7].

In the second section, we define the input language our parallelizer will admit. In particular, pointers as well as all expressions, even the most complicated ones, are allowed. In the third section, we describe how we suppress all side effects from expressions. This phase is called the *normalization* of programs. In the last section, we build the framework for semantic analysis. We have carefully designed this framework to be valid for the C complete syntax. Given this basis, we can use it to synthesize effect of instructions.

2   Input Language

The base language of our parallelizer is ANSI C [3]. However, we cannot plan to solve all problems in this study. Hence, we must apply some restrictions on the input language of our parallelizer. There are three kinds of restrictions:

1. Difficult problems. In fact, there is only one major problem: transgression of the C language type system. Hence, the *cast* operator, union types and function call have been removed from our input language.
2. Problems not specific to C, such as interprocedural analysis [12] or program restructuring [2] are not dealt with. Function calls have already been removed. In addition, all non structured constructs are removed: goto, break, return, etc.
3. Tedious problems. They are direct extensions of constructs we treat in this paper or we plan to in the future. For example, switch is a generalization of if statement. Do-while loop and switch choice are removed. We plan to treat while

and **for** loops in a near future. Another simple generalization of mechanisms presented in this paper is **struct** data type: it is an aggregate of multiple distinct objects with a common name. Hence, we remove the **struct** data type, and bit-fields.

To summarize, our input language is based on the syntax of C, and:

- has all data types (including arrays and pointers) but **struct**, **union** and the exotic bit-field,
- use all expressions operators (even cluttered ones) but cast and function call,
- has sequence of instructions, **if** statement, and **while** and **for** loops even if they are not yet presented.

which is a non-trivial subset including a large part of difficulties mentioned earlier.

We have written a syntactic analyzer for this language in C with **lex** and **yacc** tools. Programs are translated into a syntax tree written as Lisp expressions, which is our intermediate representation [6]. Time used by the translator is negligible when compared with other phases.

3 Program Normalization

We impose few restrictions on our input language so it seems difficult to parallelize when expressions contain many side effects, but they are really frequent in C programs and we must deal with them. Since semantic analysis with side effects is not a simple task, we have chosen to remove them. This section exposes the output of the program normalizer, i.e. the language our semantic analyzer expects.

This new language is basically the same as the input one. All types allowed are unchanged. No new type is introduced. The largest area of change is the expressions syntax. We must define a set of operators such as there is no side effect. Hence, we must remove some operators:

- Assignment. This is no longer an operator, but an instruction.
- Side-effect operators (++, +=, etc.). They are only short-hand notations.
- Sequential operators (&&, || and ?:). Here, the side effect is on program counter.
- Array access. Access to array elements is replaced by an explicit memory access via a pointer since both notations are equivalent.
- Comma operator. This operator is obsolete when all side effects are removed.

There are few instructions in our input language, and they differ from C:

- assignment is now an instruction. Expressions are now only part of assignments and **while** or **if** tests.
- **for** loops are replaced by equivalent **while** based code.

The program normalizer is implemented as a pattern matching filter which accepts a syntax tree in intermediate form as input and outputs a modified syntax tree. A typical function (10 lines) is processed in less than 10 seconds. When a C language program is converted to this new language, semantic analysis can be done.

4 Semantic Analysis

In this section, we present a method to synthesize the effect of a program. The analysis can be used as the dependence analysis phase of an automatic parallelizer, or as the framework of a loop analysis for normalization/parallelization. The hard work, when faced with such a complex language as C, is to build a model for analysis.

The first step is to define the classic semantic domains:

$\mathcal{N}$ ... $-1, 0, 1$ ... Natural values $\qquad$ $\mathcal{B}$ {true, false} Boolean values
$\mathcal{V}$ $\quad$ $\mathcal{N} + \mathcal{B}$ $\quad$ All possible values $\qquad$ $\mathcal{I}$ $\quad$ a, b ... $\quad$ All data object identifiers

This allows us to build address domain $\mathcal{A}$ which is included in the cartesian product $\mathcal{I} \times \mathcal{N}$. In other words, an address $a = \langle i, k \rangle$ is built from the symbol i, which identifies the start of an object in memory, and a integer offset k inside the object referenced by i. We define operations on addresses: difference, equality and inequality, addition and subtraction with integers. However, this semantic domain is too large for our purpose: there is no type notion. We introduce it by splitting $\mathcal{A}$: we state that there exists a partition of $\mathcal{A}$ in subsets $\mathcal{A}_n$ (with $n \geq 0$). What does n mean in $\mathcal{A}_n$? The idea is to include types, pointers in particular, in our formalism. A variable (addresses $\langle i, k \rangle$) is in $\mathcal{A}_n$ iff the declaration of i contains n stars. In other words, there are $n + 1$ references to get the pointed value. For example, if types of i and ppi are int and int ** respectively, then $\langle i, 0 \rangle \in \mathcal{A}_0$ and $\langle ppi, 0 \rangle \in \mathcal{A}_2$. Disjonctions of the sets $\mathcal{A}_n$ are guaranteed by the semantic rules of C and our restrictions: type violation is impossible. Hence, a variable is used as it is declared. Arrays are special pointers: they are constant pointers, and access to each cell can be done in only one memory reference. Then, a variable of type int [] [] belongs to $\mathcal{A}_0$. We could extend this partition to handle all types and re-partition each $\mathcal{A}_n$ in subsets according to the basic type ($\mathcal{A}_n^{\text{char}}$, $\mathcal{A}_n^{\text{int}}$, etc.). The implementation uses this double partitioning scheme, but it is omitted in this article for the sake of clarity.

We partition the $\mathcal{I}$ domain in the same way that we partitioned the $\mathcal{A}$ domain, and we note $ident_n$ the set of all identifiers matching simple variables (i.e. not arrays), and $const_n$ (with $n \geq 1$) the set of all array identifiers.

The $\mathcal{A}_n$ sets allow us to define the memory. Each cell contains a scalar variable, a pointer, or an array of scalars or pointers. Consider the function family $M_n : \mathcal{A}_n \to \mathcal{A}_{n-1} + \top$, where $n \geq 0$, $\mathcal{A}_{-1} = \mathcal{V}$ and $\top$ is the set containing the only element $\top$. This family associates the content of a memory cell, either a value (M_0) or an address (M_n, with $n > 0$), with an address. If the cell is neither defined nor assigned, we write $\top$ (*top*) its content. A memory is the function $M = \bigcup_{n \geq 0} M_n$. The set of all memories is called $\mathcal{M}$.

We are now able to define the syntax of expressions:

$$
\begin{aligned}
E &::= R | L & R &::= R_0 | R_1 | \ldots | R_n | \ldots \\
R_0 &::= \text{const} | ident_0 | (R_0) | R_0 \text{ binary-op } R_0 | \text{unary-op } R_0 | R_i - R_i | *R_1 \\
R_n &::= \text{const}_{n-1} | ident_n | (R_n) | R_n + R_0 | R_n - R_0 | *R_{n+1} | \&L_{n-1} \\
L &::= L_0 | L_1 | \ldots | L_n | \ldots & L_n &::= ident_n | (L_n) | *L_{n+1}
\end{aligned}
$$

Note that expressions have been split into two families: R (for *right hand side*) and L (for *left hand side*). We will use the set $\mathcal{X}$ of all expressions, and the two subsets $\mathcal{X}_l$ and $\mathcal{X}_r$ of L-expressions and R-expressions respectively. Finally, the subscript n

in R_n or L_n is the number of stars in the type of the result. All expressions evaluate in the context of a memory. Hence, the type of interpretation equations is: $E : \mathcal{X} \to \mathcal{M} \to \mathcal{A} + \mathcal{V}$. For example, the L_n function is defined by: $L_n[\![\text{ident}_n]\!] \equiv \lambda\mu.(\text{ident}_n, 0)$, $L_n[\![(L'_n)]\!] \equiv \lambda\mu.L_n[\![L'_n]\!]\mu$, and $L_n[\![*R_{n+1}]\!] \equiv \lambda\mu.R_{n+1}[\![R_{n+1}]\!]\mu$.

With the expression syntax above, assignment is simply: $L_n = R_n$. The effect of this assignment is to modify the memory. If the memory before assignment is called M, the new memory become: $M' = \lambda a.(\text{if } a = L_n[\![L_n]\!]M \text{ then } R_n[\![R_n]\!]M \text{ else } Ma)$. An assignment can be viewed as a function which modifies a memory. We call this a *transformation*, and we write: $T : \mathcal{M} \to \mathcal{M}$

Our implementation needs an easily manipulated representation of objects. We represent the transformation T (for the assignment $l = r$) by a substitution, i.e. the expressions $\langle l, r \rangle \in \mathcal{X}_l \times \mathcal{X}_r$, which is written $\sigma = [l \leftarrow r]$. In other words, the representation of a transformation is the mechanical writing of the two expressions involved in the assignment. When given a sequence of instructions, we must compose associated transformations. However, the representation we have chosen become ambiguous as soon as an indirection via a pointer appears. What is the value of i after execution of code synthesized by [i ← 1, *p ← 2]? To solve this problem, we introduce functions (*guards*) to select memory configurations. A guard is a function $G : \mathcal{M} \to \mathcal{B}$ with the form: $G = \lambda\mu.\bigwedge_{1 \leq i \leq n} Be_i\mu$ where $\bigwedge$ is the conjunction operator (*and*) and $B((\mathcal{X}_r + \mathcal{B}) \to \mathcal{M} \to \mathcal{B})$ is the function $B \equiv \lambda x.\lambda\mu.(R_0 x\mu \neq 0 \text{ if } x \in \mathcal{X}_r, x \text{ if } x \in \mathcal{B})$. It is now possible to write a *consistent* representation as:

$$\tau = \left| \begin{array}{l} \{\text{p} \text{ == } \&\text{i}\}/[\text{i} \leftarrow 2] \\ \{\text{p} \text{ != } \&\text{i}\}/[\text{i} \leftarrow 1, *\text{p} \leftarrow 2] \end{array} \right.$$

How can we be sure that our representations *represent* effectively transformations? This is accomplished by defining explicitly two operations: the *concretisation* to convert a transformation into its representation, and *abstraction* which is the reverse.

Conditionals are a simple extension of previous mechanisms. If we note T_t and T_f transformations for the *true* part and for *false* part respectively, the final transformation is thus: $TM = (\text{if } R_n[\![R_n]\!]M \neq 0 \text{ then } T_v M \text{ else } T_f M)$. Note that integration of conditional statements is very easy, thanks to the definition of a robust framework and to the introduction of *guards*.

The implementation of our semantic analyzer accepts a normalized syntax tree in intermediate form as input. It computes the corresponding transformation. There are four main steps:

1. Instruction analysis, to compute compositions of transformation associated with each instruction.
2. Guard simplification: brute composition of transformations generates a lot of impossible guards. This module removes some of these guards using the memory partitions based on the complete type system.
3. Expression simplification.
4. Expression substitution. Given a transformation and a substitution, this module compute a new transformation where all possible expressions have been substituted.

5 Conclusion

We have defined a significant subset of the C language including pointers and pointer arithmetic, as well as side effects in expressions. Next, we have translated our program to remove side effects. Then, we elaborate a framework for semantic analysis. This framework benefits from the memory we partitioned following the type system. This partition scheme allowed us a fine grain simplification of expressions and guards. All these points were implemented in order to experiment with our approach.

The techniques exposed here can be applied to other domains: program verification against semantic rules of the C norm, interprocedural parallelization, or dependence graph computation.

However, our goal is now to perform the second step toward program parallelization: loop analysis. Our approach will be, given the transformation for the loop body, to compute approximations of the iterates of this transformation until it is stable. In performing these approximations, we will recognize *true* for loops, suitable for parallelization. But this will be the subject of another paper.

Acknowledgments: I would like to thank J. Taillandier for his assistance with the preparation of this article, and Pr. P. Feautrier for his helpful comments.

References

1. Allen R., Johnson S., *Compiling C for Vectorization, Parallelization, and Inline Expansion.* ACM PLDI88, June 1988
2. Ammarguellat Z., *Restructuration des programmes Fortran en vue de leur parallélisation.* Thèse de l'Université Paris 6, Rapport MASI 90.3, 1988.
3. American National Standard Institute, *Draft Proposed American National Standard for Information Systems – Programming Langage C.* Draft X3J11/88-002., January 1988.
4. Bodin F., *Data Structure Analysis in C Programs.* Int'l Workshop on Compilers for Parallel Computers, Paris, December 1990.
5. Chase D., Wegman M., Zadeck K., *Analysis of Pointers and Structures.* ACM-PLDI90, June 1990.
6. David P., *Analyse sémantique des programmes en langage C en vue de leur parallélisation.* Thèse de l'Université Paris 6, 1991 (Rapport MASI 91.60).
7. David P., *Semantic Analysis of Straight Line C Code with Pointers.* Rapport MASI 92.39 June 1992
8. Horwitz S., Pfeiffer P., Reps T., *Dependence Analysis for Pointer Variables.* ACM-PLDI89, 1989
9. Li K., *A Note on the Vector C Language.* ACM Symp. on Compiler Construction, SIGPLAN Notices Vol. 21, No 1, January 1986.
10. Polychronopoulos C., Girkar M., Haghighat M., Ling Lee C., Leung B., Schouten D., *Parafrase-2: An Environment for Parallelizing, Partitioning, Synchronizing, and Scheduling Programs on Multiprocessors.* Int'l Conf. on Parallel Processing, 1989.
11. Thornburg J., *Number Crunching in C.* SIGPLAN Notices, Vol. 21, No 6, June 1986.
12. Triolet R., Irigoin F., Feautrier P., *Direct Parallelization of Call Statements.* ACM Symp. on Compiler Construction, SIGPLAN Notices Vol. 21, No 7, July 1986.
13. Zima H., Chapman B., *Supercompilers for Parallel and Vector Computers.* ACM Press, Addison Wesley, 1991.

This article was processed using the LaTeX macro package with LLNCS style

A Task Scheduling Algorithm for the Parallel Expression Evaluation in a Reconfigurable Fully Digit On-line Network[*]

Hong-Jin YEH

LIP-IMAG, Ecole Normale Supérieur de Lyon
46, Allée d'Italie, 69364 Lyon Cédex 07, France

Abstract. In this paper, we present a task scheduling algorithm which accounts for digit-level pipelines of on-line arithmetic units when a limited number of heterogeneous on-line arithmetic units can be connected totally with each other and the network is reconfigurable during the execution. In on-line arithmetic, an arithmetic unit can be reused after the completion of its computing process while its result is available digit by digit during the computation. Thus, a new criterion, called *the maximal delay* is introduced to take into account additional precedence constraints based on the on-line delay.

1 Introduction

In on-line arithmetic, the results as well as the operands flow through the operators serially, digit by digit, most significant digit first. This digit flow makes it possible to introduce parallelism between sequential operations by overlapping them in a digit-pipelined fashion. Thus, chaining on-line arithmetic units for a long sequence of arithmetic operations may be significantly faster than in other conventional digit-parallel environment.[1] In a fully digit on-line network, the successive operations can be overlapped by using their incomplete results.[2] The interconnection bandwidth is drastically reduced to only one digit(e.g. two bits in a radix-2 redundant system). Simpler layouts and lower circuit areas in VLSI implementation are possible.

Recently, some digit on-line networks for special numerical computations have been designed in [3, 4]. In such a system, the arithmetic units are statically connected each other. Here we deal with the on-line arithmetic units, in which the floating-point computations are performed digit-serially for both the exponent and the mantissa.[5] We assume that the network is dynamically reconfigurable for the evaluation of general expressions.

An on-line computation is characterized by the on-line delay, i.e. the value δ such that $(i + \delta)$ digits of the operands are required to generate the i-th digit of the result. Let the on-line period p be the time needed to generate a digit of the result. Then, the computation time equals to $(\delta + L)p$ where L denote the number of digits to represent a number. If n operations whose on-line delays are denoted by δ_i,

---

[*] This work is partially supported by the PRC "Architectures Nouvelles de Machines" of the French *Ministère de l'Education Nationale* and the *Centre National de la Recherche Scientifique*.

$1 \leq i \leq n$ are connected linearly, the whole evaluation time is to be $(\sum_{i=1}^{n} \delta_i + L)p$ where different operations are synchronized with the slowest one.

The main difficulties for scheduling tasks on a fully digit on-line network are due to the fact that the incomplete results can be used for the successive operations as their operands. That is, a processor(arithmetic unit) can use the result generated by another processor only after δ(on-line delay) cycles, not $(\delta + L)$ cycles. In this case, the level-based algorithms such as in [6, 7, 8] can not be applicable, because the level does not present any more the precedence relations with respect to the digit flow in on-line arithmetic. Thus, we introduce another criterion, called *the maximal delay*, to define new precedence relations. In section 2, the model of a fully digit on-line network and the task precedence graphs are defined. The scheduling algorithm using the maximal delays is described with an example in section 3. Finally, the simulated results are summarized in section 4 and we give some comments about our algorithm.

2 Problem modeling

The expression to be evaluated is given by a *directed acyclic graph*, $G = (N, E)$ where N is the set of the nodes and E is the set of the edges between nodes. A node represent an arithmetic operation to be computed. An edge e_{ij} means that the evaluated result of a node n_i is to be an operand of a node n_j. The *initial nodes* are the nodes without predecessors in G. The *final node* n_f is the only one node that will generate the evaluated value of G.

The fully digit on-line network, shown in figure 1, is composed of heterogeneous on-line arithmetic units. An on-line arithmetic unit(AU) can compute only the corresponding operations with a constant on-line delay. All pair of AUs can be connected directly through the cross-bar switch, which is locally reconfigurable during the execution. There are sufficiently many parallel/serial converters to get the operands and a serial/parallel converter to output the evaluated result. The size-variable serial buffers are used to synchronize the operands.

We assume that the on-line periods of all AUs are the same, equal to one time unit: the different operations are synchronized with the slowest one. It is also assumed that the time for a digit passing is always less than one time unit to ignore the intercommunication cost.

The parallel evaluation of G starts from the initial nodes. When the nodes are computed, their immediate successors whose operands are available are computed in the next. This step is continued repeatly until the final node is computed. If the number of AUs is fixed and the number of nodes in G is relatively very large, the reuse of AUs is unavoidable. Thus, the computation of a node can be blocked by the lack of free AUs although its operands are available. This blocking may increase the evaluation delay more than as expected. In other words, the evaluation process is dependent with the schedule of AUs due to the serial nature in on-line arithmetic. Therefore, the scheduling problem is how the evaluation delay can be minimized as much as possible.

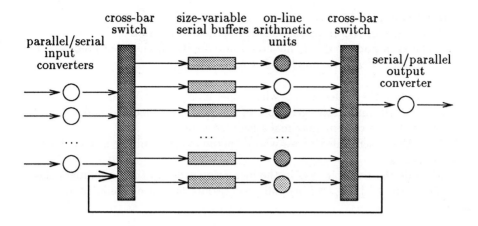

Fig. 1. A fully digit on-line network model

3 Scheduling algorithm

Let us consider a class of scheduling algorithms, called *level algorithms*. Let $NS(n_i)$ be the set of immediate successors of n_i. The level $l(n_i)$ of a node n_i is defined by $l(n_i) = \max_{n_j \in NS(n_i)} l(n_j) + 1$ where $l(n_f) = 0$. The levels allow us to decide the priority of the immediate successors as well as the partial precedence relation of the nodes. But, it is not possible to take into account the on-line delay of each type of operation. Notice that the on-line delays of different types of operations are not the same. Thus, we extend the level algorithms by introducing another criterion, called *the maximal delay*.

Let $\delta(n_i)$ be the on-line delay for computing n_i. The length of a path from n_i to n_j is defined by the sum of the on-line delays of nodes in that path except for n_j. Let Ω be the longest path in G. Then, the maximal delay $\sigma(n_i)$ of a node n_i in Ω is defined by the length of the longest path from the initial node in Ω to n_i. For the other nodes, their maximal delays are defined by the difference $\sigma(n_f)$ and the length of the longest path from them to n_f. If there is a path from n_i to n_j in G, $\sigma(n_i) < \sigma(n_j)$ means that the computation of n_i must be started not later than at time $\sigma(n_i)$ to start computing n_j at time $\sigma(n_j)$.

The key point of our algorithm is to overlap maximally the successive operations, although it might decrease the efficiency of parallel evaluation. Let $NP(n_i)$ be the set of the immediate predecessors of n_i. The scheduling algorithm is stated as below: (NC is a current subset of N)

Algorithm (Scheduling)
Begin
    choose a node n_i such that $\sigma(n_i) = 0$;
    choose a node $n_j \in NS(n_i)$ having minimally its predecessors;
    $NC = NP(n_j)$ and the time t is set to 0;

while $NC \neq \phi$ and $t < L$
    if all nodes in NC have unscheduled predecessors **then**
        choose a node $n' \in NC$ having minimally its unscheduled predecessors;
        schedule n' and its unscheduled predecessors;
    else
        schedule the nodes in NC whose operands are available;
    $NC = \{$ all immediate successors of the previous scheduled nodes $\}$;
    t is set to the current maximal scheduled time;
    $NC = \{$ the unscheduled nodes whose operands are available at time t $\}$;
    while $NC \neq \phi$
        schedule the nodes in NC in the increasing order of their maximal delay;
        $NC = \{n' \in \bigcup_{n \in NC} NS(n) \mid$ all predecessors of n' are scheduled $\}$;
End

The order among the nodes having the same maximal delay is arbitrary. Let $i(u)$ be the time expected for an AU u to be idle. The time to be able to start computing a node n is defined by $t(n) = \max_{n' \in NP(n)} (t(n') + \delta(n'))$ where $t(n) = 0$ for all initial nodes. The scheduling procedure of a node n is presented in detail:

Procedure schedule(n)
Begin
    choose the corresponding AU u to be idle as soon as possible;
    schedule n on u at time $t = max\{i(u), t(n)\}$;
    $i(u) = t + \delta(n) + L$
End

Let $\phi(n)$, $\psi(n)$ be the scheduled time and AU for the computation of a node n respectively. Then, the *schedule* of G will be represented by the set of triples $(n_i, \phi(n_i), \psi(n_i))$ for $n_i \in N$. The evaluation delay $\delta(G)$ is $\phi(n_f) + \delta(n_f)$ and the evaluation time of G is $\delta(G) + L$.

For example, we suppose that $\delta(+) = 1$, $\delta(\times) = 2$ and $L = 10$. The example is given by a task precedence graph in figure 2(the numbering of the nodes is arbitrary). The longest path is $n_1 \rightarrow n_4 \rightarrow n_7 \rightarrow \cdots \rightarrow n_{20} \rightarrow n_{22}$. The maximal delays are presented in bold style. Notice that the maximal delays in the same level are not the same.

Let us suppose that there are 5 adders and 5 multipliers in the network. The result obtained by the proposed scheduling algorithm is depicted in figure 3. The scheduled times are presented in bold style, and the scheduled AUs are omitted. $\delta(G) = \phi(n_{22}) + \delta(n_{22}) = 30$ and the evaluation time of the example is $\delta(G) + L = 40$. It is remarked that $\phi(n_{14})$ can be modified by 5 without any increasing of $\delta(G)$ to optimize the sizes of serial buffers corresponding to $e_{14,17}$, $e_{14,18}$. But, we do not consider here the optimization problem of the sizes of the serial buffers.

4 Simulated results and comments

Let us consider the evaluation of a degree-n polynomial, $P_n(x) = \sum_{i=0}^{n} a_i x^i$ and $a_i \neq 0$ for all $0 \leq i \leq n$. By using an optimal parallel algorithm, called "divide-and-conquer", $P_n(x)$ is partitioned into two polynomials $P^H(x)$, $P^L(x)$ such that

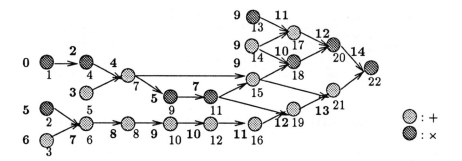

Fig. 2. An example of task graphs and the maximal delays

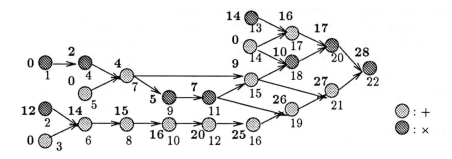

Fig. 3. The scheduled times with 5 adders and 5 multipliers

$P^H(x) = \sum_{i=k}^{n} a_i x^{i-k}$, $P^L(x) = \sum_{i=0}^{k-1} a_i x^i$, $k = \lceil \log(n+1) \rceil$. Thus, $P_n(x) = p^H(x)x^k + p^L(x)$. If we continue the partitioning recursively until all partitions are binomials or monomials, the evaluation process can be performed in the inverse order of partitioning. All binomials, including $P_n(x)$, are evaluated in parallel by overlapping the computation of powers x^{2^i}, $1 < i < k$.

This evaluation process contains n additions and $(n + k - 1)$ multiplications. Let $\delta(P_n(x))$, $\rho(P_n(x))$ be the evaluation delay and the sum of the sizes of all serial buffers used for the evaluation of $P_n(x)$ respectively. The simulated results with 5 adders and 7 multipliers are summarized in table 1. It is remarked that the proposed algorithm have been scheduled efficiently decreasing the evaluation delay and the size of serial buffers at the same time.

5 Conclusion

We have proposed a task scheduling algorithm in a fully digit on-line network. Due to the serial nature in on-line arithmetic, the maximal delay and the length(the

n(degree)		7	15	31	63	127	255	511
proposed	$\delta(P_n(x))$	17	30	61	125	247	490	985
algorithm	$\rho(P_n(x))$	33	77	496	2535	11561	49155	202711
level	$\delta(P_n(x))$	17	30	69	138	279	557	1125
algorithm	$\rho(P_n(x))$	42	205	866	3709	14648	60805	250023

Table 1. The simulated result with 5 adders and 7 multipliers

number of digits) of a number play an important role in contrast to the level and the computation/communication cost in parallel/distributed multiprocessor system. The simulations show that the scheduling is performed efficiently, and approximately minimizes the evaluation delay. It makes it possible to use fully digit on-line network as a coprocessor, conquering another parallelism.

The formal verification of the proposed algorithm is not yet finished. In general, it is difficult to specify the components of the network for general expressions. But, using the simulation, we can deduce the implementation model of a fully digit on-line network for special purpose scientific computations. The scheduling techniques for more complex expressions such as matrix computations are under investigation.

References

1. M. D. Ercegovac, "On-line arithmetic: an overview," *SPIE Vol. 495 Real Time Signal Processing VII*, pp. 86–92, 1984.
2. M. Irwin and R. Owens, "Fully digit on-line networks," *IEEE Trans. Comput.*, vol. c-32, no. 4, pp. 402–406, 1983.
3. S. P. Johansen, "A universal online bit-serial cell for parallel expression evaluation," in *Proc. of 2nd IEEE Symp. on Parallel and Dist Processing*, (Dallas, Texas, USA), pp. 335–338, Sept. 1990.
4. P. K. G. Tu and M. D. Ercegovac, "Application of on-line arithmetic algorithms to the svd computation: preliminary results," in *Proc. 10th Symp. on Comput. Arith.*, pp. 246–255, 1991.
5. J. Duprat, M. Fiallos, J. M. Muller, and H. J. Yeh, "Delays of on-line floating-point operators in borrow save notation," in *Algorithms and parallel VLSI architectures II*, pp. 273–278, North Holland, 1992.
6. D. Bernstein, M. Rodeh, and I. Gertner, "Approximation algorithms for scheduling arithmetic expressions on pipelined machines," *J. of Algorithms*, vol. 10, pp. 120–139, 1989.
7. J. Hwang, Y. Chow, F. D. Anger, and C. Lee, "Scheduling precedence graphs in systems with interprocessor communication times," *SIAM J. Comput.*, vol. 18, no. 2, pp. 244–257, 1989.
8. G. C. Sih and E. A. Lee, "Dynamic-level scheduling for heterogeneous processor networks," in *Proc. of 2nd IEEE Symp. on Parallel and Dist. Processing*, (Dallas, Texas, USA), pp. 42–49, Dec. 1990.

This article was processed using the LaTeX macro package with LLNCS style

Unimodularity Considered Non-Essential (Extended Abstract)

Michael Barnett[1] and Christian Lengauer[2]

[1] Department of Computer Sciences, The University of Texas at Austin, Austin, Texas 78712–1188, U.S.A. E-mail: mbarnett@cs.utexas.edu
[2] Fakultät für Mathematik und Informatik, Universität Passau, Postfach 25 40, D–W8390 Passau, Germany. E-mail: lengauer@fmi.uni-passau.de

Abstract. Loop transformations for parallelization are linear, invertible mappings from an iteration space to space-time; a further restriction on the mapping, unimodularity, simplifies code generation. In most previous work, non-unimodular transformations require a potentially large amount of overhead. We sketch a method for producing efficient code for non-unimodular loop transformations.

1 Introduction

Loop parallelization transforms a nested-loop source program, SP, without explicit parallelism into an explicitly parallel target program, TP, with the same input/output behaviour.

For our purposes, SP consists of r perfectly nested loops with unit steps (either $+1$ or -1). To keep the notation simple, our convention is that the lower bound is on the left and the upper bound on the right in the loop head, independent of the sign of the loop step [2]. The loop bounds are piecewise linear expressions in integer constants, integer-valued variables, and enclosing loop indices. If a left (right) bound is not linear, then it must be a maximum (minimum) of linear expressions. TP also consists of r perfectly nested loops.

Our computation model is in terms of sets of integer points in the cartesian space $\mathbb{R}^r$. IS (the *index space* or *iteration space*) is the set for SP, and TS (the *target space*) the set for TP.

The parallelization is specified by a *space-time transformation*—a linear mapping, T, from IS to TS. (It is represented by an $r \times r$ integer matrix.) T distributes the operations of SP in time and space but preserves the data dependences; operations that are mapped to the same time but to different places are executed in parallel in TP. TP enumerates the points of TS with one loop per dimension. It is not relevant here which loops iterate sequentially and which in parallel; but the idea of loop parallelization is that as many loops as possible are parallel.

The syntactic restrictions on the source program ensure that IS is a convex polyhedron; the convexity enables the automatic derivation of T. T must be invertible. Otherwise, more than one iteration of SP may be mapped to the same space-time point, creating parallelism at a finer grain than intended.

The convexity of IS also ensures that the images of the boundaries of IS under T are the boundaries of the convex closure of TS. When T is unimodular (to be defined later), TS is also convex.

2 Preliminaries

Let A be a $p \times r$ integer matrix and b an integer vector in $\mathbb{Z}^p$; (A, b) denotes the set of (integer) points $x \in \mathbb{Z}^r$ such that $A x \leq b$. e_i denotes the unit vector in dimension i, i.e., the constant vector in which component i is 1 and every other component is 0. $a \stackrel{c}{=} b$ stands for $(a \bmod c) = (b \bmod c)$.

We begin by deriving an explicit description of the polyhedron $\mathcal{IS}$ derived from the loop bounds of $\mathcal{SP}$. Following the notation of Ribas [6], a matrix E (G) is constructed from the coefficients of the loop indices in the left (right) bounds, and a vector f (h) is constructed from the parts of the left (right) loop bounds that are independent of the loop indices (the integer constants and integer variables). E and G are strictly lower triangular matrices since loop bounds may only depend on the indices of enclosing loops. Then $\mathcal{IS}$ is the set of points x such that:

$$\begin{bmatrix} E - I_E \\ I_G - G \end{bmatrix} x \leq \begin{bmatrix} -f \\ h \end{bmatrix}.$$

We call this the *normal form* of the polyhedron and refer to the matrix as A and the vector as b:

$$A = \begin{bmatrix} E - I_E \\ I_G - G \end{bmatrix} \qquad b = \begin{bmatrix} -f \\ h \end{bmatrix}.$$

Each row in I_E and I_G is a unit vector. If the corresponding row in E (G) is for loop ℓ, then the vector is e_ℓ. When all loop bounds are linear, there is only one row per loop, and $I_E = I_G = I$. The distinction between I_E (I_G) and I is necessary only for piecewise linear loop bounds; these can arise in a target program even when they are not present in the source program.

Since T is required to be invertible, T^{-1} exists and the explicit description of the image of the boundaries of $\mathcal{IS}$ under T can be derived as follows:

$$\begin{aligned} & A x \leq b \\ = \quad & \{ \ T^{-1} y = x, \text{ for } y \in T\mathcal{S}, \text{ associativity of matrix product } \} \\ & (A T^{-1}) y \leq b. \end{aligned}$$

That is, $T\mathcal{S} \subseteq (A T^{-1}, b)$. But not every point within the boundaries necessarily corresponds to a point in $\mathcal{IS}$; when T^{-1} has rational components, only a subset of the (integer-valued) points map back to points in $\mathcal{IS}$. In addition, the matrix $A T^{-1}$ does not share the structure of A; it is not straight-forward to convert it to loop bounds.

3 Unimodularity

A transformation is *unimodular* if and only if 1) it is invertible, 2) it maps integer points to integer points, and 3) its inverse maps integer points to integer points. An integer matrix is unimodular if and only if it has a unit determinant. Thus, when T is unimodular, then T^{-1} is also in $\mathbb{Z}^{r \times r}$. A unimodular transformation has the benefit that $T\mathcal{S}$ is also convex: $T\mathcal{S} = (A T^{-1}, b)$. To enumerate the points in $T\mathcal{S}$, it suffices to enumerate every integer-valued point within the boundaries.

But the description of TS by AT^{-1} is not suitable for the creation of loops: all inequalities can depend on all components of y (which are to be loop indices), whereas loop bounds may only depend on indices of enclosing loops. We must transform the polyhedron (AT^{-1}, b) to an equivalent one, (A', b'), where A' has a structure from which the loop bounds can be read off:

$$A' = \begin{bmatrix} E' - I_{E'} \\ I_{G'} - G' \end{bmatrix} \qquad b' = \begin{bmatrix} -f' \\ h' \end{bmatrix} .$$

Several algorithms for calculating A' and b' have been proposed [1, 4, 6, 7]. They proceed by eliminating variables from the inequalities. Geometrically, this projects the polyhedron on the different axes of TS to obtain the bounds in each dimension. The derived bounds may be inexact because redundant inequalities are generated; a mechanical elimination may remove some but not necessarily all of them. In this paper, we use the Fourier-Motzkin method promoted by Ancourt and Irigoin [1].

4 Non-Unimodularity

A non-unimodular transformation produces a non-convex target space. This leads to "holes" in TS: integer points within the convex closure of TS that are not elements of TS. The holes create "jagged" borders. We propose a three-step procedure for coping with non-unimodular transformations: 1) use the Fourier-Motzkin method to derive the loop bounds for the convex closure of TS, 2) perturb the solutions using piecewise linear functions to describe the jagged boundaries of TS, and 3) use non-unit steps for those loops that would otherwise enumerate holes.

Instead of applying the Fourier-Motzkin method to AT^{-1}, we first transform T^{-1} to an integer matrix by a change of basis: let m be the least common multiple of the denominators in T^{-1}. Then, let $T' = mT^{-1}$. T' is an integer matrix by construction. The polyhedron defined by the resulting matrix A' and vector b' is defined over a new set of coordinates, y', which is a transformation of the coordinates of TS, y; they are related by: $y = my'$. Although the loop bounds can be read off from A' and b', the resulting target program is phrased in terms of y' and must be transformed into one in terms of y, by scaling with a factor of m (i.e., by multiplying b' by m and dividing each point by m).

5 Example

We take the loop structure of, e.g., the polynomial product and the matrix-vector product. Figure 1 shows the loops and the index space along with the matrices and vectors derived from the loop bounds and the normal form of the index space.

A non-unimodular transformation T and its inverse are shown in Fig. 2. After obtaining T' by multiplying each element of T^{-1} with the factor $m = 3$, the Fourier-Motzkin method yields A' and b', in which two more inequalities (the first and the fourth row) provide bounds for the outer loop; d_1 is the projection axis. The other four rows are from AT'. The inequalities at the bottom of the figure are the normal form of the convex closure of TS. (In the figure, TS is depicted with its precise

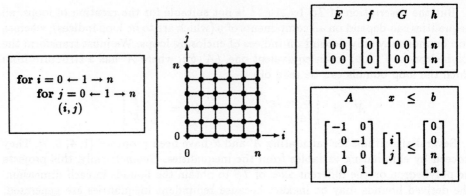

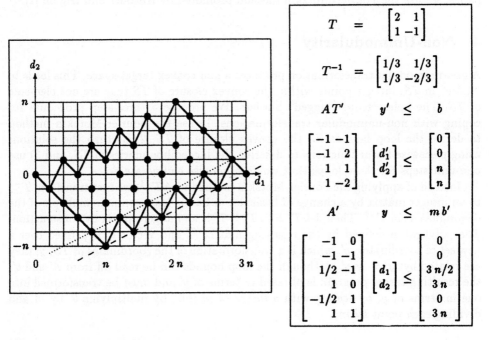

Fig. 1. The source program and index space.

Fig. 2. A non-unimodular transformation.

bounds.) The first three rows of A' form $E' - I_{E'}$, the last three $I_{G'} - G'$. The first three rows of $m\,b'$ form $-f'$, the last three h'.

The loop bounds of $T\mathcal{P}$ are composed directly from E', G', f', and h'; multiple rows for a left (right) loop bound are combined with the max (min) function. The steps reflect the scaling by m. $T\mathcal{P}$ is:

for $d_1 = 0 \leftarrow 1 \rightarrow 3\,n$
    for $d_2 = \max(-d_1, (d_1 - 3\,n)/2) \leftarrow 3 \rightarrow \min(d_1/2, 3\,n - d_1)$
        $((d_1 + d_2)/3, (d_1 - 2\,d_2)/3)$.

These loop bounds define the convex closure of $\mathcal{TS}$. For a unimodular transformation, it suffices to coerce fractional points defined by these bounds to the nearest integer-valued point inside, since $\mathcal{TS}$ is convex. But, for a non-unimodular transformation, this is not so. The nearest integer-valued point may be a hole; consider the lower boundary from n to $3n$ in Fig. 2. Even integer-valued points on the convex boundaries may be holes (though there are none in the example). The bounds need to be perturbed to follow the jagged edges shown in the figure.

In previous work [2], we described jagged boundaries by guarded commands in which each clause is a linear function. Crucial to this approach was the separate analysis of time in the space-time transformation. The description of jagged boundaries that we present here, is based on the traditional view of the space-time transformation as a whole. Which of the two methods is more suitable in the context of systolizing compilation remains to be studied.

Space limitations prevent us from describing the method in general, but we illustrate it with an example. Take the top boundary of $\mathcal{IS}$ (Fig. 1). Its points are of the form (i, n), for i ranging from 0 to n. T maps (i, n) to $(2i + n, i - n)$. These are the points on the lower right convex boundary of $\mathcal{TS}$ (the dashed line in Fig. 2). Points in $\mathcal{TS}$ have the coordinates (d_1, d_2). The first coordinate of the image of the top boundary of $\mathcal{IS}$ under T must satisfy the equation $d_1 \overset{2}{=} n$. That is, every second grid line of the d_1-axis qualifies. The second coordinate must satisfy the equation for the respective convex boundary of $\mathcal{TS}$. The third row of $(A', m\,b')$ is the image of the inequality that describes the top boundary of $\mathcal{IS}$ (the fourth row in the normal form of $\mathcal{IS}$). Thus, the equation is $d_2 = (d_1 - 3n)/2$. For values of d_1 that do not satisfy $d_1 \overset{2}{=} n$, the correct boundary point of $\mathcal{TS}$ is identified by an equation that specifies a line parallel to the convex boundary that lies inside the convex hull of $\mathcal{TS}$ (the dotted line in Fig. 2). In general, there can be several equidistant parallel lines; their number, including the convex boundary, is equal to the modulus. We can also determine the distance of neighbouring lines; in this case, it is $3/2$.

Jagged boundaries are specified by modifying the convex boundary with an added (subtracted) modulo term $lmod$ ($umod$) for lower (upper) bounds. In this case:

$$\textbf{for } d_1 = 0 \;\leftarrow 1 \rightarrow\; 3n$$
$$\quad\textbf{for } d_2 = \max(-d_1, (d_1 - 3n)/2 + lmod) \;\leftarrow 3 \rightarrow\; \min(d_1/2 - umod, 3n - d_1)$$
$$\quad\quad ((d_1 + d_2)/3, (d_1 - 2d_2)/3)$$

where

$$lmod = (3/2)\,((n - d_1) \bmod 2)$$
$$umod = (3/2)\,(d_1 \bmod 2) .$$

In general, the parallel lines containing the points on the jagged boundary are ordered either by increasing distance or by decreasing distance to the convex boundary. This ordering is derived directly from the way T skews $\mathcal{IS}$. It is encoded into the orientation of the subtraction in the modulo term. When 2 is the modulus, there is only one parallel line to the convex boundary and either ordering yields the same result.

The above loop bounds require exact arithmetic, i.e., the divisions by 2 must produce a fractional result. They cannot be implemented by integer division as in many programming languages [3]. An alternative is to combine the fractions; our theory guarantees that, if the numerators are added first, the result of the division is an integer.

6 Conclusion

Not all loop transformations used in parallelizing compilation are unimodular [7]. Also, many systolic arrays are the result of non-unimodular transformations. In previous work [2], we have presented an unconventional way of approaching non-unimodularity. Here, we have recast it in a more conventional setting.

Others that include non-unimodular transformations generate loops that represent the convex closure of TS and then use a test in each iteration to weed out the holes [5]. One of the aims of parallelizing compilation is to reduce the amount of run-time testing that tells a processor what to do. Our more precise description of the target space avoids run-time tests for coping with non-unimodularity.

Acknowledgements

The first author is grateful to Corinne Ancourt for helpful ideas. Financial support was provided by the Science and Engineering Research Council (SERC), grant no. GR/G55457.

References

1. C. Ancourt and F. Irigoin. Scanning polyhedra with DO loops. In *Proc. Third ACM SIGPLAN Symp. on Principles & Practice of Parallel Programming (PPoPP)*, pages 39–50. ACM Press, Apr. 1991.
2. M. Barnett. *A Systolizing Compiler*. PhD thesis, Department of Computer Sciences, The University of Texas at Austin, May 1992. Technical Report TR-92-13.
3. R. T. Boute. The Euclidean definition of the functions div and mod. *ACM Trans. on Programming Languages and Systems*, 14(2):127–144, Apr. 1992.
4. P. Feautrier. Semantical analysis and mathematical programming. In M. Cosnard, Y. Robert, P. Quinton, and M. Raynal, editors, *Parallel & Distributed Algorithms*, pages 309–320. North-Holland, 1989.
5. L.-C. Lu and M. Chen. New loop transformation techniques for massive parallelism. Technical Report YALEU/DCS/TR-833, Department of Computer Science, Yale University, Oct. 1990.
6. H. B. Ribas. *Automatic Generation of Systolic Programs from Nested Loops*. PhD thesis, Department of Computer Science, Carnegie-Mellon University, June 1990. Technical Report CMU-CS-90-143.
7. M. Wolf and M. Lam. A loop transformation theory and an algorithm to maximize parallelism. *IEEE Trans. on Parallel and Distributed Systems*, 2(4):452–471, Oct. 1991.

This article was processed using the LaTeX macro package with LLNCS style

PEPSIM-*ST*: a Simulator Tool for benchmarking

Michael M. Gutzmann and Klaus Steffan

Institut für Mathematische Maschinen und Datenverarbeitung VII,
Universität Erlangen-Nürnberg, Martensstr. 3, D-8520 Erlangen, Germany

email: gutzmann@immd7.informatik.uni-erlangen.de

Abstract

A simulator for performance evaluation of SIMD type computers is presented. Different architecture models are defined and simulated, using a high level hardware description. Basic problems are programmed in an architecture independent pseudo code and interpreted by the simulator for different architecture configurations. The simulator observes the execution of the program and finally presents all performance data as specified by the user. The results from the simulation are used to find bottlenecks in massively parallel computers, due to a given problem. Examples are presented for DAP-like architectures. Maspar MP-1 and Wavetracer DTC simulations are in preparation.

1   Introduction

Many different massively parallel computers will be available in the next years: the manufacturers offer all types of elementary processors, varying in bit length, instruction set, stages of pipelining, and in cycle usage. Synchronous architectures, e.g. vector, array or systolic array computers, and asynchronous architectures, e.g. loosely, tightly or memory coupled multiprocessor systems result from connecting many or even thousands of processors. The interconnection networks have different bandwidths, are irregular or regular and either static or dynamically switchable. An overview is given by Erhard [6] and Giloi [9]. A comparison of the DAP, MP-1 and DTC is given by Reinartz [18].

In this field of different parallel architectures, the need for a global benchmark for massively parallel computers that affects both, industrial applications and research, becomes more and more important, many approaches to performance evaluation of parallel architectures are known, presented for instance by Erhard et al [7].

The first difficulty is to characterize all the examined architectures in a common and homogenous way; this is an important basic step for defining parallel performance metrics, as shown by Worlton [27]. One main problem in defining parallel performance metrics is to gain fairness and objectivity for the comparison of the architectures, as discussed by Sun and Gustafson [23].

Defining a benchmark is a challenge because of the amount of parameters which have to be evaluated (e.g. problem size, chosen algorithm, efficiency of program, compiler, operating system and architecture parameters). For more details see Dongarra et al [5]. The possibilities of separating efficient, problem solving commands from those for organizing purposes are discussed by Riganati and Schneck [19] and Paul and Martin [17]. The question to decide whether a command is efficient for the concrete problem solution or not - this does not affect any hardware specific optimizations - is carried out by Hockney [14]. As a result of the complexity of defining a benchmark for more than one architecture, up to now no benchmark has become known to be suited for comparing massively parallel computers of different types. Instead of this, the benchmarks are defined for specific problems on architectures of special type. Some examples are given:

- Livermore Loops and Livermore Fortran Kernels, (McMahon) [16]
- Argonne LINPACK Benchmark, (Dongarra) [4]
- Los Alamos Benchmark, (Griffin and Simmons) [10]
- Dhrystones and Dhrystones-2, (Weiker) [25]
- Whetstones, (Cornow and Wichman) [3]

The characteristics of each benchmark have to be worked out carefully in order to evaluate its quality for the examined architectures and for the given problem (Berry et al) [1]. Characteristic points, while comparing and evaluating the results of different benchmarks - most of them are very hardware specific - are shown by Worlton [26]. It seems to be likely that a common benchmark – for e.g. a class of problems on synchronous and asynchronous types of architectures – will not be available within the next years at some level of fairness.

As a result of that, our approach to benchmarking massively parallel computers focuses on architectures of the following types next to:

- massively parallel architecture (more than 10^3 processors)
- single type of processors (in one architecture model)
- synchronous computing (instructions may be different)
- synchronous communication (directions may be different)
- regular, static interconnection networks (no routing)
- local memory for each processor (no communication via shared memory)

This class of architectures is similar to SIMD, although the hardware models are not restricted to the parallel execution of the same single instruction. Therefore, they can briefly be characterized as *Parallel Synchronous Instruction* (PSI) *Models*. In our project *Performance Evaluation of Parallel Synchronous Instruction Models* (PEPSIM), we concentrate on these architecture models. As far as the class of SIMD architectures is the most public subclass of PSI architectures, we reduce PSI models to SIMD models next to. Investigations on SIMD architectures with multiple different instruction streams, very close to the PSI models, are done by Gutzmann [11].

The class of problems we concentrate on is typically characterized by algorithms which are massively **data parallel** and static in **data mapping** and very **computing & communication intensive**. The algorithms are analyzed and transformed due to the SIMD principle, then they are mapped data-parallel onto a target architecture. Thus, efficient programs for different models are generated automatically, following a basic transformation rule system to guarantee comparability.

The programs and the input values are given to the simulator in order to be interpreted, executed and observed. The results which are obtained from the simulator are then analyzed and evaluated. The *Simulator Tool* (ST) offers important possibilities for the observation of the execution of basic algorithms on different architecture models, examined in our project PEPSIM. So far, the ST is planned to fulfill the requirements of fairness in the specified area of performance analysis.

2 Basic Concept

The concept of our approach is based on the automatically derivation of SIMD programs, first shown by Gutzmann [12]. The concept can be divided into two main parts: **program generation** (fig. 1, left) and **program interpretation** (fig. 1 right). The program generation is discussed in this section whereas the program interpretation and the associated simulator are carried out in more detail in the next sections.

2.1 The main properties of the concept

For the specified class of architectures and problems we focus on, two demands describe the main effort of PEPSIM: **comparability** and **efficiency**. The first goal guarantees comparability in evaluating the performance of one problem on different machines. The second goal means to guarantee the efficient usage of the underlying hardware resources in each investigation. The following points are regarded as subgoals to be fulfilled in this concept:

- use a high level language for defining the architecture models, easy to modify and easy to extend,
- analyze the efficiency of the architectures due to any algorithm with any problem size in each dimension,
- find bottlenecks and balance the hardware resources in communication and computation (*instead of defining virtual tera flop machines*).

In order to overcome these problems basically, we suggest the automatically generation of efficient programs for different architectures, using deterministic abstract transformation and mapping rules.

2.2 The ASL language

The carrier language for the algorithm description in all steps of transformation is called *Algorithm Specification Language* (ASL) and is mainly based on RGL, which was introduced by Thalhofer [24]. The language ASL, developed by Xiong and Gutzmann [28], is well suited for the description of the problems we are investigating: An ASL specification is an abstract description of the mathematical

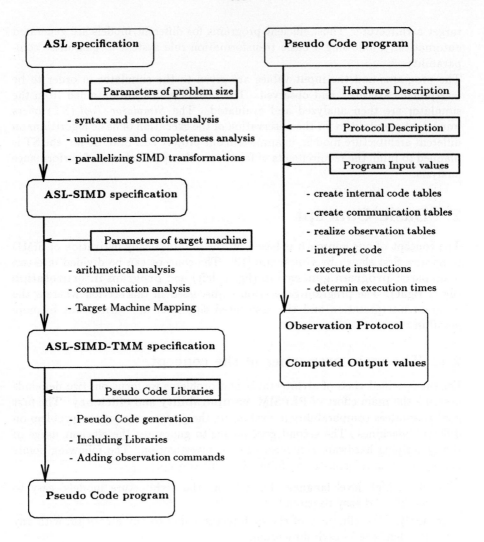

Figure 1: steps of the basic concept

relation between input and output parameters in terms of recurrence equations. Recurrence equations are widely used in the area of particular parallel numerical algorithms. Due to the single assignment principle for the identifiers (not variables) of the equations, artificial dependencies - which would suppress parallelization - are avoided. The resulting algorithm specification is independent of an underlying architecture or problem size.

An ASL specification does not contain any operational description on how (i.e. which order) to compute results and intermediate values from the input parameters. This offers the chance to rearrange and transform the equations in order to meet the requirements of the SIMD operation principle. ASL allows to carry out such transformations automatically.

2.3 Generating the ASL-SIMD specification

Starting from the user ASL specification and the parameters of the current problem size, the system analyzes the syntax and the semantics, (Xiong [28]). Not before this step the parameters of the current problem size are required. The sizes of the identifiers are used for the semantically analysis, e.g. for checking the validity of operations in each given dimension.

Analyzing the uniqueness and the completeness is important to guarantee the correctness of the specification for the following steps. Completeness in this context means that all required information (identifiers, constants) is available. The transformations for checking uniqueness and completeness were outlined by Helm [13].

The parallelizing SIMD transformations generate the architecture independent ASL-SIMD specification. These transformation steps are performed to meet the requirements of the SIMD operation principle, since the equations are divided into calculation and communication. Several elementary textual and structural transformation steps are performed. Important SIMD transformations are e.g. the **adaptation of index expressions** and the **compression** of problem data, due to the processors. In both of them the ASL equations are broken up and new communication equations are generated due to the SIMD operation principle. The transformation steps of this process were carried out in detail by Stroiczek [22].

2.4 Transformation to the ASL-SIMD-TMM specification

The architecture dependent transformation requires special parameters of the target machine in order to decide for an efficient mapping and to generate the *Target Machine Mapped* (ASL-SIMD-TMM) specification. As far as we concentrate on static mapping problems, a deterministic and decidable analysis of the algorithm demands - especially depending on the given problem size - is regarded to be possible: the class of subproblems, for which we can generate an optimal mapping automatically (in reasonable time) has to be defined. The termination of our mapping algorithm has to be proved.

Mapping data-parallel algorithms onto synchronous SIMD type architectures requires a data dependency analysis to determine the order of execution and the degree of parallelism. Very similar strategies are discussed by mapping recurrence equations onto synchronous Systolic Array architectures. In was shown in these investigations that an important subclass of algorithms, the same which describe data dependencies by affine index expressions, can be efficiently analyzed. Investigations in this context were done by Clauss [2] and Sedukhin [20].

2.5 Translation to the Pseudo Code program

The pseudo code for the simulator can be generated automatically from the final representation of the algorithm in ASL syntax, the ASL-SIMD-TMM specification. Different pseudo code libraries, including macros for general communication patterns which are implemented for different interconnection networks, are provided to support code generation and to minimize compilation effort. The idea is to have a minimum of code by realizing an abstract execution mode. This means that complex functions which are often used and supported by any target architecture being simulated, are described by their names, input and output values, and by their cycle usage, as far as known. The concept is to be modular and hierarchical as far as possible in the task of code generation, shown by Kern [15].

The user can specify the degree of observation detail in the ASL specification by making use of special bounded comments including Pseudo Code instructions. The pseudo code generation is independent of any underlying target architecture, all architecture dependent transformations are done in ASL before code generation. At this point, in general the concept allows to generate any code e.g. *DAP Fortran* or *Maspar MPL* or *Wavetracer MultiC* or anything else, due to the class of target architectures.

3   The Simulator

The simulator is the most important part of the concept, pointed out in this paper. The simulator simulates any target architecture due to a specified hardware description and it interprets and executes any pseudo code program which is generated for that architecture. While doing this, the simulator observes the program execution and determines all performance data which are demanded for the analysis.

3.1   The I/O Interface

The simulator can be characterized briefly by focusing on its input, used for e.g. configuration and simulation and on its output. The simulator is configured by two input description files:

  – the hardware description for the target architecture

  – the protocol description for the observation of program execution

For program execution, the interpreter requires further input:

  – the pseudo code program for the specified hardware

  – the input values which are required from the pseudo code program

The outputs of the simulator are:

  – the result of the program execution and the computed output values

  – an observation protocol including information about the program flow

3.2   Hardware description

The hardware of the target architecture is described in an abstract high-level language, thus the description is not based on details e.g. register transfer or gate level of the specific hardware. Typical parameters which are required for the configuration are shown in fig. 2.

The simulator allows the specification of the standard cycle usage for each instruction and additionally a minimum and maximum cycle usage for 8 bit or 32 bit arithmetic in integer mode and 16 bit or 64 bit arithmetic in floating point mode. There are three different possibilities of declaring neighborhood connections and broadcast buses:

1. functions: $i,j \Rightarrow i,j+1$ *(connects each $PE_{i,j}$ with its right neighbor)*
2. explicit tables: **0 TO 31, 0 TO 992** *(specifies two cyclic connections)*
3. musical bits: $\{3,2,1,0\} \Rightarrow \{2,1,0,3\}$ *(perfect shuffle connection)*

Musical bits, described by Flanders [8], are also used for the efficient description of the connectivity in e.g. hypercubes. Direct connections or buses can be defined using name aliases for comfortable application. An example of typical information which is used for hardware description, e.g. for an architecture which is very close to the DAP 510 (2^5 PEs in each dimension, 10 Mhz clock) and called XDAP 510, is given as a subset in fig. 2.

1. **PROCESSORS** 32 ∗ 32 .	6. **OPCODES**
2. **SCALAR MEMORY** 2024 ; 2 Kbyte	*the definition of the execution cycle usage for some instructions*
3. **PE MEMORY** 4096 ; 32 Kbit	*integer = 16 bit, float = 32 bit*
4. **CONNECTIONS:**	6.1 *ARITHMETIC (int,float)*

4. **CONNECTIONS:**
ALIAS SHEC; PORT 0: 32
$\{ i , j \} \Rightarrow \{ i , (j+1) \% 32 \}$
shift east cyclic 8 bit
ALIAS SHSC; PORT 3: 32
$\{ i , j \} \Rightarrow \{ (i+1) \% 32 , j \}$
shift south cyclic 8 bit

5. **BROADCASTS:**
ALIAS BUSns; HIGHWAY 0: 10
$\{ C , j \} \Rightarrow \{ i , j \}$
using a function
ALIAS BUSwe; HIGHWAY 1: 10
$\{9 ,8, 7, 6, 5, -4, -3, -2, -1, -0\}$
using musical bits

6.1 *ARITHMETIC (int,float)*

instruction	scalar	parallel
ADD:	16	72
MUL:	45	725
DIV:	121	950

6.2 *TRANSCENDENT (float)*

instruction	scalar	parallel
EXP:	2200	2100
SQR:	1180	970

6.3 *COMPARE (int,float)*

instruction	scalar	parallel
CMPEQ:	12	51

6.4 *OTHERS ..*

Figure 2: extract of a hardware description (XDAP 510)

3.3 Protocol description

Different levels of detail can be defined for program observation. This can be done by selecting single instructions (IN_k) and choosing entire groups of instructions (IG_l).

Thus the protocol description is defined by a set of keywords I_i ($I_i\epsilon$ [IN, IG], i=k+l: number of keywords). All information which is not required is filtered out. The following parameters are used for the protocol:

– I_activity: set to the number of active PEs for each instruction group I_i
– I_count: set to the number of calls for each instruction group I_i
– I_cycle: set to the accumulated cycles for each instruction group I_i

The information held in I_activity, I_count and I_cycle is available at each time step of program execution and can be stored as defined.

3.4 The Pseudo Code

The pseudo code provides a high-level and architecture independent assembler like language for interpretation by the simulator. The instruction names are the same for all different machine models. The instruction set can be extended for special applications by adding the required functions to the instruction table. Two data types, *integer* and *float* are supported for using constants and variables. A modifier, defined by two characters, is used to describe the data type of each operand. Additional modifiers, using one character, describe the functionality of non arithmetic operands:

	all		scalar	parallel
communication	C	integer	SI	PI
organization	O	floating point	SF	PF

Activity bits are used when executing parallel commands on the PE array to allow for masking special PEs (parameter ACTIVITY in the protocol description). The simulator distinguishes between two addressing modes:

1. immediate addressing (e.g. ADD.SI #5,x), that means: {x=x+5}
2. direct addressing (e.g. MUL.SF x,y), that means: {y=x*y}

Indirect addressing (e.g. using pointers) is supported, but not needed yet in our architecture examples. Pseudo code instructions are classified in three main groups, listed below, depending on their expressiveness and functional context.

- **high-level instructions**, obtained from the ASL specification
- **internal instructions**, generated for the machine language
- **observing commands**, added to the pseudo code instructions

3.5 Interpreter

Before interpreting and executing the pseudo code program, the simulator has to organize internal structures and tables. Due to these demands, the simulator evaluates the hardware and the protocol description.

The simulator initialization is mainly based on the generation of an internal opcode table. The table is filled with default values next to. By reading the hardware description, the table contents is substituted by all given information. The parser uses this table in order to check and identify the instructions of the pseudo code program. The following steps are performed:

- the opcode table with default values for all instructions is generated
- the hardware description is read, checked and analyzed
- all given hardware information substitutes the default values
- the connection tables are realized by evaluating the given expressions

Apart from the generation of the opcode table, the protocol description is read, analyzed and an internal table is created, due to the specified groups IG and their instructions IN.

The pseudo code interpreter is the kernel of the simulator. After the internal configurations, the interpreter requires the pseudo code program for execution and the input values for computation.

4 Results

The investigations in this paper are concentrated on a typical matrix multiplication algorithm which is characterized by integer arithmetic and communication demands. The implementation of the problem is based on the following algorithm:

$$
\begin{aligned}
&for\ \ (i = 1;\ i \leq side_length;\ i++) \\
&\quad mr = genmatrix\ (row\ (i),\ m1) \\
&\quad mc = genmatrix\ (col\ (i),\ m2) \\
&\quad mx = mx + mr * mc \\
&end
\end{aligned}
$$

Figure 3: algorithm for the matrix multiplication

The algorithm was chosen because it describes a very general and simple problem. The function *genmatrix* which duplicates either rows or columns to a matrix is based on recursive doubling and uses the nearest neighbor connections.

We present the results from the simulation of DAP-like architectures as for the XDAP 410 (2^4 PEs in two dimensions $= 2^{4^2}$), the XDAP 510 (2^{5^2} PEs) and the XDAP 710 (2^{7^2} PEs). The results underline earlier investigations which have discussed the communication overhead in large SIMD architectures, outlined by Strey [21].

	XDAP 410			XDAP 510			XDAP 710		
Instr.	calls	cycles	%	calls	cycles	%	calls	cycles	%
ADD.PI	16	1968	2.5	32	3936	1.9	128	15744	0.8
MUL.PI	16	30400	38.7	32	60800	29.0	128	243200	11.8
LOOP.O	16	240	0.3	32	480	0.2	128	1920	0.1
MOVE.C	48	5184	6.6	84	9072	4.3	284	30672	1.5
SHIFT.C	198	38768	49.4	456	131072	62.6	2316	1739552	84.8
MASK.O	185	1665	2.1	428	3852	1.8	2194	19746	1.0
$\sum$.PI	32	32368	41.2	64	64736	30.9	256	258944	12.6
$\sum$.C	246	43952	56.3	540	140144	67.0	2600	1770224	86.3
$\sum$.O	201	1905	2.4	460	4332	2.1	2322	21666	1.0
total	479	78225	100	1064	209212	100	5178	2050854	100

Table 1: matrix multiplication on the XDAP 410/510/710

Table 1 shows elementary performance characteristics of the three different architecture sizes. The results show that the communication overhead grows by a factor x faster than the arithmetical computation. The factor x depends on the communication demands, in our case x is approximately 2.

This is not surprising because the communication distance grows by scaling the architecture size. The large mesh based network causes the break down of the communication: in the third case the communication uses 84.8 % of the total program execution time.

Our first and very simple experiment demonstrates effects which occur when scaling problem size and architecture size without modifying the architecture, the algorithm is the same in all cases too.

Instr.	calls	COMMUNICATION: factor 4			ARITHMETIC: factor 4		
		cycles	%	PE use	cycles	%	PE use
ADD.PI	32	3936	3.5	100.0	992	0.6	100.0
MUL.PI	32	60800	54.7	100.0	15200	9.4	100.0
LOOP.O	32	480	0.4	–	480	0.3	–
MOVE.C	84	9072	8.2	49.9	9072	5.6	49.9
SHIFT.C	456	32768	29.5	36.4	131072	81.4	36.4
MASK.O	428	3852	3.5	–	3852	2.4	–
$\sum$.PI	64	64736	58.2	100.0	16192	10.1	100.0
$\sum$.C	540	41840	37.8	39.2	140144	87.2	37.3
$\sum$.O	460	4332	3.9	–	4332	2.7	–
total	1064	110908	100	73.1	160668	100	42.6

Table 2: matrix multiplication on the modified XDAP 510

In our second experiment we change the power of communication and computation of the XDAP 510: In the first case the processor communication bandwidth is enlarged by factor 4, in the second case the processor arithmetic is faster by a factor 4.

This experiment is done to investigate the effects when changing the power balance of an architecture. The importance and relevance of a balanced system, mainly concerning communication and arithmetic, is outlined by these examples: in contrast to quite small architectures, the *balance of power* in massively parallel architectures requires more effort for efficient communication than for computation, this is ignored by many manufacturers up to now. We observe these effects in our current work many times.

The **validation** of our results has been done by comparison with the DAP 510, installed in our institute. The simulation based performance data presented in table 1 are conform with real measurements on the DAP 510 by more than 95%. In other test cases we obtained more than 98% conformity.

5   Current and future Work

The next steps to be done concentrate on defining other architectures, e.g. Maspar-like or Wavetracer-like. An interesting research field in describing other architectures is seen in the interconnection networks. Not only different bandwidths but alternative connectivities have to be investigated while increasing the amount of processors.

We hope that our investigations will be supported soon by the automatically derivation of pseudo code programs, based on ASL specifications, as described in the project PEPSIM.

References

[1] M. Berry, G. Gybenko, and J. Larson. Scientific benchmark characterizations. *Parallel Computing*, 17(10,11):1173–1194, December 1991.

[2] Ph. Clauss and G.R. Perrin. Synthesis of Process Arrays. In C.R. Jesshope and K.D. Reinartz, editors, *CONPAR 88*, pages 743–753, Cambridge, 1988. Cambridge University Press.

[3] H.J. Cornow and B.A. Wichman. A Synthetic Benchmark. *Computer Journal*, 19(1):43–49, 1976.

[4] J.J. Dongarra. The LINPACK Benchmark: An Explanation. *Supercomputing, 1st Int. Conf., Athens*, 456-74, June 1987.

[5] J.J. Dongarra, J.L. Martin, and J. Worlton. Computer benchmarking: paths and pitfalls. *IEEE spectrum*, 7:38–43, 1987.

[6] W. Erhard. *Parallelrechnerstrukturen*. Teubner–Verlag, Stuttgart, 1990.

[7] W. Erhard, A. Grefe, M. Gutzmann, and D. Pöschl. *Vergleich von Leistungsbewertungsverfahren für unkonventionelle Rechner*, Arbeitsberichte des IMMD (Informatik), Universität Erlangen–Nürnberg, 24(5). 1991.

[8] P.M. Flanders. Musical Bits – A Generalized Method for a Class of Data Movements on the DAP. Technical Report CM 70, ICL, 1980.

[9] W.K. Giloi. *Rechnerarchitektur*. Springer–Verlag, Berlin, Heidelberg, New York, 1981.

[10] J.H. Griffin and M.L. Simmons. Los Alamos National Laborator Computer Benchmarking 1983. *Tech. Report LA 10151-MS, Los Alamos Nat. Lab.*, June 1984.

[11] M.M. Gutzmann. Algorithmenbasierte Untersuchung der Einführung mehrerer Befehlsströme am DAP. Master's thesis, Universität Erlangen–Nürnberg, 1988.

[12] M.M. Gutzmann. Performance Evaluation Of Parallel SIMD-Systems by Interpreting Automatically Transformed Algorithms On Simulated Architectures. In N.N.Mirenkov, editor, *Proceedings of the International Conference Parallel on Computing Technologies*, pages 395–406. Computing Center Novosibirsk, USSR, World Scientific, September 1991.

[13] M. Helm. Analyse und Transformation von RGL–Gleichungsschablonen mit affinen Indexausdrücken. Master's thesis, Universität Erlangen–Nürnberg, IMMD VII, 1989.

[14] R. Hockney. Performance parameters and benchmarking of supercomputers. *Parallel Computing*, 17(10,11):1111–1130, December 1991.

[15] R. Kern. Automatische Generierung von Programmen aus RGL-Spezifikationen in SIMD-Normalform und maschinenunabhängige Interpretation des erzeugten Pseudocodes. Master's thesis, Universität Erlangen–Nürnberg, IMMD VII, Mai 1991.

[16] F.H. McMahon. The Livermore FORTRAN Kernel Test of the numerical performance range. *Performance Evaluation of Supercomputers, Amsterdam*, 143-86, 1988.

[17] G. Paul and J.L. Martin. Aspects of performance evaluation in supercomputers and scientific applications. *Int. Workshop on Modeling Techniques and Performance Evaluation, Paris*, 1987.

[18] K.D. Reinartz. Quasireguläre Kommunikation in Multiprozessoren. In *Verbindungsnetzwerke für Parallelrechner und Breitband-Übermittlungssysteme*, pages 35–41. ITG/GI Workshop, Stuttgart, 1991.

[19] J.P. Riganati and P.B. Schneck. Supercomputing. *Computer*, 17(10):97–113, 1984.

[20] S.G. Sedukhin and E.V. Trishina. An Automated Procedure For Synthesis Of SystolicWavefront Arrays. In C.R. Jesshope and K.D. Reinartz, editors, *CONPAR 88*, pages 735–742, Cambridge, 1988. Cambridge University Press.

[21] A. Strey. *Ein Vergleich von Verbindungsnetzwerken für große SIMD Parallelrechner*. PhD thesis, Arbeitsberichte des IMMD (Informatik), Universität Erlangen–Nürnberg, 1991.

[22] J. Stroiczek. Automatische Transformation von RGL-Spezifikationen mit affinen Indexausdrücken in eine SIMD-Normalform. Master's thesis, Universität Erlangen–Nürnberg, IMMD VII, März 1991.

[23] X. Sun and J.L. Gustafson. Toward a better parallel performance metric. *Parallel Computing*, 17(10,11):1093–1109, December 1991.

[24] K. Thalhofer. *Automatische Generierung von Programmen für SIMD-Parallelrechner aus Spezifikationen*. PhD thesis, Arbeitsberichte des IMMD (Informatik), Universität Erlangen–Nürnberg, 1989.

[25] R.P. Weiker. Dhrystone Benchmark: Rationale for Version 2 and Measurement Rules. *SIGPLAN Notices*, 23(8), 1988.

[26] J. Worlton. Understanding Supercomputer Benchmarks. *Datamation*, 121-30, September 1984.

[27] J. Worlton. Toward a taxonomy of performance metrics. *Parallel Computing*, 17(10,11):1073–1092, December 1991.

[28] X. Xiong. Erweiterung und Implementierung der algorithmischen Spezifikationssprache ASL zur automatischen Erzeugung von Programmen für SIMD Parallelrechner. Master's thesis, Universität Erlangen–Nürnberg, IMMD VII, 1992.

Performance Modeling of Sparse Matrix Methods for Distributed Memory Architectures.

Roldan Pozo

Department of Computer Science, University of Tennessee
Knoxville, TN 37919, USA
pozo@cs.utk.edu

Abstract. We present analytical performance models for the numerical factorization phase of the multifrontal method for sparse matrices. Using a concise characterization of parallel architectures, we provide upper-bound estimates for the speedups observed on actual test problems taken from scientific and engineering applications. Representative architectures include an iPSC/2, iPSC/860, various clusters of workstations, and supercomputers connected by HIPPI interfaces. Simulation results suggest that the effective parallelism of these problems is quite sensitive to the communication bandwidth of the underlying architecture and load imbalances in the computational graph due to irregular data patterns.

1 Introduction

The solution of large sparse linear systems constantly arises in many large scale scientific applications, including computational fluid dynamics, structural engineering, weather forecasting, computational physics, circuit simulations, and biomedicine. Because these problems require significant computational resources, there has been much interest to solve large sparse linear systems on parallel architectures. Recent attention has focused on distributed memory architectures that can scale with increasing problem sizes, with growing interest in small clusters of powerful workstations as a cost-effective means of synthesizing large computational engine.

Various efforts have been directed at solving large sparse systems using direct solvers on distributed memory architectures; a good survey appears in Heath, et. al. [7]. One technique, the **multifrontal** method has exhibited a good potential for parallelism on shared memory architectures [3] and is particularly well-suited for high performance computer architectures since it involves no indirect addressing in its innermost loops . The multifrontal method was originally motivated by problems in structural finite element applications but it is also applicable to a larger class of scientific and engineering domains.

In this paper we address how the communication and computational characteristics of a given computer architecture affect the performance of the numerical factorization phase of the multifrontal method. The computational graphs associated with such algorithms typically resemble an unbalanced tree with hundreds or thousands of independent paths, and the granularity of each task increasing towards the root. Thus an efficient implementation onto distributed memory architectures requires the **partitioning** (or parallelization) of large nodes near the tree root, and the **clustering** of small leaf nodes onto a single processor due to their fine granularity.

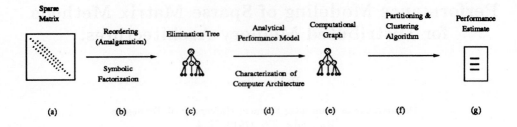

Fig. 1. Overview of the analysis and performance modeling phases for a mutlifrontal sparse matrix solver.

We present analytical performance models which characterize the communication and computation aspects of this algorithm. By utilizing such models in software simulations, we can study the performance characteristics of the multifrontal method on various architecture characterizations and provide upper bounds for the optimal speedups observed for various engineering and scientific problems taken from the Harwell-Boeing Test Suite[4]. This collection includes structural finite-element problems with irregular grids. Our architecture representations include conventional distributed memory parallel machines, such as the iPSC/860 and iPSC/2, and various distributed networks, such as a cluster of SUN-3's on standard Ethernet, a dedicated LAN of RS/6000s, various SPARC-2 on a dedicated high-speed network, and multiple supercomputers connected by a 50 MB/sec HIPPI interface. The intent is not to benchmark one architecture against another (after all, these are only approximations), but to understand how the communication and computation aspects of a particular architecture affects the obtainable parallelism in distributed sparse matrix methods.

2 Direct Sparse Matrix Factorizations

Although our study focuses on the multifrontal method, some of its characteristics are typical of other direct methods, such as the column-submatrix Cholesky factorization. In particular, the computational kernel of the multifrontal method is quite similar to the right-looking LU decomposition algorithm [2] for dense matrices. A full introduction to the multifrontal method is beyond the scope of this paper; here we briefly discuss issues relevant to the performance modeling and direct the reader to [6] for details of the numerical algorithm.

We focus on the numerical factorization phase of parallel multifrontal methods since it is the most computationally intensive section and generally dominates the overall execution time. By comparison, the ordering, and symbolic factorization phases of the solution are generally smaller and have limited benefits from parallelization [7]. Furthermore, in many practical cases multiple factorizations are performed on matrices with identical sparsity structure, thereby requiring the ordering and symbolic factorization phases be executed only once.

2.1 Multifrontal Method

Given a sparse matrix A, the reordering and amalgamation phases produce an **amalgamated elimination tree** which describes the data dependencies between the elimination steps (figure 1-b). That is, processing begins at the leaves of the tree and the elimination step at each node cannot begin until its child nodes have completed. Each node in this elimination tree factors a small dense matrix and ships a portion of this matrix up to its father node. The amalgamation phase combine various elimination variables into a single factorization step to increase the granularity of each node and enhance vectorization of the computational kernels. Each node i is annotated with two values: K_i the size of the frontal matrix, and P_i, the number of elimination variables.

Using the analytical models discussed in section 3, one can transform this elimination tree into a **computational graph** (figure 1-e) whose nodes represent computational requirements and edges denote the communication requirements between tasks. The structure of the elimination and computation tree are the same – the computation tree simply has these extra annotations. Coupled with characterizations of machine architectures (figure 1-f), such computational graphs then need to be **mapped** onto a given parallel architecture where nodes of the computational graph are assigned to individual processors.

3 Analytical Performance Models

The reordering and amalgamation phase (figure 1-b) produces an annotated tree where each node i is labeled with its number of pivots (P_i) and the frontal matrix size (K_i), where $P_i \leq K_i$. The size of the of contribution block is $(K_i - P_i)$ x $(K_i - P_i)$, and the size of the frontal matrix is K_i x K_i. As discussed in Duff & Johnson [5], the sequential multifrontal factorization code consists of the following basic steps. At each node in the elimination tree we perform assembly of contribution blocks from child nodes; for each pivot in frontal matrix, (1) determine the pivot (within the fully-summed variables 1,2, ..., P_i), (2) divide pivot column, and (3) update trailing submatrices in frontal matrix. Let n be the number of nodes in the amalgamated elimination tree, and let γ represent the average to time execute a logical or floating point operation. We can characterize the time required to complete the frontal factorization at node i as follows. The assembly portion consists of receiving the contribution block from the child nodes and adding them into the local frontal matrix. Thus the time required for this is given by

$$A_i = \gamma (\sum_{j \in S_i} (K_j - P_j)^2) \tag{1}$$

where S_i denotes the nodes which are children of node i. Similarly, the factorization time F_i of the frontal matrix is given by

$$F_i = \gamma \left(\underbrace{\sum_{j=1}^{P_i}(K_i - j + 1)}_{\text{scan for pivot}} + \underbrace{\sum_{j=1}^{P_i}(K_i - j)}_{\text{scaling}} + 2\underbrace{\sum_{j=1}^{P_i}(K_i - j)^2}_{\text{rank-1 updates}} \right). \tag{2}$$

The computation at each node consists of the assembly part A_i and the numerical elimination part, F_i (step 2 above.) Thus, the sequential time, T_i, spent at elimination tree node i is given by

$$T_i = A_i + F_i \tag{3}$$

where A_i denotes the assembly portion involving indirect additions during the processing of a contribution block. Assuming that logical comparisons, floating point multiplies, adds, and divides all take roughly the same time we have, as shown in [5],

$$F_i = \gamma \left[P_i(1 + 2K_j(K_j + 1)) - \frac{2}{3}(P_j + 1)(3K_j - P_j + 1) \right]. \tag{4}$$

The overall sequential complexity, then, is simply the sum of work on all nodes in the elimination tree:

$$T^*_{\text{seq}} = \sum_{i=1}^{n} (A_i + F_i) \tag{5}$$

3.1 Tree Parallelism

To exploit the natural parallelism of the computational tree, we run a sequential version frontal factorization code in each node but process various nodes in parallel. From the program development point of view, this approach is quite attractive since it involves little modification of the sequential code. The node subroutines essentially remain unchanged.

Under ideal conditions with zero communication costs and an unbounded number of processors, the time complexity is simply the longest execution path from leaf to node of the computational tree,

$$T^*_{\text{root}} = \max_{\ell} \sum_{i \in \text{path}_\ell} (A_i + F_i) \tag{6}$$

Unfortunately, since most of the computational bulk lies near the root nodes where parallelism is limited, speedups using only this parallelizing strategy are rather small. In Duff & Johnson[5], for example, this speedup varied from 1.9 to 4.0 for various 30x30 sample problems, even when an unbounded number of processors is allowed. In our test cases we found these speedups to remain unchanged for larger 200x200 examples. (See table 3.)

With realistic communication considerations these speedups drop even further. Typically, large clusters of nodes near the leaves get mapped to a single processor. This is necessary because for small nodes it essentially takes much longer to ship the contribution block between processors that to compute it the frontal factorization. Remember that the communication at node i consists of shipping a $(K_i - P_i) \times (K_i - P_i)$ contribution matrix to the father node. We assume the communication cost of moving n words of data between two processors is given by

$$M(n) = \alpha + w\beta * n \tag{7}$$

where α is the startup cost, β per-byte transmission cost and w is the number of bytes per word (typically four for single precision, eight for double precision). This linear model fits many distributed memory machines rather well for point-to-point communication [10]. The communication time required for node i is given by

$$C_i = M([K_i - P_i]^2) \tag{8}$$
$$= \alpha + w\beta * (K_i - P_i)^2 \tag{9}$$

The communication cost is incurred only if the father node is located on a different physical processor. Thus, if $\mathbf{f}(i)$ denotes the processor assigned to node i, the actual communication time is then given by

$$C_i^* = (1 - \delta_{\mathbf{f}(i),\mathbf{f}(S_i^{-1})}) \left(\alpha + w\beta * (K_i - P_i)^2 \right) \tag{10}$$

where δ is the Kronecker delta symbol ($\delta_{i,j} = 1$ if $i = j$ or 0 otherwise) and S_i^{-1} is the father node of i. The total time required to process the complete computational tree, therefore, depends on the processor mapping, $\mathbf{f}()$, and the optimal time is given by

$$T_{\text{tree}}^* = \min_{\mathbf{f}()} \left[\max_{\ell} \sum_{i \in \text{path}_\ell} (A_i + F_i) + (1 - \delta_{\mathbf{f}(i),\mathbf{f}(S_i^{-1})})(\alpha + w\beta * (K_i - P_i)^2) \right] \tag{11}$$

The speedup of the **tree parallelism** over the sequential implementation is given by $s_{\text{tree}} = T^*{}_{\text{seq}}/T^*{}_{\text{tree}}$

3.2 Node Parallelism

An alternative is to exploit node-level parallelism while processing the computational tree sequentially. This approach is more typical of shared-memory paradigms, since we effectively keep the same sequential code but parallelize the inner loops of the computational kernels.

This approach is still effective in the distributed memory environment because nodes near the root of the computation tree will dominate the execution time and will have to be decomposed in parallel to achieve significant speedups. Modelling the dense LU parallel factorization of a single node, however, can be rather complicated since the best parallel algorithms rely on the effective overlapping of communication with computation for their successful implementation .

The assembly process, however, is more difficult to parallelize since it involves combining results from child nodes. Here we assume that only the factorization phase ($O(n^3)$) is parallelized, i.e. the assembling of the contribution blocks ($O(n^2)$) occurs sequentially. We also make the simplifying assumption that most of the internal communication is involved in the original distribution of the frontal matrix over various processors.

Let p denote the number of processors. At each node i the factorization phase, F_i now becomes a function of p, the number of processors it is distributed over. The

$K_i \times K_i$ matrix must be broken up into p pieces and sent to respective processors. Thus,

$$F_i(p) = \underbrace{2(p-1)\left[\alpha + w\beta\frac{K_i^2}{p}\right]}_{\text{communication}} + \underbrace{\frac{F_i(1)}{p}}_{\text{computation}} \tag{12}$$

where $F_i(1)$ is simply F_i defined above. The factor of 2 appears in the first term because the subproblems are again brought back to the original processor before computation continues to the next father node. The $(p-1)$ factor occurs since the $(p-1)$ panels must be dealt out to subsequent processors. The optimal time required to perform the assembly and parallel factorization at each node i is given by

$$T_i = \min_{1 \leq p \leq K_i}\left(\underbrace{A_i}_{\text{assembly}} + \underbrace{2(p-1)M(\frac{K_i^2}{p})}_{\text{communication}} + \underbrace{\frac{F_i(1)}{p}}_{\text{computation}}\right). \tag{13}$$

Since we are still processing the elimination tree sequentially, the optimal time for the complete computation is simply this sum over all nodes in the elimination tree

$$T_{\text{node}}^* = \sum_{i=1}^{n} T_i. \tag{14}$$

3.3   Combining Node and Tree Parallelism

Clearly, the best solution combines both tree and node levels of parallelism. The analytical expression looks similar to Eq. 11, except that the F_i term has been replaced by $F_i(p)$ and the optimization space is over three dimensions,

$$T_{\text{combined}}^* \equiv$$

$$\min_{\substack{\mathbf{f}() \\ 1 \leq i \leq K_i}} \max_{\ell}\left(\sum_{i \in \text{path}_\ell} A_i + 2(p-1)M(\frac{K_i^2}{p}) + \frac{F_i(1)}{p} + (1 - \delta_{i,\mathbf{f}(s_i^{-1})})M((K_i - P_i)^2).\right)$$

Computing this combinatorical optimization is computationally unfeasible due to the large search space; in Section 4.3 we describe an heuristic solutions to this problem.

4   Computational Performance Models

This section presents experimental results obtained by applying the previous analytical models to various test problems from the Harwell-Boeing Sparse Matrix Suite. Using an concise parameterization of distributed computer architecture, we provide optimistic estimates on the performance of the parallelized multifrontal method on various computing platforms. The speedups presented here are for an unbounded number of processors, since were are interested in studying the communication and granularity effects of the algorithm under highly scalable architectures.

4.1 Example Parallel Architectures

We characterize distributed computer architectures by the three classical parameters: γ, the average time to perform a logical or floating point operation, α, the communication startup cost and β, the communication bandwidth, or the per-byte cost of sending a large message. Having a simple parameterization of a parallel architecture (α, β, γ) allows us to study the effects of each component and experiment with various hypothetical situations. Rather than study random combinations of (α, β, γ), however, we have focused on combinations that typify existing architectures as well as architectures of the future. Besides conventional distributed memory parallel machines, such as the iPSC/860 and iPSC/2, we have included various networks of popular workstations including: a cluster of SUN-3's on standarded ethernet, a dedicated LAN of RS/6000s, various SPARC-2 on a fiber optic network, and multiple Cray supercomputers connected together by a 50 MB/sec HIPPI interface. The list of example architectures used in this study is shown in Table 1 and includes examples from a wide range of computing resources. Megaflop numbers are for double precision operations. Some of performance numbers, such as the iPSC/860 and iPSC/2, were taken from direct experimentation [10] while others were based on reasonable approximations. We approximated Ethernet speeds at 100 KBytes/sec over an average load. The performance numbers for the HIPPI channel bandwidth is, at best, a reasonable estimate.

Table 1. Parameterization of example parallel architectures.

Simulated Architecture	Computation (Mflops)	Comm. Startup ($\mu secs$)	Comm. Bandwidth (MB/sec)
Sun-3 on Ethernet	0.4	5,000	0.1
Intel iPSC/2	0.3	321.8	2.8
SPARC-2s on Ethernet	4.0	5,000	0.1
Intel iPSC/860	4.0	321.8	2.8
SPARC-2s on HIPPI	4.0	2,000	50.0
RS/6000 Dedicated LAN	20.0	5,000	1.0
Crays on Ethernet	100.0	5,000	0.1
Crays on HIPPI	100.0	5,000	50.0

4.2 Example Sparse Matrix Problems

To make our study relevant to practical situations, we have utilized matrices taken from real scientific and engineering applications. These test matrices are part of the the Harwell-Boeing Test Suite [4], and include a linearized Navier-Stokes problem, an example from nuclear reactor modelling, various structural engineering examples of power stations, offshore platforms, and an automobile steering mechanism. Some of these larger examples are indicative of the medium-scale computing problems many scientists and engineers encounter on a daily basis. The Harwell-Boeing Test Suite was chosen because it is a widely used reference for the design, validation, and benchmarking of sparse matrix solvers and allows for comparison between various machine architectures. A list of the various problems used in this study in shown in Table 2. Furthermore, we have included 5pt and 9pt Laplacian discretization examples which allow us to construct sparse matrix problems of arbitrary size. Finally, we have purposely included a small-scale problem, NCC1374, to illustrate how problem size limits effective parallelism.

Table 2. Example matrices from the Harwell-Boeing Test Suite.

#	Name	Size	nz	Description
1	9pt70x70	4900	43264	5-point of Laplacian operator (70x70 grid)
2	9pt200x200	40,000	198802	9-point of Laplacian operator (200x200 grid)
3	BCCSTK15	3948	177816	offshore platform
4	BCCSTK18	11948	149090	nuclear power station
5	BCCSTK24	3562	159910	Calgary Olympic Arena
6	BCCSTK33	8738	591904	automobile steering mechanism
7	LNS3937	3937	25407	Linearized Navier-Stokes equations
8	NNC1374	1374	8606	Nuclear reactor core modelling

4.3 Simulations

The simulation process consists of three basic parts: (1) given the original matrix, we perform reordering, amalgamation, and symbolic factorization to generate an amalgamated elimination tree representing data dependencies between the elimination varaibles, (2) using the analytical models developed in the previous sections, together with an (α, β, γ) architecture description, we annotate the nodes the elimination tree with the respective computation and communication times, and (3) perform clustering and partitioning algorithms (see below) to determine possible speedups and performance times.

The elimination trees for these problems were produced using the MUPSAD() subroutine from the MUPS[1] software package for shared-memory parallel multifrontal solvers. In all our test matrices we use the minimum degree ordering algorithm together with an amalgamation process (setting the amalgamation parameter to 4) which generally enhances performance by increasing node granularity. All results reported here are for double precision (8 bytes) floating point format.

With the amalgamted tree in place, we then annotate its nodes with the respective computation times (Eqs. 1, 2, 3) and the edges with communication times (Eq. 8). Because we model communication time as $\alpha + \beta n$ between any two nodes, we imply that the underlying virtual architecture behaves like a completely connected graph. This is a reasonable for assumption for LANs or worm-hole routine topologies, e.g. iPSC/2 and iPSC/860 [10].

Next, we consider the clustering and partioning algorithms to the map the computational tree onto the virtual architecture. For the tree-parallelism case, we utilize a mapping algorithm similar to **dominant sequence clustering** (DSC) algorithm of Yang & Gerasoulis[11].

The algorithm is based on stepwise refinement, and optimizes for ideal parallelism, making no concessions for load balancing or any other **limited resource** considerations. Because we are only interested in modeling speedup, we do not require the algorithm to produce a schedule, but simply the resulting time required to execute the corresponding computation graph. It is thus ideal for establishing upper bounds on the available parallelism exhibited by a given application problem.

5 Results

The results of these simulations are given in tables 3 through 6. The optimal speedup of the amalgamated elimination trees (Eq. 6) for our test problems is given in table 3. Here we have assumed ideal conditions; there are no communication costs. Even under such ideal conditions, these speedups are between 1 and 3 due the imbalance of the respective elimination trees. This suggests we need to utilize node parallelism as well for effective parallelization.

In table 4 we list the results on node-only parallelism. Here we traverse the nodes of the tree sequentially but perform large frontal factorizations within each node in parallel (eq. 13). This provides better speedups with systems such as the iPSC/2 and a SPARC-2/HIPPI network achieving speedups of 34 and 15, respectively.

Significant improvement can be achieved by combining both node-leve land tree-level parallelism. This is shown in table 5, with the corresponding execution times in table 6. We have also included a single 100 Mflop supercomputer as a reference point to compare against conventional vector-pipelined technologies.

As expected, the results in table 5 illustrate that the larger problems provide the best speedups. Well balanced systems such as the iPSC/2 in which the time to compute a floating point result is comparable to the time required for sending one, show particular good speedups. Unfortunately, the overall execution times are not as high, due to the conservative power of its processors. We can also see from this table that the communication bandwidth of Ethernet severly limits a large cluster of workstations to be utilized effectively. For example, utilizing various SPARC-2s connected by Ethernet (a popular configuration in scientific and research environments) provides speedups less than three, even for the large LA200x200 and BCCSTK24 examples.

6 Conclusions

We have derived analytical performance models for the numerical factorization phase of the mutlifrontal method and have applied these models to large examples from the Harwell-Boeing Sparse Matrix Suite to give an indication of the speedups obtainable

Table 3. Optimal elimination tree speedup of example problems.

	LA70x70	LA200x200	BCCSTK24	BCCSTK33	LNS3937	NNC1374
Speedup	3.14	2.65	2.75	1.74	2.01	3.57

Table 4. Speedups due to the parallelization of individual nodes wihtin the elimination tree.

Simulated Architecture	LA70x70	LA200x200	BCCSTK24	BCCSTK33	LNS3937	NNC1374
Suns/Ethernet	1.04	1.63	1.20	2.68	1.03	1.00
iPSC/2	5.24	14.49	9.74	33.66	5.84	1.75
SPARC-2/Ethernet	1.00	1.00	1.00	1.00	1.00	1.00
iPSC/860	1.45	2.96	1.96	5.43	1.53	1.01
RS/6000 LAN	1.03	1.71	1.22	2.96	1.02	1.00
SPARCS/HIPPI	2.02	5.56	3.30	14.61	2.28	1.02
Crays/HIPPI	1.02	1.68	1.19	2.98	1.01	1.00

on various distributed memory architectures. Given an unbounded number of processors, some well-balanced systems, such as the iPSC/2, showed moderate speedups; most simulations of workstation clusters, however, rarely produced speedups greater than ten.

The results from these simulations suggest that multifrontal methods share similar characterizations with other parallel direct solvers –they are quite effective at achieving reasonable speedups on shared memory architectures and small clusters of workstations, but they may prove more challenging to adapt to massively parallel

Table 5. Combined speedup of various architectures

Simulated Architecture	LA70x70	LA200x200	BCCSTK24	BCCSTK33	LNS3937	NNC1374
Suns/Ethernet	3.45	7.56	4.09	7.50	2.11	2.60
iPSC/2	37.67	127.21	56.14	125.19	24.28	9.83
SPARC-2/Ethernet	1.51	2.44	1.38	1.57	1.57	1.00
iPSC/860	6.62	18.74	9.21	18.66	4.25	3.23
RS/6000 LAN	3.31	7.91	4.15	8.23	2.06	1.58
SPARCS/HIPPI	11.13	46.96	18.37	53.50	7.10	3.56
Crays/HIPPI	3.17	7.64	3.95	8.14	2.00	1.23

Table 6. Execution times (in seconds) due to the combined node and elimination tree parallelism.

Simulated Architecture	LA70x70	LA200x200	BCCSTK24	BCCSTK33	LNS3937	NNC1374
Single Cray-2	0.22	7.73	0.71	23.05	0.20	0.01
Suns/Ethernet	16.01	255.77	43.56	768.01	23.42	0.55
iPSC/2	1.95	20.24	4.23	61.31	2.71	0.20
SPARC-2/Ethernet	3.65	79.30	12.97	366.69	3.14	0.14
iPSC/860	0.83	10.32	1.94	30.89	1.16	0.04
RS/6000 LAN	0.33	4.89	0.86	14.01	0.48	0.02
SPARCS/HIPPI	0.50	4.12	0.97	10.77	0.69	0.04
Crays/HIPPI	0.07	1.01	0.18	2.83	0.10	0.00

distributed systems with thousands of processors.

One source of difficulty lies in the imbalance of elimination trees for sparse matrices with irregular patterns. By comparison, one typically sees better performance for similar algorithms on structured problems [8][9]. The coarse-grained parallelism offered by the elimination tree of irregular patterns is rather poor (less than 4 in our examples) and the significant communication costs on distributed architectures limit the amount of parallelism available to decompose single frontal factorization into finer grained tasks. It should also be noted that the multifrontal method is already highly efficient on a single processor, since it employs dense linear algebra in its computational kernel. This efficient computation section, however, also serves to make the communication bandwidth limitation even more visible.

Another difficulty arises from the need to explicitly deal with task mapping and scheduling issues. In shared-memory environments, such concerns can be handled quite effectively by simple task-queue scheduling techniques. In distributed memory environments with considerably higher communication costs and fragmented memory pools, such approaches are not as effective. In practice, a static mapping, predetermined scheduling, or some hybrid static-dynamic mapping is required before the numerical factorization begins. Such mapping problems have been shown to be NP-complete and can be quite expensive to calculate, although various hueristics exist for suboptimal solutions. Nevertheless, this computation is also part of solving the problem and must also be properly accounted for in the overall execution time. In our study, we have not addressed how the sparse matrix is generated or its initial distribution within the parallel machine. This is a critical issue but impossible to study in isolation, since it requires an understanding of how the matrix data is distributed by the driving application.

Finally, we should remind the reader that these conclusions are preliminary and the results from these simulations are not meant to be definitive. Some of the architecture representations are, at best, reasonable estimates; execution timings, particularly for the distributed networks, are meant only as a rough guide. Our heuristics have been partially validated by independent static scheduling packages [11], but further work is needed to compare simluation results with actual multifrontal timings on exisiting architectures. Although we have attempted to model realistic situations, we have not explored all possible considerations; the field of distributed direct solvers for large sparse systems is still developing and contains various areas of active research, such as generating good elimination trees for parallel execution, finding efficient partitioning/clustering hueristics for the processor- assignment problem, and dealing with scattered input matrices. We hope that by careful performance modeling and experimental testing we can better understand these subtle issues.

7   Acknowledgments

The author wishes to thank Iain Duff and Patrick Amestoy for numerous discussions on the multifrontal method and their helpful comments and suggestions which have improved the presentation of this paper. This study was conducted during a visiting appointment to CERFACS in Toulouse, France.

References

1. P. R. Amestoy, *MUPS: Subroutine Library Specification*, CERFACS, June 1991.
2. J. J. Dongarra, I. S. Duff, D. C. Sorensen, H. A. van der Host, *Solving Linear Systems on Vector and Shared Memory Computers*, SIAM, 1991.
3. I. S. Duff, "Parallel implementation of multifrontal schemes," *Parallel Computing*, North-Holland, Vol. 3, pp. 193-204, 1986.
4. I. S. Duff, R. G. Grimes, J. G. Lewis, "Sparse Matrix Problems," *ACM Trans. Math. Softw.*, Vol 14, pp. 1-14, 1989.
5. I. S. Duff, L. S. Johnson, "Node Orderings and Concurrency in Structurally-Symmetric Sparse Problems," *Parallel Supercomputing: Methods, Algorithms, and Applications*, John Wiley & Sons Ltd., 1989.
6. I. S. Duff, J. K. Reid, "The Multifrontal Solution of Unsymmetric Sets of Linear Equations," *SIAM J. Sci. Stat. Comput.*, Vol. 5, No. 3, pp 633-641.
7. M. T. Heath, E. Ng, B. W. Peyton, "Parallel Algorithms for Sparse Linear Systems," *SIAM Review*, Vol. 33, No. 3, pp 420-460, 1991.
8. R. Lucas, T. Blank, J. Tiemann, "A Parallel Solution Method for Large Sparse Systems of Equations," *IEEE Transactions on Computer-Aided Design*, Vol. CAD-6, No. 6, November 1987, pp. 981-991.
9. L. S. Ostrouchov, M. T. Heath, C. H. Romine, "Modeling Speedup in Parallel Sparse Matrix Factorization," Technical Report ORNL/TM-11786, Oak Ridge National Laboratory, Oak Ridge, TN, 1990.
10. R. Pozo, "Performance Modeling of Parallel Architectures for Scientific Computing", Ph. D. Thesis, University of Colorado, Boulder, 1991.
11. Yang and A. Gerasoulis, "PYRROS: Static scheduling and code generation for message passing multiprocessors," *Proc. of 6th ACM Inter. Conf. on Supercomputing*, Washington D.C., July, 1992.

This article was processed using the LaTeX macro package with LLNCS style

ParSim: A Tool for the Analysis of Parallel and Distributed Programs

Thomas Schnekenburger
Michael Friedrich
Andreas Weininger
Thomas Schoen

Institut für Informatik, Technische Universität München
Orleansstr. 34, D–8000 München 80, Germany

Abstract

ParSim is an efficient software simulator for parallel and distributed programs on virtual parallel machines. ParSim provides the system specification language ParSpec, which allows the description of a large class of parallel systems on an abstract level.

ParSim produces a deterministic simulation. By instrumenting the binary code of the program, ParSim counts CPU cycles to determine the runtime of short fragments of code.

Explicit control of the processor and I/O utilization can be used to insert nonintrusive monitoring facilities into the program.

1 Introduction

Programming parallel and distributed systems adds a lot of problems to sequential programming for several reasons:

- The nondeterministic behavior of parallel programs makes debugging more difficult [LM87].
- First versions of a parallel program often show a poor performance because the parallelization has an inappropriate granularity or there is a severe load imbalance in the program.
- Monitoring tools can have a substantial influence on the execution of parallel programs [Gai86].
- The behavior of a parallel program on different architectures often depends severely on the relationships between processor speed, network bandwidth and I/O performance. So new performance problems may appear when a parallel program runs on a new parallel machine.

ParSim is a new tool which helps the programmer in the analysis of programming errors, performance problems and the performance prediction of parallel programs. The principle of ParSim is to simulate the execution of parallel programs on different parallel systems by interleaving pieces of compiled user code, and evaluating the utilization of the resources of the parallel system. The technique of simulating the program execution allows a deterministic execution and nonintrusive monitoring.

ParSim provides the very simple language *ParSpec* for specification of a large class of parallel systems on a coarse–grain level. The goal of ParSpec is not the performance evaluation of parallel hardware. It is designed to manipulate the *characteristic* properties of a parallel system which have a visible influence on the execution of a parallel program.

Although ParSim was designed to simulate programs written in the parallel and distributed programming language ParMod–C [WSF91], it is not restricted to a specific programming language. ParSim provides an interface, called the *Virtual Operating System* which is used by the runtime system of the parallel programming language to implement the parallel language constructs on the simulated system.

A first version of ParSim, called PMSIM is described in [FZ89]. This first version could not simulate I/O–operations. In addition, it was not possible to determine resp. control the overhead of the runtime system and the simulation was nondeterministic.

To motivate the design decisions of ParSpec, section 2 gives a brief summary of ParMod–C and the corresponding hardware model. Section 3 describes Par-Spec and section 4 presents the ParSim simulator. We show some examples of ParSpec specifications in section 5. Finally we describe our future work, and give a conclusion in section 6.

2 The Language ParMod–C

ParMod [Eic87] is a set of language independent constructs for parallel and distributed programming which can be added to different sequential procedural languages. In 1989, the ParMod constructs where added to the the language C. The resulting language was called ParMod–C [WSF91].

2.1 Structure of a ParMod–C Program

A ParMod–C Program consists of several *distributed modules*. When a ParMod–C program starts, all *modules* are started in parallel. The modules are assumed to run in different address spaces. A module itself consists of *tasks* running in parallel in a common address space.

The modules communicate by a *remote service invocation* mechanism[1]: A module contains global procedures which can be called by every module of the program. The call of a global procedure generates a new *task* in the module where the global procedure is defined running in parallel to the other tasks of the called module. The caller of the global procedure proceeds immediately, and has the possibility to wait for the results of the global procedure call.

---

[1]A similar mechanism is used in [AOC+86]

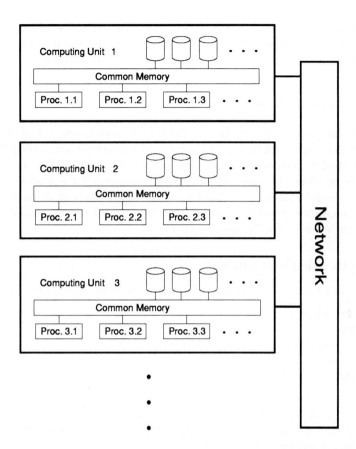

Figure 1: The Virtual ParMod Machine (VPM)

2.2 The Virtual ParMod Machine

The structure of a ParMod–C program implies a corresponding model of the underlying hardware, called the *Virtual ParMod Machine* (VPM), see figure 1. The VPM consists of an unbounded number of computing units corresponding to the modules. Each computing unit is connected with each other by a network. A computing unit consists of an unbounded number of processors corresponding to the tasks of the program. The processors have access to a common memory and the external devices of the computing unit. By adding external devices to the model introduced in [FZ89] we can simulate I/O latencies, which are important for many data intensive programs like e.g. parallel database applications [BBDW83].

2.3 Implementation of ParMod–C

Since of course, the number of computing units and processors of any existing hardware is fixed, it is necessary to provide multitasking. Furthermore the m

ParMod–C modules have to be mapped on n computing units, where m may be greater than n. A *runtime system* has to implement the ParMod constructs on top of the underlying operating system or directly on the hardware.

3   The Language ParSpec

To specify the parallel system for the ParMod–C simulation, called the *virtual system*, we developed the language ParSpec. Our interests are mainly the analysis of ParMod–C programs but not the performance evaluation of the virtual system. So we have designed a very simple language for a system specification on an abstract level. A ParSpec specification consists of definitions of the network, processors, external devices, scheduling mechanisms, and computing units. Below we describe ParSpec in detail.

3.1   Network Description

We distinguish two kinds of networks: A *bus system* and a *network system*:

> **network** |
> [**bus**
>   **busstartup** ⟨ start up time ⟩
>   **busrate** ⟨ transfer rate ⟩
> **end**]

The difference between these systems is that in a bus system there is only one common resource *bus* that is required for the transmission of a message, whereas in the *network system* each computing unit has an own *link* which is required for a message transmission.

We do not specify the topology of the network in detail, we always assume a (virtual) point to point connection from every computing unit to each other. This restriction can be justified by the fact that particularly the recent distributed systems often are virtually full connected but not physically. This means that there is only a small difference of the transfer times between a direct transmission between two nodes and a transmission which has to do several *hops*[2].

3.2   Processor Description

ParSpec assigns three attributes to a processor:

> **processor** ⟨ processor name ⟩
>   **speed** ⟨ processor speed ⟩
>   **comstartup** ⟨ start up time ⟩
>   **comproc** ⟨ transfer rate ⟩
> **end**

---

[2] See [Dun91] for a detailed analysis of the communication data rates of different hypercube computers.

The speed of a processor is more a qualitative than a quantitative number. It has to match the time measurement for the processor utilization (see below) and it serves to specify the relative speed of different processors. In addition to the speed of a processor, we have to specify the processing time for a communication which is split up into a constant part (start up time) and a part which grows linearly with the number of bytes transmitted (transfer rate).

3.3 External Devices

An external device is characterized by its speed. The time to transfer data to the device is split up into a constant (latency time) and a linear (transfer rate) part:

> **iodevice** ⟨ device name ⟩
>> **latency** ⟨ latency time ⟩
>> **transferrate** ⟨ transfer rate ⟩
> **end**

3.4 Scheduling Description

ParSpec offers three different scheduling strategies for the multitasking management: *first come first served* (fcfs), *shortest elapsed time* (set) and *random select* (random). Although ParMod–C requires a preemptive scheduling, we can simulate a nonpreemptive scheduling to observe the behavior of the program.

> **schedule** ⟨ schedule name ⟩
> [**nonpreemptive** | **preemptive** ⟨ time slice ⟩]
> [**fcfs** | **set** | **random**]
> **end**

3.5 Computing Unit Description

A computing unit consists of several processors with a common memory and several I/O–devices. In addition, we have to specify the scheduling strategy of the computing unit, and in the case of a network system the speed of the link according to the model above.

> **cu** ⟨ cu name ⟩ ⟨ number ⟩
>> **processor** ⟨ processor name ⟩ ⟨ number ⟩
>> **iodevice** ⟨ device name ⟩ ⟨ number ⟩
>> **schedule** ⟨ schedule name ⟩
>> **linkstartup** ⟨ start up time ⟩
>> **linkrate** ⟨ transfer rate ⟩
> **end**

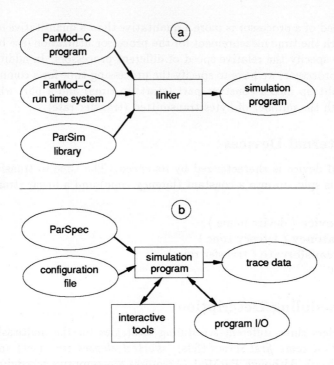

Figure 2: Usage of ParSim

4   The ParSim Simulator

Figure 2 shows the usage of the ParSim simulator. A ParMod–C program is linked with a ParMod–C runtime system and the ParSim library to executable code, called *simulation program* (figure 2a). When this program starts it scans the ParSpec specification of the virtual system and a configuration file which specifies the mapping of the ParMod–C modules to the computing units of the virtual system[3]. If no errors occur, the simulation of the ParMod–C program starts (figure 2b). To simulate the execution of a ParMod–C program, ParSim simulates the utilization of the resources of the virtual system. The following sections describe how we can determine the resource utilization, and give an overview of the simulation principles and the possible applications of the ParSim simulator.

4.1   Resource Utilization

In our system model we have to determine the utilization of the resources network, processors, and I/O–devices.

---

[3] We can use the same configuration file also to specify the mapping to real parallel systems

4.1.1 Network Utilization

To determine the network utilization, it is sufficient to know the number of the transferred bytes in a message. This number is passed explicitly with each request for a message transmission to the simulator.

If the virtual system has a bus architecture (see above), the exclusive resource *bus* is requested for a period of time corresponding to the ParSpec attributes of the bus. For a network architecture the exclusive *links* of the sending and receiving computing units are requested according to the given ParSpec specification.

4.1.2 Processor Utilization

A problem which is more difficult than the network utilization is the analysis of the processor utilization. As described below, the simulator executes short sections of task code. We have to determine the execution time of these code sections on a given processor. There are several methods for this analysis[4].

In our approach we count the number of instruction cycles on the simulating machine during the execution of a code section. This is done by instrumenting the binary code of the program[5]: At the end of each basic block we add the number of processor cycles for this basic block to a global *cycle counter* variable. The cycle counter is used to compute the corresponding execution time on the simulated processor.

This method is based on the assumption that all simulated processors have the same relative speed for all operations. This can be justified by the fact that we are not interested in the performance evaluation of processors. Moreover, it is not possible to simulate fine–grain shared variable conflicts, vector facilities or the memory access speed, but this method allows a very simple description of the hardware and an efficient simulation which is sufficiently detailed for the analysis of the behavior of parallel programs.

We provide statements for the explicit control of the cycle counter, for example a task can *switch off* the cycle counter during some statements. By this, it is possible to insert code e.g. for the generation of trace information without influencing the simulated execution.

4.1.3 I/O–Device Utilization

For the analysis of the I/O–device utilization we provide the *sim_io* macro. For example, to execute the library routine *io_routine*, which writes some data on a disk d, the expression

$$\text{sim\_io(bytes, ''w'', d, io\_routine(\langle parameters \rangle))}$$

is used: the call io_routine($\langle$parameters$\rangle$) is executed, but we do not analyze the disk utilization of this call. Instead we use the expression *bytes* as the number of bytes written on the I/O–device d. So we can insert real I/O operations

---

[4]For a survey see [SJF91].

[5]A similar technique is used by the performance analysis tool Pixie, offered by MIPS corporation.

without any change of the simulated execution simply by omitting the corresponding device–statement, or we can simulate I/O operations which are not really executed to speed up the simulation of I/O intensive programs.

4.2 Simulation Principles

The simulator executes a ParMod–C program by interleaving the execution of code sections of the running tasks. By executing a code section, the simulator determines the resource utilization of this section.

The simulation of ParMod–C programs can be separated in three logical levels:

- The first level is the ParMod–C program with the VPM as the corresponding hardware model.

- The second level is the virtual system according to the ParSpec description. We call the operating system of the virtual system the *Virtual Operating System* (VOS). The VOS provides an interface which is independent of the properties of the virtual system.

- The third level is the machine where the simulation takes place, and the operating system on this machine.

Following this hierarchical model, the simulation of ParMod–C programs can be split into the following subtasks:

- The modules of the ParMod–C program are mapped on the computing units of the virtual system. This is done before the program starts by drawing up a special configuration file (see figure 2b).

- The ParMod constructs (e.g. conditional critical regions) are implemented by a runtime system. The runtime system uses calls to the VOS. Because the VOS provides always the same interface, we can use one runtime system for all kinds of virtual systems.

- The running tasks of the ParMod–C program are executed on the simulating machine by interleaving.

Calls to a *break–routine* are inserted in the ParMod–C program and the runtime system by a precompiler to ensure that each loop contains at least one call to the break–routine. In addition, implicit break–routine calls are executed within every synchronization statement, every message passing statement, and every I/O–statement.

The purpose of the break–routine is to fix the locations of an interrupt of the simulated tasks. The break–routine is executed in the following way:

1. The execution of a task is stopped by a break–routine call.
2. The runtime of the task since the last break–routine call is computed using the cycle counter.

3. ParSim decides to continue the execution of the task or to interrupt the task and to continue another task.

Because the runtime is computed deterministically, this method leads to a deterministic scheduling and therefore to a deterministic simulation.

The user may add break–routine calls to his program if he needs a finer granularity of simulation steps for some sections of the program.

4.3 Applications of the ParSim Simulator

ParSim simulates the execution of ParMod–C programs on many different interesting parallel systems. As mentioned above, the simulation is deterministic. By this, we can reproduce a certain execution, although the execution on a real machine would be nondeterministic.

We can insert monitoring routines which have no influence on the behavior of the simulated execution. This monitoring routines can be included into the runtime system to produce execution traces with a predefined format for different *post mortem* analysis tools [EA88], or they can be written by the ParMod–C programmer himself to produce test output without disturbing the program execution. They can be used also to co–operate with interactive analysis tools like debuggers or visualization tools (see figure 2b).

Another interesting aspect of ParSim is the investigation of efficient ParMod–C implementations on existing machines[6]. ParSim makes it possible to determine the overhead of the ParMod–C runtime system. By this we can test the suitability of different runtime system versions for the individual parallel systems.

5 Examples

To illustrate ParSpec we present three hardware specifications of the Virtual Parmod Machine, a shared memory computer and a distributed memory computer.

5.1 The Virtual ParMod Machine

ParSpec allows us to describe the Virtual ParMod Machine. Although this architecture is not realistic, our experiences show that it is well suited to investigate the fundamental behavior of a ParMod–C program without regarding hardware restrictions.

The links between the computing units are assumed to have infinite speed. Since the number of processors is unbounded, we can omit the schedule directive in the computing unit description.

---

[6]This was done for iPSC/2 Hypercubes and on a workstation network.

```
network
processor vpm_proc
   speed 1                    /* e.g. 1 MIPS */
   /* no communication time, see above */
end
iodevice disk                /* unbounded speed */
   latency 0 ms
   transferrate *
end
                             /* schedule not necessary */
cu vpm_cu *                  /* unbounded */
   processor vpm_proc *      /* unbounded */
   iodevice disk
   linkrate *                /* unbounded network */
   linkstartup 0             /* unbounded network */
end
```

5.2 Shared Memory Computer

The following ParSpec code specifies a shared memory computer: There is one computing unit and eight processors. This system is similar to an Alliant FX/2800:

```
                             /* network not necessary */
processor i860
   speed 40                  /* 40 MIPS */
   /* no communication */
end
                             /* no external devices */
schedule standard
   preemptive 100 us
   fcfs
end
cu fx2800                    /* one computing unit */
   processor i860 8          /* eight processors */
   schedule standard
                             /* no communication */
end
```

Since there is only one computing unit, we don't have to specify the communication time.

By adding the specification of a workstation computing unit, it would be possible to describe a heterogeneous system with the FX/2800 as the backend machine.

5.3 Distributed Memory Computer

Here we give the specification of a machine similar to a 64 node iPSC/860 hypercube with one I/O node. The used data stem mostly from [Dun91].

```
network
processor i860
    speed 40          /* 40 MIPS */
    comstartup 136 us /* 136 microsec. */
    comproc 2.5 MB    /* 2.5 MB per second */
end
iodevice disk
    latency 15 ms     /* average 15 millisec. */
    transferrate 0.75 MB
                      /* 0.75 MB per second */
end
schedule standard
    preemptive 100 us
    fcfs
end
cu diskless 63        /* 63 nodes diskless */
    processor proc
    schedule standard
    linkstartup 80 us  /* 80 microseconds */
    linkrate 2.6 MB    /* 2.6 MB per second */
end
cu disknode 1          /* 1 node with disk */
    processor proc
    iodevice disk
    schedule standard
    linkstartup 80 us
    linkrate 2.6 MB
end
```

6 Conclusions and Future Work

In this paper we presented ParSim, a simulator for the analysis of parallel and distributed programs on different systems. Using software simulation we can insert nonintrusive monitoring routines into the user program and the runtime system. By counting the CPU cycles of the program, evaluating the utilization for network and I/O resources, and interrupting the tasks at fixed locations, we can simulate the programs deterministically.

ParSim can be used by several analysis tools for debugging, performance analysis and visualization of ParMod–C programs.

The system specification language ParSpec can be used to describe a wide range of parallel and distributed machines. Although ParSpec does not describe hardware details, it can be used to specify those characteristic properties of a hardware which have a visible influence on the execution of a ParMod–C program.

We will use ParSim for testing large parallel applications, for example parallel and distributed implementations of relational database operators and recursive numerical algorithms. ParSim will be also used in a course for parallel programming.

References

[AOC+86] G.R. Andrews, R.A. Ollsson, M. Coffin, I. Elshoff, K. Nilson, T. Purdin, and G. Townsend. An overview of the SR language and implementation. Technical Report TR 86-6c, Department of Compuer Science, The University of Arizona, Tucson, 1986.

[BBDW83] D. Bitton, H. Boral, D.J. DeWitt, and W.K. Wilkinson. Parallel algorithms for the execution of relational database operations. *ACM Transactions on Database Systems*, 8(3):324–353, 1983.

[Dun91] T.H. Dunigan. Performance of the Intel iPSC/860 and Ncube 6400 hypercubes. *Parallel Computing*, (17):1285–1302, 1991.

[EA88] S. Eichholz and F. Abstreiter. Runtime observation of parallel programs. In *CONPAR88*, Manchester (UK), September 1988.

[Eic87] S. Eichholz. Parallel programming with ParMod. In *Proceedings of the 1987 International Conference on Parallel Processing*, pages 377–380. Pennsylvania State University Press, May 1987.

[FZ89] M. Friedrich and J. Zeiler. Simulation of hardware and multitasking for the parallel programming language ParMod. *Microprocessing and Microprogramming*, (28):19–24, 1989.

[Gai86] Jason Gait. A probe effect in concurrent programs. *Software - Practice and Experience*, 16(3):225–233, 1986.

[LM87] Thomas J. LeBlanc and John M. Mellor-Crummey. Debugging parallel programs with Instant Replay. *IEEE Transactions on Computers*, C-36(4):471–482, April 1987.

[SJF91] C.B. Stunkel, B. Janssens, and W.K. Fuchs. Address tracing for parallel machines. *Computer*, 24(1):31–38, 1991.

[WSF91] Andreas Weininger, Thomas Schnekenburger, and Michael Friedrich. Parallel and distributed programming with ParMod–C. In *First International Conference of the Austrian Center for Parallel Computation*, October 1991.

Estimating the Effective Performance of Program Parallelization on Shared Memory MIMD Multiprocessors

Jean-Yves Berthou[1] and Philippe Klein[2,3]

[1] Laboratoire MASI, Université Pierre et Marie Curie,
45 Av des Etats-Unis, 78000 Versailles, France
[2] Department of Computer Science, Yale University,
P.O. Box 2158 Yale Station, New Haven CT 06520, USA
[3] Institut Français du Pétrole, DIMA/DER,
1 & 4 Avenue de Bois-Préau BP 311, 92506 Rueil-Malmaison Cedex, France

Abstract. One of the problems the parallelization of programs poses is the evaluation of the quality of the parallelization performed. We show that the disruption generated by the target machine, which we call *noise*, has a non-negligible influence on the sequential as well as parallel execution times. The effects on the efficiency, which depends on these execution times, are investigated. We show that this performance criterion gives an altered picture of the quality of the parallelization. We present a set of criteria for estimating the *effective performance of the parallelization of programs* on one hand and the machine generated drop in efficiency on the other hand. The theoretical results exposed are illustrated by experimental measures conducted on the Encore Multimax.

1 Introduction

The Parallel Computing research group of the MASI is involved in the realization of compilers for parallel machines : the PAF (*Paralléliseur Automatique pour Fortran*, automatic parallelizer for Fortran) project [1]. Evaluating the quality of the generated code is an important issue. The performance criteria of a parallel program P depend on the single processor execution time T_1 of P and the execution time T_p of P on p processors. Traditionally, we have *speed-up*, which measures the improvement in execution time, $S(p) = T_1/T_p$ and *efficiency*, which measures the average utilization of the p processors, $E(p) = T_1/pT_p$. Amdahl's claim [2] led to the well-known *Amdahl's law* speedup formula. The limitation of parallel processing it shows was revised with Gustafson's *scaled speedup* principle [3]. Eager et al. [4] studied speedup versus efficiency. The impacts of communication and synchronization on speedup were investigated in [5]. New metrics were proposed in [6] and [7]. Hockney [8] studied in details what's wrong with speedup.

We focus on the fact that when a parallel program proves inefficient, *speedup* and *efficiency* do not explain this inefficiency:

- has the intrinsic parallelism been only partially detected or badly exploited?
- does the target machine lend itself to the parallelism of the parallelized program?

Answering these two questions is the purpose of this paper. We assume the target machine is a shared memory MIMD machine with at least a two-level memory hierarchy (a global shared memory and a local memory for each processor). Memory management, data transfers from one memory hierarchy to another and memory contention phenomena (the latter are generally not taken into account [9]) generate what we call *noise*, which is included in execution times. We showed in [10] that this machine generated noise depends on the program, the data size and the number of processors. We established that, in most cases, it increases with the number of processors, which leads to a decrease of the efficiency of the parallel program. But the efficiency of the parallelization of the program does not depend on the noise generated by the target machine. Therefore, we define the *effective efficiency of the parallelization* of a sequential program as the efficiency of the resulting parallelized program when the noise is null. Noise is considered null when each processor has all the data it needs in its local memory. But the noise cannot be directly measured. We show in section 2 how the measure of its variation between the single processor execution and the parallel execution, along with the efficiency of the parallelized program lead to an estimate of the effective efficiency of the parallelization. Then these theoretical results are illustrated by the experimental results of section 3.

2 Estimating the Effective Performance of the Parallelization of Programs

2.1 Experimentally Measurable Quantities

We consider that a parallel program P is composed of p subprograms which are executed in parallel on p processors. The subprograms execute the same parallel code, and the sequential parts of the code will be arbitrarily executed on the first processor. Each subprogram is a succession of two types of code: block of instructions describing some computation and synchronization instructions which direct the parallel execution of the subprograms. The parallel execution time T_p of the program P is the execution time of the longest subprogram. We define and measure the sequential execution time in two different ways: T_s^1 is the execution time of the parallel program on a single processor; T_s^p is the sum of the *computational* execution times of all the subprograms executed in parallel. Indeed, the sequential execution time is nothing but the sum of the execution times of all the computational instruction blocks of all the subprograms of P. Since T_s^1 and T_s^p the same computation time, the difference between these two quantities measure the variation of the noise generated by the target machine between the single processor execution and the parallel execution. We will see in 3.2 that this variation is far from being negligible. We thus define the noise variation level δ_n by:

$$\delta_n = \frac{T_s^p - T_s^1}{T_s^1} \tag{1}$$

2.2 An Estimate of the Effective Efficiency of the Parallelization

Let N_1 be the noise during the single processor execution of the parallel program. N_1 is the time spent in transferring data from the shared memory to the local memory of the processor executing the program. Let N_p be the average noise on each processor during the execution of the program on p processors. Since the subprograms execute the same parallel code, we assume that the noise is equally distributed among the processors. Then pN_p is the sum of the time spent in transferring data to all processors and the time *lost* in memory contention. The *effective sequential execution time* of P, $T_{\text{seq}}^{\text{eff}}$, is the sequential execution time when the processor executing P has all the data needed in its local memory (when N_1 is null). The *effective parallel execution time* of P, $T_{\text{paf}}^{\text{eff}}$, is the parallel execution time when each processor of the parallel execution has the data it needs in its local memory (when N_p is null). T_s^1, T_s^p, T_p and δ_n are expressed as functions of $T_{\text{seq}}^{\text{eff}}$, $T_{\text{paf}}^{\text{eff}}$, N_1 and N_p as follows:

$$T_s^1 = T_{\text{seq}}^{\text{eff}} + N_1, \quad T_s^p = T_{\text{seq}}^{\text{eff}} + pN_p, \quad T_p = T_{\text{paf}}^{\text{eff}} + N_p, \quad \delta_n = \frac{T_s^p - T_s^1}{T_s^1} = \frac{pN_p - N_1}{T_s^1}$$

The *effective efficiency of the parallelization*, which cannot be experimentally measured, is thus defined by $E_p^{\text{eff}} = T_{\text{seq}}^{\text{eff}}/pT_{\text{paf}}^{\text{eff}}$, and the *efficiency of the parallel program* is given by $E_m = T_s^1/pT_p$.

Let λ_n^1 be the noise level in the sequential execution time T_s^1. It is defined by $\lambda_n^1 = N_1/T_{\text{seq}}^{\text{eff}}$. Starting from the efficiency of the parallel program, we have:

$$E_m = \frac{T_{\text{seq}}^{\text{eff}}}{pT_{\text{paf}}^{\text{eff}}} \left(\frac{1 + \lambda_n^1}{1 + (\delta_n(1 + \lambda_n^1) + \lambda_n^1)\frac{T_{\text{seq}}^{\text{eff}}}{pT_{\text{paf}}^{\text{eff}}}} \right) = E_p^{\text{eff}} \left(\frac{1 + \lambda_n^1}{1 + (\delta_n(1 + \lambda_n^1) + \lambda_n^1)E_p^{\text{eff}}} \right)$$

It follows that:

$$E_p^{\text{eff}} = \frac{E_m}{1 + \lambda_n^1 - E_m(\delta_n(1 + \lambda_n^1) + \lambda_n^1)} \tag{2}$$

We can only measure δ_n, the noise variation level, on the target multiprocessor. However, we estimate that λ_n^1 cannot be greater than 50%. We hence assume that the time spent in transferring data during the single processor execution of the program on a shared memory MIMD machine cannot represent more than 50% of the effective sequential execution time[4]. Obviously, 0 is a lower bound for λ_n^1. Therefore, if we measure E_m and δ_n for a given execution on p processors, and set down the very wide assumption that $\lambda_n^1 \in [0.0\,;0.5]$, an interval positionning E_p^{eff} relatively to E_m can be obtained. Thus, we define the *approximate effective efficiency* $E_{p,\lambda_n^1}^{\text{eff}}$ as the effective efficiency of the parallelization for a *fixed* λ_n^1. Then, for a given execution on p processors, and thus a measure of E_m and δ_n, we position the effective efficiency of the parallelization in the interval $\left[E_{p,0.5}^{\text{eff}}\,;E_{p,0.0}^{\text{eff}}\right]$. Furthermore, *there exists a noise level $\lambda_x \in [0.0\,;0.5]$ in the sequential execution time T_s^1 such that:* $E_{p,\lambda_x}^{\text{eff}} = E_p^{\text{eff}}$.

Now we present experimental results obtained with a program for the solution of linear equations using Gauss's method, PRELG. Other results with a matrix product program can be found in [11].

---

[4] Bad coding may prove this wrong, and experiments conducted with a matrix product program and matrices of size lower than 10×10 confirmed it. But the data transfer and memory contention times highly increase with the number of processors. A λ_n^1 greater than 50% would lead to a very large δ_n, which never occurred with bigger matrix sizes.

3 Experimental Results

Our target machine is an eight-processor Encore Multimax. We used the tools presented in [10] to measure T_s^1, T_s^p and T_p. Only the most remarkable results are given, complete results can be found in [11].

3.1 Presentation of the Program Kernel

The outer loop is sequential, the two inner loops are parallel. The barrier and the distribution of the inner loops make the kernel subroutine **elim** parallel.

```
      subroutine elim(n, a, p, q, porte)
      character *56 porte
      integer n
      real a(200,200)
      integer p, q
      integer i, j, l, k0, k
      do 1 i=1, n-1
        l = 0
        do 2 j = i+1, n
          k0 = mmod(q-1, p) + i + 1
          do 3 k = k0, n, p
3            a(j,k) = a(j,k) - a(j,i)*a(i,k)/a(i,i)
          l = l + n - i
2         continue
      call fbarrier(porte)
1       continue
      return
      end
```

3.2 Noise Variation Level

Table 1 gives the noise variation level as a function of the number of processors. We clearly observe that the machine generated noise increases with the number of processors and is not negligible at all. $\delta_n = 93.04\%$ for a 10×10 matrix on 7 processors

Table 1. Variation level δ_n of the noise expressed in percentage.

Processors	10×10	20×20	50×50	100×100	200×200
2	14.59	6.76	2.94	2.21	1.72
3	29.01	13.33	5.51	3.18	2.62
4	44.06	19.00	7.82	4.07	2.62
5	56.99	24.91	10.13	5.05	3.12
6	72.48	31.81	12.60	6.07	3.64
7	93.04	38.56	14.44	7.27	4.10

for instance: the increase of the noise is equal to the program execution time itself.

3.3 Efficiency and Approximate Effective Efficiency

10 × 10 Matrix. As we can see in Table 2, for any $\lambda_n^1 \in [0.0 \, ; 0.50]$, the difference between $E_{p,\lambda_n^1}^{\text{eff}}$ and E_m is far from being negligible: $0.10 \leq E_{p,\lambda_n^1}^{\text{eff}} - E_m \leq 0.32$. There is definitely good reason to distinguish efficiency of the parallel program and effective efficiency of the parallelization. The difference between $E_{p,0.50}^{\text{eff}}$ and $E_{p,0.0}^{\text{eff}}$ is distinctly smaller: $0.02 \leq E_{p,0.0}^{\text{eff}} - E_{p,0.50}^{\text{eff}} \leq 0.08$. These two remarks show that E_m gives us an altered picture of the quality of the parallelization and that the estimate $E_{p,\lambda_n^1}^{\text{eff}}$ is relatively accurate. Thus, for four processors, $0.819 \leq E_p^{\text{eff}} \leq 0.872$, while $E_m = 0.63$. An efficiency of 0.84 ± 0.03 with a 10 × 10 matrix is quite satisfactory. Knowing only E_m could not have led us to that conclusion.

100 × 100 Matrix. Although the noise variation level is small, less than 8% (see Table 2), the difference between E_m and $E_{p,\lambda_n^1}^{\text{eff}}$, $\lambda_n^1 \in [0.0 \, ; 0.50]$, is again appreciable: $0.02 \leq E_{p,\lambda_n^1}^{\text{eff}} - E_m \leq 0.06$. The difference between $E_{p,0.50}^{\text{eff}}$ and $E_{p,0.0}^{\text{eff}}$ has become very small: $0.001 \leq E_{p,0.0}^{\text{eff}} - E_{p,0.50}^{\text{eff}} \leq 0.005$. Thus, for seven processors, $0.986 \leq E_p^{\text{eff}} \leq 0.990$, while $E_m = 0.924$. This shows that all the parallelism inherent to the program has been detected and that the machine generated noise leads to a drop in efficiency of 2% (for two processors) to 6% (for seven processors).

Table 2. PRELG efficiency and approximate effective efficiency, $\lambda_n^1 \in [0.0 \, ; 0.50]$.

Processors	\multicolumn{5}{c}{10 × 10 matrix}					\multicolumn{5}{c}{100 × 100 matrix}				
	δ_n	E_m	$E_{p,0.50}^{\text{eff}}$	$E_{p,0.10}^{\text{eff}}$	$E_{p,0.0}^{\text{eff}}$	δ_n	E_m	$E_{p,0.50}^{\text{eff}}$	$E_{p,0.10}^{\text{eff}}$	$E_{p,0.0}^{\text{eff}}$
2	14.59	0.839	0.936	0.952	0.956	2.21	0.977	0.998	0.998	0.998
3	29.01	0.725	0.883	0.911	0.918	3.18	0.967	0.997	0.997	0.998
4	44.06	0.630	0.819	0.861	0.872	4.07	0.956	0.993	0.995	0.995
5	56.99	0.562	0.762	0.814	0.828	5.05	0.946	0.990	0.993	0.993
6	72.48	0.501	0.711	0.770	0.786	6.07	0.936	0.989	0.992	0.993
7	93.04	0.445	0.678	0.742	0.760	7.27	0.924	0.986	0.990	0.991

4 Conclusion

Evaluating the quality of program parallelization consists in answering the following questions:

1. To what extent has the intrinsic parallelism of the program been detected?
2. To what extent does the target machine disrupt this detected parallelism?

Two pieces of information are needed to answer the question 1: the *expected* performance if we consider that the target machine does effect neither the sequential execution nor the parallel execution; the performance *obtained* when the machine does not effectively disrupt these executions. The user of the parallelizer holds the former. We focused in this paper on the effective performance of the parallelization, E_p^{eff}, and established with (2) a relation linking λ_n^1, δ_n and E_m to E_p^{eff}. We estimated that λ_n^1 (non measurable) could not be greater than 50%. We defined the *approximate effective efficiency* $E_{p,\lambda_n^1}^{\text{eff}}$ as the effective efficiency of the parallelization for a *fixed* λ_n^1. For a given execution on p processors, the effective efficiency of the parallelization thus belongs to the interval $\left[E_{p,0.5}^{\text{eff}}\,;\,E_{p,0.0}^{\text{eff}}\right]$.

The difference between E_m and $\left[E_{p,0.5}^{\text{eff}}\,;\,E_{p,0.0}^{\text{eff}}\right]$ answers the question 2: it gives an estimate of the machine generated drop in performance.

The experimental results allowed us to show that E_m and E_p^{eff} are two separate quantities (see 3.3). We measured the drop in efficiency due to the noise and hence estimated the effects of the machine on the execution of a program. Moreover, for small values of δ_n the estimate of E_p^{eff} is very good. More precisely, the width of the interval $\left[E_{p,0.5}^{\text{eff}}\,;\,E_{p,0.0}^{\text{eff}}\right]$ depends on the values of δ_n and E_m: the bigger δ_n and the smaller E_m are, the worse the estimate is.

Obtaining a better estimate of the effective performance of the parallelization depends on a better estimate of an upper bound for λ_n^1. We direct our efforts towards the definition of an upper bound for λ_n^1 as a function of δ_n, E_m and the parallel program. We also intend to extend our criteria to the distributed memory model.

References

1. N. Tawbi, A. Dumay, P. Feautrier. *PAF un Paralléliseur Automatique pour FORTRAN. Rapport MASI No 185*, juin 1987.
2. G. Amdahl. The Validity of the Single Processor Approach to Achieving Large Scale Computing Capabilities, *Proc. AFIPS Conf.*, 1967, pp. 483-485.
3. J. Gustafson. Reevaluating Amdahl's Law. *Commun. ACM* 31, May 1988, pp. 532-533.
4. L. D. Eager, J. Zahorjan, E. D. Lazowska. Speedup Versus Efficiency in Parallel Systems. *IEEE Transactions on Computers* 38, No. 3, March 1989, pp. 408-423.
5. H. Flatt, K. Kennedy. Performance of Parallel Processors. *Parallel Computing* 12, 1989, pp. 1-20.
6. A. Karp, H. Flatt. Measuring Parallel Processor Performance. *Commun. ACM 33*, May 1990, pp. 539-543.
7. XH. Sun, and J. Gustafson. Toward a better parallel performance metric. *Parallel Computing* 17, No. 10 & 11, December 1991, pp. 1093-1109.
8. R. Hockney. Performance Parameters and Benchmarking of Supercomputers. *Parallel Computing* 17 No. 10 & 11, December 1991, pp. 1111-1130.
9. K. Gallivan, W. Jalby, and D. Gannon. On the Problem of Optimizing Data Transfer for Complex Memory Systems. *Proc. ACM Int. Conference on Supercomputing*, 1988, pp. 238-253.
10. JY. Berthou. Des outils de mesures et d'analyse de performances de la parallélisation de programmes parallèles. *Rapport MASI No 91.10*, janvier 1991.
11. JY. Berthou, P. Klein. Estimating the Effective Performance of Program Parallelization on Shared Memory MIMD Multiprocessors. *MASI Tech. Report, to appear.*

This article was processed using the LaTeX macro package with LLNCS style

On the Simulation of Pipelining of Fully Digit On-line Floating-Point Adder Networks on Massively Parallel Computers [*]

Jean Duprat and Mario Fiallos Aguilar [**]

Laboratoire de l'Informatique du Parallélisme - IMAG
Ecole Normale Supérieure de Lyon
46 Allé d'Italie, 69364 Lyon Cedex 07, France
mfiallos@frensl61.bitnet

Abstract. This paper deals with the simulation of on-line floating-point adders networks on parallel machines. We present the first results of the simulations of pipelining at digit-level on MasPar, a massively parallel SIMD computer.

1 Introduction

The digit-pipelined (most significant bits first) mode of computation introduced by Ercegovac and Trivedi [Erc84] and studied also by Asada [NTY87], Tu [Tu90], Irwin [IO83] and others, is called *on-line* mode. In such mode, an arithmetic operation is characterized by its *on-line delay*, that is, the number δ such that n digits of the result are deduced from $(n + \delta)$ digits of the input values.

In [DFMY91], [JF92] and [JMF92] was shown that it is possible to design on-line floating-point adders, with *on-line delay*, $\delta_{add} = 3$, multipliers with $\delta_{mul} = 6$ and dividers with $\delta_{div} = 6$, where the digits both for the exponent and for the mantissa circulate in *on-line* mode (*fully digit*), exponent first.

This paper describes a preliminary work that has as its goal the simulation and conception of a massively parallel machine made up of heterogeneous *on-line* operators.

As it is well known, adders interconnected by a tree structure are the fastest way to compute the addition of numbers. In fact, in scientific computing it is interesting to have thousands of processors interconnected by a tree-like structure.

As MasPar has thousands of processors, its structure is suitable to simulate other massively parallel architectures that will have maybe, thousands of *on-line* operators.

In this paper we present the results of the simulation of pipelining between *on-line* adders. We present the simulation of a 63 adders tree as an example of the simulation of the pipelining between on-line operators.

We begin with the description of the on-line floating-point adder at block level. The second part deals with the method used to simulate pipelining at digit-level

---

[*] This work is part of a project called CARESSE which is partially supported by the "PRC Architectures Nouvelles de Machines" of the French Ministère de la Recherche et de la Technologie and the Centre National de la Recherche Scientifique.

[**] On leave from Universidade Federal do Ceará/CNPq, Brazil.

of on-line floating-point adders interconnected as a 63 nodes tree on MasPar. Two differents mappings are discussed.

2   On-line Floating-Point Adder

The process implemented on every node of the tree which simulates one on-line floating-point adder is called *addflo*.

As in the classical floating-point adders case, *addflo* performs basically three operations: exponent calculation, mantissa alignment and mantissa calculation. Figure 1 shows the different blocks of the adder[DFMY91]:

- A serial maximizer computes the maximum of the two exponents.
- A serial aligner performs the mantissa alignment with a shift register using the difference between the exponents.
- A serial adder calculates the sum of the aligned mantissas.
- A synchronizer is used to guarantee that only an unavoidable carry appearing in the sum of the mantissas will provoke the truncation of the mantissa and the incrementation of the exponent of the result.

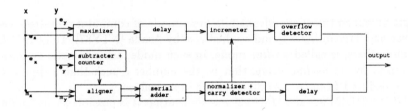

Fig. 1. The On-line Floating-Point Adder

The synchronizer must test the carry digit and the more significant digit of the mantissas sum. When these digits are equal to $1\,0$, $\bar{1}\,0$, $1\,1$ or $\bar{1}\,\bar{1}$ respectively, the incrementation of the exponent and the truncation of the mantissa (the last digit is lost) are performed. When these digits are equal to $0\,1$, $0\,\bar{1}$, $1\,\bar{1}$ or $\bar{1}\,1$, the exponent is not modified and by substituting $1\,\bar{1}$ for $0\,1$ or $\bar{1}\,1$ for $0\,\bar{1}$, if necessary, the carry digit of the sum will be 0.

The operation performed by the synchronizer is different from the systematic incrementation of the exponent during all addition proposed by Tu [Tu90]. In this last case, the truncation of the mantissa of the result leads to a needless loss of information.

3   Description of the MasPar Machine

The MasPar machine [Bla90], [Chr90], [Nic90] used in the simulation has 1024 4-bit processor elements (PEs) organized in 64 clusters. The processors are interconnected by an *xnet* toroidal neighborhood mesh and a global multistage crossbar router network [Mas91].

The programming language used is MPL (MasPar Parallel Application Language). MPL is a superset of C with commands for the data-parallel programming mode that include SIMD communication constructs between PEs.

4 Simulation of one Floating-Point Adder

In our simulation a *BS digit* is represented by two bits of a byte. The floating-point *BS* format chosen has 53 digits for the mantissa and 10 digits for the exponent.

The control of the *addflo* process is assumed by a status variable called *eadd*. The process works like a *global* automaton which controls *local* ones (maximum, overflow detector and pseudo-normalizer) and circuits (serial adder and incrementer). At each input of digit operands, the *addflo* status variable *eadd* is incremented. At the beginning, the *addflo* waits for two input digits different from 00 00; this convention will assure the synchronization of the operators when they are numerous.

In order to simulate several *addflos* with the same program code, we use pointers to differentiate each structure and indeed each adder.

5 Simulation of Several Floating-Point Adders on MasPar

The key idea to simulate several adders on Maspar is to map to several PEs, several *addflo* processes. So we can map each on-line operator and its local variables to each PE and its local memory. It is also possible to map several operators of the same or different types to each PE, but all the processors would simultaneously simulate the same type of operator since MasPar is a SIMD machine.

The conversion of the software written in C to the parallel version is straightforward: basically it is necessary to change only the declarations of some variables and functions to their *plural* [Bla90], [Chr90], [Nic90] version.

5.1 Simulation of a Pipelined 63 Nodes Complete Binary Tree

The two mapping algorithms to simulate the tree were chosen as simple as possible because our main goal was to simulate the pipeline at digit-level and not the best map of a tree on a mesh. Other mappings may be implemented and tested in future works. The first mapping is shown in figure 2. All the shadow processors performs one addition of the tree. In this mapping the number of different distances of data transmission is 9 and as MasPar is a SIMD machine, each one of this distances of communication will be executed serially, one after the other. In order to minimize the number of different distances of transmission we introduce the mapping of figure 3. In this mapping with the help of 1-cycle delay operators, the number of different distances of transmission is reduced to 2.

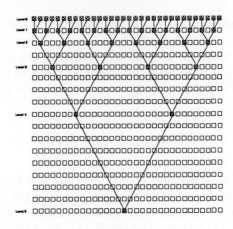

Fig. 2. The First Mapping of the 63 Nodes Tree

5.2 First Results

In the first mapping, the pipeline is full at cycle $k(\delta+1)-1$, where k is the number of levels of the tree. All the digits of an addition are produced after $length\_BS + \delta_{addflo}$ cycles. The maximum number of cycles to compute the addition of m set of 64 numbers is $k(\delta_{addflo} + 1) + m * length\_BS + \delta_{addflo}(m-1) - 1$.

In the second mapping, the pipeline is full at cycle $k(\delta + 1) + 25$, where k is the number of levels of the tree. All the digits of an addition are produced after $length\_BS + \delta_{addflo}$ cycles. The maximum number of cycles to compute the addition of m set of 64 numbers is $k(\delta_{addflo} + 1) + m * length\_BS + \delta_{addflo}(m-1) + 25$.

As we simulate the tree in a SIMD computer, each of the nine levels of the data transmission will be executed serially, one level after the other. The second mapping has reduced the number of different distances and improved the time of simulation using a larger pipe. The figure 4 shows the number of floating-point additions per second executed in the two mappings. As we can expect at the beginning the second mapping is the slowest but when the number of 64 numbers additions sets is greater than 100 it is the fastest.

6 Conclusion and Future Work

We have simulated the pipelining at digit-level for a complete binary tree of 63 on-line floating-point adders. In the first mapping, the data transmission is executed in nine steps. The second algorithm reduces the distances of communication and hence the time of the simulation.

The characteristic of massive parallelism of MasPar offers interesting possibilities of simulation of an on-line machine with hundreds or thousands of on-line operators. But, if we compute with different types of operators, like adders, multipliers, dividers, etc. all the PEs will simulate only one type of operator at once.

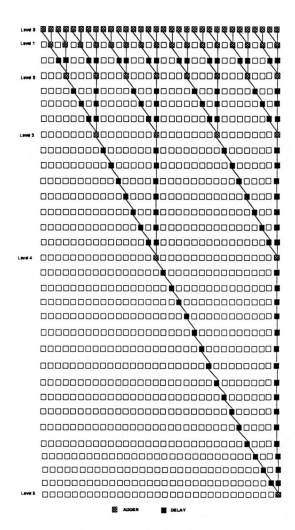

Fig. 3. The Improved Mapping of the 63 Nodes Tree

Maybe a single-program multiple data architecture, SPMD will be more efficient to our simulation. But in the first steps of our study, we look for the validation of our ideas more than for sheer performances.

Our goal is the conception of a massively parallel machine called CARESSE, the French abbreviation of Serial Redundant Scientific Computer, made up of heterogeneous on-line operators linked in a programmable network.

References

[Bla90]   T. Blank. The maspar mp-1 architecture. In IEEE, editor, *IEEE compcon*

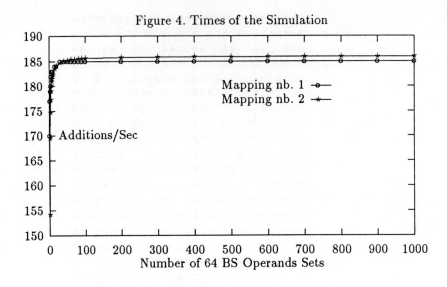

Figure 4. Times of the Simulation

spring 1990, pages pp 21–24, 1990.

[Chr90] P. Christy. Software to support massively parallel computing on the maspar mp-1. In IEEE, editor, *IEEE compcon spring 1990*, pages pp 29–33, 1990.

[DFMY91] J. Duprat, M. Fiallos, J. M. Muller, and H. J. Yeh. Delays of on-line floating-point operators in borrow save notation. In *Algorithms and parallel VLSI architectures II*, pages 273–278. Noth Holland, 1991.

[Erc84] M.D. Ercegovac. On-line arithmetic: an overview. In SPIE, editor, *SPIE, Real Time Signal Processing VII*, pages pp 86–93, 1984.

[IO83] M. J. Irwin and R. M. Owens. Fully digit on-line networks. *IEEE Transactions on Computers*, 32(4):402–406, 1983.

[JF92] J.Duprat and M. Fiallos. New on-line floating-point operators for radix 2 computations. Report (to be published), Laboratoire de l'Informatique du Parallélisme de l'Ecole Normale Supérieure de Lyon, France, 1992.

[JMF92] J.Duprat, J. M. Muller, and M. Fiallos. On-line floating-point divider. Report (to be published), Laboratoire de l'Informatique du Parallélisme de l'Ecole Normale Supérieure de Lyon, France, 1992.

[Mas91] MasPar Computer Corporation. *MasPar Parallel application language(MPL) - reference manual*, 1991.

[Nic90] J. Nickolls. The design of the maspar mp-1: A cost effective massively parallel computer. In IEEE, editor, *IEEE compcon spring 1990*, pages pp 25–28, 1990.

[NTY87] T. Asada N. Takagi and S. Yajima. A Hardware Algorithm for Computing Sine and Cosine using Reduntant Binary-Representation. *Systems and Computers in Japan*, 18(8):1–9, 1987.

[Tu90] P. K. Tu. *On-line Arithmetic Algorithms for Efficient Implemetation*. PhD thesis, Computer Science Departament, UCLA, 1990.

This article was processed using the LaTeX macro package with LLNCS style

A Parallel Expert System Using a Backward Chaining Strategy

K.R. Tout[*] and D.J. Evans

Parallel Algorithms Research Centre, Loughborough University of Technology, Loughborough, Leicestershire, U.K.

Abstract. In this paper a parallel backward chaining technique is applied to a rule-based expert system on a shared memory multiprocessor system. The results indicate satisfactory speed-up performance for a small number of processors (< 10) and a reasonably large number of rules.

1. Introduction

In this paper we propose a parallel inference mechanism based on a parallel backward chaining technique with OR-parallelism [1,3,11]. The method used is based on a parallel search of the goal tree. The idea is to divide the search tree into subtrees, where each subtree corresponds to an OR node (choice node). All the OR-nodes generated during the parallel search are maintained in a task-queue with each OR-node representing one task. The processors share the task-queue, which is resident in the shared memory of the system. Each processor collects a task from the task-queue, processes the task (this may generate new OR-nodes, which are then added to the task-queue), and becomes idle again and looks for more work. The processor which becomes idle will check the task-queue for a task to perform, and if no task is available the processor has to wait for some tasks to appear in the task-queue. Our aim is to make the model suited to 'coarse-grain' parallelism, i.e. the subtree (task) assigned to each processor has to be sufficiently large to allow the benefits of parallelism to outweigh the overheads in distributing and collecting the tasks. Thus, allowing every goal to be OR-parallel, i.e. to add its OR-nodes (Choice nodes) to the task-queue, will make the parallelism too 'fine-grained'.

The strategy followed here is to allow the processor to split up its search subtree and generate new OR-nodes, i.e. new tasks, only if there is at least one processor in a waiting state, i.e. waiting for some tasks to appear in the task-queue. Thus, before a processor generates new OR-nodes it checks the other processors status, and if it finds one or more processors waiting, it then generates the OR nodes and adds new tasks to the task-queue.

The method has the following advantages:
1. Very little communication between the processors.
2. Better usage of the shared memory architecture.
3. Minimum synchronization overhead.
4. Dynamic distribution of tasks among the processors.
5. Reasonably large size for the tasks.

*Brainware GmbH, Berlin, Germany.

2. The Backward Chaining Process

One of the reasoning mechanisms used by rule-based expert systems is that of backward chaining [8,9]. Backward chaining or 'goal-directed' inference starts with the desired goal and attempts to find evidence for this to be the case. Backward chaining is typically used in situations where the quantity of data is potentially very large, and where some specific characteristics of the system under consideration is of interest. Most typical are various problems of diagnosis, such as medical diagnosis or fault finding in electrical or mechanical equipment.

So backward chaining can be represented as searching through a branching network or tree. Trees may be searched in a number of ways. These are conveniently divided into a 'blind search' and 'informed search'. The latter is often called heuristic search. The two basic methods of blind search are called 'depth-first' and 'breadth-first' search. An AND/OR tree is a useful device for representing the behaviour of a rule-based expert system that works by problem decomposition, i.e. by decomposing high-level goals into a series of subgoals, each of which may have their own associated subgoals, and so on. Thus, to achieve high-level goals, these subgoals should be achieved first. There are two types of nodes in an AND/OR tree: OR-nodes and AND-nodes. An OR-node is satisfied if just one of its associated subgoals (child-nodes) is satisfied, whereas, in the case of an AND-node, all the associated subgoals have to be satisfied in order for the node to be satisfied.

A typical shared memory multiprocessor has a moderate number of processors (Sequent Balance, for example). We want to utilize this class of multiprocessor systems in such a way that backward chaining systems will run faster than on a single processor machine.

Among all the different types of parallelism, OR-parallelism seems to be the most promising for our problem and seems to offer a good potential for large scale and large-granularity parallelism. Moreover, parallelism in OR-parallel systems can easily be adjusted to be 'coarse-grained' and thus suitable for the current multiprocessors.

3. The PBC-D1 Model
(Parallel Backward Chaining Model using Dynamic Scheduling)

3.1 The Data Structures Used
The main data structures used are:
1. The Rule Base (RB).
2. The Data Base (DB).
3. The OR-Node-Set (ONS).
4. The Tree-Of-Nodes (TON).
5. The Processors-Status-Array (PSA).

Example 1:
As an example consider the rule r_1:

$$\text{If } C_1 \& C_2 \& C_3 \text{ THEN A}$$

The internal representation of rule r_1 is shown in Figure 1.

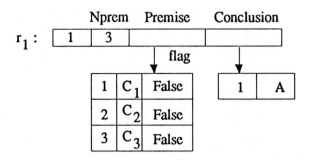

Figure 1: Internal representation of rule r_1

Note that for a condition (C_i), the field *flag* is defined as follows:

$flag(C_i)$ = TRUE IF C_i is satisfied by the elements of DB

$flag(C_i)$ = FALSE IF otherwise.

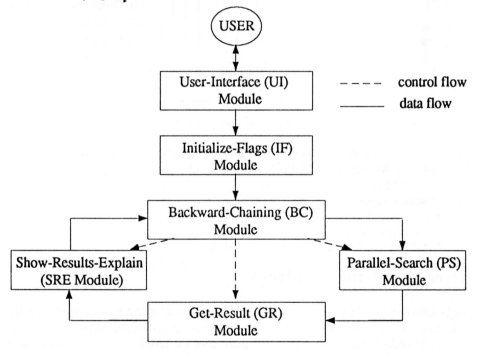

Figure 2: The main modules of PCB-D1

3.2 The Model and Its Implementation
We assume that:
. The rules are numbered from 1 to n.
. The processors are numbered from 1 to m.
. The facts needed by the system during its reasoning process are collected by the "user-Interface" (UI) module at the beginning of the consultation. This is done

for performance measurement reasons. The processors share the same 'task-queue' (this is ONS) which is resident in the shared memory of the system (see Figure 3). The processors status are determined by the content of the array PSA which also resides in the shared memory. Moreover, the processors share a global variable called 'Halt' which determines whether to halt the execution or not. At start, 'Halt' is initialized to FALSE.

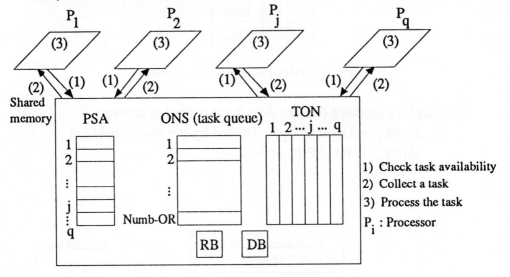

Figure 3: The concept of task partitioning in PS

The PBC-D1 model consists of 6 main modules (see Figure 2). These are:
1. The User-Interface (UI) module.
2. The Initialize-Flags (IF) module.
3. The Backward-Chaining (BC) module.
4. The Parallel Search (PS) module.
5. The Get-Results (GR) module.
6. The Show-Results-Explain (SRE) module.

4. Overview of the PS Module

The algorithm used in PS can be understood as follows: starting with a subgoal/goal, the task node, we first expand the node, always driving backward (downward in the tree) from the node to its child-nodes, and then from the child-nodes to their children and so on until no further expansion is possible. This operation, will generate the search tree for the task node, which has the structure of an AND/OR tree. This tree is represented with the structure $TON[P_i]$, where P_i is the ID of the processor which is processing the 'task-node'.

After generating the task-node tree, the system starts driving forward (upward in the tree), from the child-nodes to the parent, transfer the results from the child-nodes to their parents and updating the rules which correspond to the parents. This operation will continue until the top of the tree is reached (the task-node). The results of the intermediary nodes are broadcast to RB, and they are stored in the flags of the corresponding rules premises. The reasons behind using the rules to store the results of the nodes are:

1. To keep the degree of communication amongst the processors to a minimum.
2. An easy way to find out whether the goal is achieved or not.
3. Enable the system to explain its reasoning process, i.e. how conclusions are reached, what path is followed to achieve the goal, etc.
4. To keep each processor informed of the results procuced by the other running processors. The processors exchange information about the search process through RB, and more specifically, by using the flags in the rules.

5. Performance Analysis of PBC-D1

The model has been implemented on the Sequent Balance 8000, shared memory multiprocessor system and was tested for a Rule-Based Expert System [8], with different numbers of rules, so as to study the effects of the problem size and complexity on speed-up and efficiency [2,4,5,6,7]. The experiments are carried out with different numbers of processors, so as to determine the speed up obtained from each of the parallel implementations [10].

For performance measurement reasons, we do not time the initial loading and set up of the knowledge base (rules and facts) in any of the parallel models. Only the process of inferencing is timed.

The results from the tests of the PBC-D1 model for a rulebase of 450 rules are summarized in Table 1 and the graphical interpretation is shown in Figure 4 respectively.

Number of Processors	Computing Time (msec)	Speedup	Efficiency
1	248320	1.000	1.000
2	127850	1.942	0.971
3	87170	2.849	0.950
4	67960	3.654	0.913
5	62880	4.949	0.790
6	53030	4.683	0.780
7	48800	5.089	0727
8	47460	5.232	0.654
9	45980	5.401	0.600

Table 1: Experimental Results for the Parallel Model PBC-D1 *[Rulebase = 450 rules]*

It can be observed from the figure that the speed curve follows more closely a $\log_p$ type curve (where p is the number of processors used), when p satisfies a small number of processors (1 to 9). This is due to the fact that the bulk of the processing operations are involved with searching and matching. In addition extensive rulebase and database access by the processors involving communication overheads on the shared memory bus are involved. It is well known that the non-numerical operations of searching and matching are more difficult to parallelize than the standard scientific problems.

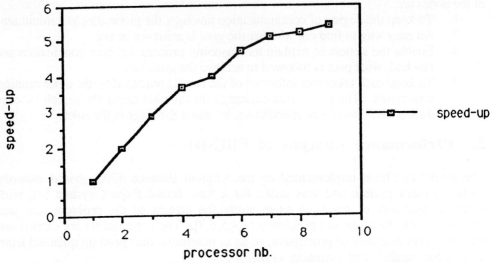

Figure 4: Speed-up graph for the model PBC-D1 *[Rulebase = 450 rules]*

References

1. K.A.M. Ali: OR-parallel execution of PROLOG on a multi-sequential machine. Int.Jour. of Parallel Programming 15, 189-214 (1986).
2. P. Arratibel, P. Glize and C. Percebois: Parallelism in the SATIN multi-expert system. In Parallel Processing and Applications, E. Chiricozzi and A. D'Amico eds., Elsevier Science Pub., North Holland 1988.
3. H.C. Fu and C.C. Chuang: An OR-parallel processing multiprocessor system for artificial intelligence. In Proc. SPIE Int.Soc.Opt.Eng., Vol. 1095, USA, 1989, pp.286-297.
4. A. Gupta: Parallelism in production systems. Pitman Pub., London, 1987.
5. T. Ishida and S.J. Stolfo: Towards the parallel execution of rules in production system programs. In Proc. Int.Conf. on Parallel Processing, IEEE, 1985, pp.568-575.
6. E.J. Krall and P.F. McGehearty: A case study of parallel execution of a rule-based expert system. Int.J. Parallel Programming 15, 5-32 (1986).
7. T. Li and C.D. Marlin: Algorithms for the parallel execution of rule-based expert systems. In Inf.Processing 89, Proc. IFIP 11th World Computer Cong., San Francisco, USA, 1989, pp.331-336.
8. G.F. Luger and W.A. Stubblefield: Artificial Intelligence and the Design of Expert Systems. Benjamin/Cummings Pub. Comp., Inc., 1989.
9. N.J. Nilsson: Principles of Artificial Intelligence. Tioga Pub.Co., Calif., 1980.
10. M.J. Quinn: Designing efficient algorithms for parallel computers, McGraw-Hill, N.Y., 1987.
11. V. Singh and M.R. Genesereth: A parallel execution model for backward-chaining deductions. Future Computing Systems 1, 271-308, (1986).

Optimal Speedup Conditions for a Parallel Back-Propagation Algorithm

Hélène Paugam-Moisy

Laboratoire de l'Informatique du Parallélisme,
Ecole Normale Supérieure de Lyon
46 allée d'Italie, 69364 LYON Cedex 07, FRANCE

Abstract. One way for implementing a parallel back-propagation algorithm is based on distributing the examples to be learned among different processors. This method provides with spectacular speedups for each epoch of back-propagation learning, but it shows a major drawback : parallelization implies alterations of the gradient descent algorithm. This paper presents an implementation of this parallel algorithm on a transputer network. It mentions experimental laws about the back-propagation convergence speed, and claims that optimal conditions still exist for performing an actual speedup by implementing such a parallel algorithm. It points out theoretical and experimental optimal conditions, in terms of the number of processors and the size of the example packets.

1 Introduction

1.1 Several Degrees of Parallelism in Multilayer Neural Networks

As pointed out by Singer [5], there are at least three degrees of parallelism in training multilayer neural networks. First, there is the parallel processing performed by the numerous nodes at each layer. Second, there is the parallel processing of the many training examples. A third parallel aspect stems from the fact that the forward and backward passes of different training patterns can be pipelined. Distributing the nodes upon all the processors requires a critical study of the network connectivity and an adapted grain of parallelism [3]. An optimal load-balancing for a given neural network in a given topology for parallel processors is not easy to achieve [7]. Distributing the examples among different copies of a neural network, each of them computed by a single processor, has been presented as a much more effective parallel algorithm [6]. The purpose of this paper is to show evidence toward disproving this claim.

1.2 The Problem with Parallel Processing of Training Examples

The training set is divided in blocks. One copy of the same multilayer neural network is fully implemented on each processor of a parallel computer. When processing examples of a packet, each processor collects the weight corrections to be applied to the weight matrix, but cannot apply them immediately, in order to keep the learning phase globally coherent. While the computations can be independent, weight updating requires synchronisation. After the complete processing of their own packets, all the processors exchange their weight corrections which are all added up everywhere. A new step can now start, with an other block of examples.

The crucial issue is : the larger the blocks, the higher the speedup, with regard to the parallel algorithm. Conversely, the smaller the blocks, the more frequent the weight updates, and the faster the convergence, with regard to back-propagation. The problem is to find the appropriate block size for achieving an optimal overall speedup for a parallel implementation. In part 2, the convergence of back-propagation learning is discussed, according to the number of examples processed between two successive weight updates. Part 3 presents performances of the parallel implementation. Part 4 emphasizes theoretical and experimental conditions for performing an actual speedup of the learning process.

2 On the Convergence of Back-Propagation

2.1 Variations on the Back-Propagation Algorithm

As a matter of fact, there exist two well-known variants of back-propagation : the total gradient descent and the stochastic gradient algorithm. Whereas, for stochastic gradient, one weight update occurs after every example presentation, total gradient descent implies that the weight matrix is updated only once after a complete presentation of the whole training set. Between these extreme cases, a smooth variant consists in updating the weights after every block of b examples. This variant will be further called a *block-gradient* algorithm.

When implementing a parallel processing of training examples, weight updates occur after the processing of a packet of k examples by each of the p processors. Hence the block size is b=kp. For instance, with a training set of 200 examples, and a net of 8 processors, packets of 5 examples each imply a block size b=40, and 5 weight updates for each epoch (an *epoch* is one presentation of each example in the training set). Total gradient descent is then performed with packets of 25 examples each. Stochastic gradient descent cannot be performed, unless p=k=1... which is not yet very parallel !

2.2 Experimental Laws on the Block-Gradient Algorithm

In the frame of another work [4], the behaviour of the block-gradient algorithm has been observed for various sizes of blocks between two successive weight updates. Applications were a classification and a character recognition problems. The neural network was a one-hidden layer, fully-connected, network. The learning rate vector was constant in time, and constant for each layer : to each cell is associated the quotient of a constant value, next called the *learning rate value*, by the fan-in.

Three laws have been stated from these experiments. The first one indicates that, in order to ensure stability along the learning phase, an adaptive learning rate has to be chosen, respecting an exponential decreasing function of the number of examples presented between two successive weight updates. The second law states that, with an adaptive learning rate, the number of epochs requisite for reaching a given level of convergence liearly depends on the block size. Derived from the previous statements, the last experimental law shows how the number of epochs, for reaching a given performance, depends on the learning rate (k is a non-negative constant) :

$$N = k\,\varepsilon^{-\frac{1}{\alpha}} \quad \text{with} \quad 0 \leqslant \alpha \leqslant 1$$

This law will be useful for deriving optimal conditions of parallel implementation.

3 Speedup of a Parallel Back-Propagation Implementation

3.1 An implementation on a net of transputers

Since one neural network has to be processed on each processor, an MIMD parallel computer, with sufficient local memory, suits well to this parallel back-propagation algorithm. Experiments have been performed on a net of 32 transputers, which can be configured to any topology of degree less or equal to 4. Since this constraint does not allow configuration of a hypercube of degree greater than three, and breaks the symmetry of a mesh, a ring has been prefered for this implementation [Fig.1].

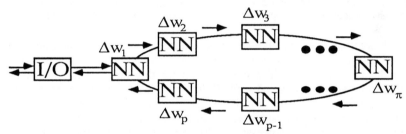

Fig.1. Parallel processing of examples, on a ring of p transputers

Since locally : $(\forall \pi \in \{1;p\})$ $\Delta w_\pi = \sum_{i=1}^{k} \Delta w(x_i(\pi))$ then globally : $\Delta w = \sum_{\pi=1}^{p} \Delta w_\pi$

Two types of communication must be considered :

- a *scattering* strategy for sending examples from the front end towards each processor : every block of b=kp examples is pipelined in p packets of k examples each. In a simpler frame, without calculation phases, this algorithm has been proved to be the optimal for scattering on an oriented ring of processors [2].

- a *gossiping* strategy for exchanging the weight corrections ΔW_π computed by each processor on the ring.

Between these two phases, each processor π keeps a packet of k examples and computes back-propagation for each of them. For communicating the weight corrections, each processor adds the content of current ΔW to its W matrix and then sends it to its successor. It also receives the corresponding ΔW from its predecessor in the ring. After p-1 steps, every processor has achieved its weight updating.

3.2 Experimental Results

Application is a classification problem. Neural network is a one-hidden layer network, with 27 input cells, 55 hidden and 3 output cells. The training set contains 1920 examples. The curves below show computational times [Fig.2] and speedups [Fig.3] for a single epoch, according to the block size, the number of processors, and the number of examples computed by each processor at each step.

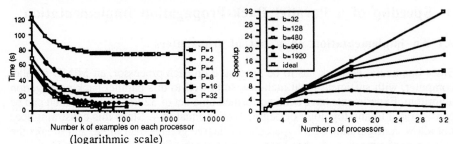

Fig.2. Computation times for a single epoch, according to the number k of examples computed by each processor

Fig.3. Speedups, according to the number p of processors, and the size b=kp of the blocks

Total computation time per epoch can be reduced from 122 seconds on a single processor (stochastic back-propagation), to 3 seconds on thirty-two processors (total gradient back-propagation). The main reason for this large variation is that the communication time for examples pipelining from the front-end to the processors becomes prominent when the ring is reduced to a single processor, or when the packets are too small. When the blocks are sufficiently large, good speedup values are obtained, such as 3.96 for 4 processors, 7.76 for 8 and 23 for 32 processors.

3.3 Modeling

The implementation described above can be modelized by adding communication time and computation time. Following Desprez and Tourancheau [1], the time for sending or receiving a message can be accurately modelized by

$\beta + L\tau$ where $\beta = 3.9\ \mu s$ and $\tau = 1.1\ \mu s$ between two transputers,
$\beta' + L\tau'$ where $\beta' = 15.4\ \mu s$ and $\tau' = 1.8\ \mu s$ between a transputer and the front-end. The communication and computation times can be modelized by

$$T_{comm} = L\tau' + \frac{1}{k}(\beta' + \gamma + \beta + w\tau) - \frac{1}{kp}(\gamma + \beta + w\tau)$$

$$T_{calc} = \frac{1}{k}Dw + \frac{1}{p}(B + Cw) + \frac{1}{kp}Aw$$

where :   p is the number of processors ;
            k is the number of examples learned by each processor at each step
            L is the length of each example message (in bytes) ;
            γ is the startup time for two parallel processes on a transputer ;
            w is the size of the weight updates.

Many experiments have been performed for w=300, 1650, 2400 (respectively 10, 55, 80 hidden cells). They show that this model is rather accurate, and that the communication time is smaller than the computation time. The computations of C and D values are the more precise. The other values must be taken as rough evaluations. Evaluations of the constants have been deduced as following :

$A \approx 2\mu s$ $B \approx 500\mu s$ $C \approx 23\mu s$ $D \approx 15\mu s$ $\gamma \approx 200\mu s$

4 Optimal Conditions for Speedup

4.1 A Theoretical Condition for Speedup

Assuming that the number of epochs necessary to reach a given threshold of convergence follows the experimental law established above, a condition for actual speedup can now be deduced. Total learning time is equal to the product of the number of epochs and the time required for a single epoch. With s being the size of the training set :

$$T = N.T_{1epoch} = N.s.(T_{comm} + T_{calc})$$

Hence :
$$T = (\lambda \, \varepsilon^{- \frac{1}{\alpha}})(T_{comm} + T_{calc}) = (\lambda \, \varepsilon(k,p)^{- \frac{1}{\alpha}}) \, \theta(k,p)$$

where λ is a parameter derived from s and from the previous constant k, $\varepsilon(k,p)$ is the learning rate, and $\theta(k,p)$ is the total execution time per example. It comes that $\partial T/\partial p$ and $\partial T/\partial k$ are identically null when $\varepsilon(k,p) = \theta(k,p)^{-\alpha}$, the expression of which differs from our experimental law for ε by the presence of a term in 1/k and a term in 1/p. This means that one may hope for T not to be constant with respect to k and p.

A condition for the existence of actual speedup is obtained by assuming that λ, $\varepsilon^{-\alpha}$ and θ are positive (verified under realistic experimental conditions), and ensuring that

$$\frac{\partial T}{\partial p} < 0 \text{ and } \frac{\partial T}{\partial k} < 0 : \qquad \frac{\frac{\partial \varepsilon}{\partial p}}{\varepsilon} > \alpha \frac{\frac{\partial \theta}{\partial p}}{\theta} \qquad \text{and} \qquad \frac{\frac{\partial \varepsilon}{\partial k}}{\varepsilon} > \alpha \frac{\frac{\partial \theta}{\partial k}}{\theta}$$

Measurements of constants in time modelings are not precise enough to verify whether these conditions are satisfied, but the next section shows that actual optimal conditions have been experimentally observed.

4.2 Existence of Optimal Conditions : Experimental Results

From the numbers of epochs experimentally computed and from the measured times, the following histograms [Fig.4] have been obtained, for a fixed number of processors p=32. This figure shows how, with a given number of processors, the optimal size of blocks can be chosen. For the experiment herein described, optimal speedups are obtained for block size b in the range [192,384]. Since p=32, the best values for the size k of example packets are in the range [6,12]. This packet size provides convergence to 80% and to 90% of learning success about four times faster than small packet size k=1, and at least three times faster than a large packet size k=120. Moreover, several evaluations show that the number p=16 of processors provides optimal speedup for small sizes k of example packets, and p=8 becomes better when k grows.

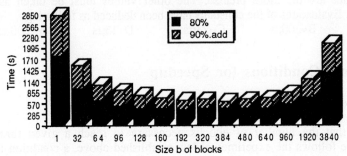

Fig.4. Convergence times, function of the block size, for 32 processors

5 Conclusion

In order to make efficient a parallel implementation of back-propagation by distributing the training set, it is important to be aware of the alterations which the parallel algorithm implies for the gradient descent method. In this paper, theoretical conditions for the existence of an actual speedup have been derived from experimental laws on the convergence of a block-gradient algorithm for back-propagation. Experimental results confirm the existence of these optimal conditions, in terms of the number of processors and the size of example packets.

In conclusion, speedup is effectively achievable for a parallel back-propagation algorithm based on the parallel processing of the training set. However caution must be exercised when choosing the number of processors, and hence when partitionning the training set. Performances are far weaker than the number of Mips [6] would lead one to imagine.

References

[1] F.Desprez, B.Tourancheau, Modélisation des performances de communication sur le Tnode avec le Logical system transputer toolset, *La lettre du transputer et des calculateurs distribués* 7 (Lab. d'Info. de Besançon, 1990) 65-72

[2] P.Fraigniaud, S.Miguet, Y.Robert, Scattering on a ring of processors, *Parallel Computing* 13 (North Holland, 1990) 377-383

[3] J.Ghosh, K.Hwang, Mapping neural networks onto message-passing multicomputers, *Journal of Parallel and Distributed Computing* 6 (Academic Press, 1989) 291-330

[4] H.Paugam-Moisy, On the convergence of a block-gradient algorithm for back-propagaton learning, *Proc. of IJCNN'92-Baltimore* (1992) III-919-924

[5] A.Singer, Implementations of artificial neural networks on the Connection Machine, *Parallel Computing* 14 (North-Holland, 1990) 305-316

[6] A.Singer, Exploiting the inherent parallelism of artificial neural networks to achieve 1300 M interconnects per second, *Proc. of INNC-90-Paris* (1990) 656-660

[7] S.Wang, Communication problems in simulating neural networks on a hypercube machine, *1st European Workshop on Hypercube and Distributed Computers* (1988)

A time-bounded binding access with low task-switching cost in an OR-Parallel Prolog

H. BOURZOUFI, G. GONCALVES, B. TOURSEL

Université de LILLE1 Laboratoire L.I.F.L. (UA 369 CNRS)
59655 Villeneuve d'Ascq Cedex - FRANCE -
e-mail : bourzouf@lifl.lifl.fr

Abstract : A new binding scheme for OR-multisequential execution of prolog programs is presented. The proposed scheme is a shared binding environment one, between the binding arrays scheme which has a constant time dereferencing and the hash-windows scheme which has low task-switching. The proposed scheme enables to have a bounded dereferencing time and a constant task-switching time. We show then this scheme allows to use various scheduling strategies and in particular leftmost strategy which enables to handle efficiently speculative work.

1 Introduction

One of the main problem in OR-parallelism implementation is how to manage multiple bindings of a same variable. Because several processors can explore distinct branches of a program search tree emanating from a common ancestor node, one must provide a mechanism to manage the binding of a single ancestor Prolog variable to multiple alternative bindings. Important issues in binding scheme are the cost of parallel task installation and the dereferencing time.

Usually, OR-parallel computational models based on multisequential approach, are classified as follows : the shared binding environment family [Lus88] and the non-shared binding environment[Ali90]. The first family is well suited for shared-memory architecture, while the second family can also be implemented on NORMA architecture [Bri90].

We have chosen the first family of computation because models based on shared-environment have a low task-switching cost (i.e no copying overhead) and allow free scheduling strategies as deepmost or leftmost one which are specialy well adapted to the handling of side-effects predicats and speculatif work [Hau90]. The major drawback of shared-environnement models is the overhead introduced by their binding accesses. In the next part, we propose a new mechanism to handle multiple bindings, which seems a good compromise between the binding arrays scheme (SRI model [War97]) which has a constant dereferencing time and the hash-windows scheme [Bar88] which has unbounded dereferencing time.

2 Computation model

We present rapidely in this section the main difference of our approach with regard to the classical OR-parallel model based on multisequential approach. A more detailed description of this approach could be found in [Bou91]] or [Bou92].

2.1 Execution control

In our model, each processor acts as a sequential Prolog engine with its own three Wam stacks : a local stack, a heap stack and a trail stack. When an active processor Pi execute an OR-parallel predicate, a choice point in local stack and a new entry in a fourth stack called "job stack" are created. Each entry in the job stack points to the corresponding choice point created in local stack and means that the choice point can be done in a parallel way. So when a processor is idle, it looks for a new task by examinating each entry of all the job stacks of active processors until it finds a choice point in which there is an available alternative. The scheduling strategy determine the way with which the choice points are examinated by an idle processor.

2.2 A backtracking process

When a processor has finished its current alternative, it backtracks to its last choice point. Depending on the state of the choice point and the processors working under it, the processor makes the appropriate action as follows:

If there are alternatives left (i.e live choice point), it executes the next alternative.

If there are no available alternatives and if all the other alternatives have been terminated (i.e dead choice point), the processor continues its backtracking to the next choice point after removing the corresponding entry in its job stack.

In the case there are no alternatives left but some processors are still working under this choice point (i.e full choice point), the processor must wait to terminate before it can backtrack over the choice point. The backtracking process can not be done because some shared informations are still accessed by other processors, so the corresponding task is temporarily suspended. In order to optimize the use of the processor, this one is allowed to help the processors working under the backtracking node. By this way, we minimize the elapsed time of suspended task, and we greatly simplify the management of each processor stacks (i.e no holes appear in memory).

Doing that, a processor can bind a same variable no more than once and the total number of bindings of a variable is always less or equal than the number of processor.

2.3 A key-based binding sharing model

To get fast task switchings, conditional bindings are shared through a global memory space. All conditional bindings are tagged with a private CPN (Choice Point Number) which relates to the total number of choice points created by a processor. This CPN plays the same role as OBL in the PEPSys implementation : to determine the scope of an OR shared variable binding.

The problem now is how a processor can determine conditional bindings made by other ancestor processors and which are valid for itself. In this way, the processor Pk use a private set of key registers $Sk = [K_0, K_1, ..., K_{N-1}]$ (where N is the number of processors) which will define its scope over bindings made by the others. Each key register Ki contains the number of choice points created by processor Pi and corresponding to the last ancestor node of processor Pk. In fact, the key register Kk of a set Sk represents the CPN of the processor Pk.

To dereference a non local variable several accesses are generally needed. A first access is made to cell value of the processor Pj stack creating this variable in order to check if the binding is unconditional or not. If it is the dereferencing is over, otherwise one must check if there is a valid conditional binding for Pk. So a searching operation is started over ancestor processors Ph which are in the scope of Pk. This operation returns a success if there is a deep binding made by Ph with a value tag which is less or equal to the corresponding key register Kh of Pk. Otherwise the searching operation fails and the variable is declared free. Thus deep binding dereferencing requires a maximum of N+1 memory accesses.

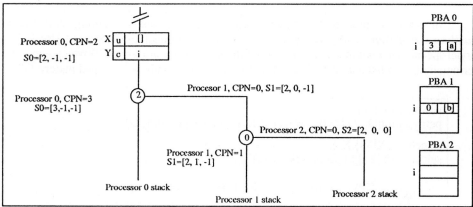

figure 1: conditional bindings in arrays

The figure 1 shows a possible storage implementation of the key based-binding sharing model which uses local processor binding array (PBA) to store conditional bindings. In this implementation, all conditional bindings are deep ones and every time a variable is created, its value is assigned with an index to the PBA as in SRI model.

In the example of figure 1, the processor P0 has created an environment in which variable X has been unconditionally bound to empty list [] (i.e. flag u is set) and variable Y was still unbound at the next choice point creation (i.e. flag c is set). After this point, the variable Y has been conditionally bound by both processor P0 and processor P1. When the processor P2 wants to dereference the variable Y, a search operation for a valid binding selects only the binding made by processor P1 which is in the scope of processor P2.

3 Speculative work

This model and its binding mechanism described above, have been developed and integrated in an OR-parallel simulator of Prolog programs extending a Prolog sequential interpreter [Bou92]. The program has been written in Le_Lisp programming language and it runs on SUN workstation.

OR-parallel Prolog models in which all the branches of the search tree can be executed in parallel, provide needless speculative works. A speculative task is one that may be pruned by a cut operator, rendering any work done on that task to be wasted. The binding mechanism described above has a bounded task-installation cost whatever the scheduling strategy used. So we have tested several of them and in particular a strategy which minimize speculative work.

3.1 Scheduling strategies

Three different scheduling strategies have been implemented in our OR-parallel simulator. The first one called "leftmost dispatching" consists to execute in prior branches situed in the left part of the search tree. The second one is called "deepmost dispatching" in which a idle processor attempts to grab work at the bottom of the search tree. Finally a third strategy called "topmost dispatching" consists to pick off work at the top of the search tree.

3.2 Modelling speculative work

In order to compare the effectiveness of the previous scheduling strategies in handling speculative work, we have used the same approach as Beaumont [Bea91] to model speculative computation. This modelling uses a program (figure 2) which generates permutations of a list and tests them to find if they match with a given goal pattern GP.

```
permutation([],[]).
permutation(X, [Z|Zs]) :- select(Z,X,Y), permutation(Y,Zs).

select(X, [X|Xs],Xs).
select(X,[Y|Ys],[Y|Zs]):-select(X,Ys, Zs).

query (List, GP) :- permutation (List, Lperm),  Lperm= GP, !.
```

figure 2: a program with speculative work

To have a good idea of how much wasted work have been done, we measure both the number of total resolutions made by all the processors for each above strategy and the number of resolutions provided by one processor using the classical depth first scheduling strategy (i.e sequential strategy). The difference between the two number give us the amount of wasted work corresponding to the scheduling strategy used (i.e leftmost, deepmost or topmost dispatching). We can vary the amount of speculative work by changing the value of goal pattern (GP = [1,...], [2,...], [3,...], [4,...], [5,...], [6,...], [7,...], [8,...]) in the initial goal query([1,2,3,4,5,6,7,8], GP). The configuration we used for these results was composed of ten processors. In all scheduling strategies tested, the cut operators implemented in a simple way based on a suspension mechanism. When a processor encounters a cut operator, it is temporarily suspended until its branch becomes the leftmost the search tree.

The figure 3 shows the results we obtained for the four preceding scheduling strategies.

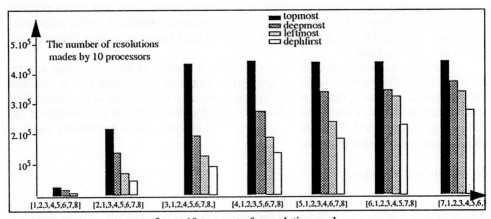

figure 10: amount of speculative work

The leftmost strategy leads to very little wasted work. The amount of wasted work does not exceed one time the amount of work in depth first strategy.

The figure 4 shows the performances corresponding to the above executions.

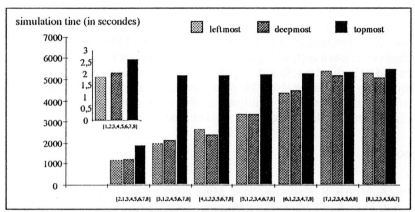

figure 4 : performances of the three scheduling strategies

The dispatching on the bottom-most (leftmost and deepmost) give much better performance results than dispatching on the top-most for programs with cuts.

Indeed, the leftmost strategy selects works which have the smallest probability to be pruned, and moreover dispatching in the left part speeds up the cut reaching, so reduces the amount of the speculative work.

The drawback of the bottom-most strategies is their small granularity. In order to get some idea about the granularity of the different scheduling strategies, we have measured the number of task-switching made by all the processors, in the case where the goal pattern GP is [8,7,6,5,4,3,2,1].

In the figure 5 the leftmost strategy gives an average number of task-switching which is 400 times greater than the one obtained by using the topmost scheduling.

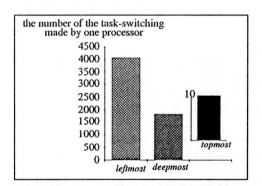

figure 5 : task-switchings (GP=[8,7,6,5,4,3,2,1])

For these reasons, we have suggest to avoid copying environments during task installation, and we think environments haringis a good approach to handle efficiently the speculative work.

4 Conclusion

An OR-parallel execution model for Prolog program has been presented. The main characteristic of this model is its new binding scheme which allows an efficient management of conditional bindings. This binding scheme is based on conditional binding sharing by tagging these ones. Furthermore conditional binding accesses are bounded-time operations (i.e. a searching operation over a fixed number of PBA), and task installation cost is cheaper (i.e just a copy of register keys), so it allows us to study various scheduling strategies and in particular leftmost dispatching which minimizes the amount of wasted work provided by speculative tasks. We plan in the forthcoming months to implemente our model on a real shared-memory multiprocessor in order to compare the effectiveness of our approach over the other shared environment models.

References

[Ali90] K. A. M. Ali, R. Karlsson : "The Muse approach to OR-Parallel Prolog".
Int. Journal of Parallel Programming, Vol 19, n?2, 1990, pp 129-162.
[Bar88] U. Baron, J. Chassin De Kergommeaux, M. Hailperin, M. Ratcliffe, P. Pobert.
"The Parallel ECRC Prolog System PEPSys : an overview and evaluation results". FGCS'88, Nov-Dec 88, pp 841-850
[Bea91] A. Beaumont "scheduling Strategies and Speculative Work"
Proceeding ICLP'91 Pre-conference Workshop on Parallel Execution of logic programs.
[Bou91] H. Bourzoufi, G. Goncalves, P. Lecouffe, B. Toursel.
"an efficient bindin management in OR-parallel model"
Proceeding ICLP'91 Pre-conference Workshop on Parallel Execution of logic programs.
[Bou92] H. Bourzoufi.
" Definition et Evaluation d'une Machine Abstraite Parallèle pour un Modèle OU-parallèle Multiséquentiel de PROLOG".
Thèse de doctorat, Février 1992, No 877, Université de Lille1.
[Bri90] J. Briat, M. Favre, C. Geyer.
"OPERA: OU Parallélisme et Régulation Adaptative en Prolog". SPLT 90
[Hau90] B. Hausman.
"Handling of speculative work in OR-Parallel PROLOG Evaluation Results"
Proceeding of NACLP 1990, pp 721-736
[Lus88] E. Lusk, R. Butler, T. Disz, R. Olson, R. Overbeek, R Stevens, D. H. Warren, A. Calderwoodd, P. Szeridl, S. Haridi, P. Brand, M. Carlson, A. Ciepielewski, B. Hausman
"The Aurora OR-Parallel Prolog System". FGCS'88, Nov-Dec 88, pp 819-830.
[War87] D. H. D. Warren "The SRI model for OR_Parallel execution of Prolog- Abstract design and implementation issues"
4th symp on Logic Programming, San Francisco, Sept 87, pp 92-102

Threads and Subinstruction Level Parallelism in a Data Flow Architecture

Theo Ungerer and Eberhard Zehendner

Department of Mathematics, University of Augsburg
Universitaetsstr. 2, W-8900 Augsburg, Germany
Email: {ungerer,zehendner}@mathi4.informatik.uni-augsburg.de

Abstract. This paper presents a data flow architecture that utilizes task level parallelism by the architectural structure of a distributed memory multiprocessor, instruction level parallelism by a token-passing computation scheme, and subinstruction level parallelism by SIMD evaluation of complex machine instructions. Sequential threads of data instructions are compiled to data flow macro actors and executed consecutively using registers.

1 Introduction

Multiprocessors are well suited for exploiting task level parallelism provided that communication is relatively sparse and granularity of tasks coarse. However, an architectural design based on extensive exploitation of parallelism should not neglect the potential fine-grain parallelism that might be available in an algorithm but cannot be efficiently exploited by coarse-grain techniques. The main problem for the exploitation of fine-grain parallelism, i.e., when utilizing instruction level parallelism or executing sequential threads with about 20 instructions, is that most conventional processors incur a very large overhead during a context switch. Multi-threaded von Neumann architectures [1, 2, 3] and data flow architectures [4, 5, 6] are two approaches to exploit fine-grain parallelism.

In a multi-threaded von Neumann architecture each processing element is equipped with a processor that can perform a very fast context switch between several threads already loaded. Moreover creation of threads is not too costly. Each thread consists of several instructions; instruction level parallelism is not supported.

When using the data flow scheme, programs are compiled into data flow graphs that represent the data dependences among instructions. Scheduling is data-driven: an instruction is ready to execute as soon as all required operands are available. The availability of operands is signaled by tokens that conceptually are propagated on the arcs of the data flow graph. Data flow architectures use token matching prior to each instruction execution. This synchronization scheme is able to exploit all possible parallelism at instruction level but, unfortunately, leads to superfluous overhead when executing sequences of instructions.

To reduce the number of synchronization events in data flow architectures three techniques have been proposed: large-grain data flow joins the von Neumann and the data flow model of computation by processing sequences of instructions in von Neumann style, but activating them as data flow macro actors [7, 8]; repeat-on-input techniques [4, 5, 6] statically schedule instructions for consecutive execution; complex machine operations, for instance vector operations [9] or relational data bank operations [10], are used as data flow macro actors that are processed in SIMD mode but activated by the data flow scheme.

The ASTOR (*Augsburg Structure-Oriented*) architecture [11, 12] is a data flow architecture organized as a distributed memory multiprocessor to exploit task level parallelism. The language interface of the ASTOR architecture is a procedural intermediate language [13] enriched by parallel control constructs (process call, parallel loop, parallel choice, and dependency constructs) [12]. In this paper we focus on the dependency construct, only.

A *dependency construct* describes the partial order in the execution of instructions. It can be visualized by a *dependency graph*, that resembles a data flow graph [12]. The nodes in a dependency graph represent control constructs or data instructions; the directed arcs denote control dependences between the nodes. Tokens are propagated on the arcs of the dependency graph. To distinguish different activations of a dependency graph, a tag is assigned to each token. We apply the firing rule of dynamic data flow: a node is enabled as soon as tokens with identical tags are present on all its input arcs. However, in the ASTOR architecture tokens do not carry data.

To increase efficiency a node in a dependency graph can denote a macro data instruction that represents a complex machine operation or a sequence of simple data instructions, executed as a sequential thread.

Complex machine operations allow to exploit parallelism at the subinstruction level: the machine partitions the complex machine operation into suboperations that can be executed in parallel. A typical example are vector operations, that are executed by a pipeline of data transformation units. Structured data is referenced in block rather than element-wise, and is supplied in a burst mode for the execution of complex machine operations. This deviates from the I-structure scheme [14] of data flow architectures where each data element within a complex data structure must be fetched individually. The use of a complex machine operation usually spares several nested loops needed in classical programming; parallelism is thereby transferred from the block level (do-across loops) to the subinstruction level.

2 The ASTOR Architecture

The ASTOR architecture consists of processing elements connected by a communication network to transfer procedure calls and another communication network for parameter passing. No global storage is used.

Figure 1 shows the structure of an ASTOR processing element. Each processing element consists of two loosely coupled parts: the *program flow control part* and the *data object processing part*. The term *manager* is used to characterize an abstract component within a processing element. All managers in an ASTOR processing element work in parallel to each other. Asynchronous processing and decoupling of the managers is achieved by buffering the messages on the links between them.

The control construct managers (individually named call, loop, choice, and dependency manager) are specialized in executing the corresponding control constructs. Each control construct manager is connected by bidirectional links to the static and the dynamic code access manager, respectively.

The *static code storage* contains the compiled code. The *dynamic code storage* contains so-called *dynamic control constructs*, that represent the state of control constructs during execution of a process. Dynamic control constructs are tagged. The tag binds a dynamic control construct to its run-time environment, similar to a tag in a dynamic data flow machine.

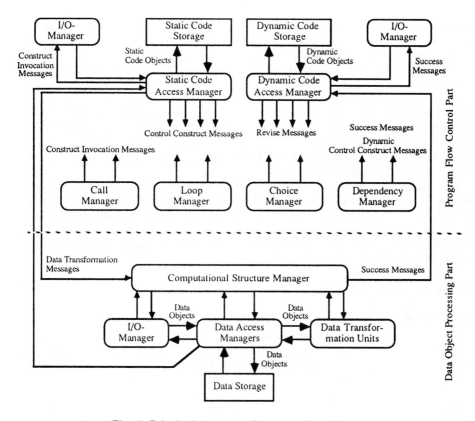

Fig. 1. Principal structure of a processing element

Data is only moved and transformed within the data object processing part, that receives data transformation messages from the program flow control part. Such a message consists of a data instruction (simple data instruction or macro data instruction) and its tag.

Access to data is performed by *data access managers* that can be configured to form a pipeline together with the *data transformation units*. Since data instructions and in particular macro data instructions can denote very complex transformation algorithms, this configuration and other organizational work is left to the *computational structure manager*.

Access to the two communication networks that connect the various processing elements is organized by the three input/output managers contained in every processing element. A dynamic load balancing strategy and throttling of abundant parallelism to prevent from an overflow in a processing element or in the whole machine caused by an excess of intermediate results is done automatically [12].

We illustrate the operational principle of a single processing element by execution of a dependency construct: The dependency manager checks the dependency construct for the existence of nodes that can be activated. For every such node it sends a construct invocation message that refers to the represented construct to the static code access manager. The dependency construct is updated to reflect the actual state of execution, and sent as part of a dynamic control construct message to the dynamic code access manager that puts it into the dynamic code storage.

For every construct invocation message the static code access manager copies the demanded construct from the static code storage and sends it, according to its construct kind, as part of a control construct message to the responsible control construct manager or as part of a data transformation message to the computational structure manager, respectively. The latter sets up some data access managers and data transformation units to work cooperatively and initiates the execution of the operations. The data is pipelined via the data access managers from the data storage to the data transformation units, and back to the data storage.

After completion of a data instruction or macro data instruction a success message is sent to the dynamic code access manager by the computational structure manager (or by a control construct manager when the execution of a control construct has been finished). The dynamic control construct that has initiated the completed construct is retrieved from the dynamic code storage by the dynamic code access manager and sent to the corresponding manager for further processing.

3 Sequential Threads

In an ASTOR processing element a token cycle is constituted by the dependency, static code access, computational structure, and dynamic code access managers. A dependency construct can be degenerate to a sequence of data instructions, or may exhibit only a low degree of instruction level parallelism. In this case passing tokens through the cycle induces a high delay since the successive data instruction is activated after a token has been passed through the whole cycle.

Data instructions that have to be executed consecutively can be compounded to a macro data instruction that constitutes a sequential thread. Experimental studies [4, 5, 6] suggest to serialize also blocks of data instructions that exhibit a low degree of parallelism. A macro data instruction is stored like an ordinary data instruction in the static code storage. Dependency and static code access managers do not distinguish between macro data instructions and ordinary data instructions.

The computational structure manager consecutively executes the instructions contained within a macro data instruction. A single success message is generated when the macro data instruction terminates. Data passed between instructions from the same thread may be stored in registers instead of writing them back to memory. These registers may be referenced by any succeeding instruction in the thread. Access time to data values is optimized by use of registers.

By this mechanism cycling of tokens through the different managers for the activation of the next instruction is suppressed. Thereby single-thread performance is improved. The total number of tokens needed to schedule the instructions of a program is reduced thus saving hardware resources. The matching operation, done by the dependency manager, to activate the succeeding instruction is eliminated for the instructions within a macro data instruction.

4 Experimental Results and Conclusions

A software simulation of a single ASTOR processing element has been conducted to reveal which managers might constitute bottlenecks and thus would need refinement. It was not possible, however, to run complex application problems on the simulator. Also, the performance gains by use of sequential threads are still to determine. Due to the abstract level of the architecture design achieved so far, we disclaimed precise timing characteristics for the architecture components, which would have been needed for a quantitative performance measurement. The simulation results proved the following statements about the utilization of the architecture components within a single ASTOR processing element:

- For each activation of the static code access manager, the dynamic code access manager is activated twice.
- The computational structure manager is activated less often as the static code access manager but has to control complex data operations and macro data instructions that can be very time-consuming.
- The number of activations of all control construct managers lies between the number of activations of the static code access manager and that of the dynamic code access manager.
- The dependency manager usually is the most activated among all control construct managers.

In consequence, bottlenecks have to be expected for the dynamic code access manager, the computational structure manager, and in a smaller degree the dependency manager. These managers thus should be replicated, or implemented in faster technology. Replication causes no principal problem since all managers are stateless and the messages in the input stream of a single manager are completely independent. Several identical managers can be served from the same input queue. The simulation also showed that the utilization of the different control construct managers depends strongly on the application program. To prevent the control construct managers from idling their functionality could be comprised into a common control construct manager.

The ASTOR architecture shares the use of complex machine operations and threads as data flow macro actors with the large-grain data flow architectures Decoupled Graph/ Computation Architecture [9] and the LGDG Machine [15]. As a major difference to conventional data flow architectures the messages of the ASTOR architecture, like the tokens in the LGDG architecture, do not carry data.

The proceeding just described is similar to the repeat-on-input in the Epsilon-1 and Epsilon-2 processors [4], to the strongly connected arc model of EM-4 [5], and the direct recycling of tokens in Monsoon [6]. Instructions from a single thread can only be executed once every 8 cycles in HEP [2] and Monsoon. The cycle-by-cycle interleaving of HEP and Monsoon cannot run applications with low parallelism efficiently, in particular if processor load consists of a single thread, only. To optimize single-thread performance the computational structure manager in the ASTOR architecture executes instructions from a macro data instruction, encapsulating a single thread, consecutively. While in the Epsilon-processors and the EM-4 each instruction of a thread is separately tagged, the instructions of a macro data instruction in the ASTOR architecture share a common tag, thus saving memory and communication capacity. In the multi-threaded architectures HEP [2] and APRIL [3] the number of the activated threads is bounded by the hardware. In the ASTOR architecture an arbitrary number of threads can be activated.

References

1. Dally, W.J., et al.: The J-Machine: A Fine-Grain Concurrent Computer. In: Ritter, G.X. (ed.): Information Processing 89, North-Holland 1989, pp. 1147-1153.

2. Smith, B.J.: A Pipelined, Shared Resource MIMD Computer. Proc. 1978 Int. Conf. Parallel Processing, Bellaire, MI, 1978, pp. 6-8.

3. Agrawal, A., et al.: APRIL: A Processor Architecture for Multiprocessing. 17th Ann. Int. Symp. Comp. Arch., Seattle, 1990, pp. 104-114.

4. Grafe, V.G., Hoch, J.E.: The EPSILON-2 Multiprocessor System. J. Parallel and Distributed Computing 10 (1990) pp. 309-318.

5. Yamaguchi, Y., et al.: An Architectural Design of a Highly Parallel Dataflow Machine. In: Ritter, G.X. (ed.): Information Processing 89, North-Holland 1989, pp. 1155-1160.

6. Papadopoulos, G.M., Culler, D.E.: Monsoon: an Explicit Token-Store Architecture. 17th Ann. Int. Symp. Comp. Arch., Seattle, 1990, pp. 82-91.

7. Iannucci, R.A.: Toward a Dataflow / von Neumann Hybrid Architecture. 15th Ann. Int. Symp. Comp. Arch., Honolulu, 1988, pp. 131-140.

8. Bic, L.: A Process-Oriented Model for Efficient Execution of Dataflow Programs. J. Parallel and Distributed Computing 8, 12 (Dezember 1990), pp. 42-51.

9. Evripidou, P., Gaudiot, J.-L.: The USC Decoupled Multilevel Data-Flow Execution Model. In: Gaudiot, J.-L., Bic, L. (eds.): Advanced Topics in Data-Flow Computing, Prentice Hall, Englewood Cliffs, 1991, pp. 347-379.

10. Glueck-Hilltop, E., Ramlow, M., Schuerfeld, U.: The Stollmann Data Flow Machine. In: Odijk, E., Rem, M., Syre, J.-C. (eds.): Proc. PARLE ´89, Parallel Architectures and Languages Europe, Eindhoven, 1989, Vol. 1, pp. 433-457.

11. Zehendner, E., Ungerer, T.: The ASTOR Architecture. 7th Int. Conf. Distributed Computing Systems, Berlin, 1987, pp. 424-430.

12. Zehendner, E., Ungerer, T.: A Large-Grain Data Flow Architecture Utilizing Multiple Levels of Parallelism. 6th Annual European Computer Conference (COMPEURO 92), The Hague, 1992, pp. 23-28.

13. Ungerer, T., Zehendner, E.: A Parallel Programming Language Directed Towards Top-Down Software Development. Int. Conf. Parallel Processing, St. Charles, Illinois, 1989, Part II, pp. 122-125.

14. Arvind, Iannucci, R.A.: Two Fundamental Issues in Multiprocessing. DFVLR Conference 1987 on Parallel Processing in Science and Engineering, Bonn, Germany, June 1987, pp. 61-88.

15. Dai, K., Giloi, W.K.: A Basic Architecture Supporting LGDF Computation. 1990 Int. Conf. Supercomputing, Amsterdam, 1990, pp. 23-33.

A Hybrid Dataflow Architecture with Multiple Tokens

Boyan Bonchev and Miroslav Iliev

Laboratory for Distributed Systems and Computer Networks
Bulgarian Academy of Sciences, 1113 Sofia, Bulgaria

Abstract. In the paper, dataflow architecture with multiple tokens is proposed. By supporting nodes with several inputs and more than two successors, with by-reference data access, the redundant synchronization is eliminated, when treating composite data. The model provides asynchronous function activations, thus the potential asynchronous activity is increased. Distinction of tokens of different contexts is accomplished by a direct matching schema for synchronization of multiple tokens. In order to facilitate effective execution of sequential code, the architecture can deal with clusters of instructions using a controlflow scheduling mechanism, executing the clusters without any pending.

1 Introduction

Dataflow archtecture appears attractive for building scalable, general purpose multiprocessor systems because the concept exploits intrisic parallelism in programs at machine level. By using fine grain parallelism, dataflow scheduling mechanism tolerates large and often unpredictable memory and synchronization latencies in program execution.

A handful of prototypes based on pure dataflow concept have been built [2]. Despite their significant peak performance, they suffer from high cost-performance ratio relative to the commercially available multiprocessors. Among their main shortcomings are great synchronization costs, a high token traffic imposed by the by-value data transfer mechanism, and large amount of noncomputation instructions. Moreover, in dataflow the only way to achieve synchronization is data-driven scheduling, and this significantly decreases the performance when executing programs with strong sequential component.

To remove such inefficiencies typical for the pure dataflow concept, two main approaches are investigated:
- combining dataflow with controlflow computations within hybrid models [1,3,4,5,6];
- introducing simplifications into dataflow model with preserving its benefits [4,6].

Dataflow model presented here makes use of the both approaches mentioned above. It extends dyadic dataflow node into one with more operands presented with multiple tokens. In this way, for processing composite data, such as multiple precision data and vectors, both synchronization and communication overhead are reduced. Additionlly, token traffic is decreased by using nodes with multiple outputs, which eliminates the need for redundant copying of the result. Instructions which are performed in strong sequential order, and do not depend on other ones, are composed into a cluster during compile time. By dyrect matching of multiple tokens, a dynamical menaging of multiple code instantiations is provided. Starting a function is performed with only one of the arguments needed, thus a greater potential asynchrony and performance are achieved.

2 A Hybrid Dataflow Model with Multiple Tokens

2.1 Nodes Processing Multiple Tokens

The main goal of the model is to decrease both the token traffic in machine realization and the redundant synchronization, while preserving dataflow benefits. In the model, a node may present code of an operation or whole function. Nodes with multiple inputs let us to substitute sequential executions of one operation over an array of data. Thus, at least token transmission between sequential operators is avoided, and if input tokens are delivered simultaneously, the time for synchronization between operations is eliminated.

Tokens for nodes with more input arcs can be treated as vector elements within a multiple token which are processing sequentially. Multiple tokens, or vectors, are composed and transmitted between nodes in a simple way, at that a vector element, or groups of elements, can be reffered but without changing the vector. Fig. 1 presents operation over two vectors. When executing traditional dyadic nodes, no one addition can be started before the four tokens arrive, as both operand parts are delivering together. Here, the multi-input node reduces both token traffic and memory latency needed for the addition of higher word with the carry. Such multi-input node can be viewed as a dyadic node processing multiple tokens. Operator *add* is extended with suffix 'c' signifying spreading of the carry. In cases of vectors addition without carry spreading, operator *addv* is used. An additional effect of using multitoken operators is a decrease of the large control dataflow overhead of conditionaly executed code blocks.

2.2 Grouping Nodes in Clusters for Sequential Execution

The model composes nodes into groups (clusters), like in [3,4], to resolve the communication and syncronization overhead, when executing sequential code. In contrast to the previous approaches, here clusters are acyclic graphs which cannot interact each other and have input arcs only to the head node activating the cluster. In this way, the partition algorithm is simpler, without any need for preserving deadlock avoidance, and there is no explicit synchronization introduced by arcs crossing cluster boundary [4]. Once started, the cluster is performed in a strongly sequential manner, without any pending and context saving. Each cluster has only one

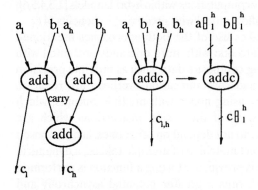

Fig. 1: Treating Multiple Precision Data

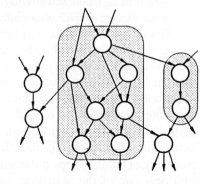

Fig. 2: A Sample Grouping into Clusters

head, in order to avoid the redundant synchronization among several threads for clusters with more heads, which reduces the number of parallel threads needed for keeping the pipeline full.

A sample grouping into clusters is shown in fig. 2. Instructions exchanging data with others activations (dataflow procedures) are not included within clusters. A cluster may include several parallel computation threads. This does not restrict the actual parallelism used as activation is running on one processing element (PE). To save the context when switching between them, registers are used. The use of registers allows to include into a cluster nodes sharing input arcs with the head, and to form a single cluster for expressions like $x*(x+1)*(x-1)$. The cluster size can be controlled by the number of registers.

2.3 Asynchronous Activation of New Instantiations

The model is designed as a dynamical one, i.e. it provides means for multiple instantiations of iterations within cycles, and of recursive function calls. Distinction among tokens produced by different code instantiations is accomplished on the base of activation frames [3,5] where the tokens are residing. When a function is invoked, an activation frame is allocated explicitly to provide needed storage for tokens of this context. Every token transmits its data and a tag, comprising pointer to activation frame and offset in this frame.

Code activation is accomplished asynchronously, i.e. immediately after delivering one of the arguments, for achieving greater potential asynchrony, and hence performance. When calling a function, the storage for the new context is allocated by the operator *alloc*. In unconditional calls *alloc* is activated by operator *first* (fig. 3), which possesses inputs for all function arguments and produces an only output token after delivering first of them. Subsequent input tokens do not make *first* to produce another output. In conditional function activation, *alloc* is started through the token produced by the conditional operator. As the other operators, *first* and *alloc* may be executed only once within a given context - multiple executions are accomplishing each in its own context. *alloc* delivers pointer to the newly created frame to *send* operators transmitting the function arguments, and to a *Send Current Frame* (*SCF*) operator which sends to the callee pointer to the current frame and destination address within it (determined in compile time). The frame occupied by the callee is deallocated by operator *free*.

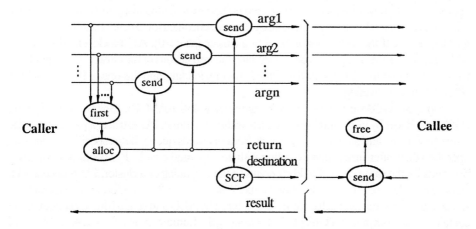

Fig. 3: Asynchronous Unconditional Function Call

3 Hybrid Dataflow Architecture

The architecture uses the direct matching [1,4], or explicit storage [5],synchronization concept but extended for multiple tokens (fig. 4). Node *opc* has *n* input arcs delivering tokens for composing a multiple token, or vector. Each token transmits its value, a tag with destination addresses, and one address for the result, *res*, as the data access is by reference. The tag comprises a frame pointer (FP), an instruction pointer (IP), and a base pointer (BP).Frame storage includes Activation Memory (AM) containing one slot for each instruction of the corresponded activation, and Operation Memory(OM). Activation in Instruction Memory (IM) starts from address shown by BP. The sample instruction contains operation code (*opc*), number of needed operands (*vn*), offset for vector begin (*vo*) in OM, its result address *res*, and a list of destinations (*dests*).By every receiving of a token, the value of received operands (*ro*) is incremented if *vn* is greater than it. By equality, execution of this instruction starts, and its operands will be delivered from OM starting from address *vo*. The frame slots are set to zero by execution of operator *free*.

The machine is constructed with a collection of pipelined PEs (fig. 5), communicating each other and with the structure memory (SM) modules via a packed switching interconnection network which controls the frame distribution. New contexts are initiated in underloaded PE, and both the intra- and intercontext parallelism are used only to keep the pipeline full. Although support multiple destinations is provided by the proposed model, PE instructions are disigned with fixed sized:

$$< opc, cls, type, vn, vo1, vo2, res, ndest, dest >$$

Field *cls* specifies the number of instructions included in cluster, or the registers for preserving operands and result. Field *type* contains information about constants, if any; vo1 and vo2 specify the relative addresses of both multitoken operands in OM; *ndest* is shows the number of destinations addresses allocated in Destination Memory (DM).DM is addressed by decrementing *ndest* and incrementing *dest*. For instructions having one successor, *dest* contains its address in IM.

The addresses of successors for the current result are sent to IM and Activation Unit (AU). AM includes a frame for each context currently in use. FP addresses the frame containing slots for *ro* in the current context, and IP selects the slot within the frame. The whole instruction enters the AU but here only fields *opc*, *type* and *vn* are taken in use, for forming number of needed operands, *no*. In case of nonequality between *no* and *ro*, *ro* is updating, and other successor's address is entering AU. Otherwise, the instructions is scheduled for execution, and the operands fetching begins. If the instruction is head of a cluster (*cls* < >0), AU blocks entering of new addresses from DM, and proceeds with fetching the instructions of the cluster. The input from Communication Unit (CU) is used for initial program loading, and this one of Processing Unit (PE) - for frame cleaning.

Operands in OM are addressed in the same way as slots in AM. The Operand Feching Unit (OFU) produces by incrementing the offsets within the frame. PU extracts a packet from the instruction queue and a couple of operands from operands queue. If *opc* specifies multitoken operation then, after instruction execution with first operand couple, PU continues extracting operands for the same code. If field *cls* points to the beginning of a cluster, PU proceeds with extracting packets only from instruction queue. When the result is a vector, the incomming tag will be attached to the last vector element, produced by ALU and sent to the result queue. PU contains a Tag Computation Unit (TCU) menaging the frame store in OM and AM. TCU and ALU are working in parallel.

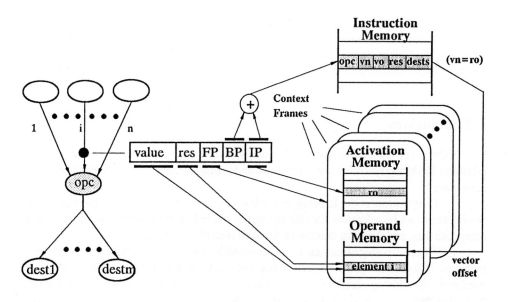

Fig. 4: Synchronization with Multiple Tokens

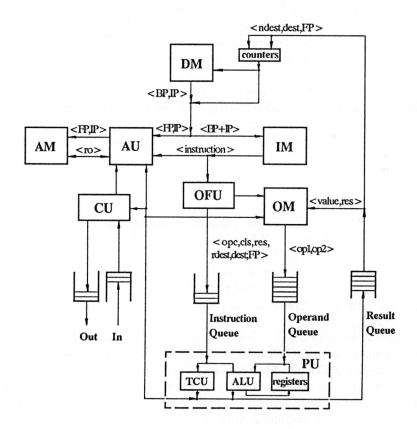

Fig. 5: Processing Element Architecture

The PE communicates with SM and other PE via Communication Unit (CU). Access to data structures in SM is accomplished through split-phase, token based transactions. For interPE data exchange, CU supports a Link Menagement Table, where the addresses of outher frames are preserving. If the queues in the PE are going to be overcrowded, and there are underloaded PE in the system, the next frame will be created on an other PE suitable loaded.

4 Conclusions

In this paper, a hybrid dataflow with multiple tokens, and its machine architecture, were proposed. Reducing synchronization overhead and communication traffic was reached in two main ways:

1) supporting nodes handling multiple tokens and having more than two successors, sharing the result by-reference, for eliminating the redundant synchronization when treating composite data, and the great amount of dataflow control operations;

2) by composing istructions into clusters which cannot interfere each other, an effective execution of sequential program sectors was obtained. Starting a cluster does not impose synchronization among parallel threads, as clusters are shaped with one head each. Though supporting more threads within a cluster, there is no loss of parallelism in it, as the cluster can include one frame at most, and a frame is running on one PE. At the same time, this approach is better than coarse grained scheduling because sequential clusters do not include instructions causing synchronization or memory latency.

The machine architecture presented matches directly multiple tokens in given context frame. Frames are creating and removing in a simple way, without need of additional garbage collection. Function arguments are delivered asynchronously, which leads in many cases to greater performance than by synchronous function activation. The coarsed grained load balancing among processors is realized through distribution of context frames among all processors in the system, whereas the perallelism within a frame, and this one between frames allocated on one processor, is used for context swiching in order to avoid the latency of external memory.

References:

1. Amamiya, M., R. Taniguchi. An Ultra-Multipracessing Machine Architecture for Efficient Parallel Execution of Functional Languages. Lecture Notes in Computer Science, No. 491, 1990, pp. 257-281.

2. Boyanov K., at al. Dataflow organisation of the computational process. Automatics and Computational Technics. No. 3, 1983, pp. 25-38.

3. Grafe, V., J. Hoch. The Epsilon-2 Hybrid Dataflow Architecture. Proc. of COMPCON90, March 1990, pp. 88-93.

4. Iannucci, R. Toward a Dataflow/von Neumann Hybrid Architecture. Proc. of 15th Ann. Int'l Symp. on Comp. Architecture, Honolulu, Hawaii, 1988, pp. 131-140.

5. Papadopoulos, G., D. Culler. Monsoon: an Explicit Token-Store Architecture. Proc. of 17th Ann. Int'l Symp. on Comp. Architecture, Seattle, WA, 1990, pp. 82-91.

6. Treleaven, P., R. Hopkins and P. Rautenbach. Combining Data flow and Control Flow Computing. Computer Journal, Vol. 25, No. 2, 1982.

Parallelism Control Scheme
in A Dataflow Architecture

Shigeru KUSAKABE, Takahide HOSHIDE,
Rin-ichiro TANIGUCHI and Makoto AMAMIYA

Department of Information Systems, Kyushu University
Kasuga, Fukuoka, 816 Japan

{kusakabe,hoshide,rin,amamiya}@is.kyushu-u.ac.jp

Abstract   We propose execution control scheme to realize an efficient multi-processing environment in dataflow architecture. With a unified software and hardware mechanism, we can detect states of processes at run time, which are treated as control information. We control the process level parallelism according to the hardware capacity, and virtualize high speed memory in dynamic data-driven computation where context changes in every instruction execution. We apply this scheme to the **Datarol** architecture, an optimized version of dynamic dataflow architecture, and evaluate them through software simulation.

1   Introduction

Dataflow computing has many attractive features for parallel processing[2, 3, 5]. For example, it allows long latencies associated with accesses to distributed resources to be automatically overlapped by independent computation without explicit management of parallel execution. The **Datarol** machine[1], an optimized version of dynamic dataflow, can execute multi-thread control flow programs, which are compiled from functional programs through data flow analysis to exploit operand sharing mechanisms[6], with high performance by supporting an efficient ultra-multi-processing environment for tiny concurrent processes. However, the Datarol machine, as well as other dataflow machines, may possibly waste hardware resources, like activation names, working memory areas and token queues, during the execution of highly parallel programs, since dataflow computation eagerly tries to exploit all the parallelism inherent in the programs.

In order to implement an efficient multi-processing environment with restricted hardware resources, the Datarol machine has following control mechanisms:

1. The expansion of process-level parallel activities in a PE are controlled in a depth-first way, while maintaining high PE working ratio. The PE-network controls the processor work load among PEs.

2. High speed memory is virtualized by using data-driven paging mechanism. It allows the memory management operations to be overlapped by the regular instruction executions.

3. In order to detect process states as control information at run time, we unify static analysis by compiler, and dynamic detection by hardware mechanism.

In this paper, we mainly discuss the memory management mechanisms. An outline of the Datarol is presented in section 2. In section 3, execution control mechanism in the Datarol PE is described. Finally, in section 4, we evaluate our execution control mechanism by software simulation and demonstrate their effectiveness.

2 Outline of the Datarol

The Datarol machine is constructed with a thousand PEs, which execute Datarol programs, and a thousand SM (Structure Memory) banks(see Fig.1). Structure data such as lists and arrays are stored in SM, and pointers to structure data are treated as operand data within a PE. The PEs are connected by multi-stage packet switching networks(based on the omega network) called inter-PE net. The PE-net controls the processor work load balance among PEs. The PE-SM connection network, called PE-SM net, realizes equi-distant packet communications for any PE-SM pairs.

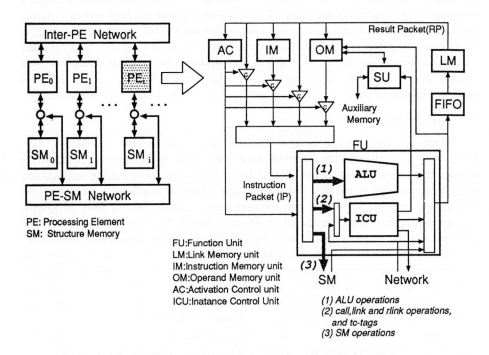

PE: Processing Element
SM: Structure Memory

FU:Function Unit
LM:Link Memory unit
IM:Instruction Memory unit
OM:Operand Memory unit
AC:Activation Control unit
ICU:Inatance Control Unit

(1) ALU operations
(2) call,link and rlink operations,
    and tc-tags
(3) SM operations

Fig. 1: Datarol machine.

The Datarol PE is constructed as a circular pipeline of three-stages, Fetch, Execution and Distribution stages. Fetch module consists of IM (Instruction Memory unit), AC (Activation Control unit), and OM(Operand Memory unit). The IM stores Datarol instructions and manages instruction fetch. The OM stores operand data, and manages operand fetch and result-data write. The AC checks whether or not the partner operand has been written in OM for some types of two operand instructions specified by compiler. In the Distribution stage, LM (Link Memory unit) manages the linkage of the multiple continuation points. Execution unit consists of FU (Function Unit), COM (COMmunication control unit) and SMC (SM Communication unit). FU executes Datarol instructions, and controls parallel activities.

3 Execution control in the Datarol

3.1 Control of process-level parallelism

To realize an efficient multi-processing environment, we control the process-level parallelism in the Datarol machine. In a Datarol PE, the number of active processes, N_a, is maintained at predefined number, N_t.

- **Freeze function call.** If $N_a \geq N_t$, a `call` operation to create a new function instance is pushed into the CS(Call Stack) in the ICU(Instance Control Unit) to implement the depth-first execution control. In this case, the result of the `call` operation is a logical activation name with a "frozen" tag.

- **Thaw function call.** When $N_a < N_t$, a "frozen" `call` is popped up from the CS to thaw the function application. A register file is allocated to the instance as working memory, and then parameters are sent to the pipeline. During this "thaw" process, if all the arguments are not available yet, the ID of the register file allocated to the instance is recorded in the TT(Trap Table) using the instance activation name as a key entry.

Parameter passing in Datarol is asynchronous, and *freezing* and *thawing* of function calls are performed regardless of the existence of their arguments. Therefore, in order to pass the arguments consistently under the system of parallelism control, operations which pass arguments are executed using the TT.

For the load balancing, each PE in the multi-PE system has a four-states load level computed from N_a and the number of frozen call. Each switch in the PE-net knows the load level of its output. To invoke a remote function call, a PE sends a request message to the network. The requesting PE sends a packet to create a new process after receiving the acknowledge from the PE of least load.

3.2 Memory management

There exist a lot of "suspended" instances during the program execution, which have the following features:

- No data or token of the instance is in the hardware pipeline, but all of them are stored in operand memory.

- The instance never accesses its operand memory until it receives the token it is waiting for.

Therefore, it is clever to re-allocate the memory area of the "suspended" instance to another activated or resumed instance.

- **Swap-out.** When no register file is available, an activating, thawing or swap-in transaction of a certain instance will cause the *swap-out* of a "suspended" instance. In this case, data of a "suspended" instance are swapped out from the register file to the auxiliary memory, so that the register file can be re-allocated to another "active" instance.

- **Swap-in.** A *swap-in* transition is triggered by a packet returned to a "swapped" instance. The data of the "swapped" instance are swapped into the available register file, and data in the returned packet from the callee instance is fed to the pipeline.

This memory management is performed as a split transaction, memory management operations can be overlapped by the regular instruction executions.

3.3 Detecting suspension

One of the problems, in implementing our parallelism control and memory management schemes, is how to detect the "suspended" state of instances at run time in an instruction-level parallel execution environment. Although a method of detecting the states of a process by counting the number of all tokens in the process has been proposed[7], we use a new suspension detection method, in which suspension points are predicted at compilation time. A similar idea of parallelism control partially supported by compiler has been proposed[4], but that method can detect only the process termination, whereas our method operates in a more sophisticated situation, and aims to detect the temporal suspension.

Although it would be ideal if we could specify the exact suspension point at compilation time, it is actually very hard to do that during the instruction-level parallel execution. However, it is possible to detect a suspension by observing only some kinds of operations, without knowing the exact number of tokens. It is possible to extract at compilation time the operation nodes whose execution may cause suspension. We call such operations "terminal operations". There are two kinds of terminal operations:

1. An operation which passes a token to another instance.
2. A two-operand operation whose operands depend on the result value sent from another instance.

The ICU manages terminal operation counter, $tc(i)$, in order to detect the suspension of an instance i.

- The $tc(i)$ is set to an initial value, which is the number of terminal operations to be executed in the instance i.
- The $tc(i)$ is decreased by 1, either when a type-1 terminal operation is executed, or when a type-2 terminal operation fails in operand matching in the instance i.
- When the $tc(i)$ becomes 0, the instance i is in "suspended" state.

4 Evaluation of execution control

We present the simulation results of parallelism control and memory management. A software simulator was designed and implemented using C++ on a Sparc station to execute the Datarol programs, and to simulate the Datarol system in each clock.

4.1 Evaluation of process-level parallelism control

We present the results of the parallelism control system during the execution of the *8-queen (all solutions)* programs, which generates a rather complex process tree. The effectiveness of parallelism control in a PE(where $N_t = 6$, and the number of PEs is 1) are shown in Fig.2. Unless parallel activities are controlled, *8-queen* program cannot be executed by one PE. This parallelism control system works rather well, because the increase of N_a is maintained within a limited range.

The effectiveness of load balancing in the context of multi-processor system (where $N_t = 6$, and the number of PEs is 64) are shown in Fig.3. This is not an example of special excellence. During the execution of the program, requests to invoke a function are distributed evenly in the system, and N_a in each PE is

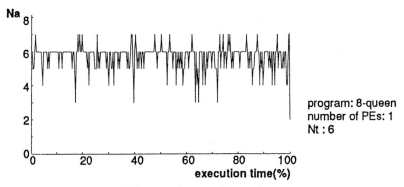

Fig. 2: Transition of N_a under parallelism control(*8-queen* program).

maintained at N_t.

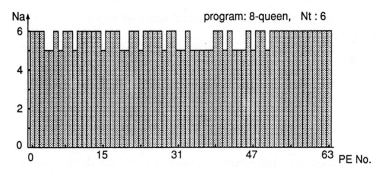

Fig. 3: A snap shot of N_a in the multi-processor system(64 PEs).

4.2 Evaluation of memory management

Fig.4 shows the simulation results of the memory management system. The simulation data is *relative execution time* $= (T_{MM}/T_{NOMM})$, where, $T_{MM} =$ *execution time under memory management*, and $T_{NOMM} = $ *execution time without memory management*. In this simulation, parameters are the number of the register files in a PE and the number of PEs. A register file consists of 32 registers, and it takes about 150 clocks to swap a register file. In the execution with no memory management, it was assumed that there might exist 1k register files.

In dataflow computation, contexts may be switched each time an instruction is executed, and, therefore, many localities of computation cannot be used. During the execution of the Datarol programs, the number of immediately changeable contexts amounts to the number of register files. If the number of register files is small, context may not be changed immediately, since context change may require swap-in or/and swap-out. Although register file management operations are overlapped by independent instruction executions, frequent swap operations cannot be overlapped.

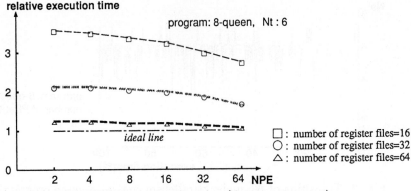

Fig. 4: Relative execution time(*8-queen* program).

5 Conclusions

We proposed parallel execution control and memory management methods in dataflow architecture:

- Control of process-level parallel activities both in a PE and in the multi-PE system.
- Virtualizing the high-speed memory with low overhead, in dynamic data-driven computation where context changes each time an instruction is executed.

And we evaluated these methods in the Datarol machine.

In order to realize parallelism control and memory management, we considered a unified software and hardware mechanism that can detect the unpredictable states of a process as control information at run time.

References

[1] M.Amamiya, and R.Taniguchi : "Datarol: A Massively Parallel Architecture for Functional Language", Proc. IEEE 2nd SPDP, pp.726-735 (Dec. 1990).

[2] V.G.Grafe and J.E.Hoch : "The Epsilon-2 Multi-Processor System", Journal of Parallel and Distributed Computing, **10**, pp.309-318 (Oct. 1990).

[3] G.M.Papadopoulos and E.C.Culler : "Monsoon: an Explicit Token-Store Architecture", Proc. 17th ISCA, pp.82-91 (June 1990).

[4] C.A.Ruggiero and J.Sargeant : "Control of Parallelism in the Manchester Dataflow Machine", Proc. FPCA (Lecture Notes in Computer Science 274, Springer- Verlag), pp.1 -15, (Sep. 1987).

[5] S.Sakai, Y.Yamaguchi, K.Hiraki, Y.Kodama and T.Yuba : "An Architecture of a Dataflow Single Chip Processor", Proc. 16th ISCA, pp.46-53 (May 1989).

[6] T.Tachibana, R.Taniguchi and Amamiya,M. : "Compiling Method of Functional Programming Language *Valid* by Data Flow Analysis -Extraction of Datarol Program-", Journal of Information Processing(in Japanese), Vol.30, No.12, pp.1628-1638 (Dec. 1989).

[7] M.Takesue : "A Unified Resource Management and Execution Control Mechanism for Data Flow Machines", Proc. 14th ISCA, pp.90- 97 (Jun. 1987).

A Petri-Net-based method to the design of parallel programs for a multiprocessor system

Herwig Unger; Khaled Ben Achour
Institute of Technology Ilmenau
PSF 327; O-6300 Ilmenau, Germany

Abstract

Petri-Nets have been proven to be an effecient tool to represent complicated systems. Nevertheless, in general it is not easy to transform a technical system, given as a Petri-Net, for implementation on a multiprocessor-system. The main purpose of the present contribution is to construct a general procedure for doing so. Our method can be realized in a purely automatic way as an algorithm having the original Petri-Net as its input and the resulting System of Concurrent State Machines (or, equivalenty, an implementation of these system) as its output.

1 Petri-Nets and parallel processes

A lot of technological and technical processes are characterized by two operating principles:

- a sequential one, i.e. a series of working or transport processes and
- a parallel one, because there exist more than one sequential process. These processes are executed independently, sometimes, however, these processes are connected with each other.

The demands for modelling such processes are satisfied by Petri-Nets. Moreover, there exist formal algorithms for analyzing Petri-Net models, e.g. for searching deadlocks in the system. When using parallel microcomputer architectures in conventional data processing, we often try to find parallel parts in existing sequential programs ([1]). The realization of this way seems to be impossible when implementing control units for technical or technological processes. The reason for this fact consist in the high number of parallel parts, which does not make it the possible to describe the problem in form of a sequential algorithm. Therfore, according to the following instructions will provide a better -but not the best- way of solving the development task:

- All sequential parts of the technical or technological process are described with State Machines (a special kind of Petri-Nets, which do not contain parallelly executing parts/transitions)

- The pairwise disjoint state machines are connected only with additional places in such a way, that none of the places is contained in any State Machine and every place is connected to transitions in at least two State Machines. These connections result from the relations between the controlled processes.

Such a structure is called System of Concurrent State Machines (SCS).

2 Methods and algorithms for the processing of Petri-Net models

2.1 Fundamentals

The specification and verification of the Petri-Net model is followed by the process of the implementation, i.e. the adequate transformation of the model description into the syntax of a programming language, for instance ANSI-C. The quality and efficiency of the whole program arising from a Petri-Net in the process of implementation depend on the determination of the parallel working parts - the so called parallelization of an algorithm. That is why effective methods and algorithms are demanded especially in this field. In the following chapter we want to show that the process of implementation can be realized in a purely automatic way as an algorithm having the original Petri-Net as its input and an implementation of this net as its output. It is easy to do so, if we have got an SCS after a process specification according to the described method, because of state machines are another form of sequential processes and can immediately be transformed into sequential processes. However, this paper is to demonstrate an idea of a transformation of common Petri-Nets and High Level Nets into SCS, because these nets give better possibilities for modelling than SCS.

2.2 Main ideas for the transformation of an arbitrary Petri-Net into an SCS

In the beginning of the transformation it is necessary to determine the active (parallel working) parts in the Petri-Net. Depending on the structures of net transitions, places or marks can be selected as active parts. The usual way is to make each transition an active part ([3]), but this idea is definitely not the best one. That is why every transition is modelled by a really parallel process, and so the number of parallel processes and the expenditure for communication is much too high. Thus programs based on this solution often works uneffectively. However, in this and every following case it is possible to simplify the arising results from the Petri-Net $PN = \{P, T, F, K, V, m_0\}$ and to increase the quality of the whole program. The method based on the determination of one special place p for every transition t with $(p, t) \in F$. Such a place is called an original place $u(t)$. Resulting from the fire rule of the transitions, the original place

$u(t)$ must contain one ore more marks, if the transition t should be able to fire. This also means, that all other firing conditions of a transition t must not be tested before the first mark arrives in the original place $u(t)$. This additional condition leads to important simplifications. The selection of the original places plays an important role concerning the extent of these simplifications. Special algorithms are demanded for this task. When using the second idea, the marks play the active role in the Petri-Net. The firing of a transition is understood as a transport of marks from the pre- to the post-places (included a virtual place ende, if the number of marks is not equal before and after firing) of the transition; the transition can be compared with "synchronous parts" or "switches". This solution is justified by the experience that, at least in many Petri-Nets arising from practical problems, the number of circulating marks is much smaller than the number of transitions. One State Machine is built for every mark in the result of the transformation algorithm. In every State Machine we find one place corresponding to one place in the original net which shows the loaction of the corresponding mark in the Petri-Net. Nonexistenting marks are represented by a State Machine having a mark on the special place p_{end}^i. The theoretical foundation of such a transformation from an arbitrary Petri-Net into an SCS is the definition of so called mark-paths. Let us consider a transition $t \in T$ of our original Petri-Net PN. The pre- and post-places of t are $p_{j1}, .., p_{j|In(t)|}$ and $p_{k1}, .., p_{k|Out(t)|}$. (with $out(t) = \{p|(t,p) \in F\}$ and $in(t) = \{p|(p,t) \in F\}$) In order to explain the definition of mark-paths ist useful to apply the following construction: Let be

$$M_{j1} = \{1, .., V((p_j1, t))\},$$
$$N_{k1} = \{1, .., V((t, p_{k1}))\}.$$

For $2 \le \alpha \le |In(t)|$ and $2 \le \beta \le |Out(t)|$ we built

$$M_{j,\alpha} = \{\sum_{n=1}^{\alpha-1} V((p_{jn}, t)) + 1, .., \sum_{n=1}^{\alpha} V((p_{jn}, t))\}$$

and

$$N_{k,\beta} = \{\sum_{m=1}^{\beta-1} V((t, p_{km}))) + 1, .., \sum_{m=1}^{\beta} V((t, p_{km}))\}.$$

Finally let be

$$M_{end} = \{\sum_{n=1}^{|In(t)|} V((p_{jn}, t)) + 1, ..\}$$

and

$$N_{end} = \{\sum_{m=1}^{|Out(t)|} V((t, p_{km})) + 1, ..\}.$$

If and only if

$$M_a \cap N_b \ne 0$$

a triple $(p_a, t, p_b), p_a, p_b \in (P \cup (end))$ (end:virtual place) is called a flowing path of a mark (mark-path). The set of mark paths represents all possible ways, on which a mark is moved. That is the reason , why one transition in every state machine has to correspond to each of these paths . The number of state machines is equal to the maximal number of marks existing in the whole Petri-Net. The additional places in the SCS and the edges from or to these places synchronize the flow of all marks if a transition fires. We get a dual transformation, if places are considered as active parts. There exists one state for every possible marking of any place. That means, that we have to built $|P|$ state machines with $\sum K(p) + 1$- states.

3 Implementation

3.1 Hardware

The typical hardware system we use for the implementation is a system of transputers T800 included in a host-PC. Each transputer consists of an T800-CPU, a storage device and 4 links connecting it to the other transputers and the host-PC, respectively. Exactly one of the transputers is linked with the host-PC, thus all processes performing in- or outputs must be implemented on this one. The remaining links can be chosen by the user in accordance to the system to be implemented. The programming language we use is inmos-ANSI-C ([4]). Consequently, the communication between the transputers is performed by channels. It should be noted that it is not hard to modify our methods for implementing on other hardware systems.

3.2 Implementing state machines

3.2.1 Preliminaries

Every state machine will be implemented as a single process. Each of these processes is sequentially since any marking of an ordinary state machine contains exactly one mark. To implement a transition is a tedious task, and, in general, there are two different possibilities to do it ([6]). The first one is to implement one function for all transitions, that takes all informations needed from the storage cells corresponding to the transition in consideration. The second one is to implement a single function for each transition, which contains the specific data and has a specific structure. In general, the first possibility consums fewer space in the memory than the second one. However, to implement a single function for each transition yields more efficient programs especially if there are many different types of transitions in the state machines to be implemented. The latter is the reason that we prefer the second possibility. The function corresponding to the transitions are divided into two parts, one part that tests whether the transition can be fired and the second that execute the process of firing. ([7]). Here the actual marking is stored in global integer-data-objects. The communication places will be implemented as special communication structures connecting the respective processes, and so testing additional places is a specific operation. Using ANSI-C these structures are carried out as semaphores or events.

3.2.2 State machines

Any marking of a state machine contains exactly one mark, using this fact, we translate a state machine into code starting with the initial marking step by step and following the flow of the mark. In the resulting program a self-contained part corresponds to any substructure of the state machine. In picture 1 a list of typical substructures of a state machine and their corresponding program instructions is given. In more detail our algorithm can be described as follow:

(0)   Generate the head of the process, the transition functions and the data structures.

(1)   Translate the first substructure starting with the place that is marked in the initial marking.

(2)   Take the next substructure following the flow of the mark if it has not been translated so far (If the last substructure was an alternative take one of the adjacent places which has not been translated so far.). If the next substructure has already been translated or, in case of an alternative, if all adjacent places have already been translated go back up to the next alternative that is adjacent to a place that has not been translated so far and take this one. If there is no alternative stop.

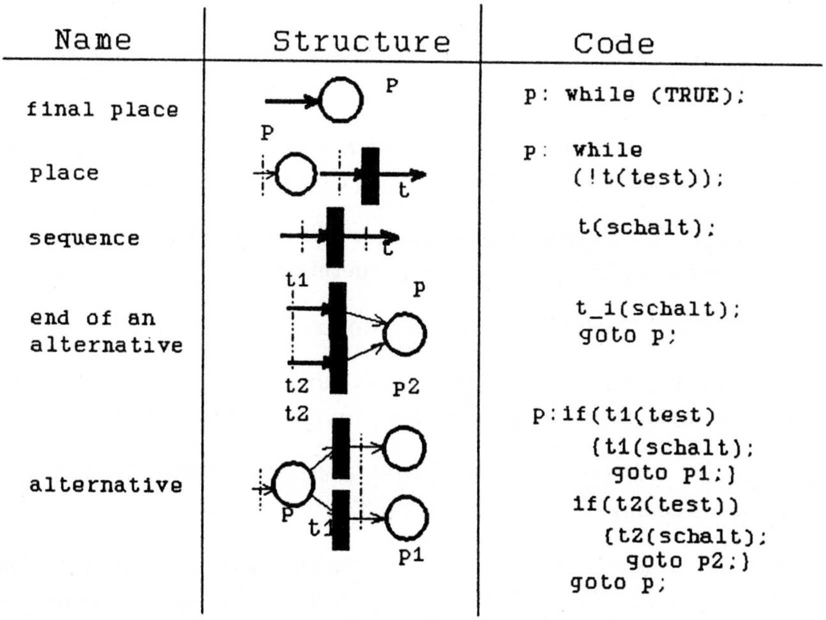

Name	Structure	Code
final place		p: while (TRUE);
place		p: while (!t(test));
sequence		t(schalt);
end of an alternative		t_i(schalt); goto p;
alternative		p:if(t1(test) {t1(schalt); goto p1;} if(t2(test)) {t2(schalt); goto p2;} goto p;

Picture 1: Structures of an SCS

Since in a system of concurrent state machine any transition is connected to some communication places transitions will be carried out by functions (described above), but, in contrast to arbitrary Petri-Nets they serve to control the semaphores corresponding to the communication places only. A process related to a state machine ZM^i, in which the place corresponding to p_{end} is marked, will be suspended; it must be reactivated if some transition in ZM^i is fired. The reader should note that we have only explained the basic idea and various improvements can still be made. For example, one can involve more subtle HLL-structures as if-then-else- constructions or loops ([5]). The latter permits the possibility to generate a program to control some technical systems represented by a Petri-Net involving w_a, w_y and w_x functions ([2]) automatically.

4   Summary

We have demonstrate, that the use of Petri-Nets improve the efficiency of the development process especially the design of parallel programs. When using Petri-Nets as a model description of our control unit we can generate software processes by a formal algorithm. That means, that the number of mistakes in the implementation process is sinking and so the costs and development times of the whole software product will be lower. In order to get an optimal solution it is useful to work with an interactive tool which allows to design a complete parallel program from its modelling to its implementation.

References

[1] Boillat, J. E. et al: *Parallel computing in the 1990's*, Universitaet Basel, Institut fuer Informatik, (1991)

[2] Fengler, W.; Philippow, I.: *Entwurf industrieller Mikrocomputersysteme*, Carl Hanser Verlag Muenchen Wien, (1991)

[3] Hartung, C.A.: *Programmierung einer Klasse von Multiprozessorsystemen mit hoeheren Petrinetzen*, Aachen, Huethig-Verlag, (1987)

[4] inmos:*ANSI-C toolset user manual*, inmos Limited, (1990)

[5] Lichtblau, U.: *Graphtransformationen zur Erkennung adaaehnlicher Kontrollstrukturen*,Dortmund, DFG-Forschungsbericht, (1980)

[6] Syrbe, H.: *Mikroprozessor-Geraete-Betriebssysteme*,TH Ilmenau, WB Computertechnik, Diplomarbeit, (1982)

[7] Unger, H.: *Moeglichkeiten der Softwaregenerierung auf der Basis von Petrinetzen*, TH Ilmenau, WB Computertechnik, Diplomarbeit, (1991)

A Parallel Structure for Static Iterative Transformation Algorithms

Fethi A. Rabhi

Department of Computer Science
University of Hull, Hull HU6 7RX (UK)
Email : far@uk.ac.hull.cs

Abstract. Parallel functional programming could be made more efficient if the paradigm used was clearly identified. A paradigm can be expressed by defining a template called a parallel algorithmic structure. As a case study, this paper addresses the issue of defining a parallel structure for the static iterative transformation paradigm. It shows how a specification can be successively turned into a sequential functional program, then into a parallel program, and finally into a program that maps on a specific parallel architecture.

1 Introduction

Functional languages are attractive candidates for parallel programming because they focus on the problem to be solved rather than on how to exhibit and exploit parallelism. Two major problems are hampering the acceptance of functional languages as a means of programming parallel systems. First is the difficulty in writing some programs with sufficient inherent parallelism. Second is the unpredictable performance of programs due to problems of load-balancing, grain size, and locality of references. One potential solution to both these problems involves the use of constructs known as *parallel algorithmic structures* [4]. Such structures capture the behaviour of an entire class of parallel algorithms. Any algorithm that obeys a known paradigm can then be specified by using its corresponding parallel algorithmic structure as a template, leaving the lower level details of exploiting parallelism to the implementation.

This paper addresses the issue of defining a parallel algorithmic structure for a specific class of parallel algorithms, called *static iterative transformation* algorithms [5]. These algorithms operate on a fixed number of homogeneous data objects. These objects are transformed through several *iteration* steps. During an iteration step, each object performs a computation using local data, local data from other objects, or global data. Global information may be obtained by combining local data contained in the objects. These algorithms are specifically used in numerical analysis, image processing, parallel branch and bound and graph problems. In other classifications, they correspond to *geometric parallelism* [2] or *domain partition* algorithms [3].

The next section describes the components of the structure which form the problem specification. The rest of the paper shows how this specification can be successively converted into a sequential functional program (Section 3), then into a parallel program (Section 4), and finally into a program that maps on a specific parallel architecture (Section 5).

2 Parallel Algorithmic Structure

The structure presented here is restricted to only one transformation in each cycle. A more general form is presented in [4]. This section provides the type definitions (in a functional style) of all the components in the specification.

First, the information held by the objects is described. Each object carries p items of information in a tuple of type $State$ and the set of objects is of type $Wset(State)$. The set has a fixed size $WsetSize$ of type $Size$ and each object can be identified with a unique identifier of type $Coordinates$. At this stage, all the constants needed in other definitions are also declared.

$$\textit{type Coordinates}$$
$$\textit{type State} = S_1 \times \ldots \times S_p$$
$$\textit{type Wset(State)}$$

Given a coordinates value, the function $access$ returns the corresponding object's state and the function sel_i accesses individual components of type S_i in a state. Global operations on the set are allowed. For example, the function $setReduce$ reduces a value from all the objects' states to compute a new value in the same way as a folding operator operates on a list. For simplicity, we assume that $setReduce$ always takes an associative function as an argument. Values can be selected from the object's state by using the function $setMap$ which applies a function to the state of each object. Another useful function is $setMapCoord$ which applies a function to the state and the current coordinates of each object. There is also a function $setMk$ used to build the initial set.

$$
\begin{array}{lll}
access & :: Wset(State) \times Coordinates \rightarrow State & \\
sel_i & :: State \rightarrow S_i & (1 \leq i \leq p) \\
setReduce & :: (a \times a \rightarrow a) \times a \times Wset(a) \rightarrow a & \\
setMap & :: (State \rightarrow a) \times Wset(State) \rightarrow Wset(a) & \\
setMapCoord & :: (State \times Coordinates \rightarrow a) \times Wset(State) \rightarrow Wset(a) & \\
setMk & :: Size \times (Coordinates \rightarrow State) \rightarrow Wset(State) &
\end{array}
$$

A set of functions $c_1 \ldots c_m$ called *communication primitives* are associated with the set of objects, giving for each object the coordinates of its closest neighbours, or the objects it needs to communicate with. In addition, there is a need to identify the inverse of these functions $c_1^{-1} \ldots c_m^{-1}$. The inverse functions could be either specified by the user or derived using a transformation system. Finally, it is useful to define some predicates $p_1 \ldots p_r$ that identify particular objects in the communication pattern.

$$
\begin{array}{lll}
c_i & :: Coordinates \rightarrow Coordinates & (1 \leq i \leq m) \\
c_i^{-1} & :: Coordinates \rightarrow Coordinates & (1 \leq i \leq m) \\
p_i & :: Coordinates \rightarrow Boolean & (1 \leq i \leq r)
\end{array}
$$

For simple communication patterns such as grids, toruses, trees and hypercubes, all these declarations should be provided in a library.

During an iteration step, a function *lcycle* produces the new state for an object of state $(s_1, \ldots, s_p)$ and of coordinates *coord*. The body of the definition of *lcycle* may contain variables from the input state, global variables and variables from the state of its closest neighbours in the form of $s_i@c_j(coord)$ called *external variables*. The initial state for each object needs also to be specified using the function *initState*.

$$
\begin{aligned}
lcycle \quad &:: Wset(State) \times State \times Coordinates \rightarrow State \\
initState &:: Coordinates \rightarrow State
\end{aligned}
$$

Global values are grouped into one type *Global*, and a function *gcycle* indicates how the global values are modified during an iteration step. Computing global values can be done using global operations on the set. The user also needs to specify the initial global values *initg* and the termination function *terminate*.

$$
\begin{aligned}
type\ Global &= Gtype_1 \times \ldots \times Gtype_q \\
gcycle \quad &:: Wset(State) \times Global \rightarrow Global \\
initg \quad &:: Global \\
terminate \quad &:: Global \rightarrow Boolean
\end{aligned}
$$

3 Constructing the sequential program

Once the specification is completed, a sequential functional program can be derived from it. This is important in identifying the errors that would otherwise be difficult to detect in a parallel environment. The sequential program is modelled as to generate a succession of sets and global variables and finishes when the termination condition is satisfied.

The first step is to transform the body of the function *lcycle* by applying a transformation called S that removes the "syntactic sugar" present in the external variables of the form $s_i@c_j(coord)$.

$$
\begin{aligned}
S\ &[[lcycle\ wset\ (s_1, ..., s_p)\ coord\ =\ \ldots (s_i@c_j(coord))\ldots]] \\
\Rightarrow\ &[[lcycle_S\ wset\ (s_1, ..., s_p)\ coord\ =\ \ldots (sel_i\ (access\ wset\ c_j(coord)))\ldots]]
\end{aligned}
$$

Then, the final program is constructed:

$$
\begin{aligned}
iterate\ wset\ g\ =\ &if\ (terminate\ g) \\
&then\ wset \\
&else\ iterate\ (cycle\ wset)\ newg \\
&\qquad where\ cycle\ wset = setMapCoord\ (lcycle\ wset)\ wset \\
&\qquad\qquad newg\ =\ (gcycle\ wset\ g)
\end{aligned}
$$

$$
\begin{aligned}
seqProgram\ \ =\ &iterate\ initWset\ initg \\
&where\ initWset\ =\ setMk\ wsetSize\ initState
\end{aligned}
$$

4 Constructing the parallel program

Static iterative transformation algorithms show a great deal of locality so they are particularly suitable for distributed memory architectures. We first assume an architecture that has as many processor/memory pairs (called reduction agents) as there are objects in the problem. We also assume that there is a processor called the *host* that synchronises the iteration steps in the algorithm. The host also holds global data and is in charge of the global operations.

We define a transformation called $\mathcal{P}$ that transforms the function *lcycle* into a version *lcycle$_\mathcal{P}$* that runs on every reduction agent and the function *gcycle* into a version *gcycle$_\mathcal{P}$* that runs on the host. This transformation needs to remove all references to external variables from the body of the function *lcycle*. One possibility is to transform variables of the form $s_i@c_j(coord)$ into references to *input nodes* with a *blocked* status. An attempt to read such nodes causes the current task to be blocked and a request message to be sent to the corresponding reduction agent. This value is then sent back in an update message that will overwrite the input node that corresponds to this value and reactivate the suspended task.

This technique causes unnecessary communication overheads because, as all reduction agents are executing the same task, it is possible to predict the data requirements of the task. This means that request messages can be eliminated by generating update messages in advance. To achieve this, we associate with each object a list ρ where each element is called an *update list* and has the following form:

$$update(s_i, [(v_{i_1}@d_{i_1}), \ldots, (v_{i_r}@d_{i_r})])$$

It means that the value of s_i should overwrite all input nodes v_{i_k} located in reduction agents d_{i_k} with $(1 \le k \le r)$. Therefore, the aims of the $\mathcal{P}$ transformation is to transform references to external variables to references to input nodes in the body of the *lcycle* function and to produce the list ρ.

$$\mathcal{P}\,[[lcycle\ wset\ s\ coord\ =\ \ldots(s_i@c_j(coord))\ldots]]$$
$$\rho[update(s_i, l)]\ \rho'$$
$$\Rightarrow$$
$$[[lcycle_\mathcal{P}\ (v_1, \ldots, v_p)\ s\ coord\ =\ \ldots v_k \ldots]]$$
$$\rho[update(s_i, (v_k@c_j^{-1}(coord)) : l)]\ \rho'$$

For every occurrence of the form $s_i@c_j(coord)$, the transformation creates an update list for the variable s_i if not already created, then adds the expression $(v_k@c_j^{-1}(coord))$ in the update list, where v_k is a new input variable, and finally replaces the external reference $s_i@c_j(coord)$ by v_k.

The transformation means that if a reduction agent is expected to request the value of the variable s_i from its neighbour $c_j(coord)$, then this processor has to send the value of its local variable s_i to processor $c_j^{-1}(coord)$. The external variable reference $s_i@c_j(coord)$ can then be replaced with an input node denoted v_k, which is the destination of the update message. If c_j^{-1} is not defined on the argument *coord* (boundaries), no update message is generated. A restriction imposed is that each c_i^{-1} must be the same to only one c_j with $(1 \le i, j \le m)$. The reason is that each destination must have one origin only [5].

The $\mathcal{P}$ transformation also takes an additional parameter ρ' which corresponds to the list of update lists of the host. It contains update lists of the form:

$$update(g_i, [v_i @all])$$

This means that the value of the global variable g_i is broadcasted to all reductions agents, overwriting the input node v_i. The identifier *all* refers to all possible coordinates. Therefore, the $\mathcal{P}$ transformation converts each reference to a global variable in the body of *lcycle* into a reference to the corresponding input variable and generates a broadcasted update in ρ'.

$$\mathcal{P} \, [[lcycle \ wset \ s \ coord \ = \ \ldots g_i \ldots)]] \qquad \rho \ \rho'$$
$$\Rightarrow \quad [[lcycle_{\mathcal{P}} \ (v_1, \ldots, v_p) \ s \ coord \ = \ \ldots v_i \ldots]] \ \rho \ \rho'[update(g_i, [v_i @all])]$$

The $\mathcal{P}$ transformation replaces any reference to the global set of objects from the body of the function *gcycle* by a reference to a *set of input nodes* denoted *iset*. If s is the state of an object of coordinates *coord*, it also adds an update operation $update(s, iset(coord)@host)$ in ρ so that each node in the set of input nodes located on the host is updated with the corresponding object's state. A special address called *host* identifies the host.

$$\mathcal{P} \, [[gcycle \ wset \ g \ = \ \ldots wset \ldots]] \ \rho \qquad\qquad\qquad \rho'$$
$$\Rightarrow \quad [[gcycle_{\mathcal{P}} \ iset \ g \ = \ \ldots iset \ldots]] \ \rho[update(s, [iset(coord)@host])] \ \rho'$$

Instead of replicating the whole set of objects, it is always desirable to use *setMap* or *setMapCoord* first to select only the values in the state that are needed. The next rules reduce communication costs and computing overheads for the host by sending processed information instead of the whole state.

$$\mathcal{P} \, [[gcycle \ wset \ g \ = \ \ldots(setMap \ f \ wset)\ldots)]]$$
$$\rho \ \rho'$$
$$\Rightarrow \quad [[gcycle_{\mathcal{P}} \ iset \ g \ = \ \ldots iset \ldots]]$$
$$\rho[update((fs), [iset(coord)@host])] \ \rho'$$

$$\mathcal{P} \, [[gcycle \ wset \ g \ = \ \ldots(setMapCoord \ f \ wset)\ldots)]]$$
$$\rho \ \rho'$$
$$\Rightarrow \quad [[gcycle_{\mathcal{P}} \ iset \ g \ = \ \ldots iset \ldots]]$$
$$\rho[update((f \ s \ coord), [iset(coord)@host])] \ \rho'$$

5 Mapping the problem on a physical architecture

In this section, we show how the parallel program could be adapted to a specific physical architecture. We assume that q objects of coordinates $coord_1 \ldots coord_q$, with states $S_1 \ldots S_q$, are mapped on a reduction agent of coordinates *pcoord*, and that there is a function *cmap* which converts logical coordinates into physical coordinates.

$$type \quad Pcoordinates$$
$$cmap :: Coordinates \rightarrow Pcoordinates$$

All that is needed is to uniquely identify states and input nodes within a single reduction agent using a transformation called $\mathcal{M}$. Each reference to an input node v_k located in an object $coord_i$ is named $v_{(coord_i, k)}$. Then each list of update lists ρ associated with an object $coord_i$ becomes ρ_{coord_i} and each reference to a state variable s_j in ρ_{coord_i} becomes $(sel_j\ S_{coord_i})$. Finally, each logical destination d_k in ρ_{coord_i} becomes a physical destination $(cmap\ d_k)$.

$$\mathcal{M}\ [[lcycle_{\mathcal{P}}\ (v_1, \ldots, v_p)\ s\ coord\ =\ \ldots v_k \ldots]]$$
$$\rho[\ update(s_i, [(v_{i_1}@d_1), \ldots, (v_{i_r}@d_r)])\ ]$$
$$\rho'$$

$\Rightarrow$

$$[[lcycle_{\mathcal{M}}\ (v_{(coord,1)}, \ldots, v_{(coord,p)})\ S_{coord}\ coord\ =\ \ldots v_{(coord,k)} \ldots]]$$
$$\rho_{coord}[update((sel_i\ S_{coord}), [(v_{(d_1,i_1)}@(cmap\ d_1)), \ldots, (v_{(d_r,i_r)}@(cmap\ d_r))])])]$$
$$\rho'$$

6 Conclusion

In this paper, we advocated a "paradigm-first" approach to the design and implementation of parallel functional programs. This is inspired by an idea described in [1]. As a case study, the use of a parallel structure for iterative transformation algorithms allows for static allocation of tasks to processors, partitioning the data in the processor's local stores, and even generating update messages in advance. A complete implementation based on the graph reduction model is described in [5] with examples.

The drawback of this approach is that a compiler-based implementation is generally not as efficient as a direct implementation of the program on a specific machine configuration. However, our approach ensures not only that a functional program contains sufficient parallelism but also provides crucial information for the run-time system about the nature of this parallelism. In addition, the use of a parallel algorithmic structure to express an algorithm makes it clear, easy to modify, and allows for formal analysis and transformation into a variety of forms (sequential, parallel or adapted to a particular machine) thus making it highly portable.

References

1. M. Cole, Higher-Order functions for parallel evaluation, In Proc. Workshop on Functional Programming, C. Hall et al. (Eds), Glasgow, August 1988, pp. 8-20.
2. A.J.G. Hey, Experiments in MIMD parallelism, In PARLE'89 Conference, LNCS 266, pp. 28-42.
3. H.T. Kung, Computational models for parallel computers, In Scientific Applications of Multiprocessors, R.J. Elliott and C.A.R. Hoare (Eds), Prentice Hall International, 1989, pp. 1-15.
4. F.A. Rabhi, Parallel Programming Paradigms: A Functional Programming Approach, Internal report, Department of Computer Science, University of Hull, May 1992.
5. F.A. Rabhi, A "Paradigm-First" Approach in the Design and Implementation of Parallel Functional Programs, Internal report, Department of Computer Science, University of Hull, May 1992.

This article was processed using the LaTeX macro package with LLNCS style

The Construction of Numerical Mathematical Software for the AMT DAP by Program Transformation.

James M. Boyle ‡[1], Maurice Clint, Stephen Fitzpatrick [2], Terence J. Harmer

The Queen's University of Belfast
Department of Computer Science
Belfast BT7 1NN
Northern Ireland

‡Mathematics and Computer Science Division
Argonne National Laboratory
Argonne IL60439
USA

1 Introduction

The general advantages of functional programming - naturalness of expression (in some problem areas), ease of proof, and clarity - are well known. In the field of numerical mathematical computation, however, these advantages are normally outweighed by functional programming's main disadvantage - inefficient execution. In this paper, we show how a functional style can be used for the elegant specification of numerical algorithms while still obtaining highly efficient implementations through the application of program transformations.

2 Notation: A Functional Specification Language

For our functional specification language we use a (very) small subset of the language constructs available in Standard ML (SML) [9]. The specifications that we express in this language are high-level. They are, however, algorithmic and, in fact, executable. Indeed, we occasionally execute them in specification form in order to carry out rapid prototyping.

We provide a standard library of vector/matrix operations to facilitate the specification of numerical mathematical algorithms. The transformational derivation must provide an implementation for each primitive operation tailored for the hardware architecture in use. In addition, a numerical mathematical algorithm is expressed using the following general-purpose vector/matrix functions.

Generate :$shape \times (Index \rightarrow \alpha) \rightarrow Matrix(shape, \alpha)$
where $shape$ is a descriptor of vector/matrix of α type elements and Index is position in that vector/matrix shape. The $generate$ function returns a vector/matrix with shape given by its shape argument and where each element of the vector/matrix is defined by the function that is an argument to the $generate$ function.

---

[1] This work was supported by the Applied mathematical sciences subprogram of the Office of Energy Research, U.S. Department of Energy, under Contract W-31-109-Eng-38.

[2] This work is supported by a research studentship from Department of Education, Northern Ireland.

$Map : Matrix(shape, \alpha) \times (\alpha \rightarrow \beta) \rightarrow Matrix(shape, \beta)$

$$map(V, \lambda x.B) \stackrel{def}{=} generate(Shape(V), \lambda k.(\lambda x.B)(element(V, k)))$$

$Reduce : Shape \times (Index \rightarrow \alpha) \times (\alpha \times \alpha \rightarrow \alpha) \times \alpha \rightarrow \alpha$

A *reduce* function combines the elements of a vector/matrix by means of a binary function to produce a single value.

3 The Parallel Orthogonal Transformation(POT) Algorithm

The POT algorithm calculates the eigenvectors, Q, and eigenvalues, Λ of a real symmetric matrix A. The algorithm is based on the construction of a sequence of symmetric matrices as shown below:

1. $U_0 = I$

2. $U_{k+1} = ortho(A.U_k.transform(B_k), diagonal(B_k)), k \geq 0$, where the sequence B_k is constructed as follows:

3. $B_0 = A$

4. $B_k = U_k : T.A.U_k$

Then $\lim_{k \rightarrow \infty} U_k = Q$ and $\lim_{k \rightarrow \infty} B_k = \Lambda$ [7]. The function *ortho* orthonormalizes the columns of its non-singular matrix argument using the standard Gram-Schmidt method. An SML function *Pot* may be defined thus:

```
fun Pot( A: real Array, U: real Array) : real Array * real Array =
let B = multiplymatrix(transpose(U), multiplymatrix(A, U))
in
if ( is`satisfactory(B) )
then (U, B)
else
  Pot(A,
     orthogonalize(multiplymatrix(A, multiplymatrix(U, transform(B))),
        diagonal(B))
end;
```

The operation *transform* produces from its matrix argument a matrix, T_k, each column of which is an approximation to an eigenvector of B_k. The components of T_k are computed by an SML function thus:

```
fun Transform( M : real Array) : real Array
= let
fun Calculate(M: real Array, i: int, j: int) : real
= let val d = M@[j, j] - M@[i, i]
in
  2*M@[i,j]/(d+sign(d)*sqrt(sqr(d)+4*sqr(M@[i,j])))
end
in
```

```
generate(Shape(M), fn(i, j)=¿
  if ( i ¿ j ) then Calculate(M, i, j)
  else if i = j then 1.0
  else ^Calculate(M, j, i))
end;
```

A *generate* function is used to construct the transformation matrix from its argument matrix, M. A local function *Calculate* defines the value of the (i, j)th element of the transformation matrix. The generating function embodies the cases required by the algorithm specification.

A similar development may be used for the ortho function. We claim that we have not intentionally biased these definitions. Indeed, we would further claim that they represent a natural SML formulation of the algorithm specification.

4 Deriving Efficient Programs from Functional Specifications

Of course, our goal is not simply to execute our functional specifications as *ML programs*, where execution can often be excruciatingly slow. POT has been designed with large matrices in mind and is interesting because it permits implementations tailored for execution on computers having novel advanced architectures [6, 10, 11, 7]. Efficient ML implementations are not likely to be available for such computers.

We use the TAMPR program transformation system [3, 4] to apply a sequence of sets of program transformations that produce an efficient Fortran or C program from the higher-order functional specification. Most of the transformations are basic; that is, they can be employed in the efficient implementation of any functional specification. These transformations form the framework for the derivation. (Used alone, they are highly effective [4].) We intersperse the basic set of transformation with a few sets of other transformations that perform either problem-domain-oriented or hardware-oriented optimizations. These transformations, few in number but powerful in effect, guide the derivation in the direction of producing code that will exploit the specialized hardware of the ADT DAP.

4.1 DAP-Specific Transformations

Earlier we defined two primitive vector/matrix functions: *generate* and *reduce*. These functions do not have equivalents in DAP Fortran: in order to implement an *arbitrary generate* or *reduce* in DAP Fortran we must use an explicit loop where expressions involve manipulations of individual matrix elements. However, certain simple forms of *generate* and *reduce* do have equivalents in DAP Fortran (and in other languages for array processors). Also, to make the most effective use of the processor array the aim is to produce an implementation where whole vector/matrix manipulations are used rather than giving alternative manipulations expressed as a sequence of simple vector/matrix element operations.

The strategy that the transformation set for the DAP adopts is *to propagate generate functions into expressions until the function argument of each generate is a value that is either independent of the generation index, or is a vector/matrix element operation.* This strategy aims to remove occurrences of vector/matrix element operations and arises from the desire to realize computations as whole vector/matrix operations.

The strategy requires an algebra that defines how a *generate* may be propagated into expressions. This propagation algebra has 5 rules:

1. A *generate* applied to a function the value of which is the vector/matrix element at the generating index is replaced by the vector/matrix - the identity *generate*;
   $generate(Shape(M), \lambda((i,j).M@[i,j])) \iff M$.

2. A *generate* applied to a function the value of which is independent of the generating index is replaced by an *expand* function that creates a vector/matrix in which all the elements have that independent value; e.g.,
   $generate(Shape(M), \lambda((i,j).2)) \longrightarrow expand(2, n, n)$, where matrix M is of shape $n \times n$.

3. A *generate* with a scalar generating function that has a componental equivalent is converted to that componental equivalent. The arguments to which the componental function is applied must be vectors/matrices, so the *generate* is propagated inward and applied to the arguments of the componental function; e.g.,
   $generate(Shape(A), \lambda((i,j).A@[i,j] + A@[i,j])) \longrightarrow$
   $generate(Shape(A), \lambda((i,j).A@[i,j])) + generate(Shape(A), \lambda((i,j).A@[i,j]))$

4. A *generate* of a conditional expression becomes an application of a data-parallel conditional - a *join* function. The *generate* is propagated inwards to the limbs of the conditional and applied to the conditional guards and the guarded results. The *join* function combines (*joins*) the results to form a single composite result for the conditional expression.

5. A *reduce* for which an aggregate function is defined is replaced by an application of that aggregate function.

The transformation strategy uses the a number simplification/optimization transformations that remove duplicate computation and to make use of standard arrangement/rearrangement being performed to the vector/matrix elements (- the interested reader is referred to [5]).

The transformations outlined above are not specific to the DAP or any other array processor architecture: they target the set of operations that may be implemented efficiently on architectures of this kind. Thus, most of the transformations above may be used in a derivation aimed at deriving efficient code for the Cray X-MP.

5 Derived DAP Code

Space does not permit us to trace the operations of the transformations that implement this algebra - the interested reader is referred to [5]. The derived DAP code for the *Transform* function given above that is the result of their

```
g371598 = patlowertri( n ) .and. .not. patunitdiag( n )
g371651 = patlowertri( n )
g371652 = patunitdiag( n )
g22( g371651 .and. g371652 ) = 1
g371651( g371652 ) = .false.
g371652 = g371598
g371597 = matr( g371600 , n ) - matc( g371600 , n )
g371629 = 1
g371629( g371597 .lt. 0 ) = - 1
g22( g371651 .and. g371652 ) = ( - 2 * b ) / (
&      g371597 + g371629 * sqrt( g371597 * g371597 +
&      4 * ( b * b ) ) )
g22( .not. patlowertri( n ) ) = - tran( g22 )
```

Figure 1: Derived DAP Code for the Transform Function.

application is given in Figure 1. The variable g22 contains the transformation matrix. The resulting program may appear to be rather ugly, but it is not intended that *this* form should be read. The identifier names are chosen for convenience rather than for understandability or readability.

6 Comparison with Hand-Crafted Versions of POT

There are two versions of DAP Fortran: Fortran-Plus [1] and Fortran-Plus Enhanced [2]. The former requires all arrays to be the size of the processor grid (32 by 32); the latter allows any size of array to be used, with the compiler automatically sectioning arrays into 32 by 32 arrays.

In Table 1 the execution time (for each approximation) [3] for the implementation of POT derived by automatic program transformation is shown together with times for two hand-crafted versions - the first is written in Fortran-Plus and the other written in Fortran Plus Enhanced. These hand-crafted versions have been analysed in [8, 11]. A hand-crafted Fortran-Plus version of POT is between 12% and 13% faster than a hand-crafted Fortran-Plus Enhanced version. As reported in [8] the code produced by the Fortran-Plus Enhanced compiler for frequently occurring linear algebra operations (e.g. matrix product) is very efficient but it is less so on more specialized operations (e.g. Gram-Schmidt orthogonalization).

The hand-crafted and automatically derived versions have execution times that are almost identical. For the large matrix examples the derived implementation is marginally slower than the time for the hand crafted version (between

---

[3] The time is constant for generation of each approximation

0.1% and 0.6%). This discrepancy arises from a minor optimization made possible by the particular way the hand-crafted version produces the *transform* matrix. We could write a transformation that could perform this optimization, but it appears to be too special-purpose to be of general use.

Matrix Size	Time per iteration (sec)		
	Hand Crafted Fortran Plus	Hand Crafted Fortran Plus Enhanced	Automatically Derived Fortran Plus Enhanced
64	1.2	1.35	1.35
128	8.23	9.30	9.31
256	60.92	69.86	70.30

Table 1: Hand-Crafted POT versus Mechnically Derived POT

7 Conclusion

We have shown that it is possible mechanically to produce a highly efficient implementation tailored for execution on the AMT DAP 510 of a high-level functional specification. The functional specification is not biased in ways that would permit its efficient execution on a particular machine architecture, but is expressed in a way that gives a clear statement of the algorithm. Indeed, the functional specification may be used as the starting point for producing implementations tailored for execution on other machines (and will be used in this way in future investigations).

The transformations used to produce the implementation discussed in this paper are not particular to this problem and are currently being applied in the transformation of functional specification for other algorithms where an implementation tailored for the DAP processor is required. However, there is still development work to be undertaken for these derivations. This includes tailoring the generated code for the compiler (for example, producing sectioned array operations) and tailoring for particular data sets (for example, sparse matrices or banded matrices).

References

[1] *Fortran-Plus Language*, AMT, man 00202, 1988.

[2] *Fortran-Plus Language Enhanced*, AMT, man 102.01, 1988.

[3] *A Transformational Component for Programming Language Grammar*, J. M. Boyle, ANL-7690 Argonne National Laboratory, July 1970, Argonne, Illinois.

[4] *Abstract programming and program transformations - An approach to reusing programs.* James M. Boyle, Editors Ted J. Biggerstaff and Alan J. Perlis in Software Reusability, Volume I, Pages 361-413, ACM Press (Addison-Wesley Publishing Company), New York, NY, 1989

[5] *Deriving efficient programs for the AMT DAP 510 using Program transformation*, J.M. Boyle, M. Clint, S. Fitzpatrick and T.J. Harmer, QUB Techical Report, June 1992.

[6] *Towards the construction of an eigenvalue engine*, Clint M. et al, Parallel Computing, 8, 127-132, 1988.

[7] *A Comparison of two Parallel Algorithms for the Symmetric Eigenproblem*, Clint M. et al, Intern'l Journal of Computer mathematics, 15, 291-302, 1984.

[8] *Fortran-Plus v. Fortran-Plus Enhanced: A comparison for an Application in Linear Algebra*, M. Clint et al, QUB Technical Report, 1991 (submitted for publication).

[9] *Functional Programming using Standard ML*, Wilstöm, A, Prentice Hall, London 1987.

[10] *The parallel computation of eigenvalues and eigenvectors of large hermitian marices using the AMT DAP 510*, Weston J. et al, Concurrency Practice and Experience, Vol 3(3), 179-185, June 1991.

[11] *Two algorithms for the parallel computation of eigenvalues and eigenvectors of large symmetric matrices using the ICL DAP*, Weston J., Clint M., Parallel Computing, 13, 281-288, 1990.

On Using Object Oriented Parallel Programming to Build Distributed Algebraic Abstractions

Dennis Gannon, Jenq Kuen Lee, Srinivas Narayana

CICA and Department of Computer Science
Indiana University

Abstract. This paper considers the problem of designing numerical linear algebra computations with a parallel object oriented programming language. An extension to C++ based on a *Concurrent Aggregate* concept is used to describe a hierarchy of distributed structures including dense matrices, sparse matrices, banded matrices, vectors and the associated linear algebra. We show that these abstractions are ideal for describing BLAS3 style blocked computation. As an example we show how to build a distributed conjugate gradient algorithms for sparse matrix (based on the NAS sparse benchmark and we show results for four different parallel machines.

1 Introduction

There are two major problems with parallel computation as it applies to scientific programming. First, automatic parallelization of old Fortran programs is not showing the types of speed-ups necessary to scale to hundreds or thousands of processors. Second, the alternative to compiling old programs is either to rewrite them in a machine specific, low level language or to wait for solutions like the HPC Fortran90-D [5] effort to become available. While the later alternative is not bad, one is still left with a Fortran program with a structure that is a long way from the mathematical models that go into the design of the computations.

In this paper we propose a methodology for using object-oriented style to build portable parallel programs that allow users to express computation completely in terms of the basic mathematical operators that describe the underlying algorithms.

Our approach is to extend the C++ language with a new construct called the distributed collection. This new language is called pC++ [3, 4] and it currently runs on several different parallel processing platforms. To illustrate the ideas behind pC++ in the context of scientific computation we will outline a design for a *distributed linear algebra collection-class hierarchy*. By "distributed", we mean structures that have been partitioned among the available processors in such a way that local memory and cache have been used to optimal advantage. In the last section of this paper we describe a large benchmark that we have implemented with this "object parallel" library and show some early results.

2 Parallel C++ (pC++) and the Collection Construct

The *Collection* construct is similar to class construct in the C++ language[6]. The difference is that a collection is a structured set of objects from some standard C++ class type that has been distributed over a set of processors. The idea is very simple. Let C be a class of the form

```
Class C{
    float data;
    ....
  public:
    C operator +(C x);
    float foo();
}
```

C has an overloaded binary operator + and two functions. The collection class *DistributedArray* is part of the standard pC++ library. To define a 2-dimensional m by n array X of objects of type C which are distributed over a "vector" of processors of size P, one writes

```
DistributedArray<C> X([P], [m, n], [Block, Whole]);
```

The key words *Block* and *Whole* describe how each dimension of the array is mapped to the 1-D array of processors. (This is identical to the Fortran-D, HP-Fortran model.)

Parallelism now comes from two possible sources. First, the operation

```
X.foo();
```

means the parallel invocation of the C class function *foo* on each element of the collection. Because foo returns a float, the value returned by this call is of type *DistributedArray* < *float* > with the same shape and distribution as X. Similarly, the operator $X + X$ is a parallel, pointwise application of the + operator to every member of the collection.

The second source of parallelism is the invocation of parallel operators associated with the global Collection structure. For distributed arrays this includes global data movement and reduction operators.

3 Inheritance and A Distributed Matrix Class Hierarchy

The most powerful feature of C++, or any other object oriented language, is the ability to define a class hierarchy where one class is defined in terms of properties that are inherited from another. Our implementation for a parallel linear algebra system begins with such a C++ class hierarchy for standard sequential linear algebra. In what follows we assume that there is a class *vector* which can be defined over the reals or complex numbers (single or double precision). In addition, we will make use of a class *matrix* with subclasses *dense_matrix*, *sparse_matrix* and *banded_matrix* and all the associated operators. (For the complete details, the full version of this paper is available from gannon@iuvax.cs.indiana.edu.)

In the same manner as C++ classes, pC++ collections form an inheritance hierarchy. To build a distributed vector collection we derive it from the DistributedArray class as

```
Collection Dvector: DistributedArray{
   public:
      Dvector operator +(Dvector x);
      ....
   };
```

The collection *Dvector* has all the basic operators associated with a *vector* in the standard linear algebra. Consequently we can define a distributed vector V as

```
Dvector<float> V(...);
```

In our case we create a large-grain distributed vector by the declaration

```
Dvector<vector> V(...);
```

We use a very simple method to build a distributed matrix. We view the processor set as a 1-D array and partition the c columns into c/P blocks where P is the total number of available processors in exactly the same way as we have described for distributed vectors. as shown in Figure 1. The collection that implements this is called a Dcol_matrix.

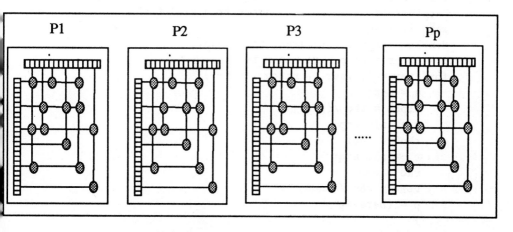

Dcol_matrix< sparse_matrix > M(..)

Fig. 1. A Distributed Column matrix of Sparse Matrices.

By using the algebraic abstractions provided by this hierarchy a programmer can easily specify the type and structure for distributed vectors and matrices. For example, to define a distributed sparse matrix A, and a pair of distributed vectors, x and y and to do a matrix vector multiply, one writes

```
Dcol_matrix<sparse_matrix> A(n,n);
Dvector<vector> x(n), y(n);

y = A*x;
```

4 A Benchmark Experiment

To illustrate the utility of these concepts we have rewritten the NASA Ames NAS Sparse Conjugate Gradient Benchmark to use these distributed matrix and vector abstractions. This benchmark uses the CG algorithm to compute an approximation of the smallest eigenvalue of a large, sparse, symmetric positive definite matrix. According to the NASA team that designed the benchmark, this computation is typical of unstructured grid computations in that it tests irregular long distance communication in parallel machines by employing unstructured matrix vector multiplication.

The benchmark code builds a large randomly sparse matrix and then makes frequent calls to a CG solver, which when translated into pC++ is shown below.

Our implementation uses one distributed sparse matrix and six distributed vectors. There is a great deal more to this benchmark, but the following routine is the key component.

```
void cgsol(int n, Dcol_matrix<sparse_matrix>& S, Dvector<vector>& b,
        Dvector<vector> & x, int nitcg, Dvector<vector> & r,
        Dvector<vector> & p, Dvector<vector> & q) {
    int  i, iter;
    double   alpha, beta, rho, rho0, dinv;
    x = 0;  r = b;  p = r;  rho = r*r;
    for(iter = 1; iter <= nitcg; iter++){
        q = S*p;
        alpha = rho /(p*q);
        x += alpha*p;
        rho0 = rho;
        r -= alpha*q;
        rho = r*r;
        beta = rho / rho0;
        p = (beta)*p + r;
        }
    r = S*x;
    r = b - r;
    resid =  r.norm();
}
```

While we would like to say that our compiler can handle this routine as shown, there are still a few basic transformations that we have not completed. The most important of these involves the use of expressions of the form

    p = (beta)*p + r;

A standard C++ compiler would allocate two temporary arrays: one to compute the product (beta)*p and another to return the value of the sum. In pC++ we must be more careful, because such an allocation would generate a distributed allocation and a lot of unnecessary copying. We plan to have these optimization implemented in the next version of the compiler.

We have run the pC++ version of the program on four different machines. The BBN GP1000, the BBN TC2000, the Alliant FX/2800 and the Thinking Machines CM-5. With the exception of the current CM-5 implementation (discussed below), the program is completely portable, so no no changes in the source code was needed in moving from one machine to another. The problem size can be set by a parameter. We selected the largest problem that would run on all four machines. The matrix size 2400 by 2400 with a total of 135238 random zeros. Execution time and speed-up numbers are given in the table below. The times are in seconds and the horizontal axis is the number of processors.

Machine	P= 5	P= 10	P= 12	P= 20	P= 25	P= 40
GP1000 time	439	244	215	146	135	128
speed-up	4.98	8.95	10.16	14.95	16.19	17.07
FX/2800 time	76.5	43.6	40.8			
speed-up	4.6	8.01	8.6			
TC2000 time	91	54	49	36.5	35	
speed-up	4.8	8.1	8.9	12	12.5	

As is clear from the experiments, the program is far from showing unbounded speed-up. One reason for this is that the problem size is still relatively small. Consequently, the large number of inner products in the CG algorithm will cause it to have a sublinear speed-up if there is not enough computation to mask the $log(p)$ cost of the reductions. But we can still put these results in perspective In the case of the Alliant FX/2800, we have access to an automatic parallelizing and vectorizing compiler for Fortran. In the table below, we have included the results of running the optimized Fortran program on the benchmark test data size of 1400 by 1400 with 78148 non-zeros. The Fortran program was compiled with full vector concurrent optimization.

Machine	P= 2	P= 5	P= 10	P= 14
FX/2800 pC++ time	112.8	47.9	27.0	22.33
FX-Fortran time	78.38	73.45	73.63	72.98
ratio Fort/pC++	0.69	1.5	2.7	3.2

As can be seen, the Alliant Fortran compiler is not able to extract any significant parallelism from this computation. On the other hand,the pC++ program, which has no vectorization within code that runs on each I860, runs slower for small numbers of processors but over three times faster than the Fortran code on 14 processors. We must also add one more caveat. While the pC++ performance may look good, the absolute performance was less than 10the original benchmark when run on a Cray YMP.

More recently we have completed a partial port of our compiler to the Thinking Machines CM-5 and we have tested this computation on a machine with 128 processors. In this case we have executed the benchmark at its full size of 14000 by 14000 with 1853104 non-zeros. The speed of the computation is 18.9 Mflops which is equal to 0.27 times the speed of a 1 processor Cray Y/MP on the Fortran version of this benchmark. We emphasize that the machine is an early version without the floating point vector hardware and a very early version of the communications library. By a "partial port" of the compiler we mean that the main vector and matrix routines had to be modified by hand to use message passing primitives provided by TMC. On the other hand, the CGM application code did not need any modification. (On the other machines discussed here none of the basic library code for vector and matrix operations had to be modified in going from one machine to another.) We also note that 80% of the time consumed by CGM on the CM-5 is spent in the data communication routines in the Matrix times vector computation. We hope to report better performance numbers as the Thinking Machines Software communications software improves.

References

1. Andrew A. Chien and William J. Dally. *Concurrent Aggregates (CA)*, Proceedings of the Second ACM Sigplan Symposium on Principles & Practice of Parallel Programming, Seattle, Washington, March, 1990.

2. Charles Koelbel, Piyush Mehrotra, John Van Rosendale. *Supporting Shared Data Structures on Distributed Memory Architectures*, Technical Report No. 90-7, Institute for Computer Applications in Science and Engineering, January 1990.

3. J. K. Lee and D. Gannon, *Object Oriented Parallel Programming: PC++*, Proceedings of Supercomputing 91 (Albuquerque, Nov.), IEEE Computer Sciety and ACM SIGARCH, 1991, pp. 273–282.

4. D. Gannon and J. K. Lee, *Object Oriented Parallelism: pC++ Ideas and Experiments*, Proceedings of 1991 Japan Society for Parallel Processing, pp. 13–23, 1991. Also Bit V.24, no. 1 (1992) (in Japanese).

5. G. Fox and S. Hiranandani and K. Kennedy and C. Koelbel and U. Kremer and C. Tseng and M. Wu, *Fortran D language specification*, Rice University, Department of Computer Science TR 90079, 1991

6. Bjarne Stroustrup. *The C++ programming Language*, Addison Wesley, Reading, MA, 1986

This article was processed using the LaTeX macro package with LLNCS style

Implementation of the Self-Organizing Feature Map on Parallel Computers

V. Demian, J.-C. Mignot
Laboratoire de l'Informatique du Parallèlisme
Ecole Normale Supérieure de Lyon, 46 Allée d'Italie,
LYON CEDEX 07, FRANCE
mail : vdemian@lip.ens-lyon.fr, mignot@lip.ens-lyon.fr

1 Introduction

The Kohonen's Self-Organizing Feature Map (SOFM) is a reliable and widely used vector quantization algorithm [1]. As stated by Wu and al. [2] the main problem with this algorithm (and generally speaking with neural network) is the increase of computation time associated with an increase in the number of neurons. In [2] a method is proposed for implementing SOFM on a transputer network following two guidelines : maintaining a high degree of load balancing and keeping communications to a minimum. In this paper, we propose a new mapping of the neurons on any number of processors and any topology maintaining an asymptotically optimal load balancing. We propose a modified learning method for the SOFM which allows to exploit the high performance level of the new generation of parallel computers.

2 Parallel Implementation

We shall focus on a geometric partition of the map onto a network of processors. We suppose that each processor has a copy of the base of examples and a number of neurons to simulate. For each example, we have to determine the neuron that is closest to the input over the whole map. This involves communications among all the processors to determine the global minimum distance. Then, the neurons in the neighborhood of the winner must modify their weight vector according to the Kohonen's algorithm [3]. The main problem is to distribute the SOFM on the processors in such a way that we can determine the global winner quickly and that the load balancing remains at a high level during the modification of the weights. Computation of the distances to the example has to be done for the whole map at each iteration step and its cost linearly depends on the number of neurons per processor. Modification of the weights has to be calculated for the neurons in the neighborhood of the winner. So the load balancing of the whole computation only depends on the way the neighborhood of the neurons will be mapped on the processors.

3 Reducing the Communication Time

New generation of very powerful microprocessors (Intel i860 for example) have high performance computation capabilities with respect to communication. In order to increase the efficiency we should increase the size of the computation done during two communication phases.The only communications involved in the algorithm are those that permit to determine the global winner. This is done by determining a global minimum over all the processors. The communication time between two processors can be expressed as $\alpha+\beta L$ where α represents a fixed start-up overhead, β is the incremental transmission time per byte, and L length of the message.

The goal is to minimize the number of exchanges by packing the messages. Each processor processes a certain number of inputs, called a block , determining the local winners associated to these inputs. Then, all the processors determine the global winners associated to each input of the block. Hence they can determine the neighborhoods and modify the weights. Note that this is quite different from the classical SOFM since all the winners in a block are evaluated with an unchanged map. For N examples per block, this allows to decrease the communication time between two computation phases from $N(\alpha+\beta L)$ to $(\alpha+N*\beta L)$. For big maps, as the communication time becomes neglectable with respect to the computation one, the use of block looses its interest. One may choose to put more examples inside a block according to the size of the map and to the problem to solve.

4 Optimizing the Load Balancing

The load balancing only depends on the way the neighborhood of the neurons is mapped on the processors. That is, the goal is to distribute the neighborhoods on a maximum number of processors. Consider the mapping which allocates neuron N whose coordinates are x,y on the processor whose number is $(n*y+x)$ modulo n^2 where n^2 is the total number of processors. It optimizes the load balancing and moreover the neurons which lie on the lower or upper border of the map, which have less probability to be modified, are equally distributed over the processors.

5 Conclusion

We have introduced a new mapping and a block strategy for the SOFM allowing to increase the speed-up of the parallel implementation. This method has been implemented on a iPSC/860 MIMD parallel computer. It performs well on learning dots randomly chosen in the unit square, i.e. it learns as well as the classical algorithm. Its performances outperform the parallel implementation of the classical algorithm since the achieved speed-up is increased from 2-3 to 7. The SOFM has been implemented on a SIMD computer, namely the MasPar MP1 exhibiting an almost perfect matching between Kohonen maps, the grid architecture and the synchronous programming model of the MasPar system

References

1. Chwan-Hwa Wu, Russel Hodges, Chia-Jiu Wang, "Parallelizing the Self-Organizing Feature Map on multiprocessor systems", Parallel Computing 17, pp. 821-832, 1991.

2. A. Ultsch, H.P. Siemon, "Exploratory Data Analysis : Using Kohonen networks on Transputers", Dpt Comp. Sc. , University of Dortmund, Dec. 89.

3. Teuvo Kohonen, "Self-Organization and Associative Memory", Springer-Verlag, Berlin, 1984.

Candela – A Topology Description Language

Herbert Kuchen*   Holger Stoltze*   Friedrich Lücking**

Abstract. The declarative language Candela allows to describe the topology of a transputer system elegantly, clearly, and concisely. It offers a set of basic operations suited for the generation of graphs and borrows control structures from programming languages. The Candela compiler transforms a Candela script into a format, which is accepted by the boot program of the distributed operating system Helios. Candela is essentially a graph description language, which can be adapted to many other contexts.

Candela was developed to describe the requested hardware topology on a dynamically configurable multiprocessor system with distributed memory and with point-to-point connections (links) between the processors, e.g. the Parsytec Supercluster[1] [4]

Such a description is, for instance, needed by the operating system, in our case Helios. Existing languages for the description of hardware topologies (e.g. the Helios Resource Map Language RML [7], the Occam configuration sublanguage [3]) and software topologies (e.g. the Helios component description language CDL [8]) include only very few structuring features. The description of a non-trivial topology can be very tedious, hard to modify, and, most of all, hard to understand, since the connection structure cannot be adequately represented. This is especially true in the case of RML, where the processors have to be declared one by one. Graphical design tools like Gracia [5] are limited by the size of the screen. Closest to our approach comes the imperative language SDT (developed as part of the TéNOR++ project [1]) which offers similar control structures but has only basic operations to add or remove a single processor or connection.

A *network topology* or *net* is an undirected graph where the nodes are numbered processors and the edges represent links. A network just consisting of one processor is described by: *processor(type)*, where *type* specifies the processor's properties (as in [7]). Using *replication*, a net consisting of several identical subnets can be defined, for instance "[4] *processor(type)*" describes a network of four unconnected processors. The processors of a network are internally *numbered*. Using these numbers, the basic operation *connect* allows to add connections to a net. For instance, a vector of four processors can be defined by:

connect([4] processor(type), [1,2,3], [2,3,4])

connect takes three arguments: a net and two lists of processor numbers. It produces a net like that given as the first argument, but where additionally the processors at corresponding list positions are connected. *Functions* define parameterized nets, e.g.

function vector(n, type) {*connect([n]processor(type), [1..n − 1], [2..n])*}

Using a *conditional*, also *recursive functions* can be defined, e.g.

---

* RWTH Aachen, Lehrstuhl für Informatik II, Ahornstraße 55, D-5100 Aachen, Germany
** Parsytec Computer GmbH, Jülicher Str. 338, D-5100 Aachen, Germany
[1] In this paper, we mention the following registered trademarks: Helios (of Perihelion Software Ltd), Supercluster (of Parsytec GmbH), occam and transputer [2] (of INMOS).

$$function\ matrix(n,\ m,\ type)$$
$$\{if\ n = 1\ then\ vector(m,\ type)$$
$$else\ join(vector(m,\ type),$$
$$matrix(n - 1,\ m,\ type))\}$$

$$function\ hypercube(dim,\ type)$$
$$\{if\ dim = 0\ then\ processor(type)$$
$$else\ join(hypercube(dim-1,\ type),$$
$$hypercube(dim-1,\ type))\}$$

The basic operation *join* combines two nets by connecting equally numbered processors. Then, the processors (of the second net) are renumbered as shown in Fig. 1.

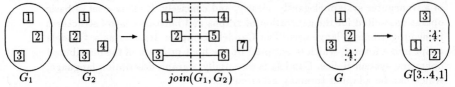

Fig. 1. (a) Joining two Graphs; (b) Changing the Visibility.

One way to specify a hierachical topology like cube-connected-cycles (ccc) is to use the *substitute* operation (assuming *cycle* to be already defined):

$$function\ ccc(dim,\ type)\ \{substitute(hypercube(dim,type),\ all,\ cycle(dim,\ type))\}$$

In general, $substitute(net_1,\ list,\ net_2)$ replaces all processors of net_1, mentioned in *list*, by (new copies of) net_2. The keyword *all* represents the list of all processors.

Normally, all processors of a net may be connected by a *connect* or *join* operation. Sometimes, it is convenient to make processors *"invisible"*, i.e. to prohibit that they are connected to others by the above operations.

For instance, if one wants to define a binary tree which may only be connected at the root, this can be done by making only the root visible:

$$function\ tree(height,\ type)$$
$$\{if\ height = 0\ then\ processor(type)$$
$$else\ (join(join(processor(type),$$
$$tree(height-1,\ type)),$$
$$tree(height-1),\ type)))\ [1]\}$$

In general, $net[list]$ causes all processors of *net* which are mentioned in *list* to be visible and the remaining ones to get invisible. Furthermore, the processors are renumbered. The visible processors get the numbers corresponding to their positions in *list*, while the invisible ones get the subsequent numbers. Note that visible processors may get invisible as well as vice versa. An example is shown in Fig. 1 (b).

A detailed explanation of Candela including other features like loops, local definitions, collapsing a net to a node, and explicit link numbers is found in [6].

References

1. J.M. Adamo, C. Bonello: TéNOR++: A Dynamic Configurer for SuperNode Machines, CONPAR'90, LNCS 457, 640-651, 1990.
2. INMOS Ltd: Transputer Instruction Set: Compiler Writer's Guide, Prentice Hall, 1988.
3. INMOS Ltd: occam 2 Reference Manual, Prentice Hall, 1988.
4. F.D. Kübler, F. Lücking: A Cluster Oriented Architecture for the Mapping of Parallel Processor Networks to High Performance Applications, ACM Proceedings of the International Conference on Supercomputing, St. Malo, 1988.
5. O. Krämer-Fuhrmann: Gracia: A Software Environment for Graphical Specification, Automatic Configuration, and Animation of Parallel Programs, Supercomputing, 1988.
6. H. Kuchen, H. Stoltze, F. Lücking: The Topology Description Language TDL, Aachener Informatik Berichte, Nr. 91-22, RWTH Aachen, 1991.
7. Perihelion Software Ltd: The HELIOS Operating System, Prentice Hall, 1989.
8. Perihelion Software Ltd: The helios Parallel Operating System, Prentice Hall, 1991.

Parallelism in generation of sequences for Monte Carlo simulation.

Boris Shukhman

Among the problems in organization of Monte Carlo simulation in parallel computers one of the most important is the restrictions of the parallelism in recurrent scheme of typical pseudo-random point generators. Some attempts to overcome this drawback result unpredictably in the characteristics of multi-dimensional distribution. Sequences of quasi-random points which may be used instead pseudo random points in algorithms with finite constructive dimension represent one of the possible solutions.

The idea of quasi-random points originates from uniformly distributed sequences introduced by H.Weyl. Their application to statistical simulation problems initiated a new branch in statistical analysis often called "Quasi Monte Carlo". That is the high quality of uniform distribution that allows to detach three types of such sequences constructed by I.Sobol (LP_τ), H.Faure and J.P.Halton correspondingly.

The particular implementation of Sobol's sequences for parallel computers is scatched here.

It was shown in Ref.1 that points of LP_τ sequences being applied instead of random points in Monte Carlo algorithms with finite constructive dimension supply better convergence. Thus while the probable error for traditional Monte Carlo can be written as $const/\sqrt{N}$, where N is the number of Monte Carlo steps. The corresponding non-random estimates of the error are of merit $const \cdot N^{-1} \ln^{-m} N$.

The recurrence, stipulating limitations of the effective parallelism, in general, can virtually be useful when the computational process has already been distributed through, for example, MIMD parallel structure. In this case a part of the process (say, one realization of the Monte Carlo step) can be executed independently in separately taken sequential subprocessor. The offered algorithm combines self-adjustably facilities of the recurrent generation with the ability to produce points of LP_τ sequences in arbitrary order.

It was speld out in Ref.2, presenting theoretical foundation for the problem of uniformly distributed sequences, how to precalculate the set of constants V_j^n usually called "direction numbers". Denote $\{Q_1, Q_2, \ldots, Q_p\}$ the sequence of n-dimensional uniformly distributed quasi-random points. If the binary representation of the number i of the point Q_i is $i = e_m e_{m-1} \ldots e_1$, then Cartesian co-ordinates of the point $Q_i = (q_{i,1}, q_{i,2}, \ldots, q_{i,n})$ are defined by the formula:

$$q_{i,j} = e_1 V_j^1 \oplus e_2 V_j^2 \oplus \ldots \oplus e_m V_j^m$$

where $\oplus$ means bit-wise addition modulo 2.

If the point Q_{i-1} is available, the next point Q_i can be computed from the recurrent correlation:

$$q_{i,j} = q_{i-1,j} \oplus V_j^1 \oplus V_j^2 \oplus \ldots \oplus V_j^{k_i+1}$$

where k_i is the number of zeros in the "tail" of binary expansion for i. The "super-fast" modification of the discussed algorithm using the single bit-wise addition is also available.

The implementation of the algorithm in C programming language uses the recurrent scheme while it is possible and the full scheme of computation in general case. This approach being used in the massive Monte Carlo simulation problems may substantially increase performance not only for MIMD-like parallel structures, but in some extend, for the ordinary computers supplying von Neumann architecture.

H.Faure [3] has constructed uniformly distributed sequences that can be used in the same applications as LP_τ sequences. According to Sobol's terminology Faure's sequences are r-adic LP_0. Comparing performance of the dyadic LP_τ sequences (S) and r-adic LP_0 sequences (F) the following conclusions could be claimed:

. At the large dimension discrepancy estimates for (F) are better than for (S);

. The additional uniformity properties are in favour of (S).

. Favourable quantities for (S) are 2^p while for (F) only $r*p$ (p - integer, $r > p$).

. Dyadic computations utilized for (S) are much more faster than the r-adic and don't depend on round-off errors.

Thus (F) sequences may be expected to perform better then (S) in multi-dimensional problems which depend on large number of equally important variables. On the contrary, the (S) sequences could be more efficient for problems depending on function $f(x_1, x_2, \ldots)$ where the influence of x_j falls down with the increase of j.

References

[1] I.M.Sobol' "Quasi Monte Carlo methods", International youth workshop on Monte Carlo methods and parallel algorithms (1-st Primorsko, Bulgaria), 24-30 September 1989, Ed. Bl.Sendow, I.Dimov.

[2] I.M.Sobol' "Multi-dimensional Quadrature Formulas and Haar Functions", Nauka, Moscow 1969. (in Russian)

[3] H.Faure "Discrepance de suites associees a une systeme de numeration (en dimension s)", Acta Arithmetica, 41, 1982, 337-351

Data Parallel Evaluation-Interpolation Algorithm for Solving Functional Matrix Equations

Chen Pin and E. V. Krishnamurthy

Computer Science Laboratory
The Australian National University
GPO Box 4, ACT 2601, Canberra, Australia

A data parallel algorithm is described for solving functional matrix equations, using evaluation and rational interpolation based on Thiele's reciprocal differences.

1 Introduction

Let us denote a linear functional matrix equation by
$$A(x)F(x) = G(x) \qquad (1.1)$$
where simply we assume that $A(x) = \{a_{ij}\}$ be a square functional matrix, $G(x) = \{g_i\}$ and $F(x) = \{f_i\}$ be functional vectors for $i, j = 1, 2, \cdots, m$ and that a_{ij} and g_i be any known natural functions and defined over the real field, $f_i(x)$ be an unknown function.

In this paper we describe an evaluation-interpolation technique that results in a data-parallel algorithm to obtain the solution for a linear functional matrix equation as rational functions. For a given equation as (1.1), in a SIMD architecture , the algorithm described here requires $O(max(km, (n+1)^2)$ using at most $(m^2(n+1))$ processors, where $(n+1)$ is the number of data points for interpolation, and k is the number of iterations to obtain an inverse(or Moore-Penrose inverse).

2 Solving a functional matrix equation – Principles

In a given field in which the functional matrix $A(x)$ and the functional vector $G(x)$ are contained, we can rewrite the equation (1.1) as
$$F(x) = A^{-1}(x)G(x) \qquad (1.2)$$
The procedure used for solving functional matrix equation is based on evaluation-interpolation [1]. This procedure consists of three main stages: (i) evaluates the given functional matrix $A(x)$ and function vector $G(x)$ at a certain number of required points $x = x_i$ to obtain a set of numerical matrices; (ii) obtains the Moore-Penrose inverses $A(x)^+$ of these numerical matrices of $A(x_i)$ instead of $A^{-1}(x_i)$; (iii) uses the values of the corresponding elements (the evaluated vectors of unknown vector $F(x_i)$), for rational interpolation of the solution of the equation $F(x)$.

Assuming that a set of numerical matrices and vectors are available at a certain number $n+1$ of points specified, we can express these matrices and vectors as $A(m, m, n+1)$ and $G(m, n+1)$ respectively. Then we have $A = \{a_{ijk}\}$ and $G(x) = g_{ik}$ where for $1 \leq i, j \leq m$, and $1 \leq k \leq n+1$. It is noted that the ith plane $A_3^{(i)}$ of A along the third dimension and the ith column $G_3^{(i)}$ of G corresponds to the evaluated values of $A(x)$ and $G(x)$ respectively at a given point x_i.

This algorithm carries out a cubic speed-up convergent iteration to find a Moore-Penrose inverse[3], that is , $Y_{k+1} = Y_k(I + \Delta Y_k + (\Delta Y_k)^2)$, here $\Delta Y_k = (I - AY_k)$. The iterative step begins with $Y_0 = \alpha A^T$ where $0 < \alpha < 2/trace(AA^T)$(where trace is the sum of the diagonal elements of a matrix). Some distinct advantages including reliability and stability of such a process are discussed in [6].

A extended version of the systolic algorithm [5] for rational interpolation is achieved to obtain a set of continued fraction $r_i(x)$ for $i = 1, 2, \cdot, n+1$ as the following, which corresponds to the solution of $F(x)$.

$$r_i(x) = p_0 + \frac{x - x_0}{p_1+} \frac{x - x_1}{p_2 - p_0+} \frac{x - x_2}{p_3 - p_1+} \cdots \frac{x - x_{n-1}}{p_n - p_{n-2}}$$

Then the rational interpolant $r_{k,l}(x)$ can be derived from the construction of the Pade approximant using the following recurrences: $g_{i+1} = g_i(p_{i+1} - p_{i-1}) + g_{i-1}(x - x_i)$;
$q_{i+1} = q_i(p_{i+1} - p_{i-1}) + q_{i-1}(x - x_i)$

where $1 \leq i \leq n-1$, and with initial values $g_0 = p_0; g_1 = p_0p_1 + (x - x_0); q_0 = 1; q_1 = p_1$.

3 Algorithms

Using matrices $U(m, 1, n+1)$ and $P(m, 1, n+1)$, we have $U_3^{(i)} = (A_3^{(i)})^+ \cdot G_3^{(i)}$ which corresponds to $F(x_i)$ and $\{p_{i11}, p_{i12}, \cdots, p_{i1(n+1)}\}$ of P for $r_i(x)$. Then, the procedure solving a functional matrix equation through rational interpolation can use data-level-parallelism, thus:

- The computation of the inverse of a matrix is achieved by inverting its point-wise evaluation matrix. This operation can be done independently in parallel at each selected point.

- The computation for rational interpolation is based on the fact that there are two vectors which are $\{x_0, x_1, \ldots, x_n\}$ and $\{u_{i11}, u_{i12}, \ldots, u_{i1n}\}$ for each element of the vector $F(x)$. Hence, in the stage 3 of the procedure all vectors along the direction of the dimension 3 of matrix $U(m, 1, n+1)$ can be used to generate the matrix P in parallel.

With these features, we provide two algorithms for the stage 2 and 3 of the procedure respectively.

a. g−Inversion

$Begin$
$\quad for \ l = 1, n + 1 \ do \ in \ parallel$
$\quad Begin$
$\qquad \alpha = 2/trace(A_3^{(l)} A_3^{(l)^T})$
$\qquad X0^{(l)} = \alpha_l A_3^{(l)^T}$
$\qquad X2^{(l)} = X0_3^{(l)}$
$\qquad while \ \epsilon \leq max \mid X1_3^{(l)} - X2_3^{(l)} \mid do$
$\qquad Begin$
$\qquad\quad X2_3^{(l)} = (I_3^{(l)} - A_3^{(l)} X0_3^{(l)})$
$\qquad\quad X1_3^{(l)} = X0_3^{(l)}(I_3^{(l)} + X2_3^{(l)}(I_3^{(l)} + X2_3^{(l)}))$
$\qquad\quad X2_3^{(l)} = X0_3^{(l)}$
$\qquad\quad X0_3^{(l)} = X1_3^{(l)}$
$\qquad End$
$\qquad X2 = 0.0$
$\qquad X2_2^{(l)} = G$
$\quad for \ i = 1, n + 1 \ do \ in \ parallel$
$\quad Begin$
$\qquad X1_3^{(i)} = X1_3^{(i)} X2_3^{(i)}$
$\quad End$
$\quad U = X1_2^{(1)}$
End

b. Rational Interpolation

$Begin$
$\quad if \ (u_{pqk} \neq u_{pql}) \ then \ subroutine \ ABORT$
$\quad \backslash * \ for \ 1 \leq p, q \leq m, j + 1 \leq k, l \leq n, k \neq l. * \backslash$
$\quad R = U$
$\quad P_3^{(0)} = 0$
$\quad for \ j = 1, n + 1 \ do$
$\quad Begin$
$\qquad P_3^{(j)} = R_3^{(j)}$
$\qquad for \ i = j + 1, n + 1 \ do$
$\qquad Begin$
$\qquad\quad S_3^{(i)} = R_3^{(j)}$
$\qquad Enddo$
$\qquad R_3^{(j+1,n+1)} = R_3^{(j+1,n+1)} - S_3^{(j+1,n+1)}$
$\qquad for \ h = j + 1, n + 1 \ do$
$\qquad Begin$
$\qquad\quad M_3^{(h)} = x_h - x_j$
$\qquad\quad R_3^{(h)} = M_3^{(h)}/R_3^{(h)}$
$\qquad\quad R_3^{(h)} = R_3^{(h)} + P_3^{(j-1)}$
$\qquad Enddo$
$\quad Enddo$
End

4 Implementation and Remarks

The algorithms in section 3 run on the Connection Machine in CM FORTRAN. Note that the most expensive part of the algorithm g−Inverse is the matrix multiplication and that the computations for all those plans $A_3^{(1)}, A_3^{(2)}, \cdots, A_3^{(n+1)}$ actually are able to be done in parallel independently, An extension of Cannon's algorithm has been developed to suit our application.

A simple modification of this algorithm can be used for solving (1.2) where $F(x)$ is a matrix by using a three dimension virtual processor set for rational interpolation. The use of the virtual processor set does not increase the complexity of the algorithm. For a more detailed discussion about the selection of given points for rational interpolation and the properties of Moore-Penrose inverses, see [6].

References

[1] E. V. Krishnamurthy, 'Error-Free Polynomial Matrix Computations' (Springer-Verlag, New York 1985).

[2] V. K. Murthy, E. V. Krishnamurthy and Pin Chen, 'Systolic Algorithm For Rational Interpolation and Padé Approximation', Parallel Computing, Vol. 18, pp.75-83, January 1992.

[3] E. V. Krishnamurthy and S. K. Sen, 'Numerical Algorithms'(Affiliated ,East-West Press, New Delhi 1986).

[4] A. Ben-Israel and T. N. E Greville, 'Generalized Inverses: Theory and Applications',(Wiley, New York, 1974).

[5] E. W. Cheney,'Introduction to Approximation theory',(McGraw Hill, New York, 1966).

[6] E. V. Krishnamurthy and Pin Chen, 'Polynomial Matrix Computation Using Data Parallel Evaluation-Interpolation' to appear in the Sixteenth Australian Computer Science Conference 1993.

Dynamic Tree Embeddings into de Bruijn Graphs

Sabine Öhring

Lehrstuhl Informatik I, Universität Würzburg, D-8700 Würzburg, Germany.
email : oehring@informatik.uni-wuerzburg.de

1 Definitions and Fundamental Results

Definition 1. : An *embedding* of a guest graph $G = (V_G, E_G)$ into a host graph $H = (V_H, E_H)$ is defined as tuple (f, g), where $f : V_G \to V_H$ and $g : E_G \to \mathcal{P}_H$ (set of paths in H), such that $g(\{u, v\})$ is a path in H connecting $f(u)$ and $f(v)$.

We present *dynamic task allocation* embeddings to map a dynamically developing task graph onto the host–nodes during runtime of the system, such that once a guest–node is placed on a processor, it cannot be moved. The quality of an embedding is measured by the values for *load, expansion, dilation* and *edge congestion*. (cf.[MS90])

Definition 2. : The *directed de Bruijn graph* $GDG(d, k)$ of base d and order k is the graph $(V_{d,k}, R_{d,k})$ with $V_{d,k} = \{x_{k-1} \ldots x_0 \mid x_i \in \mathbf{Z}_d$ for $0 \le i \le k-1\}$ and $R_{d,k} := \{(x_{k-1} \ldots x_0, x_{k-2} \ldots x_0 p) \mid p, x_i \in \mathbf{Z}_d, 0 \le i \le k-1\}$.

$SL_i(x) := x_{k-2} \ldots x_0 i$ is called the i-th Shift–Left neighbor of $x = x_{k-1} \ldots x_0 \in V_{d,k}$. For $d = 2$ we call $SL_i(x)$ SL–neighbor (SEL–neighbor) if $i = x_{k-1}$ ($i = \overline{x_{k-1}}$).

Definition 3. : A *complete d–ary tree* $CT(d, n) = (V_n^d, E_n^d)$ of height n is defined by $V_n^d := \{x_j \ldots x_0 | x_k \in \mathbf{Z}_d, 0 \le k \le j, 0 \le j \le n-1\} \cup \{e\}$ and $E_n^d := \{\{x, xa\} | x \in \mathbf{Z}_d^j, a \in \mathbf{Z}_d, 0 \le j \le n-1\}$, where e is the empty string. An *arbitrary d–ary tree* of height n is a connected subgraph of $CT(d, n)$ with at least one node at level n.

We add some new results concerning the structure of the de Bruijn graph to the properties already shown for example in [BP89], [Ö91], [SP89].

Lemma 4. : *The directed de Bruijn graph $GDG(d, k) = (V_{d,k}, R_{d,k})$ $(d \ge 2)$ can be represented as (V, R) with $V = \{0, 1, \ldots, d^k - 1\}$ and $R = \bigcup_{i=0}^{d-1} R_i$, where*
$R_i = \{\{x, y\} | y \in \{dx \bmod d^k, (dx + 1) \bmod d^k, \ldots, (dx + d - 1) \bmod d^k\},$
$\quad i \cdot d^{k-1} \le x \le (i + 1) \cdot d^{k-1} - 1\}$ *for* $0 \le i \le d - 1$.

(V, R_i), $0 \le i \le d - 1$, is a d-ary tree of height k with root $(i)^k$. Lemma 4 also induces that i different $CT(d, k - 1)$ can be embedded in $GDG(d, k)$ with dilation, edge congestion, and load simultaneous equal 1, and furthermore with expansion $\doteq \frac{d-1}{i}$ for $1 \le i \le d - 1$.

Lemma 5. : $GDG(d, k + n)$ *can be compressed into* $GDG(d, k)$ *with dilation 1, load d^n, and edge congestion d^n, for $n \in \mathbb{N} = \{0, 1, \ldots\}$.*

2 Dynamic Embeddings of Trees into de Bruijn Graphs

In many tree–structured algorithms the task graph develops in a way such that in each step a whole new level of leaves is generated or deleted, respectively.
With the help of Lemma 4 and Lemma 5 we can prove

Theorem 6. : *For $1 \leq i \leq d-1$, i different complete d-ary trees $CT(d,n)$ of height n can be dynamically embedded into a $GDG(d,k)$ with dilation 1, edge congestion $1 + i \cdot \max\left(0, \frac{d^{(n+1-k)}-1}{d-1}\right)$, and load $1 + i \cdot \max\left(0, \frac{d^{(n-k)}-1}{d-1}\right)$.*

Next we consider the situation that a d-ary tree to be embedded is dynamic in the sense that in each step only one tree–node is inserted or deleted. For that we develop a *randomized* embedding algorithm.

Theorem 7. : *There exists a dynamic embedding f of an arbitrary d-ary tree with M nodes into a $N := d^k$–node $GDG(d,k)$ with dilation 1, expansion $\frac{N}{M}$ and with high probability load and edge congestion of at most $\mathcal{O}(\frac{M}{N} + \log_d^2 N)$.*

Proof scheme : In the dynamically growing d-ary tree $T(d,M) = (V_M, E_M)$ of height h for each node v a permutation–value π_v of v is generated with $\pi_v : \mathbf{Z}_{d-1} \rightarrow \mathbf{Z}_{d-1}$. Dependent on π_v the (at most d) children of a node v are randomly mapped to one of the sons $SL_j(f(v))$, $j \in \mathbf{Z}_d$. $\pi_v(i) = i'$ means that the i-th son vi of the tree–node v, if it is ever generated, is mapped to $SL_{(y_{k-1}+i') \bmod d}(f(v))$, where $f(v) := y_{k-1} \ldots y_0$. The son $v(d-1)$ is mapped on the remaining Shift–Left neighbor of $f(v)$. f starts with mapping the root of $T(d,M)$ to the host–node $(0)^{k-1}1$.

For $d = 2$, we call π_v the flip-bit of v that decides whether the left son or the right son of the tree–node v is mapped to the SL- or to the SEL–neighbor of $f(v)$.

One verifies easily that the expected number of nodes $x \in S_l = \{x \in V_M | level(x) = l\}$ that are mapped on any processor is $\frac{|S_l|}{d^k}$. In addition, we have that the assignment of processors to tree–nodes in $S_{l+q_1 \cdot k}$ is independent from the assignment to nodes in $S_{l+q_2 \cdot k}$, for $q_1 \neq q_2; q_1, q_2 \in \{0, \ldots, \lfloor \frac{h-l}{k} \rfloor\}$. Therefore, the expected value of the number of tree–nodes in $\cup_{q=0}^{\lfloor \frac{h-l}{k} \rfloor} S_{l+q \cdot k}$ that are mapped to a single processor, is $\frac{M_{\bar{l}}}{N}$, where $M_{\bar{l}} = \sum_{q=0}^{\lfloor \frac{h-l}{k} \rfloor} |S_{l+q \cdot k}|$. Analogously to [LNRS89] we can conclude that f does not assign to any processor more than $\mathcal{O}(k^2 + \frac{M}{d^k})$ tree–nodes with high probability. The exhaustive proof can be found in the full version of this paper [Ö92].

References

[BP89]   J.C. Bermond and C. Peyrat. de Bruijn and Kautz networks : a competitor for the hypercube ? In *Hypercubes and Distributed Computers*, North–Holland, 1989. Elsevier Science Publishers.

[LNRS89] F.T. Leighton, M. Newmann, A.G. Ranade, and E. Schwabe. Dynamic Tree Embeddings in Butterflies and Hypercubes. In *Proceedings of the 1989 ACM Symposium on Parallel Algorithms and Architectures*, Santa Fe, NM, June 1989.

[MS90]   B. Monien and H. Sudborough. Embedding one Interconnection Network in Another. In *Computational Graph Theory*, Wien, 1990. Springer Verlag.

[Ö91]   S. Öhring. The de Bruijn Network : An Efficient Host for Static Embeddings of Various Program Structures. Technical report, TR 1028-91, Universität Würzburg, Lehrstuhl Informatik 1, 1991.

[Ö92]   S. Öhring. Dynamic Embeddings of Arbitrary Trees in de Bruijn Graphs. Technical report, TR 0307-92, Universität Würzburg, Lehrstuhl Informatik 1, 1992.

[SP89]   M.R. Samatham and D.K. Pradhan. The De Bruijn Multiprocessor Network: A Versatile Parallel Processing and Sorting Network for VLSI. In *IEEE Transactions on Computers, Vol. 38, No. 4*, April 1989.

Memory Access in Shared Virtual Memory *

Rudolf Berrendorf **

Zentralinstitut für Angewandte Mathematik
Forschungszentrum Jülich (KFA)
Postfach 1913, D-5170 Jülich, Germany

Abstract. Shared virtual memory (SVM) is a virtual memory layer with a single address space on top of a distributed real memory on parallel computers. We examine the behavior and performance of SVM running a parallel program with loop-level parallelism on top of it. A simulator for the underlying parallel architecture can be used to examine the behavior of SVM more deeply. The influence of several parameters, such as the number of processors, page size, cold or warm start, and restricted page replication, is studied.

1 Simulation of SVM

Examining the behavior of shared virtual memory on real machines is restricted to system parameters such as hardware page size or compiler and linker assistance in generating parallel programs. To study the behavior of SVM in detail, we have implemented a simulator that models the behavior of SVM on an abstract parallel machine. In the first step of the simulation process an appropriate parallel program trace is generated. In the second step the simulator takes this trace and several parameters and simulates the behavior of shared virtual memory on an abstract parallel machine. More details on our work can be found in [Ber92].

2 Simulation Results

As the input program for our simulations we used a parallel matrix multiply for a square matrix of size 64 × 64. An *jik* loop order was chosen, the two outer loops were parallelized. We express all execution times in multiples of *memory ticks*, where one memory tick should be seen as the cost to access one word in local memory on a node of the parallel machine. We distinguish between two types of initial page distributions. In the first type, which we call *cold start*, all pages are distributed uniformly over all nodes. In the *warm start* type, we run the simulation twice. The final page distribution of the first run gives the start distribution for the second run, which gives the overall result.

---

* This work was supported by the Applied Mathematical Sciences subprogram of the Office of Energy Research, U.S. Department of Energy, under Contract W-31-109-Eng-38.

** This work was performed when the author worked as a visiting scientist at the Mathematics and Computer Science Division, Argonne National Laboratory, Argonne, Ill.

2.1 Variation in page size

Most of the execution time with small page sizes (4-16 words) in the cold-start model is spent in getting pages the first time , because the initial data distribution is different from the initial demand of data on nodes. While small page sizes have this cold-start effect, large page sizes (1024 words) have contention problems as the number of processors increases. In the warm-start model, speedup results are up to 23 times higher than cold-start results. The reason is that, since all nodes already have copies of the read-only arrays, these pages do not need to be fetched. Problems preventing higher speedups are contention and false-sharing for the write-array, as well as parallel loop overhead. While loop overhead is due to our abstract machine model, the other problems are affected by large page sizes.

2.2 Different Access Order

For loop order *jik* in the matrix multiply, accesses to the write-array are done in subsequent order in memory under Fortran memory mapping of arrays. As loop iterations are spread in blocks over available processors, blocks of memory are written by the same processor such that write-sharing of pages is reduced. For an *ijk* loop order, written memory locations are accessed in smaller blocks in an interleaved fashion, and thus write sharing of pages occurs more often. In cold-start simulation, only medium to large page sizes with a small number of nodes show a significant performance reduction compared with the base case. For warm-start simulations, 64-node speedups show a significant performance degradation for medium to small page sizes. The reason is that now all iterations of the outer loop are spread over distinct nodes and subsequent memory locations are written by different processors.

2.3 Restriction of Page Copies

The space complexity for full information in a straightforward bit-vector approach means a quadratic increase with the number of processors. Agarwal et al. [ASHH88] proposed with their Dir_i—schemes a limitation of copies, thus restricting the information to be kept on each node; after this limit is reached, copies have to be invalidated. The results show that, for our implementation of matrix multiply, the limitation of copies means a severe restriction, as all nodes need partial copies of the read-only arrays. As long as the number of nodes is smaller than the copy limit, there is no difference from the base case. As soon as the number of nodes is larger than the copy limit, however, the system is blocked with invalidating pages, as pages are shared heavily between nodes. For a large number of nodes, page sharing is reduced, since smaller portions of the whole data are needed on every node.

References

[Ber92] Rudolf Berrendorf. Memory Access in Shared Virtual Memory. Technical report KFA-ZAM-IB9202, Forschungszentrum Jülich, 1992.

[ASHH88] Anant Agarwal, Richard Simoni, John Hennessy, and Mark Horowitz. An evaluation of directory schemes for cache coherence. In *15th Intl. Symposium on Computer Architecture*, pages 280–289. IEEE, 1988.

Parallel Implementations of Jacobi's Algorithm for the Eigensolution of Large Matrices using Array Processors.

J. S. Weston, Department of Computing Science, University of Ulster at Coleraine, Coleraine BT52 1SA, Northern Ireland.
M. Clint, Department of Computer Science, The Queen's University of Belfast, Belfast BT7 1NN, Northern Ireland.
C.W. Bleakney, Parallel Computer Centre, The Queen's University of Belfast, Belfast BT7 1NN, Northern Ireland.

Abstract. In this paper two distinct ways of implementating a parallel version of Jacobi's algorithm are examined and each is implemented in two ways using a language which permits the use of a virtual array processor of arbitrary size. The performances of the four implementations of the algorithm for the computation of the eigensolution of matrices of maximum order 512 are compared when executed on an AMT DAP 510 and on an AMT DAP 610.

1. Introduction.

The language Fortran-Plus Enhanced [1], together with its compiler, enables the implementation of an algorithm to be tailored to fit a virtual array processor whose edge size corresponds to that of either (i) the specific target machine or (ii) the maximum dimension of matrix or vector used in the application. In order to assess the relative efficiency of the code generated by the two approaches each was used to develop an implementation of Jacobi's algorithm in the modified form described by Modi and Pryce [2] and the execution times were compared.

2. Jacobi's Algorithm in the Modified Form of Modi and Pryce.

The Modi and Pryce version of Jacobi's algorithm for the computation of the eigensolution of a given matrix A, of order N, may be stated as follows:
Construct the sequence of parallel similarity transformations A_k and B_k according to

$$A_0 = A, \quad B_k = U_k^T * A_{k-1} * U_k, \quad A_k = V_k^T * B_k * V_k \qquad (1)$$

where U_k and V_k are symmetric tridiagonal matrices of order N, each of which represents an appropriately permuted set of parallel plane rotations. At each stage of construction the parallel plane rotations are chosen so that $INT(N/2)$ elements of B_k and $INT((N-1)/2)$ elements of A_k (and their main diagonal images) are reduced to zero. The permutations are required to ensure that all of the upper triangular elements of the matrix A are visited in a systematic fashion during the course of construction of each set of N similarity transformations. Whenever either A_k or B_k is diagonal to the required precision then the diagonal of whichever matrix has been diagonalised yields the eigenvalues of A, and the columns of either $Q_1 = U_1*V_1*U_2*V_2* \ldots \ldots *U_k*V_k$ or $Q_2 = U_1*V_1*U_2*V_2* \ldots \ldots *U_k$ are the eigenvectors of A.

3. Implementations of the Modi-Pryce Algorithm.

Initially, two implementations (PV1 and EV1) of the Modi-Pryce algorithm were constructed. The first is tailored specifically to the edge size of the target machine - 32 in the case of the DAP 510 and 64 in the case of the DAP 610. The second is tailored to suit a virtual array processor whose edge size corresponds to that of the given matrix A. In each case it was possible to develop special DAP multiplication routines for the computation of the matrices A_k, B_k, Q_1, and Q_2 which utilised the structure of the matrices U_k and V_k to great advantage. An analysis of A_k and B_k also revealed that, instead of using multiplication routines to evaluate their elements explicitly, it is possible to use algebraic expressions to evaluate them. Hence, two further implementations (PV2 and EV2) of the algorithm were developed from the corresponding earlier versions in that the computation of the matrices A_k and B_k was accomplished by the use of appropriate formulae rather than by matrix multiplications. Each implementation was used to compute the eigenvalues of a variety of real symmetric matrices of order N, $96 \le N \le 512$, using the AMT DAP 510 and the AMT DAP 610 array processors.

4. Conclusions.

The results suggest that the PV1 and PV2 implementations are significantly more efficient than their corresponding EV1 and EV2 implementations and that the difference in performances between them becomes more pronounced as the order of the given matrix increases. Further, each of these implementations appears to exhibit scaleable performance in that an array processor with twice the dimension of another improved the performance of each implementation by a factor which approaches the value four as the order of the matrix increases. The PV1 implementation is clearly the most efficient of the four implementations in all cases.

5. Acknowledgement.

The work was carried out using the facilities of the Parallel Computer Centre at the Queen's University of Belfast and the Centre for Parallel Computing, Queen Mary and Westfield College, London.

References.

1. Fortran-Plus Enhanced, man 102.01, AMT (1990)
2. Modi, J. J., and J. D. Pryce, Efficient Implementation of Jacobi's Diagonalisation Method on the DAP, Numer. Math. 46, (1985) 443-454.

A Parallel Architecture for a VLSI-Hardware-Realization of a Numerical Stable Variant of the Simplex-Method

Bernd Schütz, Reinhard Rauscher
University of Hamburg, Dept. of Computer Science
Troplowitzstr. 7, 2000 Hamburg 54, Germany
E-mail: schuetz@rz.informatik.uni-hamburg.dbp.de

Abstract. A hardware realization of the Simplex Method is represented. We customised the algorithm regarding numerical stability (arithmetics) and hardware proximity. The resulting hardware (VLSI custom chips, FPUs, RAM) of our accelerator is based on a parallel architecture with up to eight processing units.

1. Introduction

We present a hardware realization of the Simplex-Method, the most common and most efficient solution algorithm for linear programming [2]. Our objective was a fast and numerical stable implementation running in a PC/AT. This goal can only be achieved by using additional hardware. To overcome the limitation of commercially available software for such computers with our LP-accelerator hardware and to achieve a suitable numerical stability, we customized the implemented algorithm for our class of problems, also regarding alternative arithmetics. Next the algorithm has been parallized and transformed to a hardware-suited representation. By doing this a specialized tag-oriented parallel hardware architecture was developed [3]. Here the tag indicates zero-values. This was done due to the fact that typically 80 per cent of the operands in our problem-class are zero valued.

2. Architecture

The selected architecture as mentioned above consists of several PUs (Processing Units) connected to a shared memory for floating point values and controlled by the MCU (Master-Control-Unit). Each PU contains one FPU (Floating-Point-Unit), one LPU (Local-Processing-Unit), and a BSW (Bus-SWitch). The BSW realizes an interface between the LPU, the FPU and the floating point memory interface. The LCU consists of the program-ROM, register-file, integer-unit, status register and so on. The MCU only coordinates the PUs and contains the memory-management-unit. The MCU, LPU, and BSW are realized as custom chips.

In fig. 1 a typical configuration of the accelerator based on four PUs is sketched. The number of PUs can range from one to eight. Computer simulations of the architecture on the register-transfer-level showed that four floating-point-units give a suitable compromise of cost and performance. The realization of the architecture is currently under work at the University of Hamburg using the design systems from ES2 [1].

3. Results

Simulations of this architecture show that an IBM PC/AT equipped with one accelerator card gives a better performance than a SUN SPARCstation 2 running with our algorithm. Furthermore, the comparison with the Apollo demonstrates the speed-up that can be achieved by an application-specific architecture.

Problemsize	CPU-time/Pivotstep [ms]		
(constraints x variables)	LPA-4	Apollo DN3000	SUN SS2
61 x 69	11.7	318	8.4
118 x 52	13.9	625	20.5
88 x 116	12.1	524	14.1
166 x 77	67.2	1899	59.3
292 x 251	201.7	4168	230.8
94 x 88	32.0	692	38.0

Table 1: Some performance analyses

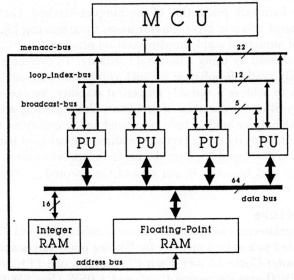

Figure 1: Overview of the accelerator architecture

References

[1] European Silicon Structures Ltd. *SOLO 2030 Release 3.1 Reference Manual.* Berkshire, 1991.

[2] Karl Heinz Borgward. *The Simplex Method - A Probabilistic Analysis.* Springer-Verlag, Berlin, 1987.

[3] A. Klindworth. *Entwurf, Simulation und Realisierung einer parallelen Rechnerarchitektur für ein revidiertes Simplex-Verfahren.* Diploma Thesis, Department of Computer Science, University of Hamburg, 1992

Generating Physical Channel Access Protocol Data Unit of CCSDS Recommendation by use of the Transputers and OCCAM

ZHANG.Lichen, GALINDO.Michel, MARQUIE.Daniel and RAYNAUD.Yves

IRIT/SIERA,
Université Paul Sabater
118 ROUTE DE NARBONNE
31062 TOULOUSE, FRANCE

Abstract: The basic goal of the project reported in this paper is to design an experimental multiprocessor system dedicated to the parallel simulation of the generation of Physical Channel Access Protocol Data Unit of CCSDS "Avanced Orbiting Systems". This paper first describes the characteristics of the application, and then presents the main problems and the actual design of the prototype system which is realized on the VLSI component Transputers and with the OCCAM language.

1. Introduction

CCSDS Advanced Orbiting Systems [1] will include manned and man-tended space stations, unmanned space platforms, free flying spacecraft and advanced space transportation systems operating at a very wide range of user data rates in an environment of extensive onboard and ground computer networking. In such systems, it is obvious that applications require surpersystem performance and also impose severe size, weight, power, and reliability constraints on acceptable solutions.

In this paper, we describe our research which aims at building a prototype which generates the Physical Channel Access Protocol Data Unit [1] that complies to the CCSDS Recommendations. We use the Transputers and OCCAM [2] to realize the prototype because they help to solve many problems dealing with concurrency and communication.

2. Prototype system

The simulator must be able to provide the Physical Channel Access Protocol Data Unit that complies to the CCSDS Recommendations and is identical with the Physical Channel Access Protocol Data Unit which is produced by an onboard generator. The primary requirements for this simulator are as follows:

1) to simulate application data and to create source packets, 2) to multiplex these different packets on a virtual channel, 3) to generate the transfer frame, 4) to add CRC or R-S code, insert the Synchronization marker and to serialize messages to generate Physical Channel Access Protocol Data Unit.

In our simulator, the system consists of five transputers made up from a Volvox 1/A board [3], which fits inside an IBM PC AT, containing one T425 processor and a Volvox 4/A board [3] containing four T425 processors. The executive software is written in the OCCAM language. This concurrent programming language and the VLSI component Transputer offer an effective solution for the application because they bridge the gap between the levels of specification, software architecture and hardware architecture. The fourth function is realized by a serial generator. This hardware communicates with Transputer network by an Inmos C012 link adaptor.

One important characteristic of the application is the great amount of communication between the Transputers. This causes message transfer delay. We evaluate the influence of various parameters on message delay. The following factors are of great importance to message delay: the number of processes on a processor, the message size, the probability of transfer message of processes, and the programming language constructs. Another problem is the allocation of processes[4] . The heuristic method is used in our application because it provides fast and effective algorithms for a suboptimum solution.

3.Conclusion

The experience acquired in the experimental process has shown that the amount of communication of our application is too great, the link between Transputer network and the serial generator is the bottleneck of the system and dynamic allocation of processes on Transputer network is difficult to realize.

References

1. CCSDS 700.0-G-2, Adavanced Orbiting Systems, Networks and Data links, October 1989.
2. E. Hirsh, Les Transputers: Application à la programmation concurrente, Editions Eyrolles 1990.
3. ARCHIPEL, VOLVOX-1/A Board and VOLVOX-4/A board, October 1990.
4. T.Muntean, E.Talbi, Méthodes de placement statique des processus sur architectures parallèles, T.S.I, Vol.10.n°5.1991.
5. Zhang.L, Galindo.M, Marquie.D, Raynaud.Y, Methodology of real-time system design with multiprocessors, In Proceedings of the Seventh Symposium on Microcomputer and Microprocessor Applications, Budapest, Hungary, April 1992.

Manifold: Concepts and Implementation

F. Arbab, I. Herman, P. Spilling
Centre for Mathematics and Computer Sciences
Department of Interactive Systems
Kruislaan 413, 1098 SJ Amsterdam, The Netherlands
Email: farhad@cwi.nl, ivan@cwi.nl, per@cwi.nl

June 11, 1992

ABSTRACT

Management of the communications among a set of concurrent processes arises in many applications and is a central concern in parallel computing and distributed computing. In this paper we introduce MANIFOLD: a coordination language for managing complex interconnections among sets of independent, concurrent, cooperating processes. The MANIFOLD system is suitable for massively parallel environments.

Keywords and Phrases: coordination language, MIMD, models of computation.

1 Introduction

MANIFOLD is a language whose sole purpose is to manage complex interconnections among independent, concurrent processes. Separating communication issues from the functionality of the component modules in a parallel system makes them more independent of their context, more reusable, and enables component modules to be programmed as a traditional sequential program which makes it easier to reuse existing sequential software. It also allows delaying decisions about the interconnection patterns of these modules, which may be changed subject to a different set of concerns. This idea is one of the main motivations behind the development of the MANIFOLD system.

2 The Manifold Language

The basic components in the MANIFOLD model of computation are *processes, events, ports,* and *streams.* A process is a *black box* with well defined ports of connection through which it exchanges *units* of information with the other processes in its environment. The internal operation of some of these black boxes are indeed written in the MANIFOLD language, which makes it possible to open them up, and describe their internal behavior using the MANIFOLD model. These processes are called *manifolds.* Other processes may in reality be pieces of hardware, programs written in other programming languages, or human beings. These processes are called *atomic processes* in MANIFOLD. In fact, an atomic process is any processing element whose external behavior is all that one is interested to observe at a given level of abstraction. In general, a process in MANIFOLD does not, and need not, know the identity of the processes with which it exchanges information. Figure 1 shows an abstract representation of a MANIFOLD process.

Interconnections between the ports of processes are made with *streams.* A stream represents a flow of a sequence of units between two ports. Streams are constructed and removed dynamically between ports of the processes that are to exchange some information.

Independent of the stream mechanism, there is an event mechanism for information exchange in MANIFOLD. Contrary to units in streams, events are *atomic* pieces of information that are *broadcast* by their sources in their environment. In principle, *any* process in an environment can pick up such a broadcast event. In practice, usually only a few processes pick up occurrences of each event, because only they are "tuned in" to their sources.

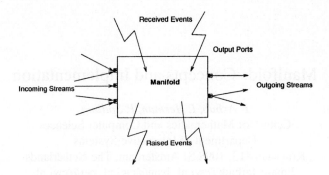

Figure 1: The model of a process in Manifold

Once an event is raised by a source, it generally continues with its processing, while the event occurrence propagates through the environment independently. Event occurrences are active pieces of information in the sense that in general, they are observed asynchronously and once picked up, they preemptively cause a change of state in the observer. Communication of processes through events is thus inherently asynchronous in MANIFOLD.

Each state in a manifold defines a pattern of connections among the ports of some processes. The corresponding streams implementing these connections are created as soon as a manifold makes a state transition (caused by an event) to a new state, and are deleted as soon as it makes a transition from this state to another one. The coexistence of event driven- and data driven control gives MANIFOLD a unique flavour.

3 Implementation

Due to space limitations not much can be said about the implementation. Our current implementation platform is Concurrent C++ [1]. The MANIFOLD system consists of a compiler which translates the MANIFOLD source code into an implementation independent intermediate format. This intermediate format is then translated by a macro processor into Concurrent C++ code, compiled by the Concurrent C++ compiler and linked with a run-time library.

4 Conclusions

The unique blend of event driven and data driven styles of programming, together with the dynamic connection graph of streams and the separation of coordination from compuation seem to provide a promising paradigm for parallel programming.

References

[1] N.H. Gehani and W.D. Roome, *Concurrent C++: Concurrent Programming with Class(es)*, Software - Practice and Experience, 1988, vol. 18, p. 1157-1177.

[2] F. Arbab, *Specification of Manifold*, Report in preparation, Centrum voor Wiskunde en Informatica, Amsterdam, 1992.

[3] F. Arbab and I. Herman, *Manifold: A Language for Specification of Inter-Process Communication*, Proceedings of the EurOpen Autumn Conference, A. Finlay ed., Budapest, September 1991, p. 127-144.

How to compile systems of recurrence equations into networks of communicating processes

M.C. EGLIN-LECLERC, J. JULLIAND, G.R. PERRIN

Laboratoire d'Informatique
Université de Franche-comté
25030 BESANCON Cedex
Phone : (33).81.66.64.51
Fax : (33).81.66.64.50
e-mail : julliand@comte.uucp

<u>Keywords</u> : parallel programming, asynchronous interpretation, program translation

Introduction –

The recent development realized about parallel and distributed architectures has given rise to lots of activities of research. Some of these ones try to define new formal methods for the design of algorithms implemented on such machines. Thus regarding synchronous ones, we could talk about lots of works (for example systolic network design). Whereas, regarding asynchronous machines, it seems that few tools of design, of parallelization, of debugging and of evaluation exist.

Then we propose to enrich the knowledge in this domain by bringing forth a new method. It derives parallel asynchronous algorithms implemented on a communicating processes architecture from a problem expression written as a set of recurrence equations in the LEQ language.

The LEQ language –

Syntax –

 Variables are sequences of values as in LUSTRE : $y = nat \times 2$.

 Equations can be recurrent : $nat = 1 \rightarrow pre\ nat + 1$.

 A program is a system of uniform recurrence equations

$$\begin{cases} nat = 1 \rightarrow pre\ nat + 1 \\ y = nat \times 2 \end{cases}$$

Semantics –

 asynchronous interpretation.

Formal method –

goal : *Compiling equations in communicating processes.*

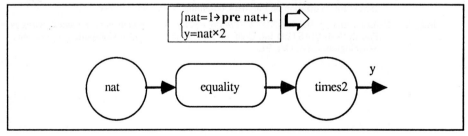

Principle : *Transforming an equational system by analysing the data-flow dependences graph.*

Steps :

 Spliting the equations into communications and calculations.

 Creation of a new equational system based on producer-consumer systems :

product :

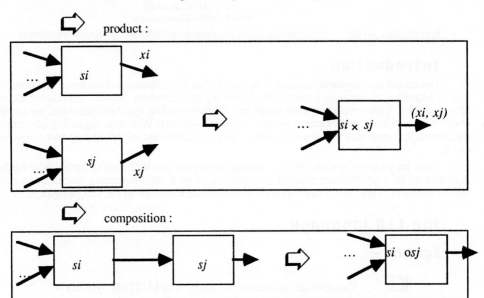

composition :

Introduction of equality communication and identity calculation.

 Compiling recurrence equations into processes.

Implementation –

This derivation method is implemented on SUN station with the programming language development software Centaur.

Réfèrences –

M.C. EGLIN-LECLERC. *Compilation de systèmes d'équations récurrentes en réseaux de processus communicants*. Thèse de doctorat, Université de Franche-Comté, 1991.

M.C. EGLIN-LECLERC, J. JULLIAND - *Translating equational system into communicating processes.* ISMM Int. Workshop on Parallel Computing, Trani, Italie, 1991.

M.C. EGLIN-LECLERC. J. JULLIAND - *Compiling equations in asynchronous communicating processes.* Fourth ISMM/IASTED Int. Conf. on Parallel & Distributed Computing & Systems, Washington, USA, Oct. 91.

PARALLEL ALGORITHMS SIMULATION APPLIED TO DIFFERENTIAL - ALGEBRAIC SYSTEMS, AND ELECTRICAL NETWORK APPLICATION.

M.Bahi.
Scientific Calculus Laboratory. Besançon

Introduction. In this paper a differential algebraic problem is considered. the convergence of asynchronous iterations follows from [1]. A simulation of parallel computation is shown, and the results are applied to electrical networks.

1.The problem considered.

The problem considered here is in the form:

$$\begin{cases} f(x'(t),x(t),y(t),t) = 0 \\ g(x(t),y(t),t) = 0 \quad ; \text{ where}: t \in [t_0,t_0+\eta] \\ \quad\quad x(t_0) = x_0 \quad\quad \eta > 0 \end{cases}$$

This problem can be write in the shape of blocks:

$$\begin{cases} F(X'(t),X(t),Y(t),t) = 0 \\ G(X(t),Y(t),t) = 0 \; . \\ \quad\quad X(t_0) = X_0 \end{cases}$$

2.The fixed point mapping.

Under some hypotesis on F and G, we define the mapping: $T(W,U,V) = (Z,X,Y)$ such that:

$$\begin{cases} F_i(W_1,\ldots,W_{i-1},X'_i,W_{i+1},\ldots,W_\alpha;U_1,\ldots,U_{i-1},X_i,U_{i+1},\ldots \\ \quad\quad\quad\quad\quad\quad\quad\quad\quad ;V;t) = 0 \\ G_i(U;V_1,\ldots,V_{i-1},Y_i,V_{i+1},\ldots,V_\beta,t) = 0 \\ \quad\quad\quad\quad\quad\quad Z_i(t) = X'_i(t) \\ \quad\quad\quad\quad\quad X_i(t_0) = X_{i0} \end{cases}$$

Theorem.

If η is sufficiently small, then every asynchronous algorithm corresponding to T converges to the solution of the problem .

3.Numerical results.

We considered a simple electrical network and we computed the totaly time, the communication time and the computation time. A and E are respectively the accelearation and the efficiency .

Numbre of processors	With Communication		Without Comm.	
	A	E	A	E
2	1.57	0.79	1.43	0.71
4	2.84	0.71	2.38	0.60

fig 1. Acceleration and efficiency

References.

1.M.Bahi:Algorithmes asynchrones pour des systèmes différentiels algébriques. Simulation numérique sur des exemples de circuits électriques.Thesis University of Franche-Comté (1991).
2.H.T.Kung: Synchronized and asynchronous parallel algorithms for multiprocessors. Algorithms and Complexity, ed.J.F.Traub, New York Academic Press (1976), 153-200.
3.E.Lelarasmee, A.Ruehli, A.Sangiovanni :The waveform relaxation method for time domain analysis of VLSI circuits.Univ.California, Berkley, UCB/ERL-M81/75 (1981).

Optimal Performances and Scheduling for Parallel Algorithms with Equal Cost Tasks

Z. Mahjoub and F. Karoui-Sahtout

Faculte des Sciences de Tunis
Dept Informatique - Belvedere 1060 - TUNISIA

Abstract. (PA) being a parallel algorithm involving n equal cost tasks, we study the $P(\tau)$ problem of determining the minimum required number of processors π to execute (PA) in minimum time τ regardless of communication costs. We use a binary search strategy based on a critical path oriented scheduling heuristic. $O(n+m)$ to $O([n\log n+m]\log n)$ steps are required to compute a near optimal solution where m is the number of precedence constraints. A generalization to the problem $P(t)$ ($\forall t > \tau$) and to the non equal cost tasks case is then easily introduced.

1 Introduction

(PA) is a parallel algorithm involving n tasks assumed for sake of clearness to be of same cost c and related by a linear precedence order, G its m-arcs redundancy-free DAG and τ the cost of a critical path in G. Our aim (an NP-Complete problem) is to compute the minimum required number of processors π to reach τ. We refer to [1], [3] for more details on these points.

2 Earliest/Latest Schedulings and Bounds

Let $h=\tau/c$ be the height of G, De(G) and Dl(G) its earliest and latest decompositions of widthes we and wl. If De(G)$\equiv$Dl(G), G is a critical DAG, all the tasks are critical and we=wl=π. If not, G involves a critical subgraph Gc of width wc and we have wl=max(wc, $\lceil n/h \rceil$)$\leq\pi\leq$min(we,wl)=w2. Hence π is to be searched within [w1,w2].

3 Binary Search Strategy (BSS)

We adopt a binary search strategy to find π. Let [lb,ub] be the current search interval (we start with [w1,w2-1]). We have to design a scheduling of length τ with $p=\lfloor(lb+ub)/2\rfloor$ processors. If this can be achieved we set ub=p-1 else lb=p+1 and the procedure is iterated whilst lb≤ub. If no scheduling can ever be designed then π=w2.

4 Predecessor Oriented Heuristic (POH)

The τ-scheduling needed at each step of (BSS) is designed by means of a predecessor oriented heuristic (POH) similar to the critical path method. Let G'=G\Gc and L the list of the tasks of G' sorted in increasing latest starting times (ILST) [1,2]. (POH) constructs a decomposition of G of width p by assigning each task in L to an appropriate one among the h levels of G (note that the tasks of Gc are directly assigned once De(G) and Dl(G) are known). Once a task cannot be assigned (POH) is left.

5 Complexity Analysis & Generalization

O(n+m) steps are needed to get De(G) and Dl(G). In (POH) we need in addition O(nlogn) steps to get L and O(n+m) for the assignement. As w2-w1= O(n), thus the whole algorithm requires O(n+m) to O([nlogn+m]logn) steps.
For any t>τ, the P(t) problem can be easily solved by applying the above approach to an "expanded" DAG Ge of G of height he=t/c unstead of h. When the tasks of G are not of same cost but mutually commensurable, each task is splitted into equal cost subtasks and the above study may be applied with a slight modification [1,2].

References

1. M.Cosnard and Y.Robert, Tech. & Sc. Inf 6, 115-125 (1987)
2. K.Hwang and F.Briggs, Computer Architecture and Parallel Processing (Mc Graw-Hill,1984)
3. Z.Mahjoub and F.Karoui-Sahtout, Par. Comp. 17, 471-481 (1991)

Load Balancing in a Neighbourhood-based Multiprocessor

Gary Tan and Wei-Ngan Chin

Department of Information Systems and Computer Science
National University of Singapore, Singapore 0511

1 Introduction

The Flagship project started with the aim of harnessing the power of a multiprocessor to exploit the parallelism inherently available in declarative languages. As the project developed, the Flagship machine was envisaged to be a complete declarative multiprogramming system [1]. This paper discusses a neighbourhood scheduling scheme, where processes with insufficient parallelism are restricted to execute only on a subset (neighbourhood) of the processors. A novel method of propagating activity levels is described which enables load balancing within the neighbourhoods to be performed.

2 The Flagship Parallel Reduction Machine

The Flagship Machine executes programs using graph reduction, implemented using a SuperCombinator Model of computation. The architecture of the machine comprises a collection of tightly-coupled processor-store pairs interconnected by a multi-stage *delta* message-passing communication network, formed using identical stages of perfect shuffle interconnections of 2x2 crossbar switches.

Because of the dynamic nature of graph reduction, Flagship distributes work dynamically to 'map' sub-graphs produced at run-time over the processors. This requires a means of ascertaining the global busyness of the system so that a processor can send work to a less busy one. This is achieved by propagating *activity* information backwards through the network. A register termed the *local activity level* (LAL) register holds the activity information for each processor. Each output port of a network switch has a register which holds the activity information. At each switch the two activities are compared and the minimum is transmitted to the preceding stage. In this way the minimum activity is progressively propagated backwards through the switches until it reaches the processors; here it is stored in the *global activity level* (GAL) register for each processor. By comparing the LAL and the GAL each processor can determine whether other processors are less busy than itself to export work.

3 The Neighbourhood Scheme

A possible way of executing the processes will be to allow each process to be exportable to all processors. This may not be desirable for programs with insufficient parallelism as it may result in performance degradation; such programs may give rise to excessive overheads associated with exporting work to other processors, viz. increased remote copying and system software overheads associated with the setting up of a process in each processor.

It is more efficient if such programs are restricted to run on only a subset of the processors. In [1], Sargeant proposes a scheme which partitions the processors into neighbourhoods (nbh) based on their binary identifiers. In a machine with N processors, each processor can be given a k-bit binary identifier, where $2^{k-1} < N \leq 2^k$. The m-nbh of a processor is a subset of the N processors whose identifiers differ only in the least significant m bits, e.g. in an 8-pe machine, for pe 0, the 0-nbh is {000}, the 1-nbh is {000,001}, the 2-nbh is {000,001,010,011}, and the 3-nbh is all eight processors. Each program is initially loaded into a processor of its chosen m-nbh. When a task needs to be exported, the switches will route the message according to the bits of the preferred processor upto the last m significant bits (i.e. the last m stages); thereafter the load balancing scheme will take over the routing. In this way, the process is confined to execute within its neighbourhood.

However, the present scheme lacks a method for load balancing within each neighbourhood. Currently, only the minimum activity of the entire machine is known. This information is inadequate for making decisions about exporting work within each neighbourhood. We propose a method of propagating activities backwards through the network which will enable the minimum activity of each neighbourhood to be determined, thus allowing load balancing to be carried out.

---

[1] multiprogramming the machine was investigated in the 1st author's Ph.D research at Manchester University.

Instead of having only a single global activity register (GAL), each processor must now have a set of activity registers - one for each possible neighbourhood. In a delta-network which is connected via perfect shuffling at each stage, the minimum activities of all m-nbhs can be obtained by performing *comparisons* during the first m stages of the switches. Here, each switch compares its two activities and propagates the minimum. After m stages of comparisons, the minimum activities of the m-nbhs will have been computed. These can then be propagated *straight-through* the remaining $k - m$ stages of switches to reach their respective neighbourhoods.

Figure 1 shows the propagation of the 1-nbh activities (from right to left), where comparisons are doned in the first stage followed by straight-through propagation in the last two stages. Note that minimum activity levels of the m-nbhs are obtained after m stages of comparisons. Straight-through propagation after the m-th stage simply sends these activity levels to the processors of each neighbourhood.

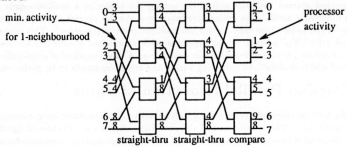

Figure 1: Propagating 1-neighbourhood minimum activities through the network

4 Preliminary Results

To evaluate the neighbourhood scheme, two sets of experiments were conducted on a Flagship simulator. In the first set, two each of four benchmark programs, nfib(20), 8-queens, matrix multiply(20) and binary integration, were multiprogrammed in an 8-pe machine. These programs were loaded into a processor and allowed to be exported to all the processors.

It is known that nfib and queens give near to ideal speedups, matmult gives the worst while binint is intermediate between the two cases. This gives an idea of how to restrict the programs within neighbourhoods. In an 8-pe machine, it would be possible to restrict matmult to a 1-nbh, binint to a 2-nbh, and both nfib and queens can be allowed to run on all the processors. Another set of experiments using this configuration was performed.

The results show that the mean turnaround is reduced by 11.5%, and the network activity is reduced by 39.4% for the machine employing the neighbourhood scheme. This is because when a program with insufficient parallelism (e.g. matmult) is restricted within a subset of the processors, less work is performed in the setting up of the process tables. There is also increased locality of data and code, resulting in less work being exported and less remote-copying.

5 Conclusion and Further Work

This paper has described a neighbourhood scheme for a declarative multiprocessor with a delta network. With this scheme, a process with insufficient parallelism can be constricted to execute on a subset of the processors, with load balancing applied within the subset. Preliminary results show that such a scheme leads to reduced mean turnaround time, system overheads and network activity.

One area currently under investigation is the expansion and contraction of neighbourhoods, depending on the load of the machine. With the neighbourhood scheme, a situation may arise where processes with larger neighbourhoods complete their execution, while a process with a smaller neighbourhood is still running. It may be useful in this case to expand the neighbourhood of the process to utilise the other processors which will otherwise be left idle.

References

[1] J.Sargeant, "Multiple Processes in the IRM", Internal Report, Dept. of Computer Science, University of Manchester, UK, Jan 87.

A DAP-based Implementation of a Portable Parallel Image Processing Machine

D Crookes and A P McHale

Department of Computer Science, The Queen's University of Belfast, Belfast BT7 1NN, UK

N Beney

Institut de Mathematique et d'Informatique, Universite de Neuchatel, Switzerland

Abstract The IAL machine is a simple hypothetical architecture designed to support the high level image processing language IAL, developed at Queens University Belfast. IAL is intended to be a machine independent programming language capable of parallel implementation on a range of different parallel architectures. The IAL portable compiler generates code for the IAL portable parallel abstract machine (PPAM). This paper discusses a prototype implementation of the IAL PPAM on the AMT DAP. An interpretive approach has been adopted, using Fortran-Plus Enhanced as the implementation language.

1   Introduction

Portability with efficiency is an important and much sought after goal, even if it is not immediately attainable. In addressing this problem, we have deliberately adopted an application-specific approach. To date, we have concentrated on image processing applications, and have considered the design of an abstract machine specifically for parallel image processing.

The IAL PPAM[1] is a very simple abstract machine whose instruction set is based on aspects of Image Algebra Language (IAL[2]), which in turn was based on Image Algebra. In IAL, operations are specified at the complete image level (rather than the individual pixel level). The language recognises the fundamental role of neighbourhood operations in low level image processing, in which a small window (or *template*) is passed over the whole image. IAL provides templates as basic operands, and has a set of built-in operators which take an image and a template and produce an image result in a single neighbourhood operation. IAL was originally implemented on a transputer network by translating IAL into occam[3]. As a means of developing a portable implementation of IAL, we have adopted the abstract machine approach by designing the IAL PPAM, and developing interpreters for this machine to run on a range of different parallel architectures, including the AMT DAP. The interpretive approach does not necessarily involve significant overheads as opposed to generating object code, since many of the IAL PPAM instructions are very powerful and involve a lot of computation.

2   Architecture of the IAL PPAM

The overall design for our portable parallel pseudo-architecture is to have a (scalar) front end, with a parallel co-processor (in rather the same way that a microprocessor might have a floating point co-processor to speed up arithmetic operations).

PPAM Data Objects

In addition to typical data structures for abstract machines, the PPAM supports several image processing-specific types of data object, including *Images* and *Templates*.

PPAM Instruction Set

In addition to sequential control and scalar operations, the PPAM instruction set supports operations on the above application-specific data structures, including:

> *For creating data structures, dynamically*
> *For performing image-level calculations*
> > e.g. point-to-point, and neighbourhood operations such as convolution.
> *For image input and output*

3   Implementation on the DAP

The above model of the IAL PPAM (controller+co-processor) maps well on to the usual configuration in which a DAP is front-ended by a SUN workstation. The SUN acts as the (sequential) controller, and the DAP itself acts as the parallel co-processor.

Data Storage

All scalar data (integers, reals, strings, etc., and non-parallel arrays) and templates are held on the SUN host. Images are held, as 2–D arrays, on the DAP (the co-processor). Our implementation represents all images internally as *real* (floating point) images.

Operations

All scalar operations are carried out on the SUN controller. Only for operations involving images is the DAP co-processor invoked. The co-processor provides a set of routines which can be called remotely by the controller, with parameters being passed in a COMMON block prior to call. (Image parameters are merely reference numbers).

To minimise the number of routines which are resident on the DAP (to reduce code space overheads), there is a relatively small number of co-processor operations. The main ones are as follows:

> *image_image*   (the operator is passed in a common block)
> *image_scalar*   (the operator is passed in a common block)
> *image_template*   (the neighbourhood operator is passed in a common block)
> *image_function*   (a number representing the function to be applied is passed)

References

1   D Crookes and P J Morrow, 'Design considerations for a portable parallel abstract machine for low level image processing', Proc. BCS Workshop on Abstract Machine Models for Highly Parallel Computers, Vol 2. Leeds, March 1991. pp.107–110.

2   D Crookes, P J Morrow and P J McParland, 'IAL: a parallel image processing programming language', IEE Proceedings, Vol 137, No. 3, June 1990. pp. 176–182.

3   P J Morrow, D Crookes and P J McParland, 'Notes on implementing an algebra-based image processing language on a multi-transputer network', Proc. International Conference on Applications of Transputers, Liverpool, August 1989.

The design of a parallel algorithm to solve the word problem for free partially commutative groups

Joaquim Gabarró *

Dept. de Llenguatges i Sistemes Informàtics, Universitat Politècnica de Catalunya
Pau Gargallo 5 , 08028 Barcelona, Spain

The study of algorithms implemented in fine-graned machines is a fundamenel domain in today computer science. A basic parallel computational model are boolean circuits Given $k > 0$ the class NC^k is defined as the class of problems solvable by uniform family of circuits of *size* $n^{O(1)}$ and *depth* $O(\log^k n)$. NL is the class of problems solvables in nondeterministic log space. Finally we consider the closure under NC^1 reductions of NL called NL^*. Finally AC^0 is the class of solvable problems with unbounded fan-in circuits of constant depth.

Free partially commutative groups were introduced by C. Wrathall [Wr88] to extend free partially commutative monoids [Ma88] to groups. To do this, consider a pair (Σ, θ) where Σ is a finite and $\theta \subseteq \Sigma \times \Sigma$ is a symmetric and irreflexive relation and extend Σ as $\hat{\Sigma} = \Sigma \cup \overline{\Sigma}$ with $\{(x\overline{x}, \lambda), (\lambda, x\overline{x}) \mid x \in \Sigma\}$ and extend θ as $\hat{\theta} = \theta \cup \{(\overline{x}, y), (x, \overline{y}), (\overline{x}, \overline{y}) \mid (x, y) \in \theta\}$. Therefore $f \sim g$ when

$$(f = f_1 x\overline{x} f_2 \wedge g = f_1 f_2) \vee (f = f_1 \overline{x} x f_2 \wedge g = f_1 f_2) \vee (f = f_1 uv f_2 \wedge g = f_1 vu f_2 \wedge (u, v) \in \hat{\theta}).$$

Writting the transitive reflexive closure as $\overset{*}{\sim}$ the *word-problem* takes $(\hat{\Sigma}, \hat{\theta})$ and $f, g \in \hat{\Sigma}^*$ as input asking if $f \overset{*}{\sim} g$ holds. A dependency graphs [Ma88] is a triple $\gamma = (V, R, \varphi)$ over (Σ, θ) where V is a finite set called the nodes of γ, $R \subseteq V \times V$ is the set of arcs and $\varphi : V \to \Sigma$ is the labelling, if the following conditions two hold $R \cup R^{-1} \cup \{(v, v) \mid v \in V\} = \{(v, v') \in V \times V \mid (\varphi(v), \varphi(v')) \in \overline{\theta}\}$ (dependence connectivity) and $R^+ \cap \{(v, v) \mid v \in V\} = \emptyset$ (acyclicity). We write $\Gamma(\Sigma, \theta)$ for the set of dependency graphs. Two dependency graphs γ and δ are isomorphic, $\gamma \simeq \delta$, when there exists a bijection of nodes preserving labelling and arc connections. Given a word $w = x_1 \ldots x_n \in \Sigma^*$ we define the dependency graph associated to w as $d(w) = (V_w, R_w, \varphi_w)$ where $V_w = \{1, \ldots, n\}$, $\varphi_w(i) = x_i$ and $R_w = \{(i, j) \mid (i < j) \wedge (x_i, x_j) \in \overline{\theta}\}$. A linearization of γ is a word w such that $\gamma \simeq d(w)$.

Lemma 1:

- Given (Σ, θ) and $\gamma = (V, R, \varphi)$ verify if $\gamma \in \Gamma(\Sigma, \theta)$ it is NL^* complete.

- Given $\gamma = (V, R, \varphi)$ and $\delta = (V', R', \varphi')$ we have that $\gamma \simeq \delta$ iff for all i such that $0 \leq i \leq \max\{\#(\gamma), \#(\delta)\}$ we get (*rank* (v) is the length of longest path arriving to v).

$$\{\varphi(v) \mid v \in V, rank\ (v) = i\} = \{\varphi'(v) \mid v \in V', rank\ (v) = i\}$$

* Research supported by the ESPRIT II Basic Research Actions Program of the EC under contract No. 3075 (project ALCOM). E-mail contact: gabarro@lsi.upc.es

- Given (Σ, θ) and $\gamma = (V, R, \varphi)$ and $\delta = (V', R', \varphi')$ test if $\gamma, \delta \in \Gamma(\Sigma, \theta)$ and $\gamma \simeq \delta$ is an NL^* complete problem.

- Given (Σ, θ) and $\gamma \in \Gamma(\Sigma, \theta)$ we can find in NL^* a word $w \in \Sigma^*$ such that $d(w) \simeq \gamma$.

- Given (Σ, θ) and $w \in \Sigma^*$ we can find in AC^0 the graph $d(w)$.

Consider $(\hat{\Sigma}, \hat{\theta})$ and write the set of dependency graphs as $\Gamma(\hat{\Sigma}, \hat{\theta})$. Given $\gamma = (V, R, \varphi)$ we write $\overline{\gamma} = (V, \overline{R}, \overline{\varphi})$, where $\overline{R} = R^{-1}$ and $\overline{\varphi}(z) = \overline{\varphi(z)}$. Let us transform $\Gamma(\hat{\Sigma}, \hat{\theta})$ in a reduction system $(\Gamma(\hat{\Sigma}, \hat{\theta}), \Rightarrow)$. Given $\gamma, \delta \in \Gamma(\hat{\Sigma}, \hat{\theta})$ such that $\gamma = (V, R, \varphi)$, we write $\gamma \Rightarrow \delta$ when there are $v, v' \in V$ (called a pair of reducible elements) and $z \in \hat{\Sigma}$ such that: first, $\varphi(v) = z$, $\varphi(v') = \overline{z}$, second, the longest directed path connecting v and v' has length 1 and third $\gamma \setminus \{v, v'\} \simeq \delta$. We write the set of all irreducible elements as $IRR(\Gamma)$ and $IRR(\gamma)$ is the set of irreducible elements obtained from γ.

Lemma 2: The basic properties of $(\Gamma(\hat{\Sigma}, \hat{\theta}), \Rightarrow)$ are:

- When $\mu \Leftarrow \gamma \Rightarrow \delta$ then or $\mu \simeq \delta$ or exists γ' such that $\mu \Rightarrow \gamma' \Leftarrow \delta$.

- Any element γ has one irreducible written as $IRR(\Gamma)$.

- Given $(\hat{\Sigma}, \hat{\theta})$ and $\gamma = (V, R, \varphi)$ test if $\gamma \in IRR(\Gamma)$ it is NL^* complete.

- Given $\gamma, \delta \in IRR(\Gamma)$, we have $\gamma \circ \delta \Rightarrow \rho$ iff there exist $z \in \hat{\Sigma}$ and $\gamma', \delta' \in IRR(\Gamma)$ such that $\gamma \simeq \gamma' \circ z$, $\delta \simeq \overline{z} \circ \delta'$ and $\rho \simeq \gamma' \circ \delta'$.

- Given $\gamma, \delta \in IRR(\Gamma)$ and $k \geq 1$ we have $\gamma \circ \delta \overset{k}{\Rightarrow} \rho$ iff there exist $\mu, \gamma', \delta' \in IRR(\Gamma)$ such that $\#(\mu) = k$ and $\gamma \simeq \gamma' \circ \mu$, $\delta \simeq \overline{\mu} \circ \delta'$ and $\rho \simeq \gamma' \circ \delta'$.

- The inverses verify $\overline{\gamma \circ \delta} = \overline{\delta} \circ \overline{\gamma}$, $IRR(\gamma \circ \overline{\gamma}) = \lambda$, $IRR(\overline{\gamma \circ \delta}) = IRR(IRR(\overline{\delta}) \circ IRR(\overline{\gamma}))$.

- Given $(\hat{\Sigma}, \hat{\theta})$ and $\gamma, \delta \in IRR(\Gamma)$ we can find in NL^* the graph $IRR(\gamma \circ \delta)$.

- Fixed (Σ, θ), and given any $\gamma \in \Gamma(\Sigma, \theta)$ we can find in NC^3 the graph $IRR(\gamma)$.

Theorem 3: The word problem for free partially commutative groups belongs to NC^3.

Sketch of the proof. Given $(\hat{\Sigma}, \hat{\theta})$ and γ, δ, first we verify whether $\gamma, \delta \in IRR(\Gamma)$, second we find $IRR(\gamma)$ and $IRR(\delta)$ and finally we test if both graphes are isomorphic. All this process can be done in NC^3.

References.

[Ma88] Mazurkiewicz, A.: *Basic Notions of Traces*, Lecture Notes in Computer Science **354** (1989) 285–363.

[Wr88] Wrathall , C.: The word problem for free partially commutative groups. *J. Symbolic Computation* **6** (1988) 99–104.

A VLSI Multigrid Poisson Solver Amenable to Biharmonic Equation

Marián Vajteršic
Institute of Control Theory and Robotics
Slovak Academy of Sciences
Bratislava, Czecho-Slovakia

Abstract. A VLSI parallel algorithm for solving discretized Poisson equation on an NxN grid is proposed. A standard multigrid algorithm is adopted which allows a parallel solution of this problem in $T = O(logN)$ time steps. A special network consisting of NxN processor elements and of $O(NlogN)$ interconnection lines in each direction results in a design the area of which is $O(N^2 log^2 N)$. Thus, the AT^2 estimation for this Poisson solver is $O(N^2 log^4 N)$ which improves the best result known until now by factor of $O(N/logN)$.

An application of the multigrid Poisson solver is made to a VLSI semidirect biharmonic solver. The VLSI layout needs an area $A = O(N^3 logN)$ and the time of algorithm is $O(\sqrt{N} log^2 N)$. The total complexity for the VLSI biharmonic solver is $AT^2 = O(N^4 log^5 N)$ which is of the same order as for the best algorithms developed until now.

1 Introduction

Elliptic partial differential equations belong to a class of those large scale problems which are amenable for parallel computing. Among them, Poisson and biharmonic equation are frequently solved in computational practice.

Reflecting a variety of parallel computer architectures there exist effective algorithms for numerical solving these model problems [5,7]. A new trend in parallel algorithm design is oriented towards exploiting the advantages of the VLSI (Very Large Scale Integration) technology. Besides the parallel computational time (T), an additional attitude occuring in the classification of VLSI algorithms is area(A) of a chip which is needed for a layout of the algorithm in a silicon.

2 A VLSI Poisson Solver

A VLSI solver developed is based on the standard multigrid algorithm [3]. The multigrid principle which is widely used for solving grid-like problems can be effectively parallelized. In order to implement it in VLSI, one has to pay a special attention to the interprocessor communication lines. We have designed a special network which allows to solve an NxN Poisson problem on a chip with an area of size $O(NlogN)xO(NlogN)$. Since the time of the algorithm is proportional to the number of grids which is $O(logN)$, the global area-time complexity of the Poisson multigrid solver is $AT^2 = O(N^2 log^4 N)$. This result represents a significant improvement against the best designs published hitherto ($O(N^3 log^4 N)$ and $O(N^3 log^3 N)$ in [1] and [6] respectively).

3 A VLSI Biharmonic Solver

A natural consequence of a development of a fast Poisson solver is to try to implement it in solving the biharmonic equation. It is due to fact that one group of effective biharmonic solvers is based on the semidirect approach which treats the biharmonic operator in a splitted form as a coupled pair of Laplace operators. The semidirect method computes the solution iteratively where one iteration consists of solving two discrete Poisson equation and two smoothing vector formulas [2,5,7].

The VLSI multigrid Poisson solver developed is used in a VLSI design for semidirect solution of the biharmonic equation on an NxN grid. The design is of aa length $O(NlogN)$ according to the length of each of the two VLSI Poisson solvers. However, the height is $O(N^2)$ because of the wiring needed to transmit an NxN array of data to an other array of the same size. Since the time for solving one Poisson equation is $O(logN)$, one iteration of the semiderect process costs $O(logN)$ time steps. The number of iterations required to obtain a solution with an initial error reduced by $O(N^{-2})$ is $O(\sqrt{N}logN)$ [2]. Hence, the total time for the VLSI biharmonic solver based on the Poisson multigrid solvers is $O(\sqrt{N}log^2N)$. The global estimation in AT^2 complexity measure for this design is $O(N^4log^5N)$. This result equals to the best upper bound known for solving the biharmonic equation in VLSI [4].

4 Conclusions

Despite of the lower bound for solving Poisson equation in VLSI remains an open problem it is to be expected that this result is very close to the optimal solution of this problem. One promising solution for the biharmonic equation could be a design where instead of the chain of blocks with the size $O(NlogN)$ x $O(NlogN)$ and $O(N)$ x $O(N)$ respectively only one block of the size $O(NlogN)$ x $O(NlogN)$ will be considered. This design will need a rather complicated internal structure. It will be a matter of our future research work.

References

1. B.Codenotti, G.Lotti, F.Romani: VLSI implementation of fast solvers for band linear systems with constant coefficient matrix. Information Processing Letters 21, 159-163 (1985)
2. L.W.Ehrlich: Solving the biharmonic equation as coupled finite diference equations. Siam J.Numer.Anal.8, 278-287, (1971)
3. W.Hackbusch, U.Trottenberg (eds.): Multigrid Methods. Lecture Notes in Mathematics 960, Berlin: Springer-Verlag 1982
4. G.Lotti, M.Vajteršic: The application of VLSI Poisson solvers to the biharmonic problem. Parallel Computing 18, 11-19, (1992)
5. J.Mikloško, M.Vajteršic, I.Vrťo, R.Klette: Fast Algorithms and their Implementation on Specialized Parallel Computers. Amsterdam:North-Holland 1989
6. M.Vajteršic: VLSI implementation of fast Poisson solver. In:Proc. CONPAR 88, Cambridge University Press, Cambridge 1989, pp. 695-702
7. M.Vajteršic: Modern Algorithms for Solving Some Elliptic Partial Differential Equations. Bratislava: VEDA Publishing House (in Slovak) 1988

MONOCHROME IMAGE CODING USING HIERARCHICAL CLOSED LOOP VECTOR QUANTIZER ON A MULTIPROCESSING SYSTEM

P.J.Kulkarni   N.R.Phadnis
Walchand College of Engineering
Sangli India 416415

Vishwas Udpikar
Centre for Development of Advanced Computing
Pune University Campus Ganeshkhind
Pune India 411 007

ABSTRACT :   This paper presents a normalized hierarchical Vector Quantizer with performance feedback scheme for monochrome image data compression. The scheme includes results of the decoder within the coder to compute error due to higher block size of coding for onward decomposition of the block. The closed loop nature guarantees minimization of the overall error. The scheme is implemented on a multiprocessing system. Results indicate superiority of the coding scheme at low bit rates.

1. INTRODUCTION

The concept of Vector Quantizer (VQ) involves partitioning an input image block into multidimensional vector space. Each block vector is then compared to a codebook of standard vectors and a codeword identifying the best match is transmitted. A receiver reconstructs the image using the corresponding standard vectors. The block vectors are usually normalized to reduce dynamic range of the input. In the overall scheme, the block size is very crucial in deciding the performance as large block typically offers higher compression ratio but also increases distortion. Adaptive methods for optimization of the compression ratio for a given pictorial fidelity can be designed by varying the block size.

2. NORMALIZATION AND THE CLOSED LOOP VECTOR QUANTIZATION

Murakami et al [1] presented a VQ coding scheme that removes the block mean (M) and normalizes the block vectors by the block standard deviation (SD). M and SD need separate coding by two scalar quantizers. A scheme proposed here uses half the difference between the block higher mean (HM) and block lower mean (LM) instead of (SD) for the normalization. Since M, HM and LM exhibit high correlation, they are jointly coded by another 3-D vector quantizer. The above two schemes will be referred here as scheme-1 and scheme-2 respectively for comparision. Figure-1 indicates the block schematic for the proposed quantizer. Codebooks are designed using LBG approach [2] with large training set which is extracted from the "GIRL" image of 256 x 256 x 8 bit resolution. Each of the codebook contains 256 standard vectors. The closed loop scheme begins coding with a large block size (8 x 8) and reduces the block size using quadtree approach until the mean square error (mse) of coding the block becomes less than a threshold which is defined by desired percentage of block composition (%8 or %4). The smallest block of size 2 x 2 is not tested for its mse. The scheme is implemented on a multiprocessing system which is built around INMOS T-800 transputers (processors). Figure-2 shows the pipeline architecture used for the implementation. The processor 0 partitions an input image and assigns them to the worker processors 1 to n. The block schematic of Figure-1 is executed on each of the worker processors in parallel.

3. RESULTS AND CONCLUSIONS

Coding is carried out for input images of 256 x 256 in size. From the results shown in Table-1 for normalization procedure, it is seen that the scheme- 2 has comparable performance with the scheme-1. Moreover scheme-2 makes use of only first moment block statistics, hence it is computationally simpler. Table-2 indicates performance of the coder for various values of bits per pixel (bpp). The performance of the coder for "COUPLE" image, which is outside the training set also exhibited good results. Refer pictures in Figure-3. It is concluded that the closed loop nature of mse feedback gurantees minimization of the overall mse. The adaptation in this scheme of VQ leads to optimization of mse against compression ratio across different regions of an image. Each element within a given processor in the pipeline performs identical processes which is a part of the coding algorithm. As shown in Table-3, this yields linear scale up (time) over increased number of processors (n). The scheme is attractive for low bit rate image data transmission and storage applications.

References :

[1] Murkami, Asai, Yamazaki; "*Vector quantizer of video signals*" Electronics Letters Vol. 16. Nov. 82. pp 1005-1006.
[2] Linde Y, Buzo A and Gray R.M "*An algorithm for vector quantizer design*" IEEE Trans. 1980 COM-28 pp 84-95.

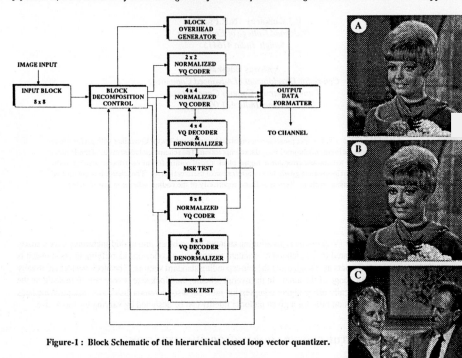

Figure-1 : Block Schematic of the hierarchical closed loop vector quantizer.

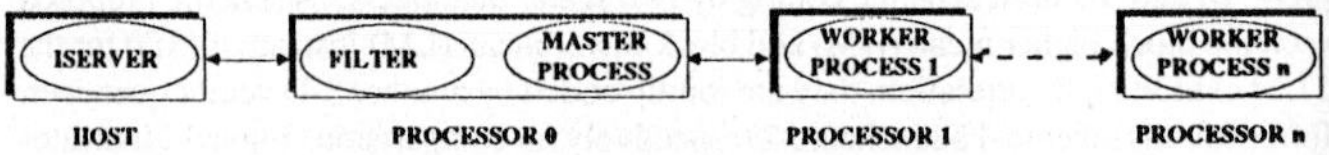

Figure-2 : Transputer Pipeline architecture.

Figure-3 : Coding Performance ⟶

A. Original "GIRL" image (Inside training set)
B. Result at bpp = 0.87, mse = 22.48
C. Original "COUPLE" image (Outside training set)
D. Result at bpp = 0.97, mse = 26.87

Table-1 Normalization

Scheme	Size	bpp	mse
Scheme-1	4 x 4	1.50	26.89
Scheme-2	2 x 2	4.00	06.67
	4 x 4	1.00	34.06
	8 x 8	0.25	80.66

Table-2 Coding Results

%8	%4	bpp	mse
65%	95%	0.64	31.31
60%	90%	0.75	26.24
60%	85%	0.81	24.14
60%	80%	0.87	22.48

Table-3 Coding Time

n	time (Sec)
1	90.47
2	46.37
4	23.93

Superscalar floating-point vector computation in Scheme

Suresh Srinivas and *Kent Dybvig***

Department of Computer Science, Indiana University
Lindley Hall 215, Bloomington, IN 47405

1 Introduction

Scheme is a dialect of Lisp that is based on the lambda calculus, is statically scoped, and has good facilities for abstraction with macros and higher order functions [1]. Numerical applications are written in Scheme using vector objects and operations provided on them. In practice these vectors often contain only floating-point numbers (henceforth referred to as *flonums*) and common operations are referencing an element, adding two sets of vectors, *etc.*, [2]. The vectors in Scheme are heterogenous structures and so their elements can be any Scheme data objects. Since Scheme is a latently typed language, every element of the vector has a tag describing the type of data object therein [3]. This being the case, using generic (heterogenous) vectors for numerical applications is inefficient for the following three reasons. Operations performed on the elements involve manipulation of the tags. A level of indirection is introduced to fetch or store the data since flonums and the tags cannot be stored in a single word. Also vector-based numerical operations (scalar reduction, vector addition *etc.*,) are hard to optimize as they require complex static and dynamic analysis.

These problems are resolved by introducing new datatypes (*flovec*'s) and associated operations (scalar reduction, vector addition *etc.*,) to handle homogenous vectors of single and double precision flonums. By virtue of their being homogenous the need for tagging each element is eliminated and along with it the first two problems. Also, since the operations that are provided are specific to the datatype, they can be optimized for speed. This allows elegant and efficient implementation of numeric intensive programs in Scheme. A prototype implementation generating code for Intel's i860 superscalar RISC processor running on the Alliant FX 2800 at University of Illinois has been completed and has yieled good speedup.

2 Flovecs and their compilation

Flovecs are "typed objects" in the Scheme system. Each Scheme object is represented by a 32-bit memory word. The object is tagged with three tag bits. The lower 3 bits

---

* *email: ssriniva@cs.indiana.edu*
** *email: dyb@cs.indiana.edu*

of the object contain the tag bits and the upper 29 bits contain either immediate data or a pointer to data. The first word in the flovec data object has a length and tag field (for distinguishing "typed objects"). Each word following that corresponds to an element of the flovec and contains a single/double precision flonum. Flovecs are allocated on an eight element boundary for speeding up certain operations.

Operations on flovecs include those that create flovecs, reference an element of a flovec, modify an element of a flovec, elementwise add two flovecs, scale a flovec, combine the elements of a flovec *etc.,*. Flovec operations are compiled to take advantage of the two forms of parallelism available in most superscalar RISC processor. The first form is because the RISC core and the floating-point unit operate on a multistage pipeline. The second form is due to the superscalar nature in which the RISC core and the floating-point unit operate simulaneously. These are utilized by scheduling instructions to hide memory latencies, interleaving floating-point loads with computations *etc.,*. Complete details of the flovec data type and the compilation issues will be available in the technical report [4].

3 Performance results

Performance evaluation was done using three programs (iterative generic vector addition, iterative flovec addition and elementwise flovec addition). The elementwise flovec addition achieves a peak of 3.1 megaflops and runs at around 7 times faster than the iterative generic vector addition and 5 times faster than the iterative flovec addition. Preliminary comparisions with the Alliant C vectorizer shows that vectorized addition in C yields 2.1 megaflops as compared to 3.1 megaflops for the elementwise flovec addition. More performance details can be found in [4]. Work is underway to incorporate the operations described here into *Chez Scheme* in order to better study overall system performance for real applications.

4 Acknowledgements

We would like to thank The University of Illinois at Urbana-Champaign for allowing access to Alliant FX2800 to undertake the research described here. We dedicate this paper to the memory of Bob Hieb who pointed out a problem with one of our techniques and provided valuable comments on many portions of the full paper.

References

1. W.Clinger and J.Rees (editors). Revised[4] Report on the Algorithmic language Scheme. In Lisp Pointers, vol 4, no 3, July-Sep 1991.
2. Scheme numerical library, MIT 1987.
3. Peter A. Steenkiste. "The implementation of tags and run-time type checking". In *Topics in advanced language implementation* ed Peter Lee, chapter 1, pages 3-24. MIT Press, 1991.
4. Suresh Srinivas and Kent Dybvig. "Superscalar floating-point vector computation in Scheme". Technical Report Indiana University 1992. Forthcoming.

An efficient Parallel Algorithm for Maximal Matching

ALAK K. DATTA[1] AND RANJAN K. SEN[2]

[1]Department of Mathematics
[2]Department of Computer Science and Engineering
Indian Institute of Technology, Kharagpur 721302,INDIA

Abstract: We present a parallel algorithm for maximal matching of an undirected graph. The algorithm runs in $O(log^3 n)$ time and uses $O(m + n)$ processors on a EREW-PRAM, where m and n are the number of edges and vertices in the graph, respectively.

1. Introduction: Matching of a graph is a set of edges, no two of which are incident on a common vertex. A maximal matching is one which is not contained in any other matching. The best EREW-PRAM algorithm to find a maximal matching in a graph takes $O(log^4 m)$ time and $O(m^3/log\ m)$ processors [1], where m and n are number of edges and vertices of the graph respectively. The best CRCW-PRAM algorithm takes $O(log^3 m)$ time and uses $O(m + n)$ processors [2]. Our algorithm takes $O(log^3 n)$ time and $O(m + n)$ processors on a EREW-PRAM. The algorithm works in different phases. In each phase of our algorithm a degree reduction procedure (which employes list ranking) is used on subgraphs of the given graph iteratively to get a graph of maximum degree five. A special matching algorithm, MAXMATCH5, is used to get a matching of this bounded degree graph. The matched vertices are deleted and the resulting graph is the input to the next phase. The union of the matchings obtained in different phases is a maximal matching.

2. Degree Reduction Procedure: The Degree Reduction Procedure (DRP) takes G as input and produces grarh G_r such that $\Delta(G_r) \leq \Delta(G)/2 + 2$, where Δ denotes the maximum degree of G. It uses two procedures described below.

2.1. Partitioning into Edge Disjoint Directed Cycles (PEDDC): Given an Eulerian graph $G = (V, E)$, PEDDC partitions the edges of G into edge disjoint directed cycles. Each edge is replaced by two anti-parallel directed edges to get a graph G'. For each vertex v of degree d_v, let $S((v_i, v)) = (v, v_{(i+d_v/2)mod\ d_v})$, where v_i is the vertex of rank i in the linked list of v. S defines a partition of the edges of G' into edge disjoint directed cycles. For each cycle there is also an anti-parallel cycle. Delete one of the two anti-parallel cycles. Represent each cycle by the lexicographically smallest edge in it and mark that edge if the corresponding cycle is of odd length.

2.2. Odd Cycle Reduction (OCR): For all the vertices the set of all marked edges adjacent to a vertex are paired. The odd cycles corresponding to each pair of marked edges are merged into a single even cycle. In this manner an independent set (just one marked edge on each vertex) of mark edges is produced.

The degree reduction procedure (DRP) is described below. First, the graph is made Eulerian by adding an auxiliary vertex v^* and connecting it to all odd degree vertices. Then procedures PEDDC and OCR are used to get a partition. Label the edges in each cycle alternately by 0 and 1 starting with 0 (start labeling from a marked edge, if possible). Edges with label 1 and v^* are deleted. It can be readily proved that $\Delta(G_r) \leq \Delta(G)/2 + 2$. Also, it is easy to prove that DRP can be executed in $O(log\ n)$ time using $O(m + n)$ processors on EREW-PRAM.

3. A maximal matching algorithm for a degree constraint graph:
Algorithm MAXMATCH5
Input: A graph $G = (V, E)$ of maximum vertex degree five.
Output: M, a maximal matching of G.
Repeat until there remains an edge in the graph

> Compute F, a spaning forest of G (simulate the spanning forest algorithm in [3] on EREW-PRAM). Compute M', a maximum matching of F. Set $M = M \cup M'$. Update G by deleting the vertices in M'.
> Delete isolated vertices, if produced.

end MAXMATCH5

Lemma 3.1: *The algorithm MAXMATCH5 correctly computes a maximal matching of the graph G of maximum vertex degree five in $O(\log^2 n)$ time using $O(n)$ processors on EREW-PRAM.*

4. The Maximal Matching Algorithm: For a graph $G = (V, E)$, let k be the smallest integer satisfying $2^k - 1 \leq \Delta(G) \leq 2^{k+1} + 1$, where $\Delta(G)$ is the maximum vertex degree of the graph. We call a vertex v *live* if its degree is greater than or equal to $2^k - 1$.

Algorithm MAXMATCH

Input: A graph $G = (V, E)$.
Output: M, a maximal matching of G.
While $G \neq \Phi$ do steps 1 to 3

 1. $G' \leftarrow G$
 2. *While $\Delta(G') > 5$ do*
Compute the set of all live vertices of G', construct the subgraph G_l induced by the edges adjacent to live vertices. Execute algorithm DRP with G_l as input. Let S be the set of all edges deleted. Set $G' = G' - S$.
 3. Execute MAXMATCH5 with G' as input to get a maximal matching M' of G' and set $M \leftarrow M \cup M'$. Update G by deleting the vertices of M' and isolated vertices, if produced.

end MAXMATCH

Theorem 4.1 *Algorithm MAXMATCH correctly computes a maximal matching of the graph G.*
proof. First we can show that after $O(\log n)$ phases of step 2, $\Delta(G') \leq 5$. So MAXMATCH5 can be used in step 3. We can also show that the set of all vertices in M at the end of algorithm *MAXMATCH* is a vertex cover of the graph. This implies that the matching obtained is maximal.

5. Complexity issues of algorithm MAXMATCH: Let G_i be the graph input to the i-th phase of MAXMATCH and L_i be the set of all live vertices at the end of step 2 of that phase. Then
Lemma 5.1: L_i *is a vertex cover of G_i. Also, $| L_i/G_{i+1} | \leq (8/9) | L_i |$, where $| L_i/G_{i+1} |$ is the set of all vertices of L_i remaining in G_{i+1}.*
proof. Omitted.
Theorem 5.1: *Algorithm MAXMATCH terminates after $O(\log n)$ phases.*
Proof. Using lemma 5.1, it can be shown that the graph G_{i+1} has a vertex cover C_{i+1} such that $| C_{i+1} | \leq (16/17) | C_i |$, for any arbitrary vertex cover C_i of G_i.
Theorem 5.2: *Algorithm MAXMATCH takes $O(\log^3 n)$ time using $O(m + n)$ processors.*
Proof: Each phase takes $O(\log^2 n)$ time using $O(m + n)$ processors and there are $O(\log n)$ phases.

Acknowledgement: The first author acknowledges Prof. J P Agarwal and CSIR, India.

References

 1. Karp, R.M. and Wigderson, W., A fast parallel algorithm for Maximal Independent Set problem, Proc. 16-th Ann. ACM Symp. on Theory of Computing, 1984, pp.266-272.

 2. Israeli, A. and Shiloach, Y., An improved parallel algorithm for maximal matching, Information Processing Letter, 22(1986), pp.57-60.

 3. Awerbuch, B.and Shiloach, Y., New connectivity and MSF algorithms for suffle-exchange network and PRAM, IEEE Tran. on Computers, Vol. C-36, No. 10, Oct. 1987, pp. 1258-1263.

Minimal, Adaptive and Deadlock-free Routing for Multiprocessors

J.M. Adamo and N. Alhafez,

Laboratoire LIP, Ecole Normale Supérieure de Lyon, 46 Allée d'Italie, 69364 Lyon cédex 07, France.

Abstract.This paper reviews methods for minimal, adaptive and deadlock-free routing. Some are based on the direct construction of a buffer graph. The other ones consist in deriving a minimal, adaptive and deadlock-free routing function f1 from a function f a priori given. The methods are compared and applied to a set of usual regular topologies.

1. Introduction

The development of a parametrable router for the C_NET programming environment required attention to be paided to the general routing methods. This paper reviews minimal, adaptive, deadlock-free routing methods for mutliprocessors. In the second section, the deadlock problem is precisely identified. The third one is devoted to the presentation of general methods for deadlock prevention. They are based either on the direct construction of buffer graphs or on the construction of link dependency graphs. All are intended to provide in the end a virtual cycle-free buffer-graph, thereby preventing any circularity in resource (i.e. buffer) requests from occuring.

2 Deadlock prevention methods: direct construction of buffer graphs

2.1 Routing through cycle-free buffer graphs

Let us consider a processor network $G = (P, L)$ where P is a set of processors and L is a set of physical links. Let B be a set of buffers and E be a set of virtual links that connect elements in B, the buffer graph $G_B = (B, E)$ is assumed to cover G and to be cycle-free. G_B is intended to provide a virtual structure applied onto G so that a deadlock-free routing function in G_B can easily be built. The question that naturally comes up is that of finding methods for deriving cycle-free buffer-graphs from processor graphs. The solution of the derivation problem is not unique. In fact it depends on the properties of the routing strategy one wants to achieve in the end. Several methods have been proposed in the literature for constructing buffer graphs that allow minimal, adaptive and dead-lock free routing. They are briefly described below.

2.2 Structured buffer pool

This method is one of the earliest ones [12, 15]. Given a processor graph G with diameter M, the method suggests M + 1 buffers be assigned to each processor. Let B_0^k, ..., B_M^k be the buffers assigned to processor p_k. For any pair (p_k, p_l) of connected processors, the edges in the buffer graph are constructed in such a way that B_i^k is connected to B_{i+1}^l for any i = 0, ..., M-1. It is very easy to show that the so constructed buffer graph is cycle-free and provides a minimal, adaptive and deadlock-free routing.

2. 3 Virtual graphs

This method proposed in is based on the construction of a set of disconnected buffer-graphs that are called virtual graphs. As we noticed earlier for the general method, the solution of the problem of assigning a set of virtual graphs to a given processor graph is not unique and depends on the property of the routing strategy we want to achieve in the end. The virtual graph method is particularly well suited to the mesh family. In this case the lattice of all the shortest paths can be covered up by four lattices only. This method has been implemented on silicon.

3 Deadlock prevention methods based on the construction of link dependency graphs

The methods based on these graphs provide another means for constructing cycle-free buffer graphs. They are based on coloured partitioning, valley counting and acyclical partitioning [1,2].

Conclusion

The performances of methods have been assessed and compared. They have been applied to a set of usual regular topologies [1, 2]. Acyclical partitioning has been shown to provide solutions well suited (constant or log space complexity) for ring, hypercubes and CCCs, whereas virtual graphs are more attractive for mesh and torus topologies (high values of the dimensions).

References

1   J.M. Adamo, J. Bonneville, C. Bonello, C-NET, A High Level Programming Environment for SuperNode, Proc. of the PCA Workshop, Bonn, May, 1991.

2   N. Alhafez, Etude et Mise en Oeuvre de Routages non Blocants dans les Architectures Multi-processeurs, thèse de doctorat, to appear.

A Theoretical Study of Reconfigurability for Numerical Algorithms on a Reconfigurable Network

F. DESPREZ and B. TOURANCHEAU

LIP/IMAG - CNRS, ENS Lyon, 69364 Lyon Cedex 07, France,
e-mail: [desprez,btouranc]@lip.ens-lyon.fr

1 Introduction

Using todays new supercomputers, programming is often a problem because of the lack of tools and libraries. Some people have tried to develop linear algebra libraries which can be easily used on a broad range of supercomputers. In the case of distributed memory multicomputers, those numerical routines are not sufficient, communication routines have to be added for the data movements, load and unload of the machine.

In this poster, we show, for distributed memory multicomputers, the major interests and limitations of the communication network reconfigurability. For each of the basic operations studied, we compare one algorithm on a classical fixed topology and one algorithm issued of the reconfiguration of the network for its execution. The chosen fixed topology is the two-dimensional torus which gives good average results and thus allows to chain efficiently successive operations. If it is possible to configure the network before the execution of one routine, we try to determine the best topology.

The cost of the (re-)configuration with a quasi-dynamic reconfigurable network is taken into account in our complexity analysis. It can range from one topology configuration during the whole computation to one topology reconfiguration for each computation or communication subroutine.

The algorithms studied are matrix transposition, broadcast and scattering operations and their chaining with a matrix product (rank-2k updates). We tune the parameters of our analysis regarding the Inmos T800 caracteristics.

2 Broadcast and scattering algorithms

The broadcast and the scattering are two of the basic operations of many parallel algorithms.

For the two operations, we compare one method using a two-dimensional torus, one using only one reconfiguration of the network in a tree and one using a multiple reconfiguration algorithm where each time a node obtains its data, it forwards it by making a connection to k other nodes (where k is the nodes degree).

For the broadcast operation, with 25 nodes and for messages of length under 80 the best solution is the multiple reconfiguration algorithm regardless the reconfiguration cost. After 80 bytes the fixed topology pipeline algorithm is better. With

81 nodes, the fixed topology pipeline algorithm starts to be better after length 210 bytes.

For the scattering operation, when we consider the complexity analysis of our 3 solutions, the two reconfiguration solutions cost almost the same and are interesting only in the case of big messages.

3 Matrix transposition algorithms

This operation is used in a broad range of linear algebra algorithms on distributed memory multicomputers in order to modify the data repartition of sub-matrices on the network.

For the reconfiguration solution, we use a direct network where diagonaly opposed processor are directly connected. We use a macro-pipeline method where internal re-arrangment of sub-matrices are done in parallel with exchanges between processors.

We show that this algorithm is more interesting than the classical torus algorithm.

4 Rank-2k updates algorithms

In this part, we consider one of the routines of the level 3 BLAS: the rank-2k updates of a symmetric matrix C.

This operation is an interesting example of the use of all the previously studied routines.

The modularity of this algorithm leads directly to a phases decomposition which fits very well to the reconfiguration solution on a quasi-dynamic reconfigurable network. we decompose the algorithm into four phases, each one corresponding to an algorithmic/topology strategy (multiple reconfigurations, multiple reconfigurations, 2D Torus and direct network). Hence each phase corresponds to an algorithm described in the preceding sections.

5 Conclusion and future work

In this poster, we have shown that with our model and parameters, the reconfiguration solution must be of interest for several algorithms if its cost is not too important and especially if one can overlap the reconfiguration with the computations/communications of the algorithm. This capability of the switching architecture must be taken into account in further researchs.

However, we pointed out that good parallel algorithmic solutions on the 2D Torus are better than many others on special topologies especially when the problem size is big and/or when pipeline or macro-pipeline solutions are possible. This demonstrates that research in this area is not obsolete and will still be used in message passing DMPC with the possibility of an underlying 2D Torus network.

This article was processed using the LaTeX macro package with LLNCS style

Multiprocessor Simulation Using Object-Oriented Programming

Annick Fron

Thomson Sintra Activités Sous-Marines
Parc de Sophia-Antipolis, BP 138 06561 Valbonne Cedex France
E-mail: fron@sophia.inria.fr

Abstract : In order to model the behaviour of an application running on a MIMD architecture, an interactive environment has been designed in an object-oriented programming language on a process-based simulation kernel, with animated graphics showing key resource occupation. The model can account for both synchronisation aspects and asynchronous events, and has been used on several industrial projects.

1. Introduction

For MIMD embedded systems, simulation of a large parallel application before integration on the target system is too costly as such on a host computer. An interactive graphical modelling environment has been designed to validate interprocessor communications within the application and tune target system parameters.

2. The Mustang architecture and programming system

The Mustang is a Mimd architecture with several racks of up to 44 processors. Mustang programs consist in large-grain communicating processes, through communication and synchronisation variables of different nature: Fifos, buffers, events. The semantics of the communication is encoded in the type and the attributes of these so-called communication objects. Moreover, the software application graph is static, and each task is allocated on a specific processor, but several tasks may share the same one.

2. Modelling environment

The modelling environment provides graphical editors to capture both the interconnection hardware architecture and the software graph, as well as task allocation on processors. Configuration code relevant to these topologies can be automatically generated and ensures global coherence. Moreover, these graphs serve as documentation for the project and libraries for next projects.

3. Simulation kernel

The simulation relies on concurrent processus and monitors. Both resource sharing and synchronisation between tasks can be simulated. The simulated time is managed by an event-driven scheduler and the simulation kernel handles both active (process) and passive (monitors) entities, representing software or hardware physical objects. Simulation objects have high-level semantics, thus it is possible to generate automatically the simulation model from the graphical capture.

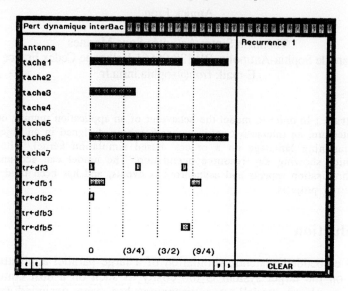

Fig. 1 Animated trace of tasks and communication between tasks

Conclusion

This system has been used in several industrial projects, in order to:
- validate the communication scheme for each task and ensure no starvation or blocking appears
- tune up regulation parameters for communication links, and try several possible task allocation.
The simulation kernel is well adapted to large-grain parallel applications, and both hardware and software entities could be captured in the same model.

References

[Dim 64] DIMSDALE, B., MARKOWITZ, H., M., A description of the language Simscript, IBM System Journal, vol. 3, n°1

[Hoa 74] HOARE C A R, Monitors: An operating system structuring concept, CACM, vol 17, n° 10, Oct. 1974

[Kaubisch 76] KAUBISCH,W.H, PERROT, R.H, HOARE, C.A.R, Quasi-Parallel Programming, Software Practice and Experience, Vol. 6, N° 3, pp. 341-356, July-September 1976

[Nel 91] NELSON, J.M., Concurrency & Object-Oriented Programming, ACM Sigplan Notices, Vol 26, No 10, October 1991

Real–Number Codes for Fault–Tolerant Matrix Inversion on Processor Arrays

M. K. Stojčev, I. Ž. Milovanović, E. I. Milovanović and G. S. Jovanović

Faculty of Electronic Engineering, University of Niš
P.O. Box 73, 18000 Niš, Yugoslavia

Abstract. This paper consider the problem of fault–tolerant (FT) inverting of triangular matrices based on linear checksum (LC) approach. Iterative Shultz' method adapted for parallel implementation on triangular processor array (PA) was used.

1 Introduction

For a large PAs faults are very likely to occur during operation. It is therefore essential to provide in such systems on–line FT processes which include detection/correction of errors. Algorithm based fault–tolerance (ABFT) provides an efficient means to implement FT matrix computations on PA [1].

2 Theory

In the focus of our interest is developing an algorithm for LC inversion of triangular matrices based on iterative Shultz' method. A procedure for LC matrix inversion of regular square matrix $A_{n \times n}$ can be decomposed into three steps: 1) Linear–checksum LU decomposition of matrix A; 2) LC inversion of matrices L and U and 3) LC multiplication of triangular matrices. We will concentrate on step 2. If $\mathbf{a}^T = [a_1, \ldots, a_n]$ is an arbitrary vector and $\mathbf{e}^T = [e_1, \ldots, e_n]$ is linear checksum vector, than coded vector $\mathbf{D}$ has the following form $\mathbf{D} = [a_1, \ldots, a_n, CS]$, where $CS = \mathbf{a}^T \mathbf{e} = a_1 e_1 + \ldots + a_n e_n$. Similarly, the row, column and full checksum matrices of an $n \times n$ matrix A are defined as follows:

$$A_c = \begin{bmatrix} A \\ \mathbf{e}^T A \end{bmatrix} , \quad A_r = [A \quad A\mathbf{e}] , \quad A_f = \begin{bmatrix} A & A\mathbf{e} \\ \mathbf{e}^T A & \mathbf{e}^T A\mathbf{e} \end{bmatrix} .$$

Now, we will give the procedures for calculating checksum inverse matrix of matrices L and U. We assume that matrix U is with unit diagonal.

a) Computing U_f^{-1}

a.1. $X^{(0)} = \text{diag}(1, 1, \ldots, 1)_{n \times n}$

a.2. $R_c^{(0)} = I_c - X_c^{(0)} U$

a.3. $P_c^{(i)} = I_c + R_c^{(i)}$

a.4. $X_f^{(i+1)} = P_c^{(i)} X_r^{(i)}$ $\Big\}$ $i = 1, k$

a.5. $R_f^{(i+1)} = R_c^{(i)} R_r^{(i)}$

b) Computing L_f^{-1}

b.1. $Y^{(0)} = \text{diag}\left(\frac{1}{l_{11}}, \ldots, \frac{1}{l_{nn}}\right)_{n \times n}$

b.2. $R_c^{(0)} = I_c - Y_c^{(0)} L$

b.3. $P_c^{(i)} = I_c + R_c^{(i)}$

b.4. $Y_f^{(i+1)} = P_c^{(i)} Y_r^{(i)}$ $\Big\}$ $i = 1, k$

b.5. $R_f^{(i+1)} = R_c^{(i)} R_r^{(i)}$

After k iteration steps we obtain $X_f^{(k+1)} = U_f^{-1}$, i.e. $Y_f^{(k+1)} = L_f^{-1}$. In both cases, a) and b), matrix $R^{(0)}$ is strictly triangular matrix of order $n \times n$, for which the following is valid:

$$i) \quad \left(R^{(0)}\right)^n = 0 \quad \text{and} \quad ii) \quad R^{(k)} = \left(R^{(k-1)}\right)^2 = \left(R^{(0)}\right)^{2^k}.$$

So, in both cases, the number of iteration steps, k, is the smallest integer that satisfies the inequality $2^k \geq n$. When this inequality is satisfied then $R^{(k)} = 0$, and $R_c^{(k)} = 0$. According to that it follows that $X^{(k+1)} = X^{(k)}$, i.e. $X_r^{(k+1)} = X_r^{(k)}$. Since $P_c^{(k)} = P_c^{(k+1)} = I_c$, it follows that

$$X_f^{(k+2)} = P_c^{(k+1)}X_r^{(k+1)} = I_c X_r^{(k)} = X_f^{(k+1)}.$$

This means that iterative process a.4. (b.4.) reaches fixed point for final number of iteration steps, k. In the third phase LC inverse matrix A_f^{-1} of matrix A is obtained according to the product $U_c^{-1}L_r^{-1}$.

3   Experimental Results

The execution of the proposed algorithm was simulated on IBM PC/AT using C^{++}. Simulation was performed for matrices of dimension 8, 16 and 32. Error injection was performed during operations of addition and multiplication. During the experiment random number generator was used for generating matrix element values in the range of 1.00 to 2.00. Table 1 summarizes obtained results for FP data represented in single and double precision (given in brackets). In Table 1 column "bit position" points to the position of error injection. Columns "addition" and "multiplication" corresponds to percentages of single error detection and correction.

Table 1.

bit posi- tion	$n = 8$ $EPS1 = 2^{-15}$ $EPS1' = 2^{-45}$		$n = 16$ $EPS2 = 2^{-14}$ $EPS2' = 2^{-42}$		$n = 32$ $EPS3 = 2^{-12}$ $EPS3' = 2^{-41}$	
	addition%	multipl.%	addition%	multipl.%	addition%	multipl.%
4	−(14.28)	1.66(7.50)	−(−)	−(−)	−(−)	−(−)
5	13.09(44.04)	15.41(41.66)	1.76(−)	−(−)	−(−)	−(−)
6	50.00(64.28)	45.41(68.75)	10.88(−)	7.17(−)	0.22(0.03)	−(−)
7	63.09(88.09)	66.25(84.16)	39.55(13.82)	36.70(8.64)	0.89(0.98)	0.29(0.61)
8	84.52(97.61)	87.50(98.75)	63.97(41.03)	64.40(41.42)	13.56(14.75)	11.28(10.48)
9	98.80(100.0)	99.58(100.0)	87.35(67.64)	86.33(62.13)	42.66(40.67)	41.50(40.07)
10	100.0(100.0)	100.0(100.0)	98.38(90.14)	99.14(91.23)	64.58(65.70)	62.73(64.53)
11	100.0(100.0)	100.0(100.0)	100.0(99.26)	100.0(99.87)	86.03(89.40)	90.09(90.75)
12	100.0(100.0)	100.0(100.0)	100.0(100.0)	100.0(100.0)	98.58(99.67)	99.91(99.99)
13	100.0(100.0)	100.0(100.0)	100.0(100.0)	100.0(100.0)	100.0(100.0)	100.0(100.0)

References

1. V.S.S. Nair, J.A. Abraham, Real–Number Codes for Fault–Tolerant Matrix Operations on Processor Arrays, *IEEE Trans. Computers*, Vol. 39, No. 4, 426–435 (1990).

Automatic Mapping of Parallel Programs onto Processor Networks

Jürgen W. Meyer

AB Technische Informatik 2, Technische Universität Hamburg–Harburg
Harburger Schloßstraße 20, DW 2100 Hamburg 90
j-meyer@tu-harburg.dbp.de

Abstract. Many heuristics have been created to solve the mapping problem. A set of mapping heuristics has been integrated into a program development system, such that mapping becomes an automatic step of program generation. The system serves as a basis for development, analysis, and comparison of mapping heuristics as well as as program development tool with selectable mapping heuristics for program configuration.

The system is implemented on a flexible transputer based parallel computer, which is able to emulate a large variety of problems for mapping heuristics. Runtime monitoring of configured programs allows a detailed evaluation of mapping heuristics.

1 Introduction

A basic problem of the generation of programs for parallel computers is the assignment of the parallel processes and their logical communication links onto the available processing units and the physical interconnection network. We call it the mapping of an image architecture onto a host architecture, or the configuration of a parallel program for a particular computing system. The problem is NP-complete, thus a lot of heuristics aiming at either minimal runtime or optimal use of resources have been created and offer reasonable solutions.

An approach is presented to integrate different heuristics into a program development system, such that configuring with a selectable heuristic is done automatically, similar to compiling. Two main objectives are pursued:

1. A base is built for development, analysis, evaluation, and comparison of mapping heuristics. A flexible interface allows the inclusion of a wide range of mapping heuristics. Monitoring by detailed measurements during runtime allows an extensive study of the heuristics' properties.
2. Program development is supported by automatic program configuration and the choice of the heuristic which is taken for configuring.

2 The Mapping Heuristic Interface

Integrating of different heuristics into a development system must take into account the different representations of image architecture and host architecture used by the heuristics. We have conceived generalized representations, i.e. they contain sufficient information for a wide range of mapping heuristics and can be transformed for each particular heuristic into adequate structures. The representations are weighted graphs with all nodes and edges labeled by a descriptor containing a set of single weights.

The interface of each mapping heuristic consists of three modules, two of them transform the graphs into adequate structures and the third transforms the output of the heuristic into a uniform program configuration record. Thus mapping heuristics implemented in different programming languages can be integrated with the small effort of writing three interface modules.

3 Generation of Graphs

Knowing the hardware and the status report about available resources the graph representing the host architecture can be produced easily. The generation of the graph representing the image architecture requires some effort. The nodes and edges can be determined automatically by analyzing the program source code. However, the weights of the graph's elements cannot always be predicted, because they might depend on the program's input data. Thus we estimate the weights during source code analysis. More precise weights are produced within an iterative procedure including a phase of monitoring.

Based on the estimated weights a mapping heuristic will establish a first program configuration. With this initial configuration the program is monitored during runtime. The results of the measurements serve to adjust the estimated weights. With improved weights the mapping heuristic is started again to repeat the phases of mapping, monitoring, and adjusting the weights, until the weights reach a stable state.

4 Implementation

The system is implemented on a Parsytec SC 128, a distributed memory system consisting of 128 transputers and a configurable interconnection network, financed by the Deutsche Forschungsgemeinschaft (DFG). Configuring, compiling, and linking parallel programs is done by Unix-Workstations, which serve as front-ends for the SC 128. Supported program development systems are Inmos OCCAM 2 Toolset and Inmos ANSI C Toolset. The software monitor [3] allowing an automatic program instrumentation and off-line analysis, was developed at the University of Paderborn.

References

1. S. Antonelli, F. Baiardi, S. Pelagatti, M. Vanneschi, *A Static Approach to Process Mapping in Massively Parallel Systems*, in Parallel Processing, M. Cosnard, M.H. Barton, M. Vanneschi (Eds.), Elsevier Science Publishers, Amsterdam, 1988
2. H. Shen, *Occam Implementation of Process-to-Processor Mapping on the Hathi-2 Transputer System*, Transputing '91, Proc. WOTUG, Sunnyvale, California, IOC Press, Amsterdam, 1991
3. E. Maehle, W. Obelöer, *Monitoring-Werkzeuge zur Leistungsmessung in Multi-Transputersystemen*, Proc. RISC '91, Karlsruhe, Germany, VDE-Verlag, Berlin, 1991

Dynamic Allocation on the Transputer Network

Peter Zaveršek and Peter Kolbezen

Jožef Stefan Institute, Jamova 39, 61111 Ljubljana, Slovenia

Abstract. Transputer based systems eliminate most of the problems associated with multiprocessor systems design using conventional microprocessors and centrally shared resources. This paper proposes a torus based array architecture which consists of multiple, unidirectional rings. Such a system can be made very flexible by combining the proposed architecture, adequate program graph presentation, and a suitable allocation algorithm.

1   Introduction

Efficient execution of parallel algorithms on a parallel system is, no doubt, conditioned by proper preparation and mapping of a program algorithm.

The topic of this paper is a multiprocessor system which could perform efficient, dynamic, run-time process allocation while having weak knowledge of process time characteristics and incomplete knowledge of the network. The aim of our work is to examine the possibility of mapping irregular algorithms onto a fixed regular structure.

2   Algorithm Presentation

A program algorithm which is presented in a traditional, sequential way must be carefully analyzed and decomposed into a set of processes to exploit parallelism. This may be performed by using appropriate tools[2]. Assuming that a program algorithm possesses several parallel paths, we may obtain a suitable data flow graph (DFG). Nodes in DFG are processes with the execution time T_{exe} and transfer time T_{trans}. The ratio T_{exe}/T_{trans}, which influences the multiprocessor system's behaviour, we call *transmission time ratio*.

We assume that algorithms are presented in so-called *hierarchical acyclic data flow graph* form (HADFG). A HADFG can be derived from acyclic and simple DFG's where no communication between concurrent nodes is permitted. HADFG consists of alternating sequential and parallel levels and exactly matches the mathematical description of a simple[1] DFG. Parallel HADFG levels consist of branching nodes with branches that can be executed concurrently. Sequential levels include the nodes with the outgoing sequential branches.

We define the HADFG's concurrent node to be *sorted* if the longest execution time branch is placed to the leftmost and the shortest one to the rightmost position within the node. The whole HADFG is sorted if all of its concurrent nodes are sorted [3].

3   Physical Configuration and Message Passing

The proposed multi-processor network is a torus. Processing elements can be transputers which perfectly fit into this type of topology, fully employing their four-link connection capabilities. Communication between processors is based on a token-passing principle. Two types of tokens are employed. *Control* tokens pass the control commands and system status words, and data tokens pass the data packets respectively. Division of each two-way communication-capable, torus-shaping ring into two, one-way communication and control rings should improve system response time.

4 Proposed Allocation Algorithm

We propose an allocation algorithm which is completely and directly instructed by explicit HADFG's interprocess time relations. The allocation procedure starts in the topmost node of HADFG. Crawling down the graph it allocates sequential branches one after another and parallel branches concurrently to idle processors. Available processes are primarily allocated within the two rings that the current processor members in, and secondarily to all the remaining idle processors of the network. Each processor which was allocated a HADFG tree or subtree onto is called a root processor. HADFG is being partitioned in each parallel node and, consequently, several root processors may appear in the network, each containing a partition of the original HADFG. After accomplishing the process execution, the results are returned to identical root processors as they were derived from. If there are no more resources available, the concurrent processes are forced to be executed sequentially.

5 Simulation

Simulation results lead us to the following conclusions. The square network form is generally better than the standard rectangle one. Better results (e.g. execution time, network utilization) can be achieved by executing sorted HADFG's in contrast to unsorted ones. Transmission time ratio value should be higher than 10 for a 4×4 network; in general it should be as high as possible. The ratio is processing-element dependent, which we must bear in mind during the algorithm-granulation phase.

6 Conclusion

A possible approach towards execution of irregular algorithms employing a regular network architecture has been exposed. HADFG presentation form and the proposed allocation algorithm together provide an efficient dynamic run-time process allocation.

The proposed system may be found useful for asymmetric HADFG's and variable process execution times, although better results can be achieved if the execution time is predictable. Multiple network entry points may be established if concurrent execution of several tasks is desired. Damaged devices may be harmlessly removed from the network without affecting the system's functionality. When so, the connections must be revised to maintain the general torus network shape.

References

1. Hwang, K.H., Briggs, F.A.: Computer Architecture and Parallel Processing, McGraw-Hill Book Company, 1984, Chaps. 7 & 8
2. Katti, R.S., Manwaring, M.L.: Executing Sequential Programs in Parallel on a Multiprocessor Architecture, Proceedings of the 3rd Annual Parallel Processing Symposium, March 29-31, 1989, California State University, Fullerton, California, 385-400
3. Kolbezen, P., Zaveršek, P.: A Hierarchical Multimicroprocessor System, Informatica, A Journal of Computing and Informatics, The Slovene Society Informatika, Vol.15, Nr.1, Feb. 1991, 65-76

This article was processed using the LaTeX macro package with LLNCS style

BLOCK IMPLEMENTATIONS OF THE SYMMETRIC QR AND JACOBI ALGORITHMS

Peter Arbenz and Michael Oettli

Institut für Wissenschaftliches Rechnen,
ETH Zürich, 8092 Zürich, Switzerland

Abstract. We discuss block variants of QR and Jacobi algorithms for computing the spectral decomposition of symmetric matrices. We report on numerical tests, which have been performed on an ALLIANT FX/80.

1   Introduction

On modern supercomputers with vector- and/or parallel-processing capabilities, it is very important to avoid unnecessary memory references, as moving data between different levels of memory (registers, cache, main memory) is slow compared to arithmetic operations on the data. This fact has led to the development of block algorithms based on matrix-matrix operations.

2   Description of the Methods

Block QR Algorithm. The starting point of this algorithm is an article by Bai and Demmel [2], which describes a block QR algorithm for real *nonsymmetric* matrices based on a multishift iteration.

The initial reduction to tridiagonal form is usually done by a sequence of Householder transformations. Each one is chosen to introduce zeros in one column below the subdiagonal and in the corresponding row to the right of the superdiagonal. To achieve better memory utilization, a sequence of p transformations may be aggregated to introduce the zeros block-wise.

The tridiagonal QR iteration may be modified to a block method by choosing k shifts simultaneously. Thus, k iteration steps are performed at a time. This can be considered as a generalization of the double shift QR method used for unsymmetric matrices. The usual nonzero element, which arises outside the tridiagonal band during one iteration and which has to be chased down the diagonal by Givens rotations is now replaced by a $k \times k$ bulge of nonzero elements. It is easy to see, that this bulge may be chased down the diagonal by the same block reduction method used in the initial tridiagonalization.

Block Jacobi Algorithm. Veselić and Hari [3] proposed the following one-sided Jacobi algorithm for symmetric positive definite matrices A (any symmetric matrix can be made positive definite by an appropriate spectral shift). Compute the Cholesky decomposition $A = LL^T$ and set $\tilde{A} = L^T L$. Apply the Jacobi algorithm to $\tilde{A}$, constructing a sequence $\tilde{A}_k = L_k^T L_k = Q_k^T L^T L Q_k$, $(k \rightarrow \infty)$. The sequence

$\{L\}_{k=0}^{\infty}$ ($\tilde{A}$ is not explicitly used) converges to the eigenvector matrix of A. The norms of the columns of this matrix give the eigenvalues.

The algorithm may be executed in blocked form as follows. The rotations of one $m \times m$ block matrix are aggregated and performed on block columns of L. A parallel version of this one-sided block method is readily derived, if the ordering of the rotations is chosen appropriately.

3 Results

To analyze the performance of our block algorithms, we compared them with TRED2/TQL2 from EISPACK and an implementation of the classical Jacobi algorithm RUTISH.

In Table 1, the performance on an eight-processor ALLIANT FX/80 is given. While both classical algorithms were executed sequentially, the block QR algorithm BTRED/BQR as well as the block Jacobi algorithm VESBLK exploited parallelism and ran on all eight processors. The timing results show, that BTRED/BQR is fastest. The

Size	Algorithm	t(sec)	$\max_i \|Tq_i - \lambda_i q_i\|_2$	$\max_i \|[q_1, \ldots, q_n]^T q_i - e_i\|_2$
100	TRED2/TQL2	2.66	0.59093E-12	0.62630E-14
	BTRED/BQR	2.97	0.16983E-11	0.64044E-14
	RUTISH	14.9	0.10199E-12	0.26609E-14
	VESBLK	2.79	0.45009E-12	0.26723E-14
200	TRED2/TQL2	19.4	0.22968E-11	0.10263E-13
	BTRED/BQR	12.7	0.29786E-11	0.81243E-14
	RUTISH	120.0	0.30690E-12	0.36766E-14
	VESBLK	17.1	0.90176E-12	0.31513E-14
400	TRED2/TQL2	153.0	0.45461E-11	0.15090E-13
	BTRED/BQR	71.5	0.96399E-11	0.11459E-13
	RUTISH	1020.0	0.10427E-11	0.48764E-14
	VESBLK	110.0	0.27734E-11	0.25046E-14

Table 1. Total time and accuracy of results on ALLIANT FX/80.

reason is a high speedup in the tridiagonalization. We did not get any speedups over TQL2 with our implementation of the multishift QR iteration. Although, classical Jacobi is not competitive with the QR algorithm, the blocked parallel Jacobi implementation VESBLK is even faster than TRED2/TQL2. In situations where the original matrix is close to diagonal, block Jacobi may be superior to QR.

On a CRAY Y-MP/464 the blocked algorithms performed poorer than the non-blocked ones, on one as well as on four processors [1].

References

1. Arbenz, P. and Oettli, M.: Block implementations of the symmetric QR and Jacobi algorithms. Research Report 178, Departement Informatik, ETH Zürich, June 1992.
2. Bai, Z. and Demmel. J.: On A block implementation of Hessenberg multishift QR iterations. Int. J. High Speed Comput.,1 (1989), 97–112
3. Veselić, K. and Hari, V.: A note on a one-sided Jacobi algorithm. Numer. Math.,56 (1989), 627–633

This article was processed using the LaTeX macro package with LLNCS style

An Improved Parallel Algorithm for the Solution of Molecular Dynamics Problems on MIMD Multiprocessors

Ralf Knirsch and Klaus Hofmann

Lehrstuhl für Rechnerstrukturen (IMMD 3), Universität Erlangen-Nürnberg
Martensstr. 3, D-8520 Erlangen

Abstract. We consider the solution of molecular dynamics problems on MIMD computers. We focus especially on the data partitioning approach. By means of a model we show that a straightforward parallelization can only obtain poor efficiencies. To overcome this drawback a modified algorithm is presented. Results obtained by implementations on two message-passing architectures underpin our theoretical results.

1 Introduction

The simulation of molecular dynamics (MD) problems is based on particle models. Depending on the characteristics of the problem under consideration different models are used (see e.g. [1]). We use the particle-particle model with short-range forces. The parallelization is achieved by assigning $\frac{N}{P}$ particles to each processor. Since the enumeration of the particles is arbitrary, a processor has to check the distance to *all* particles of the other processors. It can be observed that with this strategy data exchanges between all pairs of processors are necessary.

2 The Sequential Algorithm and Two Parallel Versions

The state S of a physical system can be characterized by the positions $\mathbf{x}_i$ and the velocities $\mathbf{v}_i$ of the N particles $i = 1, \ldots, N$. The movement of the particles in time is simulated by integrating the equation of motion using the forces of interaction. The force $\mathbf{f}_{ij}$ between two particles i and j are computed by

$$\mathbf{f}_{ij} = \frac{\mathbf{x}_i - \mathbf{x}_j}{|\mathbf{x}_i - \mathbf{x}_j|} \left. \frac{d\phi}{dr} \right|_{d = |\mathbf{x}_i - \mathbf{x}_j|} . \tag{1}$$

For the potential function ϕ we use the well-known Lennard-Jones potential. We observe that a total number of $\frac{1}{2}N(N-1)$ calculations of force interactions is needed if Newton's 3. law is taken into account. A first parallelization for P processors, where processor p_k has the particles $b_k, \ldots, e_k$, is as follows ($PAR1$):

Exchange particle positions x_i with all other processors p_k, $k = 1, \ldots, P$;
Compute forces between particles $b_k, \ldots, e_k$;
Compute forces between particles $0, \ldots, b_k - 1$ and $e_k + 1, \ldots, N$;
Update positions of own particles;

Table 1. Comparison between measured and modeled efficiencies for $N = 4000$

	SUPRENUM				Transputer			
	PAR1		PAR2		PAR1		PAR2	
P	meas.	mod.	meas.	mod.	meas.	mod.	meas.	mod.
2	0.67	0.67	0.67	0.67	0.67	0.67	0.67	0.67
4	0.58	0.57	0.76	0.80	0.58	0.57	0.77	0.80
8	0.54	0.53	0.84	0.89	0.54	0.53	0.85	0.88
16	0.52	0.52	0.88	0.94	0.52	0.51	0.89	0.93
36	-	0.51	-	0.97	0.50	0.50	0.86	0.91
48	-	0.50	-	0.97	0.50	0.50	0.84	0.88

In this case $\mathbf{f}_{ij}$ and $\mathbf{f}_{ji}$ are computed by p_k and p_l. To overcome this redundancy (since $\mathbf{f}_{ij} = -\mathbf{f}_{ji}$) p_k could compute only half of the interacting forces with its particles. The other components are computed by other processors and communicated after the force calculation. For processor p_k this results in $PAR2$:

Exchange particle positions with $\frac{P}{2}$ processors p_l, $l = k + 1, \ldots, k + P/2$;
Compute forces between own particles $b_k, \ldots, e_k$;
Compute forces with particles of $\frac{P}{2}$ processors;
Exchange forces with other processors;
Update positions of own particles;

The time can be modeled by the following formulas (for more details see [2]):

$$T^{PAR1} = \frac{N(N(2P - 1) - P)}{2P^2} t_{force} + Pt_{setup} + (2P - 2)t_{block} \qquad (2)$$

$$T^{PAR2} = \frac{N(N(P + 1) - P)}{2P^2} t_{force} + Pt_{setup} + [(P - 1) + \frac{P(P + 2)}{8}]t_{block} \qquad (3)$$

where t_{setup} and t_{block} are the setup time for a communication and the transmission time for a block of size $\frac{N}{P}$, respectively. With t_{force} we denote the time to compute the interacting force f_{ij}.

We implemented the algorithms on a SUPRENUM and a Transputer system. For specific values of the model parameters the results are shown in Table 1. It can be seen that there is a close match between the modeled and the measured values. A more thorough discussion of the algorithms can be found in [2].

References

1. R.W. Hockney and J.W. Eastwood: Computer Simulation using particles, McGraw-Hill, New York, 1981
2. R. Knirsch and K. Hofmann: An Improved Parallel Algorithm for the Solution of Molecular Dynamics Problems on MIMD Multiprocessors, Internal Report No. 8/92, IMMD3, Universität Erlangen-Nürnberg, 1992

This article was processed using the LaTeX macro package with LLNCS style

Computational Models for Image Processing: Towards a Concise Parallel Language

Neucimar J. LEITE and Gilles BERTRAND

Groupe ESIEE   Laboratoire IAAI - France

Abstract

A cellular automaton is an array of identical cells operating in parallel in a SIMD fashion. These cells may be interconnected in different ways like the two-dimensional cellular architecture. This paper is concerned with computational models and languages for iterative cellular automata for image processing applications. We present some formal models with different computational resources that can be useful for solving certain algorithmic problems. These models lead to a very readable parallel language structure that can express low-level image processing algorithms in a clear and concise way.

1   Some Cellular Automata Models

A cellular automaton is a set C of cells, each of them being, at any given time, in one of a set of states. A configuration of the automaton is an application from C to Q, Q being the set of states. The evolution of the automaton is represented by a *transition function* δ which is an application from Q^{n+1} to Q, n is the neighborhood cells. Let us define a set $\Delta = \{\delta_1, \delta_2, ..., \delta_p\}$, where δ_i is an application from Q^{n+1} to Q. A *program* of the automaton is a sequence of the kind $(\delta_{i_1}, \delta_{i_2}, ..., \delta_{i_r})$, with $\delta_{i_q} \in \Delta$. We get the final transformation after applying $\delta_{i_1}, \delta_{i_2}, ..., \delta_{i_r}$, successively. A *general automaton* for image processing is a cellular automaton with memory $Q = P \cup P'$ (P is the set of states (or memory) of the same size as the original image and P' is the "auxiliary memory"), and a set Δ of transition functions. Some special cases of this automaton, defined previously in [1], are:

- *memory plane automaton*: a general automaton with $Q = P \cup Q^1 \cup Q^2 \cup ... \cup Q^j$, $(P, Q^1, Q^2, ..., Q^j$ are the respective memory planes), where a function $\delta_i \in \Delta$ is:
  - either a neighborhood application of the type $X^{n+1} \rightarrow Y$ with X, Y $\in$ {P, $Q^1, ... Q^j$}. We note this function $\delta_i(X \rightarrow Y)$.
  - or a point-wise application of the type $X \times Y \rightarrow Z$ with X, Y, Z $\in$ {P, $Q^1, ... Q^j$}. We note this function $\delta_i((X, Y) \rightarrow Z)$. A function δ_i whose execution depends on parameters $p_1, p_2, ..., p_j$ will be noted $\delta_i(; p_1, p_2, ..., p_j)$.

- *conditional function automaton*: a memory plane automaton, in which the execution of a transition function depends on the state of a memory plane $S \in \{Q^1, Q^2, ..., Q^j\}$. A conditional function δ_i of the form $\delta_i(; \text{if } S = k)$ is a function which is executed by a cell only if the state of S is k.

- *dynamic neighborhood automaton*: a memory plane automaton with a special plane V that memorizes the active points of a cell's neighborhood. The size of this plane is then the $(n+1)$ bits used to indicate whether or not a neighborhood cell is an active point. A neighborhood function whose domain depends on V is noted $\delta_i(; \text{on } V)$.

- *supervised cellular automaton*: a general automaton to which we associate a supervisor processor. This processor executes a predicate function which is the number of times a given value occurs in a memory plane, i.e., it knows the number of cells in state q, $\forall q \in Q$.

2 Programming the Cellular Automata

The program:

```
Begin
/* compute neighborhood variance of image P and store result in Q */
      variance(P → Q)
/* search cell with minimum value in Q and memorize its direction in V */
      min(Q → V)
/* define the 3x3 neighborhood convolution */
      conv(P → Q ; 1/9, 1/9, 1/9,
                   1/9, 1/9, 1/9,
                   1/9, 1/9, 1/9)
/* replace original image P by value pointed by V */
      transf(Q → P ; on V)
End
```

gives an example of the implementation of an algorithm using the dynamic neighborhood automaton model. It corresponds to a version of Nagao's smoothing filter [2], which can not be naturally expressed in a 2-D automaton that does not support high-level functions dealing with indirect addressing. Besides being concise and readable, the automaton language structure suggests a more direct way to pass from the conceptual level of programming to the implementation one. The program below illustrates this:

```
Begin
      conv(I → S ; 1, 0, 1,
                   0, 1, 0,
                   1, 0, 1)
      thresh(S → I ; 1)
End
```

It makes a diagonal expansion of image plane I in which the state of the pixel I(i,j)=0 iff one of its neighbors in position I(i+1,j+1), I(i+1,j-1), I(i-1,j-1) or I(i-1,j+1) is in state 1. I(i,j) is unchanged otherwise.

The set of instructions:

```
*REPEAT
<transition functions>
*UNTIL HIST(<image plane> = <state>) <relational operator> <arithmetic
                                                             expression>
```

is controled by the supervised automaton. The next example presents a general convergence test useful in iterative algorithms such as the relaxation ones:

```
Begin
      *REPEAT
      transf(P → Q) /* transfer image P to Q */
      δᵢ(P → P) /* execute function δᵢ ∈ Δ */
      diff((P, Q) → Q) /* place difference between P and Q in Q */
      thresh(Q → Q ; ε) /* thresholding of Q by ε */
      *UNTIL HIST(Q=0) > n₀ /* execute program till number of cells in state
                               Q=0 is greater than n₀ */
End
```

References

[1] Bertrand, G. and Leite, N. J. "Quelques Modèles d'Automates Cellulaires Pour le Traitement d'Images", in 8 RFIA, Lyon, 1991, pp.1125-1130.

[2] Nagao, M. and Matsuyama. "Edge Preserving Smoothing", Computer Graphics and Image Processing 9, 1979, pp.394-407.

Broadcasting in Faulty Cube-Connected-Cycles with Minimum Recovery Time

Jie Wu and Eduardo B. Fernandez
Department of Computer Science and Engineering
Florida Atlantic University
Boca Raton, FL 33431, U.S.A.

Abstract

We propose a broadcasting algorithm for a faulty Cube-Connected-Cycles multiprocessor. The broadcasting algorithm delivers a message to all the nodes non-redundantly using a binomial tree. The traffic generated because of the recovery is guaranteed to be minimum.

1 Introduction

The Cube-Connected-Cycles (CCC) [3] is a parallel network that consists of $n = h2^h$ PEs. The PEs are grouped into 2^h cycles, where each cycle has h PEs each of which has an address that can be expressed as a pair of integer (l, p), where $l = 0, 1, ..., 2^{h-1}$ and $p = 0, 1, ..., h - 1$. Each PE has three ports: two ports connect two adjacent nodes in the same cycle, and the remaining port connects to a node from an adjacent cycle.

Although the broadcasting problem has been extensively studied, [1] and [2], the design of fault-tolerant distributed broadcasting is still a challenging topic. The proposed algorithm uses the concept of binomial tree. The type of node fault considered is fail-stop, where a node either works properly or stops completely. This algorithm can generate a faulty subtree, induced by a faulty node, though a leaf node in the binomial tree with *minimum traffic*, where the traffic is quantified as the number of links visited during the regeneration process.

We consider here non-redundant broadcasting, where each node receives exactly one copy of the broadcast data. When a node generates a broadcasting message the node first sends the message to the nodes in the same cycle and then to the neighboring nodes in another cycle. The nodes that receive the message in turn broadcast the message to the nodes to which they are connected. To enforce non-redundancy within a cycle, the message can be sent clockwise or counterclockwise until it meets its origin.

2 Fault-Tolerant Broadcasting

To enforce that each cycle is visited exactly once, a *direction* is introduced. When a PE broadcasts a message to another PE which belongs to a different cycle (say cycle i), then the node address of the source PE is a direction to cycle i. Among the PEs in cycle i, only those PEs whose node addresses are greater than the current direction in the cycle can further broadcast the message to PEs in other cycles. The connection of those cycles forms a special structure called *binomial tree*.

When a fault is detected the node which detects the fault becomes the fault handler in charge of the regeneration process. The method used is to regenerate a faulty subtree from a leaf node that contains the same node set as the faulty subtree. A leaf node is defined as a node that is not connected to a node in another cycle in the binomial tree. A special message for subtree regeneration is sent to the leaf node through a path starting from the node that detects the fault.

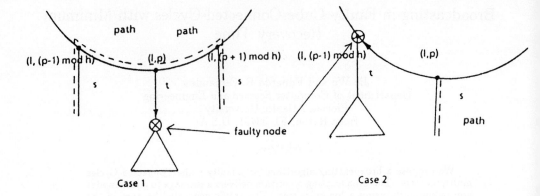

Figure 1: Two types of faulty node conditions

$c = \{c_1, c_2, ..., c_n\}$ is called a *path coordinate sequence* defined on CCC with $0 \leq c_i \leq h - 1$ $(1 \leq i \leq n)$. $(l, p)^c$ is a path defined by the coordinate sequence c with a starting address (l, p). $(l, p)^c$ is used to regenerate the faulty subtree and is recursively defined as:

$$(l,p)^c = \begin{cases} (l,p) & \text{if length}(c) = 0 \\ \{(l,p), (l^{\text{first}(c)}, p)^{\text{rest}(c)}\} & \text{if length}(c) > 0 \wedge \text{first}(c) = p \\ \{(l,p), (l, \text{first}(c)), (l^{\text{first}(c)}, \text{first}(c))^{\text{rest}(c)}\} & \text{if length}(c) > 0 \wedge \text{first}(c) \neq p \end{cases}$$

where $first(c) = c_1, last(c) = c_n$, and $rest(c) = \{c_2, c_3, ..., c_n\}$.

If (l, p) is the fault-handler (for both cases in Fig.1), c is defined as $\{s, t\}$ if $s > t \wedge d \neq s$ and is defined as $\{s, t, s\}$ if $s < t \vee d = s$, where s is defined as $(p + 1) \bmod h$ or $(p - 1) \bmod h$ in case 1 and $s = p$ in case 2. Also s is the node address of the node leaving the cycle l in the path for regeneration. In case 1 there are two possible s (or two paths for generation), t is defined as p in case 1 and as $(p - 1) \bmod h$ in case 2 and it is the direction entering the faulty subtree. d is the direction entering the cycle where (l, p) is located. Let $(T, (l, d), d)$ denote a binomial subtree formed by a root node (l, d), where d is the direction followed by the message into the root node and T is a set of cycles in the tree. We then have the following result:

Theorem: The faulty subtree $(T, (l^t, t), t)$ can be regenerated by $(T', last(l, p)^c, t)$ or $T = T'$, where t and c are as defined as above. The path $(l, p)^c$ is in the binomial tree except for the last node $(last(l, p)^c)$ of the path . This path is the shortest (in terms of the number of cycles and links visited) that can be used for this regeneration.

References

[1] S. L. Johnsson and C.-T. Ho. Optimal broadcasting and personalized communication in hypercubes. *IEEE Trans. on Computers.* 38, (9), Sept. 1989, 1249-1268.

[2] D.S. Meliksetian and C.Y. R. Chen. Communication aspects of the cube-connected cycles. *Proc. 1990 International Conference on Parallel Processing.* I579-580.

[3] F.P. Preparata and J. Vuillemin. The cube-connected cycles, a versatile network for parallel computation. *Communications of ACM.* May 1981, 30-39.

Parallel robot motion planning in a dynamic environment [1]

E-G.Talbi & P.Bessière
LGI / IMAG
e-mail: ghazali@mistral.imag.fr

J.M.Ahuactzin & E.Mazer
LIFIA / IMAG
e-mail: jma@lifia.imag.fr

Institut National Polytechnique de Grenoble
BP 53 X 38041 Grenoble cedex, France

1 Introduction

Today most of the robot motion planners are used offline: the planner is invoked with a model of the environment, it produces a path which is passed to the robot controller which in turn execute it. In general, the time necessary to achieve this loop is not short enough to allow the robot to move in a dynamic environment. Our goal is to try to reduce this time in order to be able to move a robot among moving obstacles. The use of parallel genetic algorithms can be an alternative to this problem.

Genetic algorithms are stochastic search techniques, introduced by Holland twenty years ago, inspired by adaptation in evolving natural systems. Development of massively parallel architectures made them very popular in the very last years. Standard genetic algorithms with large populations take a long time to execute. We have therefore proposed a parallel algorithm to speed up the genetic process. The purpose of this paper is to prove that the robot motion planning problem may be solved quite efficiently by a parallel genetic algorithm.

2 A Parallel genetic algorithm (PGA)

Genetic algorithms compose a very interesting family of optimization algorithms based on biological principles [1]. Their basic principle is quite simple. A population of individuals representing solutions is maintained. Search proceeds by applying genetic operators (crossover, mutation) on selected individuals of the population. Given that the size of the population is constant, we will inevitably have a competition for survival of the individuals in the next generation. We have a Darwinian "survival of the fittest" situation. A "replacement" phase is then performed; it consists in replacing the worse individuals of the population by the best individuals produced. The genetic process is iterated on the new population until a solution is found.

Considering distributed memory parallel machines with numerous processors, we chose a fine-grained parallel genetic model, where the population is mapped on a connected processor graph, one individual per processor [2]. The selection is done locally in a neighbourhood of each individual. Selection depends only on local information.

The choice of the neighbourhood is the adjustable parameter. To avoid overhead and complexity of routing algorithms in parallel distributed machines, a good choice may be to restrict neighbourhood to only directly connected individuals. Another motivation behind local selection is biological. In nature there is no global selection. Instead, natural selection is a local phenomenon, taking place in an individual's local environment.

The population is placed on a torus. Given the four links of the transputer, each individual has four neighbours. We do not consider the best solution found globally since the communication involved in determining this solution would be considerable. We only pick up the best solution routing through a "spy process" placed on the "root processor".

3 Parallel planning for an holonomic mobil robot

Designing a path planner is a classical exercice in robotic research and it remains a very active field in robotics. A review of the existing approaches can be found in Latombe's book [3]. In this section we describe the application of PGA to the problem of planning a collision free path for an holonomic mobile robot. The search space is a subspace of all the possible paths starting from the origin, however the paths are directly coded as a list of "rotate" and "move" commands. Figure 1 shows a successful path planned with PGA. Since this planner

---

[1] This work has been made possible by : Esprit Project P2528 "SuperNode", le Centre National de la Recherche Scientifique and Consejo Nacional de Ciencia y Tecnología.

does not make use of a precomputed representation of the configuration space it may be suitable to plan paths in a dynamic environment.

Figure 2 measures the CPU time used function of the number of processors of the target architecture. The search time is measured in hundredth of seconds and is the mean of 10 program runs.

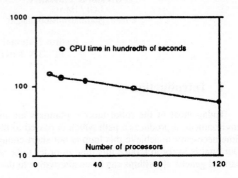

Fig.1 A path planned with the PGA.   *Fig.2* CPU time used function of architecture size.

An environment is dynamic if an obstacle can move during path planning. A routing protocol has been implemented to broadcast the change occured in the robot environment from the host processor to the workers. The message representing the environment change was routed through a balanced spanning tree of the torus. Figure 3 shows a successful path planned with PGA in a dynamic environment. The obstacle moved during path planning is the coloured one.

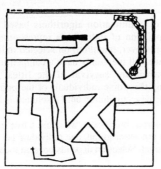 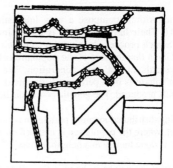

Fig.3   Parallel planning in dynamic environment.

4   Conclusion

In order to achieve fast motion planning for a robot we have chosen the genetic algorithms for the following reasons:

- they are well adapted to search for solutions in high dimensionality search space. The algorithm can be used without reduction of its efficiency for arms with more than six degree of freedom,

- they are very tolerant to the form of the function to optimize, for instance these functions do not need to be neither differentiable or continuous. They make no assumptions about the problem space that they are searching. We are using them to solve other optimization problems: graph partitioning, quadratic assignment, ...

- they are easy to implement on massively parallel distributed memory architectures. The parallel algorithm proposed achieve near-linear speed-up.

References

[1]   D.E.Goldberg, "Genetic algorithms in search, optimization, and machine learning", *Addison-Wesley, 1989*
[2]   E-G.Talbi, T.Muntean, "A parallel genetic algorithm for process-processors mapping", *Int. Conf. on High Speed Computing II, Montpellier, M.Durand and F.El Dabaghi (Editors), Elsevier Science Pub., North-Holland, pp.71-82 Oct 1991.*
[3]   J-C.Latombe, "Robot motion planning", *Ed. Kluwer Academic Publisher, 1991.*

A hypergraph-based interconnection network for large multicomputers.

L.M. Mackenzie, M. Ould-Khaoua, R.J. Sutherland.

Department of Computing Science, University of Glasgow,
Glasgow G12 8QQ.

T. Kelly.

Motorola Ltd.

Abstract. The bandwidth constraints placed on architectures by implementation technology are a critical determining factor in how well the theoretical properties of a particular topology can be exploited. However, great care must be taken in deciding which constraint is applicable in a particular technology and due attention given to examining whether a topology may, by its nature, be able to exploit partitioning and interconnection design to alleviate the effects of that constraint. This paper reviews current thinking on these matters, and introduces a new hypermesh architecture called COBRA, together with an associated interconnection scheme which permits it to reduce substantially the effects of conventional bandwidth limitations.

1. Introduction.

The evaluation of a multicomputer topology must involve not only a consideration of its fundamental graph theoretic properties, but also the bandwidth restrictions placed on it by the technology in which it is implemented. For example the relative performance of low and high-dimensional k-ary n-cubes has been studied under constraints imposed by fixed section width [2] and fixed node pinout [1], conditions which would apply in very different situations, and which lead to opposite conclusions.

In fact the applicability of the constant maximum section width constraint in real situations is somewhat questionable [1]. The constraints which actually apply will be very dependent on the properties of packaging and inter-chip connections, and not merely on the silicon medium itself.

2. COBRA.

A COBRA system [3] is an n-cube with a crossbar handling communication in each k-processor *cluster*. This crossbar has a *1* to *k-1* broadcast capability, and, extending the terminology of [4], we call the Cartesian product a *B-hypermesh*. The crossbar is distributed across the nodes of a cluster as follows: every node possesses a uniquely owned unidirectional bus-like output link which connects it to one of the multiplexer inputs of each other element in the cluster. At each of the *k-1* destinations, there is a *k-1* to *1* multiplexer with buffered inputs and a select controlled by a round-robin *k-1* way arbiter. Unlike a binary hypercube, *n* need adopt only modest values, typically only 2 or 3, even in very large implementations, so that COBRA systems will have very low diameters. It has already been established that the topological properties of more restricted forms of this network are very favourable: many common structures such as binary trees, hypercubes, meshes of two, three or more dimensions can be efficiently embedded, while omega and inverse omega permutations can be emulated in minimum distance and one pass [4].

Due to the multiplexing down at each node, a 2-D or 3-D COBRA network can benefit from separation of processing and network functions via a number of interconnected structured layers linked by narrow channels. Using this technique, wiring densities within a communication layer can be much higher than at layer interfaces. It follows that implementations of COBRA networks are possible which are constrained not by section width or even node pinout, but by relay bandwidth between communicating dimensions.

3. Performance

We have developed mathematical and discrete event models for COBRA systems and have compared performance with other topologies under constraints of fixed maximum section width, fixed node pinout and fixed node relay bandwidth. In comparison with the mesh, for example, we find that low-dimensional COBRA networks provide superior uniform traffic performance under all constraints except fixed maximum section width at very low node decision times. The COBRA network is much less sensitive to decision time variation than higher diameter structures like the mesh or torus. If traffic includes even a small broadcast component, the advantage of the COBRA network increases and superior performance is obtained under all constraints.

4. Conclusions.

With careful interconnection design it should be possible to implement B-hypermesh architectures with inherently desirable properties. These architectures can largely escape the effects of the wiring density and pinout constraints which might be expected to limit such highly connected structures, yet they retain totally regular and physically compact form.

References.

1. S. Abraham and K Padmanabhan: *Performance of Multicomputer Networks under Pinout Constraints.* In: J. Parallel & Dist. Systems 12, Aug 1991, pp 237-248.

2. W.J. Dally: *Performance Analysis of k-ary n-cube interconnection networks.* In: IEEE Trans. Comp. 39(6)-, June 1990, pp 775-785.

3. L.M. Mackenzie, M. Ould Khaoua, R.J. Sutherland, T. Kelly: *COBRA: A High-Performance Interconnection for Large Multicomputers*, Research Report 1991/R19, Dept. of Comp. Sci, Glasgow University, October 1991.

4. T. Szymanski: *A Fiber Optic Hypermesh for SIMD/MIMD Machines.* In Proc. 1990 International Conference on Parallel Processing, pp 710-718.

GREEDY PERMUTATION ROUTING ON CAYLEY GRAPHS

Miltos D. Grammatikakis[1]
Ecole Normale Superieure de Lyon, LIP
Lyon 69364, France

Jung-Sing Jwo
Providence University, Dept. of Information Science
Shalu 43309, Taiwan R.O.C.

EXTENDED ABSTRACT:

Greedy permutation routing on three proposed multicomputer architectures is evaluated, using a previously designed discrete-event simulator [3]. The following architectures are examined:

1. Generalized Hypercube (GH_k^b)

An $N = b^k$ - node, base - b, hypercube of dimension k consists of N nodes, with each node x can be represented as $x = x_1 x_2 \cdots x_{k-1} x_k$, where $x_i \in <b> = \{ 0, 1, 2, \cdots, b-1 \}$, for $1 \le i \le k$. Two nodes of the hypercube $x = x_1 x_2 \cdots x_{i-1} x_i x_{i+1} \cdots x_{k-1} x_k$ and $y = y_1 y_2 \cdots y_{i-1} y_i y_{i+1} \cdots y_{k-1} y_k$, are connected by an edge, if and only if $x_i \ne y_i$, and $x_j = y_j$ for all $j \ne i$ and $1 \le j \le k$ [2].

2. Star Graph Architecture (ST_k)

Let $X = \{1, 2, \cdots, k\}$ where $k \ge 2$. Define $p = p_1 p_2 \cdots p_k$ as a permutation over the set X, that is, $p_i \in X$ for $1 \le i \le k$ and $p_i \ne p_j$ if $i \ne j$. Let S_k be the set of all possible permutations over X. Then, S_k is known as symmetric group. Let $1 \le i < j \le k$, we say that p_i and p_j introduce an inversion if and only if $p_i > p_j$. A permutation is said to be even, if it contains even number of inversions. All the even permutations of S_k form a subgroup of S_k, which is called alternating-group A_k.

A k-dimensional star graph ST_k is a Cayley graph obtained from symmetric group S_k, and the generator set $\Omega_1 = \{T_{1j} \mid 2 \le j \le k\}$, where T_{ij} is a permutation that swaps the ith element and the jth element [1]. Examples of the the star graph are given in Figure 2.1, for $n = 3$ and 4.

3. Alternating-Group Graph Architecture (AG_k)

A k-dimensional alternating-group graph AG_k is a Cayley graph obtained from the alternating-group A_k and the generator set $\Omega_2 = \{T_{12} \cdot T_{2j} \mid 3 \le j \le k\} \cup \{T_{2j} \cdot T_{12} \mid 3 \le j \le k\}$. Examples of AG_k for $k = 3$ and 4 are given in Figure 3.1.

4. Greedy Routing Algorithms for Proposed Architectures

We assume that an arbitrary packet Ψ originates at source node $x = x_1 x_2 \cdots x_{k-1} x_k$ for destination node $x' = x'_1 x'_2 \cdots x'_{k-1} x'_k$. The routing algorithm always chooses the minimum distance path from source to destination. It also operates asynchronously; if the corresponding source and destination digits are the same, the next dimension in increasing order ($i = 1, 2, .., k$, is considered. Let $x : (x_j \Leftarrow m)$ represent the node obtained from x, when the jth digit of x's b-ary representation is changed to m. All packets, not in their final destination ($x \ne x'$), basically perform a greedy sorting from the current source node $x = x_1 x_2 \cdots x_{k-1} x_k$ to the destination $x' = x'_1 x'_2 \cdots x'_{k-1} x'_k$ by applying the appropriate generator.

(1) *Hypercube routing.*
   Transmit Ψ from x to $x : x_i \Leftarrow x'_i$, where $x_i \ne x'_i$

(2) *Star graph routing.*
   if $x_1 = x'_1$ then transmit Ψ from x to $x \cdot T_{1i}$, where $x_i \ne x'_i$
   else transmit Ψ from x to $x \cdot T_{1i}$, where $x_1 = x'_i$

(3) *Alternating-group graph routing.*
   if $x_1, x_2 \in [x'_1, x'_2]$ then transmit Ψ from x to $x \cdot T_{12} T_{2i}$, where $x_i \ne x'_i$
   else if $x_2 \notin [x'_1, x'_2]$ then transmit Ψ from x to $x \cdot T_{12} T_{2i}$, where $x_2 = x'_i$
   else if $x_1 \notin [x'_1, x'_2]$ then transmit Ψ from x to $x \cdot T_{2i} T_{12}$, where $x_1 = x'_i$

---

[1]*Currently with the Institute for Computer Science, Heraklion 71110, Greece*

5. Results and Comparisons

Using discrete-event simulation, the performance of greedy permutation routing on the three proposed multicomputers is evaluated. In Figures 5.1 and 5.2, we show the expected routing delay time and maximum queue length versus the logarithm of the number of nodes ($\log_2 N$) for the case of random permutations, d-port communication, and furthest-first queuing dicipline. Similar results have been obtained for 1-port communication mode, and random queuing dicipline.

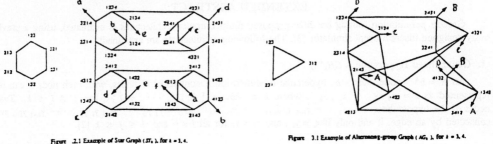

Figure 2.1 Example of Star Graph (ST_k), for $k = 3, 4$.   Figure 3.1 Example of Alternating-group Graph (AG_k), for $k = 3, 4$.

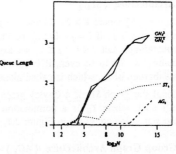

Figure 5.1   Expected time delay vs. Logarithm of Number of Nodes ($\log_2 N$), d-port   Figure 5.2   Expected max queue length vs. Logarithm of Number of Nodes ($\log_2 N$), d-port

Results from the figures show that greedy routing performs very well on the expected case on all three graphs. In particular, for relatively large systems ($N \geq 120$), the alternating-group graph offers the best performance, with smaller cost (fewer edges), and near-optimal (close to diameter) expected delay time and maximum queue length, as illustrated in the following table. From the point of routing, the star graph offers a nice trade-off between the alternating-group graph, and the generalized hypercube.

Architecture	Nodes (N)	Edges	Diameter	Outdegree	Avg. Distance	Time Delay	Queue Length
ST_7	$k! = 5040$	$(k-1) k! = 30240$	$\frac{3(k-1)}{2} = 9$	$k-1 = 6$	5.88	9.04	1.93
AG_7	$\frac{k!}{2} = 2520$	$(k-2) k! = 25200$	$\frac{3(k-2)}{2} = 7$	$2(k-2) = 10$	5.64	7.0	1.06
GH_{12}^2	$2^{12} = 4096$	$N \log_2 N = 49152$	$\log_2 N = 12$	$\log_2 N = 12$	6	11.94	3.02
GH_6^4	$4^6 = 4096$	$3 N \log_4 N = 73728$	$\log_4 N = 6$	$3 \log_4 N = 18$	4.5	9.32	3.08
GH_4^8	$8^4 = 4096$	$7 N \log_8 N = 114688$	$\log_8 N = 4$	$7 \log_8 N = 28$	3.5	7.55	3.03

REFERENCES

[1] S. B. Akers, D. Harel, and B. Krishnamurthy, "The Star Graph, an attractive alternative to the n-cube", *1987 International Conference on Parallel Processing*, pp. 393-400.

[2] L. N. Bhuyan and D. P. Agrawal, "Generalized Hypercube and Hyperbus Structures for a Computer Network", *IEEE Transactions on Computers*, C-33 (4), April 1984, pp. 323-334.

[3] M. D. Grammatikakis and J. S. Jwo, "A Discrete Event Simulator of Communication Algorithms in Interconnection Networks", *1992 Symposium on Theoretical Aspects of Computer Science*, Paris, France, pp. 609-610.

Experimenting upon the CG Algorithm within the C_NET Programming Environment

Adamo J.M., Trejo L.

Laboratoire LIP-IMAG, Ecole Normale Supérieure de Lyon
46, allée d'italie, 69364 LYON cedex 07 FRANCE.

Abstract. An experimentation upon the conjugate gradient algorithm is carried out within the C_NET programming environment. C_NET has specially been designed to take advantage of the dynamic reconfiguration facility available on SuperNode. A phase-reconfigurable and a static implementation of the conjugate gradient algorithm are developed. Time models are built for both implementations which are checked against the results provided by program runs performed on a 32-node SuperNode. The models are ultimately used for extrapolation purposes.

1 Introduction

Our group has developed a high level programming environment: C_NET, specially designed to take advantage of the dynamic reconfiguration facility available within the SuperNode multiprocessor. The environment allows the implementation of variable-topology programs that are referred to as phase-reconfigurable programs. Phase-reconfigurable programming relies on the idea that most useful algorithms can be decomposed into series of elementary data movements. As a consequence, these algorithms can be implemented as series of phases, so that each phase can be efficiently executed on the graph which is best suited to the corresponding data movement. For a detailed description of C_NET the reader is referred to [1][2]. Currently, C_NET is intensively used to experiment phase-reconfigurable algorithms on this machine. The conjugate gradient algorithm (CG) presented in this paper is part of such an experimental work.

2 Implementing the Conjugate-Gradient Algorithm as a Phase-Reconfigurable Program.

Let us consider the system of linear equations $Ax = b$, where A is a $S*S$ definite-positive matrix. The CG method [3], pictured in Fig. 6, can be used to solve this problem. It is well known that the algorithm converges in S steps at most. The implementation of the CG algorithm as a phase reconfigurable program on a 8x4 processor organisation is presented. The data are distributed on the matrix of processors. Each processor is assigned a copy of the scalars α and β, a $S/32$ sub-vector of the x, d and r vectors, a $(S/8)*(S/4)$ sub-matrix of the matrix A, and a $S/8$ sub-vector of the Ad vector. The first phase is devoted to data loading, initialisation and initial computation of the $r.r$ scalar product. It is executed on the tree shown in Fig. 2. The $r.r$ scalar product is computed by aggregating the processor contributions up the tree and broadcasting the final result down the same tree. The second phase is devoted to computing the contribution of each processor in the matrix to the Ad product. Each processor broadcasts the d part it possesses to all the others on the same column (all-to-all exchange on each column). This phase is executed on the four chordal rings represented in Fig. 3 (*P/4+1* chord-length chordal rings remain optimal when the number P of processors involved in the all-to-all operation is greater than eight). The third phase completes the computation of the *Ad* vector by summing, on the family of trees pictured in Fig. 4 the partial results computed on each processor within the previous phase. At the end of this phase, the result of the *Ad* multiplication is gathered in the eight processors: 0, 5, 10, 15, 16, 21, 26, 31. The fourth phase performs the scattering of the results generated in the previous phase from the last group of processors to the other processors so that each of them is attributed the *S/32* part it has responsibility. This data movement is performed on the family of trees pictured in Fig. 5. Note that these actually are subtrees of the tree pictured in Fig. 2 so that no reconfiguration is required for executing the next phase. The last phase utilises the same tree as that of phase 1. This tree is used to compute the value of the scalar product *d.Ad* in the same way as for the *r.r* scalar product. Each processor is then able to compute the new value of α used to update the part of *x* and *r* for which the processor has responsibility. Then the new value of the scalar product *r.r* is computed. At this point, each processor can compute the new value of β and *d*, just before starting the next iteration if *S* has not yet been reached.

3 Assessment

For comparison purposes, CG has also been implemented on a fixed topology: a 8x4 torus. After assessing the performance of both algorithms, time models were built and used for extrapolation purposes. Full details on the achieved speed-up are given in [2].

References

1   Adamo J.M., Bonello C., Trejo L., The C_NET Programming Environment: An Overview, CONPAR 92, Lyon September 1-4 1992.
2   Adamo J.M., Trejo L., Programming Environment for Phase-Reconfigurable Parallel Programming on SuperNode, submitted to the 4th IEEE Symp on PDP.
3   Minoux M., Prog. mathématiques, théorie et algorithmes, tome 1, Dunod, 1983.

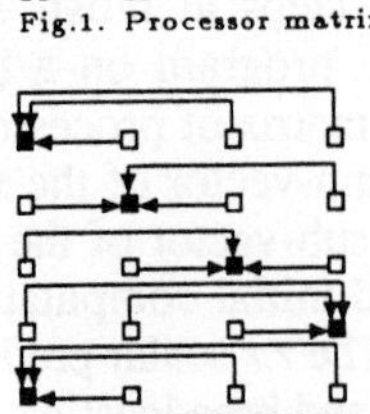

Fig.1. Processor matrix 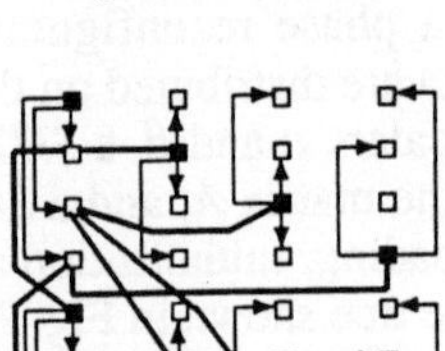   Fig.2. First phase 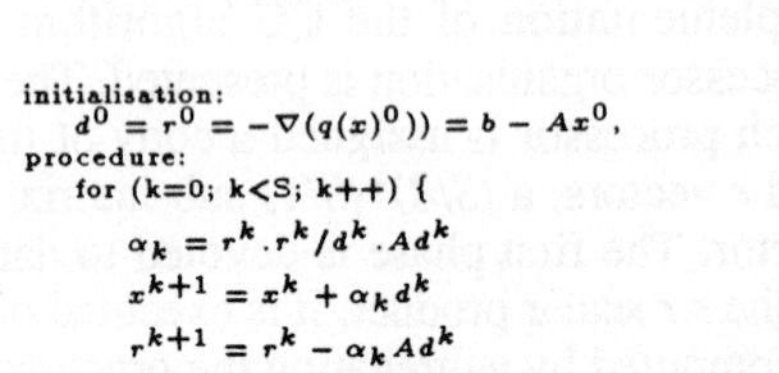   Fig.3. Second phase

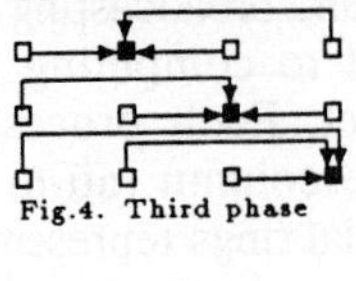

Fig.4. Third phase 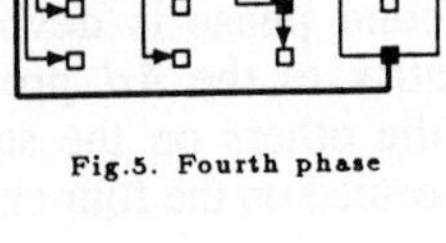   Fig.5. Fourth phase

initialisation:
$$d^0 = r^0 = -\nabla(q(x)^0)) = b - Ax^0,$$
procedure:
for (k=0; k<S; k++) {
$$\alpha_k = r^k.r^k/d^k.Ad^k$$
$$x^{k+1} = x^k + \alpha_k d^k$$
$$r^{k+1} = r^k - \alpha_k Ad^k$$
$$\beta_k = r^{k+1}.r^{k+1}/r^k.r^k$$
$$d^{k+1} = r^{k+1} + \beta_k d^k$$
}

Fig.6. The conjugate-gradient method

An Algorithm of Broadcasting in the Mesh of Trees

Dominique Barth

LaBRI, Université de Bordeaux I,
351 cours de la Libération
33405 Talence Cedex, France

Abstract. The mesh of trees is an interesting topology of distributed-memory parallel machine to implement severall parallel algorithms (sorting, algorithms on matrices,..) [3]. In this way, we study communication problems in this topology, and in particular we want to find good methods to broadcast a message in [2]. Because the mesh of trees is constructed from complete binary trees [3], we first present different broadcasting schemes in trees, and then we use this schemes to define an efficient algorithm of broadcasting in the mesh of trees [1] in at most $5n + \lfloor \frac{n}{2} \rfloor + 1$ communication steps.

1 Introduction

Here we deal with interconnection networks, discribing parallel architectures or parallel algorithms, modelized by graphs. The one we study in this paper is the mesh of trees. Because it is used to implement different algorithms, it is interesting to study good methods of broadcasting a message from a node in this network. To present it, we must precise two hypothesies [2]. First, at each communication step a vertex can inform at most one neighboor (*processor bound* model). Secondly, we just count here the number of communication steps needed to realize the broadcast (*constant time* hypothesis).

2 Definitions

- The mesh of trees, denoted by $MT(n)$, is defined as follows:
  - the vertices are all the couples $(u; v)$ of words of $\{0,1\}^k$, with $0 \le k \le n$, where $|v| = n$ or $|u| = n$ ($|u|$ is the length of u); we denote by e the empty word. The number of vertices of $MT(n)$ is equal to $2^{n+1}(2^{n+1} - 2^{n-1} - 1)$.
  - $((v; u), (vx; u))$ and $((u; v), (u; vx))$ are edges of $MT(n)$ iff $|u| = n$, $|v| < n$ and $x \in \{0, 1\}$. The maximal degree of $MT(n)$ is equal to 3 and the diameter is equal to $4n$.

- We denote by $T(n)$ the complete binary tree of depth n in which the leaves are numbered continuously from the left to the right. The ith leaf is noted $l(i)$. Note that in $MT(n)$, each vertex of form $(u; e)$ or $(e; u)$, $|u| = n$, is the root of a subtree isomorphic to $T(n)$ which we denote also by $T(n)$.

3   Broadcasting in $T(n)$

We broadcast a message in $T(n)$:

- *(a)* from the root in $2n$ steps; $l(i)$ is informed at time $t(i) = n + w(i)$ where $w(i)$ is the Hamming weight of the binary representation of i,
- *(b)* from $l(1)$ in $3n - 1$ steps; $l(1)$ is called *extremal leaf*,
- *(c)* from the leaves, where each leaf $l(i)$ begins to broadcast the same message at time $t(i) - n$, in n steps,
- *(d)* from a vertex of depth d in $2n + d - 1$ steps.

4   Broadcasting in $MT(n)$

First we show, by using automorphisms of $MT(n)$, that without loss of generality, we only have to study the broadcasting from vertices $(v; u)$ where $v = 0^n$ and $u = 0^k$, $0 \le k \le n$, in $MT(n)$. We propose two different schemes depending on k.

- If $k = 0$, we broadcast a message from $(v; e)$ in $n + 3n - 1 + n = 5n - 1$ steps by applying successively the methods *(a)*, *(b)* and *(c)* to the different subtrees $T(n)$ composing $MT(n)$.
- If $k \ne 0$, we elaborate the following algorithm depending of $|u|$:
  1. Broadcasting from $(v; u)$ in the tree $T(n)$ of root $(v; e)$ like in *(d)*; we give a precise strategy of broadcasting in each subtree of this tree $T(n)$.
  2. Broadcasting in all trees $T(n)$ of root $(e; v')$ from the extremal leaf $(v; v')$, like in *(b)*, except for $v' = 1^n$.
  3. Broadcasting in all left subtrees of trees $T(n)$ of root $(w; e)$, $w \ne v$, like in *(c)*.
  4. We give a new algorithm of broadcasting in the right subtree of the tree $T(n)$ of root $(e; 1^n)$ in $MT(n)$. In this tree, each leaf $(w; 1^n)$ is also a leaf of the tree $T(n)$ of root $(w; e)$. We use this to finish the broadcast.

It gives an algorithm of broadcasting in at most $5n + \lfloor \frac{n}{2} \rfloor + 1$ steps.

5   Conclusion

So we show that the number Nb of steps needed to broadcast in $MT(n)$ is $4n \le Nb \le 5n + \lfloor \frac{n}{2} \rfloor + 1$. With a similar method, we show that the number Ng of communication steps needed to realize the gossiping [2] is $4n \le Ng \le 7n + 2$.

References

1. D. Barth : *An Algorithm of Broadcasting in the Mesh of Trees.* Research Report, LaBRI, Université de Bordeaux I, 1992.
2. P. Fraigniaud, E. Lazard : *Methods and problems of communication in usual networks.* Research Report n.701, L.R.I., Université Paris Sud, Centre d'Orsay, 1991.
3. F.T. Leigthon : *Introduction to Parallel Algorithms and Architectures.* Morgann Kaufmann Publishers, 1992.

Complexity Estimation in the PIPS Parallel Programming Environment

Lei Zhou
Centre de Recherche en Informatique
Ecole Nationale Supérireure des Mines de Paris

Abstract

In order to choose the best optimized version of a real Fortran program, we have to compare the execution times of different optimized versions of the same Fortran program. Since real scientific Fortran programs can run for hours on expensive machines, it is useful to perform a static analysis that predicts the running-time. In this paper, we introduce our complexity model, which is a part of the PIPS project. This model is composed of a library of polynomial models of program performance and dynamically-derived program statistics to estimate the running time of Fortran programs. Then, complexity results of a real example from the PERFECT Club are presented.

1 Introduction

PIPS (Paralléliseur Interprocédural de Programmes Scientifiques) is a source-to-source parallelizing compiler [1]. Using a combined static and dynamic approach, the complexity tool of the PIPS project is composed of two elements: a library of polynomial mathematical models and counters which measure statistical information used to estimate complexity when exact information cannot be computed.

In our complexity model, we use a cost table which depends entirely on the machine, which contains all the execution times of basic operations, memory accesses, function calls, etc. Each Fortran statement is converted to a polynomial that represents the execution time of that statement, that is the sum of the basic execution times of all the components of that statement. For some statements, the running-time can not be predicted statically, e.g., for a branch statement, we resort to statistical counters to estimate the probability of each branch. Once the polynomial is derived, it is evaluated using values from the cost table specified.

2 Estimation Process

Currently, the static evaluation component of the complexity tool has been implemented for sequential Fortran programs. It has the following features:

Different Cost Table The user can choose from a set of machine description cost tables. So far two cost tables are available: one models all operations as unit cost; and the other only takes floating-point operation into account.

Symbolic Parameters In some cases, the variables in the polynomial describing the complexity remain unevaluated. For example, PIPS identifies variables which must remain unevaluated because they are free parameters of a module, e.g., formal parameters in a subroutine call or dynamic input data. In addition, the user may specify that certain variables remain unevaluated.

Interprocedural Preconditions PIPS uses preconditions, that is information acquired before the current statement, to resolve analysis problems. As it is obtained , precondition information is stored in a library for later use.

Simplifying Complexity Results Analysis is performed to minimize the number of free parameters which are local to the module. In addition, intermediate variables are removed from final result after use.

3   A Real Example

Our complexity estimator has been tested on real Fortran programs. We have estimated the running-time of a medium-sized 2000-line Fortran program *TFS.f* from the PERFECT Club [2]. We broke up the program into 27 routines, and generated complexity results for most of them. In a few cases, large matrix inversions were required which caused overflows. However, we believe this implementation problem can be resolved easily.

4   Conclusion

We think the method of half-static and half-dynamic evaluation described here will be more powerful than either approach alone. We have implemented a prototype of the static evaluator. In the future, we will extend it to more precise machine models and add dynamic evaluation to the tool.

References

[1] F. Irigoin, P. Jouvelot and R. Triolet *"PIPS overview"*, ICS'91 Paris, France

[2] G. Cybenko, *"Supercomputer Performances Trends and the Perfect Benchmark"*, Supercomputing Review, April 1991

A Graphical Petri Net Based Editor for a Visualization of Distributed and Parallel Systems

Nikolay Anisimov, Aleksey Kovalenko
Pavel Postupalski, Aleksey Simanchuk

Laboratory of Computer Networks. Institute of Automation & Control Processes
5 Radio Street, Vladivostok, 690032, Russia

Abstract. This paper is a presentation of the ongoing research project being under development at the Institute of automation and control processes (Vladivostok, Russia). The main purpose of the project is to develop a prototype of computer aided tools for specification development in a graphical mode based on Petri nets. The project includes a development of two-level editor that consists of a Petri net editor with algebraic facilities and an architectural editor. Some outcomes of the project are reported.

1. Introduction

As a rule, the specifications of real-world parallel and distributed systems are very complex. To work with the specifications successfully, one needs in special formal techniques and computer-aided tools for supporting these techniques. In this paper we suggest such techniques which are based on Petri nets [3]. The main purpose of the project is to develop a prototype of computer aided tools for specifying, storing, learning and distribution of the parallel and distributed systems specifications. These tools must support hierarchical structure of specifications, possess compositional facilities to construct specifications from the simpler ones, allow one to simulate (animate) specifications in order to learn their dynamic properties.

2. Two-Level Specification Editor.

The prototype is being developed under the graphical operation system WINDOWS 3.0. At the bottom level a Petri net editor is implemented. It offers general facilities for editing Petri nets either by drawing Petri net including places, transitions, arcs directly onto computer screen or by using the algebraic facilities of the editor. The top level is an architectural editor that supports a common description of the specifications. The relationships between both levels are established.

2.1 Petri Nets Editor with Algebraic Facilities.

The basic Petri net editor allows one to draw Petri nets on the screen of the computer in a graphical form. Petri nets may have a hierarchical structure where each place or transition can be associated with some internal net. The use of algebraic techniques for a Petri net construction allows one to be saved from tiresome manipulations. From our opinion, the algebraic style of a system construction is more adequate to human's way of thinking. As a formal basis, we use a variant of Petri net algebra (PNA) reported in [2] where a sufficient amount of net operations was suggested.

A basic element of PNA is a Petri net, that being supplemented with the sets of head and tail places to indicate explicitly initial and final states of a net. The following set of operations is available: *atomic net, sequential composition, prefix, choice, parallel composition, iteration, and recursion.*

The recursion operation allows one to establish references between transitions and places of one net with other nets. Such elements of net are considered to be not atomic but structured ones. In particular, structured transition can be interpreted as recursive call while structured place can be used for representation of a "disruption" construction [2].

2.2 Architectural editor.

At the level of architecture one can construct and describe the architecture of specification using some high-level constructs by means of *architectural specification language* (ASL).

The basic element of ASL is an entity [1]. Each entity has two sets of access points: p-access points and t-access points.

In ASL entities can be connected by drawing a line between their access points. An access point can be connected only with access point of the same type.

A set of entities with interconnections between them forms an entity configuration. Some facilities for representing hierarchical configurations are available. An entity can be of two parts - simple and structured. A simple entity is considered to be elementary or indivisible at the level of architecture. A structured entity has an entity configuration which graphically drawn inside the entity rectangular box. Access points of structured entity are connected with access points of inside configuration.

REFERENCES

1   Anisimov N.A. A Notion of Petri Net Entity for Communication Protocol Design. Institute for Automation and Control Processes, Vladivostok. To be published in: Proc.IFAC Workshop on Discrete Event System Theory (Chenyang, June 25-27), 1991.

2   Anisimov N.A. An Algebra of Regular Macronets for Formal Specification of Communication Protocols. Computers and Artificial Intelligence, Vol.10, No.6. pp.541-560 (1991)

3   Brauer W., Reisig W., Rozenberg G. (Eds). Petri Nets. Part I and II. Proc. of an Advanced Course, Bad Honnef. Lecture Notes in Computer Sciences, Vol.254,255 (1987)

Automatic Parallelization of Divide–and–Conquer Algorithms

Bernd Freisleben and Thilo Kielmann

Department of Computer Science (FB 20), University of Darmstadt, Alexanderstr. 10, D–6100 Darmstadt, Germany

Abstract. In this paper we present a system that automatically partitions sequential divide–and–conquer algorithms programmed in C into independent tasks, maps these to a MEIKO transputer system and executes them in parallel. The feasibility of our approach is illustrated by parallelizing several example algorithms and measuring the resulting performance speedups.

1 General Approach and System Description

Our approach for mapping divide–and–conquer algorithms to a multiprocessor architecture is to use the partitioning information inherently included in the algorithm and let one processor divide the initial problem into two subproblems, pass one of these to a further processor and keep the other one to itself [2]. Every processor repeats this step recursively until the problem size is sufficiently small and performs the computation assigned to it, which logically constitutes a mapping to a binomial tree topology. The results are propagated up the tree and combined in the reverse order in which the subproblems were passed down.

The fundamental communication pattern used in our system is based on a master/slave organization in which a unique master task distributes the work to a set of slave tasks via an asynchronous remote procedure call mechanism. In addition to the master task, which is responsible for the particular problem to be solved, there is a unique *scheduler* task which controls the pool of available processors and is thus the only entity that knows the physical topology of the network. The master and the scheduler are assigned to the same dedicated processor, while each slave runs on a unique processor of the pool.

A few language extensions are required for generating code which is able to operate in parallel. Besides a keyword indicating parallel compilation, additional declarations are required for specifying input and output parameters of the (possibly remotely) called function and a synchronization point after which the results of the subproblems are available.

The source code is restructured into three parts: the master part with the original `main()` function, the function part which replaces the recursive function calls by directing them to a stub, and the slave part which contains code for receiving the parameters, calling the function and returning the results. The function part is concatenated with both the master and slave part. These parts are separately compiled with the C compiler of the target system, resulting in two object files.

In a last step, the object files produced so far are linked together with appropriate main programs and a communications library which essentially contains the implementation of an asynchronous RPC mechanism and provides the interface to the runtime system of the target architecture.

2 Implementation and Performance

Our system was implemented in C on a SUN Sparcstation, using the MEIKO cross compiler. The computation time required for transforming a sequential divide–and–conquer algorithm to concurrently executable code is about 1–2 seconds.

The algorithms selected as test cases are the well known quicksort, an algorithm for matrix multiplication, an algorithm for adaptive numerical integration [1] and an algorithm for the knapsack problem. The four programs have been automatically parallelized with our system and executed on the MEIKO transputer system consisting of 72 transputers T800. The physical topologies used were hypercubes for up to 8 processors and cube–connected cycles (with 2 processors in each corner) for 16 and 32 processors. The programs have also been compiled to run sequentially on one processor. The runtimes measured for the sequential programs (T_s) were used to compute the speedup $S = T_s/T_n$, where T_n is the runtime of the parallel execution with n processors. The speedup factors achieved are shown in Figure 1.

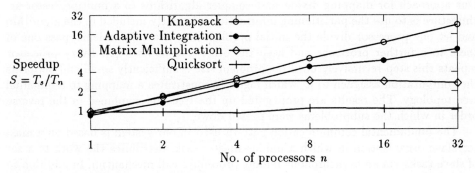

Fig. 1. Speedups relative to sequential programs

The speedups achieved for the individual problems differ significantly and thus indicate the suitability of the different algorithms for parallel execution in a message–passing multicomputer environment. For the quicksort algorithm with a relatively low sequential time complexity of $O(n \log n)$ the communication overhead clearly dominates the total cost. With increasing dominance of computation over communication, the results become better. A peak value of 23 for 32 processors is achieved by the parallelized knapsack algorithm.

References

1. G. R. Andrews. Paradigms for Process Interaction in Distributed Programs. *ACM Computing Surveys*, 23(1):49–90, 1991.
2. V. M. Lo, S. Rajopadhye, S. Gupta, D. Keldsen, M. Mohamed and J. Telle. Mapping Divide-and-Conquer Algorithms to Parallel Architectures. In *International Conference on Parallel Processing*, Vol. III, pages 128–135, CRC Press, 1990.

Author Index

Lecture Notes in Computer Science

For information about Vols. 1–544
please contact your bookseller or Springer-Verlag

Vol. 545: H. Alblas, B. Melichar (Eds.), Attribute Grammars , Applications and Systems. Proceedings, 1991. IX, 513 pages. 1991.

Vol. 546: O. Herzog, C.-R. Rollinger (Eds.), Text Understanding in LILOG. XI, 738 pages. 1991. (Subseries LNAI).

Vol. 547: D. W. Davies (Ed.), Advances in Cryptology – EUROCRYPT '91. Proceedings, 1991. XII, 556 pages. 1991.

Vol. 548: R. Kruse, P. Siegel (Eds.), Symbolic and Quantitative Approaches to Uncertainty. Proceedings, 1991. XI, 362 pages. 1991.

Vol. 549: E. Ardizzone, S. Gaglio, F. Sorbello (Eds.), Trends in Artificial Intelligence. Proceedings, 1991. XIV, 479 pages. 1991. (Subseries LNAI).

Vol. 550: A. van Lamsweerde, A. Fugetta (Eds.), ESEC '91. Proceedings, 1991. XII, 515 pages. 1991.

Vol. 551:S. Prehn, W. J. Toetenel (Eds.), VDM '91. Formal Software Development Methods. Volume 1. Proceedings, 1991. XIII, 699 pages. 1991.

Vol. 552: S. Prehn, W. J. Toetenel (Eds.), VDM '91. Formal Software Development Methods. Volume 2. Proceedings, 1991. XIV, 430 pages. 1991.

Vol. 553: H. Bieri, H. Noltemeier (Eds.), Computational Geometry - Methods, Algorithms and Applications '91. Proceedings, 1991. VIII, 320 pages. 1991.

Vol. 554: G. Grahne, The Problem of Incomplete Information in Relational Databases. VIII, 156 pages. 1991.

Vol. 555: H. Maurer (Ed.), New Results and New Trends in Computer Science. Proceedings, 1991. VIII, 403 pages. 1991.

Vol. 556: J.-M. Jacquet, Conclog: A Methodological Approach to Concurrent Logic Programming. XII, 781 pages. 1991.

Vol. 557: W. L. Hsu, R. C. T. Lee (Eds.), ISA '91 Algorithms. Proceedings, 1991. X, 396 pages. 1991.

Vol. 558: J. Hooman, Specification and Compositional Verification of Real-Time Systems. VIII, 235 pages. 1991.

Vol. 559: G. Butler, Fundamental Algorithms for Permutation Groups. XII, 238 pages. 1991.

Vol. 560: S. Biswas, K. V. Nori (Eds.), Foundations of Software Technology and Theoretical Computer Science. Proceedings, 1991. X, 420 pages. 1991.

Vol. 561: C. Ding, G. Xiao, W. Shan, The Stability Theory of Stream Ciphers. IX, 187 pages. 1991.

Vol. 562: R. Breu, Algebraic Specification Techniques in Object Oriented Programming Environments. XI, 228 pages. 1991.

Vol. 563: A. Karshmer, J. Nehmer (Eds.), Operating Systems of the 90s and Beyond. Proceedings, 1991. X, 285 pages. 1991.

Vol. 564: I. Herman, The Use of Projective Geometry in Computer Graphics. VIII, 146 pages. 1992.

Vol. 565: J. D. Becker, I. Eisele, F. W. Mündemann (Eds.), Parallelism, Learning, Evolution. Proceedings, 1989. VIII, 525 pages. 1991. (Subseries LNAI).

Vol. 566: C. Delobel, M. Kifer, Y. Masunaga (Eds.), Deductive and Object-Oriented Databases. Proceedings, 1991. XV, 581 pages. 1991.

Vol. 567: H. Boley, M. M. Richter (Eds.), Processing Declarative Kowledge. Proceedings, 1991. XII, 427 pages. 1991. (Subseries LNAI).

Vol. 568: H.-J. Bürckert, A Resolution Principle for a Logic with Restricted Quantifiers. X, 116 pages. 1991. (Subseries LNAI).

Vol. 569: A. Beaumont, G. Gupta (Eds.), Parallel Execution of Logic Programs. Proceedings, 1991. VII, 195 pages. 1991.

Vol. 570: R. Berghammer, G. Schmidt (Eds.), Graph-Theoretic Concepts in Computer Science. Proceedings, 1991. VIII, 253 pages. 1992.

Vol. 571: J. Vytopil (Ed.), Formal Techniques in Real-Time and Fault-Tolerant Systems. Proceedings, 1992. IX, 620 pages. 1991.

Vol. 572: K. U. Schulz (Ed.), Word Equations and Related Topics. Proceedings, 1990. VII, 256 pages. 1992.

Vol. 573: G. Cohen, S. N. Litsyn, A. Lobstein, G. Zémor (Eds.), Algebraic Coding. Proceedings, 1991. X, 158 pages. 1992.

Vol. 574: J. P. Banâtre, D. Le Métayer (Eds.), Research Directions in High-Level Parallel Programming Languages. Proceedings, 1991. VIII, 387 pages. 1992.

Vol. 575: K. G. Larsen, A. Skou (Eds.), Computer Aided Verification. Proceedings, 1991. X, 487 pages. 1992.

Vol. 576: J. Feigenbaum (Ed.), Advances in Cryptology - CRYPTO '91. Proceedings. X, 485 pages. 1992.

Vol. 577: A. Finkel, M. Jantzen (Eds.), STACS 92. Proceedings, 1992. XIV, 621 pages. 1992.

Vol. 578: Th. Beth, M. Frisch, G. J. Simmons (Eds.), Public-Key Cryptography: State of the Art and Future Directions. XI, 97 pages. 1992.

Vol. 579: S. Toueg, P. G. Spirakis, L. Kirousis (Eds.), Distributed Algorithms. Proceedings, 1991. X, 319 pages. 1992.

Vol. 580: A. Pirotte, C. Delobel, G. Gottlob (Eds.), Advances in Database Technology – EDBT '92. Proceedings. XII, 551 pages. 1992.

Vol. 581: J.-C. Raoult (Ed.), CAAP '92. Proceedings. VIII, 361 pages. 1992.

Vol. 582: B. Krieg-Brückner (Ed.), ESOP '92. Proceedings. VIII, 491 pages. 1992.

Vol. 583: I. Simon (Ed.), LATIN '92. Proceedings. IX, 545 pages. 1992.

Vol. 584: R. E. Zippel (Ed.), Computer Algebra and Parallelism. Proceedings, 1990. IX, 114 pages. 1992.

Vol. 585: F. Pichler, R. Moreno Díaz (Eds.), Computer Aided System Theory – EUROCAST '91. Proceedings. X, 761 pages. 1992.

Vol. 586: A. Cheese, Parallel Execution of Parlog. IX, 184 pages. 1992.

Vol. 587: R. Dale, E. Hovy, D. Rösner, O. Stock (Eds.), Aspects of Automated Natural Language Generation. Proceedings, 1992. VIII, 311 pages. 1992. (Subseries LNAI).

Vol. 588: G. Sandini (Ed.), Computer Vision – ECCV '92. Proceedings. XV, 909 pages. 1992.

Vol. 589: U. Banerjee, D. Gelernter, A. Nicolau, D. Padua (Eds.), Languages and Compilers for Parallel Computing. Proceedings, 1991. IX, 419 pages. 1992.

Vol. 590: B. Fronhöfer, G. Wrightson (Eds.), Parallelization in Inference Systems. Proceedings, 1990. VIII, 372 pages. 1992. (Subseries LNAI).

Vol. 591: H. P. Zima (Ed.), Parallel Computation. Proceedings, 1991. IX, 451 pages. 1992.

Vol. 592: A. Voronkov (Ed.), Logic Programming. Proceedings, 1991. IX, 514 pages. 1992. (Subseries LNAI).

Vol. 593: P. Loucopoulos (Ed.), Advanced Information Systems Engineering. Proceedings. XI, 650 pages. 1992.

Vol. 594: B. Monien, Th. Ottmann (Eds.), Data Structures and Efficient Algorithms. VIII, 389 pages. 1992.

Vol. 595: M. Levene, The Nested Universal Relation Database Model. X, 177 pages. 1992.

Vol. 596: L.-H. Eriksson, L. Hallnäs, P. Schroeder-Heister (Eds.), Extensions of Logic Programming. Proceedings, 1991. VII, 369 pages. 1992. (Subseries LNAI).

Vol. 597: H. W. Guesgen, J. Hertzberg, A Perspective of Constraint-Based Reasoning. VIII, 123 pages. 1992. (Subseries LNAI).

Vol. 598: S. Brookes, M. Main, A. Melton, M. Mislove, D. Schmidt (Eds.), Mathematical Foundations of Programming Semantics. Proceedings, 1991. VIII, 506 pages. 1992.

Vol. 599: Th. Wetter, K.-D. Althoff, J. Boose, B. R. Gaines, M. Linster, F. Schmalhofer (Eds.), Current Developments in Knowledge Acquisition - EKAW '92. Proceedings. XIII, 444 pages. 1992. (Subseries LNAI).

Vol. 600: J. W. de Bakker, C. Huizing, W. P. de Roever, G. Rozenberg (Eds.), Real-Time: Theory in Practice. Proceedings, 1991. VIII, 723 pages. 1992.

Vol. 601: D. Dolev, Z. Galil, M. Rodeh (Eds.), Theory of Computing and Systems. Proceedings, 1992. VIII, 220 pages. 1992.

Vol. 602: I. Tomek (Ed.), Computer Assisted Learning. Proceedings, 1992. X, 615 pages. 1992.

Vol. 603: J. van Katwijk (Ed.), Ada: Moving Towards 2000. Proceedings, 1992. VIII, 324 pages. 1992.

Vol. 604: F. Belli, F.-J. Radermacher (Eds.), Industrial and Engineering Applications of Artificial Intelligence and Expert Systems. Proceedings, 1992. XV, 702 pages. 1992. (Subseries LNAI).

Vol. 605: D. Etiemble, J.-C. Syre (Eds.), PARLE '92. Parallel Architectures and Languages Europe. Proceedings, 1992. XVII, 984 pages. 1992.

Vol. 606: D. E. Knuth, Axioms and Hulls. IX, 109 pages. 1992.

Vol. 607: D. Kapur (Ed.), Automated Deduction – CADE-11. Proceedings, 1992. XV, 793 pages. 1992. (Subseries LNAI).

Vol. 608: C. Frasson, G. Gauthier, G. I. McCalla (Eds.), Intelligent Tutoring Systems. Proceedings, 1992. XIV, 686 pages. 1992.

Vol. 609: G. Rozenberg (Ed.), Advances in Petri Nets 1992. VIII, 472 pages. 1992.

Vol. 610: F. von Martial, Coordinating Plans of Autonomous Agents. XII, 246 pages. 1992. (Subseries LNAI).

Vol. 611: M. P. Papazoglou, J. Zeleznikow (Eds.), The Next Generation of Information Systems: From Data to Knowledge. VIII, 310 pages. 1992. (Subseries LNAI).

Vol. 612: M. Tokoro, O. Nierstrasz, P. Wegner (Eds.), Object-Based Concurrent Computing. Proceedings, 1991. X, 265 pages. 1992.

Vol. 613: J. P. Myers, Jr., M. J. O'Donnell (Eds.), Constructivity in Computer Science. Proceedings, 1991. X, 247 pages. 1992.

Vol. 614: R. G. Herrtwich (Ed.), Network and Operating System Support for Digital Audio and Video. Proceedings, 1991. XII, 403 pages. 1992.

Vol. 615: O. Lehrmann Madsen (Ed.), ECOOP '92. European Conference on Object Oriented Programming. Proceedings. X, 426 pages. 1992.

Vol. 616: K. Jensen (Ed.), Application and Theory of Petri Nets 1992. Proceedings, 1992. VIII, 398 pages. 1992.

Vol. 617: V. Mařík, O. Štěpánková, R. Trappl (Eds.), Advanced Topics in Artificial Intelligence. Proceedings, 1992. IX, 484 pages. 1992. (Subseries LNAI).

Vol. 618: P. M. D. Gray, R. J. Lucas (Eds.), Advanced Database Systems. Proceedings, 1992. X, 260 pages. 1992.

Vol. 619: D. Pearce, H. Wansing (Eds.), Nonclassical Logics and Information Proceedings. Proceedings, 1990. VII, 171 pages. 1992. (Subseries LNAI).

Vol. 620: A. Nerode, M. Taitslin (Eds.), Logical Foundations of Computer Science – Tver '92. Proceedings. IX, 514 pages. 1992.

Vol. 621: O. Nurmi, E. Ukkonen (Eds.), Algorithm Theory – SWAT '92. Proceedings. VIII, 434 pages. 1992.

Vol. 622: F. Schmalhofer, G. Strube, Th. Wetter (Eds.), Contemporary Knowledge Engineering and Cognition. Proceedings, 1991. XII, 258 pages. 1992. (Subseries LNAI).

Vol. 623: W. Kuich (Ed.), Automata, Languages and Programming. Proceedings, 1992. XII, 721 pages. 1992.

Vol. 624: A. Voronkov (Ed.), Logic Programming and Automated Reasoning. Proceedings, 1992. XIV, 509 pages. 1992. (Subseries LNAI).

Vol. 625: W. Vogler, Modular Construction and Partial Order Semantics of Petri Nets. IX, 252 pages. 1992.

Vol. 626: E. Börger, G. Jäger, H. Kleine Büning, M. M. Richter (Eds.), Computer Science Logic. Proceedings, 1991. VIII, 428 pages. 1992.

Vol. 628: G. Vosselman, Relational Matching. IX, 190 pages. 1992.

Vol. 629: I. M. Havel, V. Koubek (Eds.), Mathematical Foundations of Computer Science 1992. Proceedings. IX, 521 pages. 1992.

Vol. 630: W. R. Cleaveland (Ed.), CONCUR '92. Proceedings. X, 580 pages. 1992.

Vol. 631: M. Bruynooghe, M. Wirsing (Eds.), Programming Language Implementation and Logic Programming. Proceedings, 1992. XI, 492 pages. 1992.

Vol. 632: H. Kirchner, G. Levi (Eds.), Algebraic and Logic Programming. Proceedings, 1992. IX, 457 pages. 1992.

Vol. 633: D. Pearce, G. Wagner (Eds.), Logics in AI. Proceedings. VIII, 410 pages. 1992. (Subseries LNAI).

Vol. 634: L. Bougé, M. Cosnard, Y. Robert, D. Trystram (Eds.), Parallel Processing: CONPAR 92 – VAPP V. Proceedings. XVII, 853 pages. 1992.

Vol. 635: J. C. Derniame (Ed.), Software Process Technology. Proceedings, 1992. VIII, 253 pages. 1992.